Social Cognition

McGraw-Hill Series in Social Psychology

CONSULTING EDITOR
Philip G. Zimbardo

Social Cognition

Second Edition

Susan T. Fiske
University of Massachusetts at Amherst

Shelley E. Taylor
University of California at Los Angeles

McGraw-Hill, Inc.
New York   St. Louis   San Francisco   Auckland   Bogotá
Caracas   Lisbon   London   Madrid   Mexico City   Milan
Montreal   New Delhi   San Juan   Singapore
Sydney   Tokyo   Toronto

To Edward, Geoffrey, and Lydia,
and
To Mervyn, Sara, and Charlie

This book was set in Palatino by the College Composition Unit
in cooperation with Black Dot, Inc.
The editors were Christopher Rogers and Fred H. Burns;
the production supervisor was Denise L. Puryear.
The cover was designed by Carla Bauer.
R. R. Donnelley & Sons Company was printer and binder.

Photo credit: Page v—Michael Zide.

Cover painting credit: "Ball at the Moulin de la Galette" by Pierre Auguste Renoir, Musée
d' Orsay in Paris.

This book is printed on acid-free paper.

SOCIAL COGNITION

9 0 DOC DOC 9 0 9

ISBN 0-07-021191-4

Library of Congress Cataloging-in-Publication Data

Fiske, Susan T.
    Social cognition / Susan T. Fiske, Shelley E. Taylor.—2nd ed.
        p.   cm. — (McGraw-Hill series in social psychology)
    Includes bibliographical references and index.
    ISBN 0-07-021191-4
    1. Social perception.   2. Cognition.   I. Taylor, Shelley E.
    II. Title.   III. Series.
    HM132.F573   1991
    302'.12—dc20   90-24234

About the Authors

❖

Susan T. Fiske has been a professor of social psychology at the University of Massachusetts at Amherst since 1986. She earned her bachelor's degree in 1973 at Harvard University, working in the interdisciplinary Social Relations department. In her senior year she met Shelley Taylor, and they began their work on salience. Fiske earned her doctoral degree from Harvard in 1978, working with several faculty on stereotyping, person perception, and research methodology. After that she was an assistant and associate professor at Carnegie-Mellon, where she absorbed more cognitive psychology. This background sparked her interest in the emerging field of social cognition. In 1982 she coedited the volume *Affect and Cognition*, which helped to interest social cognition researchers in affect. The first edition of this book was published in 1984. Fiske's research has typically combined social issues and social cognition. Her primary interests focus on motivation and stereotyping; to that end, she has conducted a program of studies on informational and motivational circumstances that encourage and discourage stereotyping. In 1984, she testified in a landmark employment discrimination case that was reviewed by the Supreme Court in 1988. Her testimony about the psychology of stereotyping was favorably cited in the decisions by the trial court, the appeals court, and the Supreme Court. Fiske also studies political cognition, focusing on perceptions of politicians, nuclear threat, and other political phenomena. In all her work, Fiske enjoys the challenge of synthesizing superficially contradictory ideas into more comprehensive insights that deepen our understanding of the human social situation.

Shelley E. Taylor has been a professor of social psychology at the University of California at Los Angeles since 1979. She earned her Ph.D. from Yale University in 1972, pursuing interests in interpersonal attraction and attribution theory with several faculty members there. She then joined the faculty at Harvard and began a program of research in social cognition, examining the impact of salient stimuli on attributions, memory, and interpersonal perceptions. In this context, she and her colleague, Susan Fiske, identified the implications of the salience phenomenon for minority group members, noting that "solos," or those in minority positions, such as women or blacks in work organizations, may be subject to disproportionate scrutiny, exaggerated inferences, and pernicious stereotypes as a result of their highly visible status. From 1975 on, Taylor's work also focused on social cognitions under threat, and in 1980 she initiated a program of health psychology research to identify the cognitive factors that may promote or impede recovery from threatening events such as cancer, AIDS, heart disease, and other stressful health events. In this context, she has led the Health Psychology Program at UCLA since 1979. Currently, Taylor's work focuses heavily on the role of positive illusions in maintaining well-being, that is, the role that self-aggrandizing beliefs can play in enabling people to enhance their mental health. Her other books, *Health Psychology* and *Positive Illusions*, develop these and related themes. Taylor's work has successfully combined the pursuit of theoretical issues in the context of important social issues, and thereby enhanced both theory and research in social psychology, as well as pointed in the direction of many applications that help people to cope more successfully with stressful life events.

Contents

———— ❖ ————

Foreword

———————— ❖ ————————

During the many decades when American psychology was held captive by a limited scientific doctrine of behaviorism, the pathfinders who dared to venture beyond these intellectually limited boundaries and explore new horizons were largely social psychologists. They valued the personal perspectives of the human actor in life's dramas, honored the alternative interpretations of reality held by different observers, and defended the subtle interplay of dynamic forces between and within cultures, social situations, and individual psyches.

Long relegated to a subordinate position within psychology's status hierarchy for these points of view, social psychology has steadily moved to the center of contemporary psychology. It did so by establishing a cognitively flavored brand of psychology, which, in recent years, has become the banner flown by mainstream psychology. Social psychology was the home of generalists within psychology, a haven for scholars interested in understanding the depth and breadth of the nature of human nature. It was neither too shy to ask the big questions that have intrigued social philosophers for centuries, nor too orthodox to venture into alien territories with new methodologies that have provided empirically grounded answers to the more vital questions of our time. Finally, social psychologists have become the vanguard of the movement to extend the boundaries of traditional psychology into realms vital to contributing solutions for real-world problems, the areas of health, ecology, education, law, peace and conflict resolution, and much more. Indeed, it is not immodest to declare that nothing of human nature is too alien to social psychological inquiry and concern.

Our McGraw-Hill Series in Social Psychology celebrates the fundamental contributions being made by researchers, theorists, and practitioners of social psychology to a richer understanding of the human condition. The authors of each book in the series are distinguished researchers and dedicated teachers, committed to sharing a vision of the excitement inherent in their particular area of investigation with their colleagues, graduate students, and seriously curious undergraduates. Taken as a whole the series will cover a wide path of social psychological interests, allowing instructors to use any of them as supplements to their basic textbook or, for the more daring, to organize a challenging course around a collection of them.

In every area of knowledge there are some books that stand out as the criteria against which all competing efforts are judged. This text by Susan Fiske and Shelley Taylor has been the standard resource for scholars and students interested in the fullest understanding of the area of social cognition. Now in its thoroughly revised second edition, *Social Cognition* goes even further in organizing and critically evaluating the theories, evidence, and practical applications centered around the basic issue of how people make sense of their social environment. By combining new developments in cognitive psychology on attention, memory, and inference, with those emerging from the study of attitudes, affect, and motivation, Fiske and Taylor give us the "state of the art" manual for appreciating that aspect of human nature which focuses on how people think about themselves and about others. In that sense, it is surely the Thinking Person's ideal travel guide to understanding the thoughtful—or not-so-thoughtful—person.

Philip G. Zimbardo
Series Editor

$\mathcal{P}$reface

———— ❖ ————

Writing a second edition is a bit like producing Star Trek II; Henry the IV, Part II; or any sequel. If the first production enjoys any success, then its offshoots inevitably risk disappointment when compared to the original. The first edition had its day, but inevitably time passed and a fresh perspective was needed. Undertaking the second edition was a potentially daunting enterprise. Fortunately, the field of social cognition, and its parent, social psychology, have provided more than enough excitement in the last six years to make writing the sequel just as lively as the original. We hope that readers have the same experience, whether or not they are new to the book.

The second edition contains, on a guess, from 40 to 80 percent new material in each chapter. Historical background and the early theories do not change much, but every subsequent area of social cognition has exploded with new ideas and new research. We see growth in three particular areas, and these are reflected in this edition: the social emphasis, the technical side, and the sheer complexity of the findings.

Social cognition has indisputably become more emphatically social in its concerns. Every area has seen a return of motivation, affect, behavior, and interpersonal context (communication, interaction, mutual perception). In a sense, much of social cognition research is coming back into the fold of mainstream social psychology, bringing new perspectives gained from the new pastures, but also recognizing anew the enduring concerns of the discipline.

On the technical side, social cognition researchers (not usually the same ones) are developing the full potential of computer simulation, psychophysiology, detailed models of cognitive representation, and cognitive measures sensitive practically down to a nanosecond. As these efforts evolve, they bear closer and closer resemblance to purely cognitive psychology and potentially contribute to its basic research and theory as well.

The sheer quantity of results and intricate complexity of the findings result from both the social and technical developments in the field. Both the social concerns and the technical advances have demanded greater precision in the generalizations one can make; nevertheless, we have worked to keep our review accessible to a wide audience. The increased complexity of the field is of course inevitable. As any research domain develops, it moves from the first intriguing, perhaps counterintuitive, findings to the subsequent qualifications on those findings. Sometimes that growth in complexity can lead to confusion and despair, but sometimes that growth represents real progress. In the case of social cognition, we are convinced that, as a field, we now know more than we did before, and some puzzles have been genuinely solved. Of course, new ones are being posed as well, and there is plenty to keep us all busy for years to come.

Finally, a word about our increased coverage of European material. Our first edition was admittedly parochial, reflecting the ingroup biases of many American social psychologists at the time. The field has subsequently recognized and benefited considerably from European contributions, particularly in the areas of attribution theory and intergroup perception. This edition expands its horizons to include more of our overseas colleagues.

Despite all these changes, the second edition has aimed to be as scholarly and entertaining as the field it reviews. We thank our colleagues for providing the conceptual and empirical material that makes this effort possible.

Acknowledgments

This book benefited from the help of many colleagues. The following people commented on all or parts of one or more chapters: James Averill, John Bargh, Reuben Baron, Roy Baumeister, Seymour Berger, Paul Blaney, Galen Bodenhausen, Charlie Bond, Marilynn Brewer, Jonathon Brown, Nancy Cantor, Shelly Chaiken, Margaret Clark, Anton Dijker, Alice Eagly, Phoebe Ellsworth, Seymour Epstein, Russell Fazio, Friedrich Forsterling, Daniel Gilbert, John Harvey, Tory Higgins, William Ickes, Saul Kassin, Arie Kruglanski, Ziva Kunda,

Ellen Langer, Patricia Linville, Diane Mackie, Hazel Markus, John Mayer, Steven Neuberg, Brett Pelham, Richard Petty, Pierre Phillepot, Tony Riley, Janet Ruscher, Peter Salovey, Constantine Sedikides, Eliot Smith, Charles Stangor, William Swann, Abraham Tesser, Yaccov Trope, James Uleman, Robin Vallacher, Frank Van Overwalle, Daniel Wegner, Gary Wells, David Wilder, Timothy Wilson, Robert Wyer, Mark Zanna, and Leslie Zebrowitz.

Several students—Eric Depret, Stephen Merther, Hillary Morgan, John Murray, Robert Schatz, Abhijit Sanyal, James Wilson—read and commented on the entire book.

We are grateful to all these people for their help, and also to Melanie Bellenoit, Garrett Gafford, and Stacie Melcher for their careful and considerate word-processing assistance. Stephen Merther and Holly Von Hendy helped greatly with the references. In addition, Holly Von Hendy helped in countless other respects too numerous to list. Many thanks, too, to our parents for their support and inspiration.

Susan T. Fiske
Shelley E. Taylor

1

Introduction

— ❖ —

*T*ry telling someone at a party that you are a psychologist or even that you are simply studying psychology. It does no good to say you do research and do not read minds. The inevitable reaction is either that the person draws back in horror of being analyzed on the spot or that the person leans over to disclose all sorts of intimate secrets. One psychologist we know avoids these situations by claiming to be a computer programmer. We have hit upon a different strategy, which is to say calmly, "I study how people make first impressions on strangers." That is a real conversation stopper.

Suppose, however, that the conversation did not end right there. Suppose the person began to talk about what makes people tick, about his or her impressions of various friends, relatives, and strangers at the party. That would be the kind of raw data with which this book is concerned. Social cognition is the study of how people make sense of other people and themselves. It focuses on how ordinary people think about people and how they think they think about people.

People's understanding of the social world can be studied, first, by *asking* them how they make sense of others (Heider, 1958). This is the route of phenomenology: to describe systematically how ordinary people say they experience their world. If people are right, one can build formal theories by making their insights scientific, by pulling together patterns across many people's intuitions. Even if people are wrong, one can study people's common-sense theories in and of themselves; how people think, not their accuracy, is the phenomenon of interest. Social cognition research is concerned, second, with common-sense theory or "naive psychology" for its own sake. That is, people's everyday theories about each other are themselves interesting to study. Thus, if the per-

1

son at the party has some ideas about how people form impressions of each other, the person's informal ideas are interesting in their own right. Hence, common-sense psychology is useful for two reasons.

Research on social cognition also goes beyond naive psychology. The study of social cognition entails a fine-grained analysis of how people think about themselves and others, and it leans heavily on the theory and methods of cognitive psychology. The influx of fine-grained or detailed models from cognitive psychology is one of the hallmarks of the current approaches to social cognition. Cognitive psychology's models are important because they precisely describe mechanisms of learning and thinking that apply in a wide variety of areas, perhaps including social perception. Because these models are general and because cognitive processes presumably influence social behavior heavily, it makes sense to adapt cognitive theory to social settings.

Both the naive psychology viewpoint and the cognitive viewpoint are important themes in social cognition research. These two viewpoints characterize the double appeal of social cognition: the entertaining part of studying how people think about others is its appeal to your intuitions; it resembles what is fun and absorbing about sitting around with a friend after midnight, speculating about human nature. The fine-grained part forces you to be accurate and precise; its appeal resembles that of a favorite intricate puzzle. Whether your taste runs to crosswords, math games, jigsaw puzzles, or mystery novels, there is considerable pleasure in getting all the pieces to fit.

APPROACHES TO STUDYING THE SOCIAL THINKER

Two broad intellectual approaches to the study of social cognition—elemental and holistic—can be traced to psychology's origins in philosophy. Knowing something of social cognition's intellectual history will give perspective to its current efforts. The elemental approach is characterized by breaking scientific problems down into pieces and analyzing the pieces in separate detail before combining them. The holistic approach is characterized by analyzing the pieces in the context of other pieces and focusing on the entire configuration of relationships among them. The distinction will become clearer as the two approaches are described.

The Elemental Origins of Social Cognition Research

Until the beginning of this century, psychology was a branch of philosophy, and philosophers provided some basic principles of mind that still carry weight today (Boring, 1950). In the elemental tradition of the British philosophers, the mind is likened to chemistry, in which ideas are the elements. Any concept, whether concrete like "salt" or abstract like "shame," is a basic element. Any element can be associated with any other element. The bonds between concepts create mental chemistry (Locke, 1690/1979).

In the elemental view, ideas first come from our sensations and perceptions. Then they are associated by contiguity in space and time (Hume, 1739/1978). That is, if salt is next to pepper on the table, the two can become a unit through contiguity. Repetition is the key to moving from simple contiguity to a mental compound (Hartley, 1749/1966). If salt and pepper are on the table together every day of your life, then when you think of salt you will automatically think of pepper. Salt-and-pepper becomes a mental "compound." Similarly, if the concept "professor" often comes up (on television, for example) at the same time as the concept "absent-minded," they are likely to be associated simply as a function of repeated pairings. People consciously use the principles of repetition and contiguity in daily life, too; think of the last time you attempted to memorize the seven contiguous digits of a phone number by repeating them until they became a unit. Frequency of repetition is a major factor that determines the strength of an association (J. Mill, 1869; J. S. Mill, 1843/1974).[1]

Around the turn of the century, psychology began to emerge as a discipline separate from philosophy, and at that time the notions of mental chemistry were first put to empirical test. The first laboratory psychologists, such as Wilhelm Wundt and Hermann Ebbinghaus, trained themselves and their graduate students to observe their own thought processes: to introspect on how they committed ideas to memory and on how they retrieved ideas from memory (Ebbinghaus, 1885/1964; Wundt, 1897). Their method was to analyze experience into its elements, to determine how they connect, and to determine the laws that govern the connections. These themes that started with the British philosophers continue to form the basis of modern experimental psychology. Shortly, we will see how the elemental approach is currently represented within the study of social cognition.

The Holistic Origins of Social Cognition Research

In reaction to the elemental approach, the German philosopher Immanuel Kant (1781/1969) argued for an emphasis on tackling the

---

[1]Other principles of association were proposed at various times and then dropped in favor of repeated contiguity. These included similarity and causality as creating associations, and vividness as strengthening associations (Boring, 1950).

whole mind at once. In his view of the mind, mental phenomena are inherently subjective. That is, the mind actively constructs a reality that goes beyond the original thing in and of itself. A bunch of grapes is perceived as a unit, but that perception is a construction of the mind. Perceiving a "bowl of grapes" differs from perceiving each individual grape separately. Similarly, if someone cuts off some grapes and the remaining ones topple out of the bowl, the two movements are perceived as linked in a cause-effect relationship. Again, that perception is furnished by the mind; it is not inherent in the stimulus. The intellect organizes the world, creating perceptual order from the properties of the surrounding field.

Gestalt psychology drew on these initial holistic insights (Koffka, 1935; Kohler, 1938/1976). In contrast to analysis into elements, psychologists who use Gestalt methods first describe the phenomenon of interest, the immediate experience of perception, without analysis. This method, called phenomenology, focuses on systematically describing people's experience of perceiving and thinking. It later became one of the major foundations of social cognition research: the reliance on asking people how they make sense of the world.

Although both the elemental and holistic groups drew on introspections, Gestalt psychologists focused on people's experience of dynamic wholes, and elementalists focused on the expert's ability to break the whole into pieces. As an illustration of the difference between Gestalt and elemental approaches, think of a song in your mind. A song can be perceived as a series of individual notes (elemental) or as a melody that emerges from the relationships among the notes (Gestalt). The emergent structure is lost by analyzing it into its sensory elements, in the Gestalt view. Gestalt psychologists saw the mental chemistry metaphor of the elementalists as misguided because a chemical compound has properties not predictable from its isolated elements. Similarly, the perceptual whole has properties not discernible from the isolated parts. For example, the note middle C can seem high in the context of many lower notes or low in the context of many higher notes, but it would not stand out at all in the context of other notes close to it. Psychological meaning goes beyond raw sensory parts to include the organization people impose on the whole.

Kurt Lewin (1951) imported Gestalt ideas to social psychology and ultimately to social cognition research (Boring, 1950; Bronfenbrenner, 1977; Deutsch, 1968). Like other Gestalt psychologists, Lewin focused on the person's own subjective perceptions, not on "objective" analysis. He emphasized the influence of the social environment *as perceived by the individual*, which he called the "psychological field." A full understanding of a person's psychological field thus cannot result from an "objective" description by others of what surrounds the person. The crucial factor is the person's own interpretation. This is not to say that the person can necessarily verbalize his or her perceived environment, but that the person's own reports typically provide better clues than do the researcher's intuitions. For instance, a researcher may objectively report that Barb complimented Ann on her appearance. The researcher may even have strong hunches about why Barb did it. But Ann's reaction will depend on her own perception of Barb's intent: ingratiation, envy, reassurance, or friendliness. A prime way to find that out is to ask Ann to describe what happened in her own terms. Just as in Gestalt psychology generally, then, Lewin emphasized the individual's phenomenology, the individual's construction of the situation.

Another theme imported from Gestalt psychology to social psychology was Lewin's insistence on describing the total situation, not its isolated elements. A person exists within a psychological field that is a *configuration of forces*. One must understand all the psychological forces operating on the person in any given situation in order to predict anything. For example, some forces might motivate one to study (an upcoming exam, the sight of one's roommate studying), but other forces might motivate one to spend the evening another way (a group of friends suggesting a movie). No one force predicts action, but the dynamic equilibrium among them—the everchanging balance of forces—does predict action.

The total psychological field (and hence behavior) is determined by two pairs of factors. The first pair consists of the *person* in the *situation*. Neither alone is sufficient to predict behavior. The person contributes needs, beliefs, perceptual abilities, and more. These act on the environment to constitute the psychological field. Thus, to know that a particular person is motivated to study does not predict whether or how much he or she will study. But a motivated person in a library is extremely likely to study a lot. Ever since Lewin, social psychologists have seen both the person and the situation as essential to predicting behavior. The study of social cognition focuses on perceiving, thinking, and remembering as a function of who and where one is.

The second pair of factors cuts across the psychological field to determine what behavior will be; it consists of *cognition* and *motivation*. Both are joint functions of person and situation. Both are essential to predicting behavior. Cognition provides the perceiver's own interpretation of the world; without clear cognitions, behavior is not predictable. If a person has incomplete cognitions or confused cognition about a new setting, behavior will be unstable. For example, if you do not have the foggiest cognition about what an upcoming exam in music composition will be like, you may behave erratically and hence unpredictably; you may try several study strategies, none of them very systematically. Cognitions help determine *what* a person will do, which direction behavior will take. If a musician friend explains what composition exams typically contain, your cognitions and hence your studying will settle down along the lines laid out. But this assumes that you actually do study. The second feature of the psychological field is motivation; its strength predicts *whether* the behavior will occur at all and, if it does, how much of it will occur. Knowing what to do does not mean you will do it; cognition alone is not enough. Motivations provide the motor for behavior.

To summarize, Lewin focuses his analysis on psychological reality as perceived by the individual; on confronting a whole configuration of forces, not single elements; on the person and situation; and on cognition and motivation. These major themes that date back through Gestalt psychology to Kant are theoretical points that still survive in modern approaches to social cognition, as well as in psychology as a whole.

Conclusion

We have characterized the historical origin of current approaches to social cognition as a contrast between the elemental and the holistic viewpoints. The elemental approach aims to build up from the bottom, combining smaller pieces into larger ones until the whole puzzle is assembled. The piecemeal nature of this approach contrasts sharply with the holistic nature of the Gestalt alternative. To describe a person's active construction of reality, in the holistic view, it is necessary to tackle the entire configuration as seen by the perceiver. The tension between the elemental and configural or holistic approaches will surface again. The score, however, is perpetually tied. In direct confrontations, both sides often can account for the other's data.[2] It is ultimately more useful for each side to develop its own theories in as much detail as possible, attempting to assimilate evidence and criticism from the other side, and modifying the theory where it is proved wrong. An integration of the two approaches probably is superior to either one alone. There are no dominant solutions, then, merely different but complementary approaches to common continuing problems. The central issues of both elemental and Gestalt theories are how to understand structures and processes occurring inside the mind.

THE EBB AND FLOW OF COGNITION IN PSYCHOLOGY

Psychologists have not always agreed that it is important to get inside the mind. The study of cognition has received both good and bad re-

---

[2]For examples of such controversies that can be interpreted essentially as a debate between holistic and elemental approaches, see Chapter 4, pp. 100–102; Ostrom, 1977, or Chapter 8, pp. 318–320; and J. R. Anderson, 1978. For an approach that explicitly integrates holistic and elemental views, see S. T. Fiske and Neuberg, 1990; S. T. Fiske and Pavelchak, 1986.

views over time. To prevent an overly myopic view of the importance of cognition, we will take a brief look at its place in experimental and social psychology. Early psychologists, whether elemental or holistic, relied heavily on introspection as a central tool for understanding human thought. As we will see, however, introspection developed a bad reputation, and with it cognition fell into disrepute. Experimental psychology rejected cognition for many years, while social psychology did not. The next two sections present the contrasting histories of cognition in the two subfields, experimental and social psychology.

Cognition in Experimental Psychology

Wundt's work at the dawn of empirical psychology, as already described, relied heavily on trained introspection.[3] The use of introspection was linked to the fact that Wundt's goal was emphatically cognitive: people's experience was the subject matter of interest. Wundt and others gathered data about mental events and constructed theories to account for those data. However, introspection was ultimately abandoned as a methodology in experimental psychology because it did not conform to the principles appropriate to scientific investigation. By usual scientific standards, one's data should be publicly reproduceable. Other scientists ought to be able to examine the data, replicate them following the same procedures, and analyze the data to see if they confirm the theory. In early experimental psychology, theories were required to account for introspections (i.e., self-observations), and therein lay the problem. If the criteria for a theory's success depended on private experience, the evidence could not be produced in public. The research could not be checked by others. The most absurd version of the problem would be this: if my theory accounts for my introspections and your theory accounts for yours, how do we decide who is right?

When introspection was abandoned because of problems such as this, the study of cognition was neglected too. There was a shift away from studying internal (cognitive) processes and toward external, publicly observable events. The ultimate development of this approach was American behaviorist psychology in the early decades of this century. Behaviorists held that only overt, measurable acts are sufficiently valid objects for empirical scrutiny. One of the founders of this approach was Edward L. Thorndike. B. F. Skinner and others further developed Thorndike's work. For example, Thorndike's theory of instrumental

---

[3]He also took measures that did not rely on people's own reports of their internal processes; for example, he also emphasized the measurements of reaction time, which is the time between stimulus and response. If you ask me how old I am, I can respond instantly. If you ask me how old my brother is, I have to calculate it, and that takes longer. Thus, from reaction time one could infer more or less intervening thought. Such measures supplemented introspective data.

learning (1940) held no place for cognition. According to the theory, behavior has certain rewarding and punishing effects, which cause the organism to repeat or avoid the behavior later. In short, "the effect becomes a cause." Both effect and cause are observable, and cognition is thought to be irrelevant (Skinner, 1963). One behaviorist even called the idea of cognition a superstition (Watson, 1930).

Behaviorists argue that specifying an observable stimulus (S) and response (R) for every part of one's theory is the strict scientific discipline necessary to the advancement of psychology, including social psychology (Berger & Lambert, 1968). For example, a behaviorist might approach the topic of racial and ethnic discrimination by noting that some children are punished for playing with children of certain other ethnic groups and rewarded for playing with children of the family's own ethnic group. A simplified model of this would include "the other ethnic group" as the stimulus and "not playing together" as the response. A behaviorist would not consider the possible role of stereotyping (cognition). In experimental psychology generally, one net effect of behaviorism was that ideas about cognition fell into disrepute for about half a century and behaviorist theories dominated.

Several events caused experimental psychologists to take a fresh interest in cognition during the 1960s (J. R. Anderson, 1980a; Holyoak & Gordon, 1984). First, linguists criticized the failure of the stimulus-response framework's attempts to account for language (cf. Chomsky, 1959, criticizing Skinner, 1957). It became clear that the complex, symbolic, and uniquely human phenomenon of language would not easily yield to behaviorist approaches.

Second, a new approach called *information processing* arose out of work on how people acquire knowledge and skills (Broadbent, 1958). Information processing refers to the idea that mental operations can be broken down into sequential stages. If you ask me when my niece was born, I think back to the circumstances surrounding the event and recall that it was August 1979. An information-processing theory might represent my cognitive operations as: understand the question's meaning → search for information on that topic → verify answer → state answer. The point of an information-processing theory is that one tries to specify the steps intervening *between* stimulus (question) and response (answer). From this point of view, the important feature is the sequential processing of information. Information-processing approaches entail the effort to specify cognitive processes, which behaviorists would not do.

New scientific tools have developed that allow cognitive psychologists to trace the nonobservable processes presumed to intervene between stimulus and response. The most important of these tools is the computer, which has become a methodological tool as well as a theoretical metaphor. It serves as a tool in that cognitive scientists actually use computers to simulate human cognitive processes; they write complex programs that play chess, learn geometry, and summarize the news (J. R. Anderson, 1976; Newell & Simon, 1972; Schank & Abelson, 1977). Social cognition researchers have even developed computer simulations of how people form impressions and memories of each other (Hastie, 1988; Linville, Fischer, & Salovey, 1989; E. R. Smith, 1988). The computer is also a metaphor in that it provides a framework and a jargon for characterizing mental processes; psychologists talk about input-output operations or memory storage and retrieval, with respect to human cognition. More important, most current theory builds on the idea that human cognition resembles computer information processing in important ways.

To summarize, experimental psychology began with introspection as a legitimate method for gaining insight into thinking and with cognition as a legitimate focus for theory. Behaviorists virtually eliminated such techniques and concerns for decades, and cognition fell into disrepute. Recently, cognitive psychology has re-emerged as a scientifically legitimate pursuit (J. R. Anderson, 1990; Neisser, 1967; D. A. Norman, 1976).

Cognition in Social Psychology

In contrast to experimental psychology, social psychology has consistently leaned on cognitive concepts, even when most psychology was behaviorist. Social psychology has always been cognitive in at least three ways. First, since Lewin, social psychologists have decided that social behavior is more usefully understood as a function of people's perceptions of their world, rather than as a function of objective descriptions of their stimulus environment (Manis, 1977; Zajonc, 1980a). For example, an objective reward like money or praise that people perceive as a bribe or as flattery will influence them differently than a reward they perceive as without manipulative intent. What predicts their reaction, then, is their perception, not simply the giver's actions.

Other people can influence a person's actions without even being present, which is the ultimate reliance on perceptions to the exclusion of objective stimuli. Thus, someone may react to a proffered bribe or to flattery by imagining the reactions of others ("What would my mother say?" "What will my friends think?"). Of course, such thoughts are the person's own fantasies, having perhaps tenuous connection to objective reality. Thus, the *causes* of social behavior are doubly cognitive; our perceptions of others actually present and our imagination of their presence both predict behavior (cf. G. W. Allport, 1954).[4]

---

[4]One might well ask, what is the logical alternative to this approach? Who does research on reactions to the objective as opposed to the cognized world? The answer is behaviorists, as described, and some perceptual theorists (Gibson, 1966; see Chapter 7).

Social psychologists view not only causes but also the end *result* of social perception and interaction in heavily cognitive terms, and this is a second way in which social psychology has always been cognitive. Thought often comes before feeling and behaving as the main reaction that social researchers measure. A person may worry about a bribe (thought), hate the idea (feeling), and reject it (behavior), but social psychologists often mainly ask: "What do you think about it?" Even when they focus on behavior and feelings, their questions are often, "What do you intend to do?" and "How would you label your feeling?" These arguably are not behavior and feelings but cognitions about them. Thus, social psychological causes are largely cognitive, and the results are largely cognitive.

A third way in which social psychology has always been cognitive is that the person in-between the presumed cause and the result is viewed as a *thinking organism;* this view contrasts with viewing the person as an emotional organism or a mindless automaton (Manis, 1977). Many social psychological theories paint a portrait of the typical person as reasoning (perhaps badly) before acting. In attempting to deal with complex human problems, as social psychology always has, complex mental processes seem essential. How else can one account for stereotyping and prejudice, propaganda and persuasion, altruism and aggression, and more? It is hard to imagine where a narrowly behaviorist theory would even begin. A strict stimulus-response (S-R) theory does not include the thinking organism that seems essential to account for such problems. In several senses, then, social psychology contrasts with strict S-R theories in its reliance on S-O-R theories that include stimulus, organism, and response. Consequently, the thinker, who comes in-between stimulus and response, has always been paramount in social psychology.

The social thinker has taken many guises in recent decades of research. These guises describe the various roles of cognition in social psychology. Besides the varied roles of cognition, motivation has played different roles in the view of the social thinker. Keeping in mind these two components, cognition and motivation, we can identify four general views of the thinker in social psychology: consistency seeker, naive scientist, cognitive miser, and motivated tactician.

The first view emerged from the massive quantities of work on attitude change after World War II. In the late 1950s, several theories were proposed, all sharing some crucial basic assumptions. The consistency theories, as they were called, viewed people as *consistency seekers* motivated by perceived discrepancies among their cognitions (e.g., Festinger, 1957; Heider, 1958; see Abelson et al., 1968, for an overview). For example, if David knows he is on a diet and knows that he has just eaten a hot fudge sundae, he must do some thinking to bring those two cognitions into line.

Chapter 11 on attitudes will deal more thoroughly with consistency theories, but for the moment two points are crucial. First, these theories relied on perceived inconsistency, which places cognitive activity in a central role. For example, if would-be dieters can convince themselves that one splurge will not matter, eating a sundae is not inconsistent for them. Objective inconsistency, then, is not important. Subjective inconsistency—among various cognitions or among feelings and cognitions—is central to these theories. Actual inconsistency that is not perceived as such does not yield psychological inconsistency.

Second, once inconsistency *is* perceived, the person is presumed to feel uncomfortable (a negative drive state) and to be motivated to reduce the inconsistency. Reducing the aversive drive state is a pleasant relief, rewarding in itself. This sort of motivational model is called a drive reduction model. Less formally, the sundae-consuming dieter will not be free from anxiety until he manufactures some excuse. Hence, consistency theories posit that people change their attitudes and beliefs for motivational reasons, because of unmet needs for consistency. In sum, motivation and cognition both were central to the consistency theories.

Ironically, as they proliferated, consistency theories ceased to dominate the field, partly because the variants on a theme became indistinguishable. Moreover, it was difficult to predict what a person would perceive as inconsistent and to what degree, and which route to resolving inconsistency a person would take. Finally, people do in fact tolerate a fair amount of inconsistency, so the motivation to avoid it—as an overriding principle—was called into doubt (cf. Kiesler, Collins, & Miller, 1969).

Research in social cognition began in the early 1970s, and with it two new models of the thinker emerged. Cognition and motivation played rather different roles in these two models, compared to the roles they played in the consistency seeker model. In both new models, motivation is secondary in importance to cognition. Both views are central to social cognition research, and they will be covered in more detail throughout the book. At present, however, a brief look is useful.

The first new model within the framework of social cognition research is the *naive scientist,* a model of how people uncover the causes of behavior. Attribution theories concern how people explain their own and other people's behavior; they came to the forefront of research in the early 1970s (see Chapters 2–3). Attribution theories describe people's causal analyses of or attributions about the social world. For example, an attribution can address whether someone's behavior seems to be caused by the external situation or by the person's internal disposition. If you want to know why your acquaintance Bruce snapped at you one morning, it would be important to decide if there were mitigating circumstances (his girlfriend left him; you just backed into his car) or if he has an irritable disposition (he always behaves this way and to everyone).

Attribution theorists at first assumed that people are fairly rational in distinguishing among various potential causes, as we will see in subsequent chapters. In part, this was a purposeful theoretical strategy designed to push a rational view of people as far as possible, in order to discover its shortcomings. The theories started with the working hypothesis that, given enough time, people resemble naive scientists, who will gather all the relevant data and arrive at the most logical conclusion. In this view, you would think about your friend's behavior in a variety of settings and carefully weigh the evidence for a situational cause or a dispositional cause of his behavior. Thus, the role of cognition in the naive scientist model is as an outcome of fairly rational analysis.

If you are wrong about why Bruce was irritable, the early theories would have viewed your error as an emotion-based departure from the normal process or as a simple error in available information. For example, if you attribute Bruce's unpleasant behavior to his irritable disposition, it may be because you are motivated to avoid the idea that he is angry at you. Hence, errors arise, mainly as interference from nonrational motivations. In the early attribution theories, motivation enters mainly as a potential qualification on the usual process.

Recall that in consistency theories, in contrast, motivation drives the whole system. The role of motivation in consistency theories is quite central; it acts as an aversive drive state that persists until inconsistencies are resolved. Attribution theorists traditionally have not viewed unresolved attributions as causing an aversive drive state. Motivations for predicting and controlling one's social world presumably set attributions in motion; in that sense, motivation does help to catalyze the attribution process, just as it catalyzes the entire consistency-seeking process. Nevertheless, motivation is far more explicit in consistency theories than in attribution theories.

The usual attributional process, then, is viewed as a quasi-scientific cognitive analysis of causes, with an occasional motivation-based departure. As such, attribution theories at first set forth a prescriptive or *normative* model: what sensible people ought to do, given complete data and full leisure. Under some circumstances, people clearly do proceed as attribution theories suggest, and the theories have led to quantities of research, as will be seen in Chapters 2–3. Much of this research views the person as a naive scientist in careful pursuit of truth.

Unfortunately, people are not always so careful. On an everyday basis, people often make attributions in a relatively thoughtless fashion (see Chapter 3). The cognitive system is limited in capacity, so people take shortcuts. The limitations of the cognitive system can be illustrated by such trivial problems as trying to keep a credit card number, an area code, and a telephone number in your head as you dial, or by more serious problems such as working poorly when you are distracted. The impact of cognitive limitations shows up in social inferences, too. To illustrate, in deciding why Bruce was irritable, you may seize on the easiest explanation rather than the most accurate one. Rather than asking Bruce whether there is something disturbing him, you may simply label him as unpleasant, without giving it much thought. Quite often, people simply are not very thorough.

Hence, the third general view of the thinker (and the second major type of model in social cognition research), comes under the rubric of a *descriptive* model: what people actually do, rather than what they should do. One name for this is the *cognitive miser* model (S. E. Taylor, 1981). The idea is that people are limited in their capacity to process information, so they take shortcuts whenever they can (see especially Chapters 4–9). People adopt strategies that simplify complex problems; the strategies may not be normatively correct or produce normatively correct answers, but they emphasize efficiency. The capacity-limited thinker searches for rapid adequate solutions, rather than slow accurate solutions. Consequently, errors and biases stem from inherent features of the cognitive system, not necessarily from motivations. Indeed, the cognitive miser model is silent on the issue of motivations or feelings of any sort. The role of cognition is central to the cognitive miser view, and the role of motivation has vanished almost entirely, with isolated exceptions.

As the cognitive miser viewpoint has matured, the importance of motivations and emotions has again become evident. Having developed considerable sophistication about people's cognitive processes, researchers are beginning to appreciate anew the interesting and important influences of motivation on cognition, and this recent research is described throughout the book. In addition, affect has been a continued source of fascination, as Chapter 10 indicates. With growing emphasis on motivated social cognition (Showers & Cantor, 1985; also Tetlock, 1990), researchers are returning to old problems with new perspectives gained from studying social cognition. The emerging view of the social perceiver, then, might best be termed the *motivated tactician,* a fully engaged thinker who has multiple cognitive strategies available and chooses among them based on goals, motives, and needs. Sometimes the motivated tactician chooses wisely, in the interests of adaptability and accuracy, and sometimes the motivated tactician chooses defensively, in the interests of speed or self-esteem. Thus, views of the social thinker are coming full cycle, back to appreciating the importance of motivation, but with increased sophistication about cognitive structure and process.

In summary, social psychology has always been cognitive, in the broad sense of positing important steps that intervene between observable stimulus and observable response. One early major set of theories viewed people as consistency seekers, and motivation played a central role in driving the whole system. With the rise of social cognition research, new views have emerged. In one major wave of research, psychologists view people as naive scientists. These psychologists see motivation mainly as a source of error. In another recent view, psychologists see people as cognitive misers and locate errors in the inherent limitations of the cognitive system, saying almost nothing about motivation. Finally, motivational influences on cognition reemerge in a revitalized view of the thinker as a motivated tactician.

WHAT IS SOCIAL COGNITION?

The study of social cognition does not rely on any one theory (for other reviews, see Higgins & Bargh, 1987; Leyens & Codol, 1988; Markus & Zajonc, 1985; Showers & Cantor, 1985; Sherman, Judd, & Park, 1989; Wyer & Srull, 1984). The object of study concerns how people make sense of other people and themselves. As a topic, it is relevant to the study of attitudes (Zimbardo & Leippe, 1991), person perception (Schneider, Hastorf, & Ellsworth, 1979), stereotyping (D. L. Hamilton, 1981a; J. M. Jones, 1972), small groups, and much more. Social cognition research on all these topics shares some basic features: unabashed mentalism, orientation toward process, cross-fertilization between cognitive and social psychologies, and at least some concern with real-world social issues (cf. Hastie & Carlston, 1980; Ostrom, 1984; S. E. Taylor, 1981b).

Mentalism: A Commitment to Cognitive Elements

The first of these assumptions, an unabashed commitment to mentalism (cognition), has just been discussed at some length. The cognitive elements people naturally use to make sense of other people constitute the first third of this book, the "what" of social cognition. Attributions, as defined above, are people's causal explanations for events in the social world. Chapter 2 presents the fundamentals of various central attribution theories. Chapter 3 describes the empirical record, showing the ways social perceivers fail to fit the normative models posited by early attribution theories, and addresses shortcomings in attribution theories themselves.

Another basic cognitive element in people's understanding of themselves and others is the social *schema*. A schema may be defined as a cognitive structure that represents one's general knowledge about a given concept or stimulus domain. For example, your knowledge about your new friend may be organized into a schema that includes your view of him as independent but not a loner, friendly but not saccharine, and athletic but not a star. A schema for a concept (e.g., this person) includes both relevant attributes (e.g., independent, friendly, athletic), and the relationships among the attributes (e.g., what his independence has to do with his friendliness). General knowledge about ourselves and others provides us with the expectations that enable us to function in the world. Chapter 4 describes the operation of people's social categories and schemas; it describes how people categorize social objects, what is contained in the schemas that are triggered by such categorization, and how schemas interact with data, as we take in, remember, and judge ourselves, others, and the situations in which we meet. Chapter 5 then discusses which schemas are used when, and why; how schemas develop and change; the ways that goals and individual differences influence schema use; and where the concept stands at present.

From cognitive representations of others, Chapter 6 moves to concepts of self, and how they influence our thinking. Regulating one's behavior and managing other people's impressions of oneself are central functions of people's self-representations. In examining our cognitive representations of self and others, and how they operate in social life, the book crosses the fuzzy line from the elements to the processes of social cognition.

Cognitive Processes in Social Settings

The second basic assumption in research on social cognition concerns cognitive process, that is, how cognitive elements are formed, used, and changed over time. A process orientation follows from the fundamental commitment to cognition. That is, concern with cognitive elements that intervene between observable stimulus and observable response requires an explanation of *how* one gets from S to R. Recall that, in their theories, behaviorists explicitly avoided discussion of internal processes, because behaviorists were concerned with predicting a publicly observable response from a publicly observable stimulus. In that sense, they were response- or outcome-oriented, rather than process-oriented.

But outcome orientations arose elsewhere, too. The early methodology of research on consistency theories, for example, used to be more outcome-oriented than process-oriented. Although the researchers originally theorized and made assumptions about process, they focused empirically on predicting outcomes from stimuli. For example, inconsistency was manipulated (stimulus) and the resulting attitude change measured (outcome). Later psychologists doing consistency research did attempt to measure the intervening process, but the initial thrust of the research methods were outcome-oriented. One of the recent shifts in attitude research and in social psychology generally has been away from outcome-oriented approaches and toward examinations of process.

In social cognition research, theories are now available to describe and tools to measure various implicit but hitherto unexamined assumptions about process. Social cognition research attempts to measure the stages of social information processing. That is, when one is confronted with a social stimulus, there are several steps posited to occur before one makes a response.

First, one must attend to the stimulus and encode it as an internal representation of external reality. Chapter 7 discusses which social stimuli typically capture attention, what occupies our consciousness besides the external world, and how much control we have over our thoughts. It also addresses how we sometimes operate without much thought.

After encoding the stimulus one can store it away in memory. Chapter 8 describes current theories of how one organizes memory for information about other people, the contents of memory for others, and the relationships among memory, judgment, and goals. What we remember and how we judge can be surprisingly independent processes.

Finally, the third chapter in the process section addresses how people make inferences about social events. Chapter 9 is concerned with how the social perceiver makes inferences by specifying relevant information, sampling that information, and combining it into some judgment. Heuristics, a rapid form of reasoning, provide efficiency at some cost to accuracy, but many errors are inconsequential, self-correcting, or subject to improvement.

Cross-Fertilization: Studying Social Cognitive Processes

So far, we have described two themes in social cognition research and in this book: a commitment to cognition or mentalism and a commitment to process analysis. The third theme, cross-fertilization between cognitive and social psychology, is another feature of social cognition research that we address. Borrowing relatively fine-grained cognitive theory and methods has proved fruitful for social psychological research. Not only do researchers specify the steps in a presumed process model, but researchers attempt to measure the steps in some detail. Various traditional and newer experimental methods allow researchers to support differing aspects of process models. Various research strategies attempt to trace the processes of attention, memory, and inference, and these are presented throughout the book.

Beyond Cognition: Real-World Social Issues

The fourth theme of social cognition research is application to the real world. Social psychologists have a long tradition of addressing important contemporary issues. Early research provided insights into crowd behavior, propaganda, anti-Semitism, military morale, and other social issues. In keeping with this tradition, research in social cognition informs us about important issues. It applies the often heavily cognitive theory and method to real-world social problems. Throughout this book, we illustrate the ways social cognition can guide work in areas such as psychotherapy, health care, the legal system, stereotyping, advertising, political campaigns, strangers helping strangers, and romantic involvements. All these applications illustrate the flexibility of social cognition research. They also demonstrate how some otherwise highly technical or abstract ideas generalize outside the laboratory.

Social cognition applications to real-world issues define some boundary conditions for cognitive processes. That is, the research reveals phenomena that do not lend themselves to a purely cognitive analysis; other factors must be considered in many interpersonal settings of consequence. For example, what happens when the cognitive miser encounters feelings? What relationship does social information processing have to situations of intense personal involvement? How do social cognitions get translated into behavior?

Part Three of the book, "Beyond Cognition," focuses more explicitly on the issues neglected by an overly narrow cognitive approach to social settings. Chapter 10 describes the links between cognitions and affect (feelings or emotions). In the study of how people think about people, affect is a crucial feature, but it has been for the most part neglected by cognitive psychology. As social psychologists became more cognitively oriented, they imported the study of affect into studies of social information processing.

Chapter 11 takes a central area of social psychology, attitudes, and shows the impact of recent cognitive approaches. Attitudes are affect-laden reactions to people, issues, or events, with important links to cognitions and behavior. The application of cognitively oriented theory and method to this well-established area focuses on old variables in new ways and makes a case for social cognition research on attitudes.

Chapter 12 tackles the question of the ways that behaviors (overt actions) influence and are influenced by cognitions, and Chapter 13, the final chapter, comments on the field as a whole and points toward future directions for research in social cognition.

To summarize, the book addresses the four major themes of social cognition research: unabashed mentalism in the study of cognitive representations of people, a commitment to fine-grained analyses of cognitive process, cross-fertilization between cognitive and social theory and methods, and a commitment to real-world social issues.

PEOPLE ARE NOT THINGS

As one reviews research on social cognition, the analogy between the perception of things and the perception of people becomes increasingly clear. The argument is made repeatedly: the principles that describe how people think in general also describe how people think about people. Many theories of social cognition have developed in ways that undeniably build on fundamental cognitive principles, as we will see. Nevertheless, in borrowing such principles, we must consider fundamental differences when applying them to cognition about people. After all, cognitive psychology is relatively more concerned with the processing of information about inanimate objects and abstract concepts, whereas social psychology is more concerned with the processing of information about people and social experience.

At this point, the reader who is new to social cognition research already may be saying, "Wait, you can't tell me that the way I think about mental arithmetic or about my coffee cup has anything to do with the way I think about my friends." The wisdom or folly of applying the principles of object perception to the perception of people has been debated for some time (Heider, 1958; Higgins, Kuiper, & Olson, 1981; Krauss, 1981; Schneider et al., 1979; Tagiuri & Petrullo, 1958). Some of the important differences between people and things include the following:

- People intentionally influence the environment; they attempt to control it for their own purposes. Objects, of course, are not intentional causal agents.
- People perceive back; as you are busy forming impressions of them, they are doing the same to you. Social cognition is mutual cognition.
- Social cognition implicates the self, because the target is judging you, because the target may provide you with information about yourself, and because the target is more similar to you than any object could be.
- A social stimulus may change upon being the target of cognition. People worry about how they come across and may adjust their appearance or behavior accordingly; coffee cups obviously do not.
- People's traits are nonobservable attributes that are vital to thinking about them. An object's nonobservable attributes are somewhat less crucial. Both a person and a cup can be fragile, but that inferred characteristic is both less important and more directly seen in the cup.

- People change over time and circumstance more than objects typically do. This can make cognitions rapidly obsolete or unreliable.

- The accuracy of one's cognitions about people is harder to check than the accuracy of one's cognitions about objects. Even psychologists have a hard time agreeing on whether a given person is extraverted, sensitive, or honest, but most ordinary people easily could test whether a given cup is heat-resistant, fragile, or leaky.

- People are unavoidably complex. One cannot study cognitions about people without making numerous choices to simplify. The researcher has to simplify in object cognition, too, but it is less of a distortion. One cannot simplify a social stimulus without eliminating much of the inherent richness of the target.

- Because people are so complex, and because they have traits and intents hidden from view, and because they affect us in ways objects do not, social cognition automatically involves social explanation. It is more important for an ordinary person to explain why a person is fragile than to explain why a cup is.

For these reasons, social cognitive psychology will never be a literal translation of cognitive psychology. It profits from theories and methods adapted to new uses, but the social world provides perspectives and challenges that are dramatic, if not unique, features of thinking about other people and oneself.

SUMMARY

The study of social cognition concerns how people make sense of other people and themselves. It focuses on people's everyday understanding both as the phenomenon of interest and as a basis for theory about people's everyday understanding. Thus, it concerns both how people think about the social world and how they think they think about the social world. It also draws heavily on fine-grained analyses provided by cognitive theory and method.

Two general approaches to social cognition date back to early modern philosophy. The elemental approach begins with ideas as elements that become linked into increasingly complex compounds. People form associations between ideas by the ideas' repeated contiguity in space or time. Early psychologists used introspective analysis as a method to break down their memory processes into those basic elements.

Gestalt psychologists had a holistic approach. They focused on the mind's active construction of reality, rather than on objective descriptions of the stimulus field. They also focused on the person's experience of dynamic wholes, rather than elements. Lewin imported such ideas to social psychology, emphasizing that the perceived environment—the psychological field—predicts behavior, and that one must consider the entire dynamic equilibrium of forces acting on an individual. The psychological field is the joint product of person and situation, and of motivation and cognition.

Cognition has not always been prominent in experimental psychology. After introspection proved to be a weak basis for an empirical science, every sort of cognition fell into disfavor with psychologists. Behaviorists dominated psychology for decades, insisting on an observable stimulus, an observable response, and no intervening cognitions. Later, behaviorist approaches seemed inadequate to explain language; at the same time, information-processing theories and computer-aided theory and technology paved the way for the reemergence of cognition in experimental psychology.

In social psychology, however, cognition has always been a respectable idea. The causes of social interaction predominantly lie in the perceived world, and the results of social interaction are thoughts, as well as feelings and behavior. In addition, social psychologists have always been cognitive in their view of the thinker who reacts to the perceived stimulus and generates a substantially cognitive response. They have viewed the social thinker at some times as a consistency seeker, motivated to reduce perceived discrepancies; at other times, they have seen the social thinker as a naive scientist who makes every effort thoroughly to ferret out the truth, with motivation contributing mainly error. But lately social psychologists have tended to see the social thinker as a cognitive miser, one who attempts to increase or maintain the efficiency of a capacity-limited cognitive apparatus, and they have had little to say about motivation. An emerging view of the social perceiver as a motivated tactician is gaining increasing acceptance.

Social cognition, as an area of study, cuts across various topics. Those who study it focus on various cognitive elements such as attributions and schemas. They analyze the processes of social cognition: attention, memory, and inference. Social cognition research also can be informative about a number of important real-world social issues.

Social cognition, of course, differs from the general principles of cognition in some ways. Compared to objects, people are more likely to be causal agents, to perceive as well as being perceived, and intimately to involve the observer's self. They are difficult targets of cognition; because they adjust themselves upon being perceived, many of their important attributes (e.g., traits) must be inferred, and the accuracy of observations is hard to determine. People frequently change and are unavoidably complex as targets of cognition. Hence those who study social cognition must adapt the ideas of cognitive psychology to suit the specific features of cognitions about people.

Elements of Social Cognition

2

$\mathcal{A}$ttribution $\mathcal{T}$heory

❖

What Is Attribution Theory? ✦ Heider's Theory of Naive Psychology ✦ Jones and Davis's Correspondent Inference Theory ✦ Kelley's Attribution Contributions ✦ Schachter's Theory of Emotional Lability ✦ Bem's Self-Perception Theory ✦ Weiner's Attribution Contributions

Why is my boyfriend acting so distant? Why did the teacher ignore my comment in class? Every day, we encounter events that require explanation. Causal analysis, that is, the attempt to identify what factors gave rise to what outcomes, is central to explaining events and consequently, to social cognition more generally.

Even the most trivial of events often contains an implicit causal analysis. Observing a classmate passing out leaflets that argue against abortion leads us immediately to assume that his own attitude must be antiabortion as well. Under these circumstances, the attribution process may be almost automatic, and we may have little awareness that we have actually made a causal attribution for the classmate's behavior (e.g., Gilbert, Pelham, & Krull, 1988; Winter & Uleman, 1984).

But there are many circumstances in which causal analyses are more intentional, deliberate, and time-consuming. The imputation of causality becomes a more self-conscious process when people are surprised or threatened by unexpected or negative events that undermine their beliefs and expectations (Abele, 1985; Bohner, Bless, Schwarz, & Strack, 1988; Hastie, 1984; Pittman & Pittman, 1980; Pyszczynski & Greenberg, 1981; Schoeneman, van Uchelen, Stonebrink, & Cheek, 1986; Weiner, 1985a; Wong & Weiner, 1981). For example, receiving a surprising rebuff from a friend produces more analysis (Did I offend him? Is he in a bad mood? Did I misunderstand the conversation last night?) than does receiving the warm greeting one expected. Other conditions that promote causal analysis include the presence of questions that inquire about the causes of behavior (Enzle & Schopflocher, 1978), a person's dependence on another for desired outcomes (e.g., Berscheid, Graziano, Monson, & Dermer, 1976; Erber & Fiske, 1984; Harvey, Yarkin, Lightner, & Town, 1980; Monson, Keel, Stephens, & Genung, 1982), and the perceived loss of control (e.g., Pittman & D'Agostino, 1985; Pittman & Pittman, 1980; see Hastie, 1984, for a review).

*W*HAT IS ATTRIBUTION THEORY?

Psychologists have made the distinction between attribution theory and attributional theories. Attribution theory is a collection of diverse theoretical and empirical contributions that share several common concerns (see Harvey & Weary, 1981; Kelley & Michela, 1980; Ross & Fletcher, 1985, for extensive reviews of the attribution field). Attribution theory deals with how the social perceiver uses information to arrive at causal explanations for events. It examines what information is gathered and how it is combined to form a causal judgment. Attributional theories are theories about particular content domains, such as achievement behavior, helping, coping with threatening events, and so on, that draw on the principles of attribution theory in generating predictions about how people respond in these particular domains. Thus, attribution theory is concerned with the generic causal principles that people employ that might be used in a wide variety of domains, whereas attributional theories are concerned with the specific causal attribution processes that people employ in a particular life domain. While one might be tempted to think of attributional theories as applied attribution theory, in fact, several of the attributional theorists, most notably Weiner (1986), have made fundamental contributions to our understanding of the basic generic principles of causal inference.

Why do people make causal attributions? Research has generally assumed either implicitly or explicitly that causal analysis is initiated by people's needs to predict the future and to control events (Heider, 1958; Jones & Davis, 1965; Kelley, 1967). Presumably, understanding what factors give rise to a certain outcome enables one to control the likelihood of that outcome, or at least to predict when it will happen. Following from this point is the observation that causal attribution is important for the pursuit of goals. One must know how things happen in order to make them happen (Forsterling & Rudolph, 1988). Perhaps the most fundamental assumption of attribution research is that causal attributions are important. Presumably social perceivers do not merely entertain themselves by constructing causal analyses of the world. Psychologists believe that causal analysis can be tied in important ways to attitudes and fundamental values (Feather, 1985); causal attributions can be the basis of behavior, other cognitions, and feelings (see E. E. Jones et al., 1972).

Six different theoretical traditions form the backbone of what is now called attribution theory. The first is Heider's analysis of common-sense psychology (1958). His work strongly influenced both E. E. Jones and Davis's analysis of correspondent inference (1965), a theory of how people form inferences about other people's attributes, and Kelley's work on covariation and causal schemas (1967), which are general models of causal inference. Schachter's theory of emotional lability (1964) and D. J. Bem's self-perception theory (1967, 1972) extended attribution ideas into the arena of self-perception. Bernard Weiner's (1979; 1985b) attributional theory, conducted largely in the domains of achievement and helping, articulated a dimensional structure for understanding causal inference.

HEIDER'S THEORY OF NAIVE PSYCHOLOGY

The work of Fritz Heider (1944, 1958) spearheaded the field of attribution theory. Heider maintained that a systematic understanding of how people comprehend the social world can be enlightened by common-sense psychology: the ways in which people usually think about and infer meaning from what occurs around them. This common-sense psychology, or, as some call it, naive epistemology, can best be learned through the natural language that people employ for describing their experience. To oversimplify, if I listen to you talk for a while about other people, I should gain some insight into how you think about what causes people to behave as they do; and if I listen to enough people talk, the common elements in how they understand others should help me construct a theory of causal inference. Heider believed that what motivates this inference process is people's need to predict and control the environment. People, he maintained, have a need to anticipate and influence what will happen to them and to others around them, and the best way of doing this is through understanding the causes of behavior.

Heider based his theory on the "lens" model of perception originally developed by Brunswik (1956) to explain how people perceive objects. According to Brunswik, objects are never directly perceived; instead, how they are perceived by an individual depends on the attributes of the object itself, on the context in which the object is perceived, on the manner in which it is perceived (e.g., through a fog, a tunnel, or a prism), and on characteristics of the perceiver. The final perception, then, is based on all these components—object, context, mediation, and perceiver.

Heider believed that object perception and person perception have much in common and maintained that person perception processes involve many of the same inferential tasks and problems that exist with object perception. As in object perception, perception of another individual (e.g., your reaction to your new college roommate) will be a function of the person's behavior (how pleasant he or she is), the context in which it was enacted (whether your roommate was pleasant before or after the parents left), the manner in which the perceiver experienced it (learning about your roommate from others or deciding about him or her based on your mutual interactions), and the perceiver's own characteristics and preconceptions about how and why others behave as they do (whether or not this type of person generally appeals to you and whether or not you see any offensive behaviors as redeemable). However, as we noted before, people also differ from objects in important ways: people cause actions; they have intentions, and they have abilities, desires, and sentiments; they are aware of being perceived and are, in turn, perceivers themselves. As a consequence of these factors, their status as causal beings is particularly central in the attribution process.

Fundamental to the question of why someone behaves as he or she does, according to Heider, is whether the locus of causality for that behavior is in the person (internal) or in the environment (external), or both. Internal locus or personal factors consist of *motivation* (trying) and the *ability* to accomplish that action. For example, I may be able to complete my calculus homework, but without any motivation to do so I may leave it undone. Alternatively, I may want to do my calculus homework but lack the skill to do so. Moreover, motivation and ability are not necessarily enough. To these factors must be added or subtracted situational forces that favor or oppose the outcome. For example, if my calculus homework is easy, my motivation and ability may be sufficient to do the work. If it is hard, they may not be. Whether one can succeed at a task, then, is a joint feature of task difficulty and ability; whether one does succeed is additionally determined by the motivational factors of intention and effort. The social perceiver uses what information he or she has about motivational factors, ability, and situational factors to infer the cause of the event. If I successfully complete my calculus homework, then ability, motivation, and situational forces have obviously been adequate for the task.

Heider was also concerned with perceptions of responsibility for outcomes. Under many circumstances, it not only matters what caused an event to happen, it also matters who is responsible for it (see Shaver, 1985; Shaver & Drown, 1986). If someone tells you that I shot my neighbor, the causality question of "who" has been answered but not the responsibility question. Did I shoot him by accident or on purpose? Heider hypothesized that there are varying levels of responsibility that determine how accountable one is for one's actions. The most removed level of responsibility is *association*, whereby a person is held accountable for an action with which he or she is not causally involved. If my neighbor shot himself, but his son tells me I "shot" him for not having noticed his darkening mood or erratic behavior, then I have been labeled responsible by association. *Causal responsibility*, the next level of responsibility, occurs when a person performs an action, but neither intended nor foresaw it. If I shoot at an intruder in the brush, and my neighbor, who happens to be walking there unbeknown to me, is hit, then I am causally responsible for the shooting. If I knew he was in the brush, but fired anyway, expecting to hit the intruder instead, then I bear a greater amount of responsibility because I should have anticipated the possible outcome (*foreseeability*). If I intended to shoot my neighbor and used the intruder as an excuse, then my behavior is *intentional*, and I bear a great deal of responsibility for the outcome. Finally, if I shoot at my neighbor because he shot at me first, then my behavior would be thought by most people to be *justifiable*; although I would be held responsible for my behavior, the behavior would be considered justified by the situation. Heider's analysis has generated considerable research, both on how people develop conceptions of credit and blame for actions (e.g., V. L. Hamilton, Blumenfeld, & Kushler, 1988) and for how people use information in situations to distinguish among causality, responsibility, and blame (e.g., Fincham & Roberts, 1985; B. Harris, 1977; Karlovac & Darley, 1988; Shaver & Drown, 1986).

It is important to note the obvious parallels between naive judgments of responsibility and legal categories for the dispensation of justice. Such terms as *criminal negligence, involuntary manslaughter*, and *first-degree murder* reflect in their definitions many of the same distinctions contained in the different levels of responsibility outlined by Heider. This is one example demonstrating that attributions are not only personally enlightening, they also reflect distinctions that societies find meaningful as a basis for collectively interpreting and acting upon experience.

Heider's major contribution to attribution theory was to define many of the basic issues that would later be explored more systematically in further theoretical ventures. In particular, his thinking on causality and responsibility gave rise to subsequent theoretical work by E. E. Jones and Davis (1965) and Kelley (1967).

JONES AND DAVIS'S CORRESPONDENT INFERENCE THEORY

One model of attributional processes that was heavily influenced by Heider concerns how the social perceiver makes attributions about the causes of other people's behavior. This model is termed *correspondent inference theory* (E. E. Jones & Davis, 1965) and concerns how people make stable attributions about the dispositional qualities of people. Other people, unlike objects, have intentions and the capacity to act on them; because of this, their actions are meaningful and are most likely to be the objects of our attributional interest.

Jones and Davis began with the assumption that we search for meaningful explanations for others' behavior that are both stable and informative. According to the theory, the behavior of another person will be most informative when it is judged to be intentional, and further, to have been produced by a consistent underlying intention, not one that changes from situation to situation. Whims tells you less about a person than do regularities in intentions. The goal of the attribution process, according to Jones and Davis, is the ability to make *correspondent inferences* about another person: to reach the conclusion that the behavior and the intention that produced it correspond to some underlying stable quality in the person, that is, a disposition. Knowing the dispositional attributes of others presumably enables one both to understand and to predict their behavior. For example, it is informative to know that a professor who treated you nicely genuinely enjoys working with students, whereas it would not be so informative to know that the professor was simply in a good mood.

Jones and Davis maintained, as did Heider, that the ability to impute intentions depends on knowing whether or not the person committing the behavior (actor) knew the effects that the behavior would produce and had the ability to produce the behavior. One would not, for example, infer an intention if a three-year-old child shut off the house lights during a concert, but one would certainly infer an intention if the chief custodian did so. Hence the imputation of intention requires the minimum assumptions of knowledge and ability on the part of the actor.

The Analysis of Noncommon Effects

To infer that an intention is based on an individual's underlying disposition or preference requires further analysis. One tool by which this task is accomplished is the *analysis of noncommon effects*. That is, when more than one course of action is available to an individual, one can ask: What did the chosen behavior produce that some other behavior would not have produced? By comparing the consequences of the action that is actually taken with the consequences of actions that are not taken, one can often infer the strength of the underlying intention by looking for distinctive consequences. For example, if I am offered two jobs that are very similar except that one has sports facilities, and I choose that one, then you may infer that sports facilities are important to me. Furthermore, if many relatively negative elements are incorporated into the chosen alternative relative to the unchosen ones, you may infer that the positive elements are especially important to me. Thus, if I choose the job with the sports program, despite the fact that it is at a less prestigious organization and in an undesirable part of the country, you can infer that sports facilities are very important to me indeed. Figure 2.1 provides another example of how the analysis of noncommon effects is used to reach conclusions about an individual's intentions.

One can also infer dispositions more confidently when there are fewer noncommon effects between the chosen and unchosen alternative (Ajzen & Holmes, 1976). If the only thing that distinguishes the two jobs is that one has sports facilities, then you can more confidently infer my interest in sports facilities than if the two jobs differ in several ways.

In conclusion, then, the analysis of noncommon effects leads to correspondent inferences by identifying the distinctive consequences of an actor's chosen course of action. The fewer the distinctive consequences, the more confidently one can make an inference. The more negative the elements incorporated into the chosen alternative, the more one can infer the importance of the distinctive consequence. Of course, alternative courses of action, as well as their consequences and their noncommon effects, may be very difficult to ascertain. Hence, the analysis of noncommon effects can be fraught with ambiguity.

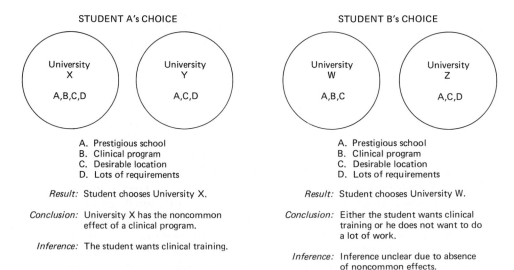

FIGURE 2.1 The analysis of noncommon effects choosing a graduate school. (After E. E. Jones & Davis, 1965.)

Other Bases for Forming Correspondent Inferences

Because the analysis of noncommon effects can produce ambiguous conclusions concerning an actor's dispositional qualities, the social perceiver must draw on other cues as well. These include choice, social desirability, social role, and prior expectations. We will consider each in turn.

One basis for resolving the ambiguity of action is the *social desirability* of the behavior. With the decreasing social desirability of the action, one is able to infer more confidently an underlying disposition. For example, if a job candidate knew that being extraverted and having people skills were important requirements of a prospective job and she then behaved in an extraverted, socially skilled manner, it might be difficult for the job interviewer to ascertain whether she was really extraverted and skilled or whether these were behaviors she had adopted for the purpose of creating a positive impression in the job interview. However, if the job called for extraversion and social skills and the candidate behaved in an introverted fashion, the job interviewer could infer with some confidence that the candidate was, in fact, an introverted sort; else, why would she behave in that way when the situational constraints so clearly called for different behavior? (E. E. Jones, Davis, & Gergen, 1961; see E. E. Jones & McGillis, 1976.) Social desirability is an important criterion for determining causality, because so often behavior is constrained by social propriety. When people are willing to break with norms or conventions to act in a certain way, one can be reasonably certain that their behavior reflects their true beliefs because by so doing they are risking socially aversive consequences, such as rejection.

Another potential basis for inferring an actor's dispositions is whether the behavior of the actor is situationally constrained or whether it occurs from the actor's *choice*. Suppose you are asked to take part in a classroom debate and the teacher assigns you the position of arguing in favor of capital punishment. Knowing that you had been assigned this side of the debate, it would be unwise of your audience to infer that your statements reflected your true beliefs. If, however, you had chosen to argue in favor of capital punishment, then the audience might appropriately conclude, with some confidence, that your statements do reflect your underlying beliefs.

Although choice is a variable that ought to have an impact on whether or not people draw correspondent inferences, research suggests that people do not take choice into sufficient account when judging another person's attributes or attitudes. There is a pervasive tendency for people to assume that when an actor engages in an activity, such as arguing against capital punishment, the statements made are indicative of the person's underlying beliefs, even when there are clear situational factors that constrain the behavior (E. E. Jones & Harris, 1967; Reeder, Fletcher, & Furman, 1989; see also L. Ross, Amabile, & Steinmetz, 1977). Research suggests that part of the reason for this tendency is that people have a strong expectation that when others are asked to express attitudes on a controversial position, they will make statements that are at least somewhat reflective of their own attitudes on the issue (Miller, Jones, & Hinkle, 1981; Miller & Rorer, 1982; Miller, Schmidt, Meyer, & Colella, 1984; Reeder & Brewer, 1979; Reeder, Fletcher, & Furman, 1989). Research also suggests that dispositional attributions based on constrained behavior can occur when there are cues in the setting, suggesting that the person intended the behavior. Thus, for example, if an essay writer is constrained to write in a particular direction and facial expressions suggest that the person is contented with this assignment, then dispositional attributions for the essay's position may result even when the situational constraints are high (Fleming & Darley, 1989).

Perceivers can even be unaware of the impact of situational forces on an actor's behavior when they themselves are the situational force that has caused the behavior. Thus, for example, in one study (Gilbert & Jones, 1986a), subjects either assigned an actor to present a liberal (or a conservative) set of arguments regarding abortion or they observed another subject assigning the actor to present a particular set of arguments. Subjects were then asked to estimate the actor's true attitudes. The subjects inferred the actor's true attitudes to be consistent with the statements he made, just as observers did, even when the subject had brought the actor's behavior about by assigning him the position.

Even when subjects can be induced to notice their own impact on a target actor's behavior, they may fail to ignore other situational forces on the target's behavior, inferring that the target's own dispositions are the only other predominant force on the target's behavior (Gilbert, Jones, & Pelham, 1987). In fact, it seems to require fairly explicit cues suggesting that situational factors may have elicited an actor's behavior for people to properly subdue their tendency to make dispositional attributions for an actor's behavior (Ginzel, Jones, & Swann, 1987; J. T. Johnson, Jemmott, & Pettigrew, 1984; E. F. Wright & Wells, 1988). A similar error can be identified at the group level. People have a tendency to use a group's decision to attribute correspondent attitudes to the group's members, even when there is information to indicate that all members do not support the decision or there is situational information to suggest that the group decision was made for situational reasons (Allison & Messick, 1985; Mackie & Allison, 1987).

A third condition that can help resolve the ambiguity of an action's meaning is whether the behavior is part of a *social role*. Behavior that is constrained by a role is not necessarily informative about an actor's underlying beliefs or behaviors. For example, when firefighters put out a fire, we do not infer that they are helpful; they are simply doing their job. But when people in well-defined social roles display out-of-role behavior, those actions can be used to infer underlying dispositions, since explanations related to role are effectively ruled out. For example, if a priest argues in favor of a woman's right to an abortion, you may infer confidently that his behavior reflects his true beliefs, since it so clearly contradicts the abortion attitudes one expects in a priest.

However, like choice, role is also a situational factor that may be overlooked when attributing causes for behavior. L. Ross, Amabile, and Steinmetz (1977) demonstrated this point particularly well in a study that simulated a television quiz show. College student subjects were randomly assigned to the role of questioner or contestant. The questioner was told to compose a set of general knowledge questions of some difficulty (e.g., "What do the letters *D. H.* stand for in D. H. Lawrence?") that would be posed to the contestants and could be scored as correct or incorrect. The contestant was merely supposed to answer as many of the questions as he or she could. Of course, the questioner was at a decided advantage in displaying his or her range of knowledge, whereas the contestant was at a distinct disadvantage, at the mercy of whatever questions the questioner posed. Needless to say, contestants were able to answer relatively few of the questions posed to them. Despite the clear advantage of the questioner role conferred by the task, however, both the questioner and the contestant rated the questioner as more generally knowledgeable than the contestant; the effect was strongest for the contestant's beliefs about the questioner (see also Block & Funder, 1986; Davies, 1985).

Prior expectations about a target individual can help the social perceiver identify the person's dispositional qualities (e.g., E. E. Jones & McGillis, 1976). Some expectations are based on knowledge of what is normative for a situation (*population-based* expectations). This type of expectation derives from the social desirability concerns just described (e.g., "She'll be polite because everybody's polite in this situation"). Other expectations are *category-based* and involve beliefs about a target based upon his or her category membership (e.g., "She's a Southerner, so of course she'll be polite"). People also have expectations about others when they have interacted with them on more than one occasion. These expectations are *target-based*, because they relate to the specific target rather than the category of which he or she might be a member (e.g., "She'll be polite because she's always that way"). Thus, knowing something about an individual's background, having information about prior behavior, or perceiving consistency in behavior or intentions over time can lead to a dispositional attribution. Deviations from expected patterns of behavior or intention may also help the social perceiver refine prior dispositional attributions. For example, if Sue knows that one of her colleagues is a very conscientious worker but observes that he stays home when his children are sick, she can make more precise inferences about his priorities. People can also use expectations to dismiss the significance of information: When information is too discrepant with prior expectations, people downplay its veracity or significance (E. E. Jones & McGillis, 1976).

There are at least two biases that perceivers hold that can sometimes interfere with an accurate assessment of another person's dispositional qualities. *Hedonic relevance* refers to the impact that an actor's behavior has on the perceiver, such as whether the action obstructs or promotes the perceiver's goals or interests. Generally, perceptions of correspondence increase as hedonic relevance increases. For example, if your roommate leaves your suite unlocked and your money and camera are stolen, you are more likely to infer that she is careless than if no harm was done. Neutral actions may also be assimilated to the hedonic value of the target action, thereby strengthening the inference. For example, you may also see her other actions, such as her chronic lateness to class, as further evidence of this dispositional characteristic of carelessness.

Personalism is the perceiver's perception that the actor intended to benefit or harm the perceiver. In this case, not only is the actor's action hedonically relevant for the perceiver, but it is seen by the perceiver as intending to be so. For example, if your roommate hogs the phone so that you cannot talk to your girlfriend (hedonic relevance) and you perceive that to be the reason for the behavior (personalism), you are more likely to infer that he is an obnoxious, mean individual than if he were simply talking for reasons unrelated to your interests. The latter circumstance might elicit some annoyance, but not a dispositional attribution of unkindness.

In summary, then, correspondent inferences can be drawn or further refined by determining whether or not a given behavior is freely chosen, socially desirable, or consistent with social roles or prior expectations. However, the perceiver's attributions are not always unbiased, and two factors that can influence the attribution process are the hedonic relevance of the action for the perceiver and the judgment that the action was intended to benefit or harm the perceiver (personalism).

KELLEY'S ATTRIBUTION CONTRIBUTIONS

Harold Kelley developed two formulations of the attribution process. For cases in which people have access to multiple instances of the same or similar events, he formulated the covariation model (1967). For cases in which information is limited to a single event, he formulated the concept of causal schemata (Kelley, 1972b). Kelley's attribution formulations differ from that of Jones and Davis in several important ways. First, as just noted, Kelley's models cover both multiple events and single events. Second, his models detail the processes for making attributions of causality not only to other people but to environmental factors and to the self as well.[1]

Kelley began with the observation that knowledge about the world, especially the social world, is often elusive or ambiguous. Although people usually have enough information to function effectively on a social level (see Thibaut & Kelley, 1959), under some circumstances, the information level is not adequate. This situation can occur when one's beliefs or opinions receive little support from others, when problems exist that are beyond one's capabilities, when information about an issue is poor or ambiguous, when one's views have been labeled as untrue or inappropriate, or when one encounters some other experience that produces low self-confidence. When any of these conditions occurs, attributions for events become uncertain (Kelley, 1967). Under these circumstances, people are especially susceptible to social influence, and they are likely to seek out additional information to validate a tentative impression of what is occurring or to develop an explanation of what is occurring. In short, uncertainty prompts causal analysis.

The Covariation Model

Under many circumstances, an individual will have access to multiple instances of the same or similar events. For example, we see our friends interacting with many different people or we observe our own repeated interactions with others. With information about multiple events, we can employ a covariation principle to infer the causes of events. Covariation is the observed co-occurrence of two events. If my roommate gets cold and distant every time I bring home a friend, that is a high covariation. If she is cold and distant only sometimes when I bring home a friend and also some times when I don't bring home a friend, that is a low covariation. In trying to understand the cause of some effect (e.g., cold and distant behavior), we observe its covariation with various potential causes and attribute the effect to the cause with which it most closely covaries. If my roommate's behavior is only cold and distant when I bring a friend in, I can infer that she does not like being disturbed by outsiders.

According to Kelley, people assess covariation information across three dimensions relevant to the entity whose behavior they are trying to explain. An entity may be another person or a thing. As an example, consider a young man who goes with a young woman (entity) to a

---

[1]The E. E. Jones and McGillis (1976) update of E. E. Jones and Davis (1965), and Kelley's later work (1972a) make the theories now much more similar in their predictions and in the phenomena they encompass than was originally true.

party only to find himself ignored while she flirts with several other men. He is likely to wonder why she bothered to go out with him in the first place and to be (at least) curious about why this has happened. The three dimensions along which he will test his attributions, according to Kelley, are:

Distinctiveness

Does the effect occur when the entity (the young woman) is there and not when it is not? (For example, is she the only woman to have behaved this way toward him in the past, or have other women done the same thing?)

Consistency over time/modality

Does the effect occur each time the entity is present and regardless of the form of the interactions? (For example, has she done this to him before and at other events as well as at parties?)

Consensus

Do other people experience the same effect with respect to this entity? (For example, has she done this to other people?)

According to Kelley, one is able to make a confident entity attribution with the combination of high distinctiveness, high consistency, and high consensus information. In this case, one may conclude that this entity, the young woman, is an impossible hussy if she is the only person who treats the wretched young man this way (high distinctiveness), if she has always done this in the past (assuming he has been foolish enough to take her out before) (high consistency), and if others have had similar experiences with her (high consensus).

Other combinations of information can also yield meaningful causal inferences. For example, suppose we learned that the young lady has never ignored other dates before (low consensus), she has always ignored this date in the past (high consistency), and most other women have also ignored this young man (low distinctiveness). One might be inclined to think there is something rather offensive about the young man, such as rude manners or bad breath. The combination of low distinctiveness, high consistency, and low consensus reliably produces this kind of person attribution (McArthur, 1972).

Covariation principles can also be employed to form joint attributions of causality. Suppose we learned that the young man has never been ignored by another date (high distinctiveness), the young lady has never ignored any other date (low consensus), but she has always ignored this fellow every time they have gone out together (high consistency). Under these circumstances, we would be inclined to attribute responsibility to them jointly, concluding that they are a fatal combination as well as gluttons for punishment (McArthur, 1972). Table 2.1

TABLE 2.1 USING KELLEY'S COVARIATION MODEL TO ANSWER THE QUESTION: WHY DOES RALPH (PERSON) TRIP OVER JOAN'S (ENTITY) FEET WHILE DANCING?

High distinctiveness

	High consistency		Low consistency	
Distinctiveness	Ralph does not trip over almost any other partner's feet.			
Consistency	In the past, Ralph has almost always tripped over Joan's feet.		In the past, Ralph has almost never tripped over Joan's feet.	
	High consensus	*Low consensus*	*High consensus*	*Low consensus*
Consensus	Almost everyone else who dances with Joan trips over her feet.	Hardly anyone else who dances with Joan trips over her feet.	Almost everyone else who dances with Joan trips over her feet.	Hardly anyone else who dances with Joan trips over her feet.
Attribution	Joan is not coordinated. She is at fault. An *entity* attribution should be made.	Ralph and Joan are jointly responsible. Both are *necessary* to produce the outcome. A *person-entity* attribution is warranted.	Usually Ralph is able to overcome Joan's uncoordination, but not today. A *circumstance* attribution is warranted.	It's a bad day. A *circumstance* attribution is warranted.

Low distinctiveness

	High consistency		Low consistency	
Distinctiveness	Ralph trips over lots of partners' feet.			
Consistency	In the past, Ralph has almost always tripped over Joan's feet.		In the past, Ralph has almost never tripped over Joan's feet.	
	High consensus	*Low consensus*	*High consensus*	*Low consensus*
Consensus	Almost everyone else who dances with Joan trips over her feet.	Hardly anyone else who dances with Joan trips over her feet.	Almost everyone else who dances with Joan trips over her feet.	Hardly anyone else who dances with Joan trips over her feet.
Attribution	Ralph and Joan are jointly responsible. Either is *sufficient* to cause the outcome. A *person-entity* attribution is warranted.	Ralph is uncoordinated and is at fault. A *person* attribution should be made.	Ralph and Joan are both uncoordinated. Usually they overcome it. But not today. Attribution is ambiguous.	Ralph is uncoordinated. Joan is usually able to overcome it. But not today. Attribution is ambiguous.

shows how the covariation model can be used to reach different causal attributions.

Attributions can also provide guidelines for future behavior (McArthur, 1972). Specifically, entity attributions produce *response generalization*. For example, if the young man decides that the young lady is at fault for the unpleasant evening, then several responses will follow: he will be unlikely to date her again, call her, or even speak to her. The attribution to her (i.e., to the entity) suggests numerous responses for dealing with her in the future. Person attributions, in contrast, provoke *stimulus generalization*. For example, if the young man decides that he is at fault for being ignored, then he can infer that not only this young lady, but other "stimuli," namely, other women, will behave in the same way. Kelley's model, then, is highly flexible: the information obtained in a causal search can yield any of several multiple meaningful patterns that in turn define guidelines for behavior. It should be noted that Kelley's covariation model has also been referred to as the ANOVA model. That is, the process of assessing covariation across several categories of information corresponds to similar processes in the formal statistical model known as analysis of variance (ANOVA).

Empirical investigations have supported certain aspects of the covariation model (e.g., Chen, Yates, & McGinnies, 1988; Ferguson & Wells, 1980; Hazlewood & Olson, 1986; Lord & Gilbert, 1983; McArthur, 1972; Orvis, Cunningham, & Kelley, 1975; Pruitt & Insko, 1980; Zuckerman, 1978). Researchers have found distinctiveness, consistency, and consensus to be relevant dimensions on which people base attributions. However, some studies using either hypothetical or real-world attributional dilemmas have revealed qualifications (Stevens & Jones, 1976; Tillman & Carver, 1980). For example, studies that have let subjects select their own information when faced with an attributional dilemma have found mixed support for the model; although subjects examine consensus, distinctiveness, and consistency information, their search is not as thorough or systematic as the ways the covariation model would suggest. When given the opportunity, people sometimes choose to acquire additional information about the actor (such as information about his or her personality) or information about the situation in which the act occurred (e.g., various situational constraints) rather than the types of information suggested by the covariation model (Garland, Hardy, & Stephenson, 1975).

It appears, then, that the three types of information are not equally influential. Consistency information is typically preferred over distinctiveness (e.g., Kruglanski, 1977), and consensus is typically least utilized (e.g., Kruglanski, Hamel, Maides, & Schwartz, 1978; Major, 1980; Olson, Ellis, & Zanna, 1983). Consensus information may require additional tests of its value for the attribution process, such as whether the other people are similar or dissimilar (e.g., Nisbett, Borgida, Crandall, & Reed, 1976). The consensus of similar others may strengthen some inferences, whereas other inferences may be stronger given the consensus of dissimilar others (Alicke & Insko, 1984).

Jaspars and his associates (Jaspars, Hewstone, & Fincham, 1983; Hewstone & Jaspars, 1987) argue that many of these apparent deviations from Kelley's model result from the fact that the particular constellations of consensus, consistency, and distinctiveness information relevant to the causal judgment may not be available to subjects in experimental investigations. Although Kelley conceptualized his attribution theory as an analog to the statistical procedure of analysis of variance, as Jaspars et al. (1983) and others (Pruitt & Insko, 1980; Forsterling, 1989) have noted, when one attempts to fit the theory into the analysis of variance model, some of the cells are empty. In particular, the theory provides no guidelines for interpreting how other people perform at other tasks, what Pruitt and Insko (1980) call "comparison object consensus." Many of the recent refinements to Kelley's theory (Jaspars et al., 1983; Hilton & Slugoski, 1986; Pruitt & Insko, 1980) have developed primarily to address how people take this absent information into account.

In their natural logic model, Jaspars et al. (1983) maintain that when people encounter an event that requires attributional explanation, the person, the stimulus, and the circumstances that gave rise to the event are all regarded as potential causes. People detect cause-effect relationships by examining whether the effect generalizes across the possible antecedents of person, stimulus, and circumstances. In this way, consensus, consistency, and distinctiveness information are used to determine whether or not the event occurs in the presence of each of the possible causes. By analyzing the covariation information that is available, the person can identify the necessary and sufficient conditions for the occurrence of an effect, thereby precisely locating its cause (Hewstone & Jaspars, 1987). If an effect occurs when a particular cause is present, this cause will be considered sufficient to produce the effect. If the effect is absent when the cause is absent, the cause is perceived to be a necessary one. When several kinds of relevant antecedent information are available to a social perceiver, the various causal objects will be combined. Thus, for example, if Mary is the only student to fail a test but she has never failed a test before, then one assumes that something unique about the combination of Mary and this test produced the effect.

According to Jaspars and his associates, the social perceiver follows formal inference rules to deduce a cause from the particular configuration of covariation information (see also Jaspars, 1983). The model details explicit predictions for each of the eight possible combinations generated by the interaction of these three information variables. Although the predictions of the natural logic model explain some of the contradictory data generated by Kelley's model, they do not account for all deviations. For example, Jaspars and his associates (Hewstone & Jaspars, 1987; Jaspars et al., 1983) predict that no attributions will be made for certain of the consensus/distinctiveness/consistency configurations. In fact, data show that subjects do make attributions under these conditions (Hilton & Slugoski, 1986; but see Hilton & Jaspars, 1987).

Recently, investigators have questioned a more fundamental assumption, namely whether the assessment of covariation is necessarily the main process by which causal attributions are formed or validated when information is ambiguous (Hilton & Knibbs, 1988; Hilton & Slugoski, 1986; E. R. Smith & Miller, 1978). We will defer extended discussion of this issue to the next chapter.

The Discounting and Augmenting Principles

Often when a person is trying to understand the causes of an event, evidence is not available about its consistency over time, its distinctiveness, and other people's experiences with it. Rather, the only information is a single occurrence of the event. In such cases, the social perceiver must fall back on other strategies or rules of causal inference than covariation. One such rule noted by Kelley (1972b) is the *discounting principle*. The discounting principle maintains that a social perceiver discounts any one candidate as a potential cause for an event to the extent that other potential causal candidates are available. For example, if I wreck my car at 2:00 A.M., you may be less inclined to conclude that I was tired and not paying careful enough attention if you learn that it was raining. Research conducted on the discounting principle suggests that sometimes it is strong (e.g., E. E. Jones, Davis, & Gergen, 1961), sometimes weak (E. E. Jones & Harris, 1967), and sometimes virtually absent (Messick & Reeder, 1974; Napolitan & Goethals, 1979; see Reeder, 1985, for a review). Under many conditions, the social perceiver appears insufficiently to discount situational information that constitutes an alternative cause for an actor's behavior. That is, you may assume I am a poor driver even if it was raining and the visibility was poor. In essence, this finding is much like that of Jones and his colleagues who found that social perceivers do not take sufficient account of situational constraints determining whether or not an actor freely chose an action in inferring a correspondent inference.

In addition, any cause can facilitate or inhibit a particular effect. An *inhibitory cause* interferes with the occurrence of a given event, whereas a *facilitative cause* increases the likelihood of its occurrence. When an effect occurs in the presence of both a facilitative cause and an inhibitory cause, people give the facilitative cause more weight in producing the outcome, because it had to be strong enough to overcome the inhibitory cause; this generalization is termed the *augmenting principle*. For example, if you learn that Sam was the winner of the skateboarding contest, you infer that he must be good. If I then explain that Sam is only six years old (inhibitory cause), you will probably infer that he is especially good to have successfully eliminated a field of older and presumably more experienced contestants.

Hansen and Hall (1985) examined the impact of discounting and augmentation information on people's causal attributions and concluded that discounting is more potent than augmentation. That is, the addition of other potential causes for an effect weakened the inferred strength of the target causal factor more than the addition of the same number of opposing forces strengthened it. Similarly, the magnitude of the effect produced by facilitative as opposed to inhibitory forces was considered to be more informative regarding facilitative forces than of those inhibitory forces. Thus, for example, if Sam won by a large margin, he would be judged more likely than a narrow-margin winner to win again in the future, but if he lost big, he would be judged no more likely than a narrow-margin loser to lose again in the future. What these data suggest, then, is that the social perceiver may be more attuned to causal factors that promote a particular effect than to causal factors that may weaken or undermine it.

Causal Schemas

Another method a person may use to infer causality for single events involves the application of *causal schemas*. "A causal schema is a general conception the person has about how certain kinds of causes interact to produce a specific kind of effect" (Kelley, 1972b, p. 151). Each of us, in our experiences with cause-effect relations in the world, develops certain abstract conceptions about how causes work together to yield effects; we can use these so-called schemas when we wish to explain effects for which causal information is ambiguous and unclear.

Kelley described two types of causal schemas in particular: the multiple necessary causes schema and the multiple sufficient causes schema. We may know, for example, that when a particularly difficult or extreme effect is involved (such as winning a marathon), multiple causes will be needed to produce the outcome (such as ability, effort, good training, and favorable course conditions). We term this the *multiple necessary causes schema*. To fail such a task would not be very informative, because any one of the necessary conditions could be absent and the effect would not occur. To succeed in performing a difficult task is informative about the presence of several causes.

On the other hand, a *multiple sufficient causes schema* accounts for less extreme outcomes and assumes that any one of several causes could be sufficient to produce the effect. If I beat my four-year-old niece at checkers, you can attribute my victory to my ability, my effort, the fact that the task is familiar to me, or the fact that I can cheat and she does not know enough to catch me. Any one of the causes will do equally well, and to the extent that any one is present, the social perceiver should employ the discounting principle to downplay the significance of the others (J. D. Cunningham & Kelley, 1975). For outcomes that are not extreme or difficult, then, success is not surprising or informative; any of a number of factors could have produced it. On the other hand, failure is somewhat informative, since failure on an easy task suggests that a variety of factors must not have been present.

Perceivers use not only information about the presence or absence of cause but also information about the relative *strength of causes* to judge cause-effect relationships. For example, if you know that I had a lot of money riding on the outcome of the checkers game with my niece and you also know that I tried hard, you may infer that I probably won by a handy margin. *Strength of effect* also provides information about cause-effect relationships. For example, if I beat my niece at checkers but just barely, you may infer that my ability is low, my effort was weak, the task may be novel, and I did not cheat very much.

Research on causal schemas has been plentiful (J. D. Cunningham & Kelley, 1975; DiVitto & McArthur, 1978; Karniol & Ross, 1976; Kun & Weiner, 1973; Leddo, Abelson, & Gross, 1984; Locksley & Stangor, 1984; M. C. Smith, 1975), although the adequacy of this research has been challenged conceptually (Fiedler, 1982) and empirically (Surber, 1981). Nonetheless, causal schemas are thought to be important aspects of causal inference for several reasons. First, causal schemas help people to make causal inferences when information is incomplete, sketchy, or derived from only one incident or observation. Second, they represent general conceptions about patterns of cause-effect relationships that may apply across a wide range of specific content areas. Causal schemata, in essence, give the social perceiver a causal shorthand for accomplishing complex inferential tasks quickly and easily. Based on our knowledge of causal schemata, we are able to use information about presence, absence, or strength of causes to infer effects when information is less than complete. And we are also able to use presence, absence, or strength of effects to infer causes and their relative strength.

Attribution Theory: A Note

The reader accustomed to viewing theories competitively may wish to know which one is right. The answer is that all of them have some validity, but under different circumstances and for different phenomena. The theories cannot be pitted against each other in the usual scientific manner. Rather, each outlines a series of processes that can be used to infer attributions if the appropriate circumstances are present. For example, if one has the opportunity to view an individual's behavior over time, then one can employ Kelley's covariation model to infer that person's dispositional qualities. If not, then one may have to infer the person's dispositions from knowledge of the social desirability of the act and whether or not the person chose it. Despite the best efforts to compare and contrast the theories (e.g., Howard, 1985; E. E. Jones & McGillis, 1976; K. G. Shaver, 1975), relatively little has emerged in the way of theoretical refinement. The theories adopt different slants rather than differing hypotheses or stands on fundamental issues.

The ideas of Heider, Jones and Davis, and Kelley constitute the early and focal theoretical contributions to attribution theory. In many respects, these theories detail an idealized manner in which the social perceiver might make attributions. Psychologists call such theories normative, because they outline the appropriate norms or guidelines for how a process should proceed. But, as will be seen shortly, research in attribution theory revealed that the social perceiver does not always follow these normative guidelines. Sometimes the process of making attributions occurs spontaneously, without the kind of detailed causal analysis that Heider, Jones and Davis, and Kelley describe. In certain cases, the social perceiver appears to seize upon a sufficient causal explanation without performing the additional cognitive work to determine if it is an accurate or the best causal explanation. Moreover, the attribution process appears to be marked by certain persistent biases. The contributions of Heider, Jones and Davis, and Kelley's models, then, have been held up as normative theories against which actual attributional processes can be compared.

In the next section, we consider three additional attributional formulations developed by Stanley Schachter, Daryl Bem, and Bernard Weiner. Schachter's work is notable for extending attribution ideas to self-perception, especially the self-perception of emotion. Bem's theory is also concerned with self-perception, and he argues that people often infer their own beliefs from environmental factors that provide cues about their beliefs. What Schachter's and Bem's theories have in common are the ideas that the attribution process can occur quite quickly with a fairly cursory examination of the environment, and the belief that as a consequence of its rapidity and simplicity, the attribution process can be subject to misattribution and faulty inference. Finally, Bernard Weiner's attributional theories of achievement and helping have been useful in identifying a set of focal dimensions along which attributions may be inferred, and in integrating attributional dimensions with emotional responses.

SCHACHTER'S THEORY OF EMOTIONAL LABILITY

In his early work on affiliation, Schachter (1959) observed that when people expect to undergo a stressful experience, they sometimes choose to affiliate with others who will also be undergoing similar stressful experiences. After ruling out several possible explanations for this effect, he concluded that people have a need to compare their emotional state with that of similar others so as better to understand and to label their own reactions. If this is true, Schachter reasoned, then the internal physiological cues on which people normally draw to help interpret their arousal must be relatively ambiguous and subject to multiple interpretations. Consequently, people's perceptions of their emotions may be indirect and relatively labile (unstable). If people have direct access to their emotions, why would they need to compare them with others?

These and other observations led Schachter (1964, 1971; Schachter & Singer, 1962) to posit that there are two necessary conditions for emotion: a state of psychological *arousal*, nonspecific with respect to a particular emotion, and *cognitions*, which label the arousal and determine what emotion is experienced. Under some circumstances, cognitions precede arousal (for example, knowing that mambas are the most deadly snakes and then becoming aroused when one encounters one in the brush). Under other circumstances, a state of arousal may occur first, which then prompts a cognitive search for a causal explanation of that aroused state. Under these circumstances, cues from the immediate environment then become likely candidates for labeling arousal as a particular emotion.

To see if the interpretation of arousal is indeed malleable, Schachter and Singer (1962) conducted a now-classic experiment. One group of undergraduate students was injected with epinephrine: half were told its true side effects (e.g., rapid breathing, flushing, increased heart rate), and half were told to expect effects that are not, in fact, produced by epinephrine (e.g., dizziness, slight headache). A control group of subjects was given no drug. Subjects were then placed in a room with a confederate of the experimenter and were instructed to fill out some papers. After a brief time (during which the epinephrine took effect in those who had received it), the confederate began to act in either a euphoric manner (engaging in silly antics and making paper airplanes) or in an angry manner (ripping up the papers and stomping around the room).

Schachter and Singer reasoned that if physiological experience is indeed subject to multiple interpretations, then those subjects who had been misinformed about the side effects of epinephrine and who later found themselves in a state of arousal would be searching for an explanation for their state. For these subjects, the behavior of the confederate could act as a salient cue for explaining their arousal, suggesting to those subjects in the euphoric condition that they were also euphoric and to those in the angry condition that they were angry. Subjects who had been informed about the side effects of epinephrine, in contrast, already had an adequate explanation for their arousal state and could remain amused or annoyed by the confederate without acquiring his mood. Subjects in the control condition would have no arousal state to explain and also should not catch the mood of the confederate. Generally speaking, this is what Schachter and Singer found. A description of their experiment is presented in Table 2.2. Schachter's ideas and the results of this experiment extensively influenced both the study of emotion and the understanding of causal attribution. As our present concern is with attribution, we will not cover the work on emotions until Chapter 10.

One of the most important aspects of Schachter's work is the point that attributions for arousal are malleable. This point is significant in part because it suggests that emotional reactions induced by a threatening experience can be reattributed to a neutral or less threatening source. The idea has profound clinical implications because it provides a potential general model for the treatment of emotional disorders (Valins & Nisbett, 1972). Consider the fact that there are a great many people who are anxious over real or imagined faults. An adolescent boy may believe he is unable to talk to girls and so avoids them. A middle-aged woman returning to work after years of child rearing may doubt her ability to convey a good impression and thus avoid tackling the job market. In such situations, a cycle of emotional exacerbation may occur (Storms & McCaul, 1976). The adolescent, fearful that he will ruin his chance with a girl, becomes so anxious that his hands get sweaty and he stutters just saying "hello." Or the middle-aged woman may think of so many things that could go wrong in a job interview that she cannot even get up the courage to check the newspaper listings.

TABLE 2.2 THE MISATTRIBUTION OF AROUSAL

	Subject informed of true side effects of epinephrine	Subject misinformed of side effects of epinephrine	No arousal
Exposure to angry confederate	Subject correctly labels arousal; does not infer that he is angry	Subject interprets own arousal as anger	Subject has no arousal and infers no emotion for the self
Exposure to euphoric confederate	Subject correctly labels arousal, does not infer that he is euphoric	Subject interprets own arousal as euphoria	Subject has no arousal and infers no emotion for the self

SOURCE: After Schachter and Singer, 1962

The misattribution paradigm (Valins, 1966) suggests that by inducing people to reattribute their arousal to some nonthreatening source, the exacerbation cycle can be broken. Consequently, they will function more effectively in the settings that currently make them anxious. The woman contemplating a return to work might be told that changes in schedule, strange settings, and trying to get to new places on time all produce some change in heart rate and breathing, and therefore, if she finds herself experiencing these changes, she should realize that they are normal physiological responses to changes in daily activities. Now having a safe, external stimulus to account for her arousal, the woman might calm down enough to schedule an interview and follow through on it. A number of experiments using this kind of intervention have yielded support for the reattribution approach (e.g., Brodt & Zimbardo, 1981; G. C. Davison & Valins, 1969; Nisbett & Schachter, 1966; Olson, 1988; L. Ross, Rodin, & Zimbardo, 1969; Storms & McCaul, 1976; Storms & Nisbett, 1970; Valins & Ray, 1967; Worchel & Brown, 1984).

After the early work supporting Schachter's ideas, some researchers criticized both the theory and its potential clinical applications. One criticism concerns whether environmental cues are easily accepted as bases for inferring one's own emotions, as Schachter implies (e.g., Maslach, 1979; Marshall & Zimbardo, 1979; Plutchik & Ax, 1967). People's efforts to understand an unexplained state of arousal appear to involve more extensive search than a quick examination of salient cues in the surrounding environment (Maslach, 1979). People also seem to be more likely to interpret unexplained arousal negatively—for example, as feelings of unease or nervousness—than positively (Maslach, 1979; Marshall & Zimbardo, 1979). These results question the extent of emotional lability (see also Schachter & Singer, 1979).

Researchers have also criticized the misattribution effect (see Parkinson, 1985, for a review). They point out that it is not completely reliable (e.g., J. W. Duncan & Laird, 1980; M. Ross & Olson, 1981; Slivken & Buss, 1984), that it may be rather short-lived (Nisbett & Valins, 1972), and that some attempts to demonstrate it have failed (e.g., Conger, Conger, & Brehm, 1976; Kellogg & Baron, 1975; Singerman, Borkovec, & Baron, 1976; see Reisenzein, 1983, for a review). Even when people have successfully been induced to reattribute their arousal to a nonthreatening source and accordingly experience reduced symptoms or anxiety, it is not clear that attributions mediate these effects (Girodo, 1973; S. C. Thompson, 1981). For misattribution effects to occur, the alternative arousal source must be plausible, unambiguous, and salient (e.g., Olson & Ross, 1988; Sterling & Gaertner, 1984), the actual cause of the arousal must not be obvious, and the subjects must believe that the misattribution source is having more impact on their arousal than it actually is (Olson & Ross, 1988; Ross & Olson,

1981). Misattribution effects also appear to occur only for a limited range of emotion-inducing stimuli (Parkinson, 1985).

Moreover, laboratory investigations of the misattribution effect seem to be more successful than actual clinical investigations (e.g., Nisbett et al., 1976; Parkinson, 1985). It may be that a person with a real problem already has a stable explanation for his or her arousal and does not search for alternative explanations; hence, he or she may not be vulnerable to misattribution efforts. Or perhaps people with real problems test out the misattributions they are given for their problems more fully than do people with laboratory-induced or short-term problems. In so doing, they may learn that the misattribution feedback is not true or at least not completely true. Suppose, for example, that our anxious job hunter has been told that her arousal is due to her change in schedule. She then decides to have several dress rehearsals for her job interview to rid herself of the arousal. She rises in the morning, dresses, drives to the spot where the interview will be held, and takes the elevator up to the office so that she is completely comfortable with the route. On the morning of the job interview itself, however, she is still terrified, because it is in fact the job situation that makes her nervous, not the changes in her schedule.

To summarize, although Schachter and Singer's emotional lability hypothesis has had a substantial impact on the development of attribution theory, twenty years of research suggest that its ability to explain or modify emotional experience has limitations. One can conclude that, within limits, people can be induced to reattribute arousal from one stimulus to another, particularly when the circumstances are short-term and relatively uninvolving. However, people have multiple methods for understanding their own emotional experiences, and when they are motivated to use them, misattribution effects may be weak.

*B*EM'S SELF-PERCEPTION THEORY

Another important contribution to attribution theory was Daryl Bem's work on self-perception (1967, 1972). Bem was concerned, as Schachter was, with how people infer their own reactions, emotions, and attitudes. And he argued, as Schachter did, that people's internal cues to their reactions are neither as directly accessible nor as unambiguous as they usually think they are. Instead, as Schachter argued, Bem argued that people often infer their internal reactions from environmental factors that provide cues about their beliefs.

Specifically, Bem's (1972) theory of self-perception posits that the processes people use to infer their own attitudes are not substantially different from those they apply in trying to infer other people's attitudes. He argues that people know their own internal states, such as attitudes or emotions, in part by inferring them from the observation of their behavior and the circumstances in which the behavior occurs.

Suppose someone asks me if my roommate likes rock music. I may have never heard him state a preference, but I will likely think over what tapes or records he chooses to play and what radio stations he selects. If he plays Mozart and Brahms all day, I am likely to conclude that he does not like rock. If he never turns off the rock station on the radio, I am likely to conclude that he does. Bem's point is that we often infer our own attitudes in the same way that we infer those of others, namely, by observing behavior. If someone asks me if I like rock, according to Bem, I may well employ the same process I would apply to others. I think over how often I choose to listen to rock and decide on that basis if I like it.

One of the most fruitful applications of Bem's self-perception theory has been to the study of motivation. Bem's theory predicts that when people are attempting to understand why they perform particular tasks, they look to see if their behavior is under the control of external forces or under the control of their own desires. Behavior attributed to external factors, such as being paid for a job, will produce an external attribution, whereas performing the same task for a minimal reward will lead to an assumption of intrinsic interest: "I couldn't have done it for the money, so I must have done it because I enjoyed it." This analysis has been applied to the paradoxical situation that minimal rewards lead to high interest in a task and that extrinsic rewards for intrinsically satisfying interests actually undermine intrinsic interest. This phenomenon has been termed the *overjustification effect*.

The earliest demonstration of the overjustification effect was conducted by Lepper, Greene, and Nisbett (1973) with nursery school children. Some children were told that they would get a "good player award" with a gold star and ribbon if they would draw pictures with a felt-tip pen for a few minutes. Other children were not told about the award. All children then drew for several minutes and the first group was given their awards. A few days later, all the children were observed in a free-play situation, and the felt-tip pens were among the materials provided. Children who had been given the awards spent half as much time drawing as the children who had not been given awards. The intrinsic interest of the children receiving awards had been undermined by the extrinsic reward. This finding has been replicated many times (see Deci & Ryan, 1985).

The consequences of overjustification extend beyond attributions for performance. People given an external reward for performing an intrinsically interesting task choose simpler tasks and are less efficient in using available information to solve problems. They tend to be answer-oriented rather than process-oriented, and they are less logical in their problem-solving strategies. Although they work harder and produce more activity, the output is of lower quality, contains more errors, and is more stereotyped and less creative than the work of non-rewarded people performing the same tasks. Finally, people are less likely to return to a task they at one time thought was interesting after they have been rewarded to do it well. These findings generalize across a wide range of people performing a wide range of tasks (Condry, 1977; see also Amabile, Hennessey, & Grossman, 1986; Boggiano, Harackiewicz, Bessette, & Main, 1985; J. Newman & Layton, 1984; Pittman, Emery, & Boggiano, 1982; Pretty & Seligman, 1984; Seta & Seta, 1987). See Table 2.3.

Research on Bem's theory has concerned the self-perception of attitudes as well, and empirical work has suggested some qualifications to these effects. Behavior must be perceived to be directly relevant to the attitude in question for self-perception effects to occur (C. A. Kiesler, Nisbett, & Zanna, 1969). Self-perception processes also may apply in only a limited range of settings. Imagine that you are asked what television program you would like to watch tonight. You may think about

TABLE 2.3 AN ANALYSIS OF THE OVERJUSTIFICATION EFFECT: REWARDS UNDERMINE INTRINSIC INTEREST

Reason for performing a task	Example	Will be the dominant reason for performing the task if:	Consequences
Intrinsic interest	Working at one's job because one loves it	Intrinsic interest is salient; extrinsic reasons for not performing the task are salient; rewards signify competence, rather than efforts at control; rewards are contingent upon good performance	Take more pleasure in the task; show more efficient and logical problem solving; maintain task performance in the absence of rewards; select more challenging subsequent problems; solve problems with fewer errors and more creativity
Extrinsic rewards	Working at one's job because it pays well	Rewards are salient or undesirable; rewards constitute efforts at control; rewards are not contingent on a high level of performance; rewards are not seen as given to reward competence	Work hard; generate more activity; show less enjoyment of task; show reduction in performance if rewards are withdrawn; choose easier subsequent tasks; solve problems less efficiently and less logically; be less creative, more error-prone, more stereotyped in performance; quality will be lower

what show you watch most often and answer, "Star Trek," overlooking the facts that "Star Trek" reruns always come on after the news (which you always watch with dinner) and that you usually have not finished eating when "Star Trek" comes on. Now imagine that a newly incarcerated convict who will have limited viewing time is asked the same question. The convict is unlikely to make the same mistake. He or she may think over the merits of different shows more carefully and decide on the basis of something other than chance factors (i.e., not based on what comes on after the news), since his or her choice of shows involves higher stakes (see S. E. Taylor, 1975).

Bem's self-perception approach has been important in the development of attribution theory for several reasons. First, it posited a very simple model of self-perception, which, although not the whole picture, is an important mechanism in understanding how people perceive and understand their own beliefs. Second, the simplicity of Bem's model and lack of complex assumptions regarding the thought processes of the social perceiver foreshadows the cognitive miser perspective that currently dominates much thinking within social cognition. The emphasis on the capacity limitations of the social perceiver and the need to use shortcuts to solve problems quickly and efficiently are implicit in Bem's work.

WEINER'S ATTRIBUTION CONTRIBUTIONS

The Structure of Causal Experience

Whether a cause is internal (generated by the person) or external (caused by the situation) is an important dimension of causality in many of the early attribution formulations (Heider, 1958; Rotter, 1966). For example, if you fail a test, it is important to know whether you lacked the ability to do well or whether the test was particularly difficult, but knowing the locus of a cause (i.e., whether it is internal or external) is not enough. Even if you decide that failing the test was your fault, it makes a big difference to you whether or not this will happen again. Thus, the stability of the behavior is also important, for it helps you further to refine what you are to make of this test failure. As the contributions of Kelley (1967) and E. E. Jones and Davis (1965) make clear, causal analysis is most informative when stable causes are uncovered, such as dispositional qualities that do not change from situation to situation. Thus, at the very least, two dimensions of causality seem to be important: locus (internal, external) and stability (stable, unstable).

But recall that people do not make causal attributions solely to understand why something happened. People also make causal attributions to understand what controls future events (Heider, 1958; Kelley,

1967). Thus, a third dimension, controllability, may also be important for understanding the implications of causal analysis. For example, if the cause of your failure is something you can control, its implications for your worklife are very different than if the cause of your failure is beyond your control.

Drawing upon these observations and assumptions, Bernard Weiner and his associates have integrated the three dimensions of locus, stability (Weiner et al., 1972), and controllability (Weiner, 1979) into a model of causal attributions that they have explored in the context of achievement, helping behavior, and several other domains (see Weiner, 1986). Using an achievement situation as an example, Weiner maintains that people assess whether they have failed or succeeded at a task and react in a general emotional way (positively or negatively) to that judgment. These general emotions are followed by a search for the cause of the outcome along the three dimensions of locus, stability, and controllability. The outcome of the causal search, that is, the causal attribution, then dictates future achievement expectations and more specific emotional reactions, such as pride or shame (Weiner, 1986). Expectations and emotions, then, jointly determine subsequent achievement-related performance. This model is depicted in Figure 2.2 and is described in more detail in the sections that follow.

Causal Attribution and the Example of Achievement

Several years ago, a little-known predominantly Hispanic high school in East Los Angeles, California, startled the testing world by achieving mathematics scores on standardized exams that greatly exceeded both their past performance and those of most other schools in the nation. The dramatic rise in scores has since been credited to the teaching of one remarkable and dedicated teacher and the responsiveness of his students. However, at the time, testing officials were so surprised by the outcome that they forced all of the students to take their exams over, feeling that cheating must have taken place.

This example illustrates several important points about causal attribution in achievement situations. First, unexpected results prompt causal analysis. Had the students achieved the scores that were expected for their high school, no one would have found it necessary to explain the outcome. Second, the dimensions of locus, stability, and controllability help us to understand the perceived cause of behavior. The test administrators inferred that a test that normally taps stable, internal, uncontrollable qualities such as student aptitude had instead tapped an unstable, external, but controllable, factor, namely cheating. Third, causal attributions have implications for the future. Expectations for future behavior, actual performance, and affective reactions may all

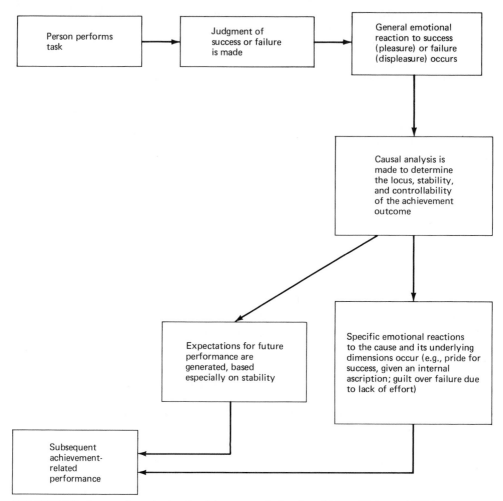

FIGURE 2.2 A causal analysis of achievement behavior. (After Weiner, 1979.)

be determined by causal analysis. Thus, attributing good performance to possible cheating implied that upon retaking the test (without the possibility of cheating), the students' test scores would reflect their presumed actual ability and likely future performance.

Table 2.4 presents the three dimensions of the causes of achievement and examples of each kind of cause. Consider first the internal causes. *Aptitude* is both stable and uncontrollable, presumably because it is determined by raw intelligence. *Mood* is also uncontrollable, but it is unstable: one's mood varies from situation to situation, but generally not as a function of one's own attempts to control it. *Effort* is controllable, but it may be either stable or unstable. The typical effort one puts into a task (e.g., studying three hours each night) is stable, but the

TABLE 2.4 POSSIBLE CAUSES OF ACHIEVEMENT OUTCOMES
ACCORDING TO LOCUS, STABILITY, AND CONTROLLABILITY

| Controllability | Internal | | External | |
	Stable	Unstable	Stable	Unstable
Controllable	Typical effort exerted	Temporary effort exerted (for this particular task)	Some forms of teacher bias	Unusual help from others
Uncontrollable	Aptitude	Mood	Task difficulty	Luck

SOURCE: After Rosenbaum, 1972, p. 21; Weiner, 1979

effort exerted for a particular task (e.g., studying extra hard for this test) is unstable.

When we consider external causes, objective task difficulty is stable and uncontrollable: the task cannot be changed. Luck is both unstable and uncontrollable. Some external factors are controllable, however. A teacher's belief in your inherent ability, for example, is stable and under personal control. And finally, unusual help from another person is controllable but unstable. For example, a friend may offer to help you study for a particular test, but he may or may not make the same offer again.

Much of Weiner's analysis has focused on how causal attributions influence future expectations, emotions, and performance. Thus, the model is a dynamic one; that is, it focuses on change over time. Weiner maintains that expectations about the future are determined primarily by the stability of one's causal attributions. For example, if I expect to succeed but fail on a test, my expectations should shift little in response to the failure if I attribute the failure to unstable factors such as effort or luck; I would expect the unstable factors not to be present again, so I would simply try again, expecting to succeed. On the other hand, if I expected to succeed and failed, but attribute the failure to my lack of ability or to task difficulty (stable factors), my expectations should now shift in response to the failure; neither the task's difficulty nor my ability are going to change the next time I try the task (Graham & Brown, 1988; for a review, see Weiner, 1986).

Specific emotional reactions to an attribution are influenced by such factors as its locus, its controllability, and who is the recipient of the outcome. Some emotions depend upon locus. For example, one might feel pride if one performed a positive act (internal locus). But the controllability of the outcome is also important for understanding emotions. For example, if a negative outcome hurts either oneself or another person, and that outcome is under the control of another person, one is likely to be angry. Likewise, if a positive outcome is due to the voluntary help of another (controllable, external), one is likely to be grateful to that person. Guilt is the emotion probably experienced by one who brings about negative outcomes for others or one's self, when the factors are within his or her control. Stability seems to intensify affect. If a cause is seen as stable, the resulting affect will be more pronounced than if the cause is unstable (Weiner, 1979). Stability may also relate to future-oriented emotions, such as hopelessness or anxiety. Several studies using a variety of methodological techniques attest to the temporal sequence that attributions can evoke specific emotional responses which, in turn, alter expectations. We will cover affective reactions to attributions more fully in Chapter 10. The important point here is that, according to Weiner's model, locus, controllability, and stability determine the emotional consequences of attributions.

Performance, in turn, typically parallels expectations and affect, being jointly determined by them (Covington & Omelich, 1979). For example, one may try harder when one attributes one's prior failing performance to unstable rather than stable factors, and these effects may be enhanced by feelings such as guilt over one's prior performance. Alternatively, one may cease trying if expectations of future success are low and feelings of hopelessness are high.

So far, we have focused primarily on people's self-attributions for behavior and their implications for future expectations and performance. Attributions are also important in determining how one responds to another person. For example, one may need to decide whether or not to offer that person help or how to evaluate the person. Weiner (1979, 1980c) argues that the controllability dimension carries special weight in making such decisions. For example, teachers are often especially hard on students who are clearly able but perform badly. Presumably the teacher sees the student's behavior as being under the student's control, and thus the teacher believes that the able student who performs poorly has failed to make the necessary effort. On the other hand, a teacher may be inclined to help students whose difficulties are beyond their control (Brophy & Rohrkemper, 1981; Reisenzein, 1986; Schmidt & Weiner, 1988).

To summarize Weiner's model briefly, three dimensions underlie the causal attributions that are made for the achievement outcomes of success and failure. The stability dimension indicates whether or not the cause will change and is strongly associated with subsequent expectations of success or failure. The locus dimension concerns whether an individual attributes performance to internal or external factors and is tied to changes in self-esteem-related emotions such as pride and shame. The controllability dimension relates to whether or not a person has control over the outcome; people often use it as a basis for evaluating themselves or someone else or offering a person help. In the typical achievement situation, people first access whether or not they succeeded or failed and feel happiness or unhappiness accordingly. They then make a causal attribution for that outcome, which leads to more specific emotional responses, for example, guilt over an effort attribution for failure or pride over an ability attribution for success. People then generate expectations of the probability of subsequent success, and these expectations are again followed by predictable emotional responses; for example, an attribution of failure to low ability produces low expectations of subsequent success as well as feelings of hopelessness. Expectations and emotional reactions jointly determine subsequent performance.

Weiner's model has been popular and widely supported. That success has not precluded criticism, however. Although researchers have generally agreed that locus is an important dimension of causal experience, and many concur that stability is also important, some question whether controllability contributes much to the model (Abramson, Seligman, & Teasdale, 1978; de Jong, Koomen, & Mellenbergh, 1988; Ickes & Kidd, 1976; Passer, 1977; Phares, 1976; Vallerand & Richer, 1988). It may be that controllability is an important dimension for understanding some domains such as helping or achievement behavior (Meyer, 1980), but it may not be as important for other domains of attribution (see Weiner, 1985b).

Critics have also focused on Weiner's hypothetical temporal sequence of events (see Figure 2.2). Some research suggests that changes in performance or changes in expectations may precede or be independent of causal attributions (see, for example, Covington & Omelich, 1979). Other researchers suggest that general affective changes may also be caused by attributions rather than solely determined by the outcomes of success or failure (McFarland & Ross, 1982). Thus, critics have questioned both the temporal sequence itself and the place of attributions in it (see also D. Russell & McAuley, 1986).

Some of the evidence for Weiner's model comes from studies using role playing or scenario methodologies. Researchers ask subjects how they think they or others would behave in particular situations such as failing a test. Because Weiner's model makes sense intuitively, the danger exists that subjects merely report what makes sense to them, rather than reporting how they would actually behave in the situation, thus providing only apparent support for the model. Studies that examine causal attributions in real situations, such as actual achievement settings of success and failure, provide converging support for the validity of the model (e.g., Vallerand & Richer, 1988).

In the net evaluation, Weiner's model fares quite well. Overall, the model is admirably specific in its hypotheses, and hence, easily subject to empirical validation. Although not all studies have supported all contentions of the theory, that in part may be due to measurement problems (e.g., Elig & Frieze, 1979; D. Russell, 1982).

Weiner's model was originally developed to encompass attributions about achievement-relevant behaviors and to predict changes in subsequent motivation, emotions, expectations, and performance. It is a mark of the theory's success that aspects of it have now been applied in other domains as well, including sex stereotyping (Deaux, 1976), emotional development (Graham & Weiner, 1986), helping (Ickes & Kidd, 1976; G. Schmidt & Weiner, 1988), loneliness (Michela, Peplau, & Weeks, 1983), parole decision making (Carroll & Payne, 1976), excuse making (Weiner, Amirkhan, Folkes, & Verette, 1987), personal problem solving (Baumgardner, Heppner, & Arkin, 1986), perceptions of sports events (Tenenbaum & Furst, 1986), reactions to hyperactivity medication (e.g., Henker & Whalen, 1980), reactions to perceived lack of control (Abramson et al., 1978), programs to improve academic performance (Van Overwalle, Segebarth, & Goldchstein, 1989; Forsterling, 1985), and reactions to stigmatized others (Graham, 1984; D. Russell et al., 1985; Weiner, Perry, & Magnusson, 1988) including people with AIDS (Weiner, 1988a). In addition, it has exerted considerable influence on researchers in many countries, and a number of its basic principles have received substantial cross-cultural support (Fletcher & Ward, 1988; Schuster, Forsterling, & Weiner, 1989; Stipek, Weiner, & Li, 1989).

SUMMARY

Attribution theory is a collection of ideas about when and how people form causal inferences. It examines how individuals combine and use information to reach causal judgments. Although the impetus for the attribution process is thought to be motivational, causal analysis itself is believed to proceed cognitively. Psychologists consider attributions to be important because they are the underpinnings of further judgments, emotional reactions, and behavior.

Attribution theory began with Heider's work on naive psychology, which maintained that the natural language people use to characterize causal action can form a basis for a theory of causal inference. Drawing on Brunswik's lens model of perception, Heider maintained that social perception is much like object perception in its need to consider attributes of the target person, attributes of the perceiver, and the context and manner in which the perception occurs. Heider thought causal inference depends on perceptions of an actor's motivation and ability and on situational factors that impede or promote an action. In addition to his work on causal inference, Heider heavily influenced theoretical and empirical research on attributions of responsibility.

Jones and Davis's theory of correspondent inference, a second cornerstone of attribution theory, maintains that the goal of the causal inference process is to locate the stable underlying attributes of individuals that explain their behavior across situations. Behaviors that are believed to be unconstrained and freely chosen, those that are out of role, actions that are not socially desirable, actions that violate prior expectations, and actions that produce distinctive consequences are all believed to reveal underlying attributes. The perceiver's needs also influence the interpretation of action; actions that are hedonically relevant for the perceiver and those perceived as produced for the perceiver's benefit (personalism) are regarded as more correspondent than actions that do not directly affect the perceiver.

Harold Kelley developed the covariation model of how individuals form causal inferences when they have access to multiple instances of similar events. According to the model, individuals employ a covariation principle to determine how the outcome in question varies across entities (distinctiveness), across time and modality (consistency), and across people (consensus). The goal of this process is to attribute the outcome to a stable cause or pattern of causes. When only a single occurrence of an event is known to a perceiver, the covariation principle cannot be used, and other rules or strategies of causal inference must be employed. One such rule is the discounting principle, which maintains that the role of any one potential cause of an event is discounted to the extent that other causal candidates are available. The perceiver may also employ complex causal schemas that tie patterns of causes to patterns of effects, including the multiple necessary causes schema for difficult or extreme events and the multiple sufficient causes schema for easy or more common events.

Three other lines of work also heavily influenced early attribution formulations. Schachter's theory of emotional lability examines attributions for emotional states. He argued that internal physiological cues are often ambiguous and consequently may be labeled as consistent with any of several emotions or sources of arousal. This emotional lability makes arousal subject to misattribution, a finding that has prompted therapeutic work inducing people to reattribute their arousal from threatening internal sources to nonthreatening external sources. Support for the emotional lability argument, however, is mixed.

In a formulation similar to Schachter's, Bem's theory of self-perception argues that people infer their own attitudes using substantially the same processes as they employ to infer others' attitudes, that is, the observation of behavior. When asked one's attitude, one considers one's previous behavior, determines whether or not it was freely chosen, and infers one's attitude accordingly. With this line of work, Bem extended attribution ideas to include causal inferences about the self.

Weiner's work on attribution theory is notable primarily for developing the dimensions of attributional experience, integrating attributions with emotional processes and enlightening the attributional and affective experiences that underlie achievement behavior, helping, and other concrete domains of experience. Weiner proposed three underlying dimensions: locus (internal, external), which is associated with changes in self-esteem and other affects; stability (stable, unstable), which is associated with changes in expectations and performance; and controllability (controllable, uncontrollable), which is associated with social affects (such as guilt, anger, pity, and gratitude), and behaviors (such as decisions to intervene in one's own or another's plight). Although Weiner's work was developed initially to explain achievement behavior, several attributional formulations have made use of these dimensions in their analyses of different situations.

3

Attribution Theory: Theoretical Refinements and Empirical Observations

❖

Empirical Contributions to Attribution Theory ✦ *Errors and Biases*
in the Attribution Process ✦ *Individual Differences in the Attribution Process*

The previous chapter detailed the main theoretical viewpoints that have guided attribution research for the last two decades. The heuristic value of these contributions has been enormous. Hundreds of empirical studies were prompted by these theories, and many real-world phenomena have been analyzed from the standpoint of theories of causal attribution. Moreover, the impact of these attribution theories has been felt on fields as disparate as law, medicine, politics, and prejudice.

EMPIRICAL CONTRIBUTIONS TO ATTRIBUTION THEORY

As would be expected in any empirical science, the research record has confirmed many of the points made by the early attribution theorists and has contradicted or added others. In this chapter, we review the major empirical trends that research has identified. Some of these empirical contributions represent alternative formulations regarding the processes associated with causal attribution. For example, some researchers have argued that the early attribution theories proposed idealized models detailing processes that are substantially different from the processes people actually go through when they attempt to infer causality. This is not to suggest that there is now consensus among researchers as to what those processes may be. The research record merely demonstrates that there are a number of ways in which people infer causality in different situations, and in the first portion of this chapter, we will review some of those alternative formulations. Other empirical contributions suggest conceptual distinctions that were not made in the early theories that must now be incorporated, inasmuch as they guide the processing of information in different ways.

In addition to the alternative processes for causal attribution that were uncovered by empirical research, a great many studies have revealed some of the systematic biases that perceivers appear to employ in their causal reasoning. Chief among these are the tendencies to attribute the actions of other people to their dispositional qualities and to infer causality in defensive or self-serving ways. We review these biases in the second part of the chapter. Finally, there are robust individual differences in how people infer causality, and we cover this topic at the end of the chapter.

Basic Principles of Causation

Developmental research on attributional processes has highlighted some of the basic principles of causation that children learn early in their efforts to understand cause-effect relations (see Kassin & Pryor, 1985; P. A. White, 1988, for reviews). It is worth considering these principles in detail, first, because they form the underpinnings of children's causal judgments and second, because adults continue to make use of them in inferring causality in ambiguous settings (Kelley & Michela, 1980).

The first fundamental principle of cause-effect relations is that *causes precede effects*. This principle appears to be well-established by the time a child is three and is virtually never contradicted in spontaneous causal attribution (see Kassin & Pryor, 1985, for a review). A second basic principle is that people perceive as causal those factors that have *temporal contiguity* with the effect. We are more inclined to attribute a factor as causal if it occurred immediately before an effect took place, but not if it took place some time before. People also draw on *spatial contiguity* in inferring cause-effect relations. Thus, for example, a suspect in a robbery would be dismissed from consideration if it were found that he had been in a city 40 miles away at the time of the bank robbery. *Perceptually salient stimuli* are more likely to be perceived as causal than stimuli that are in the visual background (S. E. Taylor & Fiske, 1975, 1978). Finally, simple principles of *covariation* are acquired relatively early in young children (Kassin & Pryor, 1985). Reviewing this literature, Kassin and Pryor (1985) and P. A. White (1988) argue that priority, contiguity, and salience, but not covariation, are fundamental principles for causal attribution, inasmuch as they appear to prompt its automatic activation.

Research suggests that these basic principles continue to be employed by adults, at least under some circumstances (Einhorn & Hogarth, 1986; S. E. Taylor, 1982). Among cancer patients who were unaware of the causes of their cancers, for example, these principles were used to infer probable cause of a malignant tumor. Drawing on the concept of spatio-temporal contiguity, for example, a cancer patient inferred that her breast cancer had been caused by an automobile accident in which she had been involved several days prior to the detection of the malignancy. Drawing on the principle of spatial contiguity, a woman in a dress shop who carried hangers over her arm inferred that the wear and tear against that side of her breast led to the development of the tumor (S. E. Taylor, Lichtman, & Wood, 1984).

To the list of basic principles of causation elaborated by Kassin and Pryor (see also Kassin & Baron, 1985), one might add the following: (1) *Causes resemble effects:* for example, people generally assume that big effects are produced by big causes, and that little effects are produced by little causes (see also Kelley & Michela, 1980). Thus, the development of a malignancy might be attributed to a traumatic divorce, but would be less likely to be attributed to the small cumulative day-to-day hassles of life (S. E. Taylor, 1982). (2) *Representative causes* are attributed to effects (Tversky & Kahneman, 1982). In trying to find an explanation for a situation, people may look at similar outcomes and infer that the cause of the current outcome is similar to the causes for the previous related outcomes. Thus, for example, a patient unfamiliar with the causes of cancer may attribute a malignant lump to a blow, since other kinds of lumps are caused by blows (S. E. Taylor, 1982).

The fundamental principles of causation, then, not only characterize the causal inferences of young children from age three on, but continue to characterize and indeed may be sufficient to characterize some adults' processes of causal inference as well. Typically, adults have been thought of as moving beyond these basic principles to include understanding of distal or delayed causality, multiple causality, and other, more complex causal rules. Unquestionably, adult perceivers have this ability at least in certain causal domains. In domains in which they are not well-informed, however, they may resort to these very primitive causal principles in attempting to make causal sense of the events they experience (S. E. Taylor, 1982).

Knowledge Structures and Causal Inference

The previous section suggested that when people have limited experience with a particular life domain, they may draw on very rudimentary principles of causality to guide the inference process. An alternative situation arises in considering causal domains about which people have considerable experience.

One of the major qualifications that empirical research has made to the study of attributions is in emphasizing the role of knowledge structures in defining potential causes (e.g., D. J. Hilton & Slugoski, 1986). The basic models of attribution, such as those developed by Kelley and by Jones and Davis are generic content-free processes that could be used to infer causality in a broad range of domains, including romantic breakups, academic failures, skirmishes initiated by warring nations, or the development of a serious disease. But there is now evidence that, at least under some circumstances, when people are faced with a causally ambiguous situation (e.g., a romantic breakup), they think through what they know about the causes *in that specific domain* (e.g., one partner found someone else, the two were incompatible in fundamental ways, the relationship died of boredom) (R. D. Hansen, 1980); then they attempt to eliminate inappropriate explanations (e.g., did they fight a lot? is one of them now with a new partner and how quickly did that happen?) (E. R. Smith & Miller, 1978). The important qualification for the purpose of understanding attributional inference is that people bring their world knowledge to bear on their causal attributions and do not necessarily employ content-free attributional principles in making those inferences. We will return to this issue shortly.

Occurrences versus Actions

Causal attribution processes and assumptions made by the attributor vary also depending upon characteristics of the event requiring explanation. Kruglanski (1975) proposed a distinction between *occurrences* (which are not completely voluntary) and *actions* (which are voluntary). He argued that, although occurrences can be caused by either internal (person) or external (situational) factors, actions cannot; actions are always internally caused. He further maintained that actions consist of two subtypes: *endogenous acts* (acts that are committed as ends in themselves) and *exogenous acts* (acts that are committed in service of other goals). For example, if I read a paper you have written because I am interested in the topic, my action would be endogenously based, whereas if I read through it because you are a student in my class, then my action is exogenously based. Figure 3.1 illustrates the distinction.

Kruglanski's theory predicts that exogenously attributed acts are

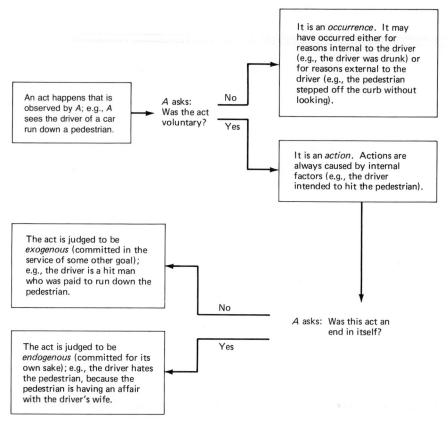

FIGURE 3.1 The layman's explanation of action. (After Kruglanski, 1975.)

seen as less freely chosen and yield less pleasure. These predictions have received some empirical support (see Calder, 1977, and Zuckerman, 1977, for critiques of Kruglanski's position). Brown and Fish (1983), for example, suggested that people tend to attribute their own actions to themselves but their experiences (things that simply happen to them) to external circumstances. Whereas Brown and Fish attributed this pattern to the self-perception of personal choice in the case of actions (a prediction consistent with Kruglanski's position), Gilovich and Regan (1986) suggest instead that the differential attribution of actions versus experiences stem from different causal schemas that people hold to explain actions and experiences (see also D. Locke & Pennington, 1982). Consistent with this explanation, Zuckerman and Evans (1984) found evidence for different kinds of causal schemas to explain actions versus occurrences.

The distinction between action and occurrence is not merely an intuitively sensible one. The distinction implies that different kinds of information will be useful for interpreting the different kinds of behaviors. Zuckerman and Feldman (1984), for example, hypothesized and found that consensus information is sought out for occurrences to infer their cause, whereas distinctiveness information is sought out to understand the reasons underlying voluntary behavior (actions). Emotional responses are considered to be occurrences not under voluntary control. Thus, to understand why John lost his composure when he saw Bob, the perceiver determines if other people reacted to Bob the same way (consensus information). In contrast, knowing that "John hit Bob when he came into the room" (a voluntary action) leads people to find out whether John has hit other people (distinctiveness information) (see also Zuckerman & Evans, 1984; R. D. Hansen, 1980).

Kruglanski's fundamental point (1975, 1977) is that one must distinguish between causal explanations (which account for what caused an act to occur) and teleological explanation (why was the action accomplished, i.e., to what end). Attribution theory has been heavily concerned with "what" questions (the "cause"), sometimes to the exclusion of "why" (the "reason") questions. Although one can sometimes infer why a person committed an action from the context in which it occurs, attribution theory is largely lacking formal statements about teleological explanation (see Brickman, Coates, & Janoff-Bulman, 1978; A. R. Buss, 1978, 1979; S. T. Fiske, 1989a; Harvey & Tucker, 1979; Kruglanski, 1979; D. Locke & Pennington, 1982).

Communication and Causal Explication

Another dominant trend in attribution research of the last decade has been an increasing focus on the communicative aspects of attributions (e.g., Antaki, 1985; Antaki & Fielding, 1981; Hewstone, 1983; Semin & Manstead, 1984). In the models developed by Kelley and by Jones and Davis, the social perceiver was implicitly characterized as completing the attribution process substantially alone by accessing the logic of causal structure and applying it to the situation at hand. But often attributional activity occurs in social settings. The search for a causal attribution may be a collective process, as when recently fired workers or disappointed fans meet over beer to figure out why they were laid off or why their team lost and to identify prospects for the future. Sometimes causal attributions are provided in full by conversational exchange, as when one person notes that mutual friends have separated and another comments on how difficult the husband is to live with. Account-making, the process by which people develop coherent descriptions and causally explain important events, is receiving increasing empirical attention (Semin & Manstead, 1983; Harvey et al., 1986; Harvey, Turnquist, & Agostinelli, 1988).

True interaction regarding causal attribution has not received research attention. We know little about social exchange around issues of causality (see Ickes, Robertson, et al., 1986; Ickes & Tooke, 1988). Certain points are self-evident. Often when people experience the conditions that give rise to attributional activity, such as unexpected negative events, they do not engage in an elaborate cognitive search for a cause; they simply ask someone. A common response to attributional uncertainty is to find someone who is more knowledgeable, such as an expert. Although sick people engage in some attributional processes to understand the causes of their symptoms, they also visit physicians, often quite quickly after the symptoms appear. An argument with a friend may produce calls to other friends to solicit explanations of the event. While one may argue that social contact is a vehicle for filling out missing information in an attributional search (such as consensus or consistency information), it is also evident that sometimes the motive is simply to acquire a ready-made causal explanation from someone who is better informed.

Some of the research on communication and attributions has focused on how causality may be communicated through the language used to express the causal interpretation. Verbs are especially informative regarding causality (McArthur, 1972). Verbs that express particular states such as "hate" or "love" evoke attributions to the objects of those states (Fiedler & Semin, 1988). If Elizabeth loves Peter, one assumes that there is something special about Peter. Action verbs that involve interpreting the meaning underlying behavior such as "cheat" or "help" produce subject attributions. If Ivan cheats Michael, one infers negative dispositional qualities about Ivan (Fiedler & Semin, 1988; see also Abelson & Kanouse, 1966; Roger Brown & Fish, 1983).

Research has made clear, then, that much causal inference must be understood not solely as the inner workings of the mind attempting to impose causal order on ambiguity, but also as a social process by which people solicit causal explanations from others and communicate their explanations to others (e.g., Fincham & Jaspars, 1980; Hewstone, 1983; Hewstone & Jaspars, 1982; Tedeschi & Riess, 1981). Accompanying this trend has been a call for methods enabling researchers to cull causal explanations from natural discourse (e.g., Stratton et al., 1986; Sousa & Leyens, 1987)

Hilton and Slugoski's Abnormal Conditions Model

Criticisms of normative theories of attribution—focusing on the assumed complexity of the attribution process, the failure of theories to incorporate knowledge structures, and their failure to incorporate communication into the process—led to the development of alternative models. Chief among these has been D. J. Hilton and Slugoski's (1986) abnormal conditions model (see also D. J. Hilton, 1990; D. J. Hilton & Knibbs, 1988).

Hilton and Slugoski (1986) suggest that the idea of a perfect content-free causal attribution process is unlikely, given what we know about human inference. Essentially, they argue that when the social perceiver encounters an event that requires causal explanation, the social perceiver defines his or her task as finding the abnormal condition that produced the unexpected event, which will be perceived as the cause. Consensus, consistency, and distinctiveness information are used to characterize contrasting cases against which to evaluate the target event so as to identify the abnormal condition that produced it. These contrastive cases can be created because the social perceiver brings to the situation world knowledge that dictates what the situation ought to have been, had there not been some abnormal condition that produced the to-be-explained event.

The contrastive criterion of causal ascription, then, interacts with world knowledge about the normal state of affairs in the world to enable the social perceiver to select as a cause conditions that deviate from those expected conditions. For example, if Jane becomes ill after eating an omelette, the social perceiver may ask if others became ill as well. If so, the food would be regarded as the cause. If not, the social perceiver might inquire as to whether Jane has become ill from eating other foods. If so, the social perceiver might infer that Jane is sick and should not be eating anything. As implied by these examples, the counterfactual contrast case for evaluating the causal role of the person is produced by consensus information, whereas for evaluating the stimulus, one employs distinctiveness information (D. J. Hilton, Smith, & Alicke, 1988). According to the theory, to determine if something about Jane produced her upset after the consumption of the omelette, one needs to know if other people were sick as well. To determine if the omelette was the event, one needs to know if other foods produce the same response in Jane (but see R. D. Hansen, 1980; Ferguson & Wells, 1980).

The theory also differentiates between scripted events, which involve detailed knowledge as to how people normally behave in a particular situation, versus unscripted events, about which the perceiver may have no prior expectations. In the case of scripted events, deviant actions are highly informative, prompting a search for the abnormal event. In nonscripted situations for which there may be no expectations, attributions may not be forthcoming. In making this distinction, Hilton and Slugoski point out how fundamental existing world knowledge is to the process of making causal attributions.

Several assumptions of the abnormal conditions model correspond to a discourse analysis of causal explanation Turnbull & Slugoski (1988) argues that explanations are sought when there is a gap between what is expected and what has occurred. In providing an explanation, a speaker will volunteer only points that are informative to a listener, that is, points that close a gap in the listener's knowledge. Essentially, the communicator defines his or her task as providing that piece of information that will explain the abnormal condition that produced the event. The parallels between intrapersonal processes of causal inference and interpersonal processes of causal inference are consistent with a viewpoint that the two follow quite naturally from each other. Causal explanations provided by one person to another or by the person to the self both seek to identify the factor that makes the difference between the target case and a counterfactual contrast case. In explaining to a friend that Jane got sick after eating an omelette and observing that "everyone got sick," the conversational exchange involving causality essentially mirrors the internal cognitive process.

In comparing this model to those of Kelley (1967) and of Jaspars, Hewstone, & Fincham (1983), it is useful to distinguish between their focal questions. The covariation model (Kelley, 1967) and the natural logic model (Jaspars, Hewstone, & Fincham, 1983) are concerned with the question, "Why did this event occur rather than not occur?" whereas the abnormal conditions model focuses on the question, "Why did this event occur rather than the normal case?"

Several points of resolution remain to be sorted out by subsequent evidence and debate. What question does the social perceiver ask when confronted with those conditions most likely to produce causal attributions, namely, unexpected or negative events? Does the process of making attributions for causality differ between unexpected events and expected ones? A recent article by Forsterling (1989) maintains that many of the recent points made by Hilton and Slugoski can actually be subsumed within Kelley's ANOVA model. He argues that previous tests of Kelley's ANOVA model have not truly conceptualized the attribution process as an analogy to analysis of variance. By strictly following the assumptions underlying the statistical model of analysis of variance model, one would arrive at different predictions as to the attributions to be expected with different combinations of high versus low consensus, distinctiveness, and consistency than have been made by prior research (e.g., McArthur, 1972). In an empirical test of this expanded ANOVA conception, subjects generated attributional predictions in line with the model. Perhaps, more important, the model provides a basis for integrating some of the observations made by Jaspars and his associates (see Chapter 2) and by Hilton and Slugoski within the ANOVA framework (see also Cheng & Novick, 1990). One suspects, however, that this debate is not yet at an end.

To summarize, then, explorations of how people actually infer causality across a broad range of situations have suggested some qualifications to the generic naive scientist models proposed by the early attribution researchers. Some of these modifications depend upon the knowledge state of the social perceiver, such as whether or not the causal domain is one about which the social perceiver has substantial information. Under circumstances of limited knowledge, people may fall back on basic fundamental principles of causation, whereas in domains about which they have more information, they may employ their world knowledge to define likely causes for a particular action. Moreover, different kinds of events yield different kinds of explanations. For example, the information that people seek for actions versus occurrences varies, as does the domain of potential causal factors. A third trend involves an increasing understanding of the role of communication both in soliciting causal explanations for events and in constraining the nature of causal explanations offered for events. Some of these investigations have focused on the nature of language itself and the ways in which language conveys causal information, whereas other analyses have focused more on the rules and goals of conversational processes and how causal inference fits those rules and goals. An alternative model to the covariation principles of Kelley and Jaspars, developed by Hilton and Slugoski, argues that people use their world knowledge to define an expected event and find it necessary to explain events to the extent that they deviate from the expected case. Consensus, distinctiveness, and consistency information are used to identify the abnormal condition which differentiates the state of affairs from the expected situation. Whether these processes can be understood within Kelley's ANOVA model remains at issue.

ERRORS AND BIASES IN THE ATTRIBUTION PROCESS

Research suggests that the attribution process is marked by a number of persistent errors and biases. Deviations from normative processing are called "errors" if what the social perceiver does is wrong. These deviations are termed "biases" if the social perceiver systematically distorts (overuses or underuses) some otherwise accurate or appropriate procedure. Some of these errors and biases derive from limitations on cognitive processes, others stem from individual motivations, and a few may derive from both motivational and cognitive factors. Until recently, these so-called errors and biases were thought of as perplexing, persistent departures from appropriate rules of causal inference. As will be noted throughout this section, however, opinion has now changed to suggest that they may be adaptive for reasons that serve larger epistemic goals than the logical imputation of local causality for specific events.

The Fundamental Attribution Error

Under most circumstances, behavior results from a mix of an individual's personal characteristics and situational factors. For example, at a cocktail party, everybody stands around with a drink in one hand, hors d'oeuvres in the other, and no way to shake hands with newcomers. One is expected to make pleasant and polite small talk with those whom one encounters. But individual differences are important too. Some people at the cocktail party are no doubt bored, others may be nervous, while others may hold forth with great enthusiasm on their latest exploits and interests. Despite the clear importance of both individual and situational factors in behavior, the social perceiver often does not see things this way.

Perhaps the most commonly documented bias in social perception, one that has accordingly been called the *fundamental attribution error*, is to attribute another person's behavior to his or her own dispositional qualities, rather than to situational factors (Heider, 1958; L. Ross, 1977). Instead of realizing that there are situational forces, such as social norms or roles, that produce particular behavior, people generally see another's behavior as freely chosen and as representing that other person's stable qualities. We already noted the propensity to make correspondent inferences about others' behaviors in considering Jones and Davis's attributional position. In that context, we noted that the perceiver often fails to take into account moderating information about the causes of another person's behavior, such as whether the person chose to engage in it or whether the behavior was constrained by a social role. Even when situational factors can or do fully account for another person's behavior, the social perceiver tends to attribute behavior to enduring dispositions, such as attitudes or personality traits (E. E. Jones & Harris, 1967; E. E. Jones et al., 1971; A. G. Miller, Jones, & Hinkle, 1981; L. Ross, Amabile, & Steinmetz, 1977; Schuman, 1983; M. L. Snyder & Jones, 1974; Yandrell & Insko, 1977).

What leads to the fundamental attribution error? One important factor may be that behavior engulfs the field (Heider, 1958). That is, what is dominant when one observes another person is that person behaving: the person moves, talks, and engages in other actions that attract attention. Background factors, social context, roles, or situational pressures that may have given rise to the behavior are, by contrast, relatively pallid and dull and unlikely to be noticed in comparison to the dynamic behavior of the actor. Accordingly, the social perceiver may simply underrate or not notice these less-salient factors when trying to comprehend the meaning of behavior. Because the person is dominant in the perceiver's thinking, aspects of that person come to be overrated as causally important (see S. E. Taylor & Fiske, 1978).

The fact that the fundamental attribution error is ubiquitous and that it may result from behavior engulfing the field has led a number of researchers to suggest that dispositional attribution may be a virtually automatic outcome of perceptual experience. McArthur and Baron (1983), for example, suggest that certain stimulus configurations evoke automatic inferences because the structure resides in the stimulus itself and not in the process of imputing structure to the experience. The fundamental attribution error may represent just such a case. The process of attributing causality to stimuli that engage attention, i.e., that are salient, appears to be acquired quite early (Kassin & Pryor, 1985), and it is one of the most robust findings in causal perception.

Several points, however, argue against the idea that dispositional attribution is an automatic outgrowth of perceptual experience. The first is the fact that it needs to be learned. Regardless of whether children's attention is automatically drawn to salient stimuli and salient stimuli are more likely to be perceived as causal, young children do not explain human behavior in dispositional terms. Rather, they explain action in concrete situational terms. As they reach late childhood, they learn to make dispositional explanations (e.g., Rholes, Jones, & Wade, 1988; see Kassin & Pryor, 1985; P. A. White, 1988, for reviews). The fundamental attribution error is also not universal. In their review of the literature on cross-cultural studies of attribution processes, Fletcher and Ward (1988) suggest that, although the fundamental attribution error is a ubiquitous part of Western causal inference, it is not as dominant in non-Western cultures. Consequently, there appears to be a substantial amount of learning involved in the attribution of dispositional causes to salient human stimuli. Moreover, research suggests that the fundamental attribution error may be observed more readily in some individuals than in others (Block & Funder, 1986), and that its magnitude is reduced if the social perceiver expects to have to account for his or her attributions for another person's behaviors (Tetlock, 1985). Its malleability further questions the idea that it is an automatic consequence of perception.

The fundamental attribution error is also strong when paper and pencil descriptions of other people's behaviors are used, settings that preclude the dominance of the perceptual field by the actor's behavior (Winter & Uleman, 1984; Winter, Uleman, & Cunniff, 1985). Research now suggests that attribution of dispositional qualities to another person on the basis of behavior may be made at encoding spontaneously, without awareness, and quite rapidly, upon learning that another person has committed a particular behavior, but it need not depend upon behavior literally engulfing the perceptual field (Winter & Uleman, 1984; Winter et al., 1985; see also Bargh, 1982; Bassili & Smith, 1986). As noted in Chapter 2, there may be inferential processes that can account for the fundamental attribution error. People have strong schema-based expectations that when others are asked to express attitudes on a position, they will make statements that reflect their own attitudes. Any expression of an attitude, even one constrained by situational factors, is viewed as falling within a range of the actor's acceptantly consistent beliefs and thus will be attributed to dispositional factors (A. G. Miller, Jones, & Hinkle, 1981; A. G. Miller et al. 1984; Reeder & Brewer, 1979; Reeder, Fletcher, & Furman, 1989).

In further efforts to understand the fundamental attribution error, researchers have attempted to break down the process of dispositional attribution into its component parts. Trope (1986) suggests a two-stage model that views judgment about one's own or others' dispositions as an end product of a spontaneous identification process and a deliberate inferential process. At the identification stage, the actor's immediate behavior, the situation in which it occurs, and any prior information about the actor are identified in terms of disposition-relevant categories. For example, at this stage perceivers may categorize the immediate behavior as aggressive or nonaggressive, the situation as facilitating or inhibiting aggression, and the actor as being aggressive or nonaggressive in the past. The identification of each of these informational cues may be influenced by expectancies generated by the other cues. Most important, prior information about the actor and information about the immediate situation may influence how behavior is identified. For example, information indicating that the actor has been aggressive in the past and that the situation facilitates aggression may bias perceivers toward identifying the immediate behavior as aggressive.

Biased or unbiased, the identifications are used as data for subsequent inferences regarding the actor's true dispositions. At this stage, situational expectancies are subtracted from the disposition implied by the identified behavior. By this *subtractive rule*, inhibiting situational inducements augment and facilitating situational inducements attenuate the diagnostic value of the identified behavior regarding the corresponding disposition. For example, perceivers will see aggressive behavior as less diagnostic of dispositional aggression when the situation facilitates aggression than when it inhibits aggression. The diagnostic value of the immediate behavior is combined with prior information about the actor to yield the actual judgment about the actor's dispositions. The model is illustrated in Figure 3.2.

The two-stage model suggests that, depending on how situational, behavioral, and prior information are utilized at the identification stage, their effect on dispositional judgment may reflect or may fail to reflect their utilization at the inferential stage. Situational information illustrates this logic. Situational information has opposite effects on dispositional judgment at the identification stage and at the inferential stage. At the identification stage, situational information may lead perceivers to categorize the behavior in terms of the dispositional category. Thus,

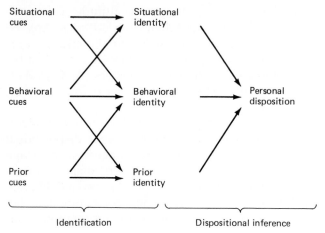

FIGURE 3.2 A two-stage model of dispositional attribution.

a situation viewed as facilitating aggression augments the perception that the behavior is an aggressive one. The subsequent reliance on this identification as evidence for the corresponding disposition may or may not offset the subtraction of the situation at the inferential stage. Thus, even though the impact of the situation may attenuate the perception of dispositional aggression at the inference stage, this may not totally cancel the facilitative impact of the situation on perceptions of aggressiveness at the identification phase.

The stronger the effect of situational information on behavior identification, the greater the likelihood that situational information will produce no effect or additive effects rather than subtractive effects on dispositional judgments. A series of studies by Trope and his colleagues varied one determinant of the effect of situational information on behavior identification, namely, the ambiguity of the behavior (Trope, 1986; Trope, Cohen, & Maoz, 1988). In one of the studies, subjects saw ambiguous or unambiguous facial reactions to positive or negative emotional situations and were asked either to identify what the face expressed or to infer the target's emotional dispositions (Trope, 1986). The identification and dispositional inference data supported the model. For example, the identification of unambiguous facial expressions was unaffected by situational provocation and, as required by the subtractive rule, inferences of dispositional anger from such faces were attenuated by situational provocation. In contrast, situational provocation biased the identification of the ambiguous faces as expressing even more anger than justified by the provocation. Instead of attentuating inferences of dispositional anger, provocation only enhanced such inferences. These results suggest that ambiguity allows the situation to bias behavior identification which, in turn, masks the subtraction of the situation at the inferential stage.

Quattrone (1982), in a similar model, argues that the attribution process consists of three stages: the categorization stage, in which the individual asks, "What is the stimulus configuration?"; the characterization stage, in which dispositional qualities are attributed to the action; and a correction phase, in which situational and other sources of information may be used to discount or augment the initial dispositional attribution. Most researchers now concur in the belief that dispositional attribution to human action can occur very early on in the perception of human action, and that it is at least spontaneous. Some have gone so far as to suggest that this rapid process of imputing dispositional qualities to people should not be considered a truly attributional process (D. L. Hamilton, 1988).

To examine this phase model of dispositional attribution, Gilbert, Pelham, and Krull (1988) employed the concept of cognitive busyness, the extent to which people's cognitive processes are devoted to multiple tasks. Cognitively busy, or active perceivers, may be attempting, for example, to manage impressions, predict a partner's behavior, evaluate alternative courses of action, and think about what is coming up in the future, all at the same time. As such, attention is diverted by several tasks at once. In contrast, a nonbusy or passive perceiver is one who is devoting full attention to the interaction at hand. Gilbert et al. argued that if drawing dispositional inferences about an actor is a simple and relatively spontaneous process, it should not be influenced by whether or not the social perceiver is cognitively busy. If the correction process of adjusting dispositional inferences with additional information is a more complex, relatively controlled process, then it should be disrupted when the person is cognitively busy.

To test this hypothesis, subjects listened to a person read either a pro- or anti-abortion speech that he had been assigned to read. Subjects in the nonbusy condition simply listened to the speech, whereas subjects in the busy condition listened to the speech, knowing that later they would also be asked to read and write a speech. One can infer that these latter subjects were cognitively busy because, as they observed the other reciting his speech, they were presumably thinking about what their own speeches would be like. The subjects who were not busy made use of the situational information, namely, the fact that the actor had been assigned his essay position, to discount the importance of the actor's attitude. In contrast, the busy perceivers were unable to make use of this situational information and discount appropriately, and instead their dispositional attributions heavily relied upon the target's behavior and not on the situational information at hand.

The results of this study are clearly consistent with the idea that dispositional attribution is a relatively spontaneous and simple process, whereas the use of situational information to qualify or discount the role of dispositional factors is a more complex process, requiring a greater commitment of cognitive resources (see also Gilbert & Krull, 1988). In an intriguing replication of this effect, Gilbert, Krull, and Pelham (1988) demonstrated that when people are self-regulating, that is, monitoring their own behavior, they act as cognitively busy subjects do. In other words, they are less able to make use of situational information than people who are not self-monitoring to correct their dispositional characterizations of a target. These results suggest that social interaction, in which people are usually both forming impressions of other and self-regulating as well, may usually proceed with people making dispositional attributions with relatively little qualification on the basis of situational information.

The question arises as to exactly how much of an error or bias the fundamental attribution error is. On the face of it, it would seem to be so because people appear to ignore important qualifying situational information when drawing inferences about others' dispositional characteristics. Yet several factors argue that there are adaptive aspects of the fundamental attribution error. When people draw dispositional attributions, they may not mean exactly the same thing by those attributions as researchers studying trait inferences think they mean. They may not, for example, assume that if behavior is attributed to a certain trait, the person will necessarily evidence behavior consistent with that underlying trait across a broad variety of situations. This is the psychologist's meaning of disposition, not the layperson's. Rather, the layperson may be seeking circumscribed accuracy (Swann, 1984), asking such questions as, "If this person were put in the same situation again, would the person do the same thing?" A dispositional attribution leads one to generate a prediction for the situation, whereas an attribution to situational factors would not. If the goal of the perceiver's attributional quest is circumscribed predictability, then making a dispositional attribution for the behavior probably results in quite accurate attributions. If asked to make a statement that opposes abortion at a later date, the subject very probably would do it again, having done it once. Dispositional attributions, then, may serve the goal of circumscribed accuracy rather than global accuracy, enabling perceivers to make confident predictions to similar situations.

The Actor-Observer Effect

Imagine the last time you encountered an irritable bus driver or a surly clerk. You may have thought, "What a hostile person." Now think of the last time you snapped at someone. Did you infer that you are a hostile person? Almost certainly not. No doubt you were just in a bad mood. This example illustrates the actor-observer effect, the tendency to explain others' behavior as due to dispositional factors and one's own behavior as due to situational or unstable factors. As such, it is related to the fundamental attribution error.

Why does this difference exist? One possible explanation follows from the behavior engulfing the field explanation for the fundamental attribution error. As an actor, one literally cannot see one's self behaving, and so one's own behavior or activity is not particularly salient. Rather, the situational forces impinging on one's behavior are salient, and so they are perceived as exerting a causal influence. In contrast, when one is observing another person, that person's behavior is figural or dynamic against a more pallid and dull situational background, and so causality is attributed to the person. This explanation draws on the perceptual experience of the social perceiver, a topic to be covered in Chapter 10 (see Storms, 1973; S. E. Taylor & Fiske, 1975, 1978).

Another explanation for the actor-observer effect relies on the differing information that the actor and the observer have regarding the events for which they attribute causality (E. E. Jones & Nisbett, 1972). Actors know their feelings with respect to an event, what their intentions were, and what factors gave rise to those intentions, including temporary ones. Consequently, they may more properly attribute their behavior to these short-term factors, of which observers may be unaware (e.g., P. A. White & Younger, 1988). Actors also have direct access to their own history and may know whether or not they have behaved similarly in the past. An understanding of variability in one's own behavior may discourage dispositional attributions. Observers, in contrast, have little information available to them about an actor and must infer what they can from the immediate environment. Hence, they may be in a poor position to appreciate the subtle contextual factors that influence the actor's behavior, and instead infer that the actor always or usually acts in this way. Empirical support exists for both the perceptual explanation (e.g., Storms, 1973; see also Wyer, Henninger, & Hinkle, 1977) and the informational explanation (Eisen, 1979), and it is likely that both types of factors contribute to this effect (see also Van Heck & Dijkstra, 1985).

Evidence for the actor-observer effect is plentiful (e.g., Goldberg, 1978; E. E. Jones & Nisbett, 1972; Nisbett et al., 1973; Schoeneman & Rubanowitz, 1985; Zaccaro & Lowe, 1985; see E. E. Jones, 1976; Kelley & Michela, 1980; Monson & Snyder, 1977; and L. Ross, 1977, for reviews). Nearly two decades of research on the effect has produced some extensions and qualifications. Actors not only see their own behavior as less dispositionally based than do observers, they also see their own behavior as less stable and predictable (Baxter & Goldberg, 1988; Sande, Goethals, & Radloff, 1988). As observers, we see others' behavior as more likely to be similar from situation to situation, whereas in recognizing the variable forces that impinge on our own behavior, we see it as less stable. Moreover, as actors, we have an appreciation of our own rich, multifaceted, and adaptive personalities, and thus often see ourselves as possessing both a trait and its opposite (e.g., serious and carefree) (e.g., J. T. Johnson et al., 1985). This presumed richness in our own personality contributes to seeing ourselves as less predictable and more variable from situation to situation (Sande et al., 1988). The variability that people see in their own behavior may also result from the fact that they are more likely to perceive mood, a transitory factor, as responsible for their behavior, than for that of others (White & Younger, 1988).

The actor-observer effect can be weakened or even reversed when valued outcomes, whether positive or negative, are involved. Positively valued outcomes (such as being helpful to another person) are more often attributed to people, while negatively valued outcomes (such as being late for a social occasion) are more often attributed to situational factors (S. E. Taylor & Koivumaki, 1976; Tillman & Carver, 1980). Moreover, at least under some conditions, actors may attribute their positive behaviors more to dispositional factors than observers do (Chen, Yates, & McGinnies, 1988; McCallum & Schopler, 1984; Schlenker, Hallam, & McCown, 1983), and attribute their own negative qualities or behaviors to situational factors more than observers would (Chen, Yates, & McGinnies, 1988; Lord & Zimbardo, 1985; but see C. A. Anderson, 1985).

At least two additional factors can reverse the usual actor-observer effect. If an actor's behavior actually is due to some dispositional quality, the actor may know this fact better than the observer and make more competent dispositional attributions. For example, if George takes home a lost puppy, he may know that he is a sucker for friendly dogs, and that he has taken puppies home in the past. Consequently, he may be more likely to attribute his behavior to his enduring qualities than would an observer, who might assume that other people would take the puppy home as well (see Monson & Hesley, 1982; Monson & Snyder, 1977; Quattrone, 1982). The actor-observer effect can also be reversed with empathy set instructions. For example, being told to pretend that one is observing one's self as another person might or being induced to take the role of another person changes attributions for behavior. Actors who are induced to see their behavior as observers become more dispositional in their attributions and observers induced to empathize with actors become more situational in their explanations (Gould & Sigall, 1977; Regan & Totten, 1975; Wegner & Finstuen, 1977; Frank & Gilovich, 1989). Personal involvement in an actor's plight yields similar effects (Chen, Yates, & McGinnies, 1988).

Researchers have also compared the attributions of active observers, namely, people who are simultaneously interacting with the actor, with those of passive observers who are uninvolved onlookers. D. T. Miller and Norman (1975) suggest that active onlookers would be even more inclined than passive observers to attribute an actor's behavior to dispositional factors. The reason is that since active observers are involved in the action, they have greater needs to predict and control the situation, especially the actions of others; dispositional attributions produce more stable inferences and hence produce a greater sense of control. According to this reasoning, then, if Joan misses a shot in a volleyball game, Carol is more likely to think Joan is uncoordinated when Carol is also playing than when she is watching the game from the sidelines.

Although studies have supported this hypothesis (D. T. Miller & Norman, 1975; D. T. Miller, Norman, & Wright, 1978; M. L. Snyder, Stephan, & Rosenfield, 1976; Stephan, Rosenfield, & Stephan, 1976), there are some qualifications to the finding. While active observers usually may be more likely to attribute an actor's behavior dispositionally than passive observers, this will not occur if the behavior in question is neutral (i.e., without any hedonic relevance for the active observer). Moreover, active observers may actually be less likely than passive observers to make dispositional attributions for an actor's behavior if they empathize with him or her (Wolfson & Salancik, 1977). If Carol has just missed a shot and then Joan does the same, Carol may empathize with Joan's situation and see her error as more due to situational factors than would an onlooker.

Overall, the actor-observer effect is modest in size (L. R. Goldberg, 1981), and, as just noted, can be undone or reversed depending upon the orientation of the observer or the type of behavior for which attributions are made. Nonetheless, the actor-observer has been heavily researched and, as a consequence, knowledge of self-attribution, attributions about others, and how the two differ in some important ways has been enlarged.

The False Consensus Effect

Kelley (1967) noted that one of the criteria the social perceiver uses in assessing the accuracy of his or her causal perceptions is consensus information, that is, the evaluations or judgments of others. However, as previously noted, the consensus criterion appears to be underutilized by subjects in experiments when they are testing the accuracy or stability of an attribution. Other researchers have also noted the apparent failure of consensus information to have an impact on attributions and related inferences (Nisbett, et al., 1976; see Kassin, 1979b, for a review).

One possible reason why consensus information is underutilized may be that most social perceivers prefer self-generated consensus information. This false consensus, or self-based consensus effect, is the tendency to see one's own behavior as typical, to assume that under the same circumstances others would have reacted the same way as oneself. In the first study to demonstrate this effect, L. Ross, Greene, and House (1977) asked college students if they would walk around their college campus for 30 minutes wearing a large sandwich board with the message, "Eat at Joe's." Some of the students agreed and others did not. The students were then asked to estimate the percentage of students who would make the same choice they made. Those who agreed to wear the sandwich board estimated that 62 percent of their peers would also have agreed, whereas those who refused estimated that 67 percent of their peers would also have refused. Over 100 empirical studies now bear testimony to the robust nature of this effect (Lord, Lepper, & Mackie, 1984; see Marks & Miller, 1987; Mullen & Hu, 1988; Mullen et al., 1985; for reviews).

Several possible explanations for the false consensus effect have been offered (see Marks & Miller, 1987; Wetzel & Walton, 1985). One possibility stems from the fact that people seek out the company of others who are similar to them and who behave as they do (selective exposure). Thus, estimates of how others would behave may reflect the biased sample of people available as a basis for social inference. That is, people who agree with us are more likely to come to mind when we attempt to infer what others will believe, and consequently, we may overestimate the degree to which others share our opinions.

Another possibility is that one's own opinions are especially salient and when a person focuses exclusively on a particular opinion, perceived consensus is increased because that position is the only one in consciousness (Marks & Miller, 1987). Were one to consider the validity of two or more positions, the estimate of the consensus for any one of them might be diluted by considering the alternatives (Marks & Miller, 1987; Nisbett et al., 1976).

A third possibility is that, in trying to predict how we would respond in a situation, we resolve ambiguous details in our mind in a way that favors a preferred course of action over a less-preferred course of action. For example, the person who imagines that others will point and laugh if she appears in a sandwich board will probably decline and assume others, anticipating the same harrassment, would do the same. In contrast, the person who sees the sandwich board caper as a lark that others will also find funny would likely agree to wear the sandwich board and would expect that others would do the same. A fourth possibility is that people have a need to see their own beliefs and behaviors as good, appropriate, and typical, and so they attribute them to others to maintain high self-esteem (L. Ross et al., 1977; see also Sherman et al., 1984).

A number of investigations have been conducted in an effort to discriminate among various possible explanations for the false consensus effect. In a review of these efforts, Marks and Miller (1987) suggest that all of the mechanisms have some validity and may explain the false consensus effect under certain conditions. Moreover, two or three of the specific mechanisms by which false consensus effects occur may operate in concert. There appears, then, to be no one single explanation for this robust effect, but rather, a variety of cognitive and motivational factors that contribute to its strength (see also Mullen et al., 1985; Sherman et al., 1984; Wetzel & Walton, 1985).

Research has identified some of the factors that increase or decrease the magnitude of the false consensus effect. False consensus effects appear to be particularly strong when situational or environmental factors are seen as causally responsible for a behavior and are weaker when dispositional attributions are made for the behavior (Marks & Miller, 1987). False consensus effects are stronger when the issue under consideration is important to the subject. People assume that others are more likely to agree with them on issues they care about than on issues about which they care little (e.g., Granberg, 1987). Certainty of one's opinion increases the strength of the false consensus effect (Marks & Miller, 1985). False consensus effects are weak or even absent when people have no belief about how others might respond, and when this is the case, they may seek consensus information (D. J. Hilton, Smith, & Alicke, 1988). Threat also appears to increase the strength of the false consensus effect because it may augment people's needs to normalize and seek support for their own beliefs (S. J. Sherman, Presson, & Chassin, 1984). False consensus effects appear to be stronger when positive qualities are involved because people assume that positive others share their positive qualities (van der Pligt, 1984). Perceived similarity of others also evokes a false consensus effect (S. J. Sherman et al., 1984). In group situations, the minority is more likely to exhibit a false consensus bias than the majority, which is actually somewhat more likely to underestimate the degree to which its opinions are shared (Sanders & Mullen, 1983; Wetzel & Walton, 1985).

On certain personal attributes, people show a *false uniqueness effect* (Marks, 1984; C. R. Snyder & Fromkin, 1980; Tesser, 1988; Tesser & Paulhus, 1983). For example, when people are asked to list their best abilities and estimate how others stand on these abilities, they underestimate their peers' abilities. In order to value an ability and to consider it special, people seem to need to feel distinctive and uniquely good at the ability. On attitude issues, in contrast, people overestimate the frequency with which others agree with their own position, thereby providing false consensus for their beliefs. Attitudes and opinions, then, appear to show false consensus effects, whereas one's own highly valued skills and abilities tend to show false uniqueness effects (Kernis, 1984).

The false consensus effect has profound implications for how people interpret social reality. Not only do people overestimate how typical their own behavior is, they also overestimate the typicality of their feelings, beliefs, and opinions. The false consensus effect may be a chief vehicle by which people maintain that their own beliefs or opinions are right. It may, for example, lead people to assume that there are a lot of others out there who feel the same way they do, which may not be the case (e.g., Granberg, 1987; Judd & Johnson, 1981). Consequently, under certain conditions, the false consensus effect may function as a justification for the imposition on others of political, moral, and religious beliefs. More commonly, however, the false consensus effect may simply provide a false sense of security regarding how common and widely shared one's own beliefs are (e.g., Fields & Schuman, 1976; Harvey, Wells, & Alvarez, 1978).

Recent work has questioned how biased the "false" consensus effect is. R. Dawes (1989) argues that estimating the consensus of others from a sample of one, namely one's own response, may be a perfectly rational strategy, the falsity of which cannot be judged by its simple departure from the actual distribution of opinions in the population. If people are unaware of the opinions of others, then using their own opinion as a basis for estimating that opinion is a rational strategy. The imputation of one's own opinions to others can be judged as false only if subjects can be observed to weight their own response more than they would that of another randomly chosen person from the group whose response is known to them.

The rationality or irrationality of the false consensus does not override the important conclusion: people impute their attitudes and judgments to others to a greater degree than is true across a large variety of attitude issues and behaviors and for an apparent variety of motivational and cognitive reasons. Thus, what Ralph Waldo Emerson said may be relevant: "To believe in your own thought, to believe what is true for you in your private heart, is true for all men—that is genius" (Emerson, *Self-Reliance*).

Self-Serving Attributional Biases

After you have soundly beaten an opponent on the tennis court, how often do you hear a gratifying, "Gee, you're much better than I am, aren't you?" Usually you hear that it was a bad day, his serve was off, he is still working on his backhand, or the sun was in his eyes. On the other hand, when you have just been badly beaten, the smug look and condescending "Bad luck" from the opponent are particularly grating, because you know he does not believe it was "bad luck" for a moment. He simply thinks he is better. This tendency to take credit for success and deny responsibility for failure is known as the self-serving attributional bias (see, for example, Bradley, 1978; D. T. Miller & Ross, 1975; M. L. Snyder, Stephan, & Rosenfield, 1978; Zuckerman, 1979; cf.

Knight & Vallacher, 1981). It is a robust effect that has been documented cross-culturally (Fletcher & Ward, 1988). Self-serving attributional biases also appear to increase with time. Whereas initial explanations for success or failure may be relatively modest, dispositional attributions for success and situational attributions for failure appear to become more pronounced with time (Burger, 1986; Burger & Huntzinger, 1985).

Overall, there is more evidence that people take credit for success—the self-enhancing bias—than that they deny responsibility for failure—the self-protective bias (D. T. Miller & Ross, 1975). People are sometimes willing to accept responsibility for failure, particularly if they can attribute it to some factor over which they have future control, such as effort. For example, if I lose badly at tennis and blame it on the condition of the court, that will not do much to help me improve my game. But if I realize I faulted on nearly every one of my first serves, I have something to work on at my next lesson (see Weiner et al., 1972).

Another reason for the relative lack of evidence for self-protective biases may stem from the different impact that positive and negative events have on people of low and high self-esteem. Negative events appear to potentiate self-esteem differences, whereas positive events do not (Campbell, 1986). Thus, for example, whereas both high and low self-esteem people tend to attribute positive events to internal factors, they diverge in their explanations of negative events. Whereas those high in self-esteem attribute negative events to external and unstable factors, those low in self-esteem are more likely to attribute failure internally. The variability introduced by self-esteem differences in attributions for failure, then, may explain why the self-protective bias is not in evidence as much as the self-enhancing bias (Campbell & Fairey, 1985; cf. Baumgardner, Heppner, & Arkin, 1986).

Much of the work on self-serving biases has assumed that the biases stem from a need to protect the ego from assault (e.g., M. L. Snyder, Stephan & Rosenfield, 1978). Presumably, one feels better about oneself if one causes good things to happen and not bad ones. However, ego-enhancing needs would seem to be more threatened by accepting blame for failure than by denying credit for success; given that accepting blame for failure is relatively common, researchers began to question whether ego-relevant needs could adequately explain the bias.

D. T. Miller and Ross (1975) argue that in the absence of a clear self-protective bias (i.e., denying blame for failure), the self-enhancing bias (i.e., accepting credit for success) can be explained by cognitive factors. First, people expect to succeed and may accordingly accept responsibility for success because it fits their expectations. Second, people strive to succeed, and when they do, their apparent self-enhancing explanation for it may reflect nothing more than the perceived covariation between their effort and the outcome. Finally, when people estimate the amount of control they have in a situation, they utilize instances in which they have been successful more often than ones in which they have been unsuccessful and hence overestimate the amount of control they have exerted (e.g., H. M. Jenkins & Ward, 1965). All of these factors can, then, explain the self-enhancing bias with reference to cognitive factors (D. T. Miller & Ross, 1975).

However, the idea that ego-defensive needs underlie self-serving biases is too appealing to be dismissed so easily. Indeed, the adequacy of these cognitive explanations has been challenged and rebutted several times (e.g., Bradley, 1978; D. T. Miller, Norman & Wright, 1978; Riess & J. Taylor, 1984; Sicoly & Ross, 1977; Zuckerman, 1979). Weary (formerly Bradley, 1978) has pointed out that, although ego needs are sometimes met by one's taking responsibility for success and denying responsibility for failure, at other times the opposite is true (see, for example, Schlenker, Weigold, & Hallam, 1990). For example, when one's success is too obvious to be denied, as in the case of a public heroic act, a strategy of modesty may be more self-serving. One may also back off from taking too much credit for success if others will know that one is being self-serving or if one's future performance will be scrutinized by others (R. S. Miller & Schlenker, 1985; Reiss et al., 1981; van Knippenberg & Koelen, 1985; Weary et al., 1982). Given that public scrutiny or other contextual factors (see also Arkin, Appelman, & Burger, 1980) can reverse the expected self-serving biases, pinning down their causes and concomitants has been difficult (see, for example, Hull & Levy, 1979).

In response to D. T. Miller and Ross's argument favoring cognitive over motivational factors, several tests of the self-serving bias were conducted in which possible cognitive explanations for self-serving effects were, for the most part, ruled out. For example, if one can arouse subjects' ego involvement in a task *after* a task has been performed, then certain of the nonmotivational explanations (centering on expectations of success and observed covariation between one's efforts and outcomes) can be eliminated (D. T. Miller, 1976; Sicoly & Ross, 1977; M. L. Snyder et al., 1976; Weary, 1980). In all these tests, subjects took more credit for successful than for unsuccessful outcomes. It seems likely that both cognitive and motivational factors contribute to self-serving biases, and the effort to rule out one or the other set of factors may be misplaced (C. A. Anderson & Slusher, 1986; Tetlock & Levi, 1982; Pyszczynski & Greenberg, 1987).

Self-serving biases can extend beyond explanations of one's own behavior to include perceptions of one's intimates, close friends, and other groups with which one is allied, even temporary ones (e.g., Burger, 1981; Lau & Russell, 1980; Schlenker & Miller, 1977; Winkler & Taylor, 1979). At the group level, this bias has been termed the ethnocentric or group-serving bias, and refers to the tendency of in-group members to attribute internal causes to positive in-group behavior and negative out-group behavior and to attribute negative in-group behavior and positive out-group behavior to external causes (Hewstone & Jaspars, 1982; Hewstone, 1989). The group-serving attributional bias has been particularly examined in the context of sports events. In a meta-analysis examining 91 tests of the hypothesis, Mullen and Riordan (1988) concluded that ability is the attribution dimension that exhibits the strongest self-serving attribution effect. That is, we explain our own team's success as being due to internal, stable abilities rather than to effort, the difficulty of the game, or luck. The corresponding tendency to attribute one's own team's failure to lack of effort, the difficulty of the game, or luck, is quite small, and consistent with the general finding that self-enhancing attributions for success are more common than self-protective attributions for failure (D. T. Miller & Ross, 1975). Group-serving biases appear to be more pervasive and robust in Western cultures than in non-Western cultures (Fletcher & Ward, 1988).

Self-serving attributional biases may be quite adaptive, despite their apparent tendency to play fast and loose with the facts. Attributing success to one's own efforts, particularly one's enduring characteristics, creates expectations that may make one more likely to attempt related tasks in the future (see S. E. Taylor & Brown, 1988). Schaufeli (1988) reported evidence that a self-serving motivational bias actually resulted in more labor market success for unemployed workers who were optimistic about their chances of becoming reemployed and motivated to find a job. Moreover, there may be some social cache to self-serving attributional biases. Carlston and Shovar (1983) found that people who made internal attributions for their performance were actually better liked than those who made external attributions. On the surface, these findings may seem to conflict with evidence suggesting that people become more modest and less self-serving when faced with an audience, because they perceive that the audience will like them better for so doing. While it is clear that attributing poor performance to external factors may produce less liking in others (Carlston & Shovar, 1983), internal attributions for either success or failure, particularly if they are moderate and backed up by evidence, may actually enhance liking (Carlston & Shovar, 1983).

To summarize, people generally assume more credit for success than responsibility for failure, although researchers find accepting credit for success is more common than denying responsibility for failure. Some of the findings can be explained by cognitive factors, such as expecting success; however, motivational needs both to preserve one's ego and to present oneself in the best light to others seem to be important too (Reiss et al., 1981). Furthermore, self-serving biases extend beyond explanations for one's own behavior to include the people and institutions with which one is allied. However, the self-serving bias may be attenuated by such factors as public scrutiny of the outcome or of the actor's behavior, ambiguity of the outcome, or competing motives such as the desire to appear modest (see also Wetzel, 1982).

The Self-Centered Bias

If two roommates are asked to estimate how much of the housework each does, each may well see his or her own share as larger than the other's. If two collaborators are asked who should be the first author listed on a paper, each may say, "I should." The *self-centered bias* consists of taking more than one's share of responsibility for a jointly produced outcome. It is useful to distinguish the self-centered bias from the self-serving bias. The self-serving bias is taking credit for success, but not for failure. The self-centered bias consists of taking more responsibility for a joint outcome than is one's due, regardless of whether the outcome is successful or unsuccessful.

In one study (M. Ross & Sicoly, 1979), researchers asked married couples to indicate the extent to which they or their spouses had responsibility for each of twenty household chores. The subjects were then asked to provide some examples of their own and their spouse's contributions for each of the chores listed. When the researchers added the responsibility scores of each member of the couple, in most cases the total exceeded 100 percent; each thought he or she had contributed more than the other thought he or she had. Furthermore, each person provided more examples of his or her own contributions than of the spouse's. A similar pattern has been found across a variety of joint experiences (see M. Ross & Sicoly, 1979; Thompson & Kelley, 1981). Why does this bias occur?

M. Ross and Sicoly (1979) suggest several possibilities, some of which are cognitively based, others of which are motivational. First, it is easier to notice one's own contributions than those of another person. That is, one may be distracted from another's contributions through one's own thoughts; one may spend more time attending to one's own contributions than those of another; and one's own contributions fit with one's conception of the project or one's past values or experience better than do another's contributions. Second, it may be easier to recall one's own contributions than those of another person. Recalling more of one's own contributions can lead to the inference that one did more. Third, there may be informational disparities that favor one's own contributions over another's. For example, if I am not in the house when my roommate does his share of the housework, I may underestimate how much he actually did. Fourth, there may be motivational factors involved in the self-centered bias. For example, thinking about how much I have contributed can increase my self-esteem. Finally, each individual may think of the self as the kind of person who does a given activity and infer greater responsibility from the match of the task to his or her dispositions (Thompson & Kelley, 1981).

Which of these explanations is correct? Clearly, not all of them apply in all instances. For example, I may take more credit for messing up the house than my roommate, but dwelling on the fact is unlikely to raise my self-esteem. Indeed, the fact that people often take as much credit for negative as for positive outcomes argues generally against the motivational explanation (M. Ross & Sicoly, 1979). Likewise, in an effort to rule out differential attention, you could force me to list every single thing my roommate does to help around the house, but I would still believe that I do more (Thompson & Kelley, 1981). Moreover, highly visible, desirable, or stressful activities do not contribute disproportionately to overestimating responsibility, thus also questioning the attention explanation (Thompson & Kelley, 1981). Even under conditions of information equivalency, the self-centered bias thrives (M. Ross & Sicoly, 1979). Overall, differential recall (i.e., the fact that one can bring to mind instances of one's own contributions more easily than those of another person) and match to prior dispositions (i.e., the self-perception that one is the kind of person who does this kind of task) appear to be the strongest among the contenders for producing the self-centered bias (M. Ross & Sicoly, 1979; Sandelands & Calder, 1984; Thompson & Kelley, 1981).

Attributions of Responsibility or Blame

So far, our discussion of attributions has centered largely around issues of causality, that is, who or what caused an event to occur. But many times, the social perceiver goes beyond this attribution to credit an actor with responsibility or blame for an action as well (Heider, 1958; Fincham & Jaspars, 1980). An attribution of responsibility points to who or what can be held accountable for an event, usually a positively or negatively valenced event (K. G. Shaver, 1975, 1985; K. G. Shaver & Drown, 1986). Responsibility for an action tends to be attributed when there is an identifiable source of an action (i.e., a particular person), the belief that the person should have been able to foresee the outcome, the perception that the person's actions were not justified by the situation, and the perception that the person operated under conditions of free choice. Thus, for example, a motorist who caused a fatal accident would not be held responsible if some mechanical failure of which he could not possibly have been aware brought about the accident. However, if he was aware that his brakes were beginning to give and failed to have them checked, then one might see him as responsible for the action in that he should have been able to foresee a potential accident, his failure to check the brakes was unjustified, and he clearly had the choice of whether or not to have the brakes checked. An attribution of blameworthiness is typically reserved for cases in which a causal agent is regarded as subject to censure or punishment for a negative event. Blame attributions tend to be made only when an actor is seen as intending to produce an outcome, and achieving a negative outcome was the actor's purpose. Thus, attributions of responsibility presuppose a judgment of causality (McGraw, 1987b), and attributions of blame presuppose judgments of both causality and responsibility.

Are these the criteria that people use when they use the terms "responsibility" and "blame"? Unfortunately, this is a difficult question to answer. There is some evidence that people do indeed perceive causality, responsibility, and blameworthiness as distinct concepts (Fincham & Bradbury, 1987; Kelman & Lawrence, 1972), and that the ability to draw such distinctions increases with age (Fincham & Jaspars, 1979; see also Fincham & Jaspars, 1980). In a critique of the literature, Shaver and Drown (1986) noted that researchers investigating attributions of blame and responsibility often use the terms interchangeably and fail to consider the specific conditions that would lead to one or another of these more qualified attributions. Consequently, comparing results across studies that have purported to assess responsibility and blame has been difficult. For example, in an investigation of reactions to rape, Janoff-Bulman (1979) reported on two types of self-blame: behavioral self-blame, involving perceptions that the rape had been caused by one's own actions, and characterological self-blame, which involved attributing blame to one's internal qualities (e.g., "I'm the sort of person to get raped"). She found that those who attributed the rape to characterological self-blame were regarded as less well-adjusted than those who attributed self-blame to their behavior. However, Janoff-Bulman's use of the term "blame" did not incorporate the criteria of foreseeability, intention, or goal-directedness. Similarly, S. E. Taylor et al. (1984) assessed "self-blame" for the cause of cancer, and found that women who perceived themselves to have brought on the cancer themselves were neither better nor more poorly adjusted than women who did not make this attribution. However, the interpretation of the results is ambiguous because, as in the Janoff-Bulman investigation, blame was not defined in terms of foreseeability, intention, and goal-directedness. Consequently, S. E. Taylor et al.'s results may more properly speak to the women's perception of their causal role rather than their responsibility or blame for the cancer.

Attributions of responsibility have been examined in the context of defensive attributional biases, phenomena related to the self-protective biases just considered. Defensive attribution refers to the idea that people attribute more responsibility for actions that produce severe rather than mild consequences (K. G. Shaver, 1970a, 1970b; Walster, 1966). Suppose you observe a friend light a cigarette and toss the lighted match to the ground. You might consider this a careless action and watch the match as it gradually flickered out, thinking it was a risky thing to do since there was so much dry brush around. But suppose the lighted match had ignited the brush and begun a major fire requiring the presence of firefighters from several departments. Might your attributions for your friend's behavior not change? He is no longer simply careless, he is now foolishly responsible for a major conflagration that could have been avoided. The defensive attribution formulation suggests that as the consequences of an action become more severe, they become more unpleasant, and the notion that they might be accidental becomes less tolerable: the fear that the same thing might involve the self becomes a realistic possibility. Seeing the actions as avoidable and blaming a person for their occurrence makes the actions more predictable and hence avoidable by the self.

Empirical evidence for the defensive attribution hypothesis has been equivocal from the outset (see Burger, 1981, for a review). By way of reconciliation, K. G. Shaver (1970a, 1970b) hypothesized that situational and personal similarities account for its occurrence. Specifically, he argued that if you, as an observer, are never going to find yourself in a situation like that of the accident perpetrator (e.g., low situational similarity: you do not smoke, barbecue, or camp, so it is unlikely you will be tossing matches around outside), the accident may not arouse a great deal of defensiveness in you. But, if you are likely to be in a similar situation (e.g., high situational similarity: you smoke, barbecue, and camp out a lot), your defensiveness could be aroused and you may attempt to deny personal similarity to the perpetrator. However, if personal similarity is high, denying personal similarity may be difficult. When personal similarity is high, Shaver predicts, you will attribute the accident to chance or bad luck to minimize implications for similar future outcomes befalling you.

Burger (1981) examined 22 studies that tested the defensive attribution hypothesis and found support for Shaver's predictions. When subjects were personally and situationally similar to the accident perpetrator, they attributed less responsibility to the perpetrator as severity of the consequences increased; presumably these defensive attributions served to avoid the threatening implications for the subjects. When subjects were situationally or personally dissimilar to the perpetrator, they attributed more responsibility as the accident's severity increased. More involving manipulations (e.g., having subjects hear about the accident from the perpetrator versus reading about it) also tended to increase the likelihood of defensive attributions. Moreover, as implied in the formulations of Shaver (1970a, 1970b) and Walster (1966), defensive attribution appears to be mediated by the arousal that occurs in response to the threatening nature of the situation (Thornton, 1984; Thornton et al., 1986).

In a formulation related to defensive attribution, Melvin Lerner suggested that people have a need to see the world as a controllable place in which good things happen to good people and bad things happen to bad people. Lerner suggested that the basis for this belief in a just world is a defensive need to ward off threats to the self. If you see another person experience a negative event, such as being struck by a car or developing an incurable disease, it is psychologically more comforting to believe that person deserved it (e.g., "She walked right in front of the car" or "He burned himself out working too hard"), than to believe that the event could be chance-determined; after all, if negative events are random, they could befall oneself as well. Hence, when observing another's misfortune, one will blame the other's actions for bringing on the event; if no faulty action can be found, one will blame the person's character, assuming that he or she is a bad person who deserved the misfortune (Lerner, 1970). Empirical research generally supports this position (e.g., Lerner, 1965, 1970; Lerner & Matthews, 1967; Simmons & Lerner, 1968).

Defensive attribution processes and the belief in a just world appear to have important consequences for social interaction. Lerner and others (e.g., Ryan, 1971) have suggested that such beliefs often provide a justification for the oppression of society's victims.

> As a nation, we have the money and technology to virtually eliminate poverty and to provide the kind of professional facilities and services which would dramatically enhance the life chances of a parentless child or the emotionally ill person. Yet...we seem not to care enough, possibly we do not care at all...we tend to assume that the other man's suffering is probably a result of his own failures (Lerner, 1970, pp. 205–206).

INDIVIDUAL DIFFERENCES IN THE ATTRIBUTION PROCESS

The previous section considered some of the biases that most social perceivers have when they attempt to infer causality in social settings. The present section examines individual differences in attributional tendencies, that is, chronic propensities to interpret causality in particular ways that discriminate among perceivers.

Rotter's Locus of Control

Rotter (1966) argued that people differ in the expectations they hold about the sources of positive and negative reinforcements for their behavior. Some people, termed *internals*, credit themselves with the ability to control the occurrence of reinforcing events. Others, termed *ex-*

ternals, perceive reinforcing events as under the control of luck, chance, or powerful other individuals—factors external to themselves. Each of us no doubt knows people who embody the extremes of this dimension. Some people's sense of control is so great that they almost seem to believe they make the sun come up in the morning and set at night, whereas other people seem never to see a connection between their own behavior and what happens to them.

Although Rotter does not suggest that locus of control will operate equally strongly in all situations, he regards it as a general, relatively stable propensity to see the world in a particular way. Locus of control is assessed using a 29-item scale that includes items like those in Table 3.1. If you answer option *a* for all or most items, then you would be on your way to a high internal locus of control score, whereas more option *b* answers would push you toward the external extreme. Studies have shown that locus of control influences perceptions of experiences as diverse as political beliefs (e.g., Gurin et al., 1969), achievement behavior (e.g., Crandall, Katkovsky, & Crandall, 1965), reactions to illness and hospitalization (Seeman & Evans, 1962), and learning (Wolk & DuCette, 1974), among others (Strickland, 1988).

Some criticisms of the locus of control concept have been made. The scale is not composed of a single dimension, as Rotter had originally proposed, but rather consists of a number of control-related beliefs. Belief that the world is just, for example, need not predict belief in a po-

TABLE 3.1 THE ASSESSMENT OF LOCUS OF CONTROL

(Choose one option for each question)

1. a. Promotions are earned through hard work and persistence.
   b. Making a lot of money is largely a matter of getting the right breaks.

2. a. In my experience, I have noticed that there is usually a direct connection between how hard I study and the grades I get.
   b. Many times the reactions of teachers seem haphazard to me.

3. a. When I am right I can convince others.
   b. It is silly to think that one can really change another person's basic attitudes.

4. a. In our society, a man's future earning power is dependent upon his ability.
   b. Getting promoted is really a matter of being a little luckier than the next guy.

5. a. If one knows how to deal with people, they are really quite easily led.
   b. I have little influence over the way other people behave.

SOURCE: From Rotter, J. B. External control and internal control. *Psychology Today*, 1971, 5, 37–42, 58–59. Reprinted from *Psychology Today* magazine. Copyright © 1971 American Psychological Association.

litically responsive world, which in turn may be independent of a belief that the world is difficult or merely unpredictable (B. E. Collins, 1974). Yet, each of these factors speaks to some aspect of perceived controllability in the world. Another criticism hinges on the fact that the scale may be more suited to white middle-class norms and values than to the values of minority-group members or lower social classes (Gurin et al., 1969; Phares, 1976; see also Strickland, 1988). A third criticism stems from the fact that the internal locus of control items include those that assess both effort (controllable) as well as ability (uncontrollable), thereby confounding locus and controllability (Weiner, 1986).

Despite these criticisms, work on locus of control has been both prevalent and fruitful within attribution research. As noted in Chapter 2, Rotter's work is chiefly responsible for the formal articulation of the internal/external dimension that is so prominent a part of attribution research and attributional theories, such as Weiner's theory of achievement behavior. Work on locus of control is also one of the few systematic efforts to examine how the perceiver's own personality or style influences social perception, a factor Heider (1958) considered essential in understanding the attribution process. And finally, the locus of control concept has generated hundreds of empirical studies documenting the importance of this individual difference.

Attributional Style

Attributional style is "a tendency to make particular kinds of causal inferences, rather than others, across different situations and across time" (Metalsky & Abramson, 1981, p. 38). Research has especially focused on the pessimistic attributional style, characterized by a tendency to regard aversive events as caused by internal, stable, and pervasive (global) factors. This characteristic, identified by Seligman and his colleagues (Abramson, Seligman, & Teasdale, 1978; Metalsky & Abramson, 1981; C. Peterson & Seligman, 1984; Seligman et al., 1979), is thought to be important because of its mediating role between negative events and adverse health and mental health outcomes. According to Seligman and his associates, when one believes that desirable outcomes are unlikely, when one expects the undesirable outcomes to occur, and when one sees no way to change this situation, helplessness, depression, and adverse health consequences can occur (see also Crocker, Alloy, & Kayne, 1988).

How severe these consequences are and how much of a toll they take on self-esteem depend upon the attributions for the uncontrollable events. Internal attributions lead to greater loss in self-esteem, global attributions produce more pervasive consequences, and stable attributions produce longer adverse consequences (Alloy et al., 1984). Global, stable, internal attributions for events, then, produce the most far-reaching adverse consequences. Seligman and his associates argue that there are people who chronically see positive events as due to external, unstable, and specific factors and failures as due to stable, internal, and global factors. When these individuals are exposed to lack of control or perceive that they have no control in a situation, their chronic attributional style makes them vulnerable to depression as well as other health and mental health disorders (Abramson, Seligman, & Teasdale, 1978; C. A. Anderson, Horowitz, & French, 1983; Fincham, Diener, & Hokoda, 1987; Hammen, 1987; D. C. Klein, Fencil-Morse, & Seligman, 1976; Kuiper, 1978; Metalsky & Abramson, 1981; C. Peterson & Seligman, 1984; Seligman et al., 1979). A meta-analysis of 104 studies involving 15,000 people found moderate support for the relation of attributional style to depression (P. D. Sweeney, Anderson, & Bailey, 1986; see also Robins, 1988; but see Cochran & Hammen, 1985). See Table 3.2.

In addition to its association with depression, explanatory style has been explored in a wide variety of other settings, ranging from college students' explanations for their good or poor grades and consequent academic success; students' depression, shyness, and loneliness; life insurance salesmen's explanations for their success or lack of it and its impact on quitting and sales records; and the content of Presidential candidates' speeches (e.g., Anderson & Arnoult, 1985b; Mikulincer, 1988; Zullow & Seligman, 1990).

In a study by C. Peterson, Seligman, and Vaillant (1988), interviews conducted with graduates of the Harvard University classes of 1942 to 1944 a few years after graduation were analyzed to see how the men habitually attributed the negative events in their lives. The men were asked about difficult experiences they had encountered during the Second World War, such as combat or relations with superiors, and they were asked whether or not they had dealt successfully or unsuccessfully with those situations. Their answers were then coded as reflecting an optimistic or pessimistic attributional style. An example of explaining a negative event in terms of a pessimistic explanatory style was provided by one young man who later died before the age of 55: "I cannot seem to decide firmly on a career . . . this may be my unwillingness to face reality." In contrast, one of the healthy young men referred to his Army career: "My career in the Army has been checkered, but on the whole, characteristic of the Army." The difference between these responses is that the first man referred to negative events in terms of his own stable qualities with no apparent hope for escape. In contrast, the second man also described negative experiences, but with reference to external factors ("that's the Army"). Overall, the authors found that those men who explained negative events by referring to their own internal, stable, pervasive, negative qualities had significantly poorer

TABLE 3.2   PERCEIVED CAUSES OF LACK OF CONTROL AND THEIR
EMOTIONAL CONSEQUENCES

	Global		Nonglobal	
	Stable	*Unstable*	*Stable*	*Unstable*
Internal	Pervasive, stable, low self-esteem; potentially serious depression (e.g., I am unlovable)	Temporary, but pervasive loss of self-esteem (e.g., 1983 was a really bad year for me)	Loss of self-esteem but confined to limited aspect of one's life (e.g., I cannot do athletics to save my life)	Some short-lived loss of self-esteem (e.g., I look terrible today)
External	Pervasive and long-term ennui or displeasure but no loss of self-esteem (e.g., The economy is lousy, and there are no jobs)	Temporary, but pervasive ennui with no loss of self-esteem (e.g., It's a wretched day, the electricity is out, and there's nothing to do)	Long-term ennui or displeasure confined to limited aspect of one's life (e.g., My tennis partner has moved out of town and now I have no one to play with)	No depression, little emotional disruption (e.g., He's in a bad mood today. Better wait until tomorrow)

SOURCE: After Abramson, Seligman, and Teasdale, 1978

health between ages 45 through 60, some 25 to 30 years later. This was true even when physical and mental health at age 25 were taken into account. Thus, the pessimistic explanatory style in early adulthood seems to be a risk factor for poor health in middle and late adulthood.

Debate concerning attributional style has centered on several factors (Brewin, 1985). Some argue that depression produces attributional changes rather than the reverse (Barnett & Gotlib, 1988; Cochran & Hammen, 1985). Others have questioned whether the onset of depression requires a precipitating stressful event for which depressive attributions are made (Williams, 1985) or whether the presence of the attributional style is sufficient for the development of depression. The cross-situational consistency, validity, and measurement of attributional style has also been debated (e.g., Cochran & Hammen, 1985; Cutrona, Russell, & Jones, 1985). Whether controllability is also an important dimension in the perceptions of outcomes is a concern as well (J. D. Brown & Siegel, 1988). Consensus appears to be settling on a modest yet definite role for attributional style in explaining reactions to positive and negative events and its resulting impact on depression and other adverse outcomes (e.g., C. A. Anderson, Jennings, & Arnoult, 1988). Attributional style may not be as general or as cross-situationally consistent as was originally hypothesized, but neither is it so situationally specific as to preclude its value as an individual difference predictor (C. A. Anderson, Jennings, & Arnoult, 1988).

Reattribution Training

In Chapter 2, we considered the therapeutic application of misattribution, the idea that negative emotional states such as anxiety can be reduced by providing people with nonemotional cognitive explanations for their arousal in emotional situations. As we noted in that section, clinical efforts to apply the misattribution approach to anxiety-based problems, such as stuttering, insomnia, or impotence, have generally yielded poor results.

Attribution retraining represents a different therapeutic approach that does not involve the reattribution of arousal. Rather, it derives from attributional theories of action, such as Weiner's model of achievement motivation, Seligman's work on the pessimistic explanatory style, and Bem's self-perception theory. The central concept is that many behaviors, affects, or beliefs are the consequences of causal attributions that people make about events, such as the reasons underlying their success or failure in an achievement domain or in an effort to meet other people. Interventions using attributional retraining often identify behaviors considered to be undesirable (such as reduced performance following a failure) that are believed to be caused by attributions, such as perceiving failure as due to low ability. During the training intervention, people are taught to make more "favorable" causal attributions, such as learning to ascribe failure to insufficient effort (Forsterling, 1985). Another technique involves altering the situation so that success will be achieved in an unobtrusive way that leads people to interpret their success as due to their internal qualities (Haemmerlie & Montgomery, 1984; Montgomery & Haemmerlie, 1986).

In a representative study (T. D. Wilson & Linville, 1982; 1985), college student subjects who reported being dissatisfied with college and who were performing badly and worrying about their performance went through an attributional retraining program designed to change their attributions for their performance. The intervention involved providing the students with statistical information about the fact that college students' grade point averages improve over time and fake videotaped interviews with students who had done poorly early on in college but whose grades had improved over the four years. The procedure yielded substantial improvements in performance. The students performed better on the Graduate Record Examination immediately and one week after training, and after one year, their grade point averages had improved. The drop-out rate in the group exposed to the intervention was lower than that of a comparison group not exposed to the intervention, and their expectations of achieving better grades in the future were higher than those of the comparison group. Mood was also substantially improved in the week following the intervention.

Reviewing 15 studies that made use of attributional retraining principles, Forsterling (1985) concluded that such programs typically produce changes in both cognitions and behavior. For example, in the achievement domain, subjects' attributions for failure usually shift to lack of effort (a controllable, internal, and unstable dimension), they show improved performance, and their persistence is increased as well. As such, attributional retraining procedures appear to have considerable promise as a general technique for cognitive intervention.

SUMMARY

Decades of empirical work on attribution theory have confirmed many of the important points made by early attribution theories and have added or contradicted others. Research with children has identified basic principles of causation, including temporal ordering (causes precede effects), spatio-temporal contiguity (causes are in close physical and temporal proximity to effects), and salience (perceptually salient stimuli tend to be perceived as causal). Principles of covariation are acquired somewhat later and do not appear to be as fundamental to causal perception. Causes also resemble effects, and representative causes are attributed to effects. These developmental principles are important not only because they characterize the causal thinking of children, but because adults continue to use them, particularly in situations about which they may be poorly informed.

Research has also identified an important role for knowledge structures in causal inference. The attribution theories developed by the early theorists were, for the most part, generic ones. Research suggests that, in domains in which people are knowledgeable, experienced, or well-informed, they may entertain several specific content-based causes and eliminate inappropriate ones.

Characteristics of the to-be-explained events also influence causal inference. Kruglanski proposed a distinction between attributions for occurrences, which are not completely voluntary, and actions, which are voluntarily initiated by an actor. Occurrences and actions appear to elicit different kinds of attributions (internal or external factors for occurrences, internal factors for actions), and also prompt the use of different kinds of information. Consensus information is sought out for occurrences whereas distinctiveness information is sought out to understand the reasons underlying voluntary behavior.

The importance of communication in the causal attribution process has also been increasingly uncovered. The conditions that elicit causal activity may also elicit social activity for the purpose of extracting explanations from others. Research on communication and attributions has also focused on how causality can be communicated through language, especially verbs that evoke attributions to the subject or object of a sentence.

An attribution theory that incorporates the importance of knowledge structures and communication into the attribution process is Hilton and Slugoski's abnormal conditions model. They argue that when the social perceiver encounters an event that requires causal explanation, the perceiver will use consensus, consistency, and distinctiveness information to develop contrasting cases against which to evaluate the target event so as to identify the abnormal condition that produced it. According to the model, the social perceiver essentially poses the question, "Why did this event occur instead of the normal case?"

Research testing attribution theory has pinpointed a number of persistent biases that people employ in the attribution process. Foremost among these is the fundamental attribution error, which maintains that people overattribute the behavior of others to dispositional causes, ignoring contributing situational factors such as context or role. This bias may result in part from behavior engulfing the perceptual field, but it also seems to be a spontaneous ascription of traits to the behaviors of others.

The actor-observer effect, a related phenomenon, reveals that whereas people's explanations for others' behavior are heavily dispositional, explanations for one's own behavior are more situational. The actor-observer effect appears to be due both to perceptual factors (i.e., what is salient when offering causes for one's own or another's behavior) and to differences in information one has about one's own versus another's behavior. However, when perceptual experience is equated, when valenced actions are involved, when information is equivalent, or when an empathy set is engaged, actor-observer effects are weakened or reversed; active observers also make different attributions than passive observers.

Another bias centers on the use of consensus information. Researchers consistently find that consensus information (i.e., the opinions or experience of others) is relatively underutilized in the judgment process. Instead of using real consensus information, people often use self-based consensus information, that is, what they think others believe or will do in a given situation. In so doing, they exaggerate the extent to which others share their own beliefs.

The self-serving attributional bias refers to the fact that people are more likely to take credit for good outcomes than for bad ones. However, accepting credit for success is more common than denying responsibility for failure. Reasons for this bias are both cognitive (e.g., it is easier to perceive a covariation between an intended outcome such as success and one's efforts) and motivational (e.g., a need to preserve self-esteem). Self-serving biases can also be seen in the explanations offered for the behavior of one's close associates and social groups. The bias can be moderated or eliminated by such factors as competing motives or public scrutiny of one's explanations.

Research also distinguishes attributions of causality from attributions of responsibility and blame. Defensive attributions refer to the idea that people attribute more responsibility for actions that produce severe rather than mild consequences. This bias appears to result from the threat engendered by the possibility that the same severe accidental outcome could befall the self. Lerner's just world formulation, which is related to defensive attribution, suggests that when another person experiences a negative event, people tend to attribute the event to that person's action or character, so as to distance the self from the threatening circumstances.

Individual differences in attribution processes are chronic propensities to interpret causality in particular ways. In Rotter's locus of control formulation, individuals are judged to be primarily oriented toward the environment (externals) or toward the self (internals) as a source of reinforcement. This chronic individual difference leads people to make systematically different attributions for the outcomes that befall them. Attributional style is a tendency to make particular patterns of causal inference rather than others. Research has especially focused on the pessimistic attributional style, characterized by a tendency to regard aversive outcomes as caused by internal, stable, and global factors. This style is believed to help maintain and perhaps even contribute to the development of adverse health and mental health outcomes, including depression.

The legacy of research on attributional processes has been rich and varied. As one of social cognition's most popular exports to other fields, it has been used as a basis for many attributional theories that analyze a variety of social and personal issues including: how people perceive and interpret the causes of physical symptoms and decide or not to seek treatment (see Michela & Wood, 1986, for a review); what some of the causal biases are that foreign policy decision makers engage in when they attempt to make sense of the geopolitical field (Jervis, 1976; Tetlock & McGuire, 1986); how people can explore and alter their attributions for personal problems through therapeutic processes (Forsterling, 1985, 1986; Harvey & Galvin, 1984; Weiner, 1988b); how the causal attribution biases of therapists induced through training and experience influence the therapeutic process (Jordan, Harvey, & Weary, 1988; Plous & Zimbardo, 1986); how stereotypes about gender and other individual differences result in prejudicial attributions for behavior (Deaux, 1984); why people are depressed, lonely, or shy, how they interpret situations in ways that perpetuate these adverse reactions, and how attributions can be used to ameliorate these problems (Anderson & Arnoult, 1985a); what causes people infer for the work they do and how such attributions influence satisfaction, performance, and creativity (e.g., Boggiano & Main, 1986; Crano, Gorenflo, & Schackelford, 1988; Harackiewicz & Manderlink, 1984; Sansone, 1986; see Kassin & Lepper, 1984, for a review); and how people react to victimizing or threatening events (Bulman & Wortman, 1977; D. T. Miller & Porter, 1983; S. E. Taylor et al., 1984; Thompson & Janigian, 1988); among many others (Frieze, Bar-Tal, & Carroll, 1979; Harvey, Ickes, & Kidd, 1976, 1978, 1981). Clearly, many fruitful avenues of investigation for attribution research remain.

4

Social Categories and Schemas

❖

The streets were all deserted and dark; he walked a few yards and came out almost opposite her house. Amid the glimmering blackness of all the row of windows, the lights in which had long since been put out, he saw one, and only one, from which overflowed, between the slats of its shutters, closed like a winepress over its mysterious golden juice, the light that filled the room within, a light which on so many evenings, as soon as he saw it, far off, as he turned into the street, had rejoiced his heart with its message: "She is there—expecting you," and now tortured him with: "She is there with the man she was expecting." He must know who; he tiptoed along by the wall until he reached the window, but between the slanting bars of the shutters, he could see nothing; he could hear, only, in the silence of the night, the murmur of conversation. What agony he suffered as he watched that light, in whose golden atmosphere were moving, behind the closed sash, the unseen and detested pair. . . .

He drew himself up on tiptoe. He knocked. They had not heard; he knocked again; louder; their conversation ceased. A man's voice—he strained his ears to distinguish whose, among such of Odette's friends as he knew, the voice could be— asked:

"Who's that?"

He could not be certain of the voice. He knocked once again. The window first, then the shutters were thrown open. It was too late, now, to retire, and since she

96

must know all, so as not to seem too contemptible, too jealous and inquis-
itive, he called out in a careless, hearty, welcoming tone:

"Please don't bother; I just happened to be passing, and saw the light. I
wanted to know if you were feeling better."

He looked up. Two old gentlemen stood facing him, in the window, one
of them with a lamp in his hand; and beyond them he could see into the
room, a room that he had never seen before. (Proust, 1914/1956, pp. 353,
356)

Categories and schemas are ways of talking about expectations and
their effects. Like it or not, we all make assumptions about other people, ourselves, and the situations we encounter. Sometimes, like the
hero in the excerpt, we are dramatically misled by our expectations. His
expectations about Odette, that she will be the only one awake in her
building and that she will be entertaining a visitor, lead him to misinterpret what he sees and hears. However, much of the time our expectations are functional, and indeed, we would be unable to operate
without them. Such expectations, assumptions, and generic prior
knowledge allow us some sense of prediction and control, which is essential to our well-being (Chapter 6; also see S. T. Fiske & Taylor, 1984,
Chapter 5). Note that the hero in the story is motivated to discover his
imagined rival's identity, information that would grant him the ability
to predict, if not control, his situation. Categories and schemas allow us
the comforting sense that we understand our world, and often they are
accurate enough, although sometimes they are sadly mistaken.

Could we do without them? Consider the seemingly objective alternative of operating within situations and with people about whom one
has virtually no expectations or prior knowledge. Arriving on a new
campus the first day, coming into an unfamiliar culture for the first
time, or meeting a stranger whose gender, age, and role are mysterious—these all are disorienting encounters that challenge one's ability to
function without the normal level of prediction and control provided by
schemas. Prior knowledge about the campus (a map, for instance), expectations about the culture (from guidebooks), or an introduction to
the stranger (by a mutual friend) would facilitate each encounter. Of
course, our inevitable reliance on such prior knowledge is not perfectly
adaptive, as when one relies on the wrong assumptions, or when one's
assumptions are overly rigid. But on the whole, such schemas are useful.

In this chapter and the next, we will concentrate on schemas and
categories, in this chapter defining them and giving some theoretical
context. We will also discuss what is contained in your schemas: what
kinds of information you store in schemas, how schemas might be organized, how you acquire them. We then describe what schemas do for
you: how they affect what you perceive, remember, and infer; in particular, how they affect your stereotypes of people belonging to social
groups other than your own; as well as how they affect your interpre-

tations of other people's personalities. We will also discuss other kinds of schemas, such as people's scripted ideas about social events and their rules about social relationships. In the next chapter, we will examine the limits on schematic understanding; we will examine how people make sense of things when they do *not* rely on their expectations, and we will describe the kinds of circumstances that encourage and discourage schematic processes.

DEFINITION AND EXAMPLES OF SCHEMAS AT WORK

A schema may be defined as a cognitive structure that represents knowledge about a concept or type of stimulus, including its attributes and the relations among those attributes (W. F. Brewer & Nakamura, 1984; S. T. Fiske & Linville, 1980; Hastie, 1981; Rumelhart & Ortony, 1977; S. E. Taylor & Crocker, 1981). In the excerpt that opened the chapter, the hero applies a schema for deceit that includes attributes (false excuses, a late-night rendezvous, whispered conversation) and their relationships (e.g., the excuse was given to enable the rendezvous). Similarly, as a reader, one can come in on the middle of a story, figure out that it concerns jealousy, and understand the events as they unfold, all because of one's schemas. They also allow one to fill in any missing details (e.g., the expression on the hero's face as the shutters opened) and remember the story's highlights (ever since high school French class).

Schemas facilitate what is called top-down, conceptually driven, or theory-driven processes, which simply means processes heavily influenced by one's organized prior knowledge, as opposed to processes that are more bottom-up or data-driven (Abelson, 1981b; Bobrow & Norman, 1975; Rumelhart & Ortony, 1977). As people's theories and concepts about the world, schemas are concerned with the general case, abstract generic knowledge that holds across many particular instances. The basic message of schema research has been that people simplify reality by storing knowledge at a molar, inclusive level, rather than squirreling away, one-by-one, all the original individual experiences in their raw forms, which would be pure data-driven processing.

Recently, however, social and cognitive psychologists have taken a closer look at data-driven processes by focusing on their interplay with schema-driven processes. Data-driven processes demonstrate ordinary people's sensitivity to the specific qualities of another individual or situation. Purely schematic theories have, in the extreme cases, portrayed people as blithely glossing over important details, as stubbornly refusing to see the information in front of them, and as maintaining their schemas at any cost. In contrast, data-driven approaches show that people do indeed care about the information given (Higgins & Bargh, 1987). We will consider both types of phenomena in these two chapters, beginning with schematic processes.

WHERE DOES THE SCHEMA CONCEPT COME FROM?

Our perceptions of the world reflect an interplay between what's out there and what we bring to it. We are, paradoxically, more aware of the contributions of the world out there than of our own contributions to our cognitive processes. As structured knowledge that we bring to everyday perceptions, schemas emphasize our active construction of reality. This is not to say that we are unconstrained by the stimuli themselves; in the words of one friend, "there is a 'there' out there." But studying the impact of schemas is interesting because it emphasizes the part of the interplay—our own contribution—that is mostly preconscious and that defies common sense.

We experience the world as if our schemas have added nothing to it, so common sense tells us that we perceive an unchanged or literal copy of the environment. We experience perception as instantaneous and direct, as if our brains were simply videotaping the surroundings. The hero in the Proust story, for example, was not aware that his jealous expectations caused him to construe the only lighted window as belonging to his lover. Ordinary people and some philosophers both have held this common-sense view that perceptions are unfiltered and veridical (Aristotle, 1931; J. Mill, 1869). An emphasis on the importance of unfiltered experience continues in the present-day study of exemplars (covered in this chapter) and direct perception (in Chapter 7).

In contrast, Gestalt psychology encouraged a different view of perception (Brunswik, 1956; Koffka, 1935). Gestalt psychologists argued that perception is constructive and that perceptions are mediated by the interpretive faculties of nerves and brain. What we "see" in any given stimulus depends on context; for example, the "l"'s in "1952" and in "life" objectively are quite similar, but we interpret them differently because of their respective contexts. Context provides a different Gestalt or configuration that alters the meaning of the individual elements. Hence, the whole is more than the simple combination of its parts. The Gestalt emphasis on people's perception of configurations in context anticipates the schema as a configuration-in-context actively contributed by the perceiver. The schema, as organized prior knowledge, shapes what is perceived and remembered, in much the same way that context-based Gestalt configurations do, but schemas are generally more complex types of configurations involving people and situations.

Origins of the Schema Concept in Person Perception Research

The importance of Gestalt stimulus configurations guided two theoretical developments that directly precede current schema theories: Solomon Asch's (1946) configural model of how we form impressions of others and Fritz Heider's (1958) theory of social configurations that produce psychological balance. Both theories endorse a schematic type of approach, positing that people have organized expectations about what goes with what, and both describe a more data-driven alternative.

The configural model. In his pioneering work, Asch (1946) examined how people combine the components of another person's personality and come up with an integrated overall impression. In so doing, he set the stage for much of person perception research (D. J. Schneider, Hastorf, & Ellsworth, 1979), and he also specifically anticipated social schema research. In his analysis of how people form impressions of others, Asch theorized that we experience another person as a psychological unit, that we fit the person's various qualities into a single unifying theme, which in many cases resembles a schema. Asch originally made this point in an impressive series of twelve studies (Asch, 1946). The subjects' task was to form an impression of someone described by one or another list of personality traits. One group, for example, was told about someone who was "intelligent, skillful, industrious, cold, determined, practical, and cautious." (Form an impression of this person before reading on.) Another group of subjects was told about someone who was "intelligent, skillful, industrious, *warm*, determined, practical, and cautious." The simple manipulation of the traits *warm* and *cold* created large differences in people's descriptions of the target person. For example, the cold, intelligent person was seen as calculating, and the warm, intelligent person was seen as wise.

Asch proposed two models to account for these results: the *configural model* and the *algebraic model*. Consider the configural model first. It hypothesizes that people form a unified overall impression of other people, and that the unifying forces work on individual elements to bring them in line with the overall impression. Thus, the pressure toward unity may change the meaning of the individual elements to fit better in context. As an example, suppose that you generally value intelligence. Would you always value intelligence? That is, would you rather encounter a smart or a stupid con artist? The configuration as a whole changes the meaning of the individual trait "intelligent." An intelligent con artist is *sly;* an intelligent child is *clever;* an intelligent grandmother is *wise.* To return to the previous example, out of the configuration *cold* and *intelligent* comes a negative inference of *calculating* and a correspondingly negative evaluation (see Fig. 4.1). In addition to meaning *change*, people use a variety of strategies to organize and unify the components of an impression; they not only change the meaning of ambiguous terms, but they also resolve apparently discrepant terms with considerable ingenuity (Asch & Zukier, 1984). All of this mental activity results, according to the configural model, in an impression made up of traits and their relationships, just as a schema later would be defined as consisting of attributes and their relationships.

The alternative, the algebraic model, directly contrasts with the configural model and, by extension, with the subsequent schema models. The algebraic model takes each individual trait, evaluates it in isolation from the others, and combines the evaluations into a summary evaluation (see Fig. 4.1). It is as if, upon meeting someone new, you were simply to combine together all the person's pros (e.g., intelligence) and cons (e.g., coldness) to form your impression. The algebraic model of information averaging boasts an impressive program of research (N. H. Anderson, 1974, 1981a), as does a related algebraic model of combining beliefs to form an overall attitude (Fishbein & Ajzen, 1975).

The configural and algebraic models represent respectively the holistic and elemental approaches to social cognition described in Chapter 1. As such, they represent two fundamentally different ideas about how people form impressions of others. These two competing approaches originally proposed by Asch were thoroughly researched and, as you might imagine, hotly debated for a number of years (D. L. Hamilton & Zanna, 1974; Schumer, 1973; Wyer, 1974; Wyer & Watson, 1969; Zanna & Hamilton, 1972, 1977, versus N. H. Anderson, 1966; N. H. Anderson & Lampel, 1965; Kaplan, 1971, 1975). However, from a theoretical per-

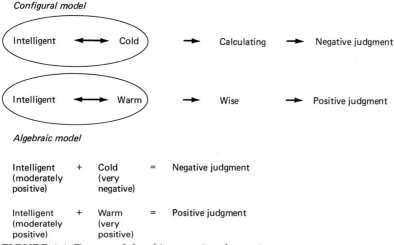

FIGURE 4.1 Two models of impression formation.

spective, the contest was essentially a draw because both models were flexible enough to account for each other's data and neither was stated in a strictly falsifiable form. This led to a consensus on the "futility of the adversarial approach" (Ostrom, 1977) and pleas for more theory development. Schema approaches supplied one remedy to the need to develop theory on the configural side, and recent work has also developed the elemental approach, as we shall see, but both approaches no longer focus on "disproving" the other side (e.g., Lydon, Jamieson, & Zanna, 1988; Schul, 1983; Watkins & Peynircioglu, 1984). Indeed, one recent proposal for resolving this old debate is that both models are right, but that people follow each under different informational and motivational circumstances that, not surprisingly, mimic the respective research paradigms of the two approaches (S. T. Fiske & Pavelchak, 1986; S. T. Fiske & Neuberg, 1990).

Balance theory. Within social psychology, another theoretical forebear of schema models is Heider's (1946, 1958) balance theory. We will discuss it in more detail later (Chapter 11; cf. Markus & Zajonc, 1985, pp. 198–201), but here it usefully illustrates another Gestalt-derived theory that anticipates current schema work. Balance theory proposes three cognitive elements in a triad: a perceiver (P), another person (O), and an attitude object (X). They may be linked by positive or negative relationships. For example, if you (P) like medieval music (X) and you meet someone else (O) who also likes it, both the P-X and O-X relationships are positive. With this shared attitude, the chances of your liking this other person, that is, of P-O also being positive, are much enhanced. Three positive relationships, as in this example, create a psychologically balanced triad that seems like a good comfortable fit. Conversely, if there is someone you quite dislike (P-O is negative), it should not surprise you that the other person likes music that you hate (O-X is positive but P-X is negative); consequently, that triad is psychologically balanced as well. Whenever the relationships' three signs multiply out to a +, the triad is balanced and provides a good psychological configuration, a "good unit" in the Gestalt sense. One way to summarize the idea is that agreeing friends and disagreeing enemies make neat cognitive packages, which might be termed schemas. One essential similarity between a balanced triad and a schema is that both specify elements (here, P, O, and X) and the typical relationships among them; hence, researchers sometimes refer to a *balance schema*.

In contrast, triads that are not balanced are not good psychological units. When friends disagree (and, to a lesser extent, when enemies agree), the triad somehow does not fit together, and the individual elements do not form a unified whole. When people attempt to learn stories about balanced and imbalanced triads, the balanced triads are learned more easily (DeSoto, Henley, & London, 1968; Press, Crockett,

& Rosenkrantz, 1969; Zajonc & Burnstein, 1965a), recalled more accurately (Gerard & Fleischer, 1967; Picek, Sherman, & Shiffrin, 1975), and recognized faster (Sentis & Burnstein, 1979). Thus, having a balance schema helps people to make sense of particular social configurations, anticipating later schema research.

Summary. Both Asch's configural model of impression formation and Heider's balance theory of relationships are Gestalt-oriented approaches to person perception that posit people's tendency to form unified overall impressions out of discrete social elements. These theories and the resulting research testify to the power of the ideas, which anticipate the later burst of research on schemas.

Origins of the Schema Concept in Nonsocial Memory Research

Whenever one encounters a new concept or theory, it is helpful to ask (silently, if not aloud): "Compared to what? What's the alternative?" The configural model of person perception was best understood in contrast to the algebraic model. In balance theory, the balanced triads, which form good units, contrast with the imbalanced triads, which are perceived merely as separate elements. A third approach to the schema concept, this time in cognitive psychology, is best understood in contrast to early traditions in memory research. Traditional "associationist" models viewed memory as built up entirely from simple links or associations between pairs of impoverished stimuli such as nonsense syllables (Ebbinghaus, 1885/1964). In this view, associations are strengthened by repetition (L. R. Peterson & Peterson, 1959). For example, black and white would be elements linked by their frequent contiguity. Traditional associationist models were a basic part of the elemental approach to psychology, as we noted in Chapter 1.

Cognitive schema theories first fully emerged in Bartlett's (1932) work on memory for figures, pictures, and stories. His position was explicitly in opposition to the then-dominant view that knowledge was represented as a collection of isolated elements (see W. F. Brewer & Nakamura, 1984; Hastie, 1981; Markus & Zajonc, 1985, for historical overviews). He was attempting to describe how people organize past experience and behavior into patterns that facilitate subsequent understanding and behavior. Bartlett's theory did not catch on until 40 years later, but then it received a real welcome. Taking up Bartlett's ideas, modern cognitive schema theories attempt to explain how people understand and remember complex material by drawing on abstracted general knowledge about how the world works. It was difficult for traditional associationist theories to explain how people went beyond the information given, without the generic prior knowledge proposed by such schema theories.[1]

The role of such expectations, generalizations, and inferences is intuitively clear. Consider the following passage:

> Nancy woke up feeling sick again and she wondered if she really were pregnant. How would she tell the professor she had been seeing? And the money was another problem. . . .
>
> Nancy went to the doctor. She arrived at the office and checked in with the receptionist. She went to see the nurse who went through the usual procedures. Then Nancy stepped on the scale and the nurse recorded her weight. The doctor entered the room and examined the results. He smiled at Nancy and said: "Well, it seems my expectations have been confirmed." When the examination was finished, Nancy left the office. . . .
>
> Nancy arrived at the lecture hall and decided to sit in the front row. She walked down the aisle and sat down in the seat. The professor went to the podium and began the lecture immediately. All through the talk, Nancy couldn't concentrate on what was being said. The talk seemed especially long, but finally the speaker finished. The professor was surrounded with people so Nancy quickly left the building. (Owens, Bower, & Black, 1979, p. 189)

As one reads the story, the meaning of certain events seems self-evident: the usual procedures at the doctor's office, the doctor's smile and confirmed expectations, why she has difficulty concentrating during the lecture, and why she cannot possibly talk to the professor with all those other people around.

Now consider the same story with a different opening paragraph and a different name for the main character:

> Jack woke up wondering how much weight he'd gained so far. His football coach had told him he would start in the game Saturday only if he gained enough weight and got a passing grade on his chemistry test. (Now reread the story, from the doctor visit onward, substituting Jack for Nancy and he for she.)

Suddenly, the meaning of the "usual procedures" is completely different, as are the nature of the doctor's sympathetic reactions, the reason for fidgeting through the lecture, and the motivation for speaking to the professor alone. Our prior knowledge on the one hand, about unwanted pregnancy and perhaps sexual harassment on campus, or on the other hand, about college sports and academic standards, guides

---

[1]Newer associationist models are far more complex (J. R. Anderson & Bower, 1973; A. M. Collins & Quillain, 1972; Rumelhart, Lindsay, & Norman, 1972), in part so they can account for some of the findings from schema research (J. R. Anderson, 1982; Alba & Hasher, 1983; Reder & Anderson, 1980).

our ability to link the events into a coherent story, to fill in the gaps, and to remember the passage afterward.

Cognitive psychologists have demonstrated the impact of schemas by examining the quantity and accuracy of people's memory, which is superior whenever people are given an appropriate organizing theme as compared to when they are not (e.g., Bransford & Franks, 1971; Bransford & Johnson, 1972). People can also recognize events from the story faster when they apply a schema (e.g., E. E. Smith, Adams, & Schorr, 1978). And they especially remember schema-relevant details more than irrelevant details (e.g., R. C. Anderson & Pichert, 1978; Pichert & Anderson, 1977). In understanding a story, people construct a coherent summary of its gist, in effect a story schema (Kintsch & van Dijk, 1978).

To summarize, in cognitive psychology, the schema concept developed in reaction to early research on memory, in order to explain people's understanding and memory for complex materials, such as text passages. It has proved useful to social psychologists looking for explicit models of cognitive structure and process.

WHAT AND HOW DO PEOPLE CATEGORIZE?

Before you can apply schematic prior knowledge to social perception, you have to classify the person or situation as fitting a familiar category. Once you recognize someone as filling a particular role (e.g., gas station attendant) on the basis of particular attributes (probably male, maybe wearing a jump suit, maybe with an oily rag in pocket, maybe approaching your car, perhaps helping others get gas), then you can apply your knowledge about the role to guide the subsequent interaction (this person can help you with your car). The issue is how to identify things and people as members of one category, similar to others in that category and different from members of other categories, and how categorization is functional. You cannot apply a schema without first having categorized the stimulus, and the process of categorization itself is of considerable interest.

Basic Principles

As an example of the problem: How would you classify something as a game? What are its defining attributes? Perhaps you would answer: A game is played for fun. (Yes, but if someone is bored, does that mean it is no longer a game?) A game has rules. (Yes, but so does a meeting; is that a game? And rolling down a grassy hill might be considered a game, but where are the rules?) A game has no external purpose. (Yes, but what about the Olympic Games and international good will? What about the war games that soldiers play for training?) A game involves people together. (Yes, but what about solitaire?) The example could continue, but the point is that natural categories—such as *game, chair, gas station attendant, extravert*—do not seem to have necessary and sufficient defining attributes. The common-sense view and the classical view had been that one could precisely define the boundaries of everyday categories (E. E. Smith & Medin, 1981), just as one imagines being able to do in science or mathematics (although even there, the classical assumption is questioned). On closer examination, this proves not possible. Building on principles first noted by Wittgenstein (1953), several principles derived in cognitive psychology (Mervis & Rosch, 1981; Rosch, 1978, 1987) and social-personality psychology (N. Cantor & Mischel, 1979) describe how people categorize things, situations, and other people.

One core notion is that natural categories do not have necessary and sufficient attributes. Instead, the category members fall within fuzzy boundaries, so it is not always clear which instances belong in the category; that is, Monopoly, baseball, and charades are good examples of the category "games," but what about playing house, torturing ants, and betting on the Superbowl? The perception that some instances are more typical than others led to the idea that instances range from being quite typical to atypical, with a most typical or prototypical instance best representing the category. The prototype is the "central tendency" or average of the category members.[2]

People may never actually encounter their prototypes in real life because they are abstracted from experiences with examples. Even though none of the instances may itself be a perfect prototype, people abstract out the most typical or average features (Hayes-Roth & Hayes-Roth, 1977; Posner & Keele, 1968, 1970; Reed, 1972). People then decide if a new instance fits the category by assessing its similarity to the prototype.

In this view, category members are related by the criterion of family resemblance. Any given pair of category members will share some features with each other and other features with other category members. For example, twenty questions and baseball both include a certain number of turns (the 20 questions or the nine innings), while tag and Monopoly do not. On the other hand, twenty questions and tag are both played without specific equipment, while baseball and Monopoly both require specialized equipment. The more features an instance shares with other category members, the more consistently, consensually, and

---

[2]This central tendency could, of course, come from the arithmetic mean or mode, depending on whether the particular dimension is continuous (e.g., height) or discrete (color).

quickly it is identified as a category member (McCloskey & Glucksberg, 1978; E. E. Smith, Shoben, & Rips, 1974; Rosch, 1978). Thus, any given feature is not necessarily present in all category members, only more or less probably so. The point is that the internal structure of categories is more fluid than the classical view would have it, and that it can be well described as a fuzzy set centering around a prototype.

Moving from within-category to between-category structure, categories are thought to be organized hierarchically, at varying levels of inclusion. That is, under the broad category "entertainment," one might include (at least) *games, parties, television, books,* and *movies.* Under each of these subcategories, one would have several more subordinate categories, such as *car games, board games, outdoor games.* Different levels of categorization are useful for different purposes (Rosch et al., 1976). For example, people propose "let's play a game" or "let's go to a movie" (intermediate level) more often than the generic "let's have some entertainment" and more often than the specific "let's play a car game." In this view, such "basic-level" or intermediate categories for objects are rich in the attributes people associate with them, are easily distinguished from related categories, and involve well-practiced everyday behaviors.

Applications to Social Perception

Just as we categorize different kinds of things and activities, so we also categorize different kinds of people, often according to their personalities. When people are exposed to another person's prototypically extraverted attributes, such as being energetic, entertaining, and friendly, people later may be unsure that they did *not* also see other prototypical attributes, such as outgoing and lively (N. Cantor & Mischel, 1977; Tsujimoto, 1978). In effect, people seem to extract a trait prototype from exposure to category-consistent information. Social categories thus may be viewed as fuzzy sets centering on a prototype.

Social categories have been viewed as being hierarchically organized, with categories becoming more inclusive as they become broader (N. Cantor & Mischel, 1979); that is, people can list more instances and more attributes that go with broader categories (Goldberg, 1986; Hampson, Goldberg, & John, 1987). In a strict *class-inclusion hierarchy,* attributes are inherited from upper levels to lower levels, so that a zealous, committed person's attributes (e.g., single-mindedness) are also true of a more specific religious devotee, whose attributes are also true of a Buddhist monk (see Fig. 4.2). The converse, of course, is not true; a Buddhist monk may have many specific attributes (e.g., a shaved head) not true of religious devotees in general or of committed people in general. Various social categories have been usefully viewed as hier-

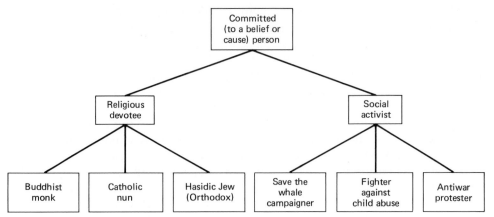

FIGURE 4.2 Hierarchy of categories for the committed person. (After N. Cantor & Mischel, 1979.)

archies. Besides hierarchies of persons, people's scripts for common events (going on a date) may be arranged by upper-level acts (e.g., they meet for the first time) and lower-level scenes (they discuss common interests; they plan a date) (Abelson, 1981b; Pryor & Merluzzi, 1985; Wyer & Gordon, 1984; Wyer et al., 1985). Similarly, people's categories for their own current behavior appear to operate hierarchically (from the higher level of an action's purpose to the lower levels of an action's operation; Vallacher & Wegner, 1987). And even people's political views may be arranged in a hierarchy (from general values to specific attitudes; Sears, Huddie, & Schaffer, 1986).

If people do use social prototypes, what is the most useful kind, suited for everyday use? Although person categories operate at varying levels of inclusiveness, just as object categories do (see Fig. 4.2), they apparently have a most common, basic level. For example, one basic-level person category might be religious devotee, under the general category "committed person," over the more specific categories of "Buddhist monk," "Catholic nun," and "Hasidic Jew" (N. Cantor & Mischel, 1977, 1979). As in object categories, the basic-level person category is simultaneously rich in associations, differentiated from similar categories, and concrete in its application.

Not surprisingly, we also categorize social situations (e.g., ceremonies, including graduations, weddings, funerals, each with its own subordinate categories), and the results are similar to object and person categories (Schutte, Kenrick, & Sadalla, 1985). How are person and situation categories related? The prototypical member of a social category (e.g., "religious devotee") exhibits the typical attributes (e.g., prays a lot) with particular intensity and consistency in the appropriate situations. Because people belong to multiple categories and because people vary their behavior to fit different contexts, the most useful everyday way to categorize people may be a compound person-in-situation episode (N. Cantor & Kihlstrom, 1987; N. Cantor, Mischel, & Schwartz, 1982a, 1982b). That is, one can most easily imagine a religious devotee in specific situations—at a worship service, visiting a shrine, or working in charity—rather than merely in the abstract.

Such rich, consensual prototypes may also help us in everyday decision making. That is, to decide which dorm or major or job to choose, you can consider your prototypic self and your prototype of people who choose that situation, and assess the degree of match. If you are reduced to a heap of giggles or a slough of despond at that image of self compared to the typical person in that dorm, major, or job, it is probably best to turn elsewhere. Certain people are most likely to use this type of decision-making strategy: those especially attuned to their "true selves" (those termed low self-monitors, M. Snyder, 1979; see Chapter 12), those whose goals are social and personal rather than practical, and people who are generally uncomfortable across social situations (N. Cantor, Mackie, & Lord, 1984; Niedenthal, Cantor, & Kihlstrom, 1985).

Categories and prototypes also help people to decide what is important in forming impressions of other people. Attributes perceived as diagnostic of category membership influence impressions most heavily. The informativeness of a particular cue comes from its ability to distinguish between different categories. For example, negative and extreme behaviors are perceived to be particularly diagnostic, so this is one way to explain why they carry particular weight in people's impressions of each other (Skowronski & Carlston, 1987; 1989; see Chapter 7 for others). Some behaviors—such as threatening murder to extort money, getting lost in your own house, refusing a two-million-dollar bribe, or getting three Yale Ph.D.s in four years—are so extreme that they are seen as "perfectly diagnostic" of their respective categories (dishonesty, stupidity, honesty, intelligence) (Skowronski & Carlston, 1990). The diagnosticity of negative behaviors holds for individuals and tightly knit groups, for which one's schematic expectations hold, but not for loose aggregates of people, for which schematic expectations are less relevant (Coovert & Reeder, 1990; cf. Reeder & Coovert, 1986).

Critiques and Extensions

Because the prototype approach has included some of the most widely cited work in social cognition, its assumptions have been closely examined, modifying the neat outlines of the original proposal, in several respects. First, people may not represent categories only in terms of prototypes. One modification of the basic approach suggests that social categories are more often represented by ideals or extremes (Barsalou, 1985; Chaplin, John, & Goldberg, 1988). That is, the best example of a nun may in fact be the ideal nun, rather than an average nun. In this view, ideals are especially likely to be used for goal-oriented categories, that is categories with a particular purpose intrinsic to them, in which the best example is one that most completely fulfills the category's goal. It may also be that people have separate representations of the best category member and the average category member; if you ask "could you suggest the best example of a local restaurant?" my interpretation of the question may lead to my recommending either the best restaurant or the most typical (not at all the same!).

A more drastic critique of prototypes rejects altogether the idea of a summary representation (ideal *or* typical), arguing that categories are represented as a collection of exemplars previously encountered. As it is rather a strong critique, we will discuss this perspective later. For now, the point is that prototypes may not be the only way that categories are stored.

Second, recall that the basic or intermediate levels of nonsocial categories apparently dominate people's everyday usage; the same may not be so true for social categories (Holyoak & Gordon, 1984). In using social categories, people's specific goals and expertise most likely determine which levels they choose to use (N. Cantor & Kihlstrom, 1987; Hampson, John, & Goldberg, 1986). This raises the further possibility that goals and expertise also determine people's choice of levels in nonsocial categories. In both social and nonsocial categories, however, some (basic) levels may function as default options, all else being equal.

A third issue is the extent to which social categories form a clear hierarchy, with higher levels subsuming lower levels. Many social categories are not so neat, representing a fuzzy hierarchy in which class inclusions do not work strictly. For example, some data indicate that being stingy (lower level) is clearly one specific way of being unkind (upper level), which would fit a hierarchy, but not all traits are structured so neatly. Subjects report that being passive (more concrete, lower level) is not necessarily one specific way of being introverted (more abstract, upper level). Accordingly, the vertical connections between upper and lower levels are not always clear-cut (Hampson, John, & Goldberg, 1986). Moreover, for some categories such as gender, the upper levels (male) do not provide richer associations than do the lower levels (the stereotypic businessman) (Deaux et al., 1985), contrary to hierarchical predictions.

Perhaps the hierarchy notion needs to be discarded altogether; people may not think in hierarchies at all, except when psychologists constrain them to do so. People actually make associations in complex networks that resemble a tangled web rather than a hierarchy (N. Cantor & Kihlstrom, 1987). Imagine a neat hierarchy, from extravert at the top level, to politician, comedian, and bully at the intermediate level, with specific attributes (socially skilled, self-confident) at the lowest level. In a strict hierarchy, of course, some attributes are true of the super-ordinate level and they are inherited by each of the lower levels. However, some data indicate that people's associations are not so neat (Andersen & Klatzky, 1987; see Fig. 4.3). Attributes perceived to hold for the top-level category (e.g., extraverts are self-confident) do not always hold for all the intermediate-level categories (politicians are self-confident, but comedians and bullies are not). Moreover, some intermediate-level categories (bullies) are associated with other intermediate-level categories (politicians) but not with the overarching category (extravert). The overlapping nature of social categories differentiates them from object categories (Lingle, Altom, & Medin, 1984), at least as nonsocial categories have been studied so far.

To summarize, the prototype approach has introduced several ideas, namely, that social categories do not have rigid boundaries but rather operate as fuzzy sets, organized around a prototypical or average category member, against which other members are judged for typicality, so that category members are related by family resemblance rather than by necessary and sufficient rules for inclusion. However, some social categories may be organized around ideal or extreme cases, rather than prototypes. The prototype approach originally proposed that social categories are arranged hierarchically, with a most useful intermediate level functioning as basic. But organization in terms of hierarchies

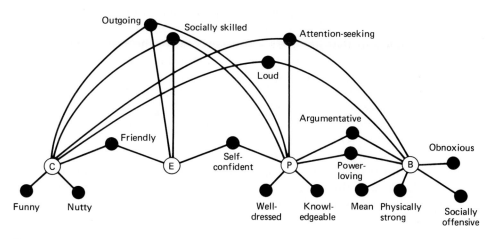

FIGURE 4.3 Tangled web of trait category (extravert) and three social stereotypes: comedian, politician, bully. (After Andersen & Klatzky, 1987.)

and basic levels has been questioned, suggesting that social categories are related in more flexible and complex ways.[3]

Social categories seem to be messier than nonsocial categories, at least according to current research on nonsocial categories. Of course, it is possible that nonsocial categories are messier than indicated by existing research, and that cognitive psychologists will borrow back from social cognition researchers some insights about loose hierarchies in tangled webs. But assuming that social categories do prove to be less neat and well-ordered than nonsocial categories, why might this be the case? If people are indeed more variable, changeable, complex, subtle, and uncontrollable than objects, as enumerated in Chapter 1, then it makes sense for social categories to be more flexible than nonsocial categories. Moreover, social perceivers may have more idiosyncratic reactions than do nonsocial perceivers, again limiting the utility of overly rigid category structures. In short, if social categories are messier than nonsocial categories, it is not useless mess.

An Elemental Alternative: Exemplars

Just as the prototype view of categories was developed in reaction to the shortcomings of the classical view, so the exemplar view has developed in reaction to the shortcomings of the prototype view (e.g., Brooks, 1978; Hintzman, 1986; Medin & Schaffer, 1978; J. H. Walker, 1975; see E. E. Smith & Medin, 1981, for a review), and it may be best understood in that light. As a counterpoint to the prototype perspective, the exemplar approach suggests that one remembers separate instances or exemplars one has actually encountered, rather than some average prototype one has abstracted from experience. One has several exemplars for a category and, in this view, people categorize a thing by seeing whether it resembles a lot of remembered exemplars from a single category.

The exemplar view has several advantages. First, it most directly accounts for people's knowledge of specific examples that guide their understanding of the category. To illustrate, if asked whether restaurants typically contain equal numbers of tables for two or tables for larger

---

[3]Besides the criticisms specific to social cognition just discussed, the prototype approach has been criticized on three basic points: (1) people know more about a concept than simply its features, for they also know which features tend to go together; for example, birds that sing tend to be small and to fly, but large birds tend neither to sing nor to fly; (2) people also know the constraints, that there are limits on what features may be posited; for example, one does not posit how many pistons a bird has; and (3) context matters; for example, "bird" in the woods suggests a different sort than "bird" in a nursery school classroom (Lingle, Altom, & Medin, 1984; Murphy & Medin, 1985; E. E. Smith & Medin, 1981).

groups, one may have to consult several specific mental examples of restaurants to answer the question. Or if someone asserts that all restaurants have cashiers, one may retrieve a specific counter-example to refute the statement. This reliance on concrete instances suggests (but of course does not require) the idea of exemplars. (The prototype view does not dispute that people can remember some specific instances.)

More importantly, people know a lot about the possible variation of members within the category, as in the big variety of Chinese restaurants versus the sameness of a particular fast-food chain. A true prototype theory cannot represent information about variability. It is easy to describe people's knowledge of such variation by positing exemplars, although equivalents might be possible within the prototype approach.

Another major advantage of the exemplar view, and probably the best argument for it, is its ability to account for correlations of attributes within a category. For example, people know that within the category "restaurant," formica tables tend to go with paying the cashier directly, while tablecloths tend to go with paying through the server. They know this through their theories about inexpensive, convenience-oriented businesses, as compared to other kinds (Murphy & Medin, 1985). A single summary prototype does not easily handle this knowledge. The knowledge of which attributes tend to be correlated among category members is especially important in social perception, as people have implicit theories about which traits go together (e.g., ambitious and hard-working) and which do not (e.g., ambitious and kind; D. J. Schneider, 1973).

Finally, the exemplar view makes it easier to modify existing categories with new instances. In the exemplar approach, the new instance may be added as yet another exemplar, which will then contribute to subsequent category judgments (Lingle, Altom, & Medin, 1984). In comparison, it is less clear how prototypes are modified, but we will return to this issue later.

Within social cognition, the evidence for exemplars is limited but growing. For example, although not interpreted in terms of exemplars, one series of studies (Gilovich, 1981) showed that people's judgments are affected by irrelevant similarities to specific past examples; a new football player from the same hometown as a famous football player may be considered a good bet, even though hometown is not especially diagnostic of athletic ability. People's political judgments are also shaped by advocates drawing lessons from history, even when the prior example is similar to the current one only in nondiagnostic ways. As another example, people's judgments about a member of a foreign culture are more heavily influenced by the foreigner's irrelevant similarity to a previously encountered exemplar, rather than by general rules they have learned about the culture (Read, 1983, 1984, 1987); if people have causal theories (i.e., that the exemplar somehow influences the new instance), they are even more likely to use the exemplar. And in more everyday settings, people deciding which of two strangers is more approachable will choose the one most superficially similar to another stranger who was recently kind to them (or, conversely, least similar to a recently mean person), without apparently being aware of the reasons for their choice (Lewicki, 1985). Familiarity, that is, similarity to a previously known individual, whether consciously perceived or not, may create a sense of shared attitudes, attraction, predictability, and safety (S. T. Fiske, 1982, pp. 62–66; Genero & Cantor, 1987; G. L. White & Shapiro, 1987). While some of these studies were explicitly based on exemplar models from cognitive psychology and some were not, they all demonstrate the effect of a single concrete prior experience on subsequent judgments and behavior, and as such they provide a counterpoint to studies documenting the influence of more global, abstract categories.

Some more direct discussion of the evidence for exemplars comes from work on the perceived variability of social categories. For example, people perceive increased variability in groups, as their impressions become more differentiated (Linville, Salovey, & Fischer, 1986); as you learn more about a particular group of foreigners through an exchange program, you perceive them to come in more different varieties than you did beforehand (and they view citizens of your country as more variable as well). Linville, Fischer, and Salovey (1989) have explicitly argued that this effect can be best described by exemplar models. Some effects of abstract, category-level information can be explained in terms of pure exemplar models, to show that the abstract representations are not necessary, although they certainly may be involved (E. R. Smith, 1988; see Chapter 8).[4] People do seem to use both abstract and exemplar information when provided; that is, they consider both their generalizations about the other nationality as well as specific citizens they have known. Moreover, when people are first given abstract information, followed by information about specific instances, they perceive less variability and make their judgments based on such prototypes, more than when the order is reversed or when they are given no abstract information (Medin, Altom, & Murphy, 1984; Park & Hastie, 1987; E. R. Smith & Zarate, 1990).

However, the evidence for exemplars is not at all clear-cut. That is, people do understand that some groups are more variable than others, and they use this information, first, in deciding whether to generalize from an individual to the group and, second, in classifying new individuals. This might seem to argue for exemplars, but knowledge about variability does not seem to be based on memory for exemplars (Park & Hastie, 1987). Similarly, people perceive minimal variability in out-

---

[4]One may also reinterpret earlier work on the retrieval of behavioral instances versus global traits as compatible with this view (e.g., Lingle et al., 1979; see Chapter 8).

groups (i.e., groups of which they are not a member), but differences in exemplar frequencies may (Linville, Salovey, & Fischer, 1986; Linville, Fischer, & Salovey, 1989; Ostrom & Sedikides, 1988) or may not (Judd & Park, 1988) be responsible. Research and theory development will clarify the role of exemplars.

One intriguing possibility is that people may be most likely to use exemplars when they are trying to account for something out of the ordinary. Sometimes we need to know whether something that has just happened is normal or not; that is, we need an immediate check on how surprising it was (assuming we do not already have a relevant schema). For example, being involved in an accident makes one think of similar accidents in one's past and of the events leading up to the incident, in order to judge how surprising or avoidable it was, and even how upset to be. An elegant and explicit model of exemplars was recently developed to describe just this process of people's post hoc normality judgments (Kahneman & Miller, 1986). Recall that the category models (and the schema models) focus on anticipation and prediction, based on what seems typical or probable in the future, given one's abstracted prior experience. In contrast, norm theory focuses on post hoc interpretation, based on an encounter with a particular stimulus in a particular context, with the aim of judging whether the stimulus was retrospectively normal or surprising. While category and schema theories describe reasoning forward, this describes reasoning backward. According to norm theory, people consider a particular stimulus in light of exemplars it brings to mind. These exemplars allow one to compare the instance to the sum of the previous experiences to see the degree to which the instance is normal or surprising. One computes this sum on the fly, so it is ad hoc knowledge, rather than explicit prior knowledge. We will return to this particular model in Chapter 9, but for present purposes, norm theory illustrates the uses of exemplars in active judgment processes.

Prototypes or Exemplars: A Resolution?

Although work on exemplars is on the increase, it is already clear that exemplar models will not be sufficient by themselves any more than prototype models have been sufficient by themselves. It seems most likely that people rely on a mixture of representations (cf. M. B. Brewer, 1988a; N. Cantor & Kihlstrom, 1987; J. B. Cohen & Basu, 1987; Lingle, Altom, & Medin, 1984; Linville, Salovey, & Fischer, 1986; Linville, Fischer, & Salovey, 1989; Messick & Mackie, 1989; E. E. Smith & Medin, 1981). People clearly do recall specific instances and use them to classify new instances, but specific instances also give rise to category generalizations that in turn facilitate classification of new instances, so they are using both (Elio & Anderson, 1981). People can rely on direct experi-

ence with exemplars or on previously provided prototypes to classify
new instances, depending on the task and the information available
(Medin, Altom, & Murphy, 1984). Moreover, because use or development of abstract representations depends on the demands of the task,
abstraction of a prototype is not automatic (Whittlesea, 1987). Indeed,
exemplars may be more basic (and therefore more likely to be automatic), because they are used (a) when people's cognitive capacity is
strained, (b) for more complex concepts, and (c) especially by younger
children (Kossan, 1981; cf. Nelson, 1984). Similarly, it has been argued
that people use exemplars and prototypes to represent groups to which
they belong, but only prototypes to represent groups to which they do
not belong and about which they therefore know less (Judd & Park,
1988).

In contrast to the idea that exemplars are relatively basic, some research suggests that exemplars represent elaborated processing. People
may use exemplars to represent both their own and other groups, having more exemplars available for their own group (Linville, Fischer, &
Salovey, 1989). In another proposal, people start out by representing others in pictoliteral (i.e., wholistic, nonverbal) prototypes and then move to
exemplars as they individuate other people (M. B. Brewer, 1988a).

Clearly, people can use either abstract category-level information,
such as prototypes, or they can use instances and memory for exemplars to make categorical judgments. Which people do when is the interesting question at this point (cf. M. B. Brewer, 1988a; Park & Hastie,
1987; Sherman & Corty, 1984, pp. 237–245; E. R. Smith & Zarate, 1990).
Doubtless, which people do when depends on task demands and individual differences; the capacity and the motivation to be accurate or to
focus on individuals would probably encourage exemplar-based processes over prototype-based processes (S. T. Fiske & Neuberg, 1990;
Kruglanski, 1990; Messick & Mackie, 1989).

When all is said and done, what ultimate use are fuzzy concepts
and concrete exemplars in loose hierarchies in tangled webs? N. Cantor
and Kihlstrom (1987) argue that this framework (a) captures the social
perceiver's need to represent both the gist of a category and its variability, allowing an economical, functional core representation, as well as
acknowledging the variability of instances within the category, and (b)
describes the multiple paths people need in responding flexibly to the
fluidity of social interaction.

WHAT IS CONTAINED IN OUR SCHEMAS?

Social schema research picks up where categorization research leaves
off, although the boundary here too is fuzzy. In its essence, categorization research is more concerned with the classification of instances,

while schema research is more concerned with the application of organized generic prior knowledge to the understanding of new information.

A Note on Schemas versus Prototypes

The specific notions of prototypes and schemas are often used by social cognition researchers as if the terms were interchangeable. For some purposes they may be, but it is useful to define the differences. Prototypes resemble instances and many conceptions of exemplars, in that all their known attributes are filled in, even if all the attributes are not directly relevant to category membership (J. R. Anderson, 1980b, 1990). The prototypic extrovert comes with a particular face and body type, even if actual category members vary so much on these dimensions that they are meaningless for classification. Nevertheless, the prototype specifies all the particular features. For example, the most prototypic category members are used to draw inferences about the category as a whole, even for features that are irrelevant to their prototypicality (Rothbart & Lewis, 1988). The schema concept raises the alternative possibility that some features may be ignored, if they are not meaningfully associated with the schema (J. R. Anderson, 1980a). Although one *could* generate a "typical" face and body for an extravert, the schema concept implies that these features are not usually stored with the abstract knowledge more relevant to being an extravert.

In addition, prototypes are usually described as unorganized lists of features, while schemas are described as having internal organization, namely, links specifying the relations between attributes (Wyer & Gordon, 1984). Thus, because a schema is more organized and because many features are left unspecified, it could be a more flexible and efficient representation than is a prototype, given that the schema contains fewer but more focal and more organized details (cf. J. Mandler, 1979). For most purposes of social cognition, however, the overlap between schemas and prototypes is more important than these representational differences; the bigger issue is how abstract representations guide encounters with new instances.

Types of Social Schemas

Social schema research has generated various typologies of schemas, but we will illustrate a few central types of these generic knowledge structures (S. E. Taylor & Crocker, 1981). All types serve similar functions, for they all influence the encoding (interpreting and taking in) of new information, memory for old information, and inferences about missing information. We will briefly describe some types. Then, in the remainder of this chapter and in the next, we will discuss the functions of schemas, as well as puzzles posed by the research.

Person schemas. Person schemas contain people's understanding of the psychology of particular individuals, focusing on their traits and goals. We have already discussed the importance of trait categories in classifying extraverts, religious devotees, and the like. We also examined the impact of person-in-situation episodes. Schemas about people and people-in-situations aid in encoding, memory, and inferences about individual people.

Another kind of person schema is a goal schema, and it merits an example, as we have not discussed it before. Consider the following scenario that was used in one study. Subjects were shown a skit in which a student had the goal of enrolling in classes to complete the requirements for his major. Some subjects were told the student's major was chemistry; others were told his major was music; still others were told his major was psychology. The student dropped his books and papers upon entering the room, picked them up, and then tried to register for several classes. When told the student's goal was to complete a major in music, subjects recalled more music-related items, such as the Beethoven sheet music he had dropped and the music classes he wanted. When subjects thought his major was psychology, they recalled psychology-related items, and when they thought it was chemistry, they recalled chemistry-related items (Zadny & Gerard, 1974). Thus, people recalled schema-consistent information (cf. R. C. Anderson & Pichert, 1978; Owens, Bower, & Black, 1979). Just as we earlier saw the effects of person schemas on the processes of categorizing new information, here and in the remainder of this chapter, we see their effects on the processes of understanding new information.

Self-schemas. How outgoing do you consider yourself to be? How hard-working are you? How honest? How dependent? Perhaps you have immediate, confident answers for some traits and slower, less confident answers for others. Trait dimensions along which we have clear self-conceptions are those on which we are *self-schematic*, while dimensions along which we are less clear are those on which we are *aschematic* (Markus, 1977). Applying the schema idea to oneself suggests that we manage information about ourselves in some ways that are similar to how we manage information about other people. Of course there are important differences too, but the idea of a self-schema suggests that our encoding, memory, and inferences about information pertinent to ourselves will be influenced by our generic self-knowledge. We will delay a discussion of self-schemas until Chapter 6.

Role schemas. A social role is the set of behaviors expected of a person in a particular social position, so a role schema is the cognitive structure that organizes one's knowledge about those appropriate behaviors. Role schemas function as do other kinds of schemas, to influence people's understanding of schema-relevant information. There are *achieved roles* that one acquires by effort and intent (job, sports team membership, club membership, special training). For example, a doctor has an achieved role that entails diagnosing and treating disease; as such, a doctor asks you in detail about your symptoms, conducts tests, and prescribes drugs. A doctor is supposed to behave in a warm but professional manner. A doctor has about the only role (except for a movie director) that can ask strangers to disrobe on demand.

There are also *ascribed roles* that one acquires at birth or automatically (age, race, sex). Each of these characteristics carries certain role-based expectations for behavior; these may be organized in other people's minds as schemas. Role schemas based on such ascribed roles are one plausible way to account for stereotyping. As we will see, stereotypes are "nouns that cut slices"; they are the cognitive culprits in prejudice and discrimination (Allport, 1954; Pettigrew, 1979). One can think about stereotypes as a particular kind of role schema that organizes people's expectations about other people who fall into certain social categories. Partly because of their implications for real-world issues such as stereotyping and partly because of social psychology's tradition of studying stereotyping, role schemas have been studied extensively, as we shall see.

Event schemas or scripts. In addition to person, self-, and role schemas, there are event schemas or scripts that describe appropriate sequences of events in well-known situations (Abelson, 1981b; Schank & Abelson, 1977). For example, many people in a given culture share expectations about what happens in a restaurant, at a sports event, on a job interview, and the like. Event schemas point out the effects of schemas on activity, such as complex sequences of behavior, typical procedures for getting things done, and so on. Consider the following example: "John was seated in the restaurant. He looked over the menu and decided to order lobster. Later, when he had paid his waiter, he left immediately." This is a standard sequence of events for a restaurant meal. The script comprises several sequential steps common to eating in most restaurants (sitting down, looking at the menu, ordering, etc.). Scripts contain props (such as the menu), roles (such as the waiter), and sequence rules (such as reading the menu before ordering).

To appreciate the importance of scripts, imagine seeing a movie of the following actual native American folktale. The hero participates in a battle, is shot with an arrow, but feels nothing; his allies turn out to be ghosts, and he returns home; he tells the story, a black thing comes out of his mouth, and he dies at sunrise. In trying to understand, remember, and flesh out this story, people who are not native Americans may have difficulty making sense of the story because it does not fit their event schemas for what happens in stories. In contrast, a native American knowledgeable about such traditions might understand that the hero did not feel the arrow because he was in the company of ghosts and beyond normal pain, and that the black thing coming out of his mouth was his departing soul. Different cultures supply people with different schemas for a good story, and these event schemas guide encoding, memory, and inference (Bartlett, 1932; Black, Galambos, & Read, 1984; Kintsch & van Dijk, 1978; Perrig & Kintsch, 1985). Without the right schema, it is difficult to make sense of what happened, but with the right schema, one can recall easily; for example, without looking back, what did John eat at the restaurant? (If you answer "lobster," your restaurant script perhaps made you assume, quite reasonably, that if he ordered and paid for it, he must also have eaten it. But we never actually said that he *ate* the lobster. That was your schema at work.)

Scripts are not limited to restaurants and folktales, for people seem to have scripts for events as varied as illness (Lau & Hartman, 1983; Meyer, Leventhal & Gutmann, 1985), persuasion (Rule, Bisanz, & Kohn, 1985), and nuclear war (S. T. Fiske, Pratto, & Pavelchak, 1983). Regardless of the particular script, they all serve to organize people's expectations regarding a likely sequence of events.

Content-free schemas. Besides person schemas, self-schemas, role schemas, and event schemas, there are types that operate like a processing rule, which specifies the links among elements but not much rich informational content. One such schema is the balance schema, already discussed as precedent-setting for current schema research.

In addition, a linear-ordering schema (Tsujimoto, Wilde, & Robertson, 1978) organizes transitive, hierarchical relationships. Size, weight, speed, and other attributes fit into a transitive relationship that may be viewed as a content-free schema. For example, suppose Geoff bats better than Edward, who bats better than Susan, then Geoff bats better than Susan. The schema is impoverished in content, for it only specifies a rule (i.e., transitivity) that links the elements. As another example, chains of authority in organizations fit linear-ordering schemas. Linear-ordering schemas are widely applicable in social settings (DeSoto, 1961; DeSoto, London, & Handel, 1965; T. B. Rogers, Kuiper, & Rogers, 1979) and in nonsocial settings (Potts, 1974; Holyoak & Patterson, 1981).

A causal schema (Kelley, 1972b), discussed in Chapter 2 as a part of attribution theory, is another example that resembles a content-free rule more than a rich knowledge structure (S. E. Taylor & Crocker, 1981, discuss others).

Comment. These particular different types of schemas are in some sense arbitrary, for other typologies are also plausible (e.g., Hastie, 1981), and this one leaves out some possible types of schemas. To name just one other kind, people seem to have "place schemas" (i.e., for particular kinds of locations, W. F. Brewer & Treyens, 1981), and one could easily generate others; people can have schemas for just about anything. Moreover, different types of schemas overlap considerably: both person schemas (for traits, person-in-situation, and goals) and role schemas (for social groupings) refer to expected behaviors. And role schemas refer to person schemas, as when a group stereotype specifies expected personality traits. Nevertheless, the distinctions among schemas for individual persons, oneself, social groups, and events remind us of the variety of general knowledge we bring to everyday experiences, and each type operates in similar ways.

WHAT DO SCHEMAS DO?

So far, we have examined how people categorize instances, in order to apply their schemas, and we have examined what kinds of schemas there might be. It is high time we described schematic effects on social cognition: that is, what do schemas do? Schemas influence the encoding of new information, memory for old information, and inferences where information is missing. These effects of schemas illustrate the interplay between organized prior knowledge and the data at hand. Most of our research examples in the following pages come from work on role schemas or stereotypes, as that has been the most active area of research, but the principles generally apply across different types of schemas.

Encoding

People often cue schemas from *visually prominent physical features*. Features indicating race, sex, and the like allow people to sort other people into categories more rapidly than they could otherwise (McCann et al., 1985). Because they are physically perceptible and culturally meaningful, age and sex may be universal dimensions for differentiating people (M. B. Brewer, 1988a). Indeed, physical features may have priority over other features of social schemas (Deaux & Lewis, 1984; cf. Ashmore & Del Boca, 1979; M. B. Brewer & Lui, 1989), and certain physical characteristics may act almost like schematic labels. For example, once a person is categorized as black or white, male or female, young or old, the stereotypic content of the schema is likely to apply regardless of how much or how little the person looks like the typical category member

(Secord, 1959; Secord, Bevan & Katz, 1956). The same is probably true of more specialized categories or subtypes, such as housewife, career woman, middle-class black, or elder statesman.

Once cued, schemas affect how quickly we perceive, what we notice, how we interpret what we notice, and what we perceive as similar and different. Thus, another principle of schematic encoding is its operation from the *earliest moments of perception*. People instantly use age, race, sex, attractiveness, job titles, and prior trait descriptions ("You'll like her; she's very funny") to form impressions. For example, if you expect to meet an "athlete" or a "farmer," you can actually react to stereotypic athletic or farm faces faster than others, within the first fraction of a second; if there is a mismatch between expectations and faces, one is even more dramatically slowed down in reacting (Klatzky, Martin, & Kane, 1982). Similarly, white subjects recognized positive stereotypic words ("smart," "ambitious," "clean") faster when they were preceded by "whites" than by "blacks" (Gaertner & McLaughlin, 1983). White subjects were faster to respond that negative or stereotypic traits "could ever be true of" blacks and similarly that positive or stereotypic traits "could ever be true of" whites than the reverse (Dovidio, Evans, & Tyler, 1986). This suggests that, whether or not they believed the stereotypes to be true, those traits were closely linked in their minds. Indeed, fairly automatic stereotypic reactions to race categories are equally characteristic of high and low prejudice people (perhaps by virtue of both living with the culture's stereotypes); what differs is that, under normal circumstances that allow controlled processing, low-prejudice people may actively reject the automatic stereotypic responses and replace them with equality-oriented thoughts (Devine, 1989).

At present, the point is that categorizing and labeling makes the person seem even more like other category members than would otherwise be true. When a bigot says, "Oh them. They're all alike," the person is *minimizing the variability* within the group. This is likely to mean the person will have trouble telling the group members apart (Malpass & Kravitz, 1969; Malpass, Lavigueur, & Weldon, 1973); this is an unpleasant but common experience for those treated as interchangeable, usually people who form a minority in a particular setting. Nor does it only take a bigot to misperceive members of a given group as all alike. Simply categorizing people into groups minimizes within-group variability and maximizes between-group differences (Capozza & Nanni, 1986; McGarty & Penny, 1988; Tajfel, Sheikh, & Gardner, 1964; Tajfel & Wilkes, 1963; Wilder, 1978b, 1981). People are particularly sensitive to new information that enhances between-group differences (Krueger, Rothbart, & Sriram, 1989). Although people are sensitive to actual differences in variability within groups, they also perceive a group as less variable when they receive a schematic label for the group before learning about its members rather than after, indicating that schemas can reduce perceived variability (Park & Hastie, 1987). Moreover, people appear to "calculate" variability as a natural part of forming impressions, rather than from memory only as a specific need arises. Variability thus can be an integral part of schemas.

People especially perceive themselves and their own group to be different from the other group (Allen & Wilder, 1979), and they seek information that confirms this perception (Wilder & Allen, 1978). Categorization's effect of reducing perceived variability is even stronger when people are considering groups to which they do not belong. A group of outsiders (an outgroup) appears less variable than one's own group (ingroup). This *outgroup homogeneity* effect occurs regardless of whether the group is students at a neighboring college, members of another profession, or people who prefer the modern painter Klee when one prefers Kandinsky (Doise, Deschamps, & Meyer, 1978; Goethals, Allison, & Frost, 1979; Linville, Salovey, & Fischer, 1986; Linville, Fischer, & Salovey, 1989; E. E. Jones, Wood, & Quattrone, 1981; Judd & Park, 1988; Park & Rothbart, 1982; Quattrone, 1986; Quattrone & Jones, 1980; Rothbart, Dawes, & Park, 1984; Wilder, 1986, 1984b). Minimizing the variability of members within an outgroup means that they are not being recognized as distinct individuals as much as they would be if they were perceived as ingroup members. Across studies, the outgroup homogeneity effect is larger and more reliable than the ingroup heterogeneity effect, and it is even stronger for preexisting, real-world groups than for artificially created laboratory groups (Mullen & Hu, 1989). Perceiving the outgroup as relatively less variable may serve to make them seem more predictable, even as individuals (Nisbett et al., 1983; Quattrone & Jones, 1980).[5]

People not only perceive outgroup members as less variable than ingroup members, they also have *less complex conceptualizations* of them. For example, young people think about old people along fewer dimensions than they do other young people, and the same is true across racial groupings (Linville, 1982b; Linville & Jones, 1980). Once a person is categorized, the person often becomes just another example of the relevant schema. If the person fits an outgroup schema, the fit is seen as particularly tight, because outgroup schemas are less variable and less complex than ingroup schemas.

In addition to variability and complexity, categorizing someone as an instance of the schema slants encoding of the content of what the person does. One child taking an eraser from another may be seen as mean and threatening if black, but not so if white (S. L. Duncan, 1976;

---

[5]The one exception may occur when the ingroup forms a minority within the society; to preserve a sense of group cohesion, the *ingroup* may be seen as more homogeneous, relative to the majority group and other minority groups (B. Simon & Brown, 1987).

Sagar & Schofield, 1980). A colleague being sarcastic may be seen as spiteful if female but cynical if male (S. E. Taylor et al., 1978; cf. V. Brown & Geis, 1984). A normal person may seem maladjusted simply by virtue of the label "mental patient" (e.g., Langer & Abelson, 1974). *Stereotypic perceptions* thus can occur even when the same behavior is performed by members of different categories. In one study, a child was identified as well-off or poor, according to social class cues provided by her home, school, and playground. When she then performed ambiguously on a test, she was perceived as more able if wealthy (Darley & Gross, 1983). Similarly, once having categorized a person as being suited to a particular job, one subsequently judges the person on that basis, rather than based on the person's previously provided attributes (Lingle & Ostrom, 1979; cf. Carlston, 1980b; Hoffman, 1985; McCann & Hancock, 1983; Wyer, Srull, & Gordon, 1984). In summary, numerous studies attest to the stereotypic content of perception based on gender, race, ethnicity, social class, age, physical attractiveness, and mental health (A. G. Miller, 1982).

So far, it might seem that the force of people's social schemas would prevent them from perceiving the actual person or situation confronting them. But people are in fact attentive to information inconsistent with their schemas (J. D. White & Carlston, 1983); for example, people *take longer to encode inconsistent information* (Belmore, 1987; M. B. Brewer, Dull, & Lui, 1981; Burnstein & Schul, 1982, 1983; S. T. Fiske & Neuberg, 1990; S. T. Fiske & Pavelchak, 1986; Hemsley & Marmurek, 1982; Jamieson & Zanna, 1989; Stern et al., 1984). Inconsistent information requires more time and capacity to assimilate (Bargh & Thein, 1985; Hastie & Kumar, 1979; Sentis & Burnstein, 1979; Srull, 1981; Srull, Lichtenstein, & Rothbart, 1985, but see Hashtroudi et al., 1984) and apparently generates more fine-grained attention (Wilder, 1984a, cited in Wilder, 1986). The less attention people pay to inconsistent information, the more schematic their processing (J. L. Hilton, Klein, & von Hippel, 1991; J. D. White & Carlston, 1983). As we will see, when people are confronted with information that dramatically undercuts their schemas, their memory and judgments indicate that they paid attention. Particularly when the schema is weak or first developing, people do notice and respond to inconsistencies (for reviews, see S. T. Fiske & Neuberg, 1990; Higgins & Bargh, 1987; Ruble & Stangor, 1986). Accordingly, people's encoding processes balance between the biasing effects of schemas and the effects of the data at hand.

Memory

All kinds of schemas shape memory in a schema-relevant direction. To illustrate the importance of schemas to memory, think of a friend's house. Now take a mental tour of the house, with burglary in mind. What details are important? You know that burglary includes looking for expensive, easily disposable items such as televisions, stereos, and jewelry, so that focuses your memory of your friend's house. To see the impact of burglary as a schema, mentally walk again through the friend's house with the goal of possible purchase or rental. Suddenly, the leaking basement and sagging stairs matter more than the TV and the stereo. A shift in schemas allows one to recall details not easily re-called from the other perspective (R. C. Anderson & Pichert, 1978; cf. Owens, Bower, & Black, 1979). This suggests the impact of a schema on memory.

Encoding vs. retrieval. Before cataloging the many effects of schemas on memory—probably the biggest area of their application—it is important to distinguish between encoding effects, just described, and memory effects, as in the burglary example of schema-guided memory. Similar predictions hold for memory and for encoding infor-mation in the first place. If you had actually, rather than mentally, walked through someone's house with burglary in mind, you would have noticed different details at the time, compared to being on a house-hunting tour. Thus, schemas have similar effects on memory when present at initial encoding or later retrieval. For example, person schemas such as traits and goals can be attributed to an individual early in an interaction—as in labeling someone with the trait "outgoing" or as having the goal of being ingratiating—but schemas can also be attrib-uted to a person after interaction. One interesting issue is which effect is stronger. The schemas' effects could be stronger when they affect both how information gets in (initial encoding) and how it is later lo-cated in memory or reconstructed from memory (subsequent retrieval). Alternatively, schematic effects could be equally strong when they af-fect only memory. Some research has pitted the encoding and retrieval effects against each other (see Fig. 4.4). It generally does this by provid-ing schematic structure either before or after subjects encounter ambig-uous stimuli. For example, one set of subjects might watch two people talking and be told beforehand that one person's goal is to obtain a fa-vor from the other, while other subjects would be told afterward. Knowing the person's goal provides a relevant schema at encoding (be-forehand) or at retrieval (afterward).

Effects of providing schematic structure beforehand are typically stronger (Howard & Rothbart, 1980; Rothbart, Evans, & Fulero, 1979; Wyer et al., 1982; Zadny & Gerard, 1974) because the prior framework allows the schema to shape the information that gets encoded into memory in the first place, and it influences how it is retrieved from memory. Reorganizing material already in memory is more difficult, and the effects of providing a schema after the fact are controversial,

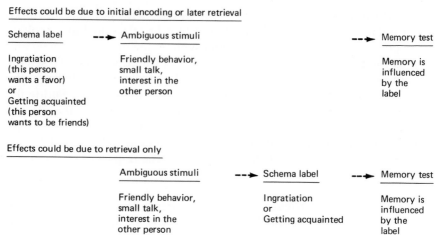

FIGURE 4.4 Two sequences that show schematic effects.

with some obtaining an effect (R. C. Anderson & Pichert, 1978; C. E. Cohen, 1981b; Pyszczynski, LaPrelle, & Greenberg, 1987; M. Synder & Uranowitz, 1978) and others not obtaining an effect (Bellezza & Bower, 1981; Bodenhausen, 1988; L. F. Clark & Woll, 1981; Rothbart, Evans, & Fulero, 1979; Wyer et al., 1982). Even when one does obtain effects at retrieval, it is not always clear whether they reflect the content of people's memory or guessing on the memory test; studies with the appropriate controls heavily implicate guessing as the mechanism in retrieval effects. Overall, it seems fair to conclude that the effects of schemas on memory are strongest when they are invoked ahead of time, so both encoding and retrieval processes are involved.

Categorization effects on memory. People tend to remember schema-relevant information and forget irrelevant information (e.g., Hastie, 1981). Many social schemas are naturally present from the very outset of an interaction, allowing them to affect the encoding of information into memory. Many role schemas, such as age, race, sex, and social class, are invoked by visual cues; other role schemas are customarily provided by labels introduced early ("This is my boss." "This is Jennifer; she's a doctor.") Similarly, person schemas are often provided ahead of time by mutual acquaintances ("Watch out for him; he's pushy." "This is Steve, who wants to find out more about graduate school."). And event schemas are usually labeled ahead of time ("It's going to be an informal cookout."). Providing plausible schemas ahead of time allows people to encode relevant information in terms of the schema, as we have seen, and to organize the material for later reference.

In a group setting, such as a meeting, people apparently use such immediately available cues to "tag" other people's comments by race, sex, and the like; this results subsequently in a likelihood of confusion about *which* woman or *which* black person made a certain comment (S. E. Taylor et al., 1978). Such intracategory errors are increased by redundant categorization (e.g., all the women are teachers, and all the men are students; Arcuri, 1982). They are also correlated with stereotyping those same individuals (C. T. Miller, 1986, 1988), although they are not necessarily correlated with prejudice (S. E. Taylor & Falcone, 1982; but see Walker & Antaki, 1986); thus, one could explain this phenomenon in purely cognitive terms. Sorting people by such superficial cues allows one to remember more about the group as a whole than one would otherwise (McCann et al., 1985), which may explain why people persist in this encoding strategy, despite the inevitable memory confusions it creates.

Memory is also affected by ingroup/outgroup status; for example, blacks and whites have particular trouble making cross-race identifications (Brigham & Malpass, 1985; see Chapter 8). People also recall more details about an ingroup member than an outgroup member (Park & Rothbart, 1982). Moreover, people tend to recall negative things about disliked outgroups (Dutta, Kanungo, & Freibergs, 1972; Higgins & King, 1981; J. W. Howard & Rothbart, 1980; Kanungo & Dutta, 1966). And they tend to recall how the outgroup differs from the ingroup, more than how they are similar (Wilder, 1981). Memory for the outgroup thus tends to support people's stereotypic biases.

Overall, people remember schema-relevant information and tend to forget irrelevant information (e.g., Hastie, 1981). Within schema-relevant information, moreover, one can distinguish consistent and inconsistent information. Under many ordinary circumstances, well-established schemas bias memory toward consistency with one's expectations. Afterward, people report schema-consistent features more than irrelevant ones. For example, in one study, subjects observed a videotape of a woman having a birthday dinner with her husband. If told she worked as a waitress, subjects afterward reported her drinking beer and owning a television. Other subjects watching the same videotape were told she worked as a librarian; they reported her wearing glasses and owning classical records (C. E. Cohen, 1981b). Thus, memory can be focused on consistency by the role schema applied to the person (cf. O'Sullivan & Durso, 1984; Rothbart, Evans, & Fulero, 1979), as also occurs for person schemas (Berman, Read, & Kenny 1983; Cantor & Mischel, 1977; Tsujimoto, 1978; Zadny & Gerard, 1974) and event schemas (Owens, Bower, & Black, 1979).

However, people do not always preferentially remember schema-consistent information (e.g., Hastie & Kumar, 1979; Srull, 1981; Wyer, Bodenhausen, & Srull, 1984). Figuring out when people's memory favors consistent information and when it favors inconsistent information has been a major puzzle in recent years, but some principles are emerging, as follows.

Schematic memory depends on the schema's strength. Schemas that are weak, tentative, or developing seem to make social perceivers especially open to inconsistent information. The development of children's gender schemas shows an initial advantage for remembering *schema-inconsistent* information, with consistent information having an advantage as knowledge increases (Ruble & Stangor, 1986). Parallel patterns are found for schema development in the short-term: When adults are first forming an impression of another person and they are introduced to a few initial personality traits followed by sample behaviors, they focus on inconsistencies. In contrast, when impressions are well-developed and judgments have been made, people are in effect validating their already formed impressions, and they focus on consistencies (Higgins & Bargh, 1987). Finally, when people use relatively well-established categories such as gender and ethnicity, the schema seems to dominate subsequent irrelevancies. However, when people use weak categories such as occupations, majors, or novel groupings ("day people" vs. "night people," or the "typical" child abuser), the schema seems to be weakened by subsequent irrelevancies (S. T. Fiske & Neuberg, 1990). In each case, an impoverished schema alerts perceivers to inconsistent or even irrelevant information, while a well-developed schema focuses perceivers toward consistent information. While these conclusions are based on reconciling findings across studies, providing only indirect but strongly suggestive support, an initial test of the idea within one study is also supportive (Stangor & Ruble, 1989). Similarly, concrete, specific (and perhaps undeveloped) schemas favor inconsistent information, while abstract, general (well-established) schemas do not (Pryor, McDaniel, & Kott-Russo, 1986).

Memory for schema-inconsistent information depends on making connections. People cannot remember what they do not at least minimally notice and consider. Accordingly, it makes sense that schematic memory partially depends on thought. Thought is often induced by surprise. In forming impressions based on traits (person schemas) and behaviors, people remember schema-relevant behavior that is unusual: whether consistent or inconsistent behavior has the *smaller set size* (i.e., which is in the minority) generally determines which is better remembered (Bargh & Thein, 1985; Hemsley & Marmurek, 1982). Of course, inconsistencies by definition are usually in the minority or else they become the dominant theme in the developing impression. Studies that create a smaller set size for schema-consistent information do so by providing a series of trait descriptors at the outset, then having the majority of behaviors inconsistent with the traits, while the minority is consistent. In any event, the underlying principle seems to be that people think about and remember the exceptions.

One of the most important effects of thinking about exceptional behavior is *making links* among elements of a developing impression (Hastie, 1980; Srull & Wyer, 1989; Wyer & Srull, 1986). As people explain the inconsistencies, they make links to other inconsistencies and to consistent information as well, which improves memory for the well-connected inconsistent information. Paradoxically, the presence of inconsistency also improves memory for consistent information, as the impression develops more internal links (O'Sullivan & Durso, 1984; Srull, Lichtenstein, & Rothbart, 1985). Whatever one explains in an impression is then better remembered (Hastie, 1984).

Moreover, people have to be motivated to make sense out of the inconsistency in order to build a coherent impression. Only when people have the explicit goal of *forming an impression,* rather than, say, the goal of remembering the material, does inconsistent information have a memory advantage (Srull, 1981; Srull & Wyer, 1989; Wyer, Bodenhausen, & Srull, 1984; Wyer & Gordon, 1982). (We will have more to say about goals in the next chapter.)

As previously noted, encoding inconsistent information takes more time than encoding schema-consistent information. One way to think about this is that encoding inconsistent information requires creating a compatible niche for it, whereas for consistent information the schema provides a ready-made niche. Because encoding inconsistent information *requires effort,* interfering with this process should reduce memory for inconsistent information; studies indeed show that attention overload does reduce memory for inconsistency (Bargh & Thein, 1985; Srull, 1981).

Because remembering inconsistent information requires effort, those with more cognitive capacity in a particular domain ought to be better able to do so. And, indeed, *experts* and chronics (people for whom a particular trait dimension is habitually accessible) notice and use inconsistent information, while novices and nonchronics do not (Bargh & Thein, 1985; Borgida & DeBono, 1989; S. T. Fiske, Kinder, & Larter, 1983; cf. Srull, Lichtenstein, & Rothbart, 1985). Having the capacity on-line allows one to notice and consider the inconsistent information, which increases memory.

This last point may seem incompatible with one made earlier, namely, that weak schemas encourage memory for inconsistency. The next chapter will discuss schema development in more detail, but for the moment it may be easiest to think of schema development at three stages (cf. Belmore, 1987; Srull, Lichtenstein, & Rothbart, 1985; Stangor & Ruble, 1989): Initially, people do not have much of a schema, so incongruencies may not even be perceived as such. As people form schematic hypotheses, they focus on reconciling inconsistencies and so remember them (the weak schemas noted earlier). Once formed, people attempt to validate their schemas, focusing at this stage on consistent information (the novices and nonchronics above). When schemas are firmly in place, people who are particularly expert have the capacity and so the option to notice and use inconsistent information, in addition to consistent information. In short, it may take some minimal experience for people to notice inconsistencies, and then they tend to focus on the inconsistent material, but when they are validating their schemas, they focus on the consistent material. Experts are more flexible, able to use inconsistent material because of their increased capacity. This is then a curvilinear (U-shaped) pattern, with inconsistent material favored at hypothesis formation and at high levels of expertise, but not in in the middle, at hypothesis validation, when consistent material is better remembered.

Memory for schema-consistent information depends on second thoughts. As people are thinking about their developing impressions, different thoughts lead to different biases. When people *reprocess the expectancy,* that is, explicitly think about the expectancy again, that strengthens memory for it and information consistent with it (O'Sullivan & Durso, 1984; Wyer et al., 1982).

Remembering consistent information also occurs when people think afterward. Musing about one's impression of another individual gives consistent material an advantage over inconsistent material (Wyer & Martin, 1986), a process sometimes called *bolstering* (Srull & Wyer, 1989). After-the-fact thought can easily make impressions more coherent (Tesser, 1978), causing people to reinterpret or forget the inconsistencies if they ultimately have dwelt on the coherent impression to a greater extent. Also, some types of inconsistent information fade over time, as people rely more on the generic schema and less on the particular encounter (Graesser & Nakamura, 1982; D. A. Smith & Graesser, 1981).

One specific way that people resolve inconsistency and do not consider it further, therefore forgetting it, is to *attribute it to situational factors.* If a behavior inconsistent with a schema can be dismissed as due to temporary situational factors, then it may not be remembered (Crocker, Hannah, & Weber, 1983; Kulik, 1983). For example, if a Hispanic person commits the crime of assault or if a Northeastern WASP commits the crime of embezzlement, that may fit some people's stereotypes. In the reverse combination (the Hispanic embezzles or the WASP assaults), the crime may be inconsistent with people's role schemas. However, if the crime could be attributed to transitory situational factors (embezzling committed because of needing cash for his pregnant wife or assault committed because of experiencing extraordinary frustration in his personal life), one might dwell on and recall such mitigating life circumstances (Bodenhausen & Wyer, 1985), thereby downplaying the effect of the inconsistency. In short, when there are ready-made situational attributions, people are more likely to remember consistent information because they can discount the inconsistent material.

Memory for schema-consistent information makes things simple. People are more likely to remember schema-consistent information when they are making *complex* judgments (as suggested by Berman, Read, & Kenny, 1983; for more direct evidence, see Bodenhausen & Wyer, 1985; Bodenhausen & Lichtenstein, 1987).

Having developed a schematic representation of another person by making a judgment about the person, people are subsequently more likely to remember and use information that *fits their own prior judgment* (Carlston, 1980b; Higgins & Rholes, 1978; Lingle et al., 1979; Lingle & Ostrom, 1979; McCann & Hancock, 1983; Wyer, Srull, & Gordon, 1984; but see Futoran & Wyer, 1986).

People tolerate more inconsistency in a group of people than in an individual. As suggested by Rothbart, Evans, and Fulero (1979), exceptions to a group are acceptable, so inconsistent information is not so surprising and therefore not preferentially recalled. Indeed, people are more likely to recall schema-consistent information about a *loosely aligned group,* because the inconsistent material does not attract any notice. People recall inconsistent information about individuals and close-knit groups because the inconsistent material is not tolerated and must be integrated (Stern et al., 1984; Srull, 1981; Srull, Lichtenstein, & Rothbart, 1985; Wyer, Bodenhausen, & Srull, 1984; Wyer & Gordon, 1982; Wyer & Martin, 1986). Similarly, people are more likely to remember inconsistent information if they focus on the individual (Devine & Ostrom, 1985), perhaps because people are so good at making connections that integrate inconsistencies into their impressions of individuals (Asch & Zukier, 1984), which makes the inconsistent material more memorable.

Schema-consistent information also has more of an advantage when the degree of fit is *ambiguous, mixed, weak, or nonevaluative.* When the inconsistency is unambiguous, persistent, strong, or evaluative, then the inconsistent information captures attention and is remembered (Pyszczynski, LaPrelle, & Greenberg, 1987; Srull, Lichtenstein, & Rothbart, 1985; Wyer, Bodenhausen, & Srull, 1984; Wyer & Gordon, 1982).

Summary. The effects of schemas on memory are strongest when the schema is present from the beginning, as many social schemas are, being cued by customary labels or by physical features. Merely categorizing a person or an event can cause confusions within the category, and ingroup members are recalled in more positive terms than outgroup members. People often remember schema-inconsistent information when they are first forming an impression or developing a tentative schema. The inconsistency advantage occurs as people attempt to explain the inconsistency, making links to other features of their developing impression. If they do not have time or capacity to attend to the inconsistent information, however, it is not well-recalled. Moreover, when people have time to consider their impressions afterward, they remember consistent information better, as they further synthesize the material. And people remember schema-consistent information when the judgment is complicated, particularly when they are using well-established schemas of the kind that cause stereotyping. However, if they are expert, they have the capacity also to notice, use, and remember inconsistent information. Whether people remember consistent or inconsistent information, it is important to note that they neglect information irrelevant to the schema.

Inference and Evaluation

Having just reviewed the material on schematic memory, one might assume that when people remember schematic consistencies, they also make judgments in line with the schema, and comparably when they remember inconsistent information, they do not rely so much on the schema. However, even when people remember inconsistent information, their impressions may still reflect the schema (Hastie & Kumar, 1979; Hemsley & Marmurek, 1982; cf. Higgins & Bargh, 1987). The connection between what people remember and their judgments is not straightforward, and we will return to this issue in Chapter 8. For the moment, we will note that people make many important judgments "on-line," as they encode information, and in those cases, memory and judgments are unrelated because the judgment is not based on what is recalled; in other cases, when a judgment only has to be generated afterward, people will base the judgment on what they can remember, and their memory and judgment, not surprisingly, will correspond (Hastie & Park, 1986; cf. N. H. Anderson & Hubert, 1963; Bargh & Thein, 1985; Dreben, Fiske, & Hastie, 1979; S. T. Fiske, 1982; Lingle et al., 1979; Ostrom et al. 1980). This relative independence of memory and judgment being so, how do schemas affect inferences, evaluations, and other judgments?

Category-based affect. Some schemas are emotionally laden, such as one's role schema for a mugger in the night. Such schemas can have direct, immediate effects; if an instance fits the schema, one reacts affectively in an apparently automatic fashion (S. T. Fiske, 1982; S. T. Fiske et al., 1987; S. T. Fiske & Pavelchak, 1986; Neuberg & Fiske, 1987; Pavelchak, 1989; see S. T. Fiske & Neuberg, 1990, for a review). The prototypic mugger elicits fear; similarly, someone resembling one's prototypic old flame or high school principal can, unknowingly, elicit their respective emotional responses (S. T. Fiske, 1982). The phenomenon of schema-triggered affect thus can operate for one's idiosyncratic schemas, as in a phenomenon therapists call "transference" (Westen, 1988), or it can operate for culturally shared schemas, as in classic cases of ethnic or racial prejudice (Allport, 1954). For example, ethnic categories can trigger specific emotional reactions such as anxiety, irritation, or concern (Dijker, 1987), particularly in those predisposed to avoid contact (Ickes, 1984).

The nature of prejudiced reactions to sexual and racial outgroups is not always simple, however. That is, prejudiced people do not necessarily react negatively to all racial and ethnic outgroup members, nor do they necessarily undervalue the competence of all women. For example, in 123 studies subjects evaluated identical materials attributed to a male or female author, but average findings indicate only negligible prejudice against women in this particular paradigm (Swim et al., 1989). Nevertheless, it would be erroneous to conclude that women are not the objects of prejudice. Rather, category-based evaluations occur at the level of subtypes (Deaux, 1985; S. E. Taylor, 1981a; Weber & Crocker, 1983). Thus, it is the interaction of the person's category and own particular attributes that causes perceivers to recategorize and evaluate accordingly. A woman whose behavior is aggressive is evaluated more negatively than a comparable man (V. Brown & Geis, 1984; Costrich et al., 1975), perhaps because she is recategorized as a masculine woman and is disliked for it.

Another type of more subtle category-based affect occurs because many people attempt to disguise their prejudice, allowing it to emerge mainly in situations that provide an excuse for their reactions. For example, racial prejudice often emerges when people have ostensibly nonracial reasons for their reactions, "reasons" that would not cause them to react negatively against a member of their own racial group (Crosby, Bromley, & Saxe, 1980; Gaertner & Dovidio, 1986; Katz, Wackenhut, & Hass, 1986; McConahay, 1986).

Thus, category-based affect can be obvious and immediate, in the case of the old flame or the mugger. Alternatively, it can be more subtle, interacting with attributes of the particular outgroup member or the specific situation (S. T. Fiske, 1989b).

Ingroup favoritism. Abstracting beyond particular racial, sexual, or ethnic categories, the most fundamental type of categorization that elicits affective or evaluative responses is "us" vs. "them." Previously, we saw that people's perception and memory of outgroups is that "they are all alike, different from us, and bad besides." If so, it is not surprising that any given "us" category is liked better than any given "them" category, under most circumstances (M. B. Brewer, 1979; M. B. Brewer & Kramer, 1985; Tajfel, 1978, 1982; Wilder, 1981, 1986; cf. Sherif et al.,

1961). When a teacher arbitrarily assigns students to teams for a course project, each team soon sees its own advantages and potential superiority; students quickly forget that they were divided up by the highly selective criterion of preferring to sit in the front left corner of the classroom rather than front right. Merely telling them that they are now a group leads them to want to reward their own group more, and to see its members as having better personalities, nicer looks, less responsibility for any failures, and more responsibility for successes.

For example, the ingroup's failures follow the self-serving attributional bias (see Chapter 3): Our group's failures are due to external circumstances beyond our control, while our successes are our own doing; their group's failures show how incompetent they really are, while any successes must be due to chance or extraordinary effort (Bond et al., 1985; Deaux, 1976; Hewstone, Bond, & Wan, 1983; Hewstone & Jaspars, 1982; Hewstone, Jaspars, & Lalljee, 1982; D. M. Taylor & Jaggi, 1974; Wang & McKillip, 1978; for reviews, see M. B. Brewer & Kramer, 1985; D. L. Hamilton & Trolier, 1986; Hewstone & Jaspars, 1984; Pettigrew, 1979). We encode and communicate our desirable behaviors and their undesirable behaviors abstractly, implying that they are more informative, stable, schematic, and less falsifiable than our undesirable behaviors and their desirable behaviors, which are viewed concretely (Maass et al., 1989). Even arbitrary ingroup members are seen as being more similar to oneself (Allen & Wilder, 1975, 1979; Billig & Tajfel, 1973; M. B. Brewer & Silver, 1978; D. L. Hamilton, 1979; J. W. Howard & Rothbart, 1980; Wilder & Cooper, 1981).

The apparent ease with which intergroup bias can be created is striking, and it occurs even when subjects do not personally benefit or did not personally contribute to the group product (J. D. Brown, Schmidt, & Collins, 1988); people apparently are motivated to give the ingroup as a whole a relative advantage over the outgroup (Wilder, 1986). Ingroup favoritism is a clear and persistent bias, probably stronger in the world than in the laboratory. Competition and status differences between groups (typical in the real world) exaggerate ingroup favoritism, as does being outnumbered (Gerard & Hoyt, 1974) or drawing attention to group membership (D. Abrams, 1985). Coercion is perceived to influence the outgroup, but conciliation is perceived to influence the ingroup (Rothbart & Hallmark, 1988).

There are also limits to the effect: it is minimally necessary for the experimenter to refer to the arbitrary divisions as "groups" (Billig & Tajfel, 1973). Moreover, even loyal ingroupers do pay some attention to fairness (Ng, 1984; Wilder, 1986) and do maintain some sense of personal identity within the group (Ng, 1986). The effects also can be undercut by introducing a second, extreme outgroup (Wilder & Thompson, 1988), as in the frequent dictum that enemy nations would get along better the instant some Martians landed (R. A. Levine & Campbell, 1972). We will come back to these issues in the next chapter.

Extreme inferences and evaluations. People are not simply predisposed to favor their own group. Sometimes people will evaluate an outgroup member more extremely than a comparable ingroup member. For example, white admissions committees who encounter a good application from a black student (i.e., an outgrouper) are likely to perceive the application as better than the same application coming from a white student (ingrouper). But they are also likely to see a weak application coming from a black student as worse than if it came from a white. Thus, the *outgroup polarization* effect cuts both ways: good outsiders are better and bad outsiders are worse than comparable insiders (Linville, 1982b; Linville & Jones, 1980).

This type of outgroup polarization appears to be caused by the simple-minded ideas people have about the outgroup. One bit of favorable or unfavorable information has much more impact when little else is already known about the outgroup, but when a lot is already known, one bit of information is only minor by comparison, so it has limited impact. The simplicity of people's understanding of outgroups may be due to their thinking about them along few dimensions (Linville, 1982b; Linville & Jones, 1980), especially if those dimensions are uncorrelated (Judd & Lusk, 1984). More specifically, people's simple-minded views of outgroups may be reflected in their having few exemplars for the outgroup (Linville, Fischer, & Salovey, 1989; Linville, Salovey, & Fischer, 1986; but for a debate, see Judd & Park, 1988; vs. Linville et al., 1989; Ostrom & Sedikides, 1989). Lack of familiarity with the outgroup can lead to extremity, as indeed can any kind of oversimplified secondhand information (Gilovich, 1987). Familiarity leads to greater differentiation and perceived variability, and thus to more moderate judgments, all else being equal.

But all else is rarely equal. When the ingroup/outgroup comparison motivates people especially to think about their own particular group identity, then *ingroup polarization* may occur. Returning to the previous example, if members of the white admissions committee focus on their identity as whites (for example, if they are resisting a well-publicized lawsuit to integrate), they may overwhelmingly reject white applicants who do not measure up to the standards they (chauvinistically) expect of whites. When the comparisons are explicitly intergroup rather than interpersonal, centrally relevant to people's identities as group members, as well as incontrovertible, then negative ingroupers can be more decisively rejected than are comparable outgroupers (and positive ingroupers are more emphatically valued), a phenomenon dubbed the Black Sheep Effect (Marques, Yzerbyt, & Leyens, 1988; Marques & Yzerbyt, 1988; cf. M. B. Brewer et al., 1987).

Schemas versus Evidence

The litany of schematic effects on inferences and evaluation makes one wonder if people are not attuned to reality, leaning on expectancies and schemas, rather than confronting the data. Yet, people actually do respond to the data. Indeed, some research has been interpreted to mean that people simply do not use schemas at all when they have any additional information whatsoever. It has even been read as saying that people readily ignore their schemas even when they have information that is nondiagnostic (irrelevant) and therefore, objectively should not dilute the schema (Locksley et al., 1980; Locksley, Hepburn, & Ortiz, 1982; Nisbett, Zukier, & Lemley, 1981; Zukier, 1982; Zukier & Jennings, 1983–84).

In light of the demonstrable effects of schemas in the laboratory and stereotypes in the outside world, these results have been closely scrutinized (R. Brown, 1986; Deaux & Lewis, 1984; S. T. Fiske & Neuberg, 1990; Grant & Holmes, 1981, 1982; Higgins & Bargh, 1987; J. L. Hilton & Fein, 1989; Krueger & Rothbart, 1988; Rasinski, Crocker, & Hastie, 1985). The evidence suggests that schemas may be totally eliminated mainly when (a) the potentially diluting behavioral information is clearly, unambiguously judgment-relevant, to the point of redundancy with the judgment; (b) the potentially diluting behavioral information is typically diagnostic in other contexts, even if it is not diagnostic in this particular case; (c) the categorical information is quite weak (ill-formed or tangential to the judgment); (d) the perceivers guess what is expected of them and respond accordingly; (e) the researcher substitutes the culture's shared stereotypes and diagnosticity for the perceiver's own views, possibly resulting in a mismatched comparison. Moreover, (f) the extremity of the schema itself may matter; moderate stereotypes, for example, easily assimilate various data to themselves, while more extreme stereotypes can provide such a contrast to the data that they are seen as not fitting at all (Manis, Nelson, & Shedler, 1988; Manis & Paskewitz, 1984, 1987; Manis, Paskewitz, & Cotler, 1986). And (g) the extremity of the data also matters, with extreme instances being viewed as clearly discrepant from a moderate stereotype. Finally, (h) people expect more consistency within some stereotyped targets (i.e., a single individual) than others (i.e., a random group) and assimilate behavior to the schema accordingly (J. L. Hilton & von Hippel, 1990).

In short, people are no fools. When they interpret the data as supporting the schema, they do use the schema, but when they interpret the data as undermining the schema, then they rely relatively more on the data. People seem to use a *continuum of impression formation* processes, ranging from more category-based or schematic processes to more attribute-based or individuating processes, and one can specify the information configurations that move people from one end of the continuum to another (e.g., S. T. Fiske et al., 1987; for a review, see S. T. Fiske & Neuberg, 1990). People initially categorize each other automatically on the basis of noticeable physical cues and labels. As Figure 4.5 indicates, people will use these initial categories when that is all they have (see "category label only") or when the data are easily categorized. If sufficiently motivated to attend to the other person, people

Continuum of Processes

Initial Categorization	Examples of Information Types
category label only (no data)	John V., an engineering major Swedish people in general
easily categorized data	a student who never meets deadlines and cannot master the course content a physical, active, competitive, fit, nonintellectual person

↓

Confirmatory Categorization	
label + category-consistent data	a loan shark who is opportunistic, shady, greedy, shrewd, heartless a male who is forceful, strong, assertive
label + mixed data	a disadvantaged student who performs sometimes poorly, sometimes well a male who is sometimes assertive and sometimes passive
strong label + irrelevant data	a male who gets a haircut early in the day a female who gets a high score on a completely meaningless test a violent criminal who has two dependents and is 28 years old

↓

Recategorization	
weak label + irrelevant data	an artist who is medium height, brown-haired, employed, and watches TV a child abuser who runs a hardware store
label + inconsistent data	a male who is the primary caretaker for the couple's children a female who consistently reacts in a forceful fashion a doctor who is uneducated, inefficient, bored, obedient, and unenterprising

↓

Piecemeal Integration	
uncategorizable data only	a person who is studious, cultured, and outgoing a person who is curious; energetic, perceptive, aggressive, and liberal

FIGURE 4.5 A continuum of impression formation, from category-based to individuating processes. (After S. T. Fiske & Neuberg, 1990.)

attempt to confirm these initial categories. Category confirmation is generally successful (a) if the data fit (i.e., if there is a label plus category-consistent data); (b) if the data are mixed (i.e., equally consistent and inconsistent, therefore objectively neutral) or (c) if the data are irrelevant to a strong category (cf. p. 128).

If category confirmation fails, people recategorize, generating new, better-fitting categories, subcategories, exemplars, or self-reference. The information configurations that encourage recategorization are illustrated in the figure: if the category is weak, even irrelevant data will undermine it. And, of course, clearly inconsistent data will undermine most categories, also causing recategorization. Finally, when it is not easy to recategorize, people will proceed piecemeal, attribute by attribute, through the data. Figure 4.5 gives examples of information contingencies that encourage these processes. As it indicates, people rely on schemas when there are good reasons to do so, but they also know when to quit using the schema.

A related way of conceptualizing people's use of expectancies versus data is to view them as branching off into different strategies as the situation demands, rather than proceeding through a continuum of processes. According to this *dual-process* perspective (M. B. Brewer, 1988a), people initially identify a person automatically, and stop there if the person is not motivationally relevant. If the person is relevant and if the perceiver is sufficiently involved, people personalize the other, using individually tailored schemas in a propositional network of memory (see Chapter 8). If not sufficiently involved, perceivers first categorize, using pictoliteral prototypes (wholistic, nonverbal patterns), unless the category fit is poor. In that case, they individuate, using category subtypes or exemplars.

There are some important differences between the dual-process and continuum approaches; for example, the dual-process model proposes distinct types of cognitive representations at different stages, while the continuum model posits stable kinds of information across its stages. In addition, the dual-process model posits specific rules for passing each processing stage, while the continuum model proposes constant rules, namely, ease of categorization depending on information (as just described) and motivation (to be described in the next chapter). There are other differences (S. T. Fiske, 1988; M. B. Brewer, 1988b; for other commentary, see Srull & Wyer, 1988), but both approaches integrate the holistic Asch configural model with the algebraic, elemental model of impression formation (described at the beginning of this chapter), which were originally pitted against each other. Moreover, both the continuum and dual-process models emphasize people balancing off their prior categories and the present data. People clearly use both schemas and data.

Moreover, schemas and data each can cue the other. Given a schema label, people are able to generate attributes, and given attributes, they generate a label. To take an example from the health domain, when diagnosed as having high blood pressure (one kind of event schema), people generate the appropriate data, namely symptoms, even though none are objectively present, as well as possible causes and an expected time-course for the disease (Baumann et al., 1989). Similarly, given symptoms, people generate a label (think of the last time you experienced unfamiliar symptoms and how quickly and perhaps wrongly you diagnosed the possibilities without a doctor's help). A variety of evidence illustrates the interplay between schemas and data, as this chapter indicates (for more on this point, see S. T. Fiske & Neuberg, 1990; Higgins & Bargh, 1987).

SUMMARY

Schemas are defined as people's cognitive structures that represent knowledge about a concept or type of stimulus, including its attributes and the relations among the attributes. Schemas facilitate top-down or conceptually driven processing, as opposed to bottom-up or data-driven processing. The schema concept comes from multiple sources that emphasize our active construction of reality. In person perception, Solomon Asch's configural model of impression formation and Fritz Heider's balance theory of interpersonal relationship triads both anticipate more recent schematic approaches. In nonsocial memory research, Frederick Bartlett's schema theory of memory for stories directly preceded modern schema research.

Before people can apply their schemas, they have to know what category fits the specific stimulus they encounter. Categorization processes describe how we classify and identify individual instances as members of larger familiar groupings. Basic principles of categorization include a rejection of the classical idea that natural categories have necessary and sufficiently defining attributes. Instead, category members are related by family resemblance. Categories have atypical instances at their fuzzy boundaries, with a prototype at the center, representing the most typical or average category member. Between categories, in this view, there are hierarchical connections, with an intermediate level being the most common, basic level. These principles apply to social perception as well, as people categorize others on the basis of traits or as persons-in-situations. Such prototypes aid in everyday decision making. The prototype view has been modified to include the possibility of ideals as prototypes, flexibility in the use of basic levels, and tangled webs instead of hierarchies.

A more dramatic alternative is the exemplar view, namely, that people represent categories in terms of specific instances, and judge category membership by similarity to these remembered exemplars. The exemplar view nicely accounts for people's knowledge of specific instances, variation within a category, correlated attributes, and easy category revision. Evidence within social and nonsocial cognition suggests the viability of the exemplar view. The most likely resoluton of the debate on prototypes versus exemplars is that each is used, to different ends.

Once instances are classified, people apply their schemas, which include person schemas (traits, person-in-situation, goals), self-schemas, role schemas (stereotypes), event schemas (scripts), and content-free schemas (balance, linear ordering, causal schemas). All types of schema influence encoding, memory, and inference.

Encoding is affected by schemas from the earliest moments, especially on the basis of physical cues such as sex, age, and race. Schemas reduce perceived complexity and variability within categories, especially for outgroups, and they bias the content of perception in stereotypic directions. Nevertheless, schemas also cause people to attend to schema-inconsistent information as well.

Memory effects are strongest when the schema is present from the outset at initial encoding. People categorize each other by salient cues such as race and sex, confusing category members with each other and remembering more, especially positive features, about ingroup members. People remember schema-relevant material more than irrelevant material. Whether they remember schema-consistent or schema-inconsistent material better depends on several factors. Schematic memory depends on the schema's strength, with weak schemas favoring inconsistent information, but stronger schemas favoring consistent information. Experts' schemas allow them the capacity to focus again on inconsistencies. Memory for schema-inconsistent information depends on making connections from the inconsistent material to other material in memory, as people attempt to integrate the inconsistency. If people have a chance to think about the material afterward, they tend to bolster their original schemas, then remembering schema-consistent information. Memory for schema-consistent information makes things simple, as people manage complex decisions, utilize prior judgments, think about loose groupings of people, and manage ambiguous, mixed, and weak information in their daily lives.

People's schematic inferences and evaluations are surprisingly independent of their memory, as many such reactions occur quickly upon the initial encounter, not relying on memory afterward. Category-based affect occurs when an instance immediately fits an affect-laden schema, sometimes at the level of a broad category, but more often at the level of subcategories in specific situations. People also routinely favor their own ingroup. However, people's reactions to outgroup members can be polarized, as when negative *or* positive responses to an outgrouper are exaggerated by oversimplified schemas.

People use their schemas initially and quickly, and they tend to stay with them until the data contradict the schema. When the schema and the data conflict, people generally rely on a mix of the two. We have learned a lot about how these processes operate. In the next chapter, we turn to the conditions of schema usage.

5

Conditions of Schema Use

---- ❖ ----

Which Schemas Do People Actually Use? ✦ *Schema Acquisition and
Development* ✦ *Schema Change* ✦ *Goals and Schema Use* ✦ *Social Identity
Theory* ✦ *Individual Differences in Schema Use* ✦ *Critiques and Shortcomings
of the Schema Approaches*

Schemas potentially have a massive impact on people's understanding of
their social world, but we have only recently begun to know something of
the boundary conditions of schema use. It is crucial to explore when
schemas are more or less likely to be used, which of several possible schemas
will be put into play, how they grow and change, what their sociocultural contexts are, and what individual differences influence their use. Moreover, the
schema concept has also come under heavy criticism, which we will raise and
discuss here.

WHICH SCHEMAS DO PEOPLE ACTUALLY USE?

People, situations, and events possess many features, so it is not obvious which
features will be used to categorize them, and consequently which schemas will
actually apply. This rather fundamental issue was neglected in early schema research, as investigators made sure that particular schemas were obviously applicable and competing schemas were in the background. The multiple-schema
problem is most striking for person and role schemas. For example, supposing
a person possesses all the following attributes, when is she primarily considered in terms of a perceiver's schema for being Hispanic, Cuban, a business major, extraverted, feminist, cultured, or scatter-brained? Recent work identifies
several principles that suggest which schemas are likely to apply in initial impressions.

Predictability: People Probably Use Roles First, Then Traits

People may use social stereotypes, such as the clown-type or the politician-type, rather than traits, such as outgoing, to make sense of people (Andersen & Klatzky, 1987). There are simply too many ways to be extraverted (e.g., like a comedian, a politician, or a bully), but there apparently are fewer ways to fulfill a concrete role schema, such as being a politician. Role schemas, thus, are more informative. Such stereotypes are richer (generate more associations) and better-articulated than traits, leading to more nonredundant features across a range of psychological, physical, behavioral, and demographic dimensions. And social stereotypes are more distinctive than traits, leading to more unique associations. Moreover, role schemas surpass traits in cuing memory for one's acquaintances (C. F. Bond & Brockett, 1987; C. F. Bond & Sedikides, 1988). To see this, think of all the people in a particular seminar, all your immediate coworkers at your job, or all your close neighbors at home. How easy was that? Now think of all the cheerful people you know, or all the self-centered people you know. How easy is that? Chances are, the social groupings generated more names more quickly than did the traits. People seem to remember their acquaintances first within a context (including a role) and then according to personality.

Finding a Level: People Habitually Use Subtypes

At what level do people habitually categorize each other? Stereotyping research and the popular media have historically emphasized blanket categories such as male and female, black and white, Hispanic and Anglo, gay and straight. Powerful as these categories may be, it is not clear that people habitually think at this level (S. E. Taylor, 1981a; Weber & Crocker, 1983). Rosch's work on object categories, covered earlier, suggested that people may think in terms of a basic-level "chair" rather than the superordinate "furniture" or the subordinate "desk chair" (Rosch, 1978; Mervis & Rosch, 1981). Similarly, in the social domain, people at least initially think in terms of basic-level "career women" rather than upper level "females" or lower-level "female lawyers" (Ashmore, 1981; Clifton, McGrath, & Wick, 1976; Deaux et al., 1985; Noseworthy & Lott, 1984). People use these basic-level subcategories to reconcile the general category membership with a limited amount of individuating information they may have. For example, women whose behavior contradicts their gender role may be viewed as lesbians or as unlikable macho women (Costrich, et al., 1975; Deaux & Lewis, 1984; Jackson & Cash, 1985). Similarly, subtypes describe young people's perceptions of older people as elder statesmen or grandmothers (Brewer, Dull, & Lui, 1981; Linville, 1982b). And whites commonly partition blacks into middle-class blacks and street-wise blacks (Pettigrew, 1981). More personal subtypes are also possible; former Secretary of State Henry Kissinger apparently categorized political leaders into such types as the Revolutionary, the Patriot, the Personal Friend, and the Able Adversary (Swede & Tetlock, 1986).

Of course, there can be several levels of subtypes, so describing the idea of subtypes does not solve the problem of which one people use. The point is merely that people do not typically operate at the very most general or the very most specific levels. However, it still remains open what level of subtypes people use. People are likely to operate at the most convenient, highest level of categorization that works well enough for their present purposes (S. T. Fiske & Neuberg, 1990). Unless that level of abstraction creates a problem, people are unlikely to move down to lower levels (see also Vallacher & Wegner, 1987).

Immediate Access: People Rely Heavily on Visual, Physical Cues

Many common social categories are based on easily perceived physical features such as age, race, sex, and attractiveness (Ashmore & Del Boca, 1979; M. B. Brewer & Lui, 1989; Kalick, 1988; McArthur, 1982; McCann et al., 1985; Milord, 1978; S. E. Taylor et al., 1978), as noted in the previous chapter. Appearance seems to be a particularly important feature of people's gender stereotypes, for instance, with appearance acting equivalently to a gender label (Deaux & Lewis, 1984; Freeman, 1987). Other social categories, such as economic class and occupation, can be based on uniforms, styles of clothing, and personal artifacts (e.g., a briefcase, a toolbox). Some role categories (e.g., the bad guys) may even be associated with wearing certain colors (e.g., black); for example, athletes dressed in black uniforms as opposed to nonblack uniforms are viewed by themselves and others as more aggressive (Frank & Gilovich, 1988). Similarly, traits (person schemas) are commonly attributed on the basis of physical features (Secord, 1958).

Visual cues generally are prominent in person perception (S. T. Fiske & Cox, 1979; D. J. Schneider, Hastorf, & Ellsworth, 1979) and object perception (Posner, Nissen, & Klein, 1976), so it stands to reason that many role schemas and subtypes are cued by physical features. One type of person schema, trait ascription, apparently shows the most interjudge agreement if evidence for the trait is more easily visible (Funder & Dobroth, 1987). For example, traits related to extraversion (cheerful, self-confident, likable, assertive, talkative) are more visible and more consensually judged than are traits related to neuroticism (daydreaming, self-defensive, over-reactive, blaming, anxious) (see also Kenny, 1991).

Thus, physical features are important in cuing all different kinds of schemas. Physical features are not only visually accessed but also they are present immediately in face-to-face interactions, providing schema-based expectations from the outset.

Early Labeling: People Use Primacy

Whatever information is present early on is likely to cue relevant schemas. Whether the information is a role label ("This is my friend Doug, the discrimination lawyer"), or a trait in a letter of recommendation ("Jane is first of all brilliant"), the early information helps to organize subsequent information (Asch, 1946; E. E. Jones & Goethals, 1972). In the previous chapter, we saw that schematic effects are stronger when people have the organizing structure from the outset; the schema then influences the interpretation of information as it is taken in, more powerfully than if the schema is applied afterward.

Salience: People Use Schema Cues That Catch Attention

The category that sets a person apart from others in context is especially likely to cue a schema (S. E. Taylor, 1981a). For example, the only woman in an all-male firm is more likely to be gender-stereotyped than is a woman in a more balanced environment (Kanter, 1977; Pettigrew & Martin, 1987; S. E. Taylor, et al., 1977; Wolman & Frank, 1975). We will address these issues in more detail in the chapter on encoding, but at present, the point is that the schema most likely to be operable is one that distinguishes the person from others.

Accessibility: People Use Schemas That Are Already Primed

People rely on categories that they have used frequently (Bargh, 1982; Bargh, Bond, Lombardi, & Tota, 1986; Bargh, Lombardi, & Higgins, 1988; Bargh & Pratto, 1986; Bargh & Thein, 1985; Higgins & King, 1981; Higgins, King, & Mavin, 1982) or recently in the past (Higgins, Rholes, & Jones, 1977; Srull & Wyer, 1979, 1986; Wyer & Srull, 1980, 1981). For example, one could be in the habit of categorizing people as "fun" or "not fun," with an eye to stimulating one's social life; one then would be more likely to apply that dimension in other perhaps less appropriate contexts, such as assessing whether a given lecturer provides a good time. (Indeed, such habits of schematic accessibility have damaged more than one set of teaching ratings.) Individual differences in schemas' accessibility spontaneously encourage people to use certain stereotypes; for instance, people whose gender schemas are accessible are more likely to respond in gender stereotypic ways (Stangor, 1988). We will discuss this phenomenon in more detail (Chapter 7), but here it points to a prominent basis for cuing schemas.

Mood: People Use Schemas Congruent with Their Current Feelings

All else being equal, people in a good mood are more likely to see the good sides of other people, and sometimes people in bad moods see others' bad sides (Bower, 1981; M. S. Clark & Isen, 1982; Isen, 1984). More specifically, moods seem to cue mood-congruent schemas for other people (Erber, 1991; see Chapter 10).

Power: People Use Schemas Relevant to Controlling Their Outcomes

People have schemas for others who matter to them. By definition, leaders and superiors in a status hierarchy control other people's outcomes (i.e., much of what happens to them), so it makes sense that people would develop schemas for people in power. Although no research seems to have pitted power-based schemas against other kinds, it is clear that people have well-developed schemas for those in control (e.g., Rush & Russell, 1988; Sande, Ellard, & Ross, 1986). Moreover, people's treatment of those who are without power overlaps across specific examples of such people—such as children, retarded adults, and foreigners—(DePaulo & Coleman, 1986, 1987) or, historically, women and minority groups (Hacker, 1951), suggesting that people may have power-based schemas that go down the hierarchy as well as up.

One also sees that power is central among the critical dimensions of personality traits (John, Angleitner, & Ostendorf, 1988), suggesting an important dimension of person schemas (see Osgood, Suci, & Tannenbaum, 1957, on potency in person perception). Moreover, people are likely to be especially accurate on this dimension and related dimensions such as aggressiveness (J. C. Wright & Dawson, 1988), suggesting their power schemas are carefully developed from experience. People pay particular attention to those with power over their outcomes

(Erber & Fiske, 1984; Neuberg & Fiske, 1987; Ruscher & Fiske, 1990), and they ignore those they see as having little relevance to their outcomes (M. J. Rodin, 1987). Well-developed schemas for those with power are likely to result.

Conclusion

Although people potentially belong to multiple categories, there are numerous bases for predicting which categories will predominate and therefore, which schemas will apply. This section has just noted some of the applicable principles, namely, roles will be used before traits, subtypes over broader categories, physical and visual cues over less tangible ones, early cues over subsequent cues, salience over nonsalience, accessibility over nonaccessibility, mood-relevance over mood-irrelevance, and power-relevance over power-irrelevance. Doubtless other determinants will prove to matter, but the task of predicting which schemas operate, while daunting, is far from hopeless.

SCHEMA ACQUISITION AND DEVELOPMENT

Schemas develop from encounters with instances or from abstracted communications of the schema's general characteristics. For example, one can learn about fraternity or department parties by attending a few, or one can learn about such parties by being told what typically occurs. It is easier to learn a schema when someone provides the general characteristics in the abstract beforehand ("We're going to a fraternity party, and here's what it's going to be like ... "), but there is a cost, in that one will perceive less variability across the specific examples than if one figured it out for oneself from the examples (Park & Hastie, 1987).

People are also extremely good at learning complex schemas from experience, although they may overdo it and become biased toward schema consistency (J. D. Mayer & Bower, 1986). When people generalize a schema from experience (J. R. Anderson, 1982; J. R. Anderson, Kline, & Beasley, 1979; N. S. Johnson, 1981), it typically becomes more *abstract*. The critical shift in abstraction may occur after two exposures, at which point people can begin to generalize about the commonalities between the two experiences (J. Martin, 1982; Nelson, 1980). Although the schema itself may well become more abstract, it is also possible that people store all the original encounters (exemplars) and then, as needed, they extract abstract principles from their accumulated experience (Hintzman, 1986). In either case, the resulting descriptions of the schema become more abstract with experience. For example, as people's impressions of other people develop, their descriptions rely more on abstract traits than on concrete behaviors or specific contexts (S. T. Fiske & Cox, 1979; Park, 1986).

Schemas also become richer and more *complex* as they develop (Linville, 1982b; Linville & Jones, 1980). The more fraternity parties or the more department parties one attends, the more dimensions one recognizes in them. One moves beyond the quality of the food and drink to notice the quality of the conversation, the music, the setting, who speaks (or doesn't speak) to whom, and so on. Moreover, the more one knows, the more one can describe details of the schema (Lurigio & Carroll, 1985).

Schemas also become more tightly *organized* as they develop. The "paradox of the expert" is that as one learns more, the knowledge is simultaneously more complex and more usable (E. E. Smith, Adams, & Schorr, 1978). That is, an expert's well-developed schema is more accessible (easier to remember and use) and more richly interconnected (its internal structure is more organized). Thus, at a party where one has known everyone for quite a while, one can quickly gauge the meaning of the pairs that form and other pairs that may form in response (or retaliation), but a newcomer would simply see an undifferentiated mass of people entertaining themselves. The well-developed schemas of experts contain more links among the elements and more complex organization (Chase & Simon, 1973; Chi & Koeske, 1983; Larkin, McDermott, Simon, & Simon, 1980; McKeithen et al., 1981), so they are in effect richer.

One consequence of experts' well-developed schemas is that, despite the greater amount and complexity of expert knowledge, their well-organized quality makes them more cognitively *compact*. As schemas develop with practice, they may become "unitized," that is, a single mental construct activated in an all-or-nothing manner (Burnstein & Schul, 1982, 1983; S. T. Fiske & Dyer, 1985; Hayes-Roth, 1977; Thorndyke & Hayes-Roth, 1979; Schul, 1983; Schul, Burnstein, & Martinez, 1983; Sentis & Burnstein, 1979). For example, when a new pledge attends a college fraternity party, the student may attempt to take in all the various elements separately (loud music, kegs of beer, dancing, exuberance), but with experience, the fraternity party becomes a single compact unit where everything just inevitably goes together. The unitization process is even more obvious with motor skills: consider the difference between learning to drive, struggling to master the separate elements of clutch, brake, accelerator, steering, etc., versus being a well-practiced driver who can use all those elements at once, without even thinking. The efficiency of a unitized schema emerges when one tries to do two things at once (e.g., drive and have a serious conversation). A unitized schema takes up less mental capacity, so it frees one to attend to other matters. Consequently, experts can organize schema-consistent information quickly (Pryor & Merluzzi, 1985), and they can evaluate schema-consistent evidence quickly, consistently, and confidently (Lurigio & Carroll, 1985). As noted in Chapter 4, experts have the capacity to notice and use schema-inconsistent information more than novices do (S. T. Fiske, Kinder, & Larter, 1983); novices, in contrast, focus on consistency (Borgida & DeBono, 1989).

As schemas develop, they become more *resilient* to inconsistency. As they become more abstract, complex, organized, and compact, they more easily incorporate exceptions. As noted earlier (see also S. T. Fiske & Neuberg, 1990; Higgins & Bargh, 1987; Ruble & Stangor, 1986), people first forming a schema focus on inconsistency to make sense of it, while the experts focus on it because they have the capacity to notice and use it. In contrast, intermediate in-between these two groups, the novices have their attention full just focusing on the consistencies. Thus, it seems likely that schema development is not a simple linear progression, but it may represent both gains and losses at different points, resulting in a curvilinear pattern.

On the whole, all else being equal, schemas should become more *accurate* as they develop. The accuracy issue in perceiving other people has a long and difficult history (e.g., Kruglanski, 1989b; D. J. Schneider, Hastorf, & Ellsworth, 1979), but our point here is relatively simple and all too obvious. If people learn from their experiences with acquaintances, social situations, and certain social roles, then such well-developed knowledge ought to reflect reality fairly well (see also Swann, 1984). In order for people to function adaptively, increasing knowledge ought more and more to fit the stimulus world, at least well enough, if not perfectly. For example, friends' judgments of their mutual friends and themselves agree more than do strangers' judgments of the same person (Funder & Colvin, 1988), which may indicate greater accuracy (cf. Kenny, 1991). This point merely serves as another reminder that "there is a 'there' there."

SCHEMA CHANGE

The initial burst of enthusiasm for studying schemas emphasized their persistence despite evidence to the contrary. Accordingly, we know more about the ways that schemas are maintained, and we are only beginning to learn what causes them to change.

Pressures Toward Maintaining the Status Quo

For dear me, why abandon a belief
Merely because it ceases to be true.
Cling to it long enough, and not a doubt
It will turn true again, for so it goes. (Frost, 1915, p. 54)

Stable schemas lend a sense of order, structure, and coherence to social stimuli that otherwise would be complex, unpredictable, and overwhelming. Having a schema confers many benefits, so it is not surprising that there are considerable pressures to maintain one's schema (Crocker, Fiske, & Taylor, 1984).

Belief perseverance. Well-developed schemas generally resist change and can even persist in the face of disconfirming evidence. Belief perseverance was originally demonstrated in a study in which people were (falsely) informed that they were especially socially sensitive; naturally, they began to think about all the reasons this was true (wouldn't you?), in effect to build or reinforce a self-schema around social sensitivity. When informed that the feedback was not in fact genuine, they nevertheless continued to believe themselves socially sensitive (L. Ross, Lepper, & Hubbard, 1975). Even though the original feedback was subsequently disqualified, by that time it was only one piece of evidence among many the subjects had recruited for themselves (C. A. Anderson, Lepper, & Ross, 1980). It turns out that, often, when people are asked to imagine an event, to explain how it might occur, or to consider how a judgment might be true, they perceive it as more likely (C. A. Anderson, 1983; Carroll, 1978; Fischhoff, 1975; Gregory, Cialdini, & Carpenter, 1982; L. Ross et al., 1977; S. J. Sherman et al., 1981), especially if it is easy to imagine (S. J. Sherman et al., 1985).

A further variant on perseverance is that people not only ignore some exceptions to the schema, they sometimes perversely interpret the exception as proving the schema. When people with strong prior beliefs encounter mixed or inconclusive evidence, they may reinterpret the evidence as if it were firm support for their schema, causing their beliefs to persevere or become even more extreme. People who believe abortion is murder, for example, might read research demonstrating the fetus's lack of independent viability. If they have a well-established schema on the topic, they are likely to perceive the research as either irrelevant or unconvincing: "If this lousy study is the best they can do, their evidence is pretty weak, so I know I'm right." Conversely, people who believe abortion is a woman's own choice might discredit research showing a woman's post-abortion regret and ambivalence. Research on one's own side of the issue seems flawless and extraordinarily relevant by comparison to evidence for the other side (C. A. Anderson, 1983; Lord, Ross, & Lepper, 1979). One implication of this phenomenon is that an impartial observer, who describes both sides as having strong and weak points, will be perceived as biased and hostile by each side. In pointing out the weaknesses of our side (and strengths of the other), the observer is viewed as hostile, but in pointing out the strengths of our side (and weaknesses of the other), the observer is viewed as merely reporting the objective merits of the case (Vallone, Ross, & Lepper, 1985).

Perseverance can be undercut in at least a couple of ways: by asking people to consider the opposite possible perspective or outcome (C. A. Anderson, 1982, 1983; C. A. Anderson, New, & Speer, 1985; C. A. Anderson & Sechler, 1986; Koriat, Lichtenstein, & Fischhoff, 1980; Lord, Lepper, & Preston, 1984; Slovic & Fischhoff, 1977); or by asking people to judge the implications of the available evidence before prematurely endorsing a particular outcome and explaining how it could be true (S. J. Sherman et al., 1983), especially if they are expert (Hirt & Sherman, 1985). Asking people simply to disregard certain evidence is only superficially effective; they may take a shortcut, just estimating how much to adjust the judgment itself rather than going back to form it afresh from the applicable evidence (Schul & Burnstein, 1985b; W. C. Thompson, Fong, & Rosenhan, 1981; Wegner, Coulton, & Wenzlaff, 1985; Wyer & Budesheim, 1987; Wyer & Unverzagt, 1985); the judgment becomes an integrated whole that is not afterward unpacked into its discredited and valid parts, with people then using only the valid parts. Apparently, people have to adopt the more active strategies of explaining or imagining, rather than merely ignoring, evidence in order to form a new judgment from the appropriate data and undo belief perseverance.

Mere thought. Schemas also seem to become more robust over time, simply by mere thought. If one has a well-developed schema, thinking about the concept and one's opinions about it polarizes judgments in whatever direction they initially tended (Tesser, 1978), and more thought polarizes judgments further (Sadler & Tesser, 1973; Tesser & Conlee, 1975), especially if one is committed to one's initial evaluation (Millar & Tesser, 1986b), if one's evaluations are unambivalent (Millar & Tesser, 1986b), and if one's evaluations and beliefs are consistent (Chaiken & Yates, 1985). The mechanism here, as with the perseverance effect, appears to be mustering evidence in favor of one's schematic stance. The more expert one is in a particular area of knowledge, the easier this is (Tesser & Leone, 1977).

Secondhand judgments. Besides actually thinking up new bits of supporting evidence for their schema, people also just continue to use it, failing to reexamine the original data on which it was based. Many judgments are simply based on one's earlier judgments, without much regard for whether the original evidence still supports the derived secondhand judgments (Carlston, 1980b; Higgins & Lurie, 1983; Lingle & Ostrom, 1979; McCann & Hancock, 1983; Schul & Burnstein, 1985a; Wyer, Srull, & Gordon, 1984). Once having said that you feel a new acquaintance has no sense of humor, you are unlikely to rethink that judgment. Moreover, you may later decide that the person is also unemotional, solely based on the prior judgment that the person is humorless, rather than going back to your original encounter with the person to decide about degree of passion. One particularly poignant example of this phenomenon occurs when people distort their descriptions (e.g., of another person) to fit what a particular listener wants to hear, and then they end up believing the version they told (Higgins & Rholes, 1978). This occurs in another version when people hear someone else's judgment of a third party; when people hear gossip, their judgment of others is more extreme (Gilovich, 1987). Fortunately, when they encounter the target's behavior for themselves, such reputation-based expectancies can be undercut (E. E. Jones, Schwartz, & Gilbert, 1983–84).

Pressures Toward Change

The effects of perseverance and explanation, mere thought, and secondhand judgments all seem to indicate that schemas will be difficult to change. And indeed this is often the case. In fact, many of the information-processing advantages of schemas would be lost if schemas changed at each encounter with slightly discrepant information.

Theoretical reasons to expect schema change. Having an incorrect schema is costly, so it behooves the social perceiver to be alert to the possibility of being wrong (Crocker, Fiske, & Taylor, 1984). Having the wrong schema can make people inefficient problem solvers, wasting time as they pursue misleading clues (S. E. Taylor, Crocker, & D'Agostino, 1978). The wrong schema can lead one to be inaccurate, biasing encoding, memory, and inference, as the previous chapter indicates. And the wrong schema can become a self-fulfilling prophecy that alters reality to fit its misconceptions (Chapter 12).

How do schemas change when they do change? Three models of schema change have been proposed (Rothbart, 1981): the *bookkeeping model,* which suggests that schema revision is a gradual process of incrementally tuning the schema with each new piece of discrepant information; the *conversion model,* which suggests that schemas resist small changes but can change massively and suddenly, given sufficient disconfirmation; and the *subtyping model,* which suggests that subcategories develop in response to isolated cases that disconfirm the schema. Research testing the viability of all three models generally supports the subtyping model (Weber & Crocker, 1983), and the prevalence of subtypes throughout social perception provides indirect support for this perspective (as noted earlier in this chapter, e.g., Deaux & Lewis, 1984; S. E. Taylor, 1981a).

Schemas vary in their potential for change; some are more easily disconfirmed than others (Crocker et al., 1984). A *logically disconfirmable* schema specifies what instances would be inconsistent with the schema; for example, honest people do not cheat. On the other hand, a schema that is not so logically disconfirmable would be one that permits a wide range of instances to be consistent with it. For example, a mental patient expected to be unpredictable would have a difficult time disconfirming the stereotype; similarly, a person accused of hypocrisy has a difficult time producing behavior that disconfirms that perception. Reeder and Brewer (1979) proposed a typology of traits that can describe their logical disconfirmability. To illustrate, hypocrisy and unpredictability are only "partially restrictive" traits in that they permit a rather wide range of behaviors, so they are difficult to disconfirm. A "hierarchically restrictive" trait is one that permits behaviors at one extreme but not the other; an intelligent person may behave intelligently or stupidly, but a stupid person cannot behave intelligently and still be consistent. A "fully restrictive" trait permits only a narrow range of behavior, so it is easily disconfirmed; neatness is a fully restrictive trait.

Schemas also vary in how *practically disconfirmable* they are. Independent of its logical disconfirmability, how likely is the perceiver to encounter discrepant instances? As Rothbart and Park (1986) point out, some traits are displayed frequently in daily life (e.g., friendliness), but opportunities to display others are rare (e.g., cowardice).

For all these theoretical reasons then, one would expect schemas to change under specifiable circumstances. Some of these have been identified from research on attempts to change role schemas, that is, stereotypes, as viewed from a cognitive perspective (for reviews, see Rose, 1981; Rothbart & John, 1985; Stephan, 1987, 1989; Wilder, 1986). In particular, the contact hypothesis holds that bringing together members of different social categories will break down their mutual stereotypes, at least under certain specifiable conditions. The contact hypothesis subscribes to certain underlying informational premises, namely, that the stereotypes are not true and that they are responsive to the disconfirming evidence provided by contact with members of the other group. The former point, the truth or falsity of stereotypes, is not within the scope of this book (but see Allport, 1954, for an excellent discussion). On the latter point, stereotypes are only sometimes undercut by disconfirming data. Research indicates some cognitive conditions under which people's stereotypes do change with contact (for other conditions, see Amir, 1976; N. Miller & Brewer, 1984; Stephan & Brigham, 1985).

Alternative schemas. As noted earlier, some categories, based on easily-perceived features such as sex, age, race, and ethnicity, seem to be important in initial encounters. What happens when these categories combine? That is, a person may be in your ingroup for one category and in an outgroup for another category. Preliminary evidence indicates a

hierarchical pattern of cross-categorization, such that sensitivity to category differences increases for targets who are ingroup members on another dimension; that is, for some purposes, one distinguishes between
gender categories more for members of one's own ethnicity than for another ethnicity; for other purposes, gender may be primary and
ethnicity secondary (M. B. Brewer et al., 1987; see also Park & Rothbart,
1982).

Schemas may be neglected if particular alternative schemas are
made salient in the contact context (Rose, 1981; Wilder, 1981), as when
people are divided into groups that cut across racial or ethnic categories
(Arcuri, 1982; Commins & Lockwood, 1978; Deschamps & Doise, 1978;
Rehm, Lilli, & Van Eimeren, 1988; Vanbeselaere, 1987). Another way to
make alternative schemas salient is to make the ingroup and the
outgroup into one big superordinate group, as when opposing groups
develop a common goal that unites them (M. Sherif & Hovland, 1961).

Seeing people as individuals. One can also encourage people to
see the outgroup as individuals, by emphasizing the variability of their
opinions or their separate responses (Quattrone, 1986; Wilder, 1978b) or
by emphasizing each outgroup member's unique personal attributes
(N. Miller, Brewer, & Edwards, 1985). The superordinate group strategy (above) and the individuating strategy (here) discourage categorization in different ways: the superordinate group strategy improves
perceptions of the outgroup members, while the individuating strategy
downgrades favoritism toward ingroup members (Gaertner et al.,
1989).

Other conditions. Both strategies—providing alternative schemas
and focusing on the other as an individual—essentially encourage people to ignore their stereotypes when considering individual group
members. But that does not mean that their stereotype of the group as
a whole has changed. People all too easily generalize their stereotype-
confirming experiences from an individual to the group as a whole
(e.g., Quattrone & Jones, 1980). Getting people to generalize their
stereotype-*dis*confirming experiences with one outgroup member to the
group as a whole is not easy. It helps to change the group stereotype if
people adopt an interpersonal rather than task orientation (N. Miller,
Brewer, & Edwards, 1985; Quattrone, 1986). It helps to provide counter-
stereotypic information spread across various individuals so that exceptions are not simply subtyped and "fenced out" out of the group stereotype (Weber & Crocker, 1983). Generalizing from the individual to
the group is also more likely if the counter-stereotypic individuals are
otherwise typical of the group so that the discrepancy is associated with
the group label in people's minds (Rothbart & John, 1985; Rothbart &
Lewis, 1988). It also may help if the discrepancies occur over time, for

then the perceiver may view the group as changing (for evidence of this in person schemas, see Silka, 1984). Perceptions of the group are also helped to change if the discrepancies cannot be "attributed away" to temporary situational factors (Crocker, Hannah, & Weber, 1983). It presumably helps if people have time to consider the discrepant information and its implications (for evidence of this in undercutting stereotypic perceptions of individuals, see S. T. Fiske & Neuberg, 1990). The perceiver's goals also matter, as we will see next.

GOALS AND SCHEMA USE

So far, we have examined information-processing factors that encourage people to maintain or change their schemas. People's goals when they examine information are at least as important as the information itself. People's use of prior knowledge (schemas) to make sense of new information (data) presumably assists them in everyday functioning. Schemas develop for a reason, namely, to guide understanding and behavior, so in many cases they should be accurate enough for most purposes. Under many circumstances, using and maintaining one's schema proves useful in predicting and controlling one's outcomes. To put it bluntly, if you know what to expect, then you know what to do to try to get what you want.

Depending on what you want, however, the accuracy of your schematic expectations may or may not matter. For example, if all you want is to complain to a close friend about some obnoxious third party neither of you will ever see again, it does not matter much (to you) whether or not the rather nasty schema you've applied is correct. Conversely, if you are trying to decide how best to approach your new boss to get her permission to do something not normally allowed, then it matters quite a lot whether your schema for the boss is correct. It essentially depends on your goal. Various motivations and situations evoke different degrees of schema and data use, resulting in different degrees of accuracy, depending on the specific goals of the perceiver.

The guiding principle behind people's relative use of schemas and data seems to be the needs of the particular interaction and the costs of being wrong. People interacting with other people enact specific social roles, within particular social settings, and these limit the information necessary and useful to the social perceiver. "Social interactions are rarely communicative free-for-alls which require large amounts of information to be intelligently maintained....Our main requirement, therefore, is for information *relevant* to adequate role performance, and, fortunately for cognitive economy, we need not be indiscriminately attentive to all the cues provided by the other actor(s)" (E. E. Jones & Thibaut, 1958, p. 152).

For many interactions then, our schematic expectancies will be sufficiently accurate, but sometimes the interaction requires a more detailed look at the other person due to the potential cost of being wrong. In either case, people's perceptions are typically functional and accurate enough for the purposes at hand. Thus, people appear to work toward *circumscribed accuracy,* that is, toward being accurate about other people within the constraints of their typical interactions (Swann, 1984). It is not usually necessary for people to be accurate about other people's behavior in interactions not involving the perceiver, that is, to have *global accuracy.* There is various evidence supporting people's pragmatic approach to accuracy and their typically functional tradeoffs between schemas and data, as we shall see. One underlying principle behind people's reliance on prior schemas versus available data is the cost of being wrong.

Increasing the Cost of Being Wrong

Various features of interactions tend to emphasize the potential costs of being wrong and consequently, to motivate people to examine the fit between the data given and their expectancies. Under many circumstances, people are careful when their outcomes depend on the target person, when they are accountable for their judgments, when self-presentational concerns are paramount, when they have been instructed in how to reduce bias, or when targets insist on an identity that contradicts the schema. Of course, being more careful and using the data do not guarantee accuracy, but they often help.

Outcome dependency and the motivation to be accurate. If your outcomes (rewards, benefits, costs, and punishments) depend on someone else's actions as well as on your own, you are outcome-dependent on that person; when the outcome dependency is mutual, it is called interdependence (Kelley & Thibaut, 1978). The degree to which people are contingent on another affects their perceptions of that person (E. E. Jones & Thibaut, 1958). When people are outcome-dependent, they pay more attention to the other person (Berscheid, Graziano, Monson, & Dermer, 1976), and they especially attend to schema-inconsistent information (Erber & Fiske, 1984), apparently because it is potentially informative. When people are outcome-dependent, they also draw more dispositional implications from the other person's behavior, apparently to increase their sense of prediction and control (Berscheid et al., 1976; Erber & Fiske, 1984), or perhaps simply to have a clear explanation for the other's behavior, even afterward, when prediction and control are less at issue (E. E. Jones & DeCharms, 1957).

Outcome dependency, such as being on a team together, can create a goal to be more accurate about the other person, causing one to go beyond one's initial stereotypes (Neuberg & Fiske, 1987). Outcome dependency causes people to probe for more information from the other person, even someone about whom they have a negative expectancy (Darley et al., 1988), and an explicit accuracy goal has the same effect (Neuberg, 1989), causing people to revise their impressions accordingly. The perceiver's motivation to be more accurate even communicates itself to the target as well; negative-expectancy targets actually perform better when interviewed by someone motivated to be accurate (Neuberg, 1989). This effect of an accuracy goal on the target's behavior is especially surprising because negative stereotypes and expectancies usually act as self-fulfilling prophecies, causing the target to perform poorly (e.g., Word, Zanna, & Cooper, 1974; see Darley & Fazio, 1980; Jussim, 1986; D. T. Miller & Turnbull, 1986; see also Chapter 12). One type of accuracy goal ("find out as much as you can about the other person") can even make people feel that the interaction is going more smoothly (Leary, Kowalski, & Bergen, 1988). Explicitly directing people's attention to the individual targets as people has effects similar to accuracy instructions (Baxter, Hill, et al., 1981; Touhey, 1972). Thus, outcome dependency, along with its more specific goal of being accurate, often reduces people's reliance on their schemas.

However, if one is already committed to a potentially positive relationship with another—for example, to go on a series of dates or to be roommates for a summer—one may be positively biased in one's assessments (Berscheid et al., 1976). And if one is involuntarily committed to a potentially uncomfortable or aversive relationship—for example, to blind-date someone who turns out to come from a different racial or ethnic group—one may be negatively biased (Omoto & Borgida, 1988). Outcome dependency does not always make people more accurate, and involuntary, long-term social commitments may form one boundary on its effectiveness. Doubtless, there are others (e.g., Pepitone, 1950).

Most of the effects of outcome dependency have been examined under cooperative interdependence. Nevertheless, outcome dependency's effects of undercutting schema use can even occur for competitive interdependence. When people are competing, they are outcome-dependent in an interfering fashion, just as cooperators are outcome-dependent in a facilitating fashion. Consequently, competing individuals attend more to their opponents and make more dispositional inferences about them, just as do cooperatively outcome-dependent individuals, compared to independent ones (Ruscher & Fiske, 1990). And competitors remember more about members of the outgroup than do noncompetitors (Judd & Park, 1988). But it is important to remember that in competition people's outcomes are negatively correlated (you win, they lose, or vice versa), so there are also likely to be less benign effects of competitive interdependence, especially in intergroup rather than interpersonal competition, where competition typically enhances stereotyping (N. Miller & Brewer, 1984; Ruscher et al., 1990). Nevertheless, one-on-one outcome dependency, whether competitive or cooperative, enhances data-driven processing.

Outcome dependency generally motivates people to pay closer attention to other people than they would when not outcome-dependent. In one sense, of course, it would be odd to describe any interaction as not outcome-dependent (E. E. Jones & Thibaut, 1958). However, interactions can be more or less interdependent, depending on how much people influence each other's outcomes. And people probably carry generic interpretations of who is likely to be motivationally relevant across situations. For example, beyond an initial category, people attend to others who are their own age or who are attractive to them (Rodin, 1987), and people probably attend to ingroup members more generally, as they are often outcome-dependent on each other. Thus, people attend to, and perhaps go beyond their initial schemas for, other people who are of natural relevance to them.

Accountability. Sometimes people have to justify their decisions to other people, and such accountability makes for more careful, complex (although not necessarily more accurate) decision making. In general, when people are accountable, they go beyond the schema to use more of the data. For example, accountable perceivers are less likely to base their decisions on initial impressions and more likely to use subsequent evidence in a murder trial (Tetlock, 1983b). Similarly, when perceivers expect to check their personality predictions against accurate information, their judgments become more complex, more accurate, and less overconfident (Tetlock & Kim, 1987). Accountable and responsible perceivers also agree with each other more than perceivers usually do, suggesting greater accuracy (Rozelle & Baxter, 1981). Conversely, when people can avoid accountability by sharing responsibility with a crowd, they use less complex judgment strategies than when they are deciding alone (Weldon & Gargano, 1985, 1988). Accountable perceivers seem to engage in "pre-emptive self-criticism" (Tetlock, 1983a) by becoming more receptive to the full range of information they are receiving, thinking in a more balanced and varied fashion. In effect, accountability makes people more vigilant (Janis & Mann, 1977): they consider a variety of alternatives, tolerate more inconsistency, and are receptive to new evidence.

Accountability is not a cure-all for people's biases, however; there are important boundary conditions on its effectiveness. First, because its effectiveness depends on people encoding information in a more open-minded fashion, people have to know they are going to be accountable before getting the relevant information (Tetlock, 1983a;

Tetlock, 1985). Second, people have to be accountable to an audience whose biases they do not know (or whom they expect to be unbiased); otherwise, they tend to conform (Tetlock, 1983b; Tetlock, Skitka, & Boettger, 1989). These strategically shifted attitudes show little complexity, suggesting that the very process through which the attitudes were formed seems more schema-based. (Thus, it is not just a temporary, audience-pleasing report, but a more fundamental change.) Third, when people are accountable for a position to which they feel previously committed, they invest their effort in justifying or defensively bolstering the position (Tetlock, Skitka, & Boettger, 1989). Finally, accountability does not always make people more accurate; it simply makes their decision making process more complex (Tetlock & Boettger, 1989). If the information at hand is indeed not diagnostic and they use it anyway, being more complex may actually undermine their accuracy. In summary, for accountability to encourage more accurate responses, people have to be accountable from the outset to an unbiased or unknown audience, without having made a previous commitment, and their information must be diagnostic.

Self-presentation and fear of invalidity. Increasing the perceived costs of being wrong makes people try to be more careful, as the interdependence and accountability research indicate. More generally, when the costs are raised in other ways, people rely less on their schemas and attend more to the data at hand. For example, in one series of studies, subjects thought their judgments would reflect fundamental abilities that were important to them, they thought their judgments would be compared to public or objective standards, or they thought they would have to explain their judgments to peers (Freund, Kruglanski, & Shpitzajzen, 1985; Kruglanski & Freund, 1983; Kruglanski & Mayseless, 1988). Under these conditions, if subjects were not under time pressure or not being pressured to make a simplistic yes/no judgment, they based judgments less on their schemas. Similarly, the costs of being wrong can be increased by emphasizing how important one's decisions are to the life of the person being judged (Freund, Kruglanski, & Shpitzajzen, 1985). Moreover, when people are in a deliberative, decision-making frame of mind, before they have committed themselves to implementing the decision, they are motivated to be accurate (Gollwitzer & Kinney, 1989).

Debiasing instructions. People's false schemas about themselves and others, although often resistant to disconfirming evidence, can be undermined when the experimenter emphasizes the personal costs of perseverance or emphasizes exactly how it is to be avoided (L. Ross, Lepper, & Hubbard, 1975). One interpretation of these results is that perceivers must be given explicit "how-to" knowledge in order to successfully undercut their erroneous impressions; in this view, perceivers simply lack specific enough knowledge about procedural aspects of debiasing. In addition, telling people about the costs to themselves clearly arouses a motivation not to appear foolish. Debiasing techniques, as noted earlier, include instructing perceivers to consider the opposite apparently counterfactual outcome (Lord, Lepper, & Preston, 1984), making the opposite outcome extremely salient to them (Lord, Lepper, & Preston, 1984), and instructing them to explain how the opposite outcome could have occurred (C. A. Anderson, 1982). In each case, the "how-to" knowledge may be critical but ineffective without the motivation to use it, which is provided by the experimenter. A related technique is to train subjects in "mindfulness" (see Chapter 7), which can decrease their stereotypic perceptions of other individuals (Langer, Bashner, & Chanowitz, 1985).

Socially negotiated realities. People often cooperate in their interactive and judgmental goals. Perceivers usually are motivated to perceive targets in terms that the targets themselves are willing to accept (Swann, 1984, 1987). That is, the targets themselves can increase the costs of being wrong by resisting erroneous judgments. For example, when targets are quite certain of their self-concepts, perceivers have a harder time imposing their own schematic expectancies on them (Swann & Ely, 1984; Swann, Pelham, & Chidester, 1988). Similarly, when targets know perceivers have a "bad attitude" toward them, their behavior can undercut the other person's negative expectancy (J. L. Hilton & Darley, 1985). Chapter 6 reviews this research in detail, but at present, the main point is that targets have some "damage control" over the ways they are perceived and can themselves increase the perceiver's cost of being wrong.

Increasing the Cost of Being Indecisive

While interaction can raise the cost of being wrong, motivating people to be more careful, the demands of social life often require that one instead make quick, efficient judgments. When decisiveness is required, people's judgments are often accurate enough for present purposes, but sometimes they are plain wrong. Several circumstances alert people to the increased costs of being slow or vague in their responses; that is, they are motivated by the perceived costs of being indecisive. Experimenters tend to arrange situations to demonstrate how people's motivations to be efficient lead them astray, as we will see. But the broader message is that people can often be motivated to make fast, good-enough decisions.

Time pressure and need for closure. Perceivers sometimes are motivated to adopt a judgment, *any* judgment, immediately, so as not to be left wavering. This need for closure (or for structure) can lead perceivers to cling to an initial hypothesis and limit their search for additional information (Kruglanski, 1989a). For example, in one study, time pressure caused male perceivers, as well as female perceivers with conservative attitudes toward women, to discriminate against female job applicants. Conversely, time pressure also caused females with liberal attitudes toward women to discriminate more against male applicants (Jamieson & Zanna, 1989). Similarly, the combination of a difficult task and high performance pressure (a timed achievement test) fostered a reliance on person schemas, that is, on traits as opposed to concrete actions (Koller & Wicklund, 1988). Time pressure inhibits people's search for diagnostic information (Kruglanski & Mayseless, 1988). Moreover, the pressure to implement a decision has similar effects (Gollwitzer & Kinney, 1989).

There are several possible explanations for time pressure effects. Going beyond one's schema takes time, as we noted earlier (also see Jamieson & Zanna, 1989). Thus, one possible explanation for the time pressure effect is that subjects are simply using the most efficient, schema-based judgment because they do not have time for slower, more data-based processes. However, one other possible mediator of the time pressure effect is physiological arousal, which has been found to enhance some kinds of stereotypic thinking (Kim & Baron, 1988). Finally, the time pressure effects could be caused by the self-presentational concern of appearing decisive. For example, time pressure (or needing an oversimplified judgment) undercuts the beneficial effects of the fear of invalidity described earlier (Freund, Kruglanski, & Shpitzajzen, 1985; Kruglanski & Freund, 1983). That is, while fear of invalidity can make people abandon an inappropriate schema, time pressure and consequent need for closure can make people stick to one. Both motivations have important self-presentational and self-esteem components, as judgments are made partly to make oneself look good.

Self-esteem threats. Although fear of public humiliation can motivate people to be more careful (or sometimes to be more precipitous), once someone has been humiliated, caution apparently vanishes. Specifically, when one's self-esteem is publicly undermined, one may utilize schematic judgments in order to bolster one's image. For example, when high self-esteem subjects were threatened by (false) feedback that they had failed, they showed greater ingroup favoritism than did subjects who received no feedback (Crocker et al., 1987). Notably, this favoritism occurred for ingroups that were evaluatively relevant (people who had taken the same test), but not for ingroups that were irrelevant (arbitrary groups and the average student). However, high self-esteem subjects who were told they had failed did not derogate outgroups. Preservation of their public image thus can lead perceivers categorically to favor their ingroup.

Threats to one's self-esteem or well-being produce anxiety, which can be (among other effects) distracting. When people are made anxious by expecting public criticism or embarrassment, they may adopt simplifying strategies for perceiving others. For example, subjects expecting to be publicly belittled were both more anxious and more likely to assimilate an exceptional outgroup member back into the negative group (Wilder & Shapiro, 1989b). Similarly, in another set of studies, some college students were made anxious by expecting public embarrassment (having to speak publicly about some aspect of their bodies they would like to change or being photographed in a playpen, wearing a baby bonnet and a bib, sucking on a pacifier). Compared to subjects who were not made anxious, the anxious subjects assimilated either a competent or incompetent individual to other group members present; these results are consistent with the idea that anxiety is distracting and impairs data-driven processes (Wilder & Shapiro, 1989a). Finally, the presence of an audience can be distracting and impair people's coherent cognitive functioning (e.g., C. E. Seta et al., 1988).

Communication sets. When people expect to have to explain something to others, they need to adopt some minimally acceptable framework. Perceivers expecting to have to communicate information to others form more organized, more polarized, more fixed, and often more category-oriented impressions than do those expecting to receive information (e.g., A. R. Cohen, 1961; Higgins, McCann, & Fondacaro, 1982; Hoffman, Mischel, & Baer, 1984; Leventhal, 1962; Zajonc, 1960[1]). In addition, communicators also tend to utilize stereotypic information more than do receivers (Hoffman, Mischel, & Baer, 1984). While these results could be interpreted as reflecting communicators' attempts to adhere to a rule of communication requiring them to present information in an organized manner (Higgins, 1981), it may also be the case that the anticipation of public scrutiny makes the communicator more willing to adopt conveniently packaged schematic structures.

Narrative and paradigmatic modes. Sometimes people simply want to tell a good story and sometimes they want to satisfy the rules for being a good scientist. In the former case, people operate in a narrative mode, which is also the mode of clinical judgment, demonstrating emotional sensitivity and intuitive understanding (Zukier, 1986). In-

---

[1]In the classic study by Zajonc, 1960, one must convert the percentages given back to the raw data in order to see this result.

ternal coherence is critical to a good story, which is provided by understanding the actors' motivations and intentions, as these make the story flow smoothly and provide themes to follow; the richness of the description is important here. In contrast, when people are thinking like scientists, the things that matter are rigorous classification and explanation, according to consensual rules of acceptable evidence; details and their logical, hierarchical relationships combine to form general laws. People can move between these two modes based on instructions to role-play a counselor (narrative) or a scientist (paradigmatic), and medical training seems to make people more paradigmatic (Zukier & Pepitone, 1984). Similarly, subjects asked to judge a person's traits may sometimes follow a scientific mode, operating in a data-driven fashion, but subjects asked to judge a person's guilt may follow a paradigmatic mode, operating in a more schematic fashion (Bodenhausen & Lichtenstein, 1987). People in a narrative mode use prior schemas more than do people in the paradigmatic mode (cf. Leyens, 1983).

Perceiver Intent

We have seen that people have the ability to be more theory-driven or more data-driven, depending on the circumstances. Some aspects of people's schematic strategies for making sense of other people are under intentional control (S. T. Fiske, 1989a; S. T. Fiske & Neuberg, 1990). Moreover, even when the costs of being wrong or being indecisive are not overtly emphasized, people can control their impression formation strategies. People can respond either in a more schema-based or in a more individuating manner, depending simply on what they perceive to be appropriate. For some people, appropriate strategies depend on what the situation requires, and for others, appropriate strategies depend on what they personally do best. Consequently, telling some people what they do best (i.e., that they have special abilities to respond in a more schema-based or more individuating fashion) motivates them to do so (S. T. Fiske & Von Hendy, in press); people who respond most to information about their own skills are low self-monitors accustomed to looking inward for cues to behavior (M. Snyder, 1979; see Chapter 12). Similarly, telling people that schematic or individuating processes are situationally appropriate motivates high self-monitors, who are accustomed to searching the situation for guides to their behavior. These changes occur even when the feedback about what is appropriate is randomly assigned (and therefore false), and the changes occur on attentional behaviors that the subjects cannot monitor simply to please the experimenter. Thus, people's intent to follow inner or outer guides to appropriate behavior influences their fundamental impression formation processes.

One might also wonder about the extent to which people's values determine how theory-driven or data-driven they are. Perceivers like to see themselves as fair-minded; people do not typically call themselves bigoted. In the United States, for example, the tension between an egalitarian self-concept and racial animosity has been labeled the "American Dilemma" (Myrdal, 1944). The ambivalence between people's values and their potentially bigoted schemas may contribute to a positive or negative over-reaction when given an excuse; that is, white people sometimes resolve their ambivalence by responding much more positively or negatively to a person of color than they would to a comparable white person (Gaertner & Dovidio 1986; I. Katz, Wackenhut, & Hass, 1986). What influence do people's values in general have on their extent of schema use? We do not have clear answers at present. People's training can make them more or less sensitive to certain kinds of inferential errors, as we shall see (Nisbett et al., 1987; see Chapter 9). And, as we shall see shortly, people's self-schemas are related to the dimensions that they notice in other people (Markus, Smith, & Moreland, 1985), so important values might have the same effect.

Perceivers do not, of course, have unlimited control over their use of schemas and data. People's rapid, initial category-based responses appear to be relatively automatic, as noted previously. Moreover, alerting people to the subjectivity of their schemas does not always cause them to be more careful (R. J. Ellis, Olson, & Zanna, 1983).

Summary

A wide variety of goals and motivations affect schema use. Generally, factors that increase the costs of being wrong motivate people to use relatively data-driven strategies. Some factors that often have this effect include outcome dependency and the motivation to be accurate, accountability, self-presentational concerns and the fear of invalidity, debiasing instructions, and socially negotiated judgments. Other factors often increase the costs of being indecisive, which encourages more schema-driven processing; these factors include time pressure and a need for closure, self-esteem threats and anxiety, a set to communicate to others, and the narrative mode. In addition to such external incentives to guard against being wrong or, alternatively, being indecisive, people also control their social judgment strategies based simply on what seems appropriate. People have some degree of intentional control over their use of schemas and data.

Although we have sorted various motivational factors into those that promote data-driven or schema-driven processing, it would be a mistake to conclude that each motivation always works in a particular direction. As described, there are frequent exceptions and qualifications. No one motivation inevitably works in only one direction, pushing people toward more theory-driven or more data-driven processes. One way to predict a priori which direction a motivation will push people is to analyze the situation in terms of what the perceiver mainly wants and who controls it. The motivating agent is the person who controls the perceiver's outcomes, and this may include the target, the perceiver, or third parties. The motivating agent's criteria for assigning the outcomes then determine the perceiver's relative reliance on schemas and data (S. T. Fiske & Neuberg, 1990). For example, members of a collaborative team are mutually dependent, and each person serves as the other's motivating agent because the other person's performance in part determines one's own outcomes. The teammate's criteria for cooperating then become important determinants of one's reliance on more schema-driven or data-driven strategies. Similarly, being accountable to someone makes that person the motivating agent, as that person determines one's outcomes (approval, votes, support, bonuses, etc.), with corresponding reliance on that person's criteria.

People's motivations can also be categorized in terms of two dimensions: their relative need for answers (closure) versus ambiguity (keeping options open), and their relative need for particular directions of knowledge (i.e., biases in types of answers or types of ambiguity; Kruglanski, 1989a, 1990).

Whatever overarching frameworks develop for thinking about motivation and the use of schemas, much of the current motivational work has the quality of being an add-on to existing ideas about how schemas operate. One exception to this treatment of motivation as an afterthought is work on social identity theory, in which people's processes of categorization and their motivations are intimately meshed.

SOCIAL IDENTITY THEORY

Social identity theory is important here because it is fundamentally a theory of social categorization, tested in real-world group relations, which necessitated the inclusion of motivational factors. Hence, it bears on the use of categories and schemas as conditioned by motivational factors. As we saw in the previous chapter's description of ingroup-outgroup biases, people are motivated to see themselves and their groups as different from other groups and as better besides. People's social groups are important to them. One's nationality, ethnicity, religion, gender, occupation, and the like, all help to define one's identity, who one is. These insights form the core of social identity theory (Tajfel, 1972, 1981; Tajfel & Turner, 1979; for reviews, see M. B. Brewer & Kramer, 1985; Messick & Mackie, 1989; Tajfel, 1982; J. C. Turner, 1981).

Social identity theory (SIT) arose out of the insight that mere categorization, while important, is not enough to explain stereotyping. That is, as we saw in the previous chapter, people categorize other people, situations, and objects as a basic part of perception, and categorization by itself maximizes between-group differences and minimizes within-group differences (Tajfel et al., 1971; S. E. Taylor et al., 1978). But when you are a member of one category yourself, that adds a motivational component otherwise missing. The phenomenon of ingroup favoritism, discussed earlier, reflects people's desire to be associated with groups that build their self-esteem. Social identity has intrinsic motivational components. Thus, strength of identification can correlate with differentiation between one's group and relevant outgroups (C. Kelly, 1988). And people favor the ingroup on dimensions particularly important to the ingroup (Mummendey & Schreiber, 1984), suggesting that identification matters. The finding that ingroup favoritism is increased when the experimenter is an outsider, rather than an insider, suggests that favoritism functions to negotiate the relative status of the ingroup when that cannot be taken for granted (Marques, Yzerbyt, & Rijsman, 1988). Moreover, people favor the ingroup even when there is no direct personal advantage or even when there is a disadvantage to doing so (J. D. Brown, Collins, & Schmidt, 1988; J. C. Turner, Brown, & Tajfel, 1979). Also, people favor the ingroup in ways that create an explicit advantage over the outgroup, rather than merely rewarding the ingroup (e.g., Allen & Wilder, 1975; M. B. Brewer & Silver, 1978; Tajfel et al., 1971).

Unfortunately, evidence for some of the motivational aspects of SIT is mixed (Hogg & Abrams, 1988; Messick & Mackie, 1989). For example, according to the theory, people who are feeling insecure should favor the ingroup even more, in an effort to rehabilitate it and themselves (J. C. Turner, 1985). Discriminating in favor of the ingroup indeed can bolster people's self-esteem (Lemyre & Smith, 1985; Oakes & Turner, 1980). And people may well favor the ingroup more when their self-esteem needs repair (Cialdini & Richardson, 1980; Finchilescu, 1986; Ng, 1985). Similarly, people whose ingroup has been derogated on a particular dimension may devalue the dimension's importance to the ingroup (U. Wagner, Lampen, & Syllwasschy, 1986). Traditionally, as well, people with low self-esteem have been found to be more prejudiced (Ehrlich, 1973; Wills, 1981), possibly because their fragile self-esteem requires picking on people outside their immediate circle or perhaps simply because they evaluate everyone (themselves and others) negatively.

However, the self-esteem predictions of social identity theory are not completely borne out (Abrams & Hogg, 1988; C. Kelly, 1988). For example, high (rather than low) self-esteem perceivers may be more likely to favor the ingroup (Crocker et al., 1987; Crocker & Schwartz, 1985). Moreover, when individual and group status combine in ways that should threaten self-esteem, the incongruity between people's *low* social and *high* personal identity yields mixed results on ingroup versus outgroup favoritism (Crocker et al., 1987; Doise, 1988; Ng, 1985; Ng & Cram, 1987, 1988). Similarly, people in power, who should feel relatively secure, may be more likely to discriminate than those not in power (Sachdev & Bourhis, 1985, 1987). The bottom line is that (a) it matters how one measures self-esteem, as global self-esteem is probably not very responsive to group identity concerns; (b) discriminatory strategies to elevate self-esteem are severely restricted by social-structural realities in real-world settings; and (c) discrimination may operate only as a last resort in the laboratory where no other strategies are available (Hogg & Abrams, 1988). Overall, the role of self-esteem has probably been over-implicated in studying intergroup categorization.

On another front, SIT also has some difficulty around the saliency of group membership. The basic theory predicts that the salience of a social categorization arouses social identity motivations. But, for example, people's degree of ingroup identification does not necessarily correlate with their degree of differentiating between groups (R. Brown et al., 1986, versus C. Kelly, 1988). And the salience of group membership does not reliably increase ingroup favoritism (Ng, 1986; Sachdev & Bourhis, 1985, 1987), although sometimes it does (Espinoza & Garza, 1985; Wilder & Shapiro, 1984), depending on how salience is operationalized. Ambiguity of membership and intergroup attitude similarity, both of which might decrease salience and therefore decrease ingroup favoritism, in fact increase it (R. Brown & Wade, 1987; Diehl, 1988).

These and other problems led to the development of a self-categorization theory (J. C. Turner, 1985, 1987; J. C. Turner & Oakes, 1986), which essentially extends SIT by emphasizing one's self-perception as necessary to group formation. The newer theory explicitly examines levels of categorizing oneself (human vs. nonhuman, member of certain social groups as apart from others, this individual self as opposed to other individuals). It argues that psychologically real groups depend on a shared sense of identity that goes beyond perceiving oneself as an isolated individual. Thus, it emphasizes one's personal identity interacting with one's social identity (J. C. Turner, 1987). For example, the salience of a category contributes to self-categorization and self-stereotyping (Hogg & Turner, 1987). Moreover, attraction can create a psychological group by acting as a cognitive criterion for group membership (Hogg & Turner, 1985a, 1985b), as in the perception that people who all like each other "belong together." Self-categorization as a group member is clearly important to the sense of belonging (also see Moreland, 1985), although the formation of a group depends on factors other than categorization (e.g., Bornewasser & Bober, 1987; Rabbie & Horowitz, 1988). Continuing research in this area emphasizes various bases for self-categorization (J. C. Turner, 1987).

INDIVIDUAL DIFFERENCES IN SCHEMA USE

People organize the world differently (G. A. Kelly, 1955); they differ in what they know and how they use it, in any given domain. For example, there are important individual differences in the perceived prototypicality of behaviors with regard to traits (Beck et al., 1988) and in specific style of stereotyping (Gardner et al., 1988). Or, to give a more concrete example, some people are experts in dating, knowing all the right moves, whereas other people have no idea what to do (Pryor & Merluzzi, 1985). This can, of course, lead to unfortunate misunderstandings, as when the dating expert assumes the dating novice knows the meaning of stopping by one's apartment at the end of the evening.

People can be more or less socially expert in general. For example, people differ in their overall *attributional complexity* (Fletcher et al., 1986; Fletcher, Grigg, & Bull, 1988), that is, in the complexity and number of their explanations for other people's behavior. People differ in their *uncertainty orientation*, which reflects their relative interest in gaining information versus clarity (King & Sorrentino, 1988; Roney & Sorrentino, 1987; Sorrentino, Short, & Raynor, 1984). Similarly, people differ in their *need for cognition* (Cacioppo & Petty, 1982), that is, in the extent to which they are intrinsically interested in thinking deeply about things, including other people. It has also long been recognized that people differ in *cognitive complexity* more generally (Crockett, 1965; Scott, Osgood, & Peterson, 1979; Streufert & Streufert, 1978). But recent social cognition research has focused more on people's domain-specific expertise, complexity, and accessibility, to which we now turn.

Self-Schemas and Perceiving Others

As the next chapter delineates, people possess organized, generic knowledge about themselves, called their self-schemas (Markus, 1977). Their self-schemas are related to their perceptions of others in ways that suggest expertise along the central dimension of their self-concept. That is, if a person's own masculinity is especially important, that person will be more sensitive to masculine behavior in others, breaking the behavior into larger chunks, i.e., more broadly organized units; "seeing" more masculine behavior in ambiguous acts; making broader inferences from behavior; and having more flexible observation strategies (Markus, Smith, & Moreland, 1985; also see Catrambone & Markus, 1987). Similarly, people give more weight to information about another person when it is relevant to their own self-schema, and when forming impressions they recall more of such material (Carpenter, 1988). In general, when a dimension is important to you in yourself, it is salient to you in others (Fong & Markus, 1982; Markus & Smith, 1981; Markus,

Smith, & Moreland, 1985; cf. Lemon & Warren, 1974), and this is especially true if you value the trait dimension in yourself (Lewicki, 1983, 1984).

The correlations between self-schematicity and perceptions of other people may go beyond traits to other types of categories. People who are members of particular social groups, such as the elderly, probably develop self-schemas of themselves along that dimension (cf. J. C. Turner's 1987 self-categorization theory, above); they certainly are more expert on the ingroup (Linville, 1982b; Linville & Jones, 1980), as defined by those category members they perceive as most similar to themselves (i.e., the subgroup that forms the real ingroup; M. B. Brewer & Lui, 1984). It is likely that other types of role schemas, particularly less common ones (minority racial status, homosexual orientation, physical stigmas) produce self-schematicity and sensitivity to that dimension in other people.

In considering this variety of ways that people's self- and other-perception are related, a couple of considerations are important. First, it is not entirely agreed that people use themselves as a reference point for judging others. Quite plausibly, the causality could go the other way (Higgins & Bargh, 1987). That is, dimensions that are central for people in general may also be central in their self-understanding. Given that self-schematicity is an individual difference variable not subject to experimental manipulation, it is difficult to establish the direction of causality between self-schematicity and sensitivity to the dimension in other people. Second, not everyone shows the same degree of correspondence between self- and other-perception (Holyoak & Gordon, 1983; Srull & Gaelick, 1983). Finally, such self-other correlations reduce with knowledge about the other (Holyoak & Gordon, 1983).

Chronicity and Construct Use

Different things come to mind easily for different people. People habitually think about different personality dimensions, regardless of whether or not the dimension happens to be part of their self-schemas. As we will see in Chapter 7, some dimensions are habitually more accessible than others due to the frequency of their use in the past (Bargh et al., 1986; Higgins, King, & Maven, 1982; Higgins, Bargh & Lombardi, 1985; Wyer & Srull, 1986). For example, one person might typically emphasize other people's kindness, while another might typically dwell on their politics. The dimensions that one typically finds accessible are those that are "chronic"; one can be chronic on kindness, shyness, extraversion, or anything else. People who are chronic on a dimension have an added sensitivity to it. Given relevant information, they are more likely to notice it (Bargh, 1982; Bargh & Pratto, 1986), and they can form rapid impressions even when other (nonchronic) people are over-loaded, i.e., cognitively overwhelmed (Bargh & Thein, 1985). Finally, people who are chronic on a particular dimension not only use it consistently, and are more sensitive to its presence, but they are also more accurate in assessing it (Park & Judd, 1989).

Chronicity, self-schemas, expertise, or some blend of them may explain why different people supposedly describing the same person often come up with rather different descriptions. Two perceivers' descriptions of the same target typically do not overlap much; indeed, *one* perceiver's descriptions of *two different* targets may overlap more (Dornbusch et al., 1965). Although people may agree on how positively or negatively to describe someone else, the actual choice of dimensions is more idiosyncratic (Park, 1986; also see Baxter, Brock, et al., 1981). In some senses, the perceiver contributes more than does the person perceived, and individual differences in chronic dimensions are one way to account for this phenomenon. People in general do tend to agree on some dimensions (e.g., extraversion) more than others (e.g., good-naturedness), perhaps because of shared stereotypes, for example, that physically attractive people are outgoing (Albright, Kenny, & Malloy, 1988; Kenny, 1991; cf. Funder & Dobroth, 1987), or perhaps because many people are chronic on the same dimensions, such as extroversion.

Gender Schemas

One specific way that people may differ in schema use is in their reliance on masculinity and femininity as concepts (S. L. Bem, 1981). According to the theory, virtually all children acquire the culture's concepts of masculinity and femininity, but sex-typed individuals (masculine males and feminine females) are more attuned to these gender schemas and more motivated to comply with them. Although there is considerable appeal to this formulation, the conception and measurement of gender schemas has been a matter of some debate (S. L. Bem, 1982; Crane & Markus, 1982; Markus et al., 1982; C. J. Mills, 1983; C. J. Mills & Tyrrell, 1983; Spence & Helmreich, 1981; Spence, 1984). Moreover, some of the initially hypothesized information-processing advantages of gender schemas have been controversial. For example, sex-typed individuals should organize incoming information in terms of gender, but two studies disagree on whether or not sex-typed individuals cluster a list of recalled words into groups of masculine and feminine items (S. L. Bem, 1981; Deaux, Kite, & Lewis, 1985). Similarly, sex-typed individuals may respond faster to the applicability of sex-relevant terms to themselves (S. L. Bem, 1981), but all individuals respond faster when describing sex-typed targets, so this may be an effect of target rather than judge (Park & Hahn, 1988).

Research using the Bem Sex Role Inventory has found evidence that sex-typed individuals do stereotype more, along gender-role related lines: they stereotype opposite-sex people more (Park & Hahn, 1988); they confuse women with other women and men with other men when trying to remember who said what (Frable & Bem, 1985; S. E. Taylor & Falcone, 1982; but see Beauvais & Spence, 1987); they respond more readily to physically attractive people of opposite sex (Andersen & Bem, 1981); and sex-typed males exposed to pornography are afterward more likely to treat a professional woman as a sex object (McKenzie-Mohr & Zanna, 1990). Nevertheless, the relationship between sex-typing and stereotyping is not entirely clear, as research using other instruments has not supported the relationship between sex-typed self-descriptions and gender stereotyping (Spence, Helmreich, & Stapp, 1975; Spence, 1984). The role of gender schemas thus continues to be of interest.

Political Expertise

In an early attempt to export social schemas to real-world thinking, it was soon discovered that how people use their political schemas depends crucially on how much they know about politics (S. T. Fiske & Kinder, 1981; S. T. Fiske, Kinder, & Larter, 1983). Although political scientists had long studied people who do and do not understand the overarching structure of ideology (Converse, 1964) and had differentiated people who participate actively in politics from those who do not (Milbraith & Goel, 1977), the specifically cognitive focus on political expertise and its effects on schema use has more recently been a matter of considerable research activity (Krosnick, 1990). The most reliable indicators of political expertise appear to be tests of accurate political knowledge (i.e., where liberals and conservatives stand on key issues), rather than actual amount of political activity or sheer personal investment in politics (e.g., as measured by interest in politics, self-schema as political, media use, opinion extremity) (S. T. Fiske, Lau, & Smith, 1990). Accurate political knowledge predicts: rapid encoding, more focused thoughts, and more relevant recall (S. T. Fiske, Lau, & Smith, 1990); ease of classifying and recalling political material, although expert recall can show a schema-consistent bias (Lodge & Hamill, 1986); facilitated placement of the President and oneself on major issues (Hamill, Lodge, & Blake, 1985); and more evaluatively organized and extreme representations of candidates (Lusk & Judd, 1988). Domain-specific expertise (e.g., on a particular topic) may differ from general sophistication (McGraw & Pinney, 1990).

The real-world context of politics offers a larger lesson for social cognition research. Most social cognition research examines subjective variations in expertise, as indicated by the other research reviewed in this section, but it might be useful to try applying the notion of social expertise as interpersonal accuracy. Unfortunately, the accuracy of social knowledge is more difficult to assess, for a variety of reasons (e.g., Schneider, Hastorf, & Ellsworth, 1979), but renewed efforts are encouraging (Kenny, 1991).

Orientations to Social Interaction

People can be expert in particular domains because of sheer information gathered, but they also are typically motivated to learn about the domain. For example, people can become expert in interpreting interactions in particular ways due to an overriding motivational orientation. A person's habitual orientation to others determines those people's perceived motivational relevance and the process of impression formation. Two crucial dimensions are a person's degree of dominance orientation (i.e., trying to control others) and degree of dependency (i.e., tendency to rely on others). Each of these is an intrinsically interactive feature of one's personality, that is, each bears on how one deals with others or the position one takes vis-à-vis others. These variables have been explored in a series of studies (for a review, see Battistich et al., 1985) suggesting that the perceiver's interactive orientations affect person perception primarily when the social context suggests the target is relevant to the perceiver's usual motives. For example, in describing another person, behaviors that are relevant to the perceiver's motives are more salient: dominant perceivers focus on assertiveness; dependent perceivers focus on affiliation. Moreover, perceivers prefer others whose interactive orientations complement their own; for example, dominant perceivers prefer a submissive target (Battistich & Aronoff, 1985). The possibility that defensive motivations underlie such phenomena is supported by the finding that dominant perceivers become aroused when observing a dominant and competent person with whom they expect to interact, and they then evaluate the person more negatively (Assor, Aronoff, & Messe, 1981, 1986). This seems a profitable avenue for research because just as situationally invoked motivations (interdependence, accountability, self-presentation) can influence the degree of schema use, so can individual differences in typical motives.

Assumptive Worlds

People's basic world views also provide operating assumptions for everyday decisions and behavior. Most of us assume that the world and the people in it are typically benevolent. We also tend to see the world as a meaningful place, in terms of justice (people get what they deserve), controllability (if people try, they can determine what happens to them), and chance (the world is not random). Analogously, we maintain a sense of self-worth as good, moral, just people; as people who effectively control what happens to us; and as people with some degree of luck. These assumptive worlds (Epstein, 1980; Janoff-Bulman & Frieze, 1983; Parkes, 1975) are crucial to people's functioning. When people are victimized by traumatic events—such as rape, incest, disabling accidents, deaths in the family, fires that destroy the home, cancer—they are forced to reexamine their views of the world as benevolent and meaningful and of themselves as worthy. Many of the strategies that victims use to cope with life-shattering events can be interpreted as efforts to find new meaning or to protect themselves from having to cope with the full implications of the event (Silver & Wortman, 1980; S. E. Taylor, 1983; Thompson & Janigian, 1988). Indeed, victims and nonvictims differ reliably in their assumptive worlds (Janoff-Bulman, 1989); it stands to reason that major life events, both negative and positive, influence the complexity, accessibility, and content of our social schemas.

Summary

In this section, we have seen that a variety of individual differences correspond to differences in schema use. People differ in those dimensions that are self-schematic and chronic, both of which correlate with their inclinations to focus on certain dimensions in other people. People differ in the extent to which they emphasize gender, in the extent to which they are knowledgeable about politics, in their typical motivational orientations toward interacting with others, and in their assumptive worlds about how reality operates. Each of these characteristics predicts differences in schema usage, as we have seen.

CRITIQUES AND SHORTCOMINGS OF THE SCHEMA APPROACHES

From the first moments of its emergence as a mainstream research topic, the schema construct has come under heavy criticism on several fronts. First, one might argue that the schema concept is simply *renaming* venerable elder concepts that are still perfectly useful (Cartwright, 1988). From this perspective, it is simply old wine rebottled: expectancies (see Zuroff & Rotter, 1985, for a historical overview), stereotypes (in particular, Allport, 1954), inferential sets (E. E. Jones & Thibaut, 1958), attitudes (see McGuire's 1985 "neutral conceptual definition," p. 239), to name a few. While acknowledging such important precursors and current areas of overlap, researchers using the schema concept generally make more explicit and fine-grained cognitive assumptions than those made by more traditional research terminologies (S. T. Fiske & Linville, 1980). Presumably, the material in this chapter and the last demonstrates the heuristic value of the schema concept, as this research has all been generated by it or by cognate notions.

The concept has also been accused of being conceptually mushy and *ill-defined* (Alba & Hasher, 1983; S. T. Fiske & Linville, 1980). Undaunted, schema researchers have forged ahead, some defining the concept more carefully, less carefully, or not all, given their own purposes. The lack of a consensual definition of other core psychological concepts such as attitudes, traits, and situations has not proved a noticeable obstacle, however, nor has it been an obstacle for the schema construct.

Moving from conceptual issues to the research itself, studies of schematic processes have emphasized perceived stability at the cost of *neglecting perceived change.* Initially, schema researchers emphasized pressures toward maintaining the status quo, as indicated by the work reviewed earlier. Even the subsequent findings on conditions of schema change make a fundamental assumption that people will generally hold onto their schemas unless motivated to do otherwise. However, people's individual schemas may not be as stable over time as is usually assumed (Berninger & DeSoto, 1985). Moreover, various lines of emerging work emphasize people's propensity to see change as well as stability (Conway & Ross, 1984; Janoff-Bulman & Schwartzberg, 1990; Klar, Nadler, & Malloy, 1991; M. Ross, 1989; Silka, 1984, 1989). Hence, the schema concept has perhaps discouraged the study of perceived change in its focus on stability.

Along with an emphasis on perceived stability, there has been an implicit message that schematic and categorical thinking is *all but inevitable.* Cognitive work on stereotyping has especially communicated that "people can't help it" (S. T. Fiske, 1987a, 1989a; cf. Billig, 1985, for a more radical solution). Nevertheless, as some of the motivationally oriented research in this chapter indicates, people do have some control over the extent to which they rely on their schemas to make sense of others. There are likely to be important situational, individual, and cultural differences in the extent to which people attempt to control their use of social schematic processes.

Schema research has also been associated with an intellectual high tide *emphasizing people's cognitive biases.* As this emphasis ebbs, researchers are more carefully examining the ways in which people are accurate, a return to some of the original issues in person perception research. Ironically, the person perception area had begun by investigating individual differences in accuracy at detecting other people's traits and emotions (see Hastorf, Schneider, & Polefka, 1970 for a review), but this line of inquiry was brought to a standstill by a cogent critique of the criteria for judging accuracy (Cronbach, 1955). Now, after a hiatus, accuracy research is restarting with an emphasis on when and how people are accurate. For example, Kenny's Social Relations Model provides a framework for specifying some interesting types of accuracy: individual accuracy, when individuals are accurately perceived by others, and dyadic accuracy, when an individual can predict a partner's behavior better than other people can (Kenny & Albright, 1987; Kenny & La Voie, 1984). As noted earlier, another kind of accuracy has been proposed, namely, circumscribed accuracy, which entails accurately judging interaction partners only in the usual settings in which one encounters them (Swann, 1984). In a related vein, Funder (1987) has argued that accuracy estimated in typical laboratory settings seriously underestimates people's abilities in the real world. Kruglanski (1990) argues that one cannot precisely answer the question of how accurate people typically are in everyday life. Instead, he suggests, accuracy depends on specific criteria in specific situations. The overall message that schemas dominate social cognition, at the cost of accuracy, is under serious revision (also see Chapter 4; Higgins & Bargh, 1987).

Schemas have been presumed to be *undesirable* in comparison to fully data-driven strategies. Because they have been viewed as leading to inaccuracy, they have typically been singled out as the culprit in a range of social crimes from stereotyping to irrational stupidity. We have seen a myriad of problems that schemas can bring when overzealously applied. Yet, there are many circumstances in which it is useful to categorize. Most importantly, we could not function if we did not rely on prior knowledge and expectations. As Allport (1954, p. 20) noted, "The human mind must think with the aid of categories...Orderly living depends upon it." Indeed, the message of much of this chapter and the last has been precisely how useful categories and schemas can be.

One further ironic example of schemas' utility occurs in the very situations in which people often are trying hardest not to overuse their prior categories. When people treat each person as a unique individual, they may not be sensitive to patterns of discrimination against particular categories of people. Viewing people's hiring and firing, promotions and demotions as unique cases would prevent one from seeing the class of people experiencing similar treatment. This piecemeal view of employment decisions, particularly when they concern oneself, helps to explain why many women see other women but not themselves as victims of discrimination (Crosby, Burris, et al., 1986; Crosby, Clayton, et al., 1986; Twiss, Tabb, & Crosby, 1989). As we have seen throughout this chapter and the last, current research provides many other examples of the importance of schemas.

In the context of research on errors and biases, however, schema research has typically assumed that the schemas themselves contain inaccuracies, or at least that applying them to a unique individual case will lead to inaccuracy. This is not necessarily so, for schemas may be *more accurate than normally credited*. For example, in the usual study, an experimenter-provided expectancy is combined with evidence that modifies it; who is to say that the subject should not rely entirely on the good information provided by the credible source, who obviously had some reason for giving it? Or if one has built up a schema from experience, who is to specify the appropriate amount of disconfirmation needed to disconfirm it? The issue of actuarial prejudice (S. B. Kiesler, 1975) captures this problem, as when a perceiver makes an assumption that is indeed on average likely to be true of a particular group (e.g., the average man is unlikely to be staying at home with his children). Schemas are presumably functional, so people are wise not to abandon them too quickly, simply for one quirky contradiction.

Schemas' *functional features are not well-specified* from a broad theoretical perspective. That is, a general conception of cognitive economy (Mischel, 1973) terms the perceiver a cognitive miser (S. E. Taylor, 1981b).[2] Schemas are supposed to be cognitively more efficient than understanding each instance afresh, and they are supposed to be relatively effective (although the research traditionally advertises their costs more than their benefits). This functional assumption has the status of a meta-theoretically given proposition, not to be questioned.

Nevertheless, alternative perspectives have emerged that ask precisely what is so functional about schemas. For example, a Gibsonian direct-perception approach argues that cognitive mediation (e.g., in terms of prior knowledge) is unnecessary, as organisms directly perceive the action possibilities that the environment affords them (McArthur & Baron, 1983). As we will see in Chapter 7, this is also explicitly a functional approach, specifying how an organism uses perception to operate in its ecological niche.

As another example, one could evaluate the functional features of social cognition from an explicitly evolutionary perspective, following sociobiology. Evolutionary theory suggests that we should rapidly, if not automatically, process information about others relevant to survival and reproduction (Kenrick, 1989). Accordingly, we should especially notice the degree of dominance and threat posed by another (in terms of survival) and the mating opportunity provided by the other (sex, attractiveness, resources, genetic fitness). Although difficult to test directly (Kenrick, 1987), such a perspective certainly adds a more specific meaning to the functional features of social cognition.

A final functional perspective addresses the individual's psycholog-

---

[2]For history hounds, this term was conjured up by the authors ten years ago in a Nashville hotel room the night before one of us needed the term for a talk. We are pleased that it has become such common parlance that people take it for granted.

ical health and maintenance of self-esteem. Schemas presumably add to one's sense of the world as a predictable, knowable place, a sense of control that contributes to basic functioning (S. T. Fiske & Taylor, 1984, Chapter 5; S. E. Taylor & Brown, 1989). Moreover, particular schemas, especially self-schemas, doubtless evolve in the service of one's well-being, but this is only beginning to be addressed directly (see Chapter 6; also discussion of social identity theory, above).

Finally, there are *important social and cultural differences* in schemas. Content clearly differs, as for example, the Chinese language has a single trait expression for someone who is worldly, experienced, socially skilled, devoted to family, and somewhat reserved, while English does not. And conversely, English has an expression for someone who is aesthetically talented, intense, moody, imaginative, and unconventional (i.e., bohemian), while Chinese does not (Hoffman, Lau, & Johnson, 1986). Specific features of a culture influence the content of people's schemas for situations as well (e.g., Forgas & Bond, 1985). Moreover, there are cultural differences in schema use as well as content (Forgas, 1985). For example, in traditional Indian society, people do not make trait attributions in the same way as in Western societies (J. G. Miller, 1984). Linguistic structure makes a difference to schema use as well within a single language (Semin & Fiedler, 1988), so it is likely that it has an impact across language groups, regardless of whether one assumes the language shapes the cognitive structures (Whorf, 1956) or vice versa. More broadly, some approaches thoroughly emphasize the social aspects of social representation (e.g., Moscovici, 1988) and social identity (e.g., Tajfel, 1981), partly in response to viewing social schema research as context-free (or context-ignorant) (for further discussion, see J. C. Turner & Oakes, 1986; and commentaries by Jahoda, 1986; Tetlock, 1986; Oakes & Turner, 1986).

SUMMARY

This chapter has addressed many conditions of schema use, some applicable to analyzing a particular situation and some applicable to changes in schema usage over time. In any given situation, several schemas potentially apply, so important progress demonstrates some principles of which schemas are most likely to be used. In the service of predictability, people tend to use role schemas first, then person schemas such as traits to specify particular versions of the role. Schemas exist at many levels of abstraction, and people find an appropriate level, often by using subtypes rather than broader, more abstract schemas. People depend on immediate access in that they rely heavily on visual, physical cues to select schemas. Early labeling helps to structure information from the outset, and people typically show primacy effects favoring the first provided schemas over later ones. Salience describes features that catch attention, which are also a likely basis for cuing schemas. People also use schemas that are already on their minds, that is, schemas that are mentally accessible. Moreover, people probably use schemas congruent with their current moods. Finally, schemas relevant to power or to controlling outcomes are also frequently used. While this is not an exhaustive compilation of the bases for selecting schemas, it illustrates many of the fundamental principles of functional schema use.

Schema usage also changes as they are acquired and develop. With experience and usage, schemas become more abstract and complex, as one would expect of increasing knowledge. In addition, they become more organized and compact, facilitating efficient usage. They also become more resilient with regard to disconfirmation, assimilating variations. All else being equal, schemas tend to be more accurate as they develop.

When do well-developed schemas change? There are various pressures toward maintaining the status quo, as demonstrated by research on belief perseverance in the face of mixed or disconfirming information. Mere thought also tends to reinforce schemas. And secondhand judgments tend to be accepted, often without consulting the original data on which they were based. On the other hand, there are theoretical reasons to expect schema change; otherwise people's cognitive systems would be inflexible and maladaptive. Pressures toward change include the presence of appropriate alternative schemas, the importance of seeing people as individuals, and other conditions uncovered in efforts to combat stereotypes.

People's goals are perhaps the most important determinants of schema use. Some goals tend to increase the costs of being wrong. For example, outcome dependency often creates a motivation to be accurate. Similarly, accountability makes people's judgments more complex and (given the right audience and correct information) more accurate. Self-presentation and fear of invalidity can make people more accurate as well. A more direct type of motivation can be induced by debiasing instructions that tell people exactly how to avoid misapplying their schemas. Finally, socially negotiated realities contribute to the costs of being wrong, as targets and third parties may pressure the perceiver to reconsider.

Other goals tend to increase the costs of being indecisive, so people readily use a schema with less concern for the possibility of being wrong. Time pressure and need for closure increase people's schema usage at the cost of data usage. Self-esteem threats and anxiety can also have this effect. A goal to communicate to others also tends to encourage schema use, as people search for organized, coherent methods of expression. Narrative modes of communication in particular, which emphasize telling a good story, also enhance schema use, compared to paradigmatic modes, which emphasize adherence to the relevant rules of scientific acceptability. Perceiver intent is an important control of schema usage; people have considerable control over the extent to which they actually use their most accessible schemas. In short, we have learned a lot about the impact of goals on schema usage.

A distinct approach to schemas and categories starts from the premise that certain types serve basic self-esteem functions. Social identity theory posits that people's division into ingroups and outgroups allows them not only to categorize and apply the relevant schemas but also to derive a sense of self-esteem from their group membership. Although some of the esteem-maintaining functions of intergroup categorization have received mixed support, self-categorization theory suggests a more detailed examination of the cognitive and motivational bases for perceiving oneself as a member of certain groups.

People also differ in their degree of using certain kinds of schemas. Individual differences in schema use include the relationship between self-schemas and perceiving others along the same dimensions. Moreover, people tend to have certain constructs chronically accessible, so they apply them to self and to others. Individual differences in gender schematicity suggest that a particular type of schematic content can influence the processing of relevant information. Political expertise is another kind of domain-specific schematicity that enhances the efficiency and effectiveness of processing relevant material. People's habitual motivational orientations to social interaction predict their schemalike sensitivity to dimensions such as dominance and dependence in others. Finally, people differ in their overall assumptive worlds, that is, their fundamental premises concerning the benevolence, controllability, and pattern of events. Each of these individual differences in schemas predisposes people to be sensitive to certain dimensions of self, others, and situations.

As research and theory concerning schemas mature, various shortcomings have been identified and addressed. Nevertheless, many social psychological phenomena, from broad and diverse areas, can be understood in terms of the schema concept. It helps to identify some basic commonalities across areas in which people's organized cognitive structures, in combination with their current motivations, play an important role in their social understanding.

6

Social Cognition and the Self

❖

The Representation of the Self ◆ *Self-Regulation* ◆ *Motivational Processes and Self-Regulation* ◆ *Awareness of the Self* ◆ *Self-Presentation and Impression Management*

*U*nderstanding the self has been one of the oldest and most doggedly pursued goals in psychology. William James's (1907) analysis laid the groundwork for many of today's leading issues, and sociologists George Herbert Mead (1934) and Charles Cooley (1902) provided a framework for understanding the self in social interaction. In the past decade, social cognition researchers have taken up the challenge of understanding the self, and in so doing, added to our fundamental understanding of its structure and functioning.

The knowledge that people have about themselves is both extensive and complex. Each of us knows ourself in many ways. We have a private self and the self we present to other people. We know the self as an active participant in the ongoing action of the environment and as a person who has already experienced many events and relationships. We know ourselves by our social roles, such as student, son or daughter, or spouse, and we have a conceptual sense of ourselves, that is, an impression of our own attributes and personal qualities (Berkowitz, 1988; Epstein, 1985; Gergen & Gergen, 1988; Markus & Wurf, 1987; Neisser, 1988). We can say quickly and with confidence whether we are outgoing or shy, rebellious or conventional, athletic or clumsy (Markus, 1977).

Sometimes, the self seems well-integrated and consistent, as when work, social life, and extracurricular activities are all running smoothly. At other

180

times, these different types of self-knowledge seem to be at war. In his book, *The Best Little Boy in the World* (1973), "John Reid" recounts in poignant and often humorous detail the difficulty he encountered as he reconciled his views of what others believed he should be with his increasing awareness of his homosexuality.

> I was all of eleven when I first "knew" what I was, in a tentative, semiconscious sort of way, hoping to be proved wrong, but knowing for certain, down deep, that it was snake eyes for keeps...I was watching *Superman* in the den. My father passed through with one of his guests. He was saying something like: "I've read that, too; but ten percent just couldn't be right. There couldn't be that many people with homosexual tendencies..." ...That is all there was to it. They passed by; I sat there with my head aimed at the TV—but my face on fire with recognition. I *knew*, I'm not sure how, but I *knew* I was in that 10 percent...All I knew about it was that it was awful (Reid, 1973, pp. 30–31).

Reid goes on to recount the painful years of pretending to be heterosexual, until at last, his sexual orientation became an integrated, positive aspect of his identity.

In this chapter, we will consider perspectives on the self that are provided by a cognitive analysis of its structure and functioning. The focus of the chapter is on self-regulation: the mental and behavioral processes by which people enact their self-conceptions, revise their behavior, or alter the environment so as to bring about outcomes in it in line with their self-perceptions and personal goals. We begin with a consideration of the structural representations of the self, namely, what the components are that make up the sense of self that most people have. We consider especially how these self-structures guide the processing of self-relevant information, enabling people to both understand the meaning of situations for themselves and promote their personal interests, goals, and values. Then we turn to a consideration of the motives that underlie self-regulation and how those motives lead people to alter or maintain their self-conceptions in social interactions. These include accuracy (the extent to which the person is motivated to have an accurate view of the self), consistency (the extent to which the person strives to maintain preexisting conceptions of the self), and self-enhancement (the tendency to maintain the most favorable self-conception possible).

*T*HE REPRESENTATION OF THE SELF

Much of the research in social cognition that concerns the analysis of the self has focused on the conceptual self, that is, the person's mental representation of his or her own personality attributes, social roles, past experience, future goals, and the like. The representation that a person holds of herself in memory appears to be similar to that held about other concepts, only more complex and varied. Kihlstrom and Cantor (1984) argue that the mental representation of the self consists of a hierarchy of context-specific self-concepts with each representing one's beliefs about oneself in a different set of situations. Thus, for example, a person may have one conception of herself in academic situations that involves the perception that she is bright, attentive, and interested in learning, and a quite different set of self-concepts for the domain of social situations, which may include being outgoing, friendly, and popular. In this viewpoint the representation of the self in memory, then, is very similar to the representation of other constructs, and may include information about both self-conceptions and specific events (episodes) that involve the self in meaningful activities.

Whether aspects of the self are organized hierarchically or not has been a topic of some debate. Some (E. E. Smith & Medin, 1981) have suggested that the self is an unordered, non-hierarchical collection of features, and others have represented the self as an associative network in memory (Bower & Gilligan, 1979). Most formulations, though, regard the self as a collection of at least semirelated and highly domain-specific knowledge structures (see, for example, Breckler, Pratkanis, & McCann, 1990; Higgins, Van Hook, & Dorfman, 1988; Kihlstrom & Hoyt, 1988; Kuiper, 1981; Markus & Sentis, 1982; T. B. Rogers, 1981). This conception of the self is presented in Figure 6.1..

Which aspect of the self influences ongoing thought and behavior depends in a large part on which aspects of the self have been accessed. The aspect of the chronic self-concept that is accessed for a particular situation is termed the *working self-concept.* In a classroom situation, the academic self is likely to be the dominant determinant of thought, feelings, and behavior, whereas if a person is reminded about a party to be held the next Friday night, the social self may be accessed. Thus, the working self-concept is important because it guides social behavior and in turn is modified by feedback from the situation.

Self-Schemas

Within the array of information and attributes that people hold about themselves, most people have clear conceptions of themselves on some attributes and less clear self-conceptions on others. Connie may feel she is hard-working and full of integrity, but when asked if she is shy or dependent, she may hedge, not knowing how to answer. Daniel may be certain about his shyness and dependency, but uncertain about whether he is a hard worker. Self-schemas are cognitive-affective structures that represent one's experience in a given domain. They organize

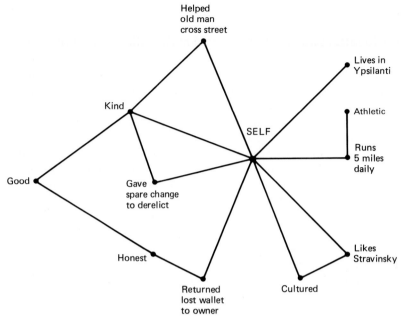

FIGURE 6.1 The self as a node in an associate memory network. (From Kihlstrom & Hoyt, 1988.)

and direct the processing of information relevant to the self-schema. People who hold self-schemas for a particular domain, whether shyness, independence, or creativity, for example, consider the domain to be personally important and typically have well-developed conceptions of themselves in these domains.

There are several criteria for deciding if someone has a schema (is *schematic*) or has no schema (is *aschematic*) on a particular dimension of his or her self-concept. People are self-schematic on dimensions that are important to them, on which they think of themselves as extreme, and on which they are certain the opposite does not hold (Markus, 1977).[1] Thus, if independence is important to you, and if you think of yourself as extremely independent and as not at all dependent, that implies that

---

[1]Some have argued that the term *self-schemas* is unnecessary, and that the older, broader term *self-conceptions* applies just as well. For example, Burke, Kraut, & Dworkin (1984) argue that measures of self-descriptiveness of trait adjectives and assessment of self-schemas produce similar results. We have elected to retain Markus' term, *self-schemas*, for several reasons. First, it explicitly ties in the research on the self with more general work on schemas and social cognition. Second, it connotes particular features of processing self-relevant information that the less precise term, *self-conceptions*, does not. Third, the term has enjoyed wide usage in the literature, and many have built on the early work that outlines a schematic approach to the self.

you have accumulated considerable knowledge about yourself on that dimension. For example, you should be certain that you would never ask for help setting up your stereo, even at the potential cost of damage to it or harm to yourself.

In contrast to schematics, aschematics are not invested in, involved with, or concerned about a particular attribute. They rate the trait as low to moderately self-descriptive, and perceive it as low to moderate in importance. Of course, people who are aschematic on one trait may well be schematic on others; everyone has some dimensions of self-concept that are idiosyncratically salient. I may think about myself predominantly in terms of independence, you may think about yourself in terms of extroversion, and a third person might be obsessed with weight. Regardless of the content of a person's self-schema, it has critical effects on perception, memory, and inference.

Perception. Being schematic on a particular dimension allows a person to filter incoming information about that dimension in much the same way that having a schema for other people guides information processing about them. Hence, we categorize ourselves much as we categorize others, with similar effects (see Markus & Sentis, 1982, for a review). Both the content and the speed of judgments about oneself show the advantages of being schematic. For example, people who are schematic on independence (called independence schematics) consistently and quickly respond "that's me" to traits related to independence. This is because they have a large, well-organized store of readily accessible knowledge about their independence. They do not show this pattern with respect to dependence traits. Aschematics on independence do not differ in the speed of their response to dependent and independent adjectives, as would be predicted. So, being schematic for a given trait means that one is a rapid judge of oneself on that trait. If independence is important to me, it is likely that I will think about my independence in a variety of circumstances, so it is useful to be able to make those judgments rapidly and efficiently (Bargh, 1982). Finally, people's self-schemas make them think harder about all kinds of schema-relevant information that comes their way. For example, people who consider themselves religious respond in more detail to religious (rather than, say, legalistic) arguments on any given topic (Cacioppo, Petty, & Sidera, 1982).

Not all self-schemas are positive. People hold well-articulated concepts about themselves on negative attributes as well (Wurf & Markus, 1983). Generally, negative self-schemas appear to function in ways similar to positive self-schemas with one exception. There is some evidence that people who are schematic on negative traits can quickly identify what they are not, but not as quickly identify what they are. For example, people who conceive of themselves as shy can quickly identify that they are not outgoing and not lively, but may be somewhat slower to identify the fact that they are reserved (Wurf & Markus, 1983).

Recently, the idea of negative self-schemas has been applied to depression, the idea being that people who are vulnerable to depression may have latent negative self-schemas that become activated by particular environmental circumstances (e.g., Dykman et al., 1989; Hammen et al., 1985; Kuiper & Olinger, 1989; Kuiper, Olinger, & MacDonald, 1988; Kuiper et al., 1985; Kuiper, Olinger, & Swallow, 1987; Segal, 1988). The application of these negative social constructs to processing information about the self appears to be automatic and unintentional (Bargh & Tota, 1988). The depressed person's use of negative social constructs is confined to self-perception and does not pervade perceptions of other people (Pietromonaco, 1985).

Memory. Self-schemas help people to remember schema-relevant information. This fact enables schematics easily to muster evidence in support of their self-concept. Independence schematics can remember many examples of independent behavior, expect to behave independently in the future, and resist people telling them that they are not independent. These self-schema effects replicate across such areas of self-knowledge as social sensitivity (Sweeney & Moreland, 1980), sex-role self-concept (Markus et al., 1982; Tunnell, 1981), and body weight (Markus, Hamill, & Sentis, 1979).

Like many knowledge structures, self-schemas are difficult to change. Of course, this is functional; if you changed your mind about your integrity every time you let a parking meter run out, you would never be sure of exactly who you were. In general, self-schemas appear to be stored in memory and to function much as do schemas about other people. Nevertheless, generally speaking, knowledge about oneself and others differs in several ways. First, knowledge about oneself seems to be more accessible in memory than knowledge about others. Imagine the difference between trying to decide whether or not you are extraverted and whether or not someone else is. Deciding about yourself should be faster, especially if you are certain that you definitely are (or are not) an extrovert. Having judged yourself and someone else, the self-judgment is far more memorable (Kuiper & Rogers, 1979; T. B. Rogers, 1981; T. B. Rogers, Kuiper, & Kirker, 1977).

The relative memorability of self-judgments decreases, the more familiar the other person being judged (G. H. Bower & Gilligan, 1979; Ferguson, Rule, & Carlson, 1983; Keenan & Baillet, 1980). One difference between judgments about the self and about most others is sheer familiarity with the knowledge on which they are based. Moreover, since we usually spend a lot of time in our own company, our self-schemas are bound to be more complex than our schemas for others (Linville, 1982a).

Schemas for oneself and others may differ in another way. Self-knowledge may be stored in verbal rather than visual form (Lord, 1980). In contrast, we may store knowledge about other people in visual form. Given the rather considerable difficulty of keeping an eye on ourselves, it makes sense that we may store limited visual information about ourselves. Debate is still ongoing concerning whether information about the self is more likely to be stored in verbal than visual form (P. Brown, Keenan, & Potts, 1986; Lord, 1987), and so this area remains one for future investigation.

Finally, knowledge about the self is more affect-laden than is knowledge about others, especially unfamiliar others. Several theorists have suggested that the advantage of self-relevant information in perception and memory accrues in large part from its *emotional importance* to people (Bargh, 1982; Ferguson, Rule, & Carlson, 1983; Greenwald & Pratkanis, 1984; T. B. Rogers, 1981). In sum, a self-schema is a familiar, affective, robust, complex, and possibly verbal self-portrait. Our schemas for others are less familiar, less accessible in memory, less affectively valenced, simpler, and may be more likely to be stored in image form.

Inference. When people are asked to predict their own behavior, they usually make predictions consistent with their self-schemas, for example, that they are independent now and always will be (Markus, 1977). In addition, people usually make self-schematic judgments rapidly (Markus, 1977; Markus et al., 1982; Pietromonaco & Markus, 1985). However, schemas do not invariably shorten the time it takes to make judgments and remember things.

Under some circumstances, self-relevant judgments take *longer* for schematics than for aschematics (Kuiper, 1981; Markus, Hamill, & Sentis, 1979; see also Mueller, Thompson, & Dugan, 1986). Since the circumstances of faster and slower self-schematic judgments have not yet been specified, one can only speculate about what they are. However, two speculations center around the novelty and/or complexity of the judgments required. For example, if you ask a person who is self-schematic on diligence whether he was working hard, you will get an immediate answer, because the answer is an integral part of his self-image. However, if you ask him a question he has not thought about before, such as how best to study for the Graduate Record Exam (GRE), he may take a long time to answer that question. Because he is a diligent schematic, he has a lot of information on the subject, and so it may take him longer to answer the novel question about GRE strategies. Someone who is not a diligent schematic would have less information and might well take a shorter time to answer the same novel question.

There is some support for this resolution of the discrepancy between the efficiency of self-schemas on familiar judgments and the apparently enormous quantities of knowledge self-schemas contain. This support comes from work on the more general problem of expertise. In that area of research, the same discrepancy between efficiency and unwieldy amounts of knowledge has been called the paradox of the expert (E. E. Smith, Adams, & Schorr, 1978): if you know many facts about a given topic, why doesn't that make you slower to retrieve any one of them? Experts resemble self-schematics in several respects (S. T. Fiske, Kinder, & Larter, 1983; Markus, Smith, & Moreland, 1985; see Chapter 5). Experts usually remember schema-relevant things more rapidly. And yet experts, like self-schematics, have more material to sort through than do novices and aschematics.

Research on expertise indicates that experts' schemas subsume large, well-integrated chunks of information, so for familiar judgments, efficiency should be increased (e.g., Chase & Simon, 1973). Instead of handling several discrete items of information, an expert schema combines several items into one. For example, as noted above, the diligence schematic can subsume all his study habits under the single familiar judgment that he is hard-working. This integration of separate bits of information speeds access (e.g., Sentis & Burnstein, 1979; E. R. Smith & Miller, 1978), minimizes confusion (e.g., S. T. Fiske & Dyer, 1985; Hayes-Roth, 1977), and creates larger perceptual units (e.g., Chase & Simon, 1973; Markus & Smith, 1981). With experts as with schematics, it seems that when a judgment is novel and requires integrating old evidence in new ways, experts and self-schematics may take longer. When the judgment draws on previously integrated judgments, experts and self-schematics should be faster. Thus, experts and self-schematics excel at both retrieving information and making judgments that are routine. A novice or an aschematic may know the same answer but may reach it more slowly and have less information to back it up.

One implication of this speculation is that extreme and familiar judgments will be processed more efficiently than moderate and unfamiliar judgments. This reasoning follows from the definition of self-schemas. Recall that people are defined as self-schematic on dimensions that are important, on which they think they are extreme, and on which they are certain the opposite does not hold. That means that extreme and familiar judgments are more likely to be schematic dimensions, by definition. Thus, such (self-schematic) self-judgments will elicit rapid responses. This speculation is consistent with the data on self-relevant judgments: reasonably familiar adjectives that are extremely like or extremely unlike the self are judged quickly, compared to moderately self-descriptive adjectives (Kuiper & Rogers, 1979). The principle appears to generalize to extreme judgments in other domains (Judd & Kulik, 1980; see S. T. Fiske, Lau, & Smith, 1990, for a review).

Perceptions of others. People who are self-schematics on a given attribute also notice it in other people. We all have friends who think about their weight and consequently inform you the instant *you* gain or lose an ounce. Noticing self-schematic traits in others seems to depend on an ability to group scattered clues into an overall pattern. A weight schematic (i.e., a person self-schematic on weight) will notice a friend eating dry toast and grapefruit for breakfast, plain yogurt for lunch, and conclude that he is dieting. Someone aschematic on weight might not associate those bits of behavior (Fong & Markus, 1982; Hamill, 1980; Markus & Sentis, 1982; Markus & Smith, 1981; Markus, Smith, & Moreland, 1985).

Self-schemas are also relevant to how people characterize others (e.g., Carpenter, 1988; Dodge & Tomlin, 1987; Hill, Smith, & Hoffman, 1988; Lewicki, 1984, 1985; Riggs & Cantor, 1984; J. P. Shapiro, 1988; see also Park & Hahn, 1988). In particular, people's self-schemas are used to organize information about others in schema-related domains, especially if drawing inferences about others requires inferences beyond the information provided (Catrambone & Markus, 1987). In one study (Markus, Smith, & Moreland, 1985), subjects with masculinity schemas chunked a film about another person's masculine behaviors into larger units than did aschematics, and in recounting the film sequence, schematics made more global judgments about the personality and motivation of the individual in the film. When told to attend to the details of the film, however, schematics were able to make smaller units than aschematics. These results suggest that self-schemas provide people with interpretive frameworks for understanding both their own and others' schema-related behavior. Exactly why self-schemas are associated with people's characterizations of others as well as the self is not entirely clear. One possibility is that people use self-relevant constructs to perceive others as well. An alternative interpretation, however, is that certain constructs are simply more accessible to people and so they use them to describe both themselves and others (Higgins, King, & Mavin, 1982; Higgins & Bargh, 1987). At present, it is difficult to distinguish between the two possibilities.

Self-schemas are not only associated with how we perceive others. Social interaction may alter both our own and others' self-concepts in ways that make us more similar to those with whom we are close. Deutsch and Mackesy (1985), for example, suggested that in the ongoing conversations that result from friendship, people become aware of the dimensions used by the friend for describing people. Over time, they incorporate some of the friend's dimensions not only for describing others, but also for describing themselves. In support of this argument, the authors found that the self-conceptions of friends were more similar than those of nonfriends, and that in interaction, each adopted the other's self-schematic dimensions for describing a target. Suggestive evidence that this is a learning process, rather than the result of similarity, was provided by pairing unacquainted partners and observing that over time their self-schemas and schemas for describing others became more similar.

In summary, people notice information relevant to their self-schemas in both themselves and others. Self-schemas enable people to remember efficiently and to judge schema-relevant information. However, sometimes self-schemas lengthen processing time; this appears to be most likely when the judgment is novel or complex. The same constructs that people use for themselves also guide the processing of information about others. Whether this is because self-schemas are used as a basis for perceiving others or whether chronically accessible constructs are used to perceive both the self and others remains unclear at present.

Possible Selves and Self-Discrepancies

The discussion to this point has concentrated on the schemas people hold about their current attributes. These schemas are abstracted from past as well as ongoing behavior. But people can have self-conceptions that are hypothetical or that do not characterize the current self, but may be self-descriptive at some time in the future. Some of these involve goals or roles to which people aspire, such as the five-year-old's desire to be a firefighter or the graduate student's expectation of becoming a professor. Others represent selves that people fear they may become, such as the suspicion that one's enthustiastic consumption of alcohol on certain occasions may eventually lead to full-blown alcoholism. Others represent conceptions of the self that one feels or others feel one ought to be, such as the homosexual youth's recognition that his parents expect him to get married (Higgins et al., 1986; Higgins, Klein, & Strauman, 1985; Markus & Nurius, 1986).

Possible selves. Possible selves, as formulated by Markus and Nurius (1986), are the future-oriented components of the self-system. They include ideas of what people may become, what they would like to become, and what they are afraid of becoming. Possible selves, then, are specific representations of the self in future states, and as such, they can serve important links to the articulation and realization of personal goals. A possible self can function as an incentive for future behavior by providing an image of the self which is to be approached or avoided. Thus, for example, the graduate student who has a clear vision of herself teaching classes, advising students, and serving on committees, has a clearer goal toward which to strive than a graduate student whose primary goal is to erase his Incompletes.

Goals are more effective guides to action when they are clear, moderate in difficulty, important, and focused around the self. Specific goals facilitate the elaboration of more distinct possible selves, and important and involving goals are perceived as more self-relevant. As a result, the desired end-state is easier to perceive and integrate into one's plans and actions (Markus & Ruvolo, 1989). In a study that supports this conceptualization, Ruvolo and Markus (1991) asked subjects to imagine themselves either being successful at work, lucky at work, failing at work despite clear effort, or failing because of bad luck. Subsequently, subjects worked on a task that measured persistence. Subjects asked to envision themselves as successful worked longer on the task than did subjects who envisioned themselves as failing, presumably because their working self-concept included the successful possible work self (see also Campbell & Fairey, 1985).

Possible selves provide focus and organization for the pursuit of goals, because they enable people to recruit appropriate self-knowledge and to develop simulations that enable them to rehearse the actions they need to undertake in pursuit of their goals (Markus & Ruvolo, 1989; see also Braun & Wicklund, 1988). Data consistent with this perspective was provided by Deutsch et al. (1988). They looked at women planning to get pregnant, who were already pregnant, or who had just had a pregnancy, and examined their self-socialization. They found that women actively sought out information in anticipation of a birth, they used the information to construct personal identities which incorporated the concept of motherhood, and after the birth, the determinants of their self-definition shifted from indirect sources of information, such as books and articles, to direct experience with children. The conception of the possible self as a mother, then, directed information-seeking activities which enabled further articulation of the "mother" as future self.

Possible selves do more than simply represent goals. They also include other self-relevant knowledge that is necessary to bring the goal about. This self-knowledge includes personal efficacy expectations, images of the self in the future setting, feelings about those situations, and an evaluative and interpretive context for the self's current status and ongoing activities (Cantor et al., 1986; Markus & Ruvolo, 1989). Thus, for example, the graduate student who has a clear conception of herself as a successful scientist may be able to picture herself in her future role, have clear beliefs concerning how to bring it about, and judge two weekdays spent at the beach reading magazines more harshly than the graduate student without such an articulated vision of the future.

The content of most possible selves appears to be positive. Markus and Nurius (1986) asked college students to describe themselves and found that about 65 percent of the students reported thinking of themselves in the future "a great deal of the time." The content of these future selves was disproportionately positive in that people were more likely to think of themselves as happily married and ensconced in won-

FIGURE 6.2 How self-schemas, ability, and possible selves interact to regulate performance. (After Markus, Cross, & Wurf, 1990.)

derful jobs than they were to regard themselves as divorced or unhappily employed.

Although the full implications of the possible selves concept may not yet be fully developed, at present it appears that conceptions of one's possible selves enable people to develop clear visions of the future, set goals that enable them to achieve or avoid those visions, and develop appropriate behaviors that enable them to reach those goals. As such, they serve an important motivational function. A diagrammatic representation of how self-schemas and possible selves interact with abilities and competencies to regulate performance is presented in Figure 6.2.

Self-discrepancy theory. Self-discrepancy theory, developed by Tory Higgins (1987, 1989a), offers another perspective on how people think about how they are and how they might be. Higgins proposes that people think about themselves in terms of their actual self (how they currently are), their ideal self (how they would like to be), and their "ought" self (what they think they should be). He argues that discrepancies between the actual self and what one would ideally like to be or ought to be are affectively involving. Sometimes self-discrepancies motivate people to take constructive action to reduce the discrepancy (E. T. Higgins et al., 1986). In cases when the actual-ideal discrepancy remains unresolved, however, the result is dejection-related emotions, such as disappointment, dissatisfaction, or sadness. Discrepancies between one's actual self and what one ought to be are associated with agitation-related emotions, such as fear, threat, restlessness, or anxiety.[2]

---

[2]Some research indicates that not all individuals actually develop an ideal-self structure and use it to make behavioral choices, even though most individuals are able to declare an ideal self if requested (Wojciszke, 1987).

A variety of evidence has been mustered that is consistent with the theory (see E. T. Higgins, 1987, 1989a, for reviews). For example, Higgins, Klein, & Strauman (1985) had undergraduates fill out a questionnaire that inquired about a variety of self-aspects, including what they would ideally like to be and what they feel they ought to be. The questionnaire was administered in two different sessions. One time the subjects filled out the questionnaire for themselves, and a second time they filled it out from the standpoint of their father, mother, and closest friend. They also rated the extent to which each particular attribute was relevant or meaningful to them. Discrepancies between own actual self and ideal self produced dejection-related emotions as predicted, as did perceived discrepancies between one's own actual self and a friend's or parent's ideal for the self. For example, wanting to be center forward on the basketball team and failing to become so produced dejection but little anxiety. In contrast, discrepancies between one's own self and others' ought self produced spells of panic and feelings of fear. For example, perceiving that one was not going to be the successful businessman of one's father's dreams produced anxiety, but little sadness. Discrepancies between one's own actual self and one's own ought self were also associated with anxiety-related emotions. The greater the magnitude and accessibility of a particular self-discrepancy, the more individuals suffered the kind of discomfort associated with that type of self-discrepancy (see also Higgins et al., 1986; Higgins, Strauman, & Klein, 1986; Strauman & Higgins, 1987). Van Hook and Higgins (1988) also found that the existence of a chronic conflict between two valued selves, namely, two self-guides (ideal or ought selves, one's own or others') that point to different standards of behavior creates an approach-avoidance conflict characterized by feeling muddled, indecisive, distractable, unsure of oneself or of one's goals, rebellious, and confused about one's identity.

Recently, Higgins (1989a; Higgins, Tykocinski, & Vookles, 1989) has incorporated a future dimension into his theory, looking at self-ideal discrepancies in terms of whether an individual believes that he or she can ever resolve the discrepancy. Some people who experience discrepancies between what they are and what they would like to be perceive themselves as having the ability to close that gap, but have not actually done so. Others, in contrast, realize that no matter how hard they work or try, they will never to able to close the gap between what they are and what they would like to be. Perceiving that one will not attain one's ideal but has the ability to do so is associated with depression marked by listlessness and fatigue, a motivation-related depression. In contrast, perceiving a discrepancy between one's actual and ideal self as not amenable to closure produces a sense of hopelessness or discouragement, an ability-related depression.

Self-Complexity

So far, in our analysis of self-structures, we have considered the attributes and dimensions that are important to self-conceptions. Another attribute of self-structures that influences thoughts, feelings, and behavior involves the *complexity* of the self-concept. Some people think of themselves in one or two predominant ways, whereas others think of themselves in terms of a variety of qualities. An unmarried farmer whose days are spent rising at dawn to work on his farm until bedtime may think of himself primarily as a farmer and not think much about other qualities he may have. In contrast, a married, employed woman with children may think of herself as a lawyer, a mother, a wife, a volunteer worker, and a patron of the arts. Linville argues that the complexity of people's self-conceptions influences their affective appraisals of their situation. Specifically, she hypothesizes that the less complex a person's cognitive representation of the self, the more extreme will be the person's swings in affect and self-appraisal in response to life's ups and downs. For example, the farmer confronted with a breakdown in his equipment may be very upset, more so than he would be if there were other aspects of his life to which he could devote his attention. Similarly, on a day of unexpected but badly needed rain, he may be jubilant in the extreme. In contrast, the lawyer who is unable to complete her work because of illness among her research staff may experience only modest distress because she has other aspects of her life that she can feel good about (e.g., her daughter's soccer success, her recent election to the board of directors of the symphony).

To measure self-complexity, people are given a list of personality traits and asked to sort them into groupings of traits that describe different aspects of themselves. The number of independent groupings is indicative of self-complexity. In one study, Linville (1985) had subjects complete this measure, and she divided her subjects into those high in complexity and those low in complexity. Subjects were then asked to complete an analytical reasoning task and were later given feedback suggesting that they had either done well or done poorly on the task. Consistent with the self-complexity predictions, those who were high in self-complexity were less adversely affected by the failure experience than were those low in self-complexity. Those high in complexity were also somewhat less positively affected by a success experience than those low in complexity.

Linville has argued that self-complexity acts as a buffer against the negative impact of stressful life events. In particular, it may help prevent people exposed to such events from becoming depressed or ill (Linville, 1987). If one has other aspects of one's life that are rewarding and satisfying, then a setback in one area of life is not as devastating as if one derives most of one's identity from a single set of tasks, roles, or personal qualities.

Summary

In the preceding pages, we have considered cognitive perspectives on the structure and organization of the self. In this context, we have considered self-schemas as cognitive/affective structures representing experience in a domain that organize and direct the processing of self-relevant information. We have also considered the fact that the self is not merely a stable representation of existing self-conceptions, but a dynamic structure representing what one may become or fears one may become as well. People also experience discrepancies between what they currently are and what they feel they ought or would like to be. Such possible selves and self-discrepancies guide behavior and govern affect. Finally, we have considered the complexity of the self-structure and the degree to which people think of themselves according to a few or a large number of attributes. All of these factors underlying the organization of the self guide the processing of self-relevant information, govern the individual's plans and behavior for future situations, and help determine the affect experienced in those settings.

Researchers have debated whether the self is a unique cognitive structure. Several sources of data have been mustered to suggest that it may be. Some have argued for a unique structure on the grounds that learning new material with reference to the self produces a deeper and semantically richer encoding than other types of encoding, leading to strong, elaborated, and integrated memory traces that facilitate recall (see Craik & Lockhart, 1972; see Chapter 8). Self-relevant information processing biases, such as the self-serving biases described in Chapter 3, have been another basis for suggesting that the self is a unique cognitive structure (see Higgins & Bargh, 1987). In an extended discussion of this issue, however, Higgins and Bargh (1987) argue that phenomena such as these can be explained without reference to the self as a unique cognitive structure. Other highly organized and interconnected constructs could produce similar effects, as could other beliefs to which a person is highly committed or about which a person is certain. Applying the label "self" to incoming information need only signify that the information is associated with one's self, not that self-knowledge or a self-system need be invoked. At present, there appears to be insufficient information to determine whether there are unique properties of the self as a cognitive structure. Clearly, however, the self is one of the most highly articulated, differentiated, and rich constructs that any given individual has, and as such, it is clearly important, though not necessarily unique, in producing reliable effects on processing.

SELF-REGULATION

Self-regulation refers to ways in which people control and direct their own actions (Markus & Wurf, 1987). The concept of self-regulation emerges, in part, from a clinical tradition (e.g., Bandura, 1977; Kanfer, 1970; Meichenbaum & Asarnow, 1979; Thoresen & Mahoney, 1974; Turk & Salovey, 1986), which conceives of the individual as actively involved in behavior change efforts designed to eliminate dysfunctional patterns of thinking or behavior. Self-regulation also derives from more general themes in psychology and other sciences regarding the goal-directed and self-corrective quality of behavior (Masters & Santrock, 1976; Carver & Scheier, 1981a). In this view, the important components of self-regulation involve the setting of a goal, cognitive preparations for behaving in a goal-directed manner (such as planning, rehearsing strategies), and the ongoing monitoring and evaluation of the goal-directed activities (Markus & Wurf, 1987). Goals are themselves a function of the individual's needs, motives, and values. They may be explicit and specific, as when an individual decides to lose twenty pounds over a six-month period and puts into effect a strategy for so doing; or they may be more general and preconscious, as in the case of the general but customarily implicit role that the desire to be perceived as a nice person plays in guiding one's interactions with others.

In the remainder of this chapter, we will examine self-regulatory processes as they have been explored by social cognition researchers and theorists. We will begin with a discussion of the working self-concept and conceptions of self-efficacy and their role in determining behavior. Then, we consider attentional processes, specifically whether an individual is attending primarily to the self or to the environment as a determinant of self-regulation. In the next section of the chapter, we turn to some of the underlying motivational processes that are addressed in the self-regulation literature, including the desires for accuracy in self-perceptions, consistency, and self-enhancement. In the final part of the chapter, we consider self-regulation in the context of social interaction: how people perceive the social environment in terms of their own attributes, how they select situations and other people with whom to interact, and how they adopt interaction strategies that enable them to manage their impressions and present themselves in ways that are consistent with their personal goals and beliefs about themselves.

The Working Self-Concept

One of the burning questions in the literature on self-concept is how stable is the self-concept (see Berkowitz, 1988). On the one hand, one can observe considerable stability in self-perceptions over many years on certain attributes (see Backman, 1988; Markus & Nurius, 1986; S. Rosenberg, 1988). It is also evident that situational contexts, experimental manipulations, and other short-term challenges to the self-concept can lead people to think about themselves in ways that appear to be at variance with their stable self-concept (see Gergen & Gergen, 1988; McGuire & McGuire, 1986). Moreover, stable conceptions of the self may themselves contain seemingly inconsistent elements. That is, people have multiple self-conceptions which may have conflicting features, and a particular self-concept may be activated at a particular time due to situational factors that may be at variance with other stable aspects of the self-concept. Indeed, all of these perceptions of the self-concept have validity. The conceptions of self that are salient as well as the valence and content of those self-perceptions may be changed remarkably in response to situational factors.

Given the complex structure of the self, the existence of self-schemas, the possible selves that exist in one's personal representation, and seemingly limitless opportunities for complexity, how do we know what information about the self is operative in any given situation? The working self-concept (Markus & Kunda, 1986; Markus & Nurius, 1986) is drawn from the repertoire of self-representations that is available. It is continually active, shifting in response to personal needs and situational contingencies (see Damon & Hart, 1986; McGuire, McGuire, & Cheever, 1986; see McGuire & McGuire, 1986, for a review). Which features of the self are represented in one's working self-concept is important because the working self-concept regulates ongoing behavior.

But what determines which of one's self-schemas will apply at any given time? If you think of yourself as both hard-working and sociable, which will affect how you process information at any given time? *Context* is clearly a major factor in activating one self-schema rather than another. If everyone around you is lazy, you may think of yourself as the hard-working one. Evidence for the impact of context on cuing of self-schemas comes from research on self-descriptions. Although self-knowledge is remarkably resistant to change, people's self-descriptions are sensitive to short-term context. When they describe themselves, people mention whatever attributes make them distinctive in a given context (McGuire, McGuire, Child, & Fujioka, 1978; McGuire & Padawer-Singer, 1976). That is, if you are in a room full of white Anglo-Saxon Protestant students, you may not think about the fact that you are a student but you may be quite aware that you are Jewish.

Which aspects of the self-concept have been *recently activated* by previous experience will also influence which components are currently accessible for interpreting current experience (Markus & Nurius, 1986). Indeed, the activation of self-schemas parallels the activation of other kinds of schemas, and those factors that typically activate schemas will also determine which self-schemas are activated (see Chapters 5 and 6). Particular self-representations, such as a specific self-schema, become active if they are triggered by events in the environment that are relevant to that aspect of the self or when they are invoked deliberately by the individual in response to a situation.

Short-term context-based changes in self-descriptions do not necessarily mean comparable changes in fundamental self-concept (Damon & Hart, 1986), but over time one's most usual contexts might shape self-concept (cf. Higgins & King, 1981; Wurf & Markus, 1990). Consistent short-term contexts add up to long-term context over time. A child who grows up as the smartest child on the block should be acutely aware of being smart in most day-to-day contexts. Over time, that child is more likely to be self-schematic about intelligence than is a child who grows up in a neighborhood where lots of people are smart. The second child would not be so aware of being smart because it is not a distinctive attribute in most of that child's daily contexts.

The changes in self-description that depend on context have another implication for self-schemas. If people are most likely to be schematic on those traits that distinguish them from others, then people are most likely to be schematic for traits on which they fall at one extreme or the other. Consequently, the definition of self-schematic dimensions as inherently extreme would seem to follow directly from the effects of context on self-concept.

Note, however, that the dependence of self-schemas on context has implications for the difficulty of determining their accuracy as self-descriptors. That is, if self-schemas arise largely as a function of context, they are necessarily not a sole function of one's actual personality. One can be aschematic on traits that are just as true of oneself as are traits on which one is schematic. There is no necessary correlation between being schematic on a trait and it being true of oneself, nor is there any necessary correlation between being aschematic on a trait and it not being true of oneself. For example, Markus, Cross, and Wurf (1990) point out that although people may be competent on particular dimensions, these competencies will not be fully realized or integrated into goals unless people develop schemas for those competencies. Whether or not a specific competency leads to a self-schema will depend heavily on whether or not it is activated consistently by situational contexts (that is, whether it is a frequently used working self-concept). Self-schematic dimensions, then, are subjective perceptions determined in part by context. Consistent short-term contexts create dimensions on which one is usually distinctive and, therefore, probably more self-schematic in the long run.

Self-Efficacy and Personal Control

So far in our discussion of self-regulation, we have considered primarily the factors that determine which aspects of the self are accessed in particular situations. Other situation-specific expectations also influence self-regulation. One such factor concerns self-efficacy beliefs, that is, the expectations that people hold about their abilities to accomplish certain tasks. Bandura (1986) has argued that whether or not people will undertake particular actions in the environment, attempt to perform particular tasks, or strive to meet specific goals depends on whether or not they believe they will be efficacious in performing those actions. Self-efficacy beliefs are conceptualized as highly specific control-related beliefs which concern one's ability to perform a particular outcome. The stronger one's perceived self-efficacy, the more one will exert effort and persist at a task. Thus, for example, faced with a challenging intellectual task, the student who believes he has the capabilities to perform the task effectively will be more likely to undertake it and to persist at the task than will the student who has doubts about his ability to perform it successfully. Self-efficacy beliefs have been particularly explored in the context of childhood socialization (Bandura, 1986; Dweck & Licht, 1980), because it is believed that early experiences with success and failure lead people to develop fairly stable conceptions of their self-efficacy in different domains.

Control-related beliefs are also important in adulthood and have been particularly explored with reference to how people cope with stressful events. Researchers have argued that conditions of threat and/or repeated failure are especially likely to evoke self-regulatory behavior (Kanfer & Hagerman, 1981; Rosenbaum & Ben-Ari, 1985). There are many unavoidably stressful events that one encounters in one's normal life, including going to the dentist, trying out for an athletic team, being interviewed for a job, or taking a test. Under such circumstances, one may begin to feel an anticipatory loss of control, especially if one knows little about the forthcoming aversive event and has few ways to regulate or change it. A wide variety of efforts to restore control examined in both laboratory and field settings suggest that the aversiveness of such stressful events can be reduced by interventions that lead people to believe they can exert control (see Averill, 1973; S. M. Miller, 1979; and S. C. Thompson, 1981, for reviews). These efforts include behavior control, cognitive control, information control, decision control, retrospective control, and secondary control (Averill, 1973; Rothbaum, Weisz, & Snyder, 1982; S. C. Thompson, 1981). These types of control are represented in Table 6.1.

Behavior control is the ability to take some step to end an aversive event, make it less likely, reduce its intensity, or alter its timing or duration. It can include any active response that a person commits to influence an event. When people are able to control directly an aversive event through their behavior, they appear to have less anticipatory anxiety, that is anxiety that occurs prior to the occurrence of the event (Gatchel & Proctor, 1976; Geer, Davison, & Gatchel, 1970; Geer & Maisel, 1972; Glass, Reim, & Singer, 1971; Stotland & Blumenthal, 1964;

TABLE 6.1 TYPES OF CONTROL AND THEIR EFFECTS ON ADJUSTMENT TO
AVERSIVE EVENTS

Type of control	Definition	Example	Effects
Behavior control	Taking some concrete step to reduce the aversiveness of a negative event	Pressing a button that will reduce the intensity of electric shock	Actual or perceived behavior control helps to reduce anxiety prior to the negative event, increases tolerance of aversive event, may not reduce distress of aversive event, may reduce postevent distress
Cognitive control	Thinking about the aversive event differently or refocusing attention on nonnoxious aspects of aversive situation	Focusing on the benefits of a noxious medical procedure while it is occurring	Appears to improve adjustment at all phases of an aversive event
Decision control	Ability to make decisions regarding the onset, timing, occurrence, or type of aversive event	Choosing between two types of surgery	Appears to be beneficial if outcome of decision is beneficial; effect if outcome is unfavorable remains equivocal
Information control	Obtaining or seeking information about the nature of the aversive event (e.g., sensations, duration, timing, cause)	Learning the side effects associated with surgery	Warning sign and causal information have equivocal effects; sensation information and procedure information reliably reduce stress of an aversive event
Retrospective control	Beliefs that one can control an event that has already occurred	Believing that one could have forestalled the accident that has left one crippled	Effects are as yet unknown—may improve adjustment to some noxious events but not others
Secondary control	Bringing one's thoughts and behaviors in line with environmental forces	Putting oneself in expert hands and "going with the flow"	May help to improve adjustment to aversive events when control is not possible

Szpiler & Epstein, 1976). Behavior control also seems to increase tolerance of the aversive events themselves. Subjects in experiments who
have some technique available to them to reduce a noxious event (such
as shock or loud noise) are able to withstand the event better than those
without such control. The impact of behavior control on felt distress
and emotionality, however, is equivocal. It is not clear that the distress
experienced during a stressful event is lessened by behavior control (S.
C. Thompson, 1981). Postevent distress may, however, be lower when
one feels one had control (Gatchel & Proctor, 1976; R. T. Mills & Krantz,
1979). For example, if you are taking a test and a radio is blasting outside, even after the noise stops, it is often hard to return to work. However, if the radio is yours or you can control its volume, you can likely
return to your work more easily. Behavior control, then, can be an effective method of self-regulation.

 Cognitive control is the availability of some cognitive strategy that either leads a person to think differently about an aversive event or focuses the person's attention on non-noxious aspects of the aversive situation. For example, one cancer patient coping with chemotherapy
describes her self-regulatory efforts this way:

> It was kind of a game with me, depending on my mood. If I was peaceful
> and wanted to be peaceful, I would image a beautiful scene, or if I wanted
> to do battle with the enemy, I would mock up a battle and have my de-
> fenses ready.

Most of us practice some form of cognitive control in our own lives.
A student may be able to put up with four grueling years of medical
school by cognitively constructing a possible self, namely, a vision of
himself as a future physician. During an awkward encounter with an
ex-girlfriend or ex-boyfriend in a restaurant, one may become intensely
aware of how the napkin holder operates. What research there is on
cognitive control suggests that our intuitive reactions of how to reduce
stress are well-placed. Cognitive control seems to ameliorate stress during the anticipatory period (Holmes & Houston, 1974; Houston, 1977;
Langer, Janis, & Wolfer, 1975), during the occurrence of the event itself
(e.g., Chaves & Barber, 1974; Girodo & Wood, 1979; Houston, 1977;
Kanfer & Goldfoot, 1966; Spanos, Horton, & Chaves, 1975), and during
the postevent period (F. Cohen & Lazarus, 1973; Egbert et al., 1964;
Langer, Janis, & Wolfer, 1975).

 Some cognitive control strategies involve merely avoiding dealing
with an aversive event (such as thinking about something else during a
fight with a romantic partner); others are nonavoidant (such as focusing
on the potential beneficial changes in the relationship that may result
from the fight). In comparing the results of the two types of strategies,
S. C. Thompson (1981) suggests that avoidant strategies may improve

coping before or even during an event, but not necessarily afterward, whereas nonavoidant strategies may lead to increased stress prior to the event, but reduced stress afterward (see also Suls & Fletcher, 1985). Which, then, is better: avoidant or nonavoidant strategies? There is no clear answer. For some events, avoidant strategies will be preferable on balance, whereas for others, nonavoidant strategies may be preferable. S. C. Thompson (1981) concludes that if a nonavoidant strategy can be successful, it may be useful, but if not, it may arouse anxiety. Perhaps, then, the best strategy is to focus on what one can do to alleviate the aversive event, and when one has done all one can do, to put it out of mind.

Decision control is the ability to make a decision or decisions with respect to a forthcoming stressful event. It may involve the decision to engage in the event itself, the ability to choose from among a set of more or less aversive alternatives, or the ability to decide on some other aspect of an event, such as its timing or duration (Averill, 1973). Although little research has explored the implications of decision control directly, there is evidence that choice can improve adjustment to later deleterious effects of that choice. There is much literature from dissonance theory, for example, showing that when people have committed themselves to a course of action that has aversive consequences, they reduce postdecisional conflict by reappraising their situation in a more positive light (see, for example, Kiesler, Collins, & Miller, 1969; Schulz & Brenner, 1977; Zimbardo, 1969). Whether there are limits to decision control remains to be seen. Does it follow that a patient who chooses minimum surgery which is unsuccessful will be better adjusted to the consequences of that decision than will someone who received the same surgery but did not choose it? These are the kinds of questions that remain to be answered.

Information control is a sense of control that is achieved when the self obtains or is provided with information about a noxious event. Particular kinds of information seem to improve adjustment more than others. For example, when one anticipates an aversive event, whether in the laboratory or in the natural environment, information about the sensations that will be experienced or about the procedures to be followed can reduce anxiety (see J. E. Johnson, 1984, for a review). The fact that information control positively affects coping has both theoretical and practical significance. Theoretically, it implies that a person need not be actively involved in an aversive event to adjust to it, but that, in some cases, mere understanding is sufficient to promote adjustment. The exact reasons why information seems to exert these positive effects are as yet unknown (J. E. Johnson, 1984; Leventhal et al., 1979).

Retrospective control, a term coined by S. C. Thompson (1981), refers to beliefs about an event that has already occurred, beliefs that may restore or enhance the feeling that one can influence or forestall the event's recurrence. For example, victims of misfortune will sometimes construe a past event as something they brought on themselves, in a possible effort to enhance their feelings of control (Bulman & Wortman, 1977; S. E. Taylor, Lichtman, & Wood, 1984; Tennen, Affleck, & Gershman, 1986; Wortman, 1976). For example, victims of rape will sometimes blame themselves for walking alone at night, not having adequate locks on their doors, or just being in the wrong place at the wrong time; through self-blame, these victims may be attempting to reassert control by identifying things they can do to prevent a repetition of the event (Janoff-Bulman, 1979). Relatively few studies have examined retrospective control, with the exception of those just noted. Although a few additional studies have noted that victims often do blame themselves for events an outsider would attribute to external factors or chance (Abrams & Finesinger, 1953; Chodoff, Friedman, & Hamburg, 1964), most have not gone on to demonstrate that the function of such self-blame is to restore feelings of control and enhance coping (see Bulman & Wortman, 1977, for an exception). Self-blame may be an effort to find meaning in an aversive event, rather than an effort at regaining control (S. C. Thompson, 1981). The idea of retrospective control remains intriguing in that it takes the control concept beyond understanding merely how people achieve control over events while they occur, to understanding how people achieve a sense of control retrospectively over adverse events that have already occurred. Such efforts may have the goal of restoring a positive sense of self (S. C. Thompson, 1981).

Secondary control, a term coined by Rothbaum, Weisz, & Snyder (1982), is a very different type of control-restoring measure than the types of control we have considered to this point. Whereas behavior control, cognitive control, decision control, information control, and retrospective control all involve attempts to bring the environment (e.g., the aversive event) in line with one's wishes (primary control), secondary control involves relinquishing primary control and bringing one's self into line with environmental forces. It is perhaps best embodied by the phrase "going with the flow."

Secondary control can assume any of several forms. One may attempt to predict events so as to avoid disappointment (*predictive secondary control*). For example, if one decides that one is simply incompetent at a task and that one will surely fail it if one tries, one will avoid the disappointment of actually failing. *Illusory secondary control* involves allying one's outcomes with chance. Going to a fortuneteller to decide whether or not to accept a new job is an example. *Vicarious secondary control* results when one allies one's outcomes with powerful others; presumably one can sit back and relax while others achieve the desired outcomes. *Interpretive secondary control* involves thinking about events so as to extract meaning from them and to accept them. Deciding that a conspicuous failure is a growth experience is an example. In sum then, passive behavior, withdrawal, and attributions of one's behavior to external forces like chance or powerful others need not mean that an individual has relinquished control altogether. Rather, it may simply mean that primary control has been exchanged for secondary control.

The six types of control described—behavior, cognitive, decision, information, retrospective, and secondary—constitute procedurally distinct ways of providing an individual with a sense of control. However, the mechanisms by which they alleviate stress may actually reduce to two techniques: taking some action with respect to an aversive situation and thinking about the situation differently. The beneficial effects of control appear to reside in the cognitive and behavioral changes that an individual can make in reacting to an aversive event; the means for instilling feelings of control are themselves, however, quite varied.

More generally, Deci and Ryan (1987) have argued that when people function in environments that promote choice and behavioral flexibility (high control), they experience more intrinsic motivation, greater interest, less pressure and tension, more creativity, more cognitive flexibility, better conceptual learning, a more positive emotional tone, higher self-esteem, more trust, greater persistence at behavior change, and better physical and psychological health. In contrast, environments that constrain individual choice or pressure a person toward specific outcomes (low control) are associated with a lowered likelihood of attaining these outcomes (see also S. E. Taylor & Brown, 1988).

In summary, then, an important determinant of self-regulatory efforts involves the control-related or self-efficacy beliefs that people hold about situations. When a task or situation seems too difficult to master, people may withdraw or make only minimal efforts to deal with the situation. In contrast, when a task or situation is readily understood by an individual who also believes that it will be possible to achieve a positive outcome, then these self-efficacy beliefs promote goal-directed behavior.

The preceding discussion has implied that feelings of personal control are always adaptive, and this may not be true. Burger (1989), for example, has suggested several conditions that may lead people to perceive an increase in personal control as undesirable. For example, if control is associated with a decreased likelihood that a person will be able to achieve desired outcomes, it may be perceived as aversive rather than desirable. An executive who is promoted into a position involving very difficult, if not impossible tasks, may find his enhanced control to be undesirable. In this case, he might have high control but low feelings of self-efficacy. Reactions to control may also be affected by whether or not the control leads to an uncomfortable level of concern about self-presentation. For example, the executive promoted to the new position may realize that his actions will be under considerable scrutiny. Control may also be aversive if it draws a person's attention to the unpleasant aspects of the situation. The promoted executive may find that the enhanced control leads him to focus his attention increasingly on the difficulties underlying the task, rather than the positive aspect of his expanded amount of influence. Control may be experienced as aversive when people anticipate bad rather than good outcomes (Scheier & Carver, 1988). Under these circumstances, Burger argues, a person may decide to relinquish personal control, he or she may experience anxiety, depression, and reduced feelings of self-worth (J. Rodin, Rennert, & Solomon, 1980), or he or she may even reduce performance on subsequent tasks, in an effort to reduce perceived control.

S. C. Thompson, Cheek, and Graham (1988) have identified other factors that may make the experience of control aversive. For example, when control requires more effort and attention than the absence of control, it can be experienced as stressful (e.g., Solomon, Holmes, & McCaul, 1980). Control may also be experienced as aversive if the person feels that he or she has too much control in a situation. Research in health settings, for example, indicates that if a patient is both informed about the details of a medical procedure and asked to make certain choices regarding that procedure, the experience of control may be somewhat overwhelming (R. T. Mills & Krantz, 1979). Control may be undesirable if a person lacks sufficient information to evaluate alternatives effectively (Rodin, Rennert, & Solomon, 1980). Control may also be experienced as aversive by those who prefer to cope with stressful situations by denying or repressing them (see Suls & Fletcher, 1985, for a review). Finally, control may be aversive when it is unsuccessful. When people expect to be able to control a situation, make attempts to do so, and fail, they may be unprepared for the failure and be held responsible by both the self and others, thereby leading to aversive emotional states. Thus, although control generally may be beneficial for self-regulation and be especially so under stressful conditions, there are clear boundaries around this phenomenon. Certain circumstances evoke a desire to reduce one's control or to give control over to others.

Attentional Processes in Self-Regulation

Self-regulation is also influenced by whether one's attention is directed inward toward the self or outward toward the environment (S. Duval & Wicklund, 1972). When people are reminded of themselves, they are said to become aware of themselves as social objects. In this state of objective self-awareness, the self is perceived as "me," the object or recipient of reaction. The self then is the focus of attention. For example, when you first get up to give a presentation in front of a class or at a conference and you are busy wondering what they will think of you, you are objectively self-aware. In contrast, when people are distracted from thinking about themselves, they are more aware of the environment. After you get started in your presentation, you no longer focus on yourself, but on your audience and your notes. You lose yourself in your talk. The environment, not the self, is the focus of attention (see Hass, 1984, for an empirical test of the distinction).

Whether one is focused on the self or on the environment has a number of ramifications. For example, people are more likely to see themselves as causal in a situation when they are self-focused, and this increases with the priming of causally relevant information (Fenigstein & Levine, 1984). Later revisions of the theory have downplayed the distinction between environmental and self-focus for several reasons (Carver, 1979; Carver & Scheier, 1981a; see also Kernis et al., 1988). First, attention constantly and rapidly switches back and forth between self and environment, instead of focusing wholly and for long periods of time on either the self or the environment. Moreover, the dichotomy is paradoxical in that often external stimuli focus attention inward. Various environmental factors create self-attention: a mirror, a camera, an audience, a tape recording of one's voice (Wicklund, 1975), and even group composition, such as whether one's own group is in a minority position (Mullen, 1983, 1986, 1987; Mullen & Baumeister, 1987) all can make people aware of themselves.[3]

Self-focused attention does not lead to unitary consequences, because the self is a highly differentiated stimulus. When one is self-directed, one can be directed toward any facet of the self. In this context, one must consider both focus of attention and personal standards. People often find themselves in situations in which they have particular competencies or beliefs that are relevant to that situation. If a person becomes self-focused upon being in such a situation and the salient aspect of the self is the relevant standard or competency, then the induction of self-focused attention should have a motivating effect on the person (Wicklund, 1986). As long as self-focus does not stray to irrelevant aspects of the self and the person has the behavioral capabilities necessary for a dynamic fit with the exigencies of the environment, the induction of self-focus should enhance motivation and performance. A more static orientation toward the environment results when the person does not have the competencies necessary for the situation or when attention is directed away from the specific personal performance standards that are relevant to the situation; under such circumstances, the person may retreat from the demands of a situation.

Thus, self-focus can make various features of the self salient depending upon the circumstances. For example, males who are self-

---

[3]It should be noted that internal factors also produce self-focused attention, such as a chronic tendency to attend internally (Fenigstein, Scheier, & Buss, 1975) or a negative mood (J. V. Wood, Saltzberg, & Goldsamt, 1990).

focused are generally less aggressive toward females, presumably because the considerate part of their ideal selves normally is salient (Scheier, Fenigstein, & Buss, 1974). But the considerate part of their ideal selves may not always be salient. People who are self-focused sometimes are more aggressive than otherwise. This happens when the angry part of themselves is made salient (Scheier, 1976; Scheier & Carver, 1977). Clearly, then, various aspects of people's selves can become salient, including either positive norms or negative emotions. Since the self has many aspects, self-attention per se does not lead to a single outcome. Nonetheless, it has many important ramifications.

Comparing oneself to ideal standards. Imagine going out to dinner at an elegant restaurant with plush carpets, dark wood paneling, and mirrors. You are seated facing your date and also—maddeningly—you are forced to gaze directly into the mirror on the wall behind the person. Try as you might to position yourself, you keep seeing your own face as you drink, nibble, and make conversation. Despite your best efforts, you keep noticing your windblown hair, the awkward way you smile, and the unattractive way you chew. Feeling utterly foolish by the time the main course arrives, you flee to the bathroom to comb your hair and vow to change tables upon your return. Self-attention often causes people to compare themselves to their ideals, and more specifically to whatever ideal standard is salient at the time. For example, if you were seated opposite a mirror at a business meeting, you might focus more on whether you appeared competent than on whether you appeared attractive.

In comparing ourselves to an ideal, we often fall short in our own eyes (Duval & Wicklund, 1972; Wicklund, 1975, 1978, 1979; Wicklund & Frey, 1980). Consequently, objective self-awareness can be aversive. However, self-attention need not focus on positive ideal standards for the self. Some internal standards are negative, as when eight-year-old Kathy remembers her mother saying, "I certainly hope you are not as rude at Jane's house as she is when she visits here." Failing to imitate a negative ideal is obviously cause for pride, not aversion. Hence, positive or negative affect can result from one's success or failure to match behavior to standards (Carver, 1979). One may even exceed a positive standard and feel good (Wicklund, 1975).

Self-esteem also moderates the effect of self-focus, such that for positively valenced outcomes, those with high self-esteem are more likely to take credit for the outcomes when self-focused, but low self-esteem individuals are less likely to take credit for positively valenced outcomes when self-focused (J. D. Brown, 1988; see also J. L. Cohen et al., 1985). Self-focused attention is also more likely to produce emotional distress among individuals with a feminine gender type than those with a more masculine gender orientation (Ingram et al., 1988).

It should be noted that, whereas self-awareness researchers no longer consider negative affect to be a necessary consequence of self-awareness, there is still evidence that self-awareness is often aversive. In those cases in which people compare themselves to an ideal, fall short, and feel unable to do anything about it, self-attention can cause substantial distress (Steenbarger & Aderman, 1979; Carver, Blaney, & Scheier, 1979). As in the restaurant example, people often attempt to escape when confronted with their own inadequacies (Duval & Wicklund, 1972; Gibbons & Wicklund, 1976). If a speedy and dignified exit is impossible, self-aware people struggle to conform to the salient ideals, which may be their own standards or other people's. People will sometimes go to considerable lengths to escape the unpleasant consequences of self-awareness, including engaging in masochistic behavior (Baumeister, 1988), suicide (Baumeister, 1990b), and other maladaptive behavior patterns.

In general, self-aware people are likely to be more honest, more helpful, more industrious, and less punitive than others (e.g., Reis & Burns, 1982; see Wicklund & Frey, 1980, for a review). One view of self-awareness is that it civilizes us because it reminds us of our better selves; in that sense, it is a theory of the conscience or superego, according to Wicklund. The notion that self-awareness awakens one's conscience underscores the importance of motivation as a link between attentional focus and behavior.

The cybernetic theory of self-regulation. In general, self-focus appears to set in motion an adjustment process. Given a standard, either positive or negative, people automatically compare and accordingly adjust their behavior. They attempt to conform behaviorally to standards, compare their adjusted behavior with the ideal standard, and decide either that it matches the standard or that it does not; this process is called feedback. People continue adjusting and comparing in feedback cycles until they meet the standard or until they give up. A series of feedback loops set in motion by self-attention is known as the *cybernetic theory of self-regulation* (Carver & Scheier, 1981b; Scheier & Carver, 1988).

To understand the basic principle of any cybernetic model, think of the parallel with a household furnace thermostat, which monitors the discrepancy between a set standard (e.g., 72 degrees) and the existing situation (e.g., 65 degrees). When the standard and the existing situation are discrepant, the thermostat initiates a chain of events (starting the furnace) that changes the existing situation to fit the standard (warms the house to 72 degrees). When the comparison indicates that the standard and the situation are no longer discrepant, the adjustment process ceases. A similar feedback and adjustment process could operate when you try to match any standard you set for yourself, for example, getting a geometry proof right or impressing your advisor. Self-attention appears to initiate and maintain such an adjustment process within people.

The critical point is that trying to fit a standard may be a simple result of attending to a discrepancy between one's own behavior and a standard. It need not be based on a motivational aversion to one's own inadequacy, as the original self-awareness theory would have it (Carver & Scheier, 1981b; Gibbons et al., 1979). However, debate over the exact nature of the attentional interpretation continues (Ellis & Holmes, 1982; Hull & Levy, 1979; Wicklund & Hormuth, 1981). Most agree, however, that self-focus is importantly attentional and that it sets in motion an adjustment process.

Finally, the cybernetic self-regulation perspective generally posits that adjustment attempts will precede giving up. For example, if you stare at yourself in the restaurant mirror, you may smooth your hair or straighten your collar, to conform better to your ideal standard of attractiveness. If you notice a huge stain down your front, you may be tempted to leave altogether. Thus, people do not always try to escape self-focus; self-awareness causes withdrawal only when change is hopeless. When adjustment attempts are doomed to failure, people may try to escape either mentally or physically. That is, you may ask your date to leave early, or you may stay but feel self-conscious and emotionally withdrawn. The cybernetic model of self-attention is summarized in Figure 6.3.

Self-focus and failures to self-regulate. The concept of self-focus has recently been related to certain inabilities to self-regulate successfully (see Kirschenbaum, Tomarken, & Humphrey, 1985). The argument is that negative emotional states, such as anxiety or depression, may focus attention on the self, thereby interfering with the ability to monitor effectively one's performance on a specific task or in a social environment (Baumeister, 1990a; S. Strack, Blaney, & Ganellen, 1985).

S. Strack, Blaney, & Ganellen (1985) suggest that depression prompts a pessimistic self-focus which can account for some of the performance deficits that are commonly observed in this disorder. In response to failure, it appears that depressed subjects persist in self-focusing longer than do nondepressed subjects (Greenberg & Pyszczynski, 1986). Pyszczynski and Greenberg (1987) argue that depression sets into effect self-regulatory processes that in turn maintain the depression. In particular, they argue that depression prompts a self-regulatory cycle in which the individual chronically attends inwardly, focusing on the discrepancy between the actual behavior and the desired state. Given that no behaviors are found that can reduce the discrepancy, these factors eventually promote a negative self-image. The depressive self-focusing style, then, is argued to be a factor that both maintains and exacerbates depressive disorders. Interestingly, psycho-

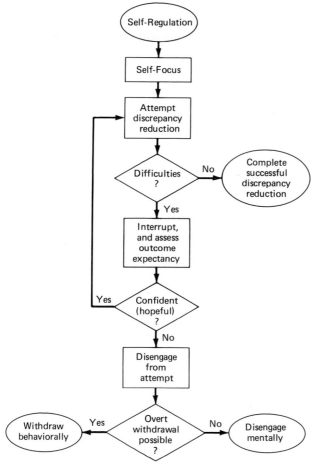

FIGURE 6.3 The cybernetic theory of self-attention
and self-regulation. (After Carver, 1979.)

therapy, too, can increase self-awareness in its own right, making people less self-enhancing (Gibbons et al., 1985).

Private and public self-consciousness. Research has emphasized
the utility of conceptualizing different aspects of consciousness about
the self. Fenigstein, Scheier, and Buss (1975) describe the public self as
consisting of observable behaviors, speech, facial expressions and physical attributes such as clothing. The private self, in contrast, consists of
internal bodily sensations, emotional feelings, thoughts, self-
evaluations, evaluations of others, and other self-produced stimuli that
cannot be observed by others. Fenigstein, Scheier, & Buss (1975) argued
that this dimension represents a chronic predisposition, such that some

people attend primarily to the public aspects of themselves, whereas others attend primarily to their own private aspects. Table 6.2 includes some of the items from the self-consciousness scale that assesses private and public self-consciousness.

Research suggests the usefulness of this distinction (e.g., Agatstein & Buchanan, 1984; Piliavin & Charna, 1988; Nasby, 1985, 1989; Kassin, 1984; see Carver & Scheier, 1985, for a review), although criticisms of the logic of the distinction remain (Gollwitzer & Wicklund, 1987; Wicklund & Gollwitzer, 1987; Carver & Scheier, 1987). People high in public self-consciousness moderate their opinions more in anticipation of a group discussion than those low in public self-consciousness. Resistance to opinion-change efforts by others is stronger among those high in private self-consciousness, whereas expressions of opinion change are associated with public self-consciousness (Scheier & Carver, 1980). Those higher in private self-consciousness resist group pressure more successfully than those low on that dimension (Froming & Carver, 1981; Santee & Maslach, 1982). And those higher in public self-consciousness are more likely than those low on the dimension to per-

---

TABLE 6.2 SELF-CONSCIOUSNESS SCALE

Indicate whether you generally agree (A) or disagree (D) with each of the following items.

_____ 1. I'm always trying to figure myself out.

_____ 2. I'm concerned about my style of doing things.

_____ 3. Generally, I'm not very aware of myself.

_____ 4. I reflect about myself a lot.

_____ 5. I'm concerned about the way I present myself.

_____ 6. I'm self-conscious about the way I look.

_____ 7. I never scrutinize myself.

_____ 8. I'm generally attentive to my inner feelings.

_____ 9. I usually worry about making a good impression.

If you answered "agree" on items 1, 4, and 8, and "disagree" on items 3 and 7, you would be scoring high on the private self-consciousness scale. If you answered "agree" to items 2, 5, 6, and 9, your score would be high on the public self-consciousness scale. Note that the entire scale is considerably longer than the excerpt above.

Source: After A. Fenigstein, M. F. Scheier, & A. H. Buss, Public and private self-consciousness: Assessment and theory, *Journal of Consulting and Clinical Psychology*, 1975, 43, 522–527. Copyright 1975 by the American Psychological Association. Adapted by permission of the authors.

ceive social situations as relevant to themselves or targeted toward themselves (Fenigstein, 1984).

MOTIVATIONAL PROCESSES AND SELF-REGULATION

We have seen that self-regulation is guided by self-conceptions, perceptions of self-efficacy and self-attention. The self-regulation process is also guided by underlying motivational processes, that is, by the desire to further some goals and avoid others. In this context, research has examined three underlying motivations that may lead people to self-regulate their mental and behavioral life, both alone and in interaction with others. The first of these is the need for accuracy, that is, the extent to which a person desires to have accurate knowledge about the self and the self's abilities. The second motivation is self-enhancement, which is the tendency to maintain the most favorable self-conception possible. The third is consistency, or what Swann calls, self-verification, namely the processes by which people strive to maintain and confirm preexisting conceptions of themselves.

The Need for Accuracy

Trope (1975, 1979, 1980, 1983) maintains that in order to make future outcomes predictable and controllable, people need to assess their abilities accurately. Achievement situations provide people with an opportunity to gain ability information. Trope predicts that, in the absence of extrinsic social or material factors that might induce people to save face or strive to succeed, people pick tasks that give them the most information about their abilities. Tasks on which differences in abilities lead to large performance differences are termed *diagnostic*; they are especially likely to be selected by a person because they will provide a lot of ability-related information (Trope, 1979). For example, if a particular individual wanted to know how good he was at spatial abilities, he would probably not pick a child's puzzle or Rubik's Cube to solve: anyone can do the first task, few people can do the second task, and those who can solve it may do so for reasons other than spatial ability. Accordingly, the kind of task this individual would pick might be a set of embedded figures graded in difficulty (e.g., triangles hiding amidst an ever more complex forest of geometric shapes). Seeing how many he can solve would then provide some information about his ability.

Other things being equal, people are most likely to pick highly diagnostic tasks on attributes about which they are most uncertain (Trope, 1979; Trope & Ben-Yair, 1982). For example, an accountant with a dubious romantic reputation is likely to choose a diagnostic social skills task over an arithmetic test, whereas the social butterfly who is trying to decide whether or not to fill out a tax form without assistance might choose the arithmetic test over the social skills test. People will also choose tasks that are maximally diagnostic at the point on which they are most uncertain (Trope, 1979). Thus, for example, if you know you are moderately good on some ability (e.g., pistol shooting), you are unlikely to choose a task that is highly diagnostic at low levels of that ability (e.g., shooting at a static target at close range); rather, you should pick a task that is diagnostic within the moderate range (e.g., shooting at a slowly moving target at moderate range).

The need to assess one's abilities extends to situations of success and failure. When subjects expect to succeed, they select tasks on which their successful performance will also be informative; likewise, when subjects expect to fail, they select tasks on which failure is diagnostic (Trope, 1979). Uncertainty and task diagnosticity also predict performance; more effort is expended when both uncertainty and task diagnosticity are high than when they are low. Consistent success or consistent failure on a diagnostic task prompts people to stop working on a task sooner (Trope & Ben-Yair, 1982). It should be noted that Trope's paradigm has been criticized by several researchers, suggesting that the case for diagnosticity has not truly been made. In particular, arguments center around ambiguities in the experimental procedures that complicate interpretation of the results and the relevance of those procedures to real-world situations (Sohn, 1984; J. D. Brown, 1990).

Overall, Trope's work suggests that self-assessment may be an important determinant of task selection, especially when knowledge of an ability is uncertain (Sorrentino & Roney, 1986; see also de Vries & van Knippenberg, 1985; Sanders, 1985; Sanders & Mullen, 1984). Presumably, accurate self-assessment enables people to anticipate and control their future performance (see also Buckert, Meyer, & Schmalt, 1979; Trope & Bassok, 1982).

Self-Enhancement

Clearly, people need to have accurate information about their abilities and opinions. Without some degree of accuracy, people would be vulnerable to a host of faulty judgments and decisions, including the likelihood of an incorrect career choice or a poor selection of a mate. Yet, research also shows that people's self-regulation processes are heavily influenced by the need to feel good about themselves and to maintain self-esteem (e.g., Greenwald, Bellezza, & Banaji, 1988). Moreover, research suggests that the impressions people hold of themselves may be falsely positive and somewhat exaggerated with respect to their actual abilities, talents, and social skills.

Most individuals possess a very positive view of the self (see Greenwald, 1980; S. E. Taylor & Brown, 1988, for reviews). When asked to indicate how accurately positive and negative personality adjectives describe them, people judge positive traits to be overwhelmingly more characteristic of self than negative attributes (Alicke, 1985; J. D. Brown, 1986). In addition, for most individuals, positive personality information is efficiently processed and easily recalled, whereas negative personality information is poorly processed and difficult to recall (Kuiper & Derry, 1982; Kuiper & MacDonald, 1982; Kuiper et al., 1985). Most individuals also show poorer recall for information related to failure than to success (Silverman, 1964) and tend to recall their task performance as more positive than it actually was (Crary, 1966). Research on the self-serving bias in causal attribution documents that most individuals are more likely to attribute positive than negative outcomes to the self (see Bradley, 1978; D. T. Miller & Ross, 1975; Ross & Fletcher, 1985; Zuckerman, 1979, for reviews; see Chapter 3). People even overvalue the letters in their own name, relative to alphabet letters that do not appear in their names (Nuttin, 1985, 1987).

Even when negative aspects of the self are acknowledged, they tend to be regarded as less consequential. One's poor abilities tend to be perceived as common, but one's favored abilities are seen as rare and distinctive (Campbell, 1986; Marks, 1984). Furthermore, the things at which people are not proficient are perceived as less important than the things at which they are proficient (e.g., Campbell, 1986; Harackiewicz, Sansone, & Manderlink, 1985; Lewicki, 1985; M. Rosenberg, 1979). And people perceive that they have improved on abilities that are important to them even when their performance has remained unchanged (Conway & Ross, 1984).

The positive self-conceptions that people hold appear to be at least somewhat unrealistic or illusory (S. E. Taylor & Brown, 1988). First, there exists a pervasive tendency to see the self as better than others. Individuals judge positive personality attributes to be more descriptive of themselves than of the average person but see negative personality attributes as less descriptive of themselves than of the average person (Alicke, 1985; J. D. Brown, 1986; Messick et al., 1985). This effect has been documented for a wide range of traits (J. D. Brown, 1986; J. D. Brown & Lord, 1990) and abilities (Campbell, 1986; Svenson, 1981; Larwood & Whittaker, 1977). Because it is logically impossible for most people to be better or less vulnerable than the average person, these highly skewed, positive views of the self can be regarded as evidence for their unrealistic and illusory nature. People also tend to use their own positive qualities when appraising others, virtually assuring a favorable self-other comparison (Lewicki, 1984). And as we saw in Chapter 3, people give others less credit for success and more blame for failure than they ascribe to themselves (Forsyth & Schlenker, 1977; Green & Gross, 1979; Mirels, 1980; Schlenker & Miller, 1977; S. E. Taylor & Koivumaki, 1976).

A second source of evidence pertaining to the illusory quality of positive self-perceptions comes from investigations in which self-ratings have been compared with judgments made by observers. Lewinsohn et al. (1980) had observers watch college-student subjects complete a group-interaction task. Observers then rated each subject along a number of personality dimensions (e.g., friendly, warm, and assertive). Subjects also rated themselves on each attribute. The results showed that self-ratings were significantly more positive than the observers' ratings. In other words, individuals saw themselves in more flattering terms than they were seen by others.

Are there any conditions under which people are more accurate or balanced in their self-appraisals? Suggestive evidence indicates that individuals who are low in self-esteem, moderately depressed, or both are more balanced in self-perceptions (see Coyne & Gotlib, 1983; Ruehlman, West, & Pasahow, 1985; Watson & Clark, 1984, for reviews). These individuals tend to (a) recall positive and negative self-relevant information with equal frequency (e.g., Kuiper & Derry, 1982; Kuiper & MacDonald, 1982), (b) show greater evenhandedness in their attributions of responsibility for valenced outcomes (e.g., Campbell & Fairey, 1985; Kuiper, 1978; Rizley, 1978), (c) display greater congruence between self-evaluations and evaluations of others (e.g., J. D. Brown, 1986), (d) offer self-appraisals that coincide more closely with appraisals by objective observers (e.g., Lewinsohn et al., 1980). In short, the individual who experiences subjective distress appears to be more likely to process self-relevant information in a relatively unbiased and balanced fashion. The differences in self-perceptions between those high and low in self-esteem appear to be enhanced when the accessibility of self-perceptions is increased (J. D. Brown, 1989).

Impressions of one's own personality and social skills are not the only factors on which people show reliable self-enhancement effects. The perception of personal control also seems to be exaggerated. In a series of studies involving gambling formats, Langer and her associates (Langer, 1975; Langer & Roth, 1975) found that people often act as if they have control over situations that are actually determined by chance, such as whether or not they can influence the roll of the dice or the flip of a coin (Fleming & Darley, 1986). Similarly, a large literature on covariation estimation indicates that people overestimate their degree of control over heavily chance-determined events (see Crocker, 1982, for a review). As is the case with perceptions of one's own personality and social skills, mildly and severely depressed individuals appear to be less vulnerable to this illusion of control (Abramson & Alloy, 1981; Golin, Terrell, & Johnson, 1977; Golin et al., 1979; M. S. Greenberg, Vazquez, & Alloy, 1988).

People are also biased in their assessments of the future. They estimate the likelihood that they will experience a wide variety of pleasant events as higher than those of their peers, such as liking their first job, getting a good salary, or having a gifted child (Weinstein, 1980). Conversely, when asked their chances of experiencing a wide variety of negative events, including having an automobile accident (Robertson, 1977), being a crime victim (Perloff & Fetzer, 1986), having trouble finding a job (Weinstein, 1980), or becoming ill (Perloff & Fetzer, 1986) or depressed (Kuiper, MacDonald, & Derry, 1983), most people believe that they are less likely than their peers to experience such negative events. Over a wide variety of tasks, subjects' predictions of what will occur in the future correspond closely to what they would like to see happen or to what is socially desirable, rather than to what is objectively likely (Cantril, 1938; Lund, 1975; McGuire, 1960; Pruitt & Hoge, 1965; S. J. Sherman, 1980). Again, mildly depressed people and those with low self-esteem appear to entertain more balanced assessments of their likely future circumstances (see Ruehlman, West, & Pasahow, 1985, for a review).

Why are people so apparently self-enhancing in their self-perceptions, and moreover, why do these self-enhancing perceptions exist if they do not conform to reality? In a review of the self-enhancement literature, S. E. Taylor and Brown (1988) argue that self-enhancing perceptions are adaptive because they appear to promote criteria associated with mental health. In their analysis, they relate positive distortions of the self, the world, and the future to the ability to be happy or contented, the ability to care about others (see also Epstein & Feist, 1988), and the ability to engage in productive, creative work, all criteria that have traditionally been regarded as evidence for successful life adjustment (cf. Deci & Ryan, 1987; Burger, 1985). Thus, for example, people who are falsely optimistic about the likelihood of succeeding on a difficult task may set higher aspirations for themselves, work harder on the task, and be more likely to succeed at it than people whose self-assessments are lower but objectively more realistic.

People are able to maintain these false assessments of their abilities, Taylor and Brown maintain, because both the social world and inferential strategies (see Chapter 9) impose filters on incoming information that distort it in a positive direction (e.g., Pyszczynski, Greenberg, & Holt, 1985; Pyszczynski, Greenberg, & LaPrelle, 1985). We elsewhere examine many of these strategies in the context of causal attributions (Chapters 2 and 3) and social inference (Chapter 9). In many ways, the strategies that people employ to maintain their unrealistically positive self-conceptions are similar to those that they employ to maintain consistency with any other schema. People can preserve their positive self-conceptions, for example, by engaging in self-serving causal attributions, that is, taking credit for good things that happen to them but not for bad ones. Under some circumstances, negative information or infor-

mation that does not fit with prior self-conceptions may be ignored, forgotten, or reinterpreted. People may assimilate ambiguous information
to preexisting positive schemas about the self (see Chapter 6). Even anticipatory pessimism about one's future performance can serve a self-
enhancing function; by leading the self to expect poor outcomes or poor
performance, one lays the groundwork for defending against loss of self-
esteem in the event of failure or experiencing elation in the case of even
moderate success. Moreover, the defensive pessimism strategy may enable a person to control anxiety during the performance of a risky task,
thereby improving performance (Norem & Cantor, 1986a, 1986b).

Negative attributes whose existence cannot be distorted or denied
may be maintained in the self-concept in as benign a fashion as possible
through negative self-schemas or acknowledged areas of incompetence
(S. E. Taylor & Brown, 1988). For example, a person may readily acknowledge a lack of talent in art but make art such a small part of his
life that the lack of competence makes little difference. People may
avoid social situations and companions who bring out these negative
aspects in themselves in order that the deficient area not loom large in
the self-concept. Just as self-esteem and depression moderate the content of the self-concept, so they also appear to moderate the strategies
employed to maintain a positive versus negative self-concept. Those
low in self-esteem and suffering from depression are less likely to engage in the strategies that preserve self-enhancing self-perceptions
(e.g., J. D. Brown, Collins, & Schmidt, 1988).

Taylor and Brown's analysis does not necessarily imply that falsely
positive self-perceptions are always adaptive. Indeed, there may be
conditions in which people's inability to appreciate objective risks and
liabilities could interfere with their goals. For example, faith in one's capacity to master situations may lead a person to persevere at tasks that
may in fact be uncontrollable; knowing when to abandon a task may be
as important as knowing when to pursue it (Janoff-Bulman & Brickman,
1982). Unrealistic optimism may lead people to ignore legitimate risks in
their environment and fail to take measures to offset those risks. Thus, the
boundary conditions around people's positive self-impressions have yet to
be fully explored. Nonetheless, the evidence is substantial that people's
self-perceptions are biased in a falsely positive direction and that, at least
in some respects, these biased self-perceptions are adaptive.

Self-Evaluation Maintenance

As we have just seen, people generally hold positive self-conceptions
and adopt cognitive and social strategies designed to maintain those
positive views. Tesser and his associates (Tesser, 1988, for a review)
have suggested another social mechanism by which people facilitate
and maintain their positive impressions of themselves, namely, how

the performances of other people in the social environment threaten or enhance one's own sense of self.

The central proposition of Tesser's model is that people evaluate themselves and need to feel good about those self-evaluations (Tesser, 1988; Tesser & Campbell, 1983; Tesser, Campbell, & Smith, 1984; Tesser & Collins, 1988; Tesser, Millar, & More, 1988; Tesser & Paulhus, 1983; Tesser & Smith, 1980). When another person in the social environment performs well or poorly on some task, the social perceiver asks, "What are the implications of this performance for me and my own abilities?" Either one can feel good by basking in the accomplishments of another (reflection), or one can feel bad in comparison, if the other has outperformed the self. Tesser argues that the cognitive and affective reactions that people have to another's performance on a task can be predicted by: the psychological closeness of the two individuals; the relevance of the task dimension to the self-evaluator's self-definitions; and the quality of one's own and the other's performance. The core of Tesser's argument is that people behave in a way that maximizes their self-evaluation or minimizes their loss in self-evaluation. They regulate their behavior and cognitions in order to maintain this positive self-regard.

Closeness refers to the relationship between the person and the target individual. For example, friends are close but strangers are not. In response to another's performance, the closer the other is, the greater the threat experienced. When a friend outperforms you on an attribute that is important to you, that is more threatening than if a stranger does so. Tesser maintains that when a close other outperforms the self, there will be a tendency for the person to reduce closeness. Each person needs to do well on his or her own turf. These effects appear to be intensified by relevance.

Relevance refers to how central a dimension is to an individual's self-definition. For example, athletic ability would be very central to an athlete's self-conception, whereas it might not be so central to the self-conception of a sedentary person. Relevance acts as an intensifier of emotional responses. When relevance is high, the comparison of the self to the other person is important, whereas when relevance is low, the comparison process is less important. When another person does well on an attribute that is central to the self, implications for .self-evaluation may be negative, and therefore the person may feel badly or take steps to undermine the other's performance. In contrast, when the dimension is of low relevance, one may not only fail to react adversely to the performance, but actually take pride in it (reflection). Thus, the athlete may be quite happy over her friend's successful piano recital, but be upset about the friend who broke the school long-jump record.

In an experimental test of these hypotheses, Tesser and Smith (1980) had college-student subjects participate in a password game. Three participants selected clues for a fourth participant, who had to guess the target word. In the high-relevance condition, performance on the task was represented as relevant to verbal ability, whereas in the low-relevance condition, performance was described as not very indicative of anything about the person. Clues that could be provided to the target individual ranged in difficulty. Under conditions of high relevance, subjects gave the target subject more difficult clues than when it was low. More interesting, the relevance effect interacted with closeness. When the target individual was a friend of the subject's, the subjects gave harder clues in the high-relevance condition but gave easier clues in the low-relevance condition.

As may be evident, closeness, relevance, and performance interact with each other. When a close individual performs well on a task, perceptions of the relevance of the task to one's own self-definition may be distorted so as to reduce perceptions of relevance. Similarly, when relevance of the dimension is high and the other does well, closeness may be altered, such that people grow apart. When relevance and closeness are both high, people may attempt to improve their performance relative to the other person. When your close friend does well on an athletic task, if athletics is important to you, you try harder than if the other is a stranger. Tesser's model also predicts that affective responses will follow the perception of threat (Tesser & Collins, 1988). When one is outperformed by another, one feels badly, and this is increasingly true the higher the relevance of the dimension and the closer the relationship. In contrast, when another does well on a dimension that is not central to self-definition, one can feel vicarious pride in the other's achievements, and this is more true with close than distant others. Indeed, emotional responses may well mediate the overt behavioral changes that occur in response to these types of events (Tesser, 1988). A schematic representation of self-evaluation maintenance theory and its impact on behavior and emotion appears in Figure 6.4.

In summary, then, Tesser's self-evaluation maintenance model is significant for several reasons. First, it adds to our comprehension of self-regulation processes by showing that interpretations of others' behavior may have implications for the self that lead to predictable changes in performance, affect, and relationship closeness (cf. Finch & Cialdini, 1989). Second, the work outlines mechanisms whereby people self-regulate so as to maintain positivity in their self-perceptions. And finally, the work shows how cognitive constructions of events can affect the relationships and interactions that people have with friends and strangers.

The Need for Consistency

In addition to the needs to have accurate self-knowledge and to have a positive sense of self, people also strive to maintain consistency in their self-impressions (Backman, 1988; Swann, 1983). They seek out and in-

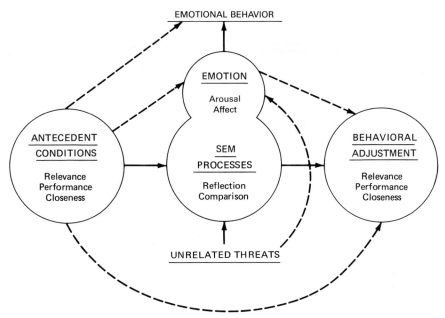

FIGURE 6.4 A schematic representation of the self-evaluation maintenance model. (After Tesser, 1988.)

terpret situations and adopt behavioral strategies that confirm their existing self-conceptions. And they avoid or resist situations or feedback
that yield information at odds with their existing self-conceptions. If I
am at a party and want to feel like and project the image of a fun-
loving, happy-go-lucky person, I will likely avoid my colleague who
makes me feel like a boring old academician in favor of the company of
other fun-loving types. At the end of the party, assuming it has been
successful, I will have one more occasion that bolsters my fun-loving
self-image.

A series of studies by Swann and Read (1981b) suggests that this
tendency is fairly widespread. In one study, subjects were led to believe
that others' evaluations of them would be either consistent or inconsistent with their own self-image. When given a chance to see these evaluations, subjects spent more time perusing the consistent than the inconsistent feedback. This was true even when the others' evaluations
were negative, such as a belief that one is basically disliked by others.
In their second study, Swann and Read found that when interacting
with others, people tend to use behavioral strategies that confirm their
self-conceptions rather than those that disconfirm them: this tendency
is especially strong when one believes others have incorrect beliefs
about the self. To take a hypothetical example, suppose you learn that

your new date, Linda, considers you a fun-loving, extroverted, party-goer. If you actually hate parties and believe yourself to be more introverted, you may go out of your way on your next date to stress your solitary qualities, even at the expense of alienating Linda (see also Swann & Read, 1981a).

If all else fails in this self-verification effort, you can, of course, preferentially recall the things you did that are consistent with your self-conception, ignoring those that were inconsistent. In Swann and Read's third study, they found that this, too, is an effective way of bolstering self-conceptions. In fact, memory may be distorted so as to maintain perceptions of consistency. Kulik and Mahler (1986), for example, had self-perceived extroverts and introverts engage in a getting-acquainted conversation. Immediately afterward or a week later, participants judged how much they had talked during the interaction. The results showed that even after controlling for the actual amount of participation time, extroverts perceived themselves as talking more, and this increased over time, whereas introverts perceived themselves as having talked less, a tendency which also increased over time. Thus, people consistently seek and recall information that confirms their self-concepts (Swann & Read, 1981a, 1981b).

People tend to see more self-confirmatory evidence than may actually exist (Swann, 1987). They attend to self-confirmatory feedback more (Swann & Read, 1981b, Study One), they encode it and recall it preferentially (Crary, 1966; Silverman, 1964; Swann & Read, 1981b, Study Three), and they interpret feedback in a consistent manner. For example, Swann et al. (1987) found that self-confirmatory feedback tended to be attributed to one's own qualities, whereas feedback that disconfirmed self-conceptions tended to be attributed to the source of the feedback (see also Kulik, Sledge, & Mahler, 1986). But, as Swann (1987) points out, there may be limits on attentional, encoding, retrieval, and interpretational processes that distort feedback about the self. People sometimes behaviorally undo others' incorrect conceptions of them. If they were able cognitively to turn all self-discrepant feedback into self-confirmatory feedback, they would never need to correct others' misconceptions. Thus, self-perception appears to be a combination of efforts to maintain self-conceptions cognitively, with social efforts to identify and undo discrepancies in others' conceptions of the self.

Social strategies of self-verification. There are a number of social strategies that people use to ensure that others will see them in the same ways that they see themselves. Selective interaction with people who see you as you see yourself is one method of maintaining self-conceptions. Swann and Pelham (1990) found, for example, that people prefer their friends and intimates to see them as they see themselves (see also Swann & Brown, 1990). In a field study of this hypothesis, Swann and Pelham (1990) found that students whose roommates' appraisals of their attributes were incongruent with their own perceptions of those attributes were more likely to plan to change roommates than were those in congruent relationships. Moreover, this was true regardless of whether people were high or low in self-esteem. Even favorable perceptions of the self by others may be avoided if they are perceived as inaccurate. People gravitate toward congruent relationships and away from incongruent ones.

Consistency in self-image is also maintained by the fact that in life, just as in some experiments (Swann & Read, 1981a, 1981b), people select and interpret their own situations and may do so, in part, to gain self-confirming feedback (Swann, 1983). People choose signs and symbols in their clothes that say a lot about who they are (Schlenker, 1985). They then attract and/or gravitate to the people who are consistent with their image, and engage in conversations that confirm their image and values (see Deaux & Major, 1987, for a discussion of this selection process in the context of gender-consistent behavior).

People also use their intimate others to protect them from discrepant feedback. In a study by Swann and Predmore (1985), subjects came into the laboratory with an intimate partner with whom they had had a relationship for an average of 18 months. The subject, hereafter referred to as the target, was given a test and then provided with bogus feedback that was either consistent or inconsistent with self-conceptions. Intimates who saw the target as the target saw himself or herself were able to help the target argue away and resolve the discrepant feedback. Incongruent intimates, that is those who held views of their partners that their partners did not hold of themselves, had some ability to help the target explain away the feedback, but were not as successful. Importantly, these processes occurred both for those with high self-esteem and low self-esteem. Thus, those who think of themselves in unflattering ways apparently enlist the cooperation of others in helping themselves to maintain these beliefs, even though their beliefs are unflattering.

The preceding sections suggest that self-verification is an active, ongoing process and that people are constantly vigilant for efforts to miscast them or disconfirm their self-conceptions. In fact, this portrait probably is not accurate (Swann, 1987). Most of the time, people are able to maintain their self-views without active or conscious effort because self-verification is routine, part of the process of interacting with friends, family, and co-workers in familiar settings, performing familiar tasks. In certain crisis situations, however, when people receive discrepant feedback, they may be motivated to focus active attention on the threat to self-conceptions and enact active self-verification efforts (Swann & Hill, 1982).

Individual differences and self-verification. Self-verification processes are clearly influenced by the certainty with which people hold their self-views, a dimension termed self-certainty. People high in self-certainty are more likely to prefer relationships with others who see them as they see themselves (Pelham & Swann, 1989; Swann & Pelham, 1990). The attitudes of those high in self-certainty are also typically very resistant to change. In a paradoxical demonstration of this effect, people who were either high or low in belief certainty were queried about their attitudes with leading questions that encouraged the respondents to make statements that were consistent with but more extreme than their actual viewpoints. Those high in belief certainty resisted the implicit persuasion effort and, in fact, changed their beliefs in the opposite direction in an apparent effort to avoid having themselves miscast (Swann, Pelham, & Chidester, 1988). Besides self-certainty, the importance of the self-relevant domain may also influence the degree to which people engage in self-verification processes. People may work harder to verify important self-conceptions than unimportant ones because the important ones are related to their goals and future plans (Pelham & Swann, 1989; see also Markus & Nurius, 1986).

Self-verification and discrepant feedback. Despite the fact that we have fixed ideas of what we are like, the environment often presents situations in which we must assess beliefs about ourselves that are discrepant with prior self-conceptions. What is the impact of assessing our standing on a self-discrepant attribute when the environment pressures us to manifest that attribute? In one study by M. Snyder & Skrypnek (1981), subjects were first tested on a sex-role inventory (S. L. Bem, 1981) to see if they were primarily masculine, primarily feminine, or androgynous (balanced in masculine and feminine attributes) in their personal attributes. The subjects were then asked to assess their suitability for a job that demanded either typically masculine attributes or typically feminine ones. Regardless of their actual sex-role identity, subjects selectively reported self-relevant information consistent with the requirements of the job, leading them to see themselves as qualified for the position. Not only was evidence supporting the discrepant belief preferentially recalled but only supportive evidence predicted final self-perceptions of the job's suitability. Thus, even when recalled, self-relevant evidence that conflicted with the attribute being tested did not affect judgments. Apparently, we can behave in ways that lead us to hold contradictory beliefs about ourselves (see also Gergen, 1977; McGuire & Padawer-Singer, 1976; Swann, 1983; Tedeschi & Lindskold, 1976; see Swann & Hill, 1982, for a discussion).

Although people may be induced to assess or entertain hypotheses about themselves that conflict with self-conceptions, both experience and extensive research on the self-concept (e.g., Block, 1981; Schein,

1956; Wylie, 1979) tell us that such changes may not last long. When do discrepant beliefs last and when are they rejected? One condition may be whether or not one has the opportunity to refute inconsistent feedback. Having been miscast by another person, the opportunity to turn him or her around by using behavioral strategies that reverse the other's impressions can undo the false conception in both the other's mind and one's own mind. When allowed to go unchallenged, however, discrepant hypotheses may be at least somewhat accepted by both the evaluator and the self (Swann & Hill, 1982).

When people do not have a chance to undo these misconceptions, how permanent are the alterations in their own self-concept? The answer seems to be: not very permanent. After a few days, any influence of miscasting effects on self-perceptions seems to disappear (Swann & Hill, 1982). Very possibly, people see themselves behaving as they always have, and fall back into their old self-evaluative ways, as the implications of miscasting fade with time. Apparently, then, even when one has temporarily convinced oneself of the appropriateness of some new self-conception (as in M. Snyder and Skrypnek's 1981 study described earlier), those alterations in self-conception have little long-term impact (see also L. Ross, Lepper, & Hubbard, 1975).

Does this mean that people never change their self-concepts? There may be circumstances that lead people to undertake a major reorganization in the way they view themselves. The research suggests that not only must people come to believe these new self-views, but their interaction partners should provide them with feedback that supports the new self-views as well (Swann, 1987). Such change may occur when people switch roles (such as making a career change), alter their status in life (such as getting married or having a baby), encounter a life-threatening event (S. E. Taylor, 1983), or encounter other conditions that motivate change in self-conceptions (such as entering therapy, attempting to take on a new identity following a move to a new city, and the like). To summarize, then, although people can be induced to consider information about the self that disconfirms the self-image, typically the self-image strays in the direction of consistency with past impressions of the self.

Reconciling Accuracy, Self-Enhancement, and Consistency

The research just reviewed suggests that three overarching goals may be guiding how self-relevant information is sought out, interpreted, and stored; how situations and interaction partners are selected; and how people self-regulate with those individuals and in those situations. These goals would seem to be at least somewhat at odds with each other. Indeed, many research efforts have gone into attempting to determine if people are accuracy-oriented or self-enhancing (e.g., de Vries & van Knippenberg, 1985; Sanders, 1985; Sanders & Mullen, 1984). Considerable research has also pitted self-enhancement theories against self-verification or consistency positions (see Swann, 1990, for a review). The needs for accuracy and consistency have generally not been pitted against each other experimentally, inasmuch as the search for consistent feedback is often also a search for subjectively accurate feedback. A less obvious point is that the search for positive feedback is also often a search for accurate and consistent feedback. Implicit social norms dictate that most people do good things most of the time, and consequently much of people's positive self-impressions may have a heavy component of consistency and accuracy. Thus, these three motives may not come into conflict as much as the literature might first suggest. Nonetheless, there are conditions in which people are more or less likely to seek accurate, self-enhancing, or self-verifying (consistent) feedback, and it is useful to consider some of the conditions under which these effects occur.

One set of conditions determining when people seek accurate, consistent, or self-enhancing feedback concerns the nature of the attributes and/or the conditions under which information is extracted. The quest for accurate feedback appears to be most dominant under conditions of instability or ambiguity regarding one's standing on a dimension (Sorrentino & Roney, 1986; Strube & Roemmele, 1985; Trope, 1979). Correspondingly, the quest for consistent information is strongest when self-certainty on the attribute is high and ambiguity is consequently low (Pelham, 1990). When a self-view is particularly important, people will seek both self-enhancing and consistent feedback. Concerning their negative qualities, people appear to choose consistent feedback for flaws of which they are highly certain, but self-enhancing feedback for flaws of which they are not so certain (Pelham, 1990). Public scrutiny of one's actions or an action that has strong implications for success or failure may make self-enhancement needs more salient. Self-enhancement effects may be more likely on attributes that have few objective standards for evaluation than on attributes where performance can be measured or closely scrutinized (J. D. Brown, 1986). Thus, for example, people may self-enhance more on their social qualities, such as how personable they are, than on their qualities that can be more readily observed, such as how well they play baseball. Highlighting past behavior may increase pressures toward consistency. Thus, much of the research effort in determining when accuracy, consistency, and self-enhancement needs will be relatively more dominant can and should focus on the dimensions of attributes and social norms that may make one or another of these overarching goals dominant, and on the individual differences that predispose people to engage in one or another kind of behavior.

Situational factors also influence whether people will seek accurate, self-enhancing, or self-verifying feedback. In his early work on social comparison processes, Festinger (1957) maintained that when objective standards of evaluation are lacking, people will evaluate themselves using social standards. Implicit in the social comparison framework was the idea that people seek accurate and stable self-appraisals. A large body of literature consistent with these propositions (see Wood, 1989, for a review) suggests that the need for accurate and self-verifying feedback does indeed drive the social comparison process under many circumstances. However, under conditions of threat, self-enhancement needs appear to become more important and individuals may downwardly compare to another worse off than the self for the purpose of feeling better (Wills, 1981; Wood, Taylor, & Lichtman, 1985). Threat, then, appears to augment the need for self-enhancement. However, S. E. Taylor and Lobel (1989) argued that social comparison processes can serve multiple needs simultaneously. Looking at comparison processes under conditions of threat, they argued that while people explicitly evaluate themselves against others doing more poorly for the purpose of self-enhancement, simultaneously people choose to affiliate with others who are the same or better off, apparently for the purpose of obtaining accurate information and improving their own situation, respectively. Self-improvement and the conditions that prompt people to strive to get better on self-relevant qualities is a fourth motive not yet fully addressed by the literature.

Another reconciliation of the needs for accuracy, consistency, and self-enhancement stems from the fact that cognitive and affective responses to feedback appear to differ. Typically, affective reactions demonstrate a self-enhancement effect: when people receive positive feedback, they feel better than when they receive negative feedback, regardless of whether or not that feedback matches their prior self-conceptions. However, when it comes to seeking out feedback or accepting it, people are more likely to want and seek self-confirmatory feedback, even when it concerns attributes about which they have negative self-conceptions (Swann et al., 1989, Study 4). Thus, the affective system appears to show self-enhancement effects and the cognitive system demonstrates self-verification effects (Swann, 1987; see also Lake & Arkin, 1985). Swann, Pelham, and Krull (1989) explored some further implications of this cognitive/affective "crossfire" effect. When seeking feedback about their attributes, people are most likely to seek feedback that will verify their positive attributes. However, when they are constrained to seeking feedback about their negative qualities, they are more likely to extract unfavorable, that is, consistent, feedback rather than the favorable but inconsistent feedback. Thus, as Swann, Pelham, & Krull (1989) suggest, even those with generally low self-esteem possess a "ray of hope," a desire to capitalize upon their positive qualities (see also Swann, Pelham, & Krull, 1989; J. D. Brown, 1989). People may generally avoid the cognitive/affective crossfire by simply trying to verify their positive attributes.

There also appear to be individual differences such that individuals with high levels of desire for feedback do not show the customary self-enhancement effect of perceiving positive feedback as more self-descriptive than negative feedback (Ruzzene & Noller, 1986; see also Aitkenhead, 1984; C. R. Snyder et al., 1982). Strube and Roemmele (1985) found that subjects low in self-esteem with ego-protective tendencies preferred tasks that were high in diagnosticity of success but low in diagnosticity of failure, thereby attempting to self-enhance their performance. Subjects with low protective tendencies preferred the highly diagnostic tasks regardless of self-esteem. Chronic defensiveness (in conjunction with self-esteem) may be a factor that predicts a chronic propensity for self-enhancing versus accurate feedback. Both the situational and the individual difference determinants of the need for accuracy, self-enhancement, and consistency will no doubt continue to occupy research attention.

A WARENESS OF THE SELF

How accurate is our self-knowledge, and to what extent are we truly aware of our qualities? The extent to which we are aware of our internal qualities has generated considerable research in recent years. Epstein (1983) suggests that usually we are not aware of the self-knowledge that guides our thoughts and behaviors. It appears to operate at a preconscious level, although situations can lead us to focus on ourselves and our self-knowledge, making at least some of it explicit and conscious (see Hart & Damon, 1986, for a developmental perspective on this issue). There are at least two other formulations that we have already considered that reach similar conclusions. In Chapter 2, we examined Bem's self-perception theory, which maintains that people infer their attitudes, at least in part, from the observation of their behavior. Bem (1972) as well as the misattribution researchers (e.g., Valins, 1966) were able to show that by manipulating people's behavior, one could lead them to infer that particular attitudes, thoughts, or feelings were characteristic of themselves. Valins (1966) extended these ideas to suggest that even false feedback can lead people to change their self-impressions. Research by Nisbett and Wilson (1977b) (see Chapter 9) likewise implies that people's access to the factors that influence their opinions, attitudes, and reactions is incomplete, and that for some purposes, people fall back on their theories of how and why people do what they do in inferring the sources of influence on their own attitudes and behavior.

Despite the fact that attitudes and emotions can be inferred directly from behavior, characteristically people seem to infer their personal attributes more from their thoughts and feelings than from their behavior (Andersen 1984, 1987; Andersen, Lazowski, & Donisi, 1986; Andersen & Ross, 1984).[4] People rate their thoughts and feelings as more diagnostic and informative about themselves (Andersen & Ross, 1984). When asked to recall either their positive cognitive and affective reactions, their positive behavioral reactions, or unspecified positive reactions to several situations in either a public or a private context, those who focused privately on their cognitive and affective reactions had higher self-esteem (Andersen & Williams, 1985), suggesting that thoughts and feelings are more central to self-esteem than is behavior. Despite this fact, when people describe themselves (versus others), they are more likely to do so in dynamic terms, mentioning what they do rather than what they think or feel. Descriptions of the self are more likely to involve the self acting alone than to involve social interaction (McGuire & McGuire, 1986).

Personal memories are another source of knowledge about the self. As we have already seen, these memories may be vulnerable to certain distortions, such as the need to represent the self in as positive a manner as possible (Greenwald, 1980; S. E. Taylor & Brown, 1988), and to maintain consistency with impressions of personal attributes (Swann, 1983). M. Ross (1989; Conway & Ross, 1984) argues that personal memories are also shaped by theories of stability and change, namely, people's ideas concerning whether particular attributes in particular situations should and do remain stable or unstable over time. For example, people assume that attitudes will remain relatively stable over time, and thus impute stability to their own attitudes, even when their attitudes have changed (M. Ross, 1989). After participating in a study skills improvement program, however, people perceive themselves as having improved even when no actual change had taken place, presumably because they regard a self-improvement program as something that should induce change (Conway & Ross, 1984). Note that Ross's argument is consistent with Nisbett and Wilson's point that social theories about personal attributes may guide self-inference just as they are used for guiding inferences about others.

The imperfect access that people have to their thoughts and feelings creates the possibility for self-deception. The literature on self-enhancement effects, especially the strategies that people have for reinterpreting negative and ambiguous information, suggests that mild self-deception does indeed exist (Gilbert & Cooper, 1985; Greenwald, 1988; S. E. Taylor & Brown, 1988). Similarly, the need to maintain con-

---

[4]However, people also put more weight on their emotional experience than on their cognitions, relative to their descriptions of others (McGuire & McGuire, 1986; see J. T. Johnson, Struthers, & Bradlee, 1988).

sistency between present and past behavior provides manifold strategies for so doing (see Swann, 1984); this implies that at least some self-deception may be going on in service of the larger goal of self-verification.

Philosophers and psychologists have wrestled for decades with the logical paradox of self-deception, namely, how a person can both know and not know something about the self at the same time. Yet, research on encoding, memorial, and inferential processes renders this paradox more tractable. As Gilbert and Cooper (1985) point out, a person can enter a social situation, behave in an appropriate manner, and extract useful information from the situation without much awareness or consciousness. Thus, although behavior can be strategic and useful, it does not require conscious planning, and consciousness may be diverted to other activities or interpretations. As such, self-deception may result from inattention to the full implications of behavior.

Greenwald (1980) suggests that the unconscious acts as a primitive front-end processor that can enable people to avoid knowing things it would be better not to know. People constantly monitor the environment for signs of what they should attend to and what they should avoid. A man interested in women can scan hundreds of faces and bodies in a few minutes, his glance resting only on the few who capture his attention. He may be virtually unaware of the hundreds rejected as inappropriate—too young, too old, unavailable, or not pretty—because the discriminations can be made in milliseconds, long before the mind can consciously respond, "She has a nice face, but she's pushing a stroller." So it is with positive and negative information more generally. Greenwald likens this front-end processing mechanism and how it prescreens material to how people avoid junk mail, namely, by scanning in a very preliminary fashion and tossing out the material without fully learning what it contains. The color of the envelope, the nature of the greeting, and other surface characteristics alert people to the fact that this is not information they need. In similar fashion, people avoid being exposed to, attending to, and understanding information that their preconscious processes tell them is not going to be useful or welcomed (Greenwald, 1980; see also Chapter 7). Indeed, many of the strategies that we have considered throughout this chapter, ranging from exposure biases (e.g., the social situations in which we choose to participate), encoding biases (the types of information we permit to have access to consciousness), memorial biases (what we remember and how we reconstruct what we remember), inferential biases (e.g., the interpretation of information), and behavioral interaction strategies (such as impression management or self-handicapping) can be thought of as having a self-deceptive quality. The full ramifications of self-deception go beyond the constraints of this chapter. For additional discussion, the reader is referred to Gur and Sackheim (1979), Erdelyi (1974), Fingarette (1969), and Greenwald (1980).

So far, our discussion has suggested that the process by which self-structures influence the processing of self-relevant information and subsequent affect and behavior are largely preconscious without conscious directive activity on the part of the self (see also Epstein, 1983). This picture is incomplete. Clearly, people have personal goals that they choose to implement and of which they are acutely aware. People also have personal projects (Little, 1983) and concerns that occupy their current attention (Klinger, 1975) and that guide and direct their behavior in social situations. N. Cantor and Kihlstrom (1985) developed the idea of life tasks, the problems that a person is working on at a particular time in his or her life. Life tasks are conceived of as broad ways of thinking about one's activities that integrate and provide a context for understanding many specific activities that the individual undertakes. Life tasks are generated by knowledge of the self, including one's abilities, values, and preferences. The way the task is defined in turn leads one to develop a particular strategy for implementing it (see N. Cantor & Kihlstrom, 1985). Thus, in addition to the preconscious aspects of the self that may guide processing, there is deliberate intentional regulation of one's activities in terms of well-articulated and fully conscious goals and plans (see Chapter 12).

SELF-PRESENTATION AND IMPRESSION MANAGEMENT

In our discussion of self-regulation to this point, we have been concerned with how the self uses social information and feedback from task performance to test, alter, and refine self-conceptions. We have suggested that these activities are primarily in service of three motives: the desire for accuracy, consistency, and self-enhancement. Another important aspect of self-regulation involves social interaction with others. Under many circumstances, we are concerned with impression management and self-presentation. Often a person has a clear idea of the image he or she wishes to present and conscientiously goes about creating it. The image may be temporary, such as trying to fit a prospective employer's idea of what the new sales director should be like, or it can be permanent, such as wanting to convey to others that one is successful, attractive, and fun-loving. Impression management is ubiquitous; it is hard to think of a social situation in which some effort to influence how others think of oneself is not going on (see Arkin & Shepperd, 1989, for a review). In Southern California, even the license plate is used to create an impression regarding occupation (ISUEM4U), friendliness (HI LA), or even how much the car cost (40 GEES). Our discussion of self-presentation and impression management strategies will of necessity be curtailed, but a brief overview of this large and complex literature is provided because of the centrality of these issues to processes of self-regulation, the central concern of social cognition views of the self.

Behavior is the vehicle through which impressions are usually enacted, and as such, impression management is much like acting. One cannot simply do it without preparation, at least not well. To create a successful impression requires the right setting, correct props, and costumes, a good deal of skill, and often some rehearsal—the same ingredients that go into any dramatic production (cf. Goffman, 1959, 1963). It requires the ability to "take the role of the other" (Cooley, 1902; Mead, 1934); that is, to be successful, one must be able to step into the shoes of the target person, see how the impression looks from his or her vantage point, and adjust one's behavior accordingly (cf. Schlenker, 1985). Usually, people strive to make a good impression, especially if they have high self-esteem (Baumeister, Tice, & Hutton, 1989). However, there are also circumstances under which an ambiguous or poor impression may be one's goal.

Making a Positive Impression

There are many reasons for wanting to create a good impression, such as increasing one's own power, obtaining desired results like a job or promotion, gaining approval from others, and the intrinsic satisfaction of projecting a positive image in both one's own and others' eyes (Schlenker, 1980; M. Snyder, 1977).

How are positive impressions created? One strategy for so doing is *behavioral matching*. If the target other is behaving modestly, usually the impression manager will too, and if the target is behaving in a self-promoting manner, so will the impression manager (e.g., Gergen & Wishnov, 1965; Newtson & Czerlinsky, 1974). However, when the target of one's impression management efforts gives no clear standard of how to behave, people generally attempt to *convey a plausible yet positive image* of the self (see Schlenker, 1980; M. Snyder, 1977).

Another basic technique of impression management is *conforming to situational norms*. As Alexander and Knight (1971) have noted, for every social setting there is a pattern of social interaction that conveys the best identity for that setting, what they term a "situated identity." For example, at a funeral, the best self-presentation involves wearing dark colors, conveying an appearance of sadness, expressing condolences in a low voice, and mentioning the positive qualities of the deceased person, regardless of how much a rogue he or she may have been. People use their knowledge of these situated identities to construct patterns of behavior for themselves (see, e.g., Gergen & Taylor, 1969; E. E. Jones, Gergen, & Davis, 1962).

In addition to behavioral matching, self-promotion, and conformity, people seek to create positive impressions by *appreciating or flattering others*. The sincere appreciation of others' abilities or accomplishments usually has its intended effect of increasing the appreciator's power in the relationship and the target's regard for him or her. However, the effects of flattery are more mixed. Flattery is, by definition, a misrepresentation of one's beliefs about another, and when it is perceived as such by the target, it can backfire. Flattery that is believed to serve the flatterer's ulterior motives is one such condition (e.g., E. E. Jones & Wortman, 1973; Mettee & Aronson, 1974). For example, when a student in a course blatantly and indiscriminately praises the instructor's lectures, the student often succeeds only in arousing the contempt of instructor and peers alike.

Flattery is most successful when it involves attributes that the target values but questions his or her own standing. For example, telling a prize-winning scientist that she is smart will likely have little effect—she already knows it—but telling her that she is charming may have its intended effect, if she values but doubts her social skills (see, for example, E. E. Jones & Wortman, 1973; S. C. Jones & Schneider, 1968; J. W. Regan, 1976). Flattery is also successful if it is given with discretion. Those who flatter everyone succeed in impressing few, and those who flatter frequently will have less impact than those who flatter at particular appropriate moments (e.g., E. E. Jones & Wortman, 1973; Mettee & Aronson, 1974). Indirect flattery may be one of the more successful forms of flattery, since ulterior motives are not so vulnerable to detection as are other forms. Imitating others, talking about their favorite topics, or even simply paying attention to them and using their names can produce the intended effect of flattery (e.g., Carnegie, 1936; E. E. Jones & Pittman, 1982; E. E. Jones & Wortman, 1973; Kleinke, Staneski, & Weaver, 1972; Schlenker & Goldman, 1982; see Schlenker, 1980, for a review).

An appearance of *consistency among beliefs or between beliefs and behavior* is another attribute of successful impression management (Tedeschi, Schlenker, & Bonoma, 1971). Generally, it is regarded as a sign of weakness to show or to admit to inconsistency, and people will often go to great lengths to justify apparent inconsistencies. The foot-in-the-door technique (Freedman & Fraser, 1966) can be viewed as an example of the need to appear consistent. This technique involves making a small request of someone (e.g., "Please place this small card in your window indicating that you have given to our charity") which then escalates some time later into a larger request (e.g., "We'd like you to place this large placard on your lawn advocating auto safety"). Frequently, those who have already complied with the smaller request will also agree to the larger one, and one possible explanation is that they wish to appear consistent in their own minds and to others.

In any successful self-presentational effort, *verbal and nonverbal behavior should match*. That is, efforts to convey a friendly impression should be accompanied by a forward lean, low interpersonal distance (e.g., sitting close to the person), smiling, and a high level of eye contact. Efforts to discourage the company of another should feature low eye contact, high interpersonal distance, a postural orientation away from the person to whom one is speaking, and little smiling (Exline, 1972; Kleinke, 1975; Mehrabian, 1972). When people are sincere in their message and feel toward the speaker as they are behaving, then verbal and nonverbal cues are usually consistent. However, when a false impression is being conveyed, frequently the nonverbal channel will "leak," giving away the speaker's true feelings (e.g., DePaulo & Rosenthal, 1979; Weitz, 1974). Sometimes, such leakage does not go unnoticed by a target (e.g., Word, Zanna, & Cooper, 1974), and hence the effort at a positive impression may be undermined (see DePaulo, 1990, for a review).

Self-presentation efforts vary, depending on how public they are. When people believe that an audience will find out how good they are at some skill, they will modify their self-presentation efforts in a modest direction, but when others are not expected to find out, self-enhancement is the rule. One of the authors attended a party years ago at which the subject of pool came up. Someone asked her if she played, and she responded that she did, implying that she had gotten rather proficient at it. "Good," replied her companion, "there's a table downstairs. Let's go shoot a few games." There ensued one of the more embarrassing public displays of incompetence within her memory, aggravated no doubt by the additional pressure that her own immodest assessment had placed on her performance.

Several individual difference factors influence the type of self-presentational efforts that people will undertake. Social anxiety, depression, shyness (Arkin, 1987), and low self-esteem (Baumeister, Tice, & Hutton, 1989) influence self-presentational strategies in similar ways (Schlenker, 1987) by evoking a self-protective presentational style. This style is characterized by less participation in social interactions, including fewer initiated conversations and talking less frequently, the avoidance of topics that might reveal ignorance, minimal self-disclosure, and self-descriptions that are modest. Interaction style centers on pleasant behaviors, such as agreeing with others or smiling, that avoid disagreement or a significant exchange of information. When a person is faced with an important goal but has low expectations that he or she will be able to meet it, self-preoccupation with limitations and physical or psychological withdrawal from the situation are most common. Accountability for one's behavior also influences self-presentational strategies. When people are highly accountable, they adopt a self-protective presentational style, if they perceive that accountability to be threatening. If instead the accountability is represented as a challenge, people present a more self-promoting style, characterized by higher achievement, commitment, determination, and efforts to control. Low account-ability, in contrast, produces indifference or overconfidence, low initia-tive, and poor performance (Schlenker & Weigold, 1989).

Overall, then, the goal of creating a positive impression is very com-mon, and a variety of impression management techniques have been identified for accomplishing this. However, their generalizability has been called into question. Many studies of impression management have been conducted with college students who apparently believe that the way to make a successful self-presentation is to be self-promoting (M. Snyder, 1977). In fact, accurate self-presentations may be more highly valued, with positive self-enhancing claims producing favorable evaluations only if the claim is congruent with a person's performance or if there is no basis for checking on whether the claims are accurate (Schlenker & Leary, 1982). Were similar studies conducted with older adults, the selection of impression management strategies might be quite different. They might include those advocated by Dale Carnegie (1936), such as being a good listener or talking about the other's inter-ests (cf. M. Snyder, 1977). Only an investigation of impression manage-ment with a variety of populations can determine if this is so.

Most of the research on impression management has implied that making a positive impression on others is done primarily to bring about positive feelings about the self in an audience. However, recently, sev-eral investigators (Arkin & Baumgardner, 1986; Breckler & Greenwald, 1986; Greenwald & Breckler, 1985; Tetlock & Manstead, 1985) have sug-gested that many impression management techniques may be under-taken not only to impress an audience but to impress the self as well. In many respects, the self is one's own best and most important audience. Evidence for this position includes the fact that self-attributions are bi-ased in a self-serving manner in private as well as in public; favorable self-attributions for performance occur even when there are strong in-centives to be honest; favorable self-judgments are made very rapidly; and self-enhancing judgments lead to predictable changes in behavior. Thus, in behavioral self-regulation under conditions when an individ-ual is attempting to create favorable impressions on others, one must entertain the hypothesis that the favorable impression on the self and the need to further maintain a positive sense of self through social in-teraction are at least as important to these impression management ef-forts as the desire to impress an external audience.

Muddying the Waters: Attribute Ambiguity

So far we have considered ways in which people try to induce a positive impression of themselves in others. Sometimes, however, people may wish to obscure the impression others form of them (M. L. Snyder et al., 1979; M. L. Snyder & Wicklund, 1981). No one likes to be categorized. Consider the statements, "You can always count on George to do more than his share," and "Linda's always happy." Although positive, they suggest a limit on the target person's behavior or abilities. People like to feel they possess a wide range of abilities and personality attributes (cf. Sande, Goethals, & Radloff, 1988). Being typed as one sort of person or another can reduce one's sense of control over one's outcomes, in that it implies that one is no longer free to do the opposite. Being typed also creates expectations in others' minds that one may not be able or may not want to live up to, that is, that constrain one's future behavior. Thus, although Linda may be pleased that others think of her as cheerful, and although George may take satisfaction from the fact that others notice his unselfishness, both may feel a bit robbed of the choice to be grumpy or piggish, respectively. Moreover, Linda may come to feel obligated to be cheerful, and George may feel that he cannot possibly be as unselfish as others now expect.

Accordingly, just as others are coming to form a stable impression of a target, the target may muddy the waters (M. L. Snyder & Wicklund, 1981). There are several ways of making one's attributes ambiguous. One can *engage in an inconsistent behavior*. Linda might choose to be publicly despondent, and George might make a token selfish gesture. One can *provide additional reasons* for the behavior, so that others will discount the importance of stable personality factors. Linda might note that her work and social life are going well, thus making her more cheerful than usual, while George might mention that he has extra time right now to do more than his share. One might *muster consensus* for his or her attributes, maintaining that one is no more happy or unselfish than anyone else. Failing these techniques, one might choose to *leave the situation* altogether or otherwise *avoid evaluating the self*.

Not all attributes constrain one's freedom. Being typed as "resourceful" or "independent" leaves one fairly unconstrained, for example. However, many attributes, both positive and negative, can constrain one's freedom, and when the potentially constraining aspects of an attribute are especially salient, one will likely make an effort to create attribute ambiguity (M. L. Snyder & Wicklund, 1981).

Managing a Poor Impression

SAM: Why is it what you just said strikes me as a mass of rationalizations?

MICHAEL: Don't knock rationalization. Where would we be without it? I don't know anyone who could get through the day without two or three juicy rationalizations. They're more important than sex.

SAM: Ah, come on. Nothin's more important than sex.

MICHAEL: Oh yeah? You ever gone a week without a rationalization? (*The Big Chill*, 1982, cited in Steele, 1988).

People are highly motivated to avoid social disapproval and pejorative impressions of the self (Baumgardner & Arkin, 1987). Making one's attributes ambiguous becomes especially important under conditions of potential or real failure, because low ability is a possible attribution for such failure. It is virtually always desirable to have others think of one as highly able. High ability is unconstraining—one can perform well or poorly as one chooses—whereas low ability is very constraining. Thus, a person will usually go to great lengths to keep both the self and others from making low ability attributions (cf. Darley & Goethals, 1980). Under these circumstances, then, attribute ambiguity is motivated not only by the need to maintain control over one's outcomes but also by the needs to save face and to maintain self-esteem. (cf. Crocker & Major, 1989).

Rendering ambiguous the attributions for failure or potential failure involves many of the same strategies described earlier: doing something inconsistent (e.g., highlighting a success), mustering consensus (e.g., everyone did poorly), or providing additional reasons (e.g., lack of effort), so that others will discount the role of ability (M. L. Snyder & Wicklund, 1981). For example, when people anticipate that they will fail in front of others, they will often exaggerate the impediments they will face to provide a rationalization for their failure (Wortman, Costanzo, & Witt, 1973). One may attribute a failure to low effort or actually engage in low effort, so as to assure an effort-related failure. One may make attributions to a short-term and/or unstable factor such as loss of sleep, but only if there will be no public scrutiny on future similar tasks. Making one's attributes successfully ambiguous, then, is more than just offering an excuse: it involves a careful consideration of what constitutes a plausible, not too damaging, nondisconfirmable reason for a poor performance (see Darley & Goethals, 1980). The tendency to engage in these kinds of behaviors appears to be enhanced by self-focused attention (Hormuth, 1986).

Self-Handicapping and Other Forms of Self-Defeating Behavior

Another way to manage a poor impression is through self-handicapping. In an intriguing analysis, E. E. Jones & Berglas (1978) suggested that the excessive and/or continual use of alcohol or drugs may sometimes be motivated by the fact that the abuser needs an excuse for failure. Presumably, attributing failure to being drunk or stoned is less threatening than attributing failure to incompetence (Kolditz & Arkin, 1982; see Arkin & Baumgardner, 1985, for a review). Since the early work, a large amount of research has examined the self-handicapping effect, which is characterized as "a response to an anticipated loss in self-esteem" (C. R. Snyder & Smith, 1982, p. 107). The overriding point of self-handicapping behavior appears to be avoiding attributions of low ability for performance and replacing them with other, less threatening attributions (Arkin & Baumgardner, 1985; cf. Duval & Duval, 1987). Self-handicapping behaviors appear to be more likely, and no doubt may be more successful, if others are unaware of any prior failures on similar tasks (Baumgardner, Lake, & Arkin, 1985).

Factors other than substance abuse can constitute self-handicapping strategies. Making excuses by attributing performance to something other than poor ability is a general strategy designed to mute negative impressions (C. R. Snyder & Higgins, 1988). T. W. Smith, Snyder, and Handelsman (1982), for example, suggest that attributing performance to test anxiety is less threatening than attributing it to lack of ability, and thereby may be used by some individuals as an explanation for poor test performance. Attributing one's poor performance to low effort (T. W. Smith, Snyder, & Handelsman, 1982), procrastination, or over-commitment may serve similar functions. Other excuses that serve a self-handicapping function include bad mood (Baumgardner, Lake, & Arkin, 1985), self-criticism (Powers & Zuroff, 1988), shyness (Shepperd & Arkin, 1989a; C. R. Snyder et al., 1985), depression (Rhodewalt & Agustsdottir, 1986; Schouten & Handelsman, 1987; C. R. Snyder, Higgins, & Stucky, 1983), or the presence of a distracting stimulus (Leary, 1986; Shepperd & Arkin, 1989b). Setting goals that are unreachable or deliberately structuring a situation to be difficult (M. L. Snyder & Frankel, 1989) and holding tenaciously to a false belief (Slusher & Anderson, 1989) may also act as self-handicapping techniques. As an example of this last strategy, the movie, "The 91st Day," tells the story of a violinist who for many years maintained the illusion that he would one day play first violin under Arturo Toscanini. While at first this belief enabled him to get through hours of painful violin lessons with untalented students, the discrepancies between his belief and his life's activities increasingly produced frustration and irritation. On the day that Toscanini died, the violinist's false belief broke down altogether, and he was hospitalized for mental illness.

Arkin and Baumgardner (1985) suggest that self-handicapping strategies may be either internal or external (i.e., pertain to the self or to the situation) and may be either acquired or claimed (i.e., actually taken on or merely asserted). This leads to four types of self-handicaps: internal acquired (such as alcohol consumption), internal claimed (such as claiming to be chronically test-anxious), external acquired (such as choosing an unreachable goal), and external claimed (such as maintaining that a task was simply too difficult to perform) (cf. Leary & Shepperd, 1986). Arkin and Baumgardner argue that acquiring a self-handicap involves more planning and greater motivation than merely claiming a handicap, since the latter may be true or false. Internal self-handicaps may be more effective than external ones, since external ones are more amenable to public scrutiny. However, internal handicaps may ultimately be more debilitating in the long term and produce more negative evaluations by others.

An early controversy in the self-handicapping research concerned whether or not self-handicapping is primarily an effort to restore one's own self-esteem or whether it is primarily an impression-management technique. Subsequent research suggests that both motives underlie the process, and that self-handicapping may be engaged either to redeem one's self in one's own eyes or to redeem one's self in the eyes of others (Arkin & Baumgardner, 1985). There is some evidence that self-handicapping may occur more for the purpose of managing social impressions than self-impressions, but this issue requires further research (Arkin & Baumgardner, 1985).

Individual differences in self-handicapping have also been explored. When males and females have been directly compared, males appear to self-handicap more than females (Harris & Snyder, 1986; Shepperd & Arkin, 1989b). People high in public self-consciousness self-handicap more (Shepperd & Arkin, 1989b), as do males uncertain in their self-esteem (Harris & Snyder, 1986). Self-handicapping behavior has also been found in females with high test anxiety and high covert self-esteem (Harris et al., 1986). Without examining a broader range of individual differences and circumstances in which self-handicapping behavior might emerge, the role of individual difference factors in producing the behavior remains equivocal.

But, ultimately, how acceptable are these excuses? One of the consequences of self-handicapping and some of the other forms of attribute ambiguity is a poor self-presentation (e.g., Gilbert & Jones, 1986b; Powers & Zuroff, 1988). Although one may avoid a low ability attribution, the price of the exchange can be high: one may look lazy, anxious, drunk, or stoned instead. On the one hand, an audience will sometimes make the kinds of attributions for a particular behavior that subjects are attempting to induce through their self-handicapping behavior. Thus, instead of attributing a poor test performance to low ability, they may accept the self-handicapper's excuse that his poor performance was due to test anxiety. However, trait attributions, as opposed to causal attributions, do not show the same effect. People infer that a person is less competent when he self-handicaps than when he does not (Arkin & Baumgardner, 1985).

A further risk of the poor self-presentation is that often, impression management efforts are internalized. People come to believe that they are the way they act (Gergen, 1968; E. E. Jones, Gergen, & Davis, 1962; E. E. Jones et al., 1981; Rhodewalt & Agustsdottir, 1986). Although positive impression management efforts can bolster self-esteem, when one has intentionally created a poor self-presentation in others' eyes, the result can be a loss of self-esteem (E. E. Jones et al., 1981). Both negative and positive self-impressions are more likely to be internalized, the stronger the prior self-beliefs that are involved in the impression man-agement effort (Schlenker & Trudeau, 1990). However, although self-handicapping may be a poor impression management technique, under some circumstances it may promote effective coping. People who are anxious, for example, may reduce their anxiety by attributing poor per-formance to a persuasive handicap, thereby laying the groundwork for improving performance at a later point in time (Arkin & Baumgardner, 1985; Brodt & Zimbardo, 1981; R. N. Harris & Snyder, 1986; Leary, 1986).

The question arises as to whether self-handicapping is always in the service of minimizing damage to one's social representation and self-esteem, or whether, under some circumstances, it can be interpreted as self-destructive behavior. Baumeister and Scher (1988) reviewed the lit-erature on self-destructive behavior, including trying to fail, choosing to suffer, self-handicapping, substance abuse, health care negligence, facework in social interactions, shyness, choking under pressure, learned helplessness, and other forms of apparently self-destructive be-havior. Their analysis suggested no evidence of primary self-destruction, that is, the ability to foresee and the intention to bring about harm to the self. Rather, sometimes when people engage in self-defeating behavior, they have exchanged long-term costs and risks for short-term benefits. Particularly when people are in the throes of some aversive emotional state or high in self-awareness (attention to the self), they are more likely to engage in behaviors that threaten long-term well-being. In other cases, such counterproductive strategies seem to derive from systematic misjudgments about the self and the world, such as misjudging contingencies, which implicate cognitive errors or malfunctions in self-destructive behavior. Deliberate self-destructive-ness among normal individuals appears to be rare. The strategies of self-presentation that have been described in this section are presented in Table 6.3.

Self-Affirmation and Compensatory Self-Inflation

Not all strategies for managing challenges or threats to the self involve the attempt to control interpretations of those threats, challenges, or failures. In some cases, the individual can manage the impact of stress-ful, threatening, or challenging events by bolstering self-conceptions in other areas of life. Thus, for example, a person may readily acknowl-edge being unathletic, but bolster his self-conception as a nice, friendly person by way of compensating for the perceived deficit. Greenberg and Pyszczynski (1985) termed such strategies compensatory self-inflation and Steele and Liu (1983; Liu & Steele, 1986) refer to them as self-affirmation (Steele, 1988). The strategy of bolstering the self may be

TABLE 6.3 STRATEGIES OF SELF-PRESENTATION

Type of impression effort	Possible motives	Representative strategies
Creating a positive impression	Increase one's power, obtain resources; obtain approval; validate a positive self-image; be liked	Match target's behavior, convey most positive image possible; conform to norms; appreciate or flatter target; appear to be consistent
Creating an ambiguous impression	Avoid stereotyping by others; maintain behavioral freedom; maintain self-esteem; save face	Engage in inconsistent behavior; provide multiple reasons for behavior; proclaim that everyone does it (i.e., muster consensus); leave the field; avoid evaluations
Controlling a negative impression	Control one's own and others' attributions for failure; avoid low-ability attributions; avoid own or others' disappointment over future anticipated failure	Exaggerate impediments to success; exert little effort; self-handicap (i.e., engage in self-destructive behavior, such as using drugs or drinking); proclaim one's failure to be due to external and/or unstable factors; make one's attributes ambiguous

done both for an audience and for one's own self-esteem, and may be an effective method for dealing with short-term threats or challenges to the self (Markus & Wurf, 1987).

In one test of self-affirmation theory, Steele and Liu (1983) had subjects write counter-attitudinal essays for insufficient justification, thus creating cognitive dissonance between their attitudes and their behavior. Some subjects were then allowed to affirm an important self-relevant value by completing a value scale immediately after having written the unrelated dissonant essay and prior to recording their attitudes on the postdissonance attitude measure. Other subjects went through the same procedure, but were selected in a way that the value affirmed by the scale was not a part of their self-concept. Completing the value scale eliminated dissonance-reducing attitude change among subjects for whom it was self-relevant. However, completion of the value scale had no effect on the dissonance-reducing attitude change of subjects for whom it was not self-relevant. The self-affirmation of personal values apparently eliminated the need to reduce dissonance, even though the value was irrelevant to the dissonance-producing inconsistency. The opportunity to affirm positive aspects of self may, then, reduce concern with more dissonant or negative self-relevant experiences.

In a similar vein, people may compensate for what they perceive to be deficiencies in one domain of their behavior by systematically making known to others or acting upon other aspects of the self that are more positive. Self-characterizations, then, can also serve a compensatory function (Gollwitzer & Wicklund, 1985a, 1985b; Wicklund & Gollwitzer, 1983). In this context, Wicklund and Gollwitzer (1982) developed the concept of "symbolic self-completion," meaning that people can use self-descriptions in the service of their self-definitional needs. When an important indicator of one's self-definition is lacking, a person may strive after alternative indicators of the self-definition. Thus, for example, in one study (Wicklund & Gollwitzer, 1981, Study One), subjects committed to various self-views, such as musician or athlete, were asked how many people they would be willing to teach. Those who had a weak educational background in the self-definition area were more invested in teaching others than those with a strong educational background. These results are interpreted as indicating that these people felt a need to substitute for their lack of educational background by instructing others and thus symbolically rounded out their self-definition. These effects were true only for subjects who were committed to this aspect of the self-definition, and presumably had a need for symbolic self-completion through the act of teaching.

Impression Management: Closing Comments

The preceding discussion is an admittedly brief introduction to the large topic of impression management (see, for example, Schlenker, 1980, for a more extended coverage). In closing, it is worth returning to an earlier point which concerns whether impression management efforts are designed to impress oneself or a social audience. This issue is part of a larger question that addresses the interplay of the private and public self in the enactment of one's identity. Self theorists are increasingly coming to the position that an arbitrary distinction between private beliefs about the self and public self-presentation is inappropriate. Instead, the sense of self influences and is influenced by both private and public enactments of its qualities. Schlenker (1986; Schlenker & Weigold, 1989), for example, refers to this as the self-identification process, and argues that people fix and express their identity both privately through self-reflection and publicly through self-disclosure and self-presentation in ways that are influenced and determined by the opportunities and constraints that they perceive in any given situation. These situations cue particular aspects of one's identity, place constraints on which aspects of identity can be manifested, and provide an evaluative context for understanding one's behavior. In like fashion, people also develop a conception of others' identities in social interactions, which in concert with their own identities, provides a basis for regulating interpersonal conduct and developing relationships (McGuire & McGuire, 1986; Schlenker, 1984). In turn, one's sense of self is modified by these interactions, so that over time, the environment that fosters particular aspects of self-identity leads to that aspect being a more central and easily referenced part of the self.

SUMMARY

People hold complex and varied representations of themselves, similar to those held about other concepts, only more so. These representations include central attributes as well as more peripheral ones. Among the central attributes are self-schemas, cognitive/affective structures that represent experience in a given domain and organize and direct the processing of information relevant to the self-concept. Self-schemas enable people to identify quickly what they are and what they are not, to remember schema-relevant information, and to predict and guide their own behavior. Self-schemas may be positive as well as negative. There is increasing evidence that people may make use of their self-schemas in drawing inferences about other people as well.

Representations of the self include not only beliefs about what one is currently like, but beliefs about what one may become in the future. These possible selves can help people to set goals and to increase motivation and activity in pursuit of those goals. Sometimes people perceive discrepancies between what they are and what they would ideally like to be or feel they ought to be. These discrepancies reliably produce affective consequences, such as depression or anxiety, respectively. People's representations of themselves differ in complexity. Those with highly complex self-representations may be more buffered against setbacks or difficulties in any one area of life than those who are not.

Self-regulation refers to the ways in which people control and direct their actions. Certain beliefs about the self are more salient than others, and environmental factors can make particular aspects of the self salient. Consequently, the working self-concept, which guides ongoing behavior, is sometimes in conflict with aspects of the stable self-concept, leading people to behave in ways consistent with situational forces but not necessarily consistent with important self-conceptions. Self-regulatory behavior is also guided by conceptions of personal control or self-efficacy. When people feel that they will be able to undertake particular actions successfully, they are more likely to do so. Beliefs in personal control may be especially adaptive under situations of stress or threat, leading people to adjust more successfully to these trying circumstances.

Self-regulation is also influenced by whether one's attention is directed inward toward the self or outward toward the environment. When people compare themselves to an ideal which they would like to achieve and they are self-focused, they may perceive a discrepancy and also experience negative emotion; these responses then can prompt self-regulatory behavior designed to reduce the discrepancy. Generally, self-focus functions to increase the correspondence between behavior and salient standards.

Self-regulation is guided by underlying motivational processes, and chief among these are three overarching goals: the need for accuracy, which is the extent to which people desire to have accurate knowledge about the self and their abilities; self-enhancement, which is the tendency to hold and maintain the most favorable self-conceptions possible; and consistency (self-verification), the process by which people strive to maintain and confirm preexisting conceptions of themselves. These goals influence how people take in, interpret, and represent information in memory, and they also influence which situations people select and which companions they choose for social interactions. All three sources of motivation have been found to have powerful effects on behavior, and each may be predominant under different situational circumstances. Despite the fact that people use their self-knowledge to guide their behavior, this process is often preconscious, that is, people are not always fully aware of the aspects of the self that exert a directive influence on behavior.

Self-conceptions are also critically important in impression management and self-presentation. Usually, people strive to create as positive an impression in others as they can. Under other circumstances, however, people may choose to make their attributes ambiguous. When people experience threat or failure, they will try to manage the poor impression as well as possible. In so doing, they may engage in apparently self-defeating or self-handicapping behaviors which involve attempting to reattribute the cause of a failure to factors other than poor ability. But in many cases, people can manage the impact of stressful or threatening events by bolstering their self-conceptions in other areas of life through compensatory self-inflation and self-affirmation processes.

Processes of Social Cognition

7

Social Encoding: Attention and Consciousness

--- ❖ ---

What Captures Our Attention? ◆ *Consciousness, Control, and*
Automaticity ◆ *The Unthinking Mind*

A friend of ours was sitting on a bench in a crowded shopping mall when
he heard running footsteps behind him. Turning, he saw two black men
being pursued by a white security guard. The first runner was past him
in a flash, but he leapt up in time to tackle the second runner, overpowering
him. From the ground, the panting black man angrily announced that he was
the store owner. Meanwhile, the thief had escaped. Our friend, who is white
and devotes his life to helping the oppressed, was mortified.

For our purposes, this case of mistaken identity illustrates the sometimes
tragic consequences of instantaneous social encoding. People rapidly take in
other people as stimuli and react to them, sometimes with little apparent
thought. At other times, people think about each other more, struggling to reconcile confusing information. However quickly or slowly it occurs, encoding
has major importance, determining much of social interaction, as people react
"on-line," in the course of their daily encounters. As artist Frank Stella put it,
"what you see is what you see."

Attention and encoding are the first steps in social information processing.
Without them, nothing else can happen: attributions cannot be made; schemas
cannot be applied. Before any internal information management can occur, the
stimuli outside the person have to be represented in the mind. The name for
this general process is *encoding*. Encoding transforms a perceived external stimulus into an internal representation. The encoding process involves considerable cognitive work, which nevertheless can be accomplished with relatively lit-

tle effort. The instant a stimulus registers on the senses, the process of interpretation begins. Immediately, some details are lost, other are altered, and still others can be misperceived. Inferences are stored in memory along with the raw data and may become indistinguishable from them. The process of encoding thus influences both memory and inference, which will concern us in the two chapters following this one.

Social encoding can be broken down into several stages (e.g., Bargh, 1984; Burnstein & Schul, 1982; Greenwald, 1988). Most theorists agree that we perform some kind of unconscious *preattentive analysis* of environmental stimuli, combining features into the objects and events we notice consciously. Once noticed, a stimulus may come into conscious *focal attention,* to be identified and categorized. As *comprehension* occurs, the stimulus is given semantic meaning. Finally, *elaborative reasoning* links the particular stimulus to other knowledge, allowing for complex inferences.

Attention thus is an integral part of encoding because attention often focuses on what is currently being encoded. If you are thinking about something external, it is at least temporarily represented in your mind. However, attention is not limited to the encoding of external stimuli; whatever occupies consciousness is defined as the focus of attention. Attention thus can also be occupied by information retrieved from memory. If you are thinking about something you remember, that memory is the focus of your attention. Thus, attention is also occupied by the current contents of the mind (often termed *active, working,* or *short-term memory*). One is attending to the internal or external stimuli that are in conscious focal awareness.

Whether attention is directed outward toward encoding external objects or inward toward memory, attention is usually seen as having two components, direction (selectivity) and intensity (effort). When you read this book, you are presumably focusing on it rather than on the radio, the conversation in the hall, the itch on your leg, or your love life. Even given your selective focus on this book, you can allocate more or less intense mental effort to it. Attention, then, is the amount of selective cognitive work you do (Kahneman, 1973; D. A. Norman, 1976; Posner, 1982).

When people are encoding external stimuli, they do not attend evenly to all aspects of their environment. They watch some things closely and ignore others altogether. In this chapter, we will examine first what captures attention in social settings because that determines what is encoded. We will examine *salience,* namely, the extent to which particular stimuli stand out relative to others in their environment, and *vividness,* which constitutes the inherent attention-getting features of a stimulus, regardless of environment. We will also consider *accessibility,* which describes how people's attention is primed for categories (or particular interpretations of stimuli) that fit what one has been thinking about recently or frequently.[1]

Next, the chapter describes the degree to which encoding dominates our consciousness. As we have said, consciousness consists of focal attention. We will consider what typically occupies people's minds, that is, what people habitually think about: we will address consciousness and its contents, examining the degree to which people focus on representing the environment or on internally generated thoughts. We will also discuss *automaticity,* namely, what encoding processes occur outside consciousness; we will focus on how much encoding and inference occurs rapidly, spontaneously, autonomously, and outside awareness. The section will also address how much people control what occupies consciousness. Moreover, we will consider the unthinking mind, processes that occur beyond conscious attention. We will examine the unconscious itself, from a cognitive perspective, and the broader consequences of behaving in a relatively unconscious or mindless fashion, namely, when one fails to attend to and encode one's environment in a fully alert fashion. Finally, we will discuss a counterpoint to the encoding literature, an approach arguing for direct unmediated perception, without complex cognitive activity at encoding.

WHAT CAPTURES OUR ATTENTION?

A person who is seven feet tall, a person in a wheelchair, and a woman in the late stages of pregnancy are all salient in most contexts, and they attract attention. However, in some contexts (respectively: on a basketball court, at a conference on ableism, or in an obstetrician's office), they will not stand out because they are not novel in those contexts. Salience, the seemingly trivial factor of attracting attention, although logically irrelevant to most social judgment, can have important effects.

Salience: A Property of Stimuli in Context

Think back to the last time you were the only one of your "kind" in a room full of other people. You may have been the only student in a crowd of professors (or vice versa), or you may have been the solo heterosexual, homosexual, youngster, oldster, male, female, black, white,

---

[1]The terms *accessibility* and *availability* have been used in two contradictory ways. We will use *accessibility* to mean ease of recall and *availability* to denote whether the information has been stored at all (Tulving & Pearlstone, 1966; Higgins & Bargh, 1987, footnote 1). Note, however, that this is inconsistent with the Tversky-Kahneman usage of *availability* to mean ease of bringing information to mind (see Chapter 9). In the current chapter, *accessibility* refers to the readiness with which stored knowledge can be used.

or whatever, in an otherwise homogeneous group. The striking experience of being a salient social stimulus is the same. One *feels* conspicuous, that all eyes have a single target, and that one's every move is over-interpreted. As a result, one may feel anxious and concerned about how the interaction is going (Ickes, 1984). Moreover, the mere belief that one is a solo can impair one's ability to take in and remember what people say (Lord & Saenz, 1985; Lord, Saenz, & Godfrey, 1987; Saenz & Lord, 1989). Research on salience supports the uncomfortable experience of the solo as being a center of attention, as looming larger than life, and as the recipient of extreme reactions (S. E. Taylor, 1981a; S. E. Taylor et al., 1977).

Antecedents of social salience. The causes of social salience all depend on the immediate or larger context (McArthur, 1981; S. E. Taylor & Fiske, 1978; see Table 7.1). In the case of the solo, attributes of a person that are novel in the immediate context cause the person to be the center of attention. Being a student is not cause for comment in a college classroom, but it will attract attention at a faculty meeting. Researchers have documented solo status as a function of novel sex, race, and other visual characteristics, such as wearing the only red shirt in a room full of blues (Crocker & McGraw, 1984; Heilman, 1980; Higgins & King, 1981, Study 1; Kanter, 1977; McArthur & Post, 1977; Nesdale & Dharmalingam, 1986; Nesdale, Dharmalingam, & Kerr, 1987; Oakes & Turner, 1986; Spangler, Gordon, & Pipkin, 1978; S. E. Taylor et al., 1977; Wolman & Frank, 1975). These forms of salience all draw on perceptual and social novelty.

TABLE 7.1 THE CAUSES OF SOCIAL SALIENCE

A person can be salient relative to the perceiver's

Immediate context
    By being novel (solo person of that race, sex, hair color, shirt color)
    By being figural (bright, complex, moving)

Prior knowledge or expectations
    By being unusual for that person (e.g., behaving in unexpected ways)
    By being unusual for that person's social category (e.g., behaving in out-of-role ways)
    By being unusual for people in general (e.g., behaving negatively or extremely)

Other attentional tasks
    By being goal-relevant (e.g., being a boss, a date)
    By dominating the visual field (e.g., sitting at the head of the table, being on camera more than others)
    By the perceiver being instructed to observe the person

Another form of salience draws on perceptual features of the stimulus that make it figural in the immediate context. Perceptual principles based on Gestalt psychology predict that stimuli will be salient if they are bright, complex, changing, moving, or otherwise stand out from their drab background (McArthur & Post, 1977). Thus, salience effects occur as a function of relative brightness (one person being literally in the spotlight), relative motion (one person rocking in a rocking chair), and relative complexity (one person in a loudly patterned shirt). Such figural people attract longer gazes than do nonfigural people (McArthur & Ginsberg, 1981).

Moving out of the immediate context to the larger social context, people are also salient if they behave in ways that do not fit other people's prior knowledge about them as individuals, as members of a particular social category, or as people in general (E. E. Jones & McGillis, 1976; see Table 7.1). As we saw in Chapter 4, people attend to schema-inconsistent information, across several types of schemas. The behavior of an introvert who suddenly runs for public office, an executive who defers to subordinates, or a person who chews his toenails will all attract attention because the behavior is unexpected for that individual, that role, or people in general. Physically disabled people attract attention in part because they are novel compared to people in general (Langer et al., 1976). All these types of salience depend on violating expectations by being out of character, out of role, or out of the ordinary.

The latter principle of salience, based on expectations about people in general, has been extended in two ways (S. T. Fiske, 1980). First, extreme social stimuli are more salient than moderate stimuli. For example, people stare at extremely positive social stimuli, such as movie stars, and at extremely negative stimuli, such as traffic accidents. Since both positive and negative extremes are more unusual than moderate stimuli, extreme stimuli are salient. Second, most people expect mildly positive stimuli in general. Most people are optimistic about the outcomes they expect from others and from life in general (Parducci, 1968). People tend to rate other individuals positively (Sears, 1983; Sears & Whitney, 1973; Nilsson & Ekehammar, 1987). Hence, negative social stimuli in general are more salient than positive ones; because most people are optimists, negative stimuli are relatively unexpected and thus, salient.[2]

A different principle of salience derives from the fact that attention depends partly on the perceiver's goals. As we saw before (Chapter 5), people attend to others on whom their outcomes depend. If two people are talking and one is your new boss, a prospective date, or a new teammate, you will watch that person more closely than the other (Berscheid et al., 1976; Erber & Fiske, 1984; Neuberg & Fiske, 1987; Ruscher & Fiske, 1990; S. E. Taylor, 1975). People attend to significant others.

---

[2]There are some exceptions as well as other explanations for the typically higher weight of negative information in impressions of likability; see Skowronski & Carlston, 1989, for a review.

Salience can also be created by more deliberate interventions into social settings. For example, salience can hinge on seating position in a group; the person directly opposite you should be especially salient because that person dominates your visual field (S. E. Taylor & Fiske, 1975). Thus, if you want to have maximum impact on the leadership of a meeting, sit opposite the chairperson at the head or foot of a long table; if you want to fade into the background, sit on the sidelines. In a videotape, increasing or decreasing the amount of time a person is on camera has similar effects (Eisen & McArthur, 1979). The most direct manipulation of attention is instructing people to watch one person rather than another (S. E. Taylor & Fiske, 1975). The sheer visual exposure effect even holds for political issues: the amount of time an issue is aired on the evening news affects how much weight people give it in subsequent decisions (Iyengar & Kinder, 1987).

Thus, a person can be salient relative to an immediate context, relative to the perceiver's prior knowledge or expectations, or relative to other attentional tasks. Note that the key word common to all these ways of creating salience is *relative*: stimulus novelty occurs relative to an immediate or broader context, a stimulus is figural relative to other stimuli present, and perceiver perspective is created relative to context. The common element in all these forms of salience is that a stimulus is distinctive in relation to other factors in the perceiver's context.

Consequences of social salience. Regardless of the way salience is created, its effects are robust and wide-ranging (McArthur, 1981; S. E. Taylor & Fiske, 1978). As suggested by the experience of the solo, salience makes a stimulus larger than life in various judgments. Prominence shows up most in perceptions of causality. Salient people are seen as especially influential in a given group. A solo is seen as having a lot of impact on the group, credited with setting the tone of the discussion, deciding on topics, and generally guiding the conversation. A salient person is, therefore, seen as intrinsically influential.

This principle extends to perceptions of causality that influence the person's own behavior. Perceptually salient behavior is seen as particularly indicative of the person's underlying disposition and as less under the control of the situation. Moreover, just as a salient person seemingly influences a group, so a salient behavior seemingly corresponds to a disposition that influences the individual. In both cases, causal attributions follow the focus of attention.

Because people generally see other people as causal agents (Heider, 1958; E. E. Jones & Nisbett, 1972; L. Ross, 1977), attention normally exaggerates this tendency (S. T. Fiske, Kenny, & Taylor, 1982). However, if a person's passivity is emphasized, attention can exaggerate perceptions of susceptibility to influence as well (F. Strack, Erber, & Wicklund,

1982). Salience exaggerates causal judgments in the direction implied by prior knowledge.

Salience also exaggerates evaluations in whichever direction they initially ténd. If a person is unpleasant, being a solo will cause dispro-portionate condemnation; similarly, a pleasant solo is exaggeratedly praised (S. E. Taylor et al., 1977). Evaluations can be nudged in one di-rection or another by prior expectations as well. For example, if a de-fendant in criminal proceedings is viewed negatively, salience should cause the person to be evaluated especially negatively. On the other hand, if the same person is viewed as a person (a more positive expec-tation), salience causes an especially positive evaluation (Eisen & McArthur, 1979; cf. McArthur & Solomon, 1978). Salience cuts both ways in evaluations.

If salient stimuli elicit attention, perceived prominence, and extreme evaluations, it would stand to reason that they also should enhance memory. Unfortunately, the data are strikingly uneven. Within social cognition research on salience, the main measure of memory has been people's free recall: sometimes recall is enhanced and sometimes not (for reviews, see McArthur, 1981; S. E. Taylor & Fiske, 1978). We will come back to this.

Although salience does not reliably enhance the quantity of recall, it does increase the organization and consistency of impressions in sev-eral ways. The more attention one pays to another person, the more coherent the impression becomes. Attention structures impressions, emphasizing features that fit and adjusting those that do not. For ex-ample, the solo student at a faculty meeting is likely to be seen as typ-ical of the student category and as presenting the "students' perspec-tive," whether or not the person truly represents most peers (S. E. Taylor, 1981a; S. E. Taylor et al., 1977). The effects of salience on ste-reotyping mean that salience combines with prior knowledge to pro-duce polarized evaluations (cf. Nesdale et al., 1987). Consequently, a solo man is perceived to be prominent and therefore a good leader, but a solo woman in an all-male group is perceived to be an intruder and is caused to feel like one (Crocker & McGraw, 1984). As noted elsewhere (Chapters 5, 11), attention (mere thought) brings into line the evaluative components of an impression, which then becomes more extreme, at least under certain conditions (Chaiken & Yates, 1985; M. G. Millar & Tesser, 1986b; Tesser, 1978).

We have seen that salience and attention have a variety of effects on judgments. Attention exaggerates evaluations and attributions of causal influence in whatever direction they initially tend. Attention sometimes increases recall. Attention can encourage stereotypic interpretations. How robust and important are these effects of temporary salience on important social judgments? Efforts to increase importance and to en-rich stimulus materials in fact enhance salience effects (Eisen &

McArthur, 1979; McArthur, 1981; McArthur & Solomon, 1978; F. Strack, Erber, & Wicklund, 1982; S. E. Taylor et al., 1979), and comparable salience effects occur in real-world organizations (Kanter, 1977; Wolman & Frank, 1975).

If they have such impact on significant decisions, it becomes especially important to know how controllable salience effects are. Despite early speculations that salience effects might be automatic (S. E. Taylor & Fiske, 1978), they apparently do not qualify as fully automatic because people sometimes can control them. That is, salience effects can be qualified by some forms of involvement, such as self-interest (Borgida & Howard-Pitney, 1983), although not simply by making the task more important (S. E. Taylor et al., 1979). And salience effects may be qualified by some instructions, such as expecting to "describe each member of the stimulus group" (Oakes & Turner, 1986), which would enhance a person-by-person accuracy goal.

A closer look at salience: What mediates its effects? It is impressive to consider the range of perceptions and behaviors guided by the seemingly trivial factor of what catches the eye (or ear). Why should attention have such pervasive effects on social judgment? Psychologists have proposed several processes to connect differential attention and differential judgments; some of these candidates for mediation (i.e., connection) have been debunked and some supported.

One potential mediator of salience effects is *sheer quantity of recall.* Consider how recall might operate as the link between attention and exaggerated judgments. At most parties, a woman dressed in magenta would stand out and attract your attention. As you notice her throughout the evening, you take in bits of her behavior and overhear fragments of her conversation. When your roommate afterward asks you what you thought of her, you may have a larger quantity of data about her than about another woman who was dressed in gray. It would seem reasonable to assume that you would have firmer opinions about the woman with the magenta dress because you recall more about her.

Much attention research has tested just such a model of mediation, that is, that salience enhances the amount of recall, which in turn influences judgments. However, we noted earlier that salience does not reliably enhance recall. Consequently, if attention does not always increase recall, large quantities of recall could not cause the standard attentional effects on judgments. Researchers have shown that judgments do not depend on the total amount of salient information people recall (S. E. Taylor & Fiske, 1975; S. T. Fiske, Kenny, & Taylor, 1982). In some cases, enhanced recall and exaggerated judgments are correlated (Harvey et al., 1980; E. R. Smith & Miller, 1979), but not always. Hence recall is not a necessary condition for the effects of attention on judgments.

A related possibility is that ease or *accessibility of recall*, rather than quantity, is facilitated by differential attention. In this view, it is not that more information is recalled about salient stimuli, but instead, that information about salient stimuli is recalled more easily. In the party example, instances of the magenta-dressed woman's behavior come to mind more rapidly than do instances of nonsalient people's behavior. Consequently, her behavior is overrepresented as evidence in subsequent causal analyses; that is, she would be seen as especially influential at the party, even if she were not, based on people's easy recall for her behavior. This recall-accessibility model of attention effects on attribution has received some support (Pryor & Kriss, 1977; Rholes & Pryor, 1982; see also Higgins & King, 1981).

Another potential reason that attention affects judgments is *channel-specific recall*. That is, if one's attention is captured by visually salient stimuli, then only visual recall will be overrepresented in memory. Thus, recall for the conversation of the woman at the party will not be enhanced, but recall for her magenta dress and accompanying gestures will be. Similarly, if Randy is salient by virtue of his loud voice, recall of what he said and how he said it should be enhanced, but not recall of his appearance. However, this channel-specific model has little support (S. T. Fiske, Kenny, & Taylor, 1982; McArthur & Ginsberg, 1981; Robinson & McArthur, 1982; S. E. Taylor et al., 1979, Study 1).

Another potential mediator of attentional effects is *causally relevant recall*. Why should people make their causal inferences from data that have no bearing on causality? In this view, people are not so inefficient as to use useless information. Helpful data such as talking time, an imposing appearance, and dominant behaviors are considered informative; remembering them in particular should predict causality. Moreover, dominant behavior and appearance seem inherently to attract attention in most contexts. Attributes relevant to perceived causality tend to have an impact perceptually as well as inferentially, and they may be well-recalled. Causally relevant data tend to be events rather than nonevents ("he talked a lot" versus " he sat silently") and to be figural rather than background ("she gestured excitedly" rather than "she smiled occasionally"; cf. Sullins, 1989). Thus, suppose your attention initially is drawn to someone because of her magenta dress. While looking at her longer than at her gray-dressed colleague, you will especially notice her causally relevant dominant behaviors rather than irrelevant behaviors or submissive behaviors. Accordingly, the judgment is in effect being made at encoding, on the basis of information that is doubly salient—salient because the person is salient and salient because the dominant behavior itself is salient. This view has received some empirical support (S. T. Fiske, Kenny, & Taylor, 1982).

To summarize, psychologists have posited several recall processes that intervene between differential attention and exaggerated causal attributions. Sheer quantity of recall and channel-specific recall do not seem to account for the effects of salience on attributions. The ease or accessibility of recall, however, is one plausible mediator. In addition, causally relevant recall, especially memory for dominant behavior and appearance, seems to be enhanced by attention. That sort of recall, in turn, leads to exaggerated attributions.

Vividness: An Inherent Property of Stimuli

Vividness is a phenomenon related to salience. Whereas salience is determined by the relation of an object to its context, vividness is inherent in a stimulus itself. Thus, for example, a plane crash is more salient during peacetime than in the context of wartime carnage. Furthermore, a plane crash is inherently more vivid than a normal flight; a detailed description of a particular accident is more vivid than the statistics about it; and an accident in your local airport is more vivid than an accident elsewhere. A stimulus is vivid, to the extent that it is "(a) emotionally interesting, (b) concrete and imagery-provoking, and (c) proximate in a sensory, temporal or spatial way" (Nisbett & Ross, 1980, p. 45). Do vivid stimuli have effects similar to those of salient stimuli? As we will see, although theory and common sense would suggest that vivid stimuli are especially impactful, research suggests that they are not.

The case for vividness effects. Vividness effects seem commonplace in daily life. Consider two versions of the same sponsor-a-child advertisement. One version describes little Felicia and her 12 brothers and sisters, orphaned and living off the sales of firewood they gather in the countryside and carry by hand into the big city. A photograph depicts her large, innocent eyes with long lashes and her brave upturned face; she is standing in a clean but ragged dress, surrounded by squalor. At this very moment, Felicia is hoping for help. Ten dollars will feed her for a month. Before you write your check, consider another version of the same ad. It merely states the statistics on world malnutrition and child neglect, listing 25 countries in which the program operates. The second appeal is rational, informative, abstract, and distant; your donation seems less likely. Why? In both cases, your conscience gives the same counsel, but the first ad seems more likely to attract your attention initially, to change your attitudes, and to elicit the desired behavior. All this is obvious, and as the idea person in an ad agency, you could have thought up the vivid ad yourself.

Psychological theorists have postulated precisely such vividness effects on several conceptual grounds. Vivid information is predicted to be more persuasive than pallid information of equal or greater validity, first, because vivid information should come to mind more easily

(Nisbett & Ross, 1980; Tversky & Kahneman, 1973). By this argument, vivid information is processed more fully at encoding, and therefore it should be more memorable. Hence, it would be recalled faster or more fully. In this view, judgments and attitudes are based on the information most easily retrieved from memory. Second, vivid information is, by definition, highly imageable, that is, likely to provoke internal visual representations. According to this argument, visual codes are especially memorable, so vivid information again would come to the forefront in memory-based judgments and attitudes. Finally, vivid information seems to have more emotional impact on the perceiver; affective overtones are hypothesized to enhance its impact on judgments. In short, the impact of vivid information on human judgment, especially persuasion, would seem to be self-evident.

Unfortunately, there is little empirical evidence for vividness effects (S. E. Taylor & Thompson, 1982). According to the research, messages that are written in concrete and colorful language are no more likely to change attitudes than are abstract and dry messages. Research shows that messages accompanied by photographs usually have no greater appeal. Similarly, videotaped messages only sometimes have enhanced impact. And finally, direct experience, which would seem the ultimate in vividness, does not necessarily change attitudes more effectively than does second-hand contact.[3] In sum, vividness does not work well empirically, although intuitively it seems as if it should.

The major exception to this pattern of negative results is that individual case histories do persuade more effectively than do group statistics. Little Felicia as a heartrending story does carry more impact than do the worldwide hunger statistics. However, it is not clear that this result speaks to the vividness effect. Other vividness research—which manipulates concrete (versus dull) language, photographs (versus none), and videotapes (versus transcripts)—holds most other information constant. However, holding information constant is more problematic when contrasting case history and statistical information. They differ in far too many ways to assume that it is only differences in vividness that cause any differences in their persuasive impact. For example, a case history communicates one particular scenario by which the existing facts could occur: a starving child might survive by selling firewood. Statistics communicate a different sort of information, such as life expectancy averaged over many instances. Hence, information nonequivalency is confounded with (not separable from) vividness. Together with the failure to find effects from other types of vividness, this problem suggests that the information difference and not vividness per

---

[3]Saying that direct experience may not change attitudes is not the same as denying that direct experience may affect the *acquisition* of attitudes or the impact of attitudes on *behavior*; it clearly does both (see Chapter 11).

se accounts for the fact that case histories are persuasive (S. E. Taylor & Thompson, 1982).

So far, we have seen no clear evidence for the effects of vivid information on persuasion and judgments, when information is held constant in other ways. One lingering possibility suggests that vivid information would have its greatest impact after a delay. By this logic, all information is relatively easy to recall immediately after receiving it. After a delay, however, the pallid information's relative weakness allows it to fade, leaving vivid information intact. Although one study has, in fact, found evidence for this hypothesis (Reyes, Thompson, & Bower, 1980), several others have not, and one (P. Wright & Rip, 1981) found the reverse. Accordingly, vividly presented information does not seem to have an effect after a delay, either.

Why does the vividness effect seem so plausible? It appears that there is, in fact, little evidence for the vividness effect. If so, what would lead people to the intuitive conclusion that there is a vividness effect? Vividness may have some effects on us that are mistaken for persuasion. For example, we believe that interesting, attention-getting messages are persuasive for other people in general, but we do not rate vivid messages as more personally convincing (R. L. Collins et al., 1988). People also recall vivid information more easily than pallid information (Lynn, Shavitt, & Ostrom, 1985), but memorability does not explain the persuasion occasionally obtained in vividness studies (Shedler & Manis, 1986; Sherer & Rogers, 1984). Moreover, vivid information may make us more confident in our opinions, without changing the actual judgment (N. K. Clark & Rutter, 1985).

Finally, vivid information is entertaining, as in the visual embellishments of rock music videos (Zillmann & Mundorf, 1987). The independence of persuasiveness and entertainment was put well by one of Carl Sagan's colleagues in describing Sagan's "gift for vividness": "Carl is very often right and always interesting. That is in contrast to most academics, who are always right and not very interesting" ("Gift for vividness," 1980). Vivid communications are frequently perceived as more graphic, more vivid, or more interesting than nonvivid communication in precisely those studies that go on to find no effect on judgments. Thus, the entertainment value of vividness does seem to be functionally distinct from its persuasive impact (S. E. Taylor & Wood, 1983). People can mistakenly infer that their attitudes have changed when they have only been entertained (R. L. Collins et al., 1988).

Future directions for vividness research. Assuming for a moment that our real-world intuitions are correct and that a vividness effect does exist, it then follows that the attempts to examine it experimentally have been flawed in some important way, or that it does occur, but only under special circumstances that most experiments have so far failed to duplicate. Several principles define the boundaries of the vividness effect (S. E. Taylor & Thompson, 1982). First, many attempts to operationalize vividness confuse vivid messages with vivid presentations. If the message context is too vivid, the gimmicks may draw people's attention away from the message itself (Eagly & Himmelfarb, 1978; Isen & Noonberg, 1979).

Second, there is some empirical evidence that pallid written material conveys more information but that vivid video or live material helps to catch people's attention, if they are relatively uninvolved (Chaiken & Eagly, 1976). Video ads do capture people's attention, but they also prompt people to deal mostly with superficial information, such as whether or not the speaker is good-looking (Chaiken & Eagly, 1983). Vivid information, thus, may work on the attentional stage, especially for uninvolved recipients.

If recipients of a message are already highly involved, vividness is not needed to capture attention. Their attention is already captured. What they need are cogent arguments and time to think about them. Written materials allow involved recipients the time to consider the message arguments in detail, which is crucial to persuading such individuals (Petty & Cacioppo, 1979; see also Chapter 11). In this view, then, vivid ads serve mainly to alert people who are uninvolved, but written information persuades people who are involved.

Accessibility: A Property of Categories in Our Heads

A phenomenon called *priming* describes the effects of prior context on the interpretation of new information. Priming is specifically a name for the fact that recently and frequently activated ideas come to mind more easily than ideas that have not been activated. Thirty years ago, Jerome Bruner (1957, 1958) pointed out that much social information is inherently ambiguous, so social perception is heavily influenced by the *accessibility* of relevant categories, that is, categories that are easily activated, given the perceiver's current goals, needs, and expectations. Priming occurs when knowledge is activated and is applicable to currently attended stimuli.

Situational priming effects. One of us knows a daughter who, in the spirit of liberation, gave her mother a subscription to *Ms.* magazine for Mother's Day, and later renewed it the second year. Just before the third year was due, the mother telephoned to request that the subscription not be renewed: "It makes me too hard to live with." Being constantly reminded of the existence of sexism creates a context in which events are more often interpreted as sexist. Similarly, being constantly reminded of competition, hostility, pollution, disease, or anything else creates a context for interpreting events. As a research example, exposing people to positive or negative trait terms (e.g., adventurous versus reckless) causes people soon afterward to interpret ambiguous behavior (e.g., shooting rapids in a canoe) as correspondingly positive or negative because of the meaning that had been primed (Higgins, Rholes, & Jones, 1977; see also Bargh et al., 1986; Bargh & Pietromonaco, 1982; Higgins, Bargh, & Lombardi, 1985; S. J. Sherman, Mackie, & Driscoll, 1990; Sinclair, Mark, & Shotland, 1987; Srull & Wyer, 1979, 1980; for a review, see Higgins, 1989b).

Priming effects are strongest, as in this example, when relevant meanings as well as positive or negative valences are primed. That is, the ambiguous behavior is more likely to be seen as reckless when relevant negative concepts, compared to irrelevant ones, have been primed. Moreover, experimenters construct the priming and stimulus contexts such that subjects do not consciously connect the two. It is crucial in priming studies that subjects do not think that the primed interpretation comes to mind because it was previously provided to them (by the accessibility of the primed construct), but instead that subjects think the primed construct comes to mind because of the stimulus itself. Because there is no conscious link between prime and stimulus, primed subjects cannot be merely responding because of what they think the experimenters want them to do (i.e., due to experimental "demand"). The apparent independence of the prime and the stimulus also means that there is no particularly rational reason for subjects to be using the prime in their interpretation of the stimulus. Priming effects can even operate automatically, without one's conscious awareness of the initial prime (Bargh et al., 1986; Bargh & Pietromonaco, 1982).

Priming is not limited to trait concepts. Other socially significant concepts can be primed. For example, several studies suggest that racial categories can be primed in an apparently spontaneous fashion (Devine, 1989; Dovidio, Evans, & Tyler, 1986; Gaertner & McLaughlin, 1983); when white subjects see words related to African-Americans, even presented below threshold for conscious recognition, they subsequently respond faster to stereotype-related words and evaluate an ambiguous (race unspecified) person as more hostile, consistent with the idea that their racial categories have been primed. On a more overt level, too, overhearing an ethnic slur can exaggerate white people's negative evaluations of a poor performance by a black person (J. Greenberg & Pyszczynski, 1985), perhaps through priming.

Similarly, other studies hint that various gender-role stereotypes are subject to priming. For example, men who had just viewed a pornographic film went on to respond more stereotypically to a woman they encountered in an apparently unrelated context: their behavior was judged to be more sexually motivated, and later they initially remembered mainly her physical features rather than the interview; but these results held only for gender-schematic men, for whom gender role is likely to be especially accessible (McKenzie-Mohr & Zanna, 1990). Relatedly, women primed with family terms remember more accurately and judge more confidently the goals of a wife/mother target person, compared to a career-woman target or compared to neutrally primed subjects (Trzebinski & Richards, 1986; cf. Trzebinski, 1985). And rock-music videos that are gender-role stereotypic seem to prime stereotypic interpretations of men's and women's interactions (Hansen & Hansen, 1988b).

Finally, a variety of other stimulus interpretations respond to priming: person categories, as a function of unconscious affective primes (Niedenthal & Cantor, 1986); reported anxiety, as a function of unconscious threatening and violent primes (Robles et al., 1987); arousal and reported mood, as a function of primed self-discrepancies from standards (Higgins et al., 1986; Strauman & Higgins, 1987); good-bad judgments of affectively loaded words, as a function of unconscious evaluatively polarized primes (Greenwald, Klinger, & Liu, 1989); perceptions of whether or not an ambiguous adult-child interaction is a kidnapping, as a function of prior exposure to a missing child poster (K. James, 1986); reported life satisfaction, as a function of relevant prior questions (F. Strack, Martin, & Schwarz, 1988); judged desirability of national policies, again as a function of relevant prior questions (Tourangeau et al., 1989); and aggressive content in stories, as a function of heat (Rule, Taylor, & Dobbs, 1987). It is striking that all kinds of responses, from temporary states to initial judgments to seemingly well-established opinions, all change with priming.

Priming subsequently has long-term as well as short-term consequences. The initial priming of a stimulus can affect its ratings as much as a week later when it is no longer in that context (Higgins & King, 1981; Higgins, Rholes, & Jones, 1977; Sinclair, Mark, & Shotland, 1987; Srull & Wyer, 1980). This is an important point. It suggests that a transitory and perhaps arbitrary juxtaposition of prime and stimulus can affect the way that stimulus is encoded permanently. If a stimulus potentially can be encoded as fitting one of several alternative categories, short-term priming may determine which category is applied in the long run.

Moreover, priming affects important social behavior. For example, subjects were primed by moderately hostile categories of then-famous people (rock singer Alice Cooper, Indiana coach Bobby Knight) in one context. Subjects next rated an ambiguous partner as more hostile and behaved more in a more hostile, competitive manner toward their partner, in line with the categories that had been primed (Herr, 1986). In another study, subjects encountered competition-related words at a level below threshold for conscious recognition; primed subjects then played more competitively, if they were relatively competitive people. In effect, the primes activated their competitive personalities (Neuberg, 1988). Moreover, one classic set of research can be further interpreted as consistent with the effects of priming on aggression. When people are angry at someone, the impulse to harm the person is more likely to be carried to action in the presence of aggressive cues. A gun lying on a nearby table provokes aggressive behavior even by other means (Berkowitz, 1974), and priming is one explanation for this.

Priming can also affect problem solving and creativity. In one study, subjects attempted to solve the following problem: given a candle, a book of matches, and a box of tacks, how can the candle be attached to the wall so it burns properly and does not drip wax on the floor? Some subjects, who had been primed into thinking of containers as separate from their contents (e.g., tray *and* tomatoes versus tray *of* tomatoes), were able to solve the problem quickly. The configuration (container and contents as separable entities) primed related configurations and facilitated problem solving (Higgins & Chaires, 1980). The solution to the problem, incidentally, is to empty the box of tacks, treating it as a box *and* tacks, and to tack up the box as a platform for the candle.[4]

Assimilation and contrast. Most of the priming research shows stimuli being assimilated to primed categories. For example, when subjects are primed with positive or negative traits, they often interpret relevant ambiguous behavior in ways that assimilate it to the category, as we have just seen. However, contrast effects have sometimes emerged. That is, when people are blatantly primed with a trait (e.g., foolhardiness), they may instead contrast their judgment of the ambiguous target, judging the fact that Donald wants to sail across the Atlantic in a sailboat as not especially foolhardy and even adventurous. If the prime is blatant enough, people may avoid using it, rating the person in the opposite or contrasting direction. Certain conditions seem to undermine the usual assimilation effects and instead, to encourage contrast.

Contrast occurs particularly when consciousness of the priming task is likely to be higher than usual (Martin, 1986). Some priming studies involve extremely rapid presentations of the prime, which subjects do not recognize consciously; others involve explicitly conscious priming, but separated into a different context, so that subjects presumably do not consciously connect the prime and the stimulus, although they do consciously perceive the prime. *Consciousness of the prime* is potentially important, for conscious priming appears to be more flexible than unconscious priming. When people are aware of a blatant prime and its potential link to a stimulus, they may resist its all-too-obvious influence

---

[4]This particular study is now interpreted as an instance of "procedural" priming (see later discussion; Higgins, 1989b).

or they may simply see it as too extreme compared to the ambiguous stimulus. In at least some circumstances, only unconscious perception of the prime assimilates the stimulus to the primed category; conscious perception of the prime, instead, can either contrast or assimilate the stimulus to the primed category (Lombardi, Higgins, & Bargh, 1987; see also L. S. Newman & Uleman, 1990). Conscious responses seem to be more variable and flexible than unconscious responses.

Assimilation and contrast also depend on features of the stimuli involved. *Overlap* between the prime and the stimulus is clearly important; moderate primes, which tend to increase overlap, are most likely to show assimilation in either conscious or unconscious priming. Contrast effects are obtained when the stimuli do not overlap much with the primed category, as when extreme primes are used (Herr, 1986; Herr, Sherman, & Fazio, 1983). Again, if there is little overlap between an extreme prime and a stimulus, people are especially likely to react against it, showing contrast.

Stimulus *ambiguity* also matters, as an ambiguous stimulus easily assimilates to a prime. Unambiguous stimuli may result in contrast effects (Herr, Sherman, & Fazio, 1983). Presumably, with an unambiguous stimulus, the complete lack of fit between prime and stimulus becomes especially obvious, and perceivers overcompensate, contrasting the two.

Importance of encoding. Priming represents primarily an encoding bias, although it can affect memory retrieval as well. Researchers suggest several reasons for this role of encoding. One reason is that priming effects decrease with wider gaps between a prime and a stimulus (see Fig. 7.1, first two rows). The wider gap presumably interferes with encoding the stimulus in terms of the prime (Srull & Wyer, 1979). In one study (Srull & Wyer, 1980), subjects worked on a priming task that

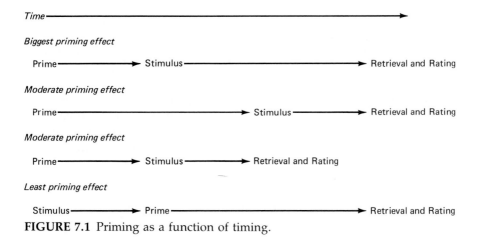

FIGURE 7.1 Priming as a function of timing.

required them to use hostile words (make a sentence out of, e.g., *leg, break, arm, his*); they then read a stimulus paragraph describing Donald's behavior, which was ambiguous with regard to hostility (e.g., demanding his money back from a store, lying to avoid a blood donation). All subjects rated Donald after the priming task and the paragraph. Subjects who experienced a delay between the stimulus and the rating (first row of the figure) showed bigger priming effects than other subjects who experienced a delay between the priming task and the stimulus paragraph (second row of the figure). This suggests that it is helpful if the prime and stimulus occur in close temporal proximity, as the effect depends on the stimulus being encoded together with the prime.

A second argument for the importance of encoding in priming comes from research holding constant the just-noted *prime-stimulus* delay but increasing the *stimulus-rating* delay. Priming effects actually increase with wider temporal gaps between the already primed stimulus and rating. Note how this differs from the effects just discussed, which compared the first two rows of Figure 7.1. The current comparison instead concerns the first and third rows: the first row shows larger priming effects than the third row. Once having encoded a stimulus in terms of the prime, the longer it sits in memory linked to that particular prime, the stronger the prime's effects. This evidence supports an encoding explanation for priming because the delayed rating must be less dependent on ability to use the initial prime itself as a retrieval cue. If it were a retrieval phenomenon, the priming effect should decrease with time because retrieval of the prime becomes more difficult over time. Instead, the effect increases with time, suggesting that the details of the original stimulus are lost and the primed representation becomes relatively more important. Thus, the delayed rating depends on the ability to use the memory of the stimulus as it has already been influenced by the prime present at encoding.

The third argument for encoding is simpler: presenting primes *after* the stimulus has little or no effect (fourth row), while presenting primes before the stimulus, which allows it to affect encoding, does show effects (first through third rows). This further supports encoding a stimulus in the context of a prime as more important than retrieving it in the context of the prime (Srull & Wyer, 1980).

Finally, prime-relevant information appears to elicit differential attention (J. S. Sherman, Mackie, & Driscoll, 1990). That is, subjects do not rate primed dimensions as more important in decision making, but they do recall them better, suggesting the primed dimension may elicit attention.

Explanations for priming. Priming can occur because of categories recently primed (e.g., Bargh & Pietromonaco, 1982; Higgins, Rholes, & Jones, 1977; Srull & Wyer, 1979, 1989) or categories frequently primed (e.g., Bargh et al., 1986; Higgins, King, & Mavin, 1982; Srull & Wyer, 1979, 1980, 1989; Wyer & Srull, 1986). Various models have been proposed to account for these effects, and an experiment was designed to clarify the models' differences by setting recency and frequency in competition against each other (Higgins, 1989b; Higgins, Bargh, & Lombardi, 1985).

One model portrays memory as a *storage bin* full of concepts (see Chapter 8). In this view, recently primed concepts are at the top of the mental heap and frequently primed concepts also are more likely to be left over on top because the odds are they will have been primed relatively recently also (Wyer & Srull, 1980, 1986); consequently, both recently and frequently primed concepts are likely to be used. If the two are pitted against each other (one concept has been primed more frequently but a competing one has been primed more recently), recency may well win.[5] Figure 7.2a depicts this graphically.

In contrast, if one views memory for each separate concept as a *storage battery*, the more often a concept is primed, the more charge it stores up. Also, the more recently it is primed, the more charge is still left before it decays (Wyer & Carlston, 1979). In this view, if recency and frequency are pitted against each other, frequency is likely to win because the frequently primed concept will have a higher overall charge (see Fig. 7.2b).

In the *synapse view*, on the other hand, timing predicts whether recency or frequency "wins" when the two are pitted against each other. In this view, there is a fixed maximum of activation. As in the other views, the more recently a concept has been activated, the more likely it is to be used again. However, the more frequently a concept is primed, the more slowly it decays (see Fig. 7.2c). In the short run, the recent concept predominates, but it decays faster than the more frequently primed concept; in the long run, the frequently primed concept predominates because of its slower decay rate.

Higgins, Bargh, and Lombardi (1985) have obtained evidence consistent with the synapse model (see also Higgins, 1989b; Wyer & Srull, 1986), so at present it seems plausible. In addition, a recent update of the storage bin model (Srull & Wyer, 1989) postulates that constructs are copied each time they are activated, resulting in multiple copies of a frequently activated concept; this allows the storage bin model to account for frequency as well as recency effects. Continued research will assess the value of the synapse and storage bin interpretations of priming.

---

[5]Note, however, that a revision of the storage bin model includes a prediction that allows for frequency as well as recency effects: when a concept is activated, the original concept keeps its place in the bin, but a copy is also placed at the top of the bin (Srull & Wyer, 1989). Thus, recent concepts are on top, but frequent concepts are scattered throughout the bin and, therefore, are also accessible. For purposes of illustrating how pure versions of the three models can be contrasted, we will consider the older model at this point in the text (see Chapter 8 for a more extensive treatment of the Srull-Wyer model).

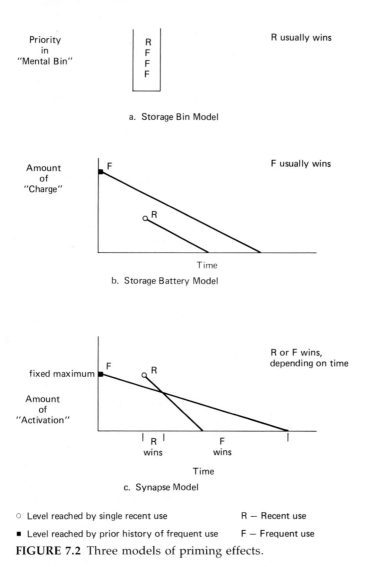

○ Level reached by single recent use   R — Recent use

■ Level reached by prior history of frequent use   F — Frequent use

FIGURE 7.2 Three models of priming effects.

Chronic sources of accessibility. Persistent differences in what is primed by one's typical situation may lead to individual differences in what is chronically primed for different people. We all know people who seem to perceive everyone in terms of how smart they are, how trustworthy, or how good-looking. People for whom a particular personality dimension is an easily and typically accessible construct are more likely to remember and describe others in those terms (Higgins & King, 1981); we discussed this phenomenon briefly in Chapter 5. For example, Higgins, King, and Mavin (1982) identified people's most typically accessible personality dimensions by recording the first and most frequent dimensions that arose in their descriptions of themselves and their friends (e.g., intelligent, witty, gracious). The dimensions that people spontaneously mention are presumably the ones that come to mind most easily, when the environment provides cues that can be interpreted in that way. Dimensions that are frequently accessed or permanently primed may become central aspects of one's personality, and one develops "chronicity" on that dimension.

Moreover, given that chronicity theoretically results from a history of frequent exposure to a category, then it should operate as does sheer frequency in situational priming, at least in any particular setting. Recall that according to the synapse model, frequently primed constructs have an advantage in the long run, although recently primed constructs predominate in the short-term (Higgins, Klein, & Strauman, 1985). Parallel results are obtained for chronicity, when it is pitted against recent priming; that is, recently primed categories predominate in the short-term, but chronically (i.e., frequently) primed categories predominate after a delay (Bargh, Lombardi, & Higgins, 1988).

Chronically accessible categories are used efficiently, allowing one to encode relevant information in less time than people who are non-chronic on that dimension (Bargh & Thein, 1985). Moreover, chronically accessible categories seem to be used without one's intention (Bargh et al., 1986; Higgins, McCann, & Fondacaro, 1982) and even outside one's control (Bargh & Pratto, 1986). As we will see, these characteristics of chronicity qualify it as truly automatic encoding (Bargh, 1984, 1989).

The automatic application of chronically accessible constructs to new information has significant social consequences. For example, the automatic, chronic processing of negative social categories regarding oneself appears to be an important component of depression (Bargh & Tota, 1988). And individual differences in gender accessibility exaggerate gender-stereotypic encoding biases (Stangor, 1988). Chronicity may also explain a positive side effect of stereotyping. People accustomed to being stereotyped (e.g., African-Americans) may show more tolerance for another potentially stereotyped person, presumably because they can see the similarity of their shared experiences, at least if their own victimization is also primed (Galanis & Jones, 1986); chronicity for stereotyping may help explain this phenomenon.

Summary

We now have some answers to what captures our attention. We especially notice things that are novel or perceptually figural in context, people or behaviors that are unusual or unexpected, behaviors that are extreme and (sometimes) negative, and stimuli relevant to our current goals; all such salience subsequently influences our reactions to other people. Our attention may also be captured by vivid stimuli, and often we are entertained, but they do not influence our reactions much. Finally, our attention also orients us to situationally or personally primed categories. Recently, frequently, and chronically encountered categories are more accessible for use, and they profoundly influence the encoding of stimuli. They are applied to relevant, moderate, ambiguous stimuli, guiding their interpretation and subsequent representation in our heads. In short, we have learned a lot about what people notice about other people and why.

CONSCIOUSNESS, CONTROL, AND AUTOMATICITY

People notice a variety of things in the external social environment, but people also attend to certain internal things, in ways that psychologists are beginning to document. Moreover, people have more control over some types of encoding and thinking processes than others, so issues of control and automaticity will come up as well.

Consciousness

What occupies people's minds? What do people think about? What is in consciousness and why? Social psychologists have not concentrated on consciousness, which has traditionally been the topic of philosophers, psychoanalysts, and (recently) cognitive scientists. Accordingly, we will not attempt a comprehensive review, but merely note some interesting points that potentially inform social cognition research and that may increasingly matter as more social cognition researchers tackle these issues.

William James described consciousness eloquently, as the stream of thought:

> Consciousness, then, does not appear to itself chopped up in bits. Such words as "chain" or "train" do not describe it as fitly as it presents itself in the first instance. It is nothing jointed; it flows. A "river" or a "stream" are the metaphors by which it is most naturally described. (W. James, 1890/1983, p. 233)

Consciousness was not only a stream to James; it was a stream "teeming with objects and relations" (p. 219), private and perpetually separate from the nearby streams belonging to other people.

Consciousness subsequently received a bad name from introspectionist experiments, in which specially trained investigators reflected on their own mental processes, in an effort to uncover basic processes such as memory retrieval. However, given the inherent inability to reproduce such introspective data publicly, and given the rise of antimentalistic behaviorism, consciousness went into hiding. With early work in cognitive psychology, it crept back in as "attention," then interpreted as what was being held in current awareness. More recently, some cognitive psychologists have rather narrowly defined consciousness; they limit it to either (a) simply being aware of (able to talk about) something, or alternatively (b) being aware of something only in the sense that it directs one's behavior, even though one might not be able to report on it (Bower, 1990).

Consciousness has also been viewed more broadly by various cognitive psychologists (G. Mandler & Nakamura, 1987). One view represents consciousness as an epiphenomenon irrelevant to ongoing mental processes. It is reminiscent of behaviorist views, and needless to say, consciousness as an epiphenomenon holds little appeal for social cognition researchers, who are by nature mentalistic. Three other perspectives are likely to be of more interest. Even these views are not terribly well-integrated with each other, but mostly represent particular attempts to solve theoretical problems using the concept of consciousness.

One idea is that consciousness is an executive that directs mental structures. When memory contents are activated sufficiently above a threshold, they are conscious, coming into short-term or working memory (see Chapter 8; D. A. Norman & Shallice, 1986; Shallice, 1972, 1978). At that point, the mental representations can be utilized under conscious control. As an executive, consciousness can inhibit and therefore control automatic associations, so it makes them responsive to one's current intents (Posner & Rothbart, 1989). A parallel social cognition account similarly labels consciousness simply as an "Executor" (Wyer & Srull, 1986; see Chapter 8).

Another perspective views consciousness as a necessary condition for human understanding and intent. Consciousness as a possible condition for intent comes into discussions of how people assign blame (K. G. Shaver, 1985) and intent (S. T. Fiske, 1987a, 1989a; Uleman, 1989). That is, one cannot discuss what people intend to do unless one assumes that they are conscious of at least some aspects of their intent.

Finally, a novel and provocative viewpoint represents consciousness as a constructed device. Consciousness as a construction requires a bit of explanation, for it would seem less obvious than the other views. In this view, consciousness is a state that makes sense of currently activated unconscious contents using a number of applicable schemas. Consciousness is constructed from the accessible schemas, within the constraints of a limited-capacity system. It operates for the purpose of furthering the needs and goals of the moment (G. Mandler & Nakamura, 1987; Marcel, 1983a, 1983b). For example, consciousness is involved in learning, as one often proceeds from the conscious to the automatic and unconscious (as in learning to drive a car). In learning, consciousness allows the formation of new associations, when previously separate things come together into awareness. Should an otherwise overlearned and automatic sequence later fail, consciousness again is implicated in troubleshooting. And consciousness is necessary for choice, which compares two alternatives held in awareness at the same time. In this view, then, constructive consciousness serves a variety of important functions in ongoing goal-directed behavior.

Cognitive psychologists generally have been concerned with the functions of consciousness. Closer to home, social-personality psychologists have focused on the contents of consciousness. They describe ongoing consciousness as the stimulus field composed of thoughts, emotional experiences, and body sensations that can compete successfully with the external world (i.e., daydreaming; J. L. Singer, 1978, 1984). Such internal landscapes (Csikszentmihalyi, 1978; Csikszentmihalyi & Larson, 1984) are often made up of unfinished business or current concerns (Klinger, 1978; Klinger, Barta, & Maxeiner, 1980; see also Srull & Wyer, 1986). These include any unmet goals, whether trivial low-level projects (getting to the bus), problems in significant relationships (will my true love marry me?), or value dilemmas (should I cooperate in my friend's tax evasion?). One study sampled college students' thoughts, finding them mostly specific, detailed, visual, unfanciful, controllable, and related to the immediate situation; only about one-fifth of the reported thoughts were strange and distorted (Klinger, 1978).

Kinds of thought. Ongoing thought may be stimulus-dependent or stimulus-independent (Antrobus et al., 1970; Klinger, 1978; J. L. Singer, 1966). That is, we sometimes think about environmental cues, i.e., in stimulus-dependent thinking. However, even when we are highly motivated to attend to the environment, we are constantly experiencing stimulus-independent thoughts (that is, our minds wander a lot). In some research demonstrating this principle, the investigators motivated subjects by paying them for correctly monitoring external signals, penalizing them for errors, and forcing them to maintain rapid responding; even then, distracting thoughts occurred 55 percent of the time (Antrobus et al., 1970; Antrobus et al., 1989). However, the nature of one's task at the time probably influences the relative amounts of stimulus-dependent and stimulus-independent thought.

A separate set of dimensions differentiates between operant and respondent thought processes (Klinger, 1977a, 1977b, 1978). As its name implies, operant thought is instrumental and problem-solving in nature; it is volitional, it monitors progress toward a goal, and one tries to protect it against external and internal distractions. Respondent thought is neither volitional nor effortful but receptive; it constitutes all the ordinary distractions of unbidden images (M. J. Horowitz, 1970) or preemptory thoughts (G. Klein, 1967) that seem to arise of their own accord. Most daily thought is operant, with respondent components, according to one study (Klinger, 1978). Doubtless, people's tasks and their stage of implementation influence the proportion of operant thoughts (e.g., Heckhausen & Gollwitzer, 1987). There are also individual differences in people's task (operant) focus (e.g., Jolly & Reardon, 1985).

While it might seem that these two dimensions of thought— stimulus-dependent versus-independent, operant versus respondent— are completely redundant, they are not. One may have operant (goal-directed) thoughts that depend on external stimuli or that are stimulus-independent and wholly internal (as when one concentrates on making a decision). Similarly, one may have respondent (spontaneous) thoughts that do or do not depend on external stimuli (funny how the word-processor keys can suddenly demand cleaning, just when one is trying to write the first sentence of a paper).

Finally, other dimensions can be used to distinguish among conscious thoughts: well-integrated or degenerative, probable or fanciful, self-involving or observation-oriented, vivid or pallid, primarily verbal or sensory, and involving particular senses (J. L. Singer, 1984; see also Klinger, 1978).

Sampling people's thoughts. In a Woody Allen scene, the moviegoer hears the dialogue between two future lovers at their first meeting and simultaneously is privy to their private thoughts as subtitles. Unfortunately, psychologists have only indirect access to people's inner worlds. Some thought-sampling studies have examined people's inner worlds while they are attempting to concentrate on a perceptual task (Antrobus et al., 1970), while others have attached people to electronic pagers that beep at random moments during the day, prompting subjects to write down their thoughts just before the signal (Klinger, 1978).

Other techniques of thought sampling ask subjects to think aloud as they are receiving information about other people (Erber & Fiske, 1984; S. T. Fiske et al., 1987; Ruscher & Fiske, 1990). As they read verbal materials describing someone, they talk into a tape recorder, providing their spontaneous and relatively unfiltered reactions, which enable researchers to observe the encoding process in detail. Although a number of methodological cautions are in order, the technique has proved useful in social cognition (S. T. Fiske & Ruscher, 1989; S. E. Taylor & Fiske, 1981).

A related series of studies has attempted the challenge of examining people's thoughts during ongoing social interaction. In these studies of naturalistic social cognition (Ickes et al., 1986; Ickes & Tooke, 1988; Ickes et al., 1988), strangers are unobtrusively videotaped as they pass the time awaiting the experimenter's return. Afterward, being informed that they have been recorded on a candid camera and granting permission for use of the tapes, subjects separately replay the tape, stopping it each time they recall having a particular thought or feeling. This research examines such dimensions of the interaction partners' thoughts and feelings as their object (self, partner, others, environment), their valence (positive or negative), and their perspective (own or other's). It finds, for example, that people's positive thoughts about their partners are related to their involvement in the interaction (as measured by both their verbal and nonverbal behavior). Moreover, in same-sex dyads, male strangers show greater convergence in their thought/feeling content than do female strangers, perhaps because they operate within a more narrow range of interactional involvement and thus, have to monitor their interaction more closely. That is, in the American culture, male strangers carefully regulate the degree of intimacy they display, and this results in their thinking and feeling similarly because their options are relatively limited. In contrast, the interactional involvement of female strangers is less constrained, but their thought/feeling content shows more convergence in taking each other's perspective and in focusing on third parties (Ickes et al., 1988).

A related paradigm also samples people's thoughts within relatively realistic social settings. Subjects role-play participation in one part of an audiotaped interpersonal encounter; that is, the tape portrays half the interaction and the subject mentally supplies the remainder. Alternatively, the tape depicts an overheard conversation, in which two people discuss a third party, and the subject then role-plays the third party as the self. At predetermined points, the tape is stopped, and subjects articulate their thoughts. People report more irrational thoughts (i.e., rigid absolute demands) in stressful, evaluative social situations, and this is especially true for the socially anxious (G. C. Davison, Feldman, & Osborn, 1984; G. C. Davison, Robins, & Johnson, 1983; G. C. Davison & Zighelboim, 1987; Kashima & Davison, 1989). The inventiveness of these various paradigms illustrates the challenge of obtaining people's thoughts during social interactions.

Conclusion. Studies that attempt to access people's thoughts must do so with their cooperation and, more importantly, within their ability to comply. As we will see (Chapter 9), there is some controversy about people's ability to access their own thought processes. People often cannot report accurately on what affects their behavior (Nisbett & Wilson, 1977b), suggesting that they have imperfect access to at least some of their own thought processes. Nevertheless, within certain limits, people can report usefully on the content of their thoughts, under certain conditions: if they do so simultaneously with their thoughts, if the relevant thoughts are already in verbal form, and if they are asked to report content and not process (Ericsson & Simon, 1980; S. T. Fiske & Ruscher, 1989; S. E. Taylor & Fiske, 1981).

In this section on consciousness, we have seen that cognition and social cognition researchers are just beginning to think about consciousness in ways that go beyond the teeming stream of William James. Consciousness may be considered an executive, a necessary condition for intent, or a construction inferred from material activated unconsciously. It tends to be occupied by unfinished business, but it may be more or less instrumental, and more or less dependent on external stimuli. Studies sampling thought during interaction are currently inventing a number of techniques to cope with this particular challenge. However, all studies of consciousness must be wary of the introspective-access problem.

Automaticity

Much important cognition occurs outside of consciousness. As perceivers, we accomplish a staggering array of encoding tasks without much bothering our intentional, voluntary, effortful, conscious selves. As we will see, people can encode rather complex material in a relatively automatic fashion. Automatic processes develop in response to people's most typical environments, and as such they show how adaptable people are.

Kinds of automaticity. Automatic processes are customarily defined according to several standard criteria: They are *unintentional*, as they do not require an explicit goal; *involuntary*, as they always occur in the presence of the relevant environmental cue; *effortless*, because they do not consume limited processing capacity; *autonomous*, for they do not need to be controlled once initiated; and *outside awareness*, as they occur without consciousness of their initiation or of the process itself (see Bargh, 1984, for a review). Your ability to recognize an upturned mouth as a smile is an automatic process, and the inference that the smiling person is friendly may be automatic as well.

There are varieties of automaticity that differ in degree of fit to the standard criteria (Bargh, 1989; see Table 7.2). *Preconscious* automaticity is the purest form of automaticity, for it fits all the standard criteria of automaticity just noted. It occurs totally prior to conscious awareness. It is unintentional and involuntary, directly triggered by the immediate environment, and it is effortless and autonomous, requiring only enough attention for the stimulus to register, but not enough to bring it into focal awareness. People react to each other preconsciously all the time, whether in trait terms, gut emotional reactions, or knee-jerk (reflexlike) stereotypes. One example would include the rapid, almost

TABLE 7.2 ANALYSES OF AUTOMATICITY AND CONTROL

Automatic Processes

    Criteria are that process be unintentional, involuntary, effortless, autonomous, outside awareness

    Forms include preconscious, postconscious, goal-dependent

    One process is proceduralization with practice, showing specific and general practice effects

Controlled Processes

    Criteria are ability to start, monitor, and terminate at will

    Forms include responsible, intentional, ruminative, spontaneous

---

effortless priming of chronically accessible categories, discussed earlier as depending on individual differences in chronicity. Another example might include "schema-triggered affect" or immediate, category-based affective responses that result instantly upon perception of another person (S. T. Fiske, 1982; S. T. Fiske & Neuberg, 1990). When stereotypes are instantly activated by physical attributes, that may also represent preconscious automaticity (McArthur, 1982). And salience effects that depend on the perceptual configuration of stimuli are also probably preconscious (McArthur, 1981; S. E. Taylor & Fiske, 1978). Finally, certain motived goals may be cued in a preconscious fashion (Bargh, 1990).

As the purest form of automaticity, preconscious automaticity effects typically provoke some controversy. In particular, there have been debates for decades around the validity of a certain research paradigm for studying preconscious automaticity, called *subliminal perception*. This is not the place to review the entire literature (see Bevan, 1964; Dixon, 1971, 1981; Erdelyi, 1974; Eriksen, 1956, 1960; Holender, 1986; Merikle, 1982; for summaries see Brody, 1987; G. Mandler & Nakamura, 1987), which ranges from debates over the existence and influence of phrases supposedly recorded backward in popular music (Vokey & Read, 1985) to highly technical accounts of the exact form of stimuli needed to produce unconscious registration. For our purposes, it suffices to note that social psychologists have demonstrated subliminal encoding of honesty, hostility, kindness, meanness, and shyness, which affect subsequent interpretation of ambiguous behaviors (Bargh et al., 1986; Bargh & Pietromonaco, 1982; Erdley & D'Agostino, 1988); subliminal encoding of threatening visual images, influencing reported anxiety (Robles et al., 1987); subliminal encoding of competitive cues, affecting competitive people's behavior on a subsequent game (Neuberg, 1988); and subliminal encoding of race-related primes, affecting interpretations of relevant but ambiguous behavior (Devine, 1989). Subliminal perception appears most likely when the subliminal cues are socially and personally relevant, not opposed by other supraliminal cues, and presented immediately before the judged stimulus.

Another form of automaticity called *postconscious* is a less pure form because it fits somewhat fewer of the standard criteria for automaticity. In particular, it occurs when initial conscious processing has unintended outcomes. One may be fully conscious of an input from the environment or of an internally generated thought, but that material may subsequently have unconscious, unintended influences on one's responses. Situational priming, described earlier, is a good example of this kind of automaticity, for one is indeed initially aware of the stimulus, but not necessarily the effects of its accessibility on later judgments. Salience effects that depend on consciously noticing a person's novelty, compared to one's expectations, are another example also described earlier in this chapter. And, as we will see later (Chapter 10), moods that are completely conscious can prime one subsequently to think in mood-congruent ways, but one may not be aware of the connection.

A third type, *goal-dependent* automaticity, is automatic according to some of the criteria, such as lack of awareness of the process itself, not needing to monitor the process to completion, and one's not intending all the specific outcomes. But it also varies by the perceiver's goals, so it is partially responsive to intentional control. Goal-dependent automaticity, thus, is not entirely automatic in that it requires intentional processing and depends on the task undertaken. One example of goal-dependent automaticity is people's spontaneous trait inferences, based on exposure to behavioral information, as described in Chapter 3. Because this occurs more under certain goals than others, it is not fully automatic. However, the trait inferences themselves do seem to occur unintentionally and without much awareness, so it is automatic once the appropriate goal triggers the process. Another example is people's schema-driven versus data-driven impression formation, which depends on their goals (see Chapter 5), but the process itself otherwise can occur without much awareness or effort. Another type of goal-dependent automaticity will be covered in Chapter 8, in discussing how people's memories for other people depend on whether they were trying to form impressions or trying to memorize their characteristics. Moreover, detecting relationships or covariation between social events (see Chapter 9) may be another example, to the extent that it depends on one's current goals, but simultaneously the process itself mostly occurs outside awareness. Finally, goal-directed processes with substantial automatic components—such as typing, driving, or perhaps rehashing the same old issues in a relationship—also illustrate this category.

Proceduralization. A crucial element of all kinds of automaticity is practice. Social inferences, such as inferring a trait from behavior, change with practice. People may start with the effortful use of general rules that are independent of the particular setting (e.g., Kelley's covariation analysis; see Chapter 2), but with practice they can make automatic inferences about certain frequently encountered stimuli (E. R. Smith, 1984). For example, if a person (e.g., a probation officer) over time judges hundreds of instances of behavior as honest or dishonest, some of those repeated inferences (e.g., shoplifting is dishonest) will show *specific* practice effects, becoming faster and easier over time.

With practice, any judgment of honesty, regardless of the particular behavior, will also speed up, showing a *general* practice effect. And even judgments of traits in general will speed up (E. R. Smith, 1989a; E. R. Smith, Branscombe, & Bormann, 1988). With consistent practice, the judgments become proceduralized so that exposure to the appropriate stimulus automatically causes the inference. In the next chapter, we will discuss different memory systems that may account for these effects (E. R. Smith, 1984), but the point here is that practice can automatize the judgment process.

Proceduralization requires repeated execution of the very same process, for example, making dispositional inferences; it does not require judging identical content, for example, judging only honesty (E. R. Smith & Lerner, 1986). Automatic or proceduralized processes can develop rapidly, within a few dozen trials, and they can last over at least a day's delay. Procedural processes constitute an alternative theoretical account of some priming effects (E. R. Smith & Branscombe, 1987, 1988; E. R. Smith, Branscombe, & Bormann, 1988), as we will see in the next chapter.

Procedural (automatic) judgments speed up people's responses, but does that matter to social interactions? E. R. Smith (1989a, 1989b) suggests that it does, for a well-practiced judgment will preempt an equally reasonable but less-practiced judgment. For example, if a teacher is used to judging intelligence, a person who is intelligent but unsociable would be viewed positively, primarily in terms of the intelligence; in contrast, a sales supervisor might emphasize the unsociability over intelligence and make a negative judgment. The speed-up of proceduralized judgments may also have implications for stereotyping, as follows: people are members of several social categories, and well-practiced reliance on sex, race, age, and the like might cause perceivers to emphasize such dimensions over others (Zarate & Smith, 1990). Another way in which the proceduralization of judgment may matter is in accounting for the speed and unconscious quality of some affective responses (Branscombe, 1988).

Necessary first steps? Immediate dispositional inferences. Perhaps as a result of practice, some significant social decisions occur instantly. Although there may be some cross-cultural differences, Americans and Europeans at least make various dispositional inferences as necessary first steps in encoding information about others. People in general rapidly identify another person as angry instead of afraid, as female instead of male, and in our culture, as kind instead of cruel. Several theorists have argued that social perceivers characterize or identify each other, in relatively automatic ways, and then they may or may not (re)-consider what they have done.

After *categorizing* another person's behavior, perceivers seem to *characterize* it quickly according to personality dispositions. This may be followed by *correction* for situational factors, if the perceiver has time and capacity (Quattrone, 1982). The processes of categorizing and characterizing, however, are relatively immune to resource limitations and thus, seem potentially automatic. That is, these first steps occur regardless of other simultaneous processes people have engaged, but the correction process may be inhibited by other concurrent tasks. In a series of experiments, Gilbert and his colleagues have suggested that the categorization and characterization step is relatively automatic, while situational correction is optional and deliberate. For example, as noted in Chapter 3, cognitively busy (overloaded) perceivers are more prone to the fundamental attribution error; that is, they readily make dispositional inferences but do not adequately correct for situational forces. This occurs whenever subjects are overloaded in any of various ways: preoccupied with a speech they will have to give, busy ignoring something prominent at the experimenter's request, or making every effort to be nice to a disliked person (Gilbert & Krull, 1988; Gilbert, Krull, & Pelham, 1988; Gilbert, Pelham, & Krull, 1988; see Gilbert, 1989, for a review).

Taking this process a substantial step further, Gilbert, Krull, and Malone (1990) suggest that a larger principle of mental systems may be at work here, namely, that the initial events of comprehending (e.g., categorizing and characterizing an action) cause one provisionally to accept the premise as true (e.g., the behavior does reflect the disposition); however, rejecting or refuting (e.g., situational correction) takes an extra step. Once comprehended, everyday propositions often *are* true (i.e., people often do behave as their personalities predict), so this relatively automatic bias would seem adaptive, but it can lead to trouble under unusual circumstances.

In a related model already discussed in Chapter 3, Trope (1986) decomposes the attribution process into two stages. In the first stage, *identification*, one classifies a behavior, using the situation as an additive cue if the behavior is ambiguous. For example, in a dangerous situation, one may interpret an ambiguous facial expression as fearful (see also Wallbott, 1988). In the second stage, *inference*, one applies a relevant causal schema to make attributions. For example, one views the (previously identified) fearful expression as normal in a dangerous situation, so one does not assume that it is a diagnostic clue to the other person having a fearful personality. Thus, in the second stage, the fear-provoking situation can act as a subtractive cue to dispositional inference, while in the first it acts as an additive cue to identifying an ambiguous behavior. Unlike Gilbert's, Quattrone's, and Uleman's work (see below), in Trope's model dispositional inference itself is not given special priority, for initial identifications can take many forms, but the identification process is seen as preconscious and automatic.

The current consensus seems to hold that dispositional inferences are necessary, perhaps automatic, first steps making sense of another person, at least in European and American cultures (Rimé et al., 1985; Zebrowitz-McArthur, 1988). The two qualifications in this consensus are worth noting. First, in other cultures, situational inferences may come first (J. G. Miller, 1984), and Westerners can also be temporarily reoriented to make situational attributions first (Quattrone, 1982). Second, although the rigorous definitions of automaticity are new, the importance of dispositional inferences is not entirely new. People perceive intention and emotion even in geometric figures that move around a screen (Bassili, 1976; Heider & Simmel, 1944; Oatley & Yuill, 1985; Rimé et al., 1985). Turning to traits, people's implicit theories about other people's personalities also are fundamental to perceiving another person as a person (D. J. Schneider, 1973). When a person is described as cold, hard, sour, and bright, it brings to mind a different configuration of meanings than when the description refers to a frozen dessert (lime sherbet perhaps?). In judging people, trait-inferencing is seen as spontaneous, coercive, and persistent (De Soto, Hamilton, & Taylor, 1985; but see S. S. Smith & Kihlstrom, 1987). Moreover, people seem to be fundamentally oriented to resolving inconsistencies in other people's personalities, at the time of the encounter (Asch, 1946; Asch & Zukier, 1984; Brewer, Dull, & Lui, 1981; S. T. Fiske et al., 1987; Stern et al., 1984), all of which suggests the priority of dispositional information.

Summary and conclusions. So far, we have seen that there are various kinds of automated responses, differing in degree. We have seen that various kinds of encoding may occur in an automated fashion, below consciousness, in subliminal perception. Practice seems to be the crucial element in developing automatic responses, as research on proceduralized inference suggests. Moreover, certain types of judgments seem especially likely to be automated: dispositional inferences seem to be necessary first steps in encoding information about others. This makes sense in that dispositional inferences allow people to predict what others will do in future encounters (Kelley, 1979; Kelley & Thibaut, 1978). Moreover, much of the time, people's behavior probably does reflect what they will do again later, at least in the situations in which we habitually encounter them.

Other types of encoding are likely to be automatic as well, although there is less accumulated evidence on these points. Self-relevant knowledge is likely to be encoded automatically, as we saw in Chapter 6, especially for certain combinations of people (e.g., the depressed) and content (e.g., negative traits; Bargh & Tota, 1988). Stimuli related to threat would be likely candidates for automatic encoding; for example, an angry face in a crowd of happy faces stands out, suggesting a preattentive search for threatening cues (C. H. Hansen & Hansen, 1988a), and negative cues may carry particular weight preconsciously (Erdley & D'Agostino, 1988). Stimuli relevant to our current needs and goals may be encoded automatically (Bruner, 1957). Finally, stimuli likely to be relevant to our interests are noticed, so that people especially notice others their own age, and males especially notice attractive females (M. J. Rodin, 1987), a process that may represent automatic encoding.

Control

The lower levels of automaticity begin to look more and more like controlled behavior. Just as there were degrees of automaticity (from preconscious to postconscious to goal-dependent), so there are degrees of controlled processes. People's degree of control over their thoughts has just recently sparked a lot of interest from social cognition researchers.

Kinds of control. It may seem simple to consider how much we control our thoughts, for after all we can focus attention on a task at hand or we can put something out of mind when necessary. Or can we? It is often not easy to concentrate, and it is even more difficult to forget at will. In what sense do we actually control our thoughts?

One treatment of this problem breaks down control into several different aspects (Uleman, 1989). Suppose one sees someone wildly waving from a distance. One may have awareness of input (i.e., a person waving), awareness of one's own current goals (trying to recognize and meet a friend from afar), awareness of means to those goals (trying to remember the color of the person's coat), metacognitions (awareness of the existence of such thought processes), and awareness of forgone alternatives (considering whether the waving person is actually a stranger asking for help). In addition, more social features of awareness and control come into thinking of oneself as a thinker ("I am thinking about all this") and awareness of one's reputation as a thinker ("am I making an accurate interpretation, and what will people think if I am wrong and that stranger really does need help?"). Control of thought refers to the capacity to initiate, terminate, and inhibit any of these components. Each of these are different ways in which one may be aware of and potentially control one's thoughts. From this perspective, then, one must be aware of a mental process in order to control it, a reasonable enough assumption.

Given this framework, social cognition researchers can derive degrees of control (Uleman, 1989). The least controlled process is automatic, as we have just seen, one that starts immediately upon encountering the stimulus and autonomously runs to completion. Of the controlled processes, the least controlled processes are *spontaneous*, occurring without intent or awareness but requiring some capacity and being subject to inhibition and termination. *Ruminative* processes are conscious but not consciously goal-directed. *Intentional* processes are directed toward some goal and are fully controlled by personal standards and goals. The most controlled processes are ones for which people are *responsible*, for which they are accountable to social as well as personal standards.

Spontaneous thoughts. As a case study, consider people's most immediate inferences about each other. We saw earlier that some social inferences seem to occur rapidly at encoding, as part of the process of understanding another's behavior. Uleman, Winter, and their colleagues have found that people reading about another person's behavior apparently encode the behavior in terms of relevant personality traits (L. S. Newman & Uleman, 1989; Uleman, 1987, 1989; Winter, Uleman, & Cunniff, 1985; Winter & Uleman, 1984). These on-line inferences are spontaneous in that they occur without explicit intent or much awareness. Spontaneous trait inferences are more likely to occur, granted, for some types of people (Bargh & Thein, 1985; Uleman et al., 1986) and some types of traits (L. S. Newman & Uleman, 1989). Moreover, this type of encoding can be increased (Bassili & Smith, 1986) or decreased (Moskowitz & Uleman, 1986, cited in Uleman, 1987) by task instructions, and it does require some short-term memory capacity (Uleman, Newman, & Winter, 1987, cited in L. S. Newman & Uleman, 1989), so it is not fully automatic. Encoding other people's behavior in trait terms appears to be a mostly unconscious, "not-intended inference" that people could avoid but usually do not. Note that at this point, this variety of control overlaps with the least automatic type of processes described earlier, goal-dependent automaticity.

Intentional thoughts. When is it fair to say that people intend a particular train of thought? This issue arose recently in considering cognitive explanations for socially significant phenomena, such as stereotyping, biased inferences, and the like. For example, consider people's propensity to categorize other people in terms of race, sex, and age, as discussed in Chapters 4 and 5. If people do not intentionally categorize, then perhaps stereotypic thinking is not strictly intentional (S. T. Fiske, 1987a, 1989a). People may be said to intend their train of thought and resulting interpretation if they perceive themselves as *having options* to think about it in other ways. Hence, if on reflection a person understood that another interpretation were possible, then the way the person thinks may be considered intentional. When a person does have options, one particular choice is likely to be easier, and others are likely to be harder. That is, the person's accustomed way of thinking is the easy way, and *making the hard choice* is likely to be seen as especially intentional, by ordinary observers, psychologists, and even legal experts. However, if the person has the capability of thinking either way, then both the hard and easy choices are intentional, by the first criterion. Finally, people implement their intended way of thinking by *paying attention*. Hence if a person wants to overcome a habitual stereotype applied to another person, paying attention to nonstereotypic attributes is the most effective route (S. T. Fiske & Neuberg, 1990). Intentional thought, thus, is characterized by having options, often by making the hard choice, and paying attention to the desired course.[6]

Control over intrusive thoughts. How often have you tried *not* to think about a certain someone while working, *not* to think about food when dieting, or *not* to think about anything at all while meditating or trying to fall asleep? One of us, as a teen-ager, discovered that being on a diet made her far more preoccupied with food than when not dieting. The cause was not just being hungry, but the fact of food being forbidden that perversely made it so preoccupying. Denial often increases thinking about the forbidden object, as people learn to their dismay in prohibiting themselves or others from seeing a particular lover, drinking alcohol, or even trivial habits such as nail-biting.

Experimental evidence supports this frustrating experience. In a pair of studies, Wegner et al. (1987) asked subjects to think aloud for five minutes while suppressing thoughts of a white bear; however, they were asked to ring a bell whenever they did think about a white bear. They were unable to suppress white-bear thoughts, as the dieter knows. Moreover, when afterward they were asked instead to think about white bears, they showed a rebound effect, thinking about white bears quite a lot; most importantly, they thought about white bears even more than did people who had been explicitly thinking about them all along. (The dieter knows all too well the potential for a post-diet binge of food thoughts and compensatory eating.) The only way out, as successful dieters and practiced meditators know, is to find a

---

[6]From intent, it is a short step to responsibility. For example, completely unintentional discrimination is not illegal, and accidentally killing someone is viewed less negatively than killing someone on purpose. Regardless, people are not held socially responsible for their thoughts, only for their actions. The intent problem matters especially when one analyzes the thoughts that provoked a particular action.

substitute thought. People who thought about a red Volkswagen as a distracter were no more successful in suppressing white-bear thoughts, but they showed no rebound afterward, suggesting that the suppression had not created the same kind of mental logjam as it had without the distracting thought.

The difficulty of thought suppression is implicated in the inability of depressed people to avoid negative thoughts, although they can suppress positive thoughts as well as control subjects can (Wenzlaff, Wegner, & Roper, 1988); as we will see later (Chapter 10), depression makes negative thoughts more accessible. For example, depressed people perseverate on (i.e., persist in ruminating about) failures longer than do nondepressed people (Carver et al., 1988). Providing depressed subjects with positive distracter thoughts seems to be helpful in the suppression of negative material (Wenzlaff, Wegner, & Roper, 1988).

When not successfully repressed, a single intrusive thought may lead the way to brooding and rumination, that is, unwanted thinking about a particular object for a long time. Repetitive, counter-productive thinking may stem both from cognitive associations cued by goal-directed thinking and from the motivation to remember uncompleted tasks (Zeigarnik, 1927). Rumination is said to entail several stages, which can be illustrated by the problem of attempting not to dwell on an unrequited attraction: initially intensified repetition of the interrupted behavior (despite rebuffs, one persists in attempts to contact the loved person), problem solving at lower and lower levels (one tries to calculate details of the person's schedule and habits, to maximize successful contact), end-state thinking (one fantasizes about the desired outcome of being together), trying to abandon the goal (one attempts to give up the person), channelized thinking (even after resolving to give up, one may persist in thinking along well-worn associative pathways that all lead to thoughts of the other), and depression from continued powerlessness (if one cannot escape from the preoccupation, one must mourn the lost ideal) (L. L. Martin & Tesser, 1989). A demonstration of the interrupted-goal aspect of rumination was obtained in one study that asked newly arrived college women about some close person they had left behind; ruminations were positively related to the number of shared activities that were interrupted by being apart from the person (K. U. Millar, Tesser, & Millar, 1988).

The studies of thought suppression and rumination suggest a solution for people who are mentally stuck on a particular issue: it may actually help to focus temporarily on the very thing that bothers them. In particular, it may be helpful to discuss the bothersome issue with another person. This, of course, is a central function of psychotherapy, confession, and good friendships. In a provocative series of studies,

Pennebaker and his colleagues have found that confiding about traumatic experiences reduces ruminations, lowers subjective distress, and enhances physical health (Pennebaker, 1988, 1989a, 1989b; Pennebaker, Kiecolt-Glaser, & Glaser, 1988; Pennebaker & Hoover, 1985; Pennebaker & O'Heeron, 1984; Pennebaker & Susman, 1988). Whether people wrote anonymously or talked to a trustworthy stranger, describing a specific negative event in detail was beneficial. Critical components of the procedure seem to include establishing rapport with the subject, emphasizing the seriousness of the request, and writing or talking in a unique, isolated environment (Pennebaker, 1989a). Of course, these are components of the more traditional methods for confiding one's innermost secrets as well, suggesting the power of the more common methods.

Conclusion. We have seen that people have varying degrees of mental control, ranging from processes that occur spontaneously, without intent or awareness, but taking up some cognitive capacity (e.g., trait inferences from behavior), to processes that occur intentionally, involving choice and active attention (e.g., controlling their tendencies to stereotype). People have difficulty suppressing unwanted thoughts, and this difficulty may lead to rumination. Effective in combating such intrusive thoughts are some well-worn cultural standbys, including distracting oneself and confiding in others.

Before leaving automaticity and control, we should note an assumption made in all of this work. Automatic and controlled processing are typically viewed as opposites or at least as endpoints of a continuum. However, a recent theory proposes that they are two separate, independent dimensions and paradoxically, that automatic processes are usually quite controlled (Logan, 1989). In this view, automatic processes are developed from consistent practice, as in the procedural view; unlike the procedural view, automatic performance is viewed as based on retrieval of *single prior instances* of the same behavior, rather than on retrieval of a general rule built up from experience (Logan, 1988). In essence, it is an exemplar view (see Chapter 4 on exemplar views of categorization). From this perspective, automatic processes are controllable in several respects: one can choose not to respond based on the retrieved memory, but instead to respond in a new fashion constructed from the retrieved instances or to respond by altering the usual response; one can change the retrieval process itself by changing one's state and, therefore, some of the relevant memory cues; one can refocus one's attention; or one can change one's goals. In this view, then, processes can be both highly automatic and quite amenable to control. Skilled behavior is both, for while experts rely on their automated skills, they can also manipulate their skills at will.

*T*HE UNTHINKING MIND

We have examined what captures attention, what enters consciousness, and what kinds of controlled and automatic processes determine people's thoughts. We now turn to examine the mind when it does not seem to be explicitly thinking. We will examine the unthinking mind in three quite different respects: the unconscious, which addresses the processes that occur and content that exists outside awareness; the state of mindlessness, which addresses people operating in a routinized, thoughtless, unalert fashion; and the Gibsonian perspective on social knowing, which takes the view that people perceive directly, without cognitive intervention, either conscious or unconscious.

Unconsciousness

Apart from research on automatic processing in general and subliminal perception in particular, social cognition research has not been much concerned with unconscious processes. Nor, for that matter, has cognitive psychology been directly concerned with it until recently. The reasons for this neglect probably stem from a variety of influences: holdovers from the behaviorist mistrust of mental processes, especially processes that could not be verbalized; spillovers from many empirical scientists' distrust of Freudian theory, including the broad role it assigns to people's unconscious life[7]; and the controversies surrounding subliminal perception (noted earlier). Nevertheless, recent efforts to integrate unconscious processes are dotting the cognitive-social-personality research terrain (for overviews, see Bower, 1990; Brody, 1987; Kihlstrom, 1987; G. Mandler & Nakamura, 1987), and this section is a preview of probable future efforts.

Theoretical perspectives on the "cognitive unconscious" differ, depending on one's overall approach to the mind (Kihlstrom, 1987). In classic information-processing approaches, unconscious processes are essentially limited to basic unattended perceptual processes, and unconscious contents are any cognitions residing in long-term memory but not currently being rehearsed. In revised information-processing approaches, unconscious contents are any cognitions that are insufficiently activated to reach awareness, and unconscious processes are essentially the well-practiced automatic procedures described earlier. A third type of model, parallel distributed processing (to be summarized in the next chapter), has yet to make inroads within social cognition, but it essentially views as unconscious (a) any processes occurring too

---

[7]This is not to exclude continuing empirical efforts to uncover the Freudian unconscious (e.g., Dahl, Kachele, & Thoma, 1989; Kline, 1987), which cannot be our concern here, for lack of space.

rapidly to reach awareness, or (b) any group of processes all occurring at once beyond the capability of consciousness to capture.

One theoretical perspective suggests that the preconscious system differs in systematic ways from the conscious system (e.g., Epstein & Erskine, 1983). In this view, the preconscious is an experiencial rather than intellective reasoning system, so it is less abstract and more affective; more action-oriented and less contemplative; more concerned with immediate personal welfare; more loosely integrated; more categorical than differentiated; and is felt as imposing itself on one's experiences, rather than being under control. These features are used to explain people's preconscious experiencial learning that may conflict with their own conscious logic.

From an empirical perspective, some would argue that unconscious processes are more powerful than conscious ones, able to detect relationships and patterns of stimuli that cannot be detected consciously (Lewicki, 1982, 1985, 1986a, 1986b; Lewicki, Czyzewska, & Hoffman, 1987; Lewicki & Hill, 1987; Lewicki, Hill, & Bizot, 1989). For example, in one pair of studies (Lewicki, 1985), subjects interacted with a kind or unkind experimenter who happened to wear glasses; they apparently acquired the inference that people with glasses were nice (or not), and they applied those principles to a subsequent encounter with a different bespectacled person. In another set of studies (Hill et al., 1990), subjects were given the task of learning to distinguish between two subtly different personality profiles. In addition to the profiles, other incidental information included a schematic drawing of the target person's face. In fact, the only difference between the two "personality types" was a tiny difference in how long or short the face appeared to be. Although subjects could not report on the differences in the schematic faces, they nevertheless were able to differentiate the two "types" and reported that it depended on the profiles themselves, which were actually random. In both social and nonsocial domains, people acquire and use complex information, without being able to report the basis for doing so, suggesting the power of processing outside awareness.

In this chapter, we have already seen evidence of relatively automatic social cognitive processes, as when people's perceptions of others are influenced by chronically accessible constructs, well-practiced inferential procedures, subliminally perceived trait categories, rapid dispositional inferences, and the like. Later, we will discuss possibly unconscious influences on affective responses (Chapter 10).

Mindlessness

We now turn our attention to a different type of unthinking process. Mindlessness refers to the state of mind when one is not especially alert, thoughtful, or creative, although one is certainly conscious in the everyday sense in that one could potentially be more aware of one's actions. For example, when one has "overlearned" a task and knows it very well (e.g., describing one's summer vacation for the twentieth time), one often performs it without thinking about it at all, in a routine, habitual fashion (Langer, 1989a, 1989b; Langer, Blank, & Chanowitz, 1978). The routinization process, according to Langer, leaves one vulnerable to certain problems or errors. Although one is still able to perform the task, if the task parameters change suddenly, it may be hard to change so as to deal mindfully with the new contingencies. Mindlessness makes people insensitive to context. Thus, to continue the vacation example, mindless processing may lead one to tell the same stories to one's great uncle as to one's college roommate, with awkward consequences. Presumably, more mindful or conscious talking might enable one to avoid the confusion.

While superficially similar, mindlessness and mindfulness differ respectively from automatic and controlled processing, in that mindfulness, according to Langer (1989a, 1989b) may actually increase capacity. That is, in this perspective, one's cognitive capacity is not fixed. The more mindful one is, the more ability one has to respond to incoming information. (The more traditional view of controlled processing is that it operates within a limited capacity system and is not greatly elastic.) Mindfulness is described as a qualitatively distinct state: alert and lively awareness, characterized by making cognitive differentiations.

Effects of Mindlessness.   Several studies have suggested that mindless processing fails to monitor task contingencies effectively. In one study (Langer, Blank, & Chanowitz, 1978), a person about to use a photocopier was interrupted by an experimental confederate who asked either, "Excuse me, may I use the Xerox machine," "Excuse me, may I use the Xerox machine, because I have to make copies," or "Excuse me, may I use the Xerox machine, because I'm in a rush." The critical result was whether or not subjects complied when the explanation ("because I have to make copies") superficially resembled a legitimate request ("because I'm in a rush"), but did not constitute as valid a reason. People complied when the request was small, presumably because they mindlessly processed only minimal information (the *form* of the request was legitimate), but they did not comply when the request was large, presumably because they (no longer mindlessly) did attend to the meaningless *content* of the explanation (everyone uses a copier to make copies). People let the other person use the copier whenever it sounded right, unless the request was inconvenient enough to make them stop and think. Mindfulness thus seems to increase with a significant interruption. Other evidence suggests that it also increases with other ways of motivating people to think twice about what they are doing: when one receives an excuse that is controllable, and therefore, illegitimate (Folkes, 1985; cf. Langer, Chanowitz, & Blank, 1985), when one encounters an explanation that is novel, and therefore, attention-getting (Kitayama & Burnstein, 1988), or when one learns labels that are conditional, and therefore, flexible (Langer & Piper, 1987).

What does this work imply about encoding, consciousness, and control? It suggests that when one knows a routine too well (i.e., requests are followed by reasons), one no longer pays attention to individual components of the routine; as a consequence, one is less aware of alternatives and exercises less control than one could. A routine for the activity substitutes for more conscious or mindful processing. Any task component that seems to satisfy the form of the routine will be accepted, perhaps wrongfully. Langer (1978) has further hypothesized that when a person has overlearned a routine, the person will perform less creatively and be less able to modify performance when external interruptions or novel task elements are suddenly introduced into the task environment. In contrast, when a task is new, attention is concentrated, leading to effective learning, better awareness of the task environment, and high accuracy (e.g., Langer & Imber, 1979). In a similar vein, Baumeister has argued that because skill entails overlearning to the point of unconscious execution of the task, conscious attention to skilled performance can be disruptive, resulting in choking under pressure. Because the conscious mind does not have the capacity to monitor skilled performance, paying attention can simply interfere (Baumeister, 1984; Baumeister & Showers, 1986).

Self-induced dependence. Another condition under which mindlessness reduces the efficacy of performance is termed self-induced dependence (Langer & Benevento, 1978). This occurs when a person who was previously able to perform a task quite successfully and mindlessly comes to doubt his or her ability because of a situation that promotes passivity, dependence, or feeling inferior. Several studies have followed a format in which subjects are initially successful on a routine task, their ability is subsequently questioned during some interim task, and performance on the initial task is reassessed. Under these circumstances, retested performance is undermined. Moreover, this is true even when the interim period of being labeled as incompetent bears no relationship to the task being evaluated (Langer & Benevento, 1978). For example, subjects in the first part of one study solved word puzzles and were led to believe that they had done quite well. In the second part of the study, subjects performed a menial clerical task, either working under another person (which connotes that one is somehow inferior) or without supervision (connoting independence and competence). In the third part of the study, subjects again solved word puzzles, and those who had just worked under a supervisor (implying incompetence) performed more poorly on the puzzle than those who had worked on their own.

Interestingly, it is overlearned tasks (i.e., those performed mindlessly) and completely new tasks that are most likely to show performance impairments following such negative labeling. For overlearned tasks, the individual parts of the task are no longer attended, and for the new tasks, the parts were never known. For moderately well-learned tasks, the task components remain more accessible to consciousness and hence are undermined less by negative labeling or irrelevant failure experiences (Langer & Imber, 1979; see also S. T. Fiske & Dyer, 1985; Hayes-Roth, 1977; and Chapters 4 and 5).

Premature cognitive commitment. A third circumstance in which mindlessness can adversely affect performance is termed *premature cognitive commitment* (Chanowitz & Langer, 1981) or single-exposure mindlessness. While most mindlessness results from well-practiced behaviors that no longer require attention, some mindlessness can result from a single event. Premature cognitive commitment refers to the fact that when one learns information for one purpose and then is called upon to use it for a different purpose, it may be hard to reorganize or restructure the information for the second purpose. Psychology students rapidly discover that one reads articles differently, depending on whether one is reading for a class discussion, reading for fun, reading to criticize, reading to explain, or reading to summarize. (We leave it to the reader's imagination which is most mindless.) Having read an article one way, it is hard to use it for another purpose without rereading it.

In a study demonstrating this effect, Chanowitz and Langer (1981) had some subjects read about a fictitious disorder they believed to be irrelevant to themselves (so they presumably read mindlessly); when subsequently told they had the disorder, they displayed more "symptoms" of the disorder, apparently because they had not planned strategies to compensate for it. Subjects who had read the original description believing the disorder might be relevant (so they presumably read mindfully) later performed better, apparently because they compensated for the disorder.

Clearly, mindlessness is not without its liabilities; under some circumstances it can lead to ineffective learning, the inability to deal with novel or interrupting conditions, and vulnerability to negative labels or failure experiences (cf. Langer & Imber, 1980; Langer & Weinman, 1981). Mindlessness is likely to be useful only under the most improbable possibilities either that one has predetermined the optimal response or that one's circumstances never change (Langer, 1989a,

1989b). Moreover, mindfulness is said to have major benefits, even including increased longevity (Alexander et al., 1989). Langer argues that it is not one's specific activities that matter so much as the state of mind with which they are engaged. For example, despite the apparent contradiction, mindful television watching may be beneficial to one's cognitive capacities (Langer & Piper, 1988).

Although the experiments on mindlessness certainly point to people overlooking things they perhaps should have noticed, none of them establish that mindlessness entails automatic behavior (nor were they so designed). "A better summary of the mindlessness studies would be that...when people exert little conscious effort in examining their environment, they are at the mercy of automatically-produced interpretations" (Bargh, 1984, p. 35).

The Gibsonian or Ecological Approach to Social Perception

This chapter opened with an example of a social perceiver unfortunately misperceiving who was chasing whom in a series of three runners. One might argue that the example reflects the automatic activation of stereotypic categorization processes (interpreting the trio as a white police officer chasing two black suspects), and one might marvel at the complexity of the inferential processes that occurred in the split second before the perceiver responded in such a misguided fashion. Alternatively, one might argue that, for that perceiver, the particular stimulus configuration effectively furnished his response. From this perspective, the perception was direct, from seeing and hearing, straight to the intrinsic behavioral possibilities. This type of analysis illustrates an ecological approach to social knowing.

Inspired by J. J. Gibson's work in object perception (1966, 1979), several theorists have suggested that much of the important activity in social understanding occurs immediately during perception (R. M. Baron, 1980a, 1980b, 1984; Kassin & Baron, 1985, 1986; Lowe & Kassin, 1980; McArthur, 1980; McArthur & Baron, 1983; Neisser, 1976, 1980; Weary et al., 1980; Zebrowitz, 1990; Zebrowitz-McArthur, 1988), rather than as the result of complex inferential activity, however automated. In particular, the ecological approach emphasizes external stimulus information and the organization inherent in it, rather than the organization constructed or imposed by the perceiver (Zebrowitz, 1990). Organization is "inherent in a stimulus" for a particular perceiver, based on that person's history of perceptual experiences. A particular stimulus *affords* or offers particular behaviors to a perceiver, and the perceiver is reciprocally *attuned* or sensitive to particular stimulus properties. The Gibsonian approach is called *ecological perception* because it emphasizes perceivers interacting with their environments and imbedded in their own characteristic niche. Perception is analyzed as adaptive for perceivers; "perceiving is for doing," in this view, so perception will typically be accurate, if perceivers are given sufficient information and context.

Example of causal perception. The Gibsonian perspective suggests, for example, that causal attributions result from segmenting the perceptual field, and that inferences and memory are irrelevant (McArthur, 1980). To illustrate, assume you overhear your neighbors quarreling. She screams at him, and he murmurs in reply; this sequence alternates for some minutes. In relating the incident to your roommate, you describe the woman as causing the argument because each segment of the interaction begins with her salient vocal behavior. Each of her loud comments marks a new perceptual unit that finishes with his soft reply. She shouts, he murmurs. Since causality requires temporal precedence, starting each unit with her then irresistibly places her in a squarely causal role (see the top of Fig. 7.3).

Now replay the fight but assume that you can see what is going on as well as hear it. (Assume further that they both do not turn on you for spying, however scientifically disinterested you might be.) The fight actually commences with him walking into the room and gesturing violently at her. She replies and retreats. He threatens her again, speaking in ominously low tones, and she backs off, arguing defensively. He threatens, and she retreats. The causal segments now commence each time with his physical gestures and her retreats. His physical gestures are perceptually big relative to her little retreats, in much the same way her shouts were loud compared to his soft murmurs. Hence, the units now begin with him: he makes big physical threats and she makes little movements of retreat. Now the man would be described as causing the argument. Note that this perceptual analysis of causal attribution

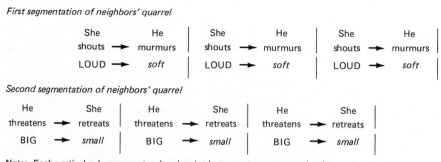

First segmentation of neighbors' quarrel

She	He	She	He	She	He
shouts → murmurs		shouts → murmurs		shouts → murmurs	
LOUD → soft		LOUD → soft		LOUD → soft	

Second segmentation of neighbors' quarrel

He	She	He	She	He	She
threatens → retreats		threatens → retreats		threatens → retreats	
BIG → small		BIG → small		BIG → small	

Note: Each vertical rule represents a breakpoint between two perceptual units.

FIGURE 7.3 Perceptual segmentation of behavioral sequences resulting in different causal judgments.

deemphasizes cognitive activity. The causal judgments are implicit in perception from the outset (McArthur, 1980).

The unitizing technique. The direct perception analysis is all the more interesting because there is considerable evidence that perceptual segmentation has important effects on social judgments. This has been shown by researchers who measure perceptual segmentation directly (for a review, see Newtson, Hairfield, Bloomingdale, & Cutino, 1987; for a critique, see Ebbesen, 1980). The technique for measuring perceptual segments or units involves subjects watching a film and pushing a button to indicate the end of each given segment and the beginning of a new one; the button push is taken to indicate what is called a breakpoint between segments. Segments are defined in whatever way seems natural to the individual (Newtson & Enquist, 1976; Newtson, Enquist, & Bois, 1977). The unitizing method (as it is called) is reliable and valid and surprisingly comfortable for subjects. People largely agree on the perceptual units in a given scene. For example, if the neighbors' quarrel were shown in a silent film, people would generally agree on the breakpoints indicated in the bottom row of Figure 7.3.

Unitizing research suggests that the breakpoints between perceptual units have special properties. The breakpoint moments of a film, when shown as a series of stills in isolation from the rest of the film, nonetheless coherently convey the story. Nonbreakpoints (at equivalent intervals) do not adequately summarize the story. Recognition memory for breakpoints is also superior to recognition for nonbreakpoints (see Newtson, 1976). The implication is that behavior is segmented at points of maximal information (Newtson, 1980; Newtson et al., 1978; but for dissent, see C. E. Cohen, 1981a; C. E. Cohen & Ebbesen, 1979; Ebbesen, 1980). Breakpoints occur at peaks of behavior complexity, when many body parts are changing at once (Newtson, Enquist, & Bois, 1977). That is, one can perceive the core of an action when it is most distinctively changing, so that is seen as a breakpoint. If action slows down to a pause or stops, that is not typically a breakpoint. Moreover, Newtson et al. (1987) suggest that the rise and fall of action complexity follows a wave pattern for individuals, and when two people are interacting, their actions jointly create a coordinated wave pattern. This suggests that basic perceptual-motor configurations could function independently of complex cognitive processes.

People can use fine-grained units or grosser units, depending on instructions to do so or on other goals. For example, people use finer units when their goal is observing nonverbal behavior (Strenta & Kleck, 1984), remembering task behavior (C. E. Cohen & Ebbesen, 1979), and observing individuals within an aggregate of people (Wilder, 1986). People also use finer units when they encounter an unexpected action (Newtson, 1973; Wilder, 1978a, 1978c, 1986) or a person about whom they have no prior information (Graziano, Moore, & Collins, 1988). Finer levels of perception are associated with measures indicating more information gained: more confident and differentiated trait inferences, more dispositional attributions (Deaux & Major, 1977; Newtson, 1973; Wilder, 1978a, 1978c), and better memory for the person observed (Lassiter, 1988; Lassiter, Stone, & Rogers, 1988). Finer unitizing even seems to be associated with greater liking of an otherwise neutral person, perhaps because of an increased sense of familiarity, independent of one's improved memory for the finely unitized other (Lassiter, 1988; Lassiter & Stone, 1984). The unitizing research as a whole addresses basic perceptual processes in ongoing interaction, suggesting how information is gained over time.

Babyfaces and other ecological phenomena. Other research from an ecological perspective examines how people make specific inferences about personality on the basis of people's physical features and other features intrinsic to the social stimulus configuration. Such appearance-based perceptions are fundamental factors in social perception. For example, old-time gangster movies often featured a ruthless criminal with a name like "Babyface" Norton. What made such figures especially sinister was the contrast between their cherubic features and their villainous behavior. Why do we expect people with babyfaced features to have equally innocent personalities? A series of studies in ecological perception indicates that babyfaced adults are perceived to have more childlike qualities than mature-faced adults; across cultures, people with large eyes, big foreheads, and short features (e.g., snub noses, small chins) are seen as less strong, less dominant, and less intellectually astute, and as more naive, more honest, kinder, and warmer, regardless of perceived age and attractiveness (Berry & McArthur, 1985; McArthur & Apatow, 1983–84; McArthur & Berry, 1987; see Berry & McArthur, 1986, for a review). Babyfaced adults are less likely to be judged guilty of crimes involving intentional criminal behavior (hence, the babyfaced gangster is disconcerting), but they are more likely to be judged guilty of crimes involving negligence (Berry & Zebrowitz-McArthur, 1988). Cross-culturally, people with childlike voices are also perceived as weaker, less competent, and warmer (Montepare & Zebrowitz-McArthur, 1987). And people with more youthful gaits are perceived to be happier and more powerful, regardless of perceived age and gender (Montepare & Zebrowitz-McArthur, 1988).

The ecological approach argues that these perceptions result from the normal covariation between babylike features and actual age, such that most babyish humans *are* more weak, submissive, intellectually undeveloped, naive, and innocent, precisely because they are very likely to be actual babies. Such perceptions based on babylike features are normally adaptive for the species' survival because it is important for adults to nurture and protect the young. Adults are, therefore, likely to perceive childlike features as needing or affording the behavioral opportunity of caretaking, which fits with perceiving a babylike person as weak, etc. To a properly attuned organism, such perceptions are biologically and socially useful. Consequently, it is not surprising that children as young as two-and-a-half can use babyface cues to judge age (Montepare & Zebrowitz-McArthur, 1986).

Implications for social cognition research. Researchers who support the direct perception or ecological view argue that it quite directly contradicts the idea that inferences depend upon complex cognitive processes. According to this view, cognitive constructs (such as observational goals or schema-based expectations) enter into the inference process only to the degree that such factors influence the initial perception of an event, as it is directly observed (Enquist, Newtson, & LaCross, 1979; Massad, Hubbard, & Newtson, 1979; see Chapter 4 for other references). With respect to causal attribution, the Gibsonian view would argue that attributions result from perceptual organization, such as temporal sequence, or the contrast of large to small stimuli, as in our earlier example of the neighbors' fight; the Gibsonian view suggests that causal inference occurs automatically during the perception of an event, an idea with which others agree (R. D. Sherman & Titus, 1982; E. R. Smith & Miller, 1979). Although there is some evidence to the contrary (Vinokur & Ajzen, 1982), the Gibsonian view is a helpful counterpoint to the standard explanations of complex cognitive processes as the only basis for social judgments.

The Gibsonian perspective is a useful antidote to some biases in mainstream research on encoding. Ecological perception recognizes the intrinsic richness of stimulus information and insists that stimuli be ecologically valid, namely, that they occur in multiple sensory modes, that they change and not be utterly static, that they be presented in configuration instead of isolation, and that they be extended in time instead of brief. The Gibsonians' frequent use of naturalistic filmed stimuli illustrates this set of concerns. The ecological approach also emphasizes the adaptive functions of perception, in particular, the link between perception and action. Hence, it examines why people would develop the perception that babyfaced people need nurturance and protection (namely that most babyfaced people are in fact babies, whom adults perceive as vulnerable). Moreover, the ecological approach explicitly acknowledges the relationship between the environment and the particular perceiver's goals, capabilities, and history. Although the social cognition literature does this as well, the Gibsonian view emphasizes the environment as full of action possibilities (affordances). Finally, it points to the relevance of cross-cultural, animal, and developmental research, for comparative purposes.

In closing, it is probably not useful to pit the ecological approach directly in competition with the cognitive approaches, for several reasons. First, each type of approach is itself a meta-theory, not intrinsically falsifiable. At the broadest levels, each can always account for the other's data in perceptual or cognitive terms, respectively. Second, in practice, it is difficult to distinguish between perception and cognition. On the one hand, perception entails taking in stimulus features in order to respond to the environment and, on the other hand, cognition can entail immediate automatic inferential activity. Whether one labels such processes "cognitive," or sometimes "perceptual" and sometimes "cognitive" depending on their rapidity or accessibility to awareness, is a matter of theoretical preference, and the distinction begins to evaporate. Third, the relative impact of perceptual and cognitive activity in any one experiment depends on the relative strengths with which each is manipulated, so any empirical "advantage" of one over the other would be a function of the particular experiment's operationalization of the perceptual process or the cognitive process, not reflecting the intrinsic relative power of the two types of process. Finally, some would argue that stimulus variation (what a particular stimulus intrinsically affords) is the mark of the ecological approach, but perceiver variation (cognitive structures that perceivers bring with them) marks the cognitive approach. If so, one is stuck comparing apples and oranges, phenomena on altogether different scales. That is, one can assess how much the stimulus contributes and how much the perceiver contributes, but they cannot be directly compared, for they come from separate populations (the population of all social perceivers or all possible stimuli).

In short, the two approaches are complementary, each with its own strengths (R. M. Baron, 1988). The ecological perception approach focuses on what people learn from particular stimulus configurations. The work on causal perception, unitizing of the behavior stream, and trait inferences from physical cues all illustrate important patterns of social stimuli that perceivers use for adaptive functioning. Social cognition focuses more on the cognitive structures and routines that people use to interpret, elaborate, and construct their memory and judgments.

SUMMARY

In this chapter, we have seen the staggering variety and complexity of activities that occur at immediate encoding. In particular, we have focused on the processes by which people create internal representations of the external world. People can attend to external stimuli or internal representations; in either case, their attentional focus constitutes the contents of their consciousness.

We first examined what captures people's attention in the external world. Salience, a property of stimuli in context, is created by whatever is distinctive or unexpected in the environment. In the immediate physical context, stimuli that are novel or perceptually figural attract attention. In terms of the individual perceiver's personal context, salient stimuli violate expectations by being unusual for the particular target, for the target's social category, or for people in general. In the context of competing demands on the perceiver, salient stimuli are relevant to the perceiver's current goals (or instructions) or they dominate the perceiver's visual field. The consequences of social salience include exaggerated perceptions of causality, extreme evaluations, and stereotypic impressions. Salience appears to be mediated by judgments made at encoding and possibly by memory accessibility or by memory for causally relevant details.

Vividness is an inherent property of stimuli. Vivid stimuli are emotionally interesting, concrete and image-provoking, and proximate to the perceiver. Although the disproportionate impact of vivid, compared to pallid, stimuli would seem intuitively obvious, evidence for vividness effects is scarce. Only case history information, compared to abstract statistics, seems to be especially impactful; however, this type of vividness confounds information equivalency with vivid presentation, so its effects are difficult to interpret. The vividness effect seems so intuitively plausible, probably because people believe vivid information is persuasive (even though it is not), it increases confidence in judgments, it is entertaining, and it may capture the attention of the uninvolved.

Another factor that predicts people's attention is accessibility, described as a property of categories in their heads. Social perception is heavily influenced by the ease of activating certain categories and applying them to currently attended stimuli, a process called priming. Situational priming occurs when it is the prior context that makes a particular construct accessible in memory. A primed trait, for example, influences the interpretation of ambiguous behavior that follows. Other categories that can be situationally primed include racial and gender stereotypes, affective states, and attitudes. Priming influences both judgments and behavior, usually assimilating the stimulus to the prime. Contrast sometimes occurs, particularly when the prime and its connection to the stimulus are conscious, when there is minimal overlap between prime and stimulus, or when the stimulus is relatively unambiguous on its own. Priming appears to operate at encoding, rather than through subsequent retrieval and rating processes. Situational priming effects have been explained by a variety of theoretical models. Priming can also occur through chronically accessible categories that differ across individuals. Chronicity results from a history of frequent exposure to a category, with results parallel to those of situational priming.

In addition to factors that influence attention to the external environment, certain factors influence attention to internally generated thoughts. Consciousness serves important cognitive functions, allowing executive control over certain processes, the implementation of intents, and the exercise of choice, as well as troubleshooting in general.

People's consciousness is typically occupied by their current concerns and unmet goals, and researchers are beginning to sample and catalog the variety of people's thoughts, both in isolation and in social interaction.

Many encoding processes are automatic, to varying degrees. The most automatic processes, preconscious ones, fit all the standard criteria: unintentional, involuntary, effortless, autonomous, and outside awareness. Subliminal perception is one paradigm for studying this type of automaticity, and social cognition researchers have demonstrated a variety of such preconscious effects. Postconscious automaticity occurs when people are aware of an initial stimulus but not of its effects on later judgment. Goal-dependent automaticity occurs when a process occurs without awareness or intent but depends on the perceiver's goals in order to be instigated. Frequent, consistent inferences create automatic responses through the process of proceduralization, showing both specific and general practice effects. One common type of relatively automatic inference may be dispositional inference, followed by situational correction, which appears to require more effort.

Just as there are degrees of automaticity, so there are degrees of control. Some thought processes are spontaneous, occurring without intent or awareness, but otherwise controllable. Rumination is not consciously goal-directed and may occur when people fail to suppress an intrusive thought. Intentional thinking occurs when one has a choice, particularly when one makes the harder choice among alternatives, and when one pays attention to the intent. The degree to which automatic and controlled processes are at opposite ends of the continuum has been recently questioned; they may be relatively independent.

Social cognition researchers have only recently begun to address the unconscious, apart from the research explicitly addressing automaticity; early results indicate various inferential processes that people cannot report. A broad perspective on unconscious thinking and behaving comes from work on mindlessness, defined as the state of being relatively unalert, unthoughtful, or uncreative. It occurs when behavior becomes routinized, when one becomes passively dependent, or when one prematurely commits information to be used for only one limited purpose. Mindlessness decreases the flexibility, adaptability, and creativity of people's responses.

As a counterpoint to the cognitively oriented work on encoding described throughout this chapter, the ecological perception approach argues for direct, unmediated perception. It has been supported as contributing to causal perception, the organization of incoming stimulus information, and the perception of dispositions based on people's physical appearance or activity. The ecological or Gibsonian perspective emphasizes the analysis of stimulus configuration in interaction with the perceiver's behavioral abilities. The ecological and social cognition approaches complement each other.

8
Person Memory

❖

How wonderful, how very wonderful the operations of time, and the changes of the human mind! . . . If any one faculty of our nature may be called *more* wonderful than the rest, I do think it is memory. There seems to be something more speakingly incomprehensible in the powers, the failures, the inequalities of memory, than in any other of our intelligences. The memory is sometimes so retentive, so serviceable, so obedient: at others, so bewildered and so weak; and at others again, so tyrannic, so beyond control. We are, to be sure, a miracle in every way; but our powers of recollecting and of forgetting do seem peculiarly past finding out (Austen, 1922, p. 172).

The human mind indeed is wonderful, but memory is no longer "peculiarly past finding out." Cognitive psychologists have made considerable progress in understanding memory. Of all the cognitive exports to social cognition research, memory ranks as a top theoretical and methodological orientation. Other chapters have already addressed issues of memory: the schema chapters (Chapters 4–5) described the impact of knowledge structures on memory for relevant, consistent, and inconsistent material; the encoding chapter (Chapter 7) described the varied impact of categories activated from memory. Social cognitive researchers infer all kinds of cognitive structures and processes from the powers and failures of memory. But memory storage and retrieval are not simple, as we will see.

This chapter examines how people remember other people, as well as complex social events (for other reviews, see L. L. Martin & Clark, 1990; Ostrom, 1989; Wyer & Srull, 1988). An eyewitness to a mugging, for example, has a lot of details to keep straight. We will first review current models of memory that use dramatically different assumptions to explain why people succeed and fail at remembering. Second, we address the wide range of content in social memory; different types (e.g., appearance, behavior, traits) may be stored in different ways. Third, we will examine the extent to which people use other people as the unit of memory; that is, when we remember the characteristics of each person separately, and when we remember people's characteristics simply as part of a particular occasion ("those people we met at Holly's party"), as one of the group who fulfill particular goals ("table servers at local restaurants"), or as an example of someone with a particular trait ("one of those self-important extraverts"). Fourth, we consider the complex relations of memory to judgment, which are centrally determined by people's observational goals when they first encounter the raw data. Finally, we will consider briefly some normative issues of accuracy and efficiency.

BASIC MODELS OF MEMORY

Suppose you are standing at a busy intersection waiting for the light to change. Across the street, you see a young man knock down an elderly woman, grab her purse, and run away. By the time you can get across the street, he is long gone, so you turn your attention to her. Just as you discover that she is angry but unhurt, a police officer arrives and takes down your description of what happened. How is this event stored in your memory?

Several models of memory have been proposed. The previous chapter, in discussing models of priming effects, referred to the storage bin model (which we will not consider further), the battery model, and the synapse model. This section details the most common and well-developed type of memory model, the associative network approach, which is potentially compatible with either the battery or synapse viewpoints. Then it describes alternative models of memory, including the model of procedural memory, exemplar models, and parallel distributed processing.

Associative Networks

The most important general principle of this approach is that the more links or associations from other concepts to any given concept in memory, the easier it is to remember that concept because there are many alternative routes to locate it in memory. The following sections elaborate this point in detail.

The basic cognitive model. In the last chapter, we noted that encoding is the process of taking in data and creating a mental representation of it. The exact format of that representation is called a *memory code*. A variety of possible codes will be discussed later, but the one most commonly discussed is called a *proposition*. There are other theories of memory structure, but the propositional model is the best developed. The most usual propositional accounts agree on some basic points (J. R. Anderson, 1976; Rumelhart, Lindsay, & Norman, 1972; Wickelgren, 1981; see J. R. Anderson, 1990, or D. A. Norman, 1976, for a more general overview of memory research). First, the usual accounts suppose the events can be stored as a series of propositions. For example, "The woman stands on the corner" is one proposition; others are "The woman is elderly," "The man knocks down the woman," and so forth. Each proposition consists of a set of nodes and links, in which each node is an idea (a noun, a verb, or an adjective), and each link is the relation between ideas.

Figure 8.1 shows the propositional model applied to part of the mugging story. Although the notation is complex (see Fig. 8.1 for details), it illustrates some critical features of many current memory models. One critical feature of these models of human memory is that they are *associative;* that is, most refer to associations between nodes (the woman) linked to other nodes (elderly). The associative feature of a propositional code has implications for important interpersonal events. Suppose you are called in to give eyewitness testimony on the mugging case. The organization of long-term memory into an associative node-link structure means that you will recall related facts together. That is, if you start out thinking about the woman herself, it may be easier to recall her attributes (e.g., elderly, standing on the corner) than to recall the man's attributes (e.g., young). One practical prediction of associative memory models, then, is that you will tend to recall related ideas together.

Another important feature of current associative theories is that the links are *labeled.* If asked who (agent) mugged whom (object), you would have the proper relationships stored in memory. Memory can be used to answer the question at hand by using the appropriately labeled links.

A third feature of propositional memory models is that the links are strengthened each time they are *activated.* That is, recall proceeds by your starting at one point (e.g., the woman) and activation spreading along links between the nodes (A. M. Collins & Loftus, 1975). Every time you recall that the woman was elderly, for example, that activates both nodes in memory ("elderly" and "woman"), strengthening the link between them. There are practical implications to the point that the links among ideas are strengthened by their joint activation. If you frequently rehearse (that is, mentally repeat) your observations, you are less likely to forget any of the practiced details because they have been activated often and the links to them are strong. Note, however, that

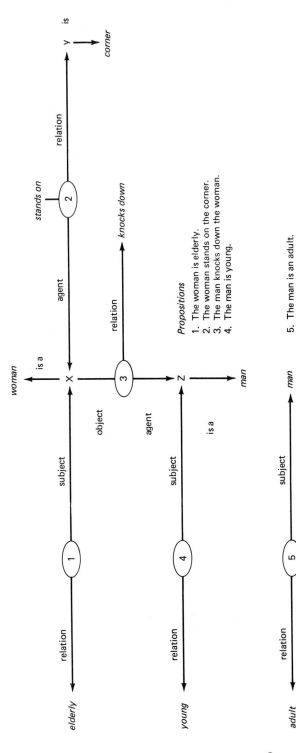

Propositions

1. The woman is elderly.
2. The woman stands on the corner.
3. The man knocks down the woman.
4. The man is young.
5. The man is an adult.

FIGURE 8.1 Propositional network model for knowledge that "The elderly woman standing on the corner is knocked down by the young man." (After J. R. Anderson, 1980a.) Each separate proposition is indicated by an ellipse. For example, the first proposition ("The woman is elderly") is represented by the nodes and links on the upper left of the figure. The numbered ellipses indicate the other propositions. Starting at ellipse 1, anything connected by arrows moving *away* from the ellipse is part of that particular proposition. For example, "elderly" and "woman" both are connected to the ellipse by arrows from it and to them. But "stands on" is not part of the first proposition; accordingly, the link from the ellipse labeled "1" to "stands on" is interrupted by an arrow pointing the wrong way. The other notation that needs explaining is the use of x, y, and z. They indicate that x is one particular woman, who is also elderly. If the proposition were "Women are elderly" (i.e., the entire category of women is elderly), the x would be replaced by the word "woman" in the figure. For example, the proposition "The man is an adult" (true of all men) would be denoted differently than "This particular man is young" (see propositions 4 and 5 in the figure). For present purposes, the notation illustrates the precision with which details of meaning can be represented in a propositional network.

298

you are also less likely to remember unrehearsed facts, since the links to those are weak in comparison to the links among the rehearsed events. The lawyer preparing you to be a witness is likely to know that frequent reviews of the testimony ahead of time will strengthen its coherence and avoid awkward surprises, such as your remembering new events on the witness stand.

In addition to strengthening links among ideas by activating them together, the more separate linkages to any given idea, the more likely it is to be recalled. More links create more *alternative retrieval routes* and enhanced memory. Thus, a smart lawyer will help you to form many alternative memory routes to any given fact, to minimize last-minute forgetfulness.

Finally, a critical feature of many network memory models is the idea that there is a distinction between *long-term memory* and *short-term* (or working) memory. Long-term memory consists of the vast store of information one can potentially bring to mind. Short-term memory refers to the information about which one is thinking at any given moment. So far, we have mainly been discussing the propositional structure of long-term memory. In many current memory models, the activated portion of long-term memory represents short-term memory or consciousness. That is, the long-term memory nodes that are currently most active make up the contents of focal attention. Memory retrieval consists of activating the appropriate nodes, which brings them to consciousness, if activation is above a certain threshold. Because the most active nodes can change rapidly, the conscious part of long-term memory (that is, what you are thinking about right now) is called the short-term memory. Things move in and out of consciousness or short-term memory as they become activated and fade from being activated. There appears to be a limited capacity for activation, which means that short-term memory is quite limited in scope. In other words, few things can be held in mind simultaneously (also see the discussion of consciousness and attention in Chapter 7).

The consequences of the rather severe limits on short-term memory can be illustrated by a lawyer's questioning a witness on the stand. A witness will be unable to keep lots of details in mind at once, so the person may contradict earlier testimony that is out of current consciousness. Short-term memory is normally assumed to hold about seven items of information. An "item" of information could be as small as a single letter or digit, or it could be a "chunk" of letters (i.e., a word on the mugger's sweatshirt) or a chunk of digits (i.e., the time on your watch). In practical terms, the limits of short-term memory mean that people can only keep in mind a few things at a time. One solution to having too many things to process simultaneously is, instead, to attend to each in turn.

In contrast to the limits of short-term memory, the capacity of the overall network of long-term memory storage seems, practically speaking, to be limitless. A lawyer who urges a witness to struggle to remember crucial details may be banking on this: the information might all be there; it is only a question of finding it. For long-term memory, the issue is not capacity (or how much one knows) but retrieval (whether or not one can find it). As we will see, many models of social memory are concerned primarily with how retrieval is influenced by the organization of long-term memory and by the links among items.

To review, associative models of memory share the assumptions that memory consists of nodes for ideas and associative links among the nodes. The associative links are posited to be labeled and strengthened by activation. The number of links to any given concept determines the number of alternative retrieval routes and hence, the concept's ease of retrieval. Long-term memory is the practically unlimited store of knowledge one has available, while short-term or working memory is the information one is actively using at any given time.

Associative network models of social memory. One associative network model of social memory describes some basic processes (Hastie, 1988, building on Hastie, 1980, 1984; Hastie & Carlston, 1980; Hastie & Kumar, 1979; Srull, 1981): in a nutshell, it predicts extra attention to impression-inconsistent material, resulting in extra associative linkages for those items, increasing their alternative retrieval paths and probability of recall. To elaborate, the encoding process invokes a limited capacity working memory, which allows one to form links among items; the stay of items in working memory depends on their relevance to the current impression judgment. A longer stay forges more links. Links are formed between items that are unexpected given the current impression, and the model posits that some links are also formed stochastically (randomly). Subsequent retrieval from long-term memory then initiates at a random point and randomly proceeds along pathways formed by inter-item links. It terminates with repeated failures to retrieve an item not already retrieved.

Finally, the model also proposes a mechanism for impression formation, simultaneous with memory encoding and storage. The anchoring-and-adjustment process (to be described more fully in Chapter 9) essentially provides for an impression that is updated with each new piece of information, based on an equally weighted average of (a) the cumulative evaluations of the items so far and (b) the new item (N. H. Anderson, 1981a; Lopes, 1982). One of this model's strong points is its linkage of the on-line impression formation process with memory storage and retrieval processes. Moreover, it has been incorporated into a working computer simulation (Hastie, 1988), which is an important test of its sufficiency (Ostrom, 1988).

Another model of social memory makes fundamentally similar assumptions. Drawing on basic models of memory as associative net-works of propositions, this comprehensive model also describes peo-ple's memory processes when forming impressions of others (Srull & Wyer, 1989). Building on previous theory (Hastie, 1980; Wyer & Srull, 1980, 1986; Srull, 1981), it specifies more precisely people's memory en-coding, organization, and judgment processes under impression forma-tion. At the most general level, the model gives an account of basic pro-cesses in forming an impression from a target's behavior, as follows: (a) first, people interpret each behavior in terms of an applicable and ac-cessible personality trait, either one provided or one that comes to mind through priming (see Chapter 7); the trait serves to summarize the be-havior; (b) next, people form a general evaluation of the other person as basically likable or dislikable, especially based on the initial information; (c) then, people interpret the person's behaviors in light of the evalua-tive impression, reviewing behaviors that are markedly inconsistent with it; and (d) when asked for a judgment, people attempt to use an already inferred trait or, if none are relevant, they review the remem-bered behaviors in order to make the judgment. The model provides a detailed analysis of these processes, which we can only introduce here, as follows.

The hypothesized memory organization of another person's behav-iors differs depending on whether or not perceivers have a trait expect-ancy. This model makes a unique (and controversial) prediction about the representation of behavioral information in memory when trait ex-pectancies are provided. In particular, it predicts that people with ex-pectations form two separate representations, one linking behaviors and traits, the other linking behaviors and an overall evaluation. Figure 8.2 depicts this proposed organization when trait expectancies are pro-vided.

People are hypothesized spontaneously to interpret behaviors in terms of relevant, applicable, accessible traits (cf. Chapter 7 on encod-ing), creating links between nodes for the behaviors and nodes for the expectancy traits, as shown on the top. Suppose, for example, that the mugging victim had been described as honest and kind, then her re-turning excess change to a store clerk would be linked to honesty and her giving money to a panhandler might be linked to kindness. How-ever, behaviors irrelevant to the honest and kind trait expectancy are not encoded in trait terms. Hence, if she could not provide her relative's exact home address (a forgetful behavior), that would be encoded as neutral, and so not represented in trait terms, in this view.

In addition to the representations linking behavior to trait expectan-cies (the top part of Fig. 8.2), people are hypothesized to form an eval-uative concept of the target, connecting all the behaviors (expectancy-relevant or not) to a person node (the bottom of Fig. 8.2). Thus, the woman's giving away money, returning change, and not knowing the

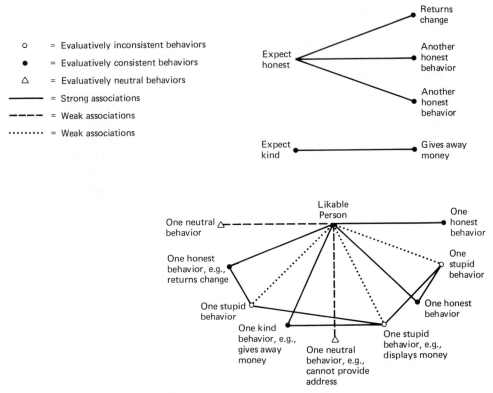

FIGURE 8.2 Dual representations of the mugging victim in person memory, when trait expectancies are provided. Trait representations are above, evaluative representation is below.

address would all contribute to an independent evaluative impression of her. In general, the strengths of association between behaviors and the evaluative person node are enhanced by the evaluative consistency of each pair. That is, if one thinks of her as a generally likable person, there will be stronger links to her positive behaviors than to her neutral or negative behaviors. Early information has the greatest influence on the evaluation formed, so learning first about her more positive attributes predisposes one toward a positive impression, a phenomenon called a *primacy effect* (cf. Asch, 1946; E. E. Jones & Goethals, 1972).

Like the Hastie model described previously, an important assumption of the Srull-Wyer model is that evaluatively inconsistent behaviors are considered thoughtfully in comparison to other behaviors (see Chapters 4 and 7); this creates stronger links between each inconsistent behavior and the remaining behaviors, compared to the links between each evaluatively consistent or neutral behavior and the remaining behaviors. This accounts for the memorability of inconsistent behaviors under some circumstances. Thus, recall that you had an impression of the mugging victim as basically likable. Suppose you then discover that she publicly displayed a handful of bills in seeking a small one; that rather careless (perhaps stupid) behavior is evaluatively inconsistent. To explain it, you might guess that she must have been pulling out her money in order to help the panhandler, and this would create an additional link for the evaluatively inconsistent behavior. Its double link, both to the person node and to the other behavior, increases its chance of retrieval.

Consider an alternative situation, namely, when people do not have a trait expectancy; in this case, they are hypothesized to form only one type of mental representation, that is, in trait terms but not in evaluative terms (shown in Fig. 8.3). When people do not have a trait expectancy (just as when they do), they are still hypothesized to interpret behaviors in terms of accessible traits. However, when people do not have a trait expectancy, *all* behaviors are interpreted in terms of an accessible trait (as there is no trait expectancy to determine which behaviors are irrelevant). To illustrate, consider how one might interpret the behaviors of another person, for example, a bystander at the mugging, assuming one has no trait expectancies about the bystander. If the person's behaviors are evaluatively mixed (e.g., the person picks up and returns all the woman's spilled money, next cannot remember the three-digit telephone number for the police, then offers his name as a witness, but does not know how to flag down a cab for her), a single

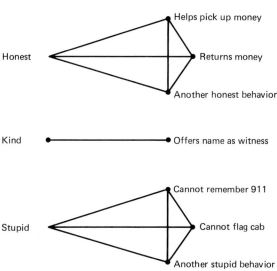

FIGURE 8.3 Representations of bystander to mugging incident, when trait expectancies are not provided.

evaluatively consistent impression cannot be formed immediately. In this case, people are hypothesized to review their trait interpretations of each behavior, thereby strengthening behavior-behavior links within each trait cluster, as indicated in Figure 8.3.

According to the Srull-Wyer model, the separate memory representations (i.e., all the various trait-behavior clusters and the evaluative person-behaviors cluster) are hypothesized to function independently, although each refers to the same particular target person. When people are asked to recall the person's behaviors, they sample one behavior inside one representation (the most accessible one) until they exhaust their memory within that representation, then move on to the next. Their retrieval is hypothesized to be sequential, beginning at the central concept node (the trait node or evaluative person node), traversing the pathways in the network, with preference given to the stronger ones. Behaviors are then recalled in the order in which they are accessed in this search process. Each time a path is traversed, it is strengthened. Thus, within any given representation, one eventually starts to retrieve the same behaviors more than once, and after a certain amount of redundant retrieval, one terminates search in that representation and moves on to another. This procedure operates both when people do and do not have a trait expectancy. That is, in the first case, when people have trait expectancies and therefore dual representations (that is, both trait and evaluative representations; Fig. 8.2), retrieval can operate through either type of representation. In the second case, when people have no trait expectancy, and therefore only independent trait representations (Fig. 8.3), retrieval can operate through each trait in turn, depending on its accessibility. Note that this model's idea of multiple representations is controversial, so we will come back to this point.

In addition to positing encoding, organization, and retrieval processes, this view describes judgment processes. Judgments are normally based on the trait concepts (either provided or inferred). That is, to decide if someone is friendly, one checks for the presence of traits relevant to friendliness and judges accordingly. However, if none of the traits is relevant, the relevant implication of the overall evaluation is used to infer the trait judgment (i.e., an honest person might be judged friendly because both traits are positive). In this case, the perceiver will also use the content of any relevant recalled behaviors (i.e., repaying a debt could be interpreted as friendly, in addition to honest; cf. a later section on specific and general social memory).

The Srull-Wyer model has some interesting implications. According to the model, people form an evaluative concept of a person, when initial information is evaluatively uniform; this impression ultimately causes them to recall evaluatively inconsistent information better than consistent, and both better than irrelevant information. The inconsistency advantage presumably occurs as people think about the inconsistencies and try to relate them to each other and to the consistent behaviors, creating associative links among them. One can infer the point at which subjects have formed their evaluative impression by observing impressions as they are being formed. That is, over blocks (sequenced groups of stimulus behaviors), one can observe the start-up and increase of the inconsistency advantage in memory. In one study, the inconsistency advantage required at least five blocks of five behaviors each (Srull, Lichtenstein, & Rothbart, 1985).

Another implication of the model is the counter-intuitive idea that adding evaluatively *inconsistent* behaviors to a list will increase memory for *consistent* behaviors; this occurs as people link the inconsistent items to the consistent ones. Moreover, the same is not true of adding consistent items, for they do not provoke thought and interitem links (Srull, 1981; Srull, Lichtenstein, & Rothbart, 1985). Similarly, interfering with the formation of interitem links should eliminate the inconsistency advantage in memory; studies in which subjects perform a competing on-line task (even rehearsing the stimulus items!) do not show the same inconsistency advantage (Srull, 1981; Srull, Lichtenstein, & Rothbart, 1985). The same is true of subjects without the capacity and time to form on-line links (Bargh & Thein, 1985). Finally, although subjects show an inconsistency advantage within the main person memory paradigm, they may preferentially recall consistent items when they have time to think over their impression afterward; this may be due to bolstering of the overall evaluative direction of the impression (Wyer & Martin, 1986; see also Chapter 4).

One major advantage of this model is its ability to summarize vast quantities of research by Srull, Wyer, and their colleagues, which will also be illustrated throughout this chapter. One disadvantage of the Srull-Wyer model is its assumption of multiple representations ("storage bins"; see Chapter 7), all pertaining to a single person. This cumbersome idea is not endorsed by other models of person memory, and it tends to make this model both counterintuitive (not as much a technical flaw as an aesthetic one) and also perhaps overly flexible, able to account for virtually any result.

To summarize, the most influential model of memory in social cognition is the node-link structure proposed by associative memory models. In this view, each concept (trait, behavior, person's name) is represented as a node, with links formed by relating two items to each other. Memory retrieval proceeds along the pathways provided by the network.

One of the prominent features of this person memory model (both the Hastie and the Srull-Wyer versions) is that it predicts a recall advantage for impression-inconsistent behaviors. The inconsistency advantage is explained by increased attention, linkages, and retrieval routes for inconsistent material. The inconsistency advantage has been a robust effect within the standard paradigm of instilling a trait impression, then presenting a series of consistent and inconsistent behaviors, and asking subjects to recall the behaviors (see Srull & Wyer, 1989, or Chapter 4 for a review). However, the inconsistency advantage is not obtained when the research paradigm departs from the standard one in any of several ways that complicate the perceiver's task: well-established expectancies (for reviews, see S. T. Fiske & Neuberg, 1990; Higgins & Bargh, 1987; Ruble & Stangor, 1986), multiple trait expectancies (D. L. Hamilton, Driscoll, & Worth, 1989), behaviors that are descriptively but not evaluatively inconsistent (Wyer & Gordon, 1982), traits and behaviors overheard in a conversation (Wyer, Budesheim, & Lambert, 1990), time to think about one's impression afterward (Wyer & Martin, 1986), and having to make a complex judgment (Bodenhausen & Wyer, 1985; Bodenhausen & Lichtenstein, 1987) (see Chapter 4 for other examples). Although the Hastie and Srull-Wyer models can account for many of these results, these findings also suggest that people use multiple processing strategies, depending on the circumstances. Future work on the node-link models will doubtless develop along these lines.

Alternative Memory Models

Most social memory researchers rely on variants of the principles described so far, that is, associative network models of memory. However, as newer models develop in cognitive psychology, they eventually tend to be imported into studies of person memory, so we will introduce them here, for future reference.

Procedural memory. In the last chapter, one explanation for automatic processing was proceduralization—that is, the speed-up of judgments with practice. However, we did not locate procedural processes within a larger model of memory. With some additional background on memory models, we can do so here. A computer simulation model called ACT* (pronounced act-star; J. R. Anderson, 1983) posits that memory includes both an associative network of concepts, as already described, and *procedural knowledge*. Procedural knowledge concerns skills, namely, how to do things, and it is represented differently from the long-term associative content knowledge ("*declarative memory*") we have been discussing up to now. Procedural knowledge is represented as condition-action pairs, or if-then statements, called *productions*. When an input pattern matches the "if" or condition part of the production, the "then" or action part immediately operates. For example, a condition might include "if the envelope is addressed to me and if the outside advertises a large cash prize." The action part of the production, for some of us, includes "then discard without opening," while for others, it must include "then open and read immediately."

Knowledge is initially represented in the declarative associative networks familiar to social cognition researchers. The advantages of declarative representation include: ease of learning, for one simply links ideas; wide availability of use, namely, in any situation that cues part of the structure; and flexibility, that is, enabling one to work in various directions among associations, depending on need (E. R. Smith, 1984). Thus, declarative knowledge is general and independent of domain, probably accessible to consciousness and verbal expression.

The disadvantages of using declarative knowledge are that it tends to be slower and to use up one's limited capacity working memory (roughly, attention or consciousness). Accordingly, as certain processes are used repeatedly, they eventually may be *compiled,* via two processes. First, certain actions that are always executed together may be combined into a single mega-step via *composition.* What began as a sequence of steps ("if envelope is addressed to me and advertises prize, then open it," followed by "if envelope advertises a prize and has just been opened, then check eligibility") may end up as one more complex step ("if envelope is addressed to me and advertises a prize, then open and check eligibility"). The second way to compile certain processes is via *proceduralization,* as when one learns to sort one's mail more rapidly, applying general procedures to specific repeated experiences. When every envelope from a certain place fails to provide an unambiguous, unconditional prize, one quickly learns the procedure: "if envelope is addressed to me from Cash Grand Prizes Clearinghouse, then discard."

In the previous chapter, we described the work of E. R. Smith and his colleagues, who have applied the principles of ACT* and procedural memory in particular to the speed-up of social inferences with practice (E. R. Smith, 1984, 1989b, 1990; E. R. Smith, Branscombe, & Bormann, 1988; E. R. Smith & Lerner, 1986); as noted, these practice effects provide one explanation for automaticity.

In addition, Smith and his colleagues propose that procedural memory provides an alternative explanation for priming effects, also discussed in the previous chapter. Recall that priming demonstrates the impact of a recently or frequently activated category on the processing of category-relevant information. Priming effects are typically interpreted in terms of category accessibility, using declarative (associative network) memory. However, studies suggest that some priming effects may be process-specific, as a procedural account would suggest (E. R. Smith & Branscombe, 1987, 1988; E. R. Smith, 1989b; cf. Higgins & Chaires, 1980). Consider the different specific processes that can prime a personality trait; for example, one might read the word and think about it, or one might generate it from an obvious behavioral instance. When a subsequent task repeats the exact operation (i.e., reading or generating), a form of priming effect occurs, namely, a speed-up of subsequent access to the word. This speed-up does not just depend on previous exposure to the concept. When the practice task uses *different* priming processes than the test task (i.e., generating at practice and reading at test), the trait concept is just as accessible as when the practice and test tasks use the *same* priming processes (i.e., generate at both or reading at both). Nevertheless, greater speed-up occurs when the same task procedure is repeated. Thus, some priming effects occur from repeated procedures, in addition to the category accessibility effects of declarative associative memory.

Other applications of procedural memory may explain the accessibility of certain attitudes (see Chapter 11), the selection of one inference or category from among many possible (cf. Chapter 5), and the learning of complex patterns that cannot be articulated (Lewicki, 1986a, b; Lewicki, Czyzewska, & Hoffman, 1987; Lewicki, Hill, & Bizot, 1988). The more a particular procedure is practiced, the more likely it is to be used again, instead of other equally applicable procedures. In this view, such procedural effects are a form of "implicit memory," which is a term for the influence of past judgmental processes on current judgments and reactions (E. R. Smith & Branscombe, 1988; see Jacoby & Kelley, 1987, for another discussion of unconscious memory). As more applications accumulate, procedural memory models will doubtless become more common in social cognition research.

Exemplar models. Another alternative account of memory focuses on memory for specific instances (exemplars) as opposed to abstract representations of concepts. Already discussed in Chapter 4, exemplar models provide a counterpoint to the prototype view of category representation. To review, the exemplar view posits that people represent categories by storing collections of instances, which they then use to infer category knowledge. General evidence for exemplars includes, as noted earlier, the facts that (a) people do remember a lot about concrete instances, (b) they have specific knowledge of variability among category members, (c) they know about correlated attributes within the category, and (d) they can easily modify their categories by the inclusion of a single instance (see Chapter 4). Within social cognition, we saw that evidence for the utility of exemplars comes from studies showing the power of single instances (e.g., Gilovich, 1987; Lewicki, 1985; S. Read, 1983), variations in the perceived variability of group members (Linville, Salovey, & Fischer, 1986; Linville, Fischer, & Salovey, 1989; Park & Hastie, 1987), and the effects of various abstract-concrete combinations (i.e., encountering abstract concepts before relevant instances, versus instances before concepts, versus instances only; E. R. Smith & Zarate, 1990). In addition, norm theory (Kahneman & Miller, 1986) uses an exemplar approach to account for people's judgments of how surprising or normal an event is (see Chapters 4, 9, 10).

Recently, an exemplar approach (Hintzman, 1986) has been tested in detail on social inference processes by comparing the usual data of human subjects and a computer simulation (E. R. Smith, 1988), with some success. The results of category priming studies are simulated by a model using only exemplars and no abstract representations. This shows at least that an exemplar approach provides a complete and sufficient account; sufficiency is one important criterion for model testing. Nevertheless, a categorization approach also provides a sufficient account. Thus, the exemplar approach is not a necessary explanation because the other is also valid. Within social cognition research, the apparently most complete approaches will combine abstract representations and exemplars, allowing perceivers some flexibility depending on individual capacities and task demands.

Parallel distributed processing. Parallel distributed processing (PDP) is a new approach to the structure of cognition that has been developing lately as an alternative to more traditional models of mental structure. For reasons that remain obscure, one of us found herself describing PDP to her eighty-year-old great-aunt, always an astute and intellectually challenging conversationalist, who demanded a sample of "the wave of the future" in cognition research. PDP seemed a safe bet, in that the great-aunt could be guaranteed to know even less about it than the author did at the time. Precariously launched on an explanation, the metaphor for PDP that came to mind was an old-fashioned time-and-temperature sign board composed of light bulbs. Such signs were made of a grid of bulbs, different combinations lighting up depending on what numerals needed to be displayed. Each light bulb contributes to all the times and temperatures displayed, by being on or off within the overall pattern.

In this PDP metaphor, individual memory units are light bulbs, each unit participating in many different memory patterns, as simply one feature of the whole. The same bulb could be part of the numeral "1" or "2." Moreover, the number "2" could appear in different positions on the board, depending on whether the time were 2:00 or 7:32. Consider how this approach differs from associative network models of memory. In such models, each node uniquely represents a concept, and when it is sufficiently activated, the concept is retrieved. In a PDP model, each unit helps to represent many different concepts, which are retrieved when the appropriate pattern of activation occurs across all the basic units. Thus, to return to the time-and-temperature sign, the specific numeral "3" could occur on the right, left, or middle of the sign, as needed, depending only on the correct configuration of light bulbs being on. Thus, no single light bulb represents "3," but instead the pattern does, and which set of bulbs does the job is arbitrary. This would differ considerably from a neon sign, for example, that had one structure dedicated to lighting up for one particular number whenever it was needed. Traditional memory models would roughly resemble a series of neon letters linked to each other. (The great-aunt was skeptical but intrigued.)

PDP models essentially deal with the subatomic particles of perception and cognition. PDP models assume that memory consists of elementary units (the bulbs, in our metaphor) that are connected with facilitative and inhibitory links to each other. The connections represent constraints about what units are associated and the connection strengths represent the type and magnitude of association. Only the strengths of connections are stored, so that the pattern can be recreated by activating parts of it and waiting for the connections to reverberate throughout the system until the entire pattern is activated.

The full theory of PDP is beyond the scope of this book (for an accessible introduction, see McClelland, Rumelhart, & Hinton, 1986), and at this writing, it has yet to influence social cognition research. For the most part, it has been applied to issues of motor control (typing, reaching) and perception at the level of individual letters in a word. One interpretation of PDP models is that they are aimed at a different and lower level than network models of memory described earlier. That is, a "node" in the network metaphor would be not a single neuron but a pattern of activation over neurons. If one considers PDP as a lower-level elaboration of network models, its implications for social cognition's level of analysis would be limited.

Nevertheless, we mention PDP to highlight its potential advantages. In the more traditional associative models, knowledge is represented as static; knowledge does not change its form between long-term and working memory, for it is simply more or less activated. In PDP models, the patterns themselves are not stored, but the strengths of connections among basic units are stored, enabling the patterns to be recreated. From a practical perspective, this allows knowledge to be implicit in the system, rather than an explicit set of stored rules. It also allows imperfect stimulus patterns to be recognized, as approximations can activate part of the pattern of connections, which subsequently generate the remaining aspects of the pattern. PDP models, thus, are good at considering several sources of information simultaneously; they are parallel processors, in contrast to the more traditional serial processing models.

One possible domain of application in social cognition is to schemas, and in particular to how schemas simultaneously interact with each other. For example, combining one's knowledge about traditional Amish farmers and progressive Montessori teachers, one can imagine someone who occupies both roles by considering their shared "back to basics" perspective and their shared emphasis on patience. Moreover, one can imagine the person's likely response to novel issues (e.g., computers in the classroom). PDP models allow for such emergent properties of previous knowledge. It remains to be seen whether and how they will influence social cognition research.

Summary

To review, many psychologists think long-term memory consists of networks of ideas, with associative links among related nodes. They assume the links are strengthened by activation. The activated nodes enter into consciousness or short-term memory, which has a rather limited capacity. In contrast, long-term memory has quite a large capacity. It is posited to be organized in hierarchical clusters of related knowledge. Alternative models of memory have been developed: procedural routines that become automated with practice, memory for specific exemplars that can aggregate to represent categories, and parallel distributed processing models that consider the simultaneous interactions among basic units of memory. These various models of memory have specific implications for what is called person memory—that is, what one remembers about other people—as we will see in the remainder of the chapter.

CONTENTS OF PERSON MEMORY

Human beings are incredibly rich stimuli. To appreciate this, imagine what you have stored in memory about your mother. Where could you begin to describe her? You could start with what she looks like, but even that is difficult. Her appearance depends on whether she is happy or sad, awake or tired, at a formal or informal occasion. And then what is her behavior like? That too depends on the situation. Your memory of her personality may be even harder to characterize. If people, especially those we know well, seem so multifaceted, how does memory do them justice?

Several attempts to catalog the contents of person memory have revealed its richness. People can retrieve from memory quantities of detail about what might be termed the Big Three of person descriptions: *appearance, behavior,* and *traits* (e.g., Beach & Wertheimer, 1961; Dornbusch et al., 1965; S. T. Fiske & Cox, 1979; Ostrom, 1975; Park, 1986; Peevers & Secord, 1973). One useful way to think about the range of person information is to consider a continuum from wholly observables (e.g., appearance) to strictly inferables (e.g., traits). People are cautious about inferables; they are more willing to report their inferences about the traits of people familiar to them than inferences about the traits of strangers. No such differences exist for appearance (S. T. Fiske & Cox, 1979). Moreover, as people become acquainted, their use of traits increases and their use of behaviors declines (Park, 1986). Even in descriptions of strangers, however, traits are more common than behaviors (S. T. Fiske & Cox, 1979).[1]

Most research on social memory concerns the traits of strangers, largely because those are the most practical stimuli for laboratory research. Because traits are the most common stimuli, we begin the next section with them, then consider behavior, and then appearance. We will also briefly address the storage of affect. One important possibility that emerges from reviewing the contents of person memory is that the propositional code most commonly assumed by memory researchers may fit trait information better than behavior, appearance, and affect information (cf. Hastie & Carlston, 1980). The section closes by returning to the issue of concrete (observable) and abstract (inferable) contents of memory.

Memory for Traits: Information Stored in Propositional Codes

Traits are not directly observable; people do not walk around with signs labeling their personalities. Traits instead are abstract; they may be inferred from appearance and behavior or from other traits. Trait inference is a complex process, and attribution theory (Chapters 2–3) is concerned largely with that complex process. Many researchers believe that traits, once inferred, are stored in propositional networks of the sort described earlier. The proposition, as noted, is the format or code in which trait information is stored. To date, there is no particular reason to assume traits differ from abstract nonsocial knowledge in the way they are encoded. We will see that other kinds of social knowledge may be stored in other codes.

At a minimum, we can safely say that behavioral information and trait information differ in level of abstraction. Behavior lies toward the concrete, observable end, and traits lie toward the abstract, inferable end of person attributes. That is, the process of remembering a behavior is influenced by its basis in direct observation. To go back to an earlier example, remembering that the mugger shouted at the elderly victim is not based on inference but on observation, which makes it a relatively concrete memory. In contrast, remembering the mugger as hostile is based on inference from his behavior, making it a more abstract memory. Because traits are more abstract, they are more econom-

---

[1]Of course, descriptions do not reflect all that people remember (Schneider, 1973). For example, people could actually make and store many trait attributions about strangers but be less confident or more reluctant to say so. Nevertheless, such open-ended descriptions illustrate the variety of information stored about others.

ical and general than behaviors (R. B. Allen & Ebbesen, 1981; Carlston, 1980b; Ostrom et al., 1980). Behavior is a less efficient piece of information to store than a trait, precisely because it is concrete. Thus, it is not surprising that people typically report traits more than behavior in describing others, and that person memory researchers study traits more often than behaviors.

The way people organize their trait knowledge in memory seems to have some unique qualities of its own. When people are asked to report which traits generally go together or which imply each other, two main dimensions emerge. Personality attributes fall along one continuum of *social desirability* and another of *competence* (Rosenberg & Sedlak, 1972; D. J. Schneider, 1973; D. J. Schneider, Hastorf, & Ellsworth, 1979). Terms such as *warm, pleasant,* and *sociable* appear near each other and those such as *intelligent, industrious,* and *determined* also appear near each other, in people's mental maps of the personality domain. For many of us, then, the two crucial things that organize our memory for someone else's traits are answers to these questions: Is this person friendly and fun? What is this person good at? However, there are some exceptions to the general rule that people organize their trait knowledge by sociability and competence; some people may group their trait knowledge instead by its relevance to integrity, attractiveness, maturity, and so on (Kim & Rosenberg, 1980). Because we have already discussed the properties of propositional networks earlier in this chapter and some properties of traits as schemas in Chapter 4, we will not elaborate on their structure here.

Memory for Behavior: A Temporal Code?

Behavioral information may be stored in a propositional code, as is trait information, but some researchers believe behavior instead may be stored another way because of the kind of information it is. Behavior has a built-in temporal feature. That is, to remember behavior requires remembering a series of things in a certain order. As with scripts or event schemas (Chapter 4), there is sequential information, and there are enabling conditions. In the mugging example, the behaviors involved are sequential (the man approached the woman, then the man knocked down the woman, etc.; see Fig. 8.4). Some of the behaviors also are enabling conditions for the next behavior (he knocked her down in order to take her purse), and some are not (he took her purse, and then he ran away). Because of the sequential and enabling aspects of a series of behaviors, it may be more convenient to think of behavior as stored in a temporal code.

A temporal code, thus, may represent a second type of memory code within declarative memory, in addition to the propositional code,

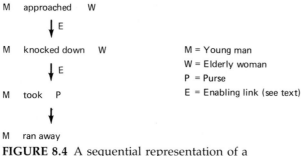

FIGURE 8.4 A sequential representation of a
                mugging.

one that preserves sequential information (cf. J. R. Anderson, 1982; Schank & Abelson, 1977). However, preserving sequential information does not mean that people recall their lives in neatly organized sequences from birth onward. (Consider how awkward it might be if someone asked you what you did over the weekend, and you had to work forward from infancy to find last weekend in memory.) People do not necessarily remember best by thinking in forward chronological order; that is, people recall some sequences of events (such as exams in a course) more easily working backward from the present than starting at the beginning and working forward (Loftus & Fathi, 1985). Moreover, not all events have equal status in memory, as when people use significant events or relationships as bench marks in their lives (Harvey, Flanary, & Morgan, 1986). People apparently recall various social action sequences, including their own personal experiences, in terms of categories for different life periods (e.g., high school, college). These categories have temporal codes indicating the sequence in which they occurred, but within period-of-life categories, people do not necessarily order the actions (Fuhrman & Wyer, 1988; Wyer et al., 1985; cf. Huttenlocher, Hedges, & Prohaska, 1988). Thus, although sequential information is preserved in various ways, the information does not necessarily have to be recalled in serial order. Whatever its exact features, this kind of temporal code would be most relevant for remembering behavioral information rather than traits.

Another possible feature of a code for behaviors is its purposive character. Prior behaviors enable subsequent behaviors, as noted, and behaviors typically entail goals suggesting a sequence of such enabling behaviors. Goals consequently are effective devices for organizing memory (G. H. Bower, 1978; Hoffman, Mischel, & Mazze, 1981; Jeffrey & Mischel, 1979). Behavior appears to have a hierarchical structure in terms of goals and subgoals (Carver & Scheier, 1981a; Newtson et al., 1987; Vallacher & Wegner, 1987); the hierarchical structure would also facilitate memory. Moreover, people may have action-oriented implicit personality theories that are organized in terms of goals—in addition to the implicit personality theories already described for traits (Trzebinski, 1985). For example, when people are primed about domains relevant to different goals (family life, peer relationships, career roles), they seem to organize their understanding of themselves and others along dimensions instrumental to the particular goal (e.g., supervising, in the case of career life; Trzebinski et al., 1985; Trzebinski & Richards, 1986). Thus goals, with their enabling relations and temporal ordering, are likely to be distinctive features of memory for behavior.

Memory for Appearance: An Analog Code?

A third type of content in person memory is appearance. Most of the standard person memory research mentioned in this chapter concerns traits (and to some extent behavior) but neglects appearance. However, memory for appearance is worth considering in some detail here because of its general neglect in the mainstream person memory research (but see Bahrick, Bahrick, & Wittlinger, 1975). The essential features of memory for appearance are that it is quite basic, extremely accurate under some conditions, and could be stored in yet a third code.

A basic and accurate type of memory. At the most concrete level of person memory, appearance constitutes a fundamental set of data that allows us to recognize the other person. For example, you may recognize the mugger in a lineup by the odd shape of his nose. Appearance also allows us to make new trait inferences and to reuse old ones. For example, if the mugger has muscular legs, you may infer that he is athletic (Secord, 1958). Alternatively, his riotously disheveled hair may remind you of an old friend who was impulsive and undisciplined, and you may transfer that assumption to the new person (Secord, 1958). As another example noted in the previous chapter, his babylike face may lead you to infer a babyish personality (e.g., Berry & McArthur, 1986). Appearance also prompts emotional reactions; for example, people assume physically attractive others to be especially sociable and competent, and they often like them as a consequence (Berscheid & Walster, 1978; Kalick, 1988; cf. Eagly et al., 1990). If the mugger were especially unattractive, you might find him even more repulsive than otherwise.

That our stored impressions of appearance are distinctive and important is further illustrated by the resilience of memory for faces. Laboratory studies reveal that people's ability to recognize faces is just short of phenomenal, with close to 100 percent accuracy over long periods of time (T. G. R. Bower, 1970; Freides, 1974; Neisser, 1967). The reason for the strength of visual memory is not entirely clear, but one possibility is that visual stimuli do not attract attention as automatically as do other stimuli. That is, a bright flash may not draw attention as quickly as a loud noise. Moreover, processing visual information requires that one actively orient one's eyes toward the stimulus, while processing auditory information does not require that one actively orient one's ears. To compensate for these weaknesses in visual information processing, people may favor encoding of visual cues, as a general strategy (Posner, Nissen, & Klein, 1976); this bias toward visual cues may enhance memory for faces.

One exception to people's phenomenal memory for faces is the finding that cross-race accuracy is far worse than own-race accuracy (Malpass & Kravitz, 1969). There are several possible explanations for this effect. People react more superficially to those of another race (Chance & Goldstein, 1981), and when people do adopt less superficial orienting strategies, their cross-race identifications are more accurate (Devine & Malpass, 1985). Indeed, superficial encoding generally hurts recognition memory for faces (G. H. Bower & Karlin, 1974; Rodin, 1987; G. L. Wells & Turtle, 1988); that is, the less thought you give to people when you meet them, the less likely you are to recognize their faces accurately. (This is the first essential trick for people who are "bad at remembering faces and names"; pay attention.) Besides paying closer attention to people of your own race, another factor that affects cross-racial identification is one's experience with members of the other race; cross-race experience improves accuracy (Brigham et al., 1982). Experience may also lead people to use more appropriate rules for cross-racial identification; white perceivers attempt to distinguish all faces by hair color, hair texture, and eye color (Ellis, Deregowski, & Shepherd, 1975). This is not the most effective strategy for distinguishing among African faces, which are more heterogenous on roundness, angularity, and feature size. Finally, if the target's face blends in with a group that all look alike to the perceiver (as can be true in cross-race encounters), identification is worse. Conversely, if the target has a distinctive face, from the perceiver's perspective, identification is facilitated (Shapiro & Penrod, 1986). Thus, difficulties in cross-race identification all stem from broader principles—superficial encoding, lack of familiarity, the wrong rules, and perceived homogeneity—all of which lower accuracy in any context. Thus, the general principle stands, namely, that most memory for faces is exceptionally accurate.

Eyewitness reports of memory. Curiously, the laboratory results on the accuracy of memory for faces are contradicted by real-world research on eyewitness testimony; people often do little better than guess when attempting to identify an alleged criminal in a lineup (Loftus, 1979). Scores of eyewitness and facial identification studies indicate that people's reliability is quite variable, depending on the specific circumstances of observing, recalling, and reporting (Cutler, Penrod, & Martens, 1987; Kassin, Ellsworth, & Smith, 1989; Shapiro & Penrod, 1986). The contradiction between skilled performance in laboratory studies of recognition memory and poor performance in real-world studies of eyewitness accuracy may be explained by differences in the two settings. (It cannot normally be explained by the problems of cross-race identification, as most crimes are perpetrated on same-race victims.) In the laboratory, stimuli are not moving, distractions are minimal, emotions and arousal are virtually absent, viewing conditions are unobscured and well-lit, no strong prior theories interfere, no one is brandishing a weapon at you, and so on. In eyewitness research, the volatile and confusing features of actual settings are retained, and memory, not surprisingly, is often garbled. The difference is roughly like that between trying to remember the face of someone who ambushed you in a dark alley and trying to recognize a face you stare at in the library, with full daylight, complete leisure, and no emotional intrusions. Of course, the library face should be easier to remember accurately. Moreover, laboratory studies tend to use the same photograph as stimulus and test item, whereas eyewitness studies tend to use real people, whose clothing and expressions vary from initial encounter to subsequent identification.

In all, because crimes against people are often rapid, unexpected, confusing, and involve real, changeable people, perhaps the variable levels of eyewitness accuracy are not surprising.[2] How can eyewitness testimony be improved? From the voluminous research, some principles have been adduced (Shapiro & Penrod, 1986). First, it is helpful to

---

[2]To make matters worse, eyewitness memory seems especially vulnerable to the way questions are asked. An unscrupulous or careless attorney may ask subtly leading questions that take advantage of abstract memory intruding on specific memory. For example, in the mugging case, an attorney might ask if you recall "the woman falling down while she was standing near the parked cars," although in fact there were no parked cars. However, it is a reasonable inference that there must have been parked cars at the corner. Even though the phrase "parked cars" is tangential to the question, and you answer simply by describing her fall, the damage has been done. If later asked whether or not there were cars parked at the corner, the typical witness may confuse the mention of them in prior questioning with their actual presence at the scene of the crime (Loftus, 1979). Similarly, if a witness examines a preliminary lineup, the person may later remember having seen one of the suspects before but not distinguish between the occasion of the lineup and that of the mugging. The (innocent) suspect may be misidentified as the mugger because he is familiar. Thus, various ways of soliciting eyewitness evidence can interfere with accurate testimony.

However, it is important to note that misleading postevent information distorts reports (testimony), but it is not clear that it necessarily distorts people's actual memories (see G. L. Wells & Turtle, 1987, for a review). Some argue that postevent information alters a witness's original memory, never to be retrieved again (Loftus, Miller, & Burns, 1978; Loftus & Hoffman, 1989), whereas others argue that witnesses merely follow the questioner's suggestion, which may leave their original memory intact for retrieval under the right conditions (Bekerian & Bowers, 1983; McCloskey & Zaragoza, 1985; Zaragoza & McCloskey, 1989; V. L. Smith & Ellsworth, 1987; Weinberg, Wadsworth, & Baron, 1983); still others argue for traces of both the original and the post-event information (Belli, 1989; B. Tversky & Tuchin; 1989).

reinstate cues associated with the original context, that is, to go back mentally to specific aspects of the scene of the crime. Second, it is also helpful if the target's face has been associated with inferences or descriptors at the time of encoding. (This is another trick for people who are "bad at faces and names": generate mental links between the person's features and name.) Third, it helps if exposure time is longer and the retention interval is shorter. Finally, of course, faces that change are harder to identify, as when someone is disguised while committing a crime or afterward.

Given all these contingencies that interfere with accurate identification, how can one know when to believe an eyewitness? Jurors and the witnesses themselves do not seem to be aware of the unreliability of eyewitness reports (G. L. Wells, Lindsay, & Tousignant, 1980). Ironically, then, people's confidence is often uncorrelated with their accuracy. Although common sense would hold that confident witnesses are more accurate, dozens of studies yield a small average correlation between confidence and accuracy (Bothwell, Deffenbacher, & Brigham, 1987; G. L. Wells & Turtle, 1987). However, witnesses with longer exposures to the other person's face show more correspondence between accuracy and confidence (as well as being more accurate). People's accuracy-confidence calibration also can be increased by making them retrospectively self-aware so that they notice clues to the reliability of their own performance (Kassin, 1985). Moreover, there are individual differences in accuracy: People who are more attuned to their environments (high self-monitors, i.e., people who attend to the social situation as a guide for behavior; see Chapter 12) may be more accurate than low self-monitors (Hosch & Platz, 1984). And people who tend to form vivid mental images of others also have more accurate memories for other characteristics and behavior (Swann & Miller, 1982). Finally and curiously, people rated as looking dishonest are easier to remember than are people who look honest (Mueller, Thompson, & Vogel, 1988), perhaps because unusual looks are considered less trustworthy than a familiar, normal appearance. If the typical suspect were to look more dishonest than most people, this suggests that the person would be easier to identify, but we know of no reputable research indicating that criminals look more dishonest than other people.

Imagery as an analog code? Even when eyewitness observation is totally wrong, however, people do retain some sort of mental images for the appearance of others. How is this visual information represented? To this point, we have assumed that a propositional code characterizes memory for traits and a sequential code may characterize memory for behaviors. Several theorists have suggested another code, such that memory for visual details is stored in what is called an *analog code* (Kosslyn & Pomerantz, 1977; Paivio, 1971; Shepard & Podgorny,

1978). Analog representations preserve the continuous quantitative relationships of the information depicted. A mercury thermometer is an analog representation of temperature; a longer column of mercury represents a greater amount of heat. A digital thermometer is not an analog representation because it simply provides a symbolic readout (in digits) whose form is unrelated to the thing it represents. Dial-faced watches are also analogs, in that each movement of the hands represents a given quantity of time; a change of 90 degrees represents twice as much time as a change of 45 degrees. Digital watches, in contrast, give a symbolic representation of time in digits. Analog representations of social information such as the mugging would include mental photographs, films, maps, or scale models of the event. Visual information may be stored in the form of such mental images, as opposed to propositions describing all the visual details in words.

Some of the more intriguing research to emerge from the analog approach to visual memory suggests that mental images may mimic reality in odd ways. To illustrate, try the following thought experiment. Form an image of the inside of your family's house or apartment. Go to the kitchen. Make sure you have a clear, complete image in mind. Count the windows in the kitchen. Now count the windows on the outside front of the building. A bit awkward, when one has to change location. Erase the whole image from your mind by thinking of your grade school building for a moment. Now imagine your family house again, but focus on the front. Form a clear, complete image of the outside front. Count the front windows again. It should seem faster and easier to count the windows on the front if you initially focus on the front rather than if you initially focus on the inside (Kosslyn et al., 1979). Scanning a mental image apparently takes time, and the time it takes is proportional to the time it would take to scan the thing itself (the percept). In a sense, when you are "inside," you have to come out to the front to count the windows, but when you are "in front" already, you can just look up and count them. The longer distance from inside to the front outside seems to be longer both actually and mentally than the shorter distance from front to front. Thus, the mental representation may retain some features of, and so is a direct analog for, the percept.

The imagery notion holds great intuitive appeal. Moreover, visual information can enhance memory for verbal information (Lynn, Shavitt, & Ostrom, 1985; Hastie, Park, & Weber, 1984; Klatzky, 1984; Swann & Miller, 1982). Despite the empirical and intuitive basis for a separate analog (image-based) memory code, it is not totally clear that it necessarily exists. Propositional and analog models both can be made to account for scanning and other related results (J. R. Anderson, 1978, 1979; Pylyshyn, 1973, 1981; Klatzky, 1984); consequently, these intriguing results neither prove nor disprove the existence of a special code for imagery. One basic problem is that although almost everyone has the experience of having mental images, the experience does not necessarily mean that images are codes for storing and processing information. However, it is sometimes theoretically convenient to consider memory as having at least three codes: one verbal and propositional; one temporal and sequential; one visual and analog (J. R. Anderson, 1982; Hastie & Carlston, 1980).

Affect: A Fourth Code?

A major aspect of people's social perception is affective, that is, emotional and evaluative reactions to social stimuli (see Chapter 10). This dominant affective factor cuts across traits, behavior, and appearance. Regardless of which other dimensions organize people's descriptions of other people (i.e., sociability, competence, integrity), the overall affective dimension emerges (Kim & Rosenberg, 1980). In their minds, people appear to group affectively positive social stimuli all together and separate from affectively negative social stimuli. The importance of the positive-negative dimension generalizes to a wide range of stimuli (Osgood, Suci, & Tannenbaum, 1957) and to virtually all analyses of people's emotions (Chapter 10). Almost anything one remembers about another person's appearance, behavior, or traits potentially has an affective reaction linked to it. Affect's property of cutting across essentially all domains suggests that it may constitute yet another type of memory code, in addition to propositional, sequential, and image codes (Hastie & Carlston, 1980; Zajonc, Pietromonaco, & Bargh, 1982; Zajonc & Markus, 1984). There is no empirical evidence directly supporting affect as a fourth code, but it seems a possible development (see Chapter 10 for some relevant theories of affect and memory).

Concrete and Abstract Information in Memory

This section on the contents of person memory began with the observation that people remember a variety of more or less directly observable information about others. Information ranges from relatively general and abstract to relatively specific and concrete. To some extent, this distinction is captured by contrasting traits (abstract) with behaviors (concrete), but not entirely. The abstract-specific point is worth discussing because these different types of content can operate differently in memory.

Semantic versus episodic memory. The distinction between *semantic* and *episodic* memory is an old distinction in cognitive psychology (Tulving, 1972). Long-term memory sometimes was viewed as containing these two types of information. Episodic memory referred to specific events or concrete personal experiences, and semantic memory referred to the meaning of concepts at a more general, abstract level. When memory is viewed as a hierarchy, episodic memory is at the most concrete, lower levels, and semantic memory is at the more general, upper levels. For example, the particular mugging you witnessed would be stored as an episodic memory, while your overall ideas about muggings would be stored as part of semantic memory. Although many cognitive psychologists no longer support this distinction (e.g., Shoben, 1984), social cognition researchers have found variants of it useful, as we will see.

Specific and general social memory. One practical result of memory ranging from single concrete experiences to general semantic concepts is that memory for the general concept is often recalled more easily, so it can shape memory for the specific episode. Thus, if you generally expect elderly mugging victims to be helpless, your memory may mistakenly emphasize the ways that this particular woman gave in to the mugger, deemphasizing her other behavior. Note that this principle also is supported by much of the research discussed as evidence for schemas (Chapters 4 and 5), as well as other research in cognitive psychology (Shoben, 1984).

There are several reasons why general memories might be recalled more easily than specific memories in social cognition (Carlston, 1980b). All of them hinge on the idea that abstract, general memories are often embedded in an elaborate network, while specific, concrete memories more often consist of relatively isolated single experiences. First, traits and trait inferences are embedded in a rich multidimensional structure very like other kinds of abstract memories. This structure is sometimes called the perceiver's *implicit personality theory* (D. J. Schneider, 1973). The structure contains the connections among various traits (e.g., "generous" is close to "sociable" but irrelevant to "intelligent" and contradictory to "selfish"). The implicit personality theory network of linkages provides many alternate retrieval routes to any given trait, so the network facilitates the accessibility of any given trait inference. Specific behaviors tend not to be embedded in as richly an interconnected structure and so should be harder to retrieve. For example, the behavior of someone who gives you a ride home may not be especially well linked to other specific behaviors in memory, compared with a trait inference such as "people who help others are generous."

Second, abstract memories may be more easily retrieved than specific memories if abstract memories are characterized by deeper levels of processing; more elaborate thought facilitates retrieval (Craik & Lockhart, 1972). When people think about something, they make new links or elaborations between it and their existing knowledge. For example, in thinking about a friend's trait of generosity, one may process it relatively deeply; in thinking about the friend giving one a ride home, one may process it in a relatively shallow manner. Although there is little evidence directly on this point, the principle would be the same as before: the links provided by deeper processing would allow many alternative retrieval routes to the trait inference, which then facilitate memory.

Third, abstract memories consist of concepts (which must be inferred), while specific memories consist of concrete experiences (which are closer to the raw data). Thus, making inferences organizes memory for experiences. The organizing function of traits enhances their impact on recall of behavior (cf. Carlston, 1980b; Lingle et al., 1979; Ostrom et al., 1980). For example, if you fit two experiences (the ride home and a loan of money) under the trait "generous," it may help to organize them in memory, and the trait will be more memorable than either behavior. All this suggests that inferences will be easier to remember than the specific data on which they are based. Thus, it seems clear that inferences often dominate specific memories.

Inferences often dominate specific memories in making judgments as well (Carlston, 1980b; Lingle et al., 1979; Wyer, Srull, & Gordon, 1984). Again, this seems to be partly because social inferences, especially traits, are embedded in the perceiver's implicit personality theory. For example, when a personality judgment is requested, one's semantic memory—composed of general abstract trait representations—may be searched initially, in order to answer the question about the other person. If a general question is asked, a general answer may be given on the basis of a simple match to semantic notions stored in memory (cf. Lingle & Ostrom, 1979). For example, someone might ask you to judge whether or not a friend is generous; there are two ways you might draw on abstract memories to answer the question. Either you may already think of your friend as generous, or you may think your friend is kind and that most kind people are generous, but in both cases you can find the general answer in memory and respond accordingly.

If the general answer has not been stored already, however, then people may make a search of the relevant specific information in memory (R. B. Allen & Ebbesen, 1981; Ebbesen & Allen, 1979). That is, you may think back to your friend's various behaviors and decide if they fit the meaning of "generous." This is a two-stage model: check abstract memories, then search for specific memories. It saves time for the decision maker, since checking for an abstract memory simply consists of retrieving the relevant trait if it is there; the initial checking stage is a simple judgment. Searching specific memories for the relevant information is more complicated because one may have to retrieve several relevant episodes and then decide what general trait applies. The more time-consuming second stage is required only when the easier judgment did not provide an answer. Note the similarity of this process to the two-stage judgment process proposed in the Srull-Wyer model, described earlier.

Other researchers have similarly proposed that judgments about people are based on memory for both prior trait inferences and specific behavioral memories (Carlston, 1980a; Lingle, 1983). Judgments will depend on prior judgments mainly if inference from the old one to the new one is easy. Thus, the similarity of the two judgments and the ease of recalling the prior judgment both encourage using the prior one (Schul & Burnstein, 1985a). On the other hand, judgments will depend on recall of specific behaviors if that is easier. In one study, Carlston and Skowronski (1986) found that when specific prior behaviors have been recently primed (or activated), then judgments will be based on memory for them instead, a relatively indirect route. In short, although the most direct route for a trait judgment may be to a prior trait judgment, it need not always be used.

Thus, people typically combine several concrete experiences into a single summary judgment. Then they access the summary rather than their memory for the individual events in later retrievals. The advantage of storing one's prior general judgments means that specific memories need not be consulted each time a general, abstract judgment is requested. Instead, people refer back directly to a prior judgment, as in the example above (Lingle et al., 1979; cf. S. T. Fiske, 1982; S. T. Fiske et al., 1987; S. T. Fiske & Pavelchak, 1986). One consequence is that once an item contributes to the initial judgment, subsequent memory for that item itself will be independent of its initial impact on the judgment (N. H. Anderson & Hubert, 1963; Dreben, Fiske, & Hastie, 1979; Riskey, 1979). That is, specific concrete memories are no longer strongly associated with the final judgment in memory. It is as if people isolate the relevant component of each item, combine it with the current judgment, and then remember the judgment. Whether or not they recall the items that contribute to the judgment is another matter. We will come back to this point.

Another consequence of using prior judgments is that if temporary contextual factors contributed to the initial judgment, those influences may persist in the stored judgment, even after the context changes. In one study, subjects tailored their description of a stimulus person to suit their audience; their own memory, impressions, and evaluations of the person were later distorted in the direction of this "context-driven" communication (Higgins & McCann, 1984). Other kinds of contextual factors can influence memory and judgment, such as when one standard is present at the initial judgment and another is present at the subsequent judgment. But people fail to make appropriate adjustments to the prior judgment in light of the new context (Higgins & Stangor, 1988a; cf. Higgins & Lurie, 1983; Higgins, McCann, & Fondacaro, 1982; Higgins & Rholes, 1978; Higgins & Stangor, 1988b). For example, evidence at a trial might be presented in one context by a defense attorney, leading jurors to make one type of inference initially, but the judge might later instruct them to reconsider the evidence under a different standard; this research suggests the jurors will insufficiently adjust their initial judgment in light of the judge's instructions; that is, they will not go back to the original data in light of the new standard.

In summary, the semantic-episodic distinction describes the differences between abstract concepts and specific experiences stored in memory. In social cognition research, abstract general memories often intrude on concrete specific memories, for several reasons, all of which relate to the difference between the elaborate network of abstract memories and the relatively isolated single experiences of specific memories. First, implicit personality theories of traits characterize general memory for people, the rich network of associations enhancing the retrieval. Second, general memories may result from more elaborate thought (deeper processing), which also facilitates retrieval. Third, general concepts in memory are often inferred, while specific memories' concrete experiences are closer to the data, with the inferences tending to organize the memory for specifics.

ORGANIZATION OF SOCIAL INFORMATION IN MEMORY

Having discussed the contents of person memory—traits, behavior, appearance, and affect, as well as the distinction between general and specific memories—we now turn to various possible organizations of memory for people. One might imagine that information about people is invariably organized around individual people, including each person's traits, behaviors, and appearance as one cluster in memory, but some research suggests that is not always the case. Information about a person does not come organized in a package; it is encountered over time and interspersed with information about other people. Unfortunately, researchers usually present subjects with a single isolated stimulus person, and in so doing, perhaps they are arbitrarily separating that person as a single unit. Subjects have little choice but to organize their memories on a person-by-person basis, in that case. However, other forms of organization are possible (Ostrom, Pryor, & Simpson, 1981; Pryor & Ostrom, 1981; Pryor et al., 1983). For example, you might have mental categories for all the premedical students you know and all the runners you know; single persons might not be the invariable units of organization. Figure 8.5 shows two ways to organize the same information.

Organization by Person

When do people organize their social memories by person? In effect, the more important and realistic the person, the more likely one is to

Stimulus presented

Jane is a movie buff.
Diane is a runner.
David is a pre-med student.
Jane is a pre-med student.
David is a runner.

Organization by interests

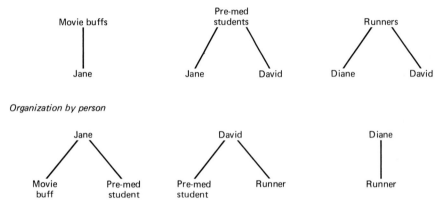

Organization by person

FIGURE 8.5 Two different organizations of person memory.

organize by person, i.e., with each person as an individual unit encompassing various characteristics. One condition appears to be *familiarity;* a familiar person is more likely to be stored as a separate unit than is an unfamiliar person (Pryor & Ostrom, 1981; Pryor et al., 1982). In one study, subjects tried to remember the facts about a person who was tall, bearded, honest, and a self-taught leader and to remember the facts about another person who was opinionated, religious, black, and a champion athlete. If Abraham Lincoln and Mohammed Ali, respectively, came to mind, the subjects' job was easy, and their subsequent memory protocols grouped the attributes in two separate clusters on a person-by-person basis. On the other hand, if the same attributes were presented in different combinations not suggesting familiar people (e.g., someone who was a tall, tough, religious, outspoken golfer), no famous people were likely to come to mind. Subjects' memory was not as likely to be organized by person when recalling information about unfamiliar others. On the whole, information about unfamiliar others is still likely to be organized by person (Sedikides & Ostrom, 1988), just less reliably so than information about familiar others. Besides increasing familiarity, stimulus people can be made more important and realistic by other means. Asking subjects to *form impressions* of people encourages person organization (Srull, 1983). *Anticipated future interaction* also increases the likelihood of organization by person (Srull & Brand, 1983).

Another factor encouraging organization by person is the salience of the person as a unit. Consider, for example, the *sequence* in which one learns personality traits and the fact that they all refer to the same person (J. R. Anderson & Hastie, 1974). If one learns the separate attributes first and only later learns that a single person possesses all of them, one is less likely to organize by person. But if one learns the characteristics knowing that they describe a single person, one is more likely to organize them that way. Similarly, *blocking* (grouping) of information by person naturally increases person organization in memory (Cafferty, DeNisi, & Williams, 1986; cf. Herstein, Carroll, & Hayes, 1980). Finally, the *redundancy* of different forms of organization increases organization by person. That is, if particular traits are distinctively associated with particular people (i.e., only one person is selfish), one organizes by person (and therefore by trait). However, if people have a lot of overlapping traits (several people are selfish), one is less likely to organize by person (Pryor, Kott, & Bovee, 1984).

Organization can also be suggested by the context in which the material is presented. For example, an *overriding situation* could be a more important category than the person; that is, some of the people who are in your psychology class may also be in your exercise class, and you may recognize them in each context, but you may not make the connection that the same person is in both classes if you do not organize by person. In addition, sheer *information overload* can overwhelm person organization, especially when stereotypic group membership provides a salient alternative (Rothbart et al., 1978; cf. S. E. Taylor et al., 1978).

The general principle seems to be that we are especially likely to organize by person when the people are significant to us (familiar, real people, with whom we expect to interact, across specific situations). However it is produced, organization by person seems to improve memory over other types of organization. When subjects are presented with information organized by person (as opposed to randomly organized), they recall more (Srull, 1983). Moreover, organization by person seems to be the preferred organization in most settings (Hastie, Park, & Weber, 1984; Sedikides & Ostrom, 1988), and it is incorporated into major models of person memory (Srull & Wyer, 1989). In sum, although person organization is the most likely format, specific circumstances affect the extent to which memory is organized by person.

Organization by Group

When people do not spontaneously organize their memory by person, they sometimes organize it by the social group to which the person belongs. As noted earlier in discussing schemas and stereotyping (Chapters 4 and 5), people seem especially likely to use physically salient categories based on sex, age, and race as a strategy for remembering information about individuals (McCann et al., 1985; S. E. Taylor et al., 1978).

One model suggests that memory retrieval starts with such social categories, recapitulating the development of acquaintance. With growing acquaintance, we learn about people first in terms of their categories and contexts, then in terms of their own specific attributes. Retrieving information about people seems to operate the same way, first accessing memory through social categories and contexts (club member, neighbor, doctor) then more specifically through individual personality traits (C. F. Bond & Brockett, 1987; C. F. Bond, Jones, & Weintraub, 1985; C. F. Bond & Sedikides, 1988). Thus, organization by group seems an important higher level structure, within which individuals are located. This, of course, is one explanation for the prevalence and resilience of stereotypes (see Chapters 4 and 5).

Other models suggest dual representations, as described at the beginning of this chapter (Srull & Wyer, 1989). In memory, some target people may be split between their group affiliations and their individual characteristics, as when one knows information about a person as an X (lawyer, Catholic, exercise nut) separately from information about the person's traits as an individual (Wyer & Martin, 1986). Or there may be multiple representations, as people initially are organized by their separate traits and the respectively associated behaviors (honest behaviors, intelligent behaviors, friendly behaviors), only later being connected as a whole person (Wyer, Bodenhausen, & Srull, 1984).

Whatever the details of the representation, people remember information about highly cohesive groups in much the same way that they remember information about individuals. Apparently, people and tightly knit groups are expected to be coherent and consistent, which makes inconsistencies stand out, so inconsistencies require thought to integrate, which in turn makes the inconsistencies memorable; the same is not true for loose aggregates of people (Srull, 1981; Srull, Lichtenstein, & Rothbart, 1985; Stern et al., 1984; Wyer, Bodenhausen, & Srull, 1984; Wyer & Gordon, 1982). Again, this has clear bearing on the perceived homogeneity of stereotyped groups (see Chapters 4 and 5).

Summary

People typically organize their memory for other people by connecting information around the person as a unit. This is especially likely to be the case when the person is familiar, when one has formed an impression, and when one anticipates future interaction. In addition, organization by person is enhanced when information about a person is presented in a context initially indicating that it will all pertain to one person, in a context grouping the information by person, or when individual persons have distinctive traits, making organization by traits and persons redundant in context. Organization by person is less likely when the situation is of overriding importance or when the perceiver is under information overload. Thus, we organize memory by persons when individuals are important to us. At a separate level, we also can organize memory by social group and role categories, perhaps as an initial entry point into memory for individuals.

MEMORY, JUDGMENT, AND GOALS

Having discussed basic models of person memory, the contents of person memory, and the organization of memory, we should consider how memory ties into the rest of the cognitive system. How does the retrieval of relevant material affect subsequent inferences and judgments? It turns out that memory, at least as measured by many traditional tests, can be surprisingly independent of many other seemingly relevant cognitive processes. The relationship between memory and judgment depends on one's goals, so we will also discuss the impact of goals on memory.

The Basic Problem of Memory and Judgment

One might expect that judgments result from information stored in memory. People encode information about others, and when they need to make a judgment, they retrieve what they know and use it as a basis for judgment. If this process accurately characterizes what people do, then there ought to be a correlation between what people recall and their judgments. Attributions, evaluations, and other judgments seemingly ought to draw on the amount and organization of relevant data in memory. Or so many psychologists thought, before complications arose.

A series of studies demonstrated that many types of judgment are surprisingly independent of recall for the data on which they were supposedly based. One of the first was a study on impression formation, in which people saw traits describing others, made likability ratings, and recalled the adjectives (N. H. Anderson & Hubert, 1963). The impact of individual traits showed dramatically different sequential patterns ("serial position effects") for likability ratings and recall; likability ratings were most influenced by the initial adjectives, while recall was strongest for the later adjectives. The respective primacy effect for liking and recency effect for recall led the authors to suggest two separate memory systems (see also N. H. Anderson, 1989a). In a subsequent study of impression formation, serial position effects again differed for the traits' impact on impressions and the traits' recallability (Dreben, Fiske, & Hastie, 1979; cf. Riskey, 1979). Moreover, various experimental tasks differentially affected the serial position effects for impressions and recall. Finally, impressions and recall were not significantly correlated. This lack of correlation was also being observed for recall and attributions (S. T. Fiske et al., 1979; S. T. Fiske, Kenny, & Taylor, 1982; S. E. Taylor & Fiske, 1975, 1978), person perception (Wyer, Srull, & Gordon, 1984), judgments of guilt (Reyes, Thompson, & Bower, 1980), and persuasion (e.g., Greenwald, 1968; N. Miller & Campbell, 1959). Why should judgments and recall be seemingly so independent?

The tangle of results began to unravel, as subsequent research specified the conditions under which judgments and recall are and are not correlated. One study showed a lack of judgment-recall correlation only for people who have time and capacity to form impressions on-line, as they initially receive the information (Bargh & Thein, 1985). In contrast, people who were overloaded as they received the information, and who presumably did not form impressions on-line, showed a clear relationship between what they recalled and their judgments, which were presumably based on memory. Other studies began to show that many judgments occur spontaneously at encoding (e.g., Winter & Uleman, 1984; see Chapter 7). And other lines of research suggested that people sometimes make an initial *stimulus-based* judgment (presumably made on-line), which also serves as a basis for later judgments, but when necessary they can also review relevant information to make a *memory-based* judgment (Carlston, 1980b; Ebbesen & Allen, 1979; Lingle & Ostrom, 1979; Lingle et al., 1979; Lingle, Dukerich, & Ostrom, 1983; Schul, 1986).

An elegant integration of this literature proposed that judgments will be uncorrelated with memory when people form impressions *on-line*, but memory and judgment will indeed be correlated when people make *memory-based* judgments (Hastie & Park, 1986). The literature as a whole indicates that people tend to form impressions on-line and that the conditions eliciting memory-based judgments are more unusual and have to be created by appropriate experimental manipulations. People can be prevented from forming judgments on-line by distraction while they receive the initial information or by afterward requesting unexpected judgments. For example, subjects might learn before receiving information that they will have to judge a person's suitability as a computer programmer (thus making it on-line), or they might only learn afterward that they have to make this unexpected judgment (in which case, it is memory-based). When judgments are made on-line, as is normally the case, memory and judgment are uncorrelated, but when judgments are memory-based, the correlation is substantial (Hastie &

Park, 1986). The on-line versus memory-based distinction is extremely useful and clarifies memory-judgment relations; it also points out the importance of perceiver goals, to which we now turn.

Goals and Memory

Perceivers approach interpersonal material with different purposes in mind, ranging from merely comprehending the information to planning an interaction. In research settings, goals are determined by experimenter instructions (e.g., "read this material and form an impression of the person described" or "read this material because we will give you a memory test later"). In natural settings, social context and individual differences determine one's goals. The goals one has for encoding and retrieving interpersonal information importantly determine the types of on-line judgments, what is remembered, and the relationship between recall and judgment (Hastie, Park, & Weber, 1984; Srull & Wyer, 1986, 1989; Wyer & Srull, 1980, 1986).

It makes sense that goals would influence whether and how one forms impressions as one first encodes information about another person. Consider the difference between forming an impression of a new graduate student for the purpose of reporting back to someone who is considering the person as a teaching assistant, and trying to empathize with the person's problems when you discover that he or she is a friend of the family and needs a shoulder to cry on. Of course, you will focus on different aspects of the person, depending on whether you are empathizing or forming an impression. You also will organize your memory differently in each case. If you are forming an impression, you need to organize your memory in terms of traits: competence, clarity, concern, wit, and the like. If you are empathizing, you need to organize your memory in terms of goals: what does the person want, what does the person feel like, and how can you help the person? As we shall see shortly, different processes of comprehending others result in markedly different memories.

As the following sections indicate, the basic principle seems to be that one's recall for information about other people appears to improve, the more psychologically engaging and less superficial the purpose with which one approaches learning about them. As we will see, instructions to memorize someone's behavior are not as helpful to recall as instructions to form an impression, which are not as helpful to recall as instructions to empathize. The most psychologically engaging task purposes of all might be comparing the other with oneself or expecting to interact with the other, and both those tasks seem to enhance recall relative to some other tasks.

A major explanation for variations in recall as a function of goals is that deeper or more elaborate processing improves recall. Borrowing a concept from cognitive psychology, researchers say that shallow depth of processing is typified by what are called *structural* tasks such as deciding if a word is written in capitals or in lower case letters. Medium depth is typified by *phonemic* tasks such as deciding if a word rhymes with another word. Deep processing is typified by *semantic* tasks such as deciding if a word is a synonym of another (Craik & Lockhart, 1972). The deeper the level of initial processing, the better one's subsequent recall, according to the depth of processing model.

An example may clarify this idea. Suppose you are proofreading a poem for a friend. In one instance, she has asked you merely to check the typefaces (a "structural" task), because her word processing system keeps mysteriously slipping into italics or capital letters. You could "read" the entire poem without really ever remembering its content. In another instance, she has asked you to check her rhymes and rhythm (a phonemic task), which would enable you to remember more than the structural task would. In still another instance, she asks you to read for her style, to see if it flows and if she picked the right words (a semantic task). You would then remember much more of the poem because you would be attending to the meanings of the words, which is called a deeper level of processing (Craik & Lockhart, 1972).

Person memory research suggests other levels of processing that depend on psychological engagement. Suppose your friend tells you the poem is all about her relationship with you; doubtless you would pay close attention and remember it rather well indeed, as you judged whether or not you thought it actually applied to you. As we will see, the more psychologically involving one's goal in processing information, the deeper or more complex the impression formed and the more recallable it is likely to be. Depth of processing is one explanation for this phenomenon, although it has some limitations, as we will see later. Person memory research has examined goals ranging from the most superficial to relatively involving: merely comprehending, memorizing, forming an impression, empathizing, comparing to oneself, or anticipating interaction.

Mere comprehension. The simplest type of social goal for encoding information about another is merely to understand what one is receiving. Under a comprehension set, when people are asked to comprehend and to judge coherence and grammar, they do not form impression judgments on-line, so they show clear judgment-recall relationships (Lichtenstein & Srull, 1987). Given the idea of mere comprehension as a lower-level depth-of-processing task, and given the plausible idea that comprehension might be a default option (i.e., what people do given no particular goal), it is surprising that more person memory studies have not examined this goal.

Memorizing versus forming impressions. One might expect that people best remember others when they are explicitly asked to memorize aspects of the other's behavior. The case turns out to be quite the contrary. People told to remember details about another person may actually remember *less* than people who are merely asked to form an impression of that person (Devine, Sedikides, & Fuhrman, 1989; D. L. Hamilton, 1981b, 1989; D. L. Hamilton, Katz, & Leirer, 1980a, 1980b; Hartwick, 1979; Srull, 1981, 1983; Srull, Lichtenstein, & Rothbart, 1985; Wyer, Bodenhausen, & Srull, 1984; Wyer & Gordon, 1982).

The superiority of an impression goal over a memory goal was first supported by a series of studies in which subjects were given instructions either to memorize or to form an impression of a person described by a series of behaviors (D. L. Hamilton et al., 1980b). Subjects read a list that included items such as "had a dinner party for some friends last week," "helped a woman fix her bicycle," "checked some books out of the library," and "wrote an articulate letter to his legislator." Subjects who simply were memorizing by rote recalled fewer items than subjects who were trying to form an impression.

Why should forming an impression enhance recall? Forming an impression of someone requires the perceiver to make sense of many individual items of information; the perceiver typically tries to form a coherent whole. For example, this may involve fitting the individual items of information to a preexisting schema involving traits or goals (Chapter 4), or it may involve temporal ordering of events (Wyer & Bodenhausen, 1985). It turns out that the same coherent organization that helps people to make sense of another person also aids recall. For example, in deciding how someone can be simultaneously helpful and articulate, one is forced to elaborate, explain, and make connections to other things in memory. One creates links among the to-be-remembered items in memory. Such links increase the alternative retrieval routes; that is, the more links one creates to an item in memory, the more likely it is to be recalled (e.g., J. R. Anderson, 1974, 1990).

A series of studies supports the idea that explicitly forming an impression causes people to organize information by linking it to prior interpersonal knowledge. In one study, subjects forming an impression organized their memories into clusters representing different categories of information, such as abilities, interpersonal characteristics, and interests (D. L. Hamilton, 1981b). In the behavior list above, for example, one might cluster together the behavior that fits with the trait "competent" (library, letter). Other research concurs that perceivers forming an impression tend to organize by trait categories (Hoffman, Mischel, & Mazze, 1981; Jeffery & Mischel, 1979). Thus, forming an impression encourages organization in terms of traits or other psychologically meaningful categories (cf. Hamilton, Katz, & Leirer, 1980b; Ostrom, Pryor, & Simpson, 1981; Srull, 1983; Srull & Brand, 1983; Srull, Lichtenstein, & Rothbart, 1985).

Under impression instructions, people focus on forming a coherent impression, on-line, as they receive the information, so it follows there is little recall-judgment relationship (Hastie & Kumar, 1979; Lichtenstein & Srull, 1987; S. J. Sherman et al., 1983). Moreover, having formed an overall impression, perceivers cannot easily "unpack" it after the fact, to examine the impact of its original elements. That is, if people are later told to disregard part of the information that went into their impression, they do not unpack and recompute the impression without the to-be-disregarded elements; rather, they simply try to adjust their current impression up and down by the apparently appropriate amount. One implication of this is that recall for the original information is independent of people's ability to disregard that information in their impression (Devine & Ostrom, 1985; Fiedler, Fladung, & Hemmeter, 1987; Schul & Burnstein, 1985b; Wyer & Budesheim, 1987; Wyer & Unverzagt, 1985).

Memory instructions have a rather different effect from impression instructions. When instructed to memorize, subjects use various strategies to organize social information; indeed, memory-task subjects appear to use more variable organizational strategies. For example, in one study, subjects told to memorize the previously described party-bicycle-library-letter list did not cluster the behavior in the same way as did impression subjects (D. L. Hamilton, 1981a). It is hard to know what organizational strategy those particular memory subjects used, but sometimes subjects think up arbitrary mnemonic devices. For example, a person might think of a key word in each sentence that matches the first four letters of the alphabet: *articulate, bicycle, checked out, dinner*. Because the mnemonic is arbitrary, it might not work very well, although it is certainly better than nothing.

Alternatively, in other studies, subjects sometimes organize by whatever is made salient by the stimulus materials, that is, by traits, situations, or goals, depending on what is most accessible (Hoffman, Mischel, & Mazze, 1981; Jeffery & Mischel, 1979; Wyer & Bodenhausen, 1985). This can lead memory subjects in some settings to outperform impression subjects, contrary to the more usual effect. One reason for this is that some materials make goals especially salient. Goals can be particularly effective devices for recall because they are specific and well-structured. Goals create direct links in memory both to a specific situation and within a sequence of behavior. For example, if you organize your memory by the idea that John had the goal to make friends with his neighbor, Jane, that creates fairly specific links in memory to his helping repair her bicycle and having a dinner party (assuming she was invited). In contrast, traits are more general and amorphous than goals, so they are less distinctive retrieval cues. If you organize your memory by a trait, for example, that someone performed several sociable behaviors, that is not much help because he could be sociable in many different situations and toward many different people. One implication of the superiority of goals over traits as aids to recall is that when memory-task subjects are given materials that fit a goal better than a trait, they may outperform impression-oriented subjects because they are flexible enough to use goals when it is more appropriate to the materials.

Thus, the impression-set advantage can be reversed (Hoffman, Mischel, & Mazze, 1981) for some people with some stimulus materials. The point, then, is that a memorizing task creates more variable and flexible organizational strategies, while an impression task encourages organization by traits. Organization by traits is likely to be superior to most arbitrary strategies that subjects think up on their own, but inferior to a goal-based strategy when the to-be-remembered material particularly fits a goal-based organization.

In summary, people forming impressions use psychologically meaningful categories—traits, in particular—to organize their memories. Most of the time, this strategy is to their advantage. Impression sets have an advantage primarily when they provide an organizational scheme for materials that previously lacked organization. Relative to psychologically irrelevant mnemonics (e.g., alphabetical order), traits appear to be an effective means of organization. Sometimes, however, traits may be relatively ineffective bases for organizing person memory; for example, goals can be more effective with some materials. In the majority of cases, though, having the explicit goal of forming an impression aids recall by encouraging people to organize in trait terms. When asked to form an impression, people organize information about others into a single coherent personality portrait (cf. Asch, 1946; D. L. Hamilton, 1981a; Ostrom, Pryor, & Simpson, 1981; Chapter 4). When asked to memorize, they use other strategies that do not necessarily depend on a coherent analysis of personality. On average, people forming impressions recall information about others better than do people memorizing. Table 8.1 summarizes this research and that of the next three sections.

Empathizing. If forming an impression requires more psychological engagement, encourages deeper processing, and is usually more effective than memorizing someone's actions, then empathizing requires even more engagement and deeper processing on the perceiver's part. Consequently, empathizing can be an even more effective recall strategy than forming an impression. Just consider the differences among (1) learning your new roommate's morning routine, so you can coordinate using the shower conveniently (memorizing); (2) deciding whether your roommate is likable, responsible, and fun (impression); and (3) trying to understand how he or she feels about the death of a parent (empathy). Empathy usually demands far more of the social perceiver than do impressions and memory. Empathy is defined as the ability to

TABLE 8.1 EFFECTS OF VARIOUS GOALS ON PERSON MEMORY

Goal	Effect
Comprehension	Limited memory
Memorizing	Variable memory, organized in an ad hoc manner, often by psychologically irrelevant categories
Forming impressions	Good memory, organized by traits
Empathy	Good memory, organized by goals
Self-reference (comparing to oneself)	Excellent memory, organized by psychological categories (traits or goals)
Anticipated interaction	Excellent well-organized memory, type of organization not yet clear
Actual interaction	Variable memory, depending on concurrent goals

share in another's feelings; empathy hence requires some effort. Accordingly, people instructed to empathize remember more about the target than do people who are detached (Harvey et al., 1980). Empathizers also make many more attributions than do detached subjects; that is, they are more likely to explain why the person behaved as he or she did. Quite probably the additional work that goes into constructing explanations improves recall; attributions provide the additional retrieval routes that enhance recall of the material explained (G. H. Bower & Masling, 1978). As with the impression-set advantage, the empathy advantage is diminished when the materials themselves provide a strong organizational structure; in that case, the structure provided by empathizing does not add as much organizational advantage over a memory task (Bodenhausen & Wyer, 1985).

People empathize with another person's perspective when both are in the same mood (G. H. Bower, Gilligan, & Monteiro, 1981), have similar personalities, share cooperative goals (Hornstein et al., 1980), or take the role of the other. As an instance of role taking, readers who keep a story character's motives in mind organize their memory on that basis; understanding someone's goals enables readers to build links among the person's various actions (Owens, Bower, & Black, 1979). If you do not know anything about Mark, then his staying up until dawn, phoning a professor, and photocopying 600 pages do not form a particularly coherent sequence. If you are told that he is trying to meet a dissertation deadline, the same disconnected actions take on new meaning. Empathy promotes a focus on the other person's goals, and as we have already noted, goals provide a strong recall aid.

Taking another person's emotional perspective is not the only way to empathize. Simply taking the other person's visual perspective provides an imaged vantage point that aids recall (S. T. Fiske et al., 1979). If Jenny tells you about a tennis match from her perspective, you remember the physical setting from her point of view (e.g., what her opponent looked like, the sun in her eyes, etc.). Imaginary perspectives can be induced in any number of ways, from direct instruction (read this story from Janet's perspective) to stylistic variations well known to novelists. A detail as subtle as "Don came in the door and brought the newspaper over to Janet" would set up the story from Janet's perspective, in contrast to "Don went in the door and took the newspaper over to Janet." A single consistent point of view aids recall for story details (Black, Turner, & Bower, 1979). Just as constructing an empathic perspective enhances recall for the person's motives and psychological vantage point, so constructing a vicarious visual perspective enhances recall for the person's physical viewpoint (R. C. Anderson & Pichert, 1978; Morrow, Greenspan, & Bower, 1987; Wyer et al., 1982).

To summarize, people's recall for other people is enhanced by empathy and role taking, perhaps because they promote a focus on the person's goals, which improves recall. Empathy can be induced by sharing a mood, personality, goal, or visual perspective.

Self-reference: Comparisons to oneself. Thus far, we have seen that increased psychological engagement (deeper processing) improves recall (cf. Greenwald & Pratkanis, 1984). In moving along a series of goals from memorizing to forming an impression to empathizing, recall typically improves at each step (see Table 8.1). One of the most psychologically engaging goals upon encountering another person might well be self-referent processing, that is, judging interpersonal information with respect to oneself. For example, in one study, subjects rated adjectives on one of four tasks: how long? (structural task), how specific? (semantic task), describes experimenter? (other-referent task), and describes self? (self-referent task). Self-referent processing produced superior recall and ratings of greater confidence and ease in making the judgment (Kuiper & Rogers, 1979). As we saw in Chapter 6, self-reference can improve memory relative to some other goals (Bellezza, 1984; P. Brown, Keenan, & Potts, 1986; Ganellen & Carver, 1985; Klein & Kihlstrom, 1986; Klein & Loftus, 1988; McCaul & Maki, 1984; Reeder, McCormick, & Esselman, 1987; Rogers, Kuiper, & Kirker, 1977). However, some researchers remain skeptical (G. H. Bower & Gilligan, 1979; Devine, Sedikides, & Fuhrman, 1989; Higgins, Van Hook, & Dorfman, 1988; Keenan & Baillet, 1980; McDaniel, Lapsley, & Milstead, 1987; for a review, see Kihlstrom et al., 1988). It may be useful to distinguish between two kinds of self-reference tasks: those requiring subjects to decide if a word describes them, which create rapid recall, and those requiring subjects to retrieve a personal (autobiographical memory), which creates slower recall (Klein, Loftus, & Burton, 1989).

There are various explanations for the usual advantage of self-relevant material in memory (also see Chapter 6). Self-relevant material may evoke deeper or more elaborate encoding of individual items, may create more organizational links among items, may involve well-developed cognitive structures (e.g., self-schemas), may enhance retrieval cues, and may involve affective desirability judgments. All of these factors potentially contribute to the advantage conferred by self-reference as a goal.

Future interaction. The depth of processing dimension so far has included comprehension, memorizing, impression formation, empathizing, and self-reference. Taking the dimension one step further, if people are learning about another person for the purpose of interacting with the person later, that should provoke even more psychological engagement, or so-called deeper processing. Expected interaction improves recall relative to the task of memorizing the other person's behavior, self-comparison, and friend-comparison (Devine, Sedikides, & Fuhrman, 1989; Srull & Brand, 1983). It appears that the expected interaction demands a more coherent impression, with many links among the items; this, in turn, aids memory retrieval. Anticipated interaction leads to greater individuation of the target from other people present; material about one's future partner is better recalled and more organized than information about others. Expected interaction especially improves recall when one has chosen one's interaction partner oneself (Beckmann & Gollwitzer, 1987); apparently, having made the decision, one is "implementation-minded" and, therefore, oriented toward enacting the chosen interaction.[3]

Actual interaction. Responding to the actual behavior of a physically present other person might seem to be the most involving of all goals, and therefore, the most beneficial to recall. But the picture is not that simple. Certainly, a responsive partner is remembered better than someone whose responses are irrelevant to the interactional flow (D. Davis & Holtgraves, 1984). Notably, however, actual interaction can also interfere with recall for information about others, as when self-presentational concerns use up capacity otherwise available for encoding (Baumeister, Hutton, & Tice, 1989; Lord & Saenz, 1985; Lord, Saenz, & Godfrey, 1987). Yet, recall differences are not always found (Gilbert & Krull, 1988; Gilbert, Pelham, & Krull, 1988), so the conditions under which actual interaction interferes with memory remain to be defined.

---

[3] Justifying one's choice (cf. dissonance theory, described in Chapter 11) does not provide an alternative explanation for this result, as more negative than positive information is remembered.

Comment on depth of processing. As more data come in, the effects of relatively high levels of psychological engagement on person memory should become clearer. The data so far are fairly consistent with a continuum of processing depth. Nevertheless, interpretations of goals based on the depth of processing idea should be qualified by the fact that depth of processing has been criticized (e.g., Baddeley, 1978), for several reasons. First, there may be nothing inherent in any given task that requires its necessarily eliciting shallow or deep processing. That is, one could expect to interact with another person but still process information about that person in a relatively shallow fashion. Similarly, one could memorize information but still process it in a relatively deep fashion. The point is that levels of processing are not absolute for any given goal; there are different levels of processing possible within any task such as memorizing, forming an impression, empathizing, self-reference, or expected interaction.

There is a second problem with the depth of processing idea and the related concept of elaborating items or making links among to-be-remembered items: there is no consensus on independent measures of processing depth or of elaboration (Baddeley, 1978). For social cognition research, these caveats suggest that the cognitive underpinnings of goal effects on recall need further clarification and should be borrowed cautiously.

Summary. Several types of goals shape people's recall for other people. The tasks vary in the implied depth of processing and level of elaboration of items or links among the to-be-remembered items. For instance, forming impressions of people requires more thorough processing and elaboration than does merely memorizing people's behavior; consequently, impression-task recall is typically enhanced. Empathizing involves imagining the other person's goals, and it facilitates recall because the imagined goals provide specific links among items in memory. Imagining another person's visual perspective facilitates recall for perceptual details apparent from that person's point of view. Self-referent encoding creates recall superior to various nonsocial tasks and sometimes superior to other-referent encoding. Future interaction may create the most detailed recall of all. Actual interaction has variable effects, depending on the perceiver's concomitant goals. In general, "deeper" processing improves recall, in requiring the elaboration of items and of links to related concepts.

Goal effects are important because a basic assumption behind social cognition researchers' use of theories and methods from cognitive psychology's memory research is that social and nonsocial settings will be essentially parallel. The direct borrowing assumes that one remembers information the same way, regardless of whether one is learning a list of words describing a person or simply learning a list of words irrelevant to a person. Thus, for example, the differences between recall under an impression task and under a memorizing task create boundaries for directly translating some of the cognitive research to social settings.

Conclusion

Recall is not correlated in any simple way with important social inferences; that is, people do not necessarily base their judgments on everything they remember. One essential explanation for this is that people make many judgments on-line, as they encode information. Consequently, what determines the impact of an item on an impression and what determines its memorability are separate issues. Whether or not people form impressions on-line partly depends on their goals. People form more elaborate impressions as their psychological involvement increases, along a rough progression from mere comprehension, memorizing, forming impressions, empathizing, self-reference, to future interaction. Actual interaction does not fit neatly into one spot along this continuum, for capacity limitations more easily intrude as people have competing goals, such as self-presentation. When people do form impressions on-line, under the more involving conditions, people may well make inferences and forget the data on which those impressions were based.

If recall and judgment are often unrelated, why, then, do psychologists study memory? The contents of people's minds are presumably major determinants of what they do (D. L. Hamilton, 1989). Judgments often occur in reaction to stimuli not currently present. In that case, the reactions must depend on some form of memory for the stimulus. Furthermore, memory helps define the range of possible responses. Certainly, if something is not in memory, it may well be outside the range of responses the person has available. Finally, the relations between memory and judgment, though often subtle, are indeed predictable, as just seen. The importance of memory structure and process is a basic premise of social cognition.

SOME NORMATIVE IMPLICATIONS

Memory processes, more than encoding processes, for instance, suggest normative criteria; that is, they lend themselves to evaluation against a standard such as efficiency or accuracy. Efficiency in memory could be defined as ease of access, the amount of wasted effort, and the degree of focus in retrieval. Accuracy in memory, of course, means whether or not one is correct. These dual standards are more complex than they appear, and they often conflict. Efficiency may interfere with accuracy, as the following quotation illustrates. Dr. Watson writes of Sherlock Holmes, who claimed to know a thing or two about the most efficient memory strategies:

> His ignorance was as remarkable as his knowledge. Of contemporary literature, philosophy and politics he appeared to know next to nothing. Upon quoting Thomas Carlyle, he inquired in the naivest way who he might be and what he had done. My surprise reached a climax, however, when I found incidentally that he was ignorant of the Copernican Theory and of the composition of the Solar System. That any civilized human being in this nineteenth century should not be aware that the earth travelled round the sun appeared to me to be such an extraordinary fact that I could hardly realize it.
>
> "You appear to be astonished," he said, smiling at my expression of surprise. "Now that I do know it I shall do my best to forget it!"
>
> "To forget it!"
>
> "You see," he explained, "I consider that a man's brain originally is like a little empty attic, and you have to stock it with such furniture as you choose. A fool takes in all the lumber of every sort that he comes across so that the knowledge which might be useful to him gets crowded out, or at best is jumbled up with a lot of other things, so that he has a difficulty in laying his hands upon it. Now the skillful workman is very careful indeed as to what he takes into his brain-attic. He will have nothing but the tools which may help him in doing his work, but of these he has a large assortment, and all in the most perfect order. It is a mistake to think that little room has elastic walls and can distend to any extent. Depend upon it there comes a time when for every addition of knowledge you forget something that you knew before. It is of the highest importance, therefore, not to have useless facts elbowing out the useful ones."
>
> "But the Solar System!" I protested (Doyle, 1930, pp. 13–14).

As it happens, Holmes was probably wrong in believing that long-term memory is inherently limited in precisely that way. But Holmes was partially right in his worry about interference among various items of information. The more related concepts one knows, the more potential there is for inefficiency. Let us examine the *accuracy* and *efficiency* criteria in turn, but first we must note a caveat that applies not only to this discussion, but also to the rest of the person memory literature.

A Note on Social Group Memory

In considering whether people's memories are sufficiently accurate and sufficiently efficient, we will discuss people as if they always struggled with memory alone. Throughout this chapter, we have discussed individual people's memory for other individuals, so we will also primarily touch on normative issues in that context. However, the normative criteria for accuracy and efficiency do depend on one's function in a social context. An entirely novel set of normative criteria emerges around group memory, that is, a dyad or more of people who jointly reconstruct the past. Wegner (1986) proposes the idea of transactive memory that connects individual memory systems. Transactive memory operates first by categorizing members' expertise ("she's the one who knows about nature"; "he's the one who's an authority on consumer goods"). If someone else in the couple or the group is responsible for remembering certain types of information, one does not have to bother remembering on one's own. As with Sherlock Holmes's brain-attic, one has less to store when one can refer to another person as an "external memory" aid. All else being equal then, groups' memories are likely to be more accurate than individuals' (Stephenson et al., 1986; Stephenson, Brandstatter, & Wagner, 1983; Stephenson, Clark, & Wade, 1986). However, interdependent memory, like any kind of interdependence, has its risks, for example, if the couple or the group splits up and the individual no longer has the requisite information available.

Of course, there is potential for inaccuracy here, too. People may be erroneously stuck with responsibility for certain expertise, if the original attribution of expertise was mistaken. The potential for accuracy and efficiency—as well as the potential for frustrations—of group memory is obvious, as anyone knows who has witnessed members of a couple trying to reconstruct a jointly experienced event or deferring to each other's domains of expertise. In any event, the accuracy and efficiency criteria are better developed for individual memory systems than for group memory.

Accuracy

Accuracy in an individual's memory for people has a limited meaning, in part because of the difficulty in determining accuracy in person memory. The general problem of accuracy in social perception has long been a problem for social and personality psychologists. Early person perception researchers were concerned with people's ability to identify correctly the traits and emotions of others (Bruner & Tagiuri, 1954; D. J. Schneider, Hastorf, & Ellsworth, 1979). But it soon became apparent that one cannot assess correctness without having a clear criterion of what makes a perception or memory correct. Given the difficulty psychologists have in establishing what people's traits and emotions actually are, it is difficult to evaluate the ordinary person's accuracy at the task of person perception. (For a more complete discussion, see D. J. Schneider, Hastorf, & Ellsworth, 1979.)

Cronbach (1955) dealt a severe blow to the person perception research on accuracy by pointing out that, theoretically, there are many different sorts of error, and each one separately contributes to accuracy (or its lack). Although Cronbach was interested in judgment accuracy, his analysis can be applied to memory accuracy just as easily. One's memory can vary in its degree of accuracy about people in general, specific people, specific attributes, or specific attributes for specific people. Current research in person memory tends to use as its accuracy criterion the most concrete of these four types—specific attributes remembered about a specific person.

The person memory laboratory is (by necessity) simplified. Subjects in memory experiments do not usually have to extract information, only to remember information they are given. That is, subjects do not have to figure out who is Republican, who is an artist, or who is boring among a group of stimulus people. Because the people's attributes are presented directly, subjects do not have to worry about the accuracy of inferring the attributes from raw data. Since the stimulus people are created with certain obvious behaviors and traits, the accuracy criterion for initial inferences is not a problem in the laboratory. The subject is accurate if he or she remembers the traits or behaviors that were presented as stimuli. Unfortunately in real life, things are more complex. You may remember a fellow we both met at a conference as being intellectual and sophisticated, while I may remember him as being pompous. Since our original perceptions shape what we recall, accuracy in real-world person memory confounds encoding biases with inferential biases to a greater degree than do less ambiguous stimuli in the laboratory.

Another accuracy issue in person memory is characterized by the balance between theory-driven and data-driven processes, discussed in Chapters 4 and 5. One could argue that theory-driven or schematic memory is almost never accurate because no single instance exactly replicates the general schema. On the other hand, one could also argue that schematic memory generally preserves the broad outlines of the most typical instances, from which it was perhaps built up in the first place, so it inevitably contains important kernels of truth. Hence, one could argue that schematic memory is "good enough." That is, one must define the degree of accuracy that matters in a normative sense. In doing so, another issue then arises: accurate enough for what? Normative standards cannot be established without knowing the function person memory will serve in a particular case, which requires knowing the person's setting, goals, and the like. For all these reasons then, accuracy raises interesting normative issues about person memory.

Efficiency

Regardless of how one defines accuracy, efficiency can be a conflicting goal. One type of memory efficiency is ease of access, which often means reaction time to retrieval or recognition. There is a tension between speed and accuracy; that is, in general, the faster people are, the more likely are they to be wrong. Efficiency and accuracy can be sacrificed for each other, then.

Another type of efficiency includes the amount of wasted effort, specifically, the ratio of inaccurate to accurate memory. In recognition tests that ask, "Have you seen this item before?" efficiency can be captured by comparing hit rates (correct yes answers) to false alarms (incorrect yes answers) in recognition; this ratio is used in what is called a signal detection index (e.g., Hartwick, 1979). In free recall tests that ask, "Tell me everything you can remember about this person," the equivalent would be the ratio of intrusion (made-up answers) to accuracies.

A third criterion for efficiency is how focused one's memory search is. For example, can related items be found clustered together? And are they in categories appropriate to the task (cf. D. L. Hamilton, 1981b)? If memory organization reflects the problem at hand, then you are halfway to solving it. To illustrate, it is typically more efficient to cluster in memory all of someone's attributes related to social behavior, separately from those related to task performance; it is usually less efficient to cluster attributes by the order in which you learned them (Ostrom et al., 1980). Efficiency, then, ultimately depends on one's purpose, just as do standards for accuracy.

SUMMARY

Memory for information about other people is a fundamental area of study within social cognition. The basic models of memory draw on associative network theories in cognitive psychology; each idea or proposition is represented by nodes linked to other nodes, and ease of retrieving any given item is determined by the number of pathways to it. Links are labeled and strengthened each time they are activated. When an item in long-term memory is sufficiently activated, it moves into short-term or working memory. Long-term memory has vast storage capacities, but short-term memory is quite limited.

An associative network model of memory predicts that expectancy-inconsistent items will attract attention; that is, they will be held relatively longer in working memory than will consistent items. With the longer stay in working memory, inconsistent items are explained and linked to other aspects of the developing impression. Consequently, inconsistent items have an advantage in recall. A related model of social memory proposes that people interpret behaviors in terms of relevant traits, form an impression of the person as basically likable or not, and interpret the behaviors in view of the evaluative impression. Evaluatively inconsistent behaviors are reviewed, adding links from them to other items, thereby enhancing the retrieval of the inconsistent items. When people have an expectancy about the target person, they are hypothesized to form two independent representations, one in terms of the trait expectancies and the other in terms of the person's overall likability. When people do not have an expectancy, they are hypothesized to form only one representation, in terms of applicable traits. Judgments are made on the basis of relevant traits, when possible; otherwise, judgments may be based on overall likability or on a review of specific behaviors. Quantities of research within the standard person-memory paradigm support many aspects of these two models, but paradigms that complicate the perceiver's task present some challenges to these theories.

Alternative memory models are less commonly used within person memory work, but they may become more developed with time. In contrast to the associative structure of long-term declarative memory, procedural memory is posited to be a separate type of memory, focused on skills, which are represented as condition-action pairs called productions. Procedural memory allows more rapid and efficient cognitive operations with practice. Procedural memory models provide an alternative account for some accessibility, automaticity, and categorization effects.

Exemplar models focus on memory for specific instances rather than abstract representations, accounting for some types of category knowledge. Parallel distributed processing models describe an alternative to associative networks as representations of knowledge in memory. Both applications are developing within cognitive psychology, although only exemplar models have so far been applied to social cognition.

Contents of person memory apparently emphasize traits, behaviors, and appearance. Memory for traits is easily explained by the propositional codes of associative network models, organized along dimensions of sociability and competence. Memory for behaviors may require an additional temporal code that preserves information about the sequential and enabling features of goal-directed behaviors. Memory for appearance can be explained by analog representations that preserve many features of the actual percept. However, propositional codes can also explain many aspects of appearance memory. In any case, memory for other people's faces is excellent, at least in the laboratory and when same-race faces are studied. Eyewitness memory, in contrast, is less reliable, perhaps because of the volatile and confusing conditions for observation. Affect has been proposed to operate in a fourth type of code, but these ideas remain to be developed (see Chapter 10).

Person memory contents range from concrete and specific (appearance, particular experiences) to the abstract and general (traits). Concrete and abstract information serve somewhat different roles in memory. Building on an old distinction between episodic and semantic memories, social cognition researchers have found that general memories can often be recalled more easily than specific memories, because the general ones are embedded in a richer network of associations. General memories often form the basis for judgment; otherwise, the judge must retrieve and combine specific memories.

The organization of social information in memory is typically assumed to depend on an individual person, and it often does. Perceivers most often organize by person when that other person is real and important or when the structure of the information encourages it. Alternative forms of organization utilize the situation or the group as a basis for memory. Group organization may provide a higher-level entry point to memory for specific individuals.

Judgments are not always related to memory for the data on which they are based. People's memory and judgment are relatively independent when people have made their judgments on-line, at the time of encoding the information. On-line judgments are typical, unless perceivers are prevented by capacity limitations or unless the judgment is unusual. Goals also influence which judgments are made on-line.

Person memory researchers have studied a continuum of goals, ranging from less to more psychologically involving. Mere comprehension goals do not facilitate memory. Memorizing produces variable memory, depending on the structure of the materials; ad hoc mnemonic strategies work less well than any structure provided by the material. Forming impressions often facilitates memory, as the material can be organized in terms of personality traits, making links among items. Empathizing promotes memory organization in terms of the other person's goals, which typically enhances memory. Self-reference usually creates excellent memory, organized in terms of traits, goals, or other structures, such as the self-concept. Anticipating future interaction also provides excellent memory, although actual interaction does not because of its multiple competing demands. Increasing levels of psychological engagement facilitate memory, and depth of processing is one explanation for this phenomenon.

Some normative implications arise when considering person memory. Social group memory depends on different individuals having responsibility for their own areas of expertise. Individual memory, however, is most commonly the focus of social cognition research. Accuracy can have several different meanings, variously referring to people in general, specific people, specific attributes, or specific attributes for specific people. Current research focuses on the latter type. Real-world accuracy considerations might be broader. Moreover, in the real world, accuracy issues necessarily implicate interpretive biases and theory-driven processes as well. Efficiency can also have several meanings, most prominently variations in accessibility, false alarms, and irrelevancies.

9

Social Inference

❖

The Process of Forming Inferences ◆ *Heuristics: A Rapid Form of Reasoning* ◆ *Inference: An Overall Evaluation* ◆ *Improving the Inference Process*

*I*nference is a central concern of social cognition. It is both a process and a product. As a process, it involves assessing what information should be gathered to address a given judgment or decision, collecting that information, and combining it in some form. As a product, it is the outcome of the reasoning process (Nisbett & Ross, 1980). In this chapter, we are concerned primarily with the social inference process, that is, how social perceivers specify what information is relevant to a given judgment, how they sample information, and whether or not they follow normative rules in combining information into a judgment. We also consider higher order processes that draw on some of these: fundamental relevancy, sampling, and combinational judgments of frequency or probability.

We have already considered the subject of inference in other chapters. Attribution theory (Chapters 2–3) is both a delineation of the methods by which people make causal inferences and an analysis of the causal inference itself. Schemas strongly influence how we process information and what inferences we draw, as we pointed out in Chapters 4–5. Memory for information about other people is composed of intermingled inferences and raw data, as we noted in Chapter 8. Attitudes are a kind of inference, and in Chapter 11 we will outline the cognitive processes underlying the way attitudes are formed and how attitudes affect other judgments. We could draw similar ties to other chapters, for the inference process is basic to all aspects of social cognition.

As will become evident, the social perceiver uses a variety of inference strategies, some quite formal and abstract, others intuitive and domain-specific. The

346

adequacy of these inferential strategies has typically been evaluated against the dictates of normative theory. By normative theories, we mean that there are believed to be standard, optimally correct ways of performing each of the steps that a social perceiver should do to form an inference (e.g., gathering and sampling data, combining information), and the social perceiver's methods and conclusions are compared with these normative models for accuracy. Why is normative theory so dominant in social inference? The reason is that research on social inference generally assumes, either implicitly or explicitly, that inference is goal-directed (i.e., made to achieve some purpose). For example, one may need to make a decision or choose from several options, or one may need to understand a situation before one can act on it. If goals dominate the inference process, then clearly some ways of reaching a goal are better than others (e.g., faster or less error-prone), at least in some circumstances. Accordingly, the social perceiver seemingly ought to use them (Einhorn & Hogarth, 1981). The normative models for making judgments and choices are known collectively as *behavioral decision theory*, and thus, it is against the principles of behavioral decision theory that social inference may be compared (Einhorn & Hogarth, 1981; Slovic, Fischhoff, & Lichtenstein, 1977). As will be seen, inferential strategies often do not match the criteria dictated by normative models. In some cases, the social perceiver may substitute an intuitive strategy that serves different goals than those dictated by normative theory, and which consequently may provide more useful or quicker answers. In other cases, normative theory would provide better answers, but the social perceiver adopts an intuitive, often well-practiced or domain-specific strategy instead that ignores important biases or errors to which the intuitive strategy may be prone.

In the first section of the chapter, we will trace temporally the process whereby the social perceiver gathers data, decides how good they are, and combines them into a judgment. Figure 9.1 presents in rough temporal fashion the sequence a perceiver goes through in forming an inference. In each section, we will consider the sources of departure from normative models and some of the reasons why intuitive strategies may be adopted over normative ones. We then consider some of the constraints on the social perceiver that may lead to the use of intuitive but occasionally flawed inferential strategies. We next consider judgmental heuristics that the social perceiver often uses to solve tasks of inference efficiently. Subsequently, we take up explicitly the question of when the social perceiver uses strategies that approximate normative models of inference. And, finally, we evaluate the consequences of naive inferential strategies and the apparent errors and biases to which they may sometimes be prone in the context of the goals of the social inference process.

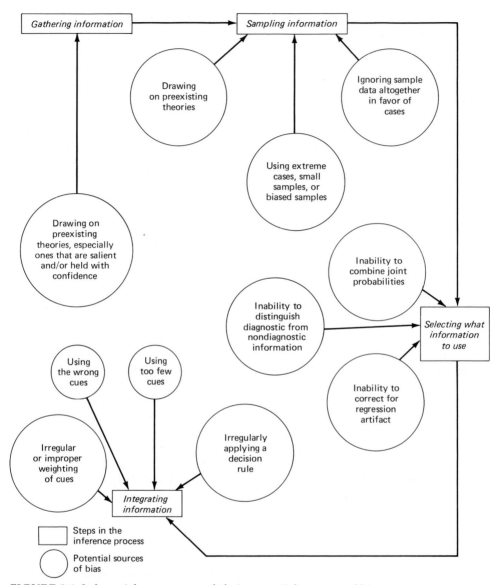

FIGURE 9.1 Inferential processes and their potential sources of bias.

THE PROCESS OF FORMING INFERENCES

Gathering Information

Every day, we as social perceivers make numerous, apparently complex, judgments. When asked by a friend what a mutual acquaintance, Rick, is like, we must decide how much and what kind of information to provide. Is his fanaticism over basketball or passion for young women relevant or should we only mention his good sense of humor, his quirk of forgetting people's names, and his love of lengthy political debates? Even the smallest inference or judgment begins with the process of deciding what information is relevant and sampling the information that is available.

According to the normative model, the social perceiver should weigh all relevant evidence in arriving at a conclusion, but, as we have already seen in our discussion of schemas (Chapters 4–5) and memory (Chapter 8), the process of deciding what information is relevant or how one is to interpret the evidence can be guided by preexistent expectations or schemas. Similarly, the information we convey to our friend about Rick will be different if our friend is an attractive 19-year-old undergraduate woman than if she is a 67-year-old Democratic party veteran.

Selecting data according to preexistent expectations or theories is perfectly appropriate under many circumstances (see Nisbett & Ross, 1980). It would be a bad doctor indeed who started from scratch with each new medical case he or she encountered, instead of letting the interpretation of symptoms be guided by the frequency of a particular illness, characteristics of the patient, knowledge of what illnesses are "going around," and the like. A slightly pudgy adolescent girl with occasional fainting spells could have a brain tumor, but it is more likely that she has low blood pressure or that she is dieting and has not eaten enough food.

Nonetheless, there are many circumstances in which characterizing information on the basis of preexistent theories is unwise. Three such conditions are as follows (Nisbett and Ross, 1980). The first is if the theory itself is faulty or suspect. For example, if the physician concludes that the fainting adolescent is possessed by demons, her parents might at least want a second opinion. Second, if an individual is characterizing data on the basis of a theory but believes his or her inferences are objectively based on raw data, problems can result. The physician who sends the girl home after a cursory examination with instructions to eat a big dinner may well have ignored other less likely causes of fainting such as diabetes or epilepsy, but the physician may believe that a thorough examination was conducted. Third, theory-guided inferences create problems when the theory overrules consideration of the data altogether. The doctor who dismisses the adolescent as an overzealous dieter prior to examining her would be guilty of this error, as well as of gross negligence.

Theories are particularly likely to guide the collection of data if the theory is held with great confidence, if it is very salient in the theory holder's mind, and if the available data are sufficiently ambiguous that they do not, in themselves, suggest an alternative theory (Nisbett & Ross, 1980). To take specific examples, suppose the physician's own daughter suffers from anorexia nervosa, a nervous disorder most common among adolescent girls that amounts to self-starvation. The sight of another adolescent, weak perhaps from hunger, might make his overzealous dieting theory so compelling that the physician ignores other possibilities. However, if other symptoms such as a history of insulin shock or seizures were present, virtually all physicians would reject any private theory in favor of one that better fits the data, such as diabetes or epilepsy, respectively.

Sampling Information

Once the social perceiver has decided what information is relevant to an inference, a task which can be biased by preexisting theories, the data must be sampled. For example, if you want to know if the students in your class enjoy the course, you must decide whom to ask and how many people to ask. When people are describing information on samples provided to them, their accuracy in estimating frequencies, proportions, or averages is quite good, so long as no prior theories or expectations are present to influence such estimates. Thus, for example, if you had students' course evaluations, you could presumably estimate their average evaluation quite easily. However, when prior theories or expectations do exist, describing data can be influenced by the theory (see Nisbett & Ross, 1980; S. E. Taylor & Crocker, 1981, for reviews).

When samples are not already available, the process of sampling and drawing inferences from samples presents other potential pitfalls. To begin with, *sample estimates can be thrown off by extreme examples* within the sample. In one study (Rothbart et al., 1978), subjects were given information about members of two groups, including the fact that some of the members had committed crimes. For one sample, only moderate crimes were listed, whereas in the other sample, a few examples of particularly heinous crimes were included. Although the actual frequency of committing crimes was the same in the two groups, subjects misremembered that more individuals committed crimes in the second group, presumably because the extreme examples had prompted a strong association between that group and crime (Tversky & Kahneman, 1974). Frequency estimation, then, is a skill crucial to correct use of sample information, but it can be misled by other, irrelevant characteristics of the sample (see also Arkes & Rothbart, 1985).

In drawing inferences from samples, *the social perceiver is often inadequately attentive to sample size.* Small samples often produce poor estimates of a population's characteristics, whereas larger samples are more reliable. This principle is called the *law of large numbers.* In apparent violation, however, people will often overgeneralize from a small unrepresentative sample (Nisbett & Ross, 1980; Tversky & Kahneman, 1974). For example, on witnessing a single instance of another person's behavior, the social perceiver will often make confident predictions about that person's behavior in the future. In this context, a friend of the authors who had spent virtually all of his early years living in Manhattan revealed that, until he was 25 years old, he believed that Queens was nothing more than a burial ground for New York City. For that entire time, his sole ventures into Queens were to Kennedy or La Guardia airports, trips that afford little more than a view of acres and acres of cemeteries. Presumably, a better sampling of the streets of Queens would have revealed more of its riches.

Kunda and Nisbett (1986) have shown that people do have some intuitive appreciation of the implication of the law of large numbers, but not for all its implications. The social perceiver shows a certain asymmetry in believing that one can use an aggregate to predict a single event with more reliability than one can use a single event to predict the aggregate. Thus, for example, people believe that a score on a short form of an intelligence test is better predicted by the score on the full test than a score on a full test is predicted from the score on the abbreviated test (Tversky & Kahneman, 1980). These perceptions are mistaken, because predicting the aggregate (full test) from a single event (short form) is identical to predicting a single event from the aggregate. This effect seems to occur because people's intuitions lead them to believe that increasing the size of the predictor sample of events increases predictability, whereas increasing the size of the predicted sample does not (Kunda & Nisbett, 1988; see also Kunda & Nisbett, 1986).[1]

In addition to size of sample, *people are sometimes insufficiently attentive to biases in samples.* When gathering his or her own sample, an individual may ask a few friends or acquaintances their opinions, forgetting that a sample of one's friends is scarcely random. Usually, one picks friends or acquaintances precisely because they are similar on at

---

[1]The main exception to this general rule is when people are using their own behavior to predict a group's behavior or vice versa. Under conditions when people know their own behavior, they are very likely to predict the aggregate's or group's behavior confidently from their own behavior or beliefs (Kunda & Nisbett, 1988). The false consensus effect described in Chapter 2 is an example of this effect.

least some dimensions, and hence, their opinions are likely to be at least somewhat similar to one's own. Under some circumstances, biased sampling may not matter. If you want to know if a movie is good so you can decide whether or not you want to see it, canvassing friends who are similar is perfectly appropriate. However, if you want to decide whether or not to take your entire assemblage of visiting relatives to a movie, the bias in the sample of your friends' opinions might matter a lot; if your friends have a penchant for motorcycles and raunchy humor but your grandparents do not, you may wish you had sampled more carefully.

When given information about a sample's typicality, people will sometimes fail to use it. In one study (Hamill, Wilson, & Nisbett, 1980), researchers told subjects they would be viewing a videotaped interview with a prison guard who was either typical of most guards or very atypical of most guards, or typicality information was not provided. Subjects then saw a tape in which the guard appeared as a highly compassionate, concerned individual or as an inhumane, macho, cruel one. Subjects were later asked a set of questions about the criminal justice system that included questions about prison guards. Results showed that, even though subjects remembered the initial typicality information, those exposed to the interview with the humane guard were more favorable in their attitudes toward prison guards than were subjects who saw the interview with the inhumane guard.

Some studies have shown that when people are reassured that the sample information is reliable and valid, they make more confident inferences about population characteristics (Kassin, 1979a; Wells & Harvey, 1977). However, it is unlikely that subjects characteristically assume that samples are representative and valid, which would explain their willingness to use small and/or biased samples. Rather, it seems more likely that questions of sample adequacy rarely arise in a person's mind. For example, people will often make stronger inferences from a small sample than a large sample, even though both samples are available to them, and the sample size problem should be readily apparent (Tversky & Kahneman, 1974). Furthermore, subjects will use biased sample information even when those sources of bias are abundantly clear, as in the "atypical guard" example above. Hence, although people do make better inferences after their attention has been called to such criteria as the representativeness or validity of a sample, these occasions might best be thought of as exceptions rather than the rule.

Rules of sampling and characteristics of samples are not the only kinds of information that people underuse when they attempt to draw inferences. Other characteristics that bear on the relevance of data to inferences also elude the social perceiver's cognitive processing. The first example of this phenomenon that we will take up is the regression effect.

Regression

Regression is a phenomenon related to prediction from probabilistic information, and it is poorly understood by most people. Regression refers to the fact that extreme events will, on the average, be less extreme when reassessed at a different point in time. To illustrate this elusive phenomenon, consider four people who take a test such as the mathematics section of the Graduate Record Exam (GRE). Suppose the four all have exactly equal mathematical ability and should all get 600 on the test. Will they all get 600? Probably not. Random factors can intrude that will affect performance, some favorably, some adversely. One person (A) may have had trouble sleeping the night before and performs more poorly than he would otherwise. A second person (B) may have studied examples similar to those on the test and thus does quite well. A third person (C) may be distracted by the gum chewer next to her and loses a few points, and the fourth person (D) may have gotten a good seat in the testing room and does well.

But if all the information one had about these four students was their performance on this one test, one might conclude that two of them (B and D) are quite bright, but the other two (A and C) are not as good. Asked to predict their future performance, the inclination would be to predict high scores for B and D and lower ones for A and C. What would, in fact, happen? In all likelihood, on a second test, B and D would not look as good as they previously did, whereas A and C would look better. Why? B and D each had random factors working in their favor that, precisely because they are random, would no longer be present at the second session. Likewise, A and C each had random error working against them that would not be present at Time 2. Although random error would still be present at Time 2, it would be equally likely to favor or disfavor each of the four students, rather than consistently favoring B and D and disfavoring A and C. Thus, at the second test, B and D should fare worse and A and C better. Table 9.1 illustrates the phenomenon of regression.

The message of regression, then, is that when one must make an inference based on limited and unreliable information, one will be most accurate if one ventures a prediction that is less extreme than the information on which it is based. A restaurant that is fabulous one night will probably not be quite as good when you drag your friends there, having raved endlessly about its cuisine. Your scathing assessment of a pitcher's potential may make you look very foolish when he pitches a shutout in his next game. Bitter experience notwithstanding, experimental evidence, as well as common observation, consistently shows that when people are provided with extreme values of predictor information, they draw extreme inferences about subsequent behavior (Jennings, Amabile, & Ross, 1982; Kahneman & Tversky, 1973).

TABLE 9.1 REGRESSION TOWARD THE MEAN: TAKING THE GRES TWICE

	Time 1			
Given four students (A, B, C, D) of equal ability, all should score a 600 on the Graduate Record Examination:	*But random factors enter in, raising or lowering their scores:*	*Actual score at Time 1:*	*Conclusion:*	
A 600	−10 (slept poorly)	590	B and D look strong:	
B 600	+15 (studied examples similar to test items)	615	A and C look weaker	
C 600	−17 (gum chewer was a distrac- tion)	583		
D 600	+12 (got a good seat in the test room)	612		

	Time 2			
Given same four students taking test again:	*Different random factors are present, raising or lowering scores:*	*Actual score at Time 2:*	*Conclusion:*	
A 600	+12 (had a good breakfast)	612	A and C look stronger and	
B 600	−10 (sat near the window)	590	B and D look weaker than at Time 1	
C 600	−4 (had a slight cold)	596		
D 600	+5 (was "on" that day)	605		

People can sometimes "learn" inappropriate rules when they fail to appreciate regression. In a study with college students, Schaffner (1985) had undergraduates use praise and reprimand to attempt to improve the promptness of two schoolboys whose arrival times at school were, in fact, randomly determined. A strong "deterioration" in promptness following reward and "improvements" in promptness following repri- mand were "found," a pattern that would be expected on the basis of regression. Nonetheless, although subjects perceived their praise to be effective in modifying the students' behavior, they perceived reprimand to be more effective.

There are rare instances in which regression, or at least something very much like it, is appreciated. For example, the response of literary critics to an author's blockbusting first novel is often to hedge their bets. Praise may be glowing, but it is often couched in cautionary language that urges readers to wait for the next product; previous experience dictates that second novels are often less stellar than first ones. However, one might well ask if an appreciation of regression underlies these conservative predictions. Although in rare cases it may, more often some theory, and not random error, is credited with the poor second showing. Authors are said to "burn themselves out" on the first novel or to have "said it all," leaving no material for a second try. Others are thought to be immobilized or blocked by their first success. Although some of these points may, in fact, be true, regression alone is fully capable of accounting for the second-book effect. Yet, how often has one read a review of a mediocre second novel in which the critic pointed out that the inferior product could have been predicted by chance?

It is difficult to determine whether people's insufficiently regressive judgments represent errors or the misapplication of a normally effective judgmental strategy. When the world is stable, people's predictions about events should show an appreciation for regression. But when the world is changing, extreme predictions generated from relevant information may be appropriate. Extreme responses can occur at random, or they can signal that there has been a change in the process. Consider, as an example, a manufacturing company that has posted large economic losses. If those losses are seen as a random perturbation in an otherwise reasonable record, then one should predict that profits will soon regress to their mean level. However, if the large losses are seen as indicating deteriorating management or worsening market conditions, even more extreme predictions on the basis of the information may be jutified. Thus, people may learn from their environment that extreme fluctuations often signal changing conditions, and thus, their failure to be regressive may be adaptive in an environment that changes. Such sensitivity to change may, however, lead them to be insufficiently regressive when random extreme values occur in stable environments (Einhorn & Hogarth, 1981).

The Dilution Effect

Under some circumstances, the social perceiver can be induced to make conservative inferences. Suppose I tell you I have a friend, Judith, who is 35, unmarried, and has lived with the same female roommate for five years with whom she has just bought a house. You may conclude that she is probably a lesbian. However, if I also tell you that she is a paralegal, takes fiction writing courses in night school, drives a blue Toyota, and is very close to her brothers and sisters, you may wonder if she is lesbian, but not immediately assume that she is. Why? The first four bits of information can be thought of as *diagnostic* with respect to whether Judith is lesbian or not, because unmarried females with constant female companions are often thought to be so. However, the extra information about her job, car, and leisure activities diluted that diagnostic information with a lot of nondiagnostic information, that is, information that would not lead you to conclude that she is lesbian or straight, but which is simply neutral with respect to the inference. In short, I reduced her similarity to the stereotype of lesbianism by deepening her characterization and making her a person, so your confidence in drawing an extreme inference about her may thereby be lessened.

A number of studies have now examined this *dilution effect,* and most have shown that when diagnostic information is diluted with nondiagnostic information, inferences are less extreme (Nisbett, Zukier, & Lemley, 1981). One cannot conclude from this evidence that people understand the phenomenon of regression, however. When diagnostic information is highly predictive of some outcome and accordingly justifies extreme inferences, nondiagnostic information still dilutes it, leading to overly conservative predictions (H. Zukier, 1982). For example, knowing that a student's grade point average (GPA) has been extremely high should lead one to predict continued high performance. However, when the high GPA information is diluted with irrelevant information, such as the fact that the student drives a Honda, always wears plaid shirts, and used to work part-time as a draftsman, the social perceiver "corrects" for the nondiagnostic information and generates overly conservative predictions about future GPA.

There are several qualifications to the dilution effect. It does not hold when prior theories about the meaning of the initial information are weak (S. T. Fiske & Neuberg, 1990; Higgins & Bargh, 1987; Ruble & Stangor, 1986). The dilution effect also appears to apply only when new nondiagnostic information is typical and not extreme (G. Zukier & Jennings, 1983–84). A study illustrating this latter point created a courtroom situation involving subjects' judgments about a defendant's guilt. In the typical information condition, the defendant was average in physical and behavioral dimensions unrelated to guilt, whereas in the atypical condition, he was extreme on these dimensions. Typical nondiagnostic information had the usual effect of diluting diagnostic information, leading to more regressive judgments of guilt, whereas atypical information actually produced more extreme judgments of guilt. The authors concluded that dilution effects are due to contrasts between diagnostic and nondiagnostic information, rather than to nondiagnosticity of information itself.

When diluting nondiagnostic information turns out to be diagnostic for some other attribute, it loses its diluting capacity for the original information, and extreme inferences again result (Gangestad & Borgida, 1981). For example, the relevance of a high GPA for future academic performance may be diluted if one also learns that the student works out at the gym three hours every day; as a consequence, when asked to predict future academic performance, an overly conservative prediction (e.g., "he will do moderately well") will result. However, if one then learns that he is on the wrestling team, "working out" becomes diagnostic for wrestling. As a consequence, it no longer dilutes the GPA information, and a prediction of high future academic performance will result.

In recent years, psychologists have developed training techniques in an attempt to reduce the kinds of errors in judgment that are frequently seen. Ironically, at least some of these efforts actually increase the dilution effect. For example, one way in which people can be induced to process social information in a more complex manner that reduces the likelihood of such biases as belief perseverance and overconfidence in judgments is demands for accountability: a need to justify one's judgments to others. In a study by Tetlock and Boettger (1989), subjects who expected to have to justify their predictions in a judgment task diluted their predictions more in response to nondiagnostic information than did subjects who were not accountable for their inferences. Thus, being accountable for their judgments may induce people to use a wider range of information in making those judgments, but it does not necessarily make them more discriminating judges of how useful the information is.

The failure to appreciate regression, then, appears to be a robust oversight in the social perceiver's inferential inventory. Usually, regression is not detected, and even when it is, as in the second-novel example discussed earlier, people often assume that logical reasons rather than random factors explain the effect. Although extreme inferences due to ignorance of regression can be guarded against by the dilution effect, the dilution effect itself constitutes a misunderstanding of the relevance of diagnostic and nondiagnostic information to the judgment process.

Bayes' Theorem

Often, people are required to make predictions to future events on the basis of limited data. You may need to decide, for example, whether or not to get season tickets to your local repertory theater based on the sample of plays you have seen them perform in the past. Or, in trying to match up a friend with a new companion, you may think through the likelihood of whether or not they will be a good match and will get along with each other.

Bayes' theorem is a normative model for making statistically optimal predictions. To illustrate, consider the following example. Suppose there are two bags of poker chips, each containing mixtures of red and blue chips. Bag A contains 10 blue and 20 red chips, and Bag B contains 20 blue and 10 red chips. The subject's task is to draw a chip three times from the bag, see what color each chip is, and put it back in the bag after he or she has seen it. The subject is further told that 80 percent of the time, the chips will be from Bag A and that 20 percent of the time, they will be drawn from Bag B. The subject must then use information from the chips, the general knowledge regarding the numbers of blue and red chips in each bag, and the knowledge that Bag A will be selected 80 percent of the time and Bag B 20 percent of the time, to decide from which bag the three chips were drawn. Suppose the subject drew three chips, and they were blue-blue-red. Which bag would they have been drawn from? Most people would assume that it was likely that the chips came from Bag B, because two-thirds of the chips in Bag B are blue. Actually, the true odds are 2 to 1 that it was Bag A.

The way in which we calculate the exact odds for this game is by using Bayes' theorem. Bayes' theorem draws on two pieces of information: The first is the prior odds that the bag is A rather than B. These odds are 4 to 1, since Bag A is chosen 80 percent of the time. The second piece of information is likelihood: the ratio of the probability that the sample comes from A to the probability that it comes from B.

Let us consider how likely the bag selected was A. The probability of drawing a blue is 1 out of 3 and a red is 2 of 3. Consequently, the probability of drawing blue-blue-red is $\frac{1}{3} \times \frac{1}{3} \times \frac{2}{3}$, which equals $\frac{2}{27}$. If, however, the bag is B, then the probability of drawing blue-blue-red is $\frac{2}{3} \times \frac{2}{3} \times \frac{1}{3}$, which equals $\frac{4}{27}$. The likelihood ratio is the probability that the sample came from A ($\frac{2}{27}$) divided by the probability that the sample came from B ($\frac{4}{27}$). This yields the odds of 1 to 2 that the sample is from Bag A rather than from Bag B. Using Bayes' theorem to combine the prior probability with the likelihood information, we multiply the prior probability ($\frac{4}{1}$) by the likelihood ($\frac{1}{2}$) which yields 2 to 1 in favor of the guess that the three chips actually came from Bag A. Most people are surprised that it is more likely that the chips came from Bag A (A. L. Glass & Holyoak, 1986). The reason for the surprise is that they ignore the base-rate information that Bag A will be selected 80 percent of the time. This robust bias, the tendency to ignore base-rate information, features in many social situations as well.

As we will see in the following sections, the social perceiver usually fails to make probabilistic judgments according to the criteria associated with Bayes' theorem. In the next section, we examine the underutilization of base-rate information.

Underutilizing Base-Rate Information

If you want to know how good a particular school's football team is, what would be your best source of information: going to one particular game or checking their win-loss record of the entire season? The answer, of course, is checking the season's win-loss record, since it provides a more reliable and valid indicator of the team's ability; a single game can be biased by many temporary factors, such as bad weather, injuries, or simply a bad day. Nonetheless, people's impressions are often overwhelmed by a particular example (e.g., a single game), when better assessments (e.g., the season record) are available. To put it more generally, even when sampling has already been done for an individual and he or she is presented with good estimates of population characteristics (such as averages, prior probabilities, or proportions), those estimates may not be appropriately brought to bear on judgment tasks. Earlier, in Chapter 3, it was pointed out that people underutilize consensus information in making causal attributions. This failure to use consensus information can be thought of as part of a larger problem. This problem is the tendency of people to ignore general, broadly based information about population characteristics (i.e., base-rate information) in favor of more concrete anecdotal but usually less valid and reliable information. Vibrant examples simply outweigh more reliable but abstract base-rate information (Bar-Hillel, 1980; S. E. Taylor & Thompson, 1982).

In one study, for example (Hamill, Wilson, & Nisbett, 1980), subjects read a colorful account of a woman who had been living on welfare with her numerous children for many years while maintaining a relatively affluent life style. This stereotypic case of welfare abuse was set in context either by base-rate statistics indicating that welfare recipients often take advantage of the system and stay on welfare a long time, or by statistics suggesting that the average welfare recipient is on the rolls only a short time, implying that the case history provided to subjects was highly atypical. Despite the available base-rate information, subjects responded as if the case history were representative of welfare recipients under both conditions, and their judgments were more influenced by it than by the more valid base-rate information (Ginossar & Trope, 1980; Hamill, Wilson, & Nisbett, 1980; S. E. Taylor & Thompson, 1982).

Perhaps people simply do not understand base-rate information or its relationship to judgment tasks. However, several studies have shown that when base-rate information is the only information available, people will draw on it as a basis for their inferences (Hamill, Wilson, & Nisbett, 1980; Nisbett & Borgida, 1975). For example, if you know a team's win-loss record and have never seen a particular game, you will clearly use the win-loss record to characterize the team's ability. Why are people so often swayed by colorful case history examples when better or qualifying base-rate information is also available?

One possibility is that people do not always see the relevance of base-rate information to a particular judgment task (Borgida & Brekke, 1981; Kassin, 1979b; Tversky & Kahneman, 1980; Zuckerman, 1979). A certain building in Los Angeles has been occupied by four different restaurants in less than three years. Each has failed, and that information should give any prospective restauranteur pause for thought. Nonetheless, as each culinary venture folds, an eager new one steps in to fill the breach, only to fail again. Presumably, each idealistic entrepreneur assumes that his or her own concept is the one that will make the place work (an Irish pub, a pasta place, soup and salad). None seemingly can appreciate the base-rate information that virtually screams out, "No one comes here!" Hence, each loses, so that the next inexperienced capitalist, ignorant of the relevance of base-rate information, can seal his or her own financial fate as well.

People do use base-rate information when its relevance is clear. For example, a number of studies demonstrate that people are more likely to use base-rate information if its causal relevance to the judgment task is made salient than if it is not (Ajzen, 1977; Hewstone, Benn, & Wilson, 1988; Manis et al., 1980; Tversky & Kahneman, 1980). In one study, subjects were told about a late-night auto accident involving a cab that an eyewitness thought might have been blue. Subjects were then informed that in that city, 85 percent of the cabs are green and 15 percent are blue. Although subjects should have concluded that the culprit's cab was probably green on the basis of the base-rate information, few did. Instead, most drew on the report of the eyewitness, and decided the cab was probably blue. However, a second group was told that 85 percent of the accidents in the city are caused by blue cabs and 15 percent by green cabs; these subjects did use the base-rate information to qualify their inferences. Presumably, people see accident rate statistics as relevant to judgments about accidents, whereas they do not perceive information about the prevalence of particular cabs as relevant to the judgment, although in fact it is. Hence, when people perceive base-rate information as relevant to a judgment, they use it in preference to colorful case history information. Interestingly enough, the mirror image of this effect is also true; when researchers manipulate case history information so it is less relevant to the judgment task, people ignore it in favor of base-rate information (Ginossar & Trope, 1980).

At least some so-called failures to use base-rate information may be attributed to experimental procedures. Formal rules of conversation dictate that people communicate primarily information that is intended to be informative and fill a gap in a recipient's knowledge (Grice, 1975; Turnbull & Slugoski, 1988). The fact that experiments emphasize individuating case information over constant base-rate information may lead subjects to perceive that the case history information but not the base-rate information is relevant to the judgment task. Hence, the appearance of overusing case history information may simply result from conditions in which it is perceived as presented to convey meaningfulness (Schwarz et al., 1991).

Several theoretical explanations for the base-rate fallacy have been offered. Kahneman and Tversky (1973) suggested that case history information is more representative of a category than base-rate information is. When people read case history information, they make immediate associations to larger categories and thus appear to overuse the case history information for drawing inferences. Drawing on the causal relevance data described earlier, Ajzen (1977) has emphasized the use of a causality heuristic, arguing that people will use base-rate information if its causal relevance to the judgment task is made salient, but not if they fail to perceive a causal connection between base-rate information and the judgment. Nisbett and Ross (1980) argued that the use of case histories over base-rate information may depend upon the greater vividness of case history information. According to this argument, the vivid quality of the more compelling case examples simply overwhelms the pallid and dull statistical information (Nisbett & Ross, 1980). However, an analysis of the so-called vividness effect suggests that this interpretation may be in error (S. E. Taylor & Thompson, 1982; see Chapter 7). Ginossar and Trope (1980) have emphasized the relative diagnosticity of base-rate versus case history information, arguing that people are better able to see the diagnostic value of case history than base-rate information, except under circumstances in which the diagnostic value of base-rate information is highlighted. Finally, Lyon and Slovick (1976) have argued that the credibility of the source is an important determinant of which information is used. As source credibility declines, faith in case history information may also decline (see also Hinsz et al., 1988).

Bar-Hillel (1980) has argued that the criterion that determines whether or not people use base-rate information in their judgments is relevance, and that causal relations, representativeness of alternative case information, and the specificity or vividness of information may all influence perceived relevance (see McGraw, 1987a). Efforts to test among these various theoretical accounts have suggested that all of them may have at least some bearing on the base-rate fallacy, with Bar-Hillel's (1980) explanation providing a more encompassing theoretical explanation than those that draw on single principles of relevance, such as vividness or causal relation.

The appropriate question regarding the use of base-rate information is *when* is it used, rather than if it is used. Clearly, there are conditions that favor the incorporation of base-rate information into judgments. Most judgments are task-specific and goal-oriented. When base-rate information is seen as relevant to the task and appropriate to a goal, it is more likely to be used than when these preconditions are not met (Bar-Hillel, 1980). Base-rate information is most likely to be used when it is perceived as causally relevant to the judgment at hand (Ajzen, 1977), or when it is made concrete (Manis et al., 1980). In this context, Brekke and Borgida (1988) examined the impact of base-rate information in a mock trial of an acquaintance rape case. They found that if base-rate information regarding rape was presented early in a trial and an example was tied directly to the specific case at hand, mock jurors were more likely to use it in reaching their judgments than if the information was presented later in the trial or not linked directly to the case. H. Zukier and Pepitone (1984) found that the subject's set also influenced the use of base-rate information. When subjects were given a scientific ("paradigmatic") orientation to a task as opposed to a clinical ("narrative") orientation, they were more likely to use base-rate information; a clinical orientation produced greater use of individualized case history information. In their study, the base-rate information was broad-based and noncausal, indicating that when problems are framed appropriately, people can make use of base-rate information even if its causal relevance or specific applicability to the problem at hand is not salient.

To summarize, then, people often do not incorporate base-rate and other statistical information adequately into an inference task. When other, less valid, but more engaging, anecdotal evidence is present, people may ignore relevant base rates (Bar-Hillel & Fischhoff, 1981; Manis, Avis, & Cardoze, 1981; Manis et al., 1980). The greater vividness or catchiness of other kinds of information, such as case histories, does not seem to be the reason why people underutilize base-rate information. Rather, it may be that people do not usually see the relevance of base rates to social judgments, in comparison with other types of information.

The base-rate fallacy has been applied to decision making (Hogarth, 1980; Nisbett & Ross, 1980) and stereotyping (Locksley et al., 1980; Locksley, Hepburn, & Ortiz, 1982; but see Rasinski, Crocker, & Hastie, 1985). The consequences of the failure to use base-rate information can be extreme.

The Conjunction Error

Many of the biases in everyday inference suggest a conservative bent that favors prior beliefs or theories over new and sometimes statistically superior evidence. However, given the task of generating future predictions from simple probabilistic information, the perceiver sometimes looks like a radical (Crandall & Greenfield, 1986). Consider the following example. Comedians make their living, in part, by sketching out highly recognizable portraits of people which make us laugh. "Consider the Nerd. He's a skinny guy, right? He walks like this? [Comedian minces across the stage.] And he carries a briefcase even if it's empty?" With each detail, the audience's laugh of recognition grows. Yet, the paradox of the well-drawn portrait is that with each detail, recognizability increases, but actual probability of occurrence decreases. One might well find a nerd on the street and he might be skinny, but the likelihood that he would also be mincing and carrying a briefcase is low. The likelihood that any two or more events will co-occur (i.e., their joint probability) is the product of their probabilities of occurring alone; accordingly, their joint probability cannot exceed the probability of the least probable event. Under some circumstances, however, people make more extreme predictions for the joint occurrence of events than for a single event. This error is termed the conjunction fallacy (Abelson & Gross, 1987; Leddo, Abelson, & Gross, 1984; Tversky & Kahneman, 1983).

In one study (Slovic, Fischhoff, & Lichtenstein, 1977), researchers gave subjects information about individuals and then asked them to predict the likelihood that particular events would occur in their lives, either jointly or singly. For example, subjects were told that an individual was gregarious and literary. When asked how likely it was that he was an engineering major, they responded that it was very unlikely. However, when asked how likely it was that he would start out as an engineering major and switch to journalism, an event with a far lower likelihood of occurrence than simply majoring in engineering, subjects gave this a much higher rating. Presumably, they could readily imagine how a gregarious, literary person would decide journalism was for him and not engineering, but they could not imagine how such a person would remain an engineer.

People appear to prefer conjunctive explanations for many events. We understand intuitively that much human action can be best understood as resulting from multiple factors that supplement each other. This seems to be particularly true for goal-directed behavior. For example, one may visit an art gallery to relax, to get away from the office, to see the work of a particularly exciting artist, to enjoy the companionship of a friend, and to have a change of scene, all of which may occur simultaneously. Thus, when people are inferring the motives underlying other people's goals, they prefer conjunctive explanations, which take into account simultaneously several possible reasons for a goal.

The preference for conjunctive explanations is a robust effect. It occurs for both important and trivial actions, it occurs whether an individual has a single goal in mind for an action or multiple goals, and it occurs whether the information involved in the conjunctive explanation is plausible or implausible (Leddo, Abelson, & Gross, 1984). Even instructions designed to induce subjects to focus on the unique aspects of a conjunction, which might be expected to reduce the effect, reveal robust preferences for conjunctive explanations (Read, 1988). Efforts to train people in the statistical principles underlying the conjunctive fallacy can lower, but do not eliminate, the conjunctive error (Crandall & Greenfield, 1986; Morier & Borgida, 1984).

Qualifications to the conjunction effect have been uncovered. Zuckerman, Eghrari, and Lambrecht (1986) found that conjunctive explanations are more likely when subjects are asked to explain an event than if they are simply asked to infer an interpretation for the event. Conjunctive explanations are also typically not found for conditions of nonaction. When actors fail to take particular actions, conjunction effects disappear; that is, people do not show a systematic preference for explanations that offer multiple explanations for inaction (Leddo, Abelson, & Gross, 1984; see also Read, 1988). Some research has found that conjunctions of causes are perceived as more likely for successful or completed actions than for failure and uncompleted actions. However, these effects may depend upon the fact that research has differentially measured causes that are individually associated with success, but omitted causes typically associated with failure, such as task difficulty. A recent investigation (McClure et al., 1989) found that conjunctions of internal causes and task-related goals were rated as more probable for success than failure, but conjunctions of external causes and competing goals were rated as more probable for failure than success. These results suggest that which causes are included in the conjunction significantly affect its perceived probability.

Several reasons for conjunction effects have been offered (Leddo, Abelson, & Gross, 1984; Read, 1988, 1989; Einhorn & Hogarth, 1986; G. L. Wells, 1985). Leddo, Abelson, & Gross (1984) argued that people generally try to understand others' actions in terms of those other persons' personal goals. Conjunctive explanations, which provide more detailed information about a particular goal or information about multiple goals, tend to be preferred because they are perceived as informative. Thus, for example, asking a friend why he treated himself to a fancy dinner alone on a week night, one may be better satisfied with a conjunctive explanation ("I needed a change of scene and I was depressed because my girlfriend and I broke up"), than with a simpler explanation ("I just wanted to get out of the house"). While the former explanation is less likely from a probabilistic standpoint (the likelihood that one both wanted a change of scene and had broken up with a girlfriend is less probable than simply wanting a change of scene), the explanation has a better fit to our beliefs about why people sometimes treat themselves to expensive dinners alone on week nights. This account of the preference for conjunctive explanations draws on knowledge structure theory (schemas) and argues that people use their knowledge of the content of a situation to construct an explanatory frame for events. Frames, like event schemas or scripts, represent people's notions about the structure of an event and provide slots for typical goals that people have and enabling conditions that make the event possible. Conjunctive explanations may simply fill out an explanatory frame for the situation better than single explanations. This explanation has been termed the *multiple goal frame interpretation*. The Leddo, Abelson, & Gross explanation has been called into question by subsequent research that has found conjunction effects for failed actions and for occurrences, which are not goal-based actions. The multiple goal frame explanation would not appear to cover these instances (Zuckerman, Eghrari, & Lambrecht, 1986; see also McClure et al., 1989).

Einhorn and Hogarth (1986) have suggested that conjunctive explanations may be perceived as more likely to be used than single explanations because they co-opt alternative explanations for the behavior. Thus, people are not motivated to consider alternative explanations because the conjunctive explanation appears to rule those alternatives out. Knowing that one's friend treated himself to a fancy dinner shortly after he and his girlfriend broke up precludes wondering whether he received a bonus at work or a gift of money in the mail.

Another possibility is that events typically have multiple necessary causes (Kelley, 1972b) and conjunctive explanations are favored over single explanations because they match the features of the multiple necessary schema. In apparent support of the multiple necessary causes argument, Locksley and Stangor (1984) found that conjunctive explanations were more likely to be preferred for rare than for common events.

The criterion of representativeness also seems to be implicated in conjunction effects (Tversky & Kahneman, 1983). As information is added to a description that rounds out a human portrait and makes the portrait seem more likely, the objective probability that the portrait is true goes down, but its resemblance to a real person goes up: it matches our general theories more closely. Consequently, use of this representativeness criterion increases the perception of probability. Wells (1985) tested the representativeness explanation for the conjunction effect and found that pairing unrepresentative events in explanations virtually eliminated the conjunction effect, whereas the pairing of a representative with an unrepresentative event or the pairing of two representative events produced substantially higher rates of the conjunction error. In short, then, when people are assessing the likelihood that several seemingly related events will occur in conjunction, they will often ignore the objective probability of their conjunction in favor of a scenario that makes the conjoint probability of the multiple events seem true.

Integrating Information

The task of bringing information together and combining it into a judgment can be problematic when evaluated against the normative model. The person's combinatorial shortcomings are particularly well illustrated when he or she is matched against a computer given the same information. The computer always does as well or better (R. Dawes, Faust, & Meehl, 1989). How can one demonstrate this fact?

First, it is necessary to find a judgment task in which roughly the same kinds of information are contained in every case; second, there must be a decision rule regarding how that information is to be combined to reach a decision for each case. Such judgment tasks are relatively common. Stock must be reordered after considering likely demand, current inventory, and cash flow. Patients must be diagnosed and treated once clinical observations, symptoms, and test results are presented. Students are admitted to or rejected from graduate school on the basis of test scores, grade point average, past work, and letters of recommendation. A normatively appropriate way of completing such a task is to take each case (e.g., student), take each of the bits of information relevant to the judgment (e.g., GPA, letters of recommendation, GRE scores), multiply each bit by its weight (e.g., count GREs twice as much as GPA and GPA half again as much as letters of recommendation), add it up for a total case score, and compare the case's score against other case scores to pick the best ones. This process employs a *linear model,* so called because the total impression is an additive combination of the available information. It is a task that can be efficiently and effectively completed by a properly programmed computer.

It should be noted that a linear combination is not the only way such repeating decisions can be reliably made. Various *nonlinear* combinations may also be reliably utilized to make decisions. The following two decision rules are nonlinear: "Place full order of stock when inventory drops to 35 percent, unless previous order was placed more than six months ago, in which case order only half as much." Or "Weigh GPA twice as heavily as letters of recommendation, unless GPA is lower than 3.0, in which case weigh it evenly with letters." The nonlinear nature of these rules makes them no less readily programmable for a computer, so they can be employed for decision-making purposes as readily as a linear combination. And, more to the point, using either type of rule is more reliable than the human decision maker.

Unfortunately, the human decision maker often has an exaggerated view of his or her ability to accomplish this task, so much so that the idea of letting it fall to a computer meets with strenuous objections. Clinical intuition, it is felt, would be sacrificed to a rigid numerical formula, and unusual instances or special cases would slip through the cracks.

Anyone who has ever sat on an admissions or membership committee and seen "clinical intuition" in operation probably knows that the process is often random and inconsistent, full of blatant stereotyping, unwarranted favoritism, and irrational dislikes. R. Dawes (1980) presents a particularly entertaining account of the process at several leading universities. A slang peculiar to the admissions process quickly develops. *Pinnochios* are applicants with high ratings from letter writers on all but one characteristic, such as maturity or independence; hence their profile has a long jag or nose. They are to be avoided, since anyone who attracts enough attention to get that low a rating on some attribute must be really bad. *Jock essays* are essays that are too short; *geos* are students that would add geographic diversity, such as a Hawaiian applying to an East coast school. And everyone seems to be looking for the proverbial "neat small-town kid." Very often, comparisons are made to apparently similar students with whom one has already had experience. "Aha. Another Smedley. He was smart, but a drudge. Not a creative bone in his body" (Abelson, 1976). Frequently, these analogies are drawn on the basis of minimal similarity, such as having a record that excels in everything except physical education.

Despite such problems, this process is loudly defended. Its advocates maintain that generally, decision makers do use the linear model, and that departures from the model are made so as to pick up the late bloomer or the prodigal child returning to the fold. Table 9.2 presents a hypothetical account of the process employed for two fictitious graduate school admissions cases given a linear decision rule, a nonlinear decision rule, and an intuitive human decision maker (see Burgess, 1941; L. R. Goldberg, 1968, 1970).

Two extensive analyses of studies have pitted the clinical judge against the computer or other mechanical aids (Meehl, 1954; J. Sawyer, 1966); both yielded the same conclusion: computers or other mechanical aids always do as well or better than clinical judges. What does the computer do, and why does it do it so well? The computer merely does more consistently what human judges believe they do. It uses the criteria established by people, but it uses them consistently, weighs them in a reliable way, combines the information accurately, and makes a judgment. What does the human decision maker do wrong? People usually believe they are using more cues and making more complex judgments than they actually are. One professor, upon reading this research, correlated her own rankings of prospective students with several admissions criteria and found, to her embarrassment and surprise, that GRE scores were virtually the sole basis of her decisions. Not only do people not use as many cues as they think they are using, they also do not weigh those cues the way they believe they do. One may believe one is giving extra weight to prior evidence of research skills when one actually is not. Thus, when it comes to combining multiple sources of information, the social perceiver is again misled by hunches about particular individuals' probable successes or failures or by attention to one, instead of multiple, cues (R. M. Dawes, 1976, 1980).

Although support for clinical judgment lingers, it is clear that for decisions that can be made using a constant decision rule, the computer

TABLE 9.2 COMPARISON OF THE LINEAR MODEL, THE NONLINEAR MODEL, AND A HUMAN DECISION MAKER: WILL STINCH AND CRABBLE BE ADMITTED TO GRADUATE SCHOOL?

	Case A: Gerald Stinch	*Case B: Amanda Crabble*
	GRE: 650 Verbal, 710 Math GPA: 3.8 Letters of recommendation: Hard-working, diligent	GRE: 620 Verbal, 590 Math GPA: 2.9 Letters of recommendation: A bit of a dreamer, hasn't come into her own
Linear model (as applied by computer)	Score = 2 (GREs)+1 (GPA) + .5 (Letter of recommendation)	
Decision:	Admit Stinch.	Reject Crabble.
Nonlinear model (as applied by computer)	Score = 2 (GREs)+1 (GPA) + .5 (Letter of recommendation), unless GPA is less than 3.0, in which case score is 3 (GREs) + .5 (GPA) + 1 (Letter of recommendation)	
Decision:	Admit Stinch.	Reject Crabble.
Human decision maker	Aha. Another Smedley. Not a creative bone in his body.	Aha. Another Woodley? She was a great theoretician—got off to a slow start, though.
Decision:	Reject Stinch.	Admit Crabble.
Probable outcome given reliable and valid admissions criteria	Stinch will do well.	Crabble will do less well.

outperforms the person. Clinical judges are, of course, important in picking out what variables need to go into the decision. However, when it comes to integrating the information to reach a decision, the person is best left out of the process (R. Dawes, Faust, & Meehl, 1989).

Assessing Covariation

Judgments of covariation, that is, how strongly two things are related, are essential to many inference tasks, both formal and informal. Much of our folk wisdom states correlations such as the adage, "Blondes have more fun," or the assumption that all work and no play leads to dullness. Mickey Gilley's observation, "Don't the girls all get prettier at closing time?" (Don't the boys, too?) assumes a correlation between time and perceived attractiveness (Pennebaker et al., 1979). Covariation is also the basis of many formal inference tasks. Kelley's covariation model of attribution (see Chapter 2) presupposes that the social perceiver is able to observe the covariation of an outcome across time, modality, persons, and entities with at least reasonable accuracy, so that an attribution can be formulated. Schemas (Chapters 4–5) are believed to be formed through the observation of co-occurring events.

Given the importance of covariation to judgment tasks, the question of how well the perceiver detects covariation is a critical one. The answer seems to be not very well (see Crocker, 1981; Nisbett & Ross, 1980, for reviews), when one compares the naive perceiver's estimates with the normative statistical model for assessing covariation (see Smedslund, 1963; Ward & Jenkins, 1965, for early references). The normative model for calculating covariation consists of several specific steps, and the research evidence to date suggests that there are sources of potential bias in each step. These steps are illustrated in Figure 9.2.

First, the perceiver must understand what data are relevant to assess covariation. For example, to test the adage, "Blondes have more fun," one needs to know the number of blonde men and women who have fun, the number of blondes who do not, the number of brunettes and redheads who have fun, and the number of brunettes and redheads who do not. Most people do not realize that all four kinds of evidence are relevant to the covariation task; rather they tend to concentrate primarily on the fun-loving blondes, believing that evidence that supports the adage is most relevant to its truth value. Indeed, this is a general propensity of the social perceiver that has been noted in other contexts; when testing the validity of an idea, people tend to seek instances that confirm the idea, rather than instances on all sides of the issue (e.g., Arkes & Harkness, 1980; G. H. Bower, Black, & Turner, 1979; Franks & Bransford, 1971; see also Fazio, Sherman, & Herr, 1982, for a related point). Yet, by nature, such statements as "Blondes have more fun" are comparative (All blondes or most? More fun than whom?), so all four types of information are needed.

The second step in assessing covariation is sampling cases, because, as in the case above, one obviously cannot check out all blonde, brunette, and redheaded men and women. As has been noted, people are very poor samplers. Their own range of acquaintances and contacts, on whom they frequently draw, is certainly biased, but most people seem to be unaware of this fact (Crocker, 1981). Small samples may be overused (Tversky & Kahneman, 1974), and when sample results disagree with one's own hunches, the sample results may be rejected or go unrecognized as contradictory (Arkes & Harkness, 1980; Crocker, 1981).

The third step in the covariation process is classifying instances as to type of evidence. Here again, prior expectations can get in the way. Negative instances, that is, cases that contradict the proposed relationship, may be mislabeled as positive if they are ambiguous, or if not, dis-

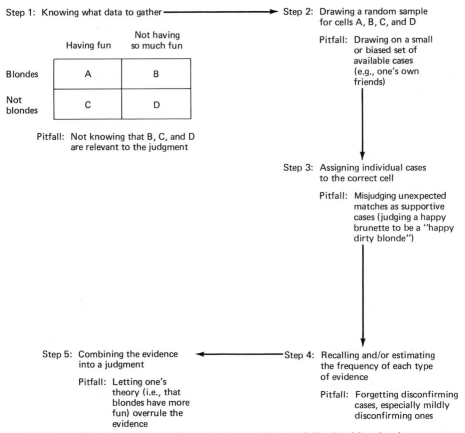

FIGURE 9.2 The assessment of covariation and its pitfalls: Do blondes have more fun?

missed as being due to error or faulty sampling. Positive instances that fit expectations are more quickly or easily identified and incorporated into the inference task (e.g., R. J. Harris, Teske, & Ginns, 1975; Owens, Bower, & Black, 1979). Nonoccurrences of the event are especially difficult for people to process (Allison & Messick, 1988).

In the fourth stage, the perceiver must recall the evidence and estimate the frequency of each type of evidence. As was evident in Chapters 4, 5, and 8, memory is certainly not infallible; it is particularly good for confirming cases and, under some circumstances, it is also good for strongly disconfirming cases. Thus, the ecstatic blonde and the deliriously happy raven-haired person may be remembered, while the three happy "mousy-browns" may be forgotten.

Finally, and only after the previous four steps have been completed, the social perceiver is ready to combine the evidence in the proper form. How successfully is this task accomplished? In fact, the ability of the social perceiver to estimate degree of covariation, once all the data have been assembled, appears to be fairly good. Previous researchers have often confused errors of perceived relevance, sampling, classification, and recall of evidence as errors in computation, thereby underestimating the social perceiver's computational abilities (Crocker, 1981). This is not, however, to suggest either that the perceiver successfully computes correlation coefficients in his or her head or that estimates of covariation, however made, are usually accurate. Perceivers' estimates of covariation generally track, though appear often to underestimate, actual covariation, as long as no strong prior expectation about the degree of relationship between the two variables exists (Jennings, Amabile, & Ross, 1982).

Certain ways of presenting covariation information favor accuracy more than others (C. A. Anderson, Lane, & Kellam, 1986; Lane, Anderson, & Kellam, 1985). People tend to be more accurate in their estimations of covariation when the actual frequencies of cases are low, when all information can be observed simultaneously rather than serially, when the data are summarized, when instructions are clear, when there is repeated exposure to the data (Cordray & Shaw, 1978; Crocker, 1982; Trolier & Hamilton, 1986), when there are no competing sources of social information (Fiedler & Stroehm, 1986), and when the concept of noncontingency (i.e., the absence of a relationship between two variables) is understood (see Crocker, 1981, for a review). Estimates of covariation are more accurate when people are highly familiar with the data in question and when the data are very codable, that is, capable of being cast into a form that would permit covariation assessment and subsequent interpretation (Kunda & Nisbett, 1986). Novices, or those unfamiliar with the task domain, appear to show the bias in favor of confirming evidence more than those expert in the task domain (Borgida & DeBono, 1989). The most important factor influencing inaccuracy in covariation estimates is whether or not individuals have a theory or prior expectation about the relationship between the two variables (Nisbett & Ross, 1980). When people have no theory, they may somewhat underestimate or not perceive a covariation, even when a statistician would consider the relationship to be quite strong (Jennings, Amabile, & Ross, 1982).

As just noted, problems in covariation estimation appear to reflect a larger problem-solving strategy, which involves the oft-noted confirmatory bias in hypothesis testing (see Chapters 4, 5, and 6). That is, when people have a hypothesis about the relationship between variables, they tend to look for evidence that confirms that hypothesis rather than assess the evidence in a more even-handed manner. Klayman and Ha (1987) argue that the confirmatory bias in covariation estimation may represent a misapplication of a generally effective strategy. They maintain that the search for positive test cases is a general strategy that cuts across many content areas and many types of inference tasks; people use it as a general problem-solving strategy: (a) when they do not have available a strategy specific to the particular problem under investigation, or (b) when task demands preclude the use of a more specific strategy. They suggest that the positive-cases strategy may result from the tendency to test cases that are expected to have the property of interest rather than cases that do not, a heuristic that generally results in, but is not equivalent to, a confirmatory bias. They point out that when people test hypotheses by looking at instances in which the target property is known to be present, i.e., positive cases, they maximize their information, particularly if the attribute they are examining is relatively rare in the population.

Moreover, a uniform prescription for seeking falsification of one's hypotheses does not exist. The strategies for disconfirming hypotheses are neither simple nor always clear. Under at least some circumstances, an examination of positive test cases may also provide evidence relevant to disconfirmation of a hypothesis. Consider, for example, the attempt to understand a rare phenomenon. Looking for an occurrence among negative test cases is like looking for a needle in a haystack. For example, looking for an AIDS victim among people not at risk for AIDS is not informative regarding who gets AIDS and who doesn't. However, finding a negative instance in a sample of positive test cases (e.g., a high-risk population) would be quite informative. Thus, in the case of rare events, the likelihood of getting useful information from negative instances among positive test cases would be higher than getting useful information by searching negative test cases for positive instances.

The previous discussion has implied that people usually test positive cases or engage in confirmatory biases when testing hypotheses. However, there appear to be conditions under which people use information relevant to falsification. People do use information about alternative hypotheses when it is made available to them (Trope & Mackie, 1987). People will use alternative information spontaneously if it is implicitly suggested by a situational context or if it has been recently or frequently activated by other inference tasks (see Ginossar & Trope, 1987; Higgins, Bargh, & Lombardi, 1985; Higgins & King, 1981; Trope & Mackie, 1987).

Alloy and Tabachnik (1984) reviewed the literature on assessment of covariation and developed an integrative model to explain covariation estimation by both humans and animals. They argue that judgments of covariation depend upon the joint influence of prior expectations about the domain and the situational information regarding the relationship (that is, data about specific instances). Data will have less impact under circumstances when prior expectations are strong. The impact of data depends upon both how much is available and whether they are presented in a form that the organism can make use of. Accuracy is dependent in a large part upon whether prior expectations and situational information converge or diverge, with greater accuracy under conditions of convergence. From this standpoint, organisms' errors in contingency judgments may stem from a generally successful inferential strategy, which in the long run preserves accuracy by not much altering contingency estimations from a general principle on the basis of a single and potentially abberant encounter (see also Alloy, 1988; Goddard & Allan, 1988).

Illusory Correlation

When a relationship between two variables is expected, subjects often overestimate the degree of relationship that exists or impose a relationship when none actually exists. This intriguing phenomenon has been termed *illusory correlation.* In an early example of the illusory correlation phenomenon, Chapman (1967) presented college-student subjects with lists of paired words such as *lion-tiger, lion eggs,* and *bacon-eggs.* Subjects were then asked to report how often each word was paired with each other word; in fact, all words were paired with each other an equal number of times. Nonetheless, subjects reported that words that were associated in meaning such as *bacon-eggs* had been paired more frequently than those not associated in meaning. Within the word list, in addition, there had been two items that were longer than the other words in the list, specifically *blossoms* and *notebook.* Subjects also inferred that these two words had more frequently been paired, apparently because they shared the distinctive quality of length. Chapman reasoned, then, that at least two factors can produce an illusory correlation: *associative meaning,* in which two items are seen as belonging together because they "ought" to on the basis of prior expectations (e.g., *bacon-eggs*); and *paired distinctiveness,* in which two items are thought to go together because they share some unusual feature (*blossoms-notebook*) (see also Chapman & Chapman, 1967, 1969).

Illusory correlation has been examined as a basis of sterotyping (D. L. Hamilton, 1979). D. L. Hamilton and Gifford (1976) argued that paired distinctiveness can explain some negative stereotypes of minority group members. Specifically, majority-group members have relatively few contacts with minority-group members, and negative behaviors are also relatively infrequent. It may be that members of the majority group make an illusory correlation between the two rare events and infer that minority-group members are more likely to engage in negative behaviors. To test this point, Hamilton and Gifford gave subjects a list of statements about members of group A and group B. Statements about group A were twice as numerous as statements

about group B, and positive statements were twice as numerous as negative ones; the relative frequency of positive and negative statements
was the same for both groups. Nonetheless, the subjects misrecalled
the uncommon, negative behaviors as more frequently paired with the
uncommon group, group B. The study was also replicated with positive
events as the more infrequent ones, and the results indicated that an
illusory correlation between minority status and positive features can
occur as well. However, since negative events are perceived to be more
rare than positive events (Parducci, 1968), the more likely situation in
real life is that minority-group members and negative events will be disproportionately perceived to covary.

Certainly, other factors than paired distinctiveness contribute to the
development of negative stereotypes. Majority-group members may
have a disproportionately negative sample of minority-group members'
behavior, because they usually encounter minority-group members in
low status roles and because the news media more frequently highlight
minority-group members' negative acts. Furthermore, majority-group
members may already hold negative stereotypes about minority
groups. Accordingly, an associative meaning basis for seeing a relationship between minority-group members' behavior and negative behavior
may also exist. Research by McArthur and Friedman (1980), in fact, confirms that both associative meaning (or prior expectations) and paired
distinctiveness contribute to the stereotyping of minority-group members.

Despite the apparent importance of associative meaning in stereotype-based illusory correlation effects, the majority of research has focused on paired distinctiveness. A meta-analysis of the paired distinctiveness illusory correlation effect suggests that the effect is highly
consistent and moderate in size (Mullen & Johnson, 1990). Extensive
research has identified the conditions under which this effect is more or
less strong. The paired distinctiveness illusory correlation is stronger
when the distinctive behaviors are negative and when memory load is
high (Mullen & Johnson, 1990). Other more specific principles are
emerging as well. People in a state of arousal may show a stronger illusory correlation effect than unaroused subjects, because arousal may
increase reliance on stereotypes and schemas, and it reduces capacity
for more elaborate problem solving (Kim & Baron, 1988). When subjects
are asked to form an impression of the individuals involved in the stimulus materials, the illusory correlation effect is attenuated, compared to
conditions under which they are simply instructed to memorize which
stimulus person had which attributes (Pryor, 1986). The illusory correlation bias is attenuated, though not eliminated, when information
about a third group is included (S. J. Sherman, Hamilton, & Roskos-
Ewoldsen, 1989). The effect also can be undermined in conditions when
subjects are presented with information about themselves and others

failing across several tasks; this result suggests that motivational needs (prompted by threats to the self) can weaken illusory correlation effects (Sanbonmatsu et al., 1987).

The illusory correlation effect appears to show a high degree of generalizability. When subjects form a negative impression of a group in one domain (e.g., the intellectual domain), the results generalize into other domains (e.g., the social domain). Thus, illusory correlations appear to produce pervasive views of a group's attributes rather than being confined to the attributes described in the stimulus materials (Acorn, Hamilton, & Sherman, 1988).

Agreement with one's own opinion can function in a manner similar to other salient information in the paired distinctiveness paradigm, such that people see their own distinctive opinions as linked to the minority position (Spears, van der Pligt, & Eiser, 1986). Conversely, the salience of one's own position can weaken the illusory correlation effect when it is pitted against distinctiveness (Spears, van der Pligt, & Eiser, 1985; see D. L. Hamilton & Sherman, 1989, for a review).

Several studies have attempted to identify exactly what the cognitive processes are whereby illusory correlations occur. There appear to be some differences between illusory correlations formed about individuals and those formed about groups. Illusory correlations about individuals appear to result from on-line impression-based judgments, whereas those for groups seem to be memory-based (Sanbonmatsu, Sherman, & Hamilton, 1987). That is, for impressions of individuals, the bias appears to operate at encoding, not at the judgment stage (D. L. Hamilton, Dugan, & Trolier, 1985), whereas group illusory correlations may be derived from recalling group attributes (Sanbonmatsu, Sherman, & Hamilton, 1987).

The twin topics of covariation estimation and illusory correlation are important for several reasons. First, as a complex operation, the estimation of covariation represents a concatenation of many of the errors and biases in the social perceiver's intuitive strategies, such as detecting what information is relevant, sampling it correctly, and recalling it accurately. Second, because covariation is often an interim inference upon which other, more complex inferences are subsequently based, the flaws that mark covariation estimation may have repercussions farther down the line in terms of the accuracy with which the social perceiver describes and acts on the environment. Third, errors in the estimation of covariation again highlight how the inference process is biased conservatively toward conclusions that people expect to be true and how the theories people have regarding the functioning of the social environment predominate in guiding the inference process. As we will see in the next section, these theories also predominate in the social perceiver's interpretation of the past. Finally, covariation estimation and the illusory correlations that may substitute for accurate assessment make their way into social interaction, shaping erroneous perceptions of reality as through the maintenance of stereotypes (D. L. Hamilton & Sherman, 1989) or the biased interpretations of patients' behavior by clinicians (e.g., Kayne & Alloy, 1988).

Learning from the Past

The maxim, "Those who ignore the past are condemned to relive it," implies that, were we scrupulously to turn our attention backward in time, rather than forward, we would learn important lessons. Although this adage may contain an element of truth, research on hindsight questions how seriously we ought to believe it. Everyone is familiar with the Monday morning quarterback who, with the advantage of retrospection, knows what could have and should have been done to win the weekend's game. He claims that the opposition's moves could have been anticipated, that the home team ought to have foreseen them, and that a particular strategy (his) clearly would have been successful.

Twenty-twenty hindsight seems to be a robust phenomenon. Work by Fischhoff and others (J. Baron & Hershey, 1988; Fischhoff, 1975, 1980, 1982b; Fischhoff & Beyth, 1975; Fischhoff, Slovic, & Lichtenstein, 1977; Janoff-Bulman, Timko, & Carli, 1985) indicates that it is very difficult to ignore knowledge of an actual outcome and to generate unbiased inferences about what could or should have happened. In retrospect, people exaggerate what could have been anticipated. Moreover, when people's predictions about future events are compared with postdictions about events that have already happened, results show that people distort and misremember their own predictions to conform with what really happened (D. J. Bem & McConnell, 1970; Fischhoff & Beyth, 1975).

A meta-analysis of 122 studies of the hindsight bias (Christensen-Szalanski & Fobian, in press) indicates that it is small but reliable. Certain factors reliably increase or decrease its strength. People are less likely to reduce in retrospect a probability assessment when told that an event did not occur than they are to increase in retrospect their probability assessment when told that the event did occur. The magnitude of the hindsight bias is reduced when people are familiar with or experienced in the domain under investigation (Christensen-Szalanski & Fobian, in press).

The social perceiver's ubiquitous theory-generating capacity is a major basis for reconstructing the past (cf. M. Ross, 1989). Even the most random sequence of events can be forced with enough thought into a logical causal chain. Once that causal chain of reasons is in place, it may be hard to see events as other than inevitable. Furthermore, interventions that would presumably have set some other causal sequence into effect may seem particularly compelling because they seem so logical. Chance or situational factors that may have heavily influenced what actually occurred may be overlooked. For example, in a football game, an opponent's series of moves may appear to be part of an overall plan, when in fact it capitalizes on chance events such as an injury or a fumble. Nonetheless, once labeled as a plan, it is likely to be seen as predictable ("They did the same thing in the Tennessee game"), and solutions to it may seem obvious ("We should have switched to a running game"). The preceding analysis implies that the hindsight bias is more motivated by cognitive factors related to the ability to construct causal explanations for events, rather than to motivational factors such as the desire to appear correct in retrospect. In fact, analyses of the hindsight bias suggest that cognitive factors probably do have more of a role in the bias than motivational ones (Christensen-Szalanski & Fobian, in press).

What ought we to learn from the past? Rarely are the lessons of history clear, since inevitably they are inextricably tinged with the advantage of hindsight. Participants in events do not know the full import of those events before they happen ("Dear Diary, The Hundred Years' War started today," Fischer, 1970, cited in Fischhoff, 1980, p. 84). Since it is hard to estimate what should have been foreseen and still harder to assess the role of environmental and chance factors in producing outcomes that have already occurred, what is actually learned from history is unclear.

In short, we are creatures of the present, trapped inferentially by what we already know. As in the case of other inference tasks, our methods of assessment can be driven by a priori or easily constructed theories, rather than by objective data. Finally, the answers themselves, that is, what we should be learning from the past, are indeterminate. Perhaps, then, a better maxim than that which opened this section might be one of Fischhoff's own: "While the past entertains, enobles, and expands quite readily, it enlightens only with delicate coaxing" (1980, p. 80).

Decision-Framing Effects

Judgments and decisions are affected not only by knowing the outcome involved but also by the ways in which the initial decision or judgment question is framed and in which the background context of the choice is described. Kahneman and Tversky (1984; Tversky & Kahneman, 1981) suggest that people often fail to recognize that problems are similar to each other and instead are distracted by surface characteristics concerning how those problems are presented. The presentation of the problem is called the *decision frame*, and constitutes the way in which the problem is represented to a person. Seemingly minor alterations in such representations can exert strong effects on decisions.

Consider the following example:

> Imagine the United States is preparing for the outbreak of an unusual Asian disease, which is expected to kill 600 people. Two alternative programs to combat the disease have been proposed. Assume that the exact scientific estimate of the consequences of the program are as follows: If Program A is adopted, 200 people will be saved. If Program B is adopted, there is a one-third probability that 600 people will be saved, and two-thirds probability that no people would be saved. Which program would you favor?
>
> Now imagine the same situation with these two alternatives: If Program C is adopted, 400 people will die. If Program D is adopted, there is a one-third probability that no one will die, and a two-thirds probability that 600 people will die (based on Tversky & Kahneman, 1981).

Tversky and Kahneman presented these problems to college students. When the problem was framed in terms of lives saved, 72 percent of the subjects chose Program A. However, when the problem was phrased in terms of lives lost, 78 percent favored Program D, and only 22 percent favored Program C.

This change in focus represents a robust principle in decision making, that people tend to avoid risks when they are dealing with possible gains (lives saved), but tend to seek risks when they are dealing with possible losses (lives lost). In the case of the problems phrased in terms of lives gained, people preferred to know that 200 lives would be saved for certain, and avoided the option that suggested a risk that no one would be saved. In contrast, when the problem was phrased in terms of lives lost, the preference was for the option providing the possibility that no one would die. The important point, of course, is that these two problems are identical, the only difference being whether the options are phrased in terms of lives gained or lives lost. Yet, the influence of framing is very pervasive, and is found for people with high levels of statistical sophistication as well as for statistical novices (see also Neale, Huber, & Northcraft, 1987; Northcraft & Neale, 1986; Levin, Schnittjer, & Thee, 1988; Slovic, Fischhoff, & Lichtenstein, 1982).

Motivated Inference

So far, we have considered primarily cognitive factors that influence how people use inferential strategies. Because the social decision maker must make many judgments in a rapid period of time, inferential strategies tend to be efficient, but not always exhaustive or accurate when contrasted with a normative model. Increasingly, research on social inference has also focused on the motivational factors that may guide the inference process. That is, the data-gathering and judgment process is assumed to be influenced not only by the cognitive strategies that people employ for sampling, combining, and interpreting information, but also by needs that inspire those judgments. This work represents the social perceiver as a motivation tactitian (Chapter 1).

Kunda (1987) suggests that people actively construct theories concerning why positive and negative events might befall them and enhance the perceived likelihood that positive events will happen to them. For example, upon learning that the divorce rate for first marriages is 50 percent, most people predict that they will not be in that 50 percent, but rather will remained married to their spouse for their lifetime. They convince themselves that this is the case by highlighting their personal attributes that might be associated with a stable marriage and downplaying the significance of or actively refuting information that might suggest a vulnerability to divorce. Thus, for example, one might point to one's parents' 50-year marriage, the close family life that existed in one's early childhood, and the fact that one's high school relationship lasted a full four years as evidence for a likely stable marriage. The fact that one's husband has already been divorced once, a factor that predicts a second divorce, might be interpreted not only as not leading to divorce in one's own case, but as a protective factor ("He does not want this marriage to fail like the last one, so he's working especially hard to keep our relationship strong"). The ability to draw seemingly rational relationships between our own assets and good events and to argue away associations between our own attributes and negative events helps us to maintain the correlations that we want to see in the world.

Summary

In the previous sections, we have reviewed the tasks of social inference as defined by normative theory. These include methods of gathering and sampling data, the use of Bayes' theorem in making predictions, methods of combining data, and assessments of covariation. In so doing, we have identified several apparently robust biases or errors, including the failure to appreciate regression effects, the dilution of diagnostic information by nondiagnostic information, the underutilization of base-rate information, the conjunction error, illusory correlation, the hindsight bias, decision-framing effects, and motivational sources of bias on inference. One conclusion that could be drawn from this comparison of the social perceiver's inferential capabilities with normative models is that we are not very good at gathering information, integrating it, and forming judgments. There are indeed many researchers who have formed precisely this conclusion.

How are we to understand these departures from normative theories of inference? One source of departure stems from capacity limitations on short-term memory. That is, the ability to process information on-line is very limited, as we noted in the discussion of short-term memory in Chapter 8. At a minimum, the inference process is often marked by a need to use strategies that move information through the system quickly though not always thoroughly. The label "cognitive miser" has developed to explain the necessary stinginess with which attention and processing time are often allocated to stimuli in the real world (S. E. Taylor, 1981b).

Long-term storage in memory, however, is quite cheap (Chapter 8), a point easily illustrated by thinking over all the songs you know or the people you can identify by sight. The advantage of so much storage space is that prior information, beliefs, and inferences can be stored in the form of schemas or other knowledge structures (Chapters 4–5) where they are accessible when new inferences must be drawn (G. H. Bower, 1977; Klatzky, 1975).

Armed with limited on-line capacity and a large amount of stored knowledge, how do these factors affect social inference? At the very least, social inference is likely to be heavily theory-driven. Using a priori theories is, generally speaking, likely to be a very effective strategy for forming judgments and making decisions, inasmuch as it represents the impact of past learning on subsequent information processing. It is efficient and effective to use our stored representations for similar situations, events, and people to interpret new and similar situations, events, and people. As such, departures from normative models of inference will tend to stray on the side of supporting already-held theories or hypotheses and against detecting sources of bias or error in the data. A second consequence is that the inference process is also often conservative, avoiding new or counterintuitive beliefs. We have already seen this principle illustrated in our discussion of attributions (Chapters 2 and 3) and schemas (Chapters 4 and 5). Related to these biases in favor of prior theories and conservative inferences is a tendency to look primarily for evidence that supports preexisting expectations, rather than to consider the full array of available evidence. As noted in the previous section, this preference for confirming instances underlies a number of the departures that intuitive inference demonstrates when compared against normative models.

A second general principle is that, given the need to process large amounts of information quickly, people's information processing strategies may lean in favor of efficiency rather than thoroughness. The criterion of efficiency is not systematically incorporated into normative models of inference, and as such, normative models may not reflect some of the most important exigencies that typically operate on the social perceiver.

A third general principle that can help explain departures of intuitive inferential strategies from normative theories concerns perceived relevance. As we have already seen, people are more likely to perceive biases in samples or appreciate the importance of base-rate information when there are cues in the situation signaling the relevance of these types of data. Under such circumstances, the social perceiver can sometimes use abstract and statistical principles appropriately. Under other circumstances, however, the content of the problem may keep the social perceiver from seeing the relevance of certain information relevant to normative models, and inference strategies may be selected on the basis of intuitive theories about the content domain of the problem instead.

Thus far, the discussion of inference has focused heavily on the ways in which social inference does not match the normative models that could be used to accomplish them. The next section focuses more heavily on what the social perceiver does, and identifies when these methods succeed and when they fail. Following our consideration of the intuitive inferential strategies, we return to a major question. Since social perceivers sometimes fall short of normative inferential strategies, how do we manage? Does the social perceiver know something that normative theories of inference do not take into account? Are normative models appropriate standards against which to compare everyday inference?

HEURISTICS: A RAPID FORM OF REASONING

As already seen, the social perceiver often must make complex judgments under conditions that may not be best suited to accuracy or thoroughness. One must figure out the best way to break the news to one's parents that one is dropping out of school and try to guess what their reactions might be. One must decide if a safe and reasonably satisfying romantic relationship should be abandoned for a new, exciting fling, the future of which is uncertain. One must decide if collaborating on a project with another is better than doing it all alone. Seemingly unlimited amounts of information could be brought to bear on any one of these decisions, but much of it would be of uncertain value. Furthermore, if thoroughly evaluated, all of these decisions could occupy the better part of a week and nothing else would get done. For these reasons—time constraints, complexity and/or volume of the relevant information, and uncertainty about the evidence itself—it is unrealistic for the social perceiver to use exhaustive strategies for making judgments. Thus, the social perceiver must be, under most circumstances, a "satisficer" who makes adequate inferences and decisions, rather than an "optimizer" who reaches the best possible inferences and decisions (March & Simon, 1958).

In a ground-breaking, highly influential paper, Tversky and Kahneman (1974) detailed some processes used by people for making judgments about uncertain events. They argued that people often use *heuristics* or shortcuts that reduce complex problem solving to more simple judgmental operations.

The Representativeness Heuristic

One such heuristic, termed *representativeness*, is used to make inferences about probability (Kahneman & Tversky, 1973; Tversky & Kahneman, 1982). It can help answer such questions as: How likely is it that person or event A is a member of category B? (e.g., Is George a football player?), or Did event A originate from process B? (e.g., Could the sequence of coin tosses H-H-T-T have occurred randomly?). For example, consider the following description. "Steve is very shy and withdrawn, invariably helpful, but with little interest in people, or in the world of reality. A meek and tidy soul, he has a need for order and structure, and a passion for detail" (Tversky & Kahneman, 1974). Suppose you are now asked to guess Steve's occupation. Is he a farmer, a trapeze artist, a librarian, a salvage diver, or a surgeon?

With adequate information about the frequency and personality characteristics of the people in these different occupations, one could conceivably tally up the probability of a meek surgeon, shy trapeze artist, and so on, and actually calculate the likelihood that Steve is in each occupation. This task would, however, take a very long time, and good information on which to base the calculations would undoubtedly be lacking. In such cases, the representativeness heuristic provides a quick solution. One estimates the extent to which Steve is representative or similar to the average person in each of the categories and makes one's judgment about his occupation accordingly. In the present case, one is likely to guess that Steve is a librarian, because the description of Steve is representative of attributes stereotypically associated with librarians.

The representativeness heuristic, then, is basically a relevancy judgment (how well do these attributes of A fit category B?) that produces a probability estimate (how probable is it that A is an instance of category B?). Using this heuristic will usually produce fairly good answers, perhaps as good as those produced by a more exhaustive analysis of the information available for the task, because relevancy is usually a good criterion for making probability judgments. However, when the representativeness heuristic is used by the social perceiver, he or she may be insensitive to other factors, independent of judged relevancy, that affect actual probability of occurrence (Kahneman & Tversky, 1973).

One such factor is *prior probability of outcomes* (base rates). If Steve lives in a town with lots of chicken farmers and only a few libraries, one's judgment that he is a librarian should be tempered by this fact; that is, it is simply more likely that he is a chicken farmer than a librarian. Nonetheless, as noted earlier, people sometimes ignore prior probabilities and instead base their judgment solely on similarity, for example, the fact that Steve resembles a librarian.

Another factor that people often ignore in judgments of representativeness is *sample size*. Suppose you are at the state fair running a booth in which you try to guess the occupation of anyone who pays a quarter. Suppose four of your first five clients are librarians, and you subsequently discover that the librarians' convention is in town. How confident should you be that the next individual in line is also a librarian? Would you be more or less confident than if twelve of the first twenty individuals you saw had turned out to be librarians? Most people making this judgment feel more confident that the next individual in line is a librarian if four of the first five individuals are librarians than if twelve of the first twenty are. Their confidence is, in fact, misplaced. As already noted, sampling theory dictates that estimates derived from a large sample are more reliable than estimates derived from a small one. Thus, even though four out of five looks like better odds than twelve out of twenty, the twelve out of twenty is the more reliable indicator.

Judgments made on the basis of representativeness may also show an *insensitivity to predictive value*, that is, insensitivity to the relevance or quality of the information as a predictor of some outcome. For example, if the description of Steve as a meek and tidy soul had been written by Steve's kindergarten teacher after a scant few weeks of class, its relevance to Steve's career choice would be weak indeed, whereas if written by Steve's adviser after four years of college, one might want to give it more weight. Nonetheless, people often behave as though information is to be trusted regardless of its source, and make equally strong or confident inferences, regardless of the information's predictive value. This *illusion of validity* may also be present when the information is a particularly good fit to the judgment. For example, if the description of Steve contained the additional sentence, "He is a bookish sort who peers intently over his wire-rimmed spectacles," our confidence in Steve's destiny as a librarian might be vastly increased. However, upon learning "he scuba dives in his spare time, and at one time in his life was a heavy cocaine user," we might begin to back off from a strong prediction. Whether the information is accurate and fully reliable or alternatively out-of-date, inaccurate, and based on hearsay may, however, matter little. Apparent fit or lack of fit can be the basis for its acceptance or rejection.

Finally, *misconceptions about chance* can also bias representativeness judgments. People have quite well-developed ideas of what chance events ought to look like. In flipping a coin several times, for example, one expects to see a sequence like H-T-H-T-T-H, not a seemingly orderly one like T-T-T-H-H-H. When asked to judge which sequence is more likely to occur, many people will erroneously pick the first one, because it looks random, whereas the second sequence is, in fact, statistically just as likely to occur.

This representativeness heuristic, then, is a quick, though occasionally fallible, method of estimating probability via judgments of relevancy. It is also perhaps our most basic cognitive heuristic. The act of identifying people as members of categories, or the act of assigning meaning to actions, is fundamental to all social inference and behavior. The question, "What is it?" must be answered before any other cognitive task can be performed.

The Availability Heuristic

Availability is a heuristic that is used to evaluate the frequency or likelihood of an event on the basis of how quickly instances or associations come to mind (Tversky & Kahneman, 1973). When examples or associations are readily accessible and easily brought to mind, this fact inflates estimates of frequency or likelihood. For example, if I am asked whether a lot of women my age are having babies now, I will likely think over the number of friends and acquaintances I know who have or are about to have babies and respond on the basis of the relative frequency of examples or ease with which examples come to mind. As is the case with the representativeness heuristic, little cognitive work need be conducted to accomplish this task. I can provide a frequency estimate on the basis of how quickly or easily instances or associations can be retrieved. If I have no trouble bringing to mind examples of pregnant friends, I will likely estimate that there is a baby boomlet in my age group, whereas if it takes me a while to think of someone who is having a baby, I will scale down my estimate of my cohorts' fertility.

Under many circumstances, use of the availability heuristic will produce correct answers. After all, when examples of something can be brought to mind easily, it is usually because there are lots of them. However, there are also biasing factors that can increase or decrease the availability of some class of phenomena or events without altering its actual overall frequency. For example, the fact that I have a newborn baby means not only that I spend time with other mothers more than I normally would, but that I am also probably more likely to notice whether someone has a child or not than I would otherwise. Thus, when I think of examples of new mothers, my available supply of examples is biased, and my estimate of the birth rate is likely to be higher than is warranted. When a class has easily retrieved instances, it will seem more numerous than will an equally frequent category that has less easily retrieved instances (Gabrielcik & Fazio, 1984).

Search biases, as well as *retrieval biases,* can skew one's frequency estimations by biasing the number of available instances. For example, for
some categories of events, it is easier to search for instances than it is for
other categories. Estimating the birth rate at a church or temple would, for
example, produce a higher estimate than would estimating the birth rate
among co-workers; because people frequently bring their children to church
or temple but rarely bring them to work, the ease with which instances can be
brought to mind varies dramatically between the two settings.

Finally, the *ease with which one can imagine* particular events can bias frequency estimates. For example, when people are asked to guess the major
causes of death in this country, they assume more deaths result from such
dramatic events as accidents, fires, drownings, or shootings than is actually the case. At the same time, they underestimate death from more common causes such as stroke or heart disease. Newspapers and television
programs have created colorful, easily imagined instances of the former
events, and hence it is easy to bring images or associations to mind,
whereas a death from disease rarely makes it past the obituary page (see
Slovic, Fischhoff, & Lichtenstein, 1976, for a discussion of this research).

Ease of retrieval of instances is one way of estimating frequency via
the availability heuristic as just seen; *strength of association* is another. As
we saw in the discussion on person memory in Chapter 8, associative
bonds are strengthened by repeated examples, and so the strength of
an association between any two things is likely to be a fairly good estimate of the frequency of some class of events. As with ease of retrieval
of instances, however, associative strength may be biased by factors irrelevant to actual frequency. For example, if I live in a small town like
Amherst that stresses family values, I may infer that the birthrate is
higher than if I lived in a city like Los Angeles, known for its wild sin-
gles' life. In the former city, the virtues and accomplishments of children may be extolled, thus creating a belief that there are many children
around, whereas in Los Angeles children keep a lower profile.

The potential biasing effects of the availability heuristic on frequency estimates were demonstrated in the context of stereotyping by
Rothbart and his associates (Rothbart et al., 1978). Subjects were given
trait information about members of a hypothetical group under one of
two conditions. They either saw the names of several different group
members (Ed, Phil, Fred, Joe) paired with a particular trait (lazy) or they
saw the same name-trait pairing (Phil is lazy) an equivalent number of
times. In addition, some subjects saw a lot of name-trait pairings (high
memory load condition), whereas other subjects saw relatively few
name-trait pairings (low memory load). After seeing the pairings, subjects were asked to characterize the group as a whole. If people are able
to remember accurately which name(s) were paired with which traits,
then inferences about the group as a whole should be stronger if several
group members have a particular trait than if only one member has the
trait. When the total number of name-trait pairings subjects were ex-

posed to was low (low memory load condition), subjects showed this caution in their inferences about the group. However, when the total number of name-trait pairings was high (high memory load condition), it was apparently difficult for subjects to keep straight how many individuals had which traits, and they began to behave as if multiple instances of the same name-trait pairing were as informative as several different names paired with that trait. Under high memory load, the group came to be characterized as lazy even when only a few of its members actually were lazy. The availability heuristic provides a potential account for the results of this study by suggesting that, under conditions of high memory load, subjects may simply have accessed the strength of their connection between the group and its attributes, which was based on the number but not the redundancy of the name-trait pairings.

The social world is often overwhelmingly informative, and as such it usually mirrors the high memory load condition more than the low memory load condition. This fact could, then, facilitate the formation of group stereotypes from the behavior of just a few individuals whose behavior shows up a large number of times. Because media are more focused on negative than positive events, these biases could favor the formation of negative group stereotypes, particularly if group membership is salient when mentioned in media coverage.

The availability heuristic has been a highly influential idea within social psychology, and it can provide an explanatory mechanism for a wide range of social phenomena, including stereotyping (D. L. Hamilton & Rose, 1980) and the perseverance of discredited beliefs (L. Ross, Lepper, & Hubbard, 1975; L. Ross et al., 1977; see S. E. Taylor, 1982, for a review). It has also been offered as an explanation for other phenomena, such as salience (S. E. Taylor, 1982; see Chapter 7), judgments of responsibility (M. Ross & Sicoly, 1979; see Chapter 3), predictions (e.g., Carroll, 1978; Slovic, Fischhoff, & Lichtenstein, 1976) and causal attributions (Pryor & Kriss, 1977). It may well have been overused. Many tasks do not require even the small amount of work engaged by use of the availability heuristic. The amount of information we already have stored in memory, as in the form of schemas for well-known types of social events or people, means that answers to many of the inferences we must form are already available, as long as we can access the correct schema. The implication of this assumption is that, generally, people will draw on the representativeness heuristic to identify what schema or category is appropriate for retrieving information more than they will draw on the availability heuristic for making judgments.

The Simulation Heuristic

One use of availability is in the construction of hypothetical scenarios to try to estimate how something will come out. This inferential technique is known as the *simulation* heuristic (Kahneman & Tversky, 1982). Consider, as an example, how you would answer the question, "What is your dad going to think when he finds out you have smashed up the car?" You may think of what you know about your father and his reactions to crises, run through these events in your mind, and generate several possibilities; the ease with which a particular ending comes to mind is used to judge what is likely to happen in real life. Your father could refuse to pay your college tuition next term, or he could ignore the whole thing, but in your judgment, it is easiest to imagine that he will strongly suggest that you find a job so that you can help pay for the car.

The simulation heuristic may be used for a wide variety of tasks, including prediction (How will Joan like Tom?) and causality (Is the dog or the kid to blame for the mess on the floor?). It is particularly relevant to situations of near misses. For example, consider the following:

> Mr. Crane and Mr. Tees were scheduled to leave the airport on different flights, at the same time. They traveled from town in the same limousine, were caught in a traffic jam, and arrived at the airport thirty minutes after the scheduled departure time of their flights.
> Mr. Crane is told his flight left on time.
> Mr. Tees is told that his flight was delayed, and just left five minutes ago.
> Who is more upset?
> Mr. Crane or Mr. Tees? (Kahneman & Tversky, 1982, p. 203)

Virtually everyone says, "Mr. Tees." Why? Presumably, one can imagine no way that Mr. Crane could have made his plane, whereas, were it not for that one long light or the slow baggage man or the illegally parked car or the error in the posted departure gate, Mr. Tees would have made it. Thus, the simulation heuristic and its ability to generate *if only* conditions can be used to understand the psychology of near misses and the frustration, regret, grief, or indignation they may produce (cf. Chapter 10).

This counterfactual construction, namely, the mental simulation of how events might otherwise have occurred, appears to have a broad range of effects on judgment. It may be used to assess causality, as by trying to identify the unique or unusual specific factor that produced a dramatic outcome (G. L. Wells & Gavanski, 1989; G. L. Wells, Taylor, & Turtle, 1987; cf. D. J. Hilton & Slugoski, 1986). It also influences the affective response to a particular event's outcome (Kahneman & Miller, 1986; Kahneman & Tversky, 1982; Landman, 1988) by providing visions of how events might have been otherwise. For example, abnormal or exceptional events lead people to generate alternatives that are normal and consequently dissimilar to the actual outcome (Kahneman & Miller, 1986). This contrast between the exceptional circumstance and the normal situation intensifies the emotional reaction to the unusual situation.

In a role-playing situation involving compensation to victims who experienced an abnormal or normal fate, Miller and McFarland (1986) found that rewards were higher for victims in the abnormal circumstances. For example, when a man had gone shopping at a convenience store far from his house and been shot during a robbery, subjects' awards of damages were higher than when he had shopped at the convenience store he normally frequented in his own neighborhood.

In counterfactual thinking, it is easier to make a downhill change, that is, to replace an unusual event with an expected one, than it is to make an upward change, that is, to replace a normal event with an abnormal one (Kahneman & Miller, 1986). This leads to the prediction that it will be easier to generate a counterfactual scenario of inaction instead of action, compared to the reverse. In fact, studies by Landman (1988) and Gleicher et al. (1990) support this prediction. Kahneman and Miller (1986) argue that people construct counterfactuals more readily in response to action than inaction because it is easier to imagine undoing an event than it is to imagine adding an action to the status quo (see Landman, 1988).[2] Thus, for example, people find it easier to imagine that Mr. Tees could have made his plane if the construction had not been blocking his lane, whereas they are less likely to generate a scenario that Mr. Tees would have reached his plane on time if there had been an alternate and faster route to the airport.

Thus, imagining an alternative via counterfactual simulation can have a broad impact on expectations, causal attributions, impressions, and the affect experienced in situations. Moreover, such situations appear to be elicited by predictable circumstances (e.g., the salience of how events might otherwise have been) and to follow rules such that probable rather than improbable elements are incorporated into the simulations (see also S. E. Taylor & Schneider, 1989).

Turning to simulations of the future rather than of the past, imagining hypothetical future events makes those events seem more likely. Consequently, it follows that if the content of a scenario is easy to imagine, it will be perceived as more likely in the future than a scenario involving difficult-to-imagine events, a prediction that has been confirmed in several studies (C. A. Anderson, 1983; C. A. Anderson & Godfrey, 1987; Anderson, Lepper, & Ross, 1980; Carroll, 1978; Gregory, Cialdini, & Carpenter, 1982; Hirt & Sherman, 1985; S. J. Sherman et al., 1985; see also J. T. Johnson, 1986). Similarly, simply imagining oneself deciding to perform or refusing to engage in a behavior leads to corresponding changes in expectations about oneself (C. A. Anderson, 1983; C. A. Anderson & Godfrey, 1987) and in subsequent attitude-relevant

---

[2]This effect was found primarily for actions involving loss. With positive consequences, only high salience of a counterfactual alternative produced exaggerated affect for outcomes associated with action versus inaction.

behavior (Gregory, Burroughs, & Ainslie 1985). Imagining someone else engaging in a behavior, however, does not increase expectations that the self will engage in the behavior (C. A. Anderson, 1983), nor does imagining the self engaging in a behavior influence one's expectations for others' behavior (C. A. Anderson & Godfrey, 1987).

Simulations are more likely to increase the perceived likelihood of a potential outcome (mental addition) than to reduce perceived likelihood of a potential consequence (mental subtraction). This asymmetry appears to occur because people give more weight to features of a particular mental simulation that serve as the subject of comparison and give more weight to factors that produce rather than inhibit a relevant outcome. So, for example, when assessing the impact of personal actions such as studying for an exam, subjects perceived more impact when the assessment was put in an additive framework (e.g., "How many more questions will you get right if you study?") as opposed to a subtractive one (e.g., "How many fewer will you get right if you do not study?"). This effect appears to be independent both of the valence of the event and by whether or not a person has personal experience in the simulation domain (Dunning & Parpal, 1989).

Anchoring and Adjustment

When making judgments under uncertainty, people will sometimes reduce ambiguity by starting with a beginning reference point or anchor and then adjust it to reach a final conclusion. If, for example, you are asked to guess how many people attended the USC-UCLA football game, and you have absolutely no idea, it is helpful to know that the previous week's game in the same stadium drew a crowd of 23,000. You may then guess 30,000, assuming that a USC-UCLA contest would draw a bigger crowd. So it is with social judgments as well, which often require anchors for making judgments about others (e.g., Wyer, 1976).

We have already discussed several phenomena that constitute instances of the anchoring and adjustment heuristic. Recall from Chapter 3 the self-based or false consensus effect in attributions. When asked to estimate how many people would perform some activity (e.g., wear a sandwich board around campus), subjects' estimates are substantially influenced by the decision they would make for themselves. Although we know intellectually that not everyone would behave as we do, our estimates of others' behavior are not adjusted sufficiently from the anchor that our own behavior provides. Likewise, self-centered estimations of responsibility may represent an inability to correct adequately for our biases in recalling our own contributions. As the two previous examples suggest, it is very possible that the most prominent anchor from which we estimate or judge others' social behavior is ourselves and our social environment (e.g., Fong & Markus, 1982; Markus & Smith, 1981). We may, for example, judge how aggressive or shy another person is as an adjusted inference from our own self-rating on these same qualities.

Judgments may also be anchored by irrelevant details of a situation that, nonetheless, suggest a beginning reference point (Schwarz & Wyer, 1985). J. Greenberg, Williams, and O'Brien (1986), for example, found that the customary instructions given by judges to juries to consider the harshest verdict first may inadvertently function as an anchoring point. When subjects in a mock trial were induced to consider the harshest verdict first, they rendered significantly harsher verdicts than subjects who were instructed to consider lenient verdicts first. Similarly, in attributing attitudes to others, you may be aware of constraints on their attitude expression (e.g., a reporter had to write an anti-Castro article, because his editor told him to); nonetheless, with the communication itself as an anchor, you may fail to correct sufficiently for the constraints (and thus infer that the writer is indeed anti-Castro). Quattrone, Finkel, and Andrus (1982) have suggested that this robust correspondence bias—failing to correct for situational constraints in the attribution of attitudes—can be understood as anchoring and insufficient adjustment effects.

The anchoring and adjustment heuristic has been applied to a variety of social situations. In one study, Plous (1989) found that an arbitrary anchor offered in a survey substantially influenced people's subjective estimates of nuclear war (see also Lilli & Rehm, 1986). Zuckerman et al. (1984) found that when subjects judged the attitudes of a target, thereby anchoring their impressions of that target, their ability to distinguish whether or not the target was telling the truth was impaired. As another example closer to the self, Cervone and Peake (1986) had subjects judge their abilities to perform a problem-solving task after having been exposed to random anchoring values representing very low or very high performance. This exposure led them to develop corresponding high or low self-efficacy judgments, which actually produced differences in subsequent task persistence when subjects performed the task. Personal experience can also function as an arbitrary anchor. McCauley et al. (1985) found that failed and successful transplant patients gave lower and higher estimates, respectively, of the population's success rate for transplantation as a result of their own outcomes.

Examples of anchoring and adjustment are ubiquitous in social situations, perhaps precisely because social behavior is so ambiguous and relatively free of objective yardsticks. When we can, we use ourselves as anchors, but when our own reference points are ambiguous, we may use the behavior and attributes of others, or we may be anchored by irrelevant details of a situation.

Heuristics: A Postscript

The heuristics discussed by Tversky and Kahneman (1974; Kahneman & Tversky, 1982) are described in Table 9.3. Psychologists have sometimes behaved as if these few—representativeness, availability, simulation, anchoring—are the main ones people use. Yet, the overall point made by this influential line of work is that the social perceiver is virtually always using heuristics to a greater or lesser extent, including general ones like representativeness that can be applied across a wide variety of situations, and idiosyncratic ones that apply only to one's particular job or hobbies. Certainly, there are circumstances in which people become more thoughtful and less reliant on heuristics, and under such circumstances, better inferences may sometimes be reached. But heuristics are fundamental to inference, making rapid information processing possible. Thus, an investigation of the abundant heuristics of daily life in addition to those already outlined would be extremely useful for understanding both the wisdom and flaws of everyday thinking (see for example, Kahneman & Tversky, 1982; Nisbett et al., 1983).

Why do heuristic strategies exist? Holyoak and Nisbett (1988) offer a perspective on this issue. They point out that any method of inferring general rules from limited data needs to be biased to generate hypotheses that are plausibly useful. Otherwise, there is no basis for constraining the induction task, and numerous false leads could result. Heuristics and a wealth of the so-called biases just documented in the inference process impose precisely these constraints. Perhaps the best example is the bias that people show in favor of evidence that confirms their hypotheses. Were we to approach every induction task without preconceptions, the manifold number of hypotheses that we could come up with to be tested in any given set of data would make the inference process totally unmanageable. Thus, heuristics and so-called inferential bias point the social perceiver in a direction that constrains the inference process to be manageable.

Statistical Heuristics and Pragmatic Reasoning Schemas

People's heuristics meet the goal of efficient processing quite well. Moreover, they often produce accurate answers. However, there are also occasions when it is important for the social perceiver to make judgments that more closely approximate those that would result from following normative models of inference. The question that arises in this context is whether people solve problems in everyday life using abstract inferential rules or whether they use rules specific to the problem domain. A number of researchers have concluded that problem-solving

TABLE 9.3 SOME HEURISTIC STRATEGIES FOR MAKING JUDGMENTS UNDER UNCERTAINTY

Representativeness	Probability judgment	Representativeness is a judgment of how relevant A is to B; high relevance yields high estimates that A originates from B	Deciding that George (A) must be an engineer because he looks and acts like your stereotype of engineers (B)
Availability	Frequency or probability judgments	Availability is the estimate of how frequently or likely is a given instance or occurrence, based on how easily or quickly an association or examples come to mind	Estimating the divorce rate on the basis of how quickly one can think of examples of divorced friends
Simulation	Expectations, causal attributions, impressions, and affective experience	Simulation is the ease with which a hypothetical scenario can be constructed	Getting angry because of a frustrating event on the basis of how easily one can imagine the situation occurring otherwise
Anchoring and adjustment	Estimates of position on a dimension	Anchoring and adjustment is the process of estimating some value by starting with some initial value and then adjusting it to the new instance	Judging another person's productivity based on one's own level of productivity

strategies follow domain-specific rules (e.g., D'Andrade, 1989; Golding, 1981; Johnson-Laird, 1983; Reich & Ruth, 1982). However, evidence that people do use some statistical concepts in solving particular problems suggests that the question might better be phrased: when do people use statistical concepts to solve particular kinds of problems (Jepson, Krantz, & Nisbett, 1983; Nisbett et al., 1982, 1983)?

Nisbett and his colleagues argue that people have both intuitive and abstract versions of statistical rules. For example, Nisbett and Kunda

(1985) demonstrated that people have some intuitive appreciation for the nature of distributions of social variables. They examined accuracy levels in estimating means, standard deviations, and distribution shapes for a variety of social behaviors, such as marijuana use, mild depression, and movie-going. Subjects were surprisingly accurate, showing only moderate overestimations of dispersions and means, as well as a modest self-consensus effect (that is, the tendency to attribute their own behavior readily to others).

People also seem to have an appreciation for more complex statistical principles, which Nisbett refers to as *statistical heuristics*. He argues that people use statistical heuristics when a problem has features that are readily encoded in terms of statistical rules, when there are cues in the situation that signal the presence of chance or random factors, and when the culture recognizes the events in question as associated with random variation (e.g., gambling), suggesting that the use of statistical principles is appropriate. Consistent with this point, a variety of apparent statistical errors, such as regression effects and the failure to properly use base-rate information, virtually disappear when the situational applicability of the statistical information to the problem at hand is made clear (Kruglanski, Friedland, & Farkash, 1984). By arguing that statistical heuristics are abstract, Nisbett and his colleagues explain the failure to use such rules as a difficulty in coding the problem in terms that make the application of the rules clear, rather than as ignorance of the abstract rules per se.

Consistent with this reasoning, Fong, Krantz, and Nisbett (1986) explored whether or not subjects were able to use the law of large numbers appropriately for a variety of problems. Spontaneously, subjects were able to see that a small sample of a slot machine's behavior would be a poor guide to its overall behavior, but they were less likely to understand that a small sample of an athlete's behavior might not be typical of his or her overall performance, or more subjectively still, that a small sample of a person's friendliness might not be typical of his or her friendliness in general. These and similar results suggest that people are not only capable of holding abstract statistical concepts but that they use them spontaneously. However, they are not always able to employ them correctly in appropriate situations because they sometimes fail to see the applicability of the rule.

In a similar vein, Cheng and Holyoak have discussed people's use of pragmatic reasoning schemas (Cheng & Holyoak, 1985; Cheng et al., 1986). Pragmatic reasoning schemas are clusters of rules that are very general and abstract but nonetheless defined with respect to particular classes of goals and types of relationships. The causal schemas described by Harold Kelley and discussed in Chapter 2 constitute examples of pragmatic reasoning schemas; they deal with a specific class of situations, namely, ones requiring causal inferences, but the rules themselves are quite abstract and general (rules for determining multiple necessary versus multiple sufficient causes), and consequently can be applied across a broad range of specific causal dilemmas. Similarly, people often use heuristics or intuitive rules of thumb that constitute the informal equivalents of statistical rules, such as the law of large numbers, the regression principle, and the like. However, because the principles are developed to deal with particular classes of events, their full applicability may not be evident and therefore, they may not be used in situations where they would be appropriate.

In summary, then, when we examine the processes social perceivers actually use for forming inferences, as opposed to focusing on the deviations from normative models, we see that people possess a wide variety of flexible strategies that may approximate but not fully match the normative models that are assumed to apply in typical inference situations. The strategies appear to be midrange ones, neither specific to a particular content domain nor totally abstract. Rather, the strategies and principles that people spontaneously use may be applied beyond the domain which they originally explained to the extent that the features of the inference problem match the conditions under which the strategy is believed to apply.

INFERENCE: AN OVERALL EVALUATION

Overall, how do we as social perceivers fare on tasks of social inference? The evidence reviewed suggests that, like the proverbial adolescent in his first amorous forays, we may be fast, but we aren't very good. Most of our shortcuts such as using judgmental heuristics and relying on prior theories or schemas enable us to accomplish inference tasks quickly, but level of accuracy, as compared against normative models, is sometimes quite poor. Indeed, there are few glowing tributes to the inferential abilities of the social perceiver. Reviews of inferential errors uniformly express dismay at our ability to solve problems correctly and wonder at the fact that we muddle through as well as we apparently do (e.g., Einhorn, 1980; Hogarth, 1980; Nisbett & Ross, 1980; Shweder, 1980; Tversky & Kahneman, 1974). Hence there is a puzzle: Why aren't inferential errors more problematic for daily living than they apparently are? If shortcuts and strategies are fraught with error, why does their use persist?

There are at least three perspectives on this puzzle. The first maintains that errors and biases in the inference process are more apparent than real, and that in the real world, subjects actually perform inferential tasks quite well. A second perspective argues that although social perceivers are prone to certain systematic errors and biases in their inferences, there are conditions in the real world that act as safeguards and checks on the inference process so that many of these biases become inconsequential or self-correcting. The third position argues that the errors and biases outlined in the inference process have considerable validity and often lead to important errors in judgments and policy, and that consequently some efforts to improve the inference process must be undertaken. Since all three positions appear to have some validity, we will discuss each.

Is the Inference Process Fraught with Error?

A first perspective on the literature documenting errors and biases in social inference maintains that these errors are more apparent than real. This perspective (McArthur & Baron, 1983; Funder 1987; Swann, 1984) makes two main points. The first is that experimental research documenting errors and biases does not create the conditions under which people normally make judgments in the real world, and therefore, it may make people look worse at inference tasks than they really are. According to this position, social perceivers' naive inference strategies are adapted to the ecological and interpersonal conditions under which inferences must be drawn; experimental studies that create conditions conducive to use of the normative model rarely exist in real-world judgment and decision-making situations. In this sense, then, judgment experiments may be designed in ways that make people look stupid. Some suggestive evidence for the validity of this position is provided by perspectives on individual errors or biases discussed earlier in the chapter. As noted in those discussions, certain of the errors, such as conjunctive errors, regression errors, and covariation errors, may represent misapplications of inferential strategies that are usually appropriate for forming judgments and making decisions.

A parallel point is that normative models, as a result, may be poor standards for evaluating intuitive inferences (Einhorn & Hogarth, 1981; Funder, 1987; Hastie & Rasinski, 1988; Hogarth, 1981; Kahneman & Tversky, 1982; Kenny & Albright, 1987; Kruglanski & Ajzen, 1983; Nisbett et al., 1982; Nisbett et al., 1983; Swann, 1984; P. White, 1984). Conditions that make it possible to use a normative model are rarely present in the real world. Often, information is not reliable, unbiased, or complete. Even if it is, it may not be presented in a clear or usable fashion. Sometimes the information may not even be available. And even if it were, use of the normative model might be prohibitively time-consuming. Suppose, for example, you suspect that terriers bite. Is it really worth it to you to get a sample of terriers, observe how often they bite, get a sample of other dogs, see how often they bite, and calculate a correlation coefficient? How many dogs would you need? How long should you wait before you decide that any given dog is not going to

bite? What breed should your comparison dogs be? Where are you going to find enough terriers? In sum, isn't it just easier (and safer) to
avoid terriers? The conditions that maximize accuracy in inferences appear infrequently in real life. Accordingly, in many situations, one
could not apply an ideal, statistical model, even if one were so inclined
(see Crocker, 1981; Nisbett et al., 1982).

Another problem with applying the normative model to most daily
inferential situations is that normative models ignore the content and
thus, the context of a decision in favor of its formal structure. Thus, for
example, deciding which of three brands of eggs to buy and deciding
which of three people to marry could easily be treated as equivalent decisions under the normative model, if the information about the three
options varied from each other in the same systematic ways. Yet, the
intuitive processes used for the two decisions would probably vary, and
rightfully so. The normative model generates inferential standards,
given a fixed time and environment (i.e., all other things being equal).
But decisions are made and inferences are drawn in dynamic environments, so predictions made for static environments may be inappropriate for changing conditions (Hogarth, 1981).

There are also circumstances under which the type of judgment to
be made suggests use of a different model than a normative one. Take
the example of a fledgling job candidate who at lunch spills his water,
sends his lamb chop flying into his neighbor's lap, and rests his elbow
in the butter (Nisbett et al., 1982). He is nervous, it is true, and his nervousness is clearly due to situational factors, not dispositional ones.
Furthermore, this is a very modest sample of his behavior, and it is
likely to be a very poor predictor of future behavior. Normatively, one
should probably discount these incidents. But consider the alternative,
practical model of the person who must make the job-hiring decisions.
He or she must select a candidate who can consistently perform well
and perform well under pressure. Wouldn't you rather have your sales
made by someone who puts his butter on his roll, instead of on his suit?
In short, statistically normative models are only one kind of model that
can be applied to social judgments. It may be the case that alternative
models held by people directly involved in making those judgments
generate useful criteria that inherently conflict with the standards generated by normative models.

Finally, it is certainly the case that judgment situations used in experimental tests are often stacked against intuitive strategies of inference (McArthur & Baron, 1983; Fischhoff, 1982a; Funder, 1987;
Kahneman & Tversky, 1982). For example, the tasks may be unfamiliar
or unfair (e.g., being set up to calculate a correlation in one's head), or
they may be misconstrued by subjects. Or information may be presented in a format conducive to use of the normative model that does
not contain the kind of contextual detail that would facilitate the use of

an effective intuitive strategy. This methodological bias in experimental evidence then, may lead to a more negative portrait of our inferential abilities than we deserve.

Yet ultimately, the task of assessing if and when a person's inferences are accurate is more complex than one might suppose. One can determine whether a judgment corresponds to some criterion (Funder, 1987; Hastie & Rasinski, 1988; Kenny & Albright, 1987); whether it is shared with others (Funder, 1987); or whether it is adaptive, pragmatic, or useful (Swann, 1984). But for many social judgments, there is no criterion for determining whether or not it is actually correct, because the judgments lack objective referents (Hastie & Rasinski, 1988). Moreover, to serve the social perceiver's needs adequately, inferences may, under some circumstances, need to depart from accuracy (S. E. Taylor & Brown, 1988), and under such circumstances, the criterion against which inferences are being compared should also reflect these needs. We do know that such factors as importance of a judgment and personal involvement in the issue lead to consideration of more information, prompt more complex judgmental strategies, and even lead to increased accuracy under some circumstances (e.g., Harkness, DeBono, & Borgida, 1985; see Chapter 5). Accountability also increases cognitive activity, such that accountable judges use more complex processing strategies than unaccountable ones (Tetlock & Boettger, 1989; Weldon & Gargano, 1988; see also Tetlock, Skitka, & Boettger, 1989). Beyond these observations, it is difficult to judge whether the social perceiver is more accurate in the real world than in the experimental laboratory. Moreover, there are no stringent criteria for defining what a "natural" situation is, and many real-world situations themselves may be quite unnatural with respect to the inferential strategies that social perceivers normally use (Kruglanski, 1989b).

Are Inferential Errors Inconsequential or Self-Correcting?

A second perspective on errors and biases in the inference process maintains that the social environment usually provides conditions whereby errors in inferential strategies become self-correcting. Some strategies are relatively robust against certain errors, and in other cases one shortcoming may cancel out another (Nisbett & Ross, 1980). As noted earlier, the dilution effect (i.e., the finding that extreme predictions can be attenuated by the presence of irrelevant information), for example, can guard against the failure to appreciate regression toward the mean. Furthermore, most of our strategies can be employed very quickly and easily, and hence, even acknowledging some error, they are likely to pay off in time and energy saved by not using the more exhaustive and exhausting normative strategies.

Some of the errors produced by faulty inferential processes will not matter. For example, if one's biased impressions will not affect one's future behavior, as in forming an incorrect impression of a person one meets only once, then the bias will be trivially important. In fact, little is known about the correspondence between inferences and behavior generally; if the correspondence is low, inferential errors may matter little. Biases may also matter little if they are constant over time. For example, if one regards one's boss as gruff, it may not matter that she is gruff only when she is in the boss role, if that is the only circumstance under which one interacts with her.

Feedback from the environment corrects some inferential errors (Einhorn, 1982; Hogarth, 1981). Most people verbalize even their most tentative judgments to others and receive some feedback as to whether they are on the right track. Thus, inferences are made in a world filled with consequences. One's commitment to any one inference can be small, because once ventured, personal experience or communication may prove it correct or show it to be wrong, and one can then change one's inferences. Thus, intuitive inferences are not choices that, once made, commit one irrevocably to a cognitive or behavioral course. Rather, in many cases, inferences may be tentative forays to be modified on the bases of the responses they evoke. Normal conversation provides a basis for reality testing one's inferences, and blatantly false conclusions with far-reaching implications are likely to be corrected. This is particularly likely to be true of errors due to self-centered biases; for example, if the assertion that one performs one's share of the housework meets with strenuous objections from one's spouse, that opinion is likely to be modified.

Biases may matter little when decisional alternatives are of near equal value. A student choosing between Harvard and Yale may make a final decision based on a biased sample of one friend's experience, but stereotypes and chauvinism aside, the student will receive a trivially better education at one place over the other. Finally, our biases may have little impact on our strategies. Consider the graduate admissions process. It is the rare graduate student who turns out to be a hotshot. If one accepts five students and they have average careers and rejects five students who also have average careers, then one can find little apparent fault with one's decision-making process, even if it was actually made with flawed methods. If one of the five rejected students goes on to excel, then one might conclude that an error was made in one case, and that that student should have been accepted. Still, one out of ten is not a bad error rate. Obviously, this reasoning is fallacious. However, it serves to underscore the fact that many of our processing errors do not yield blatantly bad results, so the processes may appear perfectly adequate.

Many sources of error will correct themselves. Whenever biases do not persist over time, the process will begin to correct itself with repeated encounters. For example, if several of one's friends have recently been divorced, one's estimate of the divorce rate may be temporarily exaggerated via the availability heuristic, but assuming that one's friends do not continue to have divorces indefinitely, one's estimated divorce rate should eventually come into line with objective data.

Are Inferential Errors Ever Consequential?

The third position, not incompatible with either of the first two, maintains that under at least some circumstances, erroneous inferential strategies have severe consequences. The contribution of inferential errors to the development and maintenance of pejorative stereotypes is one striking example. Group decision making shows marked biases in information gathering and stereotypic perceptions of one's own and another's position, indicating that severe errors can mark naturally occurring conditions of social inference (Janis, 1982; 1989). Judgmental errors have unnerving implications for fields as diverse as politics (Jervis, 1976), clinical decision making (Turk & Salovey, 1986), and education (H. A. Simon, 1980). In short, one cannot trust biases in inferential strategies to be either inconsequential or self-correcting, and accordingly, methods for the detection and correction of biased inferences are needed.

IMPROVING THE INFERENCE PROCESS

Awareness of Cognitive Processes

Were one to undertake to improve the social perceiver's inferential process, the effort would likely begin by alerting perceivers to the problem and instructing them to be attentive to inferential errors in the future. Such instructions would presuppose that people have at least some awareness of the inferential processes they are using and that they can draw on that awareness at will.

In a highly controversial paper, Nisbett and Wilson (1977b) maintained that people have little or no access to their cognitive processes. In fact, there is a substantial amount of anecdotal evidence from psychological studies indicating that many, if not most, experimental subjects have no idea of the forces in the experiment influencing their behavior. Taking these observations as their point of departure, Nisbett and Wilson conducted a series of experiments (Nisbett & Wilson, 1977a; T. D. Wilson & Nisbett, 1978) in which they systematically manipulated factors that influenced subjects' behavior and then asked the subjects to report what factors led them to behave as they did. For example, in one study, billed as an investigation of consumer preferences, subjects were asked to inspect four nightgowns, laid out on a table, and indicate which one they would choose. There is, in fact, a strong serial position effect for these kinds of tasks, such that people typically prefer the right-most item to those that are to its left. (Why this position preference exists is not fully known.) Subjects in the experiment also showed this serial position effect, but when asked why they made the particular choice they had, they offered explanations that centered on qualities of the chosen garment itself. When it was suggested that serial position might have influenced their decision, subjects expressed considerable skepticism. Such occurrences are well-known to most experimenters debriefing subjects after a social psychology experiment.

If we accept Nisbett and Wilson's interpretation that subjects have little or no access to their own cognitive processes, what are the sources for subjects' explanations for their behavior? Nisbett and Wilson argue that when people state the factors that have influenced their behavior, they are merely reporting their theories about what causes what, theories that any observer might share. For example, when one thinks about a bad or a good mood, a bad or a good night's sleep easily comes to mind as a good explanation of mood, whereas one is less likely to think, "I must be depressed because this is Tuesday." This is because theories about the relationship between sleep and mood are more common than those about the relationship between weekday and mood. Hence, when subjects are reporting what has influenced their mood, they may be actually reporting their *beliefs* about what influenced their mood, rather than actual determinants. An observer, such as one's roommate, may well share the same theory and give the same explanation: "Ralph is in a good mood because he slept well last night." When observers' explanations match those of the people involved in the behavior, the possibility that their shared explanations stem from a common theory about what influences what is a strong possibility. As Nisbett and Wilson point out, under such circumstances, there is no reason to believe that the actor has any special access to his or her own cognitive processes (see also T. D. Wilson, Hull, & Johnson, 1981).

One should not infer from the previous discussion that people are always wrong in their theories of what causes their behavior. Indeed, on many if not most occasions, people are right. If I ask you why you are crying, and you say, "Because my boyfriend left me," you are probably correct in your analysis. The fact that a theory is correct, however, or that it correctly applies to a particular case, does not imply that its holder has special access to his or her cognitive processes (T. D. Wilson, Hull, & Johnson, 1981). Everyone knows that relationship breakups can be sad. It is possible, too, that people vary in the degree to which they understand the sources of influence on their own behavior. People high in self-understanding may show a higher level of accuracy than people low in self-understanding (Warshaw & Davis, 1984).

Nisbett and Wilson's analysis touched off a heated response (e.g., Kraut & Lewis, 1982; Quattrone, 1985; E. R. Smith & Miller, 1978; P. White, 1980). Criticisms hinged on several points. First, Nisbett and Wilson's argument is hard to falsify. When subjects are wrong about what factors influenced their behavior, Nisbett and Wilson can be viewed as supported; when subjects are right, if the subjects' explanation is shared by another person, it could well be due to a shared theory; hence, Nisbett and Wilson's argument can again be construed as supported. Finally, if subjects are right about their explanation and the explanation is not shared by someone else, it may well be because subjects know things about their past behavior that others do not know, not because they have internal access to their cognitive processes.

A second problem is that, with rare exceptions (e.g., Weiss & Brown, 1977), the studies that support Nisbett and Wilson's position have asked subjects to report on trivial or obscured influences on their behavior, such as the serial position effect described earlier. Realistically, subjects could not be expected to be aware of these types of factors.

Third, it has been argued that Nisbett and Wilson's particular methodological procedures do not provide a fair test of the accuracy of subjects' reports. For example, subjects are often asked to report on factors that were manipulated experimentally, having been exposed to only one experimental condition and having no knowledge of what the other experimental conditions may have been. This fact makes it hard for subjects to infer comparatively what might have influenced their behavior (see, particularly, E. R. Smith & Miller, 1978; Nisbett & Ross, 1980).

There are also statistical problems with the interpretation of some of Nisbett and Wilson's evidence. The average of a whole group of subjects' ratings concerning what factors might have influenced their behavior are sometimes compared against actual influences on the subjects' behavior; the more appropriate statistical comparison would compare individual ratings of perceived influence with actual influence on the same individual's behavior (Kraut & Lewis, 1982).

Some have argued that, because subjects report retrospectively on the factors that influenced their decisions, memory decay may account for their apparent inability to recognize factors that influence judgments. C. K. Turner (1988), however, used concurrent reporting and found no effect on recognition of external influences on judgments, thereby belying the memory decay alternative explanation (see also Sprangers et al., 1987).

And, finally, critics say that Nisbett and Wilson have maximized the conditions under which subjects would not be able to retrieve their thought processes. When conditions more suitable to such access are created, such as an involving task or a strong motivation to be accurate, or when well-chosen probes are used to try to get at cognitive processes, evidence for access to internal thought processes may be found (Wright & Rip, 1981).

Nisbett and Ross (1980) and T. D. Wilson and Stone (1985) rebutted several of these criticisms, but the fact that the position remains hard to falsify has led to a stalemate on the issue (Quattrone, 1985; Wright & Rip, 1981; P. A. White, 1987). What is the status of their argument? Nisbett and Wilson (1977b) have clearly demonstrated the weak version of their argument: there are many causes of individual behavior of which individuals themselves are not customarily aware. It is still a matter of controversy whether the strong version of their argument is valid, that is, that people have little or no access to their cognitive processes as a rule.

Even the weak version of Nisbett and Wilson's argument has important implications for the inferential process. If we optimistically ask the social perceiver to set prior theories aside and pay attention to the many subtle but normatively important factors that ought to be influencing behavior, our optimism may well be misplaced. It seems unlikely that the task could be accomplished well or thoroughly. Self-insight into cognitive processes is surely limited, and hence, the idea that the social perceiver can describe, let alone straighten out, the inference process on his or her own is dubious.

Can We Improve the Inference Process?

Perhaps those cases in which we do strikingly well at inferential tasks could serve as models for improving the judgment process more generally. We have, after all, constructed a technological world of literally breathtaking proportions. But, as Nisbett and Ross (1980) point out, our triumphs are usually collective enterprises involving the pooling of many different kinds of expertise. They are often accomplished with the help of inferential aids such as calculators or computers. Perhaps most important, these products usually result from the cumulative effort of many years of formal research. In short, when we succeed strikingly, we do so because we use normative models and built-in devices and safeguards to ensure that we adhere to those models and because we make judgments collectively by pooling expertise. Our successes, then, may be successful precisely because we do not use our intuitive inferential strategies.

This point suggests several possible approaches for improving inferential strategies. Perhaps we should try to make the naive perceiver more like the formal scientist. Education in statistics and methodology, buttressed by the use of formal memory aids, is one approach (Einhorn, 1980; Nisbett et al., 1982). Bringing normative models into folk wisdom via catchy maxims that embody normative or statistical principles is another possibility ("It's an empirical question." "Which hat did you draw that sample out of?" Nisbett & Ross, 1980). With formal training or constant reminders of appropriate inferential techniques, formal methods may creep into everyday inference. Another solution is to get people to give up their attachment to hunches, theories, or clinical intuition by more often turning problems over to experts or computers. This is no small task. There is already sufficient evidence to justify such a move in many decision-making domains, but the evidence has been largely ignored. Moreover, none of these recommended methods is foolproof. Collectively made decisions have their own unique types of errors (e.g., Janis, 1972; Shaw, 1971), and trained statisticians and other experts are sometimes just as vulnerable to inferential errors as laypersons (Kahneman & Tversky, 1973; Tversky & Kahneman, 1974).

Teaching Reasoning

One way of improving the inference process generally is through education, by teaching reasoning in a formal educational curriculum. Nisbett and his colleagues have explored the value of teaching reasoning to see if and when learning rules applicable to specific problems generalize to a wider array of problems. In one study, Fong, Krantz, & Nisbett (1986) trained subjects in the law of large numbers, which maintains that information derived from large samples is more trustworthy than information derived from small samples. Some subjects were given formal training in the law of large numbers, others were shown how to apply the law for several concrete example problems, a third group received both types of training, and a fourth group received no training. Results indicated that subjects receiving either rule-training or training by examples were more likely to reason statistically than those who received no training; the greatest amount of statistical reasoning was demonstrated by subjects who received training in both the abstract rule and the examples.

More important, using the learning-through-examples approach (guided induction), Fong, Krantz, & Nisbett were able to show a high degree of generalizability of the training effects, such that subjects improved as much in domains in which they were not explicitly trained as in domains in which they were trained. Training by example generalized readily to domains very different from the target domain, suggesting that the effects of teaching reasoning may be relatively broad in their implications and not narrowly successful within a given content domain. These results support the idea that statistical heuristics are invoked primarily: when features of the inferential problem match the characteristics of the rules, and when chance is made salient. People clearly possess abstract inferential rules and they can be trained through guided induction to expand upon and improve their use in a variety of settings (see also Cheng et al., 1986).

The assumption that people are able to, and do, spontaneously employ higher-order statistical heuristics is also borne out by research demonstrating that graduate training can have a marked effect on reasoning strategies. Lehman, Lempert, and Nisbett (1988) compared graduate students in four disciplines—psychology, medicine, law, and chemistry—both initially upon entrance to graduate school and two years later, to see if graduate training had any impact on a variety of statistical and methodological reasoning tasks. Consistently, psychology students and to a lesser extent, students in medicine, showed improvements in their reasoning, presumably because both of these specialties involve the interpretation of probabilistic data. However, for students in chemistry, a science that deals almost exclusively with deterministic causes, no improvement was expected or found. Legal training similarly had minimal impact on changes in statistical and methodological reasoning with the exception of conditional problems, with which the law deals frequently.

The conclusion, then, is that people are capable of using abstract statistical concepts, and that they do employ them spontaneously but not always entirely correctly in relevant situations. Both formal training and training by example improve the ability to see the applicability of statistical principles to a broad range of situations and make appropriate use of them.

SUMMARY

Inference is the process of collecting and combining often diverse and complex information into a judgment. It is a task that must be accomplished by the social perceiver daily, for even the most mundane of social observations is often based on an apparently complex inference. For many of the steps that are involved in making inferences there is a normative model that describes the ideal manner in which the steps could be accomplished and that points to a correct answer. When contrasted against the normative model, the social perceiver's judgmental processes appear flawed.

Deciding what data are relevant to a judgment is often marked by prior expectations or theories; sampling is often biased, and biases in already existing samples are often ignored. Strong inferences are frequently drawn from small and unreliable samples. When good base-rate information describing population characteristics is available, it is often overlooked in favor of less reliable, but seemingly more relevant, case history or anecdotal information. Regression—the fact that extreme events will, on the average, be less extreme when observed again—is poorly understood by the social perceiver; instead, extreme events are frequently used to predict future extreme events. People are particularly poor at using and combining probabilistic information, often manifesting great confidence in the truth of unlikely events.

There are also potential sources of error that affect the ability to combine information into a judgment. Typically, computers do a more reliable job of weighting and combining diverse bits of information than the person; people may think they are combining cues in a complex fashion, but they may actually be using very few cues and combining them unreliably.

Covariation, the estimate of degree of association between two events, is a concatenation of many of the previously described skills (e.g., detecting relevancy, sampling, combining information), so it is also subject to error. When data are already collected and clearly summarized, instructions are clear, relevance to the statistical model is clear, and no a priori theory about degree of covariation exists, the social perceiver does fairly well at estimating covariation. However, in the absence of these factors, covariation estimates are heavily biased by prior expectations. In learning from past behavior or errors, people usually overestimate what could have been foreseen. Motivational factors also intrude as a source of bias in judgments and decisions.

Given that the social perceiver often does not behave in a normatively appropriate fashion, what does he or she do? One answer is that heuristics and other shortcuts are often used to reduce complex inferential tasks to simple ones. One such heuristic is representativeness; the perceiver decides how likely it is that an object is a member of some category on the basis of whether the object's features are similar to the essential features of the category. Another heuristic is availability, which involves estimating frequency or likelihood by how quickly instances or associations can be brought to mind. The simulation heuristic uses availability to determine what outcome is most likely, given a set of circumstances. The anchoring and adjustment heuristic enables the perceiver to use an already existing anchor or adjust from that anchor to reach an estimate for some new problem. A variety of statistical heuristics and pragmatic reasoning schemas that approximate normative models are also used to accomplish inferential and decision tasks, their use being dictated by their perceived relevance to the task.

How flawed is the social judgment process? Three perspectives on this issue have been voiced. The first suggests that the experimental literature makes people look worse than they really are, and that intuitive inferential strategies are actually quite effective in the real world. A second position maintains that certain of the inferential errors may not be too serious because the social world provides communication and other forms of feedback that may correct blatantly false errors. A third position suggests that, at least under certain circumstances, judgmental errors and biases may produce severe distortions, and therefore it is advisable to find ways to correct the inference process. All three positions appear to have some validity.

What are the chances of improving the inference process? Unfortunately, recent research suggests that insight into our own cognitive limitations may be limited, thereby raising the question as to whether we are indeed capable of improving our judgmental processes. However, recent research on teaching reasoning suggests that, through training, people's inferential capabilities may be improved. The key to such training appears to be increasing the perceived relevancy of normative models to social situations. Decision-making methods that attempt to control for common biases and/or the use of tools such as statistics and computers in aiding judgment formation and decision making can correct many biases.

What is striking about social inference is that we do as well as we do. One reason we do so well is that intuitive inferential strategies take into account content, context, and change, which normative strategies do not; hence, our strategies may be particularly suited to the types of daily problems we must solve. Moreover, many errors that an individual makes in social inference may be inconsequential for behavior; others will cancel out each other; and others will be detected through communication.

Beyond Cognition

10

Affect and Cognition

---------- ❖ ----------

Differentiating Among Affects, Preferences, Evaluations, Moods, Emotions ◆ *Early Theories* ◆ *Physiological Theories of Emotion* ◆ *Social Cognitive Foundations of Affect* ◆ *Affective Influences on Cognition* ◆ *Affect versus Cognition*

*A*cognitive social psychologist was recently approached with the rather disconcerting opening, "You do affect, don't you?" This comment seemed odd for several reasons. For starters, the topics included in affect are beyond the capacity of any one person to presume to "do," for the literature sprawls across every domain of psychology. But even within the traditions of social psychology, if one identifies oneself as a *cognitive* social psychologist, affect is normally not included in what one primarily does, so the blunt question is also a bit off at least in presupposing the affect without mentioning the cognition. However, suppose the cognition is a given and that our friend is indeed a cognitive-social-psychologist-who-does-affect. This is a curious hybrid, for it results from being back-bred to achieve what originally existed as a species in the wild, natural state. In other words, cognitive social psychology is the artificial creation achieved by deliberately isolating and selecting for certain valued characteristics (e.g., a commitment to the importance of thoughts and information in social contexts). In this breeding process—some would say inbreeding—affect is one of the characteristics selected out. Hence, it is ironic that, having attained the pure-bred strain of cognitive social psychology, perhaps exemplified by the material in the person memory chapter, cognitive social psychology is reverting to its wild state, to the extent that someone in the field could be approached as "doing affect."

In this chapter, we will do affect in several respects, although we will confine ourselves to the work most linked to social cognition. In the main, we will cover early theories of emotion, that is, the precursors to current cognition and emotion debates; physiological theories of emotion, to provide a broader context to the cognitive theories; social cognitive theories that describe how cognitions underlie emotions; social cognitive theories that describe how affect influences cognitions; and, to finish, the premise that affect and cognition are separate, having little to do with each other.

Fundamental questions arise when one attempts to integrate affect and cognition. The history of research on emotion reveals long struggles over the role of cognitive processes in affect. (For reviews of cognitive and other theories of emotion, see Strongman, 1978; for recent samplings, see M. S. Clark & Fiske, 1982; P. Shaver, 1984; V. Hamilton, Bower, & Frijda, 1988.) Two questions particularly concern us here, the influence of cognition on affect and the influence of affect on cognition. Dividing the psychology of affect and cognition in this way, of course, presupposes that the two can be usefully separated. However, the separation is not sustained, for example, by one's lived experience of affect and cognition as occurring in a simultaneous mix. For analytic convenience, this chapter will divide affect and cognition, examining their reciprocal influences, but it is important to note that this separation is something of a fiction.

A final word of caution: The field of affect, and likewise affect and cognition, has spawned an encyclopedic array of theories, some of which are tested by data and some of which remain untested. This inevitably creates considerably uneven scientific status for the various theories, but it also presents opportunities for the enterprising researcher. Moreover, the sheer quantity of unrelated theories challenges the capacity of any neophyte (and even the seasoned affect expert). Hence, we will organize and compare theories where possible, but let the reader beware that the review of theories inevitably resembles a laundry list to the extent that the literature has generated multiple unrelated and often untested explanations.

DIFFERENTIATING AMONG AFFECTS, PREFERENCES, EVALUATIONS, MOODS, EMOTIONS

Defining terms forces one to think hard about what is meant by affect terms used loosely in everyday language (cf. J. D. Mayer, 1986; H. A. Simon, 1982). *Affect* is a generic term for a whole range of preferences, evaluations, moods, and emotions. *Preferences* include relatively mild subjective reactions that are essentially either pleasant or unpleasant. The preferences most frequently studied by social psychologists are interpersonal *evaluations:* that is, simple positive and negative reactions to others, such as attraction, liking, prejudice, and so forth. Such positive and negative evaluations have obvious importance in social interaction, telling us whom to approach and whom to avoid. Evaluations can also pertain to objects, of course.

Preferences and evaluations may be distinguished from affects that have a less specific target, that is, *moods*. One can have an evaluative reaction toward a person, but one does not typically have a mood directed toward someone. Moods affect a wide range of social cognitions and behaviors. Like preferences and evaluations, moods are primarily considered as simply positive or negative, at least as they are currently treated in the relevant literature. Preferences, evaluations, and moods are not normally fleeting experiences, but typically have some duration.

Simple positive and negative reactions do not capture all the intensity and complexity of affect. Think how limited our worlds would be if all we could say was, "I feel good (bad) right now" or "I feel positively (negatively) toward you." More interesting and sensitive terms are needed to differentiate between being elated and contented, between being sad and angry. For instance, one person we know insists on over a dozen distinct states of being emotionally drained: tired, fatigued, sleepy, exhausted, run-down, wiped-out, depleted, spent, weak, limp, blank, numb, spaced-out, empty. Not all of us are so subtly attuned, but most of us need more than three or four terms to describe our affective reactions. *Emotion* refers to this complex assortment of affects, beyond merely good feelings and bad, to include delight, serenity, anger, sadness, fear, and more. Emotion also can imply intense feelings with physical manifestations, including physiological arousal. Emotions can be of short or long duration, but they do not usually last over periods as long as preferences and evaluations can last.

How to characterize the rich variety of affective responses is a longstanding problem in psychology (Davitz, 1970; Ekman, 1984; Plutchik, 1980; Schlosberg, 1954; Wundt, 1897). Affects can be characterized in one of two ways that emerge consistently across analyses of the structure of emotion. As the solid lines in Figure 1 indicate, two common dimensions are pleasantness/unpleasantness and high/low arousal (engagement) (e.g., J. A. Russell, 1978, 1983). When people are asked to describe how they feel right now, or when they are asked to sort emotion words according to their similarity, these two dimensions emerge reliably. Thus, one might be feeling content, happy, and pleased, but at that same moment one is unlikely also to be feeling blue, grouchy, and lonely because those terms are at the opposite end of the same dimension. Moreover, separately, one could also be feeling aroused, astonished, and surprised, or conversely quiescent, quiet, and still. Apparently, people's common-sense theories of emotion are based on what one feels at any given point in time. In this short-run framework, the more one feels good, the less one feels bad, and this is especially true if emotions are intense (Diener & Iran-Nejad, 1986) or simple, but the de-

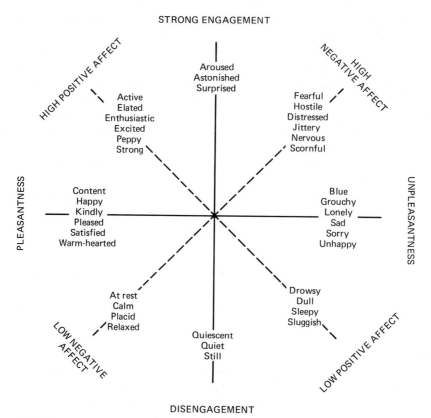

FIGURE 10.1 Two factor solutions to the structure of affect. (After Watson & Tellegen, 1985.)

gree to which one feels aroused is a separate matter. One can be happily or unhappily aroused, happily or unhappily quiescent.

In contrast, suppose people are asked about their experience of emotion over time, for example, considering their life satisfaction in general, their feelings over the last year, how they feel in close relationships over time, and even their emotional reactions to Presidential candidates over the course of the entire campaign (e.g., Abelson et al., 1982; Bradburn & Caplovitz, 1965; for reviews, see Diener, 1984; Watson & Tellegen, 1985). In the case of a longer time frame, people's reports of positive and negative affect are curiously independent. That is, over time, whether one has felt distressed, fearful, or hostile is unrelated to whether one has also at other times felt elated, enthusiastic, and excited (Diener & Emmons, 1984). Over time, with less intense, or more complex emotions, one can observe a structure of affect that is also apparent if you take Figure 1 and rotate it 45°, placing "high positive affect" at the top. In some cases, one can feel much or little "pure" positive affect, and that has little bearing on whether one also feels much or little "pure" negative affect. Thus, time frame, intensity, and complexity jointly seem to determine which of two structures captures people's emotional experiences. Intense, simple, short-term emotions show a negative correlation (i.e., inverse relation) between pleasant and unpleasant feelings, but longer-term summaries of complex and perhaps less intense emotional experience show no correlation between positive and negative emotions. In both cases, however, a two-dimensional structure captures the most consensual understanding of the structure of emotion.

Negative emotions, analyzed separately, seem to have a more complex dimensional structure than positive emotions analyzed separately (Averill, 1980; Ellsworth & Smith, 1988a, 1988b). Consider the differences among anger, sadness, fear, disgust, anxiety, shame, and hate. In contrast, love, serenity, pride, and joy seem more similar. Negative emotions vary, for example, in degree of human agency and situational control; they may also vary in degrees of certainty, attention, and anticipated effort. To take the first dimension, one feels more guilt when the human agent is self rather than another; the reverse is true for anger (Ellsworth & Smith, 1988a). However, positive emotions also have dimensional structure, although it tends to be simpler (Argyle & Crossland, 1987; Ellsworth & Smith, 1988b).

The dimensional analyses of emotion are exceedingly useful, but how do we decide what is an emotion and what is not? Is pain an emotion? What about alienation, awe, challenge, or startle? As a consequence of this issue, theorists have focused on an alternative way to characterize the concept of emotion. Deciding what is an emotion and what is not comes much more easily if one does not require emotion to be a classical concept with necessary and sufficient defining features. According to the prototype view of categories, as described in Chapter 4, category membership is a matter of degree, rather than all or nothing. Some states are more obviously emotions (e.g., happiness, anger, sadness, love, fear, hate): they come to mind easily when people list emotions, they are likely to be labeled emotions, and they fit into context as do other emotions ("He was overcome by . . . [fill in the blank]"). Moreover, the better examples of emotion share many features with other prototypic category members (heart-rate increase, perspiration, obsessive concern, tears) (Fehr & Russell, 1984).

Researchers have also applied prototypes to defining the meaning of particular emotions. Rigid definitions do not completely capture the characteristics of particular emotions; for example, what exactly is love, anger, or fear? In this view, for example, people's categorization of particular emotional facial expressions, such as anger or fear, would reflect degree of fit, not an either-or decision (Russell & Bullock, 1985, 1986; Russell & Fehr, 1987; but see Ekman & O'Sullivan, 1988 vs. Russell & Fehr, 1988).

Taking the core emotions of love, joy, anger, sadness, and fear, people indeed can specify prototypical emotion episodes that might be characterized as scripts beginning with an appraisal of events that elicit emotions, which then consist of expressions, action tendencies, subjective feelings, and physiological states (P. Shaver et al., 1987). For example, prototypic joy begins with a desired outcome, an achievement, or receiving esteem and praise; then the joyous person seeks to communicate and be with others; the person has a positive outlook and feels energetic, excited, and bubbly; the person smiles and says positive, enthusiastic things. The point here is that people conceive of a prototypic experience of joy, such that a good example contains all these elements, and less-good examples contain fewer of them but still might be classified as joy. In-depth analyses also have concentrated on prototypes for love and commitment (Fehr, 1988) and for loneliness (Horowitz, de S. French, & Anderson, 1982).

More generally, people have schemas for the typical physiological changes that occur during particular emotions, and these schemas are similar across cultures (Rimé, Philippot, & Cisamoio, 1990). People also have rules for guessing other people's affective reactions (Karniol, 1986). In all this work, one cannot be certain whether common individual experiences cause shared prototypes or whether the culture defines certain experiences as certain emotions, which individuals then enact as emotions. That is, the direction of causality between individual emotional prototypes and cultural expectations is not clear, but that does not undermine the prototype approach.

One perspective embraces the cultural determination of emotion, holding that emotions are substantially defined by culture. This social constructivist view of emotions sees emotions as transitory social roles represented cognitively in members of a shared culture. Thus, emotions are identifiable roles that people assume, each with variations on a central (or prototypic) theme (e.g., Averill, 1983). In this view, emotions (a) are constituted by social rules prescribed in cultural scripts, (b) are importantly interpersonal phenomena that are interwoven with other actors as part of the larger "play" (cf. de Rivera & Grinkis, 1986), (c) are part of a cultural story or "plot" that gives them meaning, (d) involve choice regarding one's participation as an actor, (e) require training for skilled performance, (f) require identification with the role to experience intensity, and (g) entail interpretation of the role as it fits into the larger social context (Averill, 1990c). As such, emotions entail a coherent, organized syndrome of responses (Averill, 1990b; cf. de Rivera, 1984), an entire set of characteristic responses that identify the emotion, within a certain fuzzy set of related reactions, just as prototypic features identify emotions in particular cases or emotions in general. Other social constructivist views also emphasize the individual's experience of emotion in relationship to society, but not all focus on the cognitive structures for storing social rules and roles (also see Harre, 1986; Hochs-child, 1983; and special issue of the *British Journal of Social Psychology*, 1988).

To review, affect subsumes preferences, evaluations, moods, and emotions. Preferences and evaluations are simple, long-term positive or negative reactions to a target, whereas moods are simple, long-term positive or negative feelings without a specific target. Emotion refers to the richer variety of affective states, which may be intense and short-term. Various efforts to reflect the richness of emotion have used dimensional analyses, prototype models, and social role approaches. A cautionary note is important in applying these definitional points to the work reviewed in the remainder of the chapter: many of these distinctions are not uniformly maintained by those working in the field. In fact, some of the best empirical work on affect bears little relation to the best taxonomic work on affect, an issue the field currently fails to address.

*E*ARLY THEORIES

A brief bit of historical context will help put perspective on the task of the remainder of this chapter, namely, the longstanding question of the relationship between affect and cognition. A century ago, William James (1890/1983) proposed that the feeling of autonomic feedback (heart rate, stomach tension) and muscular feedback (posture, facial expressions) itself constitutes emotion. Conrad Lange (1885/1922) invented a similar theory at the same time as James. In this James-Lange view, the physiological patterns unique to each emotion reveal to us what we are feeling. James stated that when we see a bear in the woods, we are afraid because we tremble and run away: the physical responses cause the emotion. The James-Lange theory of emotion down-played the role of cognition or mental activity as a sole basis for emotion. In a similar manner, Charles Darwin (1872) had proposed that the relevant muscular activity can strengthen or inhibit emotion.

Decades later, the James-Lange theory was undermined by Walter Cannon's (1927) arguments that visceral sensations are too diffuse to account for all the different emotions and that the autonomic system responds too slowly to account for the speed of emotional response. Following this critique, many psychologists assumed that physiological contributions to emotion were limited to diffuse arousal and did not include specific patterns of bodily sensation. We will come back to this point, but assuming this undifferentiated view of arousal for the moment, a basic problem still remained: if arousal is diffuse, and simply ranges from high to low, how can one account for the rich texture of emotional experience? One set of answers is physiological, and the other is cognitive.

PHYSIOLOGICAL THEORIES OF EMOTION

Physiology can still provide the richness of emotional experience, most importantly through that multifaceted and highly sensitive organ, the face. Another possibility is that arousal intensifies existing positive or negative feelings, in effect providing the second dimension of emotion. A third possibility is that arousal is itself differentiated, contrary to the Cannon critique. As it happens, these possibilities are not independent, for the facial and arousal possibilities are related, as we shall see. In any case, it is helpful to get a brief overview of noncognitive theories of emotion, for purposes of comparison to the cognitive theories.

Facial Feedback Theory

The original facial feedback hypothesis held that emotional events directly trigger certain innate configurations of muscles, and that we become aware of feelings only upon feedback from the face (Tomkins, 1962; cf. Gellhorn, 1964). Notice how compatible this view is with the James-Lange theory, yet without having to assume that arousal is fast and differentiated, only that facial responses are. According to facial feedback theory, development and upbringing constrain the range of expressions people adopt and so also the range of emotions they can feel (Izard, 1972, 1977). Thus, over time, people build up a repertoire of emotions, on the basis of the facial muscles society allows them to use in expressing their emotions. While variants exist, the core hypothesis is that feedback from facial expressions influences emotional experience and behavior (Buck, 1980; Winton, 1986).

Facial expressions reflect both pleasantness and intensity, two basic dimensions of emotion (Schlosberg, 1954). Moreover, facial expressions are related to other physiological responses in emotion. The pleasantness of a person's facial expression (as rated by observers, while the person is viewing evocative photographs) can be directly related to heart rate (extreme pleasantness with acceleration, extreme unpleasantness with deceleration; Winton, Putnam, & Krauss, 1984). And the rated intensity of expression can be related to skin conductance (i.e., minute differences in amount of perspiration). Thus, visceral responses in facial expression, heart rate, and skin conductance may reflect basic dimensions of emotions (Winton, Putnam, & Krauss, 1984), and they can form an integrated configuration of physiological responses in emotion (cf. Cacioppo, Petty, & Geen, 1989; Ekman, Levenson, & Friesen, 1983; McCaul, Holmes, & Solomon, 1982; Zuckerman et al., 1981). Moreover, observers agree on the core emotions communicated by certain facial expressions, even cross-culturally (Ekman, 1984). Indeed, the face reliably reflects the pleasantness and intensity dimensions of emotion, even when overt expressions are not noticeable to observers. That is, electrodes attached to the face can detect tiny muscular (electromyographic or EMG) activity too subtle or fleeting to be seen, and this activity parallels the muscles used in overt facial expressions, reflecting two basic dimensions of emotion (Cacioppo, Petty, & Geen, 1989; Cacioppo et al., 1986).

There is also evidence for the fundamental idea that facial expressions exert a direct effect on mood, emotion, and evaluations (Laird, 1984). In one typical paradigm, subjects are induced to adopt specific facial expressions (e.g., smile, frown) without labeling them as such. For example, one experiment instructed them to contract and hold the relevant muscles one-by-one, for supposed EMG recording, until they had inadvertently assumed an emotional expression (Laird, 1974). Or, supposedly to study the physical coping strategies of the disabled, another experiment asked subjects to hold a pen in their teeth, without using their lips, thereby simulating a smile (F. Strack, Martin, & Stepper, 1988). Subjects then rated the funniness of cartoons, detecting more humor when they artificially maintained a smiling facial expression than when they inhibited a smile. Other researchers have obtained similar effects (e.g., Cupchik & Leventhal, 1974; Duncan & Laird, 1977; Lanzetta, Cartwright-Smith, & Kleck, 1976; Rhodewalt & Comer, 1979; Zuckerman et al., 1981).

The facial feedback hypothesis is controversial. The effect across studies appears small (Matsumoto, 1987). Moreover, some researchers do not replicate the finding that posed facial expressions change emotion (Buck, 1980; Ellsworth & Tourangeau, 1981; Tourangeau & Ellsworth, 1979; but see Hager & Ekman, 1981; Izard, 1981; Tomkins, 1981). One likely explanation for some of the contradictory findings is that telling people simply to *exaggerate* their spontaneous facial expressions produces changes in emotion, but rigidly *posed* expressions only sometimes produce changes in emotion. The conditions under which posed expressions do produce emotion are as yet unclear. Another controversy revolves around whether or not facial feedback effects are cognitively mediated. Some maintain that the effects of facial feedback on emotion are cognitively mediated, as in the self-attribution of attitudes (e.g., Laird, 1974), while others argue that the effects are direct and cognitively unmediated (Gellhorn, 1964; Izard, 1972, 1977; Plutchik, 1962; Tomkins, 1962). Finally, throughout all the facial feedback research, even the most extreme precautions cannot completely silence critics who argue that subjects realize their expressions are being manipulated and so respond on the basis of experimental demand. Nevertheless, the facial feedback hypothesis—and related evidence regarding feedback from other nonverbal channels (Kellerman, Lewis, & Laird, 1989)—has provided one possible physiological solution to the problem of how emotions are differentiated into their complex variety.

Vascular Theory

Another, more preliminary theory makes use of the face, but differs in virtually all other respects from facial feedback theory. In the current context, it serves as an example of a fundamentally noncognitive theory of emotional differentiation. Robert Zajonc (1985a) has recently resurrected a theory posited at the beginning of the century by Israel Waynbaum (1907); briefly, Waynbaum's vascular theory of emotion held that the facial muscles serve to regulate blood flow to the brain and that these regulatory functions of facial movements have subjective (affective) consequences. This revived theory sparked considerable debate (Burdett, 1985; Fridlund & Gilbert, 1985; Izard, 1985; Zajonc, 1985b), and its pure form appears to be wrong.

Nevertheless, it provided the starting point for the Zajonc vascular theory (Zajonc, Murphy, & Inglehart, 1989). Briefly, this theory states that emotional reactions disrupt vascular blood flow to the brain (with changes in heart rate, for example). Facial expressions restore balance by changing air flow to the nasal cavity and by changing particular aspects of blood flow. Jointly, these alter the temperature of cerebral blood flow and thereby, the temperature of the brain, resulting in the subjective experiences of emotion. This theory is provocative, and the empirical support is just beginning to emerge (Zajonc, Murphy, & Inglehart, 1989). Nevertheless, it is at least a useful counterpoint to the cognitive approaches in general, and to the versions of facial feedback theory that rely heavily on cognitive mediation.

Hard Interface: Emotions Stored in the Muscles?

One of us recently was persuaded to go skating after a lapse of too many years. Wondering whether her childhood skill would come back, or whether she would be a humiliated adult clutching the guardrail as ten-year-olds whizzed past, it was comforting to let the body memories take over and give up mentally reconstructing the motions. Fortunately for pride and backside, the body remembered. Another theory posits that the body also remembers the movements of emotions.

This muscular theory of emotion makes use of the entire body, not just the face, and it posits that the body's motoric responses represent emotion (shivering with fear, drooping with sadness, jumping for joy, clenching a fist in anger) *and* cognition (subvocalizing while reading or doing mental arithmetic, raising one's eyebrows when singing or playing a high note). Thus, most relevant here, motoric "memories" act as a noncognitive, direct representation of the emotion (Zajonc & Markus, 1984; Zajonc, Pietromonaco, & Bargh, 1982; cf. Bull, 1951). In this view, postural and facial configurations are "hard representations" of internal events, just as schemas are "soft representations"; this creates an analogy to the hardware (electronics) and software (programs) of computers. In the emotion realm, the hard interface idea can be applied to people imitating each other's facial expressions and postures when empathizing, and it may account for convergence in the physical appearance of spouses over years of muscular mimicry (Zajonc et al., 1987). In less emotional realms, it also describes one's muscular memory for skating, bike riding, and antiquated dance steps. Although one may argue the cognitive or noncognitive nature of such motoric memories, this preliminary theory provides yet another contrast to more emphatically cognitive theories of emotion, and it suggests how one might move beyond the face, to the body, in physiologically accounting for the differentiated emotions.

Excitation Transfer

Thus far, we have seen several ways in which affect could be differentiated into discrete emotions, without requiring that arousal be differentiated. That is, the complexity of the human face and the entire human motoric system could provide specific patterns of emotion, while arousal need only be a diffuse intensifier. Regardless of whether arousal is differentiated or diffuse, it is important to know how arousal originates and how it influences emotion. The final physiological theory we will cover, thus, focuses on arousal.

Zillmann (e.g., 1978, 1983, 1988) suggests that arousal (that is, emotional excitation of the sympathetic nervous system) has both automatic and learned origins; for example, a startle response is unconditioned, while fear of airplane travel is a conditioned response. To explain both the learned and unlearned features of arousal, Zillmann (1983) maintains that emotion depends on three initially independent factors. The first two components create immediate emotional actions: (a) a *dispositional* component consists of learned and unlearned skeletal-motor reactions (e.g., startle responses, uncontrolled facial reactions, and involuntary emotional gestures); and then (b) an *excitatory* component energizes the organism through learned and unlearned arousal reactions. Finally, (c) the *experiential* aspect involves assessment of one's initial reactions and interpretation of the situation, which can modify one's subsequent reactions. The core of the theory, for our purposes, is that arousal is nonspecific, it is slow to decay, and people are inept at partitioning the sources of their arousal. Hence, arousal left over from a previous setting can combine with arousal in a new situation and intensify one's emotional reaction. This idea is not without practical significance. Although plying one's date with alcohol has always been a traditional mode of seduction, in theory, plying the person with coffee or getting the person to yell at a basketball game could conceivably have better effects. Dancing, too, has its proponents.

There is much evidence that arousal from otherwise innocent sources can intensify affect toward seemingly irrelevant people and objects that come into view. A classic study by Dutton and Aron (1974) shows how excitation can transfer. They arranged for an attractive woman to interview men as they ventured across a scary suspension bridge or as they crossed a relatively sturdy wooden bridge nearby. Each man was asked to tell a story about an intentionally ambiguous picture of a young woman. As predicted, the men who crossed the scary bridge and who were presumably aroused had more sexual content in their stories than did the men who crossed the safe bridge. Moreover, they were more likely to telephone the attractive woman experimenter later than were the men from the safe bridge (for similar results, see Jacobs, Berscheid, & Walster, 1971; Stephan, Berscheid, & Walster, 1971). Thus, arousal originally instigated by fear transferred to romantic or sexual attraction.[1]

Fear and romantic attraction are not the only emotions that can function in this way. When one has been angered and then is exposed to erotic stories, nude pictures, or an attractive opposite-sex confederate, reports of heightened sexual arousal often occur (e.g., Barclay, 1970; Barclay & Haber, 1965). Conversely, prior sexual arousal can increase the likelihood of aggression (e.g., Zillmann, 1971). For men, a female companion's distress at a gory horror film intensifies their own enjoyment of it (Zillmann et al., 1986). Disgust can facilitate the enjoyment of humor (J. R. Cantor, Bryant, & Zillmann, 1974) or music (J. R. Cantor & Zillmann, 1973); the latter finding may explain the appeal of certain music videos. What is provocative about these findings is that the valence of the prior experience is irrelevant; only the arousal transfers (for dissenting views, see R. A. Baron, 1977; Branscombe, 1985).

By itself, simple physical arousal can intensify anger or sexual attraction. For example, people who have just exercised respond more aggressively or more angrily when provoked than do people not previously aroused (Zillmann, 1978; Zillmann & Bryant, 1974; Zillmann, Katcher, & Milavsky, 1972). Arousal enhances romantic attraction (G. L. White, Fishbein, & Rutstein, 1981; G. L. White & Kight, 1984). Arousal even intensifies evaluations of one's alma mater (M. S. Clark, 1982), as well as one's egotistically satisfying attributions (Gollwitzer, Earle, & Stephan, 1982), and the likelihood of counterarguing a persuasive communication (Cacioppo, 1979). All these studies are consistent with the idea that excitation transfers from one source to another, in-

---

[1]Early studies of this phenomenon frequently refer to it as an analysis of heterosexual behavior, but there is no reason to think that homosexual erotic attraction would be any different.

tensifying subsequent affective responses. Their implications are broadened by the finding that, even if unable to take immediate action under transferred excitation, people may commit themselves to future actions (e.g., revenge) while excited, so that the effects of excitation transfer can last long after the actual arousal dissipates (Bryant & Zillmann, 1979). Arousal, thus, polarizes both positive and negative reactions (Stangor, 1990).

A question of particular interest to social cognition research is whether the effects of arousal depend on being cognitively aware of it. People respond emotionally—and perhaps also can be aroused—by an affect-laden stimulus without even being fully aware of the stimulus (Corteen & Wood, 1972; Niedenthal & Cantor, 1986; Robles et al., 1987; Spielman, Pratto, & Bargh, 1988). Excitation transfer theory argues that arousal influences emotion even when people do not consciously feel aroused but physiological measures indicate that they are indeed aroused. This differs importantly from Schachter and Singer's theory of emotion (1962; covered in Chapter 2 and also in the next section), as well as its derivatives, which instead posit that emotion results when people label, interpret, and identify physiological arousal for which they have no immediate other explanation. The implication in Schachter's theory is that the arousal demands explanation because it has been consciously perceived. Recent evidence from people with spinal cord injuries indicates that the perception of arousal may not be necessary for emotional experience, as Schachter's theory assumes (Chwalisz, Diener, & Gallagher, 1988). Another important difference between the two theories is that Schachter's theory originally applied only when the initial source of arousal is ambiguous (Kenrick & Cialdini, 1977), which is not the case for the Zillmann theory. Note, however, that both theories describe roles for arousal when its *current* source is otherwise ambiguous.

Summary and Comment on Physiological Contributions to Emotion

Early theories of emotion set the stage for a continuing debate over the role of cognition and physiology in affective responses. James hypothesized that unique physiological patterns occur in direct response to emotional stimuli, without cognitive mediation. His view was undermined by Cannon, who argued that visceral responses are too slow and too diffuse to differentiate the many separate emotions. Facial feedback theorists argue, as James did, that the different emotions come directly from physiological sensations. But instead of relying on the arousal system, they suggest that the sensitive facial musculature provides the different patterns for various emotions. The vascular theory of emotion

also argues that facial muscle configurations, normally called facial expressions, act to regulate cerebral blood temperature (not just to
"express" emotions). The hard interface theory suggests that a variety
of emotional and nonemotional knowledge is represented in muscular
configurations across the body and the face. Taking a different tack, the
arousal theorists have examined how arousal intensifies emotional responses that originate from learned or unlearned responses. All these
theorists downplay the importance of cognition in emotional responses,
compared to the theories covered next.

Before continuing, it is important to note that an apparently erroneous presumption motivated some of the theories just covered and some
of those that follow. That is, some of the search for facial origins of emotion, some of the original excitation transfer ideas, and certainly the
arousal-plus-cognition theories that follow, all are based on Cannon's
premise that arousal is too diffuse to account for emotional differentiation. Later evidence indicated that this conclusion may have been premature; distinct patterns of arousal can indeed occur for different emotions (e.g., Ax, 1953; Derryberry & Rothbart, 1988; Lacey, 1959, 1967;
Lacey & Lacey, 1958, 1970; G. E. Schwartz, Weinberger, & Singer, 1981;
G. E. Schwartz, Davidson & Pugash, 1976; Tourangeau & Ellsworth,
1979; Winton, Putnam, & Krauss, 1984). Note however, that Cannon
and Schachter may well have been correct in describing these patterns
as not easily distinguished on an experiential level; that question is still
open. Nevertheless, it is ironic that solving a problem that ultimately
may not require solving has been partly responsible for some of the
most crucial contributions to emotion theory.

SOCIAL COGNITIVE FOUNDATIONS OF AFFECT

Earlier, we asked how emotions could be differentiated if physiological
arousal was not; it has since become clear that both facial muscles and a
differentiated arousal system may underlie the variety of emotions.
Nevertheless, physiology is by no means the whole story in emotion,
and in social psychology, the view of arousal as undifferentiated and
inadequate to account for the variety of emotions led to a parallel effort
to see how cognition could explain emotional complexity; these ideas
worked essentially without reference to developing ideas about physiology.

In considering these ideas about how cognition leads to emotion, it
is useful to keep in mind that many social psychologists have assumed
cognition is a major basis for affective response (C. A. Kiesler, 1982), for
example, in studying stereotyping as an origin of prejudice (Allport,
1954), in proposing cognitive inconsistency as causing arousal that in-
stigates attitude change (Cooper, Zanna, & Taves, 1978), in examining

self-concept discrepancies as creating affect (Higgins, 1987), and more. Because of this broad treatment of affect and cognition within the traditions of social psychology, what follows is necessarily selective.

Emotion as Arousal plus Cognition

Most of us would like to think we are attracted to people because their unique personalities fit with our own unique personalities in significant, if not predestined, ways. We tend to downplay the importance of seemingly incidental factors such as proximity (living in the same courtyard), timing (being divorced long enough to be ready for a new relationship), convenience (being on the same work schedule), or irrelevant sources of arousal (meeting after an intense workout). Yet, all these factors can help establish a close relationship between two people. Moreover, as Schachter's theory of emotional lability proposed (see Chapter 2), when people are aroused, they explain their arousal in different ways, depending on previous experience, socialization, and context (Schachter & Singer, 1962). Thus, what one aroused person interprets as sexual attraction (Dutton & Aron, 1974), another may label love at first sight (Berscheid & Walster, 1978; Walster, 1971). Such misunderstandings have, no doubt, been the cause of much personal tragedy.

Schachter's two-component theory posits that diffuse physiological arousal catalyzes cognitive interpretation, so emotions are mediated by cognitive activity. Note how this differs from the previous views that focus more directly on unmediated physiological responses (e.g., vascular theory, hard interface theory, some versions of facial feedback theory). Despite much controversy (Reisenzein, 1983), Schachter's theory has had considerable impact on social psychological thinking about emotion, as we have already seen (see Chapter 2). Moreover, recent theories take the arousal-plus-cognition viewpoint several steps further.

Mind and arousal in emotion. Some basic features of this theory are similar to Schachter's, in that physiological arousal combines with evaluative cognition to produce emotion. Visceral activation provides the intensity and particular emotional "feel" of the experience, while evaluative cognitions provide the quality of differentiated emotional experience.

George Mandler's theory (1975, 1982, 1984, 1990), unlike Schachter's, locates an origin for arousal, namely, in discrepancy and interruption. In this view, most arousal follows from a perceptual or cognitive discrepancy or from the interruption or blocking of ongoing action. Disruptions by definition violate expectations, either preventing the easy application of one's schemas or the smooth continuation of one's goal-directed activity. Perceptual-cognitive interruptions include musical or visual patterns that diverge from the expected, story lines with an unexpected twist, jokes, and the like. Similarly, disruptions of goal-directed activity can interfere with complex sequences of intended activity. (Recall the last time you were working to meet a deadline and you were asked to take out the garbage.) The complexity of the interrupted activity corresponds to the amount of arousal one feels: if you drop your keys while trying to get in the door, that interrupts a relatively simple goal, so it should cause only a small amount of arousal; if you drop your keys while trying to impress the date of your dreams, that interrupts a potentially more complex goal, so it should create more arousal. As in other theories, arousal intensifies emotion.

Arousal also sets off cognitive interpretation. The interruption may be interpreted positively or negatively, depending on the type of schema disrupted and its interpretation. With complex action sequences, you may interpret the interruption as hindering you from your goal or unexpectedly advancing you toward it, which determines whether emotions are negative or positive. That is, if your interpretation in the key-dropping episode is that you are a hopeless, clumsy oaf, you may feel ashamed and irritated. On the other hand, if your date communicates that your nervousness is endearing, you may interpret that as unexpectedly advancing you toward your goal and feel pleased. (Admittedly, the negative emotions resulting from interruption are more intuitively compelling than the positive emotions that could result.) Whatever the cognitive interpretation, it shapes not only the quality of one's immediate affect but also one's lasting mental representation of the event.

With perceptual-cognitive schemas, the effects of interruption are more subtle. The degree of interruption (and therefore arousal) more directly determines the positivity of the response, with less need for complex interpretation (G. Mandler, 1982; Gaver & Mandler, 1987). Disconfirmations of perceptual schemas (e.g., in music, visual arts, food) range from zero (total familiarity) to extreme (total chaos and discord). On the whole, in this view, (a) familiarity is pleasant but not intense, (b) a little novelty is good, for it requires slight assimilation, and adds a bit of intensity to the pleasant recognition of the familiar, (c) more novelty is better, *if* it can be reinterpreted in familiar terms, as the required adjustment adds more intensity, and (d) complete incongruity, unsuccessfully assimilated, leads to intense negative affect. One of us recently discovered how this operates, at a formal concert, as the string quartet combined the expected classical forms with jazz, causing a sizable portion of the audience to exit at intermission, presumably because the result simply did not fit their well-worn and comfortable perceptual-cognitive schemas. If asked, no doubt they would have simply reported disliking the music; Mandler does not require that interruptions and their resolutions be wholly conscious. In any case, a little novelty is a good thing (cf. Berlyne, 1970; D. W. Fiske & Maddi, 1961; Leventhal, 1974), but too much is hard to take.

Emotion in Close Relationships

Berscheid has presented a compelling case for the application of Mandler's theory to emotion in close relationships (Berscheid, 1982, 1983). In close relationships, the more intimate the relationship, the more two people's goals depend on each other (Kelley et al., 1983). The frequency, strength, diversity, and duration of dependencies on each other define the closeness of the relationship: the more intermeshed two people's daily and long-term goals, the more seriously each person can interrupt the other. Interruptions can include unexpected facilitation, causing relief, joy, and excitement, as well as unexpected hindrance, causing disappointment, frustration, and anger. Interdependent goals can range from simple behavior sequences, such as doing the laundry together, to complex behavior sequences, such as fully sharing child care or collaborating on work. The more complex the behavior sequence, the more intense the emotion when it is interrupted. The greater the interdependence, then, the greater the potential for intense negative emotion, if one partner leaves, withdraws, or dies. Similarly, there is greater potential for positive emotions, if one partner becomes suddenly more attuned, considerate, and helpful to the other and their shared goals. If the intermeshed sequence continues to function as usual, on the other hand, there will be no interruptions and little emotion. Hence, Berscheid notes, there is the paradox that the most intimate, involved, and interdependent relationships may show as little emotion as distant, parallel, uninvolved relationships, simply because the intimate one is running fairly smoothly. An intimate relationship, thus, is defined by the potential for—but not necessarily the experience of—emotional intensity, which results from highly interdependent goals.

Thus, the theory makes the interesting prediction that the sheer amount of emotion experienced in a relationship is negatively correlated with longevity; long-term relationships are least likely to show much emotion, either positive or negative. This prediction has been confirmed in recent work (Berscheid, Snyder, & Omoto, 1989). Consider the normal course of a long-term intimacy. At first, emotions run high (both positive and negative) as two people learn all that they delightfully have in common—and all that tragically divides them. As they become better acquainted, there are simply fewer surprises (disruptions) of both the pleasant and unpleasant sort. As the novelty wears off, emotions run to fewer extremes, and either complacency or boredom may settle in. When the initial intensity fades, does that mean less potential for emotion? No. Quite the contrary. If the relationship broke up, emotional intensity would run to extremes. It is only when the long-term relationship functions smoothly that emotions seem flat and calm. The irony is that one can often only gauge the intensity of a long-term relationship when it is terminated or interrupted.

Besides implying that one can measure the intimacy of a relationship by its interdependence, this perspective explains a number of intriguing experiences in close relationships. For example, external obstacles to a relationship often heighten its passion because emotions stem from interruptions. Would Romeo and Juliet have felt as strongly if their feuding parents had not tried to prevent their relationship? Other puzzles are also resolved, such as the possibility of liking someone very much but not feeling strongly emotional because one has no goals that depend on that person, hence no interruptions, and hence no arousal. This may explain a fair number of relationships stuck on the distinction "I like you, and I even love you, but I'm not *in* love with you." There is also the devilish case in which one emphatically dislikes and would prefer to avoid someone, but nonetheless the person has the capacity to cause great emotion, even positive emotion, because the person can facilitate or interrupt one's goals. In the extreme case, this emotion can be tragically misattributed as love. Finally, how is it possible that some relationships seem to thrive on conflict? To an outsider, it may be a mystery how the relationship continues despite frequent and perhaps not-so-private quarrels. However, if a couple habitually fights, the fights may actually become an integral part of their interdependence; that is, rather than being disruptions, the fights are expected, not especially arousing, and may even meet both partners' goals.

To summarize, both Mandler and Berscheid analyze emotion as resulting from interruptions. Disrupted expectations, whether in a symphony or a relationship, create arousal and cognitive interpretations. The interpretation determines the quality of affect, while the extent of the interruption and subsequent arousal determine the intensity of affect. Because expectations (schemas or goals) are cognitive structures, the models assume that cognition is a necessary antecedent for emotion.

Cognitive Structures and Affect

Other lines of research posit that cognitive structures cue affect, but unlike the preceding theories, they emphasize the successful application of a knowledge structure, rather than its interruption and consequent arousal. Also, the preceding theories emphasize goals as cognitive structures, whereas the theories in this section emphasize more static world knowledge. This work examines cognitive structures such as social schemas, interpretations of outcomes that one has obtained, and the imagined outcomes that might have been or might yet be. Some of it also looks at the broad interplay between emotions and goals, but with little mention of interruption and arousal, the focus of the previous set of theories. One final note about the theories in this section: when they use the term "schema," they refer to knowledge about concepts (as defined in Chapters 4 and 5). In this chapter, we have already come across people's schemas for the concept of emotion in general or particular emotions. However, the schemas in this section start with other types of content that is then linked to affect by various processes.

Social schemas and affect. One approach stems in part from the observation that emotions can result from the successful application of affect-laden schemas. That is, some people (e.g., old flames, feared bosses, judgmental clergy, intrusive outgroup members) and situations (giving a talk to a large audience, receiving a call from an old friend) inspire emotion without necessarily interrupting any goals. Originally called *schema-triggered affect* (S. T. Fiske, 1981, 1982), this idea was later incorporated into the broader distinction between category-based responses and attribute-based responses (e.g., S. T. Fiske & Neuberg, 1990), already discussed in Chapters 4 and 5. The relevant point here is that schemas based on prior experiences can carry immediate affective tags. When a new instance fits the schema, not only does prior knowledge apply, but so also may prior affect. This matching effect has been demonstrated for a variety of person schemas: old flames, politicians, campus stereotypes (such as jock, nerd, artist, and gay), college majors (such as pre-med, engineering, theater), occupations (such as doctor, hotel maid, artist, loan shark), and the potentially stigmatized (schizophrenics, paraplegics) (S. T. Fiske, 1982; S. T. Fiske et al., 1987; S. T. Fiske & Pavelchak, 1986; Neuberg & Fiske, 1987; Pavelchak, 1989). The idea that old patterns match new people and situations, invoking feelings that are essentially holdovers from prior experience, also fits the literature on transference in psychotherapy (J. L. Singer, 1985, 1988; Westen, 1988). It even describes people's affective reactions to consumer products that fit familiar molds (Sujan, 1985) and to loaded political issues (Sears, Huddie, & Schaffer, 1986), and it is assumed to hold for any affect-laden category. Indeed, prototypes associated with affect may be easier to learn than those that are not (J. D. Mayer & Bower, 1986).

A related theory suggests another type of top-down determinant of affect. People have expectations about how they will feel (about a movie, for example), and if the actual experience fits their expectancy, their affective reactions are faster; if the experience is slightly discrepant, they may still assimilate it to the expectancy. When the experience is quite discrepant and they notice it, people have more trouble forming preferences (T. D. Wilson et al., 1989). This type of *affective expectancy* complements the previous work on affect-laden schemas.

Another approach focuses on the features of the schema itself and their implications for affective responses. Linville's work (1982a, 1982b; Linville & Jones, 1980; Linville, Fischer, & Salovey, 1989; Linville, Salovey, & Fischer, 1986), reviewed in Chapter 4, focuses on the affective consequences of *informational complexity*. Recall that people tend to evaluate out-group members (low complexity) more extremely than in-group members (high complexity), all else being equal. More generally, the theory predicts that the greater the complexity of a schema, the more moderate the affect it typically elicits. For example, if you know a dozen dimensions that determine whether a given football team is any good, your evaluation of any random team will include a lot of pluses and minuses. I can only think of two or three dimensions offhand, so any one bit of information about a team is more likely to sway my opinion to one extreme or the other. As we saw in Chapter 6, this analysis also applies to people with simple self-concepts, who appear prone to mood swings, compared to those with more complex self-concepts (Linville, 1985). People differ considerably in their complexity about different domains of knowledge (de Vries & Walker, 1987) and in their complexity about people in general (Sommers, 1981), with similar results.

Another view of the link between knowledge structures and evaluation is that *thought polarizes feelings* because it leads to perceiving a tighter organization of the attributes of a given stimulus, in those people who possess a schema for thinking about it (Tesser, 1978; Tesser & Conlee, 1975; Tesser & Cowan, 1977; Tesser & Leone, 1977). There is posited a general preference for cognitive consistency, so, for example, the more you consider your team's chances for the league championship, the more likely you will fit all of your team's attributes into place as consistently pro or consistently con. Over time, people can make an instance fit the schema, so evaluation becomes more extreme as the attributes become more organized. No amount of mere thought on my part about your team will polarize my evaluations of it, according to Tesser, because I have insufficient prior knowledge to rearrange and, according to Linville, because my opinion is already fairly extreme (being more easily swayed by random factors).

Linville's complexity-extremity hypothesis and Tesser's thought polarization hypothesis may seem to make contradictory predictions, in that Linville claims that complexity moderates evaluations, but Tesser claims that thought (which one might think to make schemas more complex) polarizes evaluations. However, there are several differences in the application of their theories. First, Tesser's theory states that thought makes schemas more organized, internally consistent, and evaluatively uniform, so thought indeed makes the schema (evaluatively) simpler and, therefore, more polarized, which fits Linville's predictions. Second, the complexity-extremity hypothesis refers to initial evaluations at one point in time, while the thought polarization hypothesis refers to changes over time (Linville, 1982b). Third, the thought-polarization effect occurs when subjects make an initial public commitment to their evaluations (perhaps because they are more motivated by pressures to be consistent), whereas the complexity-extremity effect obtains in the absence of such commitment (M. G. Millar & Tesser, 1986b). Finally, the thought-polarization effect occurs when the schema's dimensions are substantially correlated (i.e., ratings on one dimension predict ratings on other dimensions) because the schema's structure is more intrinsically coherent (M. G. Millar & Tesser, 1986b).

In sum, four main theories link schemas and affect. Fiske's theory of schema-triggered affect posits affective tags at the top level of knowledge structures; affective tags and Wilson's affective expectancies both facilitate evaluative responses. Linville's theory of schema complexity posits extreme responses to simple schemas, and Tesser's theory posits extreme responses as schemas become simpler over time.

Obtained outcomes and affect. Just as schema theories emphasize prior expectations about events, so other theories focus on post hoc explanations for events. Cognitions about one's already achieved outcomes underlie many common emotional experiences.

Previously (Chapter 2), we described Weiner's *attributional theory* of achievement motivation (Weiner, 1985b, 1986a), which describes basic dimensions that people use to understand their successes and failures: internal or external locus, stability over time, and controllability. These dimensions in turn provoke basic emotions, as well as expectations for future outcomes. Together, the emotions and expectations guide behavior.

One can demonstrate that specific emotions follow from specific causal attributions (Benesh & Weiner, 1982; Weiner, 1982, 1985b). For example, pride follows from a positive outcome that is attributed to oneself (i.e., internally) and that is seen as controllable, as when one works hard and succeeds, whereas guilt follows from a negative outcome attributed to internal and controllable factors, as when one neglects work and fails. Anger follows from a negative outcome that is attributed to another (i.e., externally) and that is viewed as controllable, as when one fails because another person does not follow up with expected help, whereas gratitude follows from a positive outcome attributed to external and controllable factors, as when one succeeds because the other person does indeed help. Finally, pity results from another person's negative outcome attributed to external factors (other people or the environment) that are seen as uncontrollable; one pities the person who does not succeed due to a string of bad luck. The locus and controllability factors, thus, determine the quality of emotions, and the stability factor tends to exaggerate them. This framework has been applied, with considerable success, to cognitions and emotions in achievement settings (e.g., Weiner, Russell, & Lerman, 1978, 1979; see Weiner, 1985b, for a review). Both in role-playing studies and in studies that ask subjects to reconstruct their past successes and failures, the impact of the attributional dimensions on reported emotions fits Weiner's model.

People implicitly understand these rules of attribution and emotion, so they use them to control the emotions of others. When providing excuses for interpersonal failures, people attribute their behavior to external, uncontrollable, and unintentional factors ("The dog ate my paper"; "My car broke down"). People do not provide the real reasons for being remiss, when the real reasons are internal, controllable, and intentional ("I didn't feel like doing it") or unintentional ("I forgot"). People implicitly know which excuses provoke anger and which defuse it, and experimental manipulations of the causal dimensions of excuses show that they are right (Folkes, 1982; Weiner et al., 1987). People also try to control the emotions of others when hoping to elicit their help. If the cause of one's plight is controllable, one is likely to receive only anger, but if the cause is perceived as uncontrollable, then one is likely to receive both pity and help (Meyer & Mulherin, 1980; Reisenzein, 1986; G. Schmidt & Weiner, 1988; Weiner, 1980a, 1980c). The general principles of the attribution-emotion-action relationships develop in the naive psychology of children as young as five years old (Graham & Weiner, 1986; Weiner & Handel, 1985).

This analysis extends as well to stigmatizing conditions, such as AIDS, mental illness, alcoholism, and physical disability. Physical stigmas are perceived to be stable and to have uncontrollable origins, so they elicit pity and helping, but mental and behavioral stigmas are perceived to be unstable (i.e., reversible) and to have controllable origins, so they elicit anger and neglect (Weiner, Perry, & Magnusson, 1988; cf. Brickman et al., 1982). Conflicts in people's implicit attributions about stigma doubtless cause much heartbreak; for example, depressed people sometimes view their condition as uncontrollable and expect pity, while those around them often see it as controllable and feel anger (Weiner, 1987). A major issue in caring for persons who are HIV-positive or who have developed AIDS is the perception of others regarding the extent to which the person had control over contracting the disease (Weiner, 1988a); sufferers' perceived responsibility is one of the factors contributing to whether or not they receive help. Empirical tests of Weiner's attribution-emotion-behavior theory, as well as its clear applicability, support its usefulness as a cognitively based perspective on emotion.

A second account also relates people's outcomes to emotion (Clore & Kerber, 1980; Ortony, Clore, & Collins, 1988). This is a broad, comprehensive theory not yet subjected to extensive empirical tests, although it builds on and integrates a variety of literature on affect. The *cognitive structural theory* views emotions as valenced reactions to events, agents, and objects that are relevant to one's concerns. There are three main types of emotion, in this view. The *desirability* of an event is evaluated with regard to its facilitation or hindrance of one's goals (which include everything one wants, from preserving one's health or getting a Ph.D. to refueling one's car); this class of emotions pertains to being pleased or displeased (i.e., resentment, gloating, hope, fear, satisfaction, disappointment, joy, distress). The *praiseworthiness* of an agent's action is evaluated in terms of standards (which include what ought to occur, based on morality, conventions, norms, performance expectations); this class of emotions relates to approval or disapproval (i.e., pride, shame, admiration, reproach). And the *appeal* of an object is based on one's attitudes (which include dispositional differences in taste, essentially evaluative reactions to categories of objects); this class includes liking and disliking (also loving and hating). Emotions elicited in these ways all vary in intensity according to the inducing situation's perceived reality, proximity, unexpectedness, and prior arousal. The three specific classes—goal, standard, and attitude emotions—also have specific factors that increase intensity (e.g., degree of likelihood, effort, and realization for goal-based emotions). This description of emotions is designed to give a detailed account of the cognitive antecedents of emotion, potentially suitable for computer simulation. Successful computer simulation would support its logical sufficiency as an explanation of affective processes, and empirical validation would support its psychological realism.

Weiner's work focuses on cognitions (attributions) about outcomes already obtained. Ortony et al.'s theory similarly emphasizes obtained outcomes, but it also addresses alternative possibilities (i.e., personal goals or social standards that could or could not be met). The next section describes two theories that focus more explicitly on imagined alternative outcomes.

Alternative outcomes and affect. Some psychologists studying emotion have focused on cognitions about outcomes that might have been or might yet be. This section will consider two such theories, both of which concern the affective impact of people imagining alternatives to current reality.

One theory that is well-developed conceptually and empirically relies on the simulation heuristic. As already described in Chapter 9, the simulation heuristic describes the ease of imagining alternative outcomes and its effect on post hoc inferences of probability (e.g., Kahneman & Tversky, 1982). When one can easily imagine that things might have been otherwise, one's actual state of affairs seems like more of a fluke. In contrast, when it is more difficult to imagine how things could be other than what they are, the current situation seems inevitable. For example, when you miss meeting an old friend or catching a plane by a few moments, it seems to be a quirk of fate, but when you miss by several hours, it is harder to imagine how things could have worked out differently. The emotional implications of these post hoc inferences are clear: is it more frustrating when one just barely misses the friend or the plane, or when one misses by a wide margin? Events that are retrospectively easier to undo mentally cause more intense emotion. When a person is killed by a freak accident, it somehow seems more tragic than when the person is killed in the normal course of a high-risk job or life style.

Work on *norm theory* extends these and related ideas into a theory of how people decide what is normal and, by exclusion, what is surprising and therefore emotion-producing (Chapter 4; Kahneman & Miller, 1986). An abnormal event is one that has easily imagined alternative outcomes; these alternatives may be either constructed or remembered alternative scenarios. In either case, if there seem to be many possible alternatives, the actual events are surprising. There is an interesting parallel between these ideas and ideas about expectancy effects. That is, an event inconsistent with one's implicit norms is perceived as unlikely in retrospect; an event inconsistent with one's expectations is perceived as unlikely in the future. Thus, while schema and expectancy theories consider people's reasoning before the fact, which might be called anticipatory thinking, this theory concerns people's reasoning after the fact, which might be called backward thinking.

Norm theory's relevance to emotion lies essentially in its emotional amplification hypothesis, namely, that events elicit stronger emotion when their causes are abnormal. This is especially evident for misfortunes, as in the previous examples of just-missed planes and freak accidents, both of which are particularly upsetting. Similarly, a person who wins the lottery with a ticket bought minutes before the drawing—versus one bought weeks before—feels especially lucky and happy (D. T. Miller, Turnbull, & McFarland, 1990) and probably is especially envied as well. Abnormality influences emotional reactions to other people; one feels more sympathy for someone victimized by a chance occurrence (D. T. Miller & McFarland, 1986). Again, the more easily imagined the counterfactual scenario, the more intense the emotion one experiences.

Another complementary approach examines the emotional effects of *alternative future worlds*, what might be or what ought to be (Abelson, 1981a, 1983), rather than what might have been. Certain emotions can result from the mere possibility of disruption or abnormality in a sequence of goal-directed actions; such disruption can occur when two mutually exclusive alternatives are entertained simultaneously. Incompatibility can occur at any of several stages in a sequence of events. Suppose a person decides to go away for the weekend (goal), chooses to go camping (planned action), makes reservations at a favorite camp-ground (causal instrumentality), and succeeds in staying there (out-come). If all proceeds as expected, there is little emotion. However, consider the emotional impact of incompatibility at each stage of this sequence. Feelings of conflict would result from incompatible alterna-tive goals (the person cannot decide whether to go away at all); agony results from incompatible alternative plans (the person cannot choose between camping and visiting family); hope and fear come from incom-patible alternative means or causal instrumentality (the person's camp-ground reservations may have been lost); and suspense stems from in-compatible alternative outcomes (the reserved campsite may be unusable due to flooding). Although there is as yet no research stem-ming from this framework, it illustrates another way to systematize the relationship between people's possible outcomes and their emotions.

In sum, two main theories examine people's emotional reactions to outcomes that might have been (Kahneman and Miller's norm theory) or that might yet be (Abelson's alternative future worlds). Both theories focus on the emotional impact of imagining alternatives.

Emotions as managers of goals. Another set of approaches posits that emotions essentially manage people's priorities. This perspective starts with the observation that many emotions occur when planned be-havior is interrupted, as noted in Mandler's and Berscheid's theories, could have been interrupted, as in Kahneman and Miller's theory, or could yet be interrupted, as in Abelson's theory. However, one can ex-amine not only how interruptions cause emotion, as in those theories, but also the reverse: how emotions cause interruptions.

Emotions can act as controls on cognition, alerting people to impor-tant goals. In effect, emotions are alarm signals consisting of *interruption and arousal,* and they divert people from pursuing one goal and point them toward pursuing another goal that has meanwhile increased in importance (H. A. Simon, 1967, 1982). This view follows from the premise that people are capacity-limited information processors. That is, they can pursue basically only one goal at a time, whether it is lis-tening to a lecture, thinking about a brilliant question to ask, planning what to have for dinner, or making eyes at the attractive person nearby. An information processor potentially could handle such multiple goals by ranking their relative importance and completing each in turn, at its leisure. Unfortunately, such an obsessive android might get run over by a truck if it were only attending to the goal of locomoting to work and not attending to the goal of staying intact. That is, survival depends on the organism being able to interrupt ongoing goals before completion, if other environmental contingencies demand it. Emotions, such as fear of an onrushing moving van, can prompt attention to urgent goals. Exam-ples of such high-priority items include environmental stimuli that warn of potential danger (e.g., producing fear), physiological stimuli that demand refueling (e.g., producing hunger or sleepiness), and internal cognitive stimuli that trigger unmet psychological needs (e.g., producing common negative emotions). In this view, the physiological arousal that accompanies emotion comes from the interruption itself. Note that the interrupting effect of emotion is to alter goals, rather than to disorganize one's responses. Emotions merely indicate the changing importance of one's different goals.

In a related view, emotions manage goals in another way when there is a change in the evaluation of a plan's likely success; they provide *transitions between plans*. Goals change in priority as their perceived chance of progress changes, such that impossible or completed goals are abandoned and manageable goals are pursued. Given that people have multiple goals, emotions provide a way to coordinate among them (Oatley & Johnson-Laird, 1987). Emotions are a form of internal communication about changes in the relative priority of goals, as a function of perceived likelihood of success, and a way to maintain those priorities. This theory also argues that emotions perform a similar function of external communication in coordinating goals with others. Thus, happiness communicates, both internally and externally, that subgoals have been achieved and one should continue with the plan. Sadness communicates the failure of a major plan, which suggests giving up or searching for an alternative. Anger communicates that an active goal has been frustrated, so one will attempt to remove the obstacle or aggress. Anxiety communicates a threat to self-preservation, initiating attention to the environment and possible escape. (For commentary on this theory, see Frijda, 1987a.)

These first two promising notions of emotions as interruptions or managers of changing priorities still await direct empirical test. However, some existing research supports the basic premise that intense emotions interrupt planful, ongoing cognitive activities. For example, emotionally salient material presented outside awareness quickly captures conscious attention (Nielsen & Sarason, 1981). Emotionally charged events are especially memorable (R. Brown & Kulik, 1977) and occupy much of people's daily thoughts (Klinger, Barta, & Maxeiner, 1980). Thus, emotion may well interrupt both attention and memory.

A related concept of emotion as interruption emerges from the *cybernetic theory of self-attention* and a program of research testing its premises (Carver & Scheier, 1982; see Chapter 6). Recall that the theory describes self-focused people as noticing discrepancies between their current state and the achievement of some goal or standard. When people notice the discrepancy, they attempt to adjust their behavior in order to reduce the discrepancy. The person may succeed and move on to another goal. If the person fails, the theory states that the person will keep trying. The person may try repeatedly and fail. Thus, there has to be provision in the theory for the person to give up and change goals. Otherwise, it would portray the organism as marching into a corner, without knowing when it is beaten (Scheier & Carver, 1982; Scheier, Carver, & Gibbons, 1981). An affective feedback system is posited to sense and regulate the rate at which the organism is progressing toward its goal (Carver & Scheier, 1990). Emotions, thus, interrupt ongoing behavior, causing a reassessment of one's probability of success, and one redoubles effort or withdraws accordingly. Thus, emotions in general may lead to self-focused attention (Salovey & Rodin, 1985).

Summary. To a neophyte or even to a seasoned expert, the array of cognition-affect theories is a bit overwhelming, so some retrospective orientation is useful. So far, we have seen three kinds of theories relating cognitive structure to affect. Mandler and Berscheid explore the emotional impact of interrupted schemas and relationship goals. Fiske, Wilson, Linville, and Tesser each explore the affective effects of successfully matching schemas and data. The third set of theories all share an adaptive, goal-oriented perspective: although there are important differences among them, they all address the relationship between emotions and goals. Some (Weiner; Ortony, Clore, & Collins; Kahneman & Miller; Abelson) examine the quality and intensity of emotions that result from comparing a past, present, or future reality to imagined alternatives relevant to one's goals. Others (Simon; Oatley & Johnson-Laird; Carver & Scheier) examine the interruptive functions of emotions in the service of furthering one's highest priority (most important and most attainable) goals.

Both the neophyte's and the expert's difficulty in absorbing this literature is increased by the unevenness of these theories. Some are comprehensive, reviewing scores of prior studies and theories, attempting to integrate them; others are focused and attempt to account for a narrow range of affective phenomena. Some have emerged from or been subjected to extensive empirical work, whereas others remain essentially untested. Our aim here is to provide some sense of the variety of ways in which various cognitive structures (schemas, goals, attributions, perceived outcomes) have been related to affect. The interested reader is encouraged to pursue the individual theories for more detail, as the presentations necessarily have been brief.

Appraisal Theories

The next set of theories also link cognition and emotion, but emphasize the importance of interpretation with regard to oneself and focus less on information-processing details. Most of us, when we walk into a gathering of people, scan the room to see who is there (people we are glad to see, people we are not so glad to see, or people we do not know) and what has been arranged for us and the other participants (seating, food and drink, decor). In effect, we appraise the situation to see its possible significance for us. An older set of cognitively oriented emotion theories revolves around such a concept of environmental appraisal. The shared premise is that we evaluate our environment for its likely impact on us. The first to develop the term "appraisal" was Magda Arnold (e.g., 1945, 1970), and her theory holds that we immediately and automatically appraise all that we encounter as a fundamental act of perception, producing tendencies to act. An important basis for appraisal is memory of similar past experiences, along with associated affect, and an important element of our plans for action is expectation about the consequences of our actions. All of this appraisal process typically occurs quite quickly, intuitively, and innately. Although not developed with reference to recent ideas about cognition, Arnold's theory anticipates the more current approaches.

Personal meaning. A more recent proponent of the appraisal approach is Richard Lazarus (e.g., Lazarus, 1966; Lazarus, Averill, & Opton, 1970; Lazarus & Smith, 1988). In his view, appraisal consists of evaluating any given stimulus according to its personal significance for one's own well-being. The assignment of personal meaning is viewed as a type of cognition, but not implying that cognition is necessarily conscious, verbal, deliberate, or rational. In this view, appraisal is a process of relating one's goals and beliefs to environmental realities. Appraisals begin with *primary appraisals*, in which people assess personal relevance (what is at stake for me). Primary appraisal determines both motivational relevance (that is, with regard to one's own goals and concerns) as well as motivational congruence (that is, regarding whether the stimulus facilitates or thwarts one's goals). The emotional consequences of primary appraisal are relatively primitive, being simple reactions to potential harm or benefit.

The consequences of *secondary appraisal* are more specific emotions. In secondary appraisal, people consider how to cope (what can I do, what are my options?). Two primary kinds of secondary appraisal include problem-focused coping, which attempts to change the relationship between the person and the environment, or if that fails, emotion-focused coping, which attempts to adjust one's reactions through avoidant attentional strategies or changing the meaning of the threat. Examples of relevant secondary appraisal processes include attributions of past accountability (credit or blame) and expectancies about the future's perceived motivational congruence (maybe this cloud has a silver lining). The most effective secondary appraisal coping strategies depend on the degree of realistic control one has and on the stage of the threat involved (i.e., whether information-gathering is still useful, whether one can realistically alter the situation, or whether it is too late to do anything). The core point is that appraisal leads to coping (through changes in attention, meaning, and actual circumstances), which leads to changes in person-environment relationships, which in turn lead to different emotions (Folkman & Lazarus, 1988a, 1988b).

Cognitive appraisals. Other appraisal theories focus more explicitly on people's knowledge of their circumstances and how these cognitive appraisals lead to emotion (Ellsworth & Smith, 1988a, 1988b; C. A. Smith & Ellsworth, 1985, 1987). One difference between this approach and the previous one is that this one is more explicitly cognitive, while Lazarus focuses more specifically on personal motivational meaning (Lazarus & Smith, 1988). A core idea of the cognitive appraisal approach is that people appraise various dimensions of the situation, and these dimensions determine their specific emotional reaction. In particular, once people appraise the *pleasantness* of the situation, more specific emotions result from evaluating, for example, *agency* (i.e., responsibility or control by self, other, or circumstances; how fair the situation is), *uncertainty* (how sure one is; how much understanding one has), and *attention* (attending; thinking).

Support for this explicitly cognitive approach comes from studies in which people remember experiencing particular emotions and describe their corresponding appraisals, or vice versa, as well as studies in which they report current emotions and their corresponding appraisals. Among the negative emotions, for example, self-agency goes with shame and guilt; other-agency characterizes anger, contempt, and disgust; and agency due to circumstances typifies sadness (cf. Weiner's theory, covered earlier). Thus, one feels shame or guilt when one is responsible for an unpleasant situation, such as inadvertently ruining a dinner party by one's thoughtless behavior. However, one feels anger, contempt, and disgust when another is responsible in the same way. Finally, one feels sadness when circumstances are responsible, as when the weather ruins an elaborate outdoor party. Other dimensions matter as well: for example, uncertainty characterizes fear, for one feels most intense fear in unpredictable and personally uncontrollable situations (a party at which several people become drunkenly violent). And the dimension of attention and thinking is important, for low levels of attention mark boredom and disgust; high levels of attention characterize frustration. (Consider the differences in one's attention to an interminable storyteller at a party; if the person is merely boring or disgusting, one ignores the conversational monopolist, but if the person is frustrating your attempt to tell your own story, you will attentively listen for any chance to break in.)

Among the positive emotions, people differentiate less clearly; a situation can be unpleasant in more ways than it can be pleasant, as we noted in the taxonomies at the beginning of the chapter. Pleasant situations just make people generally happy. Nevertheless, one can distinguish some specific dimensions: surprise is associated with uncertainty and external agency; interest fits with attention; hope correlates with perceived obstacles and anticipated effort; tranquility goes with certainty, an absence of obstacles, and a lack of effort; love is associated with importance, other-agency, and a lack of effort or obstacles.

Moreover, some preliminary evidence suggests that particular appraisals influence physiological concomitants of emotion, specifically, that anticipated effort influences heart rate and perceived obstacles influence eyebrow frown (C. A. Smith, 1989). Based on various types of physiological and self-report measures then, certain cognitive appraisal dimensions appear central to certain emotions.

This empirical and conceptual work is compatible with other theories that emphasize cognitive appraisal, but this discussion has emphasized the Ellsworth and Smith approach, given their accumulating body of empirical work on appraisal dimensions. The broader collection of cognitive appraisal theories all address a common process, namely, the person encountering and interpreting the environment. Unfortunately, the various appraisal theories provide a daunting variety when considered in detail, but there are some common themes (for other integrations, see Frijda, 1988; Scherer, 1988). In particular, among theories that provide taxonomies of appraisals for specific emotions, there is considerable overlap in the dimensions viewed as important in distinguishing the emotions, in particular pleasantness, agency, certainty, and attention.

These common dimensions occur in three important contributions to the nature of appraisal dimensions. Roseman's (1984) appraisal theory proposes *interpretive dimensions* that include motivational state (appetitive and reward/aversive and punishment), motive consistency (consistent and positive/inconsistent and negative), probability (certain/uncertain), agency (circumstances/other/self), and power (strong/weak); these structural dimensions reliably influenced emotion attributions in a series of vignettes. Note the overlap of Ellsworth and Smith's dimensions with Roseman's on pleasantness, certainty, and agency.

Another taxonomic approach creates *appraisal profiles* (Frijda, 1987b) of different emotions—that is, their structuring along such dimensions as valence, impact, interest, globality, uncertainty, responsibility, and relevance—all of which underlie the intuitive similarity of different affective states and the action readiness that each implies. Again, some critical dimensions overlap.

A third example is notable in that this framework compares cross-cultural consensus in people's open-ended descriptions of specific emotional experiences, their antecedents, and bodily reactions (e.g., Scherer, 1984, 1988; Scherer, Wallbott, & Summerfield, 1986; Wallbott &

Scherer, 1988). Important dimensions of the *stimulus evaluation check* (similar to appraisal) aspect include novelty, intrinsic pleasantness, significance for goals and needs, and coping potential or degree of control; these dimensions serve both social and physiological functions.

Across these cognitive appraisal theories, some central dimensions, thus, emerge: pleasantness, motive consistency, and valence; agency and responsibility; certainty, probability, and control; attention, interest, and novelty. Accordingly, all of these highly compatible cognitive appraisal theories offer conceptual (and sometimes empirical) support for each other, suggesting that appraisal theorists are homing in on the crucial cognitive dimensions by which people appraise situations, resulting in distinct emotions.[2]

Summary

This section has reviewed the literature on social cognition influencing affect. Some kinds of theory focus on arousal and cognition, particularly the interruption of schemas and goals as causing arousal and affect. Other kinds of theories examine cognitive structures successfully applied to stimuli, linking affect to schemas, attributions, standards, and goals. The final kind of theory addresses the appraisal of personal significance and its emotional consequences. It is clear that various types of cognition have a wide-ranging and discernable impact on affective responses, and moreover, that no one explanation covers all types of affect.

AFFECTIVE INFLUENCES ON COGNITION

One person, upon discovering she had lost weight, suddenly started being nicer to her dog. Another, when tired, says "no" to virtually anything. Still another, just because the janitor unexpectedly washed out her coffee cup, felt her whole day was made. And we all have found, when we are feeling cheerful, that the ideas come thick and fast. These and related phenomena illustrate the many influences of mood on be-

---

[2]Still other cognitively informed theories focus on more specific kinds of appraisal, for example, perceived self-efficacy as a cause of emotion (Bandura, 1982); illness cognitions and emotional coping (e.g., for empirical work, Ward, Leventhal, & Love, 1988; for the broader perceptual-motor theory of emotions, see Leventhal, 1982, 1984); or an accessible discrepancy between one's actual self and one's "ideal" or "ought" self (Higgins, 1987; see Chapter 6). In a related vein, Epstein's cognitive-experiential self theory (e.g., 1984) describes the preconscious construals of potential response options that give rise to specific emotions, with particular emphasis on fear, anger, sadness, joy, and affection in everyday life.

havior, memory, judgment, decision making, and persuasion (for other reviews, see M. S. Clark & Isen, 1982; Isen, 1984, 1987).

Before describing this research in detail, it is helpful to provide two bits of background. First, experiments examining these effects typically utilize relatively minor mood manipulations, such as finding a quarter in the phone booth, not major life events, such as winning a million dollars in the lottery. It does not require life-shaking affect-laden events for emotion to influence how one behaves, thinks, decides, and creates.

Second, people's perceptions and expectations have a positive bias, such that people generally rate others and their lives as moderately positive (Parducci, 1968; Sears, 1983); information processing is biased toward positive material, a finding termed the Pollyanna effect (Matlin & Stang, 1978). People remember and judge positive material more easily (e.g., Hampson & Dawson, 1985), and they make positively biased judgments. Thus, all else being equal, most people are moderately optimistic. This means that positive and negative moods are not simple opposites of each other, for positive moods fit what people feel more often and typically prefer. This asymmetry has important consequences.

We will repeatedly find that the effects of positive moods are more clear-cut than are the effects of negative moods. Across research programs, the effects of positive moods are more predictable, consistent, and interpretable than are the effects of negative moods. There are probably several reasons for the uneven effects of negative moods. Positive affect is more common than negative, as just noted, so negative affect is a bigger change from base line, more interruptive, and more distracting. Moreover, negative moods can signal situations that threaten well-being, so again, they are more disruptive. Negative emotions, in general, are more varied than positive ones, as demonstrated by studying the structure of negative and positive affect, so the effects of an angry mood and a sad mood may be less similar than the effects of a joyous mood and an excited one. And negative moods are aversive, so people try to manage their negative feelings more than their positive feelings. All this results in negative moods having more variable effects than do positive moods.

Mood and Helping

Good moods lead people to help others (as our friend who smothers the dog with affection just because she herself is feeling thin). An inspiring array of pleasant little experiences has been examined: success on a small task, finding a dime in the coin return of a pay phone, receiving a free sample, being given a cookie or candy, viewing a series of pleasant slides, listening to soothing music, being told one is helpful, experiencing good weather, and remembering positive events from the past (for reviews, see Carlson, Charlin, & Miller, 1988; Salovey & Rosenhan, 1989). These little rays of sunshine all have the salutary effect of making the world a better place: recipients will mail a lost letter; help someone pick up dropped papers, packages, or books; donate to or solicit for charity; volunteer their time; agree to donate blood; give more positive advice; or make a phone call for a stranger (for reviews, see Isen, 1987; J. D. Mayer & Salovey, 1988).

Several hypotheses have been proposed to account for these effects. In one analysis of the research, Carlson, Charlin, and Miller (1988) find strong evidence for four mechanisms, all of which bear on the principle that cheerful individuals are especially sensitive to concerns about positive reinforcement. People in good moods will help if the situation makes salient one's need for rewards and emphasizes the rewards of helping. As one view of such processes, consider how mood can alter one's *focus of attention* such that one focuses on oneself or on other people. Good moods induced by focusing on one's own good fortune promote benevolence toward others, but focusing on someone else's good fortune does not increase helping and instead may provoke envy (e.g., Rosenhan, Salovey, & Hargis, 1981). Moreover, according to the *separate process* view, people in a positive mood will help mainly if the request emphasizes the rewards of helping rather than a guilt-inducing obligation to help (e.g., M. R. Cunningham, Steinberg, & Grev, 1980). (Obligation could encourage helping, but only by a separate set of processes from the expansiveness of a good mood.) A third hypothesis holds that people can be placed in a good mood by having their *social outlook* improved (e.g., Holloway, Tucker, & Hornstein, 1977). When people are cheered by an interpersonal event, they may focus on the good sides of human nature or the benevolence of the community; such people are more likely to help than those who are cheered by an impersonal event, perhaps because an improved social outlook enhances prosocial values. Finally, people are concerned with *mood maintenance,* so cheerful people are less likely to help if it would ruin their mood (e.g., Forest et al., 1979; Isen & Simmonds, 1978). However, this does not mean that they help merely in order to boost or maintain their mood; people help for a variety of reasons, and cheerful people are simply sensitive to and avoidant of negative affect (Isen, 1987). Cheerful people help when they have salient concerns about rewards and when the rewards of helping are clear.[3]

---

[3]The *concomitance* hypothesis holds that happy people are helpful not in order to maintain their moods, but rather as a side effect of being happy, for instance, because of increased liking for others or increased optimism (Manucia, Baumann, & Cialdini, 1984). This hypothesis overlaps considerably with the social outlook hypothesis and others, so it is hard to evaluate it separately, particularly when mood-maintenance concerns are also evident (Carlson, Charlin, & Miller, 1988).

In a related vein, cheerful people are more sociable: they initiate interactions, express liking, self-disclose more, give advice, aggress less, and cooperate more, and this does not seem to be due to their being generally more compliant when cheerful (e.g., M. R. Cunningham, 1988; for a review, see Isen, 1987). People even become more cooperative negotiators, using less contentious tactics and increasing joint benefits (Carnevale & Isen, 1986). People are not only usually nicer to others, but they are also nicer to themselves when they are feeling good. They reward themselves and seek positive feedback, and this is not merely due to a loss of self-control (Isen, 1987).

What about people who are temporarily depressed? People in a bad mood are sometimes more helpful than people in a neutral mood, but only under particular conditions (for a review, see Carlson & Miller, 1987). In effect, the negative mood conditions that do encourage helping are those in which guilt rather than anger is operating. That is, according to the *responsibility/objective-self-awareness* view, unhappy people who perceive themselves to be the cause of a negative event (e.g., breaking an experimenter's equipment or being told they are responsible for their bad mood) are helpful, assuming prosocial norms are salient (e.g., M. Rogers et al., 1982). In contrast, according to the *focus-of-attention* explanation, grumpy people who perceive themselves to be the target of a negative event (e.g., imagining their own reactions to a friend dying of cancer) are less helpful to others (e.g., W. Thompson, Cowan, & Rosenhan, 1980). The attentional explanation, thus, applies to helping that is instigated by both positive and negative moods; when helping focuses attention away from one's mood, the mood is weakened, but when helping focuses attention on the conditions producing one's mood, the mood is enhanced (M. G. Millar, Millar, & Tesser, 1988).

An additional explanation for the effects of bad moods on helping is more controversial. According to a *negative state-relief* hypothesis, unhappy people help when it could dispel their negative mood (e.g., Cialdini, Darby, & Vincent, 1973; Schaller & Cialdini, 1988), and even children are aware of the personally salutary effects of helping (Cialdini & Kenrick, 1976; Perry, Perry, & Weiss, 1986). It seems clear that people attempt to regulate their moods (Baumgardner & Arkin, 1988; J. D. Mayer & Gaschke, 1988), so some version of this hypothesis is likely to hold. However, there is disagreement about interpretation of such results (Carlson & Miller, 1987; cf. Schroeder et al., 1988).

Mood and Memory

Have you ever received a piece of good news and found yourself mentally reviewing several other past experiences of being competent, good, and lovable? Present mood has important effects on memory for past experiences. Two essential phenomena have formed the core of research on mood and memory, mood-congruent memory and mood-state-dependent memory.

Mood Congruence.   Under many circumstances, people more easily remember material whose valence fits their current mood state (for reviews, see Blaney, 1986; Isen, 1987; J. D. Mayer, 1986). Dozens of studies have induced moods experimentally by having subjects undergo hypnosis, experience success and failure, read mood-relevant sentences (the "Velten" procedure), listen to mood-laden music, dwell on relevant past experiences, or assume positive and negative facial expressions (Blaney, 1986). In one study, moods were even cued by odors picked to be pleasant (similar to almond essence) and unpleasant (resembling coal tar) (Ehrlichman & Halpern, 1988). Across a variety of settings and procedures, people recall positive material in positive moods and sometimes recall negative material in negative moods (e.g., G. H. Bower, Gilligan, & Monteiro, 1981; D. M. Clark & Teasdale, 1985; Isen et al., 1978; Salovey & Singer, 1988; Teasdale & Russell, 1983). Some argue that the effect is located primarily at retrieval (Blaney, 1986; Isen, 1987), while others argue that the evidence is stronger for effects at learning (G. H. Bower, 1987; J. D. Brown & Taylor, 1986; J. D. Mayer & Salovey, 1988; Nasby & Yando, 1982; J. A. Singer & Salovey, 1988).

Most accounts assume mood-congruence effects are fairly automatic, but quite possibly some mood-congruence effects are controlled, motivated processes (Blaney, 1986). For example, subjects experiencing an induced mood without an appropriate explanation, given one of the more subtle mood manipulations (e.g., unlabeled facial expressions), might search for an explanation in the to-be-recalled material, resulting in a mood misattribution effect, caused by a motivated search. That is, if you are in an experiment, remembering a series of past events, and feeling unaccountably cheerful, you may focus on the happy memories as an explanation of your mood. Alternatively, subjects experiencing a more overt mood induction procedure (e.g., Velten or hypnosis) might be simply complying with experimental demand. In either case, mood effects would be due to controlled processes (i.e., conscious, intentional processes; see Chapter 7).

Most mood-congruence research finds uneven effects for negative moods, and motivated, controlled processes may account for these failures to obtain strong effects for induced negative moods, due to efforts at mood repair (M. S. Clark & Isen, 1982; J. A. Singer & Salovey, 1988). Alternatively, the weakness of negative mood effects may result from the store of negative material in memory being less extensive and less integrated, so negative moods may not as effectively cue congruent material (Isen, 1984, 1987). Moreover, this is especially likely to be true of repressors (people who are highly defensive), whose network of negative emotional experiences apparently is more discrete and less complex than other people's (R. D. Hansen & Hansen, 1988). Also, if negative material is less organized, it may be intrinsically harder to learn, so it is hard to equate negative and positive stimuli. Possibly, the weakness of negative mood effects is also due to there being more differentiation among negative moods (sadness, anger, fear) than among positive moods (happiness), so that the negative mood states do not match as easily and there are fewer associations to any one of them than to an overall happy glow (Laird et al., 1989).

Negative mood congruence does occur reliably in one important case, namely, for people who are depressed, for whom negative events are presumably mood-congruent and, therefore, memorable (Blaney, 1986; M. H. Johnson & Magaro, 1987). For example, when depressed and nondepressed people experience a series of experimenter-controlled successes and failures, depressed people underestimate successes (relative to control subjects; e.g., Craighead, Hickey, & DeMonbreun, 1979); the effect appears more likely to be a retrieval bias than an encoding deficit. As another example, depressed people (compared to controls) under-remember positive words and phrases or over-recall negative ones (e.g., Ingram, Smith, & Brehm, 1983). These negative mood-congruence effects may only occur when people focus on the applicability of the material to themselves (e.g., Bargh & Tota, 1988), but otherwise the conditions under which they have been obtained are numerous and varied. Depressed subjects may deliberately focus on negative material to rebut it, to improve themselves, or to confirm their self-image, so the effects may or may not be automatic (i.e., unintentional, unconscious, and rapid; see Chapter 7).

Altogether, a considerable amount of evidence supports the facilitating effects of congruence between mood and the material to be remembered. However, the research is not without its problems, namely, within-subject designs that may encourage subjects to respond to experimental demand and failures to include neutral-mood control groups (M. S. Clark & Williamson, 1989; J. A. Singer & Salovey, 1988). In addition, there are a few isolated examples of superior mood-*in*congruent memory, rather than the usual mood-congruency effects (Fiedler, Pampe, & Scherf, 1986; Forgas, Burnham, & Trimboli, 1988; Mackie et al., 1989; Parrott & Sabini, 1990). Nevertheless, there are studies that apparently circumvent demand by unobtrusively manipulating facial expressions, rather than more overtly self-induced mood states, and these studies also show mood-congruent memory (Laird et al., 1982, 1988). Moreover, the real-world effects are especially robust: clinically depressed patients reliably show the mood congruency effects, and real-life events show stronger mood-congruence effects than do experimenter-provided items (Ucros, 1989). Overall, the mood-congruence successes seem to outweigh the failures.

Mood state-dependent memory. A separate mood-and-memory phenomenon concerns the congruence between the mood context in which material is learned and the mood context in which material is retrieved. Mood-dependent memory ignores the valence of the material itself, focusing only on the fit between the two contexts. State-dependent memory apparently exists for drug-induced states; for example, something learned while intoxicated is easier to remember while intoxicated than while sober. (This should not be interpreted as a recommendation that people who cannot remember what they did while drunk should recreate the state merely in order to find out!) The reliability of drug-induced state-dependent memory led researchers to look for a similar phenomenon in mood states. Perhaps material learned while happy is best remembered while happy, regardless of the content of the particular material.

Although it is an effect that deserves to be true, evidence for it is quite weak (Blaney, 1986; G. H. Bower & Mayer, 1985, 1989; Isen, 1984, 1987). Studies that associate half the material with one mood and the other half with another mood (interference designs) have more frequently obtained effects, compared to studies that associate all the material with one mood state only. However, systematic manipulations of interference do not reliably yield the effect (G. H. Bower & Mayer, 1989), and the possibility of demand is then raised (Blaney, 1986; J. D. Mayer & Salovey, 1988; J. A. Singer & Salovey, 1988; Ucros, 1989). Moreover, mood dependence does not obtain for naturally occurring moods, which minimize demand problems (J. D. Mayer & Bremer, 1985; J. D. Mayer & Bower, 1985; Hasher, Rose, Zacks, Sanft, & Doren, 1985). One remaining puzzle may be clarified. As noted at the outset, drugs more reliably produce state-dependent effects, although mood does not. One possible explanation is that the state-dependency effects of drugs operate more similarly to arousal-dependent memory, an effect that does appear reliable (M. S. Clark, Milberg, & Ross, 1983; M. S. Clark, Milberg, & Erber, 1988).

Network model of mood and memory. One theory originally proposed to account for the various effects of mood on memory was a network model (G. H. Bower, 1981; M. S. Clark & Isen, 1982; see J. A. Singer & Salovey, 1988, for a review). The theory posits that emotion is simply a retrieval cue like any other. This means that memories or events that come to mind at the same time as a given emotion are linked to that emotion, and hence (indirectly) to other emotion-congruent memories or events. Mood-congruent memory, thus, has an advantage because the emotion provides an additional route to the item in memory. In this view, both mood-congruent memory and mood-state-dependent memory would be based on the retrieval advantages, respectively, of similar affect attached to the mood and the inherent valence of the item to be recalled, or of similar affect associated with the item at learning and at retrieval. Elaborations of this model went on to account for variations in emotional intensity by variations in activation (S. G. Gilligan & Bower, 1984) and to distinguish among emotion words, concepts, and experiences (G. H. Bower & Cohen, 1982). However, subsequent research was disappointing in its attempts to support the facilitating effects of mood on perception of similarly toned material (G. H. Bower, 1987) and on mood-state-dependent retrieval, as noted earlier. Moreover, the combined effect of conceptual and emotional relatedness in memory networks is not well-supported (E. J. Johnson & Tversky, 1983). Overall, the network model of mood and memory "has not fared well:... a few successes and several glaring failures" (G. H. Bower, 1987, p. 454), suggesting that new frameworks are needed.

In general, mood-state-dependent memory effects have been stronger when there has been more possibility of experimental demand, that is, more likelihood of the experimental subjects accurately perceiving and responding to the investigators' hypotheses. Effects have been larger for (a) the earlier studies that perhaps involved less rigorous procedures and more enthusiastic experimenters, (b) studies involving longer experimental sessions, (c) studies with older and perhaps more sophisticated subjects, (d) subjects recruited for money rather than for course credit or on a voluntary basis, and (e) studies involving fewer subjects and more intense mood inductions (Ucros, 1989).

Conclusions. One interpretation of the overall pattern of mood and memory results is that the studies work better when the induced moods are intense (J. D. Mayer & Salovey, 1988; Ucros, 1989); results are stronger when subjects are selected according to their responsiveness to the mood induction or when naturally occurring moods and real-life events are used.

As we have seen, the evidence for mood-congruent memory is strong, while the evidence for mood-state-dependent memory is weak. Despite the distinctions conventionally drawn (as here) between mood congruence and mood dependence, the distinction is not always clear (Blaney, 1986; Ucros, 1989). In real life, positive material often is acquired when one is in a positive mood or takes its positive interpretation from a positive context, thereby confounding the mood at learning with the valence of the material to be learned. Nevertheless, the two are at least conceptually distinct, and mood-congruence effects are far more reliable than mood-dependence effects.

Mood and Judgment

One of the clearest effects in the mood literature is that cheerful people like just about everything better: themselves, their health, their cars, other people, the future, and even politics (Berkowitz & Connor, 1966; M. S. Clark, Milberg, & Ross, 1983; M. S. Clark & Waddell, 1983; Erber, 1989; Fiedler, Pampe, & Scherf, 1986; Forest et al., 1979; Forgas & Bower, 1987; Isen et al., 1978; Isen & Shalker, 1982; E. J. Johnson & Tversky, 1983; Kavanagh & Bower, 1985; J. D. Mayer & Bremer, 1985; J. D. Mayer, Mamberg, & Volanth, 1988; J. D. Mayer & Volanth, 1985; Procidano & Heller, 1983; Roth & Rehm, 1980; Salovey & Birnbaum, 1989; Schiffenbauer, 1974; Schwarz et al., 1987; Strack, Schwarz, & Gschneidinger, 1985; Underwood, Froming, & Moore, 1980; J. Wright & Mischel, 1982; for reviews, see M. S. Clark & Williamson, 1989; Isen, 1984, 1987; J. D. Mayer, 1986; J. D. Mayer & Salovey, 1988). For example, people viewing their behavior in replayed social interactions rate themselves more positively when happy (Forgas, Bower, & Krantz, 1984). (This effect provides new perspective on those imaginary replays of one's behavior after a party, the interpretation of which apparently depends on the hour and condition in which one engages in such self-assessment.) The variety of cheery mood-based benevolence effects have led to the suggestion that one has multiple personalities, depending on one's current mood (G. H. Bower, 1990, in press; cf. Epstein, 1990b). However, there are some limits on this phenomenon; for example, cheerful people do not overvalue the criminal and the unattractive (Forgas & Moylan, 1987; G. L. White, Fishbein, & Rutstein, 1981), and high levels of personal involvement may moderate mood-congruence effects (Branscombe & Cohen, 1990).

Is the converse true? Do unhappy people dislike everything? Sometimes, but the evidence is more mixed, for many of the same reasons it is mixed for studies of negative mood and memory (M. S. Clark & Williamson, 1989; J. D. Mayer & Salovey, 1988). Accordingly, studies that include neutral control groups are more informative than studies that merely contrast positive and negative moods. That is, if one only compares positive and negative moods and obtains a difference, one does not know which mood had an effect. Frequently, negative mood effects do not differ from neutral mood effects and sometimes, they are even equivalent to positive mood effects, as people attempt to repair their negative moods. Hence, to detect negative mood effects, it is especially important to have a neutral control group. Some effects have emerged from negative mood studies: for example, people judge other people according to negative applicable traits more when temporarily depressed than when in a neutral mood (Erber, 1991). Similarly, both temporary depression and a chronic negative outlook lead people to perceive themselves as having less social support (L. H. Cohen, Towbes, & Flocco, 1988; Vinokur, Schul, & Caplan, 1987). Other examples are sprinkled throughout this literature, so negative mood-congruent judgments do occur.

Some other intriguing puzzles remain in this line of work. For example, not only do positive (and sometimes negative) moods show congruence in judgments, but aroused moods show judgmental congruence effects as well (M. S. Clark, Milberg, & Erber, 1984; Stangor, 1990). That is, when people are physiologically aroused (e.g., by exercise), they make arousal-congruent judgments, viewing another's ambiguously positive facial expression as more joyous than serene and interpreting ambiguous statements ("Just look at that sunset") in the same way. It will be interesting to see whether other specific dimensions of mood—in addition to valence and arousal—show mood congruence.

There is another open question: children, curiously, do not always show the same effects of positive and negative moods that adults do (Forgas, Burnham, & Trimboli, 1988; Masters & Furman, 1976; cf. Barden et al., 1985). Why this is the case is not yet clear. Is it because the arousal component of their mood overwhelms its valence? Is it because they have less-developed networks of associations? Is it because they are less well-socialized into the culturally shared effects of moods? It remains to be seen.

Another challenge for research on mood and judgment is specifying the effects of mood-incongruent stimuli. For example, mood-incongruent stimuli may interfere with information processing, causing people to evaluate others via shortcuts such as illusory correlation (Mackie et al., 1989). Certainly, some theories of emotion as an interruption (noted above) would suggest that affect, regardless of congruence, can be disruptive. The role of moods—congruent or incongruent—as interfering with judgments is not well understood. Moreover, it would be reasonable to expect some incidence of mood-*in*congruent judgment effects, with the mood creating a contrast to the judged objects, although we have not seen clear demonstrations of this.

Finally, although a network model of memory, with mood cuing mood-congruent associations, would seem a reasonable explanation for mood-congruent judgments, the evidence has not been overwhelming, and there are many other possibilities (M. S. Clark & Williamson, 1989). Moods may cue general response styles, that is, in the case of positive moods, being expansive and agreeable, and in the case of negative moods, being narrow and disagreeable. Moods may also be informative, as when one asks how someone's life is going, and they reply in part based on current mood (Schwarz, 1990; Schwarz & Clore, 1988; Schwarz et al., 1987). Moods may increase arousal, causing responses to become more polarized. Mood may consume memory capacity, leaving the more prevalent positive material in memory as the most accessible basis for judgment, accounting for the effects of positive moods. Moreover, a variety of controlled processes are likely, as people attempt to repair negative moods but to maintain positive moods. Lastly, moods may alter one's category boundaries, lowering one's threshold for seeing instances as mood-congruent and therefore, supportive of a mood-congruent judgment (J. D. Mayer, 1986). Despite all of these possible explanations, experimental demand is not a likely one, however, because mood-congruent judgments also obtain for naturally occurring moods (J. D. Mayer & Bremer, 1985; J. D. Mayer & Volanth, 1985; J. D. Mayer, Mamberg, & Volanth, 1988) and because subjects are less likely to detect the hypothesis than in many mood and memory studies.

In sum, the effects of positive mood on judgments are widespread, within reasonable limits imposed by the stimuli being judged. The effects of negative mood are quite mixed, for reasons that remain a mystery and that demand additional work; some possible reasons discussed in earlier sections on mood and memory also apply here. The effects of other mood dimensions besides valence, namely, arousal, merit additional work, as do the effects of moods on children's judgments, and the conditions under which mood-incongruent judgments will occur. The number of possible explanations for the robust effects of mood-congruent judgments has so far outstripped the research needed to choose among them.

Mood and Decision-Making Style

Mood not only influences what we remember and how positively we evaluate our worlds, but it also influences the manner in which we make judgments (for reviews, see Fiedler, 1988; Isen, 1987). Elated people are expansive, inclusive, and somewhat impulsive; they make decisions quickly (Isen & Means, 1983), they work quickly at simple tasks (J. D. Mayer & Bremer, 1985), they group more varied things into the same category (Isen & Daubman, 1984), they see more unusual connections among things (Isen et al., 1985), they have looser and less organized associations (Fiedler, 1988), they have more associations to positive words (J. D. Mayer & Volanth, 1985; J. D. Mayer, Mamberg, & Volanth, 1988), they are willing to take more risks if the possible losses are small (Isen & Geva, 1987; Isen & Patrick, 1983), but losses loom larger to them (Isen, Nygren, & Ashby, 1988). Altogether, it would seem that positive moods are associated with factors conducive to creativity, and people will even claim a bad mood as an excuse for failure (Baumgardner, Lake, & Arkin, 1985).

Mood and Persuasion

Along with being expansive and inclusive and generally pleasant to others, cheerful people are more compliant with persuasive communications, while angry uncomfortable people are generally less compliant

(R. A. Baron, 1983; Dribben & Brabender, 1979; Galizio & Hendrick, 1972; Gouaux, 1971; Griffit, 1970; Janis, Kaye, & Kirschner, 1965; Krugman, 1983; Laird, 1974; Milberg & Clark, 1988; Petty et al. 1983; Razran, 1940; Staats, Staats, & Crawford, 1962; G. L. Wells and Petty, 1980; Zanna, Kiesler, & Pilkonis, 1970; see McGuire, 1985; Petty, Cacioppo, & Kasmer, 1988, for reviews). The positive mood results may explain the effectiveness of free samples, soothing music, and friendly banter in marketing efforts, all of which increase positive moods and therefore, perhaps, persuasion. (But the effects of anger on noncompliance oddly do not seem to discourage the relentless programs of telephone promotions.)

Much of the mood and persuasion research was originally conducted under a classical conditioning paradigm, but subsequent studies have suggested some roles for cognitive processes. For example, not all persuasion is automatically enhanced by positive mood; perhaps positive mood only enhances persuasion under conditions of low involvement and low cognitive activity (Petty, Cacioppo, & Kasmer, 1988; Petty et al., 1988; Petty, Gleicher, & Baker, 1991). Positive moods themselves can be distracting and reduce cognitive capacity, leading subjects to superficial but still cognitively mediated processing of messages (Mackie & Worth, 1989; Worth & Mackie, 1987). Under conditions of moderate involvement, however, affect may enhance thought because of affect's arousing and attention-getting impact. Under conditions of high involvement, mood may serve an informative function relevant to one's possible reactions, or it may bias retrieval of relevant supporting information (Petty et al., 1988).

Summary

Good moods often lead people to be more helpful, more sociable, and nicer to themselves, to recall pleasant things, to judge things positively, to make faster and looser decisions, and to be more compliant. Bad moods have more variable effects, leading people to be more or less helpful, to remember negative things if truly depressed, sometimes to make negative judgments, and to be less often compliant.

AFFECT VERSUS COGNITION

In this chapter, we have examined research investigating some cognitive bases of emotional responses and some affective (mood) influences on cognition. In this final section, we examine the relationship between affect and cognition more explicitly, starting with the possibility that they are largely independent.

The Separate Systems View

Despite the scientific and common-sense idea that we think about things in order to know how we feel, there is a case for affect preceding cognition, rather than vice versa (Zajonc, 1980b). Indeed, some of us are constantly amazed at our own ability to make major life decisions on the basis of emotional preferences guided by no apparently relevant cognitive data. (Consider how you fell into your first serious romantic involvement or your earliest image of your career; some us can find not one iota of rational cognitive analysis in those choices.) Affective processes may operate rather independently of cognitive processes, in this view. Note that this is a controversial perspective, and it depends at a minimum on how one defines the terms "affect" and "cognition." Before detailing the objections, it is useful to present the Zajonc argument and its evidence.

The separate systems view suggests that affective and cognitive processes proceed in parallel paths without influencing each other much, under at least some circumstances. Affective processes are argued to occur at a more basic level than cognitive processes, in several respects. Zajonc suggests:

Affective reactions are primary. Evaluations are made and then justified; decisions are based on preference rather than computation. (Romantic involvements are a prime example of not choosing based on a cognitive list of pros and cons.)

Affect is basic. Evaluation is a major and universal component of virtually all perception and meaning. It is difficult to understand something without evaluating it. (Consider a lonely person scouting for a mate, unable to meet anyone in any context without evaluating the person's potential availability.)

Affective reactions are inescapable. They are demandingly present in a way that simple knowledge is not. (Attraction is harder to ignore than the other person's career plans.)

Affective reactions tend to be irrevocable, in contrast to cognitive judgments. One's feelings cannot be wrong, but one's beliefs can be; hence, affect is less vulnerable to persuasion than cognition. (As parents of adolescents constantly discover, other people's feelings of love and anger do not respond well to counterargument.)

Affect implicates the self. While cognitive judgments rest on features inherent in the object, affective judgments describe one's own reactions to the object. (One's affective response to another has everything to do with one's relationship to the other, but one's knowledge of the person does not necessarily depend on one's relationship.)

Affective judgments are difficult to verbalize. Much emotional response is communicated nonverbally; words for affective reactions always seem to fall short of the experience. (Describing the superficial features of the loved one is easy, but communicating one's actual feeling of love challenges even the poets.)

Affective reactions may not depend on cognition. The features that people use to discriminate a stimulus may not be the same features that they use to decide whether or not they like it. (Totaling up the lover's pros and cons does not necessarily predict one's feelings.)

Affective reactions may be separated from content knowledge. One sometimes remembers how one feels about a person but cannot remember the details of where or how the person was previously encountered. (One may feel strongly about someone without remembering all the reasons why.)

Overall, this stimulating line of argument has proved controversial, so we will examine some of the relevant evidence and then some of the objections.

Evidence from Mere Exposure Research

The last pair of arguments—that affect may not depend on cognition and may be separated from knowledge of content—underlie a research program demonstrating that people can know how they feel about an object before they can recognize it. The opening bars of a classic old song on the radio may be enough to let us know whether or not this is a golden oldie we like, but many of us cannot identify it right away or even be completely certain whether or not we have heard it before. Many studies document this phenomenon of feeling a warm familiar glow that is accompanied by a total lack of recognition. More generally, people grow to like an initially unobjectionable stimulus the more frequently it is encountered; this is called the *mere exposure effect* (Zajonc, 1968a; see Chapter 11).

In mere exposure studies, people typically see a series of nonsense words, Chinese characters, or yearbook photographs, either many times or few times. The more often people are exposed to the stimulus, the more they favor it, and this effect replicates consistently (Chapter 11; Kunst-Wilson & Zajonc, 1980; for a review, see Bornstein, 1989). People prefer the frequent stimuli to the less frequent stimuli, even when they can only recognize them both at levels approximating chance guessing. One study found that mere exposure to Japanese ideographs influenced affect, independent of recognition for them

(Moreland & Zajonc, 1977; for debate, see Birnbaum & Mellers, 1979a, 1979b; Moreland & Zajonc, 1979). Liking for frequently heard tone sequences was found consistently, even though the tones were only recognized as familiar at approximately chance levels (W. R. Wilson, 1979). Further evidence came from a study using a dichotic listening task, in which the experimenter presented the tones in one ear but focused subjects' attention on a literary passage presented to the other ear. Using this task, one can virtually eliminate recognition for the tone sequences, leaving affective reactions intact. Similar results have been obtained with more engaging stimuli, such as the photographs and interests of fellow students (Moreland & Zajonc, 1982). The effects are generally strongest for meaningful words (including names), polygons, and photographs, and they do not occur reliably for paintings, drawings, and matrices (Bornstein, 1989).

It would appear that affective processes more than cognitive ones underlie the mere exposure effect. A dissenting view has suggested, however, that brief repeated exposure activates a simple schema, which affects judgments of familiarity and liking, but also brightness, darkness, or any other stimulus-relevant judgment (G. Mandler, Nakamura, & Shebo Van Zandt, 1987); this view, thus, disagrees that mere exposure effects are noncognitive. At a minimum, however, mere exposure effects on liking (and perhaps on other judgments) do not depend on conscious recognition of the stimuli, itself an impressive effect.

Evidence from Person Perception and Attribution Research

A wide range of affective variables are independent of seemingly relevant cognitive variables. For example, evaluative impressions (one kind of affect) can be independent of memory for the details on which they were based (one kind of relevant cognition). This occurs when impressions are formed on-line, at the time of the initial encounter (N. H. Anderson & Hubert, 1963; Bargh & Thein, 1985; Dreben, Fiske, & Hastie, 1979; Riskey, 1979; for a review, see Hastie & Park, 1986). Thus, as you are forming an impression of someone at a party, your affective response is likely to occur independently of your later ability to remember details about the person. The exception to this apparent independence of affective responses and memory for the data on which they were based occurs when people are overloaded at the time of the encounter and do not have the motivation or the individual capacity to form an evaluative impression at the time; in this case, their impression is memory-based (Bargh & Thein, 1985). More generally, though, other social judgments and recall are often uncorrelated, as we saw in Chapter 8 (S. T. Fiske, Kenny, & Taylor, 1982; S. T. Fiske et al., 1979).

Affective judgments are not necessarily based on recallable cognitions, and instead, they often are based on evaluations formed on-line. This implies that some affective reactions are better characterized as immediate responses. One must then entertain the related possibility that affective responses are also relatively direct and noncognitive. The concept of separate stores for evaluative and cognitive content (N. H. Anderson & Hubert, 1963) is one description of this process. The notion of affective reactions as a direct result of initial categorization (S. T. Fiske & Neuberg, 1990; S. T. Fiske, 1982) is another. The idea that attitude objects can directly cue the relevant attitude is also pertinent (Fazio, 1986; Fazio, Powell, & Herr, 1983). Much other relevant work demonstrates the importance of on-line processes in affective responses (see Chapters 3, 7). And at least some emotional responses (startle and pupil dilation) are not preceded by identifying and judging of stimuli (Schmidt-Atzert, 1988).

Objections

Quite a few theorists have responded to Zajonc's (1980b) view of emotion as a system separate from cognition. The objections have centered around the existence of nonconscious cognitive processes, the possibility of subsuming affect under other forms of cognition, the definitions of both cognition and affect, and the problems in empirically comparing the two.

Among the first to respond to Zajonc was Lazarus (1982, 1984, 1990) whose emotion theory depends on the appraisal of personal meaning, as described earlier. Lazarus argues that cognition, defined as appraisal, is necessary for emotion; appraisal interprets meaningful stimuli in terms of their significance for personal well-being. In this view, appraisal is not regarded as deliberate, rational, and conscious, for it occurs from the very beginning of perceiving environmental inputs, not at the end of a long chain of serial, complete, thorough information processing. Similarly, Epstein (1983, 1984) argues that preconscious cognitions usually precede emotions, and that the Zajonc approach implicitly defines cognition as conscious, when it need not be. Thus, some form of intuitive, preconscious, unintentional cognitive appraisal is seen as an integral part of all emotion. Zajonc (1984) argues that this definition of cognitive appraisal blurs the distinction between perception and cognition and that the Lazarus concept of emotion arbitrarily requires cognitive appraisal by definition. Clearly, the two viewpoints differ as to the defining features of emotion and of cognition, and therefore, differ as to the separation between the two.

Two other critiques of the Zajonc definitions of cognition and affect begin with the observation that cognitions can be rapid, unconscious, and automatic, just as affect is presumed to be; further, like affect, cognition can be irrational and can be tied to motor involvement (Holyoak & Gordon, 1984). In this view, the distinctions are less important than the possibility of subsuming both cognition and affect within one mental system. A related proposal specifically relies on the procedural view of memory outlined in Chapter 8; recall that this view of memory depends on highly practiced mental activities that become more rapid as they are repeated. In this view, emotion can result from unconscious pattern-matching to emotional procedures, as well as from consciously accessible nonprocedural knowledge (Branscombe, 1988). Both of these efforts subsume affect under traditionally cognitive frameworks. Others have similarly argued that affect should be treated just like all other kinds of information (N. H. Anderson, 1989b).

Another possible resolution comes from recognizing two meanings of cognition (Averill, 1990a). The first, cognition$_1$, is intellective knowledge acquisition, which is the everyday (dictionary) meaning of cognition. The contrast to intellective cognition is value-laden, intuitive, or irrational thinking. The other meaning, cognition$_2$, subsumes all mental activity, as compared to behavior. This second meaning of cognition—that is, any nonbehavioral mental activity—is closer to the meaning of cognition as discussed, for example, by Lazarus in defining appraisal as a form of cognitive activity. Emotions are noncognitive in the first sense only, being nonintellective cognition, that is, more value-laden, intuitive, and irrational. Emotions are, however, cognitive$_2$ in the sense of being mental processes. The most useful point is that emotions as mental processes tend to be distinguished from intellective cognition, in typical ways:

(a). emotion concerns the person's own experience as subject or origin, rather than focusing on the object itself out there;

(b). emotion tends to influence perceived "reality," whereas thinking to a greater extent accommodates to reality;

(c). emotion views the target as important for its relationship to the person, but intellective cognition emphasizes an object's relationship to other external objects;

(d). emotion involves physiological experiences, not just environmental inputs;

(e). emotion regulates the intensity and style of behavior, rather than the goal-directed efficiency of behavior;

(f). emotion is experienced passively or in reaction to the stimulus, but people experience themselves as the source of intellective cognition;

(g).   emotion commits one to action more than does the cost-benefit calculation of intellective cognition;

(h).   emotion norms are moral and aesthetic, while intellective norms are rational;

(i).   emotion helps define the self, rather than the world.

This is not to say that intellective cognition is necessarily rational, merely that it displays all these features less often than does emotion (cf. Epstein, 1990a).

So far, we have focused on definitional issues regarding cognition and emotion or cognition per se. Of course, the resolution to this debate also depends on how one defines emotion. For example, the original Zajonc article focused on preferences (evaluations, affective judgments, liking) rather than on moods or on full-blown emotional episodes (J. A. Russell & Woudzia, 1986). Moods and emotions, many would argue, do intrinsically depend on cognitively driven appraisal processes (e.g., see theories of Lazarus; Ellsworth & Smith, covered earlier). Preferences are relatively simple affective responses, distinguished mainly by valence, so some of the Zajonc results may pertain primarily to simple preferences and not so much to full-blown complex emotions.

Others suggest that the entire distinction is largely definitional and therefore not constructively pursued as such (Leventhal, 1984; Leventhal & Scherer, 1987). Instead, they suggest viewing emotion as developing from sensory-motor processes to complex cognitive-emotional patterns, with distinct levels of memory and information processing and with continuous checks on the organism-environment relationship at all levels.

To all this, we would add only that there are inherent problems in comparing cognition and affect. Implicit in our discussion so far has been the idea that affect and cognition are somehow comparable. Judgments representing affect have included evaluation, preference, and differentiated emotions, while reactions representing cognition have included attention, inference, and memory. How does one decide what are the relevant cognitions and what are the comparable affective responses?

One study illustrates the complexity of this problem. In a mere exposure experiment, subjects rated their recognition and liking for random polygons that had been presented at varying frequencies. Although recognition accuracy was only at chance levels, subjects liked the familiar polygons better than the unfamiliar ones, confirming the standard mere exposure effect and that liking need not depend on accurate memory (Kunst-Wilson & Zajonc, 1980). But in what sense is recognition accuracy comparable to liking? The study assessed two other variables that help answer this question. Affective judgments were made more confidently and somewhat faster than recognition judgments. Nevertheless, these may not be the appropriate dimensions for comparison. The appropriate empirical tests depend on the conceptual definitions of affect and cognition, matters of some controversy, as noted earlier. For example, affect and cognition have been distinguished, respectively, as sensory vs. inferential, physiological vs. mental, motor vs. perceptual, innate vs. learned, preference vs. knowledge, and liking vs. discrimination. One's operational definitions of affect and cognition depend on which of these dimensions one emphasizes.

One can also question whether these are fair tests because people can be wrong about a recognition judgment but not about an affective judgment. One can also argue that recognition judgments are more complex. But the two types of judgment intrinsically differ in these ways, and one cannot make them more similar without destroying them as realistic judgments of their type. Affective judgments are by their nature subjective, simple, and direct. Trying to specify a cognitive response that is truly equivalent to a given affective response may be a losing proposition.

Trying to establish the independence of affect and cognition is also, essentially, trying to establish the null hypothesis. To the extent one argues that they are independent, one is trying to establish the absence of a relationship. This is a thankless task, as any statistics professor will insist if someone tries to prove the null hypothesis of no relationship. The more sensible task is to show on what each is based, if not entirely on each other (Zajonc, Pietromonaco, & Bargh, 1982). And because the separation is not complete, another task is to show the ways in which they do relate. The work reviewed in this chapter does just that.

SUMMARY

The literature on affect and cognition is moving in numerous different directions simultaneously, which do not necessarily cohere. Moreover, some theoretical efforts are supported by considerably more empirical evidence than others. Nevertheless, some central themes emerge as directing research and theory.

Affect is a generic term encompassing all kinds of evaluations, moods, and emotion. Preferences include relatively mild subjective reactions that are essentially either pleasant or unpleasant; the preferences most frequently studied by social psychologists are interpersonal evaluations. Moods typically do not have a specific target, are considered as simply positive or negative, and have some duration. Emotions are more complex and differentiated affects, often include physiological responses, and can be relatively brief. The two most common ways of distinguishing among emotions are along the two dimensions of pleasantness and arousal or along two independent dimensions of positive and negative emotions. Positive emotions, analyzed separately, have a simpler structure than negative emotions. Prototype approaches have also been applied to people's culturally shared categorization of specific emotions and to the concept of emotion in general. Emotions have also been viewed as social roles enacted according to cultural rules.

Early theories of emotion posed the question of whether physiological responses precede (James, Lange) or follow (Cannon) the experience of differentiated emotions. Following this debate, many physiological theories of emotion assumed that autonomic arousal in particular was undifferentiated and that other mechanisms must account for the complexity of emotional experience. Four theories form core contributions: *Facial feedback theory* posits that the complex and subtle musculature of the face provides the detailed patterns of feedback that underlie different emotions. The face does reliably express basic dimensions of emotion, particularly valence and intensity. There is also some evidence that manipulated facial expressions influence the experience of affect, although this evidence has sparked considerable debate. Two other physiological proposals focus, first, on the role of the facial muscles in regulating cerebral blood temperature (*vascular theory*) and, second, on the role of muscles in the body as representing and retaining emotional responses (*hard interface theory*); the data are just coming in on these two theories. *Excitation transfer theory* posits that autonomic arousal from emotions or exercise decays slowly, and that people often cannot distinguish the source of their arousal. Consequently, prior excitation can transfer or spill over to intensify new affective responses, even those of a different valence; considerable research supports this premise. All four of these modern physiological theories deemphasize the role of cognition in generating emotion.

In contrast, social cognition research has examined how cognition might contribute to affect. One set of approaches examines the interplay between arousal and cognition, building on Schachter's *two-component theory* of emotion, which states that unexplained arousal leads people to search their environment for cognitive labels for their emotions. Mandler's *theory of mind and emotion* extends this analysis in several respects: first, it explains the origins of physiological arousal in the interruption of perceptual schemas or complex goal sequences. The degree of disconfirmation of a perceptual schema determines its experienced pleasantness. The interruption of a goal sequence also prompts cognitive interpretation that determines the nature of the experienced emotion. Berscheid's theory of *emotion in close relationships* extends this analysis to complex goal sequences in which people are interdependent: the more intimate the relationship, the more interdependence, and the more potential for interruption and consequently, emotion. This theory explains various phenomena in relationships, and research is beginning to provide further support.

Other social cognition theories focus more specifically on cognitive structures and their impact on affect. A variety of work has examined social schemas and affect. The theory of *schema-triggered affect* posits that affective values are stored at the top level of a schema, accessible immediately upon categorization of an instance as matching the affect-laden schema; research supports this idea. People also have *affective expectancies* that help determine their responses. A considerable amount of research has examined the affective impact of *informational complexity;* more complex knowledge structures often lead to more moderated affect, whereas simple ones allow more extreme affect. Over time, *thought polarizes affect,* to the extent that thought organizes the relevant schema, the schema contains correlated dimensions, and the person has made a public commitment to the initial affective response; research also supports these points.

Another set of theories examines people's emotional reactions to outcomes they or others have obtained. Weiner's theory of the *dimensions of attribution* proposes that different configurations of attributions—involving internal and external locus, stability over time, and controllability—result in specific emotional and behavioral responses to self and others. This perspective has garnered a considerable amount of research support. Another account that relates outcomes to emotion is provided by a *cognitive structural theory* of emotions pertaining to goals, standards, and attitudes; this theory comprehensively organizes a variety of perspectives on emotion, and its goal is computer simulation.

Besides already obtained outcomes, some social cognition theories of emotion have emphasized alternative outcomes, what might have been or what might yet be. *Norm theory* describes the process of deciding how surprising an outcome was, compared to the alternatives. The ease of imagining alternatives determines the amount of surprise and the intensity of emotional response; research supports these ideas. A theory of *alternative future worlds* describes emotions experienced in reaction to the imagined possibility of interrupting a future goal sequence at various stages. These theories of obtained outcomes and alternative outcomes, as well as the theories of interruption as a basis for arousal, all posit that interruptions cause emotion.

However, emotions also in turn cause interruptions. Several theories describe emotions as managers of goal priorities; in these views, emotions interrupt goals to suggest changes in priorities. In one view, emotions serve as alarm signals providing *arousal and interruption* that alert the organism to an unmet need that has shifted its urgency while the organism has been pursuing another goal. In a related view, emotions provide *transitions between plans* with changes in the estimated success of the plan. Although not yet tested directly, some data are consistent with these views. A third approach, based on a *cybernetic model,* posits an affective feedback system that senses and regulates the rate at which the organism pursues the goal; a number of studies support these ideas.

A final set of theories examines ways in which cognition generates affect. The appraisal theories describe how people assess the environment to ascertain its significance for their concerns. The appraisal of *personal meaning* involves preconscious and conscious cognitive assessments of, first, personal relevance and, second, coping options; research on stress and coping is consistent with this view. *Cognitive appraisal* assesses particular dimensions of the current situation, determining particular emotional responses, and several studies of appraisal and emotions support this theory. Other theories have identified similar dimensions of appraisal leading to emotion, in particular, pleasantness, agency, certainty, and attention.

In addition to considering the various influences of cognition on affect, a considerable body of research has considered the influences of affect on cognition, and in particular, the influences of mood. This research finds clear effects even of small mood manipulations on a variety of cognitive processes. The effects for positive mood are more clear-cut than the effects of negative mood in general. Positive moods lead to more prosocial behavior. These robust effects may be explained by the cheerful person's sensitivity to positive reinforcement; helping in a good mood is enhanced by focus of attention on oneself, requests emphasizing the rewards of helping, an emphasis on a positive social outlook, and the opportunity to maintain one's positive mood. People in a negative mood may or may not be helpful, depending on the circumstances.

Mood reliably increases people's memory for mood-congruent material, due to both automatic and controlled processes. Effects for positive moods are stronger than those for negative moods, with the exception of people who are chronically depressed, who also show strong mood-congruent memory. Another mood-memory phenomenon, mood-state-dependent memory, posited that people would best recall material that was learned and retrieved in the same mood state; this hypothesis has little support. A network model to account for mood effects on memory has also received little support.

Mood generally influences judgment in a mood-congruent direction as well. Arousal similarly creates arousal-congruent judgments. Again, the effects of positive mood are more reliable than the effects of negative moods. Moreover, the effects on adults are more reliable than the effects on children. Various explanations for the effects have been proposed but, for the most part, remain to be tested. Mood also affects people's style of decision making, with positive moods making people more expansive, inclusive, impulsive, and perhaps creative. Positive moods also make people more compliant toward attempts at persuasion, at least under low involvement.

The contrast between affect and cognition has been hotly debated, leading to a proposal that they are separate systems, with affect being primary. Evidence from mere exposure and person perception research is cited in support of this perspective; people report liking frequently encountered stimuli they cannot discriminate as familiar, and people's evaluative judgments are often made on-line, without recall for the data on which they were based. Objections to this perspective have focused on the possibility of nonconscious cognitive processes, the role of affect within broader (cognitive) representational systems, the problems of defining both affect and cognition, and empirical tests of the differences. The most constructive course seems to be to examine the bases of each and to investigate the multiple ways in which they do relate, as reviewed here.

11

Cognitive Approaches
to Attitudes

❖

Background ◆ *Cognitive Features of Two Consistency Theories* ◆ *Types of
Attitude Processing* ◆ *Cognitive Analyses of Attitudes Within Social Contexts*
◆ *Attitude Change and the Self*

Suppose you have a classmate from high school coming to visit you for the
weekend, and you want to plan a little party to celebrate. Your classmate
happens to be gay, and although this has never particularly mattered to
you, you wonder how your current friends will react, if they find out. With
most of your friends, the topic of homosexuality may never have come up in
conversation. To avoid any potential awkwardness, it might be better to know
your friends' attitudes before inviting them. You could ask directly, but you
might not get an honest answer because some of your friends might try to con-
ceal antigay prejudices.

Inferring other people's attitudes is a common problem. Attitudes cannot be
observed directly, yet we all take them for granted as good predictors of important behavior, ranging from whether friends will get along to whether a race
riot will occur. Because an attitude must be inferred from an individual's response to a stimulus, it is considered a hypothetical mediating variable. An observer cannot see an attitude. Psychologists assume that an attitude intervenes
between an observable stimulus and an observable response, providing the necessary link. Even when behaviorism dominated psychology, the attitude concept
remained vital; it continued to be indispensable to almost every social psychological study. As we mentioned in Chapter 1, social psychology has always been cog-

nitive in this respect: it has always posited attitudes as a nonobservable link between an observable stimulus and an observable response.

Attitudes have been defined in many different ways by different researchers (e.g., Bagozzi & Burnkrant, 1979; Chaiken & Stangor, 1987; Fishbein, 1967; Himmelfarb & Eagly, 1974; Tesser & Shaffer, 1990). The core definition of attitudes focuses on their essential evaluative feature (e.g., Eagly & Chaiken, in press; Fazio, 1989; Fishbein & Ajzen, 1975; Greenwald, 1989; Pratkanis, 1989). However, some view this approach as too narrow. One traditional definition has viewed attitudes as having three parts: affective, cognitive, and behavioral (e.g., M. J. Rosenberg & Hovland, 1960; Zimbardo, Ebbesen, & Maslach, 1977). This definition has a certain appeal, in its having some empirical support (Breckler, 1984), in its comprehensiveness, and in its reliance on a tripartite distinction that is traditional in psychology and philosophy. However, this definition also tends to assume that the three components will necessarily be consistent with each other (Zanna & Rempel, 1988); as we will see, this is not always the case, so it is an issue to be decided theoretically and empirically (Tesser & Shaffer, 1990). An emerging consensus combines these two definitions, for example, viewing attitudes as a categorization of a stimulus along an evaluative dimension, based on cognitive, affective, and behavioral information (Zanna & Rempel, 1988). In a similar spirit, attitudes may be defined hierarchically, as a broad disposition to respond positively or negatively, inferred from more specific cognitive, affective, and behavioral responses (Ajzen, 1988; see also Breckler & Wiggins, 1989). As a final example, evaluation may be viewed as the critical feature of attitudes, with their structure representing the other components to varying degrees (Cacioppo, Petty, & Geen, 1989).

For the purposes of this chapter, the critical point is that attitudes are important elements in social cognition that are evaluative in nature and that include or are linked to cognitions (beliefs). In part of the next chapter, we will consider the links of attitudes to behavior. Attitude researchers point out the separate but interlocking status of affect, cognition, and behavioral tendencies. Note that all three must be inferred from actual behavior, both verbal and nonverbal, because attitudes cannot be observed directly, any more than any other cognitive element can be. Nevertheless, it is evidence of the importance of attitudes that scientists and ordinary people try to infer them, despite the difficulty of doing so.

BACKGROUND

Attitudes have always been accorded star status in social explanations of human behavior by lay people and professionals alike. By now, it is a textbook cliché to point out that attitudes are the cornerstone of social psychology. Over fifty years ago, Gordon Allport declared attitudes to be "the most distinctive and indispensable concept in contemporary American social psychology" (Allport, 1935, p. 798). The entire field blossomed through the attitude research motivated by World War II. Early social psychology included a variety of such work: attitudes influenced by propaganda and persuasion (Hovland, Janis, & Kelley, 1953; Hovland, Lumsdaine, & Sheffield, 1949); anti-Semitic and anti-democratic prejudice (Adorno et al., 1950); and satisfaction and deprivation in the military (Stouffer et al., 1949). These early efforts leaned heavily on attitudes both as measures and as important theoretical variables. That is, much of the effort in the first few decades of social psychology was oriented toward learning how to measure attitudes and how to define the attitude concept. This chapter cannot cover the entire field of attitude formation and change. (For other reviews, see Ajzen & Fishbein, 1980; Cialdini, Petty, & Caciopppo, 1981; Eagly & Chaiken, in press; Himmelfarb & Eagly, 1974; Kiesler, Collins, & Miller, 1969; McGuire, 1985; Petty & Cacioppo, 1981; Rajecki, 1982; Tesser & Shaffer, 1990; Zimbardo & Leippe, 1991.) Instead, this chapter will focus on a subset of attitude research that has been heavily influenced by social cognition approaches (also see Eagly & Chaiken, 1984).

Social cognition's main contribution to the field of attitude research has been a fine-grained analysis of the mediating processes involved in attitude formation and change. Traditional variables such as features of the communicator, attributes of the message, characteristics of the audience, and the persistence of attitude change are being examined in new ways, adding to the insights developed by earlier theorists. The application of social cognition theories and methods to a well-researched area like attitudes illustrates the merits of the cognitive approach; one could walk through the same exercise for other areas in social psychology as well. Focusing on such a central area as attitude research particularly illustrates what is unique about the social cognition approaches. In addition, attitude research supplements social cognition perspectives because it emphasizes the importance of affect (or at least evaluation) and behavior, which is why we have placed this chapter between the chapters on these two topics.

While social cognition research enriches current attitude research, this does not imply that cognition was absent from earlier theories. Without doubt, among the most influential approaches to attitudes have been the cognitive consistency theories (Abelson et al., 1968). Dominating social psychology journals in the 1960s, their fundamental assumption holds that inconsistencies—among cognitions, among affects, or between cognitions and affects—cause attitude change. Cognitive dissonance theory (Festinger, 1957) and balance theory (Heider, 1958) are eminent examples of this. Other major theories of attitudes also can be interpreted as reserving an important role for cognition or beliefs (Fishbein, 1963; Insko & Cialdini, 1969; Kiesler, 1971; Osgood & Tannenbaum, 1955; M. J. Rosenberg, 1956, 1960). Although we can only allude to the vast literature on attitudes, the critical point is this: cognition has been accorded a major role in practically every attitude theory, with the sole exceptions of the most narrowly construed applications of classical conditioning to attitudes (Staats & Staats, 1958) and some interpretations of mere exposure effects (e.g., Zajonc, 1980b; see Chapter 10). However, until recently, work on the role of cognition in attitude theory could not draw on the important advances in cognitive psychology and in social cognition research.

One early theory of attitude change especially foreshadows the current cognitive approaches. The theory is expressly a sequential model of information processing. Remember that Chapter 1 described information-processing models as breaking down mental operations into sequential stages. McGuire's chain of cognitive responses (1969, 1976, 1985) outlines the necessary conditions, many of them cognitive, for a persuasive communication to influence behavior; the steps include exposure, attention, comprehension, yielding, retention, retrieval, decision, and behavior. Consider, as an example, political campaign literature. In order to be effective, campaign managers must *expose* voters to the literature, say, by distributing a leaflet under people's windshield wipers. Next, the voters must *attend* to the communication, which they will not if it is raining that day and they merely use it to scrape mud off their feet upon reaching the car. If they do read the leaflet, they must *comprehend* the message; it must not be written in opaque jargon. Next, voters must *yield* to the message, that is, be persuaded by its contents (which is no mean feat for the campaign manager, of course). They must *retain* the changed attitude, in the face of competing literature, ennui, and disagreeing friends. Upon reaching the voting booth, they have to *retrieve* their attitude; the voters must remember they preferred Smedley rather than Smiley for dogcatcher. They have to *decide* to act on their attitudes despite situational forces to the contrary (perhaps the city's political machine is actively lobbying for Smiley). And finally, the voter must *behave,* write the X or pull the voting lever, thus securing the effect desired by Smedley's campaign. The entire sequence is described as a series of carefully specified cognitive steps resulting in behavior. As such, the theory anticipates more recent cognitively oriented work in attitudes. Moreover, several of the stages specified by McGuire continue to be important in current work (Eagly & Chaiken, 1984).

Comparing Older and Newer Approaches to Attitudes

The newer cognitive approaches we will discuss in this chapter build on the older attitude theories in several crucial respects. Many of the critical variables are the same. Some of the methodological procedures were established long ago and continue to form the basis of research paradigms. For example, as we will see, current researchers sometimes reuse old experimental designs, adding mainly a more detailed analysis of intervening processes. Another carry-over from older research is that many of the current theoretical issues are variants on earlier problems, as will become clearer. Finally, many of the older approaches were heavily cognitive, in the ways described above.

But there are also differences between older approaches to attitudes and the newer approaches. First, there are what might be called *meta-theoretical* differences between the two; that is, there are major conceptual differences between the overarching framework common to most consistency theories and the overarching framework behind social cognition's approach to attitude research. Most "cognitive" consistency theories rested on a strong motivational basis; the usual meta-theory behind consistency theories was that there is a drive to reduce internal discrepancies. The consistency theories were not typically designed to be theories about the cognitive system operating on its own nonmotivational principles. In contrast, cognitive approaches are based on current understandings of the cognitive system. For example, to deal with inconsistencies, a current cognitive approach might posit that people resolve discrepancies mainly for reasons of efficiency in memory storage. In contrast, a traditional consistency theory might posit that people resolve discrepancies to avoid the uncomfortable feeling of believing two conflicting things.

Second, there are specific *theoretical* differences between the older and newer approaches. The newer approaches explicitly draw on cognitive theories unavailable earlier. These theories potentially provide precise frameworks that detail the organization and processing of information in persuasion. These permit a more careful analysis of cognitive processes related to attitude change.

Third, many new *methods* for studying attitude change have evolved in directions borrowed from cognitive psychology. Attitude theories have long posited internal structures (Zajonc, 1968b), but more fine-grained analysis of cognitive organization and dynamics (typical of cognitive psychology) has become possible in attitude research, with recent advances in measurement techniques. During the 1970s, then, information-processing research on attitudes expanded in several directions, based on meta-theoretical, theoretical, and methodological developments.

In reviewing the directions of newer research, we will see that much of it draws on a framework for persuasion research described by Lasswell (1948) and elaborated by Hovland, Janis, and Kelley (1953): who says what to whom in what channel with what effect. Thus, the research tends to focus on characteristics of the communicator, the message, the audience, the modality, and the lasting effects of attitude change. Although Hovland, Janis, and Kelley's program of research did not explicitly represent an information-processing viewpoint, it did anticipate McGuire's chain of persuasion and other theories that emphasize internal processes such as attention and comprehension. Moreover, much of the current cognitive research is an effort to explain effects originally uncovered by the classic Hovland, Janis, and Kelley research.

In this chapter, we will first address some of the more strictly cognitive features of two traditional attitude theories, dissonance theory and balance theory; this work anticipates social cognition approaches. Then, we will examine three more recent cognitively oriented theories that explicitly build on social cognition ideas; each one specifies different modes of attitude processing based on cognitive principles. Next, we will look at two cognitive theories of attitude change that operate in specific social contexts: the audience's attributional response to the communicator as a person, and attitude change in groups as a function of the arguments presented. In the final section, we examine the interplay between people's attitudes and their self-concept, and in particular we will see how cognitively oriented attitude research is coming full circle to the issues of motivation that originally sparked the interest of older attitude theorists.

COGNITIVE FEATURES OF TWO CONSISTENCY THEORIES

The consistency theories of attitudes proposed in the late 1950s provide a basis for predicting the interplay between attitudes and cognitive processes, so each of the following sections begins by briefly reviewing the most relevant consistency theory as background and then describes current cognitive interpretations of its effects. The sections, thus, focus on dissonance theory and selective perception, on dissonance theory and selective learning, and on balance theory and selective recall of information about others (also see Zajonc, 1968b). These literatures show how some cognitively oriented attitude research anticipated social cognition's fine-grained analyses of information processing.

Dissonance Theory and Selective Perception

Dissonance theory (Festinger, 1957) is an account of how beliefs and behavior change attitudes; it focuses on the effects of inconsistency among cognitions. Inconsistency is explicitly viewed as causing a motivational state called dissonance. If you believe that smoking causes cancer (a cognition) and you know you smoke anyway (a conflicting cognition about behavior), you leave yourself open to cognitive dissonance. Researchers hypothesized dissonance to cause an aversive state of arousal, and recent work has shown that to be the case (e.g., Gaes, Melburg, & Tedeschi, 1986; Zanna & Cooper, 1976; see Fazio & Cooper, 1983, for a review); if you think about the inconsistency between your smoking and knowing that it causes cancer, you become uncomfortable and tense. There is a drive to reduce the arousal (or discomfort) and consequently, you rearrange your cognitions in order to reduce dissonance. Although, theoretically, one could change one's behavior to reduce the inconsistency, most dissonance research has focused on circumstances in which the inconsistent cognitions are more likely to change. This focus on cognitive change was partly an experimental strategy to investigate cognitive processes per see. But, in addition, behavior is more responsive to the constraints of reality (i.e., it entails a more public commitment), so it is often harder to change than are one's cognitions or attitudes.

Most ways to increase consistency are cognitive. Suppose that you smoke and that you have several cognitions relevant to that behavior. You may have a couple of cognitions consonant with your smoking (it tastes good; it is relaxing) and several dissonant with smoking (it causes cancer; it is expensive; it is smelly; other people dislike it). Because the number of dissonant cognitions outweigh the consonant ones, there is cognitive inconsistency, and you may experience dissonance. To reduce the dissonance, there are several changes you can make in your cognitions: for example, you can add or subtract cognitions (i.e., change your beliefs) to increase the ratio of consonant to dissonant ones (e.g., add in the idea that smoking keeps weight down and subtract the smell and the expense); or you can reduce the importance of dissonant conditions (e.g., I'll die of something anyway, so why worry about cancer). This by no means exhausts the possibilities, which are beyond our scope here (see Cooper & Fazio, 1984; C. A. Kiesler, Collins, & Miller, 1969; or Zimbardo, Ebbesen, & Maslach, 1977). To summarize, dissonance theory posits that inconsistent cognitions cause arousal; there is a drive to reduce the arousal; hence, inconsistency often leads to a change in one's attitude-relevant cognitions. Consequently, as we will see, people often avoid cognitions that are inconsistent with an attitude they hold or a behavior they have performed.

Consistency theorists in general (Abelson et al., 1968) have had much to say about selective perception as a function of consistency with prior attitudes. They posit that people seek out, notice, and interpret data in ways that reinforce their attitudes. Dissonance theory in particular predicts that people will avoid information that increases dissonance; that is, that people favor information consistent with their attitudes and behavior. For present purposes, the work on selective perception can be divided into *selective exposure* (seeking consistent information not already present), *selective attention* (looking at consistent information once it is there), and *selective interpretation* (translating ambiguous information to be consistent).

Some have argued that selective *exposure* is a principle that deserves to be true (McGuire, 1969), but much of the initial evidence was unfortunately mixed (Brehm & Cohen, 1962; Freedman & Sears, 1965; J. Mills, 1968; Wicklund & Brehm, 1976). Various early data suggested specific qualifications to dissonance theory's predictions about exposure. Notions of intellectual honesty and fairness sometimes prompt people to seek out information that is inconsistent with their attitudes (Sears, 1965). Information's utility and novelty often override dissonance in determining exposure (Brock, Albert, & Becker, 1970). However, there is strong support for *de facto* selective exposure; that is, most of us inhabit an environment that is biased in favor of positions with which we already agree (Sears, 1968; but see E. Katz, 1968). People tend to pick friends, magazines, and television shows that reinforce their own attitudes, and their attitudes, in turn, are reinforced by those agreeing others. Also, people's contacts shape their attitudes in the first place, so of course, people tend to agree with the information that surrounds them.

Thus, there was initially some support for selective exposure as a result of one's attitude, but mainly *de facto* selective exposure. Subsequent refinement of the hypothesis suggests that, when people have made a clear choice or are publicly committed (both conditions that increase dissonance), they will indeed selectively seek supportive information (Frey, 1986). Moreover, the selective exposure effect probably is strongest at intermediate levels of dissonance, rather than when the dissonance is low (and, therefore, a relatively unimportant source of motivation), or when the dissonance is high (and attitude change seems inevitable). Thus, under particular conditions, selective exposure to attitude-consonant information does occur (e.g., Sweeney & Gruber, 1984). This aspect of selective perception has proceeded without the need for social cognition theories and techniques. But it is useful to know this work because it examines an important cognitive process, namely, information seeking, and because it serves as background to the two other aspects of selective perception: attention and interpretation.

Attention to consistent and discrepant information is considerably subject to consistency pressures. People spend more time looking at consistent than inconsistent evidence under certain circumstances (Brock & Balloun, 1967; A. R. Cohen, Brehm, & Latane, 1959; Jecker, 1964). Recent work has further clarified the understanding of selective attention. For example, in one study (Olson & Zanna, 1979), subjects were divided into repressors (people who typically avoid threatening stimuli) and sensitizers (people who typically investigate threatening stimuli). Both groups reported their attitudes toward a set of paintings. The experimenter then allowed them to choose a pair which they might keep. The pairs they could choose all included one painting they liked and one they disliked.

After the decision, subjects looked at the pair they had chosen. Dissonance theory predicts that they would focus on the positive aspects of their choice, that is, the preferred painting within the chosen pair. Repressors, and not sensitizers, behaved as predicted; their looking times at the choice-consistent painting were relatively high compared to control subjects, and they avoided looking at the painting inconsistent with their expressed choice. Thus, consistent information elicited the selective attention of repressors only. Selective attention, hence, operates for some of the people some of the time. It also operates for some stimuli some of the time; for example, people selectively attend to nonsupportive arguments that are easily refuted (Kleinhesselink & Edwards, 1975). Again, this line of selective perception research did not explicitly use social cognition approaches, but rather it preceded and anticipated the social cognition focus on fine-grained analysis of information-processing strategies.

People also protect their attitudes by selective *interpretation* (as apart from exposure and attention). Here, the direct influence of social cognition research is more clear-cut. The recent work makes a complementary point to some of the work on social schemas (Chapters 4–5), showing that people's attitudes can change their interpretations of what they see. For example, viewers of the television show "All in the Family" interpreted Archie Bunker differently depending on their racial attitudes. Prejudiced viewers interpreted Archie Bunker's ethnic slurs as accurate depictions of reality, while unprejudiced viewers interpreted them as a satire on bigotry (Vidmar & Rokeach, 1974). In a similar vein, people's attitudes toward Presidential candidates influence how they judge their debate performance (Fazio & Williams, 1986); people's attitudes toward the Arab-Israeli conflict influence how they judge the fairness of its news coverage (Vallone, Ross, & Lepper, 1985); and people's attitudes toward an outgroup influence their attributions about that group's behavior (Pettigrew, 1979). Although none of these latter three examples were based precisely on dissonance theory's predictions about selective interpretation, they are consistent with it, as well as with frameworks explicitly drawn from social cognition.

To summarize, dissonance theory predicts that people are motivated to avoid information that is inconsistent with their attitudes or choices. The evidence for selective exposure is mixed, but the evidence for selective attention and interpretation is stronger. Thus, from the outset people are biased at least by attention and misperception to gather data that reinforce their beliefs. This early insight from the consistency framework fits with the social cognition emphasis on analyzing the stages of information processing, so it anticipates social cognition research in this respect. Of late, this work also has been somewhat influenced by social cognition approaches.

Dissonance Theory and Selective Learning

Proponents of dissonance and other consistency theories also predict selective learning and memory for attitude-consistent information. This prediction was not unique to dissonance theorists; selective memory for attitude consistency was one of the first questions in attitude research (J. M. Levine & Murphy, 1943; Watson & Hartmann, 1939). Thus, some earlier and later theories would all predict that if a couple is quarreling over whether to spend Christmas in Vermont or in the Caribbean, the ski addict will never learn the details of bargain snorkeling tours, while the sun worshipper will never learn the details of the ski packages. Unfortunately, evidence for selective learning is "unambiguously inconclusive" (Greaves, 1972). One reviewer concluded that the published studies yielding evidence for selective learning all must be flukes because there were so many other studies that failed to find such evidence (Greenwald, 1975). Moreover, the evidence that exists often is flawed, and recent research suggests exactly how, based in part on insights from cognitive psychology. For example, many studies have confounded the familiarity and agreeability of arguments (Zanna & Olson, 1982). It is not surprising that the ski enthusiast would recall pro-ski arguments better than pro-sun arguments, since the person has thought about the pro-ski arguments more often. Familiar arguments would be easier to recall, without having to assume any dissonance-based motivation to forget the disagreeable arguments (see also Schmidt & Sherman, 1984).

Selective learning and retention of attitudinally favorable information do seem to occur under special conditions, defined in part by the contingencies of information processing. Incidental learning, rather than intentional learning, provides clearer support for selective learning effects (Malpass, 1969). That is, people are more likely to be selective when they do not know they will be tested on the material later. A travel agent who frequently has to present the details of cruises and ski packages will remember both kinds of arguments, regardless of how he or she personally feels about them. Being sufficiently motivated also will overwhelm selective learning effects (Zanna & Olson, 1982).

Other conditions that encourage selective learning all depend on the kind of person one is (Zanna & Olson, 1982). People with high self-esteem are more biased in their attitudes, as are people with an internal locus of control. To return to our example, suppose one member of the couple is more self-confident and generally thinks she can influence events around her; she is precisely the one who will forget the other person's discrepant arguments. Finally, people who generally tend to repress unpleasant facts similarly tend to forget attitude-discrepant information (Zanna & Olson, 1982). Thus, the prediction of dissonance theorists and others about the selective learning of agreeable arguments does seem to be supported under the right circumstances for the right people. Although more research is clearly needed, work on cognition and social cognition suggests some contributing factors, such as familiarity of arguments, types of learning, and locus of control. Again, early insights have been developed by recent work. It is not that recent developments represent a dramatic shift to social cognition approaches. Rather, the recent work results from steady improvement in theory and method over the last few decades, and some of that improvement has leaned on social cognition approaches.

Balance Theory and Selective Recall of Information About Others

Another consistency theory, *balance theory* (Heider, 1958), also inspired research on learning and retention as a function of consistency (Cottrell, Ingraham, & Monfort, 1971; Picek, Sherman, & Shiffrin, 1975; Zajonc & Burnstein, 1965a, 1965b). Balance theory has influenced social cognition research on schemas (Chapters 4–5), and recently it has, in turn, been influenced by social cognition research on mental structure and processing. Balance theory is an early model of cognitive and attitudinal organization. According to the theory, structures in the perceiver's mind represent the perceiver (P), another person (O), and the mutual object (X) (see Fig. 11.1). You (P) may have an attitude toward your roommate (O) and toward his car (X), and you may perceive him as having a certain attitude toward his car. Your perceptions of the relations among you two and the old clunker may be of two sorts, either positive or negative. Liking, owning, or belonging with something is a positive relationship (+), while disliking or not belonging together is a negative relationship (−).

The combination of relationships among the three of you may be either balanced or imbalanced. Essentially, they are balanced if you are either agreeing friends or disagreeing enemies. For example, if you like your roommate (P-O is +), and he likes his car (O-X is +), then the three of you are a "balanced" trio if you develop an affection for the old car (P-X is +). It is also balanced if your roommate likes his car (O-X is +), you dislike his car (P-X is −), and on reflection you decide he is not your type either (P-O is −). Both of these relationships are shown in

Basic Cognitive Structure

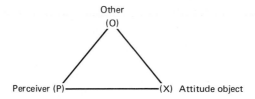

Balanced Structures

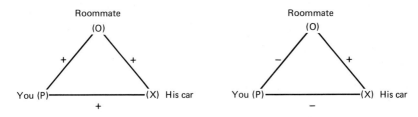

Imbalanced Structures

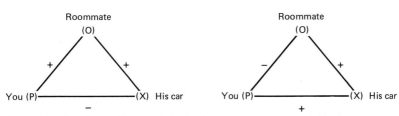

FIGURE 11.1 Balance theory triads.

Fig. 11.1. There are several other balanced possibilities besides the two shown. The basic principle is that if the three positive and negative signs multiply out to positive, the structure is balanced.

Now consider the possibility that you like your roommate (+), he adores his car (+), and you cannot stand it (−). There is trouble in store for an imbalanced relationship such as this. Similarly, it would be imbalanced if your roommate adores his car (+), and so do you (+), but you think he is an unbearable bore (−). Imbalanced relationships are under some pressure to change toward balance, and that is how the theory predicts attitude change. Your perception of any of the three relationships is likely to change in order to create balance. For example, people may interpret people they like (P-O is +) as liking what they like (P-X is +, so O-X is +) and disliking what they dislike (P-X is −, so O-X is −). For example, most people interpret close friends and favored political candidates as sharing their attitudes more closely than is the case (Berscheid & Walster, 1978; Kinder, 1978; Ottati, Fishbein, & Middlestadt, 1988; but see Judd, Kenny, & Krosnick, 1983; Krosnick, 1988b).

The theory has been influenced specifically by both older and recent work on mental structure and representation; balance research shows how cognitive constraints shape learning and memory relevant to attitudes. For example, other people hearing about you, your roommate, and his car will learn and remember the story better if it is balanced. The prediction that balanced relationships are easier to recall was derived from consistency theories and has been developed by recent schema theories (Chapters 4–5). Traditional balance research shows, for example, that people can learn and generate balanced social structures more easily than imbalanced ones (Feather, 1969; Zajonc & Burnstein, 1965a). Social schema research suggests that balanced relationships are stored in memory as a single unit. It is easier to remember that two friends agree or that two enemies disagree; this can be a compact item of memory. It is harder to recall that one of two friends like chocolate and the other hates it and which feels which way.

Recent balance researchers suggest cognitive mechanisms that explain why balanced relationships are easier to recall (Picek, Sherman, & Shiffrin, 1975; Sentis & Burnstein, 1979). Balanced and imbalanced relationships are stored differently. That is, people appear to store balanced relationships as a single cognitive unit, while imbalanced ones are stored less efficiently, in pieces. That is, suppose people initially learn an imbalanced triad. Subsequently, the time it takes them to retrieve a single relationship depends on the number of relationships (P-O, O-X, X-P) the experimenter uses as a recall cue; the more pieces of the three-way imbalanced relationship that are supplied, the faster the triad of relationships can be retrieved. However, with balanced relationships, the number of pieces supplied by the experimenter does not matter; the time to retrieve the entire balanced triad is the same regardless of the number of recall cues. This implies, then, that a balanced triad is a single cognitive unit that must be retrieved all at once, but an imbalanced triad is not (Sentis & Burnstein, 1979).

In sum, balance theorists predict that people will learn and recall balanced sets of information more easily than imbalanced ones. Such bits of information as agreeing friends and disagreeing enemies appear to form a single compact cognitive unit in memory, as opposed to imbalanced combinations.

Attitudes Organize Memory

A general principle emerges from the research inspired originally by consistency theories. Attitudes serve to organize memory under many circumstances. In particular, making an attitudinal judgment improves recall of attitude-relevant evidence and creates attitude-consistent inferences. This fits with research from person perception as well (Lingle & Ostrom, 1981; Ostrom, Lingle, Pryor, & Geva, 1980). Hence, if you judge a man's suitability as a pilot, you will remember his superior eyesight and infer that he has good spatial ability. If you judge his suitability as a comedian, on the other hand, you will recall his infectious laugh and infer that he has stage presence (Lingle, Geva, Ostrom, Leippe, & Baumgardner, 1979). The effect seems to be mediated by your recalling the attitude itself, once it is formed, rather than retrieving and resynthesizing all the individual bits of evidence. Once you have formed an attitude about somebody as a pilot instead of a comedian, that attitude organizes subsequent judgments, including recall of the data on which the judgment was based. The attitude is easier to recall than is the evidence that supports it (Lingle & Ostrom, 1979; Loken, 1984).

Summary

Traditional consistency theories were among the earliest frameworks to predict the effects of attitudes on selective perception, learning, and memory. This work both anticipated social cognition approaches and has, of late, been developed by it. Dissonance theory views people as motivated to avoid information inconsistent with their attitudes. Although the evidence for selective exposure is uneven, the evidence for selective attention and interpretation is clearer. Dissonance theorists and others also hypothesized the selective learning of attitudinally agreeable arguments, a prediction that seems to be supported under certain circumstances for certain people. In a similar vein, balanced triads (i.e., consistent interpersonal pairs with a common attitude object) are easier to learn and remember, apparently because they form a compact unit in memory. Finally, people's attitudes more generally seem to organize memory.

TYPES OF ATTITUDE PROCESSING

So far, we have examined several of the more explicitly cognitive aspects of some traditional attitude theories. Now we take up three more recent attitude theories that are themselves fundamentally cognitive in orientation. All three of these theories focus on particular modes of attitudinal processing, and in particular, on the degree to which people's attitudes form, change, and operate in relatively thoughtful or more automatic ways.

Heuristic vs. Systematic Processing of Attitudes

Many classic theories of attitudes posit that attitudes are formed and changed based on thoughtful consideration of issue-relevant information. For example, McGuire's (1969) chain of persuasion, noted earlier, assumes that people process and evaluate the arguments provided, accordingly agreeing or disagreeing with the persuasive communication. Similarly, the dominant framework for studying attitudes over a period of nearly two decades, the Yale persuasive communications approach (Hovland, Janis, & Kelley, 1953), emphasized learning of message content related to an issue and conscious acceptance or rejection. Moreover, one of the most comprehensive recent theories of attitudes and behavior, the theory of reasoned action (Fishbein & Ajzen, 1974), later elaborated into the theory of planned behavior (Ajzen, 1987), states that attitudes are importantly based on people's beliefs about the attitude object. While not specifically a theory of cognitive processes, this theory does emphasize a deliberate, thoughtful process, namely: evaluating the strengths and weaknesses of one's particular beliefs, assessing their systematic implications for one's attitude, and ultimately, along with perceived norms and control, assessing their implications for one's behavior. These traditional theories essentially focus on a relatively controlled or systematic form of attitude formation and change.

The heuristic-systematic model (e.g., Chaiken, 1980; Chaiken, Liberman, & Eagly, 1989) proposes that people only engage in such thoughtful processes when they are sufficiently motivated and have the capacity to do so. When people are relatively motivated, they indeed can engage in this thoughtful effortful mode, termed *systematic* processing, which involves evaluating the pros and cons of a message's arguments. For example, systematic processing is increased by various factors that tend to increase motivation: receiving messages on topics of high personal relevance, making attitude judgments with important consequences, having sole responsibility for message evaluation, and discovering that one disagrees with the majority position (for reviews, see Eagly & Chaiken, 1984; Chaiken & Stangor, 1987; Eagly & Chaiken, in press). Systematic processing is characterized by sensitivity to the valence and quality of a message, issue-relevant thoughts, enhanced recall for the arguments, and relatively lasting change (e.g., Axsom, Yates, & Chaiken, 1987; Chaiken, 1980; Leippe & Elkin, 1987; Mackie, 1987; McFarland, Ross, & Conway, 1984; Weldon & Gargano, 1985).

In contrast to this strategy that emphasizes relatively thoughtful processing of attitude-relevant information, people often engage in a more rapid, easy, *heuristic* form of processing. According to Chaiken's theory, people learn certain persuasion heuristics or rules (experts can be trusted; long arguments are strong arguments; attractive people are right) that provide shortcuts around more effortful processing of the actual information provided in a message. The rules are learned from experience, so they are often accurate enough. Of equal importance is the point that heuristic processing makes relatively few capacity demands. People apparently use the heuristic strategy when there is no room for the more systematic type of processing. That is, when people's cognitive capacity is reduced, they are less likely to engage in systematic processing and more likely to engage in heuristic processing (e.g., Mackie & Worth, 1989; W. Wood & Kallgren, 1988; W. Wood, Kallgren, & Preisler, 1985; Worth & Mackie, 1987).

One implication of the heuristic-systematic distinction in persuasion is that people often may not carefully process message arguments and, instead, may rely on shortcuts to form their opinions. Sometimes, people clearly do engage in the more comprehensive, analytic, systematic process. When they do each will be determined by a variety of motives; for example, accuracy motives, defensive motives, and impression-management motives all potentially influence the extent of heuristic or systematic processing (Chaiken, Liberman, Eagly, 1989). These types of motives compare to those discussed in Chapter 5 as motives that encourage more schema-driven or data-driven processing in general. Consequently, one issue for continuing research will be the degree of overlap between schematic and heuristic processing on the one hand, and data-driven and systematic processing on the other, as well as the conditions that promote each. It will also be important to specify the degree to which heuristic processing is actually automatic, as it appears to be, and the degree to which systematic processing is actually controlled, as it also appears to be. (Recall that the criteria for automatic and controlled processing were described in Chapter 7.)

Another issue for continued research is the direct identification of the persuasion heuristics. Although direct evidence for the persuasion heuristics themselves (e.g., length means strength) is currently lacking, perhaps this is not surprising, to the extent that the heuristics themselves may be relatively unconscious and automatically applied. Nevertheless, there are several profitable directions for expanded research, based on the heuristic-systematic model.

Peripheral vs. Central Routes to Persuasion

Another cognitively oriented model of persuasion also proposes that there are two routes to attitude change (Petty & Cacioppo, 1981, 1986a, 1986b). According to the elaboration likelihood model, the *central* route involves actively and carefully thinking about (i.e., elaborating) the true merits of the message arguments, and in this sense, it is similar to the systematic route proposed by Chaiken's heuristic-systematic model. The other, *peripheral*, route to persuasion includes any kind of attitude change that occurs without much thought or elaboration. As such, this route includes Chaiken's heuristic mode, but other types of superficial attitude change as well. For example, mere exposure effects on evaluations (see Chapter 10 on affect) would be a peripheral (but not a heuristic) mode of persuasion.

One basic postulate of the elaboration likelihood model is that people are motivated to hold correct attitudes. With sufficient motivation and ability to process a message, people will respond to the quality of its arguments. The balance of their favorable, unfavorable, and neutral thoughts then determines positive or negative attitude change by the central route, which is posited to be relatively enduring. Variations in the amount and type of this *cognitive elaboration* (issue-relevant thinking) depend on individual and situational factors. Elaboration includes making relevant associations, scrutinizing the arguments, inferring their value, and evaluating the overall message.

Methodologically, elaboration is assessed in various ways (Petty & Cacioppo, 1986a, 1986b). One can ask people directly how much effort they invested in processing the message, but people cannot or will not always answer accurately. Alternatively, certain physiological measures are sensitive to cognitive activity, but these techniques are in their early stages. Two other techniques have proved more successful in assessing degrees of cognitive elaboration.

The technique of cognitive response analysis derives from earlier work on the recipient's cognitions as the message is being received, and in particular on the recipient's counterarguments (Brock, 1967; Osterhouse & Brock, 1970). Early on, the favorability of the recipient's cognitive responses to persuasion was shown to be directly related to the degree of attitude change (Greenwald, 1968). More recently, the elaboration likelihood theory built on the earlier cognitive response research. As a theory, the elaboration likelihood approach has profited both from the ideas and methods of the cognitive response approach. The technique of measuring people's cognitive responses to the message, thus, is one method to document the elaboration likelihood model, in particular, by directly measuring the counterarguments and supporting arguments that presumably cause attitude change.

The cognitive response technique itself is a simple and elegant way to measure cognitive mediation. In general, cognitive mediation means that some stimulus causes a cognitive effect, which in turn causes a response. In the case of persuasive communication, cognitive mediation would entail low or high argument quality or some other variable (stimulus) causing low or high counterarguing (cognitive mediator), which in turn causes attitude change (response). Figure 11.2 depicts this model. In cognitive response research, subjects not only give an opinion on the topic at hand but also list their thoughts during or just after receiving the communication. The cognitive responses, as they are called, are scored as reactions pro and con, and thus, they presumably mediate attitude change. When researchers use the cognitive response method in concert with the elaboration likelihood model, they can show that attitude change often is caused by one's personal responses to a message.

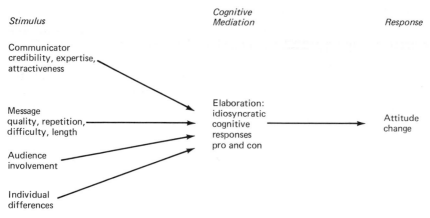

FIGURE 11.2 Cognitive response analysis.

Cognitive response analysis is a method, but it is not a theory. As a technique, cognitive response analysis is compatible with various attitude theories (as described in Petty, Ostrom, & Brock, 1981). Because it is a methodological technique, it does not guarantee theoretical advances in and of itself. The technique of cognitive response analysis has been applied to communicator, message, and audience variables (Petty, Ostrom, & Brock, 1981).

Another method for assessing elaboration involves experimental manipulation, rather than measurement, of cognitive elaboration as the proposed mediator. By manipulating the quality of the message itself, one can see whether or not subjects respond differently to the strong or weak arguments. If they are sensitive to argument quality, they are presumably thinking about what they received, so they are elaborating on it and, by definition, following the central route; if they are not sensitive to argument quality, then they are not elaborating much, and they are taking the more peripheral route. Much of the elaboration likelihood research program manipulates argument quality as well as some situational variable posited to affect elaboration, and then measures both cognitive responses and attitude change.

Armed with these methods, in particular cognitive response analysis and manipulations of argument strength, the elaboration likelihood model addresses many classic issues in persuasion research. The elaboration likelihood model provides a broad framework for understanding some basic processes in persuasive communication (Petty & Cacioppo, 1986b). As such, it has organized some comprehensive overviews of the attitude change literature (Petty & Cacioppo, 1981). The next few sections illustrate how the effects of communicator, message, and audience all can be analyzed from this perspective. As we will see, one of the major points made by this research is that many standard attitude change effects depend on how involved the audience (i.e., the subject) is with a particular persuasive message.

Communicator effects. The characteristics of the message source heavily influence the processes and outcomes of persuasion. Two features of the communicator, credibility and attractiveness, illustrate the elaboration likelihood model approach to communicator effects. On the one hand, communicator credibility and on the other hand, expertise or attractiveness, respectively, emphasize the central route and the peripheral route to persuasion.

Proponents of one model of communicator *credibility* that draws on the elaboration likelihood model maintain that persuasion is a joint function of the recipient's involvement in the outcome and the communicator's credibility (Hass, 1981). Specifically, the theorists propose that uninvolved recipients respond with more negative thoughts to a low credibility communicator than to a high credibility communicator. Involved recipients, in contrast, respond with more negative thoughts to a high credibility communicator. Thus, the model draws on the elaboration likelihood model notion that a recipient's own thoughts (pro and con) determine attitude change, although it focuses in particular on the mediating role of counterarguments.

For example, suppose you generally opposed a new federal subsidy to cattle farmers because the outcome might be higher taxes, but your concern about the issue is not particularly deep and involved because the tax increase would be trivial. According to the theory, a high school sophomore's assertion that the program would hurt our economy will produce more vigorous counterargument than will the same assertion made by a Nobel Prize-winning economist. You are willing to take the expert's word for it, while it seems all too easy to mount a counterattack against the high school student. In contrast, if you favor and care deeply about the federal student loan program because it determines whether or not people you know can attend college, and you even have written to Congress about it (i.e., you are highly involved in the outcome), then a high school student's assertion that the loan program will damage the economy elicits less counterargument than does the same opinion from a famous economist. In the second case, you actively counterargue and resist the expert's opinion because the outcome is so important to you. This type of involvement ("outcome involvement"; B. T. Johnson & Eagly, 1989) combines with credibility to produce cognitive responses (in this case, counterarguments) that, in turn, lead to attitude change.

Another example of the elaboration likelihood model's application to communicator credibility shows that credibility effects also can matter especially to people in favor of a stand. Proponents of a particular viewpoint may feel it is at best weakly represented if the communicator is only moderately credible. In one study testing this idea (Sternthal, Dholakia, & Leavitt, 1978), people who initially favored the Consumer Protection Agency heard a high or moderate credibility source argue for the agency. They then indicated their opinions and listed all thoughts pro and con that had come to mind in response to the message. The moderately credible communicator was more persuasive than the one with high credibility. Furthermore, subjects wrote more supporting arguments and fewer counterarguments for the moderate credibility source. The subjects' cognitive responses mediated the effect of moderate credibility, as the elaboration likelihood model would predict.

In general, however, communicator credibility may have the most effect on people who are relatively uninvolved in the outcomes at stake. People who are involved pay more attention to message content than to the communicator, so they generate more cognitive responses, which in turn cause attitude change, if the pros outweigh the cons (Petty & Cacioppo, 1981).

Thus, to summarize, the elaboration likelihood model shows that communicator credibility effects on attitude change may depend critically on the recipient's initial opinion and outcome involvement (see Petty & Cacioppo, 1981, for a longer review). The elaboration likelihood model shows that many thoughts pro or con on an issue are generated under the specific circumstances of high outcome involvement (see B. T. Johnson & Eagly, 1989). Cognitive response analysis allows a detailed methodological analysis and the elaboration likelihood model a theoretical specification of classic communicator credibility effects, emphasizing the central route to persuasion.

The peripheral route to persuasion is emphasized by simple cues regarding the *expertise and attractiveness* of the communicator. For example, students were told that a mandatory comprehensive exam for all seniors was advocated by an expert source (Carnegie Commission on Higher Education) or by an inexpert source (a high school class). When the issue was relevant to the students, because it would be instituted at their own school the next year, the students were more sensitive to the quality of the strong or weak arguments presented, as the elaboration likelihood model would predict. Moreover, when the issue was relevant, source expertise made little difference. However, when the issue was less relevant (the exam would be instituted elsewhere or much later), and subjects were, therefore, less outcome-involved, source expertise essentially determined their attitudes, regardless of argument quality (Petty, Cacioppo, & Goldman, 1981). Under low outcome involvement, then, source expertise can serve as a peripheral cue to persuasion, bypassing the need to process message arguments. Similar effects can be obtained for attractive or famous message sources (Chaiken, 1979, 1980; Pallak, 1983; Pallak, Murroni, & Koch, 1983; Petty, Cacioppo, & Schumann, 1983; Rhine & Severance, 1970).

To summarize, communicator credibility effects are strongest for recipients not involved in the outcomes at stake. Uninvolved recipients are most likely to respond to superficial indications of expertise. Of course, alleged expertise is not a totally reliable reason for agreeing with someone's arguments, but it is a convenient shortcut. Much of the research on communicator cues may represent only those recipients who are listening to communications at fairly shallow levels. In support of this, highly outcome-involved subjects express more message-oriented thoughts (Chaiken, 1980). Cognitive response analysis distinguishes between people who are responding superficially and those who are thinking hard in response to a message, so it allows one to distinguish between outcome-involved and uninvolved subjects' use of communicator cues.

Message effects. The elaboration likelihood model and the cognitive response technique have been applied to various features of the message, in particular number of repetitions, difficulty, number of arguments, use of rhetorical questions, number of sources, and degree of distraction in its context. In each of these areas, the model has emphasized the role of recipient thought.

The research on *message repetition* is best understood as distinguishing between two different kinds of stimuli: nonlinguistic (e.g., the Coca-Cola logo) and linguistic (e.g., the persuasive message). Cognitive response analysis suggests that the differences are due to the amount and valence (direction pro or con) of thoughts generated in each case (A. Sawyer, 1981).

We will begin with nonlinguistic stimuli. Researchers have long known that repeated exposures typically enhance liking in what is called the mere exposure effect (Stang, 1974; Zajonc, 1968a; for a review, see Bornstein, 1989; also see Chapter 10). Two major qualifications on the mere exposure effect are that the stimulus be initially unfamiliar and that people's initial reaction to the stimulus be neutral or positive (Grush, 1976; Harrison, 1977). When the stimulus is initially evaluated negatively, the exposure effect can evaporate or reverse.

In line with the peripheral route of the elaboration likelihood model, the mere exposure effect on nonlinguistic stimuli operates most clearly when recipients are essentially unthinking; that is, they cannot be generating personal responses (pro or con) to the stimulus. Hence, the more you see the Coca-Cola logo, the more you like it, assuming you do not think about it much; the logo has become as familiar as the American flag. Even animals, who presumably do not think at all, show the effect of exposure on preference. People show the effect of repetition quite plainly under circumstances of minimal cognitive processing, or as McGuire (1969) would say, when they are behaving as lazy organisms. Accordingly, the peripheral route to persuasion best describes message repetition effects with nonlinguistic stimuli.

Given nonlinguistic stimuli, there is a strong case for a nonconscious mere exposure effect on preference, and it is worth noting because it provides a stark contrast to the central route of the elaboration likelihood model and, thus, illustrates a peripheral route to persuasion. We reviewed some mere exposure research supporting nonconscious mediation in Chapter 10, when we discussed Zajonc's separate systems view of affect and cognition (Moreland & Zajonc, 1977, 1979; W. R. Wilson, 1979). Recall that subjects who do not even recognize stimuli as familiar still show exposure effects on liking (Zajonc, 1980b). Consequently, it is unlikely that the simple mere exposure effect for nonlinguistic stimuli is consciously mediated. People show the effect without recognizing the stimulus, without awareness, and without thought. Thus, message repetition effects on nonlinguistic stimuli do not appear to be mediated by conscious cognitive responses, and hence, are described by the peripheral route.

The second kind of stimulus that has been used in research on message repetition is linguistic material, that is, the persuasive message itself. This kind of material does elicit thought, and as the elaboration likelihood model would predict, amount of thought pro and con appears to determine whether or not the mere exposure effect occurs (Petty & Cacioppo, 1981; A. Sawyer, 1981). This point is illustrated by the difference between early work on message repetition and recent work using cognitive response analysis. In a study predating cognitive response analysis, W. Wilson and Miller (1968) originally found repetition effects on persuasion with prose passages; in this case the prose concerned a lawsuit for damages. Students role-played being jury members and were exposed to an attorney's arguments either one time or three times. More exposure led to more agreement. Repetition also markedly increased retention of the arguments after a week's delay. Since retention and attitude change were moderately correlated, Wilson and Miller concluded that at least some of the repetition effect was due to enhanced recall.

A decade after that effort, Cacioppo and Petty (1979) also tackled the question of what mediates message repetition effects. Armed now with cognitive response analysis, they tapped subjects' idiosyncratic responses to the communication immediately after hearing it. Subjects retrospectively listed the thoughts they had had while listening to the communication and indicated whether each thought was pro (+), con (−), or neutral (0). In a separate measure, they were asked to recall the message's arguments. Agreement with the message was completely uncorrelated with recall, but highly correlated with both favorable thoughts (positively) and unfavorable thoughts (negatively). Number of irrelevant thoughts did not correlate with agreement. Thus, cognitive responses pro and con, not recall, were shown empirically to mediate the effects of repetition on persuasion.

One important point from this line of research is that the cognitive response analysis technique of thought listing can support a different sort of cognitive process model than does a model stressing recall as the mediating process. Cognitive response analysis looks at the individual's own idiosyncratic reactions to the argument, rather than at the person's ability simply to remember the argument as given. The advantage of this is that cognitive response analysis successfully elucidates the processes intervening between exposure and agreement, consistent with the elaboration likelihood model's central route.

As elaboration likelihood model work on message repetition effects has continued, the exact nature of the mediating cognitive process has been specified further. People's cognitive responses to repeated messages support a two-stage model, in which uncertainty reduction and tedium counterbalance each other (Berlyne, 1970; Cacioppo & Petty, 1979; A. Sawyer, 1981). In other words, the first few times your friend explains his thesis to you, repetition aids understanding and convinces you the paper is right, assuming the arguments are cogent. But, after that, it is a bore, and you may begin to counterargue out of sheer perversity. In the Cacioppo and Petty study mentioned above, for example, agreement first increased with exposure, as subjects comprehended the message and thought about it. Then agreement decreased, presumably as tedium set in. Cognitive responses pro and con followed the same pattern as did agreement, that is, positive at first and then negative, which lends support to the two-factor model. Of course, this model assumes that subjects follow the central route, i.e., they bother to think about the message, which presupposes at least some outcome involvement; uninvolved subjects do not always show the pattern of initial agreement then disagreement (A. Sawyer, 1981).

Conceptually, message repetition effects illustrate several crucial points about the elaboration likelihood model: the importance of whether or not the recipient is actively thinking, and if thinking, whether those thoughts are pro or con; the possibilities for nonconscious mediation in the various peripheral routes as a contrast to the conscious cognitive mediation in the central route; and the role of the elaboration likelihood model as a highly specific theory that solves puzzles in new ways (see Cacioppo & Petty, 1985, for a review). From an applied perspective, message repetition effects might inform advertisers who air the same television commercial several times during the late show; research suggests circumstances under which they are both right and wrong to do so.

Another type of message effect is the *difficulty* of the message itself. As with repetition, cognitive response analysis and the elaboration likelihood approach have revealed that the effects of message difficulty also are influenced by outcome involvement. The number of supporting arguments and counterarguments people generate is a function of such involvement, if the message is difficult. Consider trying to understand a difficult statistics lecture. A student who hates the course content, does not care much about the final grade, and has already given up working on the material will probably ignore the lecture and daydream. When acting as an uninvolved, lazy organism, one does not make an effort to absorb message content, regardless of its comprehensibility. At intermediate levels of outcome involvement, message difficulty should have maximum impact, since a little added difficulty can make the critical difference between at least some processing and giving up. The majority of the statistics professor's students presumably are at this intermediate level, and they would be very sensitive to message difficulty. That is, message difficulty makes more difference to them than to the totally uninvolved students. At high levels of outcome involvement, message difficulty again makes little difference to comprehension, because people will be motivated to overcome message difficulty no matter what. (Ability helps, too, of course.) A new teaching assistant who has never heard the material before will make every effort to understand the lectures regardless of difficulty.

How, then, does message difficulty cause attitude change? Again, an analysis that draws on the cognitive response methods reveals that the mediating factors may well be the amount and valence of people's cognitive responses. Comprehension not surprisingly encourages persuasion, if the arguments are good (e.g., Eagly, 1974; see Eagly & Himmelfarb, 1978, for others). If you do not understand a message, you cannot easily repeat it to yourself, nor can you muster supporting arguments. Again, people's own idiosyncratic supportive cognitive responses can strengthen the argued viewpoint, but only if people comprehend the message in the first place. The more comprehensible the message, the more the professor's audience can think positively about what he or she has said (assuming the arguments are good). Consequently, the more they comprehend the lecture's good arguments, the more they will agree with the professor (W. Wood & Eagly, 1981).

Eagly proposes an alternative to the cognitive response analysis accounts of message difficulty effects. Message difficulty effects might not be mediated entirely by the build-up of supportive cognitions, as cognitive response theorists suggest. Instead, an incomprehensible argument might elicit negative affect, simply because it is frustrating not to understand something. The negative affect may then become associated with the attitude object and the persuasive attempt backfires. The frustration, in effect, spills over to discourage persuasion (Chaiken & Eagly, 1976, 1983; Eagly, 1974). In this case, message difficulty effects would be at least partially mediated by affect, without cognitive mediation. At this point, this intriguing alternative has yet to receive any firm empirical support.

In sum, message difficulty effects can be cognitively mediated, as cognitive response evidence has indicated, but they need not always be. In terms of the elaboration likelihood model, these message difficulty effects would represent, respectively, the central and peripheral routes to persuasion.

Another important feature of messages is the sheer *number of arguments*, which can act as a superficial cue for persuasion. Both the heuristic model (e.g., length means strength; Chaiken, Liberman, & Eagly, 1989) and the elaboration likelihood model support this idea. Petty and Cacioppo (1984) found that under low personal relevance (i.e., low outcome involvement), number of arguments acted as a peripheral cue to persuasion, regardless of argument quality; under high relevance, argument quality and number of arguments together determined persuasion, indicating thoughtful responses via the central route.

Cognitive response analysis has been applied to many other features of messages besides repetition, difficulty, and number of arguments (Petty & Cacioppo, 1981; Petty, Ostrom, & Brock, 1981). For example, the use of *rhetorical questions* (Burnkrant & Howard, 1984; Petty, Cacioppo, & Heesacker, 1981; Petty, Rennier, & Cacioppo, 1987), *multiple sources* (Harkins & Petty, 1981), and environmental *distractions* (Petty, Wells, & Brock, 1976) have been analyzed from this perspective. The elaboration likelihood model suggests and cognitive response methodology supports the conclusion that, in every case, the factor critical to persuasion is the amount of active cognitive elaboration pro and con done by the recipient. To generate favorable cognitive responses and to be maximally persuasive, a message should have good arguments, should be repeated a few times but not too many, should be comprehensible, and should be delivered in an atmosphere free of distraction. On the other hand, if the message has *weak* arguments (and so could produce many counterarguments), distraction and a single exposure will inhibit those negative cognitive responses and accordingly enhance persuasion.

To review, message effects depend on outcome involvement. For the linguistic part of an advertisement (as opposed to the logo), repetition cannot easily persuade people unless they bother to think about the sales pitch; the uninvolved person does not always notice even repeated messages. The same is true of message difficulty; subtle changes in comprehensibility will most affect those who are moderately involved. The totally uninvolved will not notice message difficulty because they are not paying attention (e.g., student daydreamers). The highly involved will put in the effort necessary to understand the message regardless of difficulty (e.g., the motivated teaching assistant). Nuances of the message content then should affect the vast middle more than the extremes of the outcome-involvement continuum. Thus, outcome involvement increases cognitive activity and subsequent attitude change, for moderately repeated and comprehensible messages, if the arguments are cogent. Related message effects occur for number of arguments, the use of rhetorical questions, the number of sources involved, and the presence of distractions.

Audience involvement. In discussing the elaboration likelihood model, audience involvement has combined with the effects of many other variables, in particular, communicator and message effects. Thus, a summary of elaboration likelihood research shows that, at every step of the central persuasion process, the respondent's amount and valence of cognitive response determines the type of effect that occurs. Because cognitive responses demand an actively thinking recipient, audience involvement has influenced each of the effects discussed so far. However, the discussion has not been explicit about the meaning of involvement, in part because the literature lacks consensus. Because different types of involvement appear to have different effects, it is important to examine the concept more closely.

Involvement is operationalized in various ways, without strong agreement. For example, students might be given a message advocating a change in dormitory visitation hours at their own school versus another school (Petty & Cacioppo, 1979). Or they might be told that a change in university policy will take place in one year versus in ten years (Petty, Ostrom, & Brock, 1981). Thus, the most usual manipulations include some form of personal relevance and future consequence. A variant on involvement manipulates responsibility rather than relevance; subjects are told they have sole responsibility for evaluating the message (Brickner, Harkins, & Ostrom, 1985; Petty, Harkins, & Williams, 1980).

Unfortunately for involvement research, there is also limited agreement on how to define involvement. Personal importance or relevance to one's self-concept seems to capture its general conceptual meaning (Greenwald, 1981; Greenwald & Leavitt, 1984; B. T. Johnson & Eagly, 1989), but researchers from the first identified different types of involvement. Ego involvement (M. Sherif & Hovland, 1961), issue involvement (C. A. Kiesler, Collins, & Miller, 1969), personal involvement (Apsler & Sears, 1968; C. W. Sherif et al., 1973), and vested interest (Sivacek & Crano, 1982) all imply that an issue has personal relevance or meaning, especially intrinsic importance for beliefs central to a person's identity. These terms can be contrasted with task involvement (M. Sherif & Hovland, 1961), in which the individual is concerned only with the consequences of a particular response. If a person is interested in maximizing the rewards in a given situation, that is response involvement (Zimbardo, 1960). The different types of involvement illustrate the range of factors that might make a person respond more or less thoughtfully to a persuasion attempt that is personally important (see Chaiken & Stangor, 1987, for a discussion of involvement types).

In a meta-analysis of this literature, B. T. Johnson and Eagly (1989) concluded that the involvement effects described so far in the research on elaboration likelihood apply most to *outcome-relevant involvement,* which implicates people's ability to attain desired outcomes. Their analysis of the literature indicates that such high involvement subjects are more persuaded by strong arguments, consistent with the elaboration likelihood model, but not always less persuaded by weak arguments, despite elaboration likelihood predictions. Two other types of involvement do not obtain these effects: *value-relevant involvement* (implicating one's enduring principles) just generally inhibits persuasion, and the same is somewhat true of *impression-relevant involvement* (implicating one's concern for people's opinions of self). Proponents of the elaboration likelihood model prefer to include these latter two types, involvement based on outcomes and values, in one category (Petty & Cacioppo, 1990), invoking the elaboration likelihood model postulate that (value-) involved subjects may process in a biased manner because of their prior knowledge, strong attitudes, or confidence (Petty & Cacioppo, 1986b; for disagreement, see B. T. Johnson & Eagly, 1990). Continued research should clarify these issues, but for present purposes, the distinction at least between outcome involvement and the other two types is important.

There is, thus, some consensus on the importance of the outcome-involvement effects reviewed so far. Regardless of the specific manipulation, outcome involvement stimulates thought, which can lead to increased or decreased persuasion, depending on the cognitive responses, which in turn depend on the strength of the arguments and on the subject's preexisting attitudes. Different levels of outcome involvement lead to different types of processing, which lead to greater or lesser reliance on superficial characteristics of the communication. As noted, researchers hypothesize that outcome-involved subjects employ thoughtful, systematic strategies that rely on message content, while uninvolved subjects are particularly likely to use superficial, heuristic, or shortcut strategies that depend on simple, possibly irrelevant cues such as communicator characteristics (Chaiken, 1980) rather than message content.

One overall way to think about the effects of outcome involvement on cognitive responses and on persuasion is that less involved people seem to operate "on automatic," with little conscious thought (Chaiken, 1980; Petty & Cacioppo, 1981). Highly (outcome-) involved people operate in a relatively controlled mode, with much cognitive activity (LaBerge, 1975; Langer, 1978; W. Schneider & Shiffrin, 1977; Shiffrin & Schneider, 1977). Thus, people who are outcome-involved generate more cognitive responses that are sensitive to the message they encounter: the outcome-involved listener will differentiate carefully between strong and weak arguments, and between pro- and counterattitudinal arguments (Petty & Cacioppo, 1979; Petty, Cacioppo, & Goldman, 1981). Given an airtight or a proattitudinal message, the outcome-involved recipient will not bother to counterargue, but the outcome-involved person would tend to counterargue weak or counterattitudinal communications. Someone less outcome-involved probably would generate few cognitions, regardless of the message, since the uninvolved person is attending only superficially. Thus, people who are outcome-involved use systematic, content-based processing strategies that are responsive to the quality of arguments. The less-involved rely on peripheral strategies, such as the likability of the source. Researchers have shown that outcome involvement moderates the effects of communicator and message variables (as we have seen), as well as the persistence of attitude change (Cook & Flay, 1978; Hennigan, Cook, & Gruder, 1982). However, it is important to note that the outcome-involved do not necessarily think more objectively or accurately; they think *more* and sometimes in a more biased fashion (Howard-Pitney, Borgida, & Omoto, 1986).

The other types of involvement, besides outcome involvement, tend to show different effects from those described so far. According to one review (B. T. Johnson & Eagly, 1989), involvement that implicates a person's centrally held values generally inhibits persuasion. A subsequent section focusing on conviction and importance (the chapter's next-to-last section) examines this type of involvement in more detail. Another type of involvement, impression relevance, implicates people's concerns about self-presentation, and it will be discussed in the final section of this chapter.

Individual differences in cognitive responses and persuasion. In this section on the elaboration likelihood model and on the technique of cognitive response analysis, so far we have examined various situational factors that determine the amount of thought people give to persuasive communications. Most of these situational variables interact with a recipient variable, involvement, in determining the thoughtfulness of cognitive responding, as the review has indicated. There appears to be a more general dispositional factor that determines the amount of cognitive response given. Table 11.1 shows some of the items on the scale. *Need for cognition* (Cacioppo & Petty, 1982; Cacioppo, Petty, & Morris, 1983) refers to people's chronic level of thoughtfulness in response to external stimuli such as persuasive messages. People high on the need for cognition generate more cognitive responses, both pro and con, to persuasive communications, and are consequently likely to be more or less persuaded depending on the message. People low in need for cognition are more likely to process communications heuristically (Chaiken, 1987). The need for cognition is an individual difference variable that specifically addresses the process (cognitive re-

TABLE 11.1 SUBSET OF THE NEED FOR COGNITION SCALE

1. I really enjoy a task that involves coming up with new solutions to problems.
2. I would prefer a task that is intellectual, difficult, and important to one that is somewhat important but does not require much thought.
3. Learning new ways to think doesn't excite me very much.*
4. The idea of relying on thought to make my way to the top does not appeal to me.*
5. I only think as hard as I have to.*
6. I like tasks that require little thought once I've learned them.*
7. I prefer to think about small, daily projects rather than long-term ones.*
8. I would rather do something that requires little thought than something that is sure to challenge my thinking abilities.*
9. I find little satisfaction in deliberating hard and for long hours.*
10. I don't like to have the responsibility of handling a situation that requires a lot of thinking.*

*Reverse scoring was used on this item.

SOURCE: From J. T. Cacioppo & R. E. Petty. The need for cognition, *Journal of Personality and Social Psychology*, 1982, 42, 116–131. Copyright 1982 by the American Psychological Association. Reprinted by permission of the authors.

sponses) presumed to mediate between external stimulus and attitude change. People high in need for cognition even engage in effortful cognitive processing in the absence of extrinsic motivations to do so (Petty, Cacioppo, & Kasmer, 1985).

Another individual difference variable, *uncertainty orientation* (Sorrentino et al., 1988; Sorrentino & Hancock, 1987; Sorrentino & Short, 1986), also affects persuasion. Certainty-oriented people stay with the familiar and the predictable, avoiding threats to their current understanding of the world, while uncertainty-oriented people search for meaning, attempt to make sense of their environments, and seek out novel situations. The standard elaboration likelihood effects that personal relevance or outcome-involvement leads to central processing are predicted to hold only for uncertainty-oriented people. In contrast, certainty-oriented people apparently increase their use of heuristics under high relevance, contrary to the elaboration likelihood model. Uncertainty orientation differs from need for cognition in that need for cognition apparently measures motivation to think, while uncertainty orientation measures when and what to think, in the service of increasing one's certainty versus maintaining an open-minded approach to uncertainty.

Summary and comment. Having spent considerable time on the elaboration likelihood model, we should note its limitations (Eagly & Chaiken, 1984; Eagly & Himmelfarb, 1978; Petty & Cacioppo, 1981;

Petty, Cacioppo, et al., 1987; Petty, Kasmer, et al., 1987; Stiff, 1986; Stiff & Boster, 1987). First, although it proposes that people's thoughts mediate attitude change, it does not explain why people support or counterargue what they encounter. In that sense, it is a partial theory and leans on other theories of why people agree or disagree with communications, to provide a complete explanation of attitude change.

Second, it paints a picture of people as being more oriented toward validating their attitudes than they may be. People are not only motivated to be accurate but also to feel secure, as the work on uncertainty orientation points out. Although Petty and Cacioppo note that people are often only subjectively correct when they want to be rationally correct, even the attempt to be correct may not always be paramount. (One of us has a friend who defended his right to prefer a car that would make him feel foolish.) Just as we observed with the conditions of schema use and data use, it is important to spell out when people are more and less motivated to be accurate.

Similarly, the conditions under which and the processes by which people tend to be biased by prior attitudes, knowledge, value involvement, or impression-relevant involvement need to be developed within this model's framework. Although the model does allow for biased information processing, its postulate that people are motivated to hold correct attitudes tends to limit its consideration of the conditions under which people are close-minded. For example, when people receive a communication that runs counter to an attitude that is highly accessible, they are far more likely to be intentionally or unintentionally resistant (Zanna, 1991).

Third, from an empirical perspective, it is difficult to specify a priori which variables will have which effects when. That is, some variables shift from encouraging central, "objective" processing to encouraging central but biased processing. Involvement is one such variable, and it may depend on the level of involvement (higher levels inducing more bias) or the type of involvement (B. T. Johnson & Eagly, 1989). Similarly, some variables may serve both as peripheral cues and as aids to central information processing; number of arguments is one such variable (Petty & Cacioppo, 1986b). Some of the moderating variables that determine other variables' specific effects have been identified, as this review indicates. Nevertheless, variables with multiple effects and multiple functions make it difficult to falsify the model. They also undermine its predictive power (Eagly & Chaiken, 1984). It will be important to continue specifying the moderating variables that determine which of multiple possible effects another variable will demonstrate.

Fourth, some have questioned whether cognitive responses actually cause attitude change or are merely correlated with it (Romer, 1979). That is, if attitudes change for other reasons such as reinforcement contingencies, people may justify the change with cognitive responses pro and con, but only after the fact. In this view, cognitive responses do not cause attitude change; they merely accompany it, justify it, or serve as an alternative measure of persuasion (Eagly & Chaiken, 1984). In a related vein, some have argued that the standard manipulations of argument quality (responsiveness to which reveals the central route) also manipulate argument valence (Areni & Lutz, 1988).

Finally, the elaboration likelihood model and cognitive response analysis are not well-suited to the analysis of attitude change mediated by noncognitive or nonconscious processes. For example, cognitive response analysis does not account for persuasion based on mere exposure to nonlinguistic stimuli or based on negative affect spillover from a frustratingly difficult message. And the elaboration likelihood model does not in general, detail peripheral processes of persuasion.

In summary, despite these limitations, the elaboration likelihood model and cognitive response analysis are powerful theoretical and methodological tools. Methodologically, cognitive response analysis supplies the technique of having people list their thoughts pro and con during or just after a persuasive communication. Such cognitive responses presumably mediate the effects of traditional communicator, message, and audience variables on attitude change. Theoretically, the elaboration likelihood model built on cognitive response analysis to propose that the amount and direction of people's idiosyncratic responses determine attitude change via the central or peripheral routes. The elaboration likelihood model summarized effects of communicator, message, and audience on cognitive responses and on persuasion. In addition to these situational variables, individual differences in the need for cognition and uncertainty orientation influence how much thought people devote to persuasive communications. Overall, cognitive response analysis and the elaboration likelihood model have had a major impact on the fine-grained understanding of long-standing issues in attitude research.

Automatic Activation of Attitudes

In this section on types of attitude processing, we have examined two models that each focus on two modes of persuasion, heuristic and systematic, peripheral and central, respectively. A third model that focuses on types of attitude processing examines the more automatic side in greater detail. It is not a model of persuasion (i.e., how attitudes are formed or changed), but a model of how attitudes, once formed, operate and are used. The attitude accessibility model views an attitude as an association in memory between a given object and one's evaluation of that object (Fazio, 1986, 1989, 1990). The strength of association between an attitude object and the evaluation can vary. The stronger the association, the more accessible one's attitude. The speed (latency) with which people can respond evaluatively to an attitude object is the most common way of measuring accessibility. This draws on the idea that some attitudes are activated upon mere observation of the attitude object.

Several factors contribute to the accessibility of an attitude, and they include, predictably, the same factors that contribute to the accessibility of any construct, as reviewed in Chapter 7 on encoding. Recent and frequent expression of the attitude cause it to be activated more rapidly afterward (Fazio et al., 1982; Houston & Fazio, 1989; Powell & Fazio, 1984). Moreover, reviewing one's prior attitude-congruent behavior and inferring the corresponding attitude, in a process consistent with self-perception theory (see Chapter 2), also makes attitudes more accessible (Fazio, 1987; Fazio, Herr, & Olney, 1984). In addition to these situational factors that promote accessibility, there are individual differences as well. Some people (namely, low self-monitors, who are more attuned to their attitudes, see Chapter 12) may have chronically more accessible attitudes than others (Kardes et al., 1986).

Attitude accessibility has several practical implications. Accessible attitudes influence perceptions of the attitude object, such that one is more likely to make attitude-consistent judgments about relevant information, e.g., the excellent debate performance of a favored candidate (Fazio & Williams, 1986), the high quality of scientific evidence on one's own side of an issue (Houston & Fazio, 1989), and the like. Moreover, the more accessible the attitude, the more resistent it is to contradictory information (Houston & Fazio, 1989; cf. Wu & Shaffer, 1987), so accessible attitudes are more durable. Finally, as we will see in Chapter 12 on behavior and cognition, people more consistently act on their accessible attitudes.

The mere presentation of an object linked to an accessible attitude seems to trigger an automatic process, whereby a strong evaluative association is activated (Fazio, 1989). For example, one set of studies primed people with a positive or negative attitude object immediately before presenting an evaluatively loaded adjective. Subjects' task was to respond to the evaluative content of the adjectives (preselected to be unambiguous) by pressing a key marked "good" or "bad." Subjects responded faster to the adjectives when the attitude prime and adjective stimulus were evaluatively congruent. This effect was biggest when the attitude was highly accessible (had previously elicited rapid responses) or had just been repeatedly expressed (Fazio et al., 1986).

There is some evidence that the response facilitation observed in these studies is relatively automatic: first, the sheer speed of people's responses to the adjective (about a second) would seem to preclude controlled processing. That is, the facilitation provided by the evaluatively congruent, highly accessible attitude object in responding to the adjective was relatively instantaneous. Second, the facilitation effect was eliminated when the attitude prime and adjective stimulus were separated by a full second (rather than 300 msec, as in the successful priming condition). Thus, the prime's evaluative congruence only facilitated responses if the stimulus appeared within a fraction of a second of the prime's initial appearance. The short duration of its effectiveness suggests automatic processing. Third, the subjects were instructed to focus on identifying the positive or negative valence of the adjective rather than to focus on the attitude object, which was seen as irrelevant to subject's main goal. Hence, the facilitation apparently occurred without intent, another feature of relatively automatic processes.

The degree to which the facilitating effect of an attitude depends on sheer accessibility (measured as speed of response to the initial attitude object) has been contested (Bargh et al., 1990). Instead, the effect may generalize to a variety of attitudes under a variety of circumstances. Despite such complexities, at least some attitude objects—at a minimum those with a strong association between object and evaluation—apparently automatically elicit their corresponding evaluation. This insight fits with some of the work on automatic category-based responses (Chapter 4), including schema-triggered affect (S. T. Fiske, 1982; see Chapter 10; cf. Sanbonmatsu & Fazio, 1990). Although the precise boundaries of the effect remain to be identified, the work identifies a relatively automatic form of attitude processing.

Conclusions

These three models of attitude processes, the heuristic-systematic model, the elaboration likelihood model, and the attitude accessibility approach, represent well-developed integrations of traditional attitude research and new insights from social cognition. As such, they have been called the "second generational" approach (S. J. Sherman, 1987). They are distinctive in their insistence that attitude formation, change, and operation are not entirely rational, in contrast to traditional approaches that presupposed recipients who necessarily learned and considered the message arguments, if persuasion was successful, or who necessarily consciously considered their attitudes when influenced by them. This view has been questioned in at least three ways: first, people do not have to learn and recall a message to be persuaded by it; they may instead react to it on-line, resulting in an attitude based on their own responses but not on the message arguments as given. Second, people can be persuaded by more cognitively economical methods, whether persuasion heuristics or other peripheral routes. Third, people may use their most easily accessible attitudes in relatively automatic ways. As this work continues, the cognitive processes of attitude change and use will be understood in greater detail than previously possible.

COGNITIVE ANALYSES OF ATTITUDES WITHIN SOCIAL CONTEXTS

So far, we have considered persuasion as if isolated individuals received messages from individual communicators. One alternative approach examines the perceived social context of the communicator, as it influences the perceived validity of the message. The other examines the social context of the individual receiving the communication, namely, as a member of a group. Although both approaches acknowledge the importance of social context, they fit many other cognitive approaches in their emphasis on people's careful evaluation of the information provided.

Attributional Analyses of Communicators and Their Messages

Producers of television ads are well aware that their messages have maximum impact if delivered by a gorgeous model, a respected newscaster, or a well-known millionaire; an alternative way to increase message impact is to use a communicator blatantly similar to the ordinary person, as is done in "hidden camera" testimonials. The importance of communicator attractiveness, credibility, power, and similarity were first demonstrated by Hovland, Janis, and Kelley (1953), and these variables have generated research ever since, some of which we have already reviewed.

One of the early manifestations of social cognition research influencing attitude research came from attributional approaches to persuasion (see Eagly & Chaiken, 1984, for a review). In particular, attributional perspectives have helped attitude theorists approach the problem of communicator *credibility* (Eagly, Chaiken, & Wood, 1981). For example, persuasion depends in part on the recipient's analysis of why a communicator advocates a particular position. Recipients attempt to determine the validity of a persuasive message, knowing something of the communicator's dispositional and situational constraints (see Fig. 11.3). When you hear the president of Greenpeace speaking to the local Greenpeace chapter, you know that both his own opinion (a dispositional factor) and that of his audience (a situational factor) predispose him to advocate the environmental advantages of strict auto emission controls. If this is, in fact, the message, it is appar-

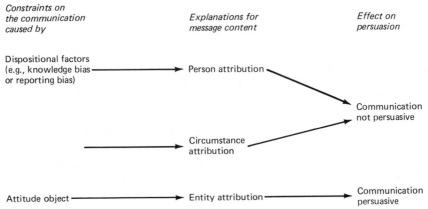

FIGURE 11.3 An attributional analysis of communicator effects in persuasion.

ently less valid and less persuasive than if it were completely independent of such dispositional and situational pressures. Messages constrained by the situation or the communicator may not validly represent
the truth, so they are not impactful. It is too easy to attribute the speaker's harangue to biases in trying to please his audience (environmental-
ists) or to his own biases; he can be biased either in what he knows
(knowledge bias) or in what he is willing to say in public (reporting
bias) (Eagly, Wood, & Chaiken, 1978). In contrast, if the president of
General Motors makes the same environmentalist point to fellow indus-
try chiefs, then he is indeed believable and persuasive.

These predictions about communicator credibility derive from
Kelley's (1967, 1972a) analysis of multiple sufficient causes, which states
that if several plausible causes exist, the weaker ones are discounted
(see Chapter 2). In this case, if both disposition (he is a crusader) and
circumstances (Greenpeace audience) conspire to produce the speech,
then the alternative cause, the facts, need not support the speech. A
careful step-by-step test of this model demonstrates that subjects' perceptions of a communicator's background (e.g., he has strong opinions)
cause the predicted attributions (e.g., he is biased). Attributions that
cast credibility into doubt then decrease opinion change (W. Wood &
Eagly, 1981). Thus, this approach focuses on the communicator-
message interaction.

Communicator *attractiveness* can also be analyzed from an attributional perspective. In one study, Eagly and Chaiken (1975) explored
the idea that attractive communicators are not only more persuasive in
general (a well-established finding) but are especially persuasive if they
advocate an undesirable position. Because attractive people are expected to advocate attractive positions, an attractive person advocating
an undesirable position must be doing so because the position is

valid. To test this, Eagly and Chaiken presented subjects with a communicator who either liked or disliked undergraduates and who made either optimistic or pessimistic statements, for example, about college graduates' employment opportunities or about the future spread of venereal disease. Attractive communicators were considerably more persuasive than unattractive communicators when advocating undesirable (pessimistic) positions (cf. Wachtler & Counselman, 1981). Messages that are unexpected, given the communicator's dispositions and the communication setting, are more persuasive than messages that are wholly predictable on the basis of who is saying them (Eagly, Chaiken, & Wood, 1981; Goethals, 1976).

Attribution theory also offers an explanation for the effects of communicator *similarity* and agreement. Those who agree with us are seen as objective and as responding to the facts of the matter, while those who disagree with us are seen as biased by their own values. Both tendencies are exaggerated by other kinds of dissimilarity between self and others (Goethals, 1976). The attributional explanation for these effects draws on Kelley's covariation model of attribution (Chapter 2) as follows. Consider two people who are discussing nonsmokers' rights. Agreement would provide support or consensus information, and *high* consensus can encourage an *entity* attribution, that is, to the attitude object (i.e., the topic being discussed). In our example, the agreeing pair attribute their shared attitude to the justice of the nonsmokers' rights. However, agreement by a dissimilar other is a particularly informative kind of consensus information (Goethals, 1976); the clearer the consensus, the more likely that the opinion is caused by the entity (the topic) in question, rather than by peculiar people or situations. Consequently, if one of the pair is a smoker and the other a nonsmoker, and if they could actually agree, each would be especially persuaded that the cause was just.

In contrast, *low* consensus, or a disagreement by another, paves the way for *person or situation* attributions. When the two people disagree, each thinks the other is not an objective judge of the facts but is letting emotional prejudices get in the way. Given that the situation is usually the same for both parties, the remaining cause has to be the other person's dispositions. However, the arguers are even more likely to believe each other biased (i.e., make a dispositional attribution) if one is a beleaguered smoker and the other an angry nonsmoker, rather than two similar individuals. Thus, a dissimilar other exaggerates the effect of disagreement as well as agreement.

To summarize, attribution theories of communicator-message interaction effects can explain when a communication will be seen as invalid and, therefore, not persuasive—that is, when a message is attributed to the dispositional biases of the communicator or the pressure of the situation, it will not be seen as valid. Conversely, attributional analyses can also explain when the communication will be perceived as valid and persuasive—that is, when it can be attributed neither to the communicator nor to the situation. When the attribution for a communication is an entity attribution (i.e., to the attitude object), the communicator is seen as presenting the objective facts, and the communicator is maximally persuasive. In sum, attributional analyses have clarified the effects of various communicator variables interacting with message variables, depending on the communicator's context.

Persuasive Arguments Theory: Attitude Change in Groups

Another cognitive analysis of attitudes examines the social context of the message recipient, rather than the communicator. In particular, it takes the recipient out of isolation and into the group context. A social cognition analysis of group-level attitude change focuses on the information provided by interaction with others. As do the approaches just covered, it also illustrates the flavor and the utility of cognitive approaches to traditional problems in attitude research.

The background for group-level attitude research comes from work in the early 1960s on group decision making. Many people think that groups represent the voice of reason and compromise; decisions made by committee are supposed to be safer than decisions made by individuals. A closer look at group decisions reveals that this is not at all the case. One research area in particular focused on the comparative riskiness of group and individual decisions (Stoner, 1961; Wallach, Kogan, & Bem, 1962). Graduate students were asked to make decisions in and out of groups on items such as the following: "A college senior planning graduate work in chemistry may enter University X where, because of rigorous standards, only a fraction of the graduate students receive the Ph.D., or may enter University Y, which has a poorer reputation but where almost every graduate student receives the Ph.D." In most cases, students who discussed this case (and others like it) emerged from the group discussion favoring a riskier alternative than when they went into the discussion. Thus, the group decision was riskier than the average of the individual decisions.

Quantities of research were generated by this counterintuitive result (Rajecki, 1982). Some of the explanations relied on traditional variables such as norms and values ("normative influences"), but one relied on a cognitive interpretation of the group interaction (an "informational influence"). As an example of the more traditional explanations, consider the possible influences of group norms. Researchers proposed that people in cohesive groups feel protected from the consequences of their decision; they can hide behind the group, in effect. This "diffusion of responsibility" hypothesis fell into disfavor when it was discovered that group attitudes do not change simply when a group feels cohesive; rather, some relevant discussion appears to be necessary (D. G. Pruitt & Teger, 1969).

Another traditional explanation was that people value risk more than caution. When people assemble in a group and compare their opinions, most of them discover that at least some others are taking riskier stands than they are. Because risk is valued, so the argument goes, the group gravitates toward the riskier extreme. This explanation in terms of social comparison and "risk as a value" faltered when researchers discovered that many groups shift toward a more cautious extreme after discussion (McCauley et al., 1973). The shift toward caution also undercut the diffusion of responsibility hypothesis. Why should a group need to diffuse responsibility for more cautious decisions?

These traditional theories and others contrast with some possible cognitive explanations, for which there is some evidence. The *persuasive arguments theory* was advanced by Burnstein and Vinokur (1973, 1975, 1977; Burnstein, Vinokur, & Trope, 1973; for a review, see Isenberg, 1986). In this more cognitive viewpoint, they proposed that attitudes in groups polarize toward relatively extreme (cautious or risky) alternatives when people are exposed to new information. Assume that there is a pool of possible arguments for any given attitude. When group members argue their positions, they may be exposed to other people's arguments that had not yet occurred to them as individuals. Group attitude change depends on whether everyone already knows similar arguments, in which case the group members are not exposed to much new information. Change also depends on how many arguments potentially could support a given position. An attitude with many good arguments supporting it has a higher probability of those arguments coming to light than does an attitude with fewer supporting arguments.

One critical test of the persuasive arguments theory comes from a study in which students were either (1) exposed to the opinions of others and given time to think about those opinions, (2) exposed to the opinions of others and not given time to think about the opinions, or (3) not exposed to the opinions of others but given time to think about the topic (Burnstein & Vinokur, 1975). Only some students' attitudes changed: those who knew the opinions of others and who had time to generate supporting arguments for them. Support for persuasive arguments theory also comes from studies in which information is exchanged in an actual discussion (Burnstein & Sentis, 1981; Rajecki, 1982). Both the number and persuasiveness of arguments affect group polarization (Hinsz & Davis, 1984). The effect may be limited to contexts that emphasize reasonableness and considered debate (McLachlan, 1986a, b).

Another explanation for group polarization effects relies on *social comparison theory.* In some cases, choice shift can be produced simply by information about others' positions (e.g., Teger & Pruitt, 1967). People apparently shifted their opinions when they learned that, relative to the opinions of others, they themselves were not as risky as they had imagined. Such comparison processes operate most strongly when people know the risk-relevant personality traits of other people, for this establishes a basis for the social comparison process (Goethals & Zanna, 1979). (For reviews of social comparison processes in group polarization, see R. Brown, 1986; Isenberg, 1986).

A variant on the social comparison theory explanation for attitude polarization in groups comes from *social identification and self-categorization* (J. C. Turner, 1987). Recall from Chapters 4 and 5 that people categorize themselves and others into distinct social groups. As a result, people stereotype members of both ingroup and outgroup, and consequently themselves. Consistent with this theory, when subjects categorize others as a group and expect to join them, they perceive the group norm to be more extreme than otherwise (Mackie, 1986). Group polarization effects seem to depend on this process of categorizing oneself as a member of the group making the arguments. That is, when an overheard discussion is attributed to a group one is to join, one perceives the group to have more extreme attitudes and one's attitude shifts in conformity with those stereotypic attitudes (Mackie, 1986; Mackie & Cooper, 1984). Attitudes clearly are one important dimension that people use in the group categorization process (Hymes, 1986).

These cognitive theories of attitude polarization in groups provide informational bases for persuasion, either as a function of exposure to persuasive arguments, as a function of social comparison information, or as a function of stereotyped and extreme ingroup opinion. These are only some of the possible explanations, and these are only one type of attitude change in groups. Nevertheless, they illustrate the utility of cognitive approaches to understanding some aspects of groups and the social context of information-based persuasion.

ATTITUDE CHANGE AND THE SELF

Cognitive theories related to attitudes have taken seriously another aspect of social context, namely, oneself. Originally, self-perception theory (D. J. Bem, 1972; see Chapter 2) posited that, when uncertain, people infer their attitudes from their own behavior. One result is that people may misrecall their own prior attitudes. After successful persuasion, people can conveniently perceive their attitudes as never having changed at all (D. J. Bem & McConnell, 1970). If a person's pre-persuasion attitudes are not salient, the person infers new attitudes from current behavior. Thus, there is a tendency to misrecall one's attitudes to bring them in line with one's behavior (cf. Fazio, Zanna, & Cooper, 1977; Wixon & Laird, 1976). One recent approach has posited a more specific role for perceptions of stability and change in one's attitudes.

Implicit Theories About Attitude Stability and Change

What were your attitudes toward religion five years ago? Fairly similar to the ones you have now? Most people assume their attitudes have been fairly stable, and in most instances they are right. However, perhaps you have undergone a conversion experience, in which case, you would answer that your attitudes toward religion have changed quite a lot. Often, we stay the same, but sometimes we change. Sometimes we perceive the stability, and sometimes not. Sometimes we perceive the change, and sometimes not.

One theory (M. Ross, 1989; M. Ross & Conway, 1986) argues that people's perceptions of stability and change depend on their implicit theories of when they do and do not change. The theory posits a two-step process, whereby people use their current attitudes as a starting point and then apply their theories to decide whether or not they would have been different in the past. Consistent with implicit theories of stability, people often do not perceive themselves to have changed, when indeed they have. Subtle forms of persuasion have this impact; people perceive their initial attitudes to be similar to their current (changed) attitudes, and they claim not to have changed (D. J. Bem & McConnell, 1970; Goethals & Reckman, 1973; M. Ross & Shulman, 1973). Even when changes spontaneously emerge over time or the course of a relationship, people do not perceive their attitudes to have changed (McFarland & Ross, 1987). Moreover, because people typically assume consistency, people base their recall of past behaviors on current attitudes. The implicit theory seems to run: (a) one behaves consistently with one's attitudes, and (b) one's attitudes are stable, therefore (c) one's current attitudes are a reliable guide to past behavior. Again, subtle persuasion can alter people's attitudes and then bias their recall of prior behavior to fit their current attitude (M. Ross et al., 1983; M. Ross, McFarland & Fletcher, 1981). When subjects do recall past behaviors just after a changed attitude, they become more committed to the new attitude (Lydon, Zanna, & Ross, 1988; M. Ross et al., 1983). Other things being equal, we expect ourselves to be stable and make inferences accordingly.

But other things are not always equal: people have conversions, join weight-loss programs, enter therapy, get divorced, move to new places, get promoted or fired, survive wars, get victimized, grow older, and so on. People expect some events to change them, so they have implicit theories about the events' propensity to change people. Have you ever heard anyone emerge from a significant amount of therapy and perceive no change whatsoever in his or her perceptions, understanding, or feelings? People in one study-skills program expected improvement, so they misperceived themselves as initially worse off than they had been, and they misrecalled their final grades as better than they were; both processes allowed them to see themselves as having improved, consistent with their theories (Conway & Ross, 1984). Such events are expected to promote change (and often do). Similarly, some attributes are expected to change (M. Ross, 1989). For example, attitudes toward social categories in general are expected to be stable across the life span, but attitudes toward one's own age group and its typical activities are expected to change with age (people do not expect attitudes toward skateboards to be stable across the life span).

Considerable evidence, thus, suggests that people's reconstruction of their own pasts are guided by implicit theories of stability and change. Although we have discussed the evidence primarily regarding perceptions of stability and change in attitudes, the theory also applies to people's construction of their own prior traits and feelings (M. Ross, 1989).

Conviction and Importance

Some attitudes centrally involve the self, for they are held with conviction. Such attitudes tend to be stable, and people know they are stable. Abelson (1988) has discussed the psychology of conviction as including, first, emotional commitment; attitudes that people hold with conviction are those about which they feel absolutely correct, cannot imagine ever changing their minds, are based on a moral sense of how things should be, and for which they would be willing to work. Second, conviction involves ego preoccupation, that is, often thinking about the issue, holding strong views, and being concerned. Third, conviction implicates cognitive elaboration, which means they have held their view for a while, see its connection to other issues, see its broad implications, know a lot about it, and find it easy to explain. For most individuals, there are only one or two such issues. But attitudes held with conviction are stable, and therefore, carry a centrality to the self, in several respects.

A related concept, attitude importance, illustrates several such respects. Attitude importance (or centrality) may be defined as a person's interest or concern about an attitude (Krosnick, 1988a). As such, it builds on work studying attitude involvement, but involvement of a different sort than the primarily outcome-relevant kind described earlier in this chapter. Attitude importance is most similar to what has been termed value-relevant involvement, which according to a meta-analytic research review, generally inhibits persuasion (B. T. Johnson & Eagly, 1989). Similarly, research on attitude importance argues that important attitudes are stable (Krosnick, 1989), accessible (Krosnick, 1989), and allow one to differentiate among relevant objects. For example, personally important policy attitudes (e.g., toward welfare, abortion, minorities, the USSR) are accessible when one evaluates political candidates, and one can discern differences among them on that issue, better than can someone for whom the attitude is not important. Consequently, important attitudes are better predictors of preferences among presidential candidates than are unimportant attitudes (Krosnick, 1988c). Other people also appreciate the impact of attitude importance. When someone says an issue is important, observers infer that the person holds extreme attitudes (Mackie & Gastardo-Conaco, 1988).

Important attitudes also show greater consistency with each other. Thus, if one holds two important attitudes, they are unlikely to contradict each other (Judd & Krosnick, 1982). Similarly, experts for whom relevant attitudes are likely to be important also show considerable consistency among their attitudes. People who know a lot about politics, report they are politically interested, or follow political news are especially consistent (for a review, see Judd & Krosnick, 1989).

Important attitudes apparently are stable, accessible, predictive of other choices, and well-connected to other attitudes. Such attitudes are central to people's values. It would seem difficult, therefore, to change attitudes that people hold to be important. One intriguing strategy does seem to change attitudes about which people are highly certain (and therefore probably the attitudes are important ones). A communicator offers statements that are even more extreme than people's own attitudes, and encourages people to endorse them. People who are certain recognize this apparent manipulation and will resist the attempt to make them more extreme. In reaction, they change their attitudes *away* from their own previous position. This technique is called a paradoxical strategy (Swann, Pelham, & Chidester, 1988), and it only works with people who are certain of their attitudes. Swann and his colleagues propose that attitudes about which one is certain are attitudes important to organizing one's experience and important to one's sense of self. Thus, people attempt to self-verify (see Chapter 6) and reject the overly extreme positions by backing away from them.

Return of the Functional Approaches

A third approach examines attitudes' relationship to self in a different way. At the beginning of this chapter, we discussed cognitive features of two consistency theories of attitudes, dissonance theory and balance theory. These traditional cognitive consistency theories have a motivational basis, in that inconsistency is assumed to be aversive, prompting people to resolve the inconsistency by various means, including attitude change. Subsequent theories of attitudes have tended to focus on their cognitive dynamics, as evident from an examination of theories emphasizing different types of attitude processing (heuristic vs. systematic, central vs. peripheral, automatic activation), attributional analyses, and persuasive arguments theories. In this section on attitude change and the self, we have so far seen recent approaches that begin more actively to take motivation into account; people's implicit theories of stability and change can have motivational underpinnings, and the approaches emphasizing conviction and importance certainly have motivational components.

Perhaps it is inevitable, then, that newer approaches are even more explicitly incorporating motivation. Recent theories of attitudes have harkened back to examine traditional theories of attitudes' motivational functions for the self (e.g., D. Katz, 1960; M. B. Smith, Bruner, & White, 1956), but with several new cognitive twists in both theory and method. The possible functions of an attitude have been divided a few ways. The simplest is to view attitudes as having knowledge functions and self functions (Greenwald, 1989; Pratkanis & Greenwald, 1989); the self functions can be broken down further into value-expressive and social-adjustive.[1]

The *knowledge function* of an attitude is fundamentally cognitive and adaptive. Attitudes help people to make sense of the world, to order and organize it. Moreover, attitudes can be instrumental and adaptive, helping people to avoid pain and receive rewards. Illustrations of recent approaches to the knowledge functions of attitudes include proposals that they act as heuristics (Pratkanis, 1988), defined in this case as simple evaluative strategies for problem solving. For example, attitudes help define attitude-consistent information as true; liked people are assumed to have good qualities and disliked people to have bad ones. Attitudes affect a range of knowledge-related problem-solving activities: interpretation and explanation, reasoning, responses to persuasion, judgment, perceived consensus, identification of facts and errors, and prediction (see Pratkanis, 1989, for a review).

Another recent illustration of the knowledge function of attitudes is the proposal that they serve schematic functions, in that they can shape attitude-relevant memory. They may have a bipolar structure, such that extreme material on either side is most easily judged and recalled (Judd

---

[1]Pratkanis and Greenwald identify a third function, social identification (adapting to a particular reference group or significant others), which we will not cover here. It is related to the social identity theory application to persuasion in groups, mentioned briefly in this chapter.

& Kulik, 1980). Or attitude schemas may have a unipolar structure, which contains well-elaborated supporting material but little or nothing on the opposing side (see Pratkanis & Greenwald, 1989, for a review).

The motivational aspect of the knowledge function has been examined in an impressive series of studies designed to heighten people's need for cognitive clarity and structure (Jamieson & Zanna, 1989). Recall from Chapter 5 that the need for structure (Kruglanski, 1990) induces people to prematurely cease information-seeking, which leads them to rely more heavily on their already-formed schemas and attitudes. People's need for structure can be enhanced by putting them under time pressure, by stress, or by increasing their arousal. Under these conditions, people form structurally simpler attitudes, and they rely more heavily on already-formed attitudes. Similar effects (simpler attitudes under pressure) can be observed in the real-world rhetoric of political leaders (Tetlock, 1985). The knowledge functions of attitudes, thus, relate to a variety of attitude operations.

Turning to one of the self functions of attitudes, their *value-expressive function* describes the importance to people of demonstrating and maintaining their long-term standards and orientations. This is similar to B. T. Johnson and Eagly's (1989) value-relevant involvement, which inhibits persuasion based on mere argument strength. It also is related to the work on attitude importance and conviction, just reviewed. People in general seem to be especially committed to attitudes that serve value-expressive functions, especially when they suffer or incur costs for holding those attitudes (Lydon & Zanna, 1990).

People differ in the value-expressive functions of their attitudes. For example, low self-monitors are people who rely heavily on their inner thoughts and feelings to guide their behavior (M. Snyder, 1974; see Chapter 12); consequently, their own attitudes are more important to them than, say, the norms of the situation or the attitudes of their friends. Such people would be expected to have a stronger motivation for value expression than other people (M. Snyder & DeBono, 1985). Indeed, low-self monitors are especially likely to appeal selectively to their long-term values in order to justify their attitudes (Kristiansen & Zanna, 1988). Low self-monitors rely more heavily on appeals to important values (DeBono, 1987). Similarly, low self-monitors are particularly attentive to expert sources, for they presumably provide reliable, value-relevant information (DeBono & Harnish, 1988).

People in general can have conflicting values about an attitude object, and this potentially causes problems for using an attitude to express their values. For example, black Americans, as targets of white Americans' attitudes, elicit core values related to humanitarian and egalitarian values, on the one hand, and to Protestant work-ethic values, on the other hand (I. Katz & Hass, 1988; I. Katz, Wackenhut, & Hass, 1986). Depending on which is primed, white racial attitudes are correspondingly more positive or negative (see Dovidio & Gaertner, 1986, for related ideas).

For people in general, attitudes are likely to be more cognitively complex when they relate to core conflicting values (Tetlock, 1986). That is, assuming value expression is important, people work especially hard to reconcile important value conflicts, creating trade-offs that result in greater attitudinal and ideological complexity. For certain ideological positions that entail (at least superficially) core conflicting values, such as liberalism, this attempt to reconcile conflicting values may result in more complex reasoning styles (Tetlock, 1984, 1986), which are not merely a function of rhetorical style (Tetlock, Hannum, & Micheletti, 1984; but see Sidanius, 1988). Upward shifts in complexity on both sides have generally preceded major American-Soviet agreements, while downward shifts have preceded major military-political interventions (Tetlock, 1988). Value expression, thus, can have global effects.

Attitudes also serve important *social-adjustive functions* for the self. That is, sometimes attitudes signal interpersonal priorities, sensitivity to others, and getting along with people in general. This function is similar to B. T. Johnson and Eagly's (1989) impression-relevant involvement, which tends to inhibit persuasion based on argument strength, presumably because that is not the most important determinant of social-adjustive attitudes. Social-adjustive attitudes are most prominent for people with a high need for affiliation, sensitivity to approval, and well-developed awareness of their self-presentation to others (Herek, 1986). For example, homophobic or egalitarian attitudes toward homosexuals can either promote acceptance by one's immediate peer group (social-adjustive functions) or demonstrate one's core moral stands (value-expressive functions). Here again, we find self-monitoring differences, in that high self-monitors, being more attuned to interpersonal settings, are more likely to have socially adjustive attitudes. High self-monitors more carefully process the message of an interpersonally attractive source (DeBono & Harnish, 1988), attend more to the images projected by consumer products (Snyder & DeBono, 1985; DeBono & Snyder, 1989), and rely more heavily on consensus information (DeBono, 1987; see Snyder & DeBono, 1987, 1989, for reviews).

The central empirical issue for functional theories has always been to identify a priori the functions served by particular attitudes for particular individuals. One approach, as we have seen, is to examine individual differences (i.e., self-monitoring) in the types of attitudes individuals are likely to hold. Another intriguing approach posits that certain attitude objects are intrinsically likely to elicit attitudes serving different functions (Shavitt, 1989). That is, the social-adjustive function of high-status clothing is more readily apparent than is the social-adjustive function of one's air conditioner. Recent research supports the predominant functions of some objects, while others appear to elicit mixed functions, brought out by different circumstances. Moreover, people show some cross-domain consistency in the functions of their attitudes, values, and even possessions (Abelson & Prentice, 1989; Prentice, 1987). The bottom line is that certain individuals, in concert with certain attitudes and certain situations, can be predicted on the basis of these interactions to hold attitudes for different functional reasons (Snyder & DeBono, 1989).

SUMMARY

An attitude is a hypothetical mediating variable assumed to intervene between stimulus and response. Attitudes involve at least an evaluation of the attitude object, and many definitions also include cognitions and behavioral tendencies. Social cognition's contribution to the field began with a meta-theoretical approach valuing a fine-grained analysis of the cognitive processes involved in attitude formation and change; it has also borrowed specific theories and methods from social cognition research. One early theory in particular foreshadowed information-processing approaches: McGuire's multistep chain of persuasion included various cognitive processes necessary for successful attitude change and enactment.

Two traditional cognitive consistency theories have profited from newer social cognition insights. Dissonance theorists' long-standing interest in selective perception to support one's attitudes has been examined in terms of selective exposure (seeking attitude-consistent information), selective attention (heeding attitude-consistent information), and selective interpretation (perceiving ambiguous information to be attitude-consistent). While evidence for selective exposure is controversial, evidence for selective attention and interpretation supports the basic premises of dissonance theory. In addition, dissonance theory has been concerned with selective learning and retention of attitude-relevant information. Incidental learning of attitude-consistent information demonstrates selectivity, but intentional learning and high degrees of motivation eliminate selectivity. People with high self-esteem, an internal locus of control, or a tendency to repress unpleasant experiences all show greater selectivity effects, consistent with dissonance theory.

Another consistency approach, balance theory, also posits that people selectively recall information, in this case information about the attitudes of self and others. People can most readily remember that friends agree (and perhaps that enemies disagree). A balanced triad of two friends who feel the same way about particular attitude objects creates a compact cognitive unit that is easier to imagine, comprehend, and remember. An unbalanced triad is more difficult and seems to be stored in separate pieces. Attitudes in general serve to organize memory for relevant information, to the extent that people may have difficulty remembering the evidence on which their attitudes were based.

More recent attitude theories have drawn heavily on social cognition theories and methods. Some new theories examine different types of attitude processing; some types are relatively thoughtful and analytic whereas others are relatively rapid and automatic. The heuristic-systematic model posits that attitudes are often changed by cognitive shortcuts or heuristics, in the form of simple persuasion rules that circumvent the need actually to process message content. Attitudes can also be changed by more systematic processing of the message arguments. Considerable research supports these ideas.

The elaboration likelihood model also proposes that attitudes can be changed by two routes, but the more automatic peripheral route includes a variety of superficial strategies, all of which share the feature of ignoring message quality. In contrast, the central route to persuasion, typical of more motivated recipients, involves thorough consideration of the merits of the arguments given. In response to message arguments, people are posited to engage in more or less cognitive elaboration, that is, idiosyncratic responses pro or con. These, as measured by cognitive response analysis, predict attitude change via the central route. Traditional variables, such as characteristics of the communicator (credibility, expertise, and attractiveness), the message (its quality, repetition, difficulty, and length), and the audience (its outcome involvement, need for cognition, and uncertainty orientation) all contribute to the degree and direction of cognitive elaboration, as well as resulting attitude change. Although open to some alternative perspectives, this approach has yielded quantities of data illuminating old problems with new sophistication.

The attitude-accessibility approach concentrates on the automatic activation of attitudes, based on the mere encounter with the attitude object. Attitudes are more easily activated when they have been recently or frequently activated in the past or when one has just reviewed attitude-relevant behavior. Low self-monitors, who are oriented to their attitudes, also seem to have more accessible attitudes. Easily activated attitudes more dramatically influence judgments about attitude-relevant information, resist contradiction, endure longer, and affect behavior more directly. The process seems to be relatively automatic, although there is some question about whether the most relevant construct is attitude accessibility. Nevertheless, some attitudes can be elicited immediately upon perception of the pertinent attitude object.

Some other social cognition approaches have emphasized the social context of persuasion. For example, attributional analyses of why the communicator is delivering a particular message influence persuasion. If a communicator delivers a message because of the audience or other situational factors, then it is suspect. Similarly, if a communicator is dispositionally biased in terms of knowledge or reporting motives, then the message is perceived as untrustworthy. Another social contextual approach examines attitude change in groups as a function of persuasive arguments raised by various group members or as a function of social comparison information.

A series of approaches integrates cognitive sophistication with the importance of the self and its motives. Implicit theories about stability and change encourage people to perceive or misperceive stability and change in their own attitudes and other dispositions. People do not typically expect their attitudes to change, so they misperceive stability, even when their attitudes have been altered by subtle means. Moreover, people misrecall their prior behavior to fit their current attitudes, again in line with the general belief that attitudes are stable and behavior accordingly follows. When people's theories suggest change, however, they also (mis)perceive change: following a conversion, a self-help program, therapy, and the like.

Conviction involves several components related to the importance of one's attitudes: emotional commitment, ego preoccupation, and cognitive elaboration. A related term for conviction is value-relevant involvement. Attitudes held with conviction are few (for most people) and resist change. Such important attitudes are stable, accessible, differentiate among attitude objects, and are consistent with other attitudes. They may be open to change only by paradoxical techniques.

Functional approaches also involve the self and its motives: attitudes serve a knowledge function, as they provide heuristics for rapid responses and schemas for organizing knowledge. As people's need for structure increases, they are more likely to rely on their ready-made attitudes or on simple attitudes quickly constructed. Attitudes can also serve a self function of value expression, allowing people to demonstrate their prized standards and orientations. The attitudes of low self-monitors are especially likely to serve value-expressive functions. When people hold core conflicting values, their relevant attitudes become more complex with the necessity of integrating them. Finally, attitudes can also serve social-adjustive self functions. They help people to fit in with other people and to demonstrate interpersonal attunement. High self-monitors, who are oriented to the social environment, are more likely to hold social-adjustive attitudes. Apart from individual differences, some attitude objects may typically elicit attitudes with particular types of functions.

The various cognitive approaches to attitudes—those elaborating traditional theories and those positing altogether new processes, those emphasizing more thoughtful or more automatic processes, those focusing almost entirely on cognition or more actively including motivation—have various implications for the relationship between cognition and behavior, as the next chapter indicates.

12

Behavior and Cognition

---------- ❖ ----------

Self-Regulation Revisited ✦ *When Are Cognitions and Behavior Related?* ✦ *How Is Behavior Related to Cognition?* ✦ *Using Behavior to Test Hypotheses About Others*

Social cognition research has sometimes been accused of leaving the person lost in thought, like Tolman's rat, with complex representations about social reality that do not necessarily correspond to behavior. But most research in social cognition assumes that cognitions develop at least in part so that people will know how to behave. For example, if a supervisor is rude to a co-worker, one tries to infer if the supervisor is a disagreeable person, if it has been a bad day, or if the co-worker has done something to deserve the treatment. Through this kind of analysis, one infers whether or not to stay out of the way of the supervisor. In this sense, cognitions give rise to behavior. Daily behaviors and interactions with others also provide a constant source of information, some redundant and much new, that must be incorporated into cognitive representations. Hence, behavior also gives rise to cognitions. In this chapter, we explore the relationships between cognitions and behavior.

SELF-REGULATION REVISITED

In Chapter 6 on the self, we introduced the concept of self-regulation, the ways in which people control and direct their behavior. Cognitions are clearly central to this process. How a person behaves in a situation depends upon how he or she defines it. For example, two people can attend a cocktail party with different goals in mind (Gorta, 1985). While one individual may have the goal of impressing his boss, another may regard the same occasion as an opportunity to grab a couple of quick drinks with friends before going home. The behavior of these individuals will be substantially shaped by these personal goals.

The first individual will no doubt scan the room quickly to see if his boss has arrived and, upon seeing him, gravitate to that part of the room. As he laughs at his boss's jokes and attempts to find opportunities in the conversation to apprise his boss of his achievements, he may well ignore other people in the room, he may be inattentive to the fact that his glass is empty, and he may lose track of time, as he pursues his goal. The other individual, in contrast, may scan the room for friendly faces, join one group for a brief conversation, drift to another, replenish his drink when it is down, and leave for home when the second drink is finished. The different behaviors of these two individuals depend on the goals they have constructed and the strategies and plans devised for meeting those goals.

Despite the close relationship between personal goals and behavior in a given social setting, people show remarkable flexibility in the ability to adjust their perceptions of a situation in response to factors that come up. They can take active control of their thoughts and their plans, especially in response to change; they can review several alternatives for interpreting the same event; and they change their knowledge through the feedback acquired by new experiences, reworking existing beliefs, values, and goals (Showers & Cantor, 1985). For example, the man intent on impressing his boss may shift his goal to impressing his co-workers if he learns that his boss has been called away from the cocktail party for a meeting. Similarly, the man planning to have a couple drinks with friends may leave the party early if he learns that none of his friends have attended. This attribute of behavioral flexibility is important and provides an antidote to some of the schema research, which implicitly suggests that behavior is automatically enacted in response to preexisting conceptions.

As we saw in Chapter 10 on affect, affective states and emotional responses to situations also strongly influence behavior. People in a good mood behave in ways that further that mood, whereas those in a bad mood will often make efforts to improve their mood, as by enjoying the companionship of others. More generally, people in a positive mood appear to have more flexibility and awareness of multiple ways of dealing with situations, whereas poor mood appears to be associated with more rigid strategies of social interaction (see Showers & Cantor, 1985). In these ways, then, cognitions and affect can have powerful joint regulatory effects on behavior (Ickes et al., 1986; Norem & Cantor, 1990; Showers & Cantor, 1985). Cognitive and affective influences on behavior are often functionally inseparable and difficult to distinguish, reciprocally influencing each other, and changing in response to behavioral feedback (Norem & Cantor, 1990).

Cantor and Kihlstrom (1985) argue that, in social situations, people implicitly ask such questions as, "What is going on here? Who are these people? What are they doing and what do they want of me? What are my own goals? Do they conflict with theirs, and if so, how do I make a choice between them? How can I achieve the goals that I select and how do I make a choice among the available strategies? What are the consequences for being wrong, and how can I recover from my mistakes? What consequences will my choices have on others and what can I do about their reactions?" The wealth of knowledge, plans, and strategies that people bring to answering these questions in social interactions is referred to as *social intelligence*. According to Cantor and Kihlstrom, it consists of concept knowledge, such as the facts one has at hand about situations and people, and rule knowledge, which includes the ways in which we categorize people, make judgments and inferences, solve problems, and perform various actions (cf. S. J. Read & Miller, 1989).[1]

The specific cognitions by which people self-regulate are, in a large part, idiosyncratic, in that individual differences in the memories that people have for themselves and for social situations and people, the concepts they hold about social situations and people, and the rules that regulate behavior in social settings, are likely to differ substantially based on past experience (Cantor & Kihlstrom, 1985). Cross-cutting these distinctions are ways of thinking about situations, including hierarchical ones (concerned with dominance and submission), territoriality (concerned with control, competence, and achievement), and identity (concerned with self-conceptions and interpersonal affiliations). Thus, for example, the first individual at the cocktail party may be using his concepts of hierarchy in relating to his boss and thinking in terms of the dominance/submission role requirements that govern how an individual relates to his boss. A secondary issue may be territoriality, in that the employee desirous of making a positive impression may also find it necessary to shove equally ambitious co-workers aside so he may achieve his goals. The second individual at the cocktail party, in contrast, may be more concerned with cementing friendships with others through a positive social occasion and finding opportunities to express his identity in ways that are consistent with his self-conceptions.

To this point, the discussion has implied that people self-regulate by defining the situations in which they find themselves and by developing appropriate plans and strategies for realizing whatever goals might be achieved within these situations. But it is important to remember that people actively choose and construct situations as well. Thus, for example, the employee who wishes to impress his boss need not wait around for a cocktail party as an opportunity to do so. He may

---

[1]Note that Cantor and Kihlstrom's use of the term "social intelligence" includes the various knowledge, talents, plans, and strategies, as well as interpersonal skills, that people bring to social situations. Others (e.g., Allport, 1935; S. J. Read & Miller, 1989) reserve the same term only for social, expressive, and communicative skills, a more restricted use of the term.

plan a dinner party to which his boss is invited, ask the boss out for lunch, hang around in the men's room waiting for him to show up, or engage in other actions that enable him to actively create and structure the situation in service of his goals (Showers & Cantor, 1985; M. Snyder, 1982).

In choosing and constructing situations that may meet personal goals, it is useful to divide the process into at least two stages, a motivational process and a volitional process (Gollwitzer, 1990; Heckhausen & Gollwitzer, 1987). The initial phase of motivation involves *deliberation* on incentives and expectations, so that people can choose between alternative goals and their implied courses of action. An employee at an office cocktail party may, for example, regard the party as an opportunity to impress her boss, to make an advance on a co-worker, or to coordinate problem-solving efforts with a member of her office team. Each of these goals would provide different incentives and imply very different courses of action during the party.

The motivational state of mind ends when a decision is made, a more or less conscious choice that then leads the person into a volitional state of mind. Volition involves the consideration of when and how to act so as to implement the intended course of action. Recognizing that the boss is already launched in conversation and that the attractive co-worker keeps looking at his watch as if he is getting ready to leave, the employee may decide to use the party as a opportunity to brainstorm with the fellow team member. After making this decision, she may be oblivious to any further actions of her boss or the attractive co-worker, instead deploying her efforts to the goal she has chosen to pursue. At this point, *planning* and *action* become important. Selection among alternative goals depends upon volitional strength, including how feasible, desirable, and urgent a particular goal is, and on how favorable the situation is for the realization of a goal.

Following the pursuit of a goal, the individual may *evaluate* whether the efforts to achieve the goal succeeded and whether the goal outcomes match the expected value of the outcomes. Such post-actional evaluation contributes to future goal setting and planning. In this analysis, then, goals are related to behavior across time, with different cognitive activities predominating and directing action at different temporal points in the motivation-action-evaluation sequence.

Although this analysis implies that self-regulation involves conscious choices and decisions, in fact, much self-regulatory activity proceeds mindlessly without awareness. That is, most of us have had so many experiences in social occasions that we are able to regulate our behavior with respect to our goals quite unconsciously, and it may take a flaw in the plan (another employee has already drawn the boss off into a private conversation) to make salient and conscious both one's personal goals for a situation and the strategies designed to achieve them. Familiar situations tend to inspire mindless behavior, whereas unfamiliar situations are more likely to evoke conscious self-regulatory efforts (Cantor & Kihlstrom, 1985; E. J. Langer, 1975). For example, the process of meeting new acquaintances in Japan may prompt a person to become intensely aware of the dynamics of social situations, inasmuch as most Westerners do not have well-developed knowledge of the norms and appropriate behaviors for many Japanese social settings.

Expertise also determines how self-consciously and how success-fully people self-regulate in social situations. People who feel uncertain or confused in social settings are more likely to try to identify the prototypic actions that are successful in social situations than people who are more aware of the competencies required in any given setting (Cantor, Mackie, & Lord, 1983–84; Wicklund & Braun, 1987; see also Showers & Cantor, 1985, for a discussion of expertise). Uncertain, con-fused people are also more likely to characterize others through the as-cription of dispositional attributions, typing them as particular sorts of people. This rigidity in perceptions may give their own behavior a cer-tain flat, unresponsive quality, compared to those who are able to main-tain a more flexible or better fit between their cognitive and behavioral repertoire and the environment (Wicklund, 1986).

Cantor and Kihlstrom (1985) argue that social intelligence regulates not only behavior in relatively mundane situations such as the cocktail party described above, but also across time and in a variety of settings, as the complexity and generality of the goal increases. People select life tasks for themselves, such as the desire to become a famous psycholo-gist or a good mother, and these conceptions, though held at a general level, may guide the choice of social situations, the selection of interac-tion patterns, and behavior in specific social settings over their lifetime.

The preceding discussion implies a degree of consistency between cognitions and behavior, assuming that the often implicit cognitions that guide behavior can be identified and made explicit. Yet, one of the most striking aspects of behavior is that under many circumstances, it does not correspond to what one would expect on the basis of appar-ently predominant cognitions. For example, most people are horrified by the prospect of a nuclear war, and yet very few people take any ac-tion to attempt to reduce its likelihood (S. T. Fiske, 1987b). We next ad-dress this issue.

WHEN ARE COGNITIONS AND BEHAVIOR RELATED?

The question, "How direct is the relationship between cognitions and behavior?" is not an easy one to answer, at least not simply. First, in the social cognition arena, there has not been a lot of research that includes behavioral dependent measures, and so opportunities to examine the relationship have been limited. When the cognition-behavior relationship is examined, sometimes the two parallel each other (e.g., Yarkin, Harvey, & Bloxom, 1981), and sometimes not (see, for example, Nisbett & Valins, 1972; Nisbett & Wilson, 1977a).

To address the cognition-behavior relationship generally, it is necessary to turn first to related literatures where similar problems exist. For example, those with an awareness of social psychological history should find the cognition-behavior problem all too familiar. Attitude change research of the 1950s and 1960s produced a similar situation: researchers initially failed to examine the attitude-behavior relationship, and when it was examined, the evidence was highly inconsistent. Some reported relatively low relationships between cognitions and behavior (e.g., Nisbett & Wilson, 1977b; Wicker, 1969), whereas others maintained that the consistency is often quite high when moderating factors are taken into account (Quattrone, 1985; Schuman & Johnson, 1976). The literature on the correspondence between personality traits and behavior, though not cognitive in its origins, is also a useful source of hypotheses: the relationship between personality traits (which have important cognitive components) and behaviors that would theoretically be expected to follow from them sometimes proves to be weak and unreliable (Mischel, 1968).

Drawing on these literatures, the attempt to clarify when cognitions and behavior go together can take several routes: specifying which behaviors are most likely to be related to particular cognitions; improving measurement procedures so that cognitions and behaviors are more comparable; determining what features of cognitions are most likely to lead to behavioral consequences; understanding the various ways people have of conceptualizing behavior; identifying situational factors that might moderate the cognition-behavior relationship; and looking for individual differences in cognition-behavior consistency.

Which Behaviors Are Related to Cognition?

One problem that arises in examining the cognition-behavior relationship is that we may expect too many and too varied behaviors to be related to any given cognition. Consider self-perceptions of friendliness as an example. Some people think of themselves as friendly, others do not. Considering only the people who consider themselves friendly, should we expect them to be friendly in *all* situations? Certainly, we would expect them to be more friendly than people who consider themselves unfriendly, but there is no reason to expect that they will be friendly every minute of the day. After all, people have to work, sleep, eat, and do many other nonsocial tasks. What, then, makes a friendly person friendly? It may well be that some people are considered friendly not because they are friendly a lot, but because they are friendly in those critical situations most relevant to friendliness. In other words, they show consistent friendliness for situations that are prototypic for friendliness.

Recall from the discussion of schemas (Chapters 4 and 5) that prototypic persons or activities are those that are most representative of their particular category. Thus, for example, prototypic activities for friendliness might be saying hello to people on campus or welcoming new people enthusiastically. To consider oneself a friendly person then, perhaps one need only show a high degree of consistency in these prototypic behaviors, and not on behaviors less centrally related to friendliness.

In fact, research supports this contention (Mischel, 1984; Mischel & Peake, 1982). In an examination of self-rated conscientiousness, undergraduates who considered themselves conscientious (or not) were studied in a wide variety of situations that might assess conscientiousness. An independent group of raters judged each of the situations for how central or prototypic it was for conscientiousness. The investigators then calculated cross-situational consistency. Individuals who rated themselves high and low in conscientiousness did not behave differently in situations that were low in prototypicality for conscientiousness. However, when prototypic conscientiousness situations were examined, the highly conscientious individuals showed significantly greater consistency in their behavior as compared with the individuals who were low in conscientiousness (Mischel & Peake, 1982).

More generally, Schutte, Kenrick, and Sadalla (1985) found that agreement among people as to which behavior a person would perform increased, the more prototypical the situation was for the behavior and the more constraints on behavior that existed in the situation. Thus, for example, ratings of probable behavior would be very consistent for a prototypic event for sadness, such as a funeral, in which behavior is also fairly constrained by social convention (e.g., quiet, tearful consolation). But following a merciful death after a long and painful illness, ratings of likely behaviors emitted by the family in the privacy of their home might be more variable, inasmuch as the situation is neither prototypic for sadness nor are there clear situational constraints.

A similar argument has been made in the context of attitudes. Attitudes are often very general representations of beliefs about particular categories of people, things, or events. Whether or not an attitude predicts behavior toward any particular member of a category is influenced by the match of that instance or member to the prototype of the category. Lord, Lepper, and Mackie (1984) argue that when people hold stereotypes about particular groups, they will manifest that attitude in specific interactions with a particular group member only if that group member meets their abstracted prototype of the group. Two experiments supported the hypothesis. When the individual was prototypically related to the group, general attitudes toward the group predicted behavior toward the individual, but the unprototypical group member was dismissed as atypical, and behavior did not match the attitude toward the group. Moreover, dismissing the unprototypical group member as atypical left the prototype intact as a source of information to guide future behavior.

What are the implications of these points for the cognition-behavior relationship generally? They suggest that consistency will be highest when one examines behaviors that are prototypically related to particular cognitions, but that cognition-behavior consistency will be lower when one examines behaviors that are less centrally related to the cognitions in question.

Measuring Cognitions and Behaviors

Another problem with studying the cognition-behavior relationship concerns how cognitions and behaviors are measured and whether or not they are measured at the same level of specificity. As this issue has been addressed substantially in the attitude-behavior literature, we will examine it in that context.

If you are asked whether you feel needy people should be helped through charity, you may well answer, "yes." If you are then accosted by a persistent beggar asking for a dollar, you may well decline. Although your attitudes and behavior would appear to be inconsistent, should one consider you to have violated your attitudes? Not necessarily. You may, for example, feel that charity should be managed by institutions, not individuals, or that begging should be discouraged. The apparent inconsistency of your attitude and behavior is caused by the fact that your attitude was assessed very generally, but your behavior was measured in a very specific situation. When attitudes and behaviors are assessed at different levels of specificity, low correspondence may be found. How, then, can attitude and behavior assessment be made more comparable?

One solution is to measure behavior through general behavioral tendencies, employing a multiple-act criterion (e.g., Epstein, 1979; Fishbein & Ajzen, 1974). That is, instead of examining the relationship between a general attitude (i.e., toward charity in the abstract) and a single act (i.e., giving money to a specific beggar), one would measure a number of specific acts to get a general behavioral measure. For example, one might measure money given to various causes, time volunteered to help the needy, and so on. Thus, although your general belief about charity may not predict your specific response to a particular panhandler, it should predict your charitable behavior more generally, if we examine how much money, time, or effort you volunteer to each of several causes.

It is unclear why the multiple-act criterion succeeds in demonstrating attitude-behavior consistency. It may succeed because (1) multiple actions provide a better estimate of the individual's typical behavior, (2) employing multiple actions succeeds in including at least one situation that can be highly predicted by attitudes (cf. Monson, Hesley, & Chernick, 1982), or (3) multiple actions include at least two situations which the individual sees as similar to each other and relevant to the attitude, thus warranting similar behavior (cf. Lord, 1982). For whichever reason, correspondence is higher when multiple-act measures of behavior are compared against global attitudes.

A debate similar to the multiple-act criterion in attitude-behavior research has emerged in the personality literature. Buss and Craik (1980, 1981) have suggested that, to aid in the assessment of personality traits, the frequency of behaviors reflecting an underlying disposition should be assessed. According to their position, specific behaviors should also be identified in terms of their centrality or not to the disposition under consideration. The framework predicts that single acts on the average correlate less well than would many acts with personality measures of the disposition in question. Moreover, responses to acts central to the disposition should correlate more highly with measures of dispositions than would responses to acts that are relatively less central to the disposition, a point consistent with the work on prototypicality just described. Although considerable attention has been given this criterion, the approach is not without critics (Block, 1989). Among these criticisms include the fact that there is little consensual agreement on what constitutes an act; many acts relevant to dispositional qualities are internal and unobservable; and by summing acts over time, one ignores the distribution of acts over time, and thereby may be tapping a temporary set of circumstances rather than an actual disposition. Finally, the analysis is largely descriptive. Consequently, it does not provide an explanation for why a person tends to exhibit multiple acts consistent with a disposition. Thus, the method may establish a criterion without necessarily enlightening the nature of dispositions.

A second solution is to measure dispositions more specifically. For example, if you had been asked about how you feel about giving money to beggars, instead of how you feel about charity generally, high correspondence between your attitude and behavior might well have been found. Many efforts to examine the attitude-behavior relationship have adopted this approach by assessing attitudes as intentions to behave in specific ways (Ajzen & Fishbein, 1977; Fishbein & Ajzen, 1974, 1975). In Chapter 11 on attitudes, we considered Fishbein and Ajzen's theory of reasoned action. To review, that theory predicts that a person's behavior can be predicted directly from his or her intention, which is, in turn, a function of attitudes toward the behavior, subjective norms about what the person thinks others think he or she should do, and the relative importance of the attitudinal and normative considerations. Specific behavioral intentions predict specific behaviors very well (see Bagozzi, 1981; Hessing, Elffers, & Weigel, 1988; Saltzer, 1981, for qualifications to this finding).

Components of Fishbein and Ajzen's model have been criticized. For example, Warshaw and Davis (1985) suggest that knowing a behavioral intention (e.g., I intend to have three cups of coffee today) may be less valuable than knowing a person's behavioral expectation (e.g., I'll probably have about three cups of coffee today, since I usually do). This distinction is important because when people commit actions mindlessly, they may have a behavioral expectation without any conscious intention. Warshaw and Davis suggest that, as a result, behavioral expectation is a better predictor of self-reported performance. Another point of debate concerned whether an attitude in the Fishbein and Ajzen model is a multidimensional or unidimensional construct (Bagozzi & Burnkrant, 1979; Burnkrant & Page, 1988; Dillon & Kumar, 1985). Burnkrant and Page (1988) have suggested that both the belief motivation to comply and the expectancy value attitude exist as multidimensional rather than unidimensional representations. The methodological details surrounding this debate go beyond the purpose of the present coverage.

Recently, Ajzen and his associates (Ajzen, 1988; Ajzen & Madden, 1986) have undertaken a revision of Fishbein and Ajzen's approach to the attitude-behavior relationship, arguing that in addition to knowing a person's attitudes, subjective norms, and behavioral intentions with respect to a given behavior, one needs to know his or her perceived behavioral control over that action. (This work ties in with Bandura's [1986] self-efficacy framework discussed in Chapter 6.) In a test of the model, they found that subjects needed not only to hold a behavioral intention toward a particular attitude object, but also needed to feel that they were capable of performing the action contemplated. Thus, feelings of perceived control or self-efficacy appear to be important in demonstrating attitude-behavior consistency, even when there is a clear behavioral intention to act upon an attitude.

To summarize, the relationship between attitudes and behavior is strongest when both are assessed at the same level of generality. General attitudes predict general behavioral intentions fairly well, and specific attitudes predict specific behaviors. Addressing similar issues in the personality literature, Kenrick and Funder (1988) conclude that traits will be most closely related to behavior when the following conditions are met: "(a) raters who are thoroughly familiar with the person being rated; (b) multiple behavioral observations; (c) multiple observers; (d) dimensions that are publicly observable; and (e) behaviors that are relevant to the dimension in question" (p. 31). Similarly, poor trait-behavior relationships will be found when "predicting (a) behavior in 'powerful' and clearly normative scripted situations from trait ratings, and (b) a single behavioral instance from another single behavioral instance" (p. 31).

Which Cognitions Predict Behavior?

One of the most frustrating aspects of the attitude-behavior relationship is that one can change attitudes that would seem to be highly related to behavior without necessarily changing those corresponding behaviors. For example, attitudes toward women in the workplace suggest that, increasingly, both men and women are more egalitarian concerning women and employment. However, as yet, most indicators of discrimination and harrassment suggest that women still experience far more of these adverse effects than men (Kahn & Crosby, 1987). There are many reasons why behavior might not match attitudes. In the example above, Kahn and Crosby suggest that attitudes may reflect ideal or socially desirable ways of responding to a group, but behavior may be influenced by other factors, such as other attitudes (i.e., seniority should determine pay), situational factors (i.e., the characteristics of a particular woman under consideration for a particular position), individual differences in the propensity to use attitudes as guides for behavior, and the possibility of getting away with harassment and discrimination (cf. Crosby, Bromley, & Saxe, 1980). In this section, we will consider the various factors that determine when attitudes are most likely to predict behavior.

Ask a person what his or her attitude on a certain topic is, and the person will likely have one (see Budd, 1987; Converse, 1964, 1970). It may be an issue the person has never thought about before and will never think about again, but for that brief moment, he or she may well have an attitude, even an apparently strong one. Clearly, if the attitude is a temporary whim, it will not predict behavior very reliably. This problem—the ubiquity of attitudes—has plagued research on attitude-behavior consistency. Attitudes seem to be everywhere, but several factors influence which attitudes matter to a person, and consequently, which predict behavior. Which attitudes are really there and which are not?

One factor that determines whether or not attitudes will predict behavior is the way they are formed. Attitudes formed from *direct experience* predict behavior better than do attitudes based on indirect experience (Fazio & Zanna, 1981). In one study, for example, college students were asked about their attitudes regarding their university's housing shortage. Only those subjects whose attitudes had been formed through direct experience (i.e., sleeping on cots in dorm lounges for several weeks because there were no rooms) showed strong attitude-behavior relationships. Overall, attitudes that are formed through direct experience are more specific; they are held more confidently; they are more stable; and they resist counterargument better than do attitudes not based on direct experience (Fazio & Zanna, 1978; Zanna & Fazio, 1982).

Why are attitudes formed through direct experience more predictive of behavior? There are several possible reasons. First, direct experiences provide a great deal of information, so the attitudes that develop as a consequence may be better informed and more robust. Second, because behavior provided an initial basis for forming the attitude, the behavioral implications of the attitude may be more clear. Third, the links between the attitude and actual experience may make the attitude more accessible in memory, and thus, it may be more likely to come to mind when one must act (Fazio & Zanna, 1981). Finally, the fact that attitudes formed through direct experience are often very specific may make specific behavioral implications clear, which may not be true for more vague general attitudes (Borgida, Swann, & Campbell, 1977).

A second feature of an attitude that influences attitude-behavior consistency is *vested interest*. To the extent that a person's attitude involves self-interest, the person is more likely to act on it. Thus, for example, 18-year-olds against it are more likely to canvass against a referendum that would raise the drinking age to 21 than are 22-year-olds also against it (Sivacek & Crano, 1982). Similarly, people who believed that the 1974 energy crisis had a strong impact on their lives were more likely to comply with governmental regulations to control energy than were those who estimated the crisis had little personal impact (Sears et al., 1978). Vested interest is more likely to predict behavior for attitudes that are personally important to an individual than for attitudes that are low in personal importance (Young et al., 1987).

Being induced to *think about the reasons* underlying one's attitudes reduces attitude-behavior consistency (T. D. Wilson, Dunn et al., 1989). When trying to come up with reasons for their attitudes, people often bring to mind thoughts that are available in memory but which may not be representative of their attitude. The reasons they come up with may come from salient situational factors or recent experiences and may imply a new attitude, leading at least temporarily to attitude change (e.g., T. D. Wilson & Dunn, 1986; T. D. Wilson et al., 1984). What is the impact of assessing the reasons for one's attitudes on one's behavior? If behavior is measured shortly after people have expressed new attitudes, then the behavior is consistent with those new attitudes. If behavior is measured some time after attitudes are analyzed for their reasons, the behavior seems to "snap back" to the original attitude, and thus, is inconsistent with the attitude reported after the reasons analysis (T. D. Wilson, Kraft, & Dunn, 1989).

It may also be that behavior is more under the control of affective aspects of an attitude than cognitive aspects. Because self-reports of attitudes are cognitively driven and behavior may be more affectively driven, then, under conditions when one has focused on the reasons underlying one's attitudes, self-reports of attitudes and behaviors may be discrepant.

Some attitudes are more vulnerable than others to the disruption produced by focusing on reasons. Attitudes that are difficult to access, weakly held, based on very little knowledge, or affectively based are more vulnerable to reasons-analysis disruption than are attitudes that are easily accessed, strongly held, based on lots of knowledge, and cognitively based (T. D. Wilson, Kraft, & Dunn, 1989; see T. D. Wilson, Dunn et al., 1989, for a review).

What are the conditions that induce people spontaneously to come up with reasons for their attitudes? This is an important question, because otherwise the effects may be experimental ones with rare analogues in the real world. T. D. Wilson and his colleagues predicted and found evidence that when people encounter unexpected reactions from others or have unexpected feelings about their attitude objects, they are motivated to engage in a reasons analysis (T. D. Wilson, Dunn et al., 1989).

In a related formulation, Tesser and his colleagues argue that the *type of behavior* in which a person is engaged also influences how focusing on affect or cognition will influence the attitude-behavior relationship (M. G. Millar & Tesser, 1986a). In its simplest form, they argue that behavior engaged in for its own sake (consummatory behavior) is driven by affect, but that behavior in service of goals (instrumental behavior) is driven by cognition. Thus, they hypothesize that if one focuses on the cognitive component of an attitude, attitude-behavior congruence should increase if the behavior is instrumental. However, focusing on the emotions or affect associated with the attitude would not increase the congruence between attitude and instrumental behavior. On the other hand, focusing on the emotional component of an attitude would increase the attitude-behavior relationship if the behavior is engaged in for its own sake (consummatory), whereas focusing on the cognitive component would have no effect on the attitude-behavior relationship if the behavior is consummatory.

To test this hypothesis, Millar and Tesser (1986b) had subjects solve difficult puzzles and led them to focus either on the cognitive component of the attitude (*why* the subject felt as he did about the puzzles) or the affective aspect of the attitude (*how* the subject felt about the puzzles). In addition, subjects were told that either they would be given a test later of their analytic ability (thus making their puzzle-solving activity instrumental), or they would later have a social sensitivity test (thus, making puzzle solving an activity undertaken in its own right, a consummatory behavior). Consistent with the predictions, subjects who engaged in the puzzle activity as instrumental behavior showed consistency between evaluations of the puzzle and time spent on the puzzles only in the cognitive focus condition; those playing with the puzzles for their own sake showed high attitude-behavior congruence only in the affective focus condition.

Millar and Tesser's (1989) argument also suggests that if the affective and cognitive components of an attitude are in evaluative agreement, then focusing on either component should produce a similar evaluation regardless of the type of behavior. However, if the two are not in agreement, then focusing on the cognitive versus the affective aspects of the attitude would lead to different evaluation, depending upon whether the behavior is instrumental or consummatory. Research supports this prediction as well (M. G. Millar & Tesser, 1989).

Attitudes also influence behavior to the extent that they can be *easily accessed* by a person (e.g., Aldrich, Sullivan, & Borgida, 1989; Fazio & Williams, 1986; Kallgren & Wood, 1986; Kiesler, Nisbett, & Zanna, 1969).[2] Sometimes, we hold attitudes as general values, but are not able to access them readily to influence our behavior. For example, we may believe in the need to protect the environment, but this attitude may be held at such a general level that it is not accessed for specific situations. Kallgren and Wood (1986) assessed subjects' attitudes toward the preservation of the environment and also assessed the accessibility of those attitudes by how many facts the person could remember relevant to the attitude and how many past behaviors he or she could remember consistent with the attitude. Two weeks later, the subjects were asked to sign and circulate a petition and to participate in a recycling project. Those subjects who were able to access their prior attitudes showed substantial congruence between their attitudes and behavior, whereas those who had little access to their attitudes demonstrated little attitude-behavior consistency.

Attitude-behavior consistency also increases as a function of the *amount of information* that is available about the attitude object. Using longitudinal data, A. R. Davison et al. (1985) found that more information about an attitude object produced greater congruence between attitudes and behavior, and this was true even when they controlled for prior experience with the attitude and for attitude certainty.

Increasingly, *values* have been examined as determinants of the attitude-behavior relationship. Some of this work builds on Rokeach's

---

[2]Interestingly, Tyler and Rasinski (1984) found that the accessibility of examples of crime victimization did not affect crime prevention behavior, whereas the informativeness and the affect did. It may be that merely having available examples of victimization does not translate into an attitude, thereby explaining the low relationship between accessible instances and subsequent behaviors.

(1973) value self-confrontation approach to behavior. Developed as a behavior change method, the theory attempts to change people's behavior by changing the value priorities that underlie that behavior. Using a method termed *self-confrontation,* people who have ranked their values and identified behaviors that they wish to change are presented with information about the value priorities that discriminate between a positive and a negative reference group with respect to that behavior change. When values relevant to the desired behavior change are made salient, behavior change can be furthered (Schwartz & Inbar-Saban, 1988; see also Homer & Kahle, 1988).

Self-schemas also determine the attitude-behavior relationship. Those whose attitudes represent self-schematic attributes are more likely to behave consistently with those attitudes than are people who hold attitudes that are not central to self-schemas (Milburn, 1987).

Overall, attitudes that matter to a person—those that are based on personal experience or values, that are held with confidence, that are accessible, that have information to back them up, and that have implications for one's future—show a stronger relationship to behavior than those that matter little (cf. Kelman, 1974). The implication for the cognition-behavior relationship more generally is that cognitions that emerge from personal rather than indirect experience, and cognitions that have implications for one's life, predict behavior better than cognitions that develop merely from mild curiosity, passing interest, or a second-hand source.

HOW IS BEHAVIOR RELATED TO COGNITION?

Action Identification

So far, in our discussion of the relationship between cognitions and behavior, we have focused largely on sources of variability that may influence the way in which attitudes are expressed. There are also factors that affect the ways in which a behavior can be labeled or identified. Actions may be identified at low levels of behavior (making idle conversation) or at high levels in the service of some goal (trying to create a positive impression). A theory that has evolved to give psychological meaning to this phenomenon is termed *action identification theory* (Vallacher & Wegner, 1987). The theory assumes that act identities, namely, the different ways of thinking about a particular action, have systematic relations to each other in an organized cognitive representation, termed the *action identity structure.* The identity structure is a hierarchical arrangement of the various identities that might be attached to a given action. Low levels identify the specifics of the action, whereas higher levels indicate a more abstract understanding of the action, indicating why it is done and what its purposes are. Putting one's feet successively in front of each other represents a very low action identity, going for a walk might represent a middle-level action identity, walking through a neighborhood to see if it is the kind of place in which one might want to live would be a high-level action identity, and planning one's future, an even higher level action identity. Together, these represent some of the different levels of identification that might be applied to the same underlying action.

The theory maintains that the level of identification that is most likely to be adopted in any given situation represents a trade-off between the need to understand action comprehensively and the need to maintain that action effectively. Actions identified at relatively low levels are subject to context effects that might cue higher levels of action identity for the purpose of understanding the meaning of the action in its context. However, when behavior is difficult to maintain with higher levels of action identity in mind, one may drop back to a lower level.

The theory argues that people have certain ideas of what they are doing or want to do and use this identification as a frame of reference for implementing that action, monitoring its occurrence, and reflecting on whether or not it is maintained. Given that a particular action can be identified either at low levels or at high levels, there is a tendency for the higher-level identity to be "prepotent," that is, to dominate the enactment and evaluation of the action. In fact, research shows that when people have only low-level understandings of what they are doing, they are predisposed to accept any higher-level identity that is suggested by the context surrounding the action (e.g., Wegner et al., 1986, 1984). Thus, for example, in one study, subjects were induced to drink coffee from a strangely shaped cup, thereby focusing their attention on very low-level aspects of the action (actually getting the coffee to their mouths); other subjects drank coffee from normal cups. Those drinking from the unusual cups were more receptive to a suggestion that they were seeking (or avoiding) self-stimulation, a higher-level action identification, than simply "drinking coffee." Moreover, they showed generalization of the self-stimulation action identification, namely, in turning up (or down) the volume of music to which they were listening (Wegner et al., 1984).

When an action cannot be maintained at a higher level, it tends to drop to a lower level of prepotency. For example, those skilled in the use of chopsticks may be able to think of consuming a Chinese meal as a delightful and tasty experience, whereas those inexperienced in the use of chopsticks may regard the experience primarily as a task of actually getting food from the plate into one's mouth. Thus, when the higher-level identities of an action cannot be automatically enacted, the tendency for actions to stay identified at the higher level is muted, and the individual moves to lower levels of action identification. More generally, actions that are successful tend to be identified and maintained at relatively high levels, whereas actions that are unsuccessful tend to be identified at lower levels (Vallacher, Wegner, & Frederick, 1987).

The level at which an action is identified depends upon several factors, including the context in which the action takes place, the difficulty experienced in carrying out the action, and the person's prior experience with the action. With respect to context, situational cues will often provide a basis for a person identifying an action at a particularly high or low level. Thus, for example, the presence of one's boss at a social gathering may define one's comments about the future directions of the company as an opportunity to impress one's boss, whereas if the boss were not present, one's observations about the company's future might simply remain gratuitous observations.

With respect to action difficulty, five factors, termed *maintenance indicators*, determine the potential disruption of an action identity. They are: the difficulty of enacting the action, familiarity with it, its complexity, the amount of time it takes to enact it, and the amount of time it takes to learn to do it well. Waiting for a bus, for example, is not difficult to enact. It is familiar to most people, it is very simple, it may take a short time, and it is not hard to learn. Consequently, the likelihood that waiting for a bus would drop to a lower level of action identification is small. However, flagging down a taxi may be somewhat more difficult to enact, less familiar, more complex, under some circumstances take longer, and in particular cities, take an inordinate amount of learning time. The novice cab-flagger in New York City, for example, may shift the identification of the task from flagging a cab to getting into the street with one's hand up to attract attention before other people do. Thus, actions seen as easy to do, familiar, short in duration, and requiring little learning time tend to be maintained at their initial level than those that fail to meet these criteria.

In terms of action experience, actions chunked at higher levels can often be enacted automatically. To the extent that this is true, they tend to be identified at higher rather than lower levels. As individuals develop more experience with a particular action sequence, they will come to identify it at a higher level than if they have little experience with the action sequence. Inexperienced Nintendo players, for example, may regard their action as attempting not to get zapped by one of the little evil men, whereas experienced Nintendo players may define their actions as "getting to the castle" or "progressing to the next level of play" (Vallacher, Wegner, & Frederick, 1987).

Whether an action is identified at a high or low level has a number of implications. The first concerns the action's stability. If an action is undertaken with a relatively low-level identity in mind, it is subject to context effects that may cue higher-level action identities. For example, an initial goal of going for a walk may give way to the identification of seeing how other people have set in plantings around their homes. However, an initially higher level of action identification, such as walking over to a friend's house, may not give way as easily to a lower level identification. One would not typically set out for a friend's house and go for a walk instead. Consequently, behaviors enacted at a higher level of action identification tend to be more stable than those enacted at low levels of action identification. Action identification also influences the flexibility of that action. Actions identified at a higher level, such as getting exercise, may be enacted in any of several ways, such as jogging, riding a bike, or swimming, whereas actions identified at a lower level, such as riding a bike, will show less flexibility.

Actions performed at the wrong level are subject to performance impairments. Specifically, difficult tasks should be performed best when identified in low-level terms, whereas easy tasks should be performed best when they are identified in high-level terms. In one study, subjects were instructed to give a speech to either an easy-to-persuade audience or a difficult-to-persuade audience, and were led either to focus on their voice during their speech or to retain the higher identification level of the speech as a persuasion effort. Subjects made fewer speech errors and were more satisfied with their speech if the task was easy and identified at a high level and if the task was difficult and identified at a low level; however, when the task was difficult and identified at a high level or when it was easy and identified at a low level, greater disruption and less satisfaction occurred (Vallacher, Wegner, & Somoza, 1989).

An action typically performed at a high level may be disrupted if one moves it to a lower level. For example, a broad jumper claims that, by asking one of her opponents why she places her right foot in a particular way, she can knock two feet off the opponent's jump. Conversely, when a behavior can be enacted automatically at a relatively low level of action identification, contextual effects that suggest a higher level of action identification can disrupt the performance of the behavioral sequence because the higher level of identification forces attention to the component parts in a way that is not true at the lower level of identification. For example, a person who normally meets new people quite easily without any great social discomfort may find that these behaviors become disrupted if a partner emphasizes the importance of making a good impression.

A relatively new development in the theory of action identification concerns the role of action identities in the production of emergent action. Emergent action is defined as behavior that people find themselves doing when they did not set out to do it. Given that low-level act identities tend to be subject to context effects suggesting higher-level action identities, emergent action is a highly likely outcome of a low-level action identification. People become subject to situational cues, suggestions from others, priming effects, and other cues in the social environment that suggest they should be thinking about their action in somewhat higher terms. More interestingly, emergent action will sometimes perpetuate itself further. Thus, for example, in one study (Wegner et al., 1986), subjects thought about participating in an experiment in terms of its details or more generally. Those who concentrated on the details were more susceptible to suggestions from others that they were either helping the experimenter, and thus, behaving altruistically, or being selfish by seeking extra course credit. These subjects who initially thought of their participation at relatively low levels came to accept these action identifications, and moreover, continued the emergent action by choosing to participate in subsequent activities that were consistent with the emergent act identity. Some of the effects of action identification are presented in Table 12.1.

There are several implications of action identification theory for other topics in social cognition. Action identification may influence the attributions made for performance. For example, when people enact behaviors at relatively low levels of action identification, they are attentive

TABLE 12.1 THE EFFECTS OF ACTION IDENTIFICATION

	Low Level of Identification	High level of Identification
Example	Bike riding	Getting exercise
Flexibility	Low (There is only one way to ride a bike)	High (There are many ways to get exercise)
Stability	Low (Action identifcation subject to context effects)	High
Impact of Context	Context may move identification to higher level (e.g., bike riding becomes labeled as getting exercise)	Little impact of context on level of identification
Disruption of Behavior Sequence	Disruption less likely to occur; when it does, action identification may move to lower level	Action identification shifts to lower level
Likelihood of Emergent Action	High, because low-level behavior is responsive to context effects	Low

SOURCE: After Vallacher & Wegner, 1987.

to situational context effects that may change the meaning of the behavior. Consequently, if such context effects occur, they may be more likely to make situational attributions for behavior. In contrast, when an action is identified at a high level, it may be perceived as dispositionally based because it is perceived as initiated and maintained by higher-level personal goals rather than situational constraints (Vallacher & Wegner, 1987).

The theory also predicts that cross-situational inconsistency in behavior need not always lead to situational attributions. If an individual has identified an action at a high level, he or she is likely to view that behavior dispositionally despite a high degree of cross-situational flexibility in enacting the goal. Similarly, the theory implies that actor and observer differences in attributions should dissipate in familiar situations, inasmuch as actors will recognize the dispositional factors that contribute to their behavior.

The theory of action identification also provides a useful perspective on the apparent consistency versus malleability of the self-concept (see Chapter 6). In particular, it suggests a resolution for those theories that argue that people maintain stability in their self-concepts but high degrees of variability in their behavior. Action identification theory suggests that only behaviors enacted at high levels will be perceived as consistent with or related to self-conceptions and that large numbers of behaviors apparently inconsistent with the self-concept will not be perceived as such because they are enacted at low levels of action identification, and thereby, judged by the actor to have few or no implications for the self-concept. In a study by Wegner et al. (1986), subjects were induced to generate five one-sentence descriptions of their behavior in either relatively low-level terms or relatively high-level terms. They were then given false feedback indicating that they were either cooperative or competitive. Subjects who had been led to think about their behavior at lower levels agreed with the bogus feedback more than those who had been led to conceptualize their behavior at higher levels. Those who were focusing at the low levels of behavior identification were susceptible to the context effects, whereas those focusing on their behavior at the higher levels were not.

Finally, action identification theory also provides a useful perspective on the identification and measurement of traits, specifically, the relatively little success that personality researchers have had in predicting behavior from traits. Action identification theory argues that people may perform an action for any of many reasons. Some of these will be at high-level identifications which may correspond to particular traits or other dispositional qualities, but others of them will be at very low levels, which need not be related to personality traits (Vallacher & Wegner, 1987).

Situational Factors Mediate Cognition-Behavior Consistency

Situational factors may also influence the cognition-behavior relationship by making particular cognitions salient as guides for behavior. Suppose you are approached by a friend who asks you to help him collect signatures on a petition that allows freshmen and sophomores to have cars on campus. What do you do? If the friend tells you he is desperate because he promised to have one hundred signatures by noon, and has only sixty at ten in the morning, you might help him out of friendship. On the other hand, if a classmate walks by muttering that there are too few parking spaces for the cars already on campus, you might reconsider, not wishing to alienate your friends. Similarly, if the parking petition is billed as a question of individual rights, you might be inclined to favor it, but if you have just read a newspaper editorial decrying the recent rise in air pollution in your community, you might not help out. This example illustrates that, in trying to examine the consistency question, one must ask, Consistency with what? Social norms? Attitudes? Which set of attitudes? Behavior is strongly influenced by situational factors that may make salient one set of cognitions over others, and one must know which concerns are salient before one can predict the nature of consistency (see Scheier & Carver, 1982).

Attitude-behavior consistency will be affected by which meaning of a particular attitude or behavior is made salient by situational cues. In a study that examined this point, Prislin (1987) measured subjects' attitudes toward capital punishment and then asked them to make a decision in a fictitious jury case. Subjects were either reminded to act in line with their attitudes (high attitude relevance) or in line with the facts (low attitude relevance). They were also told that their decision could or could not influence the decision of a real jury (high versus low behavior relevance). When external factors made neither the implications of the attitude nor the behavior especially relevant, attitude-behavior relationships were strong. However, when external factors made either the attitude or behavior relevant or both, the correlation was substantially reduced. These context effects on behavior can be very subtle, induced even by subliminal priming in a prior context (Herr, 1986; Neuberg, 1989). Berkowitz has argued that these kinds of processes may help to account for the fact that mass media presentations of antisocial behavior can, in some cases, lead to copycat events (Berkowitz, 1984).

Social norms can be strong situational determinants of behavior that overwhelm seemingly relevant attitudes (e.g., Bentler & Speckart, 1981; Fishbein & Ajzen, 1975; LaPiere, 1934; Pagel & Davidson, 1984; S. H. Schwartz & Tessler, 1972). For example, asked if you would allow Sleazy Sam into your home, you may respond with some indignation that you would not, but if he shows up at your party as a date of one of your guests, it is unlikely that you will turn him away. Your behavior, then, will be consistent with the norms surrounding the host or hostess role, though it will not be consistent with your attitudes about Sam. Social norms are likely to be especially salient when an audience is present or when one's attention is directed outward toward the situation (rather than toward oneself); accordingly, behavior is likely to be strongly affected by self-presentational concerns (Cialdini et al., 1973; S. Duval, 1976; Newtson & Czerlinsky, 1974; M. Snyder & Swann, 1976).

Other situational factors favor the use of prior attitudes as a basis for behavior. For example, if situational factors focus attention inward, a person is more likely to base his or her behavior on enduring attitudes (Wicklund, 1975): Attention to the self minimizes external influences and makes one's prior attitudes more salient (see S. E. Taylor & Fiske, 1978). When people's past behaviors that suggest a particular attitude are made salient, subsequent consistency between attitudes and behavioral intentions is high. In one study, subjects were asked to think of all the negative experiences they had had that were associated with exercise (e.g., being picked last for a team or failing to score a crucial goal). Sometime later when subjects were given a chance to participate in exercise classes, they volunteered for fewer classes than did subjects who had not reconstructed their past negative exercise-related experiences (M. Ross et al., 1983; see also Borgida & Campbell, 1982).

The priming of particular constructs also affects behavior. Making extraversion salient in a particular situation, for example, will increase expressions of extraversion among most people. However, people also differ in the extent to which a primed construct may fit their own self-conception. Thus, for example, an introverted person may behave in a more extraverted way if the primed behavior for a situation calls for extraverted behavior, but as the salience of the norm of extraversion declines, the person may revert more to his or her chronically accessible self-perception of introversion. A person who considers the self neither extraverted nor introverted might, instead, remain sensitive to the behavior normative for the situation, even when the salience of that norm declines (see Bargh, Lombardi, & Higgins, 1988).

Attitudinal expression is also heavily influenced by context. For example, in surveys assessing attitudes toward the Republican and Democratic parties, people are typically even-handed and fair if they are asked to comment on the two parties at the same time. In contrast, when each political party is considered in isolation, then the attitudes toward the two parties diverge (Schuman & Ludwig, 1983).

Why should seemingly trivial aspects of a situation have such a clear impact on people's behavior? Why should it matter what you temporarily access about your past behaviors or beliefs? Situationally induced salience can put relevant attitudes or norms in the mental foreground, making them more available as guides to action (Borgida & Campbell, 1982; C. A. Kiesler, Collins, & Miller, 1969; M. Snyder, 1977). What is salient defines the situation for the individual, reducing ambiguity and inconsistency (R. Norman, 1975); it tells you what should be relevant to your behavior if you are uncertain of what to do. Finally, when global attitudes or values are made salient, responsibility for behaving consistently with one's attitude will loom large (C. A. Kiesler, 1971; S. H. Schwartz, 1978). Thus, if cognition-behavior linkages are made salient, cognitions and behaviors may typically cohere, but when situational norms are salient, behavior may be consistent with those norms. To predict which cognitions will cohere with behavior, then, one must know which factors in a situation are salient. Self-presentational concerns may dominate behavior, or behavior may be dominated by prior beliefs, attributions, expectations, or other influences, depending on what is salient.

Individual Differences Mediate Consistency

The question, "Consistent with what?" becomes even more appropriate when we examine the role of individual differences in cognition-behavior consistency. Some people show high consistency with social norms, whereas others behave consistently with their attitudes. Some people have an overriding social goal that is manifested chronically in their behavior, whereas others show more behavioral flexibility. We now turn to these individual difference factors.

A basic question in assessing trait-behavior and attitude-behavior relations concerns the extent to which people actually think about themselves in trait terms and see behavior as highly stable across situations. Generally, researchers have assumed but not tested the idea that people believe they and others behave relatively consistently across situations ostensibly tapping the same personality domain. However, some research casts doubt on whether people actually perceive or expect high degrees of cross-situational consistency (Epstein & Teraspulsky, 1986).

Similarly, J. C. Wright and Mischel (1988) predicted and found evidence that both children and adults tend to view dispositional constructs as condition-behavior contingencies rather than as invariant traits that apply across a broad array of situations. Thus, for example, adults make dispositional attributions about others' behaviors but also modify them with conditional statements ("George is outgoing except with people he doesn't know"). One implication of this point is that people may see no need to behave in accordance with their personal dispositions, inasmuch as they perceive those dispositions as only conditionally relevant to particular situations. Thus, for example, one may believe that one is a friendly person, but believe that returning the greeting of a roadside vagrant is not required by the disposition "friendly." Consistent with this point, Mischel (1984) has found, in a series of studies examining delay of gratification, that global situation-free consistencies are rarely obtained. Rather, over time, people develop the discriminative facility to determine what behavior is required for what situation, rather than demonstrate a rigidity in the employment of well-established traits cross-situationally.

There also appear to be individual differences in the extent to which people focus on personal characteristics, such as traits, as a basis for behavior. Wicklund and Braun (1987; Wicklund, 1986) predicted and found that people who are inexperienced, incompetent, or unsure of their abilities within a given performance context are more occupied with the appropriate traits and characteristics for that performance than are experienced, capable performers (see also Cantor, Mackie, & Lord, 1983–84). This focus on the competencies required in a given performance context may lead to greater attempts to be congruent with situational demands, though not necessarily performance that more closely matches situational demands, which may instead depend on competence (Mischel, 1984).

One reason why experimental studies may show lower levels of trait-behavior consistency than would be expected is that subjects in experiments and experimenters may disagree on the relevant behaviors as well as in the difficulty that subjects have in performing behaviors ostensibly relevant to their personality or attitudes (D. J. Bem & Allen, 1974). Bem and Allen (1974) found that using self-report measures of cross-situational consistency as moderator variables could increase the size of the correlation coefficient computed among measures of two personality traits, friendliness and conscientiousness. Other research (e.g., Chaplin & Goldberg, 1984) has suggested that the effects may not be replicable or strong. Consequently, whether or not the self-perception of trait-behavior consistency is a variable that moderates actual trait-behavior consistency remains unclear.

Self-monitoring.

The Vaughts liked the engineer very much, each feeling that he was his or her special sort of person. And he was. Each saw him differently.

Mr. Vaught was certain he was a stout Southern lad in the old style, wellborn but lusty as anyone, the sort who knows how to get along with older men. Back home he would have invited the younger man on a hunt or to his poker club, where he was certain to be a favorite. The second time Mr. Vaught saw him, he took him aside ceremoniously and invited him to Jamie's birthday party.

Jamie—who, he was told, had a severe and atypical mononucleosis—saw him as a fellow technician, like himself an initiate of science, that is, of

a secret, shared view of the world, a genial freemasonry which sets itself
apart from ordinary folk and sees behind appearances.

To Mrs. Vaught elder he was as nice as he could be. His manners were
good without being too ceremonial. There was a lightness in him: he knew
how to fool with her. So acute was his radar that neither Mrs. Vaught nor
her husband could quite get it into their heads that he did not know everything they knew. He *sounded* like he did (Walker Percy, *The Last Gentleman*,
1966).

We all know people who blend into social situations easily. They
seem to know exactly what to do or say with each person. We also
know people who are themselves, regardless of what situation they are
in, who rarely bend to the norms of the social setting. Such different
patterns are termed high and low self-monitoring, respectively (M.
Snyder, 1979). Those who act as the situation demands are monitoring
themselves with respect to the situation. Those who act on their own
internal demands are not monitoring themselves with respect to the situation; they are low self-monitors (M. Snyder, 1974; M. Snyder &
Campbell, 1982; M. Snyder & Monson, 1975; M. Snyder & Tanke, 1976).

What, exactly, is self-monitoring? Self-monitoring refers to the ways
in which individuals plan, act out, and regulate behavioral decisions in
social situations (M. Snyder & Cantor, 1980). Behavioral choices utilize
a wide range of information, including knowledge of particular social
settings and knowledge of one's own abilities, resources, and stable
qualities. Snyder (1974) maintained that high self-monitors are particularly sensitive to social norms, to situations, and to interpersonal cues
regarding how to behave. Low self-monitors, in contrast, are less responsive to these environmental cues and instead, draw on salient information from their internal selves to decide how to behave. In essence, then, when faced with a new situation, high self-monitors ask,
"What is the ideal person for this situation and how can I be it?"
whereas low self-monitors ask, "How can I best be me in this situation?" (M. Snyder, 1979).

Self-monitoring is assessed by a scale (M. Snyder, 1972, 1974), some
items of which appear in Table 12.2. First, answer the items in the table.
If you answered "false" to items 1, 3, and 5, and "true" to items 2, 4,
and 6, you would tend toward the high self-monitoring side. On the
other hand, if the reverse pattern characterizes your answers, you tend
to be a low self-monitor.

High self-monitors are, in many ways, more socially skilled than
low self-monitors (e.g., Ickes & Barnes, 1977). They can communicate a
wider range of emotional states, they learn more quickly how to behave
in new situations, they are more likely to initiate conversations, and
they have good self-control (see M. Snyder, 1979). When asked to adopt
the behavior of another type of person, for example, a reserved, withdrawn, introverted type, high self-monitors are better at it than low

TABLE 12.2 SAMPLE ITEMS MEASURING SELF-MONITORING

Answer the following items true or false.

1. I find it hard to imitate the behavior of other people.	T	F
2. I would probably make a good actor.	T	F
3. In a group of people, I am rarely the center of attention.	T	F
4. I may deceive people by being friendly when I really dislike them.	T	F
5. I can only argue for ideas which I already believe.	T	F
6. I can make impromptu speeches even on topics about which I have almost no information.	T	F

SOURCE: After M. Snyder, The self-monitoring of expressive behavior. *Journal of Personality and Social Psychology*, 1974, 30, 526-537. Copyright 1974 by the American Psychological Association. Adapted by permission of the author.

self-monitors (Lippa, 1976), and they also appear to be better at discerning the meaning of nonverbal behavior than low self-monitors (see M. Snyder, 1979). When their social outcomes depend on another person, such as a potential date, high self-monitors remember more about the other person and make more confident and extreme inferences about the other (Berscheid et al., 1976). To the observer, the high self-monitor appears more friendly and less anxious than the low self-monitor (Lippa, 1976).

As might be expected, high self-monitors have great interest in social information, apparently because it is useful to them. They are more likely to seek out information that is relevant to norms for self-presentation in a situation, and they spend more time looking at it. They remember information about another person with whom they will interact better than do low self-monitors (see M. Snyder, 1974). High self-monitors are more responsive to task instructions indicating what the typical behavior is in a given situation than are low self-monitors (M. Snyder & Monson, 1975).

High self-monitors are particularly able to construct images of prototypic individuals in particular domains (e.g., the classic extravert or the perfect princess) than are low self-monitors, and are more likely to enter into a social situation when norms are clear; low self-monitors, on the other hand, are more skilled at constructing images of themselves in particular situations (e.g., how they would behave in situations calling for extravertedness), and they are more likely to enter a social situation if it fits their self-conception (M. Snyder & Gangestad, 1981).

Self-monitoring has been explored in relatively naturalistic as well as experimental settings, and the differences in style continue to hold up. For example, because of their greater interest in and attentiveness to social situations, high self-monitors are more accurate eyewitnesses than low self-monitors (Hosch & Platz, 1984). However, high self-monitors also appear to be more vulnerable to leading questions than low self-monitors, and consequently, their accuracy as eyewitnesses may deteriorate under effective cross-examination conditions (Lassiter, Stone, & Weigold, 1988). High and low self-monitoring individuals appear to respond to different aspects of advertising appeals as well. High self-monitoring individuals respond to image-oriented advertisements and are willing to pay more for products advertised with an image orientation, whereas low self-monitoring individuals react more favorably to product-quality-oriented ads, and are willing to pay more for products advertised as a quality product (M. Snyder & DeBono, 1985).

Given differences in the styles and informational preferences of high and low self-monitors, it should not be surprising that their behavior is under the control of different standards and forces. High self-monitors describe themselves as flexible, adaptive, shrewd individuals; when asked to explain the cause of their own behavior, they are likely to point to situational factors.[3] Low self-monitors, in contrast, see themselves as more consistent and principled than highs do, and they offer dispositional explanations for their behavior (e.g., M. Snyder, 1976). Low self-monitors are more likely to show the effects of temporary mood states or fatigue on their behavior than high self-monitors, who are better able to mask these sources of internal interference (Ajzen, Timko, & White, 1982; M. Snyder, 1979; see also Zanna, Olson, & Fazio, 1981). High self-monitors also appear to be more responsive to manipulations of public self-awareness (see Chapter 6 on the self), whereas low self-monitors are more sensitive to manipulations of private self-awareness (Webb et al., 1989).

These differences in self-perception are also reflected behaviorally, and as such, the self-monitoring dimension helps to unravel the attitude-behavior consistency problem. High self-monitors show high cross-situational variability in their behavior. Because they behave consistently with social norms that vary from situation to situation, high self-monitors show little consistency across situations. After being induced to perform a counterattitudinal behavior, high self-monitors are less likely to infer new attitudes from the counterattitudinal behavior

---

[3]Described this way, high self-monitoring individuals appear to be quite Machiavellian. However, Ickes, Reidhead, and Patterson (1986) have suggested that people high in Machiavellianism are self-oriented in their impression management efforts, whereas self-monitoring reflects an other-oriented, accommodative form of impression management. They tested this hypothesis by examining the conversations of individuals high and low in Machiavellianism and high and low in self-monitoring. They found that high Machiavellianism was associated with the use of first-person singular pronouns and relatively fewer second- and third-person pronouns, whereas the reverse was true of high self-monitors.

than are low self-monitors. Low self-monitors, on the other hand, show less situational variability in their behavior than high self-monitors, and their future behavior can be better predicted from knowledge of their relevant attitudes (M. Snyder & Swann, 1976). Their attitudes seem to be more accessible than those of high self-monitoring individuals, in that their response latencies to attitudinal inquiries are faster, suggesting that low self-monitoring individuals have stronger object-evaluation associations (Kardes et al., 1986).

However, there are a few situations in which high self-monitors do show attitude-behavior consistency. When the relevance of personal attitudes to behavior is made salient, they are consistent presumably because it is socially desirable to act on one's attitudes (M. Snyder & Kendzierski, 1982; cf. M. Snyder, 1982). Positive and negative feedback indicating to individuals that they either do act or generally do not act on their attitudes has different effects on high and low self-monitoring individuals. Low self-monitoring individuals, as people who have a strong sense of themselves as acting on their attitudes, are relatively unresponsive to positive or negative feedback indicating whether they have acted on their attitudes. However, when high self-monitoring individuals are provided with feedback that they generally do not act on their attitudes, they are less likely to act subsequently on their attitudes (Kendzierski, 1987).

Interestingly, self-monitoring seems to affect not only how people perceive their own characteristics and behavior, but also how they perceive the characteristics and behavior of others. Low self-monitors are attracted to people who have high attitudinal similarity; activity preference similarity is a less strong determinant of their attraction. The reverse is true of high self-monitoring individuals, who are more attracted by a person who shares activity preferences but not necessarily attitudinal similarities. These results follow from the fact that low self-monitors behave consistently across situations in line with their attitudes, and thereby may find attitudinal similarity to be more relevant than activity preference in determining friendship. Similarly, since high self-monitoring individuals show behavioral flexibility across situations, activity preference should dictate their friendship choices, as it appears to do (Jamieson, Lydon, & Zanna, 1987).

High and low self-monitoring individuals differ in what is important to them in personal relationships, and high self-monitors appear to put more emphasis on surface characteristics. A study that assessed low and high self-monitoring individuals' preferences for romantic and nonromantic partners found that high self-monitoring individuals were more influenced by physical attractiveness of the potential partners, whereas low self-monitors were influenced more by the personality characteristics of potential partners. High self-monitoring individuals reported that they have had a greater number of romantic partners than low self-monitoring individuals, and low self-monitoring individuals reported having dated their current partner for longer than is true for high self-monitoring individuals. In addition, high self-monitoring individuals indicated that they were willing to terminate current relationships in favor of alternative partners more than low self-monitors. Finally, low self-monitors' relationships appear to become more intimate, suggesting that they are more committed to their relationships than are high self-monitors (M. Snyder & Simpson, 1984). Similarly, in a study involving a role-played personnel selection task, high self-monitoring individuals placed greater emphasis on information about a job applicant's physical appearance than did low self-monitoring individuals. Low self-monitoring individuals put more weight on information about personal dispositions (M. Snyder, Berscheid, & Matwychuk, 1988).

The self-monitoring scale has come under some criticism (Briggs & Cheek, 1988; Briggs, Cheek, & Buss, 1980; Carver, 1989), and several authors (Lennox & Wolfe, 1984; Miell & Le Voi, 1985) have suggested that the subscale scores on the self-monitoring scale should be treated separately to predict behavior (but see Gangestad & Snyder, 1985; M. Snyder & Gangestad, 1986). Overall, the dimension of self-monitoring appears to be a multifaceted disposition that predicts social behavior (M. Snyder & Gangestad, 1982; M. Snyder & Kendzierski, 1982).

To summarize, then, some apparent cognition-behavior discrepancies result from stable long-term differences in the goals people have for social situations. In the case of self-monitoring, the cross-situational inconsistencies of the high self-monitor express an ability and willingness to become what is necessary to be successful in a given social setting, that is, a desire to be consistent with social norms. In contrast, the high cross-situational consistency of the low self-monitor reflects a commitment to enduring principles and beliefs and a desire to act in accord with them.

Self-consciousness. Theories of self-focused attention (Carver & Scheier, 1981a; S. Duval & Wicklund, 1972; Wicklund, 1975) suggest that people's behavior follows their attentional focus. Recall from Chapter 6 that people who focus on themselves as social objects are high in public self-consciousness (Fenigstein, Scheier, & Buss, 1975). Such people are concerned with appearances and impressions. In contrast, people high in private self-consciousness focus on their own internal states and regulate their behavior to be consistent with their thoughts and feelings (Ickes et al., 1986). People who are high on public self-consciousness or low on private self-consciousness are unlikely to act on their attitudes, either because appearances matter to them or because they are relatively unaware of their own attitudes. For example, people high on public self-consciousness are relatively discrepant in their privately held versus publicly expressed beliefs about physical punishment (Scheier, 1980). In contrast, people who are low on public self-consciousness and/or high on private self-consciousness do show somewhat greater responsiveness to their internal states, including their behavioral tendencies and their attitudes (Froming & Carver, 1981; Scheier, 1980; Scheier & Carver, 1983).

Self-monitoring and self-consciousness should also moderate the cognitive-behavior relationship in conjunction. L. E. Miller and Grush (1986) predicted that individuals high in private self-consciousness but low in self-monitoring would display high attitude-behavior correspondence, which should exceed that of other combinations of the two attributes. To test their predictions, the authors assessed attitudes, normative beliefs, and behaviors related to spending time on schoolwork in college students. The results showed clear support for the predicted personality differences. Attitude-behavior correspondence was highest for the group high in private self-consciousness and low in self-monitoring. In contrast, correspondence between social norms and behavior was higher for groups with other combinations of the two attributes.

Having learned about both self-monitoring and self-consciousness, the reader may wonder how they differ. In fact, they seem to be different measures of a somewhat similar underlying construct: the propensity to draw on one's enduring, private reactions versus the propensity to utilize social norms and the desires of a social group as standards for behavior. The two constructs seem to measure different aspects of the concept: self-monitoring emphasizes self-presentational skills (or lack of them) and self-consciousness emphasizes focus of attention. However, self-monitoring and self-consciousness are only weakly related (Carver & Scheier, 1981a; R. G. Turner et al., 1978), and it may be difficult from an empirical standpoint to try to integrate them (Schneiderman, Webb, Davis, & Thomas, 1981; M. Snyder, 1979).

Our limited coverage of individual differences should not be taken to imply that only these individual difference variables are determinants of cognition-behavior consistency (see, for example, Vallacher & Wegner, 1987). Rather, they are the ones in which the cognition-behavior relationship has been extensively explored. In reality, all individual difference variables can be interpreted as moderators of the cognition-behavior relationship in that they predict what chronic goals people have cross-situationally, what kinds of situations they prefer, and what they do when they get to those situations.

USING BEHAVIOR TO TEST HYPOTHESES ABOUT OTHERS

We learn about other people in many different ways. Sometimes we hear about them from others before meeting them or we may have hints about them based on the situations in which we encounter them. At other times, we must start from scratch, assembling an impression through information gathered from observing and talking with the person. Regardless of how an impression of another is formed, we may quickly develop hypotheses concerning what the person is like. As we are interacting with the person, how will the hypotheses influence one's behavior? Considerable research suggests that people behave toward others in ways that tend to confirm the hypotheses they hold about those others. Perceivers often employ behavioral strategies for eliciting information about others that preferentially support their hypotheses.

How might this process work? Suppose you learn that Ed has just returned from Tahiti and you quickly form an image of him as a carefree adventurer who seeks exotic places. In your subsequent interactions with him, you may inquire as to other trips he has taken or hobbies he has and learn that he once sailed the Virgin Islands with friends and fed sharks at Marineland as a summer job after high school. All this may seem fairly exotic, but note that you preferentially solicited information that confirmed this image. All of us have at least a few little things about us that make us quasi-exotic, and when those bits are elicited from us in their entirety, we look much more exciting than we really are. After dating Exotic Ed for several weeks, it may emerge that his company flew him to Tahiti for a conference, his uncle is the manager of Marineland and got him the summer job, and the "friends" with whom he sailed to the Virgin Islands were his grandparents. The point is that people have a large repertoire of behaviors and experiences and, when they are preferentially sampled by selective questioning, they may fit whatever hypothesis that selective questioning is designed to assess.

To demonstrate this point, M. Snyder and Swann (1978a) told college-student subjects they would be interviewing another student; one-half were told to find out if the other was an extravert (e.g., outgoing, sociable), and one-half were told to find out if the other was an introvert (e.g., shy and retiring). All subjects were then given a set of questions measuring introversion and extraversion, and the students were told to pick a subset of questions they would ask. Subjects who were told to assess extraversion preferentially selected a disproportionate number of extraversion questions (e.g., "What would you do if you wanted to liven things up at a party?"), and those told to assess introversion picked a disproportionate number of introversion questions (e.g., "What factors make it really hard for you to open up to people?"). These questions, in turn, made the target other appear particularly extraverted or introverted, respectively, because he or she was providing only the sample of behavior relevant to the questions. This confirmatory hypothesis testing bias has been demonstrated many times (e.g., Slowiaczek et al., 1989; M. Snyder, Campbell, & Preston, 1982). The bias exists whether the hypothesis concerns an individual's personality traits or characteristics based on group membership such as race, sex, or sexual preference. It occurs regardless of how the hypothesis originated, how likely it is to be true, and whether incentives for accuracy are offered to the hypothesis tester (see M. Snyder & Gangestad, 1981, for a review; see also Klayman & Ha, 1987; Skov & Sherman, 1986).

Perhaps more surprising is the fact that, even when people have fairly balanced information about another person, they may selectively draw on it to support a particular hypothesis. Imagine you are at a party and someone who is clearly infatuated with your roommate inquires selectively about all his or her desirable qualities. As you respond to these questions, you may find your own impression of your roommate improving in that you have highlighted for the questioner all positive attributes and none of the negative ones. M. Snyder and Cantor (1979) examined this phenomenon by giving subjects a detailed description of a woman and later asking them to assess her suitability for a particular job, either that of a real estate salesperson, which requires extraverted qualities, or that of librarian, which requires more introverted qualities. Although the initial description contained a balanced set of both extraverted and introverted behaviors, subjects selectively recalled behaviors appropriate to the particular job they were supposed to consider. When later asked to rate the woman's suitability for both jobs, each group saw her as more suited to the one for which they had mustered past evidence (see also Lingle et al., 1979; L. Ross, Lepper, & Hubbard, 1975).

The implications of confirmatory hypothesis testing are not confined solely to the impressions individuals form about each other in casual social settings, as the job interview format of Snyder and Cantor's research implies. Another study demonstrated the potential relevance of confirmatory hypothesis testing to courtroom situations, using the example of asking witnesses leading questions (Swann, Giuliano, & Wegner, 1982). Suppose, for example, that a lawyer asks you: "Tell the jury about the last time you got into a fight." The question itself may lead people to conclude that you have a history of aggressive behavior, whether or not you do. In fact, Swann, Giuliano, and Wegner found that the conjectures embodied in such leading questions can themselves be interpreted as evidence that the respondent engages in the behavior in question. Furthermore, being put in the position of answering such a leading question forces you to provide information that further confirms the behavior. Assuming you were in at least one fight in your life, you must now tell the jury about the details of the fight. Hence, leading questions are doubly biasing; the question itself is taken as evidence for the behavior (cf. Wegner et al., 1981), and the answer provides further such evidence.

When will the evidence of leading questions be ignored? In a second study, Swann, Giuliano, and Wegner (1982) made it clear that the leading questions were selected at random (drawn from a fish bowl); under these circumstances, the leading questions themselves were not taken as evidence for the existence of the behavior, but the behavioral evidence provided by the answers to those questions still was considered to be relevant. Hence, even random conjectures can create misperceptions via confirmatory hypothesis testing.

In sum, confirmatory hypothesis testing has been demonstrated under a fairly broad range of circumstances. It is important to note, however, that methodological factors may contribute to the demonstration of the confirmatory bias. First, the to-be-tested hypothesis is often made particularly salient to subjects through a vivid description of the hypothesis in question, for example, a portrait of extraversion (see Trope & Bassok, 1982). Thus, people may select questions that tend to confirm preexisting hypotheses, primarily because that hypothesis is especially salient to them. Bassok and Trope (1983–84), for example, asked subjects to assess the occurrence of a trait, the occurrence of the opposite trait, or the occurrence of both the focal trait and its opposite. Selective preference for questions about the target trait were found only in the condition when the target trait alone was described. When the alternative trait was also mentioned, subjects' questions were more balanced, perhaps because they now had a second hypothesis to test as well.

Second, in some studies, the list of questions given to subjects to test the hypothesis (e.g., extraversion) includes a heavy proportion of questions that assume that the to-be-tested hypothesis is true. Thus, instead of questions like, "Do you like parties?" (a question to which extraverts might respond "yes" and introverts "no"), the list includes questions like, "What would you do to liven up a party?" (a question to which both introverts and extraverts would be virtually forced to give information relevant only to extraversion). When subjects are allowed to create their own questions to test a hypothesis, they rarely choose such biased questions; rather, their questions may feature a behavior characteristic of the to-be-tested hypothesis, but the question itself is unbiased. That is, people will ask, "Do you like parties?" if testing extraversion, or, "Do you like to be alone?" if testing introversion (L. F. Clark & Taylor, 1983; Trope, Bassok, & Alon, 1984). It should be noted, though, that people typically answer "yes" to yes/no questions, and thus, the evidence gathered by using these less-biased questions may nonetheless preferentially support the hypothesis embodied in them (Swann & Giuliano, 1987).

However, other studies also suggest limitations to confirmatory hypothesis testing effects. Pennington (1987) found little use of confirmatory hypothesis strategies in face-to-face interaction, arguing that the personality of the individual and nature of the questions are more salient in such situations. Such findings question the conditions under which the confirmatory hypothesis testing effect would be found. Trope and Bassok (1982) found that subjects testing hypotheses about others preferred diagnostic information (i.e., information most likely to indicate whether or not the hypothesis was true), rather than confirmatory information, that is, information that preferentially supported the hypothesis (see also Kruglanski & Mayseless, 1988; Trope & Mackie, 1987). The hypothesis confirmation tendency may also be moderated by individual differences, such as the need to have valid information. Those with high fear of invalidity appear more likely to use diagnostic hypothesis-testing strategies (Kruglanski & Mayseless, 1988; see also Trope & Mackie, 1987). However, as Swann and Giuliano (1987) point out, people often perceive supportive evidence to be diagnostic evidence, and thus, the distinction may be moot in many conditions. Moreover, Skov and Sherman (1986) found that even though changes in the methodology of hypothesis-testing studies can reduce the tendency to ask hypothesis-confirming questions, it may not eliminate them altogether.

There seems little doubt that confirmatory hypothesis testing sometimes occurs, but how general it is remains at issue. It seems most likely to occur if people have a single clear hypothesis in mind, are relatively certain of its correctness (Swann & Giuliano, 1987), and have available only leading questions to test their hypothesis. When people actually select leading questions is still at issue. Klayman and Ha (1987) suggest that the hypothesis-confirmation bias in social interaction is a manifestation of the more general tendency to test cases that are expected to have a property of interest, rather than cases that will not show the property of interest (see Chapter 9 on social inference). As such, the tendency may be quite strong. However, it is also clear from recent work (Kruglanski & Mayseless, 1988; Skov & Sherman, 1986; Trope & Mackie, 1987) that the way the task is framed, the type of questions that are available, the degree of certainty of the perceiver about the hypothesis, and whether or not an alternative hypothesis is available will moderate the tendency to selectively confirm hypotheses.

An additional concern regarding the generalizability of the confirmatory bias in hypothesis testing is that rarely are conversations one-way, with one individual asking all the questions and the other merely answering. If true communication occurred, how would a target react to hypothesis testing efforts in a conversation? Would a target person recognize that he or she is being miscast or distorted by the perceiver? Under what circumstances might a target person not only confirm the perceiver's hypothesis but actually come to believe it, and under what circumstances will the target seek to disconfirm the hypothesis?

Self-Fulfilling Prophecies: When Behavior Creates Reality

As just noted, confirmatory hypothesis testing can create misperceptions of a target person in the social perceiver's mind through highlighting information that selectively favors the presentation of particular attributes. When this hypothesis-testing process also succeeds in altering the target person's behavior in the direction of the hypothesis, a self-fulfilling prophecy is said to occur. An initially false definition of a situation, then, evokes behaviors which subsequently make the false belief true (Merton, 1957; D. T. Miller & Turnbull, 1986, for a review).

A classic demonstration of the self-fulfilling prophecy was done in a classroom situation (Rosenthal & Jacobson, 1968). Teachers were told at the beginning of a school year that certain of their students were potential late bloomers who, with the proper nurturing and guidance, could be expected to excel. In fact, there was nothing to distinguish these students from their peers: they were randomly selected. However, several months later, when the so-called late bloomers' performance was examined, not only had their schoolwork improved, but their IQs had actually increased. Numerous similar investigations, many conducted in classroom settings, testify to the robustness of this "Pygmalion" effect (see Rosenthal, 1974, for a review). It holds for many different types of expectations, target persons, and situations; both positive and negative expectations can create self-fulfilling prophecies (Andersen & Bem, 1981; Fazio, Effrein, & Falender, 1981; S. C. Jones & Panitch, 1971; Jussim, 1986; Sherman et al., 1981; M. Snyder & Swann, 1978a; Zanna & Pack, 1975; see M. J. Harris & Rosenthal, 1985; D. T. Miller & Turnbull, 1986; M. Snyder, 1984, for reviews).

How do self-fulfilling prophecies come about? Rosenthal has emphasized the importance of four factors in the Pygmalion effect. First, teachers given positive expectations about students no doubt created a warmer socioemotional *climate* than would be expected for students about whom they have lower expectations. *Feedback* is also important, in that teachers give more differentiated feedback to the "special" students than to their average students. This differentiated feedback, both positive and negative, should help the student to learn correct and incorrect responses more successfully. The *input* factor refers to the tendency of teachers to try to teach more and more difficult material to the students about whom they held high expectations. Last, teachers gave the students greater opportunity for responding (*output*), such as the chance to answer questions in class. These four factors appear to be important in the mediation of positive expectancies. An expectation is also more likely to lead to a self-fulfilling prophecy if the expectation is held by a high-status person (e.g., an authority figure or older, male individual) than if the target is of relatively lower status (Darley & Fazio, 1980). For example, if a researcher tells the student sitting next to you in class that you are a potential late bloomer, that information will probably influence your behavior less than if the researcher tells your teacher the same thing.

Perhaps the most intriguing way in which an expectation can be

transmitted from perceiver to target person is through nonverbal behaviors such as eye contact, posture, smiling, nodding, and body angle.
For example, a study by Word, Zanna, and Cooper (1974) demonstrated
that negative expectations communicated nonverbally by an interviewer actually caused an interviewee to perform more poorly (see also
M. Snyder, Tanke, & Berscheid, 1977).

A substantial amount of research on self-fulfilling prophecies implies that such effects are common (see Darley & Fazio, 1980, for a review). In fact, though, several critical steps are required for the effect to
occur. As Figure 12.1 indicates, the perceiver must hold an expectation
about a target, and behave in a manner consistent with it. The target
then interprets the behavior, and responds to the perceiver with actions
that are subsequently interpreted by the perceiver as consistent with
the original expectation (Darley & Fazio, 1980; see also Harris &
Rosenthal, 1985; Jussim, 1986; D. T. Miller & Turnbull, 1986; M. Snyder,
1984).

It would seem that checks at each step could potentially erase any
self-fulfilling prophecy. However, consider, for example, the links
among the various steps. If the perceiver forms a positive expectation
about the target and behaves accordingly, the target is likely to assume
either that the perceiver especially likes him or her and has good taste
or that the perceiver is a likable person; in either case, the target is likely
to reciprocate the perceiver's behavior which will set up the self-
fulfilling prophecy. Suppose now that the perceiver holds a negative expectation about the target and behaves in a cold, aloof, or even hostile
manner. The target may decide that the perceiver is an unpleasant person, and reciprocate the negative behaviors, thus, again establishing a
self-fulfilling prophecy. Alternatively, either the perceiver or the target
may decide to have nothing further to do with the other, terminate the
interaction, and leave the interaction. Still, the self-fulfilling prophecy
will remain intact. As M. Snyder (1984) points out, there are also biases
in interpretation and recall, such that a target's behavior that may not
confirm a perceiver's expectation may nonetheless be recalled or interpreted in a manner consistent with that expectation. Under these circumstances of cognitive distortion, the self-fulfilling prophecy will also
remain intact.

The propensity for prior expectations to be confirmed in social interaction can be modified by goals or purposes that the perceiver has
regarding the target. Neuberg (1989) found that a goal to be accurate in
the perception of a target undid some of the behaviors usually associated with expectancy-based interactions. In this study, subjects were
told to evaluate two candidates for an interviewing position. They had
prior information to suggest that one of the candidates was low on attributes related to the job, specifically sociability, goal-directedness, and
general problem-solving ability. No expectations were provided about

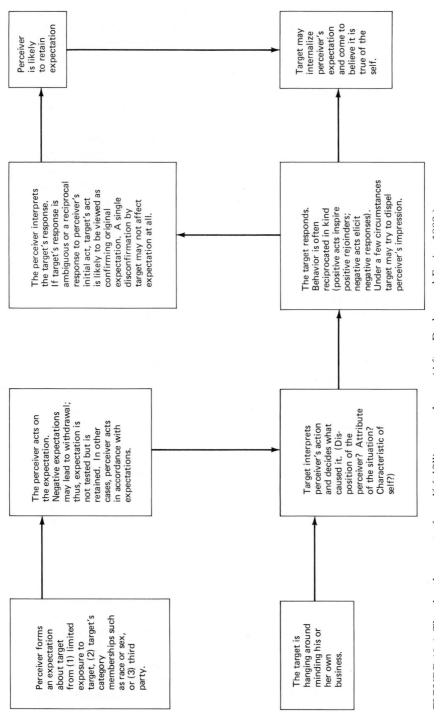

FIGURE 12.1 The development of a self-fulfilling prophecy. (After Darley and Fazio, 1980.)

Perceiver forms an expectation about target from (1) limited exposure to target, (2) target's category memberships such as race or sex, or (3) third party.

The perceiver acts on the expectation. Negative expectations may lead to withdrawal; thus, expectation is not tested but is retained. In other cases, perceiver acts in accordance with expectations.

The perceiver interprets the target's response. If target's response is ambiguous or a reciprocal response to perceiver's initial act, target's act is likely to be viewed as confirming original expectation. A single disconfirmation by target may not affect expectation at all.

Perceiver is likely to retain expectation

The target is hanging around minding his or her own business.

Target interprets perceiver's action and decides what caused it. (Disposition of the perceiver? Attribute of the situation? Characteristic of self?)

The target responds. Behavior is often reciprocated in kind (positive acts inspire positive rejoinders; negative acts elicit negative responses). Under a few circumstances target may try to dispel perceiver's impression.

Target may internalize perceiver's expectation and come to believe it is true of the self.

the other target on these variables. Subjects were then told that their goal either was to *evaluate* the target for the interviewer position or to provide an *accurate* impression of the target. Subjects who had an accuracy goal formed more positive impressions about the negative expectancy target than did subjects in the evaluation condition. Ratings of the taped interactions also suggested that in the accuracy condition, targets about whom accuracy subjects had negative expectations were given more talking time and more encouragement. The accuracy interviewers' questions provided the target with more opportunities to disconfirm the negative expectation as well. The goal of forming an accurate impression appeared, then, to prompt better information-gathering techniques on the part of the perceiver and subsequent better opportunities for the target to disconfirm the expectation. Surprisingly, however, accuracy subjects maintained slightly less favorable evaluations of the candidate about whom they had negative prior information (compared to no-expectancy subjects), even though their evaluations of the target's behavior tended to be positive. Thus, these data suggest that under conditions emphasizing accuracy, people tend to engage in better data-gathering techniques that may undermine the impact of prior expectations. These findings are also supported by a study by Darley, Fleming, Hilton, and Swann (1988), which found that when people expected to have to work with a target in the future, they asked better questions and were less likely to engage in question-asking techniques that confirmed their prior expectations.

Although the goal of accuracy or the expectation of future interaction appears to moderate the impact of prior expectations somewhat, it is likely in the real world that people employ multiple goals in evaluating others under conditions which create a heavy cognitive load. As the chapters on the use of schemas suggest (see Chapters 4 and 5), under conditions of multiple goals and heavy cognitive load, prior expectations may have an advantage, thereby giving self-fulfilling prophecies an edge, at least in the perceiver's mind.

Under what conditions can a self-fulfilling prophecy be undermined? There appear to be two main conditions: one is when a perceiver "compensates" for the expectation he or she holds about a target; the other is when a target actively tries to dispel the perceiver's false expectations (self-verification). We will consider each in turn. When a perceiver holds a negative expectation about a target, such as the belief that the target is hostile or cold, the perceiver may compensate for, rather than reciprocate, the expected behavior. Thus, for example, if you expect that another person is hostile, rather than being hostile yourself (reciprocating behavior), you may decide to be extra nice (compensatory behavior), hoping that, in so doing, you may minimize the other's unpleasant behavior (see M. H. Bond, 1972; Ickes et al., 1982; Swann & Snyder, 1980).

A study that adopted this format found that subjects who were fore-warned that their partner in a study was cold behaved in a warmer fashion toward that individual than subjects who were forewarned their partner was warm; apparently, the warmer style of the subjects expecting a cold partner was intended to minimize the unpleasantness they anticipated in the interaction. The result of the compensatory strat-egy, not suprisingly, was to elicit behaviors that contradicted the a priori expectation; target individuals who were initially labeled as cold but who were the recipients of those compensatory warm efforts, in fact, behaved more warmly toward their partners than target persons initially labeled as warm, thus canceling any possible self-fulfilling prophecy. However, as in Neuberg's study, despite the warm behavior of targets labeled as cold, perceivers clung to their original hypotheses; targets labeled as cold were perceived as more cold than targets labeled as warm (Ickes et al., 1982).

Why might this happen? As is well known from other work on schemas or theory-guided inferences and on hypothesis testing (see Chapters 5 and 9), behavior that is irrelevant to or even mildly incon-sistent with prior expectations is often, nonetheless, interpreted as be-ing consistent with prior expectations. Hence, a self-fulfilling prophecy can exist in a social perceiver's mind without it being true (see, for ex-ample, Ickes et al., 1982). Nonetheless, compensatory behavioral strat-egies generally are one important check on the development of self-fulfilling prophecies. When perceivers make an effort to avoid conflict, hostility, or other negative encounters, the unpleasantness they antici-pate may well not occur, even though in their own minds, the prophecy may have been confirmed.

Target individuals themselves can also prevent the enactment of a self-fulfilling prophecy by refusing to be miscast into some role they feel does not fit. Each of us has no doubt had the experience of finding someone typing us in a way that does not feel correct; although one may play along temporarily, after a while one is inclined to disabuse him or her, that is to engage in self-verification efforts to reaffirm one's own views of oneself. For example, if I find some acquaintance typing me as a workaholic who rarely has any fun, I will quickly do my best to counteract that impression. Such efforts may not always be successful. The target's belief about the self may be strong, but the perceiver's ex-pectation about the target may be equally strong, thus creating a battle between the perceiver's efforts to confirm expectancies and the target's efforts to self-verify.

The conditions under which a perceiver abandons an incorrect ex-pectation or a target comes to adopt a previously unheld self-attribute may depend upon a variety of moderating conditions (Major et al., 1988). One study found that in the battle between self-verification and expectancy confirmation effects, negative beliefs were more likely to change than positive beliefs (Major et al., 1988). Swann and Ely (1984) have suggested another important condition that may moderate whether targets' self-perceptions or perceivers' behavioral expectations will win out in a social interaction, namely, certainty of one's opinions. They found that self-verification always occurred when targets were certain of their self-conceptions, and it tended to occur when both perceivers and targets were uncertain of their beliefs. Behavior confirmation, namely, the tendency of the target to adopt behaviors related to the expectations held by the perceiver, occurred only when the perceivers were certain of their expectancies but the target was uncertain of his or her self-conception.

Research has suggested some other possibilities (Darley & Fazio, 1980): When the target believes that the perceiver's false impression is based on something the target did, rather than on the perceiver's own personality or on forces in the situation, then the target may be more likely to attempt to correct the misimpression. Simple awareness of the perceiver's false hypothesis can also induce targets actively to overcome perceivers' expectations. Hilton and Darley (1985) found that when targets were informed that a future interaction partner had an impression of them as having a cold personality, they acted in ways designed to overcome the expectancy and were largely successful in these efforts.

Two other factors also appear to be critical in determining whether or not a target will attempt to dispel a perceiver's false impression. The first is how important the perceiver's impression is to the target. False impressions, especially negative ones, held by others important to the target are likely to prompt some dispelling action by the target. A second condition prompting targets to dispel a perceiver's false impression concerns how discrepant the perceiver's impression is from the target's own self-impression. More discrepancy prompts more efforts to undo the impression (see, for example, Baumeister & Jones, 1978; Farina, Allen, & Saul, 1968; Gurwitz & Topol, 1978; Swann, Read, & Hill, 1981). Of course, under some circumstances, the target may find the perceiver's false impression to be so desirable that the target will attempt to fit it and come to see the self as the perceiver does. This is perhaps the most extreme case of the self-fulfilling prophecy, that is, when not only the target's behavior, but his or her own self-impression comes to fit the perceiver's initially false impression (Fazio, Effrein, & Falender, 1981; M. Snyder & Swann, 1978b).

In short, then, self-fulfilling prophecies can be created from initially false definitions of situations through a combination of factors: inferential errors and misperceptions, and reciprocal or complementary behaviors on the part of the perceiver and the target. Self-fulfilling prophecies occur for both positive and negative impressions and across a wide variety of situations. Although there are some circumstances that counter their occurrence, on the whole, biases in both the perceiver's and the target's interpretations of the meaning of behavior and social norms for reciprocating behavior would seem to favor their development.

Some Thoughts on Cognition-Affect-Behavior Relations

In recent years, within social cognition, behavior has received more attention than in its early investigative years (Wegner & Vallacher, 1987). There remains a great deal of room for additional work. For example, although the cognition-behavior relationship has been extensively investigated through such avenues of research as attitude-behavior consistency and cross-situational manifestations of personality traits, these approaches have been fairly narrowly focused on these issues to the relative exclusion of a consideration of the manifold and simultaneous mutual influences of cognitions, affect, and behavior (Quattrone, 1985). Particularly lacking in the area of cognition-behavior relationships is the influence of volitional influences on human behavior (Howard & Conway, 1986). Much research has implicitly or explicitly adopted a deterministic position, suggesting that preexisting traits and beliefs should influence behavior in specific ways. The lack of emphasis on intent and personal choice, for example, is a particular example of this oversight (S. T. Fiske, 1989a).

The complexity of cognition-affect-behavior linkages is substantial, and increasingly, we will need to develop more complex conceptualizations and appropriate methodologies for examining these linkages directly. One promising method involves the listing of covert thoughts and feelings during behavioral interaction, as originally conceptualized by Brock and Greenwald (Brock, 1967; Greenwald, 1968), and applied to dyadic interactions by Ickes and his colleagues (Ickes, Reidhead, & Patterson, 1986; Ickes et al., 1986; Ickes & Tooke, 1988). The work by Cantor and Kihlstrom (1985; 1987) on social intelligence represents another complex model for thinking about the ongoing interplay of thoughts, feelings, and actions in the context of personal goals, strategies, and plans.

Relatively little analysis has been devoted to the impact that behavior has on cognitions and feelings. The behavior-cognition relationship has been investigated in limited ways. For example, recall Bem's (1972) theory of self-perception, which suggests that people infer their attitudes and other qualities in part from the observation of their own behavior. Similarly, through false feedback and misattribution, people can come to believe that certain attitudes or beliefs are characteristic of themselves (Schachter & Singer, 1962; Valins, 1966). These observations imply that behavior and the perception of its meaning are malleable. Indeed, if you think over what you do in a day, you will discover that much of your behavior results from social roles (such as being a student or a professor), preexisting schedules (e.g., you have a class from 1:00 to 3:00), and social norms (knowing that the polite thing to do is to greet a friend in the hall and exchange a few pleasantries). Physical interrupt conditions, such as the need for food or sleep, or the need to stay home to get over the flu, also exert strong influences on what people do. In certain important ways, then, behavior takes care of itself. Yet, these behavioral enactments also shape thoughts and feelings and have often have quite long-lasting implications for one's sense of self (see Chapter 6) and one's attributions for how one behaves (see Chapters 2 and 3).

Perhaps one of the reasons why actions have not been studied as extensively as cognitions and emotions in social cognition research concerns the fact that behavior is so troublesome to interpret (Wegner & Vallacher, 1987). On the one hand, action is often obvious and mundane. Action is also ambiguous and subject to multiple interpretations. There is a propensity for people to impute goals and meaning to actions, when in fact many actions may have none. Action is also highly complex, being determined by multiple factors. Consequently, its meaning is often difficult to derive (Wegner & Vallacher, 1987). Thus, many issues remain to be explored in the manifold relations among thoughts, feelings, and behavior.

SUMMARY

The self-regulation of action is highly dependent upon cognitions and affect. How people behave in a situation depends upon how they define it and the personal goals they adopt for the situation. Affective responses are also important in the self-regulation process. People show considerable flexibility in their ability to adjust their perceptions and behavioral strategies to the exigencies of a particular situation. Much self-regulatory activity proceeds mindlessly, although interruptions in people's plans can lead people to make their goals explicit and adopt alternative methods for meeting them. Expertise, based on how much experience a person has in a social situation, will also determine that flexibility.

The cognition-behavior relationship has been especially explored in the context of research on attitudes and behavior and the circumstances under which they cohere. Attitudes may be more consistent with behaviors that are prototypic for those attitudes. Measuring attitudes and behavior at a comparable level of specificity is another approach to increasing the strength of the relationship. Attitudes formed from direct experience, that are accessible, and that reflect self-interest or values predict behavior well. Focusing on the reasons underlying one's attitudes can reduce attitude-behavior consistency, although this tendency is also moderated by whether the behavior is an end in its own right or in service of another goal.

How behavior is labeled also influences attitude-behavior consistency. Actions may be identified at relatively low levels or they may be identified at higher levels. High-level behaviors tend to be seen as dispositionally based, but they also show considerable behavioral flexibility. Low-level actions, in contrast, may show stability across situations, but may not be perceived as relating to underlying dispositions. Situational factors moderate cognition-behavior consistency by making such factors as social norms or prior attitudes salient. And finally, individual differences in how people approach a situation (e.g., self-monitoring and self-consciousness) influence what attitudes will be salient and guide behavior.

Behavior can be used to test hypotheses about both the self and others. In such cases, people are apparently biased preferentially to seek out information that confirms their hypotheses within certain limits. This bias has the effect of making even conjectural or tentative hypotheses often look more true than they really are.

Under some circumstances, testing a hypothesis about a target can lead the target to behave in ways that confirm the hypothesis; such alterations in reality are termed self-fulfilling prophecies. A self-fulfilling prophecy is most likely to occur if a high-status person holds some false positive impression toward a lower-status target and behaves toward him or her with warm verbal and nonverbal behavior; under most circumstances, the target is likely to reciprocate the behavior, thus confirming the hypothesis. Negative expectations can also produce self-fulfilling prophecies, as when one individual expects another to be unpleasant, behaves unpleasantly in turn, and so elicits the very behavior from the target he or she anticipated.

Potential self-fulfilling prophecies can also be undermined. When individuals hold negative expectations about another, instead of behaving reciprocally (i.e., negatively), they may compensate and act positively, thus eliciting the opposite behavior of what they expected. Nonetheless, perceivers may continue to perceive the target negatively, despite having elicited disconfirming behavior. Self-fulfilling prophecies can be undermined by targets themselves when they are aware that they are being miscast and wish to undo the impression.

Overall, then, the relationship between cognition and behavior is a complex one, moderated by situational factors, individual differences, biases in cognitive processes, and variations in social goals.

13

Conclusion

What Is Missing and How to Fill the Gaps ◆ *The Future of Social Cognition Research*

Taking the long view on the field of social cognition, one may find it useful to look at where the field has been and where it is going. What questions does the research answer, and what questions does it not even ask? Both sets of questions are determined by the characteristics of the field itself. Research on social cognition is guided by no single theoretical framework. Of course, the same is true of other subfields of social psychology, such as attitudes, small groups, interpersonal attraction, and more. Instead, the research consists of relatively autonomous topics, linked by some shared assumptions and a common interest.

The shared assumptions in social cognition research are those described in the opening chapter. Looking back to the beginning of the book, recall that social cognition research shares these basic features: a concentration on mentalistic explanations, a commitment to process analysis, and cross-fertilization between cognitive and social psychology. Within these broad outlines lies a rich variety of (sometimes isolated) theories and approaches.

Nevertheless, all research on social cognition is concerned with how people make sense of other people and themselves. As such, it is a fearfully complex enterprise, and researchers must exploit every useful approach. A fascinating array of insights has been gained even in the short run, and perhaps the best way to review them is to think back over the material covered. (One can reread the chapter summaries for more detail.)

In the early chapters, we saw that some elements of social cognition include attributions and schemas. Attribution theories describe how people go from observing behavior in a situation to analyzing its causes. The process is far from logical and thorough, but attributions serve the important function of granting people some sense of prediction and control over their lives. Schemas are one element that may provide a sense of prediction and control for self and others.

Schemas are abstract expectations about how the world generally operates, built up from past experience with specific examples. Schemas generally guide cognitive processes toward information relevant to prior knowledge. People seem to be conservative animals, by and large, with an emphasis on safeguarding their limited capacities. Efficiency, predictability, and generalization sometimes win out over accuracy about specific situations.

Various cognitive processes operate along these principles, although there are some checks and balances. Attention is captured by stimuli that are unexpected. Attention to discrepancies can set in motion an adjustment of expectations to close the gap. Memory is organized in terms of prior knowledge, although certainly it is not relentlessly fixed that way. Depending on the situation, memory can favor the retrieval of information discrepant with one's expectations. And, depending on one's goals and one's context, memory is flexible enough to be organized around different types of prior knowledge. Inferences also are heavily influenced by prior theories and shortcuts, but inferences are responsive to some forms of feedback. In short, cognitive processes tend to be conservative, but they have some built-in quality controls.

Cognitions carry over to affect, attitudes, and behavior, in many respects. Cognitions can give rise to affective responses, to attitude change, and to behavioral strategies. But cognitions, affect, and behavior also are fairly autonomous and often do not predict each other terribly well, at least in any simple way. Each is a complex system in its own right, with some spillover to the other three. These linkages are becoming better understood all the time.

In reviewing the insights of social cognition, one sees how the social perceiver typically simplifies the world, aiming more for sufficient, rapid understanding rather than accurate, slower understanding. As noted, however, the cognitive system provides some built-in quality controls. The motivational system, operating within a social and personal context, also determines how carefully perceivers process information about self and others. Motivation interacts with a variety of cognitive factors in attributions, schemas, self-concept, encoding, memory, inference, and attitudes. Recent research in social cognition emphasizes this interplay of motivation and cognition.

WHAT IS MISSING AND HOW TO FILL THE GAPS

Having reviewed the insights gained by the last decade of research on social cognition, it is useful to see what questions remain unanswered and what questions remain unasked. Where does the field fall short of its aims, and what is likely to be done about it? The view concerning people that more or less dominated the field up until recently, as we have said, was the cognitive miser perspective. That is, the social perceiver often compromises the thorough, logical, normatively correct procedures that the naive scientist would use. Sometimes people are smart to do this; many of the shortcuts that people develop work well most of the time. More recently, a view has emerged that depicts the perceiver as a motivated tactician, which provides a broader perspective. Nevertheless, research in social cognition sometimes depicts the social perceiver rather narrowly, in several respects (cf. Manis, 1977; S. E. Taylor, 1981b).

First, the social perceiver is viewed primarily as a thinker, motivated to understand and predict the environment fairly efficiently, where possible. Other motives and goals are all too often ignored. But people have other goals that differ from sheer understanding for its own sake. For example, what about the moral person? Sometimes people are motivated to think about the just, proper, or fair judgment to make, rather than the most efficient first approximation. Besides the moral person, there is the public person, who worries about saving face. There is also the amusing person, whose goal is to entertain the self or others, merely to make life more pleasant. This person thinks quirky thoughts, plays mental games, and passes the time in search of sheer delight or novelty. Similarly, there is the altruistic person, who thinks about others in order to help them, not to understand, predict, or control them. And there is the antisocial person, who thinks about others in order to hurt them.

The list could go on, but an exhaustive taxonomy of possible goals simply is not useful. The more important point is that cognition serves many masters, and efficient or accurate understanding is only one of them. The solution to this neglect of other motives and goals already is on the horizon in several places. Psychologists have urged research on the moral person (naive judge or naive lawyer) (Fincham & Jaspars, 1980). The public person is becoming integrated into research on social cognition by the work on impression management (Chapters 6 and 12). Person memory researchers showing the effects of goals on recall also begin to address these issues (Chapter 8). And all the goal-oriented conditions of schema use (Chapter 5) decidedly reflect this emphasis on a variety of motives.

In all fairness, the task of the field of social cognition is to help us understand how people think about other people, not to understand how they soothe their nagging consciences or protect their fragile egos. Nonetheless, the effects of various processing goals, other than simple efficient understanding, likely will continue to grow in importance, especially with the development of the motivated tactician view of the social thinker.

A related point is how efficient the thinker really is. Neglecting accuracy in the interest of enhancing efficiency is one thing, but maximizing efficiency is another. Just as certainly as people are not optimally precise naive scientists, neither are they optimally efficient information processors. A whiz-kid view of the social perceiver would be just as misguided as the naive scientist view. People's understanding processes doubtless can be highly redundant, laborious, circuitous, time-consuming, and anything but efficient. Thus, it is important not to overdo the role of efficiency as the main goal, nor is it appropriate to assume that efficiency is maximized even when it is a major goal.

In addition to being viewed primarily as a thinker, the social perceiver is often viewed as having a somewhat lunatic disregard for external reality. This fantasizer seems to operate solely on whatever convenient fictions are in his or her own head. While there is no doubt that social perceivers actively construct interpretations of the world around them, it is also true that reality imposes constraints on the process. Essentially this complaint has been raised by the Gibsonians, who argue for careful analyses of objective stimulus properties and of possible perceiver-stimulus interactions (Chapter 7). Perception is not all in the head; at least some of it is out in the world. The solution to this focus on the thinker as fantasizer is a thorough analysis of the actual stimuli confronting the perceiver.

The social perceiver also has been viewed as somewhat of a hermit, isolated from the social environment. Missing from much research on social cognition have been other people in a status other than that of stimulus. Other people are not simply targets; they reinforce, disagree, initiate, and otherwise actively inform the perceiver. Perception often is modified through social interaction. When people want to understand themselves and others, they may ask someone else. Problem solving often occurs not simply cognitively but also socially. Some solutions are emerging to counteract the omission of social interaction from social cognition research. One solution appears, for example, in the work on cognitive bases of attitude change in groups (Chapter 11). Another solution appears in theories about group memory (see Chapter 8). Elsewhere, too, social cognition research will likely begin to recognize the importance of real interaction contexts, minds in contact with other minds.

Social perception also has been viewed more or less statically. People do not take snapshots of their world; perception is not frozen in time. Perceptions are transformed as the perceiver and the environment grow and change. When the perceiver is depicted as isolated in time, he or she inevitably ends up contemplating old events, as does an archivist, because any photograph of the present immediately becomes the past. The perceiver as archivist does not contemplate the future. Yet, real people constantly speculate about the future. People often run through mental simulations to predict, control, or understand their possible future. Researchers studying plans and goals recognize this, as do those who research affect and alternative future worlds (Chapters 9 and 11).

In addition, the social perceiver often has been observed in rather impersonal, superficial, inconsequential settings, as if perceivers were dilettantes. Social perception concerning important life events and intimate relationships may differ considerably from social perception in the

lab experiment. For one thing, people dedicate more effort to social understanding when the stakes are higher. They think more, if not more accurately. Applied work on social cognition recognizes this fact explicitly.

Finally, people are not blank slates; they apply world knowledge
specific to whatever domain they are contemplating. People draw on
the resources available, and they vary in their levels of knowledge
when it comes to real-world phenomena, ranging from health to politics. People may use different information-processing strategies, depending on how much or how little they know. For example, people
who are moderately knowledgeable about an idea may be more sensitive to variations in a routine than are novices, who might skip over them.
In addition, regardless of knowledge level, some domains may elicit different strategies than others. For example, concerns about health are
more likely to implicate issues of personal control than are concerns
about international politics. Similarly, understanding a specific person
on your doorstep is more likely to implicate stimulus-based attentional
processes, while understanding one's high-school sweetheart in retrospect is more likely to implicate memory processes. Many models of social cognition are developed as if they can be independent of the particular domain of judgment, and this is clearly too narrow a view.

To summarize, social cognition research has developed models of
people as thinkers, shortchanging other possible goals; as whiz kids,
who are impossibly efficient; as fantasizers, ignoring objective reality;
as hermits, isolated from the social environment; as archivists, forever
looking backward; as dilettantes, outside of consequential social settings; and as blank slates with little domain-specific knowledge. In
these senses, work on social cognition has been overly narrow.

In another sense, work on social cognition has not been narrow
enough or, rather, precise enough. Theoretical coherence and methodological specificity are the twin goals of science. Refining both in social
cognition work is an ongoing effort. Besides the perennial adoption of
cognitive methodology that is a hallmark of this work, movements toward physiological measures, toward computer simulation, and toward
more sophisticated statistical techniques represent efforts to work toward methodological precision. A lot has been learned already; the understanding of people's social thoughts has become far deeper and
more complex than it was twenty years ago. The fine-grained methodological approach clearly has paid off, and it will continue to do so.

Theoretical coherence is a more nebulous challenge. No area of social psychology—be it attitudes, attraction, groups, stereotyping, aggression, or altruism—profits from being totally tied down to a single
theoretical perspective. Attribution theories emerged in part as a reaction to the great overarching framework formerly provided by consistency theories. Following that, an assortment of loosely linked social
cognition theories of information processing has emerged. The assortment gives the field a rich range of perspectives on which to draw, but

it may give the newcomer a dizzying sense of excess. And it gives the field a certain lack of cohesion. Nevertheless, the areas of consensus are important. There is a strong shared commitment to understanding the mental processes that occur when people try to understand themselves and others. And there is a message that people muddle along sufficiently well, trying to be efficient, but sometimes at a cost to accuracy and complexity.

THE FUTURE OF SOCIAL COGNITION RESEARCH

In two decades of concentrated research, considerable progress has been made. An exciting and fast-growing area of research came into being and created major academic enterprises (articles, books, journals) and major insightful applications (into education, health, law, politics, marketing). The applied side of social cognition research is a critical measure of its success, for two reasons. First, it provides a check on the necessarily constraining assumptions of the lab. Second, it provides a test of the usefulness of the theories. Both these points are critical to the future.

Social cognition researchers have developed elaborate models of how people make inferences when asked to do so in laboratory experiments. In the next several years researchers will probably study people's spontaneous cognitive processes when no one is asking them to think. How do people think in natural settings, when other demands are placed on them? For example, do they make as many attributions as often as social cognition researchers assume they do? When something needs explaining, it is rare that ordinary people are as thoughtful even as many social cognition models suggest. Rather, people often attend to whatever intrudes on them, remember whatever comes to mind most easily, and make inferences using very simple rules. People simplify the real world in order to get by. Stepping outside the laboratory will continue to remind researchers of these aspects of much ordinary thought.

Applications to naturalistic settings also will test the usefulness of social cognition approaches. A theory is of little use if it does not explain something of real concern. The characteristics of real-world situations in which social cognitions appear to have the most impact is important ground for future research. Where and when interventions based on social cognition research seem to work the best will continue to be a proving ground for the field of social cognition.

In a field that has witnessed an explosion of research and theory in the past twenty years, consolidation of theory and research is the next likely order of business. With it, there is likely to be increasing emphasis on the roles of social cognition in affectively and behaviorally significant areas. Applied research simultaneously provides continued tests of ideas about social cognition and opportunities for impact in important social settings.

References

Abele, A. (1985). Thinking about thinking: Causal, evaluative and finalistic cognitions about social situations. *European Journal of Social Psychology, 15,* 315–332.

Abelson, R. P. (1976). Script processing in attitude formation and decision making. In J. S. Carroll & J. W. Payne (Eds.), *Cognition and social behavior* (pp. 33–46). Hillsdale, NJ: Erlbaum.

Abelson, R. P. (1981a). *Constraint, construal, and cognitive science.* Proceedings of the Third Annual Cognitive Science Society Conference, Berkeley, CA.

Abelson, R. P. (1981b). The psychological status of the script concept. *American Psychologist, 36,* 715–729.

Abelson, R. P. (1983). Whatever became of consistency theory? *Personality and Social Psychology Bulletin, 9,* 37–54.

Abelson, R. P. (1988). Conviction. *American Psychologist, 43,* 267–275.

Abelson, R. P., Aronson, E., McGuire, W. J., Newcomb, T. M., Rosenberg, M. J., & Tannenbaum, P. H. (Eds.) (1968). *Theories of cognitive consistency: A sourcebook.* Chicago: Rand McNally.

Abelson, R. P., & Gross, P. H. (1987). The strength of conjunctive explanations. *Personality and Social Psychology Bulletin, 13,* 141–155.

Abelson, R. P., & Kanouse, D. E. (1966). Subjective acceptance of verbal generalizations. In S. Feldman (Ed.), *Cognitive consistency: Motivational antecedents and behavioral consequents* (pp. 171–197). New York: Academic Press.

Abelson, R. P., Kinder, D. R., Peters, M. D., & Fiske, S. T. (1982). Affective and semantic components in political person perception. *Journal of Personality and Social Psychology, 42,* 619–630.

Abelson, R. P., & Prentice, D. A. (1989). Beliefs as possessions: A functional perspective. In A. R. Pratkanis, S. J. Breckler, & A. G. Greenwald (Eds.), *Attitude structure and function* (pp. 361–382). Hillsdale, NJ: Erlbaum.

Abrams, D. (1985). Focus of attention in minimal intergroup discrimination. *British Journal of Social Psychology, 24,* 65–74.

Abrams, D. & Hogg, M. A. (1988). Comments on the motivational status of self-esteem in social identity and intergroup discrimination. *European Journal of Social Psychology, 18,* 317–334.

Abrams, R. D., & Finesinger, J. E. (1953). Guilt reactions in patients with cancer. *Cancer, 6,* 474–482.

Abramson, L. Y., & Alloy, L. B. (1981). Depression, non-depression, and cognitive illusions: A reply to Schwartz. *Journal of Experimental Social Psychology, 110*, 436–447.

Abramson, L. Y., Seligman, M. E. P., & Teasdale, J. D. (1978). Learned helplessness in humans: Critique and reformulation. *Journal of Abnormal Psychology, 87*, 49–74.

Acorn, D. A., Hamilton, D. L., & Sherman, S. J. (1988). Generalization of biased perceptions of groups based on illusory correlations. *Social Cognition, 6*, 345–372.

Adorno, T. W., Frenkel-Brunswik, E., Levinson, D. J., & Sanford, R. N. (1950). *The authoritarian personality.* New York: Harper.

Agatstein, F. C., & Buchanan, D. B. (1984). Public and private self-consciousness and the recall of self-relevant information. *Personality and Social Psychology Bulletin, 10*, 314–325.

Aitkenhead, M. (1984). Impression-management and consistency effects in the processing of feedback. *British Journal of Social Psychology, 23*, 213–222.

Ajzen, I. (1977). Intuitive theories of events and the effects of baserate information on prediction. *Journal of Personality and Social Psychology, 35*, 303–314.

Ajzen, I. (1987). Attitudes, traits, and actions: Dispositional prediction of behavior in personality and social psychology. In L. Berkowitz (Ed.), *Advances in experimental social psychology* (Vol. 20, pp. 1–64). San Diego, CA: Academic Press.

Ajzen, I. (1988). *Attitudes, personality, and behavior.* Chicago: Dorsey.

Ajzen, I., & Fishbein, M. (1977). Attitude-behavior relations: A theoretical analysis and review of empirical research. *Psychological Bulletin, 84*, 888–918.

Ajzen, I., & Fishbein, M. (1980). *Understanding attitudes and predicting social behavior.* Englewood Cliffs, NJ: Prentice-Hall.

Ajzen, I., & Holmes, W. H. (1976). Uniqueness of behavioral effects in causal attribution. *Journal of Personality, 44*, 98–108.

Ajzen, I., & Madden, T. J. (1986). Prediction of goal-directed behavior: Attitudes, intentions, and perceived behavioral control. *Journal of Experimental Social Psychology, 22*, 453–474.

Ajzen, I., Timko, C., & White, J. B. (1982). Self-monitoring and the attitude-behavior relation. *Journal of Personality and Social Psychology, 42*, 426–435.

Alba, J. W. & Hasher, L. (1983). Is memory schematic? *Psychological Bulletin, 93*, 203–231.

Albright, L., Kenny, D. A., & Malloy, T. E. (1988). Consensus in personality judgments at zero acquaintance. *Journal of Personality and Social Psychology, 55*, 387–395.

Aldrich, J. H., Sullivan, J. L., & Borgida, E. (1989). Foreign affairs and issue voting: Do Presidential candidates "waltz before a blind audience?" *American Political Science Review, 83*, 123–141.

Alexander, C. N., Jr., & Knight, G. W. (1971). Situated identities and social psychological experimentation. *Sociometry, 34*, 65–82.

Alexander, C. N., Langer, E. J., Newman, R. I., Chandler, H. M., & Davies, J. L. (1989). Transcendental meditation, mindfulness, and longevity: An experimental study with the elderly. *Journal of Personality and Social Psychology, 57*, 950–964.

Alicke, M. D. (1985). Global self-evaluation as determined by the desirability and controllability of trait adjectives. *Journal of Personality and Social Psychology, 49,* 1621–1630.

Alicke, M. D., & Insko, C. A. (1984). Sampling of similar and dissimilar comparison persons and objects as a function of the generality of attribution goal. *Journal of Personality and Social Psychology, 46,* 763–777.

Allen, R. B., & Ebbesen, E. B. (1981). Cognitive processes in person perception: Retrieval of personality trait and behavioral information. *Journal of Experimental Social Psychology, 17,* 119–141.

Allen, V. L., & Wilder, D. A. (1975). Categorization, belief similarity, and intergroup discrimination. *Journal of Personality and Social Psychology, 32,* 971–977.

Allen, V. L., & Wilder, D. A. (1979). Group categorization and attribution of belief similarity. *Small Group Behavior, 10,* 73–80.

Allison, S. T., & Messick, D. M. (1985). The group attribution error. *Journal of Experimental Social Psychology, 21,* 563–579.

Allison, S. T., & Messick, D. M. (1988). The feature-positive effect, attitude strength, and degree of perceived consensus. *Personality and Social Psychology Bulletin, 14,* 231–241.

Alloy, L. B. (1988). Expectations and situational information as contributors to covariation assessment: A reply to Goddard and Allan. *Psychological Review, 95,* 299–301.

Alloy, L. B., Peterson, C., Abramson, L. Y., & Seligman, M. E. P. (1984). Attributional style and the generality of learned helplessness. *Journal of Personality and Social Psychology, 46,* 681–687.

Alloy, L. B., & Tabachnik, N. (1984). Assessment of covariation by humans and animals: The joint influence of prior expectations and current situational information. *Psychological Review, 91,* 112–149.

Allport, G. W. (1935). Attitudes. In C. Murchison (Ed.), *Handbook of social psychology* (pp. 798–844). Worcester, MA: Clark University Press.

Allport, G. W. (1954). *The nature of prejudice.* Reading, MA: Addison-Wesley.

Amabile, T. M., Hennessey, B. A., & Grossman, B. S. (1986). Social influences on creativity: The effects of contracted-for reward. *Journal of Personality and Social Psychology, 50,* 14–23.

Amir, Y. (1976). The role of intergroup contact in change of prejudice and ethnic relations. In P. A. Katz (Ed.), *Toward the elimination of racism* (pp. 245–308). New York: Pergamon Press.

Andersen, S. M. (1984). Self-knowledge and social inference: II. The diagnosticity of cognitive/affective and behavioral data. *Journal of Personality and Social Psychology, 46,* 294–307.

Andersen, S. M. (1987). The role of cultural assumptions in self-concept development. In K. Yardley & T. Honess (Eds.), *Self and identity: Psychosocial perspectives* (pp. 231–246). New York: Wiley.

Andersen, S. M., & Bem, S. L. (1981). Sex typing and androgyny in dyadic interaction: Individual differences in responsiveness to physical attractiveness. *Journal of Personality and Social Psychology, 41,* 74–86.

Andersen, S. M., & Klatzky, R. L. (1987). Traits and social stereotypes: Levels of categorization in person perception. *Journal of Personality and Social Psychology, 53,* 235–246.

Andersen, S. M., Lazowski, L. E., & Donisi, M. (1986). Salience and self-inference: The role of biased recollections in self-inference process. *Social Cognition, 4,* 75–95.

Andersen, S. M., & Ross, L. (1984). Self-knowledge and social inference: I. The impact of cognitive/affective and behavioral data. *Journal of Personality and Social Psychology, 46,* 280–293.

Andersen, S. M., & Williams, M. (1985). Cognitive/affective reactions in the improvement of self-esteem: When thoughts and feelings make a difference. *Journal of Personality and Social Psychology, 49,* 1086–1097.

Anderson, C. A. (1982). Inoculation and counter-explanation: Debiasing techniques in the perseverance of social theories. *Social Cognition, 1,* 126–139.

Anderson, C. A. (1983). Abstract and concrete data in the perseverance of social theories: When weak data lead to unshakeable beliefs. *Journal of Experimental Social Psychology, 19,* 93–108.

Anderson, C. A. (1985). Actor and observer attributions for different types of situations: Causal-structure effects, individual differences, and the dimensionality of causes. *Social Cognition, 3,* 323–340.

Anderson, C.A., & Arnoult, L. H. (1985a). Attributional models of depression, loneliness, and shyness. In J. Harvey & G. Weary (Eds.), *Attribution: Basic issues and applications* (pp. 235–279). London: Academic Press.

Anderson, C. A., & Arnoult, L. H. (1985b). Attributional style and everyday problems in living: Depression, loneliness, and shyness. *Social Cognition, 3,* 16–35.

Anderson, C. A., & Godfrey, S. S. (1987). Thoughts about actions: The effects of specificity and availability of imagined behavioral scripts on expectations about oneself and others. *Social Cognition, 5,* 238–258.

Anderson, C. A., Horowitz, L. M., & French, R. D. (1983). Attributional style of lonely and depressed people. *Journal of Personality and Social Psychology, 45,* 127–136.

Anderson, C. A., Jennings, D.L., & Arnoult, L. H. (1988). The validity and utility of the attributional style construct at a moderate level of specificity. *Journal of Personality and Social Psychology, 55,* 979–990.

Anderson, C. A., Lane, D. M., & Kellam, K. L. (1986). Functional relations are not models: A note on covariation detection. *Journal of Experimental Social Psychology, 12,* 110–111.

Anderson, C. A., Lepper, M. R., & Ross, L. (1980). Perseverance of social theories: The role of explanation in the persistence of discredited information. *Journal of Personality and Social Psychology, 39,* 1037–1049.

Anderson, C. A., New, B. L., & Speer, J. R. (1985). Argument availability as a mediator of social theory perseverance. *Social Cognition, 3,* 235–249.

Anderson, C. A., & Sechler, E. S. (1986). Effects of explanation and counter-explanation on the development and use of social theories. *Journal of Personality and Social Psychology, 50,* 24–34.

Anderson, C. A., & Slusher, M. P. (1986). Relocating motivational effects: A synthesis of cognitive and motivational effects on attributions for success and failure. *Social Cognition, 4,* 250–292.

Anderson, J. R. (1974). Retrieval of propositional information from long-term memory. *Cognitive Psychology, 6,* 451–474.

Anderson, J. R. (1976). *Language, memory, and thought.* Hillsdale, NJ: Erlbaum.

Anderson, J. R. (1978). Arguments concerning representations for mental imagery. *Psychological Review, 85,* 249–277.

Anderson, J. R. (1979). Further arguments concerning representations for mental imagery: A reply to Hayes-Roth and Pylyshyn. *Psychological Review, 86,* 395–406.

Anderson, J. R. (1980a). *Cognitive psychology and its implications.* San Francisco: Freeman.

Anderson, J. R. (1980b). Concepts, propositions, and schemata: What are the cognitive units? *Nebraska Symposium on Motivation* (Vol. 28, pp. 121–162). Lincoln: University of Nebraska Press.

Anderson, J. R. (1982). Acquisition of cognitive skill. *Psychological Review, 89,* 389–406.

Anderson, J. R. (1983). *The architecture of cognition.* Cambridge, MA: Harvard University Press.

Anderson, J. R. (1990). *Cognitive psychology and its implications* (3rd ed.). New York: Freeman.

Anderson, J. R., & Bower, G. H. (1973). *Human associative memory.* Washington, D.C.: Winston & Sons.

Anderson, J. R., & Hastie, R. (1974). Individuation and reference in memory: Proper names and definite descriptions. *Cognitive Psychology, 6,* 495–514.

Anderson, J. R., Kline, P. J., & Beasley, C. M., Jr. (1979). A general learning theory and its application to schema abstraction. In G. H. Bower (Ed.), *The psychology of learning and motivation* (pp. 236–318). New York: Academic Press.

Anderson, N. H. (1966). Component ratings in impression formation. *Psychonomic Science, 6,* 179–180.

Anderson, N. H. (1974). Information integration: A brief survey. In D. H. Krantz, R. C. Atkinson, R. D. Luce, & P. Suppes (Eds.), *Contemporary developments in mathematical psychology* (pp. 236–305). San Francisco: Freeman.

Anderson, N. H. (1981a). *Foundations of information integration theory.* New York: Academic Press.

Anderson, N. H. (1981b). Integration theory applied to cognitive responses and attitudes. In R. E. Petty, T. M. Ostrom, & T. C. Brock (Eds.), *Cognitive responses in persuasion* (pp. 361–398). Hillsdale, NJ: Erlbaum.

Anderson, N. H. (1989a). Functional memory and on-line attribution. In J. N. Bassili (Ed.), *On-line cognition in person perception* (pp. 175–220). Hillsdale, NJ: Erlbaum.

Anderson, N. H. (1989b). Information integration approach to emotions and their measurement. In R. Plutchik & H. Kellerman (Eds.), *Emotion: Theory, research, and experience* (Vol. 4, pp. 133–186). New York: Academic Press.

Anderson, N. H., & Hubert, S. (1963). Effects of concomitant verbal recall on order effects in personality impression formation. *Journal of Verbal Learning and Verbal Behavior, 2,* 379–391.

Anderson, N. H., & Lampel, A. K. (1965). Effect of context on ratings of personality traits. *Psychonomic Science,* 433–434.

Anderson, R. C., & Pichert, J. W. (1978). Recall of previously unrecallable information following a shift in perspective. *Journal of Verbal Learning and Verbal Behavior, 17,* 1–12.

Antaki, C. (1985). Ordinary explanation in conversation: Causal structures and their defence. *European Journal of Social Psychology, 15,* 213–230.

Antaki, C., & Fielding, G. (1981). Research into ordinary explanation. In C. Antaki (Ed.), *The psychology of ordinary explanations of social behavior* (pp. 109–142). London: Academic Press.

Antrobus, J. S., Fein, G., Goldstein, S., & Singer, J. L. (1989). *Mindwandering: Time-sharing task-irrelevant thought and imagery with experimental tasks.* Unpublished manuscript.

Antrobus, J. S., Singer, J. L., Goldstein, S., & Fortgang, M. (1970). Mindwandering and cognitive structure. *Transactions of the New York Academy of Sciences, 32,* 242–252.

Apsler, R., & Sears, D. O. (1968). Warning, personal involvement, and attitude change. *Journal of Personality and Social Psychology, 9,* 162–166.

Arcuri, L. (1982). Three patterns of social categorization in attribution memory. *European Journal of Social Psychology, 12,* 271–282.

Areni, C. S., & Lutz, R. J. (1988). The role of argument quality in the elaboration likelihood model. *Advances in Consumer Research, 15,* 197–203.

Argyle, M., & Crossland, J. (1987). The dimensions of positive emotions. *British Journal of Social Psychology, 26,* 127–137.

Aristotle. (1931). On memory and recollection. In W. D. Ross (Ed.), J. I. Beare (trans.), *The works of Aristotle.* Oxford, England: Clarendon Press.

Arkes, H. R., & Harkness, A. R. (1980). Effect of making a diagnosis on subsequent recognition of symptoms. *Journal of Experimental Psychology: Human Learning and Memory, 6,* 568–575.

Arkes, H. R., & Rothbart, M. (1985). Memory, retrieval, and contingency judgments. *Journal of Personality and Social Psychology, 49,* 598–606.

Arkin, R. M. (1987). Shyness and self-presentation. In K. Yardley & T. Honess (Eds.), *Self and identity: Psychosocial perspectives* (pp. 187–195). London: Wiley.

Arkin, R. M., Appelman, A. J., & Burger, J. M. (1980). Social anxiety, self-presentation, and the self-serving bias in causal attribution. *Journal of Personality and Social Psychology, 38,* 23–35.

Arkin, R. M., & Baumgardner, A. H. (1985). Self-handicapping. In J. H. Harvey & G. Weary (Eds.), *Attribution: Basic issues and applications* (pp. 169–202). New York: Academic Press.

Arkin, R. M., & Baumgardner, A. H. (1986). Self-presentation and self-evaluation: Processes of self-control and social-control. In R. F. Baumeister (Ed.)., *Public self and private self* (pp. 75–97). New York: Springer-Verlag.

Arkin, R. M. & Shepperd, J. A. (1989). Strategic self-presentation: An overview. In M. Cody & M. McLaughlin (Eds.), *Psychology of tactical communication* (pp. 175–193). Clevedon, England: Multilingual Matters.

Arnold, M. B. (1945). Physiological differentiation of emotional states. *Psychological Review, 52,* 35–48.

Arnold, M. B. (1970). Perennial problems in the field of emotion. In M. B. Arnold (Ed.), *Feelings and emotions: The Loyola Symposium* (pp. 169–185). New York: Academic Press.

Asch, S. E. (1946). Forming impressions of personality. *Journal of Abnormal and Social Psychology, 41,* 1230–1240.

Asch, S. E., & Zukier, H. (1984). Thinking about persons. *Journal of Personality and Social Psychology, 46,* 1230–1240.

Ashmore, R. D. (1981). Sex stereotypes and implicit personality theory. In D. L. Hamilton (Ed.), *Cognitive processes in stereotyping and intergroup behavior* (pp. 37–81). Hillsdale, NJ: Erlbaum.

Ashmore, R. D. & Del Boca, F. K. (1979). Sex stereotypes and implicit personality theory: Toward a cognitive-social psychological conception. *Sex Roles, 5,* 219–248.

Assor, A., Aronoff, J., & Messe, L. A. (1981). Attribute relevance as a moderator of the effects of motivation on impression formation. *Journal of Personality and Social Psychology, 41*, 789–796.

Assor, A., Aronoff, J., & Messe, L. A. (1986). An experimental test of defensive processes in impression formation. *Journal of Personality and Social Psychology, 50*, 644–650.

Austen, J. (1922). *Mansfield Park*. New York: Dutton.

Averill, J. R. (1973). Personal control over aversive stimuli and its relationship to stress. *Psychological Bulletin, 80*, 286–303.

Averill, J. R. (1980). On the paucity of positive emotions. In K. Blankstein, P. Pliner, & J. Polivy (Eds.), *Advances in the study of communication and affect. Vol. 6. Assessment and modification of emotional behavior* (pp. 7–45). New York: Plenum.

Averill, J. R. (1983). Studies on anger and aggression: Implications for theories of emotion. *American Psychologist, 38*, 1145–1160.

Averill, J. R. (1990a). Emotions as episodic dispositions, cognitive schemas, and transitory social roles: Steps toward an integrated theory of emotion. In D. J. Ozer, J. M. Healy, Jr., & A. J. Stewart (Eds.), *Perspectives in personality: Vol. 3a. Self and emotion* (pp. 137–165). Greenwich, CT: JAI Press.

Averill, J. R. (1990b). Emotions in relation to systems of behavior. In N. L. Stein, B. Leventhal, & T. Trabasso (Eds.), *Psychological and biological approaches to emotion* (pp. 385–404) Hillsdale, NJ: LEA.

Averill, J. R. (1990c). Inner feelings, works of the flesh, the beast within, diseases of the mind, driving force, and putting on a show: Six metaphors of emotion and their theoretical extensions. In D. Leary (Ed.), *Metaphors in the history of psychology* (pp. 104–132). Cambridge, England: Cambridge University Press.

Ax, A. F. (1953). Physiological differentiation of emotional states. *Psychosomatic Medicine, 15*, 433–442.

Axsom, D., Yates, S., & Chaiken, S. (1987). Audience response as a heuristic cue in persuasion. *Journal of Personality and Social Psychology, 53*, 30–40.

Backman, C. W. (1988). The self: A dialectical approach. In L. Berkowitz (Ed.), *Advances in experimental social psychology* (Vol. 21, pp. 229–260). New York: Academic Press.

Baddeley, A. D. (1978). The trouble with levels: A reexamination of Craik and Lockhart's framework for memory research. *Psychological Review, 85*, 139–152.

Bagozzi, R. P. (1981). Attitudes, intentions, and behavior: A test of some key hypotheses. *Journal of Personality and Social Psychology, 41*, 607–627.

Bagozzi, R. P., & Burnkrant, R. E. (1979). Attitude organization and the attitude-behavior relationship. *Journal of Personality and Social Psychology, 37*, 913–929.

Bahrick, H. P., Bahrick, P. O., & Wittlinger, R. P. (1975). Fifty years of memory for names and faces: A cross-sectional approach. *Journal of Experimental Psychology: General, 104*, 54–75.

Bandura, A. (1977). *Social learning theory*. Englewood Cliffs, NJ: Prentice-Hall.

Bandura, A. (1982). Self-efficacy mechanism in human agency. *American Psychologist, 37*, 122–147.

Bandura, A. (1986). *Social foundations of thought and action: A social cognitive theory*. Englewood Cliffs, NJ: Prentice-Hall.

Barclay, A. M. (1970). The effect of female aggressive and sexual fantasies. *Journal of Projective Techniques and Personality Assessment, 34,* 19–26.

Barclay, A. M., & Haber, R. N. (1965). The relation of aggressive to sexual motivation. *Journal of Personality, 33,* 462–475.

Barden, R. C., Garber, J., Leiman, B., Ford, M. E., & Masters, J. C. (1985). Factors governing the effective remediation of negative affect and its cognitive and behavioral consequences. *Journal of Personality and Social Psychology, 49,* 1040–1053.

Bargh, J. A. (1982). Attention and automaticity in the processing of self-relevant information. *Journal of Personality and Social Psychology, 43,* 425–436.

Bargh, J. A. (1984). Automatic and conscious processing of social information. In R. S. Wyer, Jr., & T. K. Srull (Eds.), *Handbook of social cognition* (Vol. 3, pp. 1–44). Hillsdale, NJ: Erlbaum.

Bargh, J. A. (1989). Conditional automaticity: Varieties of automatic influence in social perception and cognition. In J. S. Uleman & J. A. Bargh (Eds.), *Unintended thought* (pp. 3–51). New York: Guilford Press.

Bargh, J. A. (1990). Auto-motives: Preconscious determinants of social interaction. In E. T. Higgins & R. M. Sorrentino (Eds.), *Handbook of motivation and cognition: Foundations of social behavior* (Vol. 2, pp. 93–130). New York: Guilford Press.

Bargh, J. A., Bond, R. N., Lombardi, W. L., & Tota, M. E. (1986). The additive nature of chronic and temporary sources of construct accessibility. *Journal of Personality and Social Psychology, 50,* 869–879.

Bargh, J. A., Chaiken, S., Govender, R., & Pratto, F. (1990). *The generality of the automatic attitude activation effect.* Unpublished manuscript, New York University.

Bargh, J. A., Lombardi, W. J., & Higgins, E. T. (1988). Automaticity of chronically accessible constructs in person X situation effects on person perception: It's just a matter of time. *Journal of Personality and Social Psychology, 55,* 599–605.

Bargh, J. A., & Pietromonaco, P. (1982). Automatic information processing and social perception: The influence of trait information presented outside of conscious awareness on impression formation. *Journal of Personality and Social Psychology, 43,* 437–449.

Bargh, J. A., & Pratto, F. (1986). Individual construct accessibility and perceptual selection. *Journal of Experimental Social Psychology, 22,* 293–311.

Bargh, J. A., & Thein, R. D. (1985). Individual construct accessibility, person memory, and the recall-judgment link: The case of information overload. *Journal of Personality and Social Psychology, 49,* 1129–1146.

Bargh, J. A., & Tota, M. E. (1988). Context-dependent automatic processing in depression: Accessibility of negative constructs with regard to self but not others. *Journal of Personality and Social Psychology, 54,* 925–939.

Bar-Hillel, M. (1980). The base-rate fallacy in probability judgments. *Acta Psychologica, 44,* 211–233.

Bar-Hillel, M., & Fischhoff, B. (1981). When do base rates affect predictions? *Journal of Personality and Social Psychology, 41,* 671–680.

Barnett, P. A., & Gotlib, I. H. (1988) Psychosocial functioning and depression: Distinguishing among antecedents, concomitants, and consequences. *Psychological Bulletin, 104,* 97–126.

Baron, J., & Hershey, J. C. (1988). Outcome bias in decision evaluation. *Journal of Personality and Social Psychology, 54,* 569–579.

Baron, R. A. (1977). *Human aggression.* New York: Plenum.

Baron, R. A. (1983). Sweet smell of success? The impact of pleasant artificial scents on evaluations of job applicants. *Journal of Applied Psychology, 68,* 709–713.

Baron, R. M. (1980a). Contrasting approaches to social knowing: An ecological perspective. *Personality and Social Psychology Bulletin, 6,* 590–600.

Baron, R. M. (1980b). Social knowing from an ecological-event perspective: A consideration of the relative domains of power for cognitive and perceptual modes of knowing. In J. H. Harvey (Ed.), *Cognition, social behavior and the environment* (pp. 61–92). Hillsdale, NJ: Erlbaum.

Baron, R. M. (1984). Distinguishing between perceptual and cognitive "groundings" for consistency theories: Epistemological implications. *Personality and Social Psychology Bulletin, 10,* 165–174.

Baron, R. M. (1988). An ecological framework for establishing a dual-mode theory of social knowing. In D. Bar-Tal & A. W. Kruglanski (Eds.), *The social psychology of knowledge* (pp. 48–82). New York: Cambridge University Press.

Barsalou, L. W. (1985). Ideals, central tendency, and frequency of instantiation as determinants of graded structure in categories. *Journal of Experimental Psychology: Learning, Memory, and Cognition, 11,* 629–654.

Bartlett, F. A. (1932). *A study in experimental and social psychology.* New York: Cambridge University Press.

Bassili, J. N. (1976). Temporal and spatial contingencies in the perception of social events. *Journal of Personality and Social Psychology, 33,* 680–685.

Bassili, J. N., & Smith, M. C. (1986). On the spontaneity of trait attribution: Converging evidence for the role of cognitive strategy. *Journal of Personality and Social Psychology, 50,* 239–245.

Bassok, M., & Trope, Y. (1983–84). People's strategies for testing hypotheses about another's personality: Confirmatory or diagnostic? *Social Cognition, 2,* 199–216.

Battistich, V. A., & Aronoff, J. (1985). Perceiver, target, and situational influences on social cognition: An interactional analysis. *Journal of Personality and Social Psychology, 49,* 788–798.

Battistich, V. A., Assor, A., Messe, L. A., & Aronoff, J. (1985). Personality and person perception. In P. Shaver (Ed.), *Review of personality and social psychology: Vol. 6. Self, situations, and social behavior* (pp. 185–208). Beverly Hills, CA: Sage.

Baumann, L. J., Cameron, L. D., Zimmerman, R. S., & Leventhal, H. (1989). Illness representations and matching labels with symptoms. *Health Psychology, 8,* 449–469.

Baumeister, R. F. (1984). Choking under pressure: Self-consciousness and paradoxical effects of incentives on skillful performance. *Journal of Personality and Social Psychology, 46,* 610–620.

Baumeister, R. F. (1988). Masochism as escape from self. *Journal of Sex Research, 25,* 28–59.

Baumeister, R. F. (1990a). Anxiety and deconstruction: On escaping the self. In J. M. Olson & M. P. Zanna (Eds.), *Self-inference processes: The Ontario Symposium* (Vol. 6, pp. 259–291). Hillsdale, NJ: Erlbaum.

Baumeister, R. F. (1990b). Suicide as escape from self. *Psychological Review, 97,* 90–113.

Baumeister, R. F., Hutton, D. G., & Tice, D. M. (1989). Cognitive processes during deliberate self-presentation: How self-presenters alter and misinterpret the behavior of their interaction partners. *Journal of Experimental Social Psychology, 25,* 59–78.

Baumeister, R. F., & Jones, E. E. (1978). When self-presentation is constrained by the target's knowledge. *Journal of Personality and Social Psychology, 36,* 608–618.

Baumeister, R. F., & Scher, S. J. (1988). Self-defeating behavior patterns among normal individuals: Review and analysis of common self-destructive tendencies. *Psychological Bulletin, 104,* 3–22.

Baumeister, R. F., & Showers, C. J. (1986). A review of paradoxical performance effects: Choking under pressure in sports and mental tests. *European Journal of Social Psychology, 16,* 361–383.

Baumeister, R. F., Tice, D. M., & Hutton, D. G. (1989). Self-presentational motivations and personality differences in self-esteem. *Journal of Personality, 57,* 547–579.

Baumgardner, A. H., & Arkin, R. M. (1987). Coping with the prospect of social disapproval: Strategies and sequelae. In C. R. Snyder & C. Ford (Eds.), *Clinical and social psychological perspectives on negative life events* (pp. 323–346). New York: Plenum.

Baumgardner, A. H., & Arkin, R. M. (1988). Affective state mediates causal attributions for success and failure. *Motivation and Emotion, 12,* 99–111.

Baumgardner, A. H., Heppner, R. P., & Arkin, R. M. (1986). Role of causal attribution in personal problem solving. *Journal of Personality and Social Psychology, 50,* 636–643.

Baumgardner, A., Lake, E. A., & Arkin, R. M. (1985). Claiming mood as a self-handicap: The influence of spoiled and unspoiled public identities. *Personality and Social Psychology Bulletin, 11,* 349–357.

Baxter, J. C., Brock, B., Hill, P. C., & Rozelle, R. M. (1981). Letters of recommendation: A question of value. *Journal of Applied Psychology, 66,* 296–301.

Baxter, J. C., Hill, P. C., Brock, B., & Rozelle, R. M. (1981). The perceiver and the perceived revisited. *Personality and Social Psychology Bulletin, 7,* 91–96.

Baxter, T. L., & Goldberg, L. R. (1988). Perceived behavioral consistency underlying trait attributions to oneself and another: An extension of the actor-observer effect. *Personality and Social Psychology Bulletin, 13,* 437–447.

Beach, L., & Wertheimer, M. (1961). A free-response approach to the study of person cognition. *Journal of Abnormal and Social Psychology, 62,* 367–374.

Beauvais, C., & Spence, J. T. (1987). Gender, prejudice, and categorization. *Sex Roles, 16,* 89–100.

Beck, L., McCauley, C., Segal, M., & Hershey, L. (1988). Individual differences in prototypicality judgments about trait categories. *Journal of Personality and Social Psychology, 55,* 286–292.

Beckmann, J., & Gollwitzer, P. M. (1987). Deliberative versus implemental states of mind: The issue of impartiality in predecisional and postdecisional information processing. *Social Cognition, 5,* 259–279.

Bekerian, D. A., & Bowers, J. M. (1983). Eyewitness testimony: Were we misled? *Journal of Experimental Psychology: Learning, Memory, and Cognition, 9,* 139–145.

Bellezza, F. S. (1984). The self as a mnemonic device: The role of internal cues. *Journal of Personality and Social Psychology, 47,* 506–516.

Bellezza, F. S., & Bower, G. H. (1981). Person stereotypes and memory for people. *Journal of Personality and Social Psychology, 41,* 856–865.

Belli, R. F. (1989). Influences of misleading postevent information: Misinformation interference and acceptance. *Journal of Experimental Psychology: General, 118,* 72–85.

Belmore, S. M. (1987). Determinants of attention during impression formation. *Journal of Experimental Psychology: Learning, Memory, and Cognition, 13,* 480–489.

Bem, D. J. (1967). Self-perception: An alternative interpretation of cognitive dissonance phenomena. *Psychological Review, 74,* 183–200.

Bem, D. J. (1972). Self-perception theory. In L. Berkowitz (Ed.), *Advances in experimental social psychology* (Vol. 6, pp. 1–62). New York: Academic Press.

Bem, D. J., & Allen, A. (1974). On predicting some of the people some of the time: The search for cross-situational consistencies in behavior. *Psychological Review, 81,* 506–520.

Bem, D. J., & McConnell, H. K. (1970). Testing the self-perception explanation of dissonance phenomena: On the salience of premanipulated attitudes. *Journal of Personality and Social Psychology, 14,* 23–31.

Bem, S. L. (1981). Gender schema theory: A cognitive account of sex typing. *Psychological Review, 88,* 354–364.

Bem, S. L. (1982). Gender schema theory and self-schema theory compared: A comment on Markus, Crane, Bernstein, and Siladi's "Self-schemas and gender." *Journal of Personality and Social Psychology, 43,* 1192–1194.

Bem, S. L. (1985). Androgyny and gender schema theory: A conceptual and empirical integration. In T. B. Sonderegger (Ed.), *Nebraska symposium on motivation 1984: Psychology and gender* (pp. 179–226). Lincoln: University of Nebraska Press.

Benesh, M., & Weiner, B. (1982). On emotion and motivation: From the notebooks of Fritz Heider. *American Psychologist, 37,* 887–895.

Bentler, P. M., & Speckart, G. (1981). Attitudes cause behaviors: A structural equation analysis. *Journal of Personality and Social Psychology, 40,* 226–238.

Berger, S. M., & Lambert, W. W. (1968). Stimulus-response theory in contemporary social psychology. In G. Lindzey & E. Aronson (Eds.), *The handbook of social psychology* (Vol. 1, 2nd ed.), Reading, MA: Addison-Wesley.

Berkowitz, L. (1974). Some determinants of impulsive aggression: Role of mediated associations with reinforcements for aggression. *Psychological Review, 81,* 165–176.

Berkowitz, L. (1984). Some effects of thoughts on anti- and prosocial influences of media events: A cognitive-neoassociation analysis. *Psychological Bulletin, 95,* 410–427.

Berkowitz, L. (1988). Introduction. In L. Berkowitz (Ed.), *Advances in experimental social psychology* (Vol. 21, pp. 1–16). New York: Academic Press.

Berkowitz, L., & Connor, W. H. (1966). Success, failure, and social responsibility. *Journal of Personality and Social Psychology, 4,* 664–669.

Berlyne, D. E. (1970). Novelty, complexity, and hedonic value. *Perception and Psychophysics, 8,* 279–286.

Berman, J. S., Read, S. J., & Kenny, D. A. (1983). Processing inconsistent social information. *Journal of Personality and Social Psychology, 45,* 1211–1224.

Berninger, V. W., & DeSoto, C. (1985). Cognitive representation of personal stereotypes. *European Journal of Social Psychology, 15,* 189–211.

Berry, D. S., & McArthur, L. Z. (1985). Some components and consequences of a babyface. *Journal of Personality and Social Psychology, 48,* 312–323.

Berry, D. S., & McArthur, L. Z. (1986). Perceiving character in faces: The impact of age-related craniofacial changes on social perception. *Psychological Bulletin, 100,* 3–18.

Berry, D. S., & Zebrowitz-McArthur, L. (1988). What's in a face? Facial maturity and the attribution of legal responsibility. *Personality and Social Psychology Bulletin, 14,* 23–33.

Berscheid, E. (1982). Attraction and emotion in interpersonal relationships. In M. S. Clark & S. T. Fiske (Eds.), *Affect and cognition: The 17th Annual Carnegie Symposium on Cognition* (pp. 37–54). Hillsdale, NJ: Erlbaum.

Berscheid, E. (1983). Emotion. In H. H. Kelley, E. Berscheid, A. Christensen, J. Harvey, T. Huston, G. Levinger, E. McClintock, L. A. Peplau, & D. Peterson (Eds.), *Close relationships* (pp. 110–168). San Francisco: Freeman.

Berscheid, E., Graziano, W., Monson, T., & Dermer, M. (1976). Outcome dependency: Attention, attribution, and attraction. *Journal of Personality and Social Psychology, 34,* 978–989.

Berscheid, E., Snyder, M., & Omoto, A. M. (1989). Issues in studying close relationships: Conceptualizing and measuring closeness. In C. Hendrick (Ed.), *Review of personality and social psychology: Vol. 10. Close relationships* (pp. 63–91). Newbury Park, CA: Sage.

Berscheid, E., & Walster, E. H. (1978). *Interpersonal attraction.* Reading, MA: Addison-Wesley.

Bevan, W. (1964). Subliminal stimulation: A pervasive problem for psychology. *Psychological Bulletin, 61,* 89–99.

Billig, M. (1985). Prejudice, categorization and particularization: From a perceptual and a rhetorical approach. *European Journal of Social Psychology, 15,* 79–103.

Billig, M., & Tajfel, H. (1973). Social categorization and similarity in intergroup behavior. *European Journal of Social Psychology, 3,* 27–52.

Birnbaum, M. H., & Mellers, B. A. (1979a). One-mediator model of exposure effects is still viable. *Journal of Personality and Social Psychology, 37,* 1090–1096.

Birnbaum, M. H., & Mellers, B. A. (1979b). Stimulus recognition may mediate exposure effects. *Journal of Personality and Social Psychology, 37,* 391–394.

Black, J. B., Galambos, J. A., & Read, S. J. (1984). Comprehending stories and social situations. In R. S. Wyer, Jr., & T. K. Srull (Eds.), *Handbook of social cognition* (Vol. 3, pp. 45–86). Hillsdale, NJ: Erlbaum.

Black, J. B., Turner, T. J., & Bower, G. H. (1979). Point of view in narrative comprehension, memory, and production. *Journal of Verbal Learning and Verbal Behavior, 18,* 187–198.

Blaney, P. H. (1986). Affect and memory: A review. *Psychological Bulletin, 99,* 229–246.

Block, J. (1981). Some enduring and consequential structures of personality. In A. I. Rabin, J. Aronoff, A. M. Barclay, & R. A. Zucker (Eds.), *Further explorations in personality* (pp. 63–91). New York: Wiley.

Block, J. (1989). Critique of the act frequency approach to personality. *Journal of Personality and Social Psychology, 56,* 234–245.

Block, J., & Funder, D. C. (1986). Social roles and social perception: Individual differences in attribution and error. *Journal of Personality and Social Psychology, 51,* 1200–1297.

Bobrow, D. G., & Norman, D. A. (1975). Some principles of memory schemata. In D. G. Bobrow & A. G. Collins (Eds.), *Representation and understanding: Studies in cognitive science* (pp. 131–150). New York: Academic Press.

Bodenhausen, G. V. (1988). Stereotypic biases in social decision making and memory: Testing process models for stereotype use. *Journal of Personality and Social Psychology, 55,* 726–737.

Bodenhausen, G. V., & Lichtenstein, M. (1987). Social stereotypes and information-processing strategies: The impact of task complexity. *Journal of Personality and Social Psychology, 52,* 871–880.

Bodenhausen, G. V., & Wyer, R. S., Jr. (1985). Effects of stereotypes on decision making and information-processing strategies. *Journal of Personality and Social Psychology, 48,* 267–282.

Boggiano, A. K., Harackiewicz, J. M., Bessette, J. M., & Main, D. S. (1985). Increasing children's interest through performance-contingent reward. *Social Cognition, 3,* 400–411.

Boggiano, A. K., & Main, D. S. (1986). Enhancing children's interest in activities used as rewards: The bonus effect. *Journal of Personality and Social Psychology, 51,* 1116–1126.

Bohner, G., Bless, H., Schwarz, N., & Strack, F. (1988). What triggers causal attributions? The impact of valence and subjective probability. *European Journal of Social Psychology, 18,* 335–345.

Bond, C. F., Jr., & Brockett, D. R. (1987). A social context-personality index theory of memory for acquaintances. *Journal of Personality and Social Psychology, 52,* 1110–1121.

Bond, C. F., Jr., Jones, R. L., & Weintraub, D. L. (1985). On the unrestrained recall of acquaintances: A sampling-traversal model. *Journal of Personality and Social Psychology, 49,* 327–337.

Bond, C. F., Jr., & Sedikides, C. (1988). The recapitulation hypothesis in person retrieval. *Journal of Experimental Social Psychology, 24,* 195–221.

Bond, M. H. (1972). Effect of an impression set on subsequent behavior. *Journal of Personality and Social Psychology, 24,* 301–305.

Bond, M. H., Hewstone, M., Wan, K.–C., & Chiu, C.–K. (1985). Group-serving attributions across intergroup contexts: Cultural differences in the explanation of sex-typed behaviours. *European Journal of Social Psychology, 15,* 435–451.

Borgida, E., & Brekke, N. (1981). The base-rate fallacy in attribution and prediction. In J. H. Harvey, W. J. Ickes, & R. F. Kidd (Eds.), *New directions in attribution research* (Vol. 3, pp. 66–97). Hillsdale, NJ: Erlbaum.

Borgida, E., & Campbell, B. (1982). Attitude-behavior consistency: The moderating role of personal experience. *Journal of Personality and Social Psychology, 42,* 239–247.

Borgida, E., & DeBono, K. G. (1989). Social hypothesis-testing and the role of expertise. *Personality and Social Psychology Bulletin, 15,* 212–221.

Borgida, E., & Howard-Pitney, B. (1983). Personal involvement and the robustness of perceptual salience effects. *Journal of Personality and Social Psychology, 45,* 560–570.

Borgida, E., Swann, W. B., Jr., & Campbell, B. (1977, August). *Attitudes and behavior: The specificity hypothesis revisited.* Paper presented at the meeting of the American Psychological Association, San Francisco.

Boring, E. G. (1950). *A history of experimental psychology.* Englewood Cliffs, NJ: Prentice-Hall.

Bornewasser, M., & Bober, J. (1987). Individual, social group, and intergroup behaviour: Some conceptual remarks on the social identity theory. *European Journal of Social Psychology, 17,* 267–276.

Bornstein, R. F. (1989). Exposure and affect: Overview and meta-analysis of research, 1968–1987. *Psychological Bulletin, 106,* 265–289.

Bothwell, R. K., Deffenbacher, K. A., & Brigham, J. C. (1987). Correlation of eyewitness accuracy and confidence: Optimality hypothesis revisited. *Journal of Applied Psychology, 72,* 691–695.

Bower, G. H. (1977). *Human memory.* New York: Academic Press.

Bower, G. H. (1978). Experiments on story comprehension and recall. *Discourse Processes, 1,* 211–231.

Bower, G. H. (1981). Emotional mood and memory. *American Psychologist, 36,* 129–148.

Bower, G. H. (1987). Commentary on mood and memory. *Behavior Research and Therapy, 25,* 443–455.

Bower, G. H. (1990). Awareness, the unconscious, and repression: An experimental psychologist's perspective. In J. A. Singer (Ed.), *Repression: Defense mechanism and personality style* (pp. 209–231). Chicago: University of Chicago Press.

Bower, G. H. (in press). Temporary emotional states act like multiple personalities. In R. Klein & B. Doane (Eds.), *Psychological concepts and dissociative disorders: Reverberating implications.* Hillsdale, NJ: Erlbaum.

Bower, G. H., Black, J. B., & Turner, T. J. (1979). Scripts in memory for text. *Cognitive Psychology, 11,* 177–220.

Bower, G. H., & Cohen, P. R. (1982). Emotional influences in memory and thinking: Data and theory. In M. S. Clark & S. T. Fiske (Eds.), *Affect and cognition: The 17th Annual Carnegie Symposium on Cognition* (pp. 291–332). Hillsdale, NJ: Erlbaum.

Bower, G. H., & Gilligan, S. G. (1979). Remembering information related to one's self. *Journal of Research in Personality, 13,* 404–419.

Bower, G. H., Gilligan, S. G., & Monteiro, K. P. (1981). Selectivity of learning caused by affective states. *Journal of Experimental Psychology: General, 110,* 451–473.

Bower, G. H., & Karlin, M. B. (1974). Depth of processing pictures of faces and recognition memory. *Journal of Experimental Psychology, 4,* 751–757.

Bower, G. H., & Masling, M. (1978). *Causal explanations as mediators for remembering correlations.* Unpublished manuscript, Stanford University.

Bower, G. H., & Mayer, J. D. (1985). Failure to replicate mood-dependent retrieval. *Bulletin of Psychonomic Society, 23,* 39–42.

Bower, G. H., & Mayer, J. D. (1989). In search of mood-dependent retrieval. *Journal of Social Behavior and Personality, 4,* 121–156.

Bower, T. G. R. (1970). Analysis of a mnemonic device. *American Scientist, 58,* 496–510.

Bradburn, N. M., & Caplovitz, D. (1965). *Reports on happiness.* Chicago: Aldine.

Bradley, G. W. (1978). Self-serving biases in the attribution process: A reexamination of the fact or fiction question. *Journal of Personality and Social Psychology, 36,* 56–71.

Branscombe, N. R. (1985). Effects of hedonic valence and physiological arousal on emotion: A comparison of two theoretical perspectives. *Motivation and Emotion, 9,* 153–169.

Branscombe, N. R. (1988). Conscious and unconscious processing of affective and cognitive information. In K. Fiedler & J. Forgas (Eds.), *Affect, cognition, and social behavior* (pp. 3–24). Toronto, Canada: Hogrefe.

Branscombe, N. R., & Cohen, B. M. (1990). Motivation and complexity levels as determinants of heuristic use in social judgment. In J. Forgas (Ed.), *Emotion and social judgment.* Oxford, England: Pergamon.

Bransford, J. D., & Franks, J. J. (1971). The abstraction of linguistic ideas. *Cognitive Psychology, 2,* 331–350.

Bransford, J. D., & Johnson, M. K. (1972). Contextual prerequisites for understanding: Some investigations of comprehension and recall. *Journal of Verbal Learning and Verbal Behavior, 11,* 717–726.

Braun, O. L., & Wicklund, R. A. (1988). The identity-effort connection. *Journal of Experimental Social Psychology, 24,* 37–65.

Breckler, S. J. (1984). Empirical validation of affect, behavior, and cognition as distinct components of attitude. *Journal of Personality and Social Psychology, 47,* 1191–1205.

Breckler, S. J., & Greenwald, A. J. (1986). Motivational facets of the self. In R. M. Sorrentino & E. T. Higgins (Eds.), *Handbook of motivation and cognition: Foundations of social behavior* (pp. 145–164). New York: Guilford Press.

Breckler, S. J., Pratkanis, A. R., & McCann, C. D. (1990). The representation of self in multidimensional cognitive space. *British Journal of Social Psychology.*

Breckler, S. J., & Wiggins, E. C. (1989). On defining attitude and attitude theory: Once more with feeling. In A. R. Pratkanis, S. J. Breckler, & A. G. Greenwald (Eds.), *Attitudes structure and function* (pp. 407–428). Hillsdale, NJ: Erlbaum.

Brehm, J. W., & Cohen, A. R. (1962). *Explorations in cognitive dissonance.* New York: Wiley.

Brekke, N., & Borgida, E. (1988). Expert psychological testimony in rape trials: A social-cognitive analysis. *Journal of Personality and Social Psychology, 55,* 372–386.

Brewer, M. B. (1979). In-group bias in the minimal intergroup situation: A cognitive-motivational analysis. *Psychological Bulletin, 86,* 307–324.

Brewer, M. B. (1988a). A dual process model of impression formation. In T. K. Srull & R. S. Wyer, Jr. (Eds.), *Advances in social cognition* (Vol. 1, pp. 1–36). Hillsdale, NJ: Erlbaum.

Brewer, M. B. (1988b). Reply to commentaries. In T. K. Srull & R. S. Wyer, Jr. (Eds.), *Advances in social cognition* (Vol. 1, pp. 177–183). Hillsdale, NJ: Erlbaum.

Brewer, M. B., Dull, V., & Lui, L. (1981). Perceptions of the elderly: Stereotypes as prototypes. *Journal of Personality and Social Psychology, 41,* 656–670.

Brewer, M. B., Ho, H. K., Lee, J. Y., & Miller, N. (1987). Social identity and social distance among Hong Kong school children. *Personality and Social Psychology Bulletin, 13,* 156–165.

Brewer, M. B., & Kramer, R. M. (1985). The psychology of intergroup attitudes and behavior. *Annual Review of Psychology, 36,* 219–243.

Brewer, M. B., & Lui, L. (1984). Categorization of the elderly by the elderly:

Effects of perceiver's category membership. *Personality and Social Psychology Bulletin, 10,* 585–595.

Brewer, M. B., & Lui, L. L. (1989). The primacy of age and sex in the structure of person categories. *Social Cognition, 7,* 262–274.

Brewer, M. B., & Silver, M. (1978). Ingroup bias as a function of task characteristics. *European Journal of Social Psychology, 8,* 393–400.

Brewer, W. F., & Nakamura, G. V. (1984). The nature and functions of schemas. In R. S. Wyer, Jr., & T. K. Srull (Eds.), *Handbook of social cognition* (Vol. 1, pp. 119–160). Hillsdale, NJ: Erlbaum.

Brewer, W. F., & Treyens, J. C. (1981). Role of schemata in memory for places. *Cognitive Psychology, 13,* 207–230.

Brewin, C. (1985). Depression and causal attributions: What is their relation? *Psychological Bulletin, 2,* 297–309.

Brickman, P., Coates, D., & Janoff-Bulman, R. (1978). Lottery winners and accident victims: Is happiness relative? *Journal of Personality and Social Psychology, 35,* 917–927.

Brickman, P., Rabinowitz, V. C., Karuza, Jr., J., Coates, D., Cohn, E., & Kidder, L. (1982). Models of helping and coping. *American Psychologist, 37,* 368–384.

Brickner, M. A., Harkins, S. G., & Ostrom, T. M. (1986). Effects of personal involvement: Thought-provoking implications of social loafing. *Journal of Personality and Social Psychology, 51,* 763–770.

Briggs, S. R., & Cheek, J. M. (1988). On the nature of self-monitoring: Problems with assessment, problems with validity. *Journal of Personality and Social Psychology, 54,* 663–678.

Briggs, S. R., Cheek, J. M., & Buss, A. H. (1980). An analysis of the self-monitoring scale. *Journal of Personality and Social Psychology, 38,* 679–686.

Brigham, J. C., Maass, A., Snyder, L. D., & Spaulding, K. (1982). Accuracy of eyewitness identifications in a field setting. *Journal of Personality and Social Psychology, 42,* 673–681.

Brigham, J. C., & Malpass, R. S. (1985). The role of experience and contact in the recognition of faces of own- and other-race persons. *Journal of Social Issues, 41*(3), 139–156.

Broadbent, D. E. (1958). *Perception and communication.* London: Pergamon Press.

Brock, T. C. (1967). Communication discrepancy and intent to persuade as determinants of counter-argument production. *Journal of Experimental Social Psychology, 3,* 269–309.

Brock, T. C., Albert, S. M., & Becker, L. A. (1970). Familiarity, utility, and supportiveness as determinants of information receptivity. *Journal of Personality and Social Psychology, 14,* 292–301.

Brock, T. C., & Balloun, J. L. (1967). Behavioral receptivity to dissonant information. *Journal of Personality and Social Psychology, 6,* 413–428.

Brodt, A., & Zimbardo, P. G. (1981). Modifying shyness related behavior through symptom misattribution. *Journal of Personality and Social Psychology, 41,* 437–449.

Brody, N. (1987). Introduction: Some thoughts on the unconscious. *Personality and Social Psychology Bulletin, 13,* 293–298.

Bronfenbrenner, U. (1977). Lewinian space and ecological substance. *Journal of Social Issues, 33,* 199–212.

Brooks, L. (1978). Nonanalytic concept formation and memory for instances. In E. Rosch & B. B. Lloyd (Eds.), *Cognition and categorization* (pp. 169–211). Hillsdale, NJ: Erlbaum.

Brophy, J. E., & Rohrkemper, M. M. (1981). The influence of problem owner-ship on teachers' perceptions of and strategies for coping with problem stu-dents. *Journal of Educational Psychology, 73,* 295–311.

Brown, J. D. (1986). Evaluations of self and others: Self-enhancement biases in social judgments. *Social Cognition, 4,* 353–376.

Brown, J. D. (1988). Self-directed attention, self-esteem, and causal attributions for valenced outcomes. *Personality and Social Psychology Bulletin, 14,* 252–263.

Brown, J. D. (1989). *Self-esteem and the accessibility of self-evaluative constructs.* Un-published manuscript, University of Washington, Seattle.

Brown, J. D. (1990). Evaluating one's abilities: Short cuts and stumbling blocks on the road to self-knowledge. *Journal of Experimental Social Psychology, 26,* 149–167.

Brown, J. D., Collins, R. L., & Schmidt, G. W. (1988). Self-esteem and direct versus indirect forms of self-enhancement. *Journal of Personality and Social Psychology, 55,* 445–453.

Brown, J. D., & Lord, K. A. (1990). *On the relation between self-appraisals and ap-praisals of others: I'm OK, you're OK?* Unpublished manuscript, University of Washington, Seattle.

Brown, J. D., Schmidt, G. W., & Collins, R. L. (1988). Personal involvement and the evaluation of group products. *European Journal of Social Psychology, 18,* 177–179.

Brown, J. D., & Siegel, J. M. (1988). Attributions for negative life events and depression: The role of perceived control. *Journal of Personality and Social Psy-chology, 54,* 316–322.

Brown, J. D., & Taylor, S. E. (1986). Affect and the processing of personal in-formation: Evidence for mood-activated self-schemata. *Journal of Experimental Social Psychology, 22,* 436–452.

Brown, P., Keenan, J. K., & Potts, G. R. (1986). The self-reference effect with imagery encoding. *Journal of Personality and Social Psychology, 51,* 897–906.

Brown, Roger. (1986). *Social psychology: The second edition.* New York: The Free Press.

Brown, Roger, & Fish, D. (1983). The psychological causality implicit in lan-guage. *Cognition, 14,* 237–273.

Brown, Roger, & Kulik, J. (1977). Flashbulb memories. *Cognition, 5,* 73–99.

Brown, Rupert, Condor, S., Matthews, A., Wade, G., & Williams, J. (1986). Ex-plaining intergroup differentiation in an industrial organization. *Journal of Occupational Psychology, 59,* 273–286.

Brown, Rupert, & Wade, G. (1987). Superordinate goals and intergroup behaviour: The effect of role ambiguity and status on intergroup attitudes and task performance. *European Journal of Social Psychology, 17,* 131–142.

Brown, V., & Geis, F. L. (1984). Turning lead into gold: Evaluations of men and women leaders and the alchemy of social consensus. *Journal of Personality and Social Psychology, 46,* 811–824.

Bruner, J. S. (1957). On perceptual readiness. *Psychological Review, 64,* 123–152.

Bruner, J. S. (1958). Social psychology and perception. In E. E. Maccoby, T. M.

Newcomb, & E. L. Hartley (Eds.), *Readings in social psychology* (3rd ed.). New York: Holt, Rinehart, & Winston.

Bruner, J. S., & Tagiuri, R. (1954). The perception of people. In G. Lindzey (Ed.), *Handbook of social psychology* (Vol. 2, pp. 634–654). Reading, MA: Addison-Wesley.

Brunswik, E. (1956). *Perception and the representative design of psychological experiments* (2nd ed.). Berkeley and Los Angeles: University of California Press.

Bryant, J., & Zillmann, D. (1979). Effect of intensification of annoyance through unrelated residual excitation on substantially delayed hostile behavior. *Journal of Experimental Social Psychology, 15,* 470–480.

Buck, R. (1980). Nonverbal behavior and the theory of emotion: The facial feedback hypothesis. *Journal of Personality and Social Psychology, 38,* 811–824.

Buckert, U., Meyer, W. U., & Schmalt, H. D. (1979). Effects of difficulty and diagnosticity on choice among tasks in relation to achievement motivation and perceived ability. *Journal of Personality and Social Psychology, 37,* 1172–1178.

Budd, R. J. (1987). Response bias and the theory of reasoned action. *Social Cognition, 5,* 95–107.

Bull, N. (1951). The attitude theory of emotion. *Archivo de Psicologia, Neuroloqia e Psichiatria, 12,* 108–114.

Bulman, R. J., & Wortman, C. B. (1977). Attributions of blame and coping in the "real world": Severe accident victims react to their lot. *Journal of Personality and Social Psychology, 35,* 351–363.

Burdett, A. N. (1985). Emotions and facial expression. [Letter in response to Zajonc, R. B. (1985). Emotion and facial efference: A theory reclaimed. *Science, 228,* 15–21.] *Science, 230,* 608.

Burger, J. M. (1981). Motivational biases in the attribution of responsibility for an accident: A meta-analysis of the defensive-attribution hypothesis. *Psychological Bulletin, 90,* 496–512.

Burger, J. M. (1985). Desire for control and achievement-related behaviors. *Journal of Personality and Social Psychology, 48,* 1520–1533.

Burger, J. M. (1986). Temporal effects on attributions: Actor and observer differences. *Social Cognition, 4,* 377–387.

Burger, J. M. (1989). Negative reactions to increases in perceived personal control. *Journal of Personality and Social Psychology, 56,* 246–256.

Burger, J.M. & Huntzinger, R. M. (1985). Temporal effects on attributions for one's own behavior: The role of task outcome. *Journal of Experimental Social Psychology, 21,* 247–261.

Burgess, E. W. (1941). An experiment in the standardization of the case-study method. *Sociometry, 4,* 329–348.

Burke, P. A., Kraut, R. E., & Dworkin, R. H. (1984). Traits, consistency, and self-schemata: What do our methods measure? *Journal of Personality and Social Psychology, 47,* 568–579.

Burnkrant, R. E., & Howard, D. J. (1984). Effects of the use of introductory rhetorical questions versus statements on information processing. *Journal of Personality and Social Psychology, 47,* 1218–1230.

Burnkrant, R. E., & Page, T. J., Jr. (1988). The structure and antecedents of the normative and attitudinal components of Fishbein's theory of reasoned action. *Journal of Experimental Social Psychology, 24,* 66–87.

Burnstein, E., & Schul, Y. (1982). The informational basis of social judgments: Operations in forming impressions of other persons. *Journal of Experimental Social Psychology, 18,* 217–234.

Burnstein, E., & Schul, Y. (1983). The informational basis of social judgments: Memory for integrated and nonintegrated trait descriptions. *Journal of Experimental Social Psychology, 19,* 49–57.

Burnstein, E., & Sentis, K. (1981). Attitude polarization in groups. In R. E. Petty, T. M. Ostrom, & T. C. Brock (Eds.), *Cognitive responses in persuasion* (pp. 197–216). Hillsdale, NJ: Erlbaum.

Burnstein, E., & Vinokur, A. (1973). Testing two classes of theories about group-induced shifts in individual choice. *Journal of Experimental Social Psychology, 9,* 123–137.

Burnstein, E., & Vinokur, A. (1975). What a person thinks upon learning he has chosen differently from others: Nice evidence for the persuasive-arguments explanation of choice shifts. *Journal of Experimental Social Psychology, 11,* 412–426.

Burnstein, E., & Vinokur, A. (1977). Persuasive argumentation and social comparison as determinants of attitude polarization. *Journal of Experimental Social Psychology, 13,* 315–332.

Burnstein, E., Vinokur, A., & Trope, Y. (1973). Interpersonal comparison versus argumentation: A more direct test of alternative explanations for group-induced shifts in individual choice. *Journal of Experimental Social Psychology, 9,* 236–245.

Buss, A. R. (1978). Causes and reasons in attribution theory: A conceptual critique. *Journal of Personality and Social Psychology, 36,* 1311–1321.

Buss, A. R. (1979). On the relationship between causes and reasons. *Journal of Personality and Social Psychology, 37,* 1458–1461.

Buss, D. M., & Craik, K. H. (1980). The frequency concept of disposition: Dominance and prototypically dominant acts. *Journal of Personality, 43,* 379–392.

Buss, D. M., & Craik, K. H. (1981). The act frequency analysis of interpersonal dispositions: Aloofness, gregariousness, dominance, and submissiveness. *Journal of Personality, 49,* 175–192.

Cacioppo, J. T. (1979). Effects of exogenous changes in heart rate on facilitation of thought and resistance to persuasion. *Journal of Personality and Social Psychology, 37,* 489–498.

Cacioppo, J. T., & Petty, R. E. (1979). Effects of message repetition and position on cognitive response, recall, and persuasion. *Journal of Personality and Social Psychology, 37,* 97–109.

Cacioppo, J. T., & Petty, R. E. (1982). The need for cognition. *Journal of Personality and Social Psychology, 42,* 116–131.

Cacioppo, J. T., & Petty, R. E. (1985). Central and peripheral routes to persuasion: The role of message repetition. In A. Mitchell & L. Alwitt (Eds.), *Psychological processes and advertising effects* (pp. 91–111). Hillsdale, NJ: Erlbaum.

Cacioppo, J. T., Petty, R. E., & Geen, T. R. (1989). Attitude structure and function: From the tripartite to the homeostasis model of attitudes. In A. R. Pratkanis, S. J. Breckler, & A. G. Greenwald (Eds.), *Attitude structure and function* (pp. 275–309). Hillsdale, NJ: Erlbaum.

Cacioppo, J. T., Petty, R. E., Losch, M. E., & Kim, H. S. (1986). Electromyographic activity over facial muscle regions can differentiate the valence and intensity of affective reactions. *Journal of Personality and Social Psychology, 50,* 260–268.

Cacioppo, J. T., Petty, R. E., & Morris, K. J. (1983). Effects of need for cognition on message evaluation, recall, and persuasion. *Journal of Personality and Social Psychology, 45,* 805–818.

Cacioppo, J. T., Petty, R. E., & Sidera, J. A. (1982). The effects of a salient self-schema on the evaluation of proattitudinal editorials: Top-down versus bottom-up message processing. *Journal of Experimental Social Psychology, 18,* 324–338.

Cafferty, T. P., DeNisi, A. S., & Williams, K. J. (1986). Search and retrieval patterns for performance information: Effects on evaluation of multiple targets. *Journal of Personality and Social Psychology, 50,* 676–683.

Calder, B. J. (1977). Endogenous-exogenous versus internal-external attributions: Implications for the development of attribution theory. *Personality and Social Psychology Bulletin, 3,* 400–406.

Campbell, J. D. (1986). Similarity and uniqueness: The effects of attribute type, relevance, and individual differences in self-esteem and depression. *Journal of Personality and Social Psychology, 50,* 281–294.

Campbell, J. D., & Fairey, P. J. (1985). Effects of self-esteem, hypothetical explanations, and verbalizations of expectancies on future performance. *Journal of Personality and Social Psychology, 48,* 1097–1111.

Cannon, W. B. (1927). The James-Lange theory of emotions: A critical examination and an alternative theory. *American Journal of Psychology, 39,* 106–124.

Cantor, J. R., Bryant, J., & Zillmann, D. (1974). Enhancement of humor appreciation by transferred excitation. *Journal of Personality and Social Psychology, 30,* 812–821.

Cantor, J. R., & Zillmann, D. (1973). The effect of affective state and emotional arousal on music appreciation. *Journal of General Psychology, 89,* 97–108.

Cantor, N., & Kihlstrom, J. F. (1985) Social intelligence: The cognitive basis of personality. In P. Shaver (Ed.), *Review of Personality and Social Psychology: Vol. 6. Self, situations, and social behavior* (pp. 15–34). Beverly Hills, CA: Sage.

Cantor, N., & Kihlstrom, J. F. (1987). *Personality and social intelligence.* Englewood Cliffs, NJ: Prentice-Hall.

Cantor, N., Mackie, D., & Lord, C. (1983–84). Choosing partners and activities: The social perceiver decides to mix it up. *Social Cognition, 2,* 256–272.

Cantor, N., Markus, H., Niedenthal, P., & Nurius, P. (1986). On motivation and the self-concept. In R. M. Sorrentino & E. T. Higgins (Eds.), *Handbook of motivation and cognition: Foundations of social behavior* (pp. 96–121). New York: Guilford Press.

Cantor, N., & Mischel, W. (1977). Traits as prototypes: Effects on recognition memory. *Journal of Personality and Social Psychology, 35,* 38–48.

Cantor, N., & Mischel, W. (1979). Prototypes in person perception. In L. Berkowitz (Ed.), *Advances in experimental social psychology* (Vol. 12, pp. 3–52). New York: Academic Press.

Cantor, N., Mischel, W., & Schwartz, J. (1982a). A prototype analysis of psychological situations. *Cognitive Psychology, 14,* 45–77.

Cantor, N., Mischel, W., & Schwartz, J. (1982b). Social knowledge: Structure, content, use, and abuse. In A. H. Hastorf & A. M. Isen (Eds.), *Cognitive social psychology* (pp. 1–32). New York: Elsevier/North-Holland.

Cantril, H. (1938). The prediction of social events. *Journal of Abnormal and Social Psychology, 33,* 364–389.

Capozza, D., & Nanni, R. (1986). Differentiation processes for social stimuli with different degrees of category representativeness. *European Journal of Social Psychology, 16,* 399–412.

Carlson, M., Charlin, V., & Miller, N. (1988). Positive mood and helping behavior: A test of six hypotheses. *Journal of Personality and Social Psychology, 55,* 211–229.

Carlson, M., & Miller, N. (1987). Explanation of the relation between negative mood and helping. *Psychological Bulletin, 102,* 91–108.

Carlston, D. E. (1980a). Events, inferences, and impression formation. In R. Hastie, T. M. Ostrom, E. B. Ebbesen, R. S. Wyer, Jr., D. L. Hamilton, & D. E. Carlston (Eds.), *Person memory: The cognitive basis of social perception* (pp. 89–119). Hillsdale, NJ: Erlbaum.

Carlston, D. E. (1980b). The recall and use of traits and events in social inference processes. *Journal of Experimental Social Psychology, 16,* 303–328.

Carlston, D. E., & Shovar, N. (1983). Effects of performance attributions on others' perceptions of the attributor. *Journal of Personality and Social Psychology, 44,* 515–525.

Carlston, D. E., & Skowronski, J. J. (1986). Trait memory and behavior memory: The effects of alternative pathways on impression judgment response times. *Journal of Personality and Social Psychology, 50,* 5–13.

Carnegie, D. (1936). *How to win friends and influence people.* New York: Simon & Schuster.

Carnevale, P. J. D., & Isen, A. M. (1986). The influence of positive affect and visual access on the discovery of integrative solutions in bilateral negotiation. *Organizational Behavior and Human Decision Processes, 37,* 1–13.

Carpenter, S. L. (1988). Self-relevance and goal-directed processing in the recall and weighting of information about others. *Journal of Experimental Social Psychology, 24,* 310–332.

Carroll, J. S. (1978). The effect of imagining an event on expectations for the event: An interpretation in terms of the availability heuristic. *Journal of Experimental Social Psychology, 14,* 88–96.

Carroll, J. S., & Payne, J. W. (1976). *Cognitive and social behavior.* Hillsdale, NJ: Erlbaum.

Cartwright, D. (1988, October). *Comment on Messick & Mackie's Annual Review chapter.* Paper presented at the meetings of the Society of Experimental Social Psychology, Madison, WI.

Carver, C. S. (1979). A cybernetic model of self-attention processes. *Journal of Personality and Social Psychology, 37,* 1251–1281.

Carver, C. S. (1989). How should multifaceted personality constructs be tested? Issues illustrated by self-monitoring, attributional style, and hardiness. *Journal of Personality and Social Psychology, 56,* 577–585.

Carver, C. S., Blaney, P. H., & Scheier, M. F. (1979). Focus of attention, chronic expectancy, and responses to a feared stimulus. *Journal of Personality and Social Psychology, 37,* 1186–1195.

Carver, C. S., La Voie, L., Kuhl, J., & Ganellen, R. J. (1988). Cognitive concomitants of depression: A further examination of the roles of generalization, high standards, and self-criticism. *Journal of Social and Clinical Psychology, 7,* 350–365.

Carver, C. S., & Scheier, M. F. (1981a). *Attention and self-regulation: A control theory approach to human behavior.* New York: Springer-Verlag.

Carver, C. S., & Scheier, M. F. (1981b). The self-attention-induced feedback loop and social facilitation. *Journal of Experimental Social Psychology, 17,* 545–568.

Carver, C. S., & Scheier, M. F. (1982). Outcome expectancy, locus of attribution for expectancy, and self-directed attention as determinants of evaluations and performance. *Journal of Experimental Social Psychology, 18,* 184–200.

Carver, C. S., & Scheier, M. F. (1985). Aspects of self and the control of behavior. In B. R. Schlenker (Ed.), *The self and social life* (pp. 146–172). New York: McGraw-Hill.

Carver, C. S., & Scheier, M. F. (1987). The blind men and the elephant: Selective examination of the public-private literature gives rise to a faulty perception. *Journal of Personality, 55,* 525–541.

Carver, C. S., & Scheier, M. F. (1990). Origins and functions of positive and negative affect: A control-process view. *Psychological Review, 97,* 19–35.

Catrambone, R. & Markus, H. (1987). The role of self-schemas in going beyond the information given. *Social Cognition, 5,* 349–368.

Ceci, S. J., Ross, D. F., & Toglia, M. P. (1987). Suggestibility of children's memory: Psycholegal implications. *Journal of Experimental Psychology: General, 116,* 38–49.

Cervone, D., & Peake, P. (1986). Anchoring, efficacy, and action: The influence of judgmental heuristics on self-efficacy judgments and behavior. *Journal of Personality and Social Psychology, 50,* 492–501.

Chaiken, S. (1979). Communicator physical attractiveness and persuasion. *Journal of Personality and Social Psychology, 37,* 1387–1397.

Chaiken, S. (1980). Heuristic versus systematic information processing and the use of source versus message cues in persuasion. *Journal of Personality and Social Psychology, 39,* 752–766.

Chaiken, S. (1987). The heuristic model of persuasion. In M. P. Zanna, J. M. Olson, & C. P. Herman (Eds.), *Social influence: The Ontario Symposium* (Vol. 5, pp. 3–40). Hillsdale, NJ: Erlbaum.

Chaiken, S., & Eagly, A. H. (1976). Communication modality as a determinant of message persuasiveness and message comprehensibility. *Journal of Personality and Social Psychology, 34,* 605–614.

Chaiken, S., & Eagly, A. H. (1983). Communication modality as a determinant of persuasion: The role of communicator salience. *Journal of Personality and Social Psychology, 45,* 41–56.

Chaiken, S., Liberman, A., & Eagly, A. H. (1989). Heuristic and systematic information processing within and beyond the persuasion context. In J. S. Uleman & J. A. Bargh (Eds.), *Unintended thought* (pp. 212–252). New York: Guilford Press.

Chaiken, S. & Stangor, C. (1987). Attitudes and attitude change. *Annual Review of Psychology, 38,* 575–630.

Chaiken, S., & Yates, S. (1985). Affective-cognitive consistency and thought-induced attitude polarization. *Journal of Personality and Social Psychology, 49,* 1470–1481.

Chance, J. E., & Goldstein, A. G. (1981). Depth of processing in response to own- and other-race faces. *Personality and Social Psychology Bulletin, 7,* 475–480.

Chanowitz, B., & Langer, E. J. (1981). Premature cognitive commitment. *Journal of Personality and Social Psychology, 41,* 1051–1063.

Chaplin, W. F., & Goldberg, L. R. (1984). A failure to replicate Bem and Allen's study of individual differences in cross-situational consistency. *Journal of Personality and Social Psychology, 47,* 1074–1090.

Chaplin, W. F., John, O. P., & Goldberg, L. R. (1988). Conceptions of states and traits: Dimensional attributes with ideals as prototypes. *Journal of Personality and Social Psychology, 54,* 541–557.

Chapman, L. J. (1967). Illusory correlation in observational report. *Journal of Verbal Learning and Verbal Behavior, 6,* 151–155.

Chapman, L. J., & Chapman, J. P. (1967). Genesis of popular but erroneous diagnostic observations. *Journal of Abnormal Psychology, 72,* 193–204.

Chapman, L. J., & Chapman, J. P. (1969). Illusory correlation as an obstacle to the use of valid psychodiagnostic signs. *Journal of Abnormal Psychology, 14,* 271–280.

Chase, W. G., & Simon, H. A. (1973). The mind's eye in chess. In W. G. Chase (Ed.), *Visual information processing* (pp. 215–281). New York: Academic Press.

Chaves, J. R., & Barber, T. X. (1974). Cognitive strategies, experimenter modeling, and expectation in the attenuation of pain. *Journal of Abnormal Psychology, 83,* 356–363.

Chen, H., Yates, B. T., & McGinnies, E. (1988). Effects of involvement on observers' estimates of consensus, distinctiveness, and consistency. *Personality and Social Psychology Bulletin, 14,* 468–478.

Cheng, P. W., & Holyoak, K. J. (1985). Pragmatic reasoning schemas. *Cognitive Psychology, 17,* 391–416.

Cheng, P. W., Holyoak, K. J., Nisbett, R. E., & Oliver, L. M. (1986). Pragmatic versus syntactic approaches to training deductive reasoning. *Cognitive Psychology, 18,* 293–328.

Cheng, P. W., & Novick, L. R. (1990). A probabilistic contrast model of causal induction. *Journal of Personality and Social Psychology, 58,* 545–567.

Chi, M. T. H., & Koeske, R. (1983). Network representations of a child's dinosaur knowledge. *Developmental Psychology, 19,* 29–39.

Chodoff, P., Friedman, S. B., & Hamburg, D. A. (1964). Stress, defenses, and coping behavior: Observations in parents of children with malignant disease. *American Journal of Psychiatry, 120,* 743–749.

Chomsky, N. (1959). Verbal behavior. [Review of Skinner's book.] *Language, 35,* 26–58.

Christensen-Szalanski, J. J. J., & Fobian, C. S. (in press). The hindsight bias: A meta-analysis. *Organizational Behavior and Human Decision Processes.*

Chwalisz, K., Diener, E., & Gallagher, D. (1988). Autonomic arousal feedback and emotional experience: Evidence from the spinal cord injured. *Journal of Personality and Social Psychology, 54,* 820–828.

Cialdini, R. B., Darby, B. L., & Vincent, J. E. (1973). Transgression and altruism: A case for hedonism. *Journal of Experimental Social Psychology, 9,* 502–516.

Cialdini, R. B., & Kenrick, D. T. (1976). Altruism as hedonism: A social development perspective on the relationship of negative mood state and helping. *Journal of Personality and Social Psychology, 34,* 907–914.

Cialdini, R. B., Levy, A., Herman, C. P., & Evenbeck, S. (1973). Attitudinal politics: The strategy of moderation. *Journal of Personality and Social Psychology, 25,* 100–108.

Cialdini, R. B., Petty, R. E., & Cacioppo, J. T. (1981). Attitudes and attitude change. *Annual Review of Psychology, 32,* 357–404.

Cialdini, R. B. & Richardson, K. D. (1980). Two indirect tactics of image management: Basking and blasting. *Journal of Personality and Social Psychology, 39,* 406–415.

Clark, D. M., & Teasdale, J. D. (1985). Constraints on the effects of mood on memory. *Journal of Personality and Social Psychology, 48,* 1595–1608.

Clark, L. F., & Taylor, S. E. (1983, August). *Hypothesis-testing under different interaction conditions: The questions people ask.* Paper presented at the annual meetings of the American Psychological Association, Anaheim, CA.

Clark, L. F., & Woll, S. B. (1981). Stereotype biases: A reconstructive analysis of their role in reconstructive memory. *Journal of Personality and Social Psychology, 41,* 1064–1072.

Clark, M. S. (1982). A role for arousal in the link between feeling states, judgments, and behavior. In M. S. Clark & S. T. Fiske (Eds.), *Affect and cognition: The 17th Annual Carnegie Symposium on Cognition* (pp. 263–290). Hillsdale, NJ: Erlbaum.

Clark, M. S., & Fiske, S. T. (Eds.). (1982). *Affect and cognition: The 17th Annual Carnegie Symposium on Cognition.* Hillsdale, NJ: Erlbaum.

Clark, M. S., & Isen, A. M. (1982). Toward understanding the relationship between feeling states and social behavior. In A. Hastorf & A. Isen (Eds.), *Cognitive social psychology* (pp. 73–108). New York: Elsevier North-Holland.

Clark, M. S., Milberg, S., & Erber, R. (1984). Effects of arousal on judgments of others' emotions. *Journal of Personality and Social Psychology, 46,* 551–560.

Clark, M. S., Milberg, S., & Erber, R. (1988). Arousal-state-dependent memory: Evidence and implications for understanding social judgments and social behavior. In K. Fiedler & J. Forgas (Eds.), *Affect, cognition, and social behavior* (pp. 63–83). Toronto, Canada: Hogrefe.

Clark, M. S., Milberg, S., & Ross, J. (1983). Arousal cues material stored in memory with a similar level of arousal: Implications for understanding the effects of mood on memory. *Journal of Verbal Learning and Verbal Behavior, 22,* 633–649.

Clark, M. S., & Waddell, B. A. (1983). Effects of moods on thoughts about helping, attraction and information acquisition. *Social Psychology Quarterly, 46,* 31–35.

Clark, M. S., & Williamson, G. M. (1989). Moods and social judgments. In H. L. Wagner & A. S. R. Manstead (Eds.), *Handbook of psychophysiology: Emotion and social behavior* (pp. 347–370). Chichester, England: Wiley.

Clark, N. K., & Rutter, D. R. (1985). Social categorization, visual cues, and social judgements. *European Journal of Social Psychology, 15,* 105–119.

Clifton, A. K., McGrath, D., & Wick, B. (1976). Stereotypes of woman: A single category? *Sex Roles, 2,* 135–148.

Clore, G. L., & Kerber, K. (1980). *Affective schemata in the person perception cycle.* Unpublished manuscript, University of Illinois.

Clore, G. L., Ortony, A., & Foss, M. A. (1987). The psychological foundations of the affective lexicon. *Journal of Personality and Social Psychology, 53,* 751–766.

Cochran, S. D., & Hammen, C. L. (1985). Perceptions of stressful life events and depression: A test of attributional models. *Journal of Personality and Social Psychology, 48,* 1562–1571.

Cohen, A. R. (1961). Cognitive tuning as a factor affecting impression formation. *Journal of Personality, 29,* 235–245.

Cohen, A. R., Brehm, J. W., & Latane, B. (1959). Choice of strategy and voluntary exposure to information under public and private conditions. *Journal of Personality, 27,* 63–73.

Cohen, C. E. (1981a). Goals and schemas in person perception: Making sense out of the stream of behavior. In N. Cantor & J. Kihlstrom (Eds.), *Personality, cognition, and social behavior* (pp. 45–68). Hillsdale, NJ: Erlbaum.

Cohen, C. E. (1981b). Person categories and social perception: Testing some boundaries of the processing effects of prior knowledge. *Journal of Personality and Social Psychology, 40,* 441–452.

Cohen, C. E., & Ebbesen, E. B. (1979). Observational goals and schema activation: A theoretical framework for behavior perception. *Journal of Experimental Social Psychology, 15,* 305–329.

Cohen, F., & Lazarus, R. S. (1973). Active coping processes, coping dispositions, and recovery from surgery. *Psychosomatic Medicine, 35,* 375–389.

Cohen, J. B., & Basu, K. (1987). Alternative models of categorization: Toward a contingent processing framework. *Journal of Consumer Research, 13,* 455–472.

Cohen, J. L., Dowling, N., Bishop, G., & Maney, W. J. (1985). Causal attributions: Effects of self-focused attentiveness and self-esteem feedback. *Personality and Social Psychology Bulletin, 11,* 369–378.

Cohen, L. H., Towbes, L. C., & Flocco, R. (1988). Effects of induced mood on self-reported life events and perceived and received social support. *Journal of Personality and Social Psychology, 55,* 669–674.

Collins, A. M., & Loftus, E. F. (1975). A spreading-activation theory of semantic processing. *Psychological Review, 82,* 407–428.

Collins, A. M., & Quillian, M. R. (1972). Experiments on semantic memory and language comprehension. In L. W. Gregg (Ed.), *Cognition and learning.* New York: Wiley.

Collins, B. E. (1974). Four separate components of the Rotter I-E scale: Belief in a difficult world, a just world, a predictable world, and a politically responsive world. *Journal of Personality and Social Psychology, 29,* 381–391.

Collins, R. L., Taylor, S. E., Wood, J. V., & Thompson, S. C. (1988). The vividness effect: Elusive or illusory? *Journal of Experimental Social Psychology, 24,* 1–18.

Commins, B., & Lockwood, J. (1978). The effects on intergroup relations of mixing Roman Catholics and Protestants: An experimental investigation. *European Journal of Social Psychology, 8,* 383–383.

Condry, J. (1977). Enemies of exploration: Self-initiated versus other-initiated learning. *Journal of Personality and Social Psychology, 35,* 459–477.

Conger, J. C., Conger, A. J., & Brehm, S. (1976). Fear level as a moderator of false feedback effects in snake phobics. *Journal of Consulting and Clinical Psychology, 44,* 135–141.

Converse, P. E. (1964). The nature of belief systems in mass publics. In D. E. Apter (Ed.), *Ideology and discontent* (pp. 206–261). New York: Free Press.

Converse, P. E. (1970). Attitudes and non-attitudes: Continuation of a dialogue.

In E. R. Tufte (Ed.), *The quantitative analysis of social problems* (pp. 168–189). Reading, MA: Addison-Wesley.

Conway, M., & Ross, M. (1984). Getting what you want by revising what you had. *Journal of Personality and Social Psychology, 47,* 738–748.

Cook, T. D., & Flay, B. R. (1978). The persistence of experimentally induced attitude change. In L. Berkowitz (Ed.), *Advances in experimental social psychology* (Vol. 11, pp. 1–57). New York: Academic Press.

Cooley, C. H. (1902). *Human nature and the social order.* New York: Scribners.

Cooper, J. & Fazio, R. H. (1984). A new look at dissonance theory. In L. Berkowitz (Ed.), *Advances in experimental social psychology* (Vol. 17, pp. 229–266). New York: Academic Press.

Cooper, J., Zanna, M. P., & Taves, P. A. (1978). Arousal as a necessary condition for attitude change following induced compliance. *Journal of Personality and Social Psychology, 36,* 1101–1106.

Coovert, M. D., & Reeder, G. D. (1990). Negativity effects in impression formation: The role of unit formation and schematic expectations. *Journal of Experimental Social Psychology, 26,* 49–62.

Cordray, D. S., & Shaw, J. I. (1978). An empirical test of the covariation analysis in causal attribution. *Journal of Experimental Social Psychology, 14,* 280–290.

Corteen, R. S., & Wood, B. (1972). Automatic responses to shock-associated words in an unattended channel. *Journal of Experimental Psychology, 94,* 308–313.

Costrich, N., Feinstein, J., Kidder, L., Marecek, J., & Pascale, L. (1975). When stereotypes hurt: Three studies of penalties for sex-role reversals. *Journal of Experimental Social Psychology, 11,* 520–530.

Cottrell, N. B., Ingraham, L. A., & Monfort, F. W. (1971). The retention of balanced and unbalanced cognitive structures. *Journal of Personality, 39,* 112–131.

Covington, M. V., & Omelich, C. L. (1979). Are causal attributions causal? A path analysis of the cognitive model of achievement motivation. *Journal of Personality and Social Psychology, 37,* 1487–1504.

Coyne, J. C., & Gotlib, I. H. (1983). The role of cognition in depression: A critical appraisal. *Psychological Bulletin, 94,* 472–505.

Craighead, W. E., Hickey, K. S., & DeMonbreun, B. G. (1979). Distortion of perception and recall of neutral feedback in depression. *Cognitive Therapy and Research, 3,* 291–298.

Craik, F. I. M., & Lockhart, R. S. (1972). Levels of processing: A framework for memory research. *Journal of Verbal Learning and Verbal Behavior, 11,* 671–676.

Crandall, C. S., & Greenfield, B. S. (1986). Understanding the conjunction fallacy: A conjunction of effects? *Social Cognition, 4,* 408–419.

Crandall, V. C., Katkovsky, W., & Crandall, V. J. (1965). Children's beliefs in their own control of reinforcement in intellectual-academic situations. *Child Development, 36,* 91–109.

Crane, M., & Markus, H. (1982). Gender identity: The benefits of a self-schema approach. *Journal of Personality and Social Psychology, 43,* 1195–1197.

Crano, W. D., Gorenflo, D. W., & Shackelford, S. L. (1988). Overjustification, assumed consensus, and attitude change: Further investigation of the incentive-aroused ambivalence hypothesis. *Journal of Personality and Social Psychology, 55,* 12–22.

Crary, W. G. (1966). Reactions to incongruent self-experiences. *Journal of Consulting Psychology, 30,* 246–252.

Crocker, J. (1981). Judgment of covariation by social perceivers. *Psychology Bulletin, 90*, 272–292.

Crocker, J. (1982). Biased questions in judgment of covariation studies. *Personality and Social Psychology Bulletin, 8*, 214–220.

Crocker, J., Alloy, L. B., & Kayne, N. T. (1988). Attributional style, depression, and perceptions of consensus for events. *Journal of Personality and Social Psychology, 54*, 840–846.

Crocker, J., Fiske, S. T., & Taylor, S. E. (1984). Schematic bases of belief change. In J. R. Eiser (Ed.), *Attitudinal judgment* (pp. 197–226). New York: Springer-Verlag.

Crocker, J., Hannah, D. B., & Weber, R. (1983). Person memory and causal attributions. *Journal of Personality and Social Psychology, 44*, 55–66.

Crocker, J., & Major, B. (1989). Social stigma and self-esteem: The self-protective properties of stigma. *Psychological Review, 96*, 608–630.

Crocker, J., & McGraw, K. M. (1984). What's good for the goose is not good for the gander: Solo status as an obstacle to occupational achievement for males and females. *American Behavioral Scientist, 27*, 357–369.

Crocker, J. & Schwartz, I. (1985). Prejudice and ingroup favoritism in a minimal intergroup situation: Effects of self-esteem. *Personality and Social Psychology Bulletin, 11*, 379–386.

Crocker, J., Thompson, L. L., McGraw, K. M., & Ingerman, C. (1987). Downward comparison, prejudice, and evaluation of others: Effects of self-esteem and threat. *Journal of Personality and Social Psychology, 52*, 907–916.

Crockett, W. H. (1965). Cognitive complexity and impression formation. In B. A. Maher (Ed.), *Progress in experimental personality research* (Vol. 2, pp. 47–90).

Cronbach, L. J. (1955). Processes affecting scores on "understanding of others" and "assumed similarity." *Psychological Bulletin, 52*, 177–193.

Crosby, F., Bromley, S., & Saxe, L. (1980). Recent unobtrusive studies of black and white discrimination and prejudice: A literature review. *Psychological Bulletin, 87*, 546–563.

Crosby, F., Burris, L., Censor, C., & MacKethan, E. R. (1986). Two rotten apples spoil the justice barrel. In H. W. Bierhoff, R. L. Cohen, & J. Greenberg (Eds.), *Justice in social relations* (pp. 267–279). New York: Plenum.

Crosby, F., Clayton, S., Alksnis, O., & Hemker, K. (1986). Cognitive biases in the perception of discrimination: The importance of format. *Sex Roles, 14*, 637–646.

Csikszentmihalyi, M. (1978). Attention and the holistic approach to behavior. In K. S. Pope & J. L. Singer (Eds.), *The stream of consciousness* (pp. 335–358). New York: Plenum.

Csikszentmihalyi, M., & Larson, R. (1984). *Being adolescent: Conflict and growth in the teenage years.* New York: Basic Books.

Cunningham, J. D., & Kelley, H. H. (1975). Causal attributions for interpersonal events of varying magnitudes. *Journal of Personality, 43*, 74–93.

Cunningham, M. R. (1988). Does happiness mean friendliness? Induced mood and heterosexual self-disclosure. *Personality and Social Psychology Bulletin, 14*, 283–297.

Cunningham, M. R., Steinberg, J., & Grev, R. (1980). Wanting to and having to help: Separate motivations for positive mood and guilt-induced helping. *Journal of Personality and Social Psychology, 38*, 181–192.

Cupchik, G. C., & Leventhal, H. (1974). Consistency between expressive behavior and the evaluation of humorous stimuli: The role of sex and self-observation. *Journal of Personality and Social Psychology, 30*, 429–442.

Cutler, B. L., Penrod, S. D., & Martens, T. K. (1987). The reliability of eyewitness identification: The role of system and estimator variables. *Law and Human Behavior, 11*, 233–258.

Cutrona, C. E., Russell, D., & Jones, R. D. (1985). Cross-situational consistency in causal attributions: Does attributional style exist? *Journal of Personality and Social Psychology, 47*, 1043–1058.

Dahl, H., Kachele, H., & Thoma, H. (Eds.) (1989). *Psychoanalytic process research strategies*. New York: Springer-Verlag.

Damon, W., & Hart, D. (1986). Stability and change in children's self-understanding. *Social Cognition, 4*, 102–118.

D'Andrade, R. (1989). Culturally based reasoning. In A. Gellatly, D. Rogers, & J. A. Sloboda (Eds.), *Cognition and social worlds* (pp. 132–143). Oxford, England: Clarendon Press.

Darley, J. M., & Fazio, R. H. (1980). Expectancy confirmation processes arising in the social interaction sequence. *American Psychologist, 35*, 867–881.

Darley, J. M., Fleming, J. H., Hilton, J. L., & Swann, W. B., Jr. (1988). Dispelling negative expectancies: The impact of interaction goals and target characteristics on the expectancy confirmation process. *Journal of Experimental Social Psychology, 24*, 19–36.

Darley, J. M., & Goethals, G. R. (1980). People's analyses of the causes of ability-linked performances. In L. Berkowitz (Ed.), *Advances in experimental social psychology* (Vol. 13, pp. 1–37). New York: Academic Press.

Darley, J. M., & Gross, P. H. (1983). A hypothesis-confirming bias in labeling effects. *Journal of Personality and Social Psychology, 44*, 20–33.

Darwin, C. R. (1872). *The expression of emotions in man and animals*. London: John Murray.

Davies, M. F. (1985). Social roles and social perception biases: The questioner superiority effect revisited. *British Journal of Social Psychology, 24*, 239–248.

Davis, D., & Holtgraves, T. (1984). Perceptions of unresponsive others: Attributions, attraction, understandability, and memory of their utterances. *Journal of Experimental Social Psychology, 20*, 383–408.

Davison, A. R., Yantis, S., Norwood, M., & Montano, D. E. (1985). Amount of information about the attitude object and attitude-behavior consistency. *Journal of Personality and Social Psychology, 49*, 1184–1198.

Davison, G. C., Feldman, P. M., & Osborn, C. E. (1984). Articulated thoughts, irrational beliefs, and fear of negative evaluation. *Cognitive Therapy and Research, 8*, 349–362.

Davison, G. C., Robins, C., & Johnson, M. K. (1983). Articulated thoughts during simulated situations: A paradigm for studying cognition in emotion and behavior. *Cognitive Therapy and Research, 7*, 17–40.

Davison, G. C., & Valins, S. (1969). Maintenance of self-attributed and drug-attributed behavior change. *Journal of Personality and Social Psychology, 11*, 25–33.

Davison, G. C., & Zighelboim, V. (1987). Irrational beliefs in the articulated thoughts of college students with social anxiety. *Journal of Rational-Emotive Therapy, 5*, 238–254.

Davitz, J. R. (1970). A dictionary and grammar of emotion. In M. B. Arnold (Ed.), *Feelings and emotion: The Loyola Symposium* (pp. 251–258). New York: Academic Press.

Dawes, R. (1989). Statistical criteria for establishing a truly false consensus effect. *Journal of Experimental Social Psychology, 25,* 1–17.

Dawes, R., Faust, D., & Meehl, P. E. (1989). Clinical versus actuarial judgment. *Science, 243,* 1668–1674.

Dawes, R. M. (1976). Shallow psychology. In J. Carroll & J. Payne (Eds.), *Cognition and social behavior* (pp. 3–12). Hillsdale, NJ: Erlbaum.

Dawes, R. M. (1980). You can't systematize human judgment: Dyslexia. In R. A. Shweder (Ed.), *New directions for methodology of social and behavioral science* (Vol. 4, pp. 67–78). San Francisco: Jossey-Bass.

Deaux, K. (1976). *The behavior of women and men.* Monterey, CA: Brooks/Cole.

Deaux, K. (1984). From individual differences to social categories: Analysis of a decade's research on gender. *American Psychologist, 39,* 105–116.

Deaux, K. (1985). Sex and gender. *Annual Review of Psychology, 36,* 49–81.

Deaux, K., Kite, M. E., & Lewis, L. L. (1985). Clustering and gender schemata: An uncertain link. *Personality and Social Psychology Bulletin, 11,* 387–397.

Deaux, K., & Lewis, L. L. (1984). Structure of gender stereotypes: Interrelationships among components and gender label. *Journal of Personality and Social Psychology, 46,* 991–1004.

Deaux, K., & Major, B. (1977). Sex-related patterns in the unit of perception. *Personality and Social Psychology Bulletin, 3,* 297–300.

Deaux, K., & Major, B. (1987). Putting gender into context: An interactive model of gender-related behavior. *Psychological Review, 94,* 369–389.

Deaux, K., Winton, W., Crowley, M., & Lewis, L. L. (1985). Level of categorization and content of gender stereotypes. *Social Cognition, 3,* 145–167.

DeBono, K. G. (1987). Investigating the social-adjustive and value-expressive functions of attitudes: Implications for persuasion processes. *Journal of Personality and Social Psychology, 52,* 279–287.

DeBono, K. G., & Harnish, R. J. (1988). Source expertise, source attractiveness, and the processing of persuasive information: A functional approach. *Journal of Personality and Social Psychology, 55,* 541–546.

DeBono, K. G., & Snyder, M. (1989). Understanding consumer decision-making processes: The role of form and function in product evaluation. *Journal of Applied Social Psychology, 19,* 416–424.

Deci, E. L., & Ryan, R. M. (1985). *Intrinsic motivation and self-determination in human behavior.* New York: Plenum.

Deci, E. L., & Ryan, R. M. (1987). The support of autonomy and the control of behavior. *Journal of Personality and Social Psychology, 53,* 1024–1037.

de Jong, P. F., Koomen, W., & Mellenbergh, G. J. (1988). Structure of causes for success and failure: A multidimensional scaling analysis of preference judgments. *Journal of Personality and Social Psychology, 55,* 718–725.

DePaulo, B. M. (1990). *Nonverbal behavior and self-presentation.* Unpublished manuscript, University of Virginia.

DePaulo, B. M., & Coleman, L. M. (1986). Talking to children, foreigners, and retarded adults. *Journal of Personality and Social Psychology, 51,* 945–959.

DePaulo, B. M., & Coleman, L. M. (1987). Verbal and nonverbal communication of warmth to children, foreigners, and retarded adults. *Journal of Nonverbal Behavior, 11,* 75–88.

DePaulo, B. M., & Rosenthal, R. (1979). Telling lies. *Journal of Personality and Social Psychology, 37,* 1713–1721.

de Rivera, J. (1984). The structure of emotional relationships. In P. Shaver (Ed.), *Review of personality and social psychology: Vol. 5. Emotions, relationships, and health* (pp. 116–145). Beverly Hills, CA: Sage.

de Rivera, J., & Grinkis, C. (1986). Emotions as social relationships. *Motivation and Emotion, 10,* 351–369.

Derryberry, D., & Rothbart, M. K. (1988). Arousal, affect, and attention as components of temperament. *Journal of Personality and Social Psychology, 55,* 958–966.

Deschamps, J.-C., & Doise, W. (1978). Crossed category memberships in intergroup relations. In H. Tajfel (Ed.), *Differentiation between social groups* (pp. 141–158). London: Academic Press.

De Soto, C. B. (1961). The predilection for single orderings. *Journal of Abnormal and Social Psychology, 62,* 13–23.

De Soto, C. B., Hamilton, M. M., & Taylor, R. B. (1985). Words, people, and implicit personality theory. *Social Cognition, 3,* 369–382.

De Soto, C. B., Henley, N. M., & London, M. (1968). Balance and the grouping schema. *Journal of Personality and Social Psychology, 8,* 1–7.

De Soto, C. B., London, M., & Handel, S. (1965). Social reasoning and spatial paralogic. *Journal of Personality and Social Psychology, 2,* 513–521.

Deutsch, F. M., & Mackesy, M. E. (1985). Friendship and the development of self-schemas: The effects of talking about others. *Personality and Social Psychology Bulletin, 11,* 399–408.

Deutsch, F. M., Ruble, D. N., Fleming, A., Brooks-Gunn, J., & Stangor, C. (1988). Information-seeking and maternal self-definition during the transition to motherhood. *Journal of Personality and Social Psychology, 55,* 420–431.

Deutsch, M. (1968). Field theory in social psychology. In G. Lindzey & E. Aronson (Eds.), *The handbook of social psychology* (Vol. 1, 2nd ed.), Reading, MA: Addison-Wesley.

Devine, P. G. (1989). Stereotypes and prejudice: Their automatic and controlled components. *Journal of Personality and Social Psychology, 56,* 5–18.

Devine, P. G., & Malpass, R. S. (1985). Orienting strategies in differential face recognition. *Personality and Social Psychology Bulletin, 11,* 33–40.

Devine, P. G., & Ostrom, T. M. (1985). Cognitive mediation of inconsistency discounting. *Journal of Personality and Social Psychology, 49,* 5–21.

Devine, P. G., Sedikides, C., & Fuhrman, R. W. (1989). Goals in social information processing: A case of anticipated interaction. *Journal of Personality and Social Psychology, 56,* 680–690.

de Vries, B., & Walker, L. J. (1987). Conceptual/integrative complexity and attitudes toward capital punishment. *Personality and Social Psychology Bulletin, 13,* 448–457.

de Vries, N. K., & van Knippenberg, A. (1985). Logical deduction and bias in self-evaluation of abilities: A reply to Sanders & Mullen. *British Journal of Social Psychology, 24,* 157–158.

Diehl, M. (1988). Social identity and minimal groups: The effects of interpersonal and intergroup attitudinal similarity on intergroup discrimination. *British Journal of Social Psychology, 27,* 289–300.

Diener, E. (1984). Subjective well-being. *Psychological Bulletin, 95,* 542–575.

Diener, E., & Emmons, R. A. (1984). The independence of positive and negative affect. *Journal of Personality and Social Psychology, 47,* 1105–1117.

Diener, E., & Iran-Nejad, A. (1986). The relationship in experience between various types of affect. *Journal of Personality and Social Psychology, 50,* 1031–1038.

Dijker, A. J. M. (1987). Emotional reactions to ethnic minorities. *European Journal of Social Psychology, 17,* 305–325.

Dillon, W. R., & Kumar, A. (1985). Attitude organization and the attitude-behavior relation: A critique of Bagozzi and Burnkrant's reanalysis of Fishbein and Ajzen. *Journal of Personality and Social Psychology, 49,* 33–46.

DiVitto, B., & McArthur, L. Z. (1978). Developmental differences in the use of distinctiveness, consensus and consistency information for making causal attributions. *Developmental Psychology, 5,* 474–482.

Dixon, N. F. (1971). *Subliminal perception: The nature of the controversy.* London: McGraw-Hill.

Dixon, N. F. (1981). *Preconscious processing.* New York: Wiley.

Dodge, K. A., & Tomlin, A. M. (1987). Utilization of self-schemas as a mechanism of interpretational bias in aggressive children. *Social Cognition, 5,* 280–300.

Doise, W. (1988). Individual and social identities in intergroup relations. *European Journal of Social Psychology, 18,* 99–111.

Doise, W., Deschamps, J.-C., & Meyer, G. (1978). The accentuation of intra-category similarities. In H. Tajfel (Ed.), *Differentiation between social groups* (pp. 159–168). London: Academic Press.

Dornbusch, S. M., Hastorf, A. H., Richardson, S. A., Muzzy, R. E., & Vreeland, R. S. (1965). The perceiver and the perceived: Their relative influence on categories of interpersonal perception. *Journal of Personality and Social Psychology, 1,* 434–440.

Dovidio, J. F., Evans, N., & Tyler, R. B. (1986). Racial stereotypes: The contents of their cognitive representations. *Journal of Experimental Social Psychology, 22,* 22–37.

Dovidio, J. F., & Gaertner, S. L. (Eds.) (1986). *Prejudice, discrimination, and racism.* Orlando, FL: Academic Press.

Doyle, A. C. (1930). *The complete Sherlock Holmes.* Garden City, NY: Doubleday, Doran.

Dreben, E. K., Fiske, S. T., & Hastie, R. (1979). The independence of evaluative and item information: Impression and recall order effects in behavior-based impression formation. *Journal of Personality and Social Psychology, 37,* 1758–1768.

Dribben, E., & Brabender, V. (1979). The effect of mood inducement upon audience receptiveness. *The Journal of Social Psychology, 107,* 135–136.

Duncan, J. W., & Laird, J. D. (1977). Cross-modality consistencies in individual differences in self-attribution. *Journal of Personality, 45,* 191–196.

Duncan, J. W., & Laird, J. D. (1980). Positive and reverse placebo effects as a function of differences in cues used in self-perception. *Journal of Personality and Social Psychology, 39,* 1024–1036.

Duncan, S. L. (1976). Differential social perception and attribution of intergroup violence: Testing the lower limits of stereotyping of blacks. *Journal of Personality and Social Psychology, 34,* 590–598.

Dunning, D., & Parpal, M. (1989). Mental addition versus subtraction in counterfactual reasoning: On assessing the impact of personal actions and life events. *Journal of Personality and Social Psychology, 57,* 5–15.

Dutta, S., Kanungo, R. N., & Freibergs, V. (1972). Retention of affective material: Effects of intensity of affect on retrieval. *Journal of Personality and Social Psychology, 23,* 64–80.

Dutton, D. G., & Aron, A. P. (1974). Some evidence for heightened sexual attraction under conditions of high anxiety. *Journal of Personality and Social Psychology, 30,* 510–517.

Duval, S. (1976). Conformity on a visual task as a function of personal novelty on attitudinal dimensions and being reminded of the object status of self. *Journal of Experimental Social Psychology, 12,* 87–98.

Duval, S., & Wicklund, R. A. (1972). *A theory of objective self-awareness.* New York: Academic Press.

Duval, T. S., & Duval, V. H. (1987). Level of perceived coping ability and attribution for negative events. *Journal of Social and Clinical Psychology, 5,* 452–468.

Dweck, C. S., & Licht, B. G. (1980). Learned helplessness and intellectual achievement. In M. E. P. Seligman & J. Garber (Eds.), *Human helplessness: Theory and applications* (pp. 197–222). New York: Academic Press.

Dykman, B. M., Abramson, L. Y., Alloy, L. B., & Hartlage, S. (1989). Processing of ambiguous and unambiguous feedback by depressed and nondepressed college students: Schematic biases and their implications for depressive realism. *Journal of Personality and Social Psychology, 56,* 431–445.

Eagly, A. H. (1974). Comprehensibility of persuasive arguments as a determinant of opinion change. *Journal of Personality and Social Psychology, 29,* 758–773.

Eagly, A. H., Ashmore, R. D., Makhijani, M. G., & Kennedy, L. C. (1990). *What is beautiful is good, but ...: A meta-analytic review of research on the physical attractiveness stereotype.* Unpublished manuscript, Purdue University.

Eagly, A. H., & Chaiken, S. (1975). An attribution analysis of the effect of communication characteristics on opinion change: The case of communicator attractiveness. *Journal of Personality and Social Psychology, 32,* 136–144.

Eagly, A. H., & Chaiken, S. (1984). Cognitive theories of persuasion. In L. Berkowitz (Ed.), *Advances in experimental social psychology* (Vol. 17, pp. 267–359). New York: Academic Press.

Eagly, A. H., & Chaiken, S. (in press). *The psychology of attitudes.* New York: Harcourt, Brace Jovanovich.

Eagly, A. H., Chaiken, S., & Wood, W. (1981). An attribution analysis of persuasion. In J. H. Harvey, W. J. Ickes, & R. F. Kidd (Eds.), *New directions in attribution research* (Vol. 3, pp. 37–62). Hillsdale, NJ: Erlbaum.

Eagly, A. H., & Himmelfarb, S. (1978). Attitudes and opinions. *Annual Review of Psychology, 29,* 517–554.

Eagly, A. H., Wood, W., & Chaiken, S. (1978). Causal inferences about communicators and their effect on opinion change. *Journal of Personality and Social Psychology, 36,* 424–435.

Ebbesen, E. B. (1980). Cognitive processes in understanding ongoing behavior.

In R. Hastie, T. M. Ostrom, E. B. Ebbesen, R. S. Wyer, Jr., D. L. Hamilton, & D. E. Carlston (Eds.), *Person memory: The cognitive basis of social perception* (pp. 179–226). Hillsdale, NJ: Erlbaum.

Ebbesen, E. B., & Allen, R. B. (1979). Cognitive processes in implicit personality trait inferences. *Journal of Personality and Social Psychology, 37,* 471–488.

Ebbinghaus, H. (1964). [*Memory: A contribution to experimental psychology.*] (H. A. Ruger & C. E. Bussenius, trans.). New York: Dover. (Originally published, 1885.)

Egbert, L. D., Batitt, E., Welch, C. E., & Bartlett, M. K. (1964). Reduction of postoperative pain by encouragement and instruction of patients. *New England Journal of Medicine, 270,* 825–827.

Ehrlich, H. J. (1973). *The social psychology of prejudice.* New York: Wiley.

Ehrlichman, H., & Halpern, J. N. (1988). Affect and memory: Effects of pleasant and unpleasant odors on retrieval of happy and unhappy memories. *Journal of Personality and Social Psychology, 55,* 769–779.

Einhorn, H. J. (1980). Overconfidence in judgment. In R. A. Shweder (Ed.), *New directions for methodology of social and behavioral science* (Vol. 4, pp. 1–16). San Francisco: Jossey-Bass.

Einhorn, H. J. (1982). Learning from experience and suboptimal rules in decision making. In D. Kahneman, P. Slovic, & A. Tversky (Eds.), *Judgment under uncertainty: Heuristics and biases* (pp. 268–286). New York: Cambridge University Press.

Einhorn, H. J., & Hogarth, R. M. (1981). Behavioral decision theory: Processes of judgment and choice. *Annual Review of Psychology, 32,* 53–88.

Einhorn, H. J., & Hogarth, R. M. (1986). Judging probable cause. *Psychological Bulletin, 99,* 3–19.

Eisen, S. V. (1979). Actor-observer differences in information inference and causal attribution. *Journal of Personality and Social Psychology, 37,* 261–272.

Eisen, S. V., & McArthur, L. Z. (1979). Evaluating and sentencing a defendant as a function of his salience and the observer's set. *Personality and Social Psychology Bulletin, 5,* 48–52.

Ekman, P. (1984). Expression and the nature of emotion. In K. Scherer & P. Ekman (Eds.), *Approaches to emotion* (pp. 319–343). Hillsdale, NJ: Erlbaum.

Ekman, P., Levenson, R. W., & Friesen, W. V. (1983). Autonomic nervous system activity distinguishes among emotions. *Science, 221,* 1208–1210.

Ekman, P., & O'Sullivan, M. (1988). Comment on Russell and Fehr. *Journal of Experimental Psychology: General, 117,* 86–88.

Elig, T. W., & Frieze, I. H. (1979). Measuring causal attributions for success and failure. *Journal of Personality and Social Psychology, 37,* 621–634.

Elio, R., & Anderson, J. R. (1981). The effects of category generalizations and instance similarity on schema abstraction. *Journal of Experimental Psychology: Human Learning and Memory, 7,* 397–417.

Ellis, H. D., Deregowski, J. B., & Shepherd, J. (1975). Descriptions of white and black faces by white and black subjects. *International Journal of Psychology, 10,* 119–123.

Ellis, R. J., & Holmes, J. G. (1982). Focus of attention and self-evaluation in social interaction. *Journal of Personality and Social Psychology, 43,* 67–77.

Ellis, R. J., Olson, J. M., & Zanna, M. P. (1983). Stereotypic personality inferences following objective versus subjective judgments of beauty. *Canadian Journal of Behavioral Science, 15,* 35–42.

Ellsworth, P. C., & Smith, C. A. (1988a). From appraisal to emotion: Differences among unpleasant feelings. *Motivation and Emotion, 12,* 271–302.

Ellsworth, P. C., & Smith, C. A. (1988b). Shades of joy: Patterns of appraisal differentiating pleasant emotions. *Emotion and Cognition, 2,* 302–331.

Ellsworth, P. C., & Tourangeau, R. (1981). On our failure to disconfirm what nobody ever said. *Journal of Personality and Social Psychology, 40,* 363–369.

Enquist, C., Newtson, D., & LaCross, K. (1979). *Prior expectations and the perceptual segmentation of ongoing behavior.* Unpublished manuscript, University of Virginia.

Enzle, M. E., & Schopflocher, D. (1978). Instigation of attribution processes by attributional questions. *Journal of Personality and Social Psychology, 4,* 595–599.

Epstein, S. (1979). The stability of behavior: I. On predicting most of the people much of the time. *Journal of Personality and Social Psychology, 7,* 1097–1126.

Epstein, S. (1980). The self-concept: A review and the proposal of an integrated theory of personality. In E. Staub (Ed.), *Personality: Basic issues and current research* (pp. 82–131). Englewood Cliffs, NJ: Prentice-Hall.

Epstein, S. (1983). The unconscious, the preconscious, and the self-concept. In J. Suls & A. Greenwald (Eds.), *Psychological perspectives on the self* (Vol. 2, pp. 220–247). Hillsdale, NJ: Erlbaum.

Epstein, S. (1984). Controversial issues in emotion theory. In P. Shaver (Ed.), *Review of personality and social psychology: Vol. 5. Emotions, relationships, and health* (pp. 64–88). Beverly Hills, CA: Sage.

Epstein, S. (1985). The implications of cognitive-experiential self-theory for research in social psychology and personality. *Journal for the Theory of Social Behavior, 15,* 283–310.

Epstein, S. (1990a). Cognitive experiential self-theory. In L.A. Pervin (Ed.), *Handbook of personality: Theory and research* (pp. 165–192). New York: Guilford Press.

Epstein, S. (1990b). The self-concept, the traumatic neurosis, and the structure of personality. In D. Ozer, J. M. Healy, Jr., & A. J. Stewart (Eds.), *Perspectives on personality* (Vol. 3, pp. 63–98). Greenwich, CT: JAI Press.

Epstein, S., & Erskine, N. (1983). The development of personal theories of realities from an interactional perspective. In D. Magnusson & V. L. Allen (Eds.), *Human development: An interactional perspective* (pp. 133–147). New York: Academic Press.

Epstein, S., & Feist, G. J. (1988). Relation between self- and other-acceptance and its moderation by identification. *Journal of Personality and Social Psychology, 54,* 309–315.

Epstein, S., & Teraspulsky, L. (1986). Perception of cross-situational consistency. *Journal of Personality and Social Psychology, 50,* 1152–1160.

Erber, R. (1991). Affective and semantic priming: Effects of mood on category accessibility and inference. *Journal of Experimental Social Psychology.*

Erber, R., & Fiske, S. T. (1984). Outcome dependency and attention to inconsistent information. *Journal of Personality and Social Psychology, 47,* 709–726.

Erdelyi, M. H. (1974). A new look at the New Look: Perceptual defense and vigilance. *Psychological Review, 81,* 1–25.

Erdley, C. A., & D'Agostino, P. R. (1988). Cognitive and affective components of automatic priming effects. *Journal of Personality and Social Psychology, 54,* 741–747.

Ericsson, K. A., & Simon, H. A. (1980). Verbal reports as data. *Psychological Review, 87*, 215–251.

Eriksen, C. W. (1956). Subception: Fact or artifact. *Psychological Review, 63*, 74–80.

Eriksen, C. W. (1960). Discrimination and learning without awareness: A methodological survey and evaluation. *Psychological Review, 67*, 279–300.

Espinoza, J. A., & Garza, R. T. (1985). Social group salience and interethnic cooperation. *Journal of Experimental Social Psychology, 21*, 380–392.

Exline, R. V. (1972). Visual interaction: The glances of power and preference. In J. Cole (Ed.), *Nebraska Symposium on motivation* (Vol. 19, pp. 163–206). Lincoln: University of Nebraska Press.

Farina, A., Allen, J. G., & Saul, B. B. (1968). The role of the stigmatized person in affecting social relationships. *Journal of Personality, 36*, 169–182.

Fazio, R. H. (1986). How do attitudes guide behavior? In R. M. Sorrentino & E. T. Higgins (Eds.), *Handbook of motivation and cognition: Foundations of social behavior* (pp. 204–243). New York: Guilford Press.

Fazio, R. H. (1987). Self-perception theory: A current perspective. In M. P. Zanna, J. M. Olson, & C. P. Herman (Eds.), *Social influence: The Ontario Symposium* (Vol. 5, pp. 129–149). Hillsdale, NJ: Erlbaum.

Fazio, R. H. (1989). On the power and functionality of attitudes: The role of attitude accessibility. In A. R. Pratkanis, S. J. Breckler, & A. G. Greenwald (Eds.), *Attitude structure and function* (pp. 153–179). Hillsdale, NJ: Erlbaum.

Fazio, R. H. (1990). Multiple processes by which attitudes guide behavior: The MODE model as an integrative framework. In M. P. Zanna (Ed.), *Advances in experimental social psychology* (Vol. 23, pp. 75–110). New York: Academic Press.

Fazio, R. H., Chen, J., McDonel, E. C., & Sherman, S. J. (1982). Attitude accessibility, attitude-behavior consistency, and the strength of the object-evaluation association. *Journal of Experimental Social Psychology, 18*, 339–357.

Fazio, R. H., & Cooper, J. (1983). Arousal in the dissonance process. In J. T. Cacioppo & R. E. Petty (Eds.), *Social psychophysiology* (pp. 122–152). New York: Guilford Press.

Fazio, R. H., Effrein, E. A., & Falender, V. J. (1981). Self-perceptions following social interaction. *Journal of Personality and Social Psychology, 41*, 232–242.

Fazio, R. H., Herr, P. M., & Olney, T. J. (1984). Attitude accessibility following a self-perception process. *Journal of Personality and Social Psychology, 47*, 277–286.

Fazio, R. H., Powell, M. C., & Herr, P. M. (1983). Toward a process model of attitude-behavior relation: Accessing one's attitude upon mere observation of the attitude object. *Journal of Personality and Social Psychology, 44*, 723–735.

Fazio, R. H., Sanbonmatsu, D. M., Powell, M. C., & Kardes, F. R. (1986). On the automatic activation of attitudes. *Journal of Personality and Social Psychology, 50*, 229–238.

Fazio, R. H., Sherman, S. J., & Herr, P. M. (1982). The feature-positive effect in the self-perception process: Does not doing matter as much as doing? *Journal of Personality and Social Psychology, 42*, 404–411.

Fazio, R. H., & Williams, C. J. (1986). Attitude accessibility as a moderator of the attitude-perception and attitude-behavior relations: An investigation of the 1984 Presidential election. *Journal of Personality and Social Psychology, 51*, 505–514.

Fazio, R. H., & Zanna, M. P. (1978). Attitudinal qualities relating to the strength of the attitude-behavior relationship. *Journal of Experimental Social Psychology, 14,* 398–408.

Fazio, R. H., & Zanna, M. P. (1981). Direct experience and attitude-behavior consistency. In L. Berkowitz (Ed.), *Advances in experimental social psychology* (Vol. 14, pp. 162–203). New York: Academic Press.

Fazio, R. H., Zanna, M. P., & Cooper, J. (1977). Dissonance and self-perception: An integrative view of each theory's proper domain of application. *Journal of Experimental Social Psychology, 13,* 464–479.

Feather, N. T. (1969). Attitude and selective recall. *Journal of Personality and Social Psychology, 12,* 310–319.

Feather, N. T. (1985). Attitudes, values, and attributions: Explanations of unemployment. *Journal of Personality and Social Psychology, 48,* 876–889.

Fehr, B. (1988). Prototype analysis of the concepts of love and commitment. *Journal of Personality and Social Psychology, 55,* 557–579.

Fehr, B., & Russell, J. A. (1984). Concept of emotion viewed from a prototype perspective. *Journal of Experimental Psychology: General, 113,* 464–486.

Fenigstein, A. (1984). Self-consciousness and the overperception of self as a target. *Journal of Personality and Social Psychology, 47,* 860–870.

Fenigstein, A., & Levine, M. P. (1984). Self-attention, concept activation, and the causal self. *Journal of Experimental Social Psychology, 20,* 231–245.

Fenigstein, A., Scheier, M. F., & Buss, A. H. (1975). Public and private self-consciousness: Assessment and theory. *Journal of Consulting and Clinical Psychology, 43,* 522–527.

Ferguson, T. J., Rule, B. G. & Carlson, D. (1983). Memory for personally relevant information. *Journal of Personality and Social Psychology, 44,* 251–261.

Ferguson, T. J., & Wells, G. L. (1980). Priming of mediators in causal attribution. *Journal of Personality and Social Psychology, 38,* 461–470.

Festinger, L. (1957). *A theory of cognitive dissonance.* Palo Alto, CA: Stanford University Press.

Fiedler, K. (1982). Causal schemata: Review and criticism of research on a popular construct. *Journal of Personality and Social Psychology, 42,* 1001–1013.

Fiedler, K. (1988). Emotional mood, cognitive style, and behavior regulation. In K. Fiedler & J. P. Forgas (Eds.), *Affect, cognition, and social behavior* (pp. 100–119). Toronto, Canada: Hogrefe.

Fiedler, K., Fladung, U., & Hemmeter, U. (1987). Short research note: A positivity bias in person memory. *European Journal of Social Psychology, 17,* 243–246.

Fiedler, K., Pampe, H., & Scherf, U. (1986). Mood and memory for tightly organized social information. *European Journal of Social Psychology, 16,* 149–164.

Fiedler, K., & Semin, G. R. (1988) On the causal information conveyed by different interpersonal verbs: The role of implicit sentence context. *Social Cognition, 6,* 21–39.

Fiedler, K., & Stroehm, W. (1986). The use of statistical, spatial-temporal, and intensional information in judgments of contingency. *European Journal of Social Psychology, 16,* 385–398.

Fields, J. M., & Schuman, H. (1976). Public beliefs and the beliefs of the public. *Public Opinion Quarterly, 40,* 427–448.

Finch, J. F., & Cialdini, R. B. (1989). Another indirect tactic of (self-) image management: Boosting. *Personality and Social Psychology Bulletin, 15,* 222–232.

Fincham, F. D., & Bradbury, T. N. (1987). Cognitive processes and conflict in close relationships: An attribution-efficacy model. *Journal of Personality and Social Psychology, 53,* 1106–1118.

Fincham, F. D., Diener, C. I., & Hokoda, A. (1987). Attributional style and learned helplessness: Relationship to the use of causal schemata and depressive symptoms in children. *British Journal of Social Psychology, 26,* 1–7.

Fincham, F. D., & Jaspars, J. M. (1979). Attribution of responsibility to self and other in children and adults. *Journal of Personality and Social Psychology, 37,* 1589–1602.

Fincham, F. D., & Jaspars, J. M. (1980). Attribution of responsibility: From man the scientist to man as lawyer. In L. Berkowitz (Ed.), *Advances in experimental social psychology* (Vol. 13, pp. 82–139). New York: Academic Press.

Fincham, F. D., & Roberts, C. (1985). Intervening causation and the mitigation of responsibility for harm doing: II. The role of limited mental capacities. *Journal of Experimental Social Psychology, 21,* 178–194.

Finchilescu, G. (1986). Effect of incompatibility between internal and external group membership criteria on intergroup behavior. *European Journal of Social Psychology, 16,* 83–87.

Fingarette, H. (1969). *Self-deception.* London: Routledge and Kegan Paul.

Fischhoff, B. (1975). Hindsight ≠ foresight: The effects of outcome knowledge on judgment under uncertainty. *Journal of Experimental Psychology: Human Perception and Performance, 1,* 288–299.

Fischhoff, B. (1980). For those condemned to study the past: Reflections on historical judgment. In R. A. Shweder (Ed.), *New directions for methodology of social and behavioral science* (Vol. 4, pp. 79–93). San Francisco: Jossey-Bass.

Fischhoff, B. (1982a). Debiasing. In D. Kahneman, P. Slovic, & A. Tversky (Eds.), *Judgment under uncertainty: Heuristics and biases* (pp. 422–444). New York: Cambridge University Press.

Fischhoff, B. (1982b). For those condemned to study the past: Heuristics and biases in hindsight. In D. Kahneman, P. Slovic, & A. Tversky (Eds.), *Judgment under uncertainty: Heuristics and biases* (pp. 335–354). New York: Cambridge University Press.

Fischhoff, B., & Beyth, R. (1975). "I knew it would happen"—Remembered probabilities of once-future things. *Organizational Behavior and Human Performance, 13,* 1–16.

Fischhoff, B., Slovic, P., & Lichtenstein, S. (1977). Knowing with certainty: The appropriateness of extreme confidence. *Journal of Experimental Psychology: Human Perception and Performance, 3,* 552–564.

Fishbein, M. (1963). An investigation of the relationship between beliefs about an object and the attitude toward that object. *Human Relations, 16,* 233–240.

Fishbein, M. (1967). A consideration of beliefs and their role in attitude measurement. In M. Fishbein (Ed.), *Readings in attitude theory and measurement.* New York: Wiley.

Fishbein, M., & Ajzen, I. (1974). Attitudes toward objects as predictors of single and multiple behavioral criteria. *Psychological Review, 81,* 59–74.

Fishbein, M., & Ajzen, I. (1975). *Belief, attitude, intention, and behavior: An introduction to theory and research.* Reading, MA: Addison-Wesley.

Fiske, D. W., & Maddi, S. R. (1961). *Functions of varied experience.* Homewood, IL: Dorsey.

Fiske, S. T. (1980). Attention and weight in person perception: The impact of negative and extreme behavior. *Journal of Personality and Social Psychology, 38,* 889–906.

Fiske, S. T. (1981). Social cognition and affect. In J. Harvey (Ed.), *Cognition, social behavior, and the environment* (pp. 227–264). Hillsdale, NJ: Erlbaum.

Fiske, S. T. (1982). Schema-triggered affect: Applications to social perception. In M. S. Clark & S. T. Fiske (Eds.), *Affect and cognition: The 17th Annual Carnegie Symposium on Cognition* (pp. 55–78). Hillsdale, NJ: Erlbaum.

Fiske, S. T. (1987a). On the road: Comment on the cognitive stereotyping literature in Pettigrew and Martin. *Journal of Social Issues, 43,* 113–118.

Fiske, S. T. (1987b). People's reactions to nuclear war: Implications for psychologists. *American Psychologist, 42,* 207–217.

Fiske, S. T. (1988). Compare and contrast: Brewer's dual process model and Fiske et al.'s continuum model. In T. K. Srull & R. S. Wyer, Jr. (Eds.), *Advances in social cognition* (Vol. 1, pp. 65–76). Hillsdale, NJ: Erlbaum.

Fiske, S. T. (1989a). Examining the role of intent: Toward understanding its role in stereotyping and prejudice. In J. S. Uleman & J. A. Bargh (Eds.), *Unintended thought* (pp. 253–283). New York: Guilford Press.

Fiske, S. T. (1989b). *Interdependence and stereotyping: From the laboratory to the Supreme Court (and back).* Invited address, American Psychological Association Convention, New Orleans.

Fiske, S. T., & Cox, M. G. (1979). Person concepts: The effects of target familiarity and descriptive purpose on the process of describing others. *Journal of Personality, 47,* 136–161.

Fiske, S. T., & Dyer, L. M. (1985). Structure and development of social schemata: Evidence from positive and negative transfer effects. *Journal of Personality and Social Psychology, 48,* 839–852.

Fiske, S. T., Kenny, D. A., & Taylor, S. E. (1982). Structural models for the mediation of salience effects on attribution. *Journal of Experimental Social Psychology, 18,* 105–127.

Fiske, S. T., & Kinder, D. R. (1981). Involvement, expertise, and schema use: Evidence from political cognition. In N. Cantor & J. Kihlstrom (Eds.), *Personality, cognition, and social interaction.* Hillsdale, NJ: Erlbaum.

Fiske, S. T., Kinder, D. R., & Larter, W. M. (1983). The novice and the expert: Knowledge-based strategies in political cognition. *Journal of Experimental Social Psychology, 19,* 381–400.

Fiske, S. T., Lau, R. R., & Smith, R. A. (1990). On the varieties and utilities of political expertise. *Social Cognition, 8,* 31–48.

Fiske, S. T. & Linville, P. W. (1980). What does the schema concept buy us? *Personality and Social Psychology Bulletin, 6,* 543–557.

Fiske, S. T., & Neuberg, S. L. (1990). A continuum of impression formation, from category-based to individuating processes: Influences of information and motivation on attention and interpretation. In M. P. Zanna (Ed.), *Advances in experimental social psychology* (Vol. 23, pp. 1–74). New York: Academic Press.

Fiske, S. T., Neuberg, S. L., Beattie, A. E., & Milberg, S. J. (1987). Category-based and attribute-based reactions to others: Some informational conditions of stereotyping and individuating processes. *Journal of Experimental Social Psychology, 23,* 399–427.

Fiske, S. T., & Pavelchak, M. A. (1986). Category-based versus piecemeal-based affective responses: Developments in schema-triggered affect. In R. M. Sorrentino & E. T. Higgins (Eds.), *Handbook of motivation and cognition: Foundations of social behavior* (pp. 167–203). New York: Guilford Press.

Fiske, S. T., Pratto, F., & Pavelchak, M. A. (1983). Citizens' images of nuclear war: Contents and consequences. *Journal of Social Issues, 39,* 41–65.

Fiske, S. T., & Ruscher, J. B. (1989). On-line processes in category-based and individuating impressions: Some basic principles and methodological reflections. In J. N. Bassili (Ed.), *On-line cognition in person perception* (pp. 141–174). Hillsdale, NJ: Erlbaum.

Fiske, S. T., & Taylor, S. E. (1984). *Social cognition.* Reading, MA: Addison-Wesley.

Fiske, S. T., Taylor, S. E., Etcoff, N. L., & Laufer, J. K. (1979). Imaging, empathy, and causal attribution. *Journal of Experimental Social Psychology, 15,* 356–377.

Fiske, S. T., & Von Hendy, H. M. (in press). Personality feedback and situational norms can control stereotyping processes. *Journal of Personality and Social Psychology.*

Fleming, J., & Darley, J. M. (1989). Perceiving choice and constraint: The effects of contextual and behavioral cues on attitude attribution. *Journal of Personality and Social Psychology, 56,* 27–40.

Fletcher, G. J. O., Danilovics, P., Fernandez, G., Peterson, D., & Reeder, G. D. (1986). Attributional complexity: An individual differences measure. *Journal of Personality and Social Psychology, 51,* 875–884.

Fletcher, G. J. O., Grigg, F., & Bull, V. (1988). The organization and accuracy of personality impressions: Neophytes versus experts in trait attribution. *New Zealand Journal of Psychology, 17,* 68–77.

Fletcher, G. J. O., & Ward, C. (1988). Attribution theory and processes: A cross-cultural perspective. In M. H. Bond (Ed.), *The cross-cultural challenge to social psychology* (pp. 230–244). Newbury Park, CA: Sage Publications, Inc.

Folkes, V. S. (1982). Communicating the causes of social rejection. *Journal of Experimental Social Psychology, 18,* 235–252.

Folkes, V. S. (1985). Mindlessness or mindfulness: A partial replication and extension of Langer, Blank, & Chanowitz. *Journal of Personality and Social Psychology, 48,* 600–604.

Folkman, S., & Lazarus, R. S. (1988a). Coping as a mediator of emotion. *Journal of Personality and Social Psychology, 54,* 466–475.

Folkman, S., & Lazarus, R. S. (1988b). The relationship between coping and emotion: Implications for theory and research. *Social Science and Medicine, 26,* 309–317.

Fong, G. T., Krantz, D. H., & Nisbett, R. E. (1986). The effects of statistical training on thinking about everyday problems. *Cognitive Psychology, 18,* 253–292.

Fong, G. T., & Markus, H. (1982). Self-schemas and judgments about others. *Social Cognition, 1,* 191–205.

Forest, D., Clark, M. S., Mills, J., & Isen, A. M. (1979). Helping as a function of feeling state and nature of the helping behavior. *Motivation and Emotion, 3,* 161–169.

Forgas, J. P. (1985). Person prototypes and cultural salience: The role of cognitive and cultural factors in impression formation. *British Journal of Social Psychology, 24,* 3–17.

Forgas, J. P., & Bond, M. H. (1985). Cultural influences on the perception of interaction episodes. *Personality and Social Psychology Bulletin, 11,* 75–88.

Forgas, J. P., & Bower, G. H. (1987). Mood effects on person-perception judgments. *Journal of Personality and Social Psychology, 53,* 53–60.

Forgas, J. P., Bower, G. H., & Krantz, S. E. (1984). The influence of mood on perceptions of social interactions. *Journal of Experimental Social Psychology, 20,* 497–513.

Forgas, J. P., Burnham, D. K., & Trimboli, C. (1988). Mood, memory, and social judgments in children. *Journal of Personality and Social Psychology, 54,* 697–703.

Forgas, J. P., & Moylan, S. (1987). After the movies: Transient mood and social judgments. *Personality and Social Psychology Bulletin, 13,* 467–477.

Forsterling, F. (1985). Attributional retraining: A review. *Psychological Bulletin, 98,* 495–512.

Forsterling, F. (1986). Attributional conceptions in clinical psychology. *American Psychologist, 41,* 275–285.

Forsterling, F. (1989). Models of covariation and attribution: How do they relate to the analogy of analysis of variance? *Journal of Personality and Social Psychology, 57,* 615–625.

Forsterling, F., & Rudolph, U. (1988). Situations, attributions and the evaluation of reactions. *Journal of Personality and Social Psychology, 54,* 225–232.

Forsyth, D. R., & Schlenker, B. R. (1977). Attributing the causes of group performance: Effects of performance quality, task importance, and future testing. *Journal of Personality, 45,* 220–236.

Frable, D. E. S., & Bem, S. L. (1985). If you're gender-schematic, all members of the opposite sex look alike. *Journal of Personality and Social Psychology, 49,* 459–468.

Frank, M. G., & Gilovich, T. (1988). The dark side of self- and social perception: Black uniforms and aggression in professional sports. *Journal of Personality and Social Psychology, 54,* 74–85.

Frank, M. G., & Gilovich, T. (1989). Effect of memory perspective on retrospective causal attributions. *Journal of Personality and Social Psychology, 57,* 399–403.

Franks, J. J., & Bransford, J. D. (1971). Abstraction of visual patterns. *Journal of Experimental Psychology, 90,* 65–74.

Freedman, J. L., & Fraser, S. C. (1966). Compliance without pressure: The foot-in-the-door technique. *Journal of Personality and Social Psychology, 4,* 195–202.

Freedman, J. L., & Sears, D. (1965). Selective exposure. In L. Berkowitz (Ed.), *Advances in experimental social psychology* (Vol. 2, pp. 58–97). New York: Academic Press.

Freeman, H. R. (1987). Structure and content of gender stereotypes: Effects of somatic appearance and trait information. *Psychology of Women Quarterly, 11,* 59–68.

Freides, D. (1974). Human information processing and sensory modality: Cross-modal functions, information complexity, memory, and deficit. *Psychological Bulletin, 81,* 284–310.

Freund, T., Kruglanski, A. W., & Shpitzajzen, A. (1985). The freezing and unfreezing of impression primacy: Effects of the need for structure and the fear of invalidity. *Personality and Social Psychology Bulletin, 11,* 479–487.

Frey, D. (1986). Recent research on selective exposure to information. In L. Berkowitz (Ed.), *Advances in experimental social psychology* (Vol. 19, pp. 41–80). New York: Academic Press.

Fridlund, A. J., & Gilbert, A. N. (1985). Emotions and facial expression. [Letter in response to Zajonc, R. B. (1985). Emotion and facial efference: A theory reclaimed. *Science, 228*, 15–21.] *Science, 230*, 607–608.

Frieze, I. H., Bar-Tal, D., & Carroll, J. S. (1979). *New approaches to social problems: Applications of attribution theory.* San Francisco: Jossey-Bass.

Frijda, N. H. (1987a). Comment on Oatley and Johnson-Laird's "Towards a cognitive theory of emotions." *Cognition and Emotion, 1*, 51–58.

Frijda, N. H. (1987b). Emotion, cognitive structure, and action tendency. *Cognition and Emotion, 1*, 115–143.

Frijda, N. H. (1988). The laws of emotion. *American Psychologist, 43*, 349–358.

Froming, W. J., & Carver, C. S. (1981). Divergent influences of private and public self-consciousness in a compliance paradigm. *Journal of Research in Personality, 15*, 159–171.

Frost, R. L. (1915). "The black cottage," in *North of Boston* (pp. 50–55). New York: Henry Holt.

Fuhrman, R. W., & Wyer, R. S., Jr. (1988). Event memory: Temporal-order judgments of personal life experiences. *Journal of Personality and Social Psychology, 54*, 365–384.

Funder, D. C. (1987). Errors and mistakes: Evaluating the accuracy of social judgment. *Psychological Bulletin, 101*, 75–90.

Funder, D. C., & Colvin, C. R. (1988). Friends and strangers: Acquaintanceship, agreement, and the accuracy of personality judgment. *Journal of Personality and Social Psychology, 55*, 149–158.

Funder, D. C., & Dobroth, K. M. (1987). Differences between traits: Properties associated with interjudge agreement. *Journal of Personality and Social Psychology, 52*, 409–418.

Futoran, G. C., & Wyer, R. S., Jr. (1986). The effects of traits and gender stereotypes on occupational suitability judgments and the recall of judgment-relevant information. *Journal of Experimental Social Psychology, 22*, 475–503.

Gabrielcik, A., & Fazio, R. H. (1984). Priming and frequency estimation: A strict test of the availability heuristic. *Personality and Social Psychology Bulletin, 10*, 85–89.

Gaertner, S. L., & Dovidio, J. F. (1986). The aversive form of racism. In J. F. Dovidio & S. L. Gaertner (Eds.), *Prejudice, discrimination, and racism* (pp. 61–90). Orlando, FL: Academic Press.

Gaertner, S. L., & McLaughlin, J. P. (1983). Racial stereotypes: Associations and ascriptions of positive and negative characteristics. *Social Psychology Quarterly, 46*, 23–40.

Gaertner, S. L., Mann, J., Murrell, A., & Dovidio, J. F. (1989). Reducing intergroup bias: The benefits of recategorization. *Journal of Personality and Social Psychology, 57*, 239–249.

Gaes, G. G., Melburg, V., & Tedeschi, J. T. (1986). A study examining the arousal properties of the forced compliance situation. *Journal of Experimental Social Psychology, 22*, 136–147.

Galanis, C. M. B., & Jones, E. E. (1986). When stigma confronts stigma: Some conditions enhancing a victim's tolerance of other victims. *Personality and Social Psychology Bulletin, 12,* 169–177.

Galizio, M., & Hendrick, C. (1972). Effect of musical accompaniment on attitude: The guitar as a prop for persuasion. *Journal of Applied Social Psychology, 2,* 350–359.

Ganellen, R. J., & Carver, C. S. (1985). Why does self-reference promote incidental encoding? *Journal of Experimental Social Psychology, 21,* 284–300.

Gangestad, S., & Borgida, E. (1981). *Intuitive prediction and intuitive regression: Accounting for predictor information.* Unpublished manuscript, University of Minnesota.

Gangestad, S., & Snyder, M. (1985). On the nature of self-monitoring. In P. Shaver (Ed.), *Review of personality and social psychology: Vol. 6. Self, situations, and social behavior* (pp. 65–86). Beverly Hills, CA: Sage.

Gardner, R. C., Lalonde, R. N., Nero, A. M., & Young, M. Y. (1988). Ethnic stereotypes: Implications of measurement strategy. *Social Cognition, 6,* 40–60.

Garland, H., Hardy, A., & Stephenson, L. (1975). Information search as affected by attribution type and response category. *Personality and Social Psychology Bulletin, 1,* 612–615.

Gatchel, R. J., & Proctor, J. D. (1976). Physiological correlates of learned helplessness in man. *Journal of Abnormal Psychology, 85,* 26–34.

Gaver, W. W., & Mandler, G. (1987). Play it again, Sam: On liking music. *Cognition and Emotion, 1,* 259–282.

Geer, J. H., Davison, G. C., & Gatchel, R. I. (1970). Reduction of stress in humans through nonveridical perceived control of aversive stimulation. *Journal of Personality and Social Psychology, 16,* 731–738.

Geer, J. H., & Maisel, E. (1972). Evaluating the effects of the prediction-control confound. *Journal of Personality and Social Psychology, 23,* 314–319.

Gellhorn, E. (1964). Motion and emotion: The role of proprioception in the physiology and pathology of emotions. *Psychological Review, 71,* 457–472.

Genero, N., & Cantor, N. (1987). Exemplar prototypes and clinical diagnosis: Towards a cognitive economy. *Journal of Social and Clinical Psychology, 5,* 59–78.

Gerard, H. B., & Fleischer, L. (1967). Recall and pleasantness of balanced and imbalanced cognitive structures. *Journal of Personality and Social Psychology, 7,* 332–337.

Gerard, H. B., & Hoyt, M. F. (1974). Distinctiveness of social categorization and attitude toward ingroup members. *Journal of Personality and Social Psychology, 29,* 836–842.

Gergen, K. J. (1968). Personal consistency and presentation of self. In C. Gordon & K. J. Gergen (Eds.), *The self in social interaction* (Vol. 1, pp. 299–308). New York: Wiley.

Gergen, K. J. (1977). The social construction of self-knowledge. In T. Mischel (Ed.), *The self: Psychological and biological issues* (pp. 139–169). Totowa, NJ: Rowman & Littlefield.

Gergen, K. J., & Gergen, M. M. (1988). Narrative and the self as relationship. In L. Berkowitz (Ed.), *Advances in experimental social psychology* (Vol. 21, pp. 17–56). New York: Academic Press.

Gergen, K. J., & Taylor, M. G. (1969). Social expectancy and self-presentation in a status hierarchy. *Journal of Experimental Social Psychology, 5,* 79–92.

Gergen, K. J., & Wishnov, B. (1965). Others' self-evaluation and interaction anticipation as determinants of self-presentation. *Journal of Personality and Social Psychology, 2,* 348–358.

Gibbons, F. X., Carver, C. S., Scheier, M. F., & Hormuth, S. E. (1979). Self-focused attention and the placebo effect: Fooling some of the people some of the time. *Journal of Experimental Social Psychology, 15,* 263–274.

Gibbons, F. X., Smith, T. W., Ingram, R. E., Pearce, K., Brehm, S. S., & Schroeder, D. J. (1985). Self-awareness and self-confrontation: Effects of self-focused attention on members of a clinical population. *Journal of Personality and Social Psychology, 48,* 662–675.

Gibbons, F. X., & Wicklund, R. A. (1976). Selective exposure to self. *Journal of Research in Psychology, 10,* 98–106.

Gibson, J. J. (1966). *The senses considered as perceptual systems.* Boston: Houghton Mifflin.

Gibson, J. J. (1979). *The ecological approach to visual perception.* Boston: Houghton Mifflin.

Gilbert, D. T. (1989). Thinking lightly about others. In J. S. Uleman & J. A. Bargh (eds.), *Unintended thought* (pp. 189–211). New York: Guilford.

Gilbert, D. T., & Cooper, J. (1985). Social psychological strategies of self-deception. In M. Martin (Ed.), *Self-deception and self-understanding: New essays in philosophy and psychology* (pp. 75–94). Lawrence, KS: University of Kansas.

Gilbert, D. T., & Jones, E. E. (1986a). Perceiver-induced constraint: Interpretations of self-generated reality. *Journal of Personality and Social Psychology, 50,* 269–280.

Gilbert, D. T., & Jones, E. E. (1986b). Exemplification: The self-presentation of moral character. *Journal of Personality, 54,* 593–615.

Gilbert, D. T., Jones, E. E., & Pelham, B. W. (1987). Influence and inference: What the active perceiver overlooks. *Journal of Personality and Social Psychology, 52,* 861–870.

Gilbert, D. T., & Krull, D. S. (1988). Seeing less and knowing more: The benefits of perceptual ignorance. *Journal of Personality and Social Psychology, 54,* 193–202.

Gilbert, D. T., Krull, D. S., & Malone, P.S. (1990). Unbelieving the unbelievable: Some problems in the rejection of false information. *Journal of Personality and Social Psychology, 59,* 601–613.

Gilbert, D. T., Krull, D. S., & Pelham, B. W. (1988). Of thoughts unspoken: Social inference and the self-regulation of behavior. *Journal of Personality and Social Psychology, 55,* 685–694.

Gilbert, D. T., Pelham, B. W., & Krull, D. S. (1988). On cognitive busyness: When person perceivers meet persons perceived. *Journal of Personality and Social Psychology, 54,* 733–739.

Gilligan, S. G., & Bower, G. H. (1984). Cognitive consequences of emotional arousal. In C. E. Izard, J. Kagan, & R. B. Zajonc (Eds.), *Emotions, cognition and behavior* (pp. 547–588). Cambridge, England: Cambridge University.

Gilovich, T. (1981). Seeing the past in the present: The effect of associations to familiar events on judgments and decisions. *Journal of Personality and Social Psychology, 40,* 797–808.

Gilovich, T. (1987). Secondhand information and social judgment. *Journal of Experimental Social Psychology, 23,* 59–74.

Gilovich, T., & Regan, D. T. (1986). The actor and the experiencer: Divergent patterns of causal attribution. *Social Cognition, 4,* 342–352.

Ginossar, Z., & Trope, Y. (1980). The effects of base rates and individuating information on judgments about another person. *Journal of Experimental Social Psychology, 16,* 228–242.

Ginossar, Z., & Trope, Y. (1987). Problem solving in judgment under uncertainty. *Journal of Personality and Social Psychology, 52,* 464–474.

Ginzel, L. E., Jones, E. E., & Swann, W. B., Jr. (1987). How "naive" is the naive attributor? Discounting and augmentation in attitude attribution. *Social Cognition, 5,* 108–130.

Girodo, M. (1973). Film-induced arousal, information search, and the attribution process. *Journal of Personality and Social Psychology, 25,* 357–360.

Girodo, M., & Wood, D. (1979). Talking yourself out of pain: The importance of believing you can. *Cognitive Therapy and Research, 3,* 21–33.

Glass, A. L., & Holyoak, K. J. (1986). *Cognition* (2nd ed.). New York: Random House.

Glass, D. C., Reim, B., & Singer, J. E. (1971). Behavioral consequences of adaptation to controllable and uncontrollable noise. *Journal of Experimental Social Psychology, 7,* 244–257.

Gleicher, F. H., Kost, K. A., Baker, S. M., Strathman, A., Richman, S. A., & Sherman, S. J. (1990). The role of counterfactual thinking in judgments of affect. *Personality and Social Psychology Bulletin, 16,* 284–295.

Goddard, M., & Allan, L. (1988). A critique of Alloy and Tabachnik's theoretical framework for understanding covariation assessment. *Psychological Review, 95,* 296–298.

Goethals, G. R. (1976). An attributional analysis of some social influence phenomena. In J. H. Harvey, W. J. Ickes, & R. F. Kidd (Eds.), *New directions in attribution research* (Vol. 1, pp. 291–310). Hillsdale, NJ: Erlbaum.

Goethals, G. R., Allison, S. J., & Frost, M. (1979). Perceptions of the magnitude and diversity of social support. *Journal of Experimental Social Psychology, 15,* 570–581.

Goethals, G. R., & Reckman, R. F. (1973). The perception of consistency in attitudes. *Journal of Experimental Social Psychology, 9,* 491–501.

Goethals, G. R., & Zanna, M. P. (1979). The role of social comparison in choice shifts. *Journal of Personality and Social Psychology, 37,* 1469–1476.

Goffman, E. (1959). *The presentation of self in everyday life.* New York: Doubleday Anchor.

Goffman, E. (1963). *Stigma: Notes on the management of spoiled identity.* Englewood Cliffs, NJ: Prentice-Hall.

Goldberg, L. R. (1968). Simple models or simple processes? Some research on clinical judgments. *American Psychologist, 23,* 483–496.

Goldberg, L. R. (1970). Man versus model of man: A rationale, plus some evidence, for a method of improving on clinical inferences. *Psychological Bulletin, 73,* 422–432.

Goldberg, L. R. (1978). Differential attribution of trait-descriptive terms to oneself as compared to well-liked, neutral, and disliked others: A psychometric analysis. *Journal of Personality and Social Psychology, 36,* 1012–1028.

Goldberg, L. R. (1981). Unconfounding situational attributions from uncertain, neutral, and ambiguous ones: A psychometric analysis of descriptions of oneself and various types of others. *Journal of Personality and Social Psychology, 41,* 517–522.

Goldberg, L. R. (1986). The validity of rating procedures to index the hierarchical level of categories. *Journal of Memory and Language, 25,* 323–347.

Golding, E. (1981). *The effect of past experience on problem solving.* Paper presented at the Annual Conference of the British Psychological Society, Surrey University, England.

Golin, S., Terrell, T., & Johnson, B. (1977). Depression and the illusion of control. *Journal of Abnormal Psychology, 86,* 440–442.

Golin, S., Terrell, T., Weitz, J., & Drost, P. L. (1979). The illusion of control among depressed patients. *Journal of Abnormal Psychology, 88,* 454–457.

Gollwitzer, P. M. (1990). Action phases and mind-sets. In E. T. Higgins & R. M. Sorrentino (Eds.), *Handbook of motivation and cognition: Foundations of social behavior* (Vol. 2, pp. 53–92). New York: Guilford Press.

Gollwitzer, P. M., Earle, W. B., & Stephan, W. G. (1982). Affect as a determinant of egotism: Residual excitation and performance attributions. *Journal of Personality and Social Psychology, 43,* 702–709.

Gollwitzer, P. M. & Kinney, R. F. (1989). Effects of deliberative and implemental mind-sets on illusion of control. *Journal of Personality and Social Psychology, 56,* 531–542.

Gollwitzer, P. M., & Wicklund, R. A. (1985a). Self-symbolizing and the neglect of others' perspectives. *Journal of Personality and Social Psychology, 48,* 702–715.

Gollwitzer, P. M., & Wicklund, R. A. (1985b). The pursuit of self-defining goals. In J. Kuhl & J. Beckmann (Eds.), *Action control: From cognition to behavior* (pp. 61–85). New York: Springer-Verlag.

Gollwitzer, P. M., & Wicklund, R. A. (1987). Fusing apples and oranges: A rejoinder to Carver & Scheier and to Fenigstein. *Journal of Personality, 55,* 555–561.

Gorta, A. (1985). Choosing situations for a purpose. *European Journal of Social Psychology, 15,* 17–35.

Gouaux, C. (1971). Induced affective states and interpersonal attraction. *Journal of Personality and Social Psychology, 20,* 37–43.

Gould, R., & Sigall, H. (1977). The effects of empathy and outcome on attribution: An examination of the divergent-perspectives hypothesis. *Journal of Experimental Social Psychology, 13,* 480–491.

Graesser, A. C., & Nakamura, G. V. (1982). The impact of a schema on comprehension and memory. In G. H. Bower (Ed.), *The psychology of learning and motivation* (Vol. 16, pp. 60–109). New York: Academic Press.

Graham, S. (1984). Communicating sympathy and anger to black and white children: The cognitive (attributional) consequences of affective cues. *Journal of Personality and Social Psychology, 47,* 40–54.

Graham, S., & Brown, J. D. (1988). Attributional mediators of evaluation, expectancy, and affect: A response time analysis. *Journal of Personality and Social Psychology, 55,* 873–881.

Graham, S., & Weiner, B. (1986). From an attributional theory of emotion to developmental psychology: A round-trip ticket? *Social Cognition, 4,* 152–179.

Granberg, D. (1987). Candidate preference, membership group, and estimates of voting behavior. *Social Cognition, 5,* 323–335.

Grant, P. R., & Holmes, J. G. (1981). The integration of implicit personality theory schemas and stereotype images. *Social Psychology Quarterly, 44,* 107–115.

Grant, P. R., & Holmes, J. G. (1982). The influence of stereotypes in impression formation: A reply to Locksley, Hepburn, and Ortiz. *Social Psychology Quarterly, 45,* 274–276.

Graziano, W. G., Moore, J. S., & Collins, J. E., II (1988). Social cognition as segmentation of the stream of behavior. *Developmental Psychology, 24,* 568–573.

Greaves, G. (1972). Conceptual system functioning and selective recall of information. *Journal of Personality and Social Psychology, 21,* 327–332.

Green, S. K., & Gross, A. E. (1979). Self-serving biases in implicit evaluations. *Personality and Social Psychology Bulletin, 5,* 214–217.

Greenberg, J., & Pyszczynski, T. (1985). The effects of an overheard ethnic slur on evaluations of the target: How to spread a social disease. *Journal of Experimental Social Psychology, 21,* 61–72.

Greenberg, J., & Pyszczynski, T. (1986). Persistent high self-focus after failure and low self-focus after success: The depressive self-focusing style. *Journal of Personality and Social Psychology, 50,* 1039–1044.

Greenberg, J., Williams, K. D., & O'Brien, M. K. (1986). Considering the harshest verdict first: Biasing effects on mock juror verdicts. *Personality and Social Psychology Bulletin, 12,* 41–50.

Greenberg, M. S., Vazquez, C. V., & Alloy, L. B. (1988). Depression versus anxiety: Differences in self and other schemata. In L. B. Alloy (Ed.), *Cognitive processes in depression* (pp. 109–142). New York: Guilford Press.

Greenwald, A. G. (1968). Cognitive learning, cognitive response to persuasion, and attitude change. In A. G. Greenwald, T. C. Brock, & T. M. Ostrom (Eds.), *Psychological foundations of attitudes* (pp. 147–170). New York: Academic Press.

Greenwald, A. G. (1975). Consequences of prejudice against the null hypothesis. *Psychological Bulletin, 82,* 1–20.

Greenwald, A. G. (1980). The totalitarian ego: Fabrication and revision of personal history. *American Psychologist, 35,* 603–618.

Greenwald, A. G. (1981). Self and memory. In G. H. Bower (Ed.), *The psychology of learning and motivation* (Vol. 15, pp. 201–236). New York: Academic Press.

Greenwald, A. G. (1988). Self-knowledge and self-deception. In J. S. Lockard & D. L. Paulhus (Eds.), *Self-deception: An adaptive mechanism?* (pp. 113–131). Englewood Cliffs, NJ: Prentice-Hall.

Greenwald, A. G. (1989). Why attitudes are important: Defining attitude and attitude theory 20 years later. In A. R. Pratkanis, S. J. Breckler, & A. G. Greenwald (Eds.), *Attitude structure and function* (pp. 429–440). Hillsdale, NJ: Erlbaum.

Greenwald, A. G., Bellezza, F. S., & Banaji, M. R. (1988). Is self-esteem a central ingredient of the self-concept? *Personality and Social Psychology Bulletin, 14,* 34–45.

Greenwald, A. G., & Breckler, S. J. (1985). To whom is the self presented? In B. R. Schlenker (Ed.), *The self and social life* (pp. 126–145). New York: McGraw-Hill.

Greenwald, A. G., Klinger, M. R., & Liu, T. J. (1989). Unconscious processing of dichotically masked words. *Memory and Cognition, 17,* 35–47.

Greenwald, A. G., & Leavitt, C. (1984). Audience involvement in advertising: Four levels. *Journal of Consumer Research, 11,* 581–592.

Greenwald, A. G., & Pratkanis, A. R. (1984). The self. In R. S. Wyer, Jr., & T. K. Srull (Eds.), *Handbook of social cognition* (Vol. 3, pp. 129–178). Hillsdale, NJ: Erlbaum.

Gregory, W. L., Burroughs, W. J., & Ainslie, F. M. (1985). Self-relevant scenarios as an indirect means of attitude change. *Personality and Social Psychology Bulletin, 11,* 435–444.

Gregory, W. L., Cialdini, R. B., & Carpenter, K. M. (1982). Self-relevant scenarios as mediators of likelihood estimates and compliance: Does imagining make it so? *Journal of Personality and Social Psychology, 43,* 89–99.

Grice, H. P. (1975). Logic and conversation. In P. Cole & J. L. Morgan (Eds.), *Syntax and semantics 3: Speech acts* (pp. 95–113). New York: Academic Press.

Griffit, W. B. (1970). Environmental effects on interpersonal behavior: Ambient effective temperature and attraction. *Journal of Personality and Social Psychology, 15,* 240–244.

Grush, J. E. (1976). Attitude formation and mere exposure phenomena: A nonartificial explanation of empirical findings. *Journal of Personality and Social Psychology, 33,* 281–290.

Gur, R. C., & Sackeim, H. A. (1979). Self-deception: A concept in search of a phenomenon. *Journal of Personality and Social Psychology, 37,* 147–169.

Gurin, P., Gurin, G., Lao, R. C., & Beattie, M. (1969). Internal-external control in the motivation dynamics of Negro youth. *Journal of Social Issues, 25,* 29–53.

Gurwitz, S. B., & Topol, B. (1978). Determinants of confirming and disconfirming responses to negative social labels. *Journal of Experimental Social Psychology, 14,* 31–42.

Hacker, H. M. (1951). Women as a minority group. *Social Forces, 30,* 60–69.

Haemmerlie, F. M., & Montgomery, R. L. (1984). Purposefully biased interactions: Reducing heterosocial anxiety through self-perception theory. *Journal of Personality and Social Psychology, 47,* 900–908.

Hager, J. C., & Ekman, P. (1981). Methodological problems in Tourangeau and Ellsworth's study of facial expression and experience of emotion. *Journal of Personality and Social Psychology, 40,* 358–362.

Hamill, R. (1980). *Selective influences of the self on social perception and memory.* Unpublished doctoral dissertation, University of Michigan.

Hamill, R., Lodge, M., & Blake, F. (1985). The breadth, depth, and utility of class, partisan, and ideological schemata. *American Journal of Political Science, 29,* 850–870.

Hamill, R., Wilson, T. D., & Nisbett, R. E. (1980). Insensitivity to sample bias: Generalizing from atypical cases. *Journal of Personality and Social Psychology, 39,* 578–589.

Hamilton, D. L. (1979). A cognitive-attributional analysis of stereotyping. In L. Berkowitz (Ed.), *Advances in experimental social psychology* (Vol. 12, pp. 53–84). New York: Academic Press.

Hamilton, D. L. (Ed.) (1981a). *Cognitive processes in stereotyping and intergroup behavior.* Hillsdale, NJ: Erlbaum.

Hamilton, D. L. (1981b). Organizational processes in impression formation. In E. T. Higgins, C. P. Herman, & M. P. Zanna (Eds.), *Social cognition: The Ontario Symposium* (Vol. 1, pp. 135–160). Hillsdale, NJ: Erlbaum.

Hamilton, D. L. (1988). Causal attribution viewed from an information-processing perspective. In D. Bar-Tal & A. W. Kruglanski (Eds.), *The social psychology of knowledge* (pp. 359–385). Cambridge: Cambridge University Press.

Hamilton, D. L. (1989). Understanding impression formation: What has memory research contributed? In P. R. Solomon, G. R. Goethals, C. M. Kelley, &

B.R. Stephens (Eds.), *Memory: Interdisciplinary approaches* (pp. 221–242). New York: Springer-Verlag.

Hamilton, D. L., Driscoll, D. M., & Worth, L. T. (1989). Cognitive organization of impressions: Effects of incongruency in complex representations. *Journal of Personality and Social Psychology, 57,* 925–939.

Hamilton, D. L., Dugan, P. M., & Trolier, T. K. (1985). The formation of stereotypic beliefs: Further evidence for distinctiveness-based illusory correlations. *Journal of Personality and Social Psychology, 48,* 5–17.

Hamilton, D. L., & Gifford, R. K. (1976). Illusory correlation in interpersonal perception: A cognitive basis of stereotypic judgments. *Journal of Experimental Social Psychology, 12,* 392–407.

Hamilton, D. L., Katz, L. B., & Leirer, V. O. (1980a). Cognitive representation of personality impressions: Organizational processes in first impression formation. *Journal of Personality and Social Psychology, 39,* 1050–1063.

Hamilton, D. L., Katz, L. B., & Leirer, V. O. (1980b). Organizational processes in impression formation. In R. Hastie, T. M. Ostrom, E. B. Ebbesen, R. S. Wyer, D. L. Hamilton, & D. E. Carlston (Eds.), *Person memory: The cognitive basis of social perception* (pp. 121–153). Hillsdale, NJ: Erlbaum.

Hamilton, D. L., & Rose, T. L. (1980). Illusory correlation and the maintenance of stereotypic beliefs. *Journal of Personality and Social Psychology, 39,* 832–845.

Hamilton, D. L., & Sherman, S. J. (1989). Illusory correlations: Implications for stereotype theory and research. In D. Bar-Tal, C. F. Graumann, A. W. Kruglanski, & W. Stroebe (Eds.), *Stereotypes and prejudice: Changing conceptions* (pp. 59–82). New York: Springer-Verlag.

Hamilton, D. L., & Trolier, T. K. (1986). Stereotypes and stereotyping: An overview of the cognitive approach. In J. F. Dovidio & S. L. Gaertner (Eds.), *Prejudice, discrimination, and racism* (pp. 127–163). Orlando, FL: Academic Press.

Hamilton, D. L., & Zanna, M. P. (1974). Context effects in impression formation: Changes in connotative meaning. *Journal of Personality and Social Psychology, 29,* 649–654.

Hamilton, V., Bower, G. H., & Frijda, N. H. (Eds.) (1988). *Cognitive perspectives on emotion and motivation.* Norwood, MA: Kluwer Academic Publishers.

Hamilton, V. L., Blumenfeld, P. C., & Kushler, R. H. (1988). A question of standards: Attributions of blame and credit for classroom acts. *Journal of Personality and Social Psychology, 54,* 34–38.

Hammen, C. (1987). Causes and consequences of attribution research in depression. *Journal of Social and Clinical Psychology, 5,* 485–500.

Hammen, C., Marks, T., deMayo, R., & Mayol, A. (1985). Self-schemas and risk for depression: A prospective study. *Journal of Personality and Social Psychology, 49,* 1147–1159.

Hampson, S. E., & Dawson, W. J. M. (1985). Whatever happened to Pollyanna? The effects of evaluative congruence on speed of trait inference. *Personality and Social Psychology Bulletin, 11,* 106–117.

Hampson, S. E., Goldberg, L. R., & John, O. P. (1987). Category-breadth and social-desirability values for 573 personality terms. *European Journal of Personality, 1,* 241–258.

Hampson, S. E., John, O. P., & Goldberg, L. R. (1986). Category breadth and hierarchical structure in personality: Studies in asymmetries in judgments of trait implications. *Journal of Personality and Social Psychology, 51,* 37–54.

Hansen, C. H., & Hansen, R. D. (1988a). Finding the face in the crowd: An anger superiority effect. *Journal of Personality and Social Psychology, 54,* 917–924.

Hansen, C. H., & Hansen, R. D. (1988b). How rock music videos can change what's seen when boy meets girl: Priming stereotypic appraisal of social interactions. *Sex Roles, 19,* 287–316.

Hansen, R. D. (1980). Commonsense attribution. *Journal of Personality and Social Psychology, 39,* 996–1009.

Hansen, R. D. & Hall, C. A. (1985). Discounting and augmenting facilitative and inhibitory forces: The winner takes almost all. *Journal of Personality and Social Psychology, 49,* 1482–1493.

Hansen, R. D., & Hansen, C. H. (1988). Repression of emotionally tagged memories: The architecture of less complex emotions. *Journal of Personality and Social Psychology, 55,* 811–818.

Harackiewicz, J. M., & Manderlink, G. (1984). A process analysis of the effects of performance-contingent rewards on intrinsic motivation. *Journal of Experimental Social Psychology, 20,* 531–551.

Harackiewicz, J. M., Sansone, C., & Manderlink, G. (1985). Competence, achievement orientation, and intrinsic motivation: A process analysis. *Journal of Personality and Social Psychology, 48,* 493–508.

Harkins, S. G., & Petty, R. E. (1981). Effects of source magnification of cognitive effort on attitudes: An information-processing view. *Journal of Personality and Social Psychology, 40,* 401–413.

Harkness, A. R., DeBono, K. G., & Borgida, E. (1985). Personal involvement and strategies for making contingency judgments: A stake in the dating game makes a difference. *Journal of Personality and Social Psychology, 49,* 22–32.

Harre, R. (Ed.) (1986). *The social construction of emotions.* New York: Basil Blackwell.

Harris, B. (1977). Developmental differences in the attribution of responsibility. *Developmental Psychology, 13,* 257–265.

Harris, M. J., & Rosenthal, R. (1985). Mediation of interpersonal expectancy effects: 31 meta-analyses. *Psychological Bulletin, 97,* 363–386.

Harris, R. J., Teske, R. R., & Ginns, M. J. (1975). Memory for pragmatic implications from courtroom testimony. *Bulletin of the Psychonomic Society, 6,* 494–496.

Harris, R. N., & Snyder, C. R. (1986). The role of uncertain self-esteem in self-handicapping. *Journal of Personality and Social Psychology, 51,* 451–458.

Harris, R. N., Snyder, C. R., Higgins, R. L., & Schrag, J. L. (1986). Enhancing the prediction of self-handicapping. *Journal of Personality and Social Psychology, 51,* 1191–1199.

Harrison, A. A. (1977). Mere exposure. In L. Berkowitz (Ed.), *Advances in experimental social psychology* (Vol. 10, pp. 39–83). New York: Academic Press.

Hart, D., & Damon, W. (1986). Developmental trends in self-understanding. *Social Cognition, 4,* 388–407.

Hartley, D. (1966). *Observations on man, his frame, his duty, and his expectations.* Delmar, NY: Scholastic Facsimiles. (Originally published, 1749.)

Hartwick, J. (1979). Memory for trait information: A signal detection analysis. *Journal of Experimental Social Psychology, 15,* 533–552.

Harvey, J. H., Flanary, R., & Morgan, M. (1986). Vivid memories of vivid loves gone by. *Journal of Social and Personal Relationships, 3,* 359–373.

Harvey, J. H., & Galvin, K. S. (1984). Clinical implications of attribution theory and research. *Clinical Psychology, 4,* 15–33.

Harvey, J. H., Ickes, W. J., & Kidd, R. F. (1976). *New directions in attribution research* (Vol. 1). Hillsdale, NJ: Erlbaum.

Harvey, J. H., Ickes, W. J., & Kidd, R. F. (1978). *New directions in attribution research* (Vol. 2). Hillsdale, NJ: Erlbaum.

Harvey, J. H., Ickes, W. J., & Kidd, R. F. (1981). *New directions in attribution research* (Vol. 3). Hillsdale, NJ: Erlbaum.

Harvey, J. H., & Tucker, J. A. (1979). On problems with the cause-reason distinction in attribution theory. *Journal of Personality and Social Psychology, 37,* 1441–1446.

Harvey, J. H., Turnquist, D. C., & Agostinelli, G. (1988). Identifying attributions in oral and written explanations. In C. Antaki (Ed.), *Analysing everyday explanation: A casebook of methods* (pp. 32–42). London: Sage.

Harvey, J. H., & Weary, G. (1981). *Perspectives on attributional processes.* Dubuque, IA: W. C. Brown.

Harvey, J. H., Weber, A. L., Galvin, K. S., Huszt, H. C., & Garnick, N. N. (1986). Attribution and the termination of close relationships: A special focus on the account. In R. Gilmour & S. Duck (Eds.), *The emerging field of personal relationships* (pp. 189–201). Hillsdale, NJ: Erlbaum.

Harvey, J. H., Wells, G. L., & Alvarez, M. D. (1978). Attribution in the context of conflict and separation in close relationships. In J. H. Harvey, W. Ickes, & R. F. Kidd (Eds.), *New directions in attribution research* (Vol. 2, pp. 236–264). Hillsdale, NJ: Erlbaum.

Harvey, J. H., Yarkin, K. L., Lightner, J. M., & Town, J. P. (1980). Unsolicited interpretation and recall of interpersonal events. *Journal of Personality and Social Psychology, 38,* 551–568.

Hasher, L., Rose, K. C., Zacks, R. T., Sanft, H., & Doren, B. (1985). Mood, recall, and selectivity effects in normal college students. *Journal of Experimental Psychology: General, 114,* 104–118.

Hashtroudi, S., Mutter, S. A., Cole, E. A., & Green, S. K. (1984). Schema-consistent and schema-inconsistent information: Processing demands. *Personality and Social Psychology Bulletin, 10,* 269–278.

Hass, R. G. (1981). Effects of source characteristics on cognitive responses and persuasion. In R. E. Petty, T. M. Ostrom, & T. C. Brock (Eds.), *Cognitive responses in persuasion.* Hillsdale, NJ: Erlbaum.

Hass, R. G. (1984). Perspective taking and self-awareness: Drawing an *E* on your forehead. *Journal of Personality and Social Psychology, 46,* 788–798.

Hastie, R. (1980). Memory for behavioral information that confirms or contradicts a personality impression. In R. Hastie, T. M. Ostrom, E. B. Ebbesen, R. S. Wyer, D. L. Hamilton, & D. E. Carlston (Eds.), *Person memory: The cognitive basis of social perception* (pp. 141–172). Hillsdale, NJ: Erlbaum.

Hastie, R. (1981). Schematic principles in human memory. In E. T. Higgins, C. P. Herman, & M. P. Zanna (Eds.), *Social cognition: The Ontario Symposium* (Vol. 1, pp. 39–88). Hillsdale, NJ: Erlbaum.

Hastie, R. (1984). Causes and effects of causal attribution. *Journal of Personality and Social Psychology, 46,* 44–56.

Hastie, R. (1988). A computer simulation model of person memory. *Journal of Experimental Social Psychology, 24,* 423–447.

Hastie, R., & Carlston, D. (1980). Theoretical issues in person memory. In R.

Hastie, T. M. Ostrom, E. B. Ebbesen, R. S. Wyer, D. L. Hamilton, & D. E. Carlston (Eds.), *Person memory: The cognitive basis of social perception* (pp. 1–53). Hillsdale, NJ: Erlbaum.

Hastie, R., & Kumar, P. A. (1979). Person memory: Personality traits as organizing principles in memory for behavior. *Journal of Personality and Social Psychology, 37,* 25–38.

Hastie, R., & Park, B. (1986). The relationship between memory and judgment depends on whether the judgment task is memory-based or on-line. *Psychological Review, 93,* 258–268.

Hastie, R., Park, B., & Weber, R. (1984). Social memory. In R. S. Wyer, Jr., & T. K. Srull (Eds.), *Handbook of social cognition* (Vol. 2, pp. 151–212). Hillsdale, NJ: Erlbaum.

Hastie, R., & Rasinski, K. A. (1988). The concept of accuracy in social judgment. In D. Bar-Tal & A. W. Kruglanski (Eds.), *The social psychology of knowledge* (pp. 193–208). Cambridge, England: Cambridge University Press.

Hastorf, A. H., Schneider, D. J., & Polefka, J. (1970). *Person perception.* Reading, MA: Addison-Wesley.

Hayes-Roth, B. (1977). Evolution of cognitive structure and processes. *Psychological Review, 84,* 260–278.

Hayes-Roth, B., & Hayes-Roth, F. (1977). Concept learning and the recognition and classification of exemplars. *Journal of Verbal Learning and Verbal Behavior, 16,* 321–338.

Hazlewood, J. D., & Olson, J. M. (1986). Covariation information, causal questioning, and interpersonal behavior. *Journal of Experimental Social Psychology, 22,* 276–291.

Heckhausen, H., & Gollwitzer, P. M. (1987). Thought contents and cognitive functioning in motivational versus volitional states of mind. *Motivation and Emotion, 11,* 101–120.

Heider, F. (1944). Social perception and phenomenal causality. *Psychological Review, 51,* 358–374.

Heider, F. (1946). Attitudes and cognitive organization. *Journal of Psychology, 21,* 107–112.

Heider, F. (1958). *The psychology of interpersonal relations.* New York: Wiley.

Heider, F., & Simmel, M. (1944). An experimental study of apparent behavior. *American Journal of Psychology, 57,* 243–259.

Heilman, M. E. (1980). The impact of situational factors on personnel decisions concerning women: Varying the sex composition of the applicant pool. *Organizational Behavior and Human Performance, 26,* 386–395.

Hemsley, G. D., & Marmurek, H. H. C. (1982). Person memory: The processing of consistent and inconsistent person information. *Personality and Social Psychology Bulletin, 8,* 433–438.

Henker, B., & Whalen, C. K. (1980). The many messages of medication: Hyperactive children's perceptions and attributions. In S. Salzinger, J. Antrobus, & J. Glick (Eds.), *The ecosystem of the "sick" child* (pp. 141–166). New York: Academic Press.

Hennigan, K. M., Cook, T. D., & Gruder, C. L. (1982). Cognitive tuning set, source credibility, and the temporal persistence of attitude change. *Journal of Personality and Social Psychology, 42,* 412–425.

Herek, G. M. (1986). The instrumentality of ideologies: Toward a neofunctional theory of attitudes. *Journal of Social Issues, 42,* 99–114.

Herr, P. M. (1986). Consequences of priming: Judgment and behavior. *Journal of Personality and Social Psychology, 51,* 1106–1115.

Herr, P. M., Sherman, S. J., & Fazio, R. H. (1983). On the consequences of priming: Assimilation and contrast effects. *Journal of Experimental Social Psychology, 19,* 323–340.

Herstein, J. A., Carroll, J. S., & Hayes, J. R. (1980). The organization of knowledge about people and their attributes in long-term memory. *Representative Research in Social Psychology, 11,* 17–37.

Hessing, D. J., Elffers, H., & Weigel, R. H. (1988). Exploring the limits of self-reports and reasoned action: An investigation of the psychology of tax evasion behavior. *Journal of Personality and Social Psychology, 54,* 405–413.

Hewstone, M. (1983). The role of language in attribution processes. In J. Jaspars, F. Fincham, & M. Hewstone (Eds.), *Attribution theory and research: Conceptual developmental and social dimensions* (pp. 1–16). London: Academic Press.

Hewstone, M. (1989). *Causal attribution: From cognitive processes to cognitive beliefs.* Oxford, England: Basil Blackwell.

Hewstone, M., Benn, W., & Wilson, A. (1988). Bias in the use of base rates: Racial prejudice in decision-making. *European Journal of Social Psychology, 18,* 161–176.

Hewstone, M., Bond, M. H., & Wan, K. (1983). Social facts and social attributions: The explanation of intergroup differences in Hong Kong. *Social Cognition, 2,* 142–157.

Hewstone, M., & Jaspars, J. (1987). Covariation and causal attribution: A logical model of the intuitive analysis of variance. *Journal of Personality and Social Psychology, 53,* 663–672.

Hewstone, M., & Jaspars, J. M. F. (1982). Intergroup relations and attribution processes. In H. Tajfel (Ed.), *Social identity and intergroup relations* (pp. 99–133). Cambridge: Cambridge University Press.

Hewstone, M., & Jaspars, J. M. F. (1984). Social dimensions of attribution. In H. Tajfel (Ed.), *The social dimension: European developments in social psychology* (pp. 379–404). Cambridge, England: Cambridge University Press.

Hewstone, M., Jaspars, J., & Lalljee, M. (1982). Social representations, social attribution, and social identity: The intergroup images of "public" and "comprehensive" schoolboys. *European Journal of Social Psychology, 12,* 241–269.

Higgins, E. T. (1981). The "communication game": Implications for social cognition. In E. T. Higgins, C. P. Herman, & M. P. Zanna (Eds.), *Social cognition: The Ontario Symposium* (Vol. 1, pp. 343–392). Hillsdale, NJ: Erlbaum.

Higgins, E. T. (1987). Self-discrepancy: A theory relating self and affect. *Psychological Review, 94,* 319–340.

Higgins, E. T. (1989a). Continuities and discontinuities in self-regulatory and self-evaluative processes: A developmental theory relating self and affect. *Journal of Personality, 57,* 407–444.

Higgins, E. T. (1989b). Knowledge accessibility and activation: Subjectivity and suffering from unconscious sources. In J. S. Uleman & J. A. Bargh (Eds.), *Unintended thought* (pp. 75–123). New York: Guilford Press.

Higgins, E. T., & Bargh, J. A. (1987). Social cognition and social perception. *Annual Review of Psychology, 38,* 369–425.

Higgins, E. T., Bargh, J. A., & Lombardi, W. (1985). The nature of priming effects on categorization. *Journal of Experimental Psychology: Learning, Memory, and Cognition, 11,* 59–69.

Higgins, E. T., Bond, R. N., Klein, R., & Strauman, T. (1986). Self-discrepancies and emotional vulnerability: How magnitude, accessibility, and type of discrepancy influence affect. *Journal of Personality and Social Psychology, 51,* 5–15.

Higgins, E. T., & Chaires, W. M. (1980). Accessibility of interrelational constructs: Implications for stimulus encoding and creativity. *Journal of Experimental Social Psychology, 16,* 348–361.

Higgins, E. T., & King, G. A. (1981). Accessibility of social constructs: Information-processing consequences of individual and contextual variability. In N. Cantor & J. F. Kihlstrom (Eds.), *Personality, cognition, and social interaction* (pp. 69–122). Hillsdale, NJ: Erlbaum.

Higgins, E. T., King, G. A., & Mavin, G. H. (1982). Individual construct accessibility and subjective impressions and recall. *Journal of Personality and Social Psychology, 43,* 35–47.

Higgins, E. T., Klein, R., & Strauman, T. (1985). Self-concept discrepancy theory: A psychological model for distinguishing among different aspects of depression and anxiety. *Social Cognition, 3,* 51–76.

Higgins, E. T., Kuiper, N. A., & Olson, J. M. (1981). Social cognition: A need to get personal. In E. T. Higgins, C. P. Herman, & M. P. Zanna (Eds.), *Social cognition: The Ontario Symposium* (Vol. 1, pp. 395–420). Hillsdale, NJ: Erlbaum.

Higgins, E. T., & Lurie, L. (1983). Context, categorization, and memory: The "change-of-standard" effect. *Cognitive Psychology, 15,* 525–547.

Higgins, E. T., & McCann, C. D. (1984). Social encoding and subsequent attitudes, impressions, and memory: "Context-driven" and motivational aspects of processing. *Journal of Personality and Social Psychology, 47,* 26–39.

Higgins, E. T., McCann, C. D., & Fondacaro, R. (1982). The "communication game": Goal-directed encoding and cognitive consequences. *Social Cognition, 1,* 21–37.

Higgins, E. T., & Rholes, W. S. (1978). "Saying is believing": Effects of message modification on memory and liking for the person described. *Journal of Experimental Social Psychology, 14,* 363–378.

Higgins, E. T., Rholes, W. S., & Jones, C. R. (1977). Category accessibility and impression formation. *Journal of Experimental Social Psychology, 13,* 141–154.

Higgins, E. T., & Stangor, C. (1988a). A "change-of-standard" perspective on the relations among context, judgment, and memory. *Journal of Personality and Social Psychology, 54,* 181–192.

Higgins, E. T., & Stangor, C. (1988b). Context-driven social judgment and memory: When "behavior engulfs the field" in reconstructive memory. In D. Bar-Tal and A. W. Kruglanski (Eds.), *The social psychology of knowledge.* (pp. 262–298). New York: Cambridge University Press.

Higgins, E. T., Strauman, T., & Klein, R. (1986). Standards and the process of self-evaluation: Multiple effects from multiple stages. In R. M. Sorrentino & E. T. Higgins (Eds.), *Handbook of motivation and cognition: Foundations of social behavior* (pp. 23–63). New York: Guilford Press.

Higgins, E. T., Tykocinski, O., & Vookles, J. (1990). Patterns of self-beliefs: The psychological significance of relations among the actual, ideal, ought, can, and future selves. In J. M. Olson & M. P. Zanna (Eds.), *Processes in self-perception: The Ontario Symposium* (Vol. 7, pp. 153–190). Hillsdale, NJ: Erlbaum.

Higgins, E. T., Van Hook, E., & Dorfman, D. (1988). Do self-attributes form a cognitive structure? *Social Cognition, 6,* 177–207.

Hill, T., Lewicki, P., Czyzewska, M., & Schuller, G. (1990). The role of learned inferential encoding rules in the perception of faces: Effects of nonconscious self-perpetuation of a bias. *Journal of Experimental Social Psychology, 26,* 350–371.

Hill, T., Smith, N. D., & Hoffman, H. (1988). Self-image bias and the perception of other persons' skills. *European Journal of Social Psychology, 18,* 293–298.

Hilton, D. J. (1990). Conversational processes and causal explanation. *Psychological Bulletin, 107,* 65–81.

Hilton, D. J., & Jaspars, J. M. F. (1987). The explanation of occurrences and non-occurrences: A test of the inductive logic model of causal attribution. *British Journal of Social Psychology, 26,* 189–201.

Hilton, D. J., & Knibbs, C. S. (1988). The knowledge-structure and inductivist strategies in causal attribution. *European Journal of Social Psychology, 18,* 79–92.

Hilton, D. J., & Slugoski, B. R. (1986). Knowledge-based causal attribution: The abnormal conditions focus model. *Psychological Review, 93,* 75–88.

Hilton, D. J., Smith, R. H., & Alicke, M. D. (1988). Knowledge-based information acquisition: Norms and the functions of consensus information. *Journal of Personality and Social Psychology, 55,* 530–540.

Hilton, J. L., & Darley, J. M. (1985). Constructing other persons: A limit on the effect. *Journal of Experimental Social Psychology, 21,* 1–18.

Hilton, J. L., & Fein, S. (1989). The role of typical diagnosticity in stereotype-based judgments. *Journal of Personality and Social Psychology, 57,* 201–211.

Hilton, J. L., Klein, J. G., & von Hippel, W. (1991). Attention allocation and impression formation. *Personality and Social Psychology Bulletin, 17,* 548–559.

Hilton, J. L., & von Hippel, W. (1990). The role of consistency in the judgment of stereotype-relevant behaviors. *Personality and Social Psychology Bulletin, 16,* 430–448.

Himmelfarb, S., & Eagly, A. H. (1974). Orientations to the study of attitudes and their change. In S. Himmelfarb & A. H. Eagly (Eds.), *Readings in attitude change* (pp. 2–49). New York: Wiley.

Hinsz, V. B., & Davis, J. H. (1984). Persuasive arguments theory, group polarization, and choice shifts. *Personality and Social Psychology Bulletin, 10,* 260–268.

Hinsz, V. B., Tindale, R. S., Nagao, D. H., Davis, J. H., & Robertson, B. A. (1988). The influence of the accuracy of individuating information on the use of base rate information in probability judgment. *Journal of Experimental Social Psychology, 24,* 127–145.

Hintzman, D. L. (1986). "Schema abstraction" in a multiple-trace memory model. *Psychological Review, 93,* 411–428.

Hirt, E. R., & Sherman, S. J. (1985). The role of prior knowledge in explaining hypothetical events. *Journal of Experimental Social Psychology, 21,* 519–543.

Hochschild, A. R. (1983). *The managed heart: Commercialization of human feeling.* Berkeley: University of California Press.

Hoffman, C. (1985). A descriptive bias in trait attributions following decisions favoring one role candidate over another. *Social Cognition, 3,* 296–312.

Hoffman, C., Lau, I., & Johnson, D. R. (1986). The linguistic relativity of person cognition: An English-Chinese comparison. *Journal of Personality and Social Psychology, 51,* 1097–1105.

Hoffman, C., Mischel, W., & Baer, J. S. (1984). Language and person cognition. *Journal of Personality and Social Psychology, 46,* 1029–1043.

Hoffman, C., Mischel, W., & Mazze, K. (1981). The role of purpose in the organization of information about behavior: Trait-based versus goal-based categories in person cognition. *Journal of Personality and Social Psychology, 40,* 211–225.

Hogarth, R. M. (1980). *Judgment and choice.* New York: Wiley.

Hogarth, R. M. (1981). Beyond discrete biases: Functional and dysfunctional aspects of judgmental heuristics. *Psychological Bulletin, 90,* 197–217.

Hogg, M. A., & Abrams, D. (1988). *Social identifications.* London: Routledge.

Hogg, M. A., & Turner, J. C. (1985a). Interpersonal attraction, social identification, and psychological group formation. *European Journal of Social Psychology, 15,* 51–66.

Hogg, M. A., & Turner, J. C. (1985b). When liking begets solidarity. *British Journal of Social Psychology, 24,* 267–281.

Hogg, M. A., & Turner, J. C. (1987). Intergroup behavior, self-stereotyping, and the salience of social categories. *British Journal of Social Psychology, 26,* 325–340.

Holender, D. (1986). Semantic activation without conscious identification in dichotic listening, parafoveal vision, and visual masking: A survey and appraisal. *Behavioral and Brain Sciences, 9,* 1–66.

Holloway, S., Tucker, L., & Hornstein, H. A. (1977). The effects of social and nonsocial information on interpersonal behavior of males: The news makes news. *Journal of Personality and Social Psychology, 35,* 514–522.

Holmes, D. S., & Houston, B. K. (1974). Effectiveness of situation redefinition and affective isolation in coping with stress. *Journal of Personality and Social Psychology, 29,* 212–218.

Holyoak, K. J. & Gordon, P. C. (1983). Social reference points. *Journal of Personality and Social Psychology, 44,* 881–887.

Holyoak, K. J. & Gordon, P. C. (1984). Information processing and social cognition. In R. S. Wyer, Jr., & T. K. Srull, (Eds.), *Handbook of social cognition* (Vol. 1, pp. 39–70). Hillsdale, NJ: Erlbaum.

Holyoak, K. J., & Nisbett, R. E. (1988). Induction. In R. J. Sternberg & E. E. Smith (Eds.), *The psychology of human thinking* (pp. 50–91). Cambridge, MA: Cambridge University Press.

Holyoak, K. J., & Patterson, K. K. (1981). A positional discriminability model of linear-order judgments. *Journal of Experimental Psychology: Human Perception and Performance, 7,* 1283–1302.

Homer, P. M., & Kahle, L. R. (1988). A structural equation test of the value-attitude-behavior hierarchy. *Journal of Personality and Social Psychology, 54,* 638–646.

Hormuth, S. (1986). Lack of effort as a result of self-focused attention. ˄r

Hormuth, S. (1986). Lack of effort as a result of self-focused attention. *European Journal of Social Psychology, 16,* 181–192.

Hornstein, H. A., Martin, J., Rupp, A. H., Sole, K., & Tartell, R. (1980). The propensity to recall another's completed and uncompleted tasks as a consequence of varying social relationships. *Journal of Experimental Social Psychology, 16,* 362–375.

Horowitz, L. M., de S. French, R., & Anderson, C. A. (1982). The prototype of a lonely person. In L. A. Peplau & D. Perlman (Eds.), *Loneliness: A sourcebook of current theory, research and therapy* (pp. 183–205). New York: Wiley.

Horowitz, M. J. (1970). *Image formation and cognition.* New York: Appleton-Century-Crofts.

Hosch, H. M., & Platz, S. J. (1984). Self-monitoring and eyewitness accuracy. *Personality and Social Psychology Bulletin, 10,* 289–292.

Houston, B. K. (1977). Dispositional anxiety and the effectiveness of cognitive strategies in stressful laboratory and classroom situations. In C. D. Spielberger & I. G. Sarason (Eds.), *Stress and anxiety* (Vol. 4, pp. 205–226). New York: Wiley.

Houston, D. A., & Fazio, R. H. (1989). Biased processing as a function of attitude accessibility. *Social Cognition, 7,* 51–66.

Hovland, C. I., Janis, I. L., & Kelley, H. H. (1953). *Communication and persuasion.* New Haven, CT: Yale University Press.

Hovland, C. I., Lumsdaine, A. A., & Sheffield, F. D. (1949). *Experiments in mass communication.* Princeton, NJ: Princeton University Press.

Howard, G. S., & Conway, C. G. (1986). Can there be an empirical science of volitional action? *American Psychologist, 41,*1241–1251.

Howard, J. A. (1985). Further appraisal of correspondent inference theory. *Personality and Social Psychology Bulletin, 11,* 467–477.

Howard, J. W., & Rothbart, M. (1980). Social categorization and memory for ingroup and outgroup behavior. *Journal of Personality and Social Psychology, 38,* 301–310.

Howard-Pitney, B., Borgida, E., & Omoto, A. M. (1986). Personal involvement: An examination of processing differences. *Social Cognition, 4,* 39–57.

Hull, J. G., & Levy, A. S. (1979). The organizational functions of the self. *Journal of Personality and Social Psychology, 37,* 756–768.

Hume, D. (1978). *A treatise on human nature being an attempt to introduce the experimental method of reasoning into moral subjects.* Fair Lawn, NJ: Oxford University Press. (Originally published, 1739.)

Huttenlocher, J., Hedges, L., & Prohaska, V. (1988). Hierarchical organization in ordered domains: Estimating the dates of events. *Psychological Review, 95,* 471–484.

Hymes, R. W. (1986). Political attitudes as social categories: A new look at selective memory. *Journal of Personality and Social Psychology, 51,* 233–241.

Ickes, W. J. (1984). Compositions in black and white: Determinants of interaction in interracial dyads. *Journal of Personality and Social Psychology, 47,* 230–241.

Ickes, W. J., & Barnes, R. D. (1977). The role of sex and self-monitoring in unstructured dyadic interactions. *Journal of Personality and Social Psychology, 35,* 315–330.

Ickes, W. J., & Kidd, R. F. (1976). Attributional analysis of helping behavior. In J. H. Harvey, W. J. Ickes, & R. F. Kidd (Eds.), *New directions in attribution research* (Vol. 1, pp. 311–334). Hillsdale, NJ: Erlbaum.

Ickes, W. J., Patterson, M. L., Rajecki, D. W., & Tanford, S. (1982). Behavioral and cognitive consequences of reciprocal versus compensatory responses to preinteraction expectancies. *Social Cognition, 1,* 160–190.

Ickes, W. J., Reidhead, S., & Patterson, M. (1986). Machiavellianism and self-monitoring: As different as "me" and "you." *Social Cognition, 4,* 58–74.

Ickes, W. J., Robertson, E., Tooke, W., & Teng, G. (1986). Naturalistic social cognition: Methodology, assessment, and validation. *Journal of Personality and Social Psychology, 51,* 66–82.

Ickes, W. J., & Tooke, W. (1988). The observational method: Studying the interaction of minds and bodies. In S. W. Duck (Ed.), *Handbook of personal relationships* (pp. 79–97). New York: Wiley.

Ickes, W. J., Tooke, W., Stinson, L., Baker, V. L., & Bissonnette, V. (1988). Naturalistic social cognition: Intersubjectivity in same-sex dyads. *Journal of Nonverbal Behavior, 12,* 58–84.

Ingram, R. E., Cruet, D., Johnson, B. R., & Wisnicki, K. S. (1988). Self-focused attention, gender, gender role, and vulnerability to negative affect. *Journal of Personality and Social Psychology, 55,* 967–978.

Ingram, R. E., Smith, T. W., & Brehm, S. S. (1983). Depression and information processing: Self-schemata and the encoding of self-referent information. *Journal of Personality and Social Psychology, 45,* 412–420.

Insko, C. A., & Cialdini, R. B. (1969). A test of three interpretations of attitudinal verbal reinforcement. *Journal of Personality and Social Psychology, 12,* 333–341.

Isen, A. M. (1984). Toward understanding the role of affect in cognition. In R. S. Wyer, Jr., & T. K. Srull (Eds.), *Handbook of social cognition* (Vol. 3, pp. 179–236). Hillsdale, NJ: Erlbaum.

Isen, A. M. (1987). Positive affect, cognitive processes, and social behavior. In L. Berkowitz (Ed.), *Advances in experimental social psychology* (Vol. 20, pp. 203–253). New York: Academic Press.

Isen, A. M., & Daubman, K. A. (1984). The influence of affect on categorization. *Journal of Personality and Social Psychology, 47,* 1206–1217.

Isen, A. M., & Geva, N. (1987). The influence of positive affect on acceptable level of risk: The person with a large canoe has a large worry. *Organizational Behavior and Human Decision Processes, 39,* 145–154.

Isen, A. M., Johnson, M. M. S., Mertz, E., & Robinson, G. F. (1985). The influence of positive affect on the unusualness of word associations. *Journal of Personality and Social Psychology, 48,* 1413–1426.

Isen, A. M., & Means, B. (1983). The influence of positive affect on decision-making strategy. *Social Cognition, 2,* 18–31.

Isen, A. M., & Noonberg, A. (1979). The effects of photographs of the handicapped on donation to charity: When a thousand words may be too much. *Journal of Applied Social Psychology, 9,* 426–431.

Isen, A. M., Nygren, T. E., & Ashby, F. G. (1988). Influence of positive affect on the subjective utility of gains and losses: It is just not worth the risk. *Journal of Personality and Social Psychology, 55,* 710–717.

Isen, A. M., & Patrick, R. (1983). The effect of positive feelings on risk taking: When the chips are down. *Organizational Behavior and Human Performance, 31,* 194–202.

Isen, A. M., & Shalker, T. E. (1982). Do you "accentuate the positive, eliminate the negative" when you are in a good mood? *Social Psychology Quarterly, 45,* 58–63.

Isen, A. M., Shalker, T. E., Clark, M. S., & Karp, L. (1978). Affect, accessibility of material in memory and behavior: A cognitive loop? *Journal of Personality and Social Psychology, 36,* 1–12.

Isen, A. M., & Simmonds, S. F. (1978). The effect of feeling good on a helping task that is incompatible with good mood. *Social Psychology, 41,* 346–349.

Isenberg, D. J. (1986). Group polarization: A critical review and meta-analysis. *Journal of Personality and Social Psychology, 50,* 1141–1151.

Iyengar, S., & Kinder, D. R. (1987). *News that matters: Television and American opinion.* Chicago: University of Chicago Press.

Izard, C. E. (1972). *The face of emotion.* New York: Appleton-Century-Crofts.

Izard, C. E. (1977). *Human emotions.* New York: Plenum.

Izard, C. E. (1981). Differential emotions theory and the facial feedback hypothesis of emotion activation: Comments on Tourangeau and Ellsworth's "The role of facial response in the experience of emotion." *Journal of Personality and Social Psychology, 40,* 350–354.

Izard, C. E. (1985). Emotions and facial expression. [Letter in response to Zajonc, R. B. (1985). Emotion and facial efference: A theory reclaimed. *Science, 228,* 15–21.] *Science, 230,* 608.

Jackson, L. A., & Cash, T. F. (1985). Components of gender stereotypes: Their implications for inferences on stereotypic and nonstereotypic dimensions. *Personality and Social Psychology Bulletin, 11,* 326–344.

Jacobs, L., Berscheid, E., & Walster, E. (1971). Self-esteem and attraction. *Journal of Personality and Social Psychology, 17,* 84–91.

Jacoby, L. L., & Kelley, C. M. (1987). Unconscious influences of memory for a prior event. *Personality and Social Psychology Bulletin, 13,* 314–336.

Jahoda, M. (1986). Small selves in small groups. *British Journal of Social Psychology, 25,* 253–254.

James, K. (1986). Priming and social categorizational factors: Impact on awareness of emergency situations. *Personality and Social Psychology Bulletin, 12,* 462–467.

James, W. (1907). *Pragmatism.* New York: Longmans-Green.

James, W. (1983). *The principles of psychology.* Cambridge, MA: Harvard University Press. (Originally published, 1890.)

Jamieson, D. W., Lydon, J. E., & Zanna, M. P. (1987). Attitude and activity preference similarity: Differential bases of interpersonal attraction for low and high self-monitors. *Journal of Personality and Social Psychology, 53,* 1052–1060.

Jamieson, D. W., & Zanna, M. P. (1989). Need for structure in attitude formation and expression. In A. R. Pratkanis, S. J. Breckler, & A. G. Greenwald (Eds.), *Attitude structure and function* (pp. 383–406). Hillsdale, NJ: Erlbaum.

Janis, I. L. (1972). *Victims of groupthink.* Boston: Houghton Mifflin.

Janis, I. L. (1982). *Groupthink: Psychological studies of policy decisions and fiascoes.* (Revised and enlarged edition of *Victims of groupthink* [1972].) Boston: Houghton Mifflin.

Janis, I. L. (1989). *Crucial decisions: Leadership in policymaking and crisis management.* New York: Free Press.

Janis, I. L., Kaye, D., & Kirschner, P. (1965). Facilitating effects of "eating while reading" on responsiveness to persuasive communications. *Journal of Personality and Social Psychology, 11,* 181–186.

Janis, I. L., & Mann, L. (1977). *Decision making: A psychological analysis of conflict, choice, and commitment.* New York: Free Press.

Janoff-Bulman, R. (1979). Characterological versus behavioral self-blame: Inquiries into depression and rape. *Journal of Personality and Social Psychology, 37,* 1798–1809.

Janoff-Bulman, R. (1989). Assumptive worlds and the stress of traumatic events: Applications of the schema construct. *Social Cognition, 7,* 113–138.

Janoff-Bulman, R., & Brickman, P. (1982). Expectations and what people learn from failure. In N. T. Feather (Ed.), *Expectations and action: Expectancy-value models in psychology* (pp. 207–272). Hillsdale, NJ: Erlbaum.

Janoff-Bulman, R., & Frieze, I. H. (1983). A theoretical perspective for understanding reactions to victimization. *Journal of Social Issues, 39,* 1–17.

Janoff-Bulman, R., & Schwartzberg, S. S. (1990). Toward a general model of personal change: Applications to victimization and psychotherapy. In C. R. Snyder & D. R. Forsyth (Eds.), *Handbook of social and clinical psychology: The health perspective.* New York: Pergamon Press.

Janoff-Bulman, R., Timko, C., & Carli, L. L. (1985). Cognitive biases in blaming the victim. *Journal of Experimental Social Psychology, 21,* 161–177.

Jaspars, J. M. F. (1983). The process of causal attribution in common sense. In M. R. C. Hewstone (Ed.), *Attribution theory: Social and functional extensions* (pp. 28–44). Oxford, England: Basil Blackwell.

Jaspars, J. M. F., Hewstone, M., & Fincham, F. D. (1983). Attribution theory and research: The state of the art. In J. Jaspars, F. D. Fincham, & M. Hewstone (Eds.), *Attribution theory and research: Conceptual, developmental, and social dimensions* (pp. 3–36). London: Academic Press.

Jecker, J. D. (1964). The cognitive effects of conflict and dissonance. In L. Festinger (Ed.), *Conflict, decision, and dissonance.* Palo Alto, CA: Stanford University Press.

Jeffrey, K. M., & Mischel, W. (1979). Effects of purpose on organization and recall of information in person perception. *Journal of Personality, 47,* 397–419.

Jenkins, H. M., & Ward, W. C. (1965). Judgments of contingency between responses and outcomes. *Psychological Monographs, 79* (1, Whole No. 594).

Jennings, D., Amabile, T. M., & Ross, L. (1982). Informal covariation assessment: Data-based vs. theory-based judgments. In A. Tversky, D. Kahneman, & P. Slovic (Eds.), *Judgment under uncertainty: Heuristics and biases* (pp. 211–230). New York: Cambridge University Press.

Jepson, C., Krantz, D. H., & Nisbett, R. E. (1983). Inductive reasoning: Competence or skill? *Behavioral and Brain Sciences, 6,* 494–501.

Jervis, R. (1976). *Perception and misperception in international politics.* Princeton, NJ: Princeton University Press.

John, O. P., Angleitner, A., & Ostendorf, F. (1988). The lexical approach to personality: A historical review of trait taxonomic research. *European Journal of Personality, 2,* 171–203.

Johnson, B. T., & Eagly, A. H. (1989). The effects of involvement on persuasion: A meta-analysis. *Psychological Bulletin, 106,* 290–314.

Johnson, B. T., & Eagly, A. H. (1990). Involvement and persuasion: Types, traditions, and the evidence. *Psychological Bulletin, 107,* 375–384.

Johnson, E. J., & Tversky, A. (1983). Affect generalization and the perception of risk. *Journal of Personality and Social Psychology, 45,* 20–31.

Johnson, J. E. (1984). Psychological interventions and coping with surgery. In A. Baum, S. E. Taylor, & J. E. Singer (Eds.), *Handbook of psychology and health: Social psychological aspects of health* (Vol. 4, pp. 167–188) Hillsdale, NJ: Erlbaum.

Johnson, J. T. (1986). The knowledge of what might have been: Affective and attributional consequences of near outcomes. *Personality and Social Psychology Bulletin, 12,* 51–62.

Johnson, J. T., Cain, L. M., Falke, T. L., Hayman, J., & Perillo, E. (1985). The "Barnum effect" revisited: Cognitive and motivational factors in the acceptance of personality descriptions. *Journal of Personality and Social Psychology, 49,* 1378–1391.

Johnson, J. T., Jemmott, J. B., III., & Pettigrew, T. F. (1984). Causal attribution and dispositional inference: Evidence of inconsistent judgments. *Journal of Experimental Social Psychology, 20,* 567–585.

Johnson, J. T., Struthers, N. J., & Bradlee, P. (1988). Social knowledge and the "secret self": The mediating effect of data base size on judgments of emotionality in the self and others. *Social Cognition, 6,* 319–344.

Johnson, M. H., & Magaro, P. A. (1987). Effects of mood and severity on memory processes in depression and mania. *Psychological Bulletin, 101,* 28–40.

Johnson, N. S. (1981, August). *The role of schemata in comprehension and memory: A developmental perspective.* Paper presented at the meeting of the American Psychological Association, Los Angeles.

Johnson-Laird, P. N. (1983). *Mental models.* Cambridge, MA: Harvard University Press.

Jolly, E. J., & Reardon, R. (1985). Cognitive differentiation, automaticity, and interruptions of automatized behaviors. *Personality and Social Psychology Bulletin, 11,* 301–314.

Jones, E. E. (1976). How do people perceive the causes of behavior? *American Scientist, 64,* 300–305.

Jones, E. E., & Berglas, S. (1978). Control of attributions about the self through self-handicapping strategies: The appeal of alcohol and the role of underachievement. *Personality and Social Psychology Bulletin, 4,* 200–206.

Jones, E. E., & Davis, K. E. (1965). From acts to dispositions: The attribution process in person perception. In L. Berkowitz (Ed.), *Advances in experimental social psychology* (Vol. 2, pp. 220–266). New York: Academic Press.

Jones, E. E., Davis, K. E., & Gergen, K. J. (1961). Role playing variations and their informational value for person perception. *Journal of Abnormal and Social Psychology, 63,* 302–310.

Jones, E. E., & DeCharms, R. (1957). Changes in social perception as a function of the personal relevance of behavior. *Sociometry, 20,* 75–85.

Jones, E. E., Gergen, K. J., & Davis, K. E. (1962). Some determinants of reactions to being approved or disapproved as a person. *Psychological Monographs, 76* (Whole No. 521).

Jones, E. E., & Goethals, G. R. (1972). Order effects in impression formation: Attribution context and the nature of the entity. In E. E. Jones, D. E. Kanouse, H. H. Kelley, R. E. Nisbett, S. Valins, & B. Weiner (Eds.), *Attribution: Perceiving the causes of behavior* (pp. 27–46). Morristown, NJ: General Learning Press.

Jones, E. E., & Harris, V. A. (1967). The attribution of attitudes. *Journal of Experimental Social Psychology, 3,* 1–24.

Jones, E. E., Kanouse, D. E., Kelley, H. H., Nisbett, R. E., Valins, S., & Weiner, B. (Eds.) (1972). *Attribution: Perceiving the causes of behavior.* Morristown, NJ: General Learning Press.

Jones, E. E., & McGillis, D. (1976). Correspondent inferences and the attribution cube: A comparative reappraisal. In J. H. Harvey, W. J. Ickes, & R. F. Kidd (Eds.), *New directions in attribution research* (Vol. 1, pp. 389–420). Hillsdale, NJ: Erlbaum.

Jones, E. E., & Nisbett, R. E. (1972). The actor and the observer: Divergent perceptions of the causes of behavior. In E. E. Jones, D. E. Kanouse, H. H. Kelley, R. E. Nisbett, S. Valins, & B. Weiner (Eds.), *Attribution: Perceiving the causes of behavior* (pp. 79–94). Morristown, NJ: General Learning Press.

Jones, E. E., & Pittman, T. S. (1982). Toward a general theory of strategic self-presentation. In J. Suls (Ed.), *Psychological perspectives on the self* (pp. 231–262). Hillsdale, NJ: Erlbaum.

Jones, E. E., Rhodewalt, F., Berglas, S., & Skelton, J. A. (1981). Effects of strategic self-presentation on subsequent self-esteem. *Journal of Personality and Social Psychology, 41,* 407–421.

Jones, E. E., Schwartz, J., & Gilbert, D. T. (1983–84). Perceptions of moral-expectancy violation: The role of expectancy source. *Social Cognition, 2,* 273–293.

Jones, E. E., & Thibaut, J. W. (1958). Interaction goals as bases of inference in interpersonal perception. In R. Tagiuri & L. Petrullo (Eds.), *Person perception and interpersonal behavior* (pp. 151–178). Palo Alto, CA: Stanford University Press.

Jones, E. E., Wood, G. C., & Quattrone, G. A. (1981). Perceived variability of personal characteristics in in-groups and out-groups: The role of knowledge and evaluation. *Personality and Social Psychology Bulletin, 7,* 523–528.

Jones, E. E., Worchel, S., Goethals, G. R., & Grumet, J. F. (1971). Prior expectancy and behavioral extremity as determinants of attitude attribution. *Journal of Experimental Social Psychology, 71,* 59–80.

Jones, E. E., & Wortman, C. (1973). *Ingratiation: An attributional approach.* Morristown, NJ: General Learning Press.

Jones, J. M. (1972). *Prejudice and racism.* Reading, MA: Addison-Wesley.

Jones, S. C., & Panitch, D. (1971). The self-fulfilling prophecy and interpersonal attraction. *Journal of Experimental Social Psychology, 7,* 356–366.

Jones, S. C., & Schneider, D. J. (1968). Certainty of self-appraisal and reactions to evaluations from others. *Sociometry, 31,* 395–403.

Jordan, J. S., Harvey, J. H., & Weary, G. (1988). Attributional biases in clinical decision making. In D. C. Turk & P. Salovey (Eds.), *Reasoning, inference and judgment in clinical practice* (pp. 90–106). New York: Free Press.

Judd, C. M., & Johnson, J. T. (1981). Attitudes, polarization, and diagnosticity: Exploring the effect of affect. *Journal of Personality and Social Psychology, 41,* 26–36.

Judd, C. M., Kenny, D. A., & Krosnick, J. A. (1983). Judging the positions of political candidates: Models of assimilation and contrast. *Journal of Personality and Social Psychology, 44,* 952–963.

Judd, C. M., & Krosnick, J. A. (1982). Attitude centrality, organization, and measurement. *Journal of Personality and Social Psychology, 42,* 436–447.

Judd, C. M., & Krosnick, J. A. (1989). The structural bases of consistency among political attitudes: Effects of political expertise and attitude importance. In A. R. Pratkanis, S. J. Breckler, & A. G. Greenwald (Eds.), *Attitude structure and function* (pp. 99–128). Hillsdale, NJ: Erlbaum.

Judd, C. M., & Kulik, J. A. (1980). Schematic effects of social attitudes on information processing and recall. *Journal of Personality and Social Psychology, 38,* 569–578.

Judd, C. M., & Lusk, C. M. (1984). Knowledge structures and evaluative judgments: Effects of structural variables on judgmental extremity. *Journal of Personality and Social Psychology, 46,* 1193–1207.

Judd, C. M., & Park, B. (1988). Out-group homogeneity: Judgments of variability at the individual and group levels. *Journal of Personality and Social Psychology, 54,* 778–788.

Jussim, L. (1986). Self-fulfilling prophecies: A theoretical and integrative review. *Psychological Review, 93,* 429–445.

Kahn, W. A., & Crosby, F. (1987). Discriminating between attitudes and discriminatory behaviors. In L. Larwood, B. A. Gutek, & A. H. Stromberg (Eds.), *Women and work: An annual review* (Vol. 1, pp. 215–328). Beverly Hills, CA: Sage.

Kahneman, D. (1973). *Attention and effort.* Englewood Cliffs, NJ: Prentice-Hall.

Kahneman, D., & Miller, D. T. (1986). Norm theory: Comparing reality to its alternatives. *Psychological Review, 93,* 136–153.

Kahneman, D., & Tversky, A. (1973). On the psychology of prediction. *Psychological Review, 80,* 237–251.

Kahneman, D., & Tversky, A. (1982). The simulation heuristic. In D. Kahneman, P. Slovic, & A. Tversky (Eds.), *Judgment under uncertainty: Heuristics and biases* (pp. 201–208). New York: Cambridge University Press.

Kahneman, D., & Tversky, A. (1984). Choices, values, and frames. *American Psychologist, 39,* 341–350.

Kalick, S. M. (1988). Physical attractiveness as a status cue. *Journal of Experimental Social Psychology, 24,* 469–489.

Kallgren, C. A., & Wood, W. (1986). Access to attitude-relevant information in memory as a determinant of attitude-behavior consistency. *Journal of Experimental Social Psychology, 22,* 328–338.

Kanfer, F. H. (1970). Self-regulation: Research, issues, and speculations. In C. Neuringer & J. L. Michael (Eds.), *Behavior modification in clinical psychology* (pp. 178–220). New York: Appleton-Century-Crofts.

Kanfer, F. H., & Goldfoot, D. A. (1966). Self-control and tolerance of noxious stimulation. *Psychological Reports, 18,* 79–85.

Kanfer, F. H., & Hagerman, S. (1981). The role of self-regulation. In L. P. Rehm (Ed.), *Behavior therapy for depression: Present status and future directions* (pp. 143–179). New York: Academic Press.

Kant, I. (1969). *Critique of pure reason.* New York: St. Martin's Press. (Originally published, 1781.)

Kanter, R. (1977). *Men and women of the corporation.* New York: Basic Books.

Kanungo, R. N., & Dutta, S. (1966). Retention of affective material: Frame of reference or intensity? *Journal of Personality and Social Psychology, 4,* 27–35.

Kaplan, M. F. (1971). Contextual effects in impression formation: The weighted average versus the meaning-change formulation. *Journal of Personality and Social Psychology, 19,* 92–99.

Kaplan, M. F. (1975). Evaluative judgments are based on evaluative information: The weighted average versus the meaning-change formulation. *Memory and Cognition, 3,* 375–380.

Kardes, F. R., Sanbonmatsu, D. M., Voss, R. T., & Fazio, R. H. (1986). Self-monitoring and attitude accessibility. *Personality and Social Psychology Bulletin, 12*, 468–474.

Karlovac, M., & Darley, J. M. (1988). Attribution of responsibility for accidents: A negligence law analogy. *Social Cognition, 6*, 287–318.

Karniol, R. (1986). What will they think of next? Transformation rules used to predict other people's thoughts and feelings. *Journal of Personality and Social Psychology, 51*, 932–944.

Karniol, R., & Ross, M. (1976). The development of causal attributions in social perception. *Journal of Personality and Social Psychology, 34*, 455–464.

Kashima, K., & Davison, G. C. (1989). Functional consistency in the face of to-pographical change in articulated thoughts. *Journal of Rational-Emotive & Cognitive-Behavior Therapy, 7*, 131–139.

Kassin, S. M. (1979a). Base rates and prediction: The role of sample size. *Personality and Social Psychology Bulletin, 5*, 210–213.

Kassin, S. M. (1979b). Consensus information, prediction, and causal attribution: A review of the literature and issues. *Journal of Personality and Social Psychology, 37*, 1966–1981.

Kassin, S. M. (1984). TV cameras, public self-consciousness, and mock juror performance. *Journal of Experimental Social Psychology, 20*, 336–349.

Kassin, S. M. (1985). Eyewitness identification: Retrospective self-awareness and the accuracy-confidence correlation. *Journal of Personality and Social Psychology, 49*, 878–893.

Kassin, S. M., & Baron, R. M. (1985). Basic determinants of attribution and social perception. In J. Harvey & E. G. Weary (Eds.), *Attribution: Basic issues and applications* (pp. 37–64). New York: Academic Press.

Kassin, S. M., & Baron, R. M. (1986). On the basicity of social perception cues: Developmental evidence for adult processes? *Social Cognition, 4*, 180–200.

Kassin, S. M., Ellsworth, P. C., & Smith, V. L. (1989). The "general acceptance" of psychological research on eyewitness testimony: A survey of the experts. *American Psychologist, 44*, 1089–1098.

Kassin, S. M., & Lepper, M. R. (1984). Oversufficient and insufficient justification effects: Cognitive and behavioral development. *Advances in Motivation and Achievement, 3*, 73–106.

Kassin, S. M., & Pryor, J. B. (1985). The development of attribution processes. In J. Pryor & J. Day (Eds.), *The development of social cognition* (pp. 3–34). New York: Springer-Verlag.

Katz, D. (1960). The functional approach to the study of attitudes. *Public Opinion Quarterly, 24*, 163–204.

Katz, E. (1968). On reopening the question of selectivity in exposure to mass media. In R. P. Abelson et al. (Eds.), *Theories of cognitive consistency: A sourcebook.* Chicago: Rand McNally.

Katz, I., & Hass, R. G. (1988). Racial ambivalence and American value conflict: Correlational and priming studies of dual cognitive structures. *Journal of Personality and Social Psychology, 55*, 893–905.

Katz, I., Wackenhut, J., & Hass, R. G. (1986). Racial ambivalence, value duality, and behavior. In J. F. Dovidio & S. L. Gaertner (Eds.), *Prejudice, discrimination, and racism* (pp. 35–60). Orlando, FL: Academic Press.

Kavanagh, D. J., & Bower, G. H. (1985). Mood and self-efficacy: Impact of joy and sadness on perceived capabilities. *Cognitive Therapy and Research, 9,* 508–525.

Kayne, N. T., & Alloy, L. B. (1988). Clinician and patient as aberrant actuaries: Expectation-based distortions in assessment of covariation. In L. Y. Abramson (Ed.), *Social cognition and clinical psychology: A synthesis* (pp. 295–365). New York: Guilford Press.

Keenan, J. M., & Baillet, S. D. (1980). Memory for personally and socially relevant events. In R. S. Nickerson (Ed.), *Attention and performance VIII.* (pp. 651–670). Hillsdale, NJ: Erlbaum.

Kellerman, J., Lewis, J., & Laird, J. D. (1989). Looking and loving: The effects of mutual gaze on feelings of romantic love. *Journal of Research in Personality, 23,* 145–161.

Kelley, H. H. (1967). Attribution theory in social psychology. In D. Levine (Ed.), *Nebraska Symposium on Motivation* (Vol. 15, pp. 192–240). Lincoln: University of Nebraska Press.

Kelley, H. H. (1972a). Attribution in social interaction. In E. E. Jones, D. E. Kanouse, H. H. Kelley, R. E. Nisbett, S. Valins, & B. Weiner (Eds.), *Attribution: Perceiving the causes of behavior* (pp. 1–26). Morristown, NJ: General Learning Press.

Kelley, H. H. (1972b). Causal schemata and the attribution process. In E. E. Jones, D. E. Kanouse, H. H. Kelley, R. E. Nisbett, S. Valins, & B. Weiner (Eds.), *Attribution: Perceiving the causes of behavior* (pp. 151–174). Morristown, NJ: General Learning Press.

Kelley, H. H. (1979). *Personal relationships: Their structures and processes.* Hillsdale, NJ: Erlbaum.

Kelley, H. H., Berscheid, E., Christensen, A., Harvey, J. H., Huston, T. L., Levinger, G., McClintock, E., Peplau, L. A., & Peterson, D. R. (1983). Analyzing close relationships. In H. H. Kelley, E. Berscheid, A. Christensen, J. H. Harvey, T. L. Huston, G. Levinger, E. McClintock, L. A. Peplau, & D. R. Peterson (Eds.), *Close relationships* (pp. 20–67). San Francisco: Freeman.

Kelley, H. H., & Michela, J. L. (1980). Attribution theory and research. *Annual Review of Psychology, 31,* 457–501.

Kelley, H. H., & Thibaut, J. W. (1978). *Interpersonal relations: A theory of interdependence.* New York: Wiley-Interscience.

Kellogg, R., & Baron, R. S. (1975). Attribution theory, insomnia, and the reverse placebo effect: A reversal of Storms and Nisbett's findings. *Journal of Personality and Social Psychology, 32,* 231–236.

Kelly, C. (1988). Intergroup differentiation in a political context. *British Journal of Social Psychology, 27,* 319–332.

Kelly, G. A. (1955). *The psychology of personality constructs.* New York: Norton.

Kelman, H. C. (1974). Attitudes are alive and well and gainfully employed in the sphere of action. *American Psychologist, 29,* 310–324.

Kelman, H. C., & Lawrence, L. H. (1972). Assignment of responsibility in the case of Lt. Calley: Preliminary report on a national survey. *Journal of Social Issues, 28,* 177–212.

Kendzierski, D. (1987). Effects of positive and negative behavioral feedback on subsequent attitude-related action. *Journal of Personality, 55,* 55–74.

Kenny, D. A. (1991). A general model of consensus and accuracy in interpersonal perception. *Psychological Review, 98.*

Kenny, D. A., & Albright, L. (1987). Accuracy in interpersonal perception: A social relations analysis. *Psychological Bulletin, 102,* 390–402.

Kenny, D. A., & La Voie, L. (1984). The social relations model. In L. Berkowitz (Ed.), *Advances in experimental social psychology* (Vol. 18, pp. 141–182). New York: Academic Press.

Kenrick, D. T. (1987). Gender, genes, and the social environment. In P. C. Shaver & C. Hendrick (Eds.), *Review of personality and social psychology: Vol. 7. Sex and gender* (pp. 14–43). Newbury Park, CA: Sage.

Kenrick, D. T. (1989). Bridging social psychology and sociobiology: The case of sexual attraction. In R. W. Bell & N. J. Bell (Eds.), *Sociobiology and the social sciences* (pp. 5–23). Lubbock, TX: Texas Tech University Press.

Kenrick, D. T., & Cialdini, R. B. (1977). Romantic attraction: Misattribution versus reinforcement explanations. *Journal of Personality and Social Psychology, 35,* 381–391.

Kenrick, D. T., & Funder, D. C. (1988). Profiting from controversy: Lessons from the person-situation debate. *American Psychologist, 43,* 23–34.

Kernis, M. H. (1984). Need for uniqueness, self-schemas, and thought as moderators of the false-consensus effect. *Journal of Experimental Social Psychology, 20,* 350–362.

Kernis, M. H., Grannemann, B. D., Richie, T., & Hart, J. (1988). The role of contextual factors in the relationship between physical activity and self-awareness. *British Journal of Social Psychology, 27,* 265–273.

Kiesler, C. A. (1971). *The psychology of commitment.* New York: Academic Press.

Kiesler, C. A. (1982). Comments. In M. S. Clark & S. T. Fiske (Eds.), *Affect and cognition.* (pp. 111–118). Hillsdale, NJ: Erlbaum.

Kiesler, C. A., Collins, B. E., & Miller, N. (1969). *Attitude change: A critical analysis of theoretical approaches.* New York: Wiley.

Kiesler, C. A., Nisbett, R. E., & Zanna, M. P. (1969). On inferring one's beliefs from one's behavior. *Journal of Personality and Social Psychology, 11,* 321–327.

Kiesler, S. B. (1975). Actuarial prejudice toward women and its implications. *Journal of Applied Social Psychology, 5,* 201–216.

Kihlstrom, J. F. (1987). The cognitive unconscious. *Science, 237,* 1145–1152.

Kihlstrom, J. F., & Cantor, N. (1984). Mental representations of the self. In L. Berkowitz (Ed.), *Advances in experimental social psychology* (Vol. 17, pp. 2–48). New York: Academic Press.

Kihlstrom, J. F., Cantor, N., Albright, J. S., Chew, B. R., Klein, S. B., & Niedenthal, P. M. (1988). Information processing and the study of the self. In L. Berkowitz (Ed.), *Advances in experimental social psychology* (Vol. 21, pp. 145–180). New York: Academic Press.

Kihlstrom, J. F., & Hoyt, I. P. (1988). Hypnosis and the psychology of delusions. In T. F. Oltmanns & B. A. Maher (Eds.), *Delusional beliefs* (pp. 66–109). New York: Wiley.

Kim, H-S., & Baron, R. S. (1988). Exercise and the illusory correlation. *Journal of Experimental Social Psychology, 24,* 366–380.

Kim, M. P., & Rosenberg, S. (1980). Comparison of two structural models of implicit personality theory. *Journal of Personality and Social Psychology, 38,* 375–389.

Kinder, D. R. (1978). Political person perception: The asymmetrical influence of sentiment on perceptions of presidential candidates. *Journal of Personality and Social Psychology, 36,* 859–871.

King, G. A., & Sorrentino, R. M. (1988). Uncertainty orientation and the relation between individual accessible constructs and person memory. *Social Cognition, 6,* 128–149.

Kintsch, W., & van Dijk, T. A. (1978). Toward a model of text comprehension and production. *Psychological Review, 85,* 363–394.

Kirschenbaum, D. S., Tomarken, A. J., & Humphrey, L. L. (1985). Affect and adult self-regulation. *Journal of Personality and Social Psychology, 48,* 509–523.

Kitayama, S., & Burnstein, E. (1988). Automaticity in conversations: A reexamination of the mindlessness hypothesis. *Journal of Personality and Social Psychology, 54,* 219–224.

Klar, Y., Nadler, A., & Malloy, T. E. (1991). Opting to change: Students' informal self-change endeavors. In Y. Klar, J. D. Fisher, J. M. Chinsky, & A. Nadler, (Eds.), *Initiating changes: Social psychological and clinical perspectives.* New York: Springer-Verlag.

Klatzky, R. L. (1975). *Human memory: Structures and processes.* San Francisco: Freeman.

Klatzky, R. L. (1984). Visual memory: Definitions and functions. In R. S. Wyer, Jr., & T. K. Srull (Eds.), *Handbook of social cognition* (Vol. 2, pp. 233–270). Hillsdale, NJ: Erlbaum.

Klatzky, R. L., Martin, G. L., & Kane, R. A. (1982). Influence of social-category activation on processing of visual information. *Social Cognition, 1,* 95–109.

Klayman, J., & Ha, Y-W. (1987). Confirmation, disconfirmation, and information in hypothesis testing. *Psychological Review, 94,* 211–228.

Klein, D. C., Fencil-Morse, E., & Seligman, M. E. P. (1976). Learned helplessness, depression, and the attribution of failure. *Journal of Personality and Social Psychology, 33,* 508–516.

Klein, G. (1967). Peremptory ideation: Structure and force in motivated ideas. In R. R. Holt (Ed.), *Motives and thought* (pp. 78–128). New York: International Universities Press.

Klein, S. B., & Kihlstrom, J. F. (1986). Elaboration, organization, and the self-reference effect in memory. *Journal of Experimental Psychology: General, 115,* 26–38.

Klein, S. B., & Loftus, J. (1988). The nature of self-referent encoding: The contributions of elaborative and organizational processes. *Journal of Personality and Social Psychology, 55,* 5–11.

Klein, S. B., Loftus, J., & Burton, H. A. (1989). Two self-reference effects: The importance of distinguishing between self-descriptiveness judgments and autobiographical retrieval in self-referent encoding. *Journal of Personality and Social Psychology, 56,* 853–865.

Kleinhesselink, R. R., & Edwards, R. E. (1975). Seeking and avoiding belief-discrepant information as a function of its perceived refutability. *Journal of Personality and Social Psychology, 31,* 787–790.

Kleinke, C. L. (1975). *First impressions: The psychology of encountering others.* Englewood Cliffs, NJ: Prentice-Hall.

Kleinke, C. L., Staneski, R. A., & Weaver, P. (1972). Evaluation of a person who uses another's name in ingratiating or noningratiating situations. *Journal of Experimental Social Psychology, 8,* 457–466.

Kline, P. (1987). The experimental study of the psychoanalytic unconscious. *Personality and Social Psychology Bulletin, 13,* 363–378.

Klinger, E. (1975). Consequences of commitment to and disengagement from incentives. *Psychological Review, 82,* 1–25.

Klinger, E. (1977a). *Meaning and void: Inner experience and the incentives in people's lives.* Minneapolis: University of Minnesota Press.

Klinger, E. (1977b). The nature of fantasy and its clinical uses. *Psychotherapy: Theory, Research and Practice, 14,* 223–231.

Klinger, E. (1978). Modes of normal conscious flow. In K. S. Pope & J. L. Singer (Eds.), *The stream of consciousness: Scientific investigations into the flow of human experience* (pp. 225–258). New York: Plenum.

Klinger, E., Barta, S. G., & Maxeiner, M. E. (1980). Motivational correlates of thought content frequency and commitment. *Journal of Personality and Social Psychology, 39,* 1222–1237.

Knight, J. A., & Vallacher, R. R. (1981). Interpersonal engagement in social peception: The consequence of getting into the action. *Journal of Personality and Social Psychology, 40,* 990–999.

Koffka, K. (1935). *Principles of Gestalt psychology.* New York: Harcourt, Brace, & World.

Kohler, W. (1976). *The place of value in a world of facts.* New York: Liveright. (Originally published 1938.)

Kolditz, T. A., & Arkin, R. M. (1982). An impression management interpretation of the self-handicapping strategy. *Journal of Personality and Social Psychology, 43,* 492–502.

Koller, M., & Wicklund, R. A. (1988). Press and task difficulty as determinants of preoccupation with person descriptors. *Journal of Experimental Social Psychology, 24,* 256–274.

Koriat, A., Lichtenstein, S., & Fischhoff, B. (1980). Reasons for confidence. *Journal of Experimental Psychology: Human Learning and Memory, 6,* 107–118.

Kossan, N. E. (1981). Developmental differences in concept acquisition strategies. *Child Development, 52,* 290–298.

Kosslyn, S. M., Pinker, S., Smith, G. E., & Schwartz, S. P. (1979). On the demystification of mental imagery. *Behavioral and Brain Sciences, 2,* 535–581.

Kosslyn, S. M., & Pomerantz, J. R. (1977). Imagery, propositions, and the form of internal representation. *Cognitive Psychology, 9,* 52–76.

Krauss, R. M. (1981) Impression formation, impression management, and nonverbal behaviors. In E. T. Higgins, C. P. Herman, & M. P. Zanna (Eds.), *Social cognition: The Ontario Symposium* (Vol. 1, pp. 323–341). Hillsdale, NJ: Erlbaum.

Kraut, R. E., & Lewis, S. H. (1982). Person perception and self-awareness: Knowledge of one's influences on one's own judgments. *Journal of Personality and Social Psychology, 42,* 448–460.

Kristiansen, C. M., & Zanna, M. P. (1988). Justifying attitudes by appealing to values: A functional perspective. *British Journal of Social Psychology, 27,* 247–256.

Krosnick, J. A. (1988a). Attitude importance and attitude change. *Journal of Experimental Social Psychology, 24,* 240–255.

Krosnick, J. A. (1988b). *Psychological perspectives on political candidate perception: A review of research on the projection hypothesis.* Paper presented at the meeting of the Midwest Political Science Association, Chicago.

Krosnick, J. A. (1988c). The role of attitude importance in social evaluation: A study of policy preferences, presidential candidate evaluations, and voting behavior. *Journal of Personality and Social Psychology, 55,* 196–210.

Krosnick, J. A. (1989). Attitude importance and attitude accessibility. *Personality and Social Psychology Bulletin, 15,* 297–308.

Krosnick, J. A. (1990a). Expertise and political psychology. *Social Cognition, 8*, 1–8.

Krueger, J., & Rothbart, M. (1988). Use of categorical and individuating information in making inferences about personality. *Journal of Personality and Social Psychology, 55*, 187–195.

Krueger, J., Rothbart, M., & Sriram, N. (1989). Category learning and change: Differences in sensitivity to information that enhances or reduces intercategory distinctions. *Journal of Personality and Social Psychology, 56*, 866–875.

Kruglanski, A. W. (1975). The endogenous-exogenous partition in attribution theory. *Psychological Review, 82*, 387–406.

Kruglanski, A. W. (1977). The place of naive contents in a theory of attribution: Reflections on Calder's and Zuckerman's critiques of the endogenous-exogenous partition. *Personality and Social Psychology Bulletin, 3*, 592–605.

Kruglanski, A. W. (1979). Causal explanation, teleological expansion: On the radical particularism in attribution theory. *Journal of Personality and Social Psychology, 37*, 1447–1457.

Kruglanski, A. W. (1988). Knowledge as a social psychological construct. In D. Bar-Tal & A. W. Kruglanski (Eds.), *The social psychology of knowledege* (pp. 109–141). Cambridge, England: Cambridge University Press.

Kruglanski, A. W. (1989a). *Lay epistemics and human knowledge.* New York: Plenum.

Kruglanski, A. W. (1989b). The psychology of being "right": On the problem of accuracy in social perception and cognition. *Psychological Bulletin, 106*, 395–409.

Kruglanski, A. W. (1990). Motivations for judging and knowing: Implications for causal attribution. In E. T. Higgins & R. M. Sorrentino (Eds.), *Handbook of motivation and cognition: Foundations of social behavior* (Vol. 2, pp. 333–368). New York: Guilford Press.

Kruglanski, A. W., & Ajzen, I. (1983). Bias and error in human judgment. *European Journal of Social Psychology, 19*, 448–468.

Kruglanski, A. W., & Freund, T. (1983). The freezing and unfreezing of lay-inferences: Effects on impressional primacy, ethnic stereotyping, and numerical anchoring. *Journal of Experimental Social Psychology, 19*, 448–468.

Kruglanski, A. W., Friedland, N., & Farkash, E. (1984). Lay persons' sensitivity to statistical information: The case of high perceived applicability. *Journal of Personality and Social Psychology, 46*, 503–518.

Kruglanski, A. W., Hamel, I. Z., Maides, S. A., & Schwartz, J. M. (1978). Attribution theory as a special case of lay epistemology. In J. H. Harvey, W. Ickes, & R. F. Kidd (Eds.), *New directions in attribution research* (Vol. 2, pp. 299–334). Hillsdale, NJ: Erlbaum.

Kruglanski, A. W., & Mayseless, O. (1988). Contextual effects in hypothesis testing: The role of competing alternatives and epistemic motivations. *Social Cognition, 6*, 1–20.

Krugman, H. (1983). Television program interest and commercial interruption. *Journal of Advertising Research, 23*, 21–23.

Kuiper, N. A. (1978). Depression and causal attributions for success and failure. *Journal of Personality and Social Psychology, 36*, 236–246.

Kuiper, N. A. (1981). Convergent evidence for the self as a prototype: The "inverted-U RT effect" for self and other judgments. *Personality and Social Psychology Bulletin, 7*, 438–443.

Kuiper, N. A., & Derry, P. A. (1982). Depressed and nondepressed content self-reference in mild depression. *Journal of Personality, 50,* 67–79.

Kuiper, N. A., & MacDonald, M. R. (1982). Self and other perception in mild depressives. *Social Cognition, 1,* 233–239.

Kuiper, N. A., MacDonald, M. R., & Derry, P. A. (1983). Parameters of a depressive self-schema. In J. Suls & A. G. Greenwald (Eds.), *Psychological perspectives on the self* (Vol. 2, pp. 191–217). Hillsdale, NJ: Erlbaum.

Kuiper, N. A., & Olinger, L. J. (1989). Stress and cognitive vulnerability for depression: A self-worth contingency model. In R. W. J. Neufeld (Ed.), *Advances in the investigation of psychological stress* (pp. 367–391). New York: Wiley.

Kuiper, N. A., Olinger, L.J., & MacDonald, M. R. (1988). Vulnerability and episodic cognitions in a self-worth contingency model of depression. In L. B. Alloy (Ed.), *Cognitive processes in depression* (pp. 289–309). New York: Guilford Press.

Kuiper, N. A., Olinger, L.J., MacDonald, M. R., & Shaw, B. F. (1985). Self-schema processing of depressed and nondepressed content: The effects of vulnerability to depression. *Social Cognition, 3,* 77–93.

Kuiper, N. A., Olinger, L.J., & Swallow, S. R. (1987). Dysfunctional attitudes, mild depression, views of self, self-consciousness, and social perceptions. *Motivation and Emotion, 11,* 379–401.

Kuiper, N. A., & Rogers, T. B. (1979). Encoding of personal information: Self-other differences. *Journal of Personality and Social Psychology, 37,* 499–514.

Kulik, J. A. (1983). Confirmatory attribution and the perpetuation of social beliefs. *Journal of Personality and Social Psychology, 44,* 1171–1181.

Kulik, J. A., & Mahler, H. I. M. (1986). Self-confirmatory effects of delay on perceived contribution to a joint activity. *Journal of Personality and Social Psychology, 12,* 344–352.

Kulik, J. A., Sledge, P., & Mahler, H. I. M. (1986). Self-confirmatory attribution, egocentrism, and the perpetuation of self-beliefs. *Journal of Personality and Social Psychology, 50,* 587–594.

Kun, A., & Weiner, B. (1973). Necessary versus sufficient causal schemata for success and failure. *Journal of Research in Psychology, 7,* 197–207.

Kunda, Z. (1987). Motivated inference: Self-serving generation and evaluation of causal theories. *Journal of Personality and Social Psychology, 53,* 636–647.

Kunda, Z., & Nisbett, R. E. (1986). Prediction and the partial understanding of the law of large numbers. *Journal of Experimental Social Psychology, 22,* 339–354.

Kunda, Z., & Nisbett, R. E. (1988). Predicting individual evaluations from group evaluations and vice versa: Different patterns for self and other? *Personality and Social Psychology Bulletin, 14,* 326–334.

Kunst-Wilson, W. R., & Zajonc, R. B. (1980). Affective discrimination of stimuli that cannot be recognized. *Science, 207,* 557–558.

LaBerge, D. (1975). Acquisition of automatic processing in perceptual and associative learning. In P. M. A. Rabbitt & S. Dornic (Eds.), *Attention and performance* (Vol. 5, pp. 50–64). New York: Academic Press.

Lacey, J. I. (1959). Psychophysiological approaches to the evaluation of psychotherapeutic process and outcome. In E. A. Rubinstein & M. B. Parloff

(Eds.), *Research in psychotherapy* (Vol. 1, pp. 160–208). Washington, DC: American Psychological Association.

Lacey, J. I. (1967). Somatic response patterning and stress: Some revisions of activation theory. In M. H. Appley & R. Trumbull (Eds.), *Psychological stress: Issues in research* (pp. 14–44). New York: Appleton-Century-Crofts.

Lacey, J. I., & Lacey, B. C. (1958). The relationship of resting autonomic activity to motor impulsivity. In H. C. Solomon, S. Cobb, & W. Pennfield (Eds.), *The brain and human behavior* (Vol. 36, pp. 144–209). Baltimore: Williams & Wilkins.

Lacey, J. I., & Lacey, B. C. (1970). Some autonomic-central nervous system interrelationships. In P. Black (Ed.), *Physiological correlates of emotion* (pp. 205–227). New York: Academic Press.

Laird, J. D. (1974). Self-attribution of emotion: The effects of expressive behavior on the quality of emotional experience. *Journal of Personality and Social Psychology, 29,* 475–486.

Laird, J. D. (1984). The real role of facial response in the experience of emotion: A reply to Tourangeau and Ellsworth, and others. *Journal of Personality and Social Psychology, 47,* 909–917.

Laird, J. D., Cuniff, M., Sheehan, K., Shulman, D., & Strum, G. (1989). Emotion specific effects of facial expressions on memory for life events. *Journal of Social Behavior and Personality, 4,* 87–98.

Laird, J. D., Wagener, J., Halal, M., & Szegda, M. (1982). Remembering what you feel: Effects of emotion on memory. *Journal of Personality and Social Psychology, 42,* 646–657.

Lake, E. A., & Arkin, R. M. (1985). Reactions to objective and subjective interpersonal evaluation: The influence of social anxiety. *Journal of Social and Clinical Psychology, 3,* 142–160.

Landman, J. (1988). Regret and elation following action and inaction: Affective responses to positive versus negative outcomes. *Personality and Social Psychology Bulletin, 13,* 524–536.

Lane, D. M., Anderson, C. A., & Kellam, K. L. (1985). Judging the relatedness of variables: The psychophysics of covariation detection. *Journal of Experimental Social Psychology, 11,* 640–649.

Lange, C. G. (1922). *The emotions.* Baltimore: Williams & Wilkins. (Originally published, 1885.)

Langer, E. J. (1975). The illusion of control. *Journal of Personality and Social Psychology, 32,* 311–328.

Langer, E. J. (1978). Rethinking the role of thought in social interaction. In J. H. Harvey, W. I. Ickes, & R. F. Kidd (Eds.), *New directions in attribution research* (Vol. 2, pp. 35–58). Hillsdale, NJ: Erlbaum.

Langer, E. J. (1989a). *Mindfulness.* Reading, MA: Addison-Wesley.

Langer, E. J. (1989b). Minding matters. In L. Berkowitz (Ed.), *Advances in experimental social psychology* (Vol. 22, 137–173). New York: Academic Press.

Langer, E. J., & Abelson, R. P. (1974). A patient by any other name . . . : Clinician group difference in labeling bias. *Journal of Consulting and Clinical Psychology, 42,* 4–9.

Langer, E. J., Bashner, R. S., & Chanowitz, B. (1985). Decreasing prejudice by increasing discrimination. *Journal of Personality and Social Psychology, 49,* 113–120.

Langer, E. J., & Benevento, A. (1978). Self-induced dependence. *Journal of Personality and Social Psychology, 36,* 886–893.

Langer, E. J., Blank, A., Chanowitz, B. (1978). The mindlessness of ostensibly thoughtful action: The role of "placebic" information in interpersonal interaction. *Journal of Personality and Social Psychology, 36,* 635–642.

Langer, E. J., & Chanowitz, B., & Blank, A. (1985). Mindlessness-mindfulness in perspective. *Journal of Personality and Social Psychology, 48,* 605–607.

Langer, E. J., & Imber, L. (1979). When practice makes imperfect: Debilitating effects of overlearning. *Journal of Personality and Social Psychology, 37,* 2014–2024.

Langer, E. J., & Imber, L. (1980). The role of mindlessness in the perception of deviance. *Journal of Personality and Social Psychology, 39,* 360–367.

Langer, E. J., Janis, I. L., & Wolfer, J. (1975). Effects of a cognitive coping device and preparatory information on psychological stress in surgical patients. *Journal of Experimental Social Psychology, 11,* 155–165.

Langer, E. J., & Piper, A. I. (1987). The prevention of mindlessness. *Journal of Personality and Social Psychology, 53,* 280–287.

Langer, E. J., & Piper, A. I. (1988). Television from a mindful/mindless perspective. *Applied Social Psychology Annual, 8,* 247–260.

Langer, E. J., & Roth, J. (1975). Heads I win, tails it's chance: The illusion of control as a function of the sequence of outcomes in a purely chance task. *Journal of Personality and Social Psychology, 32,* 951–955.

Langer, E. J., Taylor, S. E., Fiske, S. T., & Chanowitz, B. (1976). Stigma, staring, and discomfort: A novel stimulus hypothesis. *Journal of Experimental Social Psychology, 12,* 451–463.

Langer, E. J., & Weinman, C. (1981). When thinking disrupts intellectual performance: Mindlessness on an overlearned task. *Personality and Social Psychology Bulletin, 7,* 240–243.

Lanzetta, J. T., Cartwright-Smith, J., & Kleck, R. E. (1976). Effects of nonverbal dissimilation on emotional experience and autonomic arousal. *Journal of Personality and Social Psychology, 33,* 354–370.

LaPiere, R. T. (1934). Attitudes versus actions. *Social Forces, 13,* 230–237.

Larkin, J. H., McDermott, J., Simon, D. P., & Simon, H. A. (1980). Models of competence in solving physics problems. *Science, 200,* 1335–1342.

Larwood, L., & Whittaker, W. (1977). Managerial myopia: Self-serving biases in organizational planning. *Journal of Applied Psychology, 62,* 194–198.

Lassiter, G. D. (1988). Behavior perception, affect, and memory. *Social Cognition, 6,* 150–176.

Lassiter, G. D., & Stone, J. I. (1984). Affective consequences of variation in behavior perception: When liking is in the level of analysis. *Personality and Social Psychology Bulletin, 10,* 253–259.

Lassiter, G. D., Stone, J. I., & Rogers, S. L. (1988). Memorial consequences of variation in behavior perception. *Journal of Experimental Social Psychology, 24,* 222–239.

Lassiter, G. D., Stone, J. I., & Weigold, M. F. (1988). Effect of leading questions on the self-monitoring-memory correlation. *Personality and Social Psychology Bulletin, 13,* 537–545.

Lasswell, H. D. (1948). The structure and function of communication in society. In L. Bryson (Ed.), *The communication of ideas* (pp. 37–51). New York: Harper.

Lau, R. R., & Hartman, K. A. (1983). Common sense representations of common illnesses. *Health Psychology, 2,* 167–185.

Lau, R. R., & Russell, D. (1980). Attribution in the sports pages. *Journal of Personality and Social Psychology, 39,* 39–38.

Lazarus, R. S. (1966). *Psychological stress and the coping process*. New York: McGraw-Hill.

Lazarus, R. S. (1982). Thoughts on the relations between emotion and cognition. *American Psychologist, 37,* 1019–1024.

Lazarus, R. S. (1984). On the primacy of cognition. *American Psychologist, 39,* 124–129.

Lazarus, R. S. (1990). Constructs of the mind in adaptation. In N. L. Stein, B. Leventhal, & T. Trabasso (Eds.), *Psychological and biological approaches to emotion* (pp. 3–20). Hillsdale, NJ: Erlbaum.

Lazarus, R. S., Averill, J. R., & Opton, E. M., Jr. (1970). Towards a cognitive theory of emotion. In M. B. Arnold (Ed.), *Feelings and emotion: The Loyola Symposium* (pp. 207–232). New York: Academic Press.

Lazarus, R. S., & Smith, C. A. (1988). Knowledge and appraisal in the cognition-emotion relationship. *Cognition and Emotion, 2,* 281–300.

Leary, M. R. (1986). The impact of interactional impediments on social anxiety and self-presentation. *Journal of Experimental Social Psychology, 22,* 122–135.

Leary, M. R., Kowalski, R. M., & Bergen, D. J. (1988). Interpersonal information acquisition and confidence in first encounters. *Personality and Social Psychology Bulletin, 14,* 68–77.

Leary, M. R., & Shepperd, J. A. (1986). Behavioral self-handicaps versus self-reported handicaps: A conceptual note. *Journal of Personality and Social Psychology, 51,* 1265–1268.

Leddo, J., Abelson, R. P., & Gross, P. H. (1984). Conjunctive explanations: When two reasons are better than one. *Journal of Personality and Social Psychology, 47,* 933–943.

Lehman, D. R., Lempert, R. O., & Nisbett, R. E. (1988). The effects of graduate training on reasoning: Formal discipline and thinking about everyday-life events. *American Psychologist, 43,* 431–442.

Leippe, M. R., & Elkin, R. A. (1987). When motives clash: Issue involvement and response involvement as determinants of persuasion. *Journal of Personality and Social Psychology, 52,* 269–278.

Lemon, N., & Warren, N. (1974). Salience, centrality, and self-relevance of traits in construing others. *British Journal of Social and Clinical Psychology, 13,* 119–124.

Lemyre, L., & Smith, P. M. (1985). Intergroup discrimination and self-esteem in the minimal group paradigm. *Journal of Personality and Social Psychology, 49,* 660–670.

Lennox, R. D., & Wolfe, R. N. (1984). Revision of the self-monitoring scale. *Journal of Personality and Social Psychology, 46,* 1349–1364.

Lepper, M. R., Greene, D., & Nisbett, R. E. (1973). Undermining children's intrinsic interest with extrinsic rewards: A test of the "overjustification" hypothesis. *Journal of Personality and Social Psychology, 28,* 129–137.

Lerner, M. J. (1965). The effect of responsibility and choice on a partner's attractiveness following failure. *Journal of Personality, 33,* 178–187.

Lerner, M. J. (1970). The desire for justice and reactions to victims. In J. Macaulay & L. Berkowitz (Eds.), *Altruism and helping behavior* (pp. 205–229). New York: Academic Press.

Lerner, M. J., & Matthews, G. (1967). Reactions to suffering of others under conditions of indirect responsibility. *Journal of Personality and Social Psychology, 5,* 319–325.

Leventhal, H. (1962). The effects of set and discrepancy on impression change. *Journal of Personality, 30,* 1–15.

Leventhal, H. (1974). Emotions: A basic problem for social psychology. In C. Nemeth (Ed.), *Social psychology: Classic and contemporary integrations* (pp. 1–51). Chicago: Rand-McNally.

Leventhal, H. (1982). The integration of emotion and cognition: A view from the perceptual-motor theory of emotion. In M. S. Clark & S. T. Fiske (Eds.), *Affect and cognition: The 17th Annual Carnegie Symposium on Cognition* (pp. 121–156). Hillsdale, NJ: Erlbaum.

Leventhal, H. (1984). A perceptual-motor theory of emotion. In L. Berkowitz (Ed.), *Advances in experimental social psychology* (Vol. 17, pp. 118–182). Orlando, FL: Academic Press.

Leventhal, H., Brown, D., Shacham, S., & Engquist, C. (1979). Effects of preparatory information about sensations, threat of pain, and attention on cold pressor distress. *Journal of Personality and Social Psychology, 37,* 688–714.

Leventhal, H., & Scherer, K. (1987). The relationship of emotion to cognition: A functional approach to a semantic controversy. *Cognition and Emotion, 1,* 3–28.

Levin, I. P., Schnittjer, S. K., & Thee, S. L. (1988). Information framing effects in social and personal decisions. *Journal of Experimental Social Psychology, 24,* 520–529.

Levine, J. M., & Murphy, G. (1943). The learning and retention of controversial statements. *Journal of Abnormal and Social Psychology, 38,* 507–517.

Levine, R. A., & Campbell, D. T. (1972). *Ethnocentrism: Theories of conflict, ethnic attitudes and group behavior.* New York: Wiley.

Lewicki, P. (1982). Trait relationships: The nonconscious generalization of social experience. *Personality and Social Psychology Bulletin, 8,* 439–445.

Lewicki, P. (1983). Self-image bias in person perception. *Journal of Personality and Social Psychology, 45,* 384–393.

Lewicki, P. (1984). Self-schema and social information processing. *Journal of Personality and Social Psychology, 48,* 463–474.

Lewicki, P. (1985). Nonconscious biasing effects of single instances of subsequent judgments. *Journal of Personality and Social Psychology, 48,* 563–574.

Lewicki, P. (1986a). Processing information about covariations that cannot be articulated. *Journal of Experimental Psychology: Learning, Memory, and Cognition, 12,* 135–146.

Lewicki, P. (1986b). *Nonconscious social information processing.* New York: Academic Press.

Lewicki, P., Czyzewska, M., & Hoffman, H. (1987). Unconscious acquisition of complex procedural knowledge. *Journal of Experimental Psychology: Learning, Memory, and Cognition, 13,* 523–530.

Lewicki, P., & Hill, T. (1987). Unconscious processes as explanations of behavior in cognitive, personality, and social psychology. *Personality and Social Psychology Bulletin, 13,* 355–362.

Lewicki, P., Hill, T., & Bizot, E. (1988). Acquisition of procedural knowledge about pattern of stimuli that cannot be articulated. *Cognitive Psychology, 20,* 24–37.

Lewin, K. (1951). *Field theory in social science.* New York: Harper.

Lewinsohn, P. M., Mischel, W., Chaplin, W., & Barton, R. (1980). Social competence and depression: The role of illusory self-perceptions. *Journal of Abnormal Psychology, 89,* 203–212.

Leyens, J.-P. (1983). *Sommes-nous tous des psychologues? Approche psychosociale des théories implicites de la personalité* [Are we all psychologists? A social psychological apparoach to implicit personality theories]. Bruxelles: Mardaga.

Leyens, J.-P., & Codol, J. P. (1988). Social cognition. In M. Hewstone, W. Stroebe, J. P. Codol, & G. M. Stephenson (Eds.), *Introduction to social psychology: A European perspective* (pp. 89–110). Oxford, England: Basil Blackwell.

Lichtenstein, M., & Srull, T. K. (1987). Processing objectives as a determinant of the relationship between recall and judgment. *Journal of Experimental Social Psychology, 23,* 93–118.

Lilli, W., & Rehm, J. (1986). The formation of prejudicial judgments as an interaction between heuristic processes and social identity of the judge: The case of traffic accident participation. *European Journal of Social Psychology, 16,* 79–81.

Lingle, J. H. (1983). Tracing memory structure activation during person judgments. *Journal of Experimental Social Psychology, 19,* 480–496.

Lingle, J. H., Altom, M. W., & Medin, D. L. (1984). Of cabbages and kings: Assessing the extensibility of natural object concept models to social things. In R. S. Wyer, Jr., & T. K. Srull (Eds.), *Handbook of social cognition* (Vol. 1, pp. 71–117). Hillsdale, NJ: Erlbaum.

Lingle, J. H., Dukerich, J. M., & Ostrom, T. M. (1983). Accessing information in memory-based impression judgments: Incongruity vs. negativity in retrieval selectivity. *Journal of Personality and Social Psychology, 44,* 262–272.

Lingle, J. H., Geva, N., Ostrom, T. M., Leippe, M. R., & Baumgardner, M. H. (1979). Thematic effects of person judgments on impression organization. *Journal of Personality and Social Psychology, 37,* 674–687.

Lingle, J. H. & Ostrom, T. M. (1979). Retrieval selectivity in memory-based impression judgments. *Journal of Personality and Social Psychology, 37,* 180–194.

Lingle, J. H., & Ostrom, T. M. (1981). Principles of memory and cognition in attitude formation. In R. E. Petty, T. M. Ostrom, & T. C. Brock (Eds.), *Cognitive responses in persuasion* (pp. 399–420). Hillsdale, N.J.: Erlbaum.

Linville, P. W. (1982a). Affective consequences of complexity regarding the self and others. In M. S. Clark & S. T. Fiske (Eds.), *Affect and cognition: The 17th Annual Carnegie Symposium on Cognition* (pp. 79–109). Hillsdale, NJ: Erlbaum.

Linville, P. W. (1982b). The complexity-extremity effect and age-based stereotyping. *Journal of Personality and Social Psychology, 42,* 193–211.

Linville, P. W. (1985). Self-complexity and affective extremity: Don't put all your eggs in one cognitive basket. *Social Cognition, 3,* 94–120.

Linville, P. W. (1987). Self-complexity as a cognitive buffer against stress-related depression and illness. *Journal of Personality and Social Psychology, 52,* 663–676.

Linville, P. W., Fischer, G. W., & Salovey, P. (1989). Perceived distributions of the characteristics of in-group and out-group members: Empirical evidence and a computer simulation. *Journal of Personality and Social Psychology, 57,* 165–188.

Linville, P. W., & Jones, E. E. (1980). Polarized appraisals of outgroup members. *Journal of Personality and Social Psychology, 38,* 689–703.

Linville, P. W., Salovey, P., & Fischer, G. W. (1986). Stereotyping and perceived distributions of social characteristics: An application to ingroup-outgroup perception. In J. F. Dovidio & S. L. Gaertner (Eds.), *Prejudice, discrimination, and racism* (pp. 165–208). Orlando, FL: Academic Press.

Lippa, R. (1976). Expressive control and the leakage of dispositional introversion-extraversion during role-playing teaching. *Journal of Personality, 44,* 541–559.

Little, B. R. (1983). Personal projects: A rationale and method for investigation. *Environmental Behavior, 15,* 273–309.

Liu, T. J., & Steele, C. M. (1986). Attributional analysis as self-affirmation. *Journal of Personality and Social Psychology, 51,* 531–540.

Locke, D., & Pennington, D. (1982). Reasons and other causes: Their role in attribution processes. *Journal of Personality and Social Psychology, 42,* 212–223.

Locke, J. (1979). *Essay concerning human understanding.* New York: Oxford University press. (Originally published 1690.)

Locksley, A., Borgida, E., Brekke, N., & Hepburn, C. (1980). Sex stereotypes and social judgment. *Journal of Personality and Social Psychology, 39,* 821–831.

Locksley, A., Hepburn, C., & Ortiz, V. (1982). Social stereotypes and judgments of individuals: An instance of the base rate fallacy. *Journal of Experimental Social Psychology, 18,* 23–42.

Locksley, A., & Stangor, C. (1984). Why versus how often? Causal reasoning and the incidence of judgmental bias. *Journal of Experimental Social Psychology, 20,* 470–483.

Lodge, M., & Hamill, R. (1986). A partisan schema for political information processing. *American Political Science Review, 80,* 505–519.

Loftus, E. F. (1979). *Eyewitness testimony.* Cambridge, MA: Harvard University Press.

Loftus, E. F., & Fathi, D. C. (1985). Retrieving multiple autobiographical memories. *Social Cognition, 3,* 280–295.

Loftus, E. F., & Hoffman, H. G. (1989). Misinformation and memory: The creation of new memories. *Journal of Experimental Psychology: General, 118,* 100–104.

Loftus, E. F., Miller, D. G., & Burns, H. J. (1978). Semantic integration of verbal information into visual memory. *Journal of Experimental Psychology: Human Learning and Memory, 4,* 19–31.

Logan, G. D. (1988). Toward an instance theory of automatization. *Psychological Review, 95,*492–527.

Logan, G. D. (1989). Automaticity and cognitive control. In J. S. Uleman & J. A. Bargh (Eds.), *Unintended thought* (pp. 52–74). New York: Guilford Press.

Loken, B. (1984). Attitude processing strategies. *Journal of Experimental Social Psychology, 20,* 272–296.

Lombardi, W. J., Higgins, E. T., & Bargh, J. A. (1987). The role of consciousness in priming effects on categorization: Assimilation versus contrast as a function of awareness of the priming task. *Personality and Social Psychology Bulletin, 13,* 411–429.

Lopes, L. L. (1982). *Towards a procedural theory of judgment.* (Tech. Rep. No. 17, pp. 1–49). Information Processing Program, University of Wisconsin, Madison, WI.

Lord, C. G. (1980). Schemas and images as memory aids: Two modes of processing social information. *Journal of Personality and Social Psychology, 38*, 257–269.

Lord, C. G. (1982). Predicting behavioral consistency from an individual's perception of situational similarities. *Journal of Personality and Social Psychology,
42*, 1076–1088.

Lord, C. G. (1987). Imagining self and others: Reply to Brown, Keenan, and
Potts. *Journal of Personality and Social Psychology, 53*, 445–450.

Lord, C. G., & Gilbert, D. T. (1983). The "same person" heuristic: An
attributional procedure based on an assumption about person similarity.
Journal of Personality and Social Psychology, 45, 751–762.

Lord, C. G., Lepper, M. R., & Mackie, D. (1984). Attitude prototypes as determinants of attitude-behavior consistency. *Journal of Personality and Social Psychology, 46*, 1254–1266.

Lord, C. G., Lepper, M. R., & Preston, E. (1984). Considering the opposite: A
corrective strategy for social judgment. *Journal of Personality and Social Psychology, 47*, 1231–1243.

Lord, C. G., Ross, L., & Lepper, M. R. (1979). Biased assimilation and attitude
polarization: The effects of prior theories on subsequently considered evidence. *Journal of Personality and Social Psychology, 37*, 2098–2109.

Lord, C. G., & Saenz, D. S. (1985). Memory deficits and memory surfeits: Differential cognitive consequences of tokenism for tokens and observers. *Journal of Personality and Social Psychology, 49*, 918–926.

Lord, C. G., Saenz, D. S., & Godfrey, D. K. (1987). Effects of perceived scrutiny
on participant memory for social interactions. *Journal of Experimental Social
Psychology, 23*, 498–517.

Lord, C. G., & Zimbardo, P. G. (1985). Actor-observer differences in the perceived stability of shyness. *Social Cognition, 3*, 250–265.

Lowe, C. A., & Kassin, S. M. (1980). A perceptual view of attribution. *Personality
and Social Psychology, 6*, 532–542.

Lund F. H. (1975). The psychology of belief: A study of its emotional and volitional determinants. *Journal of Abnormal and Social Psychology, 20*, 63–81.

Lurigio, A. J., & Carroll, J. S. (1985). Probation officers' schemata of offenders:
Content, development, and impact on treatment decisions. *Journal of Personality and Social Psychology, 48*, 1112–1126.

Lusk, C. M., & Judd, C. M. (1988). Political expertise and the structural mediators of candidate evaluations. *Journal of Experimental Social Psychology, 24*,
105–126.

Lydon, J. E., Jamieson, D. W., & Zanna, M. P. (1988). Interpersonal similarity
and the social and intellectual dimensions of first impressions. *Social Cognition, 6*, 269–286.

Lydon, J. E., & Zanna, M. P. (1990). Commitment in the face of adversity: A
value-affirmation approach. *Journal of Personality and Social Psychology, 58*,
1040–1047.

Lydon, J. E., Zanna, M. P., & Ross, M. (1988). Bolstering attitudes by autobiographical recall. *Personality and Social Psychology Bulletin, 14*, 78–86.

Lynn, M., Shavitt, S., & Ostrom, T. (1985). Effects of pictures on the organization and recall of social information. *Journal of Personality and Social Psychology, 49*, 1160–1168.

Lyon, D., & Slovic, P. (1976). Dominance of accuracy information and neglect of
base rates in probability estimation. *Acta Psychologica, 40*, 287–298.

Maass, A., Salvi, D., Arcuri, L., & Semin, G. (1989). Language use in intergroup contexts: The linguistic intergroup bias. *Journal of Personality and Social Psychology, 57*, 981–993.

Mackie, D. M. (1986). Social identification effects in group polarization. *Journal of Personality and Social Psychology, 50*, 720–728.

Mackie, D. M. (1987). Systematic and nonsystematic processing of majority and minority persuasive communications. *Journal of Personality and Social Psychology, 53*, 41–52.

Mackie, D. M., & Allison, S. T. (1987). Group attribution errors and the illusion of group attitude change. *Journal of Experimental Social Psychology, 23*, 460–480.

Mackie, D. M., & Cooper, J. (1984). Attitude polarization: Effects of group membership. *Journal of Personality and Social Psychology, 46*, 575–585.

Mackie, D. M., & Gastardo-Conaco, M. C. (1988). The impact of importance accorded an issue on attitude inferences. *Journal of Experimental Social Psychology, 24*, 543–570.

Mackie, D. M., Hamilton, D. L., Schroth, H. A., Carlisle, C. J., Gersho, B. F., Meneses, L. M., Nedler, B. F., & Reichel, L. D. (1989). The effects of induced mood on illusory correlations. *Journal of Experimental Social Psychology, 25*, 524–544.

Mackie, D. M., & Worth, L. T. (1989). Cognitive deficits and the mediation of positive affect in persuasion. *Journal of Personality and Social Psychology, 57*, 27–40.

Major, B. (1980). Information acquisition and attribution processes. *Journal of Personality and Social Psychology, 39*, 1010–1024.

Major, B., Cozzarelli, C., Testa, M., & McFarlin, D. B. (1988). Self-verification versus expectancy confirmation in social interaction: The impact of self-focus. *Personality and Social Psychology Bulletin, 14*, 346–359.

Malpass, R. S. (1969). Effects of attitude on learning and memory: The influence of instruction-induced sets. *Journal of Experimental Social Psychology, 5*, 441–453.

Malpass, R. S., & Kravitz, J. (1969). Recognition for faces of own and other race. *Journal of Personality and Social Psychology, 13*, 330–334.

Malpass, R. S., Lavigueur, H., & Weldon, D. E. (1973). Verbal and visual training in face recognition. *Perception and Psychophysics, 14*, 285–292.

Mandler, G. (1975). *Mind and emotion.* New York: Wiley.

Mandler, G. (1982). The structure of value: Accounting for taste. In M. S. Clark & S. T. Fiske (Eds.), *Affect and cognition: The 17th Annual Carnegie Symposium on Cognition* (pp. 3–36). Hillsdale, NJ: Erlbaum.

Mandler, G. (1984). *Mind and body: Psychology of emotion and stress.* New York: Norton.

Mandler, G. (1990). A constructivist theory of emotion. In N. S. Stein, B. L. Leventhal, & T. Trabasso (Eds.), *Psychological and biological approaches to emotion* (pp. 21–43). Hillsdale, NJ: Erlbaum.

Mandler, G., & Nakamura, Y. (1987). Aspects of consciousness. *Personality and Social Psychology Bulletin, 13*, 299–313.

Mandler, G., Nakamura, Y., & Shebo Van Zandt, B. J. (1987). Nonspecific effects of exposure on stimuli that cannot be recognized. *Journal of Experimental Psychology: Learning, Memory, and Cognition, 13*, 646–648.

Mandler, J. (1979). Categorical and schematic organization in memory. In C. R. Puff (Ed.), *Memory organization and structure* (pp. 259–299). New York: Academic Press.

Manis, M. (1977). Cognitive social psychology. *Personality and Social Psychology Bulletin, 3,* 550–566.

Manis, M., Avis, N. E., & Cardoze, S. (1981). Reply to Bar-Hillel and Fischhoff. *Journal of Personality and Social Psychology, 41,* 681–683.

Manis, M., Dovalina, I., Avis, N. E., & Cardoze, S. (1980). Base rates can affect individual predictions. *Journal of Personality and Social Psychology, 38,* 231–248.

Manis, M., Nelson, T. E., & Shedler, J. (1988). Stereotypes and social judgment: Extremity, assimilation, and contrast. *Journal of Personality and Social Psychology, 55,* 28–36.

Manis, M., & Paskewitz, J.R. (1984). Judging psychopathology: Expectation and contrast. *Journal of Experimental Social Psychology, 20,* 363–381.

Manis, M., & Paskewitz, J. R. (1987). Assessing psychopathology in individuals and groups: Aggregating behavior samples to form overall impressions. *Personality and Social Psychology Bulletin, 13,* 83–94.

Manis, M., Paskewitz, J., & Cotler, S. (1986). Stereotypes and social judgment. *Journal of Personality and Social Psychology, 50,* 461–473.

Manucia, G. K., Baumann, D. J., & Cialdini, R. B. (1984). Mood influences on helping: Direct effects or side effects? *Journal of Personality and Social Psychology, 46,* 357–364.

Marcel, A. J. (1983a). Conscious and unconscious perception: An approach to the relations between phenomenal experience and perceptual processes. *Cognitive Psychology, 15,* 238–300.

Marcel, A. J. (1983b). Conscious and unconscious perception: Experiments on visual masking and word recognition. *Cognitive Psychology, 15,* 197–237.

March, J. G., & Simon, G. A. (1958). *Organizations.* New York: Wiley.

Marks, G. (1984). Thinking one's abilities are unique and one's opinions are common. *Personality and Social Psychology Bulletin, 10,* 203–208.

Marks, G., & Miller, N. (1985). The effect of certainty on consensus judgments. *Personality and Social Psychology Bulletin, 2,* 165–177.

Marks, G., & Miller, N. (1987). Ten years of research on the false-consensus effect: An empirical and theoretical review. *Psychological Bulletin, 102,* 72–90.

Markus, H. (1977). Self-schemata and processing information about the self. *Journal of Personality and Social Psychology, 35,* 63–78.

Markus, H., Crane, M., Bernstein, S., & Siladi, M. (1982). Self-schemas and gender. *Journal of Personality and Social Psychology, 42,* 38–50.

Markus, H., Cross, S., & Wurf, E. (1990). The role of the self-system in competence. In R. J. Sternberg & J. Kolligian, Jr. (Eds.), *Competence considered* (pp. 205–225). New Haven, CT: Yale University Press.

Markus, H., Hamill, R., & Sentis, K. P. (1987). Thinking fat: Self-schemas for body weight and the processing of weight relevant information. *Journal of Applied Social Psychology, 17,* 50–71.

Markus, H., & Kunda, Z. (1986). Stability and malleability of the self concept. *Journal of Personality and Social Psychology, 51,* 858–866.

Markus, H., & Nurius, P. (1986). Possible selves. *American Psychologist, 41,* 954–969.

Markus, H., & Ruvolo, A. (1989). Possible selves: Personalized representations of goals. In L. A. Pervin (Ed.), *Goal concepts in personality and social psychology* (pp. 211–242). Hillsdale, NJ: Erlbaum.

Markus, H., & Sentis, K. P. (1982). The self in social information processing. In J. Suls (Ed.), *Psychological perspectives on the self* (Vol. 1, pp. 41–70). Hillsdale, NJ: Erlbaum.

Markus, H., & Smith, J. (1981). The influence of self-schemas on the perception of others. In N. Cantor & J. F. Kihlstrom (Eds.), *Personality, cognition, and social interaction* (pp. 233–262). Hillsdale, NJ: Erlbaum.

Markus, H., Smith, J., & Moreland, R. L. (1985). Role of the self-concept in the social perception of others. *Journal of Personality and Social Psychology, 49,* 1494–1512.

Markus, H., & Wurf, E. (1987). The dynamic self-concept: A social psychological perspective. *Annual Review of Psychology, 38,* 299–337.

Markus, H., & Zajonc, R. B. (1985). The cognitive perspective in social psychology. In G. Lindzey & E. Aronson (Eds.), *The handbook of social psychology* (3rd ed.) (Vol. 1, pp. 137–230). New York: Random House.

Marques, J. M., & Yzerbyt, V. Y. (1988). The black sheep effect: Judgmental extremity towards ingroup members in inter- and intra-group situations. *European Journal of Social Psychology, 18,* 287–292.

Marques, J. M., & Yzerbyt, V. Y., & Leyens, J. P. (1988). The "black sheep effect": Extremity of judgments towards ingroup members as a function of group identification. *European Journal of Social Psychology, 18,* 1–16.

Marques, J. M., & Yzerbyt, V. Y., & Rijsman, J. B. (1988). Context effects on intergroup discrimination: In-group bias as a function of experimenter's provenance. *British Journal of Social Psychology, 27,* 301–318.

Marshall, G. D., & Zimbardo, P. G. (1979). Affective consequences of inadequately explained physiological arousal. *Journal of Personality and Social Psychology, 37,* 970–988.

Martin, J. (1982). Stories and scripts in organizational settings. In A. M. Hastorf & A. M. Isen (Eds.), *Cognitive social psychology* (pp. 255–306). New York: Elsevier/North-Holland.

Martin, L. L. (1986). Set/reset: Use and disuse of concepts in impression formation. *Journal of Personality and Social Psychology, 51,* 493–504.

Martin, L. L., & Clark, L. F. (1990). Social cognition: Exploring the mental processes involved in human social interaction. In M. W. Eysenck (Ed.), *Cognitive psychology: An international review* (Vol. 1, pp. 266–310). Sussex, England: Wiley.

Martin, L. L., & Tesser, A. (1989). Toward a motivational and structural theory of ruminative thought. In J. S. Uleman & J. A. Bargh (Eds.), *Unintended thought* (pp. 306–326). New York: Guilford Press.

Maslach, C. (1979). Negative emotional biasing of unexplained arousal. *Journal of Personality and Social Psychology, 37,* 953–969.

Massad, C. M., Hubbard, M., & Newtson, D. (1979). Selective perception of events. *Journal of Experimental Social Psychology, 15,* 513–532.

Masters, J. C., & Furman, W. (1976). Effects of affective states on noncontingent outcome expectancies and beliefs in internal or external control. *Developmental Psychology, 12,* 481–482.

Masters, J. C., & Santrock, J. W. (1976). Studies in the self-regulation of behavior: Effects of contingent cognitive and affective events. *Developmental Psychology, 12,* 334–348.

Matlin, M., & Stang, D. (1978). *The Pollyanna principle.* Cambridge, MA: Schenkman.

Matsumoto, D. (1987). The role of facial response in the experience of emotion: More methodological problems and a meta-analysis. *Journal of Personality and Social Psychology, 52,* 769–774.

Mayer, J. D. (1986). How mood influences cognition. In N. E. Sharkey (Ed.), *Advances in cognitive science* (pp. 290–314). Chichester, England: Ellis Horwood Limited.

Mayer, J. D., & Bower, G. H. (1985). Naturally occurring mood and learning: Comment on Hasher, Rose, Zacks, Sanft, and Doren. *Journal of Experimental Psychology: General, 114,* 396–403.

Mayer, J. D., & Bower, G. H. (1986). Learning and memory for personality prototypes. *Journal of Personality and Social Psychology, 51,* 473–492.

Mayer, J. D., & Bremer, D. (1985). Assessing mood with affect-sensitive tasks. *Journal of Personality Assessment, 49,* 95–99.

Mayer, J. D., & Gaschke, Y. N. (1988). The experience and meta-experience of mood. *Journal of Personality and Social Psychology, 55,* 102–111.

Mayer, J. D., Mamberg, M. H., & Volanth, A. J. (1988). Cognitive domains of the mood system. *Journal of Personality, 56,* 453–486.

Mayer, J. D., & Salovey, P. (1988). Personality moderates the interaction of mood and cognition. In K. Fiedler & J. Forgas (Eds.), *Affect, cognition, and social behavior* (pp. 87–99). Toronto, Canada: Hogrefe.

Mayer, J. D., & Volanth, A. J. (1985). Cognitive involvement in the mood response system. *Motivation and Emotion, 9,* 261–275.

McArthur, L. Z. (1972). The how and what of why: Some determinants and consequences of causal attribution. *Journal of Personality and Social Psychology, 22,* 171–193.

McArthur, L. Z. (1980). Illusory causation and illusory correlation: Two epistemological accounts. *Personality and Social Psychology Bulletin, 6,* 507–519.

McArthur, L. Z. (1981). What grabs you? The role of attention in impression formation and causal attribution. In E. T. Higgins, C. P. Herman, & M. P. Zanna (Eds.), *Social cognition: The Ontario Symposium* (Vol. 1, pp. 201–246). Hillsdale, NJ: Erlbaum.

McArthur, L. Z. (1982). Judging a book by its cover: A cognitive analysis of the relationship between physical appearance and stereotyping. In A. Hastorf & A. Isen (Eds.), *Cognitive social psychology.* New York: Elsevier North-Holland.

McArthur, L. Z., & Apatow, K. (1983–84). Impressions of baby-faced adults. *Social Cognition, 2,* 315–342.

McArthur, L. Z., & Baron, R. (1983). Toward an ecological theory of social perception. *Psychological Review, 90,* 215–238.

McArthur, L. Z., & Berry, D. S. (1987). Cross-cultural agreement in perceptions of babyfaced adults. *Journal of Cross-Cultural Psychology, 18,* 165–192.

McArthur, L. Z., & Friedman, S. A. (1980). Illusory correlation in impression formation: Variations in the shared distinctiveness effect as a function of the distinctive person's age, race, and sex. *Journal of Personality and Social Psychology, 39,* 615–624.

McArthur, L. Z., & Ginsberg, E. (1981). Causal attribution to salient stimuli: An investigation of visual fixation mediators. *Personality and Social Psychology Bulletin, 7,* 547–553.

McArthur, L. Z., & Post, D. L. (1977). Figural emphasis and person perception. *Journal of Experimental Social Psychology, 13,* 520–535.

McArthur, L. Z., & Solomon, L. K. (1978). Perceptions of an aggressive encounter as a function of the victim's salience and the perceiver's arousal. *Journal of Personality and Social Psychology, 36,* 1278–1290.

McCallum, D. M., & Schopler, J. (1984). Agent and observer attributions of influence: The effects of target response. *Personality and Social Psychology Bulletin, 10,* 410–418.

McCann, C. D., & Hancock, R. D. (1983). Self-monitoring in communicative interactions: Social cognitive consequences of goal-directed message modifications. *Journal of Experimental Social Psychology, 19,* 109–121.

McCann, C. D., Ostrom, T. M., Tyner, L. K., & Mitchell, M. L. (1985). Person perception in heterogeneous groups. *Journal of Personality and Social Psychology, 49,* 1449–1459.

McCaul, K. D., Holmes, D. S., & Solomon, S. (1982). Voluntary expressive changes and emotion. *Journal of Personality and Social Psychology, 42,* 145–152.

McCaul, K. D., & Maki, R. H. (1984). Self-reference versus desirability ratings and memory for traits. *Journal of Personality and Social Psychology, 47,* 953–955.

McCauley, C., Durham, M., Copley, J. B., & Johnson, J. P. (1985). Patients' perceptions of treatment for kidney failure: The impact of personal experience on population predictions. *Journal of Experimental Social Psychology, 21,* 138–148.

McCauley, C., Stitt, C. L., Woods, K., & Lipton, D. (1973). Group shift to caution at the race track. *Journal of Experimental Social Psychology, 9,* 80–86.

McClelland, J. L., Rumelhart, D. E., & Hinton, G. E. (1986). The appeal of parallel distributed processing. In D. E. Rumelhart, J. L. McClelland, & the PDP Research Group, *Parallel distributed processing: Explorations in the microstructure of cognition* (Vol. 1, pp. 3–44). Cambridge, MA: MIT Press.

McCloskey, M. E., & Glucksberg, S. (1978). Natural categories: Well-defined or fuzzy sets. *Memory and Cognition, 6,* 462–472.

McCloskey, M., & Zaragoza, M. (1985). Misleading postevent information and memory for events: Arguments and evidence against memory impairment hypotheses. *Journal of Experimental Psychology: General, 114,* 3–18.

McClure, J., Lalljee, M., Jaspars, J., & Abelson, R. P. (1989). Conjunctive explanations of success and failure: The effect of different types of causes. *Journal of Personality and Social Psychology, 56,* 19–26.

McConahay, J. B. (1986). Modern racism, ambivalence, and the modern racism scale. In J. F. Dovidio & S. L. Gaertner (Eds.), *Prejudice, discrimination, and racism* (pp. 91–125). Orlando, FL: Academic Press.

McDaniel, M. A., Lapsley, D. K., & Milstead, M. (1987). Testing the generality and automaticity of self-reference encoding with release from proactive interference. *Journal of Experimental Social Psychology, 23,* 269–284.

McFarland, C., & Ross, M. (1982). Impact of causal attributions on affective reactions to success and failure. *Journal of Personality and Social Psychology, 43,* 937–946.

McFarland, C., & Ross, M. (1987). The relation between current impressions and memories of self and dating partners. *Personality and Social Psychology Bulletin, 13,* 228–238.

McFarland, C., Ross, M., & Conway, M. (1984). Self-persuasion and self-presentation as mediators of anticipatory attitude change. *Journal of Personality and Social Psychology, 46,* 529–540.

McGarty, C., & Penny, R. E. C. (1988). Categorization, accentuation and social judgment. *British Journal of Social Psychology, 27*, 147–157.

McGraw, K. M. (1987a). Outcome valence and base rates: The effects on moral judgments. *Social Cognition, 5*, 58–75.

McGraw, K. M. (1987b). Conditions for assigning blame: The impact of necessity and sufficiency. *British Journal of Social Psychology, 26*, 109–117.

McGraw, K. M., & Pinney, N. (1990). The effects of general and domain-specific expertise on political memory and judgment. *Social Cognition, 8*, 9–30.

McGuire, W. J. (1960). A syllogistic analysis of cognitive relationships. In C. I. Hovland & M. J. Rosenberg (Eds.), *Attitude organization and change* (pp. 65–111). New Haven, CT: Yale University Press.

McGuire, W. J. (1969). Nature of attitudes and attitude change. In G. Lindzey & E. Aronson (Eds.), *The handbook of social psychology* (2nd ed., Vol. 3, pp. 136–314). Reading, MA: Addison-Wesley.

McGuire, W. J. (1976). Some internal psychological factors influencing consumer choice. *Journal of Consumer Research, 2*, 302–309.

McGuire, W. J. (1985). Attitudes and attitude change. In G. Lindzey & E. Aronson (Eds.), *The handbook of social psychology* (3rd ed., Vol. 2, pp. 233–346). New York: Random House.

McGuire, W. J., & McGuire, C. V. (1986). Differences in conceptualizing self versus conceptualizing other people as manifested in contrasting verb types used in natural speech. *Journal of Personality and Social Psychology, 51*, 1135–1143.

McGuire, W. J., McGuire, C. V., & Cheever, J. (1986). The self in society: Effects of social contexts on the sense of self. *British Journal of Social Psychology, 25*, 259–270.

McGuire, W. J., McGuire, C. V., Child, P., & Fujioka, T. (1978). Salience of ethnicity in the spontaneous self-concept as a function of one's ethnic distinctiveness in the social environment. *Journal of Personality and Social Psychology, 36*, 511–520.

McGuire, W. J., & Padawer-Singer, A. (1976). Trait salience in the spontaneous self-concept. *Journal of Personality and Social Psychology, 33*, 743–754.

McKenzie-Mohr, D., & Zanna, M. P. (1990). Treating women as sexual objects: Look to the (gender schematic) male who has viewed pornography. *Personality and Social Psychology Bulletin, 16*, 296–308.

McKiethen, K. B., Reitman, J. S., Rueter, H. H., & Hirtle, S. C. (1981). Knowledge organization and skill differences in computer programmers. *Cognitive Psychology, 13*, 307–325.

McLachlan, A. (1986a). The effects of two forms of decision reappraisal on the perception of pertinent arguments. *British Journal of Social Psychology, 25*, 129–138.

McLachlan, A. (1986b). Polarization and discussion context. *British Journal of Social Psychology, 25*, 345–347.

Mead, G. H. (1934). *Mind, self, and society.* Chicago: University of Chicago Press.

Medin, D. L., Altom, M. W., & Murphy, T. D. (1984). Given versus induced category representations: Use of prototype and exemplar information in classification. *Journal of Experimental Psychology: Learning, Memory, and Cognition, 10*, 333–352.

Medin, D. L., & Schaffer, M. M. (1978). Context theory of classification learning. *Psychological Review, 85*, 207–238.

Meehl, P. E. (1954). *Clinical versus statistical prediction: A theoretical analysis and review of the literature.* Minneapolis: University of Minnesota Press.

Mehrabian, A. (1972). Nonverbal communication. In J. Cole (Ed.), *Nebraska Symposium on Motivation* (Vol. 19, pp. 107–162). Lincoln: University of Nebraska Press.

Meichenbaum, D., & Asarnow, J. (1979). Cognitive-behavioral modification and metacognitive development: Implications for the classroom. In P. C. Kendall & S. D. Hollon (Eds.), *Cognitive-behavioral interventions: Theory, research, and procedures* (pp. 11–35). New York: Academic Press.

Merikle, P. M. (1982). Unconscious perception revisited. *Perception & Psychophysics, 31,* 298–301.

Merton, R. K. (1957). *Social theory and social structure.* New York: Free Press.

Mervis, C. B., & Rosch, E. (1981). Categorization of natural objects. *Annual Review of Psychology, 32,* 89–115.

Messick, D. M., Bloom, S., Boldizar, J. P., & Samuelson, C. D. (1985). Why we are fairer than others. *Journal of Experimental Social Psychology, 21,* 480–500.

Messick, D. M., & Mackie, D. M. (1989). Intergroup relations. *Annual Review of Psychology, 40,* 45–81.

Messick, D. M., & Reeder, G. D. (1974). Roles, occupations, behaviors, and attributions. *Journal of Experimental Social Psychology, 10,* 126–132.

Metalsky, G. I., & Abramson, L. Y. (1981). Attributional styles: Toward a framework for conceptualization and assessment. In P. C. Kendall & S. D. Hollon (Eds.), *Cognitive-behavioral intentions: Assessment methods.* New York: Academic Press.

Mettee, D. R., & Aronson, E. (1974). Affective reactions to appraisal from others. In T. L. Huston (Ed.), *Foundations of interpersonal attraction* (pp. 236–284). New York: Academic Press.

Meyer, D., Leventhal, H., & Gutmann, M. (1985). Common-sense models of illness: The example of hypertension. *Health Psychology, 4,* 115–135.

Meyer, J. P. (1980). Causal attribution for success and failure: A multivariate investigation of dimensionality, formation, and consequences. *Journal of Personality and Social Psychology, 38,* 704–718.

Meyer, J. P., & Mulherin, A. (1980). From attribution to helping: An analysis of the mediating effects of affect and expectancy. *Journal of Personality and Social Psychology, 39,* 201–210.

Michela, J. L., Peplau, L. A., & Weeks, D. G. (1983). Perceived dimensions of attributions for loneliness. *Journal of Personality and Social Psychology, 43,* 929–936.

Michela, J. L., & Wood, J. V. (1986). Causal attributions in health and illness. *Advances in Cognitive-Behavioral Research and Therapy, 5,* 179–235.

Miell, D., & Le Voi, M. (1985). Self-monitoring and control in dyadic interactions. *Journal of Personality and Social Psychology, 49,* 1652–1661.

Mikulincer, M. (1988). Reactance and helplessness following exposure to unsolvable problems: The effects of attributional style. *Journal of Personality and Social Psychology, 54,* 679–686.

Milberg, S., & Clark, M. S. (1988). Moods and compliance. *British Journal of Social Psychology, 27,* 79–90.

Milbraith, L. W., & Goel, M. L. (1977). *Political participation* (2nd ed.). Chicago: Rand McNally.

Milburn, M. A. (1987). Ideological self-schemata and schematically induced attitude consistency. *Journal of Experimental Social Psychology, 23,* 383–398.

Mill, J. (no date). *The analysis of the phenomena of the human mind.* New York: Kelley. (Originally published, 1869.)

Mill, J. S. (1974). *System of logic, ratiocinative and inductive.* Toronto, Canada: University of Toronto Press. (Originally published, 1843.)

Millar, K. U., Tesser, A., & Millar, M. G. (1988). The effects of a threatening life event on behavior sequences and intrusive thought: A self-disruption explanation. *Cognitive Therapy and Research, 12,* 441–457.

Millar, M. G., Millar, K. U., & Tesser, A. (1988). The effects of helping and focus of attention on mood states. *Personality and Social Psychology Bulletin, 14,* 536–543.

Millar, M. G., & Tesser, A. (1986a). Effects of attitude and cognitive focus on the attitude-behavior relation. *Journal of Personality and Social Psychology, 51,* 270–276.

Millar, M. G., & Tesser, A. (1986b). Thought-induced attitude change: The effects of schema structure and commitment. *Journal of Personality and Social Psychology, 51,* 259–269.

Millar, M. G., & Tesser, A. (1989). The effects of affective-cognitive consistency and thought on the attitude-behavior relationship. *Journal of Experimental Social Psychology, 25,* 189–202.

Miller, A. G. (Ed.). (1982). *In the eye of the beholder: Contemporary issues in stereotyping.* New York: Praeger.

Miller, A. G., Jones, E. E., & Hinkle, S. (1981). A robust attribution error in the personality domain. *Journal of Experimental Social Psychology, 17,* 587–600.

Miller, A. G., & Rorer, L. G. (1982). Toward an understanding of the fundamental attribution error. *Journal of Research in Personality, 16,* 41–59.

Miller, A. G., Schmidt, D., Meyer, C., & Colella, A. (1984). The perceived value of constrained behavior: Pressure toward biased inference in the attitude attribution paradigm. *Social Psychology Quarterly, 47,* 160–171.

Miller, C. T. (1986). Categorization and stereotypes about men and women. *Personality and Social Psychology Bulletin, 12,* 502–512.

Miller, C. T. (1988). Categorization and the physical attractiveness stereotype. *Social Cognition, 6,* 231–251.

Miller, D. T. (1976). Ego involvement and attributions for success and failure. *Journal of Personality and Social Psychology, 34,* 901–906.

Miller, D. T., & McFarland, C. (1986). Counterfactual thinking and victim compensation: A test of norm theory. *Personality and Social Psychology Bulletin, 12,* 513–519.

Miller, D. T., & Norman, S. A. (1975). Actor-observer differences in perceptions of effective control. *Journal of Personality and Social Psychology, 31,* 503–515.

Miller, D. T., Norman, S. A., & Wright, E. (1978). Distortion in person perception as a consequence of the need for effective control. *Journal of Personality and Social Psychology, 36,* 598–602.

Miller, D. T., & Porter, C. A. (1983). Self-blame in victims of violence. *Journal of Social Issues, 39,* 139–152.

Miller, D. T., & Ross, M. (1975). Self-serving biases in the attribution of causality: Fact or fiction? *Psychological Bulletin, 82,* 213–225.

Miller, D. T. & Turnbull, W. (1986). Expectancies and interpersonal processes. *Annual Review of Psychology, 37,* 233–256.

Miller, D. T., Turnbull, W., & McFarland, C. (1990). Counterfactual thinking and social perception: Thinking about what might have been. In M. P. Zanna (Ed.), *Advances in experimental social psychology* (Vol. 23, pp. 305–331). New York: Academic Press.

Miller, J. G. (1984). Culture and the development of everyday social explanation. *Journal of Personality and Social Psychology, 46,* 961–978.

Miller, L. E., & Grush, J. E. (1986). Individual differences in attitudinal versus normative determination of behavior. *Journal of Experimental Social Psychology, 22,* 190–202.

Miller, N. & Brewer, M. B. (Eds.) (1984). *Groups in contact: The psychology of desegregation.* New York: Academic Press.

Miller, N., Brewer, M. B., & Edwards, K. (1985). Cooperative interaction in desegregated settings: A laboratory analogue. *Journal of Social Issues, 41,* 63–79.

Miller, N., & Campbell, D. T. (1959). Recency and primacy in persuasion as a function of the timing of speeches and measurements. *Journal of Abnormal and Social Psychology, 59,* 1–9.

Miller, R. S., & Schlenker, B. R. (1985). Egotism in group members: Public and private attributions of responsibility for group performance. *Social Psychology Quarterly, 48,* 85–89.

Miller, S. M. (1979). Controllability and human stress: Method, evidence, and theory. *Behavior Research and Therapy, 17,* 287–306.

Mills, C. J. (1983). Sex-typing and self-schemata effects on memory and response latency. *Journal of Personality and Social Psychology, 45,* 163–172.

Mills, C. J., & Tyrrell, D. J. (1983). Sex stereotypic encoding and release from proactive interference. *Journal of Personality and Social Psychology, 45,* 772–781.

Mills, J. (1968). Interest in supporting and discrepant information. In R. P. Abelson, E. Aronson, W. J. McGuire, T. M. Newcomb, M. J. Rosenberg, & P. H. Tannenbaum (Eds.), *Theories of cognitive consistency: A sourcebook* (pp. 771–776). Chicago: Rand McNally.

Mills, R. T., & Krantz, D. S. (1979). Information, choice, and reactions to stress: A field experiment in a blood bank with laboratory analogue. *Journal of Personality and Social Psychology, 37,* 608–620.

Milord, J. T. (1978). Aesthetic aspects of faces: A (somewhat) phenomenological analysis using multidimensional scaling methods. *Journal of Personality and Social Psychology, 36,* 205–216.

Mirels, H. L. (1980). The avowal of responsibility for good and bad outcomes: The effects of generalized self-serving biases. *Personality and Social Psychology Bulletin, 6,* 299–306.

Mischel, W. (1968). *Personality and assessment.* New York: Wiley.

Mischel, W. (1973). Toward a cognitive social learning reconceptualization of personality. *Psychological Review, 80,* 252–283.

Mischel, W. (1984). Convergences and challenges in the search for consistency. *American Psychologist, 39,* 351–364.

Mischel, W., & Peake, P. K. (1982). Beyond déjà vu in the search for cross-situational consistency. *Psychological Review, 89,* 730–755.

Monson, T. C., & Hesley, J. W. (1982). Causal attributions for behavior consistent or inconsistent with an actor's personality traits: Differences between those offered by actors and observers. *Journal of Experimental Social Psychology, 18,* 426–432.

Monson, T. C., Hesley, J. W., & Chernick, L. (1982). Specifying when personality traits can and cannot predict behavior: An alternative to abandoning the attempt to predict single-act criteria. *Journal of Personality and Social Psychology, 43,* 385–399.

Monson, T. C., Keel, R., Stephens, D., & Genung, V. (1982). Trait attribution: Relative validity, covariation with behavior, and prospect of future interaction. *Journal of Personality and Social Psychology, 42,* 1014–1024.

Monson, T. C., & Snyder, M. (1977). Actors, observers, and the attribution process: Toward a reconceptualization. *Journal of Experimental Social Psychology, 13,* 89–111.

Montepare, J. M., & Zebrowitz-McArthur, L. (1986). The influence of facial characteristics on children's age perceptions. *Journal of Experimental Child Psychology, 42,* 303–314.

Montepare, J. M., & Zebrowitz-McArthur, L. (1987). Perceptions of adults with childlike voices in two cultures. *Journal of Experimental Social Psychology, 23,* 331–349.

Montepare, J. M., & Zebrowitz-McArthur, L. (1988). Impressions of people created by age-related qualities of their gaits. *Journal of Personality and Social Psychology, 55,* 547–556.

Montgomery, R. L. & Haemmerlie, F. M. (1986). Self-perception theory and the reduction of heterosocial anxiety. *Journal of Social and Clinical Psychology, 4,* 503–512.

Moreland, R. L. (1985). Social categorization and the assimilation of "new" group members. *Journal of Personality and Social Psychology, 48,* 1173–1190.

Moreland, R. L., & Zajonc, R. B. (1977). Is stimulus recognition a necessary condition for the occurrence of exposure effects? *Journal of Personality and Social Psychology, 35,* 191–199.

Moreland, R. L., & Zajonc, R. B. (1979). Exposure effects may not depend on stimulus recognition. *Journal of Personality and Social Psychology, 37,* 1085–1089.

Moreland, R. L., & Zajonc, R. B. (1982). Exposure effects in person perception: Familiarity, similarity, and attraction. *Journal of Experimental Social Psychology, 18,* 395–415.

Morier, D. M., & Borgida, E. (1984). The conjunction fallacy: A task specific phenomenon? *Personality and Social Psychology Bulletin, 10,* 243–252.

Morrow, D. G., Greenspan, S. L., & Bower, G. H. (1987). Accessibility and situation models in narrative comprehension. *Journal of Memory and Language, 26,* 165–187.

Moscovici, S. (1988). Notes towards a description of social representations. *European Journal of Social Psychology, 18,* 211–250.

Mueller, J. H., Thompson, W. B., & Dugan, K. (1986). Trait distinctiveness and accessibility in the self-schema. *Personality and Social Psychology Bulletin, 12,* 81–89.

Mueller, J. H., Thompson, W. B., & Vogel, J. M. (1988). Perceived honesty and face memory. *Personality and Social Psychology Bulletin, 14,* 114–124.

Mullen, B. (1983). Egocentric bias in estimates of consensus. *Journal of Social Psychology, 121,* 31–38.

Mullen, B. (1986). Atrocity as a function of lynch mob composition: A self-attention perspective. *Personality and Social Psychology Bulletin, 12,* 187–197.

Mullen, B. (1987). Self-attention theory: The effects of group composition on the individual. In B. Mullen & G.R. Goethals (Eds.), *Theories of group behavior* (pp. 125–145). New York: Springer-Verlag.

Mullen, B. (1991). Group composition, salience, and cognitive representations: The phenomenology of being in a group. *Journal of Experimental Social Psychology, 27.*

Mullen, B., Atkins, J. L., Champion, D. S., Edwards, C., Hardy, D., Story, J. E., & Vanderklok, M. (1985). The false consensus effect: A meta-analysis of 115 hypothesis tests. *Journal of Experimental Social Psychology, 21,* 262–283.

Mullen, B., & Baumeister, R. F. (1987). Group effects on self-attention and performance: Social loafing, social facilitation, and social impairment. In C. Hendrick (Ed.), *Review of personality and social psychology: Vol. 9. Group processes and intergroup relations* (pp. 189–206). Beverly Hills, CA: Sage.

Mullen, B., & Hu, L. (1988). Social projection as a function of cognitive mechanisms: Two meta-analytic integrations. *British Journal of Social Psychology, 27,* 333–356.

Mullen, B., & Hu, L. (1989). Perceptions of ingroup and outgroup variability: A meta-analytic integration. *Basic and Applied Social Psychology, 10,* 233–252.

Mullen, B., & Johnson, C. (1990). Distinctiveness-based illusory correlations and stereotyping: A meta-analytic integration. *British Journal of Social Psychology, 29,* 11–28.

Mullen, B., & Riordan, C. A. (1988). Self-serving attributions for performance in naturalistic settings: A meta-analytic review. *Journal of Applied Social Psychology, 18,* 3–22.

Mummenday, A., & Schreiber, H.-J. (1984). "Different" just means "better": Some obvious and some hidden pathways to in-group favouritism. *British Journal of Social Psychology, 23,* 363–368

Murphy, G.L., & Medin, D.L. (1985). The role of theories in conceptual coherence. *Psychological Review, 92,* 289–316.

Myrdal, G. (1944). *An American dilemma: The Negro problem and modern democracy.* New York: Harper.

Napolitan, D. A., & Goethals, G. R. (1979). The attribution of friendliness. *Journal of Experimental Social Psychology, 15,* 105–113.

Nasby, W. (1985). Private self-consciousness, articulation of the self-schema, and recognition memory of trait adjectives. *Journal of Personality and Social Psychology, 49,* 704–709.

Nasby, W. (1989). Private and public self-consciousness and articulation of the self-schema. *Journal of Personality and Social Psychology, 56,* 117–123.

Nasby, W., & Yando, R. (1982). Selective encoding and retrieval of affectively-valent information: Two cognitive consequences of mood. *Journal of Personality and Social Psychology, 43,* 1244–1253.

Neale, M. A., Huber, V. L., & Northcraft, G. B. (1987). The framing of negotiations: Contextual versus task frames. *Organizational Behavior and Human Decision Processes, 39,* 228–241.

Neisser, U. (1967). *Cognitive psychology.* Englewood Cliffs, NJ: Prentice-Hall.

Neisser, U. (1976). *Cognition and reality*. San Francisco: Freeman.

Neisser, U. (1980). On "social knowing." *Personality and Social Psychology Bulletin, 6*, 601–605.

Neisser, U. (1988). Five kinds of self-knowledge. *Philosophical Psychology, 1*, 35–59.

Nelson, D. G. K. (1984). The effect of intention on what concepts are acquired. *Journal of Verbal Learning and Verbal Behavior, 23*, 734–759.

Nelson, K. (1980, September). *Characteristics of children's scripts for familiar events*. Paper presented at the meeting of the American Psychological Association, Montreal.

Nesdale, A. R., & Dharmalingam, S. (1986). Category salience, stereotyping, and person memory. *Australian Journal of Psychology, 38*, 145–151.

Nesdale, A. R., Dharmalingam, S., & Kerr, G. K. (1987). Effect of subgroup ratio on stereotyping. *European Journal of Social Psychology, 17*, 353–356.

Neuberg, S. L. (1988). Behavioral implications of information presented outside of conscious awareness: The effect of subliminal presentation of trait information on behavior in the Prisoner's Dilemma Game. *Social Cognition, 6*, 207–230.

Neuberg, S. L. (1989). The goal of forming accurate impressions during social interactions: Attenuating the impact of negative expectancies. *Journal of Personality and Social Psychology, 56*, 374–386.

Neuberg, S. L., & Fiske, S. T. (1987). Motivational influences on impression formation: Outcome dependency, accuracy-driven attention, and individuating processes. *Journal of Personality and Social Psychology, 53*, 431–444.

Newell, A., & Simon, H. A. (1972). *Human problem solving*. Englewood Cliffs, NJ: Prentice-Hall.

Newman, J., & Layton, B. D. (1984). Overjustification: A self-perception perspective. *Personality and Social Psychology Bulletin, 10*, 419–425.

Newman, L. S., & Uleman, J. S. (1989). Spontaneous trait inference. In J. S. Uleman & J. A. Bargh (Eds.), *Unintended thought* (pp. 155–188). New York: Guilford Press.

Newman, L. S., & Uleman, J. S. (1990). Assimilation and contrast effects in spontaneous trait inference. *Personality and Social Psychology Bulletin, 16*, 224–240.

Newtson, D. (1973). Attribution and the unit of perception of ongoing behavior. *Journal of Personality and Social Psychology, 28*, 28–38.

Newtson, D. (1976). Foundations of attribution: The perception of ongoing behavior. In J. H. Harvey, W. J. Ickes, & R. F. Kidd (Eds.), *New directions in attribution research* (Vol. 1, pp. 223–248). Hillsdale, NJ: Erlbaum.

Newtson, D. (1980). An interactionist perspective on social knowing. *Personality and Social Psychology Bulletin, 6*, 520–531.

Newtson, D., & Czerlinsky, T. (1974). Adjustment of attitude communications for contrasts by extreme audiences. *Journal of Personality and Social Psychology, 30*, 829–837.

Newtson, D., & Enquist, G. (1976). The perceptual organization of ongoing behavior. *Journal of Experimental Social Psychology, 12*, 436–450.

Newtson, D., Enquist, G., & Bois, J. (1977). The objective basis of behavior units. *Journal of Personality and Social Psychology, 35*, 847–862.

Newtson, D., Hairfield, J., Bloomingdale, J., & Cutino, S. (1987). The structure of action and interaction. *Social Cognition, 5*, 191–237.

Newtson, D., Rindner, R., Miller, R., & LaCross, K. (1978). Effects of availability of feature changes on behavior segmentation. *Journal of Experimental Social Psychology, 14,* 379–388.

Ng, S. H. (1984). Equity and social categorization effects on intergroup allocation of rewards. *British Journal of Social Psychology, 23,* 165–172.

Ng, S. H. (1985). Biases in reward allocation resulting from personal status, group status, and allocation procedure. *Australian Journal of Psychology, 37,* 297–307.

Ng, S. H. (1986). Equity, intergroup bias and interpersonal bias in reward allocation. *European Journal of Social Psychology, 16,* 239–255.

Ng, S. H. & Cram, F. (1988). Intergroup bias by defensive and offensive groups in majority and minority conditions. *Journal of Personality and Social Psychology, 55,* 749–757.

Ng, S. H., & Cram, F. (1987). Polarization of ingroup bias in secure and insecure groups. *Journal of Social Psychology, 127,* 589–594.

Niedenthal, P. M., & Cantor, N. (1986). Affective responses as guides to category-based inferences. *Motivation and Emotion, 10,* 217–232.

Niedenthal, P. M., Cantor, N., & Kihlstrom, J. F. (1985). Prototype matching: A strategy for social decision making. *Journal of Personality and Social Psychology, 48,* 575–584.

Nielson, S. L., & Sarason, S. G. (1981). Emotion, personality, and selective attention. *Journal of Personality and Social Psychology, 41,* 945–960.

Nilsson, I., & Ekehammar, B. (1987). Person-positivity bias in political perception? *European Journal of Social Psychology, 17,* 247–252.

Nisbett, R. E., & Borgida, E. (1975). Attribution and the psychology of prediction. *Journal of Personality and Social Psychology, 32,* 932–943.

Nisbett, R. E., Borgida, E., Crandall, R., & Reed, H. (1976). Popular induction: Information is not necessarily informative. In J. S. Carroll & J. W. Payne (Eds.), *Cognition and social behavior* (pp. 113–134). Hillsdale, NJ: Erlbaum.

Nisbett, R. E., Caputo, C., Legant, P., & Maracek, J. (1973). Behavior as seen by the actor and as seen by the observer. *Journal of Personality and Social Psychology, 27,* 154–164.

Nisbett, R. E., Fong, G. T., Lehman, D. R., & Cheng, P. W. (1987). Teaching reasoning. *Science, 238,* 625–631.

Nisbett, R. E., Krantz, D. H., Jepson, C., & Fong, G. T. (1982). Improving inductive inference. In D. Kahneman, P. Slovic, & A. Tversky (Eds.), *Judgment under uncertainty: Heuristics and biases* (pp. 445–462). New York: Cambridge University Press.

Nisbett, R. E., Krantz, D. H., Jepson, C., & Kunda, Z. (1983). The use of statistical heuristics in everyday inductive reasoning. *Psychological Review, 90,* 339–363.

Nisbett, R. E., & Kunda, Z. (1985). Perception of social distributions. *Journal of Personality and Social Psychology, 48,* 297–311.

Nisbett, R. E., & Ross, L. (1980). *Human inference: Strategies and shortcomings of social judgment.* Englewood Cliffs, NJ: Prentice-Hall.

Nisbett, R. E., & Schachter, S. (1966). Cognitive manipulation of pain. *Journal of Experimental Social Psychology, 2,* 227–236.

Nisbett, R. E., & Valins, S. (1972). Perceiving the causes of one's own behavior. In E. E. Jones, E. E. Kanouse, H. H. Kelley, R. E. Nisbett, S. Valins, & B. Weiner (Eds.), *Attribution: Perceiving the causes of behavior* (pp. 63–78). Morristown, NJ: General Learning Press.

Nisbett, R. E., & Wilson, T. D. (1977a). The halo effect: Evidence for unconscious alteration of judgments. *Journal of Personality and Social Psychology, 35,* 250–256.

Nisbett, R. E., & Wilson, T. D. (1977b). Telling more than we can know: Verbal reports on mental processes. *Psychological Review, 84,* 231–259.

Nisbett, R. E., Zukier, H., & Lemley, R. E. (1981). The dilution effect: Non-diagnostic information weakens the implications of diagnostic information. *Cognitive Psychology, 13,* 248–277.

Norem, J. K., & Cantor, N. (1986a). Anticipatory and post hoc cushioning strategies: Optimism and defensive pessimism in "risky" situations. *Cognitive Therapy and Research, 10,* 347–362.

Norem, J. K., & Cantor, N. (1986b). Defensive pessimism: Harnessing anxiety as motivation. *Journal of Personality and Social Psychology, 51,* 1208–1217.

Norem, J. K., & Cantor, N. (1990). Capturing the "flavor" of behavior: Cognition, affect, and interpretation. In B. S. Moore & A. M. Isen (Eds.), *Affect and social behavior* (pp. 39–63). New York: Cambridge University Press.

Norman, D. A. (1976). *Memory and attention: An introduction to human information processing.* New York: Wiley.

Norman, D. A., & Shallice, T. (1986). Attention to action: Willed and automatic control of behavior. In R. J. Davidson, G. E. Schwartz, & D. Shapiro (Eds.), *Consciousness and self-regulation: Advances in research and theory* (Vol. 4, pp. 1–18). New York: Plenum.

Norman, R. (1975). Affective-cognitive consistency, attitudes, conformity, and behavior. *Journal of Personality and Social Psychology, 32,* 83–91.

Northcraft, G. B., & Neale, M. A. (1986). Opportunity costs and the framing of resource allocation decisions. *Organizational Behavior and Human Decision Processes, 37,* 348–356.

Noseworthy, C. M., & Lott, A. J. (1984). The cognitive organization of gender-stereotypic categories. *Personality and Social Psychology Bulletin, 10,* 474–481.

Nuttin, J. M., Jr. (1985). Narcissism beyond Gestalt and awareness: The name letter effect. *European Journal of Social Psychology, 15,* 353–361.

Nuttin, J. M., Jr. (1987). Affective consequences of mere ownership: The name letter effect in twelve European languages. *European Journal of Social Psychology, 17,* 381–402.

Oakes, P. J., & Turner, J. C. (1980). Social categorization and intergroup behavior: Does the minimal intergroup discrimination make social identity more positive? *European Journal of Social Psychology, 10,* 295–301.

Oakes, P. J., & Turner, J. C. (1986). Authors' rejoinder to Jahoda and Tetlock. *British Journal of Social Psychology, 25,* 257–258.

Oatley, K., & Johnson-Laird, P. N. (1987). Towards a cognitive theory of emotions. *Cognition and Emotion, 1,* 29–50.

Oatley, K. & Yuill, N. (1985). Perception of personal and interpersonal action in a cartoon film. *British Journal of Social Psychology, 24,* 115–124.

Olson, J. M. (1988). Misattribution, preparatory information, and speech anxiety. *Journal of Personality and Social Psychology, 54,* 758–767.

Olson, J. M., Ellis, R. J., & Zanna, M. P. (1983). Validating objective versus subjective judgments: Interest in social comparison and consistency information. *Personality and Social Psychology Bulletin, 9,* 427–436.

Olson, J. M., & Ross, M. (1988). False feedback about placebo effectiveness:

Consequences for the misattribution of speech anxiety. *Journal of Experimental Social Psychology, 24,* 275–291.

Olson, J. M., & Zanna, M. P. (1979). A new look at selective exposure. *Journal of Experimental Social Psychology, 15,* 1–15.

Omoto, A. M., & Borgida, E. (1988). Guess who might be coming to dinner? Personal involvement and racial stereotyping. *Journal of Experimental Social Psychology, 24,* 571–593.

Ortony, A., Clore, G. L., & Collins, A. (1988). *The cognitive structure of emotion.* Cambridge, England: Cambridge University Press.

Orvis, B. R., Cunningham, J. D., & Kelley, H. H. (1975). A closer examination of causal inference: The roles of consensus, distinctiveness, and consistency information. *Journal of Personality and Social Psychology, 32,* 605–616.

Osgood, C. E., Suci, G. J., & Tannenbaum, P. H. (1957). *The measurement of meaning.* Urbana: University of Illinois Press.

Osgood, C. E., & Tannenbaum, P. H. (1955). The principle of congruity in the prediction of attitude change. *Psychological Review, 62,* 42–55.

Osterhouse, R. A., & Brock, T. C. (1970). Distraction increases yielding to propaganda by inhibiting counterarguing. *Journal of Personality and Social Psychology, 15,* 344–358.

Ostrom, T. M. (1975, August). Cognitive representation of impressions. Paper presented at the meeting of the American Psychological Association, Chicago.

Ostrom, T. M. (1977). Between-theory and within-theory conflict in explaining context effects in impression formation. *Journal of Experimental Social Psychology 13,* 492–503.

Ostrom, T. M. (1984). The sovereignty of social cognition. In R. S. Wyer, Jr., & T. K. Srull (Eds.), *Handbook of social cognition* (Vol. 1, pp. 1–38). Hillsdale, NJ: Erlbaum.

Ostrom, T. M. (1988). Computer simulation: The third symbol system. *Journal of Experimental Social Psychology, 24,* 381–392.

Ostrom, T. M. (1989). Three catechisms for social memory. In P. R. Solomon, G. R. Goethals, C. M. Kelley, & B. R. Stephens (Eds.), *Memory: Interdisciplinary approaches* (pp. 201–220). New York: Springer-Verlag.

Ostrom, T. M., Lingle, J. H., Pryor, J. B., & Geva, N. (1980). Cognitive organization of person impressions. In R. Hastie, T. M. Ostrom, E. B. Ebbesen, R. S. Wyer, Jr., D. Hamilton, & D. E. Carlston (Eds.), *Person memory: The cognitive basis of social perception* (pp. 55–88). Hillsdale, NJ: Erlbaum.

Ostrom, T. M., Pryor, J. B., & Simpson, D. D. (1981). The organization of social information. In E. T. Higgins, C. P. Herman, & M. P. Zanna (Eds.), *Social cognition: The Ontario Symposium* (Vol. 1, pp. 3–38). Hillsdale, NJ: Erlbaum.

Ostrom, T. M., & Sedikides, C. (1989). *The status of theory and research on outgroup homogeneity: An analysis of cognitive approaches.* Unpublished manuscript, Ohio State University.

O'Sullivan, C. S., & Durso, F. T. (1984). Effect of schema-incongruent information on memory for stereotypical attributes. *Journal of Personality and Social Psychology, 47,* 55–70.

Ottati, V., Fishbein, M., & Middlestadt, S. E. (1988). Determinants of voters' beliefs about the candidates' stands on the issues: The role of evaluative bias heuristics and the candidates' expressed message. *Journal of Personality and Social Psychology, 55,* 517–529.

Owens, J., Bower, G. H., & Black, J. B. (1979). The "soap-opera" effect in story recall. *Memory and Cognition, 7,* 185–191.

Pagel, M. D., & Davidson, A. R. (1984). A comparison of three social-psychological models of attitude and behavioral plan: Prediction of contraceptive behavior. *Journal of Personality and Social Psychology, 47,* 517–533.

Paivio, A. (1971). *Imagery and verbal processes.* New York: Holt, Rinehart and Winston.

Pallak, S. R. (1983). Salience of a communicator's physical attractiveness and persuasion: A heuristic versus systematic processing interpretation. *Social Cognition, 2,* 158–170.

Pallak, S. R., Murroni, E., & Koch, J. (1983). Communicator attractiveness and expertise, emotional versus rational appeals, and persuasion: A heuristic versus systematic processing interpretation. *Social Cognition, 2,* 122–141.

Parducci, A. (1968). The relativism of absolute judgments. *Scientific American, 219,* 84–90.

Park, B. (1986). A method for studying the development of impressions of real people. *Journal of Personality and Social Psychology, 51,* 907–917.

Park, B., & Hahn, S. (1988). Sex-role identity and the perception of others. *Social Cognition, 6,* 61–87.

Park, B., & Hastie, R. (1987). Perception of variability in category development: Instance- versus abstraction-based stereotypes. *Journal of Personality and Social Psychology, 53,* 621–635.

Park, B., & Judd, C. M. (1989). Agreement on initial impressions: Differences due to perceivers, trait dimensions, and target behaviors. *Journal of Personality and Social Psychology, 56,* 493–505.

Park, B., & Rothbart, M. (1982). Perception of out-group homogeneity and levels of social categorization: Memory for the subordinate attributes of in-group and out-group members. *Journal of Personality and Social Psychology, 42,* 1051–1068.

Parkes, C. M. (1975). What becomes of redundant world models? A contribution to the study of adaptation to change. *British Journal of Medical Psychology, 48,* 131–137.

Parkinson, B. (1985). Emotional effects of false autonomic feedback. *Psychological Bulletin, 98,* 471–494.

Parrott, W. G., & Sabini, J. (1990). Mood and memory under natural conditions: Evidence for mood incongruent recall. *Journal of Personality and Social Psychology, 59,* 321–336.

Passer, M. W. (1977). *Perceiving the causes of success and failure revisited: A multidimensional scaling approach.* Unpublished doctoral dissertation, University of California, Los Angeles.

Pavelchak, M. A. (1989). Piecemeal and category-based evaluation: An idiographic analysis. *Journal of Personality and Social Psychology, 56,* 354–363.

Peevers, B. H., & Secord, P. F. (1973). Developmental changes in attribution of descriptive concepts to persons. *Journal of Personality and Social Psychology, 27,* 120–128.

Pelham, B. W. (1990). *On confidence and consequence: The certainty and importance of self-knowledge.* Manuscript submitted for publication.

Pelham, B. W., & Swann, W. B., Jr. (1989). From self-conceptions to self-worth:

On the sources and structure of global self-esteem. *Journal of Personality and Social Psychology, 57*, 672–680.

Pennebaker, J. W. (1988). Confiding traumatic experiences and health. In S. Fisher & J. Reason (Eds.), *Handbook of life stress, cognition and health.* (pp. 669–682). New York: Wiley.

Pennebaker, J. W. (1989a). Confession, inhibition, and disease. In L. Berkowitz (Ed.), *Advances in experimental social psychology* (Vol. 22, pp. 211–244). New York: Academic Press.

Pennebaker, J. W. (1989b). Stream of consciousness and stress: Levels of thinking. In J. S. Uleman & J. A. Bargh (Eds.), *Unintended thought* (pp. 327–350). New York: Guilford Press.

Pennebaker, J. W., Dyer, M. A., Caulkins, R. S., Litkowitz, D. L., Ackreman, P. L., Anderson, D. B., & McGraw, K. M. (1979). Don't the girls get prettier at closing time: A country and western application to psychology. *Personality and Social Psychology Bulletin, 5*, 122–125.

Pennebaker, J. W., & Hoover, C. W. (1985). Inhibition and cognition: Toward an understanding of trauma and disease. In R. J. Davidson, G. E. Schwartz, & D. Shapiro (Eds.), *Consciousness and self-regulation* (Vol. 4, pp. 107–136). New York: Plenum.

Pennebaker, J. W., Kiecolt-Glaser, J. K., & Glaser, R. (1988). Disclosure of traumas and immune function: Health implications for psychotherapy. *Journal of Consulting and Clinical Psychology, 56*, 239–245.

Pennebaker, J. W., & O'Heeron, R. C. (1984). Confiding in others and illness rate among spouses of suicide and accidental death victims. *Journal of Abnormal Psychology, 93*, 473–476.

Pennebaker, J. W., & Susman, J. R. (1988). Disclosure of traumas and psychosomatic processes. *Social Science and Medicine, 26*, 327–332.

Pennington, D. C. (1987). Confirmatory hypothesis testing in face-to-face interaction: An empirical refutation. *British Journal of Social Psychology, 26*, 225–235.

Pepitone, A. (1950). Motivational effects in social perception. *Human Relations, 3*, 57–76.

Perloff, L. S., & Fetzer, B. K. (1986). Self-other judgments and perceived vulnerability to victimization. *Journal of Personality and Social Psychology, 50*, 502–510.

Perrig, W., & Kintsch, W. (1985). Propositional and situational representations of text. *Journal of Memory and Language, 24*, 503–518.

Perry, L. C., Perry, D. G., & Weiss, R. J. (1986). Age differences in children's beliefs about whether altruism makes the actor feel good. *Social Cognition, 4*, 263–269.

Peterson, C., & Seligman, M. E. P. (1984). Causal explanations as a risk factor for depression: Theory and evidence. *Psychological Review, 91*, 347–374.

Peterson, C., Seligman, M. E. P., & Vaillant, G. E. (1988). Pessimistic explanatory style is a risk factor for physical illness: A thirty-five-year longitudinal study. *Journal of Personality and Social Psychology, 55*, 23–27.

Peterson, L. R., & Peterson, M. (1959). Short-term retention of individual items. *Journal of Experimental Psychology, 58*, 193–198.

Pettigrew, T. F. (1979). The ultimate attribution error: Extending Allport's cognitive analysis of prejudice. *Personality and Social Psychology Bulletin, 5*, 461–476.

Pettigrew, T. F. (1981). Extending the stereotype concept. In D. L. Hamilton (Ed.), *Cognitive processes in stereotyping and intergroup behavior* (pp. 303–332). Hillsdale, NJ: Erlbaum.

Pettigrew, T. F., & Martin, J. (1987). Shaping the organizational context for black American inclusion. *Journal of Social Issues, 43,* 41–78.

Petty, R. E., & Cacioppo, J. T. (1979). Issue involvement can increase or decrease persuasion by enhancing message-relevant cognitive responses. *Journal of Personality and Social Psychology, 37,* 1915–1926.

Petty, R. E., & Cacioppo, J. T. (1981). *Attitudes and persuasion: Classic and contemporary approaches.* Dubuque, IA: W. C. Brown.

Petty, R. E., & Cacioppo, J. T. (1984). The effect of involvement on responses to argument quantity and quality: Central and peripheral routes to persuasion. *Journal of Personality and Social Psychology, 46,* 69–81.

Petty, R. E., & Cacioppo, J. T. (1986a). *Communication and persuasion: Central and peripheral routes to attitude change.* New York: Springer-Verlag.

Petty, R. E., & Cacioppo, J. T. (1986b). The elaboration likelihood model of persuasion. In L. Berkowitz (Ed.), *Advances in experimental social psychology* (Vol. 19, pp. 123–205). New York: Academic Press.

Petty, R. E., & Cacioppo, J. T. (1990). Involvement and persuasion: Tradition versus integration. *Psychological Bulletin, 107,* 367–374.

Petty, R. E., Cacioppo, J. T., & Goldman, R. (1981). Personal involvement as a determinant of argument-based persuasion. *Journal of Personality and Social Psychology, 41,* 847–855.

Petty, R. E., Cacioppo, J. T., & Heesacker, M. (1981). Effects of rhetorical questions on persuasion: A cognitive response analysis. *Journal of Personality and Social Psychology, 40,* 432–440.

Petty, R. E., Cacioppo, J. T., & Kasmer, J. (1985). *Effects of need for cognition on social loafing.* Paper presented at the Midwestern Psychological Association Meeting, Chicago.

Petty, R. E., Cacioppo, J. T., & Kasmer, J. A. (1988). The role of affect in the elaboration likelihood model of persuasion. In L. Donohew, H. E. Sypher, & E. T. Higgins (Eds.), *Communication, social cognition, and affect* (pp. 117–146). Hillsdale, NJ: Erlbaum.

Petty, R. E., Cacioppo, J. T., Kasmer, J. A., & Haugtvedt, C. P. (1987). A reply to Stiff and Boster. *Communication Monographs, 54,* 257–263.

Petty, R. E., Cacioppo, J. T., & Schumann, D. (1983). Central and peripheral routes to advertising effectiveness: The moderating role of involvement. *Journal of Consumer Research, 10,* 134–148.

Petty, R. E., Cacioppo, J. T., Sedikides, C., & Strathman, A. J. (1988). Affect and persuasion: A contemporary perspective. *American Behavioral Scientist, 31,* 355–371.

Petty, R. E., Gleicher, F., & Baker, S. M. (1991). Multiple roles for affect in persuasion. In J. Forgas (Ed.), *Emotion and social judgment.* London: Pergamon.

Petty, R. E., Harkins, S. G., & Williams, K. D. (1980). The effects of group diffusion of cognitive effort on attitudes: An information-processing view. *Journal of Personality and Social Psychology, 38,* 81–92.

Petty, R. E., Kasmer, J., Haugtvedt, C. P., & Cacioppo, J. T. (1987). Source and message factors in persuasion: A reply to Stiff's critique of the elaboration likelihood model. *Communication Monographs, 54,* 233–263.

Petty, R. E., Ostrom, T. M., & Brock, T. C. (Eds.) (1981). *Cognitive responses in persuasion.* Hillsdale, NJ: Erlbaum.

Petty, R. E., Rennier, G. A., & Cacioppo, J. T. (1987). Assertion versus interrogation format in opinion surveys: Questions enhance thoughtful responding. *Public Opinion Quarterly, 51,* 481–494.

Petty, R. E., Wells, G. L., & Brock, T. C. (1976). Distraction can enhance or reduce yielding to propaganda: Thought disruption versus effort justification. *Journal of Personality and Social Psychology, 34,* 874–884.

Petty, R. E., Wells, G. L., Heesacker, M., Brock, T., & Cacioppo, J. T. (1983). The effects of recipient posture on persuasion: A cognitive response analysis. *Personality and Social Psychology Bulletin, 9,* 209–222.

Phares, E. J. (1976). *Locus of control in personality.* Morristown, NJ: General Learning Press.

Picek, J. S., Sherman, S. J., & Shiffrin, R. M. (1975). Cognitive organization and coding of social structures. *Journal of Personality and Social Psychology, 31,* 758–768.

Pichert, J. W., & Anderson, R. C. (1977). Taking different perspectives on a story. *Journal of Educational Psychology, 69,* 309–315.

Pietromonaco, P. R. (1985). The influence of affect on self-perception in depression. *Social Cognition, 3,* 121–134.

Pietromonaco, P. R., & Markus, H. (1985). The nature of negative thoughts in depression. *Journal of Personality and Social Psychology, 48,* 799–807.

Piliavin, J. A., & Charna, H-W. (1988). What *is* the factorial structure of the private and public self-consciousness scales? *Personality and Social Psychology Bulletin, 14,* 587–595.

Pittman, T. S., & D'Agostino, P. R. (1985). Motivation and attribution: The effects of control deprivation on subsequent information processing. In J. H. Harvey & G. Weary (Eds.), *Attribution: Basic issues and applications* (pp. 117–141). New York: Academic Press.

Pittman, T. S., Emery, J., & Boggiano, A. K. (1982). Intrinsic and extrinsic motivational orientations: Reward-induced changes in preference for complexity. *Journal of Personality and Social Psychology, 42,* 789–797.

Pittman, T. S., & Pittman, N. L. (1980). Deprivation of control and the attribution process. *Journal of Personality and Social Psychology, 39,* 377–389.

Plous, S. (1989). Thinking the unthinkable: The effects of anchoring on likelihood estimates of nuclear war. *Journal of Applied Social Psychology, 19,* 67–91.

Plous, S., & Zimbardo, P. G. (1986). Attributional biases among clinicians. *Journal of Consulting and Clinical Psychology, 54,* 568–570.

Plutchik, R. (1962). *The emotions.* New York: Random House.

Plutchik, R. (1962). *Emotion: A psychoevolutionary synthesis.* New York: Harper & Row.

Plutchik, R., & Ax, A. F. (1967). A critique of determinants of emotional state by Schachter and Singer (1962). *Psychophysiology, 4,* 79-82.

Posner, M. I. (1982). Cumulative development of attentional theory. *American Psychologist, 37,* 168–179.

Posner, M. I. & Keele, S. W. (1968). On the genesis of abstract ideas. *Journal of Experimental Psychology, 77,* 353–363.

Posner, M. I. & Keele, S. W. (1970). Retention of abstract ideas. *Journal of Experimental Psychology, 83,* 304–308.

Posner, M. I., Nissen M. J., & Klein, R. M. (1976). Visual dominance: An information processing account of its origins and significance. *Psychological Review, 83*, 157–171.

Posner, M. I., & Rothbart, M. K. (1989). Intentional chapters on unintended thoughts. In J. S. Uleman & J. A. Bargh (Eds.), *Unintended thought* (pp. 450–470). New York: Guilford Press.

Potts, G. R. (1974). Storing and retrieving information about ordered relationships. *Journal of Experimental Psychology, 103*, 431–439.

Powell, M. C., & Fazio, R. H. (1984). Attitude accessibility as a function of repeated attitudinal expression. *Personality and Social Psychology Bulletin, 10*, 139–148.

Powers, T. A., & Zuroff, D. C. (1988). Interpersonal consequences of overt self-criticism: A comparison with neutral and self-enhancing presentations of self. *Journal of Personality and Social Psychology, 54*, 1054–1062.

Pratkanis, A. R. (1988). The attitude heuristic and selective fact identification. *British Journal of Social Psychology, 27*, 257–263.

Pratkanis, A. R. (1989). The cognitive representation of attitudes. In A. R. Pratkanis, S. J. Breckler, & A. G. Greenwald (Eds.), *Attitude structure and function* (pp. 71–98). Hillsdale, NJ: Erlbaum.

Pratkanis, A. R., & Greenwald, A. G. (1989). A sociocognitive model of attitude structure and function. In L. Berkowitz (Ed.), *Advances in experimental social psychology* (Vol. 22, pp. 245–285). New York: Academic Press.

Prentice, D. A. (1987). Psychological correspondence of possessions, attitudes, and values. *Journal of Personality and Social Psychology, 53*, 993–1003.

Press, A. N., Crockett, W. H., & Rosenkrantz, P. S. (1969). Cognitive complexity and the learning of balanced and unbalanced social structures. *Journal of Personality, 37*, 541–553.

Pretty, G. H., & Seligman, C. (1984). Affect and the overjustification effect. *Journal of Personality and Social Psychology, 46*, 1241–1253.

Prislin, R. (1987). Attitude-behaviour relationship: Attitude relevance and behaviour relevance. *European Journal of Social Psychology, 17*, 483–485.

Procidano, M. E., & Heller, K. (1983). Measures of perceived social support from friends and from family: Three validation studies. *American Journal of Community Psychology, 11*, 1–24.

Proust, M. (1956). *Swann's way* (C. K. S. Moncrieff, trans.). New York: Modern Library. (Originally published 1914.)

Pruitt, D. G., & Hoge, R. D. (1965). Strength of the relationship between the value of an event and its subjective probability as a function of method of measurement. *Journal of Experimental Social Psychology, 5*, 483–489.

Pruitt, D. J., & Insko, C. A. (1980). Extension of the Kelley attribution model: The role of comparison-object consensus, target-object consensus, distinctiveness and consistency. *Journal of Personality and Social Psychology, 39*, 39–58.

Pruitt, D. G., & Teger, A. I. (1969). The risky shift in group betting. *Journal of Experimental Social Psychology, 5*, 115–126.

Pryor, J. B. (1986). The influence of different encoding sets upon the formation of illusory correlations and group impressions. *Personality and Social Psychology Bulletin, 12*, 216–226.

Pryor, J. B., Kott, T. L., & Bovee, G. R. (1984). The influence of information redundancy upon the use of traits and persons as organizing categories. *Journal of Experimental Social Psychology, 20*, 246–262.

Pryor, J. B., & Kriss, N. (1977). The cognitive dynamics of salience in the attribution process. *Journal of Personality and Social Psychology, 35,* 49–55.

Pryor, J. B., McDaniel, M. A., & Kott-Russo, T. (1986). The influence of the level of schema abstractness upon the processing of social information. *Journal of Experimental Social Psychology, 22,* 312–327.

Pryor, J. B., & Merluzzi, T. V. (1985). The role of expertise in processing social interaction scripts. *Journal of Experimental Social Psychology, 21,* 362–379.

Pryor, J. B., & Ostrom, T. M. (1981). The cognitive organization of social information: A converging-operations approach. *Journal of Personality and Social Psychology, 41,* 628–641.

Pryor, J. B., Ostrom, T. M., Dukerich, J. M., Mitchell, M. L., & Herstein, J. A. (1983). Preintegrative categorization of social information: The role of persons as organizing categories. *Journal of Personality and Social Psychology, 44,* 923–932.

Pryor, J. B., Simpson, D. D., Mitchell, M., Ostrom, T. M., & Lydon, J. (1982). Structural selectivity in the retrieval of social information. *Social Cognition, 1,* 336–357.

Pylyshyn, Z. W. (1973). What the mind's eye tells the mind's brain: A critique of mental imagery. *Psychological Bulletin, 80,* 1–24.

Pylyshyn, Z. W. (1981). The imagery debate: Analogue media versus tacit knowledge. *Psychological Review, 88,* 16–45.

Pyszczynski, T. A., & Greenberg, J. (1981). Role of disconfirmed expectancies in the instigation of attributional processing. *Journal of Personality and Social Psychology, 40,* 31–38.

Pyszczynski, T. A., & Greenberg, J. (1987). Self-regulatory perseveration and the depressive self-focusing style: A self-awareness theory of reactive depression. *Psychological Bulletin, 102,* 122–138.

Pyszczynski, T. A., Greenberg, J., & Holt, K. (1985). Maintaining consistency between self-serving beliefs and available data: A bias in information evaluation. *Personality and Social Psychology Bulletin, 11,* 179–190.

Pyszczynski, T. A., Greenberg, J., & LaPrelle, J. (1985). Social comparison after success and failure: Biased search for information consistent with a self-serving conclusion. *Journal of Experimental Social Psychology, 21,* 195–211.

Pyszczynski, T., LaPrelle, J., & Greenberg, J. (1987). Encoding and retrieval effects of general person characterizations on memory for incongruent and congruent information. *Personality and Social Psychology Bulletin, 13,* 556–567.

Quattrone, G. A. (1982). Overattribution and unit formation: When behavior engulfs the person. *Journal of Personality and Social Psychology, 42,* 593–607.

Quattrone, G. A. (1985). On the congruity between internal states and action. *Psychological Bulletin, 98,* 3–40.

Quattrone, G. A. (1986). On the perception of a group's variability. In S. Worchel & W. Austin (Eds.), *The psychology of intergroup relations* (Vol. 2, pp. 25–48). New York: Nelson-Hall.

Quattrone, G. A., Finkel, S. E., & Andrus, D. C. (1982). *Anchors away!: On overcoming the anchoring bias across a number of domains.* Unpublished manuscript, Stanford University.

Quattrone, G. A., & Jones, E. E. (1980). The perception of variability within ingroups and outgroups: Implications for the Law of Small Numbers. *Journal of Personality and Social Psychology, 38,* 141–152.

Rabbie, J. M., & Horowitz, M. (1988). Categories versus groups as explanatory concepts in intergroup relations. *European Journal of Social Psychology, 18*, 117–123.

Rajecki, D. W. (1982). *Attitudes: Themes and advances.* Sunderland, MA: Sinauer.

Rasinski, K. A., Crocker, J., & Hastie, R. (1985). Another look at sex stereotypes and social judgments: An analysis of the social perceiver's use of subjective probabilities. *Journal of Personality and Social Psychology, 49*, 317–326.

Razran, G. H. S. (1940). Conditioned response changes in rating and appraising sociopolitical slogans. *Psychological Bulletin, 37*, 481.

Read, S. (1983). Once is enough: Causal reasoning from a single instance. *Journal of Personality and Social Psychology, 45*, 323–334.

Read, S. (1984). Analogical reasoning in social judgment: The importance of causal theories. *Journal of Personality and Social Psychology, 46*, 14–25.

Read, S. (1987). Similarity and causality in the use of social analogies. *Journal of Experimental Social Psychology, 23*, 189–207.

Read, S. J. (1988). Conjunctive explanations: The effect of a comparison between a chosen and a nonchosen alternative. *Journal of Experimental Social Psychology, 24*, 146–162.

Read, S. J. (1989). Constructing causal scenarios: A knowledge structure approach to causal reasoning. *Journal of Personality and Social Psychology, 52*, 288–302.

Read, S. J., & Miller, L. C. (1989). Inter-personalism: Toward a goal-based theory of persons in relationships. In L. Pervin (Ed.), *Goal concepts in personality and social psychology* (pp. 413–472). Hillsdale, NJ: Erlbaum.

Reder, L. M., & Anderson, J. R. (1980). A partial resolution of the paradox of interference: The role of integrating knowledge. *Cognition Psychology, 12*, 447–472.

Reed, S. K. (1972). Pattern recognition and categorization. *Cognitive Psychology, 3*, 382–407.

Reeder, G. D. (1985). Implicit relations between dispositions and behaviors: Effects on dispositional attribution. In J. H. Harvey & G. Weary (Eds.), *Attribution: Basic issues and applications* (pp. 87–116). New York: Academic Press.

Reeder, G. D., & Brewer, M. B. (1979). A schematic model of dispositional attribution in interpersonal perception. *Psychological Review, 86*, 61–79.

Reeder, G. D., & Coovert, M. D. (1986). Revising an impression of morality. *Social Cognition, 4*, 1–17.

Reeder, G. D., Fletcher, G. J. O., & Furman, K. (1989). The role of observers' expectations in attitude attribution. *Journal of Experimental Social Psychology, 25*, 168–188.

Reeder, G. D., McCormick, C. B., & Esselman, E. D. (1987). Self-referent processing and recall of prose. *Journal of Educational Psychology, 79*, 243–248.

Regan, D. T., & Totten, J. (1975). Empathy and attribution: Turning observers into actors. *Journal of Personality and Social Psychology, 32*, 850–856.

Regan, J. W. (1976). Liking for evaluators: Consistency and self-esteem theories. *Journal of Experimental Social Psychology, 12*, 156–169.

Rehm, J., Lilli, W., & Van Eimeren, B. (1988). Reduced intergroup differentiation as a result of self-categorization in overlapping categories: A quasi-experiment. *European Journal of Social Psychology, 18*, 375–379.

Reich, S. S., & Ruth, P. (1982). Wason's selection task: Verification, falsification, and matching. *British Journal of Psychology, 73*, 395–405.

Reid, J. (1973). *The best little boy in the world*. New York: Ballantine.

Reis, H. T., & Burns, L. B. (1982). The salience of the self in responses to inequity. *Journal of Experimental Social Psychology, 18,* 464–475.

Reisenzein, R. (1983). The Schachter theory of emotion: Two decades later. *Psychological Bulletin, 94,* 239–264.

Reisenzein, R. (1986). A structural equation analysis of Weiner's attribution-affect model of helping behavior. *Journal of Personality and Social Psychology, 50,* 1123–1133.

Reiss, M., Rosenfeld, P., Melburg, V., & Tedeschi, J. T. (1981). Self-serving attributions: Biased private perceptions and distorted public descriptions. *Journal of Personality and Social Psychology, 41,* 224–251.

Reyes, R. M., Thompson, W. C., & Bower, G. H. (1980). Judgmental biases resulting from differing availabilities of arguments. *Journal of Personality and Social Psychology, 39,* 2–12.

Rhine, R., & Severance, L. (1970). Ego-involvement, discrepancy, source credibility, and attitude change. *Journal of Personality and Social Psychology, 16,* 175–190.

Rhodewalt, F., & Agustsdottir, S. (1986). Effects of self-presentation on the phenomenal self. *Journal of Personality and Social Psychology, 50,* 47–53.

Rhodewalt, F., & Comer, R. (1979). Induced-compliance attitude change: Once more with feeling. *Journal of Experimental Social Psychology, 15,* 35–47.

Rholes, W. S., Jones, M., & Wade, C. (1988). Children's understanding of personal dispositions and its relationship to behavior. *Journal of Experimental Child Psychology, 45,* 1–17.

Rholes, W. S., & Pryor, J. B. (1982). Cognitive accessibility and causal attributions. *Personality and Social Psychology Bulletin, 8,* 719–727.

Riess, M., & Taylor, J. (1984). Ego-involvement and attributions for success and failure in a field setting. *Personality and Social Psychology Bulletin, 10,* 536–543.

Riggs, J. M., & Cantor, N. (1984). Getting acquainted: The role of the self-concept and preconceptions. *Personality and Social Psychology Bulletin, 10,* 432–445.

Rimé, B., Boulanger, B., Laubin, P., Richir, M., & Stroobants, K. (1985). The perception of interpersonal emotions originated by patterns of movement. *Motivation and Emotion, 9,* 241–260.

Rimé, B., Philippot, P., & Cisamolo, D. (1990). Social schemata of peripheral changes in emotion. *Journal of Personality and Social Psychology, 59,* 38–49.

Riskey, D. R. (1979). Verbal memory processes in impression formation. *Journal of Experimental Psychology: Human Learning and Memory, 5,* 271–281.

Rizley, R. (1978). Depression and distortion in the attribution of causality. *Journal of Abnormal Psychology, 87,* 32–48.

Robertson, L. S. (1977). Car crashes: Perceived vulnerability and willingness to pay for crash protection. *Journal of Community Health, 3,* 136–141.

Robins, C. J. (1988). Attributions and depression: Why is the literature so inconsistent? *Journal of Personality and Social Psychology, 54,* 880–889.

Robinson, J., & McArthur, L. Z. (1982). The impact of salient vocal qualities on causal attributions for a speaker's behavior. *Journal of Personality and Social Psychology, 43,* 236–247.

Robles, R., Smith, R., Carver, C. S., & Wellens, A. R. (1987). Influence of subliminal visual images on the experience of anxiety. *Personality and Social Psychology Bulletin, 13,* 399–410.

Rodin, J., Rennert, K., & Solomon, S. K. (1980). Intrinsic motivation for control: Fact or fiction. In A. Baum & J. E. Singer (Eds.), *Advances in environmental psychology* (Vol. 2, pp. 131–148). Hillsdale, NJ: Erlbaum.

Rodin, M. J. (1987). Who is memorable to whom: A study of cognitive disregard. *Social Cognition, 5,* 144–165.

Rogers, M., Miller, N., Mayer, F. S., & Duval, S. (1982). Personal responsibility and salience of the request for help: Determinants of the relation between negative affect and helping behavior. *Journal of Personality and Social Psychology, 43,* 956–970.

Rogers, T. B. (1981). A model of the self as an aspect of human information processing. In N. Cantor & J. Kihlstrom (Eds.), *Personality, cognition, and social interaction* (pp. 193–214). Hillsdale, NJ: Erlbaum.

Rogers, T. B., Kuiper, N. A., & Kirker, W. S. (1977). Self-reference and the encoding of personal information. *Journal of Personality and Social Psychology, 35,* 677–688.

Rogers, T. B., Kuiper, N. A., & Rogers, P. J. (1979). Symbolic distance and congruity effects for paired-comparisons judgments of degree of self-reference. *Journal of Research in Personality, 13,* 433–449.

Rokeach, M. (1973). *The nature of human values.* New York: Free Press.

Romer, D. (1979). Distraction, counterarguing, and the internalization of attitude change. *European Journal of Social Psychology, 9,* 1–17.

Roney, C. J. R., & Sorrentino, R. M. (1987). Uncertainty orientation and person perception: Individual differences in categorization. *Social Cognition, 5,* 369–382.

Rosch, E. H. (1978). Principles of categorization, In E. Rosch & B. B. Lloyd (Eds.), *Cognition and categorization.* Hillsdale, NJ: Erlbaum.

Rosch, E. H. (1987). Wittgenstein and categorization research in cognitive psychology. In M. Chapman & M. Dixon (Eds.), *Meaning and the growth of understanding: Wittgenstein's significance for developmental psychology* (pp. 151–166). Berlin: Springer-Verlag.

Rosch, E. H., Mervis, C. B., Gray, W., Johnson, D., & Boyes-Braem, P. (1976). Basic objects in natural categories. *Cognitive Psychology, 8,* 382–439.

Rose, T. L. (1981). Cognitive and dyadic processes in intergroup contact. In D. L. Hamilton (Ed.), *Cognitive processes in stereotyping and intergroup behavior* (pp. 259–302). Hillsdale, NJ: Erlbaum.

Roseman, I. J. (1984). Cognitive determinants of emotion: A structural theory. In P. Shaver (Ed.), *Review of personality and social psychology: Vol. 5. Emotions, relationships, and health* (pp. 11–36). Beverly Hills, CA: Sage.

Rosenbaum, M., & Ben-Ari, K. (1985). Learned helplessness and learned resourcefulness: Effects of noncontingent success and failure on individuals differing in self-control skills. *Journal of Personality and Social Psychology, 48,* 198–215.

Rosenberg, M. (1979). *Conceiving the self.* New York: Basic Books.

Rosenberg, M. J. (1956). Cognitive structure and attitudinal affect. *Journal of Abnormal and Social Psychology, 53,* 367–372.

Rosenberg, M. J. (1960). An analysis of affective-cognitive consistency. In C. I. Hovland & M. J. Rosenberg (Eds.), *Attitude organization and change* (pp. 15–64). New Haven, CT: Yale University Press.

Rosenberg, M. J., & Hovland, C. I. (1960). Cognitive, affective, and behavioral components of attitudes. In M. J. Rosenberg, C. I. Hovland, W. J. McGuire,

R. P. Abelson, & J. W. Brehm (Eds.), *Attitude organization and change* (pp. 1–14). New Haven, CT: Yale University Press.

Rosenberg, S. (1988). Self and others: Studies in social personality and autobiography. In L. Berkowitz (Ed.), *Advances in experimental social psychology* (Vol. 21, pp. 57–96). New York: Academic Press.

Rosenberg, S., & Sedlak, A. (1972). Structural representations of implicit personality theory. In L. Berkowitz (Ed.), *Advances in experimental social psychology* (Vol. 6, pp. 235–297). New York: Academic Press.

Rosenhan, D. L., Salovey, P., & Hargis, K. (1981). The joys of helping: Focus of attention mediates the impact of positive affect on altruism. *Journal of Personality and Social Psychology, 40,* 899–905.

Rosenthal, R. (1974). *On the social psychology of the self-fulfilling prophecy: Further evidence for Pygmalion effects and their mediating mechanisms.* New York: MSS Modular Publications (Module 53).

Rosenthal, R., & Jacobson, L. F. (1968). *Pygmalion in the classroom.* New York: Holt, Rinehart, & Winston.

Ross, L. (1977). The intuitive psychologist and his shortcomings: Distortions in the attribution process. In L. Berkowitz (Ed.), *Advances in experimental social psychology* (Vol. 10, pp. 174–221). New York: Academic Press.

Ross, L., Amabile, T. M., & Steinmetz, J. L. (1977). Social roles, social control, and biases in social-perception processes. *Journal of Personality and Social Psychology, 35,* 485–494.

Ross, L., Greene, D., & House, P. (1977). The "false consensus effect": An egocentric bias in social perception and attribution processes. *Journal of Experimental Social Psychology, 13,* 279–301.

Ross, L., Lepper, M. R., & Hubbard, M. (1975). Perseverance in self-perception and social perception: Biased attribution processes in the debriefing paradigm. *Journal of Personality and Social Psychology, 32,* 880–892.

Ross, L., Lepper, M. R., Strack, F., & Steinmetz, J. (1977). Social explanation and social expectation: Effects of real and hypothetical explanations on subjective likelihood. *Journal of Personality and Social Psychology, 35,* 817–829.

Ross, L., Rodin, J., & Zimbardo, P. G. (1969). Toward an attribution therapy: The reduction of fear through induced cognitive-emotional misattribution. *Journal of Personality and Social Psychology, 12,* 279–288.

Ross, M. (1989). The relation of implicit theories to the construction of personal histories. *Psychological Review, 96,* 341–357.

Ross, M., & Conway, M. (1986). Remembering one's own past: The construction of personal histories. In R. M. Sorrentino & E. T. Higgins (Eds.), *Handbook of motivation and cognition: Foundations of social behavior* (pp. 122–144). New York: Guilford Press.

Ross, M., & Fletcher, G. J. O. (1985). Attribution and social perception. In G. Lindzey & A. Aronson (Eds.), *The handbook of social psychology* (3rd ed., Vol. 2, pp. 73–122). Reading, MA: Addison-Wesley.

Ross, M., McFarland, C., Conway, M., & Zanna, M. P. (1983). Reciprocal relation between attitudes and behavior recall: Committing people to newly formed attitudes. *Journal of Personality and Social Psychology, 45,* 257–267.

Ross, M., McFarland, C., & Fletcher, G. J. O. (1981). The effect of attitude on the recall of personal histories. *Journal of Personality and Social Psychology, 10,* 627–634.

Ross, M., & Olson, J. M. (1981). An expectancy-attribution model of the effects of placebos. *Psychological Review, 88,* 408–437.

Ross, M., & Shulman, R. F. (1973). Increasing the salience of initial attitudes: Dissonance vs. self-perception theory. *Journal of Personality and Social Psychology, 28,* 138–144.

Ross, M., & Sicoly, F. (1979). Egocentric biases in availability and attribution. *Journal of Personality and Social Psychology, 37,* 322–337.

Roth, D., & Rehm, L. P. (1980). Relationships among self-monitoring processes, memory, and depression. *Cognitive Therapy and Research, 4,* 149–157.

Rothbart, M. (1981). Memory processes and social beliefs. In D. Hamilton (Ed.), *Cognitive processes in stereotyping and intergroup behavior* (pp. 145–182). Hillsdale, NJ: Erlbaum.

Rothbart, M., Dawes, R., & Park, B. (1984). Stereotyping and sampling biases in intergroup perception. In J. R. Eiser (Ed.), *Attitudinal judgment* (pp. 109–134). New York: Springer-Verlag.

Rothbart, M., Evans, M., & Fulero, S. (1979). Recall for confirming events: Memory processes and the maintenance of social stereotyping. *Journal of Experimental Social Psychology, 15,* 343–355.

Rothbart, M., Fulero, S., Jensen, C., Howard, J., & Birrell, B. (1978). From individual to group impressions: Availability heuristics in stereotype formation. *Journal of Experimental Social Psychology, 14,* 237–255.

Rothbart, M., & Hallmark, W. (1988). Ingroup-outgroup differences in the perceived efficacy of coercion and conciliation in resolving social conflict. *Journal of Personality and Social Psychology, 55,* 248–257.

Rothbart, M., & John, O. P. (1985). Social categorization and behavioral episodes: A cognitive analysis of the effects of intergroup contact. *Journal of Social Issues, 41,* 81–104.

Rothbart, M., & Lewis, S. (1988). Inferring category attributes from exemplar attributes: Geometric shapes and social categories. *Journal of Personality and Social Psychology, 55,* 861–872.

Rothbart, M., & Park, B. (1986). On the confirmability and disconfirmability of trait concepts. *Journal of Personality and Social Psychology, 50,* 131–142.

Rothbaum, F., Weisz, J. R., & Snyder, S. S. (1982). Changing the world and changing the self: A two-process model of perceived control. *Journal of Personality and Social Psychology, 42,* 5–37.

Rotter, J. B. (1966). Generalized expectancies for internal versus external control of reinforcement. *Psychological Monographs, 80* (1, Whole No. 609).

Rozelle, R. M., & Baxter, J. C. (1981). Influence of role pressures on the perceiver: Judgments of videotaped interviews varying judge accountability and responsibility. *Journal of Applied Psychology, 66,* 437–441.

Ruble, D. N., & Stangor, C. (1986). Stalking the elusive schema: Insights from developmental and social-psychological analyses of gender schemas. *Social Cognition, 4,* 227–261.

Ruehlman, L. S., West, S. G., & Pasahow, R. J. (1985). Depression and evaluative schemata. *Journal of Personality, 53,* 46–92.

Rule, B. G., Bisanz, G. L., & Kohn, M. (1985). Anatomy of a persuasion schema: Targets, goals, and strategies. *Journal of Personality and Social Psychology, 48,* 1127–1140.

Rule, B. G., Taylor, B. R., & Dobbs, A. R. (1987). Priming effects of heat on aggressive thoughts. *Social Cognition, 5,* 131–143.

Rumelhart, D. E., Lindsay, P. H., & Norman, D. A. (1972). A process model for long-term memory. In E. Tulving & W. Donaldson (Eds.), *Organization of memory* (pp. 197–246). New York: Academic Press.

Rumelhart, D. E., & Ortony, A. (1977). The representation of knowledge in memory. In R. C. Anderson, R. J. Spiro, & W. E. Montague (Eds.), *Schooling and the acquisition of knowledge* (pp. 99–136). Hillsdale, NJ: Erlbaum.

Ruscher, J. B., & Fiske, S. T. (1990). Interpersonal competition can cause individuating impression formation. *Journal of Personality and Social Psychology, 58*, 832–842.

Ruscher, J. B., Miki, H., Fiske, S. T., & Van Manen, S. (1990, August). *Individuating processes in competition: Interpersonal versus intergroup.* Paper presented at the meeting of the American Psychological Association, Boston.

Rush, M. C., & Russell, J. E. A. (1988). Leader prototypes and prototype-contingent consensus in leader behavior descriptions. *Journal of Experimental Social Psychology, 24*, 88–104.

Russell, D. (1982). The causal dimension scale: A measure of how individuals perceive causes. *Journal of Personality and Social Psychology, 42*, 1137–1145.

Russell, D., Lenel, J. C., Spicer, C., Miller, J., Albrecht, J., & Rose, J. (1985). Evaluating the physically disabled: An attributional analysis. *Personality and Social Psychology Bulletin, 11*, 23–31.

Russell, D., & McAuley, E. (1986). Causal attributions, causal dimensions, and affective reactions to success and failure. *Journal of Personality and Social Psychology, 50*, 1174–1185.

Russell, J. A. (1978). Evidence of convergent validity on the dimensions of affect. *Journal of Personality and Social Psychology, 36*, 1152–1168.

Russell, J. A. (1983). Pancultural aspects of the human conceptual organization of emotions. *Journal of Personality and Social Psychology, 45*, 1281–1288.

Russell, J. A., & Bullock, M. (1985). Multidimensional scaling of emotional facial expressions: Similarity from preschoolers to adults. *Journal of Personality and Social Psychology, 48*, 1290–1298.

Russell, J. A., & Bullock, M. (1986). Fuzzy concepts and the perception of emotion in facial expressions. *Social Cognition, 4*, 309–341.

Russell, J. A., & Fehr, B. (1987). Relativity in the perception of emotion in facial expressions. *Journal of Experimental Psychology: General, 116*, 223–237.

Russell, J. A., & Fehr, B. (1988). Reply to Ekman & O'Sullivan. *Journal of Experimental Psychology: General, 117*, 89–90.

Russell, J. A., & Woudzia, L. (1986). Affective judgments, common sense, and Zajonc's thesis of independence. *Motivation and Emotion, 10*, 169–183.

Ruvolo, A., & Markus, H. (1991). Possible selves and performance: The power of self-relevant imagery. *Social Cognition.*

Ruzzene, M., & Noller, P. (1986). Feedback motivation and reactions to personality interpretations that differ in favorability and accuracy. *Journal of Personality and Social Psychology, 51*, 1293–1299.

Ryan, W. (1971). *Blaming the victim.* New York: Random House.

Sachdev, I., & Bourhis, R. Y. (1985). Social categorization and power differentials in group relations. *European Journal of Social Psychology, 15*, 415–434.

Sachdev, I., & Bourhis, R. Y. (1987). Status differentials and intergroup behaviour. *European Journal of Social Psychology, 17*, 277–293.

Sadler, O., & Tesser, A. (1973). Some effects of salience and time upon interpersonal hostility and attraction during social isolation. *Sociometry, 36,* 99–112.

Saenz, D. S., & Lord, C. G. (1989). Reversing roles: A cognitive strategy for undoing memory deficits associated with token status. *Journal of Personality and Social Psychology, 56,* 698–708.

Sagar, H. A., & Schofield, J. W. (1980). Racial and behavioral cues in black and white children's perceptions of ambiguously aggressive acts. *Journal of Personality and Social Psychology, 39,* 590–598.

Salovey, P., & Birnbaum, D. (1989). Influence of mood on health-relevant cognitions. *Journal of Personality and Social Psychology, 57,* 539–551.

Salovey, P., & Rodin, J. (1985). Cognitions about the self: Connecting feeling states and social behavior. In P. Shaver (Ed.), *Review of personality and social psychology: Vol. 6. Self, situations, and social behavior* (pp. 143–166). Beverly Hills, CA: Sage.

Salovey, P., & Rosenhan, D. L. (1989). Mood states and prosocial behavior. In H. Wagner & A. Manstead (Eds.), *Handbook of social psychophysiology* (pp. 371–391). Chichester, England: Wiley.

Salovey, P., & Singer, J. A. (1988). Mood congruency effects in recall of childhood versus recent memories. *Journal of Social Behavior and Personality, 3,* 1–22.

Saltzer, E. B. (1981). Cognitive moderators of the relationship between behavioral intentions and behavior. *Journal of Personality and Social Psychology, 41,* 260–275.

Sanbonmatsu, D. M., & Fazio, R. H. (1990). The role of attitudes in memory-based decision making. *Journal of Personality and Social Psychology, 59,* 614–622

Sanbonmatsu, D. M., Shavitt, S., Sherman, S. J., & Roskos-Ewoldsen, D. R. (1987). Illusory correlation in the perception of performance by self or a salient other. *Journal of Experimental Social Psychology, 23,* 518–543.

Sanbonmatsu, D. M., Sherman, S. J., & Hamilton, D. L. (1987). Illusory correlation in the perception of individuals and groups. *Social Cognition, 5,* 1–25.

Sande, G. N., Ellard, J. H., & Ross, M. (1986). Effect of arbitrarily assigned status labels on self-perceptions and social perceptions: The mere position effect. *Journal of Personality and Social Psychology, 50,* 684–689.

Sande, G. N., Goethals, G. R., & Radloff, C. E. (1988). Perceiving one's own traits and others': The multifaceted self. *Journal of Personality and Social Psychology, 54,* 13–20.

Sandelands, L. E., & Calder, B. J. (1984). Referencing and bias in social interaction. *Journal of Personality and Social Psychology, 46,* 755–762.

Sanders, G. S. (1985). Unbiased evaluations of performance: Artifact or research topic? *British Journal of Social Psychology, 24,* 159–160.

Sanders, G. S., & Mullen, B. (1983). Accuracy in perceptions of consensus: Differential tendencies of people with majority and minority positions. *European Journal of Social Psychology, 13,* 57–70.

Sansone, C. (1986). A question of competence: The effects of competence and task feedback on intrinsic interest. *Journal of Personality and Social Psychology, 51,* 918–931.

Santee, R. T., & Maslach, C. (1982). To agree or not to agree: Personal dissent amid social pressure to conform. *Journal of Personality and Social Psychology, 42,* 690–700.

Sawyer, A. (1981). Repetition, cognitive responses, and persuasion. In R. E. Petty, T. M. Ostrom, & T. C. Brock (Eds.), *Cognitive responses in persuasion* (pp. 237–262). Hillsdale, NJ: Erlbaum.

Sawyer, J. (1966). Measurement and prediction, clinical and statistical. *Psychological Bulletin, 66*, 178–200.

Schachter, S. (1959). *The psychology of affiliation.* Palo Alto, CA: Stanford University Press.

Schachter, S. (1964). The interaction of cognitive and physiological determinants of emotional state. In L. Berkowitz (Ed.), *Advances in experimental social psychology* (Vol. 1, pp. 49–82). New York: Academic Press.

Schachter, S. (1971). *Emotion, obesity, and crime.* New York: Academic Press.

Schachter, S., & Singer, J. E. (1962). Cognitive, social, and physiological determinants of emotional state. *Psychological Review, 69*, 379–399.

Schachter, S., & Singer, J. E. (1979). Comments on the Maslach and Marshall-Zimbarbo experiments. *Journal of Personality and Social Psychology, 37*, 989–995.

Schaffner, P. E. (1985). Specious learning about reward and punishment. *Journal of Personality and Social Psychology, 48*, 1377–1386.

Schaller, M., & Cialdini, R. B. (1988). The economics of empathic helping: Support for a mood management motive. *Journal of Experimental Social Psychology, 24*, 163–181.

Schank, R. C., & Abelson, R. P. (1977). *Scripts, plans, goals, and understanding: An inquiry into human knowledge structures.* Hillsdale, NJ: Erlbaum.

Schaufeli, W. B. (1988). Perceiving the causes of unemployment: An evaluation of the causal dimensions scale in a real-life situation. *Journal of Personality and Social Psychology, 54*, 347–356.

Scheier, M. F. (1976). Self-awareness, self-consciousness, and angry aggression. *Journal of Personality, 44*, 627–644.

Scheier, M. F. (1980). The effects of public and private self-consciousness on the public expression of personal beliefs. *Journal of Personality and Social Psychology, 39*, 514–521.

Scheier, M. F., & Carver, C. S. (1977). Self-focused attention and the experience of emotion: Attraction, repulsion, elation, and depression. *Journal of Personality and Social Psychology, 35*, 625–636.

Scheier, M. F., & Carver, C. S. (1980). Private and public self-attention, resistance to change, and dissonance reduction. *Journal of Personality and Social Psychology, 39*, 390–405.

Scheier, M. F., & Carver, C. S. (1982). Cognition, affect, and self-regulation. In M. S. Clark & S. T. Fiske (Eds.), *Affect and cognition: The 17th Annual Carnegie Symposium on Cognition* (pp. 157–184). Hillsdale, NJ: Erlbaum.

Scheier, M. F., & Carver, C. S. (1983). Two sides of the self: One for you and one for me. In J. Suls & A. G. Greenwald (Eds.), *Psychological perspectives on the self* (Vol. 2, pp. 123–158). Hillsdale, NJ: Erlbaum.

Scheier, M. F., & Carver, C. S. (1988). A model of behavioral self-regulation: Translating intention into action. In L. Berkowitz (Ed.), *Advances in experimental social psychology* (Vol. 21, pp. 303–346). New York: Academic Press.

Scheier, M. F., Carver, C. S., & Gibbons, F. X. (1981). Self-focused attention and reactions to fear. *Journal of Research in Personality, 15*, 1–15.

Scheier, M. F., Fenigstein, A., & Buss, A. H. (1974). Self-awareness and physical aggression. *Journal of Experimental Social Psychology, 10*, 264–273.

Schein, E. H. (1956). The Chinese indoctrination program for prisoners of war: A study of attempted "brainwashing." *Psychiatry, 19,* 149–172.

Scherer, K. R. (1984). Emotion as a multicomponent process: A model and some cross-cultural data. In P. Shaver (Ed.), *Review of personality and social psychology: Vol. 5. Emotions, relationships, and health* (pp. 37–63). Beverly Hills, CA: Sage.

Scherer, K. R. (1988). Criteria for emotion-antecedent appraisal: A review. In V. Hamilton, G. H. Bower, & N. H. Frijda (Eds.), *Cognitive perspectives on emotion and motivation* (pp. 89–126). Dordrecht, The Netherlands: Kluwer Academic Publishers.

Scherer, K. R., Wallbott, H. G., & Summerfield, A. B. (Eds.). (1986). *Experiencing emotion: A cross-cultural study.* Cambridge, England: Cambridge University Press.

Schiffenbauer, A. (1974). Effect of observer's emotional state on judgments of the emotional state of others. *Journal of Personality and Social Psychology, 30,* 31–35.

Schlenker, B. (1980). *Impression management: The self-concept, social identity, and interpersonal relations.* Monterey, CA: Brooks/Cole.

Schlenker, B. R. (1984). Identities, identifications, and relationships. In V. Derlega (Ed.), *Communication, intimacy, and close relationships* (pp. 71–104). New York: Academic Press.

Schlenker, B. R. (1985). Identity and self-identification. In B. R. Schlenker (Ed.), *The self and social life* (pp. 65–99). New York: McGraw-Hill.

Schlenker, B. R. (1986). Self-identification: Toward an integration of the private and public self. In R. Baumeister (Ed.), *Public self and private self* (pp. 21–62). New York: Springer-Verlag.

Schlenker, B. R. (1987). Threats to identity: Self-identification and social stress. In C. R. Snyder & C. E. Ford (Eds.), *Coping with negative life events: Clinical and social psychological perspectives* (pp. 273–321). New York: Plenum.

Schlenker, B. R., & Goldman, H. J. (1982). Attitude change as a self-presentation tactic following attitude-consistent behavior: Effects of choice and role. *Social Psychology Quarterly, 45,* 92–99.

Schlenker, B. R., Hallam, J. R., & McCown, N. E. (1983). Motives and social evaluation: Actor-observer differences in the delineation of motives for a beneficial act. *Journal of Experimental Social Psychology, 19,* 254–273.

Schlenker, B. R., & Leary, M. R. (1982). Audiences' reactions to self-enhancing, self-denigrating, and accurate self-presentations. *Journal of Experimental Social Psychology, 18,* 89–104.

Schlenker, B. R., & Miller, R. S. (1977). Egocentrism in groups: Self-serving biases or logical information processing? *Journal of Personality and Social Psychology, 35,* 755–764.

Schlenker, B. R., & Trudeau, J. V. (1990) The impact of self-presentations on private self-beliefs: Effects of prior self-beliefs and misattribution. *Journal of Personality and Social Psychology, 58,* 22–32.

Schlenker, B. R., & Weigold, M. F. (1989). Self-identification and accountability. In R. A. Giacalone & P. Rosenfeld (Eds.), *Impression management in the organization* (pp. 21–43). Hillsdale, NJ: Erlbaum.

Schlenker, B. R., Weigold, M. F., & Hallam, J. R. (1990). Self-serving attributions in social context: Effects of self-esteem and social pressure. *Journal of Personality and Social Psychology, 58,* 855–863.

Schlosberg, H. (1954). Three dimensions of emotion. *Psychological Review, 61,* 81–88.

Schmidt, D. F., & Sherman, R. C. (1984). Memory for persuasive messages: A test of a schema-copy-plus-tag model. *Journal of Personality and Social Psychology, 47,* 17–25.

Schmidt, G., & Weiner, B. (1988). An attribution-affect-action theory of behavior: Replications of judgments of help-giving. *Personality and Social Psychology Bulletin, 14,* 610–621.

Schmidt-Atzert, L. (1988). Affect and cognition: On the chronological order of stimulus evaluation and emotion. In K. Fiedler & J. P. Forgas (Eds.), *Affect, cognition, and social behavior* (pp. 153–164). Toronto, Canada: Hogrefe.

Schneider, D. J. (1973). Implicit personality theory: A review. *Psychological Bulletin, 79,* 294–309.

Schneider, D. J., Hastorf, A. H., & Ellsworth, P. C. (1979). *Person perception.* Reading, MA: Addison-Wesley.

Schneider, W., & Shiffrin, R. M. (1977). Controlled and automatic human information processing: I. Detection, search, and attention. *Psychological Review, 84,* 1–66.

Schneiderman, W., Webb, W., Davis, B., & Thomas, S. (1981). *Self-monitoring and states of awareness.* Unpublished manuscript, Marshall University.

Schoeneman, T. J., & Rubanowitz, D. E. (1985). Attributions in the advice columns: Actors and observers, causes and reasons. *Personality and Social Psychology Bulletin, 11,* 315–325.

Schoeneman, T. J., van Uchelen, C., Stonebrink, S., & Cheek, P. R. (1986). Expectancy, outcome, and event type: Effects on retrospective reports of attributional activity. *Personality and Social Psychology Bulletin, 12,* 353–362.

Schouten, P. G. W., & Handelsman, M. M. (1987). Social basis of self-handicapping: The case of depression. *Personality and Social Psychology Bulletin, 13,* 103–110.

Schroeder, D. A., Dovido, J. F., Sibicky, M. E., Matthews, L. L., & Allen, J. L. (1988). Empathy and helping behavior: Egoism or altruism. *Journal of Experimental Social Psychology, 24,* 333–353.

Schul, Y. (1983). Integration and abstraction in impression formation. *Journal of Personality and Social Psychology, 44,* 45–54.

Schul, Y. (1986). The effect of the amount of information and its relevance on memory-based and stimulus-based judgments. *Journal of Experimental Social Psychology, 22,* 355–373.

Schul, Y., & Burnstein, E. (1985a). The informational basis of social judgments: Using past impression rather than the trait description in forming a new impression. *Journal of Experimental Social Psychology, 21,* 421–439.

Schul, Y., & Burnstein, E. (1985b). When discounting fails: Conditions under which individuals use discredited information in making a judgment. *Journal of Personality and Social Psychology, 49,* 894–903.

Schul, Y., Burnstein, E., & Martinez, J. (1983). The informational basis of social judgments: Under what conditions are inconsistent trait descriptions processed as easily as consistent ones? *European Journal of Social Psychology, 13,* 143–151.

Schulz, R., & Brenner, G. (1977). Relocation of the aged: A review and theoretical analysis. *Journal of Gerontology, 32,* 323–333.

Schuman, H. (1983). Survey research and the fundamental attribution error. *Personality and Social Psychology Bulletin, 9*, 103–103.

Schuman, H., & Johnson, M. P. (1976). Attitudes and behavior. *Annual Review of Sociology, 2*, 161–207.

Schuman, H., & Ludwig, J. (1983). The norm of even-handedness in surveys as in life. *American Sociological Review, 48*, 112–120.

Schumer, R. (1973). Context effects in impression formation as a function of the ambiguity of test traits. *European Journal of Social Psychology, 3*, 333–338.

Schuster, B., Forsterling, F., & Weiner, B. (1989). Perceiving the causes of success and failure: A cross-cultural examination of attributional concepts. *Journal of Cross-Cultural Psychology, 20*, 191–213.

Schutte, N. S., Kenrick, D. T., & Sadalla, E. K. (1985). The search for predictable settings: Situational prototypes, constraint, and behavioral variation. *Journal of Personality and Social Psychology, 49*, 121–128.

Schwartz, G. E., Davidson, R. J., & Pugash, E. (1976). Voluntary control of patterns of EEG parietal asymmetry. *Psychophysiology, 13*, 498–504.

Schwartz, G. E., Weinberger, D. A., & Singer, J. A. (1981). Cardiovascular differentiation of happiness, sadness, anger, and fear following imagery and exercise. *Psychonomic Medicine, 43*, 343–364.

Schwartz, S. H. (1978). Temporal instability as a moderator of the attitude-behavior relationship. *Journal of Personality and Social Psychology, 36*, 715–724.

Schwartz, S. H., & Inbar-Saban, N. (1988). Value self-confrontation as a method to aid in weight loss. *Journal of Personality and Social Psychology, 54*, 396–404.

Schwartz, S. H., & Tessler, R. C. (1972). A test of a model for reducing measured attitude-behavior discrepancies. *Journal of Personality and Social Psychology, 24*, 225–236.

Schwarz, N. (1990). Feelings as information. In R. Sorrentino & E. T. Higgins (Eds.), *Handbook of motivation and cognition.* (Vol. 2, pp. 527–561). New York: Guilford.

Schwarz, N., & Clore, G. L. (1988). How do I feel about it? The informative function of affective states. In K. Fiedler & J. Forgas (Eds.), *Affect, cognition, and social behavior* (pp. 44–62). Toronto, Canada: Hogrefe.

Schwarz, N., Strack, F., Hilton, D., & Naderer, G. (1991). Base-rates, representativeness, and the logic of conversation. *Social cognition, 9*, 67–84.

Schwarz, N., Strack, F. Kommer, D., & Wagner, D. (1987). Soccer, rooms, and the quality of your life: Mood effects on judgments of satisfaction with life in general and with specific domains. *European Journal of Social Psychology, 17*, 69–79.

Schwarz, N., & Wyer, R. S., Jr. (1985). Effects of rank ordering stimuli on magnitude ratings of these and other stimuli. *Journal of Experimental Social Psychology, 21*, 30–46.

Scott, W. A., Osgood, D. W., & Peterson, C. (1979). *Cognitive structure: Theory and measurement of individual differences.* Washington, DC: Winston.

Sears, D. O. (1965). Biased indoctrination and selectivity of exposure to new information. *Sociometry, 28*, 363–376.

Sears, D. O. (1968). The paradox of de facto selective exposure without preferences for supportive information. In R. P. Abelson, et al. (Eds.), *Theories of cognitive consistency: A sourcebook* (pp. 777–787). Chicago: Rand McNally.

Sears, D. O. (1983). The person-positivity bias. *Journal of Personality and Social Psychology, 44*, 233–240.

Sears, D. O., Huddie, L., & Schaffer, L. G. (1986). A schematic variant of symbolic politics theory, as applied to racial and gender equality. In R. R. Lau & D. O. Sears (Eds.), *Political cognition* (pp. 159–202). Hillsdale, NJ: Erlbaum.

Sears, D. O., Tyler, T. R., Citrin, J., & Kinder, D. R. (1978). Political system support and public response to the energy crisis. *American Journal of Political Science, 22*, 56–82.

Sears, D. O., & Whitney, R. F. (1973). Political persuasion. In I. de Sola Pool, F. W. Frey, W. Schramm, N. Maccoby, & E. B. Parker (Eds.), *Handbook of communication* (pp. 253–289). Chicago: Rand McNally.

Secord, P. F. (1958). Facial features and inference processes in interpersonal perception. In R. Tagiuri & L. Petrullo (Eds.), *Person perception and interpersonal behavior* (pp. 300–315). Palo Alto, CA: Stanford University Press.

Secord, P. F. (1959). Stereotyping and favorableness in the perception of Negro faces. *Journal of Abnormal and Social Psychology, 59*, 309–321.

Secord, P. F., Bevan, W., & Katz, B. (1956). Perceptual accentuation and the Negro stereotype. *Journal of Abnormal and Social Psychology, 53*, 78–83.

Sedikides, C., & Ostrom, T. M. (1988). Are person categories used when organizing information about unfamiliar sets of persons? *Social Cognition, 6*, 252–267.

Seeman, M., & Evans, J. W. (1962). Alienation and learning in a hospital setting. *American Sociological Review, 27*, 772–782.

Segal, Z. V. (1988). Appraisal of the self-schema construct in cognitive models of depression. *Psychological Bulletin, 103*, 147–162.

Seligman, M. E. P., Abramson, L. Y., Semmel, A., & Von Baeyer, C. (1979). Depressive attributional style. *Journal of Abnormal Psychology, 88*, 242–247.

Semin, G. R., & Fiedler, K. (1988). The cognitive functions of linguistic categories in describing persons: Social cognition and language. *Journal of Personality and Social Psychology, 54*, 558–568.

Semin, G. R., & Manstead, A. S. R. (1983). *The accountability of conduct: A social psychological analysis*. London: Academic Press.

Sentis, K. P., & Burnstein, E. (1979). Remembering schema consistent information: Effects of a balance schema on recognition memory. *Journal of Personality and Social Psychology, 37*, 2200–2211.

Seta, C. E., Seta, J. J., Donaldson, S., & Wang, M. A. (1988). The effects of evaluation on organizational processing. *Personality and Social Psychology Bulletin, 14*, 604–609.

Seta, J. J., & Seta, C. E. (1987). Payment and value: The generation of an evaluation standard and its effect on value. *Journal of Experimental Social Psychology, 23*, 285–301.

Shallice, T. (1972). Dual functions of consciousness. *Psychological Review, 79*, 383–393.

Shallice, T. (1978). The dominant action system: An information-processing approach to consciousness. In K. S. Pope & J. L. Singer (Eds.), *The stream of consciousness: Scientific investigations into the flow of human experience* (pp. 117–157). New York: Plenum.

Shapiro, J. P. (1988). Relationships between dimensions of depressive experience and evaluative beliefs about people in general. *Personality and Social Psychology Bulletin, 14*, 388–400.

Shapiro, P. N., & Penrod, S. (1986). Meta-analysis of facial identification studies. *Psychological Bulletin, 100*, 139–156.

Shaver, K. G. (1970a). Defensive attribution: Effects of severity and relevance on the responsibility assigned for an accident. *Journal of Personality and Social Psychology, 14*, 101–113.

Shaver, K. G. (1970b). Redress and conscientiousness in the attribution of responsibility for accidents. *Journal of Experimental Social Psychology, 6*, 100–110.

Shaver, K. G. (1975). *An introduction to attribution processes*. Cambridge, MA: Winthrop Publishing.

Shaver, K. G. (1985). *The attribution of blame: Causality, responsibility, and blameworthiness*. New York: Springer-Verlag.

Shaver, K. G., & Drown, D. (1986). On causality, responsibility, and self-blame: A theoretical note. *Journal of Personality and Social Psychology, 50*, 697–702.

Shaver, P. (Ed.) (1984). *Review of personality and social psychology: Vol. 5. Emotions, relationships, and health*. Beverly Hills, CA: Sage.

Shaver, P., Schwartz, J., Kirson, D., & O'Connor, C. (1987). Emotion knowledge: Further exploration of a prototype approach. *Journal of Personality and Social Psychology, 52*, 1061–1086.

Shavitt, S. (1989). Operationalizing functional theories of attitude. In A. R. Pratkanis, S. J. Breckler, & A. G. Greenwald (Eds.), *Attitude structure and function* (pp. 311–338). Hillsdale, NJ: Erlbaum.

Shaw, M. E. (1971). *Group dynamics*. New York: McGraw-Hill.

Shedler, J., & Manis, M. (1986). Can the availability heuristic explain vividness effects? *Journal of Personality and Social Psychology, 51*, 26–36.

Shepard, R. N., & Podgorny, P. (1978). Cognitive processes that resemble perceptual processes. In W. K. Estes (Ed.), *Handbook of learning and cognitive processes: Vol. 5. Human information processing.* (pp. 189–237). Hillsdale, NJ: Erlbaum.

Shepperd, J. A., & Arkin, R. M. (1989a). Determinants of self-handicapping: Task importance and the effects of preexisting handicaps on self-generated handicaps. *Personality and Social Psychology Bulletin, 15*, 101–112.

Shepperd, J. A., & Arkin, R. M. (1989b). Self-handicapping: The moderating roles of public self-consciousness and task importance. *Personality and Social Psychology Bulletin, 15*, 252–265.

Shepperd, J. A., & Arkin, R. M. (1990). Shyness and self-presentation. In R. Crozier (Ed.), *Shyness and embarrassment: Perspectives from social psychology.* New York: Cambridge University Press.

Sherer, M., & Rogers, R. W. (1984). The role of vivid information in fear appeals and attitude change. *Journal of Research in Personality, 18*, 321–334.

Sherif, C. W., Kelly, M., Rodgers, H. L., Sarup, G., & Tittler, B. (1973). Personal involvement, social judgment, and action. *Journal of Personality and Social Psychology, 27*, 311–327.

Sherif, M., Harvey, O. J., White, B. J., Hood, W. R., & Sherif, C. W. (1961). *Intergroup conflict and cooperation: The Robber's Cave experiment.* Norman: University of Oklahoma Press.

Sherif, M., & Hovland, C. I. (1961). *Social judgment: Assimilation and contrast effects in communcation and attitude change.* New Haven, CT: Yale University Press.

Sherman, R. D., & Titus, W. (1982). Covariation information and cognitive processing: Effects of causal implications on memory. *Journal of Personality and Social Psychology, 42,* 989–1000.

Sherman, S. J. (1980). On the self-erasing nature of errors of prediction. *Journal of Personality and Social Psychology, 39,* 211–221.

Sherman, S. J. (1987). Cognitive processes in the formation, change, and expression of attitudes. In M. P. Zanna, J. M. Olson, & C. P. Herman (Eds.), *Social influence: The Ontario Symposium* (Vol. 5, pp. 75–106). Hillsdale, NJ: Erlbaum.

Sherman, S. J., Chassin, L., Presson, C. C., & Agostinelli, G. (1984). The role of the evaluation and similarity principles in the false consensus effect. *Journal of Personality and Social Psychology, 47,* 1244–1262.

Sherman, S. J., Cialdini, R. B., Schwartzman, D. F., & Reynolds, K. D. (1985). Imagining can heighten or lower the perceived likelihood of contracting a disease: The mediating effect of ease of imagery. *Personality and Social Psychology Bulletin, 11,* 118–127.

Sherman, S. J., & Corty, E. (1984). Cognitive heuristics. In R. S. Wyer, Jr., & T. K. Srull (Eds.), *Handbook of social cognition* (Vol. 1, pp. 189–286). Hillsdale, NJ: Erlbaum.

Sherman, S. J., Hamilton, D. L., & Roskos-Ewoldsen, D. R. (1989). Attenuation of illusory correlation. *Personality and Social Psychology Bulletin, 15,* 559–571.

Sherman, S. J., Judd, C. M., & Park, B. (1989). Social cognition. *Annual Review of Psychology, 40,* 281–326.

Sherman, S. J., Mackie, D. M., & Driscoll, D. M. (1990). Priming and the differential use of dimensions in evaluation. *Personality and Social Psychology Bulletin, 16,* 405–418.

Sherman, S. J., Presson, C. C., & Chassin, L. (1984). Mechanisms underlying the false consensus effect: The special role of threats to the self. *Personality and Social Psychology Bullentin, 10,* 127–138.

Sherman, S. J., Skov, R. B., Hervitz, E. F., & Stock, C. B. (1981). The effects of explaining hypothetical future events: From possibility to probability to actuality and beyond. *Journal of Experimental Social Psychology, 17,* 142–158.

Sherman, S. J., Zehner, K. S., Johnson, J., & Hirt, E. R. (1983). Social explanation: The role of timing, set, and recall on subjective likelihood estimates. *Journal of Personality and Social Psychology, 44,* 1127–1143.

Shiffrin, R. M., & Schneider, W. (1977). Controlled and automatic human information processing: II. Perceptual learning, automatic attending, and general theory. *Psychological Review, 84,* 127–190.

Shoben, E. J. (1984). Semantic and episodic memory. In R. S. Wyer, Jr., & T. K. Srull (Eds.), *Handbook of social cognition* (Vol. 2, pp. 213–231). Hillsdale, NJ: Erlbaum.

Showers, C., & Cantor, N. (1985). Social cognition: A look at motivated strategies. *Annual Review of Psychology, 36,* 275–305.

Shweder, R. A. (Ed.) (1980). *Fallible judgment in behavioral research: New directions for methodology of social and behavioral science* (Vol. 4). San Francisco: Jossey-Bass.

Sicoly, F., & Ross, M. (1977). Facilitation of ego-biased attributions by means of self-serving observer feedback. *Journal of Personality and Social Psychology, 35,* 734–741.

Sidanius, J. (1988). Political sophistication and political deviance: A structural equation examination of context theory. *Journal of Personality and Social Psychology, 55,* 37–51.

Silka, L. (1984). Intuitive perceptions of change: An overlooked phenomenon in person perception? *Personality and Social Psychology Bulletin, 10,* 180–190.

Silka, L. (1989). *Intuitive judgments of change.* New York: Springer-Verlag.

Silver, R. L., & Wortman, C. B. (1980). Coping with undesirable life events. In J. Garber & M. E. P. Seligman (Eds.), *Human helplessness: Theory and applications.* (pp. 279–340). New York: Academic Press.

Silverman, I. (1964). Self-esteem and differential responsiveness to success and failure. *Journal of Abnormal and Social Psychology, 69,* 115–119.

Simmons, C. H., & Lerner, M. J. (1968). Altruism as a search for justice. *Journal of Personality and Social Psychology, 9,* 216–225.

Simon, B., & Brown, R. (1987). Perceived intragroup homogeneity in minority-majority contexts. *Journal of Personality and Social Psychology, 53,* 703–711.

Simon, H. A. (1967). Motivational and emotional controls of cognition. *Psychological Review, 74,* 29–39.

Simon, H. A. (1980). Problem solving and education. In D. T. Tuma & F. Reif (Eds.), *Problem solving and education: Issues in teaching and research* (pp. 81–96). Hillsdale, NJ: Erlbaum.

Simon, H. A. (1982). Comments. In M. S. Clark & S. T. Fiske (Eds.), *Affect and cognition: The 17th Annual Carnegie Symposium on Cognition* (pp. 333–342). Hillsdale, NJ: Erlbaum.

Sinclair, R. C., Mark, M. M., & Shotland, R. L. (1987). Construct accessibility and generalizability across response categories. *Personality and Social Psychology Bulletin, 13,* 239–252.

Singer, J. A., & Salovey, P. (1988). Mood and memory: Evaluating the network theory of affect. *Clinical Psychology Review, 8,* 211–251.

Singer, J. L. (1966). *Daydreaming.* New York: Random House.

Singer, J.L. (1978). Experimental studies of daydreaming and the stream of thought. In K. S. Pope & J. L. Singer (Eds.), *The stream of consciousness: Scientific investigations into the flow of human experience* (pp. 187–223). New York: Plenum.

Singer, J. L. (1984). The private personality. *Personality and Social Psychology Bulletin, 10,* 7–30.

Singer, J. L. (1985). Transference and the human condition: A cognitive-affective perspective. *Psychoanalytic Psychology, 2,* 189–219.

Singer, J. L. (1988). Reinterpreting the transference. In D. C. Turk & P. Salovey (Eds.), *Reasoning, inference, and judgment in clinical psychology* (pp. 182–205). New York: Free Press.

Singerman, K. G., Borkovec, T. D., & Baron, R. S. (1976). Failure of a misattribution therapy manipulation with a clinically relevant target behavior. *Behavior Therapy, 7,* 306–313.

Sivacek, J., & Crano, W. D. (1982). Vested interest as a moderator of attitude-behavior consistency. *Journal of Personality and Social Psychology, 43,* 210–221.

Skinner, B. F. (1957). *Verbal behavior.* New York: Appleton-Century-Crofts.

Skinner, B. F. (1963). Operant behavior. *American Psychologist, 18,* 503–515.

Skov, R. B., & Sherman, S. J. (1986). Information-gathering processes: Diagnosticity, hypothesis-confirmatory strategies, and perceived hypothesis confirmation. *Journal of Experimental Social Psychology, 22,* 93–121.

Skowronski, J. J., & Carlston, D. E. (1987). Social judgment and social memory: The role of cue diagnosticity in negativity, positivity, and extremity biases. *Journal of Personality and Social Psychology, 52,* 689–699.

Skowronski, J. J., & Carlston, D. E. (1989). Negativity and extremity biases in impression formation: A review of explanations. *Psychological Bulletin, 105,* 131–142.

Skowronski, J. J., & Carlston, D. E. (1990). *The effect of category diagnosticity and type of processing on a cue's resistance to contradictory information.* Unpublished manuscript.

Slivken, K. E., & Buss, A. H. (1984). Misattribution and speech anxiety. *Journal of Personality and Social Psychology, 47,* 396–402.

Slovic, P., & Fischhoff, B. (1977). On the psychology of experimental surprises. *Journal of Experimental Psychology: Human Perception and Performance, 3,* 544–551.

Slovic, P., Fischhoff, B., & Lichtenstein, S. (1976). Cognitive processes and societal risk taking. In J. S. Carroll & J. W. Payne (Eds.), *Cognition and social behavior* (pp. 165–184). Hillsdale, NJ: Erlbaum.

Slovic, P., Fischhoff, B., & Lichtenstein, S. (1977). Behavioral decision theory. *Annual Review of Psychology, 28,* 1–39.

Slovic, P., Fischhoff, B., & Lichtenstein, S. (1982). Facts versus fears: Understanding perceived risk. In D. Kahneman, P. Slovic, & A. Tversky (Eds.), *Judgment under uncertainty: Heuristics and biases* (pp. 463–489). New York: Cambridge University Press.

Slowiaczek, L. M., Klayman, J., Sherman, S. J., & Skov, B. (1989). *Information selection and use in hypothesis testing: What is a good question, what is a good answer.* Unpublished manuscript.

Slusher, M. P., & Anderson, C. A. (1989). Belief perseverance and self-defeating behavior. In R. C. Curtis (Ed.), *Self-defeating behaviors: Experimental research, clinical impressions, and practical implications* (pp. 11–40). New York: Plenum.

Smedslund, J. (1963). The concept of correlation in adults. *Scandinavian Journal of Psychology, 4,* 165–173.

Smith, C. A. (1989). Dimensions of appraisal and physiological response in emotion. *Journal of Personality and Social Psychology, 56,* 339–353.

Smith, C. A., & Ellsworth, P. C. (1985). Patterns of cognitive appraisal in emotion. *Journal of Personality and Social Psychology, 48,* 813–838.

Smith, C. A., & Ellsworth, P. C. (1987). Patterns of cognitive appraisal and emotion related to taking an exam. *Journal of Personality and Social Psychology, 52,* 475–488.

Smith, D. A., & Graesser, A. C. (1981). Memory for actions in scripted activities as a function of typicality, retention interval, and retrieval task. *Memory and Cognition, 9,* 550–559.

Smith, E. E., Adams, N., & Schorr, D. (1978). Fact retrieval and the paradox of interference. *Cognitive Psychology, 10,* 438–464.

Smith, E. E., & Medin, D. L. (1981). *Categories and concepts.* Cambridge, MA: Harvard University Press.

Smith, E. E., Shoben, E. J., & Rips, L. J. (1974). Structure and process in semantic memory: A featural model for semantic decisions. *Psychological Review, 81,* 214–241.

Smith, E. R. (1984). Model of social inference processes. *Psychological Review, 91,* 392–413.

Smith, E. R. (1988). Category accessibility effects in simulated exemplar-based memory. *Journal of Experimental Social Psychology, 24,* 448–463.

Smith, E. R. (1989a). Procedural efficiency and on-line social judgments. In J. Bassili (Ed.), *On-line cognition in person perceptions* (pp. 19–38). Hillsdale, NJ: Erlbaum.

Smith, E. R. (1989b). Procedural efficiency: General and specific components and effects on social judgment. *Journal of Experimental Social Psychology, 25,* 500–523.

Smith, E. R. (1990). Content and process specificity in the effects of prior experiences. In T. K. Srull & R. S. Wyer, Jr. (Eds.), *Advances in social cognition* (Vol. 3, pp. 1–59). Hillsdale, NJ: Erlbaum.

Smith, E. R., & Branscombe, N. R. (1987). Procedurally mediated social inferences: The case of category accessibility effects. *Journal of Experimental Social Psychology, 23,* 361–382.

Smith, E. R., & Branscombe, N. R. (1988). Category accessibility as implicit memory. *Journal of Experimental Social Psychology, 24,* 490–504.

Smith, E. R., Branscombe, N. R., & Bormann, C. (1988). Generality of the effects of practice on social judgment tasks. *Journal of Personality and Social Psychology, 54,* 385–395.

Smith, E. R., & Lerner, M. (1986). Development of automatism of social judgments. *Journal of Personality and Social Psychology, 50,* 246–259.

Smith, E. R., & Miller, F. D. (1978). Limits on perception of cognitive processes: A reply to Nisbett and Wilson. *Psychological Review, 85,* 355–362.

Smith, E. R., & Miller, F. D. (1979). Salience and the cognitive mediation of attribution. *Journal of Personality and Social Psychology, 37,* 2240–2252.

Smith, E. R., & Zarate, M. A. (1990). Exemplar and prototype use in social categorization. *Social Cognition.*

Smith, M. B., Bruner, J. S., & White, R. W. (1956). *Opinions and Personality.* New York: Wiley.

Smith, M. C. (1975). Children's use of the multiple sufficient cause schema in social perception. *Journal of Personality and Social Psychology, 32,* 737–747.

Smith, S. S., & Kihlstrom, J. F. (1987). When is a schema not a schema? The "big five" traits as cognitive structures. *Social Cognition, 5,* 26–57.

Smith, T. W., Synder, C. R., & Handelsman, M. M. (1982). On the self-serving function of an academic wooden leg: Test anxiety as a self-handicapping strategy. *Journal of Personality and Social Psychology, 42,* 314–321.

Smith, V. L., & Ellsworth, P. C. (1987). The social psychology of eyewitness accuracy: Leading questions and communicator expertise. *Journal of Applied Psychology, 72,* 294–300.

Snyder, C. R., & Fromkin, H. L. (1980). *Uniqueness: The human pursuit of difference.* New York: Plenum.

Snyder, C. R., & Higgins, R. L. (1988). Excuses: Their effective role in the negotiation of reality. *Psychological Bulletin, 104,* 23–35.

Snyder, C. R., Higgins, R. L., & Stucky, R. J. (1983). *Excuses: Masquerades in search of grace.* New York: Wiley-Interscience.

Snyder, C. R., Ingram, R. E., Handelsman, M. M., & Wells, D. S. (1982). Desire for personal feedback: Who wants it and what does it mean for psychotherapy? *Journal of Personality, 50,* 316–330.

Snyder, C. R., & Smith, T. W. (1982). Symptoms as self-handicapping strate-
gies: The virtues of old wine in a new bottle. In G. Weary & H. Mirels (Eds.),
Integrations of clinical and social psychology (pp. 104–127). New York: Oxford
University Press.

Snyder, C. R., Smith, T. W., Augelli, R. W., & Ingram, R. E. (1985). On the
self-serving function of social anxiety: Shyness as a self-handicapping strategy. *Journal of Personality and Social Psychology, 48,* 970–980.

Snyder, M. (1972). Individual differences and the self-control of expressive behavior. *Dissertation Abstracts International, 33,* 4533A–4534A.

Snyder, M. (1974). The self-monitoring of expressive behavior. *Journal of Personality and Social Psychology, 30,* 526–537.

Snyder, M. (1976). Attribution and behavior: Social perception and social causation. In J. H. Harvey, W. J. Ickes, & R. F. Kidd (Eds.), *New directions in
attribution research* (Vol. 1, pp. 53–72). Hillsdale, NJ: Erlbaum.

Snyder, M. (1977). Impression management. In L. S. Wrightsman (Ed.), *Social
psychology in the seventies* (pp. 115–145). New York: Wiley.

Snyder, M. (1979). Self-monitoring processes. In L. Berkowitz (Ed.), *Advances in
experimental social psychology* (Vol. 12, pp. 86–131). New York: Academic
Press.

Snyder, M. (1982). When believing means doing: Creating links between atti-
tudes and behavior. In M. P. Zanna, E. T. Higgins, & C. P. Herman (Eds.),
Consistency in social behavior: The Ontario symposium (Vol. 2, pp. 105–130).
Hillsdale, NJ: Erlbaum.

Snyder, M. (1984). When belief creates reality. In L. Berkowitz (Ed.), *Advances in
experimental social psychology* (Vol. 18, pp. 248–306). New York: Academic
Press.

Snyder, M., Berscheid, E., & Matwychuk, A. (1988). Orientations toward personnel selection: Differential reliance on appearance and personality. *Journal
of Personality and Social Psychology, 54,* 972–979.

Snyder, M., & Campbell, B. H. (1982). Self-monitoring: The self in action. In J.
Suls (Ed.), *Psychological perspectives on the self* (Vol. 1, pp. 185–208). Hillsdale,
NJ: Erlbaum.

Snyder, M., Campbell, B. H., & Preston, E. (1982) Testing hypothesis about human nature: Assessing the accuracy of social stereotypes. *Social Cognition, 1,*
256–272.

Snyder, M., & Cantor, N. (1979). Testing hypotheses about other people: The
use of historical knowledge. *Journal of Experimental Social Psychology, 15,* 330–342.

Snyder, M., & Cantor, N. (1980). Thinking about ourselves and others: Self-
monitoring and social knowledge. *Journal of Personality and Social Psychology,
39,* 222–234.

Snyder, M., & DeBono, K. G. (1985). Appeals to image and claims about quality: Understanding the psychology of advertising. *Journal of Personality and
Social Psychology, 49,* 586–597.

Snyder, M., & DeBono, K. G. (1987). A functional approach to attitudes and
persuasion. In M. P. Zanna, J. M. Olson, & C. P. Herman (Eds.), *Social influence: The Ontario Symposium* (Vol. 5, pp. 107–125). Hillsdale, NJ: Erlbaum.

Snyder, M., & DeBono, K. G. (1989). Understanding the functions of attitudes:
Lessons from personality and social behavior. In A. R. Pratkanis, S. J.
Breckler, & A. G. Greenwald (Eds.), *Attitude structure and function* (pp. 339–
360). Hillsdale, NJ: Erlbaum.

Snyder, M., & Gangestad, S. (1981). Hypothesis-testing processes. In J. H. Harvey, W. Ickes, & R. F. Kidd (Eds.), *New directions in attribution research* (Vol. 3, pp. 171–198). Hillsdale, NJ: Erlbaum.

Snyder, M., & Gangestad, S. (1982). Choosing social situations: Two investigations of self-monitoring processes. *Journal of Personality and Social Psychology, 43,* 123–135.

Snyder, M., & Gangestad, S. (1986). On the nature of self-monitoring: Matters of assessment, matters of validity. *Journal of Personality and Social Psychology, 51,* 125–139.

Snyder, M., & Ickes, W. (1985). Personality and social behavior. In G. Lindzey & E. Aronson (Eds.), *The handbook of social psychology* (3rd ed., Vol. 2, pp. 883–948). New York: Random House.

Snyder, M., & Kendzierski, D. (1982). Acting on one's attitudes: Procedures for linking attitude and behavior. *Journal of Experimental Social Psychology, 18,* 165–183.

Snyder, M., & Monson, T. C. (1975). Persons, situations, and the control of social behavior. *Journal of Personality and Social Psychology, 32,* 637–644.

Snyder, M., & Simpson, J. A., (1984). Self-monitoring and dating relationships. *Journal of Personality and Social Psychology, 47,* 1281–1291.

Snyder, M., & Skrypnek, B. J. (1981). Testing hypotheses about the self: Assessments of job suitability. *Journal of Personality, 49,* 193–211.

Snyder, M., & Swann, W. B., Jr. (1976). When actions reflect attitudes: The politics of impression management. *Journal of Personality and Social Psychology, 34,* 1034–1042.

Snyder, M., & Swann, W. B., Jr. (1978a). Behavioral confirmation in social interaction: From social perception to social reality. *Journal of Experimental Social Psychology, 14,* 148–162.

Snyder, M., & Swann, W. B., Jr. (1978b). Hypothesis-testing processes in social interaction. *Journal of Personality and Social Psychology, 36,* 1202–1212.

Snyder, M., & Tanke, E. D. (1976). Behavior and attitude: Some people are more consistent than others. *Journal of Personality, 44,* 501–517.

Snyder, M., Tanke, E. D., & Berscheid, E. (1977). Social perception and interpersonal behavior: On the self-fulfilling nature of social stereotypes. *Journal of Personality and Social Psychology, 35,* 656–666.

Snyder, M., & Uranowitz, S. W. (1978). Reconstructing the past: Some cognitive consequences of person perception. *Journal of Personality and Social Psychology, 36,* 941–950.

Snyder, M. L., & Frankel, A. (1989). Making things harder for yourself: Pride and joy. In R. C. Curtis (Ed.), *Self-defeating behaviors: Experimental research, clinical impressions, and practical implications* (pp. 131–157). New York: Plenum.

Snyder, M. L., & Jones, E. E. (1974). Attitude attribution when behavior is constrained. *Journal of Experimental Social Psychology, 10,* 585–600.

Snyder, M. L., Kleck, R. E., Strenta, A., & Mentzer, S. J. (1979). Avoidance of the handicapped: An attributional ambiguity analysis. *Journal of Personality and Social Psychology, 37,* 2297–2306.

Snyder, M. L., Stephan, W. G., & Rosenfield, D. (1976). Egotism and attribution. *Journal of Personality and Social Psychology, 33,* 435–441.

Snyder, M. L., Stephan, W. G., & Rosenfield, D. (1978). Attributional egotism.

In J. H. Harvey, W. Ickes, & R. F. Kidd (Eds.), *New directions in attribution research* (Vol. 2, pp. 91–120). Hillsdale, NJ: Erlbaum.

Snyder, M. L., & Wicklund, R. A. (1981). Attribute ambiguity. In J. H. Harvey, W. Ickes, & R. F. Kidd (Eds.), *New directions in attribution research* (Vol. 3, pp. 199–224). Hillsdale, NJ: Erlbaum.

Sohn, D. (1984). The empirical base of Trope's position on achievement-task choice: A critique. *Motivation and Emotion, 8,* 91–107.

Solomon, S., Holmes, D. S., & McCaul, K. D. (1980). Behavioral control over aversive events: Does control that requires effort reduce anxiety and physiological arousal? *Journal of Personality and Social Psychology, 39,* 729–736.

Sommers, S. (1981). Emotionality reconsidered: The role of cognition in emotional responsiveness. *Journal of Personality and Social Psychology, 41,* 553–561.

Sorrentino, R. M., Bobocel, D. R., Gitta, M. Z., Olson, J. M., & Hewitt, E. L. (1988). Uncertainty orientation and persuasion: Individual differences in the effects of personal relevance on social judgments. *Journal of Personality and Social Psychology, 55,* 357–371.

Sorrentino, R. M., & Hancock, R. D. (1987). The role of information and affective value for social influence: A case for the study of individual differences. In M. P. Zanna, J. M. Olson, & C. P. Herman (Eds.), *Social influence: The Ontario Symposium* (Vol. 5, pp. 244–268). Hillsdale, NJ: Erlbaum.

Sorrentino, R. M., & Roney, C. J. R. (1986). Uncertainty orientation, achievement-related motivation, and task diagnosticity as determinants of task performance. *Social Cognition, 4,* 420–436.

Sorrentino, R. M., & Short, J. C. (1986). Uncertainty orientation, motivation, and cognition. In R. M. Sorrentino & E. T. Higgins (Eds.), *Handbook of motivation and cognition: Foundations of social behavior* (pp. 379–403). New York: Guilford Press.

Sorrentino, R. M., Short, J. C., & Raynor, J. O. (1984). Uncertainty orientation: Implications for affective and cognitive views of achievement behavior. *Journal of Personality and Social Psychology, 46,* 189–206.

Sousa, E., & Leyens, J-P. (1987). A priori vs. spontaneous models of attribution: The case of gender and achievement. *British Journal of Social Psychology, 26,* 281–292.

Spangler, E., Gordon, M. A., & Pipkin, R. M. (1978). Token women: An empirical test of the Kanter hypothesis. *American Journal of Sociology, 84,* 160–170.

Spanos, N. P., Horton, C., & Chaves, J. F. (1975). The effects of two cognitive strategies on pain threshold. *Journal of Abnormal Psychology, 84,* 677–681.

Spears, R., van der Plight, J., & Eiser, J. R. (1986). Generalizing the illusory correlation effect. *Journal of Personality and Social Psychology, 51,* 1127–1134.

Speilman, L. A., Pratto, F., & Bargh, J. A. (1988). Are one's moods, attitudes, evaluations, and emotions out of control? *American Behavioral Scientist, 31,* 296–311.

Spence, J. T. (1984). Masculinity, femininity, and gender-related traits: A conceptual analysis and critique of current research. *Progress Experimental Personality Research, 13,* 1–97.

Spence, J. T. & Helmreich, R. L. (1981). Androgyny versus gender schema: A comment on Bem's gender schema theory. *Psychological Review, 88,* 365–368.

Spence, J. T., Helmreich, R. L., & Stapp, J. (1975). Ratings of self and peers on sex-role attributes and their relations to self-esteem and conceptions of masculinity and femininity. *Journal of Personality and Social Psychology, 32,* 29–39.

Sprangers, M., van den Brink, W., van Heerden, J., & Hoogstraten, J. (1987). A constructive replication of White's alleged refutation of Nisbett and Wilson and of Bem: Limitations on verbal reports of internal events. *Journal of Experimental Social Psychology, 23,* 302–310.

Srull, T. K. (1981). Person memory: Some tests of associative storage and retrieval models. *Journal of Experimental Psychology: Human Learning and Memory, 7,* 440–462.

Srull, T. K. (1983). Organizational and retrieval processes in person memory: An examination of processing objectives, presentation format, and the possible role of self-generated retrieval cues. *Journal of Personality and Social Psychology, 44,* 1157–1170.

Srull, T. K., & Brand, J. F. (1983). Memory for information about persons: The effect of encoding operations on subsequent retrieval. *Journal of Verbal Learning and Verbal Behavior, 22,* 219–230.

Srull, T. K., & Gaelick, L. (1983). General principles and individual differences in the self as a habitual reference point. *Social Cognition, 2,* 108–121.

Srull, T. K., Lichenstein, M., & Rothbart, M. (1985). Associative storage and retrieval processes in person memory. *Journal of Experimental Psychology: Learning, Memory, and Cognition, 11,* 316–345.

Srull, T. K., & Wyer, R. S., Jr. (1979). The role of category accessibility in the interpretation of information about persons: Some determinants and implications. *Journal of Personality and Social Psychology, 37,* 1660–1672.

Srull, T. K., & Wyer, R. S., Jr. (1980). Category accessibility and social perception: Some implications for the study of person memory and interpersonal judgments. *Journal of Personality and Social Psychology, 38,* 841–856.

Srull, T. K., & Wyer, R. S., Jr. (1986). The role of chronic and temporary goals in social information processing. In R. M. Sorrentino & E. T. Higgins (Eds.), *Handbook of motivation and cognition: Foundations of social behavior* (pp. 503–549). New York: Guilford Press.

Srull, T. K., & Wyer, R. S., Jr. (Eds.) (1988). *Advances in soicial cognition* (Vol. 1). Hillsdale, NJ: Erlbaum.

Srull, T. K., & Wyer, R. S., Jr. (1989). Person memory and judgment. *Psychological Review, 96,* 58–83.

Staats, A. W., & Staats, C. K. (1958). Attitudes established by classical conditioning. *Journal of Abnormal and Social Psychology, 57,* 37–40.

Staats, A. W., Staats, C. K., & Crawford, H. L. (1962). First-order conditioning of meaning and the parallel conditioning of GSR. *Journal of General Psychology, 67,* 159–167.

Stang, D. J. (1974). Methodological factors in mere exposure research. *Psychological Bulletin, 81,* 1014–1025.

Stangor, C. (1988). Stereotype accessibility and information processing. *Personality and Social Psychology Bulletin, 14,* 694–708.

Stangor, C. (1990). Arousal, accessibility of trait constructs, and person perception. *Journal of Experimental Social Psychology, 26,* 305–321.

Stangor, C., & Ruble, D. N. (1989). Strength of expectancies and memory for social information: What we remember depends on how much we know. *Journal of Experimental Social Psychology, 25,* 18–35.

Steele, C. M. (1988). The psychology of self-affirmation: Sustaining the integrity of the self. In L. Berkowitz (Ed.), *Advances in experimental psychology* (Vol. 21, pp. 261–302). New York: Academic Press.

Steele, C. M., & Liu, T. J. (1983). Dissonance processes as self-affirmation. *Journal of Personality and Social Psychology, 45*, 5–19.

Steenbarger, B. N., & Aderman, D. (1979). Objective self-awareness as a nonaversive state: Effect of anticipating discrepancy reduction. *Journal of Personality, 47*, 330–339.

Stein, J. (Ed.) (1982). *The Random House dictionary of the English language* (unabridged ed.). New York: Random House.

Stephan, W. G. (1987). The contact hypothesis in intergroup relations. In C. Hendrick (Ed.), *Review of personality and social psychology: Vol. 9. Group processes and intergroup relations* (pp. 13–40). Newbury Park, CA: Sage.

Stephan, W. G. (1989). A cognitive approach to stereotyping. In D. Bar-Tal, C. F. Graumann, A. W. Kruglanski, & W. Stroebe (Eds.), *Stereotypes and prejudice: Changing conceptions* (pp. 37–58). New York: Springer-Verlag.

Stephan, W. G., Berscheid, E., & Walster, E. (1971). Sexual arousal and heterosexual perception. *Journal of Personality and Social Psychology, 20*, 93–101.

Stephan, W. G., & Brigham, J. C. (Eds.) (1985). Intergroup contact. *Journal of Social Issues, 41* (3), 1–179.

Stephan, W. G., Rosenfield, D., & Stephan, C. (1976). Egotism in males and females. *Journal of Personality and Social Psychology, 34*, 1161–1167.

Stephenson, G. M., Abrams, D., Wagner, W., & Wade, G. (1986). Partners in recall: Collaborative order in the recall of a police interrogation. *British Journal of Social Psychology, 25*, 341–343.

Stephenson, G. M., Brandstatter, H., & Wagner, W. (1983). An experimental study of social performance and delay of the testimonial validity of story recall. *European Journal of Social Psychology, 13*, 175–191.

Stephenson, G. M., Clark, N. K., & Wade, G. S. (1986). Meetings make evidence? An experimental study of collaborative and individual recall of a stimulated police interrogation. *Journal of Personality and Social Psychology, 50*, 1113–1122.

Sterling, B., & Gaertner, S. L. (1984). The attribution of arousal and emergency helping: A bidirectional process. *Journal of Experimental Social Psychology, 20*, 586–596.

Stern, L. D., Marrs, S., Millar, M. G., & Cole, E. (1984). Processing time and the recall of inconsistent and consistent behaviors of individuals and groups. *Journal of Personality and Social Psychology, 47*, 253–262.

Sternthal, B., Dholakia, R., & Leavitt, C. (1978). The persuasive effect of source credibility: Tests of cognitive response. *Journal of Consumer Research, 4*, 252–260.

Stevens, L., & Jones, E. E. (1976). Defensive attribution and the Kelley cube. *Journal of Personality and Social Psychology, 34*, 809–820.

Stiff, J. B. (1986). Cognitive processing of persuasive message cues: A meta-analytic review of the effects of supporting information on attitudes. *Communication Monographs, 53*, 75–89.

Stiff, J. B., & Boster, F. J. (1987). Cognitive processing: Additional thoughts and a reply to Petty, Kasmer, Haugtvedt, and Cacioppo. *Communication Monographs, 54*, 250–256.

Stipek, D., Weiner, B., & Li, K. (1989). Testing some attribution-emotion relations in the People's Republic of China. *Journal of Personality and Social Psychology, 56*, 109–116.

Stoner, J. A. F. (1961). A comparison of individual and group decisions involving risk. Unpublished master's thesis, School of Industrial Management, Massachusetts Institute of Technology.

Storms, M. D. (1973). Videotape and the attribution process: Reversing actors' and observers' points of view. *Journal of Personality and Social Psychology, 27*, 165–175.

Storms, M. D., & McCaul, K. D. (1976). Attribution processes and emotional exacerbation of dysfunctional behavior. In J. H. Harvey, W. J. Ickes, & R. F. Kidd (Eds.), *New directions in attribution research* (Vol. 1, pp. 143–164). Hillsdale, NJ: Erlbaum.

Storms, M. D., & Nisbett, R. E. (1970). Insomnia and the attribution process. *Journal of Personality and Social Psychology, 16*, 319–328.

Stotland, E., & Blumenthal, A. L. (1964). The reduction of anxiety as a result of the expectation of making a choice. *Canadian Journal of Psychology, 18*, 139–145.

Stouffer, S. A., Suchman, E. A., DeVinney, L. C., Star, S. A., & Williams, R. M., Jr. (1949). *The American soldier: Vol. 1. Adjustment during army life*. Princeton, NJ: Princeton University Press.

Strack, F., Erber, R., & Wicklund, R. A. (1982). Effects of salience and time pressure on ratings of social causality. *Journal of Experimental Social psychology, 18*, 581–594.

Strack, F., Martin, L. L., & Schwarz, N. (1988). Priming and communication: Social determinants of information use in judgments of life satisfaction. *European Journal of Social Psychology, 18*.

Strack, F., Martin, L. L., & Stepper, S. (1988). Inhibiting and facilitating conditions of the human smile: A nonobtrusive test of the facial feedback hypothesis. *Journal of Personality and Social Psychology, 54*, 768–777.

Strack, F., Schwarz, N., & Gschneidinger, E. (1985). Happiness and reminiscing: The role of time perspective, affect, and mode of thinking. *Journal of Personality and Social Psychology, 49*, 1460–1469.

Strack, S., Blaney, P.H., Ganellen; R.J.; & Coyne, J.C. (1985). Pessimistic self-preoccupation, performance deficits, and depression. *Journal of Personality and Social Psychology, 49*, 1076–1085.

Stratton, P., Heard, D., Hanks, H. G. I., Munton, A. G., Brewin, C. R., & Davidson, C. (1986). Coding causal beliefs in natural discourse. *British Journal of Social Psychology, 25*, 299–313.

Strauman, T. J., & Higgins, E. T. (1987). Automatic activation of self-discrepancies and emotional syndromes: When cognitive structures influence affect. *Journal of Personality and Social Psychology, 53*, 1004–1014.

Strenta, A. C., & Kleck, R. E. (1984). Physical disability and the perception of social interaction: It's not what you look at but how you look at it. *Personality and Social Psychology Bulletin, 10*, 279–288.

Streufert, S. & Streufert, S. (1978). *Behavior in the complex environment*. Washington, DC: Winston.

Strickland, B. R. (1988). Internal-external expectancies and health-related behaviors. *Journal of Consulting and Clinical Psychology, 46*, 1192–1211.

Strongman, K. T. (1978). *The psychology of emotion*. New York: Wiley.

Strube, M. J., & Roemmele, L. A. (1985). Self-enhancement, self-assessment, and self-evaluative task choice. *Journal of Personality and Social Psychology, 49*, 981–993.

Sujan, M. (1985). Consumer knowledge: Effects on evaluation strategies mediating consumer judgments. *Journal of Consumer Research, 12*, 1–16.

Sullins, E. S. (1989). Perceptual salience as a function of nonverbal expressiveness. *Personality and Social Psychology Bulletin, 15*, 584–595.

Suls, J., & Fletcher, B. (1985). The relative efficacy of avoidant and nonavoidant coping strategies: A meta-analysis. *Health Psychology, 4*, 249–288.

Surber, C. F. (1981). Effects of information reliability in predicting task performance using ability and effort. *Journal of Personality and Social Psychology, 40*, 977–989.

Svenson, O. (1981). Are we all less risky and more skillful than our fellow drivers? *Acta Psychologica, 47*, 143–148.

Swann, W. B., Jr. (1983). Self-verification: Bringing social reality into harmony with the self. In J. Suls & A. G. Greenwald (Eds.), *Psychological perspectives on the self* (Vol. 2, pp. 33–66). Hillsdale, NJ: Erlbaum.

Swann, W. B., Jr. (1984). Quest for accuracy in person perception: A matter of pragmatics. *Psychological Review, 91*, 457–477.

Swann, W. B., Jr. (1987). Identity negotiation: Where two roads meet. *Journal of Personality and Social Psychology, 53*, 1038–1051.

Swann, W. B., Jr. (1990). To be known or to be adored? The interplay of self-enhancement and self-verification. In R. M. Sorrentino & E. T. Higgins (Eds.), *Handbook of motivation and cognition: Foundations of social behavior* (Vol. 2, pp. 408–448). New York: Guilford.

Swann, W. B., Jr., & Brown, J. D. (1990). From self to health: Self-verification and identity disruption. In B. Sarason, I. Sarason, & G. Pierce (Eds.), *Social support: An interactional view* (pp. 150–172). New York: Wiley.

Swann, W. B., Jr., & Ely, R. M. (1984). The battle of wills: Self-verification versus behavioral confirmation. *Journal of Personality and Social Psychology, 46*, 1287–1302.

Swann, W. B., Jr., & Giuliano, T. (1987). Confirmatory search strategies in social interaction: How, when, why, and with what consequences. *Journal of Consulting and Clinical Psychology, 5*, 511–524.

Swann, W. B., Jr., Giulano, T., & Wegner, D. M. (1982). Where leading questions can lead: The power of conjecture in social interaction. *Journal of Personality and Social Psychology, 42*, 1025–1035.

Swann, W. B., Jr., Griffin, J. J., Predmore, S., & Gaines, B. (1987). The cognitive-affective crossfire: When self-consistency confronts self-enhancement. *Journal of Personality and Social Psychology, 52*, 881–889.

Swann, W. B., Jr., & Hill, C. A. (1982). When our identities are mistaken: Reaffirming self-conceptions through social interaction. *Journal of Personality and Social Psychology, 43*, 59–66.

Swann, W. B., Jr., & Miller, L. C. (1982). Why never forgetting a face matters: Visual imagery and social memory. *Journal of Personality and Social Psychology, 43*, 475–480.

Swann, W. B., Jr., & Pelham, B. W. (1990). *Embracing the bitter truth: Positivity and authenticity in social relationships.* Unpublished manuscript, University of Texas, Austin.

Swann, W. B., Jr., Pelham, B. W., & Chidester, T. R. (1988). Change through paradox: Using self-verification to alter beliefs. *Journal of Personality and Social Psychology, 54,* 268–273.

Swann, W. B., Jr., Pelham, B. W., & Krull, D. S. (1989). Agreeable fancy or disagreeable truth? Reconciling self-enhancement and self-verification. *Journal of Personality and Social Psychology, 57,* 782–791.

Swann, W. B., Jr., & Predmore, S. C. (1985). Intimates as agents of social support: Sources of consolation or despair? *Journal of Personality and Social Psychology, 49,* 1609–1617.

Swann, W. B., Jr., & Read, S. J. (1981a). Acquiring self-knowledge: The search for feedback that fits. *Journal of Personality and Social Psychology, 41,* 1119–1128.

Swann, W. B., Jr., & Read, S. J. (1981b). Self-verification processes: How we sustain our self-conceptions. *Journal of Experimental Social Psychology, 17,* 351–370.

Swann, W. B., Jr., Read, S. J., & Hill, C. A. (1981, August). *Bringing others to see us as we see ourselves.* Paper presented at the annual meetings of the American Psychological Association, Los Angeles.

Swann, W. B., Jr., & Snyder, M. (1980). On translating beliefs into action: Theories of ability and their application in an instructional setting. *Journal of Personality and Social Psychology, 38,* 879–888.

Swann, W. B., Jr., Wenzlaff, R. M., Krull, D. S., & Pelham, B. W. (1989). *Seeking truth, reaping despair: Depression, self-verification, and the quest for negative feedback.* Unpublished manuscript, University of Texas, Austin.

Swede, S. W., & Tetlock, P. E. (1986). Henry Kissinger's implicit theory of personality: A quantitative case study. *Journal of Personality, 54,* 617–646.

Sweeney, P. D., Anderson K., & Bailey, S. (1986). Attributional style in depression: A meta-analytic review. *Journal of Personality and Social Psychology, 50,* 974–991.

Sweeney, P. D., & Gruber, K. L. (1984). Selective exposure: Voter information preferences and the Watergate Affair. *Journal of Personality and Social Psychology, 46,* 1208–1221.

Sweeney, P. D., & Moreland, R. L. (1980, September). *Self-schemas and the perseverance of beliefs about the self.* Paper presented at the American Psychological Association annual meetings, Montreal, Canada.

Swim, J., Borgida, E., Maruyama, G., & Myers, D. G. (1989). Joan McKay versus John McKay: Do gender stereotypes bias evaluations? *Psychological Bulletin, 105,* 409–429.

Szpiler, F. A., & Epstein, S. (1976). Availability of an avoidance response as related to automatic arousal. *Journal of Abnormal Psychology, 85,* 73–82.

Taguiri, R., & Petrullo, L. (Eds.) (1958). *Person perception and interpersonal behavior.* Palo Alto, CA: Stanford University Press.

Tajfel, H. (1970). Experiments in intergroup discrimination. *Scientific American, 223,* 96–102.

Tajfel, H. (1972). Social categorization [English ms. of La categorization sociale]. In S. Moscovici (Ed.), *Introduction à la psychologie sociale* (Vol. 1, pp. 272–302). Paris: Larousse.

Tajfel, H. (Ed.) (1978). *Differentiation between social groups.* London: Academic Press.

Tajfel, H. (1981). *Human groups and social categories: Studies in social psychology.* Cambridge, England: Cambridge University Press.

Tajfel, H. (1982). Social psychology of intergroup relations. *Annual Review of Psychology, 33,* 1–39.

Tajfel, H., Billig, M., Bundy, R. P., & Flament, C. (1971). Social categorization and intergroup behavior. *European Journal of Social Psychology, 1,* 149–177.

Tajfel, H., Sheikh, A. A., & Gardner, R. C. (1964). Content of stereotypes and the inference of similarity between members of stereotyped groups. *Acta Psychologica, 22,* 191–201.

Tajfel, H., & Turner, J. C. (1979). An integrative theory of intergroup conflict. In W. G. Austin & S. Worchel (Eds.), *The social psychology of intergroup relations.* Monterey, CA: Brooks/Cole.

Tajfel, H., & Wilkes, A. L. (1963). Classification and qualitative judgment. *British Journal of Psychology, 54,* 101–114.

Taylor, D. M., & Jaggi, V. (1974). Ethnocentrism and causal attribution in a S. Indian context. *Journal of Cross-Cultural Psychology, 5,* 162–171.

Taylor, S. E. (1975). On inferring one's own attitudes from one's behavior: Some delimiting conditions. *Journal of Personality and Social Psychology, 31,* 126–131.

Taylor, S. E. (1981a). A categorization approach to stereotyping. In D. L. Hamilton (Ed.), *Cognitive processes in stereotyping and intergroup behavior* (pp. 88–114). Hillsdale, NJ: Erlbaum.

Taylor, S. E. (1981b). The interface of cognitive and social psychology. In J. Harvey (Ed.), *Cognition, social behavior, and the environment* (pp. 189–211). Hillsdale, NJ: Erlbaum.

Taylor, S. E. (1982). Social cognition and health. *Personality and Social Psychology Bulletin, 8,* 549–562.

Taylor, S. E. (1983). Adjustment to threatening events: A theory of cognitive adaptation. *American Psychologist, 38,* 1161–1173.

Taylor, S. E., & Brown, J. D. (1988). Illusion and well-being: A social psychological perspective on mental health. *Psychological Bulletin, 103,* 193–210.

Taylor, S. E., & Crocker, J. (1981). Schematic bases of social information processing. In E. T. Higgins, C. P. Herman, & M. P. Zanna (Eds.), *Social cognition: The Ontario Symposium* (Vol. 1, pp. 89–134). Hillsdale, NJ: Erlbaum.

Taylor, S. E., Crocker, J., & D'Agostino, J. (1978). Schematic bases of social problem-solving. *Personality and Social Psychology Bulletin, 4,* 447–451.

Taylor, S. E., Crocker, J., Fiske, S. T., Sprinzen, M., & Winkler, J. D. (1979). The generalizability of salience effects. *Journal of Personality and Social Psychology, 37,* 357–368.

Taylor, S. E. & Falcone, H. T. (1982). Cognitive bases of stereotyping: The relationship between categorization and prejudice. *Personality and Social Psychology Bulletin, 8,* 426–432.

Taylor, S. E., & Fiske, S. T. (1975). Point-of-view and perceptions of causality. *Journal of Personality and Social Psychology, 32,* 439–445.

Taylor, S. E., & Fiske, S. T. (1978). Salience, attention, and attribution: Top of the head phenomena. In L. Berkowitz (Ed.), *Advances in experimental social psychology* (Vol. 11, pp. 249–288). New York: Academic Press.

Taylor, S. E., & Fiske, S. T. (1981). Getting inside the head: Methodologies for process analysis in attribution and social cognition. In J. H. Harvey, W. Ickes, & R. F. Kidd (Eds.), *New directions in attribution research* (Vol. 3, pp. 459–524). Hillsdale, NJ: Erlbaum.

Taylor, S. E., Fiske, S. T., Close, M., Anderson, C., & Ruderman, A. (1977). Solo status as a psychological variable: The power of being distinctive. Unpublished manuscript, Harvard University.

Taylor, S. E., Fiske, S. T., Etcoff, N. L., & Ruderman, A. (1978). Categorical bases of person memory and stereotyping. *Journal of Personality and Social Psychology, 36*, 778–793.

Taylor, S. E., & Koivumaki, J. H. (1976). The perception of self and others: Acquaintanceship, affect, and actor-observer differences. *Journal of Personality and Social Psychology, 33*, 403–408.

Taylor, S. E., Lichtman, R. R., & Wood, J. V. (1984). Attributions, beliefs about control, and adjustment to breast cancer. *Journal of Personality and Social Psychology, 46*, 489–502.

Taylor, S. E., & Lobel, M. (1989). Social comparison activity under threat: Downward evaluation and upward contacts. *Psychological Review, 96*, 569–575.

Taylor, S. E., & Schneider, S. K. (1989). Coping and the simulation of events. *Social Cognition, 7*, 176–196.

Taylor, S. E., & Thompson, S. C. (1982). Stalking the elusive "vividness" effect. *Psychological Review, 89*, 155–181.

Taylor, S. E., & Wood, J. V. (1983). The vividness effect: Making a mountain out of a molehill? In R. P. Bagozzi & A. M. Tybout (Eds.), *Advances in consumer research* (Vol. X, pp. 540–542). Ann Arbor, MI: Association for Consumer Research.

Teasdale, J. D., & Russell, M. L. (1983). Differential effects of induced mood on the recall of positive, negative and neutral words. *British Journal of Clinical Psychology, 22*, 163–171.

Tedeschi, J. T., & Lindskold, S. (1976). *Social psychology: Interdependence, interaction, and influence.* New York: Wiley.

Tedeschi, J. T., & Riess, M. (1981). Verbal strategies in impression management. In C. Antaki (Ed.), *The psychology of ordinary explanations of social behaviour* (pp. 271–309). London: Academic Press.

Tedeschi, J. T., Schlenker, B. R., & Bonoma, T. V. (1971). Cognitive dissonance: Private ratiocination or public spectacle? *American Psychologist, 26*, 685–695.

Teger, A. I., & Pruitt, D. G. (1967). Comparison of group risk taking. *Journal of Experimental Social Psychology, 3*, 189–205.

Tenenbaum, G., & Furst, D. M. (1986). Consistency of attributional responses by individuals and groups differing in gender, perceived ability and expectations for success. *British Journal of Social Psychology, 25*, 315–321.

Tennen, H., Affleck, G., & Gershman, K. (1986). Self-blame among parents of infants with perinatal complications: The role of self-protective motives. *Journal of Personality and Social Psychology, 50*, 690–696.

Tesser, A. (1978). Self-generated attitude change. In L. Berkowitz (Ed.), *Advances in experimental social psychology* (Vol. 11, pp. 289–338). New York: Academic Press.

Tesser, A. (1988). Toward a self-evaluation maintenance model of social behavior. In L. Berkowitz (Ed.), *Advances in experimental social psychology* (Vol. 21, pp. 181–227). New York: Academic Press.

Tesser, A., & Campbell, J. (1983). Self-definition and self-evaluation mainte-
    nance. In J. Suls & A. G. Greenwald (Eds.), *Psychological perspectives on the self*
    (Vol. 2, pp. 1–32). Hillsdale, NJ: Erlbaum.
Tesser, A., & Campbell, J., & Smith, M. F. (1984). Friendship choice and per-
    formance: Self-evaluation maintenance in children. *Journal of Personality and
    Social Psychology, 46,* 561–574.
Tesser, A., & Collins, J. (1988). Emotion in social reflection and comparison sit-
    uations: Intuitive, systematic, and exploratory approaches. *Journal of Person-
    ality and Social Psychology, 55,* 695–709.
Tesser, A., & Conlee, M. C. (1975). Some effects of time and thought on atti-
    tude polarization. *Journal of Personality and Social Psychology, 31,* 262–270.
Tesser, A., & Cowan, C. L. (1977). Some attitudinal and cognitive consequences
    of thought. *Journal of Research in Personality, 11,* 216–226.
Tesser, A., & Leone, C. (1977). Cognitive schemas and thought as determinants
    of attitude change. *Journal of Experimental Social Psychology, 13,* 340–356.
Tesser, A., Millar, M., & Moore, J. (1988). Some affective consequences of social
    comparison and reflection processes: The pain and pleasure of being close.
    Journal of Personality and Social Psychology, 54, 49–61.
Tesser, A., & Paulhus, D. (1983). The definition of self: Private and public self-
    evaluation maintenance strategies. *Journal of Personality and Social Psychology,
    44,* 672–682.
Tesser, A., & Shaffer, D. R. (1990). Attitudes and attitude change. *Annual Review
    of Psychology, 41,* 479–523.
Tesser, A., & Smith, J. (1980). Some effects of friendship and task relevance on
    helping: You don't always help the one you like. *Journal of Experimental Social
    Psychology, 16,* 582–590.
Tetlock, P. E. (1983a). Accountability and complexity of thought. *Journal of Per-
    sonality and Social Psychology, 45,* 74–83.
Tetlock, P. E. (1983b). Accountability and the perseverance of first impressions.
    Social Psychology Quarterly, 46, 285–292.
Tetlock, P. E. (1984). Cognitive style and political belief systems in the Brit-
    ish House of Commons. *Journal of Personality and Social Psychology, 46,*
    365–375.
Tetlock, P. E. (1985). Accountability: A social check on the fundamental attribu-
    tion error. *Social Psychology Quarterly, 48,* 227–236.
Tetlock, P. E. (1986). Is self-categorization theory the solution to the level-of-
    analysis problem? *British Journal of Social Psychology, 25,* 255–256.
Tetlock, P. E. (1988). Monitoring the integrative complexity of American and
    Soviet policy rhetoric: What can be learned? *Journal of Social Issues, 44,* 101–
    132.
Tetlock, P. E. (1990). Some thoughts on fourth generational models of social
    cognition. *Psychological Inquiry.*
Tetlock, P. E., & Boettger, R. (1989). Accountability: A social magnifier of the
    dilution effect. *Journal of Personality and Social Psychology, 57,* 388–398.
Tetlock, P. E., Hannum, K. A., & Micheletti, P. M. (1984). Stability and change
    in the complexity of senatorial debate: Testing the cognitive versus rhetorical
    style hypotheses. *Journal of Personality and Social Psychology, 46,* 979–990.
Tetlock, P. E., & Kim, J. I. (1987). Accountability and judgment processes in a

personality prediction task. *Journal of Personality and Social Psychology, 52,* 700–709.

Tetlock, P. E., & Levi, A. (1982). Attribution bias: On the inconclusiveness of the cognition-motivation debate. *Journal of Experimental Social Psychology, 18,* 68–88.

Tetlock, P. E., & Manstead, A. S. R. (1985). Impression management versus intrapsychic explanations in social psychology: A useful dichotomy? *Psychological Review, 92,* 59–77.

Tetlock, P. E., & McGuire, C., Jr. (1986). Cognitive perspectives on foreign policy. In S. Long (Ed.), *Political behavior annual* (Vol. 1, pp. 147–179). Boulder, CO: Westview Press.

Tetlock, P. E., Skitka, L., & Boettger, R. (1989). Social and cognitive strategies for coping with accountability: Conformity, complexity, and bolstering. *Journal of Personality and Social Psychology, 57,* 632–640.

Thibaut, J. W., & Kelley, H. H. (1959). *The social psychology of groups.* New York: Wiley.

Thompson, S. C. (1981). Will it hurt less if I can control it? A complex answer to a simple question. *Psychological Bulletin, 90,* 89–101.

Thompson, S. C., Cheek, P. R., & Graham, M. A. (1988). The other side of perceived control: Disadvantages and negative effects. In S. Spacapan & S. Oskamp (Eds.), *The social psychology of health* (pp. 69–94). Newbury Park, CA: Sage.

Thompson, S. C. & Janigian, A. S. (1988). Life schemes: A framework for understanding the search for meaning. *Journal of Social & Clinical Psychology, 7,* 260–280.

Thompson, S. C., & Kelley, J. J. (1981). Judgments of responsibility for activities in close relationships. *Journal of Personality and Social Psychology, 41,* 469–477.

Thompson, W., Cowan, C., & Rosenhan, D. (1980). Focus of attention mediates the impact of negative affect on altruism. *Journal of Personality and Social psychology, 38,* 291–300.

Thompson, W. C., Fong, G. T., & Rosenhan, D. L. (1981). Inadmissible evidence and juror verdicts. *Journal of Personality and Social Psychology, 40,* 453–463.

Thoresen, C. E., & Mahoney, M. J. (1974). *Behavioral self-control.* New York: Holt.

Thorndike, E. L. (1940). *Human nature and the social order.* New York: Macmillan.

Thorndyke, P. W., & Hayes-Roth, B. (1979). The use of schemata in the acquisition and transfer of knowledge. *Cognitive Psychology, 11,* 82–106.

Thornton, B. (1984). Defensive attribution of responsibility: Evidence for an arousal-based motivational bias. *Journal of Personality and Social Psychology, 46,* 721–734.

Thornton, B., Hogate, L., Moirs, K., Pinette, M., & Presby, W. (1986). Physiological evidence of an arousal-based motivational bias in the defensive attribution of responsibility. *Journal of Experimental Social Psychology, 22,* 148–162.

Tillman, W. S., & Carver, C. S. (1980). Actors' and observers' attributions for success and failure: A comparative test of predictions from Kelley's cube, self-serving bias, and positivity bias formulations. *Journal of Experimental Social Psychology, 16,* 18–32.

Tomkins, S. S. (1962). *Affect, imagery, and consciousness* (Vol. 1). New York: Springer.

Tomkins, S. S. (1981). The role of facial response in the experience of emotion: A reply to Tourangeau and Ellsworth. *Journal of Personality and Social Psychology, 40*, 355–357.

Touhey, J. C. (1972). Role perception and the relative influence of the perceiver and the perceived. *Journal of Social Psychology, 87*, 213–217.

Tourangeau, R., & Ellsworth, P. C. (1979). The role of facial response in the experience of emotion. *Journal of Personality and Social Psychology, 37*, 1519–1531.

Tourangeau, R., Rasinski, K. A., Bradburn, N., & D'Andrade, R. (1989). Belief accessibility and context effects in attitude measurement. *Journal of Experimental Social Psychology, 25*, 401–421.

Trolier, T. K., & Hamilton, D. L. (1986). Variables influencing judgments of correlational relations. *Journal of Personality and Social Psychology, 50*, 879–888.

Trope, Y. (1975). Seeking information about one's own ability as a determinant of choice among tasks. *Journal of Personality and Social Psychology, 32*, 1004–1013.

Trope, Y. (1979). Uncertainty-reducing properties of achievement tasks. *Journal of Personality and Social Psychology, 37*, 1505–1518.

Trope, Y. (1980). Self-assessment, self-enhancement, and taste preference. *Journal of Experimental Social Psychology, 16*, 116–129.

Trope, Y. (1983). Self-assessment in achievement behavior. In J. M. Suls & A. G. Greenwald (Eds.), *Psychological perspectives on the self* (Vol. 2, pp. 93–122). Hillsdale, NJ: Erlbaum.

Trope, Y. (1986). Identification and inferential processes in dispositional attribution. *Psychological Review, 93*, 239–257.

Trope, Y., & Bassok, M. (1982). Confirmatory and diagnosing strategies in social information gathering. *Journal of Personality and Social Psychology, 43*, 22–34.

Trope, Y., Bassok, M., & Alon, E. (1984). The questions lay interviewers ask. *Journal of Personality, 52*, 90–106

Trope, Y., & Ben-Yair, E. (1982). Task construction and persistence as means for self-assessment of abilities. *Journal of Personality and Social Psychology, 42*, 637–645.

Trope, Y., Cohen, O., & Maoz, Y. (1988). The perceptual and inferential effects of situational inducements on dispositional attributions. *Journal of Personality and Social Psychology, 55*, 165–177.

Trope, Y., & Mackie, D. M. (1987). Sensitivity to alternatives in social hypothesis-testing. *Journal of Experimental Social Psychology, 23*, 445–459.

Trzebinski, J. (1985). Action-oriented representations of implicit personality theories. *Journal of Personality and Social Psychology, 48*, 1266–1278.

Trzebinski, J., McGlynn, R. P., Gray, G., & Tubbs, D. (1985). The role of categories of an actor's goals in organizing inferences about a person. *Journal of Personality and Social Psychology, 48*, 1387–1397.

Trzebinski, J., & Richards, K. (1986). The role of goal categories in person impression. *Journal of Experimental Social Psychology, 22*, 216–227.

Tsujimoto, R. N. (1978). Memory bias toward normative and novel trait prototypes. *Journal of Personality and Social Psychology, 36*, 1391–1401.

Tsujimoto, R. N., Wilde, J., & Robertson, D. R. (1978). Distorted memory for exemplars of a social structure: Evidence for schematic memory processes. *Journal of Personality and Social Psychology, 36*, 1402–1414.

Tulving, E. (1972). Episodic and schematic memory. In E. Tulving & W. Donaldson (Eds.), *Organization of memory.* New York: Academic Press.

Tulving, E., & Pearlstone, Z. (1966). Availability versus accessibility of information in memory for words. *Journal of Verbal Learning and Verbal Behavior, 5,* 381–391.

Tunnell, G. (1981). Sex role and cognitive schemata: Person perception in feminine and androgynous women. *Journal of Personality and Social Psychology, 40,* 1126–1136.

Turk, D. C., & Salovey, P. (1986). Clinical information processing: Bias innoculation. In R. E. Ingram (Ed.), *Information processing approaches to clinical psychology* (pp. 305–323). New York: Academic Press.

Turnbull, W., & Slugoski, B. R. (1988). Conversational and linguistic processes in causal attribution. In D. J. Hilton (Ed.), *Contemporary science and natural explanation: Commonsense conceptions of causality* (pp. 66–93). Brighton, England: Harvester Press.

Turner, C. K. (1988). Don't blame memory for people's faulty reports on what influences their judgments. *Personality and Social Psychology Bulletin, 14,* 622–629.

Turner, J. C. (1981). The experimental social psychology of intergroup behaviour. In J. C. Turner & H. Giles (Eds.), *Intergroup behavior* (pp. 66–101). Chicago: The University of Chicago Press.

Turner, J. C. (1985). Social categorization and the self-concept: A social cognitive theory of group behavior. In E. J. Lawler (Ed.), *Advances in group processes* (Vol. 2, pp. 77–121). Greenwich, CT: JAI Press.

Turner, J. C. (1987). *Rediscovering the social group: A self-categorization theory.* New York: Basil Blackwell.

Turner, J. C., Brown, R. J., & Tajfel, H. (1979). Social comparison and group interest in ingroup favoritism. *European Journal of Social Psychology, 9,* 187–204.

Turner, J. C., & Oakes, P. J. (1986). The significance of the social identity concept for social psychology with reference to individualism, interactionism and social influence. *British Journal of Social Psychology, 25,* 237–352.

Turner, R. G., Scheier, M. F., Carver, C. S., & Ickes, W. (1978). Correlates of self-consciousness. *Journal of Personality Assessment, 42,* 285–289.

Tversky, A., & Kahneman, D. (1973). Availability: A heuristic for judging frequency and probability. *Cognitive Psychology, 5,* 207–232.

Tversky, A., & Kahneman, D. (1974). Judgment under uncertainty: Heuristics and biases. *Science, 185,* 1124–1131.

Tversky, A., & Kahneman, D. (1980). Causal schemata in judgments under uncertainty. In M. Fishbein (Ed.), *Progress in social psychology* (pp. 49–72). Hillsdale, NJ: Erlbaum.

Tversky, A., & Kahneman, D. (1981). The framing of decisions and the psychology of choice. *Science, 211,* 453–458.

Tversky, A., & Kahneman, D. (1982). Judgments of and by representativeness. In D. Kahneman, P. Slovic, & A. Tversky (Eds.), *Judgment under uncertainty: Heuristics and biases* (pp. 84–100). New York: Cambridge University Press.

Tversky, A., & Kahneman, D. (1983). Extensional versus intuitive reasoning:

The conjunction fallacy in probability judgment. *Psychological Review, 90,* 293–315.

Tversky, A., & Tuchin, M. (1989). A reconciliation of the evidence on eyewitness testimony: Comments on McCloskey and Zaragoza. *Journal of Experimental Psychology: General, 118,* 86–91.

Twiss, C., Tabb, S., & Crosby, F. J. (1989). Affirmative action and aggregate data: The importance of patterns in the perception of discrimination. In F. A. Blanchard & F. J. Crosby (Eds.), *Affirmative action in perspective* (pp. 159–167). New York: Springer-Verlag.

Tyler, T. R., & Rasinski, K. (1984). Comparing psychological images of the social perceiver: Role of perceived informativeness, memorability, and affect in mediating the impact of crime victimization. *Journal of Personality and Social Psychology, 46,* 308–329.

Ucros, C. G. (1989). Mood state-dependent memory: A meta-analysis. *Cognition and Emotion, 3,* 139–169.

Uleman, J. S. (1987). Consciousness and control: The case of spontaneous trait inferences. *Personality and Social Psychology Bulletin, 13,* 337–354.

Uleman, J. S. (1989). A framework for thinking intentionally about unintended thoughts. In J. S. Uleman & J. A. Bargh (Eds.), *Unintended thought* (pp. 425–449). New York: Guilford Press.

Uleman, J. S., Winborne, W. C., Winter, L., & Schecter, D. (1986). Personality differences in spontaneous personality inferences at encoding. *Journal of Personality and Social Psychology, 51,* 396–403.

Underwood, B., Froming, B. J., & Moore, B. S. (1980). Mood, attention, and altruism: A search for mediating variables. *Developmental Psychology, 13,* 541–542.

Valins, S. (1966). Cognitive effects of false heart-rate feedback. *Journal of Personality and Social Psychology, 4,* 400–408.

Valins, S., & Nisbett, R. E. (1972). Attribution processes in the development and treatment of emotional disorders. In E. E. Jones, D. E. Kanouse, H. H. Kelley, R. E. Nisbett, S. Valins, & B. Weiner (Eds.), *Attribution: Perceiving the causes of behavior* (pp. 137–150). Morristown, NJ: General Learning Press.

Valins, S., & Ray, A. (1967). Effects of cognitive desensitization on avoidance behavior. *Journal of Personality and Social Psychology, 20,* 239–250.

Vallacher, R. R., & Wegner, D. M. (1987). What do people think they're doing? Action identification and human behavior. *Psychological Review, 94,* 3–15.

Vallacher, R. R., Wegner, D. M., & Frederick, J. (1987). The presentation of self through action identification. *Social Cognition, 5,* 301–322.

Vallacher, R. R., Wegner, D. M., & Somoza, M. P. (1989). That's easy for you to say: Action identification and speech fluency. *Journal of Personality and Social Psychology, 56,* 199–208.

Vallerand, R. J., & Richer, F. (1988). On the use of the Causal Dimension Scale in a field setting: A test with confirmatory factor analysis in success and failure situations. *Journal of Personality and Social Psychology, 54,* 704–712.

Vallone, R. P., Ross, L., & Lepper, M. R. (1985). The hostile media phenomenon: Biased perception and perceptions of media bias in coverage of the Beirut massacre. *Journal of Personality and Social Psychology, 49,* 577–585.

Van der Pligt, J. (1984). Attributions, false consensus and valence: Two field studies. *Journal of Personality and Social Psychology, 46,* 57–68.

Van Heck, G. L., & Dijkstra, P. (1985). The scope and generality of self-other asymmetry in person perception. *European Journal of Social Psychology, 15,* 125–145.

Van Hook, E., & Higgins, E. T. (1988). Self-related problems beyond the self-concept: Motivational consequences of discrepant self-guides. *Journal of Personality and Social Psychology, 55,* 625–633.

van Knippenberg, A. D., & Koelen, M. (1985). Attributional self-presentation and information available to the audience. *European Journal of Social Psychology, 15,* 249–261.

Van Overwalle, F., Segebarth, K., & Goldchstein, M. (1989). Improving performance of freshmen through attributional testimonies from fellow students. *British Journal of Educational Psychology, 59,* 75–85.

Vanbeselaere, N. (1987). The effects of dichotomous and crossed social categorizations upon intergroup discrimination. *European Journal of Social Psychology, 17,* 143–156.

Vidmar, N., & Rokeach, M. (1974). Archie Bunker's bigotry: A study in selective perception and exposure. *Journal of Communications, 24,* 36–47.

Vinokur, A., & Ajzen, I. (1982). Relative importance of prior and immediate events: A causal primacy effect. *Journal of Personality and Social Psychology, 42,* 820–829.

Vinokur, A., Schul, Y., & Caplan, R. D. (1987). Determinants of perceived social support: Interpersonal transactions, personal outlook, and transient affective states. *Journal of Personality and Social Psychology, 53,* 1137–1145.

Vokey, J. R., & Read, J. D. (1985). Subliminal messages: Between the devil and the media. *American Psychologist, 40,* 1231–1239.

Wachtler, J., & Counselman, E. (1981). When increasing liking for a communicator decreases opinion change: An attributional analysis of attractiveness. *Journal of Experimental Social Psychology, 17,* 386–395.

Wagner, U., Lampen, L., & Syllwasschy, J. (1986). In-group inferiority, social identity and out-group devaluation in a modified minimal group study. *British Journal of Social Psychology, 25,* 15–23.

Walker, J. H. (1975). Real-world variability, reasonableness judgments, and memory representations for concepts. *Journal of Verbal Learning and Verbal Behavior, 14,* 241–252.

Walker, P., & Antaki, C. (1986). Sexual orientation as a basis for categorization in recall. *British Journal of Social Psychology, 25,* 337–339.

Wallach, M. A., Kogan, N., & Bem, D. J. (1962). Group influence on individual risk taking. *Journal of Abnormal and Social Psychology, 65,* 75–86.

Wallbott, H. G. (1988). In and out of context: Influences of facial expression and context information on emotion attributions. *British Journal of Social Psychology, 27,* 357–369.

Wallbott, H. G., & Scherer, K. R. (1988). Emotion and economic development: Data and speculations concerning the relationship between economic factors and emotional experience. *European Journal of Social Psychology, 18,* 267–273.

Walster, E. (1966). Assignment of responsibility for an accident. *Journal of Personality and Social Psychology, 3*, 73–79.

Walster, E. (1971). Passionate love. In B. I. Murstein (Ed.), *Theories of attraction and love* (pp. 85–99). New York: Springer.

Wang, G., & McKillip, J. (1978). Ethnic identification and judgments of an accident. *Personality and Social Psychology Bulletin, 4*, 292–299.

Ward, S. E., Leventhal, H., & Love, R. (1988). Repression revisited: Tactics used in coping with a severe health threat. *Personality and Social Psychology Bulletin, 14*, 735–746.

Ward, W. D., & Jenkins, H. M. (1965). The display of information and the judgment of contingency. *Canadian Journal of Psychology, 19*, 231–241.

Warshaw, P. R., & Davis, F. D. (1984). Self-understanding and the accuracy of behavioral expectations. *Personality and Social Psychology Bulletin, 10*, 111–118.

Warshaw, P. R., & Davis, F. D. (1985). Disentangling behavioral intention and behavioral expectation. *Journal of Experimental Social Psychology, 21*, 213–228.

Watkins, M. J., & Peynircioglu, Z. F. (1984). Determining perceived meaning during impression formation: Another look at the meaning change hypothesis. *Journal of Personality and Social Psychology, 46*, 1005–1016.

Watson, D., & Clark, L. A. (1984). Negative affectivity: The disposition to experience aversive emotional states. *Psychological Bulletin, 96*, 465–490.

Watson, D., & Tellegen, A. (1985). Toward a consensual structure of mood. *Psychological Bulletin, 98*, 219–235.

Watson, J. (1930). *Behaviorism*. New York: Norton.

Watson, W. S., & Hartmann, G. W. (1939). The frigidity of a basic attitudinal frame. *Journal of Abnormal and Social Psychology, 34*, 314–335.

Waynbaum, I. (1907). *La physionomie humaine: Son mecanisme et son role social.* Paris: Alcan.

Weary, G. (1980). Examination of affect and egotism as mediators of bias in causal attributions. *Journal of Personality and Social Psychology, 38*, 348–357.

Weary, G., Harvey, J. H. Schweiger, P., Olson, C. T., Perloff, R., & Pritchard, S. (1982). Self-presentation and the moderation of the self-serving bias. *Social Cognition, 1*, 140–159.

Weary, G., Swanson, H., Harvey, J. H., & Yarkin, K. L. (1980). A molar approach to social knowing. *Personality and Social Psychology Bulletin, 6*, 574–581.

Webb, W. M., Marsh, K. L., Schneiderman, W., & Davis, B. (1989). Interaction between self-monitoring and manipulated states of awareness. *Journal of Personality and Social Psychology, 56*, 70–80.

Weber, R., & Crocker, J. (1983). Cognitive processes in the revision of stereotypic beliefs. *Journal of Personality and Social Psychology, 45*, 961–977.

Wegner, D. M. (1986). Transactive memory: A contemporary analysis of the group mind. In B. Mullen & G. R. Goethals (Eds.), *Theories of group behavior* (pp. 185–208). New York: Springer-Verlag.

Wegner, D. M., Coulton, G. F., & Wenzlaff, R. (1985). The transparency of denial: Briefing in the debriefing paradigm. *Journal of Personality and Social Psychology, 49*, 338–346.

Wegner, D. M., & Finstuen, K. (1977). Observers' focus of attention in the simulation of self-perception. *Journal of Personality and Social Psychology, 35*, 56–62.

Wegner, D. M., Schneider, D. J., Carter, S. R., III, & White, T. L. (1987). Paradoxical effects of thought suppression. *Journal of Personality and Social Psychology, 53,* 5–13.

Wegner, D. M., & Vallacher, R. R. (1987). The trouble with action. *Social Cognition, 5,* 179–190.

Wegner, D. M., Vallacher, R. R., Kiersted, G. W., & Dizadji, D. (1986). Action identification in the emergence of social behavior. *Social Cognition, 4,* 18–38.

Wegner, D. M., Vallacher, R. R., Macomber, G., Wood, R., & Arps, K. (1984). The emergence of action. *Journal of Personality and Social Psychology, 46,* 269–279.

Wegner, D. M., Wenzlaff, R., Kerker, R. M., & Beattie, A. E. (1981). Incrimination through innuendo: Can media questions become public answers? *Journal of Personality and Social Psychology, 40,* 822–832.

Weinberg, H. I., Wadsworth, J., & Baron, R. S. (1983). Demand and the impact of leading questions on eyewitness testimony. *Memory and Cognition, 11,* 101–104.

Weiner, B. (1979). A theory of motivation for some classroom experiences. *Journal of Educational Psychology, 71,* 3–25.

Weiner, B. (1980a). A cognitive (attribution)-emotion-action model of motivated behavior: An analysis of judgments of help-giving. *Journal of Personality and Social Psychology, 39,* 186–200.

Weiner, B. (1980b). *Human motivation.* New York: Holt, Rinehart, & Winston.

Weiner, B. (1980c). May I borrow your class notes? An attributional analysis of judgments of help-giving in an achievement-related context. *Journal of Educational Psychlolgy, 72,* 676–681.

Weiner, B. (1982). The emotional consequences of causal attributions. In M. S. Clark & S. T. Fiske (Eds.), *Affect and cognition: The 17th Annual Carnegie Symposium on Cognition* (pp. 185–210). Hillsdale, NJ: Erlbaum.

Weiner, B. (1985a). "Spontaneous" causal thinking. *Psychological Bulletin, 97,* 74–84.

Weiner, B. (1985b). An attributional theory of achievement motivation and emotion. *Psychological Review, 92,* 548–573.

Weiner, B. (1986a). *An attributional theory of motivation and emotion.* New York: Springer-Verlag.

Weiner, B. (1986b). Attribution, emotion, and action. In R. Sorrentino & E. T. Higgins (Eds.), *Handbook of motivation and cognition* (pp. 281–312). New York: Guilford Press.

Weiner, B. (1987). The social psychology of emotion: Applications of a naive psychology. *Journal of Social and Clinical Psychology, 5,* 405–419.

Weiner, B. (1988a). An attributional analysis of changing reactions to persons with AIDS. In R. A. Berk (Ed.), *The social impact of AIDS in the U.S.* (pp. 139–169). Cambridge, MA: Abt Books.

Weiner, B. (1988b). Attribution theory and attributional therapy: Some theoretical observations and suggestions. *British Journal of Clinical Psychology, 27,* 93–104.

Weiner, B., Amirkhan, J., Folkes, V. S., & Verette, J. A. (1987). An attributional analysis of excuse giving: Studies of a naive theory of emotion. *Journal of Personality and Social Psychology, 52,* 316–324.

Weiner, B., Frieze, I., Kukla, A., Reed, L., Rest, S., & Rosenbaum, R. M. (1972). Perceiving the causes of success and failure. In E. E. Jones, D. E. Kanouse,

H. H. Kelley, R. E. Nisbett, S. Valins, & B. Weiner (Eds.), *Attribution: Perceiving the causes of behavior* (pp. 95–120). Morristown, NJ: General Learning Press.

Weiner, B., & Handel, S. (1985). Anticipated emotional consequences of causal communications and reported communication strategy. *Developmental Psychology, 21,* 102–107.

Weiner, B., Perry, R. P., & Magnusson, J. (1988). An attributional analysis of reactions to stigmas. *Journal of Personality and Social Psychology, 55,* 738–748.

Weiner, B., Russell, D., & Lerman, D. (1978). Affective consequences of causal ascriptions. In J. H. Harvey, W. J. Ickes, & R. F. Kidd (Eds.), *New directions in attribution research* (Vol. 2, pp. 59–90). Hillsdale, NJ: Erlbaum.

Weiner, B., Russell, D., & Lerman, D. (1979). The cognition-emotion process in achievement-related contexts. *Journal of Personality and Social Psychology, 37,* 1211–1220.

Weinstein, N. D. (1980). Unrealistic optimism about future life events. *Journal of Personality and Social Psychology, 39,* 806–820.

Weiss, J. A., & Brown, P. (1977). *Self-insight error in the explanation of mood.* Unpublished manuscript, Harvard University.

Weitz, S. (Ed.) (1974). *Nonverbal communication.* New York: Oxford University Press.

Weldon, E. & Gargano, G. M. (1985). Cognitive effort in additive task groups: The effects of shared responsibility on the quality of multiattribute judgments. *Organizational Behavior and Human Development, 36,* 348–361.

Weldon, E., & Gargano, G. M. (1988). Cognitive loafing: The effects of accountability and shared responsibility on cognitive effort. *Personality and Social Psychology Bulletin, 14,* 159–171.

Wells, G. L. (1985). The conjunction error and the representativeness heuristic. *Social Cognition, 3,* 266–279.

Wells, G. L., & Gavanski, I. (1989). Mental simulation of causality. *Journal of Personality and Social Psychology, 56,* 161–169.

Wells, G. L., & Harvey, J. H. (1977). Do people use consensus information in making causal attributions? *Journal of Personality and Social Psychology, 35,* 279–293.

Wells, G. L., Lindsay, R. C. L., & Tousignant, J. P. (1980). Effects of expert psychological advice on human performance in judging the validity of eyewitness testimony. *Law and Human Behavior, 4,* 275–285.

Wells, G. L., & Petty, R. E. (1980). The effects of overt head movements on persuasion: Compatibility and incompatibility of responses. *Basic and Applied Social Psychology, 1,* 219–230.

Wells, G. L., Taylor, B. R., & Turtle, J. W. (1987). The undoing of scenarios. *Journal of Personality and Social Psychology, 53,* 421–430.

Wells, G. L., & Turtle, J. W. (1987). Eyewitness testimony research: Current knowledge and emergent controversies. *Canadian Journal of Behavioral Science, 19,* 363–388.

Wells, G. L., & Turtle, J. W. (1988). What is the best way to encode faces? In M. M. Gruneberg, P. E. Morris, & R. N. Sykes (Eds.), *Practical aspects of memory: Current research and issues* (Vol. 1, pp. 163–168). Chichester, England: Wiley.

Wenzlaff, R. M., Wegner, D. M., & Roper, D. W. (1988). Depression and mental control: The resurgence of unwanted negative thoughts. *Journal of Personality and Social Psychology, 55,* 862–892.

Westen, D. (1988). Transference and information processing. *Clinical Psychology Review, 8,* 161–179.

Wetzel, C. G. (1982). Self-serving biases in attribution: A Bayesian analysis. *Journal of Personality and Social Psychology, 43,* 197–209.

Wetzel, C. G., & Walton, M. D. (1985). Developing biased social judgments: The false-consensus effect. *Journal of Personality and Social Psychology, 49,* 1352–1359.

White, G. L., Fishbein, S., & Rutstein, J. (1981). Passionate love and misattribution of arousal. *Journal of Personality and Social Psychology, 41,* 56–62.

White, G. L., & Kight, T. D. (1984). Misattribution of arousal and attraction: Effects of salience of explanations for arousal. *Journal of Experimental Social Psychology, 20,* 55–64.

White, G. L., & Shapiro, D. (1987). Don't I know you? Antecedents and social consequences of perceived familiarity. *Journal of Experimental Social Psychology, 23,* 75–92.

White, J. D. & Carlston, D. E. (1983). Consequences of schemata for attention, impressions, and recall in complex social interactions. *Journal of Personality and Social Psychology, 45,* 538–549.

White, P. (1980). Limitation on verbal reports of internal events: A refutation of Nisbett and Wilson and of Bem. *Psychological Review, 87,* 105–112.

White, P. (1984). A model of the layperson as pragmatist. *Personality and Social Psychology Bulletin, 10,* 333–348.

White, P. A. (1987). Causal report accuracy: Retrospect and prospect. *Journal of Experimental Social Psychology, 23,* 311–315.

White, P. A. (1988). Causal processing: Origins and development. *Psychological Bulletin, 104,* 36–52.

White, P. A., & Younger, D. P. (1988). Differences in the ascription of transient internal states to self and other. *Journal of Experimental Social Psychology, 24,* 292–309.

Whittlesea, B. W. A. (1987). Preservation of specific experiences in the representation of general knowledge. *Journal of Experimental Psychology: Learning, Memory, and Cognition, 13,* 3–17.

Whorf, B. L. (1956). *Language, thought and reality* (J. B. Carroll, Ed.). Cambridge, MA: M.I.T. Press.

Wickelgren, W. A. (1981). Human learning and memory. *Annual Review of Psychology, 32,* 21–52.

Wicker, A. W. (1969). Attitudes vs. actions: The relationship of verbal and overt behavioral responses to attitude objects. *Journal of Social Issues, 41,* 41–78.

Wicklund, R. A. (1975). Objective self-awareness. In L. Berkowitz (Ed.), *Advances in experimental social psychology* (Vol. 8, pp. 233–275). New York: Academic Press.

Wicklund, R. A. (1978). Three years later. In L. Berkowitz (Ed.), *Cognitive theories in social psychology* (pp. 509–521). New York: Academic Press.

Wicklund, R. A. (1979). The influence of self-awareness on human behavior. *American Scientist, 67,* 187–193.

Wicklund, R. A. (1986). Orientation to the environment versus preoccupation with human potential. In R. M. Sorrentio & E. T. Higgins (Eds.), *Handbook of motivation and cognition: Foundations of social behavior* (pp. 64–95). New York: Guilford Press.

Wicklund, R. A., & Braun, O. L. (1987). Incompetence and the concern with human categories. *Journal of Personality and Social Psychology, 53,* 373–382.

Wicklund, R. A., & Brehm, J. W. (1976). *Perspectives on cognitive dissonance.* Hillsdale, NJ: Erlbaum.

Wicklund, R. A., & Frey, D. (1980). Self-awareness theory: When the self makes a difference. In D. M. Wegner & R. R. Vallacher (Eds.), *The self in social psychology* (pp. 31–54). New York: Oxford University Press.

Wicklund, R. A., & Gollwitzer, P. M. (1981). Symbolic self-completion, attempted influence, and self-deprecation. *Basic and Applied Social Psychology, 2,* 89–114.

Wicklund, R. A., & Gollwitzer, P. M. (1982). *Symbolic self-completion.* Hillsdale, NJ: Erlbaum.

Wicklund, R. A., & Gollwitzer, P. M. (1983). A motivational factor in self-report validity. In J. Suls & A. G. Greenwald (Eds.), *Psychological perspectives on the self* (Vol. 2, pp. 67–92). Hillsdale, NJ: Erlbaum.

Wicklund, R. A., & Gollwitzer, P. M. (1987). The fallacy of the private-public self-focus distinction. *Journal of Personality, 55,* 491–523.

Wicklund, R. A., & Hormuth, S. E. (1981). On the functions of the self: A reply to Hull and Levy. *Journal of Personality and Social Psychology, 40,* 1029–1037.

Wilder, D. A. (1978a). Effect of predictability on units of perception and attribution. *Personality and Social Psychology Bulletin, 9,* 281–284.

Wilder, D. A. (1978b). Perceiving persons as a group: Effects on attributions of causality and beliefs. *Social Psychology, 1,* 13–23.

Wilder, D. A. (1978c). Predictability of behaviors, goals, and unit of perception. *Personality and Social Psychology Bulletin, 4,* 604–607.

Wilder, D. A. (1980). *Predictions of belief homogeneity and similarity as a function of the salience of an outgroup following social categorization.* Unpublished manuscript, Rutgers University.

Wilder, D. A. (1981). Perceiving persons as a group: Categorization and intergroup relations. In D. L. Hamilton (Ed.), *Cognitive processes in stereotyping and intergroup behavior* (pp. 213–258). Hillsdale, NJ: Erlbaum.

Wilder, D. A. (1984a). *Effects of perceiving persons as a group on the information conveyed by their behavior.* Unpublished manuscript, Rutgers University.

Wilder, D. A. (1984b). Predictions of belief homogeneity and similarity following social categorization. *British Journal of Social Psychology, 23,* 323–333.

Wilder, D. A. (1986). Social categorization: Implications for creation and reduction of intergroup bias. In L. Berkowitz (Ed.), *Advances in Experimental Social Psychology* (Vol. 19, pp. 291–355). New York: Academic Press.

Wilder, D. A., & Allen, V. L. (1978). Group membership and preference for information about others. *Personality and Social Psychology Bulletin, 4,* 106–110.

Wilder, D. A., & Cooper, W. E. (1981). Categorization in groups: Consequences for social perception and attribution. In J. Harvey, W. Ickes, & R. Kidd (Eds.), *New directions in attribution research* (Vol. 3, pp. 247–277). Hillsdale, NJ: Erlbaum.

Wilder, D. A. & Shapiro, P. N. (1984). Role of out-group cues in determining social identity. *Journal of Personality and Social Psychology, 47,* 342–348.

Wilder, D. A., & Shapiro, P. (1989a). Effects of anxiety on impression formation in a group context: An anxiety-assimilation hypothesis. *Journal of Experimental Social Psychology, 25,* 481–499.

Wilder, D. A., & Shapiro, P. (1989b). The role of competition-induced anxiety in limiting the beneficial impact of positive behavior by an outgroup member. *Journal of Personality and Social Psychology, 56,* 60–69.

Wilder, D. A., & Thompson, J. E. (1988). Assimilation and contrast effects in the judgments of groups. *Journal of Personality and Social Psychology, 54,* 62–73.

Williams, J. M. G. (1985). Attributional formulation of depression as a diathesis-stress model: Metalsky et al. reconsidered. *Journal of Personality and Social Psychology, 48,* 1572–1575.

Wills, T. A. (1981). Downward comparison principles in social psychology. *Psychological Bulletin, 90,* 245–271.

Wilson, T. D., & Dunn, D. S. (1986). Effects of introspection on attitude-behavior consistency: Analyzing reasons versus focusing on feelings. *Journal of Experimental Social Psychology, 22,* 249–263.

Wilson, T. D., Dunn, D. S., Bybee, J. A., Hyman, D. B., & Rotondo, J. A. (1984). Effects of analyzing reasons on attitude-behavior consistency. *Journal of Personality and Social Psychology, 47,* 5–16.

Wilson, T. D., Dunn, D. S., Kraft, D., & Lisle, D. J. (1989). Introspection, attitude change, and attitude-behavior consistency: The disruptive effects of explaining why we feel the way we do. In L. Berkowitz (Ed.), *Advances in experimental social psychology* (Vol. 22, pp. 287–344). New York: Academic Press.

Wilson, T. D., Hull, J. G., & Johnson, J. (1981). Awareness and self-perception: Verbal reports on internal states. *Journal of Personality and Social Psychology, 40,* 53–70.

Wilson, T. D., Kraft, D., & Dunn, D. S. (1989). The disruptive effects of explaining attitudes: The moderating effect of knowledge about the attitude object. *Journal of Experimental Social Psychology, 25,* 379–400.

Wilson, T. D., & Linville, P. W. (1982). Improving the academic performance of college freshmen: Attribution therapy revisited. *Journal of Personality and Social Psychology, 42,* 367–376.

Wilson, T. D., & Linville, P. W. (1985). Improving the performance of college freshmen with attributional techniques. *Journal of Personality and Social Psychology, 49,* 287–293.

Wilson, T. D., Lisle, D. J., Kraft, D., & Wetzel, C. G. (1989). Preferences as expectation-driven inferences: Effects of affective expectations on affective experience. *Journal of Personality and Social Psychology, 56,* 519–530.

Wilson, T. D., & Nisbett, R. E. (1978). The accuracy of verbal reports about the effects of stimuli on evaluations and behavior. *Social Psychology, 41,* 118–131.

Wilson, T. D., & Stone, J. I. (1985). Limitations of self-knowledge: More on telling more than we can know. In P. Shaver (Ed.), *Review of personality and social psychology: Vol. 6. Self, situations, and social behavior* (pp. 167–183). Beverly Hills, CA: Sage.

Wilson, W., & Miller, H. (1968). Repetition, order of presentation, and timing of arguments and measures as determinants of opinion change. *Journal of Personality and Social Psychology, 9,* 184–188.

Wilson, W. R. (1979). Feeling more than we can know: Exposure effects without learning. *Journal of Personality and Social Psychology, 37,* 811–821.

Winkler, J., & Taylor, S. E. (1979). Preference, expectations, and attributional bias: Two field studies. *Journal of Applied Social Psychology, 2,* 183–197.

Winter, L., & Uleman, J. S. (1984). When are social judgments made? Evidence for the spontaneousness of trait inferences. *Journal of Personality and Social Psychology, 47*, 237–252.

Winter, L., Uleman, J. S., & Cunniff, C. (1985). How automatic are social judgments? *Journal of Personality and Social Psychology, 49*, 904–917.

Winton, W. M. (1986). The role of facial response in self-reports of emotion: A critique of Laird. *Journal of Personality and Social Psychology, 37*, 1519–1531.

Winton, W. M., Putnam, L. E., & Krauss, R. M. (1984). Facial and autonomic manifestations of the dimensional structure of emotion. *Journal of Experimental Social Psychology, 20*, 195–216.

Wittgenstein, L. (1953). *Philosophical investigations.* New York: Macmillan.

Wixon, D. R., & Laird, J. D. (1976). Awareness and attitude change in the forced-compliance paradigm: The importance of when. *Journal of Personality and Social Psychology, 34*, 376–384.

Wojciszke, B. (1987). Ideal-self, self-focus, and value-behavior consistency. *European Journal of Social Psychology, 17*, 187–198.

Wolfson, M. R., & Salancik, G. R. (1977). Observer orientation and actor-observer differences in attributions for failure. *Journal of Experimental Social Psychology, 5*, 441–451.

Wolk, S., & DuCette, J. (1974). Intentional performance and incidental learning as a function of personality and task dimension. *Journal of Personality and Social Psychology, 29*, 90–101.

Wolman, C., & Frank, H. (1975). The solo woman in a professional peer group. *American Journal of Orthopsychiatry, 45*, 164–171.

Wong, P. T. P., & Weiner, B. (1981). When people ask "why" questions, and the heuristics of attributional search. *Journal of Personality and Social Psychology, 40*, 650–663.

Wood, J. V. (1989). Theory and research concerning social comparisons of personal attributes. *Psychological Bulletin, 106*, 231–248.

Wood, J. V., Saltzberg, J. A., & Goldsamt, L. A. (1990). Does affect induce self-focused attention? *Journal of Personality and Social Psychology, 58*, 899–908.

Wood, J. V., Taylor, S. E., & Lichtman, R. R. (1985). Social comparison in adjustment to breast cancer. *Journal of Personality and Social Psychology, 49*, 1169–1183.

Wood, W., & Eagly, A. H. (1981). Stages in the analysis of persuasive messages: The role of causal attributions and message comprehension. *Journal of Personality and Social Psychology, 40*, 246–259.

Wood, W., & Kallgren, C. A. (1988). Communicator attributes and persuasion: Recipients' access to attitude-relevant information in memory. *Personality and Social Psychology Bulletin, 14*, 172–182.

Wood, W., Kallgren, C. A., & Preisler, R. M. (1985). Access to attitude-relevant information in memory as a determinant of persuasion: The role of message attributes. *Journal of Experimental Social Psychology, 21*, 73–85.

Worchel, S. & Brown, E. H. (1984). The role of plausibility in influencing environmental attributions. *Journal of Experimental Social Psychology, 20*, 86–96.

Word, C. O., Zanna, M. P., & Cooper, J. (1974). The nonverbal mediation of self-fulfilling prophecies in interracial interaction. *Journal of Experimental Social Psychology, 10*, 109–120.

Worth, L. T., & Mackie, D. M. (1987). The cognitive mediation of positive affect in persuasion. *Social Cognition, 5,* 76–94.

Wortman, C. B. (1976). Causal attributions and personal control. In J. H. Harvey, W. Ickes, & R. F. Kidd (Eds.), *New directions in attribution research* (Vol. 1, pp. 23–52). Hillsdale, NJ: Erlbaum.

Wortman, C. B., Costanzo, P. R., & Witt, T. R. (1973). Effect of anticipated performance on the attributions of causality to self and others. *Journal of Personality and Social Psychology, 27,* 372–381.

Wright, E. F., & Wells, G. L. (1988) Is the attitude-attribution paradigm suitable for investigating the dispositional bias? *Personality and Social Psychology Bulletin, 14,* 183–190.

Wright, J, & Mischel, W. (1982). Influence of affect on cognitive social learning person variables. *Journal of Personality and Social Psychology, 43,* 901–914.

Wright, J. C., & Dawson, V. L. (1988). Person perception and the bounded rationality of social judgment. *Journal of Personality and Social Psychology, 55,* 780–794.

Wright, J. C., & Mischel, W. (1988). Conditional hedges and the intuitive psychology of traits. *Journal of Personality and Social Psychology, 55,* 454–469.

Wright, P., & Rip, P. D. (1981). Retrospective reports on the causes of decisions. *Journal of Personality and Social Psychology, 40,* 601–614.

Wu, C., & Shaffer, D. R. (1987). Susceptibility to persuasive appeals as a function of source credibility and prior experience with the attitude object. *Journal of Personality and Social Psychology, 52,* 677–688.

Wundt, W. (1897). *Outlines of psychology.* New York: Stechert. (Translated 1907.)

Wurf, E., & Markus, H. (1983, August). *Cognitive consequences of the negative self.* Presented at American Psychological Association meeting, Anaheim, CA.

Wurf, E., & Markus, H. (1990). Possible selves and the psychology of personal growth. In D. Ozer, A. Stewart, & J. Healey (Eds.) *Perspectives on personality.* (Vol. 3, pp. 39–62). Grennwich, CT: JAI Press.

Wyer, R. S., Jr. (1974). Changes in meaning and halo effects in personality impression formation. *Journal of Personality and Social Psychology, 29,* 829–835.

Wyer, R. S., Jr. (1976). An investigation of relations among probability estimates. *Organizational Behavior and Human Performance, 15,* 1–18

Wyer, R. S., Jr., & Bodenhausen, G. V. (1985). Event memory. *Journal of Personality and Social Psychology, 49,* 301–316.

Wyer, R. S., Jr., Bodenhausen, G. V., & Srull, T. K. (1984). The cognitive representation of persons and groups and its effect on recall and recognition memory. *Journal of Experimental Social Psychology, 20,* 445–469.

Wyer, R. S., Jr., & Budesheim, T. L. (1987). Person memory and judgments: The impact of information that one is told to disregard. *Journal of Personality and Social Psychology, 53,* 14–29.

Wyer, R. S., Jr., Budesheim, T. L., & Lambert, A. J. (1990). Cognitive representation of conversations about persons. *Journal of Personality and Social Psychology, 58,* 218–238.

Wyer, R. S., Jr., & Carlston, D. E. (1979). *Social cognition, inference, and attribution.* Hillsdale, NJ: Erlbaum.

Wyer, R. S., Jr., & Gordon, S. E. (1982). The recall of information about persons and groups. *Journal of Experimental Social Psychology, 18,* 128–164.

Wyer, R. S., Jr., & Gordon, S. (1984). The cognitive representation of social information. In R. S. Wyer, Jr., & T. K. Srull (Eds.), *Handbook of social cognition*, (Vol. 2, pp. 73–150). Hillsdale, NJ: Erlbaum.

Wyer, R. S., Jr., Henninger, M., & Hinkle, R. (1977). An information analysis of actors' and observers' belief attributions in a role-playing situation. *Journal of Experimental Social Psychology, 13,* 199–217.

Wyer, R. S., Jr., & Martin, L. L. (1986). Person memory: The role of traits, group stereotypes, and specific behaviors in the cognitive representation of persons. *Journal of Personality and Social Psychology, 50,* 661–675.

Wyer, R. S., Jr., Shoben, E. J., Fuhrman, R. W., & Bodenhausen, G. V. (1985). Event memory: The temporal organization of social action sequences. *Journal of Personality and Social Psychology, 49,* 857–877.

Wyer, R. S., Jr., & Srull, T. K. (1980). The processing of social stimulus information: A conceptual integration. In R. Hastie, T. M. Ostrom, E. B. Ebbesen, R. S. Wyer, D. Hamilton, & D. E. Carlston (Eds.), *Person memory: The cognitive basis of social perception* (pp. 227–300). Hillsdale, NJ: Erlbaum.

Wyer, R. S., Jr., & Srull, T. K. (1981). Category accessibility: Some theoretical and empirical issues concerning the processing of social stimulus information. In E. T. Higgins, C. P. Herman, & M. P. Zanna (Eds.), *Social cognition: The Ontario Symposium* (Vol. 1, pp. 161–198). Hillsdale, NJ: Erlbaum.

Wyer, R. S., Jr., & Srull, T. K. (Eds.) (1984). *Handbook of social cognition* (Vol. 1–3). Hillsdale, NJ: Erlbaum.

Wyer, R. S., Jr., & Srull, T. K. (1986). Human cognition in its social context. *Psychological Review, 93,* 322–359.

Wyer, R. S., Jr., & Srull, T. K. (1988). Understanding social knowledge: If only the data could speak for themselves. In D. Bar-Tal & A. W. Kruglanski (Eds.), *The social psychology of knowledge* (pp. 142–193). Cambridge, England: Cambridge University Press.

Wyer, R. S., Jr., Srull, T. K., & Gordon, S. (1984). The effects of predicting a person's behavior on subsequent trait judgments. *Journal of Experimental Social Psychology, 20,* 29–46.

Wyer, R. S., Jr., Srull, T. K., Gordon, S. E., & Hartwick, J. (1982). Effects of processing objectives on the recall of prose material. *Journal of Personality and Social Psychology, 43,* 674–688.

Wyer, R. S., Jr., & Unverzagt, W. H. (1985). Effects of instructions to disregard information on its subsequent recall and use in making judgments. *Journal of Personality and Social Psychology, 48,* 533–549.

Wyer, R. S., Jr., & Watson, S. F. (1969). Context effects in impression formation. *Journal of Personality and Social Psychology, 12,* 22–33.

Wylie, R. (1979). *The self concept.* Lincoln: University of Nebraska Press.

Yandrell, B., & Insko, C. A. (1977). Attribution of attitudes to speakers and listeners under assigned-behavior conditions: Does behavior engulf the field? *Journal of Experimental Social Psychology, 3,* 269–278.

Yarkin, K. L., Harvey, J. H., & Bloxom, B. M. (1981). Cognitive sets, attribution, and social interaction. *Journal of Personality and Social Psychology, 41,* 243–252.

Young, J., Borgida, E., Sullivan, J., & Aldrich, J. (1987). Personal agendas and the relationship between self-interest and voting behavior. *Social Psychology Quarterly, 50,* 64–71.

Zaccaro, S. J., & Lowe, C. A. (1985). Effort attributions: Task novelty, perceptual focus, and cue utilization. *Personality and Social Psychology Bulletin, 11,* 489–501.

Zadny, J., & Gerard, H. B. (1974). Attributed intentions and informational selectivity. *Journal of Experimental Social Psychology, 10,* 34–52.

Zajonc, R. B. (1960). The process of cognitive tuning in communication. *Journal of Abnormal and Social Psychology, 61,* 159–167.

Zajonc, R. B. (1968a). Attitudinal effects of mere exposure. *Journal of Personality and Social Psychology, 9,* 1–27.

Zajonc, R. B. (1968b). Cognitive theories in social psychology. In G. Lindzey & E. Aronson (Eds.), *The handbook of social psychology* (2nd ed., Vol. 1, pp. 320–411). Reading, MA: Addison-Wesley.

Zajonc, R. B. (1980a). Cognition and social cognition: A historical perspective. In L. Festinger (Ed.), *Retrospections on social psychology* (pp. 180–204). New York: Oxford University Press.

Zajonc, R. B. (1980b). Feeling and thinking: Preferences need no inferences. *American Psychologist, 35,* 151–175.

Zajonc, R. B. (1984). On the primacy of affect. *American Psychologist, 39,* 117–123.

Zajonc, R. B. (1985a). Emotion and facial efference: A theory reclaimed. *Science, 228,* 15–21.

Zajonc, R. B. (1985b). Emotions and facial expression. [Letter in response to Zajonc, R. B. (1985a). Emotion and facial efference: A theory reclaimed. *Science, 228,* 15–21.] *Science, 230,* 608; 610; 687.

Zajonc, R. B., Adelmann, P., Murphy, S. T., & Niedenthal, P. M. (1987). Convergence in the physical appearance of spouses. *Motivation and Emotion, 11,* 335–346.

Zajonc, R. B., & Burnstein, E. (1965a). The learning of balanced and unbalanced social structures. *Journal of Personality, 33,* 153–163.

Zajonc, R. B., & Burnstein, E. (1965b). Structural balance, reciprocity, and positivity as sources of cognitive bias. *Journal of Personality, 33,* 570–583.

Zajonc, R. B., & Markus, H. (1984). Affect and cognition: The hard interface. In C. E. Izard, J. Kagan, & R. B. Zajonc (Eds.), *Emotions, cognition, and behavior* (pp. 73–102). Cambridge, England: Cambridge University Press.

Zajonc, R. B., Murphy, S. T., & Inglehart, M. (1989). Feeling and facial efference: Implications of the vascular theory of emotion. *Psychological Review, 96,* 395–416.

Zajonc, R. B., Pietromonaco, P., & Bargh, J. (1982). Independence and interaction of affect and cognition. In M. S. Clark & S. T. Fiske (Eds.), *Affect and cognition: The 17th Annual Carnegie Symposium on Cognition* (pp. 211–228). Hillsdale, NJ: Erlbaum.

Zanna, M. P. (1991). Message receptivity: A new look at the old problem of open- vs. close-mindedness. In A. Mitchell (Ed.), *Advertising exposure: Memory and choice.* Hillsdale, NJ: Erlbaum.

Zanna, M. P., & Cooper, J. (1976). Dissonance and the attribution process. In J. H. Harvey, W. I. Ickes, & R. F. Kidd (Eds.), *New directions in attribution research* (Vol. 1, pp. 199–217). Hillsdale, NJ: Erlbaum.

Zanna, M. P., & Fazio, R. H. (1982). The attitude-behavior relation: Moving toward a third generation of research. In M. P. Zanna, E. T. Higgins, & C. P. Herman (Eds.), *Consistency in social behavior: The Ontario symposium* (Vol. 2, pp. 283–302). Hillsdale, NJ: Erlbaum.

Zanna, M. P., & Hamilton, D. (1972). Attribute dimensions and patterns of trait inferences. *Psychonomic Science, 27,* 353–354.

Zanna, M. P., & Hamilton, D. L. (1977). Further evidence for meaning change in impression formation. *Journal of Experimental Social Psychology, 13,* 224–238.

Zanna, M. P., Kiesler, C. A., & Pilkonis, P. A. (1970). Positive and negative attitudinal affect established by classical conditioning. *Journal of Personality and Social Psychology, 14,* 321–328.

Zanna, M. P., & Olson, J. M. (1982). Individual differences in attitudinal relations. In M. P. Zanna, E. T. Higgins, & C. P. Herman (Eds.), *Consistency in social behavior: The Ontario Symposium* (Vol. 2, pp. 75–104). Hillsdale, NJ: Erlbaum.

Zanna, M. P., Olson, J. M., & Fazio, R. H. (1981). Self-perception and attitude-behavior consistency. *Personality and Social Psychology Bulletin, 7,* 252–256.

Zanna, M. P., & Pack, S. J. (1975). On the self-fulfilling nature of apparent sex differences in behavior. *Journal of Experimental Social Psychology, 11,* 583–591.

Zanna, M. P., & Rempel, J. K. (1988). Attitudes: A new look at an old concept. In D. Bar-Tal & A. W. Kruglanski (Eds.), *The social psychology of knowledge* (pp. 315–334). Cambridge, England: Cambridge University Press.

Zaragoza, M. S., & McCloskey, M. (1989). Misleading postevent information and the memory impairment hypothesis: Comment on Belli and reply to Tversky and Tuchin. *Journal of Experimental Psychology: General, 118,* 92–99.

Zarate, M. A., & Smith, E. R. (1990). Person categorization and stereotyping. *Social Cognition, 8,* 161–185.

Zebrowitz, L. A. (1990). *Social perception.* Pacific Grove, CA: Brooks-Cole.

Zebrowitz-McArthur, L. (1988). Person perception in cross-cultural perspective. In M. H. Bond (Ed.), *The cross-cultural challenge to social psychology.* (pp. 245–265). Beverly Hills, CA: Sage.

Zeigarnik, B. (1927). Das Bahalten erfedigter und unerledigter Handlungen. *Psychologoie Forshung, 9,* 1–85. Translated and condensed as "On finished and unfinished tasks" in W. D. Ellis (Ed.), *A source book of gestalt psychology.* New York: Harcourt, Brace, & World, 1938.

Zillmann, D. (1971). Excitation transfer in communication-mediated aggressive behavior. *Journal of Experimental Social Psychology, 7,* 419–434.

Zillmann, D. (1978). Attribution and misattribution of excitatory reactions. In J. H. Harvey, W. Ickes, & R. F. Kidd (Eds.), *New directions in attribution research* (Vol. 2, pp. 335–368). New York: Wiley.

Zillmann, D. (1983). Transfer of excitation in emotional behavior. In J. T. Cacioppo & R. E. Petty (Eds.), *Social psychophysiology* (pp. 215–240). New York: Guilford Press.

Zillmann, D. (1988). Cognition-excitation interdependencies in aggressive behavior. *Aggressive Behavior, 14,* 51–64.

Zillmann, D., & Bryant, J. (1974). Effect of residual excitation on the emotional response to provocation and delayed aggressive behavior. *Journal of Personality and Social Psychology, 30,* 782–791.

Zillmann, D., & Mundorf, N. (1987). Image effects in the appreciation of video rock. *Communication Research, 14,* 316–334.

Zillmann, D., Katcher, A. H., & Milavsky, B. (1972). Excitation transfer from physical exercise to subsequent aggressive behavior. *Journal of Experimental Social Psychology, 8,* 247–259.

Zillmann, D., Weaver, J. B., Mundorf, N., & Aust, C. F. (1986). Effects of an opposite-gender companion's affect to horror on distress, delight, and attraction. *Journal of Personality and Social Psychology, 51,* 586–594.

Zimbardo, P. G. (1960). Involvement and communication discrepancy as determinants of opinion conformity. *Journal of Abnormal and Social Psychology, 60,* 86–94.

Zimbardo, P. G. (1969). *The cognitive control of motivation: The consequences of choice and dissonance.* Glenview, IL: Scott, Foresman.

Zimbardo, P. G., Ebbesen, E. B., & Maslach, C. (1977). *Influencing attitudes and changing behavior.* Reading, MA: Addison-Wesley.

Zimbardo, P. G., & Leippe, M. (1991). *Psychology of social influence and attitude change.* New York: McGraw-Hill.

Zuckerman, M. (1977). On the endogenous-exogenous partition in attribution theory. *Personality and Social Psychology Bulletin, 3,* 389–399.

Zuckerman, M. (1978). Actions and occurrences in Kelley's cube. *Journal of Personality and Social Psychology, 36,* 647–656.

Zuckerman, M. (1979). Attribution of success and failure revisited, or: The motivational bias is alive and well in attribution theory. *Journal of Personality, 47,* 245–287.

Zuckerman, M., Eghrari, H., & Lambrecht, M. R. (1986). Attributions as inferences and explanations: Conjunction effects. *Journal of Personality and Social Psychology, 51,* 1144–1153.

Zuckerman, M., & Evans, S. (1984). Schematic approach to the attributional processing of actions and occurrences. *Journal of Personality and Social Psychology, 47,* 469–478.

Zuckerman, M., & Feldman, L. S. (1984). Actions and occurrences in attribution theory. *Journal of Personality and Social Psychology, 46,* 541–550.

Zuckerman, M., Klorman, R., Larrance, D. T., & Spiegel, N. H. (1981). Facial, autonomic, and subjective components of emotion: The facial feedback hypothesis versus the externalizer-internalizer distinction. *Journal of Personality and Social Psychology, 41,* 929–944.

Zuckerman, M., Koestner, R., Colella, M. J., & Alton, A. O. (1984). Anchoring in the detection of deception and leakage. *Journal of Personality and Social Psychology, 47,* 301–311.

Zukier, H. (1982). The role of the correlation and the dispersion of predictor variables in the use of nondiagnostic information. *Journal of Personality and Social Psychology, 43,* 1163–1175.

Zukier, H. (1986). The paradigmatic and narrative modes in goal-guided inference. In R. M. Sorrentino & E. T. Higgins (Eds.), *Handbook of motivation and cognition: Foundations of social behavior* (pp. 465–502). New York: Guilford Press.

Zukier, H., & Jennings, D. L. (1983–84). Nondiagnosticity and typicality effects in prediction. *Social Cognition, 2,* 187–198.

Zukier, H., & Pepitone, A. (1984). Social roles and strategies in prediction: Some determinants of the use of base rate information. *Journal of Personality and Social Psychology, 47,* 349–360.

Zullow, H. M., & Seligman, M. E. P. (1990). Pessimistic rumination predicts electoral defeat of Presidential candidates. *Psychological Inquiry, 1,* 52–61.

Zuroff, D. C., & Rotter, J. B. (1985). A history of the expectancy construct in psychology. In J. B. Dusek (Ed.), *Teacher expectancies* (pp. 9–36). Hillsdale, NJ: Erlbaum.

Name Index

701

Subject Index